D1365260

Freedom in the World 2012

Purchased with
C. Henry Smith
Peace Funds

Musselman Library
Bluffton University

The findings of *Freedom in the World 2012* include events from January 1, 2011 through December 31, 2011.

Freedom in the World 2012
The Annual Survey of Political Rights & Civil Liberties

Arch Puddington
General Editor

Aili Piano
Managing Editor

Jennifer Dunham, Bret Nelson, Tyler Roylance, Eliza Young
Associate Editors

Freedom House • New York, NY and Washington, DC
Rowman & Littlefield Publishers, Inc. • Lanham, Boulder,
New York, Toronto, Plymouth, UK

Bluffton University Library
No Longer
the Property of
Bluffton University

ROWMAN & LITTLEFIELD PUBLISHERS, INC.

Published in the United States of America
by Rowman & Littlefield Publishers, Inc.
A wholly owned subsidiary of The Rowman & Littlefield Publishing Group, Inc.
4501 Forbes Boulevard, Suite 200, Lanham, Maryland 20706
www.rowman.com

10 Thornbury Road, Plymouth PL6 7PY, United Kingdom

Copyright © 2013 by Freedom House

All rights reserved. No part of this publication may be reproduced, stored in a retrieval system, or transmitted in any form or by any means, electronic, mechanical, photocopying, recording, or otherwise, without the prior permission of the publisher.

British Library Cataloguing in Publication Information Available

Library of Congress Cataloging-in-Publication Data

Freedom in the world / —1978–
New York : Freedom House, 1978–
v. : map; 25 cm.—(Freedom House Book)
Annual.
ISSN 0732-6610=Freedom in the World.
1. Civil rights—Periodicals. I. R. Adrian Karatnycky, et al. I. Series.
JC571 .F66 323.4'05—dc 19 82-642048
AACR 2 MARC-S
Library of Congress [84101]

ISBN: 978-1-4422-1794-2 (cloth : alk. paper)
ISBN: 978-1-4422-1795-9 (pbk : alk. paper)
ISBN: 978-1-4422-1796-6 (electronic)
ISSN: 0732-6610

Printed in the United States of America

The paper used in this publication meets the minimum requirements of American National Standard for Information Sciences—Permanence of Paper for Printed Library Materials, ANSI/NISO Z39.48-1992.

Contents

Acknowledgments

Freedom in the World 2012 could not have been completed without the contributions of numerous Freedom House staff members and consultants. The section titled "The Survey Team" contains a detailed list of the writers and advisors without whose efforts this project would not have been possible.

Aili Piano served as the project director for this year's survey. Jennifer Dunham, Bret Nelson, Tyler Roylance, and Eliza Young provided extensive research, analytical, editorial, and administrative assistance, and Nicholas Bowen provided additional research and administrative support. Ronald Eniclerico, Shannon O'Toole, and Leigh Tomppert served as additional country report editors. Overall guidance for the project was provided by David J. Kramer, president of Freedom House, and Arch Puddington, vice president for research. A number of Freedom House staff offered valuable additional input on the country reports and/or ratings process

Freedom House would like to acknowledge the generous financial support for *Freedom in the World* by The Lynde and Harry Bradley Foundation, Smith Richardson Foundation, Lilly Endowment, F.M. Kirby Foundation, Walter J. Schloss, and the Freedom House Board of Trustees.

Freedom in the World 2012
The Arab Uprisings and Their Global Repercussions

Arch Puddington

The political uprisings that swept across the Arab world over the past year represent the most significant challenge to authoritarian rule since the collapse of Soviet communism. In a region that had seemed immune to democratic change, coalitions of activist reformers and ordinary citizens succeeded in removing dictators who had spent decades entrenching themselves in power. In some cases, protest and upheaval was followed by the beginnings of democratic institution building. At year's end, two countries with unbroken histories of fraudulent polling, Tunisia and Egypt, had conducted elections that observers deemed competitive and credible, and freedom of expression had gained momentum in many Middle Eastern societies.

Unfortunately, the gains that were recorded in Tunisia, and to a considerably lesser extent in Egypt and Libya, were offset by more dubious trends elsewhere in the region. Indeed, the overthrow of autocrats in these countries provoked determined and often violent responses in many others, most notably in Syria, where by year's end the Assad dictatorship had killed over 5,000 people in its efforts to crush widespread antigovernment protests. Similar if less bloody crackdowns took place in Bahrain and Yemen.

This pattern of protest and repression—with an emphasis on the latter—was echoed elsewhere in the world as news of the Arab uprisings spread beyond the Middle East and North Africa. In China, the authorities responded to events in Cairo's Tahrir Square with a near-hysterical campaign of arrests, incommunicado detentions, press censorship, and stepped-up control over the internet. The Chinese Communist Party's pushback, which aimed to quash potential prodemocracy demonstrations before they even emerged, reached a crescendo in December with the sentencing of a number of dissident writers to long terms in prison. In Russia, the state-controlled media bombarded domestic audiences with predictions of chaos and instability as a consequence of the Arab protests, with a clear message that demands for political reform in Russia would have similarly catastrophic results. In other Eurasian countries and in parts of Africa, the authorities went to considerable lengths to suppress demonstrations and isolate the democratic opposition.

The authoritarian response to change in the Middle East had a significant impact on the state of global freedom at year's end. The findings of *Freedom in the World* 2012, the latest edition of Freedom House's annual report on political rights and civil liberties, showed that slightly more countries registered declines than exhibited gains over the course of 2011. This marks the sixth consecutive year in which countries with declines outnumbered those with improvements.

The continued pattern of global backsliding—especially in such critical areas as press freedom, the rule of law, and the rights of civil society—is a sobering reminder that the institutions that anchor democratic governance cannot be achieved by protests alone. Yet if there is an overarching message for the year, it is one of hope and not of reversal. For the first time in some years, governments and rulers who mistreated their people were on the defensive. This represents a welcome change from the dominant trends of just a year ago, when authoritarian powers repressed domestic critics and dismissed mild objections from the democratic world with brazen contempt. In 2010, China conducted a bullying campaign against the Nobel committee for honoring jailed dissident Liu Xiaobo, Russia imposed a second prison term on former oil magnate Mikhail Khodorkovsky after a fraudulent judicial proceeding, and Egyptian president Hosni Mubarak's National Democratic Party claimed to have won heavily rigged parliamentary elections with well over 80 percent of the seats.

In 2011, by contrast, the signal events were the overthrow of Mubarak, Tunisia's Zine el-Abidine Ben Ali, and Libya's Mu'ammar al-Qadhafi; successful elections in Tunisia; and democratic ferment throughout the Arab world. Meanwhile, China's perpetual campaign of repression, directed at writers, lawyers, journalists, religious believers, ethnic minorities, and ordinary citizens who had spoken out against injustice and state abuses, seemed only to show the staggering fears and weaknesses of a regime that otherwise presents the image of a confident, globally integrated economic powerhouse. And in Russia, Vladimir Putin faced his first serious political crisis, as election fraud and the prospect of 12 more years without new leadership drew tens of thousands of protesters to the streets.

Whether the events of 2011 will lead to a true wave of democratic revolution is uncertain. Tunisia was clearly the greatest beneficiary of the year's changes. It experienced one of the largest single-year improvements in the history of the *Freedom in the World* report, rising from among the worst-performing Middle Eastern countries to achieve electoral democracy status and scores that place it roughly alongside such Partly Free countries as Colombia and Philippines. But much remains to be done, and there are some questions about the positions of the new leaders on such crucial issues as minority rights, freedom of belief, and freedom of expression. Egypt also made significant gains, but they have been overshadowed in many respects by the continued political dominance of the military, its hostility toward media critics, its campaign against human rights organizations, and its humiliating treatment of female protesters. In many other Arab countries, democracy movements have yet to reach even the initial milestone of forcing the resignation of their longtime rulers. The perceived success or failure of these efforts will either continue to inspire similar changes in the rest of the world, or bolster authoritarian calls for "stability" at any price.

FREEDOM'S TRAJECTORY IN 2011

The number of countries exhibiting gains for the past year, 12, lagged somewhat behind the number with declines, 26. The most noteworthy gains were in the Middle East—in Tunisia, Egypt, and Libya—and in three Asian countries—Burma, Singapore, and Thailand. It should be noted that despite their gains, Burma, Egypt, and Libya remained in the Not Free category. Moreover, while the Middle East experi-

Freedom in the World—2012 Survey

The population of the world as estimated in mid-2011 was 6,967.2 million persons, who reside in 195 sovereign states. The level of political rights and civil liberties as shown comparatively by the *Freedom House* survey is:

Free: 3,016.6 million (43 percent of the world's population) live in 87 of the states.

Partly Free: 1,497.4 million (22 percent of the world's population) live in 60 of the states.

Not Free: 2,453.2 million (35 percent of the world's population) live in 48 of the states.

A Record of the Survey (population in millions)

Year under Review	FREE	PARTLY FREE	NOT FREE	WORLD POPULATION
Mid-1992	1,352.2 (24.83%)	2,403.3 (44.11%)	1,690.4 (31.06%)	5,446.0
Mid-1993	1,046.2 (19.00%)	2,224.4 (40.41%)	2,234.6 (40.59%)	5,505.2
Mid-1994	1,119.7 (19.97%)	2,243.4 (40.01%)	2,243.9 (40.02%)	5,607.0
Mid-1995	1,114.5 (19.55%)	2,365.8 (41.49%)	2,221.2 (38.96%)	5,701.5
Mid-1996	1,250.3 (21.67%)	2,260.1 (39.16%)	2,260.6 (39.17%)	5,771.0
Mid-1997	1,266.0 (21.71%)	2,281.9 (39.12%)	2,284.6 (39.17%)	5,832.5
Mid-1998	2,354.0 (39.84%)	1,570.6 (26.59%)	1,984.1 (33.58%)	5,908.7
Mid-1999	2,324.9 (38.90%)	1,529.0 (25.58%)	2,122.4 (35.51%)	5,976.3
Mid-2000	2,465.2 (40.69%)	1,435.8 (23.70%)	2,157.5 (35.61%)	6,058.5
Mid-2001	2,500.7 (40.79%)	1,462.9 (23.86%)	2,167.1 (35.35%)	6,130.7
Mid-2002	2,717.6 (43.85%)	1,293.1 (20.87%)	2,186.3 (35.28%)	6,197.0
Mid-2003	2,780.1 (44.03%)	1,324.0 (20.97%)	2,209.9 (35.00%)	6,314.0
Mid-2004	2,819.1 (44.08%)	1,189.0 (18.59%)	2,387.3 (37.33%)	6,395.4
Mid-2005	2,968.8 (45.97%)	1,157.7 (17.93%)	2,331.2 (36.10%)	6,457.7
Mid-2006	3,005.0 (46.00%)	1,083.2 (17.00%)	2,448.6 (37.00%)	6,536.8
Mid-2007	3,028.2 (45.85%)	1,185.3 (17.94%)	2,391.4 (36.21%)	6,604.9
Mid-2008	3,055.9 (45.73%)	1,351.0 (20.21%)	2,276.3 (34.06%)	6,683.2
Mid-2009	3,088.7 (45.49%)	1,367.4 (20.14%)	2,333.9 (34.37%)	6,790.0
Mid-2010	2,952.0 (42.95%)	1,487.0 (21.63%)	2,434.3 (35.42%)	6,873.3
Mid-2011	3,016.6 (43.30%)	1,497.4 (21.49%)	2,453.2 (35.21%)	6,967.2

* The large shift in the population figure between 1997 and 1998 is due to India's change in status from Partly Free to Free.

enced the most significant improvements, it also registered the most declines, with a list of worsening countries that includes Bahrain, Iran, Lebanon, Saudi Arabia, Syria, the United Arab Emirates, and Yemen. Declines were also noted in a number of countries in Central and Eastern Europe and Eurasia, including Albania, Azerbaijan, Hungary, Kazakhstan, and Ukraine.

Among other trends:

- Glimmers of Hope for the Most Repressed: Burma, which has ranked alongside North Korea as one of the world's most closed societies, experienced what many hope will become a major political opening. The government of President Thein Sein has permitted more public discussion, tolerated a measure of press commentary, freed longtime opposition leader Aung San Suu Kyi, and cleared the path for her party's participation in elections. Another country that endured decades of brutal misrule, Libya, now has the potential for significant gains thanks to the overthrow of al-Qadhafi. Cuba, also one of the world's most repressive countries, experienced a small improvement linked to the limited reduction of economic restrictions by the government of Raúl Castro. Unlike in Burma, however, Cuba underwent no political liberalization.

• (Some) Good News in Asia: In a region whose dominant power, China, maintains the world's most sophisticated and comprehensive system of authoritarian political control, the recent trend has been largely positive. Aside from the improvements in Burma, the past year was notable for more open and competitive elections in Singapore, whose unique variant of "guided democracy" has been in place for several decades. In fact, for the countries of Asia proper, practically every indicator measured by *Freedom in the World* improved to some degree.

• Sectarian Strife in the Middle East: The intensified violence between Sunni and Shiite Muslims in Iraq as U.S. forces completed their withdrawal touched on a broader threat posed by sectarianism to democracy's future in the region. Differences among various strains of Islam complicated the crackdown on mainly Shiite protesters in Bahrain, and played a role in the crisis in Syria, principally propelled by President Bashar al-Assad's desperate efforts to remain in power. Sunni-Shiite rivalry also presents a serious threat to political stability in Lebanon, while in Egypt, anti-Christian sentiment flared into violence during the year, with notable help from the military.

• Long-Term Setbacks in Energy-Rich Eurasia: The past year featured the continuation of a decade-long trend of setbacks for the wealthiest and most "modern" former Soviet countries: Russia, Kazakhstan, and Azerbaijan. The level of freedom fell further despite rising popular demands for reform and warning signs from the Middle East. Indeed, beginning with the "color revolutions" of 2003–05, authoritarians in Eurasia have consistently responded to freedom movements outside their borders with intensified clampdowns at home. Year-end protests in Moscow and violent labor unrest in Kazakhstan should remind the world that repression does not in fact lead to stability.

• Danger Signs for New Democracies: Until recently, Ukraine, Hungary, South Africa, and Turkey were regarded as important success stories for democratic development. Now, increasingly, the democratic credentials of each is coming under question. The steepest decline in the institutions of freedom has taken place in Ukraine, where a series of negative developments was punctuated by the conviction of opposition leader Yuliya Tymoshenko on dubious charges. In the past two years, Ukraine has moved from a status of Free to Partly Free and suffered deterioration on most indicators measured by Freedom House. Developments in Turkey are also worrying, given the country's role as a model for democracy in Muslim-majority countries and its aspirations to regional leadership. While the government of Prime Minister Recep Tayyip Erdo an has instituted important reforms since coming to power, stepped-up arrests of advocates for Kurdish rights and the continued pursuit of the wide-ranging and politically fraught Ergenekon conspiracy case, which has led to lengthy detentions without charge, are both causes for concern. In Hungary, the government of Prime Minister Viktor Orbán, taking advantage of a parliamentary supermajority, has pushed through a new constitution and a raft of laws that could seriously weaken press freedom, judicial independence, and a fair election process. And in South Africa, new media regulations and evidence of pervasive corruption within the African National Congress leadership threaten to undermine the country's past achievements in peaceful democratic change.

RESULTS FOR 2011

The number of countries designated by *Freedom in the World* as Free in 2011 stood at 87, representing 45 percent of the world's 195 polities and 2,951,950,000 people—43 percent of the global population. The number of Free countries did not change from the previous year's survey.

The number of countries qualifying as Partly Free stood at 60, or 31 percent of all countries assessed by the survey, and they were home to 1,487,000,000 people, or 22 percent of the world's total. The number of Partly Free countries did not change from the previous year.

A total of 48 countries were deemed Not Free, representing 25 percent of the world's polities. The number of people living under Not Free conditions stood at 2,434,250,000, or 35 percent of the global population, though it is important to note that more than half of this number lives in just one country: China. The number of Not Free countries increased by one from 2010 due to the inclusion for the first time of South Sudan, a new state that was given a Not Free designation.

The number of electoral democracies increased by two and stands at 115. Three countries achieved electoral democracy status due to elections that were widely regarded as improvements: Niger, Thailand, and Tunisia. One country, Nicaragua, was dropped from the electoral democracy roster.

One country moved from Not Free to Partly Free: Tunisia. One country, The Gambia, dropped from Partly Free to Not Free.

The Global Trend

Year Under Review	Free	Partly Free	Not Free
1981	54	47	64
1991	76	65	42
2001	85	59	48
2011	87	60	48

Tracking Electoral Democracy

Year Under Review	Number of Electoral Democracies
2001	121
2006	123
2011	117

ANALYSIS OF REGIONAL TRENDS MIDDLE EAST AND NORTH AFRICA: THE ARAB SPRING'S AMBIGUOUS ACHIEVEMENTS

Even in a region that was notorious for its leaders' disdain for honest government and civil liberties, Tunisia had long stood out for the thoroughness of its system of control and oppression. Its longtime strongman, Zine el-Abidine Ben Ali, had seemingly smothered all significant sources of opposition. Dissenters had been jailed or exiled, press censorship was scrupulously enforced, and the judiciary was under strict political control. This country seemed a highly unlikely setting for a democratic revolution.

Yet it is Tunisia that has emerged as the most dramatic success story thus far in the series of popular uprisings that took place across the Arab world during 2011. It has been transformed from a showcase for Arab autocracy to an electoral democracy whose new leaders have pledged themselves to moderation, adherence to civil liberties, and the rule of law. The press is critical and vibrant; there are practically no taboo subjects. Civil society has proliferated, and elements within the new leadership appear committed to tackling the problem of pervasive corruption, though achieving such deep institutional reforms will likely require many years of effort.

Some gains were also made in Egypt and Libya, but in both of these societies, the future prospects for democratic reform are still very much in doubt. In Egypt, governing authority shifted from the Mubarak regime to the Supreme Council of the Armed Forces (SCAF), a group of military leaders who have dispensed justice through military tribunals, engaged in periodic crackdowns on critical media, raided the offices of civil society organizations, mistreated women activists, and engaged in violence against Christians. While a protracted election process, still under way at year's end, was conducted with an adherence to fair practices that stood in vivid contrast to the sham polls of the Mubarak regime, the dominant forces in the new parliament will be Islamist parties whose devotion to democracy is open to question. And while Libya has benefited greatly from the demise of the Qadhafi dictatorship, the country confronts an array of daunting political and security challenges, and has yet to hold its first elections.

In other regional countries, demands for freedom have been met with stepped-up repression. In the worst case, Syrian leader Bashar al-Assad responded to widespread peaceful protests with a campaign of arrests, torture, and urban fusillades that took the lives of an estimated 5,000 Syrians by year's end. In Bahrain, a prodemocracy movement consisting principally of members of the Shiite majority encountered violent repression by the monarchy and intervention by the Saudi military. The government's tactics included mass arrests, torture, and the use of military justice in cases of political activists. In Yemen, security forces loyal to President Ali Abdullah Saleh killed hundreds of civilians as Saleh repeatedly slipped out of agreements on a transfer of power. The authorities in Saudi Arabia intensified their persecution of Shiites and other Muslim sects, while Iran escalated its persecution of nongovernmental organizations (NGOs) and civic leaders who were critical of regime actions. Lebanon suffered a decline in civil liberties due to the violent treatment of protesters and punitive measures against those demanding regime change in neighboring Syria. The United Arab Emirates also experienced a civil liberties decline after the government tightened restrictions on free speech and civil society and arrested those calling for political change.

Israel's relations with Palestinians in the West Bank and Gaza Strip, and with other countries in the region, worsened as the year's tumult raised expectations and shook old assumptions. Israel also faced condemnation for a series of measures that were either introduced in the Knesset or signed into law and were seen by critics as threats to freedom of speech. One measure that was enacted called for punishment of those who support boycotts against Israel or its institutions, including universities and businesses located in West Bank settlements.

ASIA-PACIFIC: IMPORTANT GAINS, DESPITE CHINA AND CONFLICT

Over the past five years, the Asia-Pacific region has been the only one to record steady gains in the majority of indicators that are measured by *Freedom in the World*. Progress is especially noteworthy in the countries of Asia proper, excluding the small Pacific island nations. The most impressive gains have come in the institutions of electoral democracy—elections, political parties, pluralism—and in freedom of association.

The embrace of free institutions has taken place in the face of significant regional obstacles, including, most notably, the influence of China. In recent years China has accelerated its efforts to project its power beyond its borders, and its Asian neighbors have been important targets of this effort. Despite several incidents in which critics of the Chinese government and exiled Chinese minorities encountered repression in Nepal, Indonesia, and Vietnam, the allure of the so-called China model—combining state-led economic growth, a Leninist one-party political system, and strict control over the media—has gained only modest traction in the region. Meanwhile, the Chinese leadership has demonstrated no serious interest in political liberalization at home, and has devoted impressive resources to internet censorship, the suppression of minorities, and the elimination of even oblique political dissent. In 2011, the authorities carried out a major campaign of repression in the wake of the Arab uprisings by censoring public discussion of the movement for Arab democratization, prosecuting or arbitrarily detaining scores of social-media commentators and human rights lawyers, and strengthening the online censorship of domestic social-networking services.

Another regional challenge is the explosion of civil and sectarian strife in South Asia. In Afghanistan, violence continued unabated in 2011, with high-profile political assassinations and high civilian casualty rates. In Pakistan, there was growing discord over enforcement of the country's blasphemy laws, punctuated by the murders of Punjab governor Salmaan Taseer and Shahbaz Bhatti, the minister for minority affairs, both of whom had criticized the blasphemy statutes. Bangladesh also suffered a decline due to the ruling Awami League's prosecution of opposition politicians and efforts to muzzle NGOs. On the other hand, India, the world's largest democracy, showed increased room for peaceful demonstrations, particularly with the rise of an anticorruption movement that brought tens of thousands of people to the streets. Meanwhile, Indian-administered Kashmir experienced a notable improvement in the space for open public discussion amid growing use of social media and a drop in violence.

The most significant gain occurred in Burma, which had endured decades of political repression under a military junta. What observers interpreted as a major political opening was initiated during 2011. In a series of steps toward a more liberal domestic environment, the leadership allowed opposition leader Aung San Suu Kyi and her political party, the National League for Democracy, to register and compete in forthcoming by-elections, eased press censorship, and legalized political protest. At the same time, many cautioned that it was still unclear whether the changes in Burma were durable or simply cosmetic improvements by the regime. In Singapore, the system of managed democracy engineered by the former prime minister, Lee Kuan Yew, was loosened, and opposition candidates gained popular support in national elections, though the system ensured that this did not translate into significantly increased representation in the parliament. Conditions also improved in Thailand, whose deeply polarized political life had been dominated by riots and crippling demonstrations for several years. A July election led to a peaceful transfer of power to the opposition party and the installation as prime minister of Yingluck Shinawatra, the sister of controversial former prime minister Thaksin Shinawatra. However, there has been some backsliding on civil liberties since the end of November.

CENTRAL AND EASTERN EUROPE/EURASIA: STABILITY AND STAGNATION

The protests that roiled Moscow and other Russian cities in the wake of deeply flawed December parliamentary elections were stark reminders that no authoritarian leadership, no matter how sophisticated its methods, is immune to popular demands for change. While the immediate trigger for the mass demonstrations were widely circulated YouTube videos that suggested ballot-stuffing and other forms of election fraud, the protests also reflected displeasure with the earlier announcement that Prime Minister Vladimir Putin and President Dmitry Medvedev had forged an agreement to swap positions at the end of Medvedev's term in 2012. The two men had failed to fulfill long-standing promises to reform Russia's corrupt, stagnant, and unresponsive government system, and the idea of Putin's return for a third and possibly fourth presidential term helped drive ordinary Russians to the unprecedented demonstrations.

There are many questions about the ability of the forces that led the postelection protests to influence future politics in Russia. But clearly Russia is not alone in its vulnerability to popular discontent with authoritarian leadership. As the 20th anniversary of the Soviet Union's disintegration was marked at year's end, most Eurasian countries were still subject to autocratic rule of one variant or another. Whereas prior to 2011 the "president for life" phenomenon was principally associated with the Middle East, it is today more likely to apply to the long-term leaders of the former Soviet Union.

The authoritarian temptation poses a threat even in countries with recent histories of free-wheeling democracy. Thus Ukraine suffered a major decline due to President Viktor Yanukovych's moves to crush the political opposition through a variety of antidemocratic tactics, including the prosecution of opposition political leader and former prime minister Yuliya Tymoshenko. Other "color revolution" countries also faced problems. Kyrgyzstan, recovering from a 2010 revolt against an authoritarian president, held national elections that were judged to be relatively fair and competitive. Nevertheless, deep divisions lingered between the majority Kyrgyz and minority Uzbeks, and little progress was made in bringing to justice those responsible for anti-Uzbek violence in mid-2010. In Georgia, President Mikheil Saakashvili continued to face criticism for his apparent efforts to marginalize potential opposition figures.

Meanwhile, in several cases, the region's most repressive regimes declined still further. In Azerbaijan, the government of President Ilham Aliyev used force to break up demonstrations, jailed opposition activists, tried to neutralize the international press, and misused state power to evict citizens from their homes as part of grandiose building schemes. Kazakhstan suffered a decline due to the adoption of legislation that restricted religious belief. In December, conditions deteriorated further when the regime used violence in an effort to put down labor protests by oil workers. And in Belarus, the regime of President Alyaksandr Lukashenka held scores of political prisoners and adopted a series of bizarre policies—such as outlawing public clapping in unison—to prevent creative expressions of popular discontent over political repression and economic decline.

For most of Central and Eastern Europe and the Baltics, by contrast, the year was notable for the ability of most countries to weather the European economic crisis without major damage to the basic institutions of democracy. At the same time, a number of countries in the region remained highly vulnerable to precarious economies, the merging of business and political interests, and corruption. Latvia, Bulgaria, Romania, and the Western Balkans could face problems as Europe's economic woes persist.

Hungary poses the most serious problem in Central Europe. The government of Viktor Orbán has taken advantage of a two-thirds parliamentary majority to push through a new and problematic constitution without adequate input from the opposition, and a series of laws that are widely seen as threats to press freedom, judicial independence, and political pluralism. Albania experienced declines due to violence against demonstrators, flawed municipal elections, and the failure of the courts to deal effectively with major corruption cases. On the positive side, Slovakia was credited for having adopted legislation designed to shield the press from political intimidation.

The Balkans achieved mixed progress on the road to democratization and European Union (EU) accession. In July, Serbia's government finally surrendered the last of the 161 suspected war criminals indicted by the International Criminal Tribunal for the former Yugoslavia, including Ratko Mladi , a leading figure in the 1995 Srebrenica massacre who had evaded arrest for 16 years. Mladi 's extradition met with disapproval from over 50 percent of Serbia's population, triggering sizeable protests. Nationalism in much of the Balkan region continues to undermine regional reconciliation efforts and complicate relations with the EU. Pressures on free media increased across the Balkans, particularly in Macedonia, where an opposition-oriented television station and several newspapers were harassed and closed.

SUB-SAHARAN AFRICA: CIVIL SOCIETY UNDER PRESSURE

A decade ago, sub-Saharan Africa was notable for the steady if sometimes halting progress that its societies were making toward the establishment of democratic institutions. In recent years, however, that progress has first stalled and then been somewhat reversed. The year 2011 gave evidence of moderate decline, with particular problems in countries where members of the opposition and civil society made pleas for change in emulation of protests in the Arab world.

Five of the 10 countries that registered the most significant declines in the *Freedom in the World* report over the two-year period from 2010 to 2011 were in Africa: The Gambia, Ethiopia, Burundi, Rwanda, and Djibouti. Likewise, over the five-year period from 2007 through 2011, Africa as a region has exhibited declines in each of the topical subcategories measured by Freedom in the World. Particularly substantial declines were recorded for rule of law and freedom of association.

The Gambia experienced the most notable decline over the past year. Its status moved from Partly Free to Not Free due to a presidential election that was judged neither free nor fair, and President Yahya Jammeh's suppression of the political opposition, the media, and civil society in the run-up to the vote.

Five other regional countries experienced declines for the year. Ethiopia continued a decade-long trend of growing authoritarianism, with the government of Prime Minister Meles Zenawi making increased use of antiterrorism laws against the political opposition and journalists. In Sudan, the administration of President Omar al-Bashir engaged in stepped-up arrests of opposition leaders, banned a leading political party, used violent tactics against demonstrators, and persecuted the media. In Uganda, President Yoweri Museveni cracked down on critical members of the press in a year that also featured flawed national elections, repressive tactics against protesters, and continued harassment of the gay community. Malawi witnessed pressure against journalists and violence against protesters as well as violations of academic freedom. Antigovernment protests were also met with repressive tactics in Djibouti, where the intimidation of opposition political parties was followed by the election of President Ismail Omar Guelleh to a third term in office.

Two countries with recent histories of political upheaval registered gains. Conditions in Côte d'Ivoire improved somewhat after Alassane Ouattara assumed the presidency, ending months of civil strife associated with incumbent president Laurent Gbagbo's refusal to surrender power despite his defeat in 2010 elections. Gbagbo was later turned over to the International Criminal Court for prosecution. Niger experienced a major improvement in its political rights rating due to credible national and local elections that marked the end of more than a year of military rule.

AMERICAS: CONTINUITY DESPITE POPULIST THREAT

Over the past decade, left-wing populist leaders have risen to power in a number of Latin American countries, causing some to predict that the authoritarian model established by Venezuela's President Hugo Chávez would come to dominate the politics of the region. In fact, authoritarian populism has remained a minority phenomenon, as most societies have embraced the model of private-sector growth, social-welfare initiatives, and adherence to democratic standards established by leaders in Brazil, Chile, and Mexico.

Nevertheless, events in 2011 demonstrated that quasi-authoritarian populism still stands as a threat to the region's political stability. In the most serious case, Nicaragua suffered a steep decline in political rights due to irregularities in advance of and during the presidential election, which gave Sandinista leader Daniel Ortega another term in office. Likewise, Ecuador suffered a decline due to President Rafael Correa's intensified campaign against media critics, the government's use of state resources to influence the outcome of a referendum, and a restructuring of the judiciary that was in blatant violation of constitutional provisions.

Chávez himself was preoccupied with medical treatment, mostly carried out under less-than-transparent conditions in Cuba, reportedly for prostate cancer. Chávez has announced that he will seek reelection in 2012, but the campaign promises to be more competitive than in the past due to the apparent unity of the opposition.

Violent crime, much of it generated by drug-trafficking groups, continued to plague societies throughout the region, causing ripple effects in the political system and contributing to a growing trend toward the militarization of police work. In Mexico, government institutions remained unable to protect ordinary citizens, journalists, and elected officials in many areas from organized crime. Mexican journalism in certain regions remains shackled by drug-gang intimidation, with some editors significantly altering coverage to avoid violent repercussions. In Venezuela, the kidnapping for ransom of professional baseball catcher Wilson Ramos stood out as a vivid reminder of the violent criminality that more commonly affects the population at large. In Brazil, the government's efforts to bring down crime in the most troubled urban districts in advance of the 2014 World Cup soccer tournament have been met by determined resistance from organized gangs.

In other developments, Guatemala registered an improvement in political rights due to progress made by an international commission set up to investigate impunity and corruption in the country's institutions. Puerto Rico suffered a civil liberties decline stemming from reports of widespread police misconduct and brutality.

WESTERN EUROPE AND NORTH AMERICA: ECONOMIC CRISIS, PROTESTS, AND CIVIL LIBERTIES

In the face of the most serious economic crisis in the postwar period, the countries of Western Europe and North America maintained their traditionally high level of respect for democratic standards and civil liberties. This was even the case in countries that were compelled to make major cuts to social-welfare provisions in response to high levels of indebtedness. Throughout Europe, citizens mounted massive demonstrations to protest policies, often dictated by the EU and the International Monetary Fund, that called for fiscal austerity and the removal of various protections for many workers and industries. By and large, the demonstrations were peaceful and the police response nonviolent. The exception was Greece, where anarchists frequently set fires and threw projectiles at police, and the police responded with batons and tear gas.

It is unlikely that Europe's democratic standards will suffer serious setbacks in the wake of the ongoing debt crisis. Nonetheless, the region does face major challenges. A number of European countries are already confronted by problems associated with the influx of immigrants from the Middle East, Asia, and Africa, and have shown little willingness to devise rational and humane policies toward their integration. Economic decline could well exacerbate polarization over immigration policy, as migrants seek refuge from upheavals in the Arab world and unemployment levels in some European countries are at record levels. Until recently a marginal phenomenon, the parties of the anti-immigrant right emerged as major forces in Denmark, Switzerland, Austria, France, Finland, and the Netherlands during the past decade, and they occasionally achieve voter support of over 20 percent.

Many European countries have opted for policies that restrict future immigration and, in some instances, asylum applications. A growing number have taken steps to curtail customs identified with Islam that much of the population finds offensive. In 2011, women in France and Belgium were arrested in cases related to the wearing of ultraconservative Muslim female attire.

Also during the year, observers raised doubts about the durability of the current Turkish political model, in which a ruling party with moderate Islamist roots has committed itself to the norms of liberal democracy. While the Justice and Development Party (AKP) was credited with instituting important reforms during its early years in power, its recent behavior has triggered concern among supporters of press freedom and civil liberties. In the past few years, thousands of people have been arrested on charges of involvement with Kurdish terrorist organizations or participation in an alleged military conspiracy to overthrow the government. Those detained include journalists, scholars, and even defense lawyers.

Britain was rocked first by a series of urban riots, which many felt were handled poorly by the authorities, and then by a "phone hacking" case in which members of the tabloid press were accused of widespread abuse of privacy rights in pursuit of sensationalistic stories about celebrities and, most controversially, crime victims. At the same time, the coalition government of Conservatives and Liberal Democrats indicated that a law aimed at reforming the country's punitive libel laws would be introduced in 2012. The measure is meant to deal with the phenomenon of "libel tourism," in which foreign individuals use the plaintiff-friendly English courts to press libel suits against critical journalists and scholars. If adopted, the new law would place the burden of proof on the plaintiff rather than the defense in libel cases. Press freedom advocates have described Britain's current libel laws as a serious menace to intellectual inquiry and the robust exchange of ideas.

The United States endured a year of deep political polarization and legislative gridlock. Despite the efforts of a bipartisan commission and a select committee of lawmakers drawn equally from both major parties, the legislative branch and the White House were unable to reach agreement on a plan to reduce the federal deficit to manageable levels. Even as Congress and the president failed to agree on key economic measures, left-wing critics of the country's wealth disparities and ties between politics and big business came together to launch the Occupy Wall Street movement. Beginning with an encampment near the financial district in New York City, the Occupy movement spread to cities across the country, with protesters camping out in parks or other public spaces for indefinite periods. After several months, municipal authorities moved to evict the protesters, often through peaceful police actions but in some cases using batons, tear gas, pepper spray, and arrests. Some observers voiced criticism of the police for employing confrontational tactics and military-style equipment when dealing with protesters.

In fulfillment of a pledge made during his election campaign, President Barack Obama revoked the policy known as "don't ask, don't tell," under which military personnel were not asked about their sexual orientation, but openly gay and lesbian individuals were barred from military service. In another step toward observance of homosexual rights, the state of New York legalized gay marriage through legislative action, joining a small number of other states that allow same-sex marriage or civil unions.

CONCLUSION: WINNING FREEDOM, SUSTAINING DEMOCRACY

As 2011 drew to a close, officials in Egypt made headlines by conducting a series of raids on NGOs that monitor human rights and promote democracy. Most of the targeted organizations were Egyptian; a few were international groups (Freedom House was one of the latter). The authorities were insistent that the raids, which included the seizure of files and computers, were legal and technical in nature. Government officials emphasized and reemphasized that they believed human rights organizations had a role to play in a democratic Egypt. Their actions indicated otherwise.

In fact, the behavior of the Egyptian authorities, now and under Mubarak, reflects a deep-seated hostility to NGOs that support democracy and human rights. This in turn points to a broader institutional continuity between the current Egyptian state and the old regime that will present major obstacles to democratic development in the coming months and years, and similar dynamics may play out in other countries where authoritarian rule is being defied.

There were many heroes, many casualties, and many martyrs to freedom's cause in 2011. There were also many extraordinary achievements. Authoritarians who aspired to rule in perpetuity were toppled in Tunisia, Egypt, and Libya, and autocratic heads of state in Yemen and Syria seem likely to follow. But unlike in communist Eastern Europe in 1989, today's oppressive leaders have for the most part refused to go quietly, without a fight. Some have adopted a rule or ruin strategy that threatens to condemn those who would supplant them to failure.

Indeed, one of the great disappointments of the Arab Spring is that its principal lesson—that people will eventually rise up against despotism and injustice—has been almost universally rejected by the world's authoritarian powers. Rather than responding to popular demands for freedom with, at minimum, a gradual plan of moderate reforms, despots in the Middle East and elsewhere have either tightened the screws or flatly excluded changes to the status quo. China fell into the first category with its frenzied campaign against political dissent. So too did Bashar al-Assad in Syria, with his repudiation of talks with the opposition and a murderous campaign against peaceful protesters across the country. Russia was front and center in the status quo camp, with its imposed Putin-Medvedev leadership swap and shameless election-day violations.

Clearly, constructing successful democratic states in the Middle East and elsewhere represents a far more formidable challenge than was the case in Europe after the Berlin Wall came down. Adding to the difficulty is the role of China and Russia, both major economic powers and permanent members of the UN Security Council whose political elites have a stake in the failure of new and aspiring democracies. There is reason to believe that the influence of these two powers could become magnified in the near future. As the European debt crisis deepened in 2011, there were widespread reports that EU leaders were looking to Beijing for bailout assistance. Likewise, the Russian president traveled to several European capitals with a package of economic deals designed to help the beleaguered region in its time of need, with strings attached. Ultimately, China seems to have rejected serious involvement in Europe's woes, and nothing of significance materialized from Medvedev's initiative. But the very fact that the world's most successful league of democracies would countenance involving two of the world's great authoritarian powers in its financial rescue is a chilling commentary on the current state of both the global economy and the democratic world's political morality, not to mention its survival instincts.

What of the United States? Can it be relied on to stand as the international beacon of freedom given its present economic torpor and political gridlock? American politics have sent conflicting signals over the past year. The notion that it is time for America to shrug off its global commitments has been increasingly posited by foreign policy analysts and some political figures. A prominent candidate for the Republican presidential nomination has put himself squarely in favor of backing away from the world's problems, saying the United States should simply "mind its own business." Leading figures from both major political parties criticized the Obama administration for its role in the NATO campaign that helped Libyan rebels overthrow the Qadhafi regime.

On the positive side, the Obama administration has evolved from its early discomfort with democracy as a foreign policy theme to a position where it episodically places its words, and in a few cases policy muscle, behind struggles for freedom abroad. Despite the unfortunate characterization that it was "leading from behind," America's firmness in assisting NATO's Libyan campaign was an important step. After initial hesitation, the administration has also cautiously supported the process of building democratic systems in Tunisia, Egypt, and Libya. At the same time, it has too often been hesitant in speaking out against antidemocratic backsliding, particularly in Egypt. President Obama himself has made several important statements about America's commitment to democratic change around the world, but he has failed to invoke the authority of the White House on specific cases. Instead it is Secretary of State Hillary Clinton who has publicly addressed violations of human rights in Russia, Hungary, and Turkey, and aligned the administration with the forces of change in Burma and elsewhere where prospects for freedom's growth have opened up.

If the past year has demonstrated that courage and sacrifice are essential to the achievement of freedom, a somewhat different set of characteristics are required to build the democratic infrastructure that will ensure long-term observance of political rights and civil liberties. These characteristics include the self-confidence needed to accept the complexities, and occasionally irresponsibility, of a free press; the fortitude to impose restrictions on oneself as well as on one's political opponents as part of the fight against corruption; and the perspicacity to accept that the judiciary, police, and other critical institutions must function without political interference.

In far too many parts of the world, these qualities proved to be in short supply during 2011. Thus in addition to singling out the full-fledged authoritarians for special attention, it is imperative to shine the spotlight on leaders who, having come to power through legitimate democratic means, have set about systematically undermining the aspects of freedom that they find inconvenient. The temptation to create a quasi-authoritarian regime, in which standards that reinforce the leader's authority are embraced and those that complicate his goals are dispensed with, can have disastrous consequences for democracies with shallow roots. Prosecuting an opposition leader or closing a television station can be the first steps down a slippery slope, as witnessed in the careers of Vladimir Putin and Hugo Chávez, both of whom dragged seriously flawed political systems into new depths of dysfunction and stagnation.

Still, while the year 2010 ended on a pessimistic note, with authoritarianism seemingly on the march, the events of 2011 have presented more hopeful prospects. Unaccountable and oppressive rulers have been put on notice that their actions will not be tolerated forever. The year of Arab uprisings has reminded the world that ordinary people want freedom even in societies where such aspirations have been written off as futile. This is a lesson to which the world's leading democracies, especially the United States, should pay special heed. It should dispel free societies' persistent doubts about the strength and universal appeal of their institutions and values. The opportunities that have been opened up by brave people in Tunis and Cairo should prompt a reenergized democratic world to address the twin challenges of how dictatorships can be overturned, and how stable and durable fellow democracies can be built in their place.

Eliza Young and Tyler Roylance assisted in the preparation of this report.

Introduction

The *Freedom in the World 2012* survey contains reports on 195 countries and 14 related and disputed territories. Each country report begins with a section containing the following information: **population**, **capital**, **political rights** (numerical rating), **civil liberties** (numerical rating), **status** (Free, Partly Free, or Not Free), and a **10-year ratings timeline**. Each territory report begins with a section containing the same information, except for capital. The population figures are drawn primarily from the *2011 World Population Data Sheet* of the Population Reference Bureau.

The **political rights** and **civil liberties** categories contain numerical ratings between 1 and 7 for each country or territory, with 1 representing the most free and 7 the least free. The **status** designation of Free, Partly Free, or Not Free, which is determined by the combination of the political rights and civil liberties ratings, indicates the general state of freedom in a country or territory. The ratings of countries or territories that have improved or declined since the previous survey are indicated by notations next to the ratings. Positive or negative trends that do not warrant a ratings change since the previous year may be indicated by upward or downward trend arrows, which are located next to the name of the country or territory. A brief explanation of ratings changes or trend arrows is provided for each country or territory as required. For a full description of the methods used to determine the survey's ratings, please see the chapter on the survey's methodology.

The **10-year ratings timeline** lists the political rights and civil liberties ratings and status for each of the last 10 years. Each year that is included in the timeline refers to the year under review, *not* the edition of the survey. Thus, the ratings and status from the *Freedom in the World 2012* edition are listed under "2011" (the year that was under review for the 2012 survey edition).

Following the section described above, each country and territory report is divided into two parts: an **overview** and an analysis of **political rights and civil liberties**. The overview provides a brief historical background and a description of major recent events. The political rights and civil liberties section summarizes each country or territory's degree of respect for the rights and liberties that Freedom House uses to evaluate freedom in the world.

↓ Afghanistan

Political Rights: 6
Civil Liberties: 6
Status: Not Free

Population: 32,400,000
Capital: Kabul

Trend Arrow: Afghanistan received a downward trend arrow due to a steady increase in violence and further deterioration in the independence of the judiciary.

Ten-Year Ratings Timeline For Year Under Review (Political Rights, Civil Liberties, Status)

2002	2003	2004	2005	2006	2007	2008	2009	2010	2011
6,6NF	6,6NF	5,6NF	5,5PF	5,5PF	5,5PF	5,6NF	6,6NF	6,6NF	6,6NF

Overview: **In 2011, the Afghan political landscape still reverberated from the flawed 2010 parliamentary elections, and the president's ultimately unsuccessful attempts to alter the election results by means of an unconstitutional special court demonstrated the weaknesses of the judicial system. A series of high-profile assassinations further undermined the stability of the already embattled government, raising doubts about the ongoing transfer of control over security from coalition troops to the Afghan army and police. A broader increase in civilian casualties, continued government corruption, reported abuse of prisoners, and violence against women, along with sectarian attacks, further eroded the credibility of Afghan state institutions.**

After decades of intermittent attempts to assert control and ward off Russian influence in the country, Britain recognized Afghanistan as a fully independent monarchy in 1921. Muhammad Zahir Shah ruled from 1933 until he was deposed in a 1973 coup and a republic was declared. Afghanistan entered a period of continuous civil conflict in 1978, when a Marxist faction staged a coup and set out to transform the country's highly traditional society. The Soviet Union invaded to support its allies in 1979, but was defeated by U.S.-backed guerrillas and forced to withdraw in 1989.

The mujahideen guerrilla factions finally overthrew the Marxist government in 1992 and then battled one another for control of Kabul, killing more than 25,000 civilians in the capital by 1995. The Islamist Taliban movement entered the fray, seizing Kabul in 1996 and quickly establishing control over most of the country, the rest of which remained in the hands of other factions. In response to the terrorist attacks of September 11, 2001, the United States launched a military campaign to topple the Taliban regime and eliminate Saudi militant Osama bin Laden's terrorist network, al-Qaeda.

As a result of the December 2001 Bonn Agreement, an interim administration took office to replace the ousted Taliban. In June 2002, the United Nations oversaw an emergency loya jirga (gathering of representatives) that appointed a Transitional Administration (TA) to rule Afghanistan for another two years. Interim leader Hamid Karzai won the votes of more than 80 percent of the delegates to become president and head of the TA.

In 2004, Karzai won a presidential election under the country's new constitution, taking 55 percent of the vote and forming a cabinet that was a mix of technocrats and regional power brokers. Relatively peaceful elections for a National Assembly and 34 provincial councils were held in September 2005. However, a large number of warlords and others involved in organized crime and human rights abuses were elected.

The new parliament made little progress over the next several years on addressing political and economic reforms or passing key legislation. While some analysts had expressed concern that the legislative branch would be largely subservient to the executive, it was often at odds with the president, making it difficult for him to advance the government's agenda.

The UN-mandated International Security Assistance Force (ISAF), which had been managed by NATO since August 2003, completed the expansion of its security and reconstruction mission from Kabul to the rest of the country in 2006. Despite tens of thousands of additional U.S. and allied troops, and the ongoing development of the Afghan army, Afghanistan largely remained under the sway of local military commanders, tribal leaders, warlords, drug traffickers, and petty bandits. Meanwhile, the resurgent Taliban increased their attacks on the government and international forces, and steadily extended their influence over vast swaths of territory, particularly in the southern provinces of Kandahar and Helmand, but also in previously quiet areas of the north and west.

The constitution called for the 2009 presidential election to be held by April, with Karzai's term due to expire in May, but delays in passing the electoral law and slow international coordination resulted in the election being postponed until August. Fraud and manipulation during the voter registration process, low turnout, a compromised electoral management body, and insecurity across the country undermined the balloting. Karzai initially emerged as the outright winner with more than 50 percent of the vote, but the confirmation of large-scale fraud significantly reduced his total, necessitating a November runoff against his main opponent, former foreign minister Abdullah Abdullah. However, Abdullah withdrew before the vote, arguing that the flaws in the electoral system had not been adequately addressed, and Karzai was declared the winner.

Lingering doubts about the Karzai administration's legitimacy, combined with the continued deterioration in security, posed a major challenge to the central and provincial governments as they struggled to control areas under their jurisdiction, deliver basic services, and engage in vital reconstruction efforts.

The country's institutional integrity was dealt another blow when the September 2010 parliamentary elections also proved to be deeply flawed, with low voter turnout, at least 1,000 electoral workers accused of fraud, and the discovery of misplaced ballots from over 500 polling stations. Karzai did not inaugurate the new parliament until January 2011, ruling by decree in the interim. The delay was largely due to disputed votes and the establishment in December 2010 of an unconstitutional Special Election Court (SEC), with judges appointed by the president, to review complaints from losing candidates. Six months later, in June 2011, the SEC ruled that 62 candidates for the 249-seat lower house who had been considered losers or were disqualified should be reinstated. This decision triggered an international outcry which led to the SEC's dissolution in August. The Independent Election Commission, which had declared the final results in November 2010, agreed to replace only nine of the lawmakers, bringing Karzai's nine-month effort to change the parliament's makeup to an end.

Also during 2011, the government was shaken by a series of high-profile assassinations and terrorist attacks, including an assault on Kabul's Intercontinental Hotel in June; the murder of Ahmad Wali Karzai, the president's half-brother and a leading Kandahar province power broker, in July; an attack on the U.S. embassy in September; and later that month, the assassination of former president Burhanuddin Rabbani, who was leading efforts to initiate peace talks with the Taliban.

Despite such incidents, the United States announced in June that it would withdraw 10,000 troops by year's end and another 23,000 by the end of September 2012. The United States and its NATO allies proceeded in July with the transfer of responsibility for security to Afghan forces in the provinces of Bamiyan, Kabul, and Panjshir, as well as in the eastern town of Mehtar Lam, the western city of Herat, and the northern city of Mazar-e-Sharif. The second phase of security handover, announced in November, involved the handover of Balkh, Takhar, Daikundi, Samangan, Kabul, and Nimroz provinces, along with the cities of Jalalabad, Cheghcheran, Sheberghan, Faizabad, Ghazni city, Qalai-e-Naw, and Maidan Shahr.

Though the Afghan army and police met their growth targets, their competence was cast into doubt by a major jailbreak in Kandahar in April and by a UN human rights report that alleged torture and abuse of detainees. The year was also marred by an increase in Afghan civilian casualties. A separate UN report documented 1,462 Afghan civilian deaths from January to June 2011, a 15 percent increase from the same period in 2010; most of the deaths were attributed to insurgents.

Political Rights and Civil Liberties: Afghanistan is not an electoral democracy. The overall results of the 2004 presidential election and delayed 2005 parliamentary elections were broadly accepted by Afghans and the international community, despite allegations of intimidation by militias and insurgent groups, partisanship within the electoral administration, and other irregularities. However, the 2009 presidential and 2010 parliamentary elections were critically undermined by fraud and other problems, and state institutions have failed to provide effective governance or transparency. Afghanistan's district council elections, which were scheduled to take place in 2010, were canceled.

The directly elected president serves five-year terms and has the power to appoint ministers, subject to parliamentary approval. In the directly elected lower house of the National Assembly, the 249-seat Wolesi Jirga (House of the People), members stand for five-year terms. In the 102-seat Meshrano Jirga (House of Elders), the upper house, two-thirds of members are indirectly elected by the provincial councils for three- or four-year terms, and one-third are appointed by the president for five-year terms. Ten of the Wolesi Jirga seats are reserved from the nomadic Kuchi community, including at least three women, and another 65 seats are reserved for women. Provisions for women's representation have also been implemented for the Meshrano Jirga and provincial councils.

Violence, insecurity, and repression continue to restrict political activity nationwide, particularly outside urban areas. Critics have warned that vague language in the 2003 Political Parties Law could be exploited to deny registration to parties on flimsy grounds. In addition, analysts viewed the adoption of the single-nontransferable-vote system for the 2005 legislative elections as a disadvantage for new political parties. Parties lack a formal role within the legislature, which further weakens their ability to contribute to stable political, policymaking, and legislative processes.

There have been regular violent and often deadly attacks against government officials at all levels, including assassination attempts aimed at the president. The victims of assassinations in 2011 included the provincial council chairman, deputy governor, mayor, and provincial police chief of Kandahar; the former governor of Uruzgan; the police chief for a nine-province zone in the north; and the chief peace negotiator, a former president.

Corruption, nepotism, and cronyism are rampant at all levels of government, and woefully inadequate salaries encourage corrupt behavior by public employees. The international community, concerned that government corruption is crippling the counterinsurgency campaign, has pressed the administration of President Hamid Karzai to make the issue its top priority. However, a massive scandal involving fraud at Kabul Bank that emerged in 2010 continued to plague confidence in Afghan financial institutions in 2011. The International Monetary Fund withheld approval for transfers of donor funds until late in the year, when it finally acknowledged sufficient progress in Afghanistan's efforts to address the damage from the banking scandal. Afghanistan was ranked 180 of 183 countries surveyed in Transparency International's 2011 Corruption Perceptions Index.

Afghan media continue to grow and diversify but face major challenges, including physical attacks and intimidation. Though a 2007 media law was intended to clarify press freedoms and limit government interference, a growing number of journalists have been arrested, threatened, or harassed by politicians, security services, and others in positions of power as a result of their coverage. Media diversity and freedom are markedly higher in Kabul than elsewhere in the country, but some local warlords display limited tolerance for independent media in their areas. Dozens of private radio stations and several private television channels currently operate. Some independent outlets and publications have been criticized by conservative clerics for airing programs that "oppose Islam and national values," or fined by the authorities for similar reasons. The use of the internet and mobile telephones continues to grow rapidly and has broadened the flow of news and other information, particularly for urban residents, but increased Taliban attacks on mobile-phone transmission infrastructure has recently worked against this trend. In September 2011, an Afghan journalist with the British Broadcasting Corporation was killed by NATO forces who mistook him for a suicide bomber during a battle against insurgents.

Religious freedom has improved since the fall of the Taliban government in late 2001 but is still hampered by violence and harassment aimed at religious minorities and reformist Muslims. The constitution establishes Islam as the official religion. Blasphemy and apostasy by Muslims are considered capital crimes. While faiths other than Islam are permitted, non-Muslim proselytizing is strongly discouraged. A 2007 court ruling found the minority Baha'i faith to be a form of blasphemy, jeopardizing the legal status of that community. Hindus, Sikhs, and Shiite Muslims—particularly those from the Hazara ethnic group—have also faced official obstacles and discrimination by the Sunni Muslim majority. Militant groups have targeted mosques and clerics as part of the larger civil conflict, with two particularly brutal attacks against Shiites in Kabul and Mazar-i-Sharif in December 2011 that left 60 people dead and over 200 wounded.

Aside from constitutional provisions regarding the role of Islam in education, academic freedom is not officially restricted, but insurgents have attacked or destroyed schools associated with the government or foreign donors, particularly girls' schools. The quality of school instruction and resources remains poor, and higher education is subject to bribery and prohibitively expensive for most Afghans.

The constitution guarantees the rights to assembly and association, subject to some restrictions, but they are upheld erratically from region to region. Police and other security personnel have occasionally used excessive force when confronted with demonstrations or protests.

The work of hundreds of international and Afghan nongovernmental organizations (NGOs) is not formally constrained by the authorities, but their ability to operate freely and effectively is impeded by the worsening security situation and increasingly restrictive bureaucratic rules. Both foreign and Afghan NGO staff members have been targeted in a growing number of kidnappings and violent attacks by criminals and insurgents. Civil society activists, particularly those who focus on human rights or accountability issues, continue to face threats and harassment. Despite broad constitutional protections for workers, labor rights are not well defined, and there are currently no enforcement or dispute-resolution mechanisms. Child labor is reportedly common.

The judicial system operates haphazardly, and justice in many places is administered on the basis of a mixture of legal codes by inadequately trained judges. Corruption in the judiciary is extensive, and judges and lawyers are often subject to threats from local leaders or armed groups. Traditional justice remains the main recourse for the population, especially in rural areas. The Supreme Court, composed of religious scholars who have little knowledge of civil jurisprudence, is particularly in need of reform. Prison conditions are extremely poor, with many detainees held illegally. The national intelligence agency, as well as some warlords and political leaders, maintain their own prisons and do not allow access to detainees.

In a prevailing climate of impunity, government ministers, as well as warlords in some provinces, sanction widespread abuses by the police, military, local militias, and intelligence forces under their command, including arbitrary arrest and detention, torture, extortion, and extrajudicial killings. The Afghan Independent Human Rights Commission (AIHRC) receives hundreds of complaints of rights violations each year. In addition to the abuses by security forces, reported violations have involved land theft, displacement, kidnapping, child trafficking, domestic violence, and forced marriage.

U.S. forces have reportedly made some improvements to their detention practices in recent years, but Human Rights First has found ongoing violations of due process and other rights, and Afghan detainees who are handed over to Afghan authorities continue to suffer abuses. An October 2011 UN human rights report revealed egregious violations of detainee rights in the custody of Afghan security forces. U.S.-led forces have also bred popular resentment through the growing use of nighttime raids on households that are aimed at killing or capturing suspected Taliban commanders.

The Afghan security forces continued to grow in 2011, but the army and especially the police have been plagued by inadequate training, illiteracy, corruption, involvement in drug trafficking, and high rates of desertion. The intelligence service, the National Directorate of Security, lacks transparency and stands accused of serious human rights violations.

Disarmament programs have stalled, and foreign military programs to rearm informal militias as a counterinsurgency force are actively undermining efforts to curtail and regulate the distribution of weaponry. Ongoing programs aimed at reintegrating former insurgents have failed to ensure that they disarm.

As of December 2011, approximately 400,000 civilians were displaced within the country, according to the Office of the UN High Commissioner for Refugees. Humanitarian agencies and Afghan authorities are ill-equipped to deal with the displaced. Factors like the poor security situation and widespread land-grabbing have prevented refugees from returning to their homes, and many congregate instead around major urban centers. In the absence of a properly functioning legal system, the state remains unable to protect property rights.

Women's formal rights to education and employment have been restored, and in some areas, women are once again participating in public life. They accounted for about 16 percent of the candidates in the 2010 parliamentary elections, and roughly 41 percent of registered voters were women; 69 female parliamentarians were elected. There were 2 women among the 41 candidates for the 2009 presidential election, but on the whole, female participation was limited by threats, harassment, and social restrictions on traveling alone and appearing in public. Another major setback to women's rights came with the passage in 2009 of legislation that derogated many constitutional rights for women belonging to the Shiite Muslim minority, leaving questions of inheritance, marriage, and personal freedoms to be determined by conservative Shiite religious authorities.

Social discrimination and domestic violence against women remain pervasive, with the latter often going unreported because of social acceptance of the practice. In 2010, the AIHRC recorded 2,765 cases of violence against women, a 22 percent increase compared with 2009. President Karzai's controversial pardon in December 2011 of a rape victim provisional on her marrying her attacker further confirmed the precarious situation for Afghan women. The case first came to light in an EU documentary on women's moral crimes in Afghanistan, which the organization chose to withdraw in fear of security reprisals despite criticism from human rights workers who wanted to bring to light the inadequacies of the Afghan government in terms of women's rights and protections. Women's choices regarding marriage and divorce remain circumscribed by custom and discriminatory laws, and the forced marriage of young girls to older men or widows to their husbands' male relations is a problem. Nearly 60 percent of Afghan girls are married before the legal age of 16, according to UNICEF, and in 2009, UNICEF ranked Afghanistan as the world's worst country in which to be born. Though men, women, and male children have been used to perpetrate suicide bombings in Afghanistan, a June 2011 attack in Uruzgan province was committed by a young girl and one of the youngest child bombers in the decade-long conflict.

↓ Albania

Political Rights: 3
Civil Liberties: 3
Status: Partly Free

Population: 3,197,000
Capital: Tirana

Trend Arrow: Albania received a downward trend arrow due to the killing of opposition protesters in January, the politicization of electoral mechanisms surrounding municipal balloting in May, and the failure of the courts to impartially adjudicate a corruption case against a senior government politician.

Ten-Year Ratings Timeline For Year Under Review (Political Rights, Civil Liberties, Status)

2002	2003	2004	2005	2006	2007	2008	2009	2010	2011
3,3PF	3,3PF	3,3PF	3,3PF	3,3PF	3,3PF	3,3PF	3,3PF	3,3PF	3,3PF

Overview:

Polarization and deadlock between the ruling Democratic Party (PD) and opposition Socialist Party (PS) intensified in 2011, further damaging Albania's bid for European Union (EU) candidate status. In January, a corruption scandal forced the resignation of Deputy Prime Minister Ilir Meta and triggered opposition protests, during which four demonstrators were shot and killed. In municipal elections in May, a PD candidate won the crucial mayoralty of Tirana by a razor-thin margin after a highly politicized legal battle. At year's end, both Meta's trial and investigations into the January shootings remained unresolved.

Ruling from World War II until his death in 1985, communist dictator Enver Hoxha turned Albania into the most isolated country in Europe. The regime began to adopt more liberal policies in the late 1980s, and multiparty elections in 1992 brought the Democratic Party (PD), led by Sali Berisha, to power. Continuing poverty and corruption, along with unrest after the collapse of large-scale investment scams, resulted in the election of a new government led by the Socialist Party (PS) in 1997.

Former president Berisha returned to government as prime minister after the PD won the 2005 parliamentary elections. In 2007, the parliament elected PD candidate Bamir Topi as the country's president.

Berisha's government was plagued by allegations of corruption and abuse of office in 2008. Nevertheless, in June 2009 parliamentary elections, the PD took 68 of 140 seats and formed a coalition government with four smaller parties that collectively held 7 seats. The PS, in opposition with 65 seats, claimed fraud and boycotted the new parliament. Although the PS finally named a deputy parliament Speaker and committee members in June 2010, it continued to mount protests and block key legislative votes that required a three-fifths majority.

In January 2011, the media aired a video recording that showed Deputy Prime Minister Ilir Meta apparently discussing corrupt deals involving a hydropower tender. The PS mounted a large protest in Tirana on January 21, and four demonstrators were shot and killed, allegedly by Republican Guards protecting the prime minister's office. Dozens of protesters and police were injured in related clashes. Prosecutor General Ina Rama launched an investigation into the deaths, but her efforts were openly obstructed by Berisha, who set up a rival parliamentary inquiry and accused Rama, Topi, the PS, the intelligence service, and leading journalists of orchestrating an attempted coup. The prime minister promised financial rewards for those who agreed to testify in the parliamentary probe. By year's end, neither inquiry had made significant progress, and Meta's corruption trial was still under way.

Meanwhile, PD candidate Lulzim Basha, who had faced corruption allegations as a cabinet minister, won the Tirana mayoralty in May municipal elections, defeating PS leader and three-term incumbent Edi Rama (no relation to the prosecutor general). After a protracted legal battle over miscast ballots, PD-dominated electoral bodies found that Basha had won by 93 votes out of some 250,000. The PS mounted confrontational protests, boycotted the parliament over the dispute until early September, and continued to wrangle with the PD majority thereafter.

The political deadlock since mid-2009 has obstructed reforms linked to Albania's bid for European Union (EU) candidacy, with EU officials warning that candidate status will not be granted absent substantial progress.

Political Rights and Civil Liberties: Albania is an electoral democracy. International observers of the 2009 parliamentary elections hailed improvements in a number of areas, but also cited problems including media bias, abuse of state resources, political pressure on public employees, and flaws in the tabulation process. The unicameral, 140-member Kuvendi (Assembly) is elected through proportional representation in 12 regional districts of varying size. All members serve four-year terms. The prime minister is designated by the majority party or coalition, and the president—who does not hold executive powers but heads the military and plays an important role in selecting senior judges—is chosen by the parliament for a five-year term.

The sharp, personality-driven rivalry between the two main political parties, the PD and the PS, escalated significantly in 2011. The campaign for the May municipal elections featured interparty violence—including some nonfatal shootings, bombings, and property damage—as well as party-line decisions, boycotts, and acrimony within the Central Election Commission, and political pressure on public employees. Nevertheless, observers noted improvements on some issues, including abuse of administrative resources and voter list accuracy.

Corruption is pervasive, and the EU has repeatedly called for rigorous implementation of antigraft measures. Prosecutor General Ina Rama continues to pursue high-level cases with support from U.S. and EU officials, but Prime Minister Sali Berisha has regularly accused her of political bias, and the prosecutions have been thwarted by parliamentary immunity and unfavorable court rulings. In early 2011, Rama filed charges against Ilir Meta, who had resigned as deputy prime minister in January after a video showed him apparently discussing bribery, and against former economy minister Dritan Prifti, who appeared in another incriminating video. Parliamentary immunity was lifted for both men. Meta's trial was under way before the Supreme Court at year's end, though the chief justice failed to recuse herself despite Meta's alleged claims to have influence over her, and key evidentiary rulings during the trial strongly favored the defense. Albania was ranked 95 out of 183 countries surveyed in Transparency International's 2011 Corruption Perceptions Index.

While the constitution guarantees freedom of expression, the intermingling of powerful business, political, and media interests inhibits the development of independent outlets. During the 2011 municipal election campaign, most outlets were seen as biased toward either the PS or the PD. Reporters have little job security and remain subject to lawsuits, intimidation, and in some cases, physical attacks by those facing media scrutiny. Several journalists were reportedly assaulted during the protests of January 21, and Berisha's subsequent parliamentary probe briefly sought to question and seize the telephone records of four leading media figures. Berisha's government has placed financial pressure on critical outlets. In September 2011, an appeals court rejected the previous year's $500,000 judgment against the television station Top Channel, which was accused of illegally obtaining a 2009 video that showed then culture minister Ylli Pango engaging in apparent sexual harassment of a female job applicant. The government does not limit internet access, and internet penetration is estimated at over 43 percent.

The constitution provides for freedom of religion, and it is usually upheld in practice. The government generally does not limit academic freedom, though students and teachers have faced political pressure ahead of elections.

Freedoms of association and assembly are generally respected. In addition to the deaths and injuries during the January 21 protest, police reportedly beat and detained civilians in its immediate aftermath. However, most of those arrested were quickly released. Subsequent demonstrations by both major parties remained relatively peaceful. Nongovernmental organizations function without restrictions but have limited funding and policy influence. The constitution guarantees workers the rights to organize and bargain collectively, and most have the right to strike. However, effective collective bargaining remains limited, and union members have little protection against discrimination by employers. Hundreds of workers at a chromium mine mounted a three-month strike in July, successfully extracting a pay raise and new investment from the Austrian owner. Child labor is a problem, and informal child workers sometimes face hazardous conditions.

The constitution provides for an independent judiciary, but the underfunded courts are subject to political pressure. Several vacancies on the Constitutional Court and Supreme Court have gone unfilled in the last two years due to disagreements between the president, who nominates the judges for confirmation by the parliament, and the PD majority, which has demanded more influence over the appointments. Judicial immunity obstructs investigations of corruption among the country's poorly paid judges, who also face threats of violence. In September 2011, a district court judge in Vlora was killed in a bomb explosion. High court fees allegedly limit access to justice for ordinary Albanians.

Police reportedly engage in abuse of suspects during arrest and interrogation, and such ill-treatment is lightly if ever punished. Prison inmates suffer from poor living conditions and lack of adequate medical treatment. The parliament filled the vacant human rights ombudsman's position in late December 2011 after nearly two years of deadlock, during which the institution had functioned under an acting leader.

Weak state institutions have augmented the power of crime syndicates. Albania is known as a transshipment point for heroin smugglers and a key site for cannabis production. Traditional tribal law and revenge killings are practiced in parts of the north.

Roma face significant discrimination in education, health care, employment, and housing. In February 2011, local citizens destroyed a settlement of some 45 Romany families near the Tirana train station, forcing residents to flee. Two perpetrators were sentenced for relatively minor offenses. Some tensions persist between the ethnic Greek minority and the ethnic Albanian majority.

A 2010 law bars discrimination based on several categories, including sexual orientation and gender identity, but bias against sexual minorities in society and by law enforcement officials remains strong.

Women are underrepresented in most governmental institutions, and a quota for women in party candidate lists is not well enforced. Domestic violence, which is believed to be widespread, is rarely punished by the authorities. Albania is a source country for trafficking in women and children.

Algeria

Political Rights: 6
Civil Liberties: 5
Status: Not Free

Population: 35,980,000
Capital: Algiers

Ten-Year Ratings Timeline For Year Under Review (Political Rights, Civil Liberties, Status)

2002	2003	2004	2005	2006	2007	2008	2009	2010	2011
6,5NF	6,5NF	6,5NF	6,5NF	6,5NF	6,5NF	6,5NF	6,5NF	6,5NF	6,5NF

Overview: **Fearing a popular uprising similar to the Arab Spring movements sweeping the region, the Algerian government made a number of political and economic concessions in early 2011 to calm discontent. While the government also promised reforms to the constitution, the electoral law, and laws governing the media, real progress was slow to materialize, due in part to concerns about increasing extremist violence.**

Algeria secured independence from France after a guerrilla war that lasted from 1954 to 1962. The military overthrew the country's first president in 1965 and dominated Algerian politics for the next four decades, backing the National Liberation Front (FLN) for most of that time. President Chadli Benjedid permitted the establishment of legal opposition parties in 1989, and an Islamist movement quickly gained popularity in the face of the government's failures; the Islamic Salvation Front (FIS) became the main opposition faction. With the FIS poised to win parliamentary elections in 1992, the army canceled the elections, forced Benjedid from office, and imprisoned thousands of FIS supporters under a declared state of emergency.

Over the next decade, the military government and various Islamist groups engaged in a bloody civil conflict. All sides targeted civilians and perpetrated large-scale human rights abuses, causing an estimated 200,000 deaths and the disappearance of at least 7,000 people.

A military-backed candidate, former foreign minister Abdelaziz Bouteflika, easily won the 1999 presidential election after his opponents withdrew to protest alleged fraud. Bouteflika's first attempt at resolving the civil war was the Civil

Concord Law, which granted partial amnesty to combatants who renounced violence. A few thousand militants surrendered, but the more uncompromising groups—including what later became al-Qaeda in the Islamic Maghreb (AQIM)—continued to kill government personnel and civilians. The next several years saw occasional outbursts of violence, and the government continued to commit human rights abuses.

The ruling FLN gained ground against the military-backed National Democratic Rally (RND) in the 2002 and 2003 elections to the lower and upper houses of Parliament, respectively, while Bouteflika, who began to distance himself from the military, won a second term in 2004. In 2005, a referendum approved the Charter for Peace and National Reconciliation, which offered amnesty to most militants and government agents for crimes committed during the civil war. However, human rights organizations criticized the charter for not addressing the issue of the disappeared and for allowing perpetrators to escape justice.

In May 2007 lower-house elections, the FLN lost 63 seats, though it remained the largest party, with 136. The RND came in second, with 61 seats, followed by the Islamist-oriented Movement of the Society of Peace (MSP), with 52, and independent candidates, who claimed 33. The FLN and RND also placed first and second, respectively, in indirect elections for the upper house in December 2009.

Bouteflika won a third term in an April 2009 election, taking about 90 percent of the vote amid widespread accusations of fraud. After the election, reports that the ailing Bouteflika would be succeeded by his younger brother met with opposition from the intelligence services, particularly General Mohamed "Toufik" Mediène, the powerful head of the Department of Intelligence and Security. In January 2010, Mediène launched a corruption investigation into the state-owned oil and gas company Sonatrach, which was responsible for 98 percent of Algeria's foreign exchange and 40 percent of its gross domestic product. Bouteflika allies at Sonatrach were indicted for corruption and later jailed; the president also lost two key supporters in a May cabinet shuffle. Some observers interpreted the February 2010 murder of the head of Algeria's national police, Ali Tounsi, as part of the ongoing power struggle.

In early 2011, the Algerian government remained firmly in control as political change gripped its Arab neighbors. Protests over high unemployment, rising prices, and the lack of political freedoms failed to attract crowds beyond a few thousand, and were violently subdued by the police. The government quickly introduced new subsidies and wage increases to head off a more widespread uprising. It also lifted the country's long-standing emergency law in February and promised reforms to the constitution and political party laws before parliamentary polls in May 2012. Meanwhile, AQIM attacks increased starting in April, heightening concerns over security. Some analysts said that a desire for stability among a population weary of conflict after years of civil war—along with the government's ability to draw on its oil wealth to appease economic grievances—made an uprising similar to those in Tunisia, Egypt, and Libya less likely in Algeria.

In August, Algeria took in several members of deposed Libyan leader Mu'ammar al-Qadhafi's family who had fled the conflict in their home country.

Political Rights and Civil Liberties:

Algeria is not an electoral democracy. The military and intelligence services still play an important role in politics, despite their ongoing rivalries with the political establishment. The People's National Assembly, the lower house of Parliament, has 389 members directly elected for five-year terms. The upper house, the National Council, has 144 members serving six-year terms; 96 members are chosen by local assemblies, and the president appoints the remaining 48. The president is directly elected for five-year terms, and constitutional amendments passed in 2008 abolished the two-term limit, allowing President Abdelaziz Bouteflika to run for a third term in 2009. The amendments also increased the president's powers relative to the premiership and other entities, drawing criticism from segments of the press and opposition parties.

The Ministry of the Interior must approve political parties before they can operate legally. A coalition of the FLN, RND, and MSP forms the current government. While there are dozens of active political parties, movements that are deemed too radically Islamist are outlawed, and many of the Islamist groups that were banned in the 1990s remain illegal. As the next round of parliamentary elections approaches, debates have reopened over whether exiled Islamists, such as former FIS leader Anwar Haddam, should be allowed to return to Algeria. In September 2011, Haddam announced plans to return to the country, though he officially remained an outlaw.

High levels of corruption plague Algeria's business and public sectors, especially the energy sector. Sonatrach has come under particularly heavy fire in recent years; after being dismissed and arrested for corruption in 2010, its former chief executive officer, Mohamed Meziane, was sentenced to two years in prison in May 2011. Algeria was ranked 112 out of 183 countries surveyed in Transparency International's 2011 Corruption Perceptions Index.

There is an array of restrictions on press freedom, but the situation has improved since the peak of the civil war in the mid-1990s. Privately owned newspapers have been published for nearly two decades, and journalists have been aggressive in their coverage of government affairs. However, most newspapers rely on the central government for printing, giving the state a high degree of influence over them. Also, the state-owned advertising agency favors progovernment newspapers, encouraging self-censorship. Arabic- and French-language satellite channels are popular, though the government maintains tight control over national news broadcasts. Both government officials and private entities use criminal defamation laws to pressure independent newspapers. Harassment of journalists continued in 2011, especially during the protests. In September 2011, Bouteflika announced proposed reforms that would lift state regulation of television and radio, and end the practice of imprisoning individual journalists convicted of libel. A new press law adopted in December 2011 was criticized by journalists and human rights activists for containing vague language that reinforces the government's ability to block reporting on certain sensitive topics, including those deemed to undermine the country's security or economic interests.

A July 2009 cybercrime law gives authorities the right to block websites "contrary to the public order or decency." In late 2009, the information minister announced a centralized system for monitoring internet traffic. In February 2011, amid protests against the regime, activists in Algiers and the northwestern city of Annaba accused the government of shutting down the internet and disrupting social networking activities.

Algeria's population is overwhelmingly Sunni Muslim, and small non-Muslim communities do not face systematic harassment. However, non-Muslims may gather to worship only at state-approved locations, proselytizing by non-Muslims is illegal, and the government in 2008 began enforcing an ordinance that tightened restrictions on minority faiths. In May 2011, an Oran court sentenced a Christian convert to five years in prison for offending the prophet Muhammad. Also that month, the governor of Bejaia province ordered all churches in the province to be shut down, part of an ongoing legal dispute over possession of a church building in the region. Security services monitor mosques for radical Islamist activity, but Muslims are also sometimes harassed for a perceived lack of piety. Academic freedom is largely respected, though debate is somewhat circumscribed.

The police disperse peaceful assemblies, and the government generally discourages demonstrations featuring clear or implicit criticism of the authorities. As protests deposed other leaders in the region in 2011, the government forcibly disrupted public gatherings and protests, even after repealing the emergency law in February. Several people died and hundreds more were injured in clashes between the police and demonstrators.

Permits are required to establish nongovernmental organizations, and those with Islamist leanings are regarded with suspicion by the government. Workers can establish independent trade unions, but the main labor federation, the General Union of Algerian Workers, has been criticized for being too close to the government and failing to advocate aggressively for workers' interests.

The judiciary is susceptible to government pressure. International human rights activists have accused the security forces of practicing torture. In January 2011, Algerian national Saeed Farhi bin Mohammed was sent home from the U.S. military detention center in Guantanamo Bay, Cuba. Mohammed had fought the transfer, saying he feared being targeted by the regime upon his return. This was the second such transfer to Algeria in less than a year. Prison conditions in Algeria generally do not meet international standards due to overcrowding and poor nutrition and hygiene.

Algeria's ethnic composition is a mixture of Arabs and Berbers, with Arabs traditionally forming the country's elite. In recent years, following outbreaks of antigovernment violence in the Berber community, officials have made more of an effort to recognize Berber cultural demands. Tamazight, the Berber language, is now a national language. However, Berbers were not beyond the reach of government repression during protests in early 2011.

While most citizens are free to move throughout the country and travel abroad, the authorities closely monitor and limit the movement of suspected terrorists. Access to visas for non-Algerians is carefully controlled. Men of military draft age are not allowed to leave the country without government consent.

Women continue to face discrimination at both the legal and societal levels. Under the family code, which is based on Islamic law, women do not enjoy equal rights in marriage, divorce, and inheritance. They are poorly represented in Parliament, holding only 5.2 percent of the upper house and 7.7 percent of the lower house. A law requiring that female candidates comprise one-third of any candidate list for legislative elections was adopted in November 2011. However, Algeria is one of the few countries in the region to allow women to transfer their nationality to their children, regardless of the father's nationality. A law adopted in January 2009 criminalized all forms of trafficking in persons, but the government has made little effort to enforce it, according to the U.S. State Department's 2011 Trafficking in Persons Report.

Andorra

Political Rights: 1
Civil Liberties: 1
Status: Free

Population: 85,000
Capital: Andorra la Vella

Ten-Year Ratings Timeline For Year Under Review (Political Rights, Civil Liberties, Status)

2002	2003	2004	2005	2006	2007	2008	2009	2010	2011
1,1F	1,1F	1,1F	1,1F	1,1F	1,1F	1,1F	1,1F	1,1F	1,1F

Overview: **Parliamentary elections were held in April 2011 after former leader Jaume Bartumeu called for early elections to end two years of government deadlock. The Democrats for Andorra captured 20 out of 28 parliamentary seats and chose Antoni Martí as the new head of government. Also during the year, Andorra adopted the euro as its official currency.**

As a co-principality, Andorra was ruled for centuries by the French head of state and the bishop of Seu d'Urgel, Spain. The 1993 constitution retained the titular co-princes but transformed the government into a parliamentary democracy. Andorra joined the United Nations that year and the Council of Europe in 1994. While Andorra is not a member of the European Union (EU), the country began using the euro in 2002 as the country's sole circulating currency.

The April 2009 national elections brought the Social Democratic Party to power with 14 of the 28 seats in the Consell General, or parliament. Jaume Bartumeu replaced Albert Pintat Santolària as the cap de govern (head of government) in June.

After two years of government deadlock, including failing to pass a national budget, Bartumeu on February 15, 2011, requested that Andorra's two co-princes dissolve parliament and hold early elections. In the April 3 polls, the Democrats for Andorra won a decisive victory, securing 20 parliamentary seats. Antoni Martí became the new head of government.

An EU monetary agreement was signed in June that will make the euro the official, rather than merely the accepted, currency in Andorra.

In October, Martí announced that a value-added tax would go into effect as early as 2012, opening Andorra to foreign investors. He also announced a plan to legalize gambling at the start of 2013. The new tax laws were proposed to further Andorra's financial compliance with European and Organization for Economic Cooperation and Development standards.

Political Rights and Civil Liberties: Andorra is an electoral democracy. Popular elections are held every four years to the 28-member Consell General, which selects the executive council president, or head of government. Half of the members are chosen in two-seat constituencies known as parishes, and the other half are chosen through a national system of proportional representation.

The people have the right to establish and join different political parties. However, more than 60 percent of the population consists of noncitizens, who do not have the right to vote.

In June 2011, the Council of Europe's Group of States against Corruption (GRECO) released a report finding some "shortcomings" in Andorra's bribery laws, and calling for tougher penalties for bribery and influence peddling. GRECO also highlighted the fact that there are still no adequate campaign finance transparency laws.

Freedom of speech is respected across the country. There are two independent daily newspapers, *Diari d'Andorra* and *El Periòdic d'Andorra*, and two free weekday papers, *Bon Dia* and *Diari Més*. There is only one Andorran television station, operated by the public broadcaster Ràdio I Televisió d'Andorra, though residents have access to broadcasts from neighboring France and Spain. Internet access is unrestricted.

Although the constitution recognizes the state's special relationship with the Roman Catholic Church, the government no longer subsidizes the Church. Religious minorities like Mormons and Jehovah's Witnesses are free to seek converts. Despite years of negotiations between the Muslim community and the government, a proper mosque for the country's roughly 2,000 Muslims still has not been built. While requests to convert public buildings or former churches for this purpose have been denied, the government does provide the Muslim community with public facilities for various religious functions. Academic freedom is respected.

Freedoms of assembly and association are generally respected, and domestic and international human rights organizations operate freely. While the government recognizes that both workers and employers have the right to defend their interests, the right to strike is not legally guaranteed. There are also no laws in place to penalize antiunion discrimination or regulate collective bargaining. Few advances have been made in labor rights since the creation of a registry for associations in 2001, which enabled trade unions to gain legal recognition. In 2009, the government passed a law that guarantees unions the right to operate.

The government generally respects the independence of the judiciary. Defendants enjoy the presumption of innocence and the right to a fair trial. Police can detain suspects for up to 48 hours without charging them. Prison conditions meet international standards.

Under Andorra's restrictive naturalization criteria, one must marry a resident Andorran or live in the country for more than 20 years to qualify for citizenship. Prospective citizens are also required to learn Catalan, the national language. Although they do not have the right to vote, noncitizen residents receive most of the social and economic benefits of citizenship.

Immigrant workers, primarily from North Africa, complain that they lack the rights of citizens. Nearly 7,000 such immigrants have legal status, but many hold only "temporary work authorizations." Temporary workers are in a precarious position, as they must leave the country when their job contract expires.

Citizens have the right to own property. Legislation passed in 2008 fully opened up 200 key economic sectors to foreign investment. This law also gives noncitizens the right to hold up to 49 percent capital in other established sectors.

Women enjoy the same legal rights as men. Fifteen seats were captured by women in the 2011 parliamentary elections, making Andorra the first European country to elect a majority female legislature, and the second globally, after Rwanda. However, there are no specific laws addressing the problem of violence against women, nor are there any government departments for women's issues or government-run shelters for battered women. Abortion is illegal, except to save the life of the mother.

Angola

Political Rights: 6
Civil Liberties: 5
Status: Not Free

Population: 19,638,000
Capital: Luanda

Ten-Year Ratings Timeline For Year Under Review (Political Rights, Civil Liberties, Status)

2002	2003	2004	2005	2006	2007	2008	2009	2010	2011
6,5NF	6,5NF	6,5NF	6,5NF	6,5NF	6,5NF	6,5NF	6,5NF	6,5NF	6,5NF

Overview: **Antigovernment activity increased in 2011, and in September, a number of small, loosely organized protests opposing the 32-year rule of President José Eduardo dos Santos took place in Luanda, leading to a ban on demonstrations in the city center. Throughout the year, speculation rose as to whether dos Santos would lead his party in the 2012 presidential elections. Violent deportations of migrants from the Democratic Republic of Congo by Angolan security forces continued in 2011.**

Angola was racked by civil war for nearly three decades following independence from Portugal in 1975. José Eduardo dos Santos took over as president in 1979, after the death of Angola's first postindependence leader, Agostinho Neto. Peace accords in 1991 and 1994 failed to end fighting between the rebel National Union for the Total Independence of Angola (UNITA) and the government, controlled by dos Santos's Popular Movement for the Liberation of Angola (MPLA). The death of UNITA leader Jonas Savimbi in 2002 helped to spur a successful ceasefire deal later that year, and UNITA subsequently transformed itself into Angola's largest opposition party.

The conflict claimed an estimated one million lives, displaced more than four million people, and forced over half a million to flee to neighboring countries. Many resettled people have remained without land, basic resources, or even identification documents. The resettlement process was slowed by the presence of an estimated 500,000 land mines and a war-ruined infrastructure.

Legislative elections, delayed repeatedly since 1997, were finally held in September 2008. The ruling MPLA took 191 of 220 seats, and UNITA won 16 seats, placing second among 14 parties. While domestic and international observers found that the results reflected the people's will, the campaign was marred by political violence and pro-MPLA bias by both the state media and the National Electoral Commission (CNE), which denied the opposition access to the voter registry and obstructed the accreditation of domestic monitors who were not aligned with the government. In addition, the government delayed releasing state funding for opposition parties, and the MPLA abused state resources. Voting in Luanda—home to between one-quarter and one-third of registered voters—was marred by serious irregularities, including the late delivery of ballot papers and the failure to open 320 polling stations. UNITA accepted the outcome after an initial challenge of the Luanda results was rejected by the CNE.

In 2010, the MPLA-dominated parliament approved a new constitution that abolished direct presidential elections, stipulating instead that the leader of the largest party in the parliament would become the president, starting with the next elections in 2012. The last presidential election had been held in 1992, and a vote due in 1997 had been repeatedly postponed. Throughout 2011, dos Santos refrained from stating if he would lead the MPLA in the 2012 elections, resulting in significant speculation about his successor; the MPLA is almost assured victory. In September, rumors abounded that Manuel Vicente, the chairman of the national oil company Sonangol, would top the MPLA slate in 2012.

Attempts in March to organize protests against dos Santos's 32-year rule—said to be inspired by the early 2011 popular uprisings in the Arab world—were largely stifled by the government. In September, a series of small, loosely organized antigovernment protests took place in Luanda, marking a rare, if relatively minor, spate of open opposition to dos Santos's rule. In several instances, groups of a few hundred people, including many youths, organized demonstrations by text message and social media. In response, the Luanda provincial government banned demonstrations in the city center, and security forces violently dispersed the protests and arrested dozens of demonstrators, 18 of whom were jailed for between 45 and 90 days by an emergency court. Later that month, the government organized a pro-MLPA rally in Luanda attended by tens of thousands of people. In October, the Supreme Court ordered the release of the jailed protesters.

Political Rights and Civil Liberties: Angola is not an electoral democracy. The long-delayed 2008 legislative elections, while largely reflective of the people's will, were not free and fair. The 220-seat National Assembly, whose members serve four-year terms, has little power, and 90 percent of legislation originates in the executive branch. Under the 2010 constitution, the largest party in the National Assembly selects the head of state. The president is to serve a maximum of two five-year terms beginning in 2012, and directly appoints the vice president, cabinet, and provincial governors.

While five political parties are represented in the National Assembly, the ruling MPLA dominates Angola's party system. UNITA is the largest opposition party.

Corruption and patronage are endemic in the government, and bribery often underpins business activity. In 2009, President José Eduardo dos Santos called for a crackdown on corruption, declaring that MPLA members had squandered large portions of the country's oil revenues; the president himself is alleged to be one of the country's richest men. A December 2011 International Monetary Fund report stated that $32 billion in government funds from 2007 to 2010, believed to be linked to Sonangol, could not be accounted for. Angola was ranked 168 out of 183 countries surveyed in Transparency International's 2011 Corruption Perceptions Index.

Despite constitutional guarantees of freedom of expression, journalists are driven to self-censorship by the threat of dismissal, detention, and prosecution. The state owns the only daily newspaper and national radio station, as well as the main television stations, and private media are often denied access to official information and events. Libel and defamation are punishable by imprisonment and fines. Journalists endured harassment, attacks, and detentions by security forces in 2011. In October 2011, William Tonet, editor of the independent weekly *Folha 8*, was convicted of libel, given a suspended one-year jail sentence, and fined a massive 10 million kwanza (US$105,000) for a series of 2008 stories alleging corruption in the acquisition of diamond mines by close dos Santos associates. In March 2011, the Committee to Protect Journalists reported that authorities were barring journalists from covering opposition activities, including hearings in parliament and UNITA party meetings; authorities also restricted journalists' access to the August Southern African Development Community (SADC) summit in Luanda. Also in March, police detained journalists attempting to cover an antigovernment demonstration in Luanda, and security agents raided the printing presses and blocked the distribution of three independent weeklies that had run headlines about a scheduled protest. Authorities have consistently prevented the outspoken Roman Catholic radio station Radio Ecclesia from broadcasting outside the capital.

In May 2011, the government scrapped legislation that would have criminalized the electronic publication or distribution of information that could "destroy, alter, or subvert state institutions" or "damage national integrity or independence." The legislation had drawn vociferous opposition from civil society organizations and local press outlets. The government announced plans to instead incorporate clauses about internet crimes into an ongoing reform of the penal code.

Religious freedom is widely respected, despite colonial-era statutes that ban non-Christian religious groups. The educational system barely functions, suffering from underpaid and often corrupt teachers and severely damaged infrastructure.

The constitution guarantees freedoms of assembly and association, although these rights are not respected in practice. In March 2011, authorities arrested several opposition leaders and members of civil society the night before a planned antigovernment protest, while using state media outlets to warn that participants would be prosecuted for inciting violence and division; the protest did not take place. According to Human Rights Watch, opposition politicians and human rights lawyers also received death threats in advance of the protest. The antigovernment protests that successfully went ahead in March and September were violently dispersed by security forces, and dozens of protesters were arrested. In May, between 15 and 20 activists were arrested while participating in an antipoverty protest in Luanda organized by the Revolutionary Movement of Social Intervention on the social networking site Facebook.

Hundreds of nongovernmental organizations (NGOs) operate in Angola, many of them advocating for political reform, government accountability, and human rights protections. However, the government has occasionally threatened organizations with closure. In August 2011, authorities restricted the activities of a number of local and international NGOs relating to the SADC summit, including refusing NGO activists from across southern Africa entry to Angola at the Luanda airport, and confiscating publications on the human rights situation in Zimbabwe. The right to strike and form unions is provided by the constitution, but the MPLA dominates the labor movement, and only a few independent unions exist. Some 85 percent of the population engages in subsistence agriculture.

The judiciary is subject to extensive political influence, particularly from the executive, though courts occasionally rule against the government. The president appoints Supreme Court judges to life terms without legislative input. The courts in general are hampered by a lack of training and infrastructure, a large backlog of cases, corruption, and conflicts of interest. While the government has sought to train more municipal magistrates, municipal courts are rarely operational, leading to the use of traditional or informal courts.

Lengthy pretrial detention is common, and prisoners are subject to torture, severe overcrowding, sexual abuse, extortion, and a lack of basic services, including food and water. However, in 2010, seven police officers were each sentenced to 24 years in prison for killing eight suspects in Luanda's Sambizanga township, marking the first time a police officer had been convicted of an extrajudicial killing. According to Amnesty International, Angolan jails contain a number of political prisoners, mostly members of peaceful activist groups and advocates of regional autonomy. In March 2011, 30 political prisoners—activists for autonomy in the Lunda Tchokwe region—were released after being arrested and detained in 2009 and 2010.

An estimated four million weapons in civilian hands threaten to contribute to lawlessness, and both government and private security personnel have committed murders and other abuses in connection with the diamond-mining industry.

In 2006, the government signed a peace agreement with secessionists in the oil-rich northern exclave of Cabinda, hoping to end a conflict that had continued intermittently since 1975. While between 80 and 90 percent of the rebel fighters have reportedly joined the army or demobilized, some violence has continued. The military continues to arrest Cabindans for alleged state security crimes. Most of these detainees are allegedly denied basic due process rights and subjected to inhumane treatment. Citing continued attacks by rebels, the military restarted a counterinsurgency campaign in Cabinda in March 2011.

Minefields from the civil war continue to restrict freedom of movement, as does the country's rigid system of entry and exit visas. Tension involving refugees and migrants along the Angolan-Congolese border have led to a series of tit-for-tat expulsions affecting tens of thousands of people. In October 2011, Angolan soldiers allegedly attacked a village of Congolese migrants near the border, forcing 3,400 people to return to their home country. Between April and October 2011, the International Committee for the Development of Peoples reported that over 38,000 Democratic Republic of Congo nationals had been deported from Angola, with several thousand alleging physical and sexual abuse at the hands of Angolan authorities.

Since 2001, security forces have evicted thousands of people from informal settlements in and around Luanda without adequate notice, compensation, or resettlement provisions, ostensibly for development purposes. In August 2011, authorities canceled the planned evictions of some 750 families from the Arco Iris neighborhood in Lubango.

Women enjoy legal protections and occupy cabinet positions and 37 percent of National Assembly seats, but de facto discrimination and violence against women remain common, particularly in rural areas. A new law on domestic violence, which included a broader definition of sexual violence, took effect in July 2011. Child labor is a major problem, and there have been reports of trafficking in women and children for prostitution or forced labor. A recent study by Angola's National Children's Institute and UNICEF found "a significant and growing" trend of abuse and abandonment of children who are accused of witchcraft after the death of a family member, usually from AIDS.

Antigua and Barbuda

Political Rights: 3
Civil Liberties: 2
Status: Free

Population: 88,000
Capital: St. John's

Ten-Year Ratings Timeline For Year Under Review (Political Rights, Civil Liberties, Status)

2002	2003	2004	2005	2006	2007	2008	2009	2010	2011
4,2PF	4,2PF	2,2F	2,2F	2,2F	2,2F	2,2F	3,2F	3,2F	3,2F

Overview: **Antigua and Barbuda's economy continued to struggle in 2011 following the collapse of the Stanford Financial Group two years earlier and as a result of an increase in crime affecting the country's tourism industry.**

Antigua and Barbuda, a member of the Commonwealth, gained its independence from Britain in 1981. In the 2004 elections, the opposition United Progressive Party (UPP), led by Baldwin Spencer, defeated Prime Minister Lester Bird and the ruling Antigua Labour Party (ALP). The transfer of power ended the rule of the Bird political dynasty, which had governed the country continuously since 1976.

The 2009 parliamentary elections returned Spencer and the UPP to power with 9 seats in the 17-seat lower house; the ALP took 7 seats, while the Barbuda People's Movement (BPM) retained the single seat representing Barbuda. While elections were deemed fair and competitive by the Organization of American States, the voting was preceded by instances of violence, including attacks on ALP offices, and there were accusations of voter registration irregularities. In March 2010, a High Court ruling invalidated the election of Spencer and other members of Parliament due to electoral irregularities, though the Eastern Caribbean Court of Appeals overturned the verdict in October.

The collapse in 2009 of the $7 billion Stanford Financial Group, run by U.S. financier R. Allen Stanford, exposed deep ties between Stanford and the government of Antigua and Barbuda. A consortium of defrauded investors sued the government, claiming that top officials had been aware of and benefitted from a Ponzi scheme run by the company. In July 2009, the Eastern Caribbean Central Bank—the monetary authority of six independent Caribbean nations, including Antigua and Barbuda—seized control of Stanford's Bank of Antigua. A new financial entity, the Eastern Caribbean Amalgamated Bank—co-owned by the Government of Antigua and several other Eastern Caribbean private financial institutions—took over the Bank of Antigua in October 2010. No Antiguan officials connected to the Stanford fraud scheme have been brought to trial in Antigua and Barbuda. However, Stanford, who was accused of masterminding the massive fraud that led to his financial group losing more than $7 billion dollars, was in custody in the United States. In December 2011, a Texas judge ruled that he was mentally fit to stand trial.

Fallout from the collapse of the Stanford Financial Group, as well as the global economic downturn, continued to wreak havoc on Antigua and Barbuda's economy in 2011. In July, the government and the Eastern Caribbean Central Bank were forced to take over the Antigua and Barbuda Investment Bank, which was established in 1990, to save it from collapse due to liquidity problems.

In addition to the Stanford financial crisis, crime continues to be a roadblock to the country's economic recovery. Antiguan authorities attribute an increasing crime rate to drug trafficking and the deportation of expatriates from North America and Europe. In 2010, a leading cruise line canceled all calls to Antigua following the murder of one of its passengers on the island.

Political Rights and Civil Liberties: Antigua and Barbuda is an electoral democracy. The 1981 constitution establishes a parliamentary system, with a governor general representing the British monarch as ceremonial head of state. The bicameral Parliament is composed of the 17-seat House of Representatives (16 seats for Antigua, 1 for Barbuda), to which members are elected for five-year terms, and an appointed Senate. Of the senators, 11 are appointed by the governor general on the advice of the prime minister, 4 on the advice of the parliamentary opposition leader, 1 on the advice of the Barbuda Council (an 11-member local government body that runs Barbuda's internal affairs), and 1 at the governor general's discretion. Antigua and Barbuda's prime minister is typically the leader of the majority party or coalition that emerges from the legislative elections. The Antigua and Barbuda Electoral Commission (ABEC) was established in 2008 to reform the country's electoral system, including the introduction of voter identification cards. Political parties can organize freely.

The government has overseen the enactment of anticorruption and transparency legislation in recent years, but implementation has been slow. In the wake of the Stanford financial scandal, Prime Minister Baldwin Spencer's government has sought to improve its image by addressing irregularities at the ABEC, including alleged violations of electoral law by its chairman. However, complaints remain that Antigua and Barbuda has not moved quickly to cooperate with U.S. authorities to investigate and extradite officials who have committed criminal activities in connection with bank fraud.

Antigua and Barbuda generally respects freedom of the press, but in practice media outlets are concentrated among a small number of firms affiliated with either the current government or its predecessor. The Bird family continues to control television, cable, and radio outlets. The government owns one of three radio stations and the public television station. There are no restrictions on access to the internet.

The government generally respects religious and academic freedoms.

Nongovernmental organizations are active, but they lack adequate funding and are often influenced by the government. Demonstrators are occasionally subject to police harassment. Labor unions can organize freely. The Industrial Relations Court mediates labor disputes.

The country's legal system is based on English common law. During the Bird years, the ALP government manipulated the nominally independent judicial system, which was powerless to address corruption in the executive branch. However, in recent years, the courts have increasingly asserted independence through controversial decisions against the government.

The police generally respect human rights, though basic police statistics remain confidential. The country's prison is in primitive condition, and the abuse of inmates has been reported, though visits by independent human rights groups are permitted. The government has responded to higher levels of crime in recent years with increased patrols, the reintroduction of roadblocks, and stiffer fines for firearms violations.

The 2005 Equal Opportunity Act bars discrimination on the basis of race, gender, class, political affinity, or place of origin. However, societal discrimination and violence against women remain problems.

Argentina

Political Rights: 2
Civil Liberties: 2
Status: Free

Population: 40,488,000
Capital: Buenos Aires

Ten-Year Ratings Timeline For Year Under Review (Political Rights, Civil Liberties, Status)

2002	2003	2004	2005	2006	2007	2008	2009	2010	2011
3,3PF	2,2F	2,2F	2,2F	2,2F	2,2F	2,2F	2,2F	2,2F	2,2F

Overview: **President Cristina Fernández de Kirchner was reelected in a landslide in October 2011, defeating the nearest challenger by an unprecedented 37 points. Her Front for Victory coalition also regained control of both houses of Congress in concurrent legislative elections. Meanwhile, the Fernández administration continued to prosecute perpetrators of human rights violations committed during the "dirty war."**

Argentina gained independence from Spain in 1816. Democratic rule was often interrupted by war and military coups over the following century. The end of former president Juan Perón's populist and authoritarian regime in 1955 led to a series of right-wing military dictatorships that lasted until 1983. The beginning of civilian rule brought an end to Argentina's "dirty war," which was waged against real or suspected dissidents by the far-right military regime.

Carlos Menem, a populist of the Justicialist Party (PJ, commonly known as the Peronist Party) who ran on a platform of nationalism and state intervention in the economy, was elected president in 1989 amid hyperinflation and food riots. As president, however, he implemented an economic liberalization program and unconditionally allied the country with the United States. His convertibility plan, which pegged the peso to the U.S. dollar through a currency board, ended the country's chronic bouts of hyperinflation.

Buenos Aires mayor Fernando de la Rúa, of the center-left Alianza coalition, was elected president in 1999. Record unemployment and reduced government wages, effects of the highly overvalued and inflexible currency, spurred demonstrations and unprecedented economic insecurity. Government efforts to stop a run on Argentina's banking system sparked violent protests in December 2001, forcing de la Rúa to resign. He was replaced by interim president Adolfo Rodríguez Saá, who resigned less than a week later. On December 31, Congress selected Menem's former vice president, Eduardo Duhalde, as Argentina's new president. A steep devaluation of the peso and a debilitating default on its foreign debt left Argentina teetering on the brink of political and economic collapse throughout 2002.

Néstor Kirchner of the Front for Victory (FPV) coalition, a faction of the Peronists, was elected president in 2003. While working to stabilize the economy, Kirchner moved to purge the country's military and police leadership of authoritarian elements. He took steps to remove justices from the highly politicized Supreme Court—considered the country's most corrupt institution—and signed a decree that permitted the extradition of former military officials accused of human rights abuses. In 2006, Kirchner implemented a series of measures to centralize power in the executive branch. He also changed the tax system to limit the influence of historically powerful provincial governors and created new state-owned enterprises while nationalizing privatized ones.

Kirchner successfully passed his concentrated power on to his wife, Senator Cristina Fernández de Kirchner, after she was elected president in October 2007. In practice, she began to govern in tandem with her husband, and the Argentine media commonly referred to their rule as a dual presidency, or "Los K."

Fernández's once-strong political alliance and majority in Congress fractured following a standoff with Argentina's agricultural sector in 2008 over her administration's failed attempt to increase export taxes on certain farm products. Midterm legislative elections held in June 2009 in the midst of an economic downturn brought significant losses for Fernández and her party.

Beginning in mid-2010, the economy began to recover, fueled by a more benign international economic environment and increased agricultural prices. The administration also increased social welfare spending, including a grant program that provides $50 per month to approximately 3 million poor children.

To finance increased spending, Fernández pushed a law through Congress in February 2010 allowing the government to use $6.5 billion of Argentina's foreign currency reserves. The nationalization of $30 billion in private pension funds in December 2008 provided additional financial support, and also gave the Kirchner administration increased control over companies owned in part by these pension funds. Fernández continued to centralize power around the executive even after Néstor Kirchner's sudden death in October 2010.

Garnering 54 percent of the vote, Fernández was reelected on October 23, 2011. She obtained the largest margin of victory in the first round of an Argentine presidential election since the return of democracy in 1983, 37 points ahead of runner-up Hermes Binner of the socialist Progressive Broad Front (FAP) party. Fernández's FPV, with its allies, also won eight of the nine governors' races, reclaimed the lower house of Congress, and increased their majority in the Senate. A fragmented opposition contributed to Fernández's reelection, as did strong economic growth fueled by government spending and high commodity prices. Ongoing sympathy for the death of Néstor Kirchner, still wildly popular, also contributed to her landslide election. While beginning her second term with a strong mandate, monthly capital flight of $3 billion, unofficial annual inflation of 20-30 percent, and a narrowing trade surplus threatened the strength of the Argentine economy at the end of 2011.

Political Rights and Civil Liberties: Argentina is an electoral democracy. As amended in 1994, the constitution provides for a president elected for four years, with the option of reelection for one additional term. Presidential candidates must win 45 percent of the vote to avoid a runoff. The National Congress consists of the 257-member Chamber of Deputies, whose members are directly elected for four-year terms, with half of the seats up for election every two years, and the 72-member Senate, whose members are directly elected for six-year terms, with one-third of the seats up for election every two years.

The right to organize political parties is generally respected. Major parties include the Justicialist Party, which includes the center-left FPV faction, the centrist Radical Civic Union (UCR), the center-right Republican Proposal (PRO), and the socialist FAP. The Peronists have been a dominant force in politics since 1946.

Former president Néstor Kirchner's government initially made anticorruption efforts a central theme, establishing the public's right to information and other transparency guarantees. However, subsequent corruption scandals revealed the degree to which entrenched corruption plagues Argentine society. Former president Carlos Menem (and current senator) was charged in 2008 with illegally supplying weapons to Ecuador and Croatia, but he was acquitted in September 2011. Allegations of vote-buying on the part of the government arose in 2010 due to various opposition congressmen voting against opposition-led reforms. Former secretary of transportation, Ricardo Jaime, was indicted twice in 2010 on separate charges of embezzlement that reportedly occurred during his tenure from 2003 to 2009; no trial had taken place by the end of 2011. A corruption scandal emerged in May 2011 surrounding the Association of Mothers of the Plaza de Mayo, a group of women campaigning to discover the fate of their children under Argentina's military dictatorship. The government of Cristina Fernández de Kirchner had provided them with an estimated $175 million dollars in state financing to build homes for the poor; the group allegedly committed fraud, money laundering, and illegal enrichment. More than 60 members of the group faced criminal charges at year's end. Argentina was ranked 100 out of 183 countries surveyed in Transparency International's 2011 Corruption Perceptions Index.

Freedom of expression is guaranteed by law. However, while Congress decriminalized libel and slander in 2009, the Fernández government has consistently limited press freedom in practice. In 2011, it continued to manipulate the distribution of official advertising to reward supportive media and to damage critical media such as Grupo Clarín, Argentina's largest media conglomerate. A media reform bill passed in 2009 was designed to help break up Grupo Clarín and limit monopoly abuses by large media corporations. However, the bill also contained provisions limiting freedom of expression, including the creation of a politically appointed media regulatory body with control over interpreting and implementing the law. In August 2010, the government canceled the operating license of Fibertel, a broadband internet service provider owned by Grupo Clarín, based on licensing issues. The government also moved to take over Argentina's only newsprint company, Papel Prensa, and filed criminal charges against its owners for allegedly conspiring with the dictatorship to buy the company in 1976. However, a federal court ruling overturned the government's cancelation of Fibertel in September 2010—a decision that the Fernández government appealed in March 2011; the case was pending at year's end. While the Senate passed a freedom of information bill in September 2010 that would apply to all branches of the government, the bill had yet to pass the Chamber of Deputies by the end of 2011.

The constitution guarantees freedom of religion, and anti-Semitism is reportedly on the decline. In June 2010, Fernández appointed a Jewish foreign minister, the first person of the Jewish faith to become foreign minister in Argentina. Nevertheless, Argentina's Jewish community, the largest in Latin America, remains a target of discrimination and vandalism. The 1994 bombing of a Jewish cultural center continues to play a role in Argentine politics, as no convictions have been made. Academic freedom is a cherished Argentine tradition and is largely observed in practice.

The rights of freedom of assembly and association are generally respected. Civic organizations are robust and play a major role in society, although some fall victim to Argentina's pervasive corruption. Labor is dominated by Peronist unions, though union influence has diminished dramatically in recent years due to internal divisions.

While Kirchner appointed magistrates of professional quality, the tenure of scores of incompetent and corrupt judges remains a serious problem. Police misconduct, including torture and brutality of suspects in police custody, is endemic. The Buenos Aires provincial police have been involved in drug trafficking, extortion, and other crimes. Arbitrary arrests and abuse by police are rarely punished in the courts owing to intimidation of witnesses and judges, particularly in Buenos Aires province. Prisons are overcrowded, and conditions remain substandard throughout the country.

In 2005, the Supreme Court ruled that laws passed in the 1980s to protect the military from prosecution were unconstitutional. The decision laid the foundation for the prosecution of past military crimes, leading Néstor Kirchner to initiate prosecution proceedings against former officials involved in Argentina's dirty war. Prosecutions of perpetrators of human rights violations committed during the dirty war have continued under the Fernández administration. In December 2010, former military dictator and principal architect of the dirty war, Jorge Videla, was found guilty of crimes against humanity. The 85-year-old was sentenced to life in prison; more than 20 other former military and police officials were also convicted along with Videla. Twelve military and police officers, including Ricardo Cavallo and Alfredo Astiz, were convicted with torture, murder, and forced disappearance in October 2011 and sentenced to life in prison.

Argentina's indigenous peoples, who represent between 3 and 5 percent of the total population, are largely neglected by the government. Approximately 70 percent of the country's rural indigenous communities lack title to their lands. While the Kirchner administration returned lands to several communities, most disputes remain unresolved. Forced evictions of indigenous communities still occur, despite laws prohibiting this practice. In 2002, Buenos Aires became the first South American city to pass a domestic partnership law, and Argentina became the second country in the Americas—after Canada—to legalize same-sex marriage nationwide in July 2010.

Women actively participate in politics in Argentina. In addition to the 2011 reelection of Fernández as president, women were elected to 38 percent of the seats in the Chamber of Deputies in October and 39 percent of seats in the Senate. Decrees mandate that one-third of Congress members be women. However, domestic abuse remains a serious problem. Women also face economic discrimination and gender wage gaps.

Armenia

Political Rights: 6
Civil Liberties: 4
Status: Partly Free

Population: 3,123,000
Capital: Yerevan

Note: The numerical ratings and status listed above do not reflect conditions in Nagorno-Karabakh, which is examined in a separate report.

Ten-Year Ratings Timeline For Year Under Review (Political Rights, Civil Liberties, Status)

2002	2003	2004	2005	2006	2007	2008	2009	2010	2011
4,4PF	4,4PF	5,4PF	5,4PF	5,4PF	5,4PF	6,4PF	6,4PF	6,4PF	6,4PF

Overview: **Under mounting pressure from Arab Spring–inspired protests and international organizations like the Council of Europe, the Armenian authorities released the last remaining political prisoners from a 2008 postelection crackdown on the opposition. The government also lifted a ban on rallies in the capital's Freedom Square, reopened an investigation into the 10 deaths that had accompanied the 2008 crackdown, and began a dialogue with the opposition; however, there was little progress on the last two efforts by year's end. Finally, the country adopted a new electoral code, which the Council of Europe regarded as an improvement, though it did not incorporate the opposition's suggestions.**

Following a short period of independence amid the turmoil at the end of World War I, Armenia was divided between Turkey and the Soviet Union by 1922. Most Armenians in the Turkish portion were killed or driven abroad during the war and its aftermath, but those in the east survived Soviet rule. The Soviet republic of Armenia declared its independence in 1991, propelled by a nationalist movement that had initially focused on demands to transfer the substantially ethnic Armenian region of Nagorno-Karabakh from Azerbaijan to Armenia. Nagorno-Karabakh was recognized internationally as part of Azerbaijan, but by the late 1990s, it was held by ethnic Armenian forces who claimed independence. Prime Minister Robert Kocharian, a former president of Nagorno-Karabakh, was elected president of Armenia in March 1998.

On October 27, 1999, five gunmen assassinated Prime Minister Vazgen Sarkisian, Assembly Speaker Karen Demirchian, and several other senior officials. Allegations that Kocharian or members of his inner circle had orchestrated the shootings prompted opposition calls for the president to resign. Citing a lack of evidence, however, prosecutors did not press charges against Kocharian, who gradually consolidated his power during the following year.

In 2003, Kocharian was reelected in a presidential vote that was marred by fraud. During the runoff, authorities placed more than 200 opposition supporters in administrative detention for over 15 days; they were sentenced on charges of hooliganism and participation in unsanctioned demonstrations. The Constitutional Court upheld the election results, but it proposed holding a "referendum of confidence" on

Kocharian within the next year; Kocharian rejected the proposal. Opposition parties boycotted subsequent sessions of the National Assembly, and police violently dispersed protests mounted in the spring of 2004 over the government's failure to redress the problems of the 2003 vote.

The Republican Party of Armenia (HHK)—the party of Prime Minister Serzh Sarkisian, a close Kocharian ally—won 65 of 131 seats in the May 2007 National Assembly elections. Two other major propresidential parties took a total of 41 seats, giving the government a dominant majority. Opposition parties suffered from disadvantages regarding media coverage and the abuse of state resources ahead of the vote.

The 2008 presidential election was held on February 19. Five days after the balloting, the Central Election Commission announced that Sarkisian had won with 52.8 percent, and the main opposition candidate, former president Levon Ter-Petrosian, had taken 21.5 percent. The results, which the opposition disputed, allowed Sarkisian to avoid a runoff vote. Peaceful opposition demonstrations that began on February 21 turned violent a week later, when the police engaged the protesters. According to the Organization for Security and Cooperation in Europe (OSCE), 10 people were killed, and more than 200 were injured during the clashes. Outgoing president Kocharian declared a 20-day state of emergency, and more than 100 people were arrested in the wake of the upheaval.

The HHK secured a majority in May 2009 municipal elections in Yerevan, but opposition parties rejected the results as fraudulent. Meanwhile, the authorities' inadequate steps to investigate police abuses during the 2008 violence were criticized by the Council of Europe, and although a June 2009 amnesty freed 30 protesters, about a dozen remained behind bars at the end of 2010.

In the spring of 2011, inspired by ongoing uprisings in Arab countries, tens of thousands of opposition protesters took to the streets. Combined with increased international pressure, the demonstrations convinced the Armenian authorities to release the last political prisoners from the 2008 crackdown, remove a ban on rallies in Yerevan's Freedom Square that also dated to 2008, reopen the investigation into the 10 deaths during the crackdown, and begin a dialogue with opposition parties. However, the dialogue was suspended in September 2011 without any tangible results, and the investigation into the 10 deaths made no headway by year's end.

Given the negative assessments of the 2008 and 2009 elections by international observers, the government adopted a new electoral code in 2011, which the Council of Europe regarded as an improvement over the previous code. However, it did not incorporate any of the suggestions made by opposition parties, and the year's concessions overall were made under intense pressure, raising questions as to the durability and authenticity of the government's new openness to reform.

Political Rights and Civil Liberties: Armenia is not an electoral democracy. The unicameral National Assembly is elected for five-year terms, with 90 seats chosen by proportional representation and 41 through races in single-member districts. The president is elected by popular vote for up to two five-year terms. However, elections since the 1990s have been marred by major irregularities. The 2008 presidential election was seriously undermined by problems with the vote count, a biased and restricted media environment, and the abuse of administrative resources in favor of ruling party candidate Serzh Sarkisian. The Yerevan municipal elections held in May 2009 also suffered from significant violations, though international observers claimed that the fraud did not jeopardize the overall legitimacy of the results. In 2011, local elections were held in several districts, but the polls were boycotted by the opposition and not observed by international monitors.

Corruption is pervasive and systematic in Armenia. Bribery and nepotism are reportedly common among government officials, who are rarely prosecuted or removed for abuse of office. Corruption is also believed to be a serious problem in law enforcement. A five-year initiative to combat graft, announced in 2008, has not made meaningful headway against the country's entrenched culture of corruption.

There are limits on press freedom. The authorities use informal pressure to maintain control over broadcast outlets, the chief source of news for most Armenians. State-run Armenian Public Television is the only station with nationwide coverage, and the owners of most private channels have close government ties. In June 2010, the National Assembly enacted legislation that fixed the maximum number of television stations at 18—down from at least 22 operating at the time—and obliged a number of the new total to focus on content other than domestic news and political affairs. The legislation contributed to the revocation in 2011 of the license of GALA TV, the sole remaining station that regularly criticized the government. The government also continued to deny a license to the independent television company A1+, despite a 2008 ruling in its favor by the European Court of Human Rights. A1+, which had been forced off the air by a government licensing decision in 2002, made a fresh bid for a license in October 2010, but it was rejected in December, 2010 on the grounds that A1+ had submitted fraudulent documents. The authorities do not interfere with internet access.

Libel remains a criminal offense, and violence against journalists is a problem. Nikol Pashinian, editor in chief of the independent daily *Haykakan Zhamanak*, was released from prison in 2011 as part of the amnesty for those arrested during the 2008 postelection crackdown. He had reportedly been beaten while in detention and was held in solitary confinement.

Freedom of religion is generally respected, though the dominant Armenian Apostolic Church enjoys certain exclusive privileges, and members of minority faiths sometimes face societal discrimination. Jehovah's Witnesses are forced to serve prison terms for refusing to participate in either military service or the military-administered alternative service for conscientious objectors.

The government generally does not restrict academic freedom. Public schools are required to display portraits of the president and the head of the Armenian Apostolic Church, and to teach the church's history.

In the aftermath of the 2008 postelection violence, the government imposed restrictions on freedom of assembly. Under pressure from major opposition rallies in the spring of 2011, as well as criticism from the Council of Europe, the authorities ended the practice of forbidding demonstrations in the capital's Freedom Square, the traditional venue for political gatherings since the late 1980s. However, they continued to create artificial obstacles for people attempting to travel from the provinces to participate in such rallies.

Registration requirements for nongovernmental organizations (NGOs) are cumbersome and time consuming. Some 3,000 NGOs are registered with the Ministry of Justice, though many are not active in a meaningful way. While the constitution provides for the right to form and join trade unions, labor organizations are weak and relatively inactive in practice.

The judiciary is subject to political pressure from the executive branch and suffers from considerable corruption. Police make arbitrary arrests without warrants, beat detainees during arrest and interrogation, and use torture to extract confessions. Prison conditions in Armenia are poor, and threats to prisoner health are significant.

Although members of the country's tiny ethnic minority population rarely report cases of overt discrimination, they have complained about difficulties in receiving education in their native languages. Members of the Yezidi community have sometimes reported discrimination by police and local authorities.

Citizens have the right to own private property and establish businesses, but an inefficient and often corrupt court system and unfair business competition hinder such activities. Key industries remain in the hands of so-called oligarchs and influential cliques who received preferential treatment in the early stages of privatization.

According to the new election code, women must occupy every 6th position on a party's candidate list for the parliament's proportional-representation seats. Women took 12 of 131 seats in the National Assembly elected in 2007. Domestic violence and trafficking in women and girls for the purpose of prostitution are believed to be serious problems. Though homosexuality was decriminalized in 2003, homosexual individuals still face violence and persecution.

Australia

Political Rights: 1
Civil Liberties: 1
Status: Free

Population: 22,670,000
Capital: Canberra

Ten-Year Ratings Timeline For Year Under Review (Political Rights, Civil Liberties, Status)

2002	2003	2004	2005	2006	2007	2008	2009	2010	2011
1,1F	1,1F	1,1F	1,1F	1,1F	1,1F	1,1F	1,1F	1,1F	1,1F

Overview: **The Australian government continued in 2011 to struggle with an influx of asylum seekers, mostly from South Asia, and violent outbreaks at detention centers. In August, the High Court ruled against a controversial plan to exchange asylum seekers in Australia for refugees in Malaysia. In late 2011, Parliament passed a controversial package of bills that would introduce a tax on some carbon dioxide emissions.**

The British colonies in Australia, first settled in 1788, were organized as a federative commonwealth in 1901 and gradually gained full independence from Britain. Since World War II, political power has alternated between the center-left Labor Party and a conservative coalition of the Liberal Party and the smaller National Party. Labor emerged from the 2007 elections with 83 seats in the 150-seat

House of Representatives and 32 in the 76-seat Senate, allowing party leader Kevin Rudd to replace John Howard of the Liberal Party as prime minister.

The Rudd government reversed a number of its predecessor's positions, including issuing a formal apology for past laws and policies that had "inflicted profound grief, suffering, and loss" on the country's Aborigines. It also closed detention centers in Nauru and Papua New Guinea that the Howard government had created in response to an influx of asylum seekers from South Asia, and pledged to resolve asylum claims within a year. However, by the end of 2008, the government was forced to open a new detention center on Christmas Island to receive an increasing number of migrants; by the first week of December 2010, 82 boats with nearly 4,000 asylum seekers were stopped, or 1,000 more than the total for 2009. Public sentiment on both sides of the issue intensified as asylum seekers set fire to their boats, went on hunger strikes, committed suicide, or took other extreme measures to demand entry into Australia.

Rudd resigned as party leader and prime minister in June 2010, having been buffeted by the asylum crisis, a national home-insulation scheme that was linked to four deaths and many fires, a controversial proposal for a "super tax" on the booming coal and iron-ore industries, and a failed effort to adopt carbon-emissions trading. Deputy Prime Minister Julia Gillard was chosen to replace Rudd, making her the country's first female prime minister. She called snap elections for August, and the campaign centered on issues including the economy, health care, the national debt, and immigration. The number of Labor Party seats fell to 72 in the House, compared with a total of 73 seats for the conservative parties. The Greens took one seat, and four seats went to independents. After two weeks of intense negotiations, Labor secured support from the Greens' member and three independents, and Gillard announced a new cabinet in September.

In response to the continuing issue of asylum seekers, the new Labor government negotiated an agreement with Afghanistan in January 2011 for the involuntary repatriation of Afghans who fail to meet refugee criteria; however, the government had yet to carry out any such repatriations by year's end. Six months later, the Australian government announced an agreement to send 800 asylum seekers to Malaysia in exchange for receiving 4,000 refugees from Malaysia for permanent resettlement over the next four years. While authorities said the plan was intended to deter the smuggling of asylum seekers to Australia, the High Court ruled in August that it was unlawful on the grounds that Malaysia does not offer adequate refugee protection. The government dropped the plan in October. Also in 2011, asylum seekers at the Christmas Island detention facility turned to violence, suicide, and hunger strikes to voice their discontent with living conditions at the center and the pace of processing their applications. In March and July, asylum seekers on Christmas Island clashed with security personnel and burned buildings.

In October and November, the House and the Senate, respectively, passed a controversial package of bills that would introduce a tax on some carbon dioxide emissions, in an effort to reduce the country's greenhouse gas emissions. Under the bills, Australia's top 500 carbon emitters—including companies in the lucrative energy and mining sectors—would be hit by the tax starting on July 1, 2012. In 2015, the tax would be replaced with an emissions permit trading system. The bills drew strong protests from industry, the Liberal Party, and the public due to concerns about its effect on the economy and jobs.

Political Rights and Civil Liberties: Australia is an electoral democracy. A governor general, who is appointed on the recommendation of the prime minister, represents the British monarch as head of state. The prime minister is the leader of the majority party or coalition in Parliament.

Voting is compulsory, and citizens participate in free and fair multiparty elections to choose representatives for the bicameral Parliament. The Senate, the upper house, has 76 seats, with 12 senators from each of the six states and 2 from each of the two mainland territories. Half of the state members, who serve six-year terms, are up for election every three years; all territory members are elected every three years. The House of Representatives, the lower house, has 150 seats. All members are elected by popular preferential voting to serve three-year terms, and no state can have fewer than five representatives.

The Labor and Liberal parties are the two major parties. Minor parties represented in the Parliament are the left-leaning Green Party and three right-leaning factions (the Liberal National Party of Queensland, the National Party, and the Country Liberal Party).

Australia is regarded as one of the least corrupt societies in the world, ranking 8 out of 183 countries surveyed in Transparency International's 2011 Corruption Perceptions Index.

There are no constitutional protections for freedom of speech and the press, but citizens and the media freely criticize the government without reprisal. Some laws restrict publication and dissemination of material that promotes or incites terrorist acts. There are numerous public and private television and radio broadcasters, but ownership of private print media is highly concentrated. In September 2011, the government announced an inquiry to determine whether the media used illegal means to collect protected information in the wake of a phone-hacking scandal in the United Kingdom involving News Ltd., which controls some two-thirds of Australia's newspaper market.

Freedom of religion is respected, as is academic freedom. Under antiterrorism laws, mosques and Islamic schools are barred from disseminating anti-Australian messages.

Freedoms of assembly and association are not codified in law, but the government respects these rights in practice. Workers can organize and bargain collectively.

The judiciary is independent, and prison conditions generally meet international standards. Antiterrorism legislation enacted in 2005, with a 10-year sunset clause, includes police powers to detain suspects without charge, "shoot to kill" provisions, the criminalization of violence against the public and Australian troops overseas, and authorization for the limited use of soldiers to meet terrorist threats on domestic soil.

Some 40 people have been arrested on terrorism charges since 2000. Five men of Libyan, Bangladeshi, and Lebanese origin arrested in 2005 were sentenced in February 2010 to prison terms ranging from 23 to 28 years for conspiracy to commit acts of terrorism. Australian immigration has been expanding use of electronic biometric captures of fingerprints and facial images for visitors since 2011, with emphasis on those from countries deemed a high risk for Islamic extremism, such as Yemen and Somalia.

Since the beginning of 2011, the military has been embroiled in a series of scandals involving rape, homophobia, bullying, and sexual predation. More than 1,000 allegations were registered by late August. In September, a navy male cadet was convicted of raping a female cadet; in December, a navy commander was found guilty of abusing a female subordinate by spanking her. In November, the Human Rights Commissioner released an initial review stating that culture change is needed. Meanwhile, in September the government lifted a ban on women in combat roles.

Racial tensions involving South Asian and other immigrant groups have grown in recent years, especially in Melbourne, where the bulk of interracial violence has occurred in recent years. The number of South Asian applications to universities in Australia fell in the 2010 and 2011 academic years, which run from mid-January to mid-December.

Aborigines, who comprise about 2 percent of the population, are underrepresented at all levels of political leadership and lag far behind other groups in key social and economic indicators, including life expectancy and employment. Aborigines are reportedly routinely mistreated by police and prison officials, and they experience higher rates of incarceration and levels of violence, including homicide and child abuse.

Women enjoy equal rights and have attained greater parity in pay and promotion in public and private sector jobs. In September 2011, the government announced that women in the military could serve in combat positions. Violence against women remains a serious problem, particularly within the Aboriginal population. Homosexuals can serve in the military, and federal law grants legal residence to foreign same-sex partners of Australian citizens. However, there is no federal ban on discrimination based on sexual orientation, and a 2004 amendment to the Federal Marriage Act defines marriage as a union between a man and a woman. A 2010 law allows prosecution of Australians for sex crimes committed overseas and imposes prison terms of up to 25 years for sex crimes against children. In July 2011, New South Wales gave new powers to the police to order women to remove burqas and other face coverings if they are suspected of a crime; those who refuse to remove the coverings could face one year in jail or be fined A$5,500 (US$5,384).

Austria

Political Rights: 1
Civil Liberties: 1
Status: Free

Population: 8,418,000
Capital: Vienna

Ten-Year Ratings Timeline For Year Under Review (Political Rights, Civil Liberties, Status)

2002	2003	2004	2005	2006	2007	2008	2009	2010	2011
1,1F	1,1F	1,1F	1,1F	1,1F	1,1F	1,1F	1,1F	1,1F	1,1F

Overview: **In 2011, Austria saw a number of high-profile court cases centering on the balance between freedom of speech and hate speech, including one case involving a person convicted of denigration of religious teachings for statements made during a seminar on Islam. In June, the parliament repealed a constitutional provision that had denied the right of**

members of the Habsburg family to run for Austria's presidency. Meanwhile, Austria was elected to the UN Human Rights Council in May.

Modern Austria, which emerged from the collapse of the Austro-Hungarian Empire in World War I, was annexed to Nazi Germany in 1938 before being restored to independence after World War II. The country remained neutral during the Cold War and joined the European Union in 1995.

From 1986 until 2000, the two largest political parties—the center-left Social Democratic Party of Austria (SPÖ) and the center-right People's Party of Austria (ÖVP)—governed together in a grand coalition. The 1999 elections produced the first government since 1970 that did not include the SPÖ. Instead, the ÖVP formed a coalition with the Freedom Party of Austria (FPÖ), a far-right nationalist party that won 27 percent of the popular vote. Its support had risen steadily as voters became disaffected with the large parties' power-sharing arrangement. In 2000, the European Union (EU) briefly suspended ties with Austria, imposing diplomatic sanctions in response to the FPÖ's inclusion in government.

Due to the sanctions, the controversial Jörg Haider stepped down as FPÖ leader at the end of 2000, and the FPÖ withdrew from the coalition in September 2002 after an internal leadership struggle. Parliamentary elections that November saw the FPÖ's share of the vote fall to 10 percent. It rejoined the coalition with the ÖVP, but as a junior partner. Subsequent poor election performances widened rifts within the party. Most of its members of parliament, as well as Haider, left in 2005 to form the Alliance for the Future of Austria (BZÖ).

In October 2006, parliamentary elections confirmed an ÖVP decline, with the SPÖ winning by a small margin and the two parties forming another grand coalition. In the summer of 2008, the ÖVP announced its exit from the coalition amid political battles over health, tax, and pension reforms, as well as policy toward the EU.

In September 2008 elections, the SPÖ and ÖVP lost ground to the BZÖ and FPÖ, which were buoyed by xenophobic sentiment and deep skepticism toward the EU. However, both the SPÖ and the ÖVP refused to form a coalition with the far right, and in late 2008, they agreed to revive their alliance.

The February 2009 state elections suggested a continued movement toward the right, with the SPÖ suffering dramatic losses. The ÖVP retained power in Upper Austria and Vorarlberg, but the FPÖ nearly doubled its presence in both regions as it absorbed support from the much-diminished BZÖ. However, the ÖVP again ruled out a coalition with the FPÖ.

Incumbent Heinz Fischer of the SPÖ won a second term as president in an April 2010 election. He took around 80 percent of the vote, defeating FPÖ candidate Barbara Rosenkranz and Christian Party of Austria (CPÖ) candidate Rudolf Gehring, with some 16 percent and 5.5 percent, respectively.

In October 2010 state elections in Vienna, the SPÖ lost its absolute majority in the legislature for only the second time since World War II, though it still led with 44.2 percent of the vote. The FPÖ placed second with 27 percent, while the ÖVP faced its worst-ever result in Vienna with only 13.2 percent. However, the FPÖ did not achieve equal gains in the Burgenland and Styria state elections, which have small foreign-born and ethnic minority populations.

In 2009, Ulrich Habsburg-Lothringen, whose family ruled the Austro-Hungarian Empire until 1918, lobbied the Austrian Constitutional Court to end a ban prohibiting members of his family from running for Austria's presidency. After both his request and his presidential candidacy were denied, the Habsburg family filed a complaint with the European Court of Human Rights in October 2010, claiming that the ban violated their right to participate in democratic elections. In June 2011, the Austrian parliament formally repealed the constitutional provision.

In May 2011, Austria was elected as a new member of the UN Human Rights Council. As part of its candidature, the government made a series of pledges and commitments to promote and protect the rule of law and human rights, including increasing protections for religious minorities and members of the press, and advancing children's rights.

Political Rights and Civil Liberties: Austria is an electoral democracy. The lower house of the Federal Assembly, the Nationalrat (National Council), has 183 members chosen through proportional representation at the district, state, and federal levels. Members serve five-year terms, extended from four in 2008. The president, who is elected for a six-year term, appoints the chancellor, who needs the support of the legislature to govern. The 62 members of the upper house, the Bundesrat (Federal Council), are chosen by state legislatures for five- or six-year terms.

Though Austria has competitive political parties and free and fair elections, the traditional practice of grand coalitions has fostered disillusionment with the political process. The participation of Slovene, Hungarian, and Roma minorities in local government remains limited despite governmental efforts to provide bilingual education, media, and access to federal funds.

Tightened campaign donation laws have reduced political corruption in recent decades. While Austria ratified the OECD Anti-Bribery Convention in 1999, concerns were raised around a 2009 amendment to Austria's anticorruption legislation, which could weaken its laws against bribery of foreign public officials. Nonetheless, Austria was ranked 16 out of 183 countries surveyed in Transparency International's 2011 Corruption Perceptions Index.

The federal constitution and the Media Law of 1981 provide the basis for free media in Austria, and the government generally respects these provisions in practice. However, libel and slander laws protect politicians and government officials, and a large number of defamation cases have been brought by public officials, particularly from the FPÖ, over the last years. Despite a 2003 law to promote media diversity, media ownership remains highly concentrated. There are no restrictions on internet access.

While there is no official censorship, Austrian law prohibits any form of neo-Nazism or anti-Semitism, as well as the public denial, approval, or justification of Nazi crimes, including the Holocaust. However, the far-right FPÖ has been accused of anti-Semitic rhetoric in recent years. Additionally, the FPÖ has been criticized for fueling anti-Muslim feelings in Austria through controversial ad campaigns. A number of recent high-profile court cases have centered on the balance between freedom of speech and hate speech. In February 2011, Elisabeth Sabaditsch-Wolff was found guilty of "denigration of religious teachings of a legally recognized religion" for statements made in a seminar she delivered on Islam for the FPÖ and fined up to 480 (US$656). Her conviction was upheld in a higher court in December. Austria rejected the recommendations made in January 2011 by the Universal Periodic Review (UPR) of the UN Human Rights Council to develop a National Action Plan on Racism and Xenophobia and to collect and generate disaggregated data on manifestations of racism and discrimination.

Religious freedom is constitutionally guaranteed. Austrian law divides religious organizations into three legal categories: officially recognized religious societies, religious confessional communities, and associations. Many religious minority groups have complained that the law impedes their legitimate claims for recognition and demotes them to second- or third-class status. There are no government restrictions on academic freedom or cultural events.

Freedoms of assembly and association are protected in the constitution and in practice. Civic and nongovernmental organizations operate without restrictions. Trade unions are free to organize and strike, and they are considered an essential partner in national policymaking.

The judiciary is independent, and the Constitutional Court examines the compatibility of legislation with the constitution. Austria is a member of the Council of Europe, and its citizens have recourse to the European Court of Human Rights. The quality of prisons generally meets high European standards.

Residents are usually afforded equal protection under the law. However, immigration has fueled some resentment toward minorities and foreigners. Austria has one of the world's highest numbers of asylum seekers per capita, and the Office of the UN High Commissioner for Refugees has criticized Austria's strict asylum law. Some asylum seekers can be deported while appeals are pending, and new arrivals are asked for full statements within 72 hours. In addition, the number of people who have been naturalized has fallen dramatically since the establishment of a more restrictive national integration policy in 2009.

A 1979 law guarantees women's freedom from discrimination in various areas, including the workplace. However, the income gap between men and women remains significant. The 2009 Second Protection Against Violence Act increased penalties for perpetrators of domestic violence and authorized further measures against chronic offenders. A 2009 law permits civil partnerships for same-sex couples, giving them equal rights to pension benefits and alimony. However, it does not provide same-sex couples with the same adoption rights as heterosexual couples or equal access to assisted reproductive technologies. By the end of 2011, women comprised 28 percent of the lower house and 31 percent of the upper house.

Azerbaijan

Political Rights: 6
Civil Liberties: 5
Status: Not Free

Population: 9,150,000
Capital: Baku

Trend Arrow: Azerbaijan received a downward trend arrow due to widespread attacks on civil society, including the unlawful detention and imprisonment of political activists, opposition members, and local and international journalists; restrictions on and violent dispersals of public protests; and unlawful evictions of citizens from their homes.

Note: The numerical ratings and status listed above do not reflect conditions in Nagorno-Karabakh, which is examined in a separate report.

Ten-Year Ratings Timeline For Year Under Review (Political Rights, Civil Liberties, Status)

2002	2003	2004	2005	2006	2007	2008	2009	2010	2011
6,5PF	6,5NF	6,5NF	6,5NF	6,5NF	6,5NF	6,5NF	6,5NF	6,5NF	6,5NF

Overview: **A series of antigovernment protests calling for democratic reform were violently dispersed in March and April 2011, and dozens of people, including opposition leaders and well-known journalists, were detained and jailed. The government acted aggressively during the year to quash political dissent, apparently fearing an uprising akin to those unfolding in the Middle East and North Africa. In June, high-level, Russian-mediated talks on the status of Nagorno-Karabakh ended in stalemate. Separately during the summer, the government forcibly evicted many Baku residents from their homes as part of a citywide redevelopment project.**

After a short period of independence from 1918 to 1920, Azerbaijan was occupied by Soviet forces and formally entered the Soviet Union in 1922. Following a referendum in 1991, Azerbaijan declared independence from the disintegrating union.

In 1992, Abulfaz Elchibey, leader of the nationalist opposition Azerbaijan Popular Front, was elected president in a generally free and fair vote. A military coup one year later ousted him from power and installed the former first secretary of the Azerbaijan Communist Party, Heydar Aliyev, in his place. In the October 1993 presidential election, Aliyev was credited with receiving nearly 99 percent of the vote. Five leading opposition parties and some 600 independent candidates were barred from the first post-Soviet parliamentary elections in 1995, allowing Aliyev's Yeni Azerbaijan Party (YAP) to win the most seats. In 1998, Aliyev was reelected with more than 70 percent of the vote in balloting that was marred by irregularities, and the YAP won fraudulent parliamentary polls in 2000.

Heydar Aliyev collapsed during a live television broadcast in April 2003 and left Azerbaijan that summer to receive medical treatment abroad. In June, his son, Prime Minister Ilham Aliyev, was officially nominated as a candidate for the October presidential election, and the elder Aliyev withdrew his own candidacy just two weeks before the vote.

Final election results showed Ilham Aliyev defeating seven challengers with nearly 77 percent of the ballots. His closest rival, opposition Musavat Party leader Isa Gambar, received only 14 percent, while six other candidates received less than 4 percent each. According to Organization for Security and Cooperation in Europe (OSCE) observers, the vote was again tainted by widespread fraud. After violent clashes between security forces and demonstrators in Baku in October, the authorities unleashed a crackdown against the opposition in which more than 600 people were detained. Among those arrested were election officials who refused to certify fraudulent results. Heydar Aliyev died in December 2003.

Less than half of all registered voters cast ballots in the 2005 parliamentary elections, the lowest voter turnout in a decade. The opposition captured just 10 of 125 seats in the Milli Majlis (National Assembly), with a substantial majority going to the ruling YAP and its allies. The results were contested by the opposition, which organized a number of rallies in the capital.

Aliyev easily won a second term in the October 2008 presidential election, taking 89 percent of the vote amid 75 percent turnout, according to official results. Most of the political opposition chose to boycott the poll, citing barriers to meaningful media access and the overwhelming influence of administrative resources deployed by the YAP. In March 2009, a constitutional amendment that removed presidential term limits reportedly passed a referendum with more than 90 percent of the vote, allowing Aliyev to run again in 2013.

The November 2010 parliamentary elections followed the established trend of increasing manipulation, and the YAP emerged with 71 seats, up from 61 in the 2005 polls. The remainder went to 41 independents and 10 minor parties, none of which garnered more than three seats.

In March and April 2011, a series of antigovernment protests calling for democratic reforms drew a harsh crackdown by the authorities. Demonstrations were violently dispersed, and dozens of people—including well-known journalists, youth activists, and opposition members—were arrested on dubious charges.

International mediators have failed to make progress on a final settlement for the disputed territory of Nagorno-Karabakh, a region of Azerbaijan that has been ruled by ethnic Armenian separatists since the early 1990s. In June 2011, the presidents of Armenia and Azerbaijan met with Russia's president Dmitry Medvedev for talks that were hailed as the most important since the start of the conflict, but Baku refused the terms of a proposed agreement, and the negotiations ended in deadlock. No country or international organization recognizes Nagorno-Karabakh's self-proclaimed independence.

Political Rights and Civil Liberties:

Azerbaijan is not an electoral democracy. The country's constitution provides for a strong presidency, and the parliament, the 125-member Milli Majlis, exercises little or no independence from the executive branch. The president and members of parliament serve five-year terms, and a 2009 referendum eliminated presidential term limits.

Elections since the early 1990s have been considered neither free nor fair by international observers. As with previous votes, the 2010 parliamentary balloting featured the abuse of state administrative resources, including news media, to ensure the dominance of the YAP. The OSCE also cited voter intimidation and the improper disqualification of some opposition candidates.

Corruption is widespread, and wealth from the country's massive oil exports creates ever greater opportunities for graft. Because critical institutions, including the media and judiciary, are largely subservient to the president and ruling party, government officials are rarely held accountable for corruption. The 2011 crackdown on dissent in civil society further reduced the government's exposure to outside scrutiny.

While Azerbaijan's constitution guarantees freedom of speech and the press, the authorities severely limit press freedom in practice. Broadcast media, the main source of information for the vast majority of the population, generally reflect progovernment views. Most of Azerbaijan's television stations are controlled by the government, which also controls approval of broadcast licenses. While there is more pluralism in the print media, newspaper circulation and readership are relatively small. Approximately 80 percent of newspapers are owned by the state. Independent and opposition papers struggle financially and have faced heavy fines and imprisonment of their staff. State-owned companies rarely if ever advertise in such papers. Those who supply information to opposition newspapers have at times been subject to threats and arrest. Local radio broadcasts of key international news services, including the British Broadcasting Corporation (BBC), Radio Free Europe/Radio Liberty (RFE/RL), and Voice of America, were banned in 2009.

Journalists are threatened and assaulted with impunity, and several have been jailed for defamation and other offenses. Newspaper editor Eynulla Fatullayev, who was jailed on a variety of dubious charges in 2007, was released in May 2011. Another editor, Avaz Zeynalli, was arrested in October 2011 and faced up to 12 years in jail on charges of blackmail and bribery. Journalists were beaten and detained during the spring 2011 protests. During one demonstration in April, around 30 reporters were restricted from covering the protest, and two Swedish journalists were arrested and later deported.

Internet-based reporting and social networking have increased significantly in recent years as a means of sidestepping government censorship and mobilizing protesters. The government has repeatedly blocked some websites featuring opposition views, and intimidated the online community through its harsh treatment of two bloggers who were jailed from 2009 to 2010 after satirizing the leadership. In 2011, the authorities monitored the internet use of protest leaders and proposed changing the criminal code to restrict internet access.

The government restricts the practice of "nontraditional" minority religions—those other than Islam, Orthodox Christianity, and Judaism—through burdensome registration requirements and interference in the importation and distribution of printed religious materials. A 2009 law required religious groups to reregister with the authorities and religious figures to be recertified. It also barred foreign citizens from leading prayers. A 2011 amendment to the law significantly increased fines for distribution of unapproved religious material and made leaders of unsanctioned religious services subject to multiyear prison sentences.

The authorities have linked academic freedom to political activity in recent years. Some professors and teachers have reported being dismissed for links to opposition groups, and students have faced threats of lowered grades for similar reasons. In April 2011, a student was expelled from Baku State University and banned from further study after participating in protests, and a university professor was demoted after criticizing the arrest of a youth activist.

The government restricts freedom of assembly, especially for opposition parties. The authorities unlawfully denied registration for the public protests in March and April 2011, a number of which were violently dispersed. Dozens of protesters were arrested, many on false or trumped-up charges. Among them were several well-known youth activists and opposition figures. In October, the head of the unregistered Islamic Party of Azerbaijan was given a 12-year prison sentence on charges of attempting to overthrow the government, having been arrested in January after denouncing the regime at a party meeting. Six other party members received similar sentences.

Legal amendments enacted in 2009 require nongovernmental organizations (NGOs) to register their grants with the authorities and foreign NGOs to reach agreements with the government before opening offices in the country. The rules have been used to put pressure on both local and foreign NGOs. In 2011, three local NGOs in Ganja were evicted from their offices without warning, and the local branches of two international NGOs were shut down for allegedly failing to meet registration requirements. The U.S.-based National Democratic Institute (NDI) was shut down in March but allowed to reopen in September pending negotiations with the government.

Although the law permits the formation of trade unions and the right to strike, the majority of trade unions remain closely affiliated with the government, and most major industries are state owned.

The judiciary is corrupt, inefficient, and subservient to the executive branch. Arbitrary arrest and detention are common, particularly for members of the political opposition. Detainees are often held for long periods before trial, and their access to lawyers is restricted. Police abuse of suspects during arrest and interrogation reportedly remains common; torture is sometimes used to extract confessions. Prison conditions are severe, with many inmates suffering from overcrowding and inadequate medical care. Detained protesters in 2011 reported ill-treatment in custody. Most were arrested arbitrarily, and were denied legal counsel in closed pretrial hearings.

Some members of ethnic minority groups, including the small ethnic Armenian population, have complained of discrimination in areas including education, employment, and housing. Hundreds of thousands of ethnic Azeris who were displaced by the war in Nagorno-Karabakh in the early 1990s remain subject to restrictions on their place of residence and often live in dreadful conditions.

As part of a citywide redevelopment project, the government evicted many Baku residents in the summer of 2011, forcibly removing and illegally demolishing the homes of those who refused to be resettled. Significant parts of the economy are controlled by a corrupt elite, which severely limits equality of opportunity. Supporters of the political opposition face job discrimination, demotion, and dismissal.

Traditional societal norms and poor economic conditions restrict women's professional roles, and they remain underrepresented in government. Women hold 20 seats in the parliament. Domestic violence is a problem, and the country is believed to be a source, transit point, and destination for the trafficking of women for prostitution. A 2005 law criminalized human trafficking, but the U.S. State Department's 2011 Trafficking in Persons Report placed Azerbaijan on its Tier 2 Watch List for the fourth consecutive year.

Bahamas

Political Rights: 1
Civil Liberties: 1
Status: Free

Population: 357,000
Capital: Nassau

Ten-Year Ratings Timeline For Year Under Review (Political Rights, Civil Liberties, Status)

2002	2003	2004	2005	2006	2007	2008	2009	2010	2011
1,1F	1,1F	1,1F	1,1F	1,1F	1,1F	1,1F	1,1F	1,1F	1,1F

Overview: **In response to a dramatic increase in crime rates in 2011, the Bahamian government introduced reforms to key criminal justice legislation, including the Penal Code. A freedom of information bill was also introduced in Parliament in October.**

The Bahamas, a former British colony, became an independent state within the Commonwealth in 1973. Lynden Pindling served as the country's first prime minister and head of the Progressive Liberal Party (PLP) for a quarter century. After years of allegations of corruption and involvement by high-ranking officials in narcotics trafficking, Pindling and the PLP were defeated by the Free National Movement (FNM) party in the 1992 elections.

The FNM ruled the Bahamas for 10 years under Prime Minister Hubert Ingraham, until the 2002 elections brought the PLP, led by Perry Christie, back to power. In May 2007, the FNM triumphed at the polls, winning 23 parliamentary seats to the PLP's 18, thereby restoring Ingraham to the premiership. Christie retained his position as leader of the opposition by winning an overwhelming majority of votes at the PLP leadership conference in October 2009.

Following the surprise resignation in January 2010 of PLP representative Malcolm Adderley, a by-election was called for February to fill the Elizabeth constituency seat. The governing FNM, the PLP, the newly formed National Development Party, the Workers' Party, and the Bahamas Democratic Movement (BDM) all fielded candidates. The FNM was declared the winner by just two votes, a close result that was challenged by the PLP and triggered a mandatory recount. In March, an election court ruled in favor of the PLP, thus overturning the election day results.

The Bahamas has established a model service economy based on an impressive tourism sector—which accounts for a large share of national income—and offshore financial services. However, the Bahamian tourism industry continues to suffer from the global economic crisis that struck in late 2008, posing challenges for the Ingraham government. Marijuana cultivation and trafficking by foreign nationals residing in the country have led the United States to keep the Bahamas on the list of major drug-producing or drug-transit countries.

In 2011, government statistics indicated that almost all major categories of crime had risen dramatically in comparison to the previous year: murder increased by 44 percent, attempted murder by 29 percent, rape by 38 percent, and robbery by 16 percent. In an effort to address the rise in crime, the government amended existing laws and introduced new legislation related to the functioning of the criminal justice system, including amendments to the Penal Code, the Dangerous Drugs Act, the Firearms Act, the Bail Act, the Sexual Offences Bill, and the Court of Appeal Act.

Political Rights and Civil Liberties: The Bahamas is an electoral democracy. The lower house of the bicameral Parliament, the 41-member House of Assembly, is directly elected for five-year terms. The 16 members of the upper house, the Senate, are appointed for five-year terms by the governor general based on recommendations made by the prime minister and the opposition leader. The governor general represents the British monarch as head of state. The head of the majority party or coalition in Parliament typically serves as prime minister. Political parties can organize freely.

Corruption remains a problem at all levels of government. Top officials frequently face allegations of administrative graft, domestically and from abroad. A freedom of information bill was introduced to Parliament in October 2011 and was expected to be debated in early 2012.

The Bahamas has a well-developed tradition of respecting press freedom. The privately owned daily and weekly newspapers express a variety of views, as do the government-run radio station and four privately owned radio broadcasters. Strict and antiquated libel laws dating to British legal codes are seldom invoked. Access to the internet is unrestricted.

Religious and academic freedoms are respected.

Freedoms of assembly and association are protected. Constitutional guarantees of the right to form nongovernmental organizations (NGOs) are generally respected, and human rights organizations have broad access to institutions and individuals. Labor, business, and professional organizations are also generally free from government interference. Unions have the right to strike, and collective bargaining is prevalent.

The judicial system is headed by the Supreme Court and a court of appeals, with the additional right of appeal to the Privy Council in London under certain circumstances. In 2006, the Privy Council ruled that mandatory death sentences for individuals convicted of murder in the Bahamas are unconstitutional. In practice, the death penalty was last carried out in 2000. However, in light of the rising crime rate, calls for resuming capital punishment have been issued recently by government representatives.

NGOs have occasionally documented cases of prisoner abuse and arbitrary arrest. Overcrowding in the country's prison remains a major problem, and juveniles are often housed with adults, increasing the risk of sexual abuse. The correctional training institute established in 2005 has worked to segregate violent and nonviolent offenders. However, the institute continues to face problems of limited capacity, including inadequate space to segregate offenders and insufficient numbers of trained personnel.

The Bahamas remains a major transit point for migrants coming from other Caribbean islands, especially Cuba and Haiti, who are trying to reach the United States. Discrimination against Haitian immigrants persists, and at least 30,000 undocumented Haitians reside in the Bahamas. Strict citizenship requirements and a stringent work-permit system leave Haitians with few rights. While the government halted the deportation of Haitians for a short period following the Haitian earthquake in January 2010, the financial crisis and its effects on the country's tourism sector—which is a main employer of undocumented workers—led the government to resume repatriation of undocumented migrants later that year.

Although gender discrimination is not legally protected, criminal quid pro quo sexual harassment is prohibited. Violence against women, including domestic violence, is a serious problem. Despite laws against domestic violence, police are often reportedly reluctant to intervene in domestic disputes. Only 12 percent of the seats in Parliament are held by women. While sexual orientation is not criminalized, discrimination against same-sex relationships is not prohibited by the constitution. The government is strongly opposed to homosexuality, and efforts have been promoted to weave anti-gay clauses into existing marriage acts.

Bahrain

Political Rights: 6
Civil Liberties: 6*
Status: Not Free

Population: 1,336,000
Capital: Manama

Ratings Change: Bahrain's civil liberties rating declined from 5 to 6 due to the government's brutal response to the February 14 popular democracy movement, the imprisonment and torture of protesters, a clampdown on critical media, and the use of military trials for civilian activists.

Ten-Year Ratings Timeline For Year Under Review (Political Rights, Civil Liberties, Status)

2002	2003	2004	2005	2006	2007	2008	2009	2010	2011
5,5PF	5,5PF	5,5PF	5,5PF	5,5PF	5,5PF	5,5PF	6,5NF	6,5NF	6,6NF

Overview: **In February 2011, peaceful protesters launched a campaign calling for democratic political reform. The authorities responded with violence and repression, killing more than 50 people over the course of the year and wounding thousands. King Hamad imposed martial law from mid-March through June. In that time, security forces arrested hundreds of demonstrators and subjected many of them to torture. Journalists, bloggers, students, high-profile human rights and political activists, and medical personnel who treated wounded protesters all faced detention, and in many cases, lengthy prison sentences. In addition, several thousand workers were fired for supporting the protest movement. Bahrain's main opposition political society, Al-Wefaq, withdrew its 18 members from the parliament over the crackdown, and boycotted interim elections that were held in September to fill the empty seats. In November, a government-appointed commission found that Bahraini security forces used excessive force in repressing the protest movement and that, in spite of government claims to the contrary, there were no connections between Iran and the uprising. The BICI report offered a number of recommendations to resolve the country's political impasse, none of which had been implemented by year's end.**

The al-Khalifa family, which belongs to Bahrain's Sunni Muslim minority, has ruled the Shiite-majority country for more than two centuries. Bahrain gained independence in 1971 after more than a hundred years as a British protectorate. The first constitution provided for a legislative assembly with both elected and appointed members, but the monarch dissolved the body in 1975 for attempting to end al-Khalifa rule.

In 1994, prominent individuals who had petitioned for the reestablishment of democratic institutions were detained, sparking unrest that left more than 40 people dead, thousands arrested, and hundreds either imprisoned or exiled.

After Sheikh Hamad bin Isa al-Khalifa ascended to the throne in 1999, he released political prisoners, permitted the return of exiles, and eliminated emergency laws and courts. He also introduced the National Charter, which aimed to create a constitutional monarchy with an elected parliament, an independent judicial branch, and rights guaranteeing women's political participation.

Voters approved the National Charter in 2001, and the country was proclaimed a constitutional kingdom the following year. However, leading Shiite groups and leftists boycotted local and parliamentary elections in 2002 to protest campaigning restrictions and gerrymandering aimed at diminishing the power of the Shiite majority. The government barred international organizations from monitoring the elections, and Sunni groups won most of the seats in the new National Assembly.

Shiite groups that boycotted the 2002 voting took part in the next elections in 2006. Al-Wefaq, a Shiite political society, won 42 percent of the vote and 17 of the 40 seats in the Council of Representatives, the lower house of the National Assembly.

Beginning in 2007, security forces carried out an escalating crackdown on the government's most outspoken critics. Tensions increased after the January 2009 arrest of Hassan Mushaima, Abduljalil al-Singace, and Mohammed Habib al-Muqdad, three leaders of the opposition political association Haq. Protests and cycles of arrests became more frequent in 2010, and human rights organizations in Bahrain documented the use of torture against detainees.

In elections for the Council of Representatives in October 2010, Al-Wefaq won 18 seats. A combination of 17 independents and 5 Islamists—all Sunnis and supporters of the ruling family—captured the remaining 22 seats. As in 2002 and 2006, critics accused the government of accelerating the naturalization of foreign workers and non-Bahraini Arabs to boost the number of Sunni voters.

In February 2011, Bahraini activists, mostly from economically depressed Shiite communities, organized local demonstrations that called for accelerated political reform and an end to sectarian discrimination. The small groups that initially took to the streets were met with police violence. The brutal response galvanized support for the protest movement, and tens of thousands of demonstrators converged on one of Manama's most visible public spaces, the Pearl Roundabout. Military and security forces cleared the roundabout in a violent nighttime raid on February 17, establishing what would become a pattern of harsh repercussions for those who publicly challenged the regime. In March, after hundreds of thousands of Bahrainis demonstrated in various parts of Manama, the government declared martial law and summoned military and security forces from regional allies, including Saudi Arabia and the United Arab Emirates, to backstop a prolonged crackdown that aimed to clear the streets and collectively punish the Shiite community.

In the subsequent months, the authorities arrested hundreds of activists and prodemocracy demonstrators. Many were subjected to systematic torture and tried in secret by military courts. High-profile activists including Mushaima, Singace, Ibrahim Sharif, and human rights activist Abd al-Hadi al-Khawaja were sentenced to life in prison. The arrests also extended to journalists and bloggers who reported on the crackdown, and medical personnel who treated injured protesters. Thousands of people were fired from their jobs for supporting the uprising, and hundreds of students were dismissed from the University of Bahrain. Those who remained were forced to sign loyalty pledges.

The government lifted martial law in June but maintained a heavy security presence in primarily Shiite villages. Security forces restricted the movements of Shiite citizens, periodically destroyed property, and continued to arrest regime critics and activists. In late June, King Hamad appointed a Bahrain Commission of Inquiry (BICI) headed by Egyptian legal scholar Cherif Bassiouni to investigate claims of torture and human rights abuses committed during the crackdown. The commission published its report in late November and found that state security forces had used excessive force in crushing the protest movement in the spring. The Commission also concluded that there was no evidence that Iran or other foreign forces were behind the uprising, contradicting a key government claim. The report recommended that the government reinstate sacked workers, release political prisoners, and hold members of the security forces who broke the law accountable. In December, the Bahraini regime appointed a committee to investigate the report's findings and replaced the head of its National Security Agency, but had not acted on any of the main recommendations by year's end.

Political Rights and Civil Liberties: Bahrain is not an electoral democracy. The 2002 constitution gives the king power over the executive, legislative, and judicial authorities. He appoints cabinet ministers and members of the 40-seat Consultative Council, the upper house of the National Assembly. The lower house, or Council of Representatives, consists of 40 elected members serving four-year terms. The National Assembly may propose legislation, but the cabinet must draft the laws. Bahrain's main opposition party, Al-Wefaq, withdrew its 18 members from the Council of Representatives in February to protest the government's crackdown. The opposition then boycotted interim elections that were held in September to fill the seats, with the result that all 40 seats are now held by government supporters. A source of frustration for many Bahrainis is the perception that Khalifa bin Salman al-Khalifa, the prime minister since 1971, is both corrupt and a key opponent of reform.

While formal political parties are illegal, the government has generally allowed political societies or groups to operate. A 2005 law makes it illegal to form political associations based on class, profession, or religion, and requires all political associations to register with the Ministry of Justice. While the government claimed that political societies remained free to operate in 2011, it imprisoned key opposition leaders, including Hassan Mushaima (Haq), Ibrahim Sharif (Democratic Action Society), Abd al-Jalil Singace (Haq), Matar Ibrahim Matar (Al-Wefaq), and Jawad Fairuz (Al-Wefaq). Mushaima, Sharif, and Singace were sentenced to life in prison for their activism.

Bahrain has some anticorruption laws, but enforcement is weak, and high-ranking officials suspected of corruption are rarely punished. Bahrain was ranked 46 out of 183 countries surveyed in Transparency International's 2011 Corruption Perceptions Index.

Restrictions on freedom of expression intensified in 2011, as several dozen journalists, bloggers, and users of the Twitter microblogging service were imprisoned for their responses to the prodemocracy uprising and regime crackdown. Mansour al-Jamri, former editor of the popular newspaper *Al-Wasat*, was charged with falsifying reporting at his paper; other *Al-Wasat* journalists were forced to sign pledges restricting their future commentary. The government owns all broadcast media outlets, and the private owners of the three main newspapers have close ties to the government. The government and its supporters have used the press to smear human rights and opposition activists. Self-censorship is encouraged by the vaguely worded 2002 Press Law, which allows the state to imprison journalists for criticizing the king or Islam, or for threatening "national security." The prominent blogger Ali Abdulemam, a regular contributor to the popular opposition web forum *Bahrain Online*, was released February 2011, along with two dozen other activists who had been charged with terrorism offenses in 2010. However, he was rearrested later that month and sentenced by a military court to 15 years in prison in June for plotting to overthrow the regime. The government blocked a number of opposition websites in 2011, including those that broadcast live events, such as protests.

Islam is the state religion. However, non-Muslim minorities are generally free to practice their faiths. All religious groups must obtain a permit from the Ministry of Justice and Islamic Affairs to operate legally, though the government has not punished groups that operate without a permit. In 2010, amid the crackdown on Shiite activists, the government stripped Ayatollah Hussein Mirza Najati, one of the country's top Shiite clerics, of his Bahraini nationality. In the course of the regime's crackdown in spring 2011, police and military forces destroyed over 40 Shiite places of worship, including mosques, religious centers, and shrines.

Academic freedom is not formally restricted, but teachers and professors in past years tended to avoid politically sensitive issues, as scholars who criticize the government are subject to dismissal. Criticism on university campuses became much more heated in 2011, when protests spread from Manama to universities across Bahrain in February and March. Along with a number of faculty and administrators who were fired for supporting the call for democracy, hundreds of university students were also expelled. Those who remained enrolled were forced to sign loyalty pledges.

Citizens must obtain a license to hold demonstrations, which are banned from sunrise to sunset in any public arena. Police regularly use violence to break up political protests, most of which occur in Shiite villages. The 1989 Societies Law prohibits any nongovernmental organization (NGO) from operating without a permit. In 2010, the government dissolved the board of directors of the Bahrain Human Rights Society, an independent NGO, and assigned a government-appointed director to run the organization. Security forces harassed prominent members of Bahraini NGOs, including Nabeel Rajab of the Bahrain Center for Human Rights, throughout 2011. The government also prevented foreign NGOs, including Human Rights Watch and others, from entering the country to carry out investigations during the year.

Bahrainis have the right to establish independent labor unions, but workers must give two weeks' notice before a strike, and strikes are banned in a variety of economic sectors. Private sector employees cannot be dismissed for union activities, but harassment of unionist workers occurs in practice. Foreign workers are not protected by the labor law and lack the right to organize and seek help from Bahraini unions. A 2009 decision that shifted responsibility for sponsoring foreign workers from private employers to the Labor Market Regulatory Authority did not apply to household servants, who remain particularly vulnerable to exploitation. Among the several thousand people known to have been fired in 2011 for allegedly supporting the prodemocracy protests were key officials in the General Federation of Bahraini Trade Unions.

The king appoints all judges, and courts have been subject to government pressure. Members of the royal family hold all senior security-related offices. Bahrain's antiterrorism law prescribes the death penalty for members of terrorist groups and prison terms for those who use religion to spread extremism. Critics have argued that the law's definition of terrorist crimes is too broad and that it has encouraged the use of torture and arbitrary detention.

Shiites are underrepresented in government and face various forms of discrimination. Fears of Shiite power and suspicions about their loyalties have limited employment opportunities for young Shiite men and fueled government attempts to erode the Shiite majority, mostly by granting citizenship to foreign-born Sunnis. While most of those who protested against the regime in 2011 called primarily for a democratic overhaul of the political system, many were Shiites motivated by a shared sense of persecution. Although the uprising was not initially based on sectarian resentment, Shiite-Sunni tensions deepened over the course of the year because of the government's heavy-handed response and its attempts to frame the uprising as driven by sectarian sentiment.

As part of its crackdown in 2011, the government restricted the ability of key figures to travel outside of Bahrain. From March through November, few members of the opposition or those who supported the uprising were able to travel abroad. Authorities also restricted movement inside the country; those most affected were Shiite residents in the villages outside Manama. In order to prevent any attempt to stage rallies in the capital, security forces imposed a tight security cordon that prevented easy access to the city.

Although women have the right to vote and participate in elections, they are underrepresented politically. While they are often partners in family decision-making, women are generally not afforded equal protection under the law. The government drafted a personal status law in 2008 but withdrew it in February 2009 under pressure from the country's Shiite clergy; the Sunni portion was resubmitted and passed by the parliament. Personal status and family law issues for Shiite Bahrainis are consequently still governed by Sharia (Islamic law) court rulings based on the interpretations of predominantly male religious scholars, rather than by any formal statute.

Bangladesh

Political Rights: 3
Civil Liberties: 4
Status: Partly Free

Population: 150,685,000
Capital: Dhaka

Trend Arrow: Bangladesh received a downward trend arrow due to heightened political polarization and attempts by the government to improperly strengthen its hold on power, including through selective prosecutions of opposition politicians and increased harassment of nongovernmental organizations.

Ten-Year Ratings Timeline For Year Under Review (Political Rights, Civil Liberties, Status)

2002	2003	2004	2005	2006	2007	2008	2009	2010	2011
4,4PF	4,4PF	4,4PF	4,4PF	4,4PF	5,4PF	4,4PF	3,4PF	3,4PF	3,4PF

Overview:

Political dysfunction worsened during 2011, as the primary opposition and Islamist parties stepped up street protests and political violence. The government failed to address the problem of extrajudicial executions and other human rights abuses, and was accused of combating corruption in a politicized manner. Meanwhile, critical nongovernmental organizations faced increased pressure, and the judiciary showed signs of mounting political influence.

Bangladesh gained independence from Britain in 1947 as part of the newly formed state of Pakistan, and successfully split from Pakistan in December 1971, after a nine-month war. The 1975 assassination of independence leader and prime minister Sheikh Mujibur Rahman by soldiers precipitated 15 years of military rule. The last military ruler resigned in 1990 after weeks of prodemocracy demonstrations. Elections in 1991 brought the Bangladesh Nationalist Party (BNP) to power under Prime Minister Khaleda Zia.

In 1994, Sheikh Hasina Wajed's center-left Awami League (AL) party began boycotting Parliament to protest alleged corruption in Zia's government. The ensuring years of political deadlock often reflected the personal animosity between Hasina, the daughter of Rahman, and Zia, the widow of a military ruler who was allegedly complicit in his assassination. The AL boycotted the February 1996 elections, then forced Zia's resignation in March and triumphed in elections held in June. The BNP also marked its time in opposition by boycotting Parliament and organizing periodic nationwide strikes, or hartals.

In 2001, the AL was voted out of office in elections marred by political violence and intimidation, and a new BNP-led coalition that included two Islamist parties took power. The AL again turned to parliamentary boycotts, strikes, and other forms of protest. Political violence and general lawlessness mounted, partly due to attacks by Islamist extremist groups. However, two of the largest were banned in 2005, and a government crackdown in 2006 effectively crippled the organizations.

As planned 2007 elections approached, the AL demanded reform of Bangladesh's caretaker government (CG) system, in which a theoretically nonpartisan government takes power temporarily to oversee parliamentary voting. The AL also questioned the conduct and impartiality of the Election Commission (EC) and its preparation of a new voter list. Faced with the possibility of balloting that lacked credibility, in January 2007, the army pressured the president to declare a state of emergency and cancel the elections. A new, military-backed CG, headed by technocrat Fakhruddin Ahmed, announced plans to tackle endemic corruption and prepare for eventual elections. Under emergency regulations, freedoms of assembly and association were suspended, controls were placed on the media, and all political activity was banned. This "soft coup" was carried out partly within the constitutional framework, stopping short of martial law and leaving a civilian CG in nominal control.

A new Anti-Corruption Commission (ACC) investigated high-level politicians and their business allies. Dozens were arrested, and several were subsequently convicted by a special court. However, after both main parties decided to boycott pre-election talks with the EC unless their leaders were released, the CG capitulated, weakening its anticorruption campaign. The new EC also failed to address the issue of suspected war criminals' continued involvement in politics. Of particular concern was the Jamaat-e-Islami (Islamic Party, or JI), whose leaders and student wing played a role in atrocities against civilians during the 1971 war of independence.

The emergency regulations were fully lifted in mid-December 2008, and the elections followed on December 29. Although the longtime party leaders remained in place, there was a considerable infusion of new blood into the parties' candidate lists. Turnout was extremely high, at 87 percent, and included a large proportion of first-time, women, and minority voters. An electoral alliance led by the AL won an overwhelming 263 seats (230 for the AL), while the BNP-led coalition took 32 seats (29 for the BNP and just 2 for the JI). Zia accepted the results, and Hasina took office as prime minister, returning Bangladesh to elected civilian rule.

The new government moved to implement its campaign promises. Several suspected war criminals were arrested in 2009, and in 2010, the government established a tribunal that subsequently indicted and issued arrest warrants for five JI leaders. The first trial began in late 2011. However, experts remained concerned that the process would not adhere to international standards, and both witnesses and defense lawyers received threats during 2011.

Another important part of the AL's agenda was the restoration of the 1972 constitution, which would reestablish Bangladesh's character as a secular republic. In a key step toward that end, a February 2010 Supreme Court decision nullified elements of the fifth amendment to the constitution, effectively paving the way for a reinstatement of the principle of secularism and a ban on religiously based political parties. Following the ruling, the EC requested that the JI amend its charter accordingly. Meanwhile, the government took a harder line on Islamist extremism, arresting dozens of activists and those suspected of links to terrorist groups. An even wider crackdown in September 2011—in the wake of violent JI protests regarding the war crimes issue—led to the arrest of several party leaders and hundreds of activists.

The BNP-led opposition continued to intermittently boycott Parliament and rigidly oppose the AL government's initiatives. The BNP began resorting to the use of hartals in 2010, and led relatively peaceful mass protests in June that year. However, the party suffered from serious internal divisions, particularly over succession issues. General political dysfunction intensified in 2011, with more frequent opposition protests and strikes against both specific policies and the government in general.

In June 2011, following a May Supreme Court decision on the validity of interim administrations, the AL-dominated Parliament passed the fifteenth amendment to the constitution despite a BNP boycott of the vote, which effectively scrapped the CG system and replaced it with a nominally independent electoral commission. Other articles of the amendment termed any criticism of the constitution an act of sedition, and effectively forbade further amendments to large parts of the constitution. The AL suffered an electoral defeat in late October, when an independent candidate won the mayoralty of Narayanganj, just outside Dhaka. Meanwhile, a series of apparently biased decisions in corruption cases raised concerns about political influence over the judiciary.

Political Rights and Civil Liberties: Bangladesh is an electoral democracy. The December 2008 parliamentary elections were deemed free and fair by European Union (EU) observers and other monitoring groups. Terms for both the unicameral National Parliament and the largely ceremonial presidency are five years. Under provisions contained in the 15th amendment, Parliament is composed of 350 members, of whom 300 are directly elected, and 50 are women nominated by political parties—based on their share of the elected seats—and then voted on by their fellow lawmakers. The president is elected by Parliament.

A series of 2008 electoral reforms mandated that parties disband their student, labor, and overseas units; obliged parties to reserve a third of all positions for women; reduced the number of seats a parliamentary candidate could simultaneously contest from five to three; tripled campaign spending limits to 1.5 million taka (US$22,000) per candidate; and gave voters in each constituency the option of rejecting all candidates. The new regulations were designed to curtail the widespread bribery, rigging, and violence that had characterized past elections, as was a new, considerably more accurate voter registry. While the December 2008 elections were relatively clean, local government polls held in January 2009 were marred by more extensive violence and intimidation, as well as suspected rigging. The level of political violence remained relatively high in 2011; local rights group Odhikar registered 135 deaths, and more than 11,500 people injured as a result of inter- or intraparty clashes during 2011, a slight drop from the previous year. Harassment of the opposition became more widespread in 2011, and ranged from charges being filed against senior BNP members to limitations being placed on political activities, particularly rallies and processions.

Endemic corruption and criminality, weak rule of law, limited bureaucratic transparency, and political polarization have long undermined government accountability. Moreover, opposition boycotts of Parliament have regularly nullified the legislature's role as a check on the government. A 2009 Right to Information Act mandates public access to all information held by public bodies and overrides existing secrecy legislation. Bangladesh was ranked 120 out of 183 countries surveyed by Transparency International (TI) in its 2011 Corruption Perceptions Index. Under the present government, anticorruption efforts have been weakened by patchy enforcement and subversion of the judicial process, according to TI-Bangladesh. In addition, prosecutions have become considerably more politicized. Dozens of cases against Prime Minister Sheikh Hasina Wajed and other AL politicians have been withdrawn, while those against BNP politicians, including party leader Khaleda Zia and her family, have remained open. Additional charges were filed against Zia in August 2011, and an arrest warrant was issued for her son in connection with a 2004 grenade attack at a political rally. In early 2011, the cabinet approved draft amendments that would require the ACC to receive government permission before initiating new cases against officials and members of Parliament, though they had yet to be passed by the legislature at year's end. In October, the World Bank suspended a planned $1.2 billion loan for the Padma Bridge construction project, citing evidence of corruption and financial irregularities.

Bangladesh's media environment remained relatively unfettered in 2011, though the legal and regulatory framework allows for some restrictions, and the government showed signs of intolerance during the year. Print media are generally given more leeway when covering sensitive topics than broadcasters. Nevertheless, over the past several years, various employees at the oppositionist daily *Amar Desh* have been charged with defamation for articles about the ruling party. Mahmudur Rahman, acting editor of the paper and a close adviser to Zia, was released in March 2011 after spending nine months in jail on charges of fraud, publishing without a valid license, sedition, and contempt of court. Mohammad Ekramul Haq, editor of the *Sheersha News* web portal and the *Sheersha Kagoj* weekly, was arrested in July on apparently trumped-up extortion charges. He was freed after serving four months in jail, despite a court's earlier order that he be granted bail.

Journalists continue to be threatened and attacked with impunity by organized crime groups, party activists, and Islamist groups, which sometimes leads to self-censorship on sensitive topics. Although no journalists have been killed for the past six years, according to the Committee to Protect Journalists, there appeared to be an increase in harassment in 2011. In June, five journalists were injured by armed ruling party activists in the town of Comilla, and other attacks by party activists and criminal gangs were noted in September. Some journalists received threatening telephone calls from intelligence agencies seeking to prevent negative coverage. No attempts to censor internet-based content were reported in 2011.

Various forms of artistic expression are occasionally censored. In January 2011, the controversial film *Meherjaan*, which deals with events during the 1971 war, was withdrawn from theater by the distributor. The decision came as a result of objections voiced by several critics who felt that the filmmaker had failed to use historical accuracy when portraying the 1971 war.

Islam is the official religion, but about 10 percent of the population is Hindu, and there are smaller numbers of Buddhists and Christians. Although religious minorities have the right to worship freely, they face societal discrimination as well as harassment and legal repercussions for proselytizing. Members of the Ahmadiyya sect are considered heretical by some Muslims, and despite increased state protection since 2009, they have encountered physical attacks, boycotts, and demands that the state declare them non-Muslims. They are also occasionally denied permission to hold religious events, as occurred in February 2011 in Gazipur district, when local authorities abruptly cancelled a permit for a planned annual convention. In a positive step in May 2011, a court sentenced 11 men to life in prison for the gang rape of a Hindu schoolgirl during anti-Hindu violence shortly after the 2001 elections.

Religious minorities remain underrepresented in politics and state employment, but the secularist AL government has appointed several members of minority groups to leadership positions. It has also initiated curriculum reform in Islamic schools. In July 2011, Islamist groups staged violent protests against an amendment passed by the government in June that removed a reference to Islam in the constitution. An estimated 3,000 Islamist activists participated in the 30-hour protest across the nation. Not only did they argue for the constitutional re-instatement of the phrase, but they also protested that the promulgation of "secularism" as a state principle be dropped entirely.

While authorities largely respect academic freedom, research on sensitive political and religious topics is reportedly discouraged. Political polarization at many universities, including occasional clashes involving the armed student wings of the main three parties, inhibits education and access to services. In September 2011, a government attempt to withdraw public funding from Jagannath University led to widespread student protests.

The rights of assembly and association were restored in late 2008 with the lifting of emergency regulations. The authorities have sometimes tried to prevent rallies by arresting party activists, and protesters are frequently injured and occasionally killed during clashes with police. Nevertheless, demonstrations took place regularly in 2011, including a growing number of nationwide strikes and rallies called by the BNP.

Numerous nongovernmental organizations (NGOs) operate in Bangladesh. While most are able to function without onerous restrictions, they must obtain clearance from the NGO Affairs Bureau (NAB)—which reports to the prime minister's office—to use foreign funds. The bureau is also empowered to approve or reject individual projects after a review period of 45 days. NGOs seen as overly critical of the government, particularly on human rights issues, have on occasion been subject to harassment or denied permission for proposed projects. In July 2011, the NAB rejected an EU-funded project on torture by the human rights group Odhikar on the grounds that the application alluded to the fact that torture is endemic in Bangladesh. In April, Nobel Peace Prize laureate Muhammad Yunus lost a final appeal and was ousted as managing director of Grameen Bank, one of the country's largest and most influential microfinance institutions, based on an age-limit technicality; many analysts described the case as politically motivated.

Labor union formation is hampered by a 30 percent employee approval requirement, restrictions on organizing by unregistered unions, and rules against unionization by certain categories of civil servants. Labor activists occasionally encounter harassment, and worker grievances sometimes fuel unrest at factories. In the past several years, garment workers have regularly engaged in strikes and protests to demand higher pay and safer working conditions, in some instances leading to violence in which dozens of workers have been injured. In 2010, the Bangladesh Center for Workers' Solidarity (BCWS) was stripped of its legal status by the NAB for allegedly inciting labor unrest; BCWS leaders faced criminal cases that were still pending at the end of 2011 and reportedly suffered abuse in custody. Child labor is widespread.

Politicization of the judiciary remains a concern. The military-backed CG, unlike previous governments, worked to implement a 1999 Supreme Court directive ordering the separation of the judiciary from the executive. In 2007, the power to appoint judges and magistrates was transferred from the executive branch to the Supreme Court. However, political authorities have continued to make appointments to the higher judiciary, in some cases demonstrating an overt political bias. In 2011, procedural irregularities in the Grameen Bank and CG system cases added to suspicions that judicial independence had been compromised. Harassment of witnesses and the dismissal of cases following political pressure are also growing issues of concern.

The court system is prone to corruption and severely backlogged; pretrial detention is often lengthy, and many defendants lack counsel. The indigent have little access to justice through the courts. In 2009, the government launched an initiative to form small courts in 500 rural administrative councils that could settle local disputes and reduce pressure on the legal system, but this has not yet helped to reduce a backlog of nearly 2 million pending cases. Prison conditions are extremely poor, and severe overcrowding is common. According to the New Delhi–based Asian Centre for Human Rights, hundreds of juveniles are held in prisons in contravention of the 1974 Children's Act. Suspects are routinely subject to arbitrary arrest and detention, demands for bribes, and physical abuse by police. Torture is often used to extract confessions and intimidate political detainees.

Security forces including the Rapid Action Battalion (RAB), a paramilitary unit composed of military and police personnel, have been criticized for excesses like extrajudicial executions. According to Odhikar, there were 84 extrajudicial killings by law enforcement agencies in 2011, and it is estimated that more than 800 people have been killed by the RAB since its formation in 2004. The Directorate General–Forces Intelligence (DGFI), a military intelligence unit, has been responsible for a number of cases of abuse during interrogations. Although the AL government initially promised a "zero-tolerance" approach on torture and extrajudicial executions, high-level officials routinely excuse or deny the practices, and the rate of custodial deaths remains high. Abductions and disappearances are also a growing concern, according to the International Crisis Group.

Law enforcement abuses are facilitated by legislation such as the 1974 Special Powers Act, which permits arbitrary detention without charge, and Section 54 of the Criminal Procedure Code, which allows detention without a warrant. A June 2008 counterterrorism ordinance, later adopted as law in 2009, included an overly broad definition of terrorism and generally does not meet international standards.

Following a February 2009 mutiny by the paramilitary Bangladesh Rifles (BDR) force—in which some 70 officers and family members were killed—more than 3,500 BDR members were arrested, and at least 60 died in custody under suspicious circumstances, with some bodies bearing marks of torture and other abuse. The mutineers' subsequent trials have been marred by problems, including defendants' limited access to counsel, lack of individualized incriminating evidence, and the alleged use of torture to extract confessions. In July 2011, a mass trial of 666 BDR members before a military court ended in the conviction of all but nine, with prison terms ranging from four months to seven years.

The International War Crimes Tribunal Act of 1973 was revised in 2009 to meet international standards concerning the right to a fair trial, and June 2011 additions to the tribunal's procedural rules provided for victim and witness protection, the presumption of innocence, defendant access to counsel, and the right to bail. Five senior JI leaders were indicted in 2010, and after several postponements, the trial of JI leader Delwar Hossain Sayedee began in November 2011. Charges of crimes against humanity were also filed against BNP leader Salahuddin Quader Chowdhury in November. However, observers raised concerns about threats and harassment against witnesses and defense lawyers as well as other elements of the tribunal system that fell short of international standards for due process.

The National Human Rights Commission (NHRC), reestablished in 2010 under a 2009 law, is empowered to investigate and rule on complaints against the armed forces and security services, and can request reports from the government at its own discretion. In 2011, the NHRC undertook training and capacity-building programs with support from international donors, and investigated a number of complaints.

Islamist militant groups continue to operate and maintain contact with regional allies, but Islamist violence has been negligible since the 2006 crackdown. The AL government has been aggressive in arresting cadres and closely monitoring their activities. Following violent protests by Islamist groups in September 2011, hundreds of activists as well as the groups' leaders were temporarily detained. Separately, casualties from clashes involving Maoist militants have declined somewhat in the past several years; according to the South Asia Terrorism Portal, 24 people, all of them militants, were killed in 2011.

Land rights for the Hindu minority remain tenuous. Tribal minorities have little control over land decisions affecting them, and Bengali-speaking settlers continue to illegally encroach on tribal lands in the Chittagong Hill Tracts (CHT), with the reported connivance of government officials and the army. A 1997 accord ended a 24-year insurgency by indigenous groups in the CHT, but implementation of the accord has been lacking. Security forces in the area are occasionally implicated in the suppression of protests, the arrest of political activists, and extrajudicial killings. Moreover, indigenous people remain subject to physical attacks and property destruction by Bengali settlers. In July 2009, the AL government said it would immediately withdraw more than 2,000 troops from the CHT and dismantle several dozen military camps. It also announced plans to set up a commission that would allocate land to indigenous tribes. However, although this commission was reconstituted, its activities were suspended in 2011, and it did not address land disputes effectively. Clashes between settlers and indigenous people continued in 2011.

Roughly 230,000 ethnic Rohingyas who fled forced labor, discrimination, and other abuses in Burma in the early 1990s remain in Bangladesh and are subject to some harassment. Bangladesh also hosts camp-like settlements of some 300,000 non-Bengali Muslims, often called Biharis, who had emigrated from India in 1947 and were rendered stateless at independence in 1971, as many had sided with and initially sought repatriation to Pakistan. A landmark 2008 court ruling granted citizenship rights to this group. Separately, approximately 50,000 inhabitants of de jure Indian enclaves in Bangladesh and Bangladeshi enclaves in India, located near the countries' mutual border, are also effectively stateless and have difficulty accessing public services. In September 2011, India and Pakistan signed a historic agreement that demarcated the land by swapping 111 Indian enclaves in Bangladesh for 51 Bangladeshi enclaves in India, leaving only 49 extraterritorial pieces of land.

Rights activists expressed concern about a law passed in August 2011 that effectively authorized police to detain suspected vagrants and homeless people for up to two years in government-run rehabilitation centers; those refusing the confinement could face jail time.

Rape, dowry-related assaults, acid throwing, and other forms of violence against women occur regularly. A law requiring rape victims to file police reports and obtain medical certificates within 24 hours of the crime in order to press charges prevents most cases from reaching the courts. Police also accept bribes to quash rape cases and rarely enforce existing laws protecting women. The Acid Survivors Foundation (ASF), a local NGO, recorded 84 acid attacks during 2011; they affected 111 victims, most of them women. While attacks have declined since the passage of the Acid Crime Prevention Act in 2002, investigations remain inadequate. A 2010 law offers greater protection to women and children from domestic violence, including both physical and mental abuse. Giving or receiving dowry is a criminal offense, but coercive requests remain a problem, as does the country's high rate of early marriage. Local rights group Odhikar noted an increase in dowry-related violence against women in 2011, with more than 300 murders recorded during the year.

Under the legal codes pertaining to Muslims, women have fewer divorce and inheritance rights than men. In rural areas, religious leaders sometimes impose flogging and other extrajudicial punishments on women accused of violating strict moral codes, despite Supreme Court orders calling on the government to stop the practice. Women also face some discrimination in health care, education, and employment. In 2011, Islamic clergy and women's groups remained at loggerheads over implementation of the National Women Development Policy, which holds that women and men should have equal political, social, and economic rights.

Women and children are trafficked both overseas and within the country for the purposes of domestic servitude or sexual exploitation, while men are trafficked primarily for the purposes of labor abroad. The government has taken steps to raise awareness and prosecute sex traffickers somewhat more vigorously, with dozens convicted each year, and some sentenced to life in prison.

A criminal ban on homosexual acts is rarely enforced, but societal discrimination remains the norm. Transgendered people also face persecution, though a government-sponsored rally in the capital in October 2011 urged greater recognition for the group.

Barbados

Political Rights: 1
Civil Liberties: 1
Status: Free

Population: 273,900
Capital: Bridgetown

Ten-Year Ratings Timeline For Year Under Review (Political Rights, Civil Liberties, Status)

2002	2003	2004	2005	2006	2007	2008	2009	2010	2011
1,1F	1,1F	1,1F	1,1F	1,1F	1,1F	1,1F	1,1F	1,1F	1,1F

Overview: **Barbados continued to grapple with the impact of the global recession as Prime Minister Freundel Stuart faced a sluggish economy and rising crime rate. In response to a judgment by the Inter-American Court of Human Rights, Barbados began an internal debate on its mandatory death sentence in murder convictions.**

Barbados gained its independence from Britain in 1966 but remained a member of the Commonwealth. The Barbados Labour Party (BLP) under Prime Minister Owen Arthur governed from 1994 to January 2008, when the opposition Democratic Labour Party (DLP) won a clear majority of 20 seats in the lower house of Parliament. The BLP was left with the remaining 10 seats. Despite this stunning upset, the new government led by David Thompson of the DLP did not break markedly from the policies pursued by the Arthur government.

During much of the summer of 2010, Thompson remained out of office due to an undisclosed ailment, and DLP member Freundel Stuart took over as acting prime minister. While Thompson returned to office in late August, many important economic decisions, including the new budget and several proposed judicial and other reforms, were delayed. In September, the government officially acknowledged that he had pancreatic cancer. Thompson died on October 23, 2010, and was replaced by Stuart.

As Barbados struggled to emerge from the economic recession, the government was forced to cut expenditures, freeze public wages, and shore up the country's foreign reserves. According to the International Monetary Fund (IMF), Barbados experienced only 1 percent growth in 2011 despite an increase in tourism. The unemployment rate also grew to over 12 percent. Barbados is particularly weighed down by its debt-to-GDP ratio, and the IMF recommended that the country lower spending on its social partnership scheme of entitlements.

Barbados has been more successful than other Caribbean countries in combating violent crime, though the crime rate in 2011 remained at high levels. The drug trade continues to be an important problem for Barbados, as the island has become a transshipment point for cocaine originating from Venezuela, and radar monitoring cannot cover the entire island.:

Political Rights and Civil Liberties: Barbados is an electoral democracy. Members of the 30-member House of Assembly, the lower house of the bicameral Parliament, are directly elected for five-year terms.

The governor-general, who represents the British monarch as head of state, appoints the 21 members of the Senate: 12 on the advice of the prime minister, 2 on the advice of the leader of the opposition, and the remaining 7 at his own discretion. The prime minister is appointed by the governor-general and is usually the leader of the political party with a majority in the House.

Political parties are free to organize. Historically, power has alternated between two centrist parties—the DLP and the BLP. Other political organizations without representation in Parliament include the small, left-wing Workers Party of Barbados and the People's Empowerment Party (PEP), an opposition force favoring trade union rights and greater state intervention in the economy.

Barbados was ranked 16 out of 183 countries surveyed in Transparency International's 2011 Corruption Perceptions Index, the second-best ranking in the Americas after Canada.

Freedom of expression is respected. Public opinion expressed through the news media, which are free of censorship and government control, has a powerful influence on policy. Newspapers, including the two major dailies, are privately owned. Four private and two government-run radio stations operate. The single television station, operated by the government-owned Caribbean Broadcasting Corporation, presents a wide range of political viewpoints. The DLP has so far failed to make good on its promise to introduce a new Freedom of Information Act. Access to the internet is not restricted.

The constitution guarantees freedom of religion, which is widely respected for mainstream religious groups. However, members of Barbados's small Rastafarian community have protested prison regulations that require inmates to have their long dreadlocks cut off while in detention, and have also reported discrimination in the areas of education and employment. Academic freedom is fully respected.

Barbados's legal framework provides important guarantees for freedom of assembly, which are upheld in practice. The right to form civic organizations and labor unions is respected. Two major labor unions, as well as various smaller ones, are active.

The judicial system is independent, and the Supreme Court includes a high court and a court of appeals. Lower-court officials are appointed on the advice of the Judicial and Legal Service Commission. Barbados has ratified the Caribbean Court of Justice as its highest appellate court. There are occasional reports and complaints of the use of excessive force by the Royal Barbados Police Force to extract confessions, along with reports that police do not always seek warrants before searching homes.

The government has taken some positive steps to address overcrowding in the prison system and to discharge prison personnel accused of beating inmates, but there has not been substantial progress in their prosecution. The death penalty remains a mandatory punishment for certain capital crimes, although it has not been implemented since 1984. In October 2011, the government announced its plan to update the Corporal Punishment Act, the Juvenile Offenders Act, and the Prevention of Cruelty Act, in response to rulings by the Inter-American Court of Human Rights that found Barbados in violation of certain protections that are enshrined in the American Convention on Human Rights.

Barbadian authorities have been criticized for excessively restrictive migration policies, including the treatment of foreign nationals at airports. Barbados is a source and destination for human trafficking.

Women comprise roughly half of the country's workforce, although the World Economic Forum reported that in 2010 women earned 26 percent less than men for comparable work. Violence against women and children also continued to be a serious social concern. Women are underrepresented in the political sphere, comprising only 10 percent of the elected House.

Belarus

Political Rights: 7
Civil Liberties: 6
Status: Not Free

Population: 9,472,000
Capital: Minsk

Ten-Year Ratings Timeline For Year Under Review (Political Rights, Civil Liberties, Status)

2002	2003	2004	2005	2006	2007	2008	2009	2010	2011
6,6NF	6,6NF	7,6NF	7,6NF	7,6NF	7,6NF	7,6NF	7,6NF	7,6NF	7,6NF

Overview: **Public protests following the deeply flawed December 19, 2010, presidential election led incumbent Alyaksandr Lukashenka, who claimed to have won a new term, to orchestrate an extensive crackdown on all forms of dissent. Most visibly, three former presidential candidates received prison terms of five years or more for their roles in the demonstrations. Protesters continued to come into the street during 2011, but they faced prison terms even for mild forms of expression, like wordlessly clapping hands. The regime also continued to harass the media and attempted to gain tighter control over the internet. Ethnic Poles and their leaders similarly faced official harassment during the year.**

Belarus declared independence in 1991, ending centuries of rule by Poland, Russia, and the Soviet Union. In 1994, voters made Alyaksandr Lukashenka, a member of parliament with close links to the security services, Belarus's first post-Soviet president. He pursued reunification with Russia and subordinated the government, legislature, and courts to his political whims while denying citizens basic rights and liberties. A widely criticized 1996 referendum approved constitutional amendments that extended Lukashenka's term through 2001, broadened presidential powers, and created a new bicameral parliament, the National Assembly.

Lukashenka won a second term through disputed elections in September 2001, amid accusations by former security officials that the president was directing a death squad aimed at silencing his opponents. Four politicians and journalists who had been critical of the regime disappeared during 1999 and 2000.

Not a single opposition candidate won a seat in 2004 parliamentary elections (three had been elected in 2000), and voters ostensibly endorsed a parallel referendum proposal to allow Lukashenka to run again in 2006. As with previous votes, the Organization for Security and Cooperation in Europe (OSCE) declared that the parliamentary elections fell "significantly short" of Belarus's commitments.

The March 2006 presidential election, in which Lukashenka won a third term, did not meet democratic standards, according to the OSCE. The poll brought 10,000 to 15,000 protesters to Minsk's October Square on election day. However, the authorities detained and beat many activists, and opposition activity dwindled after the protests, as the government jailed opposition leaders and intimidated their rank-and-file supporters with fees and warnings. Alyaksandr Kazulin, one of three opposition candidates, was sentenced to five and a half years in prison for protesting the flawed election and the subsequent crackdown.

To bolster his international standing, Lukashenka released all political prisoners identified by the European Union (EU) and the United States by August 2008, including Kazulin. However, no opposition candidates won seats in the September 2008 parliamentary elections, and the authorities arrested a new batch of political prisoners in a February 2009 crackdown.

On December 19, 2010, Lukashenka won a fourth term as president in a deeply flawed election. The authorities' brutal treatment of the approximately 15,000 protesters who turned out to question the legitimacy of the vote cast a shadow over the country during 2011. More than 700 individuals were arrested, including seven of the nine opposition presidential candidates, and many of them remained in jail for long periods. The regime later sentenced three of the former candidates to prison: Andrei Sannikau (five years), Dzmitry Uss (five and a half years, released in October), and Mikalay Statkevich (six years). In March, Youth Front leader Dzmitry Dashkevich received two years, while another activist, Eduard Lobau, was sentenced to four. The two had been arrested before the December vote and charged with assaulting a passerby so that they would not be free to lead protest activity on election day. At least 41 people were convicted for participating in the postelection demonstrations, with 28 arrestees still in jail by mid-September.

The numerous crackdowns on antigovernment protests during 2011 drove demonstrators to adopt novel tactics, such as wordlessly clapping their hands or ringing their mobile phones in unison, in an attempt to deprive the police of a pretext for arresting them. Nevertheless, more than 100 people were arrested on July 3 (Independence Day) for engaging in such an action. At their height in the summer, the unusual forms of protest brought out thousands of people in 30 cities across the country.

Also during 2011, the KGB carried out an extensive harassment campaign against all activists who spoke out against the government or published critical material. In August, the authorities arrested Viasna Human Rights Center leader Ales Byalyatski after he circulated reports about the regime's crackdown on freedom of assembly; he was sentenced to four and a half years in jail for tax evasion.

Separately, on April 11, a bomb blast struck a Minsk subway station, killing 15 people. Two Belarusian men from Vitebsk were sentenced to death for carrying out the unprecedented terrorist act in a trial that critics claimed was flawed. The authorities harassed media outlets that criticized the emergency response and the criminal investigation into the explosion.

Russia's ongoing efforts to slash energy subsidies to Belarus caused an economic crisis during 2011, with a plummeting currency, increasing unemployment, spiraling inflation, and goods shortages. These conditions undermined Lukashenka's long-standing argument that his rule guaranteed a reasonable standard of living for Belarusian citizens.

Political Rights and Civil Liberties: Belarus is not an electoral democracy. Serious and widespread irregularities have marred all recent elections, including the December 2010 presidential poll. The 110 members of the Chamber of Representatives, the lower house of the rubber-stamp National Assembly, are popularly elected for four years from single-mandate constituencies. The upper house, the Council of the Republic, consists of 64 members serving four-year terms; 56 are elected by regional councils, and 8 are appointed by the president. The constitution vests most power in the president, giving him control over the government, courts, and even the legislative process by stating that presidential decrees have a higher legal force than ordinary legislation. The president is elected for five-year terms, and there are no term limits.

Opposition parties have no representation in the National Assembly, while propresidential parties serve only superficial functions. Young members of opposition parties report being deliberately drafted into the military; soldiers are banned from party membership. Amendments to the electoral law adopted in 2009 give parties more opportunities to campaign but do not provide for a transparent vote count. Local elections in April 2010 produced unusually large returns for proregime candidates.

The state controls 70 percent of the Belarusian economy, feeding widespread corruption. Graft is also encouraged by the overall lack of transparency and accountability in government.

President Alyaksandr Lukashenka systematically curtails press freedom. Libel is both a civil and a criminal offense, and a 2008 media law gives the state a monopoly over information about political, social, and economic affairs. Belarusian national television is completely under the control of the state and does not present alternative and opposition views. The state-run press distribution monopoly limits the availability of private newspapers. The authorities routinely harass and censor the remaining independent media outlets, including through physical force and revocation of journalists' credentials. The authorities do allow two independent newspapers to publish: *Nasha Niva* and *Narodnaya Volya*. Charges filed against the papers for "wrong coverage" were dropped without explanation in July 2011. Also that month, a Belarusian court convicted Andrzej Poczobut, an ethnic Polish Belarusian citizen who writes for Poland's *Gazeta Wyborcza*, of defaming Lukashenka. He received a suspended three-year prison sentence and was banned from leaving Belarus.

Internet penetration has doubled from a quarter to nearly half of the population over the last five years, and the number of broadband subscribers has exploded from 11,400 in 2006 to 1.8 million in January 2011. Every day, more than 400,000 Belarusians (the audience size for state television) visit news websites. To deal with this shift, the government is seeking greater control over the internet. The 2008 media law subjects internet outlets to the same restrictions as traditional media, and the government owns the country's sole internet service provider. A presidential decree that took effect in June 2010 requires internet café owners to identify users and track their activities. The authorities have repeatedly blocked access to social-networking sites, such as the Russian VKontakte and U.S.-based Facebook and Twitter. Charter97.org news editor Natalya Radina, who had been facing trial for publishing appeals to citizens to participate in the December 2010 protests, fled the country in March 2011 and sought political asylum in Lithuania. Charter97.org frequently experiences denial of service attacks, and its staff members have been threatened and arrested.

Despite constitutional guarantees of religious equality, government decrees and registration requirements have increasingly restricted religious activity. Legal amendments in 2002 provided for government censorship of religious publications and barred foreigners from leading religious groups. The amendments also placed strict limitations on religious groups that have been active in Belarus for fewer than 20 years. The government in 2003 signed a concordat with the Belarusian Orthodox Church, which enjoys a privileged position. The authorities have discriminated against Protestant clergy and ignored anti-Semitic attacks, according to the U.S. State Department.

Academic freedom is subject to intense state ideological pressures, and institutions that use a liberal curriculum, promote national consciousness, or are suspected of disloyalty face harassment and liquidation. Regulations stipulate immediate dismissal and revocation of degrees for students and professors who join opposition protests. Wiretapping by state security agencies limits the right to privacy.

The government restricts freedom of assembly for critical independent groups. Protests and rallies require authorization from local authorities, who can arbitrarily deny permission. When public demonstrations do occur, police frequently break them up and arrest participants.

Freedom of association is severely restricted. More than a hundred of the most active nongovernmental organizations (NGOs) were forced to close down between 2003 and 2005, and participation in an unregistered or liquidated political party or organization was criminalized in 2005. Registration of groups remains selective. As a result, most human rights activists operating in the country face potential jail terms ranging from six months to two years. Regulations introduced in 2005 ban foreign assistance to NGOs, parties, and individuals deemed to have promoted "meddling in the internal affairs" of Belarus from abroad. In May 2011, the Economic Court evicted the Belarusian Popular Front opposition party from premises it had used since the 1990s. Independent trade unions face harassment, and their leaders are frequently fired and prosecuted for peaceful protests. No independent trade unions have been registered since 1999. Over 90 percent of workers have fixed-term contracts, meaning they can be arbitrarily dismissed when the contract expires.

Although the constitution calls for judicial independence, courts are subject to significant executive influence. The right to a fair trial is often not respected in cases with political overtones. Human rights groups continue to document instances of beatings, torture, and inadequate protection during detention in cases involving leaders of the democratic opposition, and their trials are frequently held in secret. In May 2011, the European Parliament passed a resolution condemning the reported use of torture by the police and KGB against opposition activists and journalists. Several lawyers for the political opposition have been disbarred. The power to extend pretrial detention lies with a prosecutor rather than a judge, in violation of international norms.

Ethnic Poles and Roma often face discrimination. In 2010, the police seized the property of the unofficial Union of Poles in Belarus and arrested its activists. Uladzislau Tokarau, head of the Vitebsk branch of the Union of Poles in Belarus, fled the country in May 2011, fearing that he would be arrested on fraud charges following a police search of his apartment.

An internal passport system limits freedom of movement and choice of residence. Citizens no longer need a travel permit before going abroad, but as of 2010, at least 120,000 people were banned from foreign travel due to their possession of state secrets, pending legal cases, or outstanding financial obligations. Some opposition activists have been turned back at the border or detained for lengthy searches. Belarus's command economy severely limits economic freedom.

Women are not specifically targeted for discrimination, but there are significant discrepancies in income between men and women, and women are poorly represented in leading government positions. As a result of extreme poverty, many women have become victims of the international sex trade.

Belgium

Political Rights: 1
Civil Liberties: 1
Status: Free

Population: 10,970,000
Capital: Brussels

Ten-Year Ratings Timeline For Year Under Review (Political Rights, Civil Liberties, Status)

2002	2003	2004	2005	2006	2007	2008	2009	2010	2011
1,2F	1,1F	1,1F	1,1F	1,1F	1,1F	1,1F	1,1F	1,1F	1,1F

Overview: **After more than 500 days of negotiations following June 2010 parliamentary elections, a new Belgian government was formed in early December 2011. Elio Di Rupo took office as the first French-speaking prime minister from Wallonia in almost 40 years. Two women were arrested in July for wearing burqas after a ban on the partial or total covering of the face in public came into force earlier that month.**

Modern Belgium dates to 1830, when the largely Roman Catholic territory broke away from the mostly Protestant Netherlands and formed an independent constitutional monarchy. In the 20th century, Belgium became one of the founding members of the European Union (EU) and hosts the organization's central administration in Brussels.

Ethnic and linguistic conflicts prompted a series of constitutional amendments in 1970, 1971, and 1993 that devolved considerable power from the central government to the three regions in the federation: French-speaking Wallonia in the south; Flemish-speaking Flanders in the north; and Brussels, the capital, where French and Flemish share the same official status. Cultural and economic differences between the regions have contributed to political rifts between Flemish and Francophone parties across the ideological spectrum, with the wealthier Flemish north seeking increased self-rule and reduced taxpayer support for the less-prosperous Wallonia. Voting takes place along strict linguistic lines; with the exception of the bilingual district encompassing Brussels, parties are only permitted to run in their respective linguistic regions.

In June 2007 parliamentary elections, Flanders premier Yves Leterme's centrist

Christian Democratic and Flemish (CD&V) party—in an electoral bloc with the New Flemish Alliance (N-VA)—won 30 of 150 seats in the lower house. The remaining seats were divided among 10 other factions. Flemish and Walloon parties were unable to agree on coalition terms after an extraordinary 196 days of negotiations, and in December, the king asked outgoing prime minister Guy Verhofstadt to form an interim government with the authority to act on pressing economic and other concerns.

In February 2008, a majority of political parties agreed on an outline for limited constitutional reform, which cleared the way for Leterme to become prime minister the following month. He was unable to consolidate support after taking office, however, and lawmakers began to leave the ruling coalition during the fall. Leterme's government was ultimately brought down at the end of the year after being accused of interfering in a court case concerning the failed bank Fortis. The prime minister offered his resignation, and on December 30, the king swore in Herman Van Rompuy, also of the CD&V, to replace him.

Van Rompuy was credited with calming the recent political instability, and partly as a result of this success, he was appointed as the first permanent president of the European Council, the EU's intergovernmental decision-making body, in November 2009. Leterme returned to replace Van Rompuy as prime minister. However, his government fell in April 2010, when its coalition partner, the Flemish Liberals and Democrats (VLD), pulled out; the coalition had disagreed on proposed changes to voting rules in the district encompassing Brussels.

In national elections held in June 2010, the N-VA led with 27 seats in the Chamber of Deputies, and the Francophone Socialist Party (PS) placed second with 26 seats. Coalition negotiations again stalled over a series of issues linked to the balance of power between Flanders and Wallonia. The Leterme government remained in place for most of 2011 in a caretaker capacity. In September, the Dutch and Francophone parties reached a compromise on the fate of a contentious electoral district outside Brussels, and a final agreement was reached at the end of November. The development appeared to be prompted by the Standard & Poors downgrade of Belgium's credit rating on November 25 as well as warnings from the EU because the country had failed to meet its fiscal targets; the caretaker government was unable to pass a budget necessary to reduce the deficit. The new government, which notably does not include the N-VA, is led by Elio Di Rupo of the PS, the first French-speaking prime minister in more than 30 years; it took over from the caretaker government in December.

Political Rights and Civil Liberties: Belgium is an electoral democracy. Parliament consists of two houses: the Chamber of Deputies and the Senate. The 150 members of the Chamber of Deputies are elected directly by proportional representation. There are 71 seats in the Senate, with 40 filled by direct popular vote and 31 by indirect vote. Members serve four-year terms in both houses. The prime minister, who is the leader of the majority party or coalition, is appointed by the monarch and approved by Parliament. The party system is highly fragmented, with separate Flemish and Walloon parties representing all traditional parties of the left and right.

The xenophobic Vlaams Blok party was banned in 2004 for violating the country's antiracism laws. It changed its name to Vlaams Belang (Flemish Interest) and removed some of the more overtly racist elements from its platform. However, the party maintains its opposition to immigration and its commitment to an independent Flanders.

Corruption is relatively rare in Belgium, which was ranked 19 out of 183 countries surveyed in Transparency International's 2011 Corruption Perceptions Index.

Freedoms of speech and the press are guaranteed by the constitution and generally respected by the government. Belgians have access to numerous private media outlets. However, concentration of newspaper ownership has progressed in recent decades, leaving most of the country's papers in the hands of a few corporations. In March 2011, the European Court of Human Rights (ECHR) ruled against Belgium concerning a 2001 Belgian court injunction that delayed broadcast of a program on patients' rights, while a doctor profiled in the program brought defamation charges against the television channel in question. The ECHR said this violated the channel's freedom of expression as protected in the European Convention on Human Rights. The government does not limit access to the internet.

Freedom of religion is protected. About half of the country's population identifies itself as Roman Catholic. However, members of a number of minority religions have complained of discrimination by the government, which has been criticized for its characterization of some non-Catholic groups as "sects." In April 2010, the Chamber of Deputies approved a ban on the partial or total covering of the face in public locations; although it did not specifically mention the veils worn by some Muslim women, these were widely seen as the target. New elections were called before the Senate could vote on the measure, and implementation of the ban was delayed until July 2011. Offenders face a fine of up to 137.50 euros (US$183) or a week in jail. Two women who were fined 50 euros (US$66) in July for wearing full veils have challenged the law in court. The government does not restrict academic freedom.

Freedom of assembly is respected. Freedom of association is guaranteed by law, except for groups that practice discrimination "overtly and repeatedly." Employers found guilty of firing workers because of union activities are required to reinstate the workers or pay an indemnity. Belgian human rights groups and trade unions criticized the police for preventive arrests and using physical force against peaceful demonstrators during the September 2010 "Euromanifestation" demonstration, which was organized by European trade unions.

The judiciary is independent, and the rule of law generally prevails in civil and criminal matters. Although conditions in prisons and detention centers meet most international standards, many continue to suffer from overcrowding.

Specific antiracism laws penalize the incitement of discrimination, acts of hatred, and violence based on race, ethnicity, or nationality. While a 2009 government decision regularized 25,000 illegal immigrants, there have been complaints about the treatment of rejected asylum seekers and illegal immigrants awaiting deportation, who can sometimes be held in unsanitary conditions in the Brussels airport for several months. The Belgian League of Human Rights filed a complaint with the Labor Court in Brussels in August 2011, claiming authorities had failed to provide adequate housing for asylum seekers, particularly unaccompanied minors. In January 2011, the ECHR ruled Belgian deportations of asylum seekers to Greece were a human rights violation due to the poor detention conditions in the country. Belgium has since halted returns to Greece.

The law provides for the free movement of citizens at home and abroad, and the government does not interfere with these rights. However, individual communities may expel Roma from city limits at the discretion of the local government. In July 2010, it was reported that up to 700 Roma were forced to move from Flanders to Wallonia.

The government actively promotes equality for women. The state Institute for the Equality of Men and Women is empowered to initiate sex discrimination lawsuits. In the 2010 elections, women won about 40 percent of the seats in the Chamber of Deputies, and 37 percent of the seats in the Senate. Belgium is a destination and transit point for trafficked persons. However, according to the U.S. State Department's 2011 Trafficking in Persons Report, the country complies fully with the minimum standards for eliminating trafficking, including financing nongovernmental organizations that assist victims.

Belize

Political Rights: 1
Civil Liberties: 2
Status: Free

Population: 317,900
Capital: Belmopan

Ten-Year Ratings Timeline For Year Under Review (Political Rights, Civil Liberties, Status)

2002	2003	2004	2005	2006	2007	2008	2009	20010	2011
1,2F	1,2F	1,2F	1,2F	1,2F	1,2F	1,2F	1,2F	1,2F	1,2F

Overview: **In a controversial move, Belize's government amended the constitution in 2011 in order to guarantee the state a majority stake in water, electricity, and telecommunications companies. Meanwhile, violent crime and drug trafficking remained serious concerns throughout the year.**

Belize achieved independence from Britain in 1981 but has remained a member of the British Commonwealth. Control of the government has since alternated between the center-right United Democratic Party (UDP) and the center-left People's United Party (PUP).

Said Wilbert Musa of the PUP was elected prime minister in 1998, replacing George Cadle Prince, the cofounder of the PUP and Belize's first prime minister. Musa became the country's first prime minister to secure a second consecutive term after the PUP won again in 2003. However, the opposition UDP swept the 2008 national elections, capturing 25 out of 31 National Assembly seats, amid public dissatisfaction with corruption, increased taxation, and rising crime rates. The UDP's Dean Barrow became prime minister.

The Barrow government proposed controversial amendments to the constitution in 2008 that would allow for wiretapping, preventative detention, and the right to seize land where mineral resources are discovered. Opponents argued that this latter measure could easily be abused and did not respect the land rights of Mayan minority groups. The amendments were passed by the National Assembly in August, but the Court of Appeals ruled in March 2009 that a referendum was required as well. The Interception of Communications Act, which would allow for wiretaps and was criticized by opponents for its potential for misuse by law enforcement officials, was enacted on December 2010.

The Barrow government also faced criticism for its 2009 takeover of Belize Telemedia Limited, the country's largest telecommunications company. The Supreme Court upheld the nationalization in 2010, but ordered the government to compensate shareholders immediately. In June 2011, the Belizean Court of Appeals ruled that Telemedia's nationalization was unconstitutional. The Belizean government nationalized Telemedia a second time in July, believing that it had addressed those issues that the court had found to be illegal during the first nationalization process. In July, Prime Minister Barrow also introduced a constitutional amendment to parliament that would ensure government control of all public utilities; the amendment became law in October.

Political Rights and Civil Liberties: Belize is an electoral democracy. The head of state is the British monarch, who is represented by a governor general. Members of the 31-seat House of Representatives, the lower house of the bicameral National Assembly, are directly elected for five-year terms. The 12 members of the Senate are currently appointed to five-year terms, though Belizeans voted in a 2008 referendum to change to an elected Senate following the next general elections in 2013.

There are no restrictions on the right to organize political parties, and the interests of Mestizo, Creole, Mayan, and Garifuna ethnic groups are represented in the National Assembly.

Government corruption remains a serious problem. Belize is the only country in Central America that is not a party to the UN Convention against Corruption. In 2010, three high-ranking Belize City Council members resigned due to allegations of misconduct. A report by the auditor general claimed that the council had misused or failed to account for millions of dollars in municipal funds since 2006.

Belize has a generally open media environment. Journalists or others who question the financial disclosures of government officials may face up to three years in prison or up to US$2,500 in fines, but this law has not been applied in recent years. The Belize Broadcasting Authority has the right to prior restraint of all broadcasts for national security or emergency reasons, though this too is rarely invoked. Despite the availability of diverse sources of media, including privately owned weekly newspapers, radio and television stations, concerns over government control of the broadcast industry remain after the nationalization of Telemedia. While the government does not restrict internet access or use, internet penetration is low due to lack of infrastructure and high costs.

Residents of Belize enjoy full freedom of religion, and academic freedom is respected.

Freedoms of assembly and association are generally upheld, and demonstrations are usually peaceful. A large number of nongovernmental organizations are active, and labor unions remain politically influential despite their shrinking ranks. Official boards of inquiry adjudicate labor disputes, and businesses are penalized for labor-code violations. However, the government has done little to combat antiunion discrimination, and workers who are fired for organizing rarely receive compensation.

The judiciary is independent, and the rule of law is generally respected. However, concerns remain that the judicial system is vulnerable to political interference. A 2011 report by the American Bar Association scored Belize poorly on 16 out of 28 factors in evaluating its prosecutorial and criminal justice system. Defendants can remain free on bail or in pretrial detention for years amid a heavy case backlog; about one-fifth of the country's detainees are awaiting trial.

Violent crime, money laundering, gang violence, and drug trafficking continued to be serious concerns in 2011. Belize now has the sixth-highest homicide rate in the world. Officials estimate the perpetrators are convicted in only about 10 percent of homicides. In September, the government brokered a truce among rival gangs in response to complaints made by residents and alleged gang members of police brutality by the Gang Suppression Unit. Extrajudicial killings and the use of excessive force remain concerns. Police misconduct is investigated by the department's internal affairs office or an ombudsman's office. Belize was added to the U.S. list of "major" drug-producing and transit countries in 2011 because of large numbers of drugs and weapons seized along its border with Mexico and weak anticorruption measures. According to the International Center for Prison Studies, Belize has the world's ninth-highest prisoner-to-public ratio, with about 439 inmates per 100,000 inhabitants. Prisons do not meet minimum international standards.

While the government actively discourages ethnic discrimination, it has designated only 77,000 acres as Mayan reserves, and there has been little action on the 500,000 acres of disputed land following a 2004 Inter-American Court on Human Rights ruling in favor of Mayan property rights. However, the June 2010 Supreme Court ruling recognizing the land-use rights of 38 Mayan communities could allow them to block development on communal property. Most Spanish-speaking immigrants in the country lack legal status and face discrimination.

Violence against women and children remains a serious concern, as does the prevalence of child labor in agriculture. Gender disparities are profound; Belize ranks 100 out of 135 countries on the World Economic Forum's 2011 Global Gender Gap Report. There have been reports of discrimination against people living with HIV/AIDS, despite the government's efforts to educate the public about the illness. Lesbian, gay, bisexual, and transgender (LGBT) persons also face legal and societal discrimination. While female same-sex sexual activity is legal, male same-sex sexual activity is illegal and can result in 10 years imprisonment. The United Belize Advocacy Movement is challenging the constitutionality of this law and is scheduled to go before the Supreme Court in early 2012. Belize is the only country in the Americas that has no women in its elected lower house of government.

Belize is a source, transit, and destination country for women and children trafficked for prostitution and forced labor. The majority of trafficked women are from Guatemala, Honduras, and El Salvador. The trafficking of workers from South Asia and China for forced labor has also been uncovered in recent years. There is also concern that Belize is emerging as a sex tourism destination. The U.S. State Department's 2011 Trafficking in Persons Report removed Belize from the Tier 2 Watch List but continued to categorize it as a Tier 2 country.

Benin

Political Rights: 2
Civil Liberties: 2
Status: Free

Population: 9,100,000
Capital: Porto-Novo

Ten-Year Ratings Timeline For Year Under Review (Political Rights, Civil Liberties, Status)

2002	2003	2004	2005	2006	2007	2008	2009	2010	2011
3,2F	2,2F	2,2F	2,2F	2,2F	2,2F	2,2F	2,2F	2,2F	2,2F

Overview: **In March 2011, President Boni Yayi was reelected to a second five-year term in a vote that was considered free and fair by international observers but heavily criticized by the opposition. Demonstrations against the result led by the opposition were forcefully dispersed by police. Yayi's coalition gained a majority in free and fair April legislative elections.**

Six decades of French rule in Benin lasted until 1960. Twelve years later, Mathieu Kérékou took power, ending a series of coups and counter-coups and imposing a one-party Marxist-Leninist government that lasted nearly 20 years. However, by 1990, economic hardship and rising internal unrest forced Kérékou to hold a national conference that eventually ushered in a peaceful democratic transition. Following his defeat by Nicéphore Soglo in the 1991 presidential election, the country's human rights record improved. Kérékou returned to power in 1996 through a democratic election, and he secured another term in 2001, after his two main opponents boycotted a runoff due to administrative problems and alleged fraud. The 2003 legislative elections, which were generally considered free and fair, gave the ruling coalition a majority in the National Assembly.

The 2006 presidential election—for which both Kérékou and Soglo were ineligible due to their ages—was won by Boni Yayi, an independent candidate and former president of the regional development bank. He pledged transparency, a hard line on corruption, decentralization of government, and the privatization of state companies.

A coalition of parties supporting Yayi, led by the Cowrie Forces for an Emerging Benin (FCBE), won 35 of 83 seats in generally free and fair 2007 legislative elections. In 2009, this loose alliance began to break apart, posing a challenge to Yayi's efforts to enact electoral and economic reforms. By 2010, a number of FCBE members had defected to the opposition, causing the alliance to lose its majority and effectively blocking any new legislation.

In August 2010, more than half of the National Assembly's members called for Yayi's impeachment, accusing him of involvement in a high-profile Ponzi scheme in which a large investment firm was found to have stolen $130 million in savings from more than 100,000 people. Although parliament was unable to secure the necessary two-thirds majority to impeach Yayi, the president's reputation suffered greatly. The scandal also unified the opposition, bringing together the five major political parties of the south for the first time since independence to form the Build the Nation Union (UN), which put forward a single candidate for the 2011 election, Adrien Houngbédji.

Benin's poverty and limited infrastructure have often caused technical and logistical problems during elections. Electoral reforms have been slow to come about, but a new electronic voter list was implemented by the Autonomous National Electoral Commission (CENA) for the 2011 presidential and legislative polls. The opposition harshly criticized the new system, alleging that more than one million voters had been left off the rolls, and demanded a postponement of the February 27 presidential election. With backing from the United Nations and the African Union, the government agreed to a delay. The election was held March 13, and CENA soon after announced that Yayi had won with 53 percent. International observers deemed the election free and fair. Houngbédji, who received 36 percent, refused to accept the results and appealed to the Constitutional Court. On March 21, the court confirmed Yayi's victory, leading to mass opposition demonstrations that were dispersed with tear gas and other police violence. In July, the government convened a national consultative meeting with legislators, former CENA members, and union and civil society leaders to establish guidelines to better manage future election-related disputes.

Houngbédji's refusal to accept the results appears to have divided the opposition, undermining its campaign for the April legislative polls. Yayi's coalition gained a majority, winning 49 of 83 National Assembly seats, with 41 going to his core party, FCBE, in an election that international observers believed to be fair.

Political Rights and Civil Liberties: Benin is an electoral democracy. Despite delays, serious problems with the new electronic voting system, and doubts about the performance of CENA, the 2011 presidential and legislative polls were both considered largely free and fair by the international community. The president is elected by popular vote for up to two five-year terms and serves as both the chief of state and head of government. Delegates to the 83-member, unicameral National Assembly serve four-year terms.

Historically, Benin has been divided between northern and southern ethnic groups. President Boni Yayi's support comes primarily from the north, while the main opposition parties hail primarily from the south. All political parties, regardless of ethnic or regional affiliation, normally operate freely throughout the country.

Yayi came to power in 2006 on an anticorruption platform and subsequently enacted a number of measures to combat corruption, including an internationally praised audit of 60 state-run companies. However, these efforts were undermined by the 2010 Ponzi scheme scandal. In August 2011, the National Assembly voted unanimously to pass an antigraft law initially proposed by Yayi in 2006, which requires government employees to declare their assets when they enter and leave office.

Constitutional guarantees of freedom of expression are largely respected in practice. A pluralistic and frequently politicized press publishes articles that are highly critical of both government and opposition party leaders. While media outlets were largely able to cover the elections unhindered, a number of troubling incidents were reported. A local journalist was beaten by the National Assembly Speaker's private security in February, and another was beaten by police while covering an opposition demonstration in March. Also in March, the authorities disrupted Radio France Internationale's transmission as it was about to begin airing a popular call-in show on the disputed election; it was the second such disruption in two years. The government does not restrict access to the internet, but a 2011 regulation requires mobile phone users to register and undergo an identity check.

The government actively seeks to ensure religious and academic freedoms. While the majority of Beninese identify themselves as either Muslim or Christian, many also practice some form of voodoo. Confrontations between religious groups are rare. The state plans to provide free universal primary education by 2015.

Freedom of assembly is respected, and requirements for permits and registration have often been ignored. In 2011, demonstrations were held on a variety of issues, including problems with the voter roll and the electronic voting system, police violence against journalists, and the Constitutional Court's confirmation of Yayi's election victory. Police cracked down on the postelection demonstrations, using tear gas and batons to disperse hundreds of opposition protesters in Cotonou after the court's announcement. Police arrested a number of the protesters, including opposition officials, citing a directive from the security ministry banning such demonstrations.

Nongovernmental organizations and human rights groups operated freely in 2011. The right to organize and join labor unions is constitutionally guaranteed, even for government employees and civil servants. Unions played a central role in the country's democratization and were a vocal force supporting Houngbédji in 2011. A number of civil servant unions went on strike in June, demanding a 25 percent pay increase, halting the strike when the government agreed to negotiate.

The judiciary's independence is generally respected by the executive branch, but the courts are highly inefficient and susceptible to corruption, largely due to their serious and persistent lack of funding. Nevertheless, the constitutional court demonstrated remarkable independence in 2010 in its rulings on a number of complex issues regarding electoral reform. The court appeared to maintain this independence during the 2011 presidential election controversy. Prisons are harsh and overcrowded, and criminal cases are rarely processed on time.

Relations among Benin's ethnic groups are generally amicable, although regional divisions occasionally flare up, particularly between the north and south. Minority ethnic groups are well represented in government agencies, the civil service, and the armed forces.

Although the constitution provides for gender equality, women enjoy fewer educational and employment opportunities than men, particularly in rural areas. A family code promulgated in 2004 improved women's inheritance, property, and marriage rights, and prohibited forced marriage and female genital mutilation, but these laws have not yet been well enforced. In April 2009, to address the country's high maternal mortality rate, the government began helping women pay for caesarean births, a project that continued into 2011.

Human trafficking is widespread in Benin; the vast majority of victims are girls trafficked inside the country from rural to urban areas. A law formally outlawing the trafficking of children was passed in 2006, but there is no legislation in Benin that specifically addresses the trafficking of adults.

Bhutan

Political Rights: 4
Civil Liberties: 5
Status: Partly Free

Population: 708,000
Capital: Thimphu

Ten-Year Ratings Timeline For Year Under Review (Political Rights, Civil Liberties, Status)

2002	2003	2004	2005	2006	2007	2008	2009	2010	2011
6,5NF	6,5NF	6,5NF	6,5NF	6,5NF	6,5NF	4,5PF	4,5PF	4,5PF	4,5PF

Overview: **Local elections that had been postponed for three years took place in early 2011. While tens of thousands of Nepali-speaking Bhutanese refugees who were displaced in the 1990s have been resettled in other countries in recent years, some 54,000 remained in camps in Nepal by year's end.**

Britain helped to install the Wangchuck dynasty as Bhutan's ruling family in 1907, and a 1949 treaty allowed newly independent India to assume Britain's role in conducting the kingdom's foreign and defense policies. In 1971, Jigme Singye Wangchuck succeeded his father as king.

The government in the 1980s imposed restrictions on Nepali speakers, also known as Southern Bhutanese, to protect the culture of the ruling Ngalong Drukpa ethnic group. The newly formed Bhutanese People's Party (BPP) responded in 1990 with violent demonstrations, prompting a government crackdown. Tens of thousands of Southern Bhutanese fled or were expelled to Nepal in the early 1990s, and soldiers raped and beat many villagers and detained thousands as "antinationals."

The king launched a gradual transition to democracy in 1998. Political parties were legalized in June 2007, and elections for an upper house of Parliament were held in two rounds in December 2007 and January 2008. Elections for the lower house, the National Assembly, took place in March 2008. The Bhutan Peace and Prosperity Party (DPT) won 45 of the 47 seats, while the People's Democratic Party (PDP) took the remainder; voter turnout was nearly 80 percent. A new constitution promulgated in July provided for some fundamental rights, but it upheld the primacy of the monarchy, and did not adequately protect the rights of Nepali speakers.

Jigme Khesar Namgyel Wangchuck succeeded his father as king in November 2008, though he had been in power since the outgoing king's abdication in 2006. The monarchy remained highly popular with the public, and many Bhutanese expressed reservations about the shift toward democracy.

Local elections that had been postponed since late 2008 were finally held across the country in early 2011. Officials experienced difficulty recruiting qualified candidates to stand in the elections in a country with a small population, voter apathy, and high education requirements. All candidates were officially required to be nonpartisan and to prove that they had no party affiliations. Several candidates in the local elections ultimately were disqualified, because they did not meet the age or professional requirements. Some polls took long to open due to logistical difficulties, and turnout was relatively low, reportedly due in part to the remoteness of certain areas of the country and to voter apathy and distrust that the polls would result in concrete change.

Political Rights and Civil Liberties: Bhutan is not an electoral democracy, though the 2008 and 2011 elections represented a significant step toward that status. However, monitors in both elections found problems with freedom of expression and association during the campaign. In 2008, European Union (EU) monitors noted that a rule requiring candidates to obtain a security clearance certificate may have been an obstacle for some Nepalese. Also in 2008, Human Rights Watch reported that many ethnic Nepalese residents were barred from voting because they were among the 13 percent of the population counted as non-nationals in the 2005 census. While similar complaints were lodged during the 2011 local elections, international monitors nonetheless deemed them to have been conducted successfully.

The constitution provides for a bicameral Parliament, with a 25-seat upper house, the nonpartisan National Council, and a 47-seat lower house, the National Assembly, both serving five-year terms. The king appoints 5 members of the National Council, and the remaining 20 are elected; the lower house is entirely elected, and the head of the majority party is nominated by the king to serve as prime minister. The cabinet is nominated by the king and approved by the National Assembly. The king remains the head of state and appoints members of the Supreme Court, the attorney general, and the heads of national commissions. He can return legislation with objections or amendments, but once it has been reconsidered and resubmitted, the king must sign it into law.

Political parties, previously illegal, were allowed to begin registering in 2007, though the Bhutan People's United Party was denied registration.

The government operates with limited transparency and accountability, but steps have been taken in recent years to improve both. The 2006 Anti-Corruption Act established whistle-blower protections, and the Anti-Corruption Commission (ACC) is tasked with investigating and preventing graft. In 2011, the National Assembly passed an anticorruption law that strengthened and expanded the ACC's mandate. Bhutan was ranked 38 of 183 countries surveyed in Transparency International's 2011 Corruption Perceptions Index.

The authorities restrict freedom of expression, and a 1992 law prohibits criticism of the king and the political system. A 2006 media law led to the establishment of two independent radio stations, but it did not provide specific protections for journalists or guarantee freedom of information. The state-owned *Kuensel* and two independent weeklies, the *Bhutan Times* and the *Daily Observer*, generally publish progovernment articles but occasionally cover criticism of the government. In September 2011, Kuensel was warned by the government for printing an unlicensed version in a local language and ordered to cease publication of it. Earlier in the year, the government had allowed only one out of three applicants seeking to produce a new local-language newspaper to proceed. Applications for private television stations in Bhutan also were delayed in 2011, with the government saying it had not yet decided which applicants to allow. The internet is accessed by about 15 percent of Bhutan's population. The government monitors online content and blocks material that is seen as pornographic, but rarely blocks political content.

The constitution protects freedom of religion, and a 2007 election law bars any ordained religious figure or "religious personality" from voting or running for office. In 2010, the election commission maintained that even lay members of religious organizations would be prevented from voting, but in 2011, monks and other members of religious groups did participate heavily in the local elections. While Bhutanese of all faiths can worship relatively freely, the Drukpa Kagyupa school of Mahayana Buddhism is the official religion and reportedly receives various subsidies. The Christian minority is allegedly subject to harassment by the authorities, and permits for the construction of Hindu temples are apparently difficult to obtain. Few restrictions on academic freedom have been reported, though nongovernmental organizations (NGOs) claim that the teaching of Nepali and Sanskrit is banned. The government requires that Bhutanese wear traditional dress on certain occasions and at certain times.

The constitution guarantees freedom of assembly, but the government must approve the purpose of any protests. In recent years, security forces have arrested Southern Bhutanese refugees based in Nepal who entered Bhutan to demonstrate for the right to return home.

The constitution guarantees freedom of association, but only for groups "not harmful to the peace and unity of the country." NGOs that work on human rights, the refugee issue, or other sensitive matters are not legally allowed to operate. Under the 2007 Civil Society Organization Act, all new NGOs must register with the government. The government prohibits independent trade unions and strikes, though most of the country's workforce is engaged in subsistence agriculture.

An independent Judicial Service Council created in 2007 controls judicial appointments and promotions. However, critics have alleged that the judiciary is not fully independent. Until a new Supreme Court was finally seated in early 2010, the king served as the final arbiter of appeals. Arbitrary arrest, detention, and torture remain areas of concern, and dozens of political prisoners continue to serve lengthy sentences.

Prior to the mass expulsions of Nepali speakers in the early 1990s, the government had stripped thousands of their citizenship under a 1985 law that required both parents to be Bhutanese citizens. While the Office of the UN High Commissioner for Refugees (UNHCR) asserts that the overwhelming majority of refugees have proof of Bhutanese nationality, the government maintains that many left voluntarily or had been illegal immigrants. Some 55,000 refugees live in extremely poor conditions in Nepal and have been denied reentry to Bhutan, and the Bhutanese government continues to harshly criticize UNHCR. A resettlement effort aimed at transferring the refugees to third countries began in 2007. By the end of 2012, the refugee camps in Nepal are planned to be consolidated into just two. By the end of 2011, some 58,000 refugees had been resettled in third countries, mostly to the United States.

Women participate freely in social and economic life but continue to be underrepresented in government and politics, though they participated heavily in the 2011 elections. They also comprise nearly 50 percent of the workforce.

Bolivia

Political Rights: 3
Civil Liberties: 3
Status: Partly Free

Population: 10,088,100
Capital: La Paz (administrative), Sucre (judicial)

Ten-Year Ratings Timeline For Year Under Review (Political Rights, Civil Liberties, Status)

2002	2003	2004	2005	2006	2007	2008	2009	2010	2011
3,3F	3,3F	3,3PF	3,3PF	3,3PF	3,3PF	3,3PF	3,3PF	3,3PF	3,3PF

Overview: **President Evo Morales faced a growing wave of social protest in 2011 on issues ranging from economic policy to land rights. In September, police repression of a march by an indigenous group drew domestic and international criticism. The protesters eventually secured an agreement with the government to protect their territory from unwanted road construction and migrants. In October, the country held its first elections to fill judicial posts at the highest levels, including the Supreme Court and Constitutional Tribunal. Voters sent an unclear message by casting a high percentage of null ballots.**

After achieving independence from Spain in 1825, the Republic of Bolivia endured recurrent instability and military rule. However, the armed forces, responsible for more than 180 coups in 157 years, refrained from political intervention after 1982, allowing a regular succession of civilian presidents over the next two decades.

In 2002, Gonzalo Sánchez de Lozada won the presidency on the basis of a narrow first-round election victory and a subsequent vote in Congress. He had previously served as president in the 1990s, when he oversaw market-oriented economic reforms. The 2002 election also marked the emergence of Evo Morales as a national political leader. Known as a founder of the coca growers' federation and the Movement Toward Socialism (MAS) party, Morales received the second-largest number of votes in the first round. In 2003, Sánchez de Lozada's government confronted massive protests over economic policy and its unpopular decision to build a $5 billion natural gas pipeline to the Pacific via Chile, which was reviled for having annexed Bolivia's only coastal territory in a 19th-century war. Government repression of protests, resulting in at least 120 deaths over several months, provoked even greater opposition in the streets of La Paz. In October 2003, Sánchez de Lozada resigned and fled the country.

Vice President Carlos Mesa assumed the presidency. Despite successfully increasing state control over natural resources, he failed to quell mounting protests over gas revenues, regional autonomy, and other issues, and he ultimately resigned in June 2005. The chief justice of the Supreme Court temporarily served as president to oversee new elections. Morales won the December presidential poll, and the MAS became the largest party in Congress.

In 2006, the MAS and allied parties won a majority of delegates for a constituent assembly charged with writing a new constitution. From 2006 to 2009, recurring conflicts erupted over voting procedures in the constituent assembly and the substance of the draft constitution, pitting the government and its supporters against congressional and regionally based political opponents, especially from Bolivia's eastern departments.

As polarization increased, Morales survived a recall referendum in August 2008 with 67 percent of the vote. Political confrontations during this period sometimes turned violent; a September 2008 clash between pro-Morales peasants and followers of opposition prefect Leopoldo Fernández in Pando left at least 14 people dead and triggered a criminal indictment for Fernández.

By October 2008, the opposing sides had reached a compromise on the draft constitution that retained most of the administration's proposals, though notable changes included an easing of potentially restrictive media language, a higher bar for future constitutional amendments, expansion of the electoral commission, and the limitation of consecutive presidential terms to two. After a brief but intense campaign, over 61 percent of voters approved the new constitution in January 2009, with a turnout of over 90 percent.

In 2009 national elections, Morales's main challenger was former Cochabamba mayor Manfred Reyes Villa, who ran as the candidate of the Progressive Plan for Bolivia (PPB) party. Morales was reelected with 64 percent of the vote amid a record 95 percent turnout. Opposition leaders complained about the abuse of state resources and being targeted in criminal investigations. Monitors from the European Union characterized the elections as generally free and fair, but reported some cases of the misuse of state resources. With corruption charges pending, Reyes Villa fled abroad, as did other opposition figures and former public officials.

The MAS also dominated the concurrent legislative elections, winning majorities in the lower chamber and the Senate. Meanwhile, the remainder of Bolivia's nine departments approved regional autonomy statutes, joining four that had already done so in 2006. In April 2010 regional elections, MAS candidates won governorships in six of the nine departments, but opposition candidates from the left and right became mayors in 7 of the 10 principal cities. The MAS used its legislative majority to pass new laws during 2010, including a long-debated anticorruption law, an ambitious antiracism law, as well as legislation to implement the new constitution's articles regarding electoral processes, the judiciary, and decentralization.

While regional backlash and opposition from the right dominated Morales's first term as president, his second term has been marked by challenges from unions and social movements allied with the left. The December 2010 announcement of plans to remove state gasoline subsidies, which would lead to sharp price increases, triggered street protests, and Bolivia's largest trade union organization, the Bolivian Workers' Center (COB), scheduled another mass demonstration for January 3, 2011. This threat forced the government to rescind its proposal on December 31. In April, the government ended two weeks of protests over wages by striking a deal with the COB on wage hikes.

Also in 2011, a group of indigenous residents of the Indigenous Territory and National Park of Isiboro Sécure (TIPNIS) joined with other social organizations and opposition groups to block a planned $415 million highway through the territory that would link the cities of Trinidad and Cochabamba and facilitate exports to Brazil. Indigenous leaders argued that the Brazilian-financed highway would cause environmental damage and encourage further encroachment on their land by coca growers, Brazil's timber industry, and other migrants. The movement began by invoking the community's right to a consultation (*consulta previa*) as stipulated in the 2010 constitution. In mid-August, TIPNIS residents began a march to La Paz to demand that the government scrap the highway plan. After a failed attempt to negotiate en route, Foreign Minister David Choquehuanca was briefly detained by the protesters and forced to march with them. On the following day, the police clubbed and teargased the 1,500 marchers, leaving 70 people injured. Domestic and international human rights groups called for an investigation. Morales condemned the violence and accepted the resignations of his defense and interior ministers.

The TIPNIS protesters resumed their march and received a warm welcome from La Paz residents. In meetings with Morales and other high-ranking officials, indigenous leaders reached an agreement to protect their territory. Enacted as Law 180 in October, the legislation banned highway construction across the designated areas, prohibited illegal settlements, and authorized the use of force to remove squatters.

Also in October, Bolivia became the first country in Latin America to elect judges to its highest courts, including the Constitutional Tribunal, the Supreme Court, and the newly created Agroenvironmental Tribunal. The change was intended to remedy an appointments crisis in the judicial branch. Since 2007, the judiciary had been rocked by resignations, charges of malfeasance, and a backlog of cases. In 2010, a short-term law gave the president the power to select judges until elections could be held. However, the October voting was marred by the fact that the number of null ballots cast surpassed the number of valid votes.

A November 2011 agreement reestablished full diplomatic relations between Bolivia and the United States. Bolivia had expelled the U.S. ambassador in 2008 on the charge that he had conspired against the Morales government. Subsequently, the U.S. government had announced the suspension of trade benefits provided under the Andean Trade Promotion and Drug Eradication Act, and Bolivia then banned the U.S. Drug Enforcement Agency from the country.

Political Rights and Civil Liberties:

Bolivia is an electoral democracy. Elections and referendums since 2005 have been deemed free and fair by international observers. Under the new constitution, presidential and legislative terms are both five years, with up to two consecutive terms permitted. The Plurinational Legislative Assembly consists of a 130-member Chamber of Deputies and a 36-member Senate, in which all senators and 53 deputies are elected by proportional representation, and 70 deputies are elected in individual districts. Seven seats in the Chamber of Deputies are reserved for indigenous representatives. The 2009 constitution includes a presidential runoff provision to replace the previous system, in which Congress had decided elections when no candidate won an outright majority.

Citizens have the right to organize political parties. President Evo Morales's MAS, the most important political organization, draws support from a diverse range of social movements, unions, and civil society actors. The opposition had been led by the center-right Social Democratic Power (PODEMOS) party, but in 2008, it split over the negotiations on the draft constitution. Most prominent opposition members ran under the PPB banner in 2009 and participate in the legislative opposition alliance known as PPB–National Convergence. Following the 2010 local and regional elections, the Movement Without Fear (MSM) party, a moderate group previously allied with the MAS, emerged as a left-leaning alternative to the ruling party. It is led by former La Paz mayor Juan del Granado.

Corruption remains a major problem in Bolivia, affecting a range of government entities and economic sectors, including extractive industries. New anticorruption legislation enacted in 2010 has been criticized for permitting retroactive enforcement, which contradicts international legal standards. In September 2011, legislators voted to authorize the trial of former presidents Gonzalo Sánchez de Lozada and Jorge Quiroga for approving petroleum contracts that are alleged to have contravened national interests. Three former ministers were also included in the indictment. Separately, there have been concerns about the corruption of law enforcement bodies in connection with the illegal drug trade. In February 2011, General René Sanabria, the former chief of Bolivia's counternarcotics office, was arrested in Panama and extradited to the United States to stand trial on drug-trafficking charges. The Bolivian government responded with arrests that included five former police chiefs and the firing of the national police chief. Bolivia was ranked 118 out of 183 countries surveyed in Transparency International's 2011 Corruption Perceptions Index.

Although the constitution guarantees freedom of expression, the media are subject to some limitations in practice. Press associations have complained that the language of the 2010 antiracism law is excessively vague and contributes to a climate of self-censorship. In particularly serious cases, the law allows publication of racist or discriminatory ideas to be punished with fines, the loss of broadcast licenses, and prison sentences of up to five years. In many cases, a public apology can result in the waiver of such sanctions. The 2011 Electoral Regime Law restricted press coverage of the candidates running in the October judicial elections, making it difficult for the press to provide independent information to voters.

Most media outlets are privately owned, and radio is the leading source of information. Many newspapers and television stations tend to feature opposition rather than progovernment opinion pieces; the opposite holds true in state media. In July 2011, Morales signed a new telecommunications law requiring that state-run media control 33 percent of all broadcast licenses. Commercial broadcasters will be limited to another 33 percent, while local communities and indigenous groups will each be entitled to 17 percent of licenses. Press freedom advocates welcomed the idea of expanding media access to new groups, but expressed fears that local and indigenous outlets would lack the financial resources to operate independently and could fall under government control. The law also allows the government to access any private communication, including e-mail and telephone calls, for reasons of "national security" or any other emergency.

Freedom of religion is guaranteed by the constitution. The new constitution ended the Roman Catholic Church's official status and created a secular state. The government does not restrict academic freedom.

Bolivian law provides for the rights of peaceful assembly and freedom of association, though protests sometimes turn violent. The Morales government has been highly critical of nongovernmental organizations, especially those that supported the TIPNIS protest in 2011. The number of protests, strikes, and demonstrations increased markedly in the first half of 2011, with many actions focused on wages and price hikes. The right to form labor unions is guaranteed by the constitution. Unions are an active force in society and have significant political influence.

The judicial system remained in flux in 2011, operating with temporary appointees selected by the president. The attempt to revamp the judiciary and strengthen its legitimacy through elections was marred by procedural problems and voter discontent. Candidates for the Supreme Court, the Constitutional Tribunal, and other entities were nominated through a two-thirds vote in the legislature, which allowed the MAS to dominate the selection process. Election officials ruled that candidates were not permitted to campaign openly, and that information about the candidates would be disseminated through official channels. In results that were interpreted as a defeat for the government, voters cast null ballots in numbers that exceeded the overall valid vote. Despite opposition criticism questioning the legitimacy of the elections, the government said it would seat the new judges.

Prosecutorial independence is viewed as weak, and enforcement in 2011 at times appeared to focus on opposition members and sympathizers, with multiple former presidents and many of the country's most prominent opposition politicians facing charges ranging from graft to treason. Court cases are proceeding against 21 of the 39 defendants accused of terrorism and armed uprising for their involvement in the regional movement led by Eduardo Rózsa, who died in a shootout with police in 2009. The defendants maintain that they were seeking the autonomy of Bolivia's eastern departments and that they are not separatists.

Prison conditions are harsh. Over 70 percent of those behind bars are in pretrial detention. While the criminal procedure code recognizes indigenous conflict-resolution traditions, jurisdictional reform efforts to date have not fully resolved questions pertaining to indigenous customary law. This lack of clarity has led some perpetrators of vigilante crimes, including lynching, to misrepresent their actions as a form of indigenous justice. In May 2011, four policemen were killed in a community lynching in Potosí department.

Both the human rights ombudsman and independent human rights organizations are able to report on violations committed by the security forces. While impunity remains a problem, human rights organizations hailed the Supreme Court's landmark August 30, 2011, ruling in the "Black October" case, in which military and public officials were charged with the use of lethal force against demonstrators in 2003. Five army officers and two former ministers were found guilty and sentenced to jail terms. The Bolivian government continues to seek the extradition of former president Gonzalo Sánchez de Lozada from the United States to stand trial in the same case.

Bolivia is the world's third-largest producer of the coca leaf. By law, 12,000 hectares of land are designated for the legal cultivation of the crop. The United Nations estimates that another 19,000 hectares are used for unregulated coca production destined for the illegal cocaine trade. The Bolivian government has expressed concern about increased cocaine production in the country as well as the rising flow of Peruvian cocaine through Bolivian territory.

The new constitution recognizes 36 indigenous nationalities, declares Bolivia a "plurinational" state, and formalizes local political and judicial control within indigenous territories. However, some groups remain dissatisfied with receiving just seven reserved legislative seats. In general, racism is rife in the country, especially by mestizos and whites against indigenous groups. Despite its potential effects on press freedom, the new antiracism law includes a series of positive measures to combat discrimination and impose criminal penalties for discriminatory acts. Some rural employers keep indigenous workers in debt peonage, particularly in the Chaco region.

While the law protects and the government generally respects freedom of movement, protesters often block highways and city streets, causing serious economic losses.

The constitution prohibits discrimination based on gender and sexual orientation, but it reserves marriage only for opposite-sex couples, and there is no provision for same-sex civil unions. Women's political representation has increased in recent years. Ballot alternation requirements resulted in women winning 44 percent of the seats in the current Senate, though only 28 percent of the seats in the Chamber of Deputies. Gender parity election rules were also applied to the 2011 judicial elections. Violence against women is pervasive, and the justice system is ineffective at safeguarding women's broader legal rights. Child prostitution and child labor are problems.

Bosnia and Herzegovina

Political Rights: 4
Civil Liberties: 3
Status: Partly Free

Population: 3,843,000
Capital: Sarajevo

Ten-Year Ratings Timeline For Year Under Review (Political Rights, Civil Liberties, Status)

2002	2003	2004	2005	2006	2007	2008	2009	2010	2011
4,4PF	4,4PF	4,3PF	4,3PF	3,3PF	4,3PF	4,3PF	4,3PF	4,3PF	4,3PF

Overview: **After a 15-month deadlock following the October 2010 elections, Bosnia and Herzegovina's political parties formed a government in December 2011. In the meantime, the country experienced political stagnation, with the parliament failing to pass any significant reforms deemed necessary by the international Peace Implementation Council.**

Formerly a constituent republic within socialist Yugoslavia, Bosnia and Herzegovina (BiH) is among the most ethnically diverse countries in the region. The bulk of the population consists of three ethnic groups: Bosniaks, who are mainly Muslim; Serbs, who are Orthodox Christian; and Croats, who identify with the Roman Catholic Church. As Yugoslavia began to disintegrate in the early 1990s, BiH was recognized as an independent state in April 1992. A 43-month-long civil war ensued, resulting in the deaths of tens of thousands of people and the forced resettlement of approximately half of BiH's population.

The 1995 the Dayton Peace Accords brought an end to the war by creating a loosely knit state composed of the Bosniak-Croat "Federation of Bosnia and Herzegovina" (the Federation) and the largely Serb "Republika Srpska." The final status of the Brcko district was decided in 1999 by a special arbitration council, which defined it as a self-governing administrative unit that is formally part of both the Federation and Republika Srpska. The Dayton Accords gave significant authority to international civilian agencies such as the Office of the High Representative (OHR). However, despite years of considerable efforts by the international community to aid the country's integration, most aspects of political, social, and economic life remained divided along ethnic lines.

A coalition government formed in early 2007, following October 2006 elections, proved to be highly unstable, particularly due to a thorny working relationship between Serb leader Milorad Dodik of the Alliance of Independent Social Democrats (SNSD), who was determined to maintain Republika Srpska's autonomy, and Bosniak leader Haris Silajdžic of the Party for BiH (SzBiH), who sought to create a unitary BiH. Meanwhile, most Croat officials advocated further decentralization and the creation of a third constituent entity for Croat-majority areas. Despite these tensions, in June 2008 the European Union (EU) and BiH signed a Stabilization and Association Agreement, a key step toward EU membership.

In March 2009, Austrian diplomat Valentin Inzko was appointed as the new high representative. Long-standing tensions between the OHR and the Bosnian Serb leadership continued, with the latter challenging several of Inzko's decisions.

In a step condemned by the OHR, the parliament of Republika Srpska adopted a law in February 2010 that made it easier for the authorities to hold referendums on national issues, raising the possibility of a vote on secession. Later in February, the Peace Implementation Council (PIC), the international body charged with overseeing the postwar development of BiH, postponed the closure of the OHR due to the country's failure to meet the required conditions, including a political agreement on the census law. Serb authorities generally favored collecting census data on ethnic affiliation, but most Bosniaks opposed it, because the Bosniak population in Republika Srpska decreased during the civil conflict, in large part due to the policies of "ethnic cleansing."

Parliamentary and presidential elections took place in October 2010, bringing a power shift to several government bodies. The SNSD remained the dominant party in Republika Srpska, with Dodik stepping up his nationalist rhetoric ahead of the vote. Dodik himself was elected president of the Serb entity, having served as its prime minister since 2006. The more moderate and largely Bosniak Social Democratic Party (SDP) secured the plurality of seats in the Federation at the expense of the Party of Democratic Action (SDA) and the SzBiH, the latter of which experienced major defeats. The Croat Democratic Union of BiH (HDZ BiH) remained the most popular party among Bosnian Croats.

In the tripartite presidential election, incumbent Željko Komšic of the SDP was reelected as the Croat member of presidency. In a surprise victory, Bakir Izetbegovic of the SDA, the son of the late president Alija Izetbegovic, defeated the incumbent Silajdžic in the race for the Bosniak seat. SNSD incumbent Nebojša Radmanovic narrowly defeated Mladen Ivani of the Party of Democratic Progress (PDP) to become the Serb member of presidency.

In months following the elections, prolonged political wrangling over the formation of ruling coalitions paralyzed the country, stifling the already slow reform process. In Republika Srpska, a new government was formed in December 2010.

In the Federation, however, a new government was not formed until March 2011, and it almost immediately faced a legal challenge by the HDZ BiH and its ally, HDZ 1990,, which argued that the entity's legislature did not have a quorum when it voted to approve the new cabinet. Although the Central Electoral Commission (CEC) ruled in favor of the claim, Inzko in late March declared that the government would remain in place until the Federation's Constitutional Court provided a final ruling, and in April the two Croat parties decided to withdraw their legal challenge.

An agreement on a new central government was not reached until late December 2011, in large part due to disagreement over which party should receive the premiership and other key cabinet positions. The SDP argued that it should name the prime minister, as it won a plurality of the votes in the elections, but the HDZ BiH and HDZ 1990 claimed the right to choose the key officeholders, citing the informal system of rotating core posts among the three main ethnic groups. The December compromise agreement permitted the HDZ BiH to nominate candidates for only three out of four key ministry positions allocated to Croats, though HDZ BiH's Vjekoslav Bevanda was set to be confirmed as prime minister in January 2012.

Several rallies were held in Republika Srpska to support former Bosnian Serb military commander Ratko Mladic, who was arrested in Serbia in May after over 16 years in hiding. In June, the Republika Srpska government created a new fund to help with the legal costs of Mladic and other accused Bosnian Serb war criminals on trial before the International Criminal Tribunal for the former Yugoslavia (ICTY), which many Serbs perceive as biased against them, provoking strong criticism from other ethnic groups.

In September, in a move designed to dilute the powers of the OHR, the head of the EU mission in BiH assumed the position of EU special representative to Bosnia, a role that was previously combined with the OHR. Although some European countries see the OHR as having outlived its usefulness, the PIC has refused to set a timeline for its closure due to the lack of progress on key reforms and consistent challenges by the government of Republika Srpska to central state institutions.

Political Rights and Civil Liberties: The Republic of Bosnia and Herzegovina (BiH) is an electoral democracy. In general, voters can freely elect their representatives, although the OHR has the authority to remove elected officials if they are deemed to be obstructing the peace process. The government is led by a prime minister, and the role of head of state is performed by a three-member presidency composed of one Bosniak, one Serb, and one Croat. The Parliamentary Assembly is a bicameral body. The 15-seat upper house, the House of Peoples, consists of five members from each of the three main ethnic groups, elected by the Federation and Republika Srpska legislatures for four-year terms. The lower house, the House of Representatives, has 42 popularly elected members serving four-year terms, with 28 seats assigned to the Federation and 14 to Republika Srpska.

Corruption remains a serious problem. Enforcement of legislation designed to combat it has been weak, due in part to the lack of strong and independent anticorruption agencies and a dearth of political will to seriously address the issue. In its annual report on Bosnia's progress toward EU membership, the European Commission in 2011 identified serious flaws in the fight against corruption and noted a shortage of effective investigations, prosecutions, and convictions in corruption cases. BiH was ranked 91 among 183 countries surveyed in Transparency International's 2011 Corruption Perceptions Index.

The constitution and the human rights annex to the Dayton Peace Accords provide for freedom of the press, but this right is not always respected in practice. While a large number of independent broadcast and print outlets operate, they tend to appeal to narrow ethnic audiences, and most neglect substantive or investigative reporting. The public broadcaster BiH Radio Television (BHRT), which is designed to cater to multiethnic audiences, has faced growing political pressure in recent years. In April 2011, its Steering Committee, whose members are confirmed by the parliament, changed the broadcaster's charter to extend the committee's supervisory power over editorial and managerial policies, significantly undermining the outlet's independence. Separately, Free Media Helpline, which operates under the auspices of the BiH Federation of Journalists, found that attacks against journalists between January and September 2011 increased by 30 percent compared with the same period in 2010. The organization recorded 52 violations of journalists' rights during 2011, including four physical attacks and one death threat.

Citizens enjoy full freedom of religion, but only in areas where their particular group represents a majority. Acts of vandalism against holy sites of all three major faiths continue to occur. According to the Inter-Religious Council of Bosnia (IRCB), 56 attacks on religious sites, objects, and officials took place between November 2010 and November 2011. Police made arrests in 17 of these cases.

While the authorities do not restrict academic freedom at institutions of higher education, academic appointments are heavily politicized, with ethnic favoritism playing a significant role. Primary and secondary school curriculums are also politicized. Depending on their ethnicity, children use textbooks printed in Croatia, Serbia, or Sarajevo. In parts of the region of Herzegovina, students are divided by ethnicity, with separate classrooms, entrances, textbooks, and class times. The educational sector is among the most corrupt in BiH, with studies showing that bribery and inappropriate expenditures are pervasive.

The constitution provides for freedoms of assembly and association, and the various levels of government generally respect these rights in practice. Nonetheless, nongovernmental organizations (NGOs)—particularly those that are critical of the authorities—have faced some intimidation. Authorities in Banja Luka fined the local NGO Oštra Nula 1,400 convertible marks (US$900) in September 2011 for placing a banner in the city's main square that aimed to draw attention to the fact that a new central government had yet to be formed despite growing economic challenges facing the country. Although there are no legal restrictions on the right of workers to form and join labor unions, discrimination against union members persists.

Despite evidence of growing independence, the judiciary remains influenced by nationalist political parties and faces pressure from the executive branch. The lack of a single, supreme judicial body and the existence of four separate court systems—for the central state, Republika Srpska, the Federation, and the Brcko district—contributes to overall inefficiency. The country has made some efforts to reduce its case backlog, but the number of pending cases continues to be high. The state court—established in 2002 to handle organized crime, war crimes, corruption, and terrorism cases—made some progress in 2010 on adjudicating cases of organized crime and war crimes, and it expanded its witness-protection program. In April 2011, however, the Republika Srpska's parliament voted in favor of holding a referendum that would have disputed the jurisdiction of the state court and the state prosecutor's office on the territory of Republika Srpska. The parliament rescinded its decision in late May, after the Office of the EU Representative offered to initiate a "structured dialogue" on judicial reform in BiH.

Individuals face discrimination in employment, housing, and social services in regions that are not dominated by their own ethnic group. In December 2009, the European Court of Human Rights ruled that the constitution was discriminatory for allowing only Bosniaks, Croats, and Serbs to run for the presidency or serve in the upper house of parliament, excluding candidates from the Jewish, Romany, and other smaller minorities. However, no remedies have been implemented to date.

Women are legally entitled to full equality with men. However, they are underrepresented in politics and government and face discrimination in the workplace. The issue of sexual harassment is poorly understood, and improper behavior frequently goes unpunished. The police are still largely unresponsive to violent domestic disputes, particularly in rural areas. Women are trafficked internally for the purpose of prostitution, and BiH is to a lesser extent a transit country for trafficking to other parts of Europe.

Botswana

Political Rights: 3
Civil Liberties: 2
Status: Free

Population: 2,033,000
Capital: Gaborone

Ten-Year Ratings Timeline For Year Under Review (Political Rights, Civil Liberties, Status)

2002	2003	2004	2005	2006	2007	2008	2009	2010	2011
2,2F	2,2F	2,2F	2,2F	2,2F	2,2F	2,2F	3,2F	3,2F	3,2F

Overview: **A public sector strike of almost 100,000 workers in April and May 2011 resulted in the temporary closure of public schools and many health facilities, government firing of striking "essential" workers, and a low negotiated wage increase. Meanwhile, former minister of defense Ramadeluka Sereste was acquitted of corruption charges and immediately reinstated to his post by the president in October.**

Elected governments, all led by the Botswana Democratic Party (BDP), have ruled the country since it gained independence from Britain in 1966. Vice President Festus Mogae rose to the presidency when longtime president Ketumile Masire retired in 1998, and he was confirmed as the country's leader after the BDP easily won legislative elections in 1999. The BDP took 44 of the 57 contested seats in the 2004 elections, securing a second presidential term for Mogae.

In 2008, Mogae—like Masire before him—retired before the end of his term, leaving Vice President Seretse Khama Ian Khama to assume the presidency. Khama, the son of independence leader and first president Seretse Khama, had been appointed vice president by Mogae in 1998 and was elected chairman of the BDP in 2003. He quickly shuffled the cabinet and appointed former foreign minister Mompati Merafhe as vice president. Critics have accused the BDP of subverting democratic institutions through this "automatic succession" process.

Significant rifts within the ruling party emerged before legislative elections in October 2009. Most notably, Khama suspended his rival, BDP secretary general Gomolemo Motswaledi, preventing him from competing in parliamentary elections. In September, the High Court rejected Motswaledi's related lawsuit against Khama, citing the head of state's constitutional immunity from civil suits.

The BDP won 45 of the 57 National Assembly seats in the 2009 elections with 53.3 percent of the vote. The Botswana National Front (BNF) won six seats, while the Botswana Congress Party (BCP) took four. Two other parties each captured one seat. Parliament confirmed Khama for a full presidential term later that month, and observer reports declared the elections free and fair.

In March 2010, leaders of the so-called Barata-Pathi faction of the BDP—including Motswaledi and fellow suspended BDP parliamentarian Botsalo Ntuane—officially withdrew from the BDP and declared their intention to form a new opposition party, the Botswana Movement for Democracy (BMD). Accusing Khama of violating the party's constitution by concentrating power in the presidency and among his so called "A-Team" faction, the BMD party was officially registered in June, led by Ntuane and including some 20 former BDP MPs. However, the continued shuffling of MPs between the BMD and BDP left the former with only seven seats in parliament by year's end.

Beginning in April 2011, almost 100,000 public sector workers—including "essential" workers in the health sector—staged an eight-week strike. In mid-May, the minister of education closed all public schools following violent clashes between police and students protesting the absence of teachers. After health workers ignored a court order barring them from striking, many clinics and hospitals were forced to close or partially shutdown. Unions demanded a 16 percent wage increase but eventually settled for only 3 percent in late May. The government fired nearly 2,600 striking health workers and demanded they re-apply for their jobs following the settlement. In September, a group of unions appealed to a Gaborone court to force the government to reinstate the workers, alleging that they had been fired illegally.

Political Rights and Civil Liberties: Botswana is an electoral democracy. The 63-seat National Assembly, elected for five years, chooses the president to serve a five-year term. Of the Assembly's 63 members, 57 are directly elected, 4 are nominated by the president and approved by the Assembly, and 2—the president and the attorney general—are ex-officio members. Despite being elected indirectly, the president holds significant power. While the president can prolong or dismiss the legislature, the legislature is not empowered to impeach the president. Democracy advocates have alleged that power has become increasingly centralized around President Seretse Khama Ian Khama, with many top jobs going to military officers and family members.

A House of Chiefs, which serves primarily as an advisory body, represents the country's eight major Setswana-speaking tribes and some smaller ones. Groups other than the eight major tribes tend to be left out of the political process; under the Territories Act, land in ethnic territory is distributed under the jurisdiction of majority groups. Due in part to their lack of representation in the House of Chiefs, minority groups are subject to patriarchal Tswana customary law despite having their own traditional rules for inheritance, marriage, and succession.

Botswana's anticorruption body has special powers of investigation, arrest, and search and seizure, and the body generally boasts a high conviction rate. Nevertheless, there are almost no restrictions on the private business activities of public servants, and there have been a number of high-profile corruption scandals in recent years. Most notably, in 2010, Minister of Justice, Defense and Security (and cousin of President Khama) Ramadeluka Sereste was charged with corruption and relinquished his post in August for failing to disclose his position as a shareholder in a company—owned by his wife—which won a massive defense contract in 2009. Seretse was acquitted of all charges in October 2011 and was reinstated in his post the next day by President Khama. The Directorate of Public Prosecution intended to file an immediate appeal at years end. Minister of Finance and Development Planning Kenneth Matambo was also cleared of corruption charges in November for allegedly having indirect interests in contracting the Botswana Development Corporation

Botswana has a free and vigorous press, with several independent newspapers and magazines. The private Gaborone Broadcasting Corporation television system and two private radio stations have limited reach, though Botswana easily receives broadcasts from neighboring South Africa. State-owned outlets dominate the local broadcast media, which reach far more residents than the print media, yet provide inadequate access to the opposition and government critics. In addition, the government sometimes censors or otherwise restricts news sources or stories that it finds undesirable. A lawsuit challenging the constitutionality of the 2008 Media Practitioners Act—which established a media regulatory body and mandated the registration of all media workers and outlets—was brought by 32 representatives of media, trade ,and civil society groups in August 2010. In April 2011, BDP parliamentarian Phillip Makgalemele sued the private Yarona FM radio station over a 2008 broadcast that alleged he was willing to take bribes to orchestrate losses by the national soccer team while head of the Botswana Football Association. Botswana does not have a freedom of information law, and critics accuse the government of excessive secrecy. President Khama had yet to hold a domestic press conference by the end of 2011. The government does not restrict internet access, though such access is rare outside cities.

Freedom of religion is guaranteed, but all religious organizations must register with the government. There are over 1,000 church groups in Botswana. Academic freedom is generally respected.

The government generally respects the constitutional rights of assembly and association. Nongovernmental organizations, including human rights groups, operate openly without harassment. However, the government has barred organizations supporting the rights of the San (an indigenous tribal population) from entering the Central Kgalagadi Game Reserve (CKGR), the subject of a long-running land dispute, and demonstrations at the reserve have been forcibly dispersed. While independent labor unions are permitted, workers' rights to strike and bargain collectively are restricted, as evidenced by the 2011 mass public sector strikes.

The courts are generally considered to be fair and free of direct political interference, although the legal system is affected by staffing shortages and a large backlog of cases. Trials are usually public, and those accused of the most serious violent crimes are provided with attorneys. Civil cases, however, are sometimes tried in customary courts, where defendants have no legal counsel. The 2007 Intelligence and Security Services Act created a Directorate of Intelligence and Security in the office of the president. Critics charged that it vested too much power in the agency's director—including allowing him to authorize arrests without warrants—and lacked parliamentary oversight mechanisms.

Occasional police abuse to obtain evidence or confessions has been reported, and Botswana has been criticized by rights groups for continuing to use corporal and capital punishment. Prisons are overcrowded and suffer from poor health conditions, though the government has responded by building new facilities and providing HIV testing to inmates.

Since 1985, authorities have relocated about 5,000 San, who tend to be marginalized in education and employment opportunities, to settlements outside the CKGR. Almost all of the remaining San fled in 2002, when the government cut off water, food, health, and social services in the area. In 2006, a three-judge panel of the Lobatse High Court ordered the government to allow the San to return to the CKGR. Several hundred San have since gone back, though disagreement remains as to how many will be allowed to live in the reserve. By court order, the issue is being mediated by the Botswana Centre for Human Rights. In July 2010, those San who had returned to CKGR lost a court battle with the government to reopen a water hole on the reserve. In April 2011, an appeals court overturned the decision, ruling that the San have rights to subsurface water, which led to the reopening of the Mothomelo borehole in September and the return of many San to the area. The government insists that the San have been relocated to give them access to modern education and health facilities and have been adequately compensated, and it rejects claims that it simply wanted unrestricted access to diamond reserves in the region.

Undocumented immigrants from Zimbabwe face increasing xenophobia and are subject to exploitation in the labor market. Botswana has built a fence along its border with Zimbabwe, ostensibly to control foot-and-mouth disease among livestock, but the barrier is popularly supported as a means of halting illegal immigration; thousands of Zimbabweans have are deported from Botswana every month. In 2010, the government announced a set of new immigration policies to halt the flow of undocumented immigrants into the country, mostly from Zimbabwe. The new policies introduced an online passport system, mandated electronic permits for visitors and immigrants, and increased the number of official workplace inspections.

Women enjoy the same rights as men under the constitution, though customary laws limit their property rights, and women married under traditional laws have the same legal status as minors. The 2004 Abolition of Marital Powers Act established equal control of marriage estates and equal custody of children, removed restrictive domicile rules, and set the minimum marriage age at 18. However, enforcement of the act is not uniform and generally requires the cooperation of traditional authorities, which is not always forthcoming. Women are underrepresented in the government, comprising less than 8 percent of the National Assembly seats following the 2009 elections. Domestic violence and trafficking for the purposes of prostitution and labor remain significant problems. Same-sex sexual relations are illegal and can carry a prison sentence of up to seven years. A 2010 amendment to the Employment Act outlaws workplace dismissal based on an individual's sexual orientation or HIV status, and in October 2011, former president Festus Mogae called for Botswana to legalize homosexuality and prostitution in order to better combat HIV/AIDS.

Brazil

Political Rights: 2
Civil Liberties: 2
Status: Free

Population: 196,655,000
Capital: Brasilia

Ten-Year Ratings Timeline For Year Under Review (Political Rights, Civil Liberties, Status)

2002	2003	2004	2005	2006	2007	2008	2009	2010	2011
2,3PF	2,3F	2,3F	2,2F	2,2F	2,2F	2,2F	2,2F	2,2F	2,2F

Overview: **The new administration of President Dilma Rousseff suffered from a series of setbacks in 2011, including losing five cabinet members to corruption scandals. Although Rousseff's tough stance toward corruption weakened her position within her disparate multiparty alliance, she was able to use the crises to highlight her anticorruption credentials, which contributed to high levels of popular support by year's end. The president launched a major antipoverty program in June, and a Supreme Court ruling in May afforded homosexuals greater rights, including the right to form civil unions.**

After gaining independence from Portugal in 1822, Brazil retained a monarchical system until a republic was established in 1889. Democratic governance was interrupted by long periods of authoritarian rule, and the last military regime gave way to an elected civilian government in 1985. However, Brazil's democracy has been marred by frequent corruption scandals. One scandal eventually led Congress to impeach President Fernando Collor de Mello in 1992.

Brazilian Social Democracy Party (PSDB) leader Fernando Henrique Cardoso—a market-oriented, centrist finance minister—was elected president in 1994, and he subsequently oversaw a highly successful currency stabilization program that included fiscal reform, privatization of state enterprises, and a new currency pegged to the U.S. dollar. He also ushered in a new era of dialogue with international human rights and good-governance groups. In 1998, Cardoso handily won a second term in a rematch against his 1994 opponent, former labor leader and political prisoner Luiz Inácio Lula da Silva of the left-leaning Workers' Party (PT).

Lula finally won the presidency in 2002, promising to maintain orthodox economic policies while initiating meaningful social-welfare programs. These included "Bolsa Família," a cash-transfer program that benefited approximately one-fourth of the population, and "ProUni," a fund providing low-income students with scholarships to private colleges.

Lula was reelected by a comfortable margin in the October 2006 presidential runoff, drawing on his popularity among working-class voters. Despite the fact that the legislature was widely seen as the most corrupt in the country's history, the PT did not suffer losses in the concurrent congressional elections.

In August 2007, the government released a report outlining the fate of political dissidents who were "disappeared" by the military between 1961 and 1988. Unlike in other Latin American countries with recent histories of military rule, former officials in Brazil remain protected by a 1979 amnesty law, and none have faced charges for human rights violations. Brazil's Supreme Court upheld the constitutionality of the amnesty in April 2010. However, the Inter-American Court of Human-rights ruled in December 2010 that the amnesty law was invalid, and that Brazil was responsible for the forced disappearances of 70 members of a resistance movement during the military era.

Dilma Rousseff, Lula's chosen successor, was elected president in October 2010 with 56 percent of the vote, defeating rival PSDB candidate José Serra. The PT and its coalition partners also did well in congressional elections held in early October, strengthening their majorities in both the Senate and Chamber of Deputies.

A number of major government corruption scandals that began in 2004 continued into 2011. The affairs involved vote-buying, kickbacks for public-works contracts, and the abuse of congressional power in awarding jobs and salary increases to favored recipients. During Lula's tenure, two of his three chiefs of staff were forced to resign amid corruption scandals, and Brazil's legislature was deemed one of the most corrupt in the world. The transition to the Rousseff administration brought no immediate improvement on the corruption front. Between June and October 2011, Rousseff ousted five staff and cabinet members for corruption: her chief of staff for alleged enrichment; the transport minister for bribes and over-billing on contracts; the agriculture minister for nepotism and cronyism; the tourism minister, along with dozens of tourism ministry officials, for embezzlement; and the sports minister for alleged kickbacks.

Rousseff's "ethical cleansing" campaign earned her respect from many for taking a hard line against corruption. Indeed, by the end of 2011, her popular support levels remained high at 70 percent. However, ending the decades-old norm of tolerating some forms of official corruption raised doubts about the president's ability to maintain control over her divided coalition, made up of 10 parties of varying sizes and ideologies. The center-right Partido da Republica (PR) dropped out of the government coalition after Rousseff ousted the transport minister, who was also the party's president. The cabinet shake-ups also hindered the administration's ability to push through structural changes, such as badly needed tax reform.

In June 2011, Rousseff launched an antipoverty program known as Brasil Sem Miseria (Brazil Without Poverty)—an initiative intended to eliminate the extreme poverty that afflicts 16 million Brazilians—by 2014. The program will increase the transfer payments already provided by Bolsa Familia; provide credit, technical assistance and skills training; and increase the poor's access to health care, housing, and sanitation. She also signed a Truth Commission bill in November 2011 that will investigate human rights abuses committed during the military regime.

Political Rights and Civil Liberties: Brazil is an electoral democracy. The 2010 national elections were free and fair. The constitution provides for a president, to be elected for up to two four-year terms, and a bicameral National Congress. The Senate's 81 members serve eight-year terms, with a portion coming up for election every four years, and the 513-member Chamber of Deputies is elected for four-year terms.

The four largest political parties, accounting for more than half of the seats in the Chamber of Deputies and the Senate, are the centrist Brazilian Democratic Movement Party, the leftist PT, the conservative Democratic Party, and the center-left PSDB. Seventeen other parties are also represented in Congress. The electoral system encourages the proliferation of parties, a number of which are based in a single state. A 2007 Supreme Court decision outlawed party switching after elections, though lawmakers have continued to switch parties on occasion for financial and other inducements.

Corruption is an endemic problem in Brazil, and five members of President Dilma Rousseff's cabinet were forced to resign in 2011 in the face of various corruption scandals. The country was ranked 73 out of 183 in Transparency International's 2011 Corruption Perceptions Index.

The constitution guarantees freedom of expression, and both libel and slander were decriminalized in 2009. A long-awaited freedom of information bill, which covers all branches of government at all levels, was passed in the Senate on October 25, 2011. Rousseff signed the bill into law in November, and it will come into effect in mid-2012. The press is privately owned, and while foreigners can acquire a 30 percent stake in a media company, they are restricted in their ability to influence editorial decisions and management selection. There are dozens of daily newspapers and a variety of television and radio stations across the country. The print media have played a central role in exposing official corruption. However, journalists—especially those who focus on organized crime, corruption, or military-era human rights violations—are frequently the targets of violence. According to the International Press Institute, five journalists were killed in 2011 in probable connection to their work; at least one of the deaths was attributed to alleged government involvement. The judicial branch—especially judges outside large urban centers—remained active in 2011 in preventing media outlets from covering numerous stories, often involving politicians. The government does not impose restrictions on access to the internet.

The constitution guarantees freedom of religion, and the government generally respects this right in practice. The government does not restrict academic freedom.

Freedoms of association and assembly are generally respected, as is the right to strike. Industrial labor unions are well organized; organized labor represents 17 percent of the Brazilian workforce. Although they are politically connected, Brazilian unions tend to be freer from political party control than their counterparts in most other Latin American countries. Labor issues are adjudicated in a system of special labor courts.

The country's largely independent judiciary is overburdened, plagued by corruption, and virtually powerless in the face of organized crime. The judiciary is often subject to intimidation and other external influences, especially in rural areas, and public complaints over its inefficiency are frequent.

Brazil has one of the highest homicide rates in the world. Most violent crime in the country is related to the illegal drug trade. Highly organized and well-armed drug gangs frequently fight against the military police as well as private militias comprising off-duty police officers, prison guards, and firefighters. Drug-related violence migrated away from the major cities to some extent in 2011, increasing in Brazil's historically poor northeast—specifically the states of Bahia and Alagoas. The homicide rate for Rio—once deemed one of the world's most dangerous cities—has dropped by half in the last decade; the government's aggressive counterinsurgency against drug-related violence ahead of the 2016 Summer Olympic Games likely contributed to that reduction. Most notably, the longer-term presence of "peace police" forces successfully pacified several of the city's dangerous *favelas*, or slums. In Rio de Janeiro, 1.2 million citizens—20 percent of the population—live in favelas.

Corruption and violence remains an entrenched problem in Brazil's police forces. Torture is used systematically to extract confessions from suspects, and extrajudicial killings are portrayed as shootouts with dangerous criminals. Police officers are rarely prosecuted for abuses, and those charged are almost never convicted. However, a military police chief and seven officers were arrested on September 27, 2011, for the killing of a judge known for her tough stance against corrupt police officers.

The prison system is anarchic, overcrowded, and largely unfit for human habitation. According to official estimates, Brazil's prisons hold over 490,000 inmates, 50 percent over the system's intended capacity. Overcrowding sometimes results in men and women being held in the same facilities, and human rights groups claim that the torture and other abuses common to most of the country's detention centers have the effect of turning petty thieves into hardened criminals.

Racial discrimination, long officially denied as a problem in Brazil, began to receive both recognition and remediation from Lula during his first term. Afro-Brazilians earn less than 50 percent of the average earnings of other citizens, and they suffer from the highest homicide, poverty, and illiteracy rates. When he assumed office, Lula took the unprecedented step of naming four Afro-Brazilians to his cabinet, and appointed the country's first Afro-Brazilian Supreme Court justice. The 2010 Statute of Racial Equality Statute calls for the establishment of non-quota affirmative action policies in education and employment, as well as programs to improve Afro-Brazilians's access to health care. The law also recognized the right of *quilombos*—communities of descendants of escaped slaves—to receive title to their land.

The owners of large estates control nearly 60 percent of the country's arable land, while the poorest 30 percent of the population hold less than 2 percent. Land invasions are organized by the grassroots Landless Workers' Movement (MST), which claims that the seized land is unused or illegally held. Progress on land reform has been slow due in part to a strong farm caucus and the economic importance of large-scale agriculture.

Although Brazil abolished slavery in 1888, thousands of rural laborers still work under slavery-like conditions. Landowners who enslave workers face two to eight years in prison, in addition to fines. Mobile inspection groups established under Lula's presidency have been effective in the fight to end slave labor; they have rescued more than 39,000 workers since the 1995 creation of the program, and compensated them over $5 million. Measures to fight the impunity of employers, such as a public "black list" of offending companies and landowners, have also proven effective in reducing slave labor in rural Brazil. In December 2011, two separate cases of forced labor resulted in the prosecution of three cattle ranchers who were sentenced to five to seven years in prison.

Brazil's indigenous population numbers around 700,000. Violence and discrimination against indigenous people continues; half of the indigenous population lives in poverty, and most indigenous communities lack adequate sanitation and education services. The government promised in 2003 to demarcate large swaths of ancestral lands as the first step in creating indigenous reserves. A 2009 Supreme Court ruling defended the creation of one of the largest protected indigenous areas in the world, and the non-indigenous, farmers living there peacefully left the 1.7 million hectare reservation that year.

Brazil's Supreme Court ruled in May 2011 that homosexuals have the right to form civil unions, and that couples in civil unions have the same rights as heterosexual married couples in regards to alimony, health, and retirement benefits as well as adoption rights. While discrimination based on sexual orientation is prohibited by law, violence against homosexuals remains a problem.

In 2003, a new legal code made women equal to men under the law for the first time in the country's history. Upon entering office, President Rousseff vowed to push women's rights onto the national and international agenda. Women make up a third of Rousseff's cabinet, comprising 11 of 34 posts. Nevertheless, the government has yet to propose specific policy plans to improve women's access to health care or to ensure wage equality. Violence against women and children is commonplace, and protective laws are rarely enforced. Forced prostitution of children is widespread. More than one million children between the ages of 10 and fourteen worked in 2010. The government has sought to address the problem by cooperating with various nongovernmental organizations, increasing inspections, and offering cash incentives to keep children in school. Human trafficking continues from and within Brazil for the purpose of forced labor and commercial sexual exploitation.

Brunei

Political Rights: 6
Civil Liberties: 5
Status: Not Free

Population: 410,000
Capital: Bandar Seri Begawan

Ten-Year Ratings Timeline For Year Under Review (Political Rights, Civil Liberties, Status)

2002	2003	2004	2005	2006	2007	2008	2009	2010	2011
6,5NF	6,5NF	6,5NF	6,5NF	6,5NF	6,5NF	6,5NF	6,5NF	6,5NF	6,5NF

Overview: **Brunei, which has been ruled continuously by Sultan Hassanal Bolkiah Mu'izzaddin Waddaulah since 1967, experienced little political change in 2011. The essentially rubber-stamp Legislative Council was disbanded in March after completing its five-year term, and a new, expanded council was appointed in June.**

The oil-rich sultanate of Brunei became a British protectorate in 1888. The 1959 constitution vested full executive powers in the sultan while providing for five advisory councils, including a Legislative Council. In 1962, Sultan Omar Ali Saifuddien annulled legislative election results after the leftist and antimonarchist Brunei People's Party (BPP) won all 10 elected seats in the 21-member council. British troops put down an insurrection mounted by the BPP, and Omar declared a state of emergency, which remains in force. Continuing his father's absolute rule, Hassanal Bolkiah Mu'izzaddin Waddaulah became Brunei's 29th sultan in 1967. The British granted Brunei full independence in 1984.

In 2004, Hassanal reconvened the Legislative Council, which had been suspended since 1984. The Council passed a constitutional amendment to expand its size to 45 seats, 15 of which would be elected. However, in 2005 Hassanal appointed a new, 29-member Legislative Council, including 5 indirectly elected members representing village councils; most of the members of this body were either relatives or loyalists. Following the completion of its five-year term, the Legislative Council was disbanded in March 2011 and replaced with a newly appointed and expanded 33-member council in June.

Hassanal instituted a significant reshuffle of the Cabinet of Ministers in May 2010. While many ministers retained their positions, and the sultan continued to hold the posts of prime minister, minister of defense, and minister of finance, the changes there were instituted signified a small step toward improving governance. The new cabinet included the country's first woman cabinet member as deputy minister for culture, youth, and sports.

Energy wealth has long allowed the government to stave off demands for political reform by employing much of the population, providing citizens with extensive benefits and sparing them an income tax. Despite a declining GDP growth rate, Brunei remains the fourth-largest oil producer in Southeast Asia and the ninth-largest exporter of liquefied natural gas in the world. In December 2010, Brunei and Malaysia moved forward with a "milestone" offshore oil exploration deal in which both countries have agreed to a 50-50 sharing partnership for a period of 40 years.

Political Rights and Civil Liberties: Brunei is not an electoral democracy. The sultan continues to wield broad powers under a long-standing state of emergency, and no direct legislative elections have been held since 1962. Citizens convey concerns to their leaders through government-vetted councils of elected village chiefs.

The reform efforts of Sultan Hassanal Bolkiah Mu'izzaddin Waddaulah have been largely superficial and are designed to attract foreign investment. The unicameral Legislative Council has no political standing independent of the sultan. However, the Council's mounting oversight activity and queries aimed at the government reflect a growing demand for accountability and responsible spending. These tentative reforms were considered preparations for an eventual succession and the expected depletion of the country's oil and gas reserves, which account for about 90 percent of state revenues.

Genuine political activity remains extremely limited. In 2007, the Registrar of Societies disbanded the People's Awareness Party (PAKAR) and forced the president of the Brunei National Solidarity Party (PPKB) to resign. The PPKB was then deregistered without explanation in 2008, leaving the National Development Party (NDP) as Brunei's sole remaining political party.

The government claims to have a zero-tolerance policy on corruption, and its Anti-Corruption Bureau has successfully prosecuted a number of lower-level officials in recent years. The sultan's brother and former finance minister, Prince Jefri Bolkiah, has faced a number of legal issues, including a 2008 arrest warrant, over accusations that he misappropriated state funds, and he was ordered to return personal assets to the state. Brunei was ranked 44 out of 183 countries surveyed in Transparency International's 2011 Corruption Perceptions Index.

Journalists in Brunei face considerable restrictions. Officials may close newspapers without cause and fine and imprison journalists for up to three years for reporting deemed "false and malicious." The national sedition law was amended in 2005 to strengthen prohibitions on criticizing the sultan and the national "Malay Muslim Monarchy" ideology. The country's main English-language daily newspaper, the *Borneo Bulletin*, is controlled by the sultan's family and often practices self-censorship. A second English-language daily, the Brunei Times, was launched by prominent businessmen in 2006 to attract foreign investors. A smaller, Malay-language newspaper and several Chinese-language papers are also published. Brunei's only television station is state run, but residents can receive Malaysian broadcasts and satellite channels. The country's internet practice code stipulates that content must not be subversive or encourage illegitimate reform efforts.

The constitution allows for the practice of religions other than the official Shafeite school of Sunni Islam, but proselytizing by non-Muslims is prohibited. Non-Shafeite forms of Islam are actively discouraged, in part due to concerns about security and foreign investment. Christianity is the most common target of censorship, and the Baha'i faith is banned. Marriage between Muslims and non-Muslims is not allowed. Muslims require permission from the Ministry of Religious Affairs to convert to other faiths, though official and societal pressures make conversion nearly impossible.

The study of Islam, Malay Muslim Monarchy ideology, and the Jawi (Arabic script used for writing the Malay language) is mandatory in all schools, public or private. The teaching of all other religions is prohibited.

Emergency laws continue to restrict freedoms of assembly and association. Most nongovernmental organizations are professional or business groups. All groups must register and name their members, and registration can be refused for any reason. No more than 10 people can assemble for a purpose without a permit. Brunei only has three, largely inactive, trade unions, which are all in the oil sector and represent only about 5 percent of the industry's labor force. Strikes are illegal, and collective bargaining is not recognized.

The constitution does not provide for an independent judiciary. Although the courts generally appear to act independently, they have yet to be tested in political cases. Final recourse for civil cases is managed by the Privy Council in the United Kingdom. Sharia (Islamic law) takes precedence in areas including divorce, inheritance, and some sex crimes, though it does not apply to non-Muslims. A backlog of capital cases results in lengthy pretrial detention for those accused of serious crimes. Caning is mandatory for 42 criminal offenses, including immigration violations, and is commonly carried out, though an attending doctor can interrupt the punishment for medical reasons.

Religious enforcement officers raid homes to arrest people for khalwat, the mingling of unrelated Muslim men and women. However, most first offenders are fined or released due to a lack of evidence. The authorities also detain suspected antigovernment activists under the Internal Security Act, which permits detention without trial for renewable two-year periods. Prison conditions generally meet international standards.

Brunei's many "stateless" people, mostly longtime ethnic Chinese residents, are denied the full rights and benefits of citizens, while migrant workers, who comprise approximately one quarter of the workforce, are largely unprotected by labor laws and vulnerable to exploitation. Workers who overstay visas are regularly imprisoned and, in some cases, caned or whipped.

Islamic law generally places women at a disadvantage in cases of divorce and inheritance. All women in government-run institutions and schools are required or pressured to wear traditional Muslim head coverings. An increasing number of women have entered the workforce in recent years, comprising 57 percent of the civil service force in 2010. Brunei appointed its first female attorney general in 2009, Hayati Salleh, formerly the first female High Court judge. Brunei serves as a destination, transit and source country for the trafficking of men and women for forced labor and prostitution.

Bulgaria

Political Rights: 2
Civil Liberties: 2
Status: Free

Population: 7,476,000
Capital: Sofia

Ten-Year Ratings Timeline For Year Under Review (Political Rights, Civil Liberties, Status)

2002	2003	2004	2005	2006	2007	2008	2009	2010	2011
1,3F	1,2F	1,2F	1,2F	1,2F	1,2F	2,2F	2,2F	2,2F	2,2F

Overview: **A series of small bombings targeted opposition-oriented media and political parties during 2011, and the killing of an ethnic Bulgarian youth in September triggered a series of street protests against organized crime and the Romany minority. Nevertheless, concurrent presidential and municipal elections proceeded peacefully in late October, with Rosen Plevneliev of the ruling Citizens for the European Development of Bulgaria (GERB) party defeating Ivailo Kalfin of the opposition Bulgarian Socialist Party in a runoff vote for the presidency.**

Bulgaria gained autonomy within the Ottoman Empire in 1878 and full independence in 1908. Its monarchy was replaced by communist rule after Soviet forces occupied the country during World War II. Communist leader Todor Zhivkov governed Bulgaria from 1954 until 1989, when the broader political changes sweeping the region inspired a massive prodemocracy rally in Sofia.

Over the next 12 years, power alternated between the Bulgarian Socialist Party (BSP)—successor to the Communist Party—and the center-right Union of Democratic Forces (UDF). In 2001, the National Movement for Simeon II, led by the former monarch, won national elections and formed a governing coalition with the Movement for Rights and Freedoms (DPS), a party representing the ethnic Turkish minority. However, both parties became junior partners in a BSP-led coalition government after the 2005 elections.

Bulgaria formally joined the European Union (EU) in January 2007, and its first elections for the European Parliament in May featured the emergence of a new right-leaning opposition party, Citizens for the European Development of Bulgaria (GERB), led by Sofia mayor Boyko Borisov. The party gained popularity, as the BSP and its allies were blamed for unchecked corruption, particularly after the EU suspended hundreds of millions of dollars in aid funds over the issue in July 2008.

GERB captured 117 of 240 seats in the July 2009 parliamentary elections. Borisov took office as prime minister with the support of the ultranationalist Ataka party (21 seats), the center-right Blue Coalition (15 seats), and the new right-wing Order, Law, and Justice (RZS) party (10 seats). The BSP-led Coalition for Bulgaria was left in opposition with 40 seats, as was the DPS, with 37.

The new GERB government pledged to tackle corruption and organized crime, overseeing a series of high-profile reforms, police raids, and prosecutions that extended through 2010. However, according to EU progress reports, flawed investigations and deep-seated problems with the judiciary meant that few high-profile cases resulted in convictions.

In 2011, a succession of small bombings struck targets that had been critical of the government, including the weekly publication *Galeria* in February, the offices of RZS and a constituent party of the Blue Coalition in July, and the car of television journalist Sasha Dikov in October; there were no casualties. Both *Galeria* and RZS were reportedly linked to suspected crime boss Aleksei Petrov, who was facing racketeering charges after an arrest in the government's 2010 anticrime campaign. The government argued that the blasts, which coincided with key EU visits or reports, were meant to discredit it. In January, *Galeria* had published alleged telephone conversations that purported to show Borisov and other officials seeking favors from the customs chief, which led to an unsuccessful no-confidence vote in the parliament.

The September 23 death of a 19-year-old ethnic Bulgarian youth in the village of Katunitsa, in an apparent hit-and-run by an associate of reputed local Romany crime boss Kiril Rashkov, set off violent protests in which some of Rashkov's properties were destroyed. Over the subsequent week, demonstrations led by right-wing soccer fans and political parties were held in several cities, with overlapping slogans aimed at Roma, Turks, and criminals. Hundreds were arrested, often for carrying weapons, and Rashkov was charged with threatening those who burned his property. After the initial outbreak of violence in Katunitsa, police mobilized to protect Romany communities from protesters.

In the October presidential election, GERB candidate Rosen Plevneliev, a businessman who had served as regional development and public-works minister in Borisov's government, led the first round with 40 percent, followed by Ivailo Kalfin of the BSP with 29 percent, independent former EU commissioner Meglena Kuneva with 14 percent, Ataka leader Volen Siderov with 3.6 percent, and 14 other candidates with smaller shares of the vote. Plevneliev went on to win the runoff with about 53 percent, and was set to replace the term-limited Georgi Parvanov of the BSP. GERB also performed well in concurrent municipal elections, winning in most large cities.

Political Rights and Civil Liberties: Bulgaria is an electoral democracy. The unicameral National Assembly, composed of 240 members, is elected every four years. The president, elected for up to two five-year terms, is the head of state, but his powers are limited. The legislature chooses the prime minister, who serves as head of government. International observers generally praised the 2011 presidential and municipal elections, but found flaws in the Central Election Commission's performance, adherence to vote-counting procedures, and the accuracy of the voter list. There were widespread claims of vote-buying.

Bulgaria's multiparty system includes a variety of left- and right-leaning factions, and the ethnic Turkish minority is represented by the DPS. Roma are not as well represented, with just one Romany candidate winning a National Assembly seat in 2009, though a number of small Romany parties are active, and many Roma reportedly vote for the DPS.

Corruption is a serious concern in Bulgaria. The European Commission's July 2011 progress report found that the GERB government's anticorruption efforts had yielded insufficient results to date, noting a lack of final convictions and sentences. A new commission to handle conflict-of-interest cases involving senior officials was created in late 2010, but it was slow to begin functioning in 2011. In April, the parliament reduced public access to an official database of private sector contracts and activities, threatening transparency and obstructing investigative reporting. In July, lawmakers rejected legislation that would have enabled asset seizures in cases of suspected corruption. Bulgaria was ranked 86 out of 183 countries surveyed in Transparency International's 2011 Corruption Perceptions Index.

Bulgarian media have become more vulnerable to political and economic pressures as some foreign media firms withdraw from the struggling market and domestic ownership becomes more concentrated. Although the state-owned media have at times been critical of the government, ineffective legislation leaves them exposed to political influence. Most election coverage in 2011 was paid political content, creating a dearth of independent information. Journalists continued to face the threat of violence during the year. Reporter Mirolyuba Benatova of bTV received numerous threats and insults over her coverage of the initial anti-Roma protests in September. However, in a symbolically important ruling in February, former president Petar Stoyanov was fined for slapping a journalist in 2009. In April, the parliament passed legislation that prescribed up to four years in prison for instigating discrimination based on a broad range of categories; critics warned that the vaguely defined law could be used to curtail media freedom. The government does not place restrictions on internet access.

Members of minority faiths report occasional instances of harassment and discrimination despite constitutional guarantees of religious freedom, and authorities have blocked the construction of new mosques in certain areas. In May 2011, Ataka supporters clashed with Muslims praying outside a central Sofia mosque. Ataka's actions were widely criticized, including by three of its own lawmakers, who quit the party in protest. The mosque later agreed to curtail use of outdoor speakers and accommodate more worshippers inside. The government does not restrict academic freedom.

The authorities generally respect freedoms of assembly and association. Workers have the right to join trade unions, but public employees cannot strike or bargain collectively, and private employers often discriminate against union members without facing serious repercussions.

Bulgaria's judiciary has benefited from reforms associated with EU accession, but recent European Commission reports have noted that increased efforts to combat corruption and organized crime had often foundered in the courts, with cases subject to lengthy procedural delays and dismissal on technicalities. In 2011, this led to public pressure from the interior minister, who criticized judges for releasing organized crime suspects. The EU has also cited ongoing flaws in the judicial appointment process despite de jure improvements enacted in December 2010.

Organized crime remains a serious problem, and scores of suspected contract killings over the past decade have gone unsolved. The GERB government oversaw multiple police operations targeting criminal syndicates in 2010, and several reputed mob bosses were arrested and charged. However, most defendants were released pending trial, and there have been few major convictions to date; the EU has cited weaknesses in investigations, evidence collection, and witness protection for the lack of convictions. Incidents of mistreatment by police have been reported, and prison conditions remain inadequate in many places.

Authorities routinely hold asylum seekers in detention for many months, in violation of Bulgarian law and EU regulations.

Ethnic minorities, particularly Roma, continue to face discrimination in employment, health care, education, and housing. Sexual minorities also face discrimination.

Women remain underrepresented in political life, accounting for 21 percent of the National Assembly seats after the 2009 elections. However, the new chamber elected the first female Speaker, and Sofia elected its first female mayor that year. Domestic violence is an ongoing concern. The country is a source of human-trafficking victims, of whom Roma make up a disproportionately large share.

Burkina Faso

Political Rights: 5
Civil Liberties: 3
Status: Partly Free

Population: 16,970,000
Capital: Ouagadougou

Ten-Year Ratings Timeline For Year Under Review (Political Rights, Civil Liberties, Status)

2002	2003	2004	2005	2006	2007	2008	2009	2010	2011
4,4PF	4,4PF	5,4PF	5,3PF	5,3PF	5,3PF	5,3PF	5,3PF	5,3PF	5,3PF

Overview: **In the first half of 2011, Burkina Faso was rocked by antigovernment protests and army mutinies, followed by an increased level of violence and instability. In response, President Blaise Compaoré replaced the prime minister and declared himself minister of defense. In July, the leaders of the army mutiny were arrested and several hundred soldiers were dismissed, while three policemen responsible for the death of a student in their custody were convicted in August.**

Burkina Faso experienced a series of military coups after gaining independence from France in 1960. In 1987, army captain Blaise Compaoré ousted Thomas Sankara, a populist president who had risen to power through a coup in 1983. In 1991, a democratic constitution was approved in a referendum, and Compaoré won that year's presidential election due to an opposition boycott. Compaoré secured another seven-year term in the 1998 election.

The government undertook a series of political reforms after 1998, including the introduction of an independent electoral commission, a single-ballot voting system, public campaign financing, and a third vice presidential position in the legislature for the opposition leader. The 2002 National Assembly election were the first conducted without a significant opposition boycott, and Compaoré's Congress for Democracy and Progress (CDP) party won only half of the assembly seats.

Two-term presidential limits were reintroduced in 2000, but this law was not retroactive, allowing for Compaoré's reelection to a third term in 2005. The country's first municipal elections were held in 2006, with the CDP capturing nearly two-thirds of the local council seats. The CDP won 73 seats in the 2007 National Assembly election, while the largest opposition party, the Alliance for Democracy and Federation–African Democratic Rally (ADF-RDA), captured only 14.

In the November 2010 presidential election, six opposition candidates ran against Compaoré, who won with just over 80 percent of the vote. His closest challenger, Hama Arba Diallo, captured less than 10 percent. Only 55 percent of registered voters came out to the polls; the Burkina-based think tank, Center for Democratic Governance, estimated that over 3.5 million eligible voters remain unregistered. Although four opposition candidates challenged Compaoré's victory and called for a new election, the Constitutional Council upheld the results. The 2010 election was the last in which Compaoré was eligible to run under the current constitution. However, the CDP has stated its intention to revise Article 37 of the charter, which would allow him to run again in 2015.

In February 2011, student riots broke out in many major cities in reaction to the death of a student, Justin Zongo, while in police custody. The government ordered universities to close and cut off funding for student services. Meanwhile, army soldiers mutinied over unpaid wages from March to May, a period of looting and general violence nationwide. In April, policemen and teachers joined the protests, demanding better pay and working conditions. Compaoré responded in mid-April by replacing the prime minister and the security chiefs, and naming himself minister of defense. However, soldiers rampaged in Bobo-Dioulasso, the second-largest city, for several days in early June until elite troops arrived to quell the unrest. Later in June, Compaoré replaced all 13 of the country's regional governors. In July, 217 leaders of the army mutiny were arrested and 566 soldiers who took part were dismissed. In August, three policemen were sentenced for Zongo's death.

The crisis in neighboring Côte d'Ivoire in early 2011 caused significant disruptions in the volume of trade to and from Burkina Faso, as well as a sharp decrease in remittances from the large Burkinabè emigrant community in Côte d'Ivoire.

Political Rights and Civil Liberties: Burkina Faso is not an electoral democracy. International monitors have judged recent elections to be generally free but not entirely fair, due to the ruling CDP's privileged access to state resources and the media. Some reported problems with the 2010 presidential election include traditional leaders mobilizing voters for the incumbent, inadequate numbers of voting cards and ballots at the polls, incorrect electoral lists, and the use of state resources for President Blaise Compaoré's campaign. The 111-seat National Assembly is unicameral, and members serve five-year terms. The legislature is independent, but subject to executive influence. In July 2011, the National Assembly dissolved the National Electoral Commission at the request of the opposition, and a new commission will be formed before the May 2012 legislative and municipal elections.

The constitution guarantees the right to form political parties, and 13 parties are currently represented in the legislature. Electoral reforms in 2009 extended the right to vote in presidential elections and referendums to Burkinabè living abroad, but not until the 2015 presidential election. Reforms also included an injunction against the practice of switching parties after elections. In January 2010, the National Assembly passed a law requiring that all voters show picture identification when arriving to the polls, though there were problems with delayed distribution of the cards.

Corruption remains widespread, despite a number of public and private anticorruption initiatives. The courts have been unwilling or unable to adequately prosecute many senior officials charged with corruption. Burkina Faso was ranked 100 out of 183 countries surveyed in Transparency International's 2011 Corruption Perceptions Index.

Although freedom of expression is constitutionally guaranteed and generally respected, many media outlets practice self-censorship. Journalists occasionally face criminal libel prosecutions, death threats, and other forms of harassment and intimidation. In March 2011, student demonstrators at the University of Ouagadougou attacked journalists from the state-owned Burkinabe Broadcasting Corporation for allegedly censoring coverage of an earlier protest; later that month, RTB journalists were prevented by an angry mob from covering a labor union meeting. Along with the state-owned outlets, there are over 50 private radio stations, three private television stations, and several independent newspapers. The government does not restrict internet access.

Burkina Faso is a secular state, and freedom of religion is respected. Academic freedom is also unrestricted.

The constitution provides for the right to assemble, though demonstrations are sometimes suppressed or banned. While many nongovernmental organizations operate openly and freely, human rights groups have reported abuses by security forces. At least six people were killed in February 2011 as a result of demonstrations following the death of student Justin Zongo in police custody, as security forces used tear gas and live ammunition to subdue the protests. The constitution guarantees the right to strike, and unions are able to engage freely in strikes and collective bargaining, although only a minority of the workforce is unionized.

The judicial system is formally independent, but it is subject to executive influence and corruption. The courts are further weakened by a lack of resources and citizens' poor knowledge of their rights.

Human rights advocates in Burkina Faso have repeatedly criticized the military and police for committing abuses with impunity, which sparked the protests in February. Police often use excessive force and disregard pretrial detention limits. The sentencing in August 2011 of three police officers charged with the torture and death of Zongo was seen as a positive step.

Discrimination against various ethnic minorities occurs but is not widespread. However, homosexuals and those infected with HIV routinely experience discrimination. In an effort to address discrimination against the disabled, Burkina Faso ratified the Convention on the Rights of Persons with Disabilities in 2009 and adopted a new law on the protection and promotion of the rights of the disabled in April 2010. Civil society actors also noted increased government efforts in 2010 to provide access to health care and a decrease in costs for maternal health services.

The constitution provides for freedom of movement within the country, although security checks on travelers are common. Equality of opportunity is hampered in part by the advantages conferred on CDP members, who receive preferential treatment in securing public contracts.

While illegal, gender discrimination remains common in employment, education, property, and family rights, particularly in rural areas. There are 16 women in the 111-seat national legislature. Reforms in 2009 established a 30 percent quota for women on all party candidate lists in municipal and legislative elections, but the law is vague regarding implementation. In the north, early marriage contributes to lower female school enrollment and a heightened incidence of obstetric fistula. Human rights groups have recorded a significant drop in the prevalence of female genital mutilation since its criminalization in 1996.

Burkina Faso is a source, transit, and destination country for trafficking in women and children, who are subject to forced labor and sexual exploitation. According to the U.S. State Department's 2011 Trafficking in Persons Report, Burkina Faso does not comply with the minimum standards for eliminating human trafficking. However, the report also noted the government's reform efforts, including a 2008 law that criminalizes all forms of human trafficking and assigns more stringent penalties to those convicted. In 2010, Burkinabè authorities intercepted 660 children from traffickers.

Burma (Myanmar)

Political Rights: 7
Civil Liberties: 6*
Status: Not Free

Population: 54,000,000
Capital: Nay Pyi Taw

Ratings Change: Burma's civil liberties rating improved from 7 to 6 due to an increase in public discussion and media coverage of news and politics, as well as reduced restrictions on education.

Ten-Year Ratings Timeline For Year Under Review (Political Rights, Civil Liberties, Status)

2001	2002	2003	2004	2005	2006	2007	2008	2009	2010
7,7NF	7,7NF	7,7NF	7,7NF	7,7NF	7,7NF	7,7NF	7,7NF	7,7NF	7,6NF

Overview: **In 2011, opposition leader Aung San Suu Kyi, who had been released from prolonged house arrest in late 2010, entered into a dialogue with the government, traveled around the country to rebuild her political party, and gave interviews to the domestic media for the first time in at least 20 years. Although the new parliament elected in November 2010 was dominated by allies of the military, the new, nominally civilian president appointed a series of reformist advisers, and some independent lawmakers raised human rights issues in the parliament for the first time in decades. The government released thousands of prisoners during the year and promised to relax censorship. The National League for Democracy registered to participate in parliamentary by-elections scheduled for early 2012, and Aung San Suu Kyi planned to run for a seat. Burma also began repairing its relations with foreign countries, including the United States. Despite these initial signs of progress, it remained unclear how far the reforms would go, and numerous conflicts between the government and the country's ethnic minority militias remained unresolved.**

Burma gained independence from Britain in 1948. In 1962, General Ne Win led a coup that toppled an elected civilian government. The ruling Revolutionary Council then consolidated all legislative, executive, and judicial power and pursued radical socialist and isolationist policies. As a result of decades of misrule by the military regime, Burma, once one of the wealthiest countries in Southeast Asia, eventually became one of the most impoverished in the region.

A new military junta, eventually led by Senior General Than Shwe, dramatically asserted its power in 1988, when the army opened fire on peaceful, student-led, prodemocracy protesters, killing an estimated 3,000 people. In the aftermath, a younger generation of army commanders created the State Law and Order Restoration Council (SLORC) to rule the country. The SLORC refused to cede power in 1990 after the National League for Democracy (NLD) won 392 of 485 parliament seats in Burma's first free elections in three decades. Instead, the junta nullified the results and jailed dozens of NLD members, including party leader Aung San Suu Kyi, who spent most of the next two decades in detention.

In late 2000 the military leadership, renamed the State Peace and Development Council (SPDC), began holding talks with Aung San Suu Kyi, leading to an easing of restrictions on the NLD by mid-2002. However, the party's revitalization apparently rattled hard-liners within the regime during the first half of 2003. On May 30 of that year, scores of NLD leaders and supporters were killed when SPDC thugs ambushed an NLD motorcade. Arrests and detentions of political activists, journalists, and students followed the attack.

The largest demonstrations in nearly 20 years broke out in cities across the country in August and September 2007, triggered by a 500 percent fuel-price increase. The 88 Generation Students, a group composed of dissidents active in the 1988 protests, were at the forefront of many of the demonstrations. The protest movement expanded to include thousands of Buddhist monks and nuns, who were encouraged by the general populace. Soldiers, riot police, and members of the paramilitary Union Solidarity and Development Association (USDA) and the Swan Arr Shin militia group responded brutally, killing at least 31 people. The crackdown targeted important religious sites and included the public beating, shooting, and arrest of monks, further delegitimizing the regime in the eyes of many Burmese.

In May 2008 the government pushed through a constitutional referendum, despite the devastation caused by a cyclone that struck just a week earlier, killing over 150,000 people. Burmese political opposition and international human rights groups denounced the new charter, which was approved by an implausibly high margin and would ensure military control of the political system even after elections. In an apparent bid to remove potential obstacles prior to the voting, the authorities continued to arrest and imprison dissidents throughout 2009. More than 300 activists, ranging from political and labor figures to artists and bloggers, received harsh sentences after closed trials, with some prison terms exceeding 100 years.

The national elections held in November 2010 were neither free nor fair, as the SPDC had hand-picked the election commission and wrote election laws designed to favor military-backed parties, leading the NLD to boycott the polls. There were many allegations of rigged "advanced voting" and other irregularities. Ultimately, the Union Solidarity and Development Party (USDP), the political reincarnation of the USDA, captured 129 of the 168 elected seats in the Nationalities Assembly, or upper house, and 259 of 330 elected seats in the People's Assembly, or lower house. The USDP also secured 75 percent of the seats in the 14 state and regional assemblies. The Rakhine Nationalities Development Party and the Shan National Democracy Party earned the second-highest percentage of seats in the Nationalities Assembly and People's Assembly, respectively. However, the vote for ethnic minority parties would likely have been higher had voting not been canceled in several minority-dominated areas. The National Democratic Force (NDF), a breakaway faction of the NLD that decided to contest the elections, won just four seats in the upper house and eight in the lower.

Outgoing prime minister Thein Sein, who had shed his military uniform to register as a civilian candidate, was chosen as president by the new parliament, and took office in March 2011. The longtime head of the SPDC, Senior General Than Shwe, officially retired, but he was thought to retain influence through his allies in the new government.

Despite his military background, Thein Sein took a number of steps toward reform in 2011. He launched a dialogue with Aung San Suu Kyi, who had been released from house arrest shortly after the elections, allowing her to travel the country and meet with members of her party. The president also appointed one of her close associates as an adviser to his cabinet. Thein Sein urged political exiles to return to the country, and implicitly admitted in a speech that years of military misrule had left Burma far behind its neighbors in terms of development.

The authorities lifted restrictions on foreign media entering Burma, eased some constraints on the internet, and reduced censorship of domestic media, allowing Aung San Suu Kyi to reach Burmese audiences on a regular basis. Several independent journalists received lengthy prison sentences during the year, however. Diplomats from democratic countries were allowed to travel around Burma far more freely than at any time in the past.

The government established a national human rights commission in September, though many of its members had previously served under highly repressive military regimes. In October the government released some 6,000 prisoners, including over 100 political prisoners, but an estimated 2,000 political prisoners remained behind bars at year's end.

In December, the president signed legislation that legalized peaceful demonstrations, and the reinvigorated NLD registered to participate in parliamentary by-elections scheduled for early 2012. Aung San Suu Kyi was expected to seek a seat in the polls.

The government met with some success during the year in its long-standing effort to convince ethnic minority militias with which it had signed ceasefire agreements to give up their autonomy and join a state-led Border Guard Force. The Kachin Independence Army, one of the largest groups, had resumed fighting with the government, and the conflict continued throughout 2011. A number of other militias appeared be buying new weapons, allegedly with funds raised from drug trafficking, and several agreed to work together against the Burmese military. However, the government signed several ceasefire deals with smaller militias as 2011 drew to a close.

In part because of pressure from the ethnic minority armies, and in part because of broader public dissatisfaction with the project, in September Thein Sein's government suspended construction on the Myitsone Dam, a large Chinese-funded hydropower project on the upper portion of the Irrawaddy River. The suspension was greeted with praise and some shock by Burmese activists, and led to a short-term cooling in relations between Burma and China.

Political Rights and Civil Liberties: Burma is not an electoral democracy. The military junta long ruled by decree and controlled all executive, legislative, and judicial powers; suppressed nearly all basic rights; and committed human rights abuses with impunity. It carefully rigged the electoral framework surrounding the 2010 national elections, which were neither free nor fair. The process of drafting the 2008 constitution, which the elections put into effect, had proceeded intermittently for 15 years, was closely controlled by the military, and excluded key stakeholders. Although the charter establishes a parliament and a civilian president, it also entrenches military dominance, and allows the military to dissolve the civilian government if it determines that the "disintegration of the Union or national solidarity" is at stake.

The bicameral legislature consists of the 440-seat People's Assembly, or lower house, and the 224-seat Nationalities Assembly, or upper house. A quarter of the seats in both houses are reserved for the military and filled through appointment by the commander in chief, an officer who has broad powers and is selected by the military-dominated National Defense and Security Council. The legislature elects the president, though the military members have the right to nominate one of the three candidates, with the other two nominated by the elected members of each chamber. The charter's rights guarantees are limited by existing laws and may be suspended in a state of emergency. The military retains the right to administer its own affairs, and members of the outgoing military government received blanket immunity for all official acts. The military budget is not publicly available.

The Political Party Registration Law, announced in March 2010, gave new political parties only 60 days to register, mandated that existing parties reregister, and required parties to expel members currently serving prison terms. At the end of 2011, the government was still holding some 2,000 political prisoners, including hundreds of members of the NLD. There were a number of new high-profile arrests during the year, including the incarceration of independent journalists and rights activists, both before and after the prisoner releases in October. However, the government publicly welcomed back Burmese exiles who had fled for political reasons and allowed members of the parliament to speak about democratic rights. The legislators' time to speak was severely limited, but many of their speeches received coverage in the domestic media, and they were not harassed for their remarks. Aung San Suu Kyi and her allies were able to travel outside Rangoon with little incident, whereas in previous years, they had faced harassment and sometimes deadly violence.

In a system that lacks transparency and accountability, corruption and economic mismanagement are rampant at both the national and local levels. Burma was ranked 180 out of 183 countries surveyed in Transparency International's 2011 Corruption Perceptions Index. The new government in 2011 continued economic reforms that had begun under the military regime, including the privatization of many state assets. However, this process was marred by accusations that it primarily benefited family members and associates of senior government officials. The privatizations threatened to increase corruption and conflicts of interest by creating a new generation of business magnates whose control of industries is dependent on government connections and other forms of collusion.

The government restricts press freedom. The market for private publications and blogs is growing, and while the government censors private periodicals before publication, in 2011 it stopped censoring those that did not explicitly deal with politics. It also relaxed many restrictions on the internet and access to foreign news sources and allowed for the appearance of Aung San Suu Kyi and other opposition leaders in the press. However, the authorities closely watch internet cafes, slow or shut down internet connections during periods of internal strife, and regularly jail bloggers. Possession or use of a modem without official permission can draw a 15-year prison sentence. Websites run by Burmese exiles are frequently the targets of cyberattacks.

The 2008 constitution provides for freedom of religion. It distinguishes Buddhism as the majority religion but also recognizes Christianity, Islam, Hinduism, and animism. At times the government interferes with religious assemblies and attempts to control the Buddhist clergy. Buddhist temples and monasteries have been kept under close surveillance since the 2007 protests and crackdown. The authorities have also discriminated against minority religious groups, refusing to grant them permission to celebrate holidays and hold gatherings, and restricting educational activities, proselytizing, and construction of houses of worship.

Academic freedom has been severely limited. Under the military junta, teachers were subject to restrictions on freedom of expression and held accountable for the political activities of their students. Universities were sporadically closed, and many campuses were relocated to relatively isolated areas to disperse the student population. There were some signs of more open academic discussion in 2011, as well as eased restrictions on private education.

Freedoms of association and assembly are restricted. Authorities regularly use force to break up or prevent demonstrations and meetings, most notably during the 2007 protests. However, in 2011 the government allowed Aung San Suu Kyi and the NLD to hold meetings and public gatherings with little interference.

The government violates workers' rights and represses union activity. Some public sector employees and ordinary citizens were compelled to join the USDA during military rule. Independent trade unions, collective bargaining, and strikes are illegal, and several labor activists are serving long prison terms. However, garment workers have held strikes in Rangoon in the last two years, with fewer repercussions than in the past. The regime continues to use forced labor despite formally banning the practice in 2000. Nongovernmental organizations providing social services in remote areas regularly face threats to their activities. International humanitarian organizations have expanded their work in the country but continue to face severe restrictions and monitoring. In 2011, international organizations could more easily acquire visas for their members to visit the country.

The judiciary is not independent. Judges are appointed or approved by the government and adjudicate cases according to its decrees. Administrative detention laws allow individuals to be held without charge, trial, or access to legal counsel for up to five years if the government concludes that they have threatened the state's security or sovereignty. Political prisoners are often held incommunicado in pretrial detention, facilitating torture. About 43 prisons hold political prisoners, and there are over 50 hard-labor camps in the country, though the government allowed several large-scale prisoner releases in 2011. Impunity for crimes and human rights violations committed by state security forces is deeply entrenched.

Some of the worst human rights abuses take place in border regions populated by ethnic minorities, who comprise roughly 35 percent of Burma's population. In these areas the military kills, beats, rapes, and arbitrarily detains civilians, according to human rights groups. The Chin, Karen, and Rohingya minorities are frequent victims. Tens of thousands of ethnic minorities in Shan, Karenni, Karen, and Mon states live in squalid relocation centers set up by the military. Government confrontations with ethnic militias displaced tens of thousands of refugees in 2011, though several insurgency groups agreed to ceasefire deals by year's end.

China's sizable investments in various extractive industries in Burma, in addition to the migration of hundreds of thousands of Chinese workers and businesspeople, have led to rising anti-China sentiment. Related violence broke out in Mandalay in the summer of 2011, when a dispute between Chinese and Burmese gem traders nearly led to a riot.

Burmese women have traditionally enjoyed high social and economic status, but women remain underrepresented in the government and civil service. In the 2010 elections, only 114 out of 3,000 candidates were women. Domestic violence and trafficking are growing concerns, and women and girls in refugee camps are at an increased risk of rape, sexual violence, and being targeted by traffickers. The Women's League of Burma has accused the military of systematically using rape and forced marriage as a weapon against ethnic minorities.

Burundi

Political Rights: 5
Civil Liberties: 5
Status: Partly Free

Population: 10,216,000
Capital: Bujumbura

Ten-Year Ratings Timeline For Year Under Review (Political Rights, Civil Liberties, Status)

2002	2003	2004	2005	2006	2007	2008	2009	2010	2011
6,5NF	5,5PF	5,5PF	3,5PF	4,5PF	4,5PF	4,5PF	4,5PF	5,5PF	5,5PF

Overview: **Burundi's fragile democracy was threatened in 2011 by sporadic violence between supporters of the ruling party and opposition groups that had boycotted 2010 elections. Tensions were heightened in September by an attack that killed more than 30 people in Gatumba, likely carried out by members of the former rebel National Liberation Forces (FNL) in revenge for killings of FNL personnel.**

The minority Tutsi ethnic group governed Burundi for most of the period since independence from Belgium in 1962. The military, judiciary, education system, business sector, and news media were also traditionally dominated by the Tutsi. Violence between them and the majority Hutu has broken out repeatedly since independence. A 1992 constitution introduced multiparty politics, but the 1993 assassination of the newly elected Hutu president, Melchior Ndadaye of the Front for Democracy in Burundi (FRODEBU) party, led to sustained and widespread ethnic violence. The resulting 12-year civil war killed more than 300,000 people.

Ndadaye's successor was killed in 1994, along with Rwandan president Juvénal Habyarimana, when their plane was shot down as it approached Kigali airport in Rwanda. This event triggered the Rwandan genocide and intensified the fighting in Burundi.

A 1994 power-sharing arrangement between FRODEBU and the mainly Tutsi-led Unity for National Progress (UPRONA) party installed Hutu politician Sylvestre Ntibantunganya as Burundi's new president, but he was ousted in a 1996 military coup led by former president Pierre Buyoya, a Tutsi whom Ndadaye had defeated in the 1993 election. Peace and political stability remained elusive, as insurgents sporadically staged attacks and government forces pursued a campaign of intimidation.

In 2000, 19 groups from across the political spectrum agreed in principle on a future political solution to the conflict. A transitional government was installed in 2001, with Buyoya temporarily remaining chief of state and FRODEBU's Domitien Ndayizeye serving as vice president. Key elements of two Hutu rebel groups, the Forces for the Defense of Democracy (FDD) and the National Liberation Forces (FNL), failed to participate in the transition, resulting in both continued negotiations and additional violence.

By the end of 2002, most factions had agreed to stop the fighting and participate in transitional arrangements leading to national elections. In April 2003, Buyoya stepped down and was replaced as president by Ndayizeye, and the FDD subsequently reached an agreement with the government in October. An August 2004 agreement outlined the shape of new democratic institutions—designed to balance the interests of the Hutu and Tutsi populations—and the holding of elections.

In 2005, Burundi held the first local and national elections since 1993. The largely Hutu National Council for the Defense of Democracy (CNDD), the political wing of the FDD, emerged as the country's largest party, and Parliament chose Pierre Nkurunziza as president. Domestic and international observers generally regarded the voting as legitimate and reflective of the people's will.

A key faction of the sole remaining rebel group, the FNL, agreed to lay down its arms and participate in the political process in 2006. A tentative ceasefire agreement was reached with the last significant FNL faction in 2007, but violence involving the group flared again in 2008. Nonetheless, FNL leader Agathon Rwasa soon returned to participate in negotiations on the demobilization of his guerrillas and the transformation of the FNL into a political party. These discussions were complicated by complaints regarding repressive actions taken by the CNDD and counterclaims that the FNL was continuing to recruit military cadres.

The talks finally led the FNL to lay down its arms in 2009, leading to its recognition as a legal political party. In April of that year, an independent election commission was sworn in to prepare for elections due in 2010, and a new electoral code was adopted. However, political uncertainty and tension remained, as opposition parties accused the government of trying to manipulate the electoral process.

Local elections took place in May 2010, in which the CNDD won with almost two-third of the vote. Following increasing efforts by the CNDD to close political space, opposition candidates boycotted both the June presidential election and July parliamentary polls. Prior to the presidential poll, the government placed serious restrictions on freedom of movement for opposition leaders, arrested dozens of opposition activists, and banned all opposition party meetings. According to opposition parties and human rights organizations, the ostensibly independent election commission failed to adequately investigate allegations of preelectoral violence and make public some individual polling place results. In the legislative poll, the CNDD captured 81 percent of the vote, followed by UPRONA with almost 12 percent and FRODEBU with nearly 6 percent, while Nkurunziza was reelected president with some 92 percent of the vote. Observers viewed the elections as a missed opportunity for strengthening Burundi's democratic political culture, as political polarization increased, and several leading opposition figures—including Rwasa—fled the country fearing for their safety. It was also noted that the political rifts and violence were mainly between rival Hutu groups, and not between Hutus and Tutsis as in the past.

Sporadic violence continued throughout much of 2010, with both the CNDD and opposition parties blaming one another for the attacks. In September, at least 18 bodies, some of which had been mutilated, were found in the Ruzizi River west of Bujumbura; some were identified as FNL members. This violence continued in 2011, as supporters of the CNDD and FNL members who had again taken up arms engaged in retaliatory attacks. In September, at least 30 people were killed when gunmen opened fire in a bar in Gatumba, on the Congolese border, an attack that the intelligence services attributed to the FNL. The putative motive was retribution for government violence against its own members; along with murders of lower-level FNL supporters, three high-ranking current and former members of the group had been killed since July 2011. In December, 21 people went on trial for involvement in the massacre, in a process that apparently was seriously flawed. A number of the defendants said in court that they had been tortured to confess or implicate the FNL in the attack. The court also refused a request by the defense to call senior members of the police and intelligence services to testify. The trial was ongoing at year's end.

Political Rights and Civil Liberties:

Burundi is not an electoral democracy. The country lacks representative institutions at the national level, in both the legislative and executive branches of government. Despite citizens' ability to change their government democratically in 2005, serious electoral irregularities and repression during the May 2010 local elections led most opposition parties to boycott subsequent presidential and parliamentary polls. The 2010 presidential election was the first by direct vote for a five-year term, but without meaningful competition, the results lacked legitimacy. The president appoints two vice presidents, one Tutsi and one Hutu, and they must be approved separately by a two-thirds majority in both the lower and upper houses.

While the lower house of Parliament—the 100-seat National Assembly—is directly elected for a five-year term, locally elected officials choose members of the Senate, also for five-year terms. Each of Burundi's 17 provinces chooses two senators—one Tutsi and one Hutu. Carefully crafted constitutional arrangements require the National Assembly to be 60 percent Hutu and 40 percent Tutsi, with three additional deputies from the Twa ethnic minority, who are also allocated three senators. In both houses, a minimum of 30 percent of the legislators must be women.

There are more than two dozen active political parties in the country, ranging from those that champion radical Tutsi positions to those that hold extremist Hutu views. Most are small in terms of membership, and many Tutsi have now joined formerly Hutu-dominated parties. The government appointed in September 2010 consists of members from the three political parties represented in Parliament: the CNDD, UPRONA, and FRODEBU. Many political parties include groups of youths that are used for intimidation and violence against opponents.

Corruption remains a significant problem. Burundi was ranked 172 out of 183 countries surveyed in Transparency International's 2011 Corruption Perceptions Index, making it the most corrupt country in East Africa. The deputy head of Burundi's largest anticorruption organization, the Anticorruption and Economic Malpractice Observatory, was assassinated in April 2009, and although the case went to trial in July 2010, no verdict had been reached by the end of 2011.

Freedom of speech is legally guaranteed, but press laws restrict journalists in broad, imprecise ways, and sanctions for defamation and insult include harsh fines and imprisonment. While journalists continue to engage in self-censorship and are sometimes censored by authorities, they have been increasingly willing to express opinions critical of the government. Radio is the primary source of information for the majority of the population. The media is dominated by the government, which owns the public television and radio stations; it also runs *Le Renouveau*, the only daily newspaper. Several private broadcast media outlets also operate, though most have a limited broadcast range. The British Broadcasting Corporation (BBC), Radio France Internationale, and the Voice of America are available on FM radio in the capital. Print runs of most newspapers remain small, and readership is limited by low literacy levels. Access to the internet remains largely confined to urban areas.

Despite the recent emergence of a more pluralistic press, journalists have been arbitrarily arrested, harassed, or threatened on numerous occasions. In July 2010, the editor of an online newspaper, Jean-Claude Kavumbagu, was charged with treason after publishing an article warning that Burundi's security forces lacked the capacity to effectively counter external terror threats against the country, such as the one carried out that month by the Somali terrorist group Al-Shabaab in Uganda. He was freed in May 2011, after being acquitted of the treason charge but found guilty of publishing material "likely to discredit the state or economy." He was sentenced to time served and fined 100,000 francs (US$70), after already having served 10 months in pretrial detention. After the Gatumba attack in September 2011, the government imposed a 30-day media blackout regarding the massacre, issuing a statement banning "publishing, commenting or doing analyses in connection with the ongoing investigations into the carnage in Gatumba." After the 30-day period expired, the government harassed and intimidated journalists who attempted to report on or investigate the attack or the other murders that had occurred throughout the year.

Freedom of religion is generally observed. For many years, the ongoing civil strife and the Tutsi social and institutional dominance impeded academic freedom by limiting educational opportunities for the Hutu, but this situation has improved in recent years.

The constitution provides for freedoms of assembly and association, although members of human rights groups that criticize the government have been threatened with or subjected to surveillance. There is modest but important civil society activity with a focus on human rights. In June 2011, the members of the newly created National Independent Human Rights Commission was sworn in. However, the commission's work had been hampered by a lack of funding and support from the government.

Constitutional protections for organized labor are in place, and the right to strike is guaranteed by the labor code. The Confederation of Burundi Trade Unions has been independent since its establishment in 1995. Most union members are civil servants and have bargained collectively with the government.

Burundi's judiciary is hindered by corruption, a lack of resources and training, and executive interference in legal matters. Crimes, especially those related to political violence, often go unreported or uninvestigated. The current judicial system struggles to function effectively or independently and cannot handle the large number of pending cases, many of which are politically sensitive. Prisons remain overcrowded, unhygienic, and at times, life-threatening. In July 2011, President Pierre Nkurunziza announced the creation of a truth and reconciliation commission, designed to provide accountability for past abuses; it was set to start work in 2012.

Women have limited opportunities for advancement in the economic and political spheres, especially in rural areas. Burundi continues to have a serious problem with sexual and domestic violence, and these crimes are rarely reported. The 2009 penal code criminalizes same-sex relationships. Albinos face a particular threat from discrimination and violence.

Cambodia

Political Rights: 6
Civil Liberties: 5
Status: Not Free

Population: 14,702,000
Capital: Phnom Penh

Ten-Year Ratings Timeline For Year Under Review (Political Rights, Civil Liberties, Status)

2002	2003	2004	2005	2006	2007	2008	2009	2010	2011
6,5NF	6,5NF	6,5NF	6,5NF	6,5NF	6,5NF	6,5NF	6,5NF	6,5NF	6,5NF

Overview: **In June 2011, the UN-backed tribunal trying former leaders of the Khmer Rouge placed the remaining four defendants on trial, following the conviction of the first in 2010. But tribunal staff members resigned after the body proved unwilling to investigate other suspects still at large. Critics of the government continued to face legal harassment, while the leadership used a border dispute with Thailand to boost nationalism and consolidate the power of Prime Minister Hun Sen and his family. Separately, new incidents of land grabs by companies with links to the government, along with protests against these practices, continued in the Cambodian countryside.**

Cambodia won independence from France in 1953. King Norodom Sihanouk ruled until he was ousted in 1970 by U.S.-backed military commander Lon Nol, and the communist Khmer Rouge (KR) seized power in 1975. Approximately two million of Cambodia's seven million people died from disease, overwork, starvation, or execution under the KR before Vietnamese forces toppled the regime and installed a new communist government in 1979. Fighting continued in the 1980s between the Hanoi-backed government and the allied armies of Sihanouk, the KR, and other political contenders. The 1991 Paris Peace Accords halted open warfare, but the KR continued to wage a low-grade insurgency until its disintegration in the late 1990s.

Since entering government as part of the Vietnamese-backed regime in 1979, Prime Minister Hun Sen and his Cambodian People's Party (CPP) have played a leading role in the country's politics, generally controlling the National Assembly, military, courts, and police. Opposition figures, journalists, and democracy advocates have been given criminal sentences or faced violent attacks by unknown assailants in public spaces.

In the early 1990s, Hun Sen used his control of the security forces to coerce the royalist party, known as Funcinpec, into sharing power, even though Funcinpec won the largest number of seats in the first parliamentary elections after the peace accords, held in 1993. Hun Sen later ousted the prime minister, Prince Norodom Ranariddh of Funcinpec, in a 1997 coup, and the CPP won a majority of seats in the 1998 parliamentary elections, which were held under restrictive conditions.

The deeply flawed parliamentary elections in 2003 featured violence and voter intimidation by the CPP. Nevertheless, the party failed to obtain the two-thirds majority required to form a government. Following the formation of a CPP-Funcinpec coalition, Hun Sen turned to silencing opposition leader Sam Rainsy's attacks on government corruption and abuse. After fleeing the country, Rainsy was convicted in absentia of defaming Prince Ranariddh and Hun Sen in 2005. However, under pressure from international donors, Hun Sen negotiated a settlement in 2006 that allowed Rainsy to receive a royal pardon and return to Cambodia in exchange for a public apology and a withdrawal of his allegations.

In the 2008 elections, the CPP took 90 of 123 parliamentary seats, and Hun Sen was reelected as prime minister. Opposition parties rejected the results, citing political intimidation and violence. However, with the opposition divided and unproven in the eyes of voters, and the country enjoying relative political stability and sustained economic growth, the CPP had started to command a measure of popular credibility. Meanwhile, Rainsy returned to exile ahead of a 2010 conviction on charges related to his claims that the government had ceded territory along the border to Vietnam, and he remained outside the country at the end of 2011.

In June 2011, the Extraordinary Chambers in the Courts of Cambodia began trial proceedings against four high-ranking former KR officials on charges of genocide and other crimes against humanity. The UN-backed tribunal's efforts had been delayed for years by bureaucratic and funding obstacles following its establishment in 2007. In July 2010, the former chief of the Tuol Sleng prison, Kang Kek Ieu (also known as Duch), was found guilty of war crimes and sentenced to 35 years in prison, reduced to 19 years given time served. One of the four remaining defendants, 80-year-old former social affairs minister Ieng Thirith, was found mentally incompetent to stand trial in November 2011, but she remained in detention at year's end pending further evaluations.

While the international judges on the court have sought to charge and try additional suspects, they have been rebuffed by their Cambodian colleagues. Hun Sen allegedly does not want the tribunal to delve too deeply into the past or weaken the prevailing climate of impunity for the powerful; he has publicly called for the tribunal not to investigate any other former KR officials. Human rights organizations, including Human Rights Watch, have called on the tribunal's investigating judges to step down for failing to effectively conduct investigations of KR suspects. Several tribunal staff members, including a German investigating judge, resigned in 2011 over the body's failure to proceed with two pending cases that had not yet resulted in indictments.

Throughout 2011, the government used a growing controversy over a temple on the disputed border with Thailand to boost nationalism and place more power in the hands of Hun Sen's son, who personally oversaw Cambodian forces on the border. The authorities also took steps to restrict civil society activity. In August, the government started informing local nongovernmental organizations (NGOs) working on contentious resettlement issues that their activities would now be suspended, while the National Assembly advanced a draft law that would subject NGOs to a registration process and give the government wide latitude to reject their applications. The law was still being debated at the end of the year. Meanwhile, Cambodian courts continued to uphold tough sentences against civil society activists and opposition politicians. In July, an appeals court upheld a two-year sentence against human rights worker Leang Sokchouen for allegedly spreading disinformation. Earlier in the year, security forces had broken up multiple rallies in downtown Phnom Penh that aimed to highlight labor abuses, corruption, and the position of women in Cambodian society. Later in the year, the government sent letters to local NGOs warning and threatening them, and suspended one in August.

Political Rights and Civil Liberties: Cambodia is not an electoral democracy. Although it holds regular elections, they are conducted under often repressive conditions, and the opposition is hampered by serious legal and physical harassment. The current constitution was promulgated in 1993 by the king, who serves as head of state. The monarchy remains highly revered as a symbol of national unity, but has little political power. Prince Norodom Sihamoni, who lived abroad for much of his life, succeeded his father, King Norodom Sihanouk, in 2004, after the latter abdicated for health reasons. Some palace experts charge that Sihamoni is a virtual prisoner of the government, with no control over his own activities.

The prime minister and cabinet must be approved by a majority vote in the 123-seat National Assembly, whose members are elected by party-list voting to serve five-year terms. The upper house of the bicameral parliament, the Senate, has 61 members, of whom 2 are appointed by the king, 2 are elected by the National Assembly, and 57 are chosen by local legislators. Senators serve six-year terms. Voting is tied to a citizen's permanent resident status in a village, township, or urban district, and this status cannot be changed easily. The CPP's strong influence in rural areas, with its presence of party members and control of local and provincial government officials, gives it an advantage over the opposition Sam Rainsy Party, which finds support mainly in urban centers. Continued economic growth and political patronage in recent years has led to a rise in popular support for the CPP and Prime Minister Hun Sen.

Corruption is a serious problem that hinders economic development and social stability. Many in the ruling elite abuse their positions for private gain. While economic growth in recent years has been sustained by increased investment in mining, forestry, agriculture, textile manufacturing, tourism, hydropower, and real estate, these enterprises frequently involve land grabs by powerful politicians, bureaucrats, and military officers. Repeated efforts by international donors to promote tough anticorruption laws have been stalled and watered down by the government.

The government does not fully respect freedom of speech. Media controls are largely focused on local broadcast outlets. Print journalists are somewhat freer to criticize the government, but the print media reach only about 10 percent of the population. There are many privately owned print and broadcast outlets, including several owned and operated by the CPP and opposition parties, though broadcast licensing processes remain opaque. There are no restrictions on access to foreign broadcasts via satellite. The government has increasingly used lawsuits and criminal prosecution as means of media intimidation over the past three years. A 2010 penal code drew criticism for several vague provisions relating to freedom of expression, including one that criminalizes any action that "affects the dignity" of a public official. The internet is fairly free of government control, though access is largely limited to urban centers.

The majority of Cambodians are Theravada Buddhists and can generally practice their faith freely, but societal discrimination against ethnic Cham Muslims remains a problem. Terrorist attacks by Islamist militants elsewhere in Southeast Asia in recent years have raised new suspicions about Muslims. The government generally respects academic freedom, though criticism of the prime minister and his family is often punished.

The authorities' tolerance for freedoms of association and assembly has declined over the past two years. Civil society groups work on a broad spectrum of issues and offer social services, frequently with funding from overseas. Those that work on social or health issues, as opposed to justice and human rights, generally face less harassment from the state. Public gatherings, protests, and marches occur and are rarely violent. However, the government has used police and other forces to intimidate participants and break up demonstrations with greater frequency. In April 2011, the authorities dispersed several rallies held to commemorate Women's Day, and Sam Rainsy Party workers charged that security forces prevented them from holding rallies in Phnom Penh and other towns on multiple occasions during the year. In September, activists trying to hold a rally to stop the forced resettlement of Phnom Penh residents were severely beaten by police.

Cambodia has a small number of independent unions. Workers have the right to strike, and many have done so to protest low wages and poor or dangerous working conditions. Lack of resources and experience limits union success in collective bargaining, and union leaders report harassment and physical threats. The garment industry has made several compacts with international companies to ensure the fair treatment of workers, but these have not prevented the harassment of union leaders in the industry. Those who led strikes in late 2010 and early 2011 were targeted by the police and frequently detained, putting a damper on union activity among garment workers during 2011.

The judiciary is marred by inefficiency, corruption, and a lack of independence. There is a severe shortage of lawyers, and the system's poorly trained judges are subject to political pressure from the CPP, which has also undermined the Khmer Rouge tribunal. Abuse by law enforcement officers, including illegal detention and the torture of suspects, is common. Jails are seriously overcrowded, and inmates often lack sufficient food, water, and health care. Police, soldiers, and government officials are widely believed to tolerate, or be involved in, the trafficking of guns, drugs, and people, as well as other crimes.

The constitution guarantees the right to freedom of travel and movement, and the government generally respects this right. However, there have been reports of authorities restricting travel for opposition politicians, particularly during election campaigns. The Cambodian government closed the UN refugee center in Phnom Penh in early 2011, making it more difficult for Uighurs from China, Montagnards from Vietnam, and other people fleeing persecution to gain refugee status in Cambodia.

Land and property rights are regularly abused for the sake of private development projects. Over the past several years, tens of thousands of people have been forcibly removed—from both rural and urban areas, and with little or no compensation or relocation assistance—to make room for commercial plantations, mine operations, factories, and high-end office and residential developments. High-ranking officials and their family members are frequently involved in these ventures, alongside international investors. In the most prominent case, thousands of people in central Phnom Penh have been displaced, as the lake they lived on is filled in for a development project controlled by a wealthy investor with close ties to the prime minister. In August 2011, representatives of the displaced people protested to complain that they had received no compensation or aid. The government refused to respond to their grievances, and protests continued throughout the year. In December, the government offered to give a small number of residents title to their land, allowing them to stay, presumably in different housing. However, most of the original residents of the lake area had already fled or been forced off their land.

Women suffer widespread economic and social discrimination, lagging behind men in secondary and higher education, and many die from difficulties related to pregnancy and childbirth. Rape and domestic violence are common and are often tied to alcohol and drug abuse by men. Women and girls are trafficked inside and outside of Cambodia for prostitution, and the country has become one of the trafficking centers of Asia, according to a detailed study released in 2011 by Human Rights Watch.

Cameroon

Political Rights: 6
Civil Liberties: 6
Status: Not Free

Population: 20,050,000
Capital: Yaounde

Ten-Year Ratings Timeline For Year Under Review (Political Rights, Civil Liberties, Status)

2002	2003	2004	2005	2006	2007	2008	2009	2010	2011
6,6NF	6,6NF	6,6NF	6,6NF	6,6NF	6,6NF	6,6NF	6,6NF	6,6NF	6,6NF

Overview: **Longtime president Paul Biya easily won another term in the October 2011 election, securing approximately 78 percent of the vote. A marginalized and divided opposition offered only token resistance during the campaign. Though nearly 80 years old, Biya still has not officially anointed a successor, raising concerns that Cameroon will suffer political upheaval if he dies or becomes incapacitated before vacating office.**

Colonized by Germany in the late 19th century, Cameroon was later administered by Britain and France, first through League of Nations mandates and then as a UN trust territory after World War II. Independence for French Cameroon in 1960 was followed a year later by independence for Anglophone Cameroon, part of which opted for union with Nigeria. The rest joined Francophone Cameroon in a federation, which became a unitary state in 1972.

The country's first president, Ahmadou Ahidjo, oversaw a repressive, one-party system until his resignation in 1982. He was succeeded by Paul Biya, whose Cameroon People's Democratic Movement (CPDM) did not face multiparty legislative elections until 1992. It failed to win an absolute majority, despite a boycott by the main opposition party, the Anglophone-led Social Democratic Front (SDF). In 1992, Biya was reelected in a vote that was condemned by international observers.

A 1996 constitutional revision extended the presidential term from five to seven years, and Biya won elections in 1997 and 2004 amid numerous irregularities. The CPDM's victories in 1997 and 2002 legislative and 2002 municipal elections were similarly tainted. Electoral gerrymandering provided the CPDM with significant inroads into the SDF support base in the 2007 legislative and municipal polls, and SDF parliamentary representation decreased to 16 of 180 total seats.

In 2008, Biya secured a constitutional amendment to remove the two-term presidential limit, allowing him to stand for reelection in 2011. Approximately 100 people were killed in clashes with police during subsequent antigovernment riots, as citizens used the opportunity to protest the amendment as well as the rising cost of living.

For much of 2011, Biya refused to commit to running in the October presidential poll, officially entering the race only in early September. The SDF, after pledging to boycott the election, agreed in August to field a candidate. Nevertheless, Biya easily defeated his 22 rivals, claiming 78 percent of the vote. His closest challenger, SDF leader John Fru Ndi, received just 11 percent. However, the president's advancing age and rumored failing health fueled concerns that he would become incapacitated while in office, potentially sparking a succession crisis.

Political Rights and Civil Liberties: Cameroon is not an electoral democracy. Although the 1996 constitutional revisions created an upper chamber for the legislature, a decentralized system of regional government, and a Constitutional Court, none of these provisions have been implemented. A 2008 constitutional amendment removed the limit of two seven-year terms for the president, allowing the incumbent, Paul Biya, to run again in 2011. The president is not required to consult the National Assembly, and the Supreme Court may review the constitutionality of a law only at the president's request. Since 1992, the executive has initiated every bill passed by the legislature. The unicameral National Assembly has 180 seats and is dominated by Biya's CPDM. Members are elected by direct popular vote for five-year terms.

The National Elections Observatory has little influence. An elections commission, Elections Cameroon (ELECAM), was created in 2006, but commissioners were not named until December 2008. No civil society or opposition members were included, and 11 of the 12 appointees were reputedly CPDM loyalists. Expanded to 18 members in 2011, ELECAM continues to be dominated by CPDM partisans. In March 2010, an amendment was passed requiring ELECAM to collaborate with the Ministry of Territorial Administration and Decentralization; the move was widely criticized for placing election management into the hands of a ministry loyal to Biya and jeopardizing the commission's transparency. An opposition threat to boycott the 2011 election until the independence of ELECAM was ensured proved empty. Of the 52 individuals who sought to run for president in 2011, 29 were rejected by ELECAM due to procedural irregularities.

There are more than 250 recognized political parties, but Biya's CPDM, with its access to state patronage, dominates. Biya's grip on the CPDM remains strong; during the party's congress in September 2011, he was reelected for another five-year term as party leader. One of his few critics within the CPDM, Ayah Paul Abine, had resigned from the party in January, citing fears for his safety. Continued marginalization of the Anglophone community has fueled a campaign for independence by the Southern Cameroons National Council (SCNC). In February 2011, the security forces temporarily detained the SCNC's national chairman, Ayamba Ette Otun, and his son on charges of fomenting secessionist sentiments. Meanwhile, the northern-based Fulani, who once enjoyed political prominence under former president Ahmadou Ahidjo, still resent Biya for a bloody 1984 crackdown on northerners in the armed forces.

Corruption remains endemic in Cameroon. Biya's administration has encouraged cronyism, with members of the president's Beti ethnic group dominating many key positions. Revenues from the oil, gas, and mining sectors are not openly reported. The National Anticorruption Commission, created in 2006, is the country's principal independent anticorruption agency, though its subservience to the president and lack of autonomy undermine its effectiveness. The National Financial Investigations Unit is a separate intelligence unit that tracks money laundering. In recent years, Biya has resumed his 2004 anticorruption initiative, Opération Épervier, under which scores of government officials have been arrested on corruption charges. While the campaign maintained some public support, critics argued that it was being used to eliminate political opponents. Cameroon was ranked 134 out of 183 countries surveyed in Transparency International's 2011 Corruption Perceptions Index.

The constitution guarantees free speech, but genuine freedom of expression remains elusive. Although the 1996 constitution ended prepublication censorship, the charter's Article 17 gives officials the power to ban newspapers based on a claimed threat to public order. Libel and defamation remain criminal offenses, and judicial harassment and arrests of journalists and writers have engendered self-censorship. Author Bertrand Teyou—who had been imprisoned in November 2010 for six months, after a trial in which he had no legal representation, for allegedly insulting the president's wife in a book he had written—was released in April 2011 after a supporter paid his $4,371 fine. Author and founding member of the Cameroon Writers Association Enoh Meyomesse was arrested in November and charged with attempting to organize a coup, possessing a firearm, and aggravated theft, though he maintained that the arrest was politically motivated. He remained in prison by year's end. There were several reports of journalists being attacked, harassed, and arrested in 2011. In September, special operations police in Yaounde assaulted and seriously injured journalist Ulrich Fabien Ateba Biwole of *Le Jour* newspaper. There is no systematic internet censorship in Cameroon.

Freedom of religion is generally respected. There are no legal restrictions on academic freedom, but state security informants operate on university campuses, many professors exercise self-censorship, and some argue that entrance into university requires bribery or the support of a powerful patron.

The requisite administrative authorization for public meetings is often used to restrict freedoms of assembly and association. Meetings of the banned SCNC are routinely disrupted. In May 2010, police violently dispersed hundreds of journalists staging a sit-in to protest the death of journalist Germain S. Ngota Ngota, who died in prison from lack of proper medical care. In February 2011, eight political and civil society activists were arbitrarily arrested, apparently in response to calls for demonstrations to commemorate the deadly 2008 protests. Trade union formation is permitted, but subject to numerous restrictions.

The judiciary is subordinate to the Ministry of Justice, and the courts are weakened by political influence and corruption. Military tribunals exercise jurisdiction over civilians in cases involving civil unrest or organized armed violence. Acts of brutality against civilians by Cameroon's elite security unit, Bataillon d'Intervention Rapide (BIR), are increasing, although some troops have been dismissed for unnecessary use of force. Prison conditions are poor and sometimes life threatening, with overcrowding, poorly maintained facilities, and widespread violence by guards and among inmates being the norm. Torture and ill-treatment of detainees are routine. In May 2010, a report by the UN Committee Against Torture found that over half of Cameroon's prisoners were in provisional detention, and that many remained in jail much longer than the maximum time for pretrial detention. The absence of habeas corpus provisions in Francophone civil law further undermines due process. In the north, traditional rulers (*lamibe*) operate private militias, courts, and prisons, which are used against political opponents.

Slavery reportedly persists in parts of the north, and indigenous groups and ethnic minorities, particularly the Baka, face discrimination.

Despite legal protections, and there is widespread violence and discrimination against women, and female genital mutilation is practiced in the southwest and far north regions. Homosexuality is illegal, and in November 2011, three men received five-year prison terms for engaging in homosexual acts. Cameroon is a child labor market and a transit center for child trafficking.

Canada

Political Rights: 1
Civil Liberties: 1
Status: Free

Population: 34,468,000
Capital: Ottawa

Ten-Year Ratings Timeline For Year Under Review (Political Rights, Civil Liberties, Status)

2002	2003	2004	2005	2006	2007	2008	2009	2010	2011
1,1F	1,1F	1,1F	1,1F	1,1F	1,1F	1,1F	1,1F	1,1F	1,1F

Overview: **Following the defeat of Prime Minister Stephen Harper's Conservative minority government in a March 2011 vote of confidence over various scandals, the Conservative Party scored a major victory in parliamentary elections held two months later. The Liberal Party, Canada's dominant party throughout most of its history, suffered a crushing setback, finishing in third place behind the New Democratic Party.**

Colonized by French and British settlers in the 17th and 18th centuries, Canada was secured by the British Crown under the terms of the Treaty of Paris in 1763. After granting home rule in 1867, Britain retained a theoretical right to override the Canadian Parliament until 1982, when Canadians established complete control over their own constitution.

After a dozen years of center-left Liberal Party rule, the Conservative Party emerged from the 2006 parliamentary elections with a plurality and established a fragile minority government. Following setbacks in several of the 2007 provincial elections, the Conservatives expanded their position in the 2008 national elections. While capturing 143 seats in Parliament, the Conservatives failed to attain a majority. The Liberals, the principal opposition party, formed an alliance with the social democratic New Democratic Party (NDP) and the Quebec-based Bloc Quebecois, in an attempt to displace the Conservatives with a coalition government. Prime Minister Stephen Harper, the leader of the Conservative Party, suspended Parliament in December 2008 to prevent a confidence vote, which his government was likely to lose.

The Conservatives triumphed in the May 2, 2011, parliamentary election, winning 166 seats, well over the 155 necessary to secure a majority government. Placing second, with 103 seats—well above its previous record of 43—was the NDP, which for the first time became the leading opposition party. The Liberals finished in third place with 34 seats, while the Bloc Québécois, which favors Quebec separatism, suffered a devastating defeat, with just 4 members elected to Parliament. The Green Party captured 1 seat.

The election was called after the parliamentary opposition voted on March 25 to hold the government in contempt for allegedly failing to disclose accurate costs for key programs, as well as other minor scandals. Harper has been criticized for adopting a polarizing governing style, which is regarded as unusual for Canadian politics, and for an adversarial stance toward the media. Under Harper, however, Canada weathered the economic crisis that struck the global economy in 2008 in notably better shape than the United States or most European countries, and the government's record at economic stewardship ultimately swung the electorate in the Conservatives' direction.

Political Rights and Civil Liberties: Canada is an electoral democracy. The country is governed by a prime minister, a cabinet, and Parliament, which consists of an elected 308-member House of Commons and an appointed 105-member Senate. Senators may serve until age 75, and elections for the lower house have been held at least every five years. However, a law enacted in 2007 stipulated that lower-house elections would be held every four years, with early elections called only if the government lost a parliamentary no-confidence vote. The British monarch remains head of state, represented by a ceremonial governor-general, who is appointed on the advice of the prime minister. As a result of government canvassing, Canada has nearly 100 percent voter registration. Prisoners have the right to vote in federal elections, as do citizens who have lived abroad for fewer than five years.

Civil liberties have been protected since 1982 by the federal Charter of Rights and Freedoms, but they are limited by the constitutional "notwithstanding" clause, which permits provincial governments to exempt themselves with respect to individual provisions in their jurisdictions. Quebec has used the clause to retain its provincial language law, which restricts the use of languages other than French on signs. The provincial governments exercise significant autonomy.

Canada has reputation for clean government and has a record of vigorous prosecution of corruption cases. It also enjoys a reputation of open government, although the media have complained that the Harper government is less open in its dealings with the press than its predecessors. In 2004, the Supreme Court upheld legislation that places a limit on the amount lobbying groups can spend on advertisements that support or oppose political candidates, a measure designed to prevent corruption. Canada was ranked 10 out of 183 countries surveyed in Transparency International's 2011 Corruption Perceptions Index.

The media are generally free, although they exercise self-censorship in areas such as violence on television, and there is concern that this tendency may also apply to coverage of the country's minority groups, especially Muslims. There is a high degree of media concentration. Limitations on freedom of expression range from unevenly enforced "hate laws" and restrictions on pornography to rules on reporting. Some civil libertarians have expressed concern over an amendment to the criminal code that gives judges wide latitude in determining what constitutes hate speech on the internet. However, in 2009, the country's human rights tribunal found unconstitutional an anti-hate speech law that targeted telephone and internet messages. The decision has had the effect of restricting the Canadian Human Rights Commission's efforts to bring cases against alleged hate speech on the internet. In general, conditions for press freedom have improved in recent years. In 2010, the Supreme Court, while stopping short of issuing a blanket protection of journalists' sources in a case involving a major political scandal, sent a strong warning that judges should force journalists to identify their confidential sources only as a last resort. Also in 2010, the Supreme Court ruled for the first time that the media has the right to publish confidential information provided by a source—even when the source has no right to divulge the information or has obtained it by illegal means.

Religious expression is free and diverse. In 2010, the Court of Appeals for Ontario ruled that women had the constitutional right to wear the niqab in court. Academic freedom is respected.

Freedom of assembly is respected, and many political and quasi-political organizations function freely. Trade unions and business associations enjoy high levels of membership and are free and well organized. The Harper government, however, has adopted a tough line with unions representing public workers. After postal workers called a series of rotating strikes in June 2011, the government pushed through a law that dictated the terms of settlement and compelled the workers to return to the job. Canadian unions denounced the maneuver as a violation of the right to strike.

The judiciary is independent. Canada's criminal law is based on legislation enacted by Parliament; its tort and contract law is based on English common law, with the exception of Quebec, where it is based on the French civil code. While Canada's crime rate is low by regional standards, it has experienced a growing problem from the growth of criminal gangs, often involved in the illegal drug trade.

Canada maintains relatively liberal immigration policies. However, concern has mounted over the possible entry into Canada of immigrants involved in terrorist missions. The 2002 Immigration and Refugee Protection Act seeks to continue the tradition of liberal immigration by providing additional protection for refugees while making it more difficult for potential terrorists, people involved in organized crime, and war criminals to enter the country. Canada has an immigration policy that gives preference to applicants with higher education or certain job skills. Unlike in Europe and the United States, Canada has generally avoided high levels of political polarization over immigration. Some, however, have objected to Canada's policies of multiculturalism in education, law, and social life, and have raised questions about the high percentage of immigrants who hold dual citizenship. There is a growing controversy over the wearing of the niqab or burqa in public. In 2010, a bill was proposed in Quebec that would prohibit the wearing of either garment in public sector jobs, but it had not been enacted by the end of 2011.

The authorities have taken important steps to protect the rights of native groups, although some contend that indigenous people remain subject to discrimination. Indigenous groups continue to lag badly on practically every social indicator, including those for education, health, and unemployment. There are frequent controversies over control of land in various provinces. At the same time, government proposals to facilitate the assimilation of native groups have met with stiff opposition from the groups' chiefs.

The country boasts a generous welfare system, including national health care, which supplements the largely open, competitive economy.

Women's rights are protected in law and practice. Women hold 22 percent of seats in Parliament, have made major gains in the economy, and are well represented in such professions as medicine and law. However, women's rights advocates report high rates of violence against women in indigenous communities. Canada in 2005 became one of the few countries in the world to legalize same-sex marriage.

Cape Verde

Political Rights: 1
Civil Liberties: 1
Status: Free

Population: 496,000
Capital: Praia

Ten-Year Ratings Timeline For Year Under Review (Political Rights, Civil Liberties, Status)

2002	2003	2004	2005	2006	2007	2008	2009	2010	2011
1,2F	1,1F	1,1F	1,1F	1,1F	1,1F	1,1F	1,1F	1,1F	1,1F

Overview: **Cape Verde continued to serve as a model for political rights and civil liberties in Africa in 2011. The African Party for Independence of Cape Verde captured parliamentary elections in February, while Jose Carlos Fonseca of the opposition Movement for Democracy won the presidency in August. Both polls were considered credible and fair by international observers.**

After achieving independence from Portugal in 1975, Cape Verde was governed for 16 years as a Marxist, one-party state under the African Party for the Independence of Guinea and Cape Verde, later renamed the African Party for Independence of Cape Verde (PAICV). The establishment of the opposition Movement for Democracy (MPD) in 1990 helped to bring one-party rule to an end, and in 1991, the country became the first former Portuguese colony in Africa to abandon Marxist political and economic systems and hold democratic elections. The MPD won both the legislative and presidential elections, with candidate António Mascarenhas Monteiro elected president by a landslide victory. In 1995 legislative elections, the MPD increased its majority in the National Assembly, and Monteiro was reelected for a second term in 1996.

Presidential elections in 2001 were more competitive, with PAICV candidate Pedro Verona Rodrigues Pires narrowly defeating Carlos Alberto Wahnon de Carvalho Veiga of the MPD in the second round. The PAICV also captured a majority in the legislative elections that were held a month earlier. The January 2006 legislative elections had a similar outcome, with the PAICV taking 41 of the 72 seats, the MPD placing second with 29, and the Democratic and Independent Cape Verdean Union (UCID)—a smaller opposition party—securing the remaining 2 seats. Pires won a new five-year mandate in the February presidential election. Although his closest rival, Veiga, claimed that the results were fraudulent, they were endorsed by international election monitors.

In June 2007, the parliament unanimously passed new electoral code provisions aimed at strengthening the National Electoral Commission's transparency and independence. The opposition MPD won a marginal victory in the 2008 local elections, capturing 11 out of 22 municipalities, including the capital.

On February 6, 2011, Cape Verde held parliamentary elections that confirmed the left-leaning PAICV's dominance of Cape Verdean politics. The PAICV secured 53 percent of the vote, while the MPD garnered 42 percent, and the UCID received just 4 percent; two other parties captured less than 1 percent of the vote each. However, in the August 2011 presidential election, former foreign minister Jose Carlos Fonseca of the MPD defeated rival Manuel Sousa of the PAICV with 54 percent of the vote in a second-round runoff. International observers declared both the presidential and parliamentary elections to be free and fair. Subsequently, Fonseca and Prime Minister Jose Maria das Neves promised to put aside their political differences and work together to ensure Cape Verde's stability and increased prosperity.

Services, particularly tourism, dominate the economy with almost 80 percent share of the GDP. As a result of persistent droughts, the country experienced heavy emigration in the second half of the 20th century, and Cape Verde's expatriate population is greater than its domestic population; remittances, therefore, continue to be a major source of wealth. While the United Nations upgraded Cape Verde's classification out of the least developed countries category in 2008, the country's unemployment rate still hovers around 20 percent, and there is significant income inequality.

Political Rights and Civil Liberties: Cape Verde is an electoral democracy. The president and members of the 72-seat National Assembly are elected by universal suffrage for five-year terms. The prime minister is nominated by the National Assembly and appointed by the president.

Cape Verde received the second-highest ranking for governance performance in the 2011 Ibrahim Index of African Governance. However, the country still suffers from significant police corruption, mostly among border police who reportedly overcharge Western tourists for their visas and demand payment from poor Cape Verdeans and undocumented migrants from Africa. Cape Verde was ranked 41 out of 183 countries in Transparency International's 2011 Corruption Perceptions Index.

While government authorization is needed to publish newspapers and other periodicals, freedom of the press is guaranteed in law and generally respected in practice. The independent press is small but vigorous, and there are several private and community-run radio stations. State-run media include radio and television stations. The government does not impede or monitor internet access.

According to the 2011 U.S. Department of State's International Religious Freedom Report, there were no societal or governmental incidents of religious intolerance, and the constitution requires the separation of church and state. However, the vast majority of Cape Verdeans belong to the Roman Catholic Church, which enjoys a somewhat privileged status. Academic freedom is respected.

Freedoms of assembly and association are legally guaranteed and observed in practice. Nongovernmental organizations operate freely. The constitution also protects the right to unionize, and workers may form and join unions without restriction. Approximately a quarter of the workforce is unionized, but collective bargaining is reportedly rare.

Cape Verde's judiciary is independent. However, the capacity and efficiency of the courts are limited, and lengthy pretrial detention remains a problem. In 2010, Cape Verde signed the Dakar Initiative to fight trafficking by strengthening judicial systems, improving security forces, and increasing international cooperation. In 2011, Interpol agreed to work on a permanent basis with Cape Verdean authorities. Cape Verde is increasingly serving as a transit point for drug trafficking between Latin America and Europe. In October 2011, Cape Verdean police, working with their Dutch counterparts, made the largest drug apprehension in Cape Verde's history.

Ethnic divisions are not a salient problem in Cape Verde, although there are tensions between the authorities and West African immigrants. Work conditions for undocumented migrants in the country are often dire.

While discrimination based on gender is legally prohibited, problems such as violence against women and inequalities in the areas of education and employment persist. To address these issues, the government adopted a series of legislative reforms, including a 2010 law criminalizing gender violence, and a National Action Plan to fight gender violence (2009-2011).

Central African Republic

Political Rights: 5
Civil Liberties: 5
Status: Partly Free

Population: 4,576,000
Capital: Bangui

Ten-Year Ratings Timeline For Year Under Review (Political Rights, Civil Liberties, Status)

2002	2003	2004	2005	2006	2007	2008	2009	2010	2011
5,5PF	7,5NF	6,5NF	5,4PF	5,4PF	5,5PF	5,5PF	5,5PF	5,5PF	5,5PF

Overview: **President François Bozizé was reelected for a second term in January 2011 with 64 percent of the vote. The National Convergence Kwa Na Kwa, which backs Bozizé, won the majority of the seats in concurrent elections to the National Assembly. Although members of opposition parties challenged the results, citing irregularities at the polls, the country's Constitutional Council ruled in favor of Bozizé. Insecurity continued to plague much of the country during the year, as the Lord's Resistance Army continued its attacks against civilians, though the Convention of Patriots for Justice and Peace rebel group signed a ceasefire with the government in July.**

The Central African Republic (CAR) gained independence from France in 1960 after a period of brutal colonial exploitation. General André Kolingba deposed President David Dacko in 1981. Mounting political pressure led Kolingba to introduce a multiparty system in 1991, and Ange-Félix Patassé, leader of the Movement for the Liberation of the Central African People (MLPC), was elected president in 1993. With French assistance, he survived three attempted coups between 1996 and 1997. French forces were replaced by African peacekeepers in 1997, and the United Nations took over peacekeeping duties the following year. Patassé won a second six-year term in 1999, and UN peacekeepers withdrew the following year. Patassé was ousted by General François Bozizé in 2003, allegedly with backing from President Idriss Déby of Chad.

Bozizé initiated a transition back to civilian rule, and voters approved a new constitution in 2004. With the backing of the National Convergence Kwa Na Kwa (KNK) coalition, Bozizé ran for president as an independent, winning 65 percent of the vote in a May 2005 runoff against MLPC candidate Martin Ziguélé. The KNK won 42 of 105 seats in the National Assembly, securing a majority with the help of several smaller parties and independents. The MLPC, the second-largest grouping, won just 11 seats.

Between 2005 and 2007, several major insurgencies were launched against the government by rebel groups such as the Popular Army for the Restoration of the Republic and Democracy (APRD), supported by forces loyal to Patassé; the Union of Democratic Forces for Unity (UFDR); and the Central African People's Democratic Front (FDPC). An estimated 200,000 Central Africans were internally displaced as a result of the fighting or fled to neighboring countries as refugees.

After a series of failed attempts, the Comprehensive Peace Agreement was signed between the government, the UFDR, and the APRD in June 2008. The National Assembly also passed a law in September 2008 providing government and rebel forces with immunity for abuses committed after March 15, 2003. The Inclusive Political Dialogue, which was held between the government, the opposition, and rebel groups in December, established an interim government until 2010 elections could be held, and outlined a disarmament, demobilization, and reintegration program. By December 2009, all rebel groups, except the Convention of Patriots for Justice and Peace (CPJP), were participating in the peace process, but the demobilization of these groups has been slow and partial.

In September 2007, the UN Security Council authorized a new UN Mission in CAR and Chad (MINURCAT) and a European Union peacekeeping force in northeastern CAR. MINURCAT's mandate ended on December 31, 2010, and troops had left northeastern CAR by mid-November. The CPJP took control of Birao for one week in November, forcing many civilians to flee, but Chadian forces drove them out on November 20, 2010.

In January 2010, half of the members of the Independent Electoral Commission quit in protest over the appointment of its president, Joseph Binguimalet, whom they claimed favored Bozizé. Presidential and legislative elections were postponed twice in early 2010 as a result of inadequate funding, insecurity in the north, and incomplete voter lists. By August, all political parties and civil society groups signed onto a new election calendar scheduled for January 23, 2011. A law passed by the National Assembly in May 2010 allowed Bozizé and members of the Assembly to remain in power until elections were held.

In January 2011, President Bozizé, with the backing of KNK, ran against four candidates and won 66 percent of the vote. His closest challenger, ex-president and independent Ange-Félix Patassé, captured 20 percent of the vote. Opposition leaders and candidates challenged the results, which were upheld by the Constitutional Court, but revised by lowering the percentage of Bozizé's votes to 64 percent. MKNK won 63 out of the 105 seats in concurrent elections to the National Assembly. These elections were considered free, and security officers did not intimidate voters to the degree they had in previous elections. However, the opposition criticized both the presidential and parliamentary elections as unfair, citing fictitious and displaced polling stations, problematic electoral rolls, and numbers on voting cards not matching those in the voting stations rolls.

In June, the CPJP signed a ceasefire with the government, but no timetable was established for the implementation of its demobilization. Meanwhile, former UFDR rebels occupied the city of Sam Ouandje in July, and in September, they started fighting with CPJP rebels over control of the diamond trade. The two rebel groups signed a ceasefire on October 9.

Decades of conflict and poor governance have led to economic and social collapse. The CAR was ranked 179 out of 187 countries in the UN Development Programme's 2011 Human Development Index. However, according to the International Monetary Fund, the economy has recovered slightly, mainly as the result of investments in the diamond and forest industries.

Political Rights and Civil Liberties: The CAR is not an electoral democracy. The 2011 presidential and parliamentary elections were marked by irregularities and criticized by opposition candidates as unfair. The president, who is elected for a five-year term and eligible for a second term appoints the cabinet and dominates the legislative and judicial branches. Members of the unicameral, 105-seat National Assembly are elected by popular vote for five-year terms.

Though the KNK coalition is the country's leading political force, other parties operate freely. However, the government sometimes withheld approval for meetings of political opposition groups in 2011.

Corruption remains pervasive, despite some steps toward reform in recent years. Diamonds account for about half of the country's export earnings, but a large percentage circumvent official channels. CAR was ranked 154 of 183 countries surveyed in Transparency International's 2011 Corruption Perceptions Index.

The government generally respects the right to free speech, but many journalists practice self-censorship. It is illegal to broadcast information that is "false" or that could incite ethnic or religious tension. The state dominates the broadcast media, but private radio stations exist. Several private newspapers offer competing views, though they have limited influence due to low literacy levels and high poverty rates. There are no government restrictions on the internet, but the vast majority of the population is unable to access this resource.

The constitution guarantees religious freedom. However, the government prohibits activities that it considers subversive or fundamentalist, and the constitution bans the formation of religion-based parties. Academic freedom is generally respected.

Freedoms of assembly and association are constitutionally protected and generally upheld in practice. However, permission is required to hold public meetings and demonstrations, and authorities sometimes deny such requests on the grounds that they could stoke ethnic or religious tensions. The rights to unionize and strike are constitutionally protected and generally respected, though only a small percentage of workers are unionized, primarily those in the public sector.

Corruption, political interference, and lack of training undermine the judiciary. Judges are appointed by the president, and proceedings are prone to executive influence. Limitations on police searches and detention are often ignored. While the penal code prohibits torture, police brutality remains a serious problem. The military and members of the presidential guard continue to commit human rights abuses, including extrajudicial killings, with impunity. Prison conditions are poor.

Insecurity restricts the movement of citizens and greatly undermines the protection of private property. Attacks by the Lord's Resistance Army, a Ugandan rebel group, continued in 2011. A United Nations Development Programme report stated that thousands of villagers were displaced, 83 killed, and 334 abducted in the first three months of the year. The Office of the United Nations High Commissioner for Refugees estimates the number of internally displaced persons at 176,000, the number of refugees in CAR at 18,000, and the number of Central African refugees abroad at 130,000 as of December 2011.

Constitutional guarantees for women's rights are not enforced, especially in rural areas. There is no specific law criminalizing domestic abuse, which is widespread, and there is a high incidence of sexual violence against women by state and nonstate actors. Abortion is prohibited in all circumstances. Women were elected to only 13 percent of the seats in the National Assembly in 2011. The U.S. State Department's 2011 Trafficking in Persons Report downgraded CAR to Tier 3 as a result of the ongoing trafficking of children for forced labor and sexual exploitation, as well as their use in armed conflict.

Chad

Political Rights: 7
Civil Liberties: 6
Status: Not Free

Population: 11,500,000
Capital: N'Djamena

Ten-Year Ratings Timeline For Year Under Review (Political Rights, Civil Liberties, Status)

2002	2003	2004	2005	2006	2007	2008	2009	2010	2011
6,5NF	6,5NF	6,5NF	6,5NF	6,6NF	7,6NF	7,6NF	7,6NF	7,6NF	7,6NF

Overview: **In April 2011, longtime president Idriss Déby was reelected with 89 percent of the vote, in an election that was boycotted by the three main opposition candidates. In February, Déby's Patriotic Salvation Movement (MPS) party had retained its absolute majority in the National Assembly amid allegations of fraud by the opposition. The security situation improved during the year, although bandit attacks continued throughout the country.**

Since gaining independence from France in 1960, Chad has been beset by civil conflict and rebellions. Hissene Habre seized control in 1982 and led a one-party dictatorship characterized by widespread atrocities against individuals and ethnic groups that were perceived as threats to the regime. In 1989, Idriss Déby, a military commander, launched a rebellion against Habre from Sudan. With support from Libya and no opposition from French troops stationed in Chad, Déby overthrew Habre in 1990.

Déby won a presidential election held under a new constitution in 1996 despite the ongoing threat of rebel violence. In 1997 legislative elections, his Patriotic Salvation Movement (MPS) party won 65 of the 125 seats. International observers charged that both elections were marred by irregularities.

Déby was reelected in 2001, and the six opposition candidates were briefly detained for alleging that the election results were fraudulent. The MPS secured 113 seats in the enlarged, 155-seat National Assembly during the 2002 legislative elections, which were boycotted by several opposition parties. Voters approved the elimination of presidential term limits in a 2005 constitutional referendum, though the balloting was marred by irregularities and the government cracked down on the media during the campaign.

Security forces, assisted by French intelligence and air support, repelled an April 2006 attack on N'Djamena by the United Front for Change (FUC) rebel group. The May presidential election was then held on schedule despite an opposition boycott, and Déby secured a third term. The military, again with French support, launched a new assault on eastern-based rebel forces in September, and in November, the government declared a six-month state of emergency for the capital and most of the east, including a ban on media coverage of sensitive issues. In early February 2008, a formation of some 2,000 rebel fighters attacked the capital. Although the two sides soon agreed on a ceasefire and the rebels withdrew, Déby declared another state of emergency, suspending due process rights and tightening already harsh media restrictions. Human rights groups accused the regime of extrajudicial detention and killing of suspected rebels, their supporters, and members of the Goran ethnic group, some of whom were involved in the rebel assault. The state of emergency was lifted on March 15, but fighting continued in the east during the year.

Déby and Sudanese president Omar al-Bashir had traded accusations for several years over support for rebels on each other's territory. In May 2009, the Chadian and Sudanese governments signed the latest of several accords aimed at normalizing relations. However, shortly thereafter, the Union of Resistance Forces (UFR)—an alliance of eight rebel groups that had formed in January—launched an attack on Chad from its base in Sudan's war-torn western Darfur region. Violence along the border increased over the subsequent months, and in July, Chadian planes bombed targets in Darfur.

In April 2010, the government clashed with the rebel Popular Front for National Resistance near Tissi, reportedly killing more than 100 fighters. In May, former defense minister Mahamat Nouri announced the formation of a new rebel grouping, the National Alliance for Democratic Change. Members included dissidents from three groups that belonged to the UFR.

Relations between Sudan and Chad improved significantly in 2010, starting with a January agreement that led to a series of presidential visits. In February, the governments established a joint patrol of 3,000 troops along the border. Authorities reopened the border to civilian traffic in April after it had been closed for seven years. In May, Chad prohibited the head of a leading Darfur rebel group, the Justice and Equality Movement, from returning to Sudan. Meanwhile, the Sudanese authorities pressured Chadian rebel groups to leave Sudanese territory. In October, a reported 171 UFR fighters returned to Chad from Darfur.

After years of regular fighting in the region, Chad by the end of 2011 was home to some 130,000 internally displaced persons (IDPs) and an estimated 363,000 refugees from Darfur and the Central African Republic, according to the Office of the UN High Commissioner for Refugees (UNHCR). The UN Mission in the Central African Republic and Chad (MINURCAT) had been formed in 2007 to help care for and protect these civilians. Its original mandate was set to expire in May 2010, but was renewed until December 31. In February 2010, Déby requested that UN troops leave Chad, while humanitarian groups expressed concern about increased insecurity if the force were to withdraw. By December, MINURCAT had withdrawn all of its troops. The security situation in 2011 improved significantly, despite bandit attacks across the country. The UNHCR reported that 50,000 IDPs had returned to their areas of origin in 2011.

After years of delay, parliamentary elections were held in February 2011, the first in which opposition parties participated. In the enlarged, 188-seat National Assembly, Déby's MPS party won 117 seats, and 14 more seats went to Déby's allies, securing an absolute majority for the president. The most successful opposition party won only 10 seats. Citing irregularities before and during the parliamentary election, the three main opposition candidates boycotted the presidential poll in April, which Déby won with 89 percent of the vote. The Independent Electoral Commission (CENI) reported voter participation for the election at 64 percent, though African Union observers said the turnout was much lower.

In June, the rebel group Popular Front for Reconstruction (FPR) signed a peace agreement with the government. Also that month, the government signed an action plan with the United Nations to end the use of child soldiers by the country's security forces. Chad was one of six nations listed as a violator by the UN secretary general in an annual report on children and armed conflict.

Political Rights and Civil Liberties: Chad is not an electoral democracy. The country has never experienced a free and fair transfer of power through elections. The president is elected for five-year terms, and a 2005 constitutional amendment abolished term limits. The executive branch dominates the judicial and legislative branches, and the president appoints the prime minister. The unicameral National Assembly consists of 188 members elected for four-year terms.

The legislative elections due in 2006 had been repeatedly postponed due to insufficient equipment and staffing, and delays in voter registration. In September 2010, they were pushed back from November of that year, and finally took place in February 2011. The European Union praised the peaceful and fair conduct of the elections, despite some logistical problems. However, the opposition claimed that irregularities occurred both before the vote—due to the government's media dominance and the use of state resources to benefit the ruling party—and during the elections, including irregularities with electoral rolls and voter registration cards. They also pointed to CENI's official results page, which showed irregularities. A request by opposition parties to reprint voter registration cards was rejected.

There are more than 70 political parties, although a number were created by the government to divide the opposition. Only the ruling MPS has significant influence. Despite rivalries within Déby's northeastern Zaghawa ethnic group, members of that and other northern ethnic groups continue to control Chad's political and economic systems, causing resentment among the country's more than 200 other ethnic groups.

Corruption is rampant within Déby's inner circle. Despite becoming an oil producer in 2003, Chad remains one of the world's poorest nations. Weaknesses in revenue management and oversight facilitate the diversion of oil revenues from national development projects to private interests and growing military expenditures. Chad was ranked 168 out of 183 countries surveyed in Transparency International's 2011 Corruption Perceptions Index.

The constitution provides for freedom of the press and expression. However, both are severely restricted, and self-censorship is common. Broadcast media are controlled by the state. The High Council of Communication (HCC) exerts control over most radio content, and while there are roughly a dozen private stations, they face high licensing fees and the threat of closure for critical coverage. In 2008, the HCC banned reporting on the activities of rebels or any other information that could harm national unity. Radio is the most important means of mass communication, but the HCC has put the price for commercial broadcast channels to a prohibitively high $11,000 per year. A small number of private newspapers have circulated in the capital, and internet access is not restricted, but the reach of both print and online media is limited by poverty, illiteracy, and inadequate infrastructure. In August 2010, the National Assembly passed a media bill that eliminated imprisonment as a punishment for libel, slander, or insulting the president, but created sentences of heavy fines or prison for inciting racial and ethnic hatred and "condoning violence."

Although Chad is a secular state, religion is a divisive force. Muslims, who make up slightly more than half of the population, hold a disproportionately large number of senior government posts, and some policies favor Islam in practice. At the same time, the authorities have banned Muslim groups that are seen as promoting violence. The government does not restrict academic freedom, but funds meant for the education system have reportedly been lost to corruption. In November 2011, University of N'Djamena students protesting failed payment of their grants clashed with police in the capital, resulting in 150 arrests and injuries to 9 officers.

Despite the constitutional guarantee of free assembly, the authorities ban demonstrations by groups thought to be critical of the government. In September 2011, Amnesty International issued a report condemning the arrest of two students for allegedly planning proreform protests and demanding investigation into allegations of torture during their time in custody. The constitution guarantees the rights to strike and unionize, but a 2007 law imposed new limits on public sector workers' right to strike. Despite those limits, public sector workers went on strike for three weeks in October and November 2011, culminating in a deal with the government that significantly increased their wages.

The rule of law and the judicial system remain weak, and the courts are heavily influenced by the political leadership, with the president naming key judicial officials. Civilian leaders do not maintain effective control of the security forces, which routinely ignore constitutional protections regarding search, seizure, and detention. Human rights groups credibly accuse the security forces and rebel groups of killing and torturing with impunity. Overcrowding, disease, and malnutrition make prison conditions harsh, and many inmates are held for years without charge.

Clashes are common between Christian farmers of the various southern ethnic groups and Muslim Arab groups living largely in the north. Turmoil linked to ethnic and religious differences is exacerbated by clan rivalries and external interference along the insecure borders. Communal tensions in eastern Chad have worsened due to the proliferation of small arms and ongoing disputes over the use of land and water resources.

The government restricts the movement of citizens within the country. Insecurity has severely hindered the activities of humanitarian organizations in recent years. Despite relative stability during 2011, recurrent bandit attacks on humanitarian workers make access to the population difficult.

Chadian women face widespread discrimination and violence. Twelve of the 188

National Assembly members, or about 12 percent, are women. Female genital mutilation is illegal, but routinely practiced by several ethnic groups. Chad is a source, transit, and destination country for child trafficking, and the government has not made significant efforts to eliminate the problem. The U.S. State Department again placed Chad on the Tier 2 Watch List in its 2011 Trafficking in Persons Report.

Chile

Political Rights: 1
Civil Liberties: 1
Status: Free

Population: 17,268,000
Capital: Santiago

Ten-Year Ratings Timeline For Year Under Review (Political Rights, Civil Liberties, Status)

2002	2003	2004	2005	2006	2007	2008	2009	2010	2011
2,1F	2,1F	1,1F	1,1F	1,1F	1,1F	1,1F	1,1F	1,1F	1,1F

Overview: **President Sebastián Piñera of the center-right Coalition for Change faced growing political challenges in the second half of 2011 due principally to an impasse on education reform between the government and student leaders. The government's harsh response and inability to control the demonstrations resulted in plummeting popularity for both the president and his coalition. Separately, the Chilean government continued to promote the economic development and increased rights of the Mapuche Indians.**

The Republic of Chile was founded after independence from Spain in 1818. Democratic rule predominated in the 20th century until 1973, when General Augusto Pinochet led a military coup against President Salvador Allende. An estimated 3,000 people were killed or "disappeared" under Pinochet's regime. The 1980 constitution provided for a plebiscite in which voters could bar another presidential term for the general. When the poll was held in 1988, some 55 percent of voters rejected eight more years of military rule, and competitive presidential and legislative elections were scheduled for the following year. Christian Democrat Patricio Aylwin of the center-left bloc Concertación (Coalition of Parties for Democracy) won the presidential vote, ushering in an era of regular democratic power transfers as well as two decades of Concertación rule.

In the first step in what would become a years-long effort to hold Pinochet responsible for his regime's human rights atrocities, the former leader was detained in London in 1998 under an extradition order from Spain. After being released for health reasons in 2000, he returned to Chile, where he was eventually indicted in 2004 for tax evasion and two outstanding human rights cases. A September 2006 Supreme Court decision cleared the way for his trial, but Pinochet died in December of that year.

Michelle Bachelet, who served as health and defense minister under the outgoing Concertación president, won the 2006 presidential election. Bachelet presided over popular spending projects, including the construction of new hospitals, homes, and nursery schools.

In December 2009 congressional elections, the center-right Coalition for Change edged out Concertación in the 120-seat lower house, 58 seats to 57, with the remainder going to small parties and independents. In the Senate, the two main blocs split the 18 seats at stake, leading to a new total of 19 for Concertación, 16 for the Coalition for Change, and 3 for independents.

Sebastián Piñera of the center-right Coalition for Change was elected president in January 2010. The new administration was challenged by a massive earthquake that struck Chile in late February, but Piñera was able to carry out effective reconstruction due to Chile's sound public finances. The government also assumed full control of rescue operations after an accident trapped 33 miners in a gold and copper mine in northern Chile in August. Their successful rescue in October boosted Piñera's popularity as well as Chile's international image. In response to the incident, Chile ratified an International Labour Organization convention in April 2011 on occupational safety and health.

However, Piñera's popularity was short-lived, plummeting to a record low 26 percent approval rate by mid-2011. The government's plan to build dams in Patagonia was met with fierce resistance from environmentalists and protesters. Months of student protests and strikes beginning in April also brought hundreds of thousands to the streets of Chile's large cities with demands for a major overhaul of the education system. Students occupied more than 200 institutions of learning, calling for changes to Chile's largely privatized education system, including free public college education for low-income students. Piñera responded by replacing his education minister in July, promised $4 billion in new education spending financed by copper revenues, and a 24 percent rise in student scholarships. In October, Congress also passed a law to cut interest rates on student loans by more than half. However, the government's attempts to criminalize the protests by imposing harsh sentences for arrested protesters prompted increased student intransigence. At the end of 2011, there was still no resolution to what had easily become one of Chile's most intractable political problems in decades.

Political Rights and Civil Liberties: Chile is an electoral democracy. The president is elected for a single four-year term. The Senate's 38 members serve eight-year terms, with half up for election every four years, and the 120-member Chamber of Deputies is elected for four years. In 2005, the Senate passed reforms that repealed some of the last vestiges of military rule, ending authoritarian curbs on the legislative branch and restoring the president's right to remove top military commanders.

The major political groupings in Chile include the center-left Concertación, composed of the Christian Democratic Party, the Socialist Party, the Party for Democracy, and the Social Democratic Radical Party; the center-right Alliance coalition, consisting of the Independent Democratic Union and the National Renewal party; and the Communist Party. The Coalition for Change, encompassing the Alliance coalition, independents, and some Concertación defectors, was formed in 2009.

Congress passed significant transparency and campaign finance laws in 2003 that contributed to Chile's reputation for good governance. A 2007 law further improved transparency by offering protections for public employees who expose corruption. Chile was ranked 22 out of 183 countries surveyed in Transparency International's 2011 Corruption Perceptions Index.

Guarantees of free speech are generally respected, and the media operate without constraint, though some laws barring defamation of state institutions remain on the books. The print media are dominated by two right-leaning companies, but the television market is considered highly diverse. A freedom of information law enacted in 2008 was praised by civil society groups. However, in 2011, many members of the press—mainly photojournalists—were detained, harassed, and attacked by the police while covering the environmental and student protests. There are no government restrictions on the internet.

The constitution provides for freedom of religion, and the government generally upholds this right in practice. The government does not restrict academic freedom.

The rights to form nongovernmental organizations and to assemble peacefully are largely respected. Although the government regularly granted permits for student demonstrations in 2011, police allegedly used excessive force against participants during a number of protests. Despite laws protecting worker and union rights, antiunion practices by private employers are reportedly common.

The constitution provides for an independent judiciary, and the courts are generally free from political interference. The right to legal counsel is constitutionally guaranteed, but indigent defendants have not always received effective representation. Approximately 75 percent of the some 3,000 documented "disappearances" under military rule have been heard by courts or were under court jurisdiction by the end of 2011. Further, Chilean courts have convicted hundreds of military officers of committing heinous crimes during military rule, though sentences have tended to be lenient.

The government has developed effective mechanisms to investigate and punish police abuse and corruption. However, excessive force and human rights abuses committed by the Carabineros—a national police element of the armed forces—still occur. Chile's prisons are overcrowded and increasingly violent. Inmates suffer from physical abuse as well as substandard medical and food services.

In early 2010, the Bachelet administration introduced a bill that would remove a relic of the former regime—the Copper Reserve Law—which obliged the state-owned copper producer Codelco to transfer 10 percent of its earnings to the military. Public support for stopping the automatic military transfer increased after the massive reconstruction costs resulting from the February 2010 earthquake. Piñera sent a bill to Congress in June 2011 to repeal the Copper Law; the bill was pending at year's end.

Approximately 1 million Chileans identify themselves with indigenous ethnic groups. While they still experience societal discrimination, their poverty levels are declining, aided by government scholarships, land transfers, and social spending. In August 2010, President Piñera announced a development plan for the southern Araucanía region, one of Chile's poorest regions and the homeland of the Mapuche Indians. The "Plan Araucanía" will finance educational opportunities, tax incentives for investors, widespread road building, and construction of both a freight port and reservoir.

A 1993 law officially recognized the Mapuche and paved the way for the return of their land; but rather than appeasing the Mapuche, it prompted additional land claims, land seizures, and violence. Over 30 Mapuche accused of attacks participated in an extended hunger strike in 2010, which prompted a change to Chile's antiterrorism law. The law, which dated to the Pinochet era, allowed for secret witnesses, pretrial detention, and the use of military courts in trying Mapuches employing arson and other violent means to reclaim ancestral lands. As amended by Congress in September 2010, the law presumes innocence and carries a reduced sentence for arson. However, trials of Mapuche Indians under the antiterrorism law, and prosecutions through the military justice system continued in 2011.

President Michelle Bachelet made great strides to reduce gender discrimination, including appointing women to half of the positions in her cabinet. She also enacted new laws to increase women's labor rights and to eliminate the gender pay gap. However, violence against women and children remains a problem. In August 2011, President Piñera introduced legislation that would give same-sex couples the same rights as married couples; Congress was preparing to debate the proposed law at year's end.

↓ China

Political Rights: 7
Civil Liberties: 6
Status: Not Free

Population: 1,345,855,000
Capital: Beijing

Trend Arrow: China received a downward trend arrow due to increased Communist Party efforts to restrict public discussion of political, legal, and human rights issues, including through the systematic disappearance of dozens of leading social-media activists and lawyers and growing online censorship among domestic social-networking services.

Note: The numerical ratings and status listed above do not reflect conditions in Hong Kong or Tibet, which are examined in separate reports.

Ten-Year Ratings Timeline For Year Under Review (Political Rights, Civil Liberties, Status)

2002	2003	2004	2005	2006	2007	2008	2009	2010	2011
7,6NF	7,6NF	7,6NF	7,6NF	7,6NF	7,6NF	7,6NF	7,6NF	7,6NF	7,6NF

Overview: **With a sensitive change of leadership approaching in 2012 and popular uprisings against authoritarian regimes occurring across the Middle East, the ruling Chinese Communist Party showed no signs of loosening its grip on power in 2011. Despite minor legal improvements regarding the death penalty and urban property confiscation, the government stalled or even reversed previous reforms related to the rule of law, while security forces resorted to extralegal forms of repression. Growing public frustration over corruption and injustice fueled tens of thousands of protests and several large outbursts of online criticism during the year. The party responded by committing more resources to internal security forces**

and intelligence agencies, engaging in the systematic enforced disappearance of dozens of human rights lawyers and bloggers, and enhancing controls over online social media.

The Chinese Communist Party (CCP) took power in mainland China in 1949. Party leader Mao Zedong subsequently oversaw devastating mass-mobilization campaigns, such as the Great Leap Forward (1958–61) and the Cultural Revolution (1966–76), which resulted in tens of millions of deaths. Following Mao's death in 1976, Deng Xiaoping emerged as paramount leader. Over the next two decades, he maintained the CCP's absolute rule in the political sphere, while initiating limited market-based reforms to stimulate the economy.

The CCP signaled its resolve to avoid democratization with the deadly 1989 assault on prodemocracy protesters in Beijing's Tiananmen Square and surrounding areas. Following the crackdown, Jiang Zemin replaced Zhao Ziyang as general secretary of the party. Jiang was named state president in 1993 and became China's top leader following Deng's death in 1997. He continued Deng's policy of rapid economic growth, recognizing that regime legitimacy now rested largely on the CCP's ability to boost living standards. In the political sphere, Jiang maintained a hard line.

Hu Jintao succeeded Jiang as CCP general secretary in 2002, state president in 2003, and head of the military in 2004. Many observers expected Hu and Premier Wen Jiabao to implement modest political reforms to address pressing socioeconomic problems, including a rising income gap, unemployment, the lack of a social safety net, environmental degradation, and corruption. The government proved moderately more responsive to certain constituencies—especially the urban middle class—and undertook economic reforms with some redistributive effects. However, in the political sphere, the CCP tightened control over key institutions and intensified repression of perceived threats to its authority.

In March 2008, the National People's Congress bestowed additional five-year terms on Hu and Wen, while Shanghai party boss Xi Jinping was appointed vice president, setting the stage for him to succeed Hu as CCP general secretary in 2012 and head of state in 2013. Xi's position as heir apparent was reinforced in October 2010, when he was appointed as deputy chair of the Central Military Commission. Intraparty power struggles related to the upcoming 2012 leadership transition and the 90th anniversary of the CCP's establishment in July 2011 appeared to strengthen hard-liners. This was reflected in an upsurge of quasi-Maoist propaganda and a continued trend of heightened political repression that had begun in 2008.

Popular uprisings against authoritarian regimes in Tunisia, Egypt, and elsewhere in early 2011 led to even greater CCP hostility toward manifestations of domestic dissent. Nevertheless, growing public anger over corruption, abuse of power, and injustice fueled tens of thousands of protests during the year. Bloggers, journalists, scholars, legal professionals, workers, and religious believers tested the limits of permissible activity, sometimes effectively challenging local-level abuses of power, outpacing censors, and forcing government concessions regarding rights violations. In response, the party committed more resources to internal security forces and intelligence agencies, engaged in the systematic enforced disappearance of dozens of human rights lawyers and bloggers, enhanced controls over online social media, and increased societal surveillance. Some observers expressed concerns about the destabilizing effect of the CCP's retreat from reforms related to the rule of law in particular, as a growing number of citizens took to the streets to deal with grievances. Conditions in Tibet and Xinjiang, both home to restive ethnic and religious minorities, remained highly repressive in 2011.

After surpassing Japan in 2010 to become the world's second-largest economy, China's economy continued to expand in 2011, but inflation and signs of a slowdown toward year's end fed widespread uncertainty about the strength of future growth. Meanwhile, Chinese officials continued to demonstrate a penchant for strong-arm tactics in international relations during the year. Under apparent Chinese pressure, suppression of Tibetan refugees in Nepal intensified, and Falun Gong practitioners in Indonesia and Vietnam were jailed for broadcasting uncensored news about China. In the run-up to elections in Taiwan scheduled for January 2012, Chinese officials made various public comments warning Taiwanese voters that recently improved cross-strait economic ties could be damaged if they brought the opposition party to power.

Political Rights and Civil Liberties: China is not an electoral democracy. The CCP has a monopoly on political power, and its nine-member Politburo Standing Committee sets government policy. Party members hold almost all top posts in the government, military, and internal security services, as well as in many economic entities and social organizations. The 3,000-member National People's Congress (NPC), which is elected for five-year terms by subnational congresses, formally elects the state president for up to two five-year terms, and confirms the premier after he is nominated by the president. However, the NPC is a largely symbolic body. Only its standing committee meets regularly, while the full body convenes for just two weeks a year to approve proposed legislation. In an effort to expand representation at the grassroots level, dozens of independent candidates attempted in 2011 to compete for seats in the lowest tier of subnational congresses, with most campaigning via social media. The authorities responded with a variety of obstructions, including fraud, censorship, intimidation, and detention, causing most to abandon their campaigns or lose to CCP-backed candidates under questionable circumstances.

Opposition groups like the China Democracy Party (CDP) are suppressed, and members are imprisoned. Democracy advocate and 2010 Nobel Peace Prize winner Liu Xiaobo remained in prison in 2011, having been sentenced in December 2009 to 11 years for his role in creating the prodemocracy manifesto Charter 08. His wife, Liu Xia, was under strict house arrest in Beijing throughout the year, with communications to the outside world cut off. Similarly, two veteran democracy activists from Sichuan Province, Liu Xianbin and Chen Wei, were sentenced to 10 and 9 years in March and December, respectively. In October, the U.S. Congressional-Executive Commission on China published a partial list of over 1,400 political prisoners. The San Francisco–based Dui Hua Foundation estimated that 1,045 new arrests for "endangering state security" were made in 2010, and that over 10,000 people have been arrested and indicted for such political crimes since 1997. Tens of thousands of other people are thought to be held in extrajudicial forms of detention for their political or religious views.

Corruption remains endemic despite increased government antigraft efforts, generating growing public resentment. Each year tens of thousands of officials are investigated and punished by government or CCP entities, but prosecution is selective, with informal personal networks and internal CCP power struggles influencing the choice of targets. Party members accused of corruption are subject to a system of extralegal, incommunicado detention known as *shuanggui*. One of the most prominent cases of 2011 was the arrest of Railroads Minister Liu Zhijun on corruption charges in February, just a few months before a high-speed train crash in July that left 40 people dead and hundreds injured, sparking public outrage as efforts were made to cover up the cause. A government report in December placed much of the blame on Liu and 50 other officials and pledged to correct design flaws in rail equipment, but did not call for any systemic change in oversight. Also during the year, the authorities worked to prevent citizens from independently identifying corrupt officials, leading to the closure of several popular bribery-reporting websites.

CCP officials increasingly seek input from academics and civic groups, though without relinquishing control over the decision-making process. New open-government regulations took effect in 2008, but implementation has been incomplete. Some agencies and local governments have been more forthcoming in publishing accounting details or official regulations, but many continue to withhold vital public information, including on topics such as food safety, home demolitions, and smog levels. The state-run Chinese Academy of Social Sciences found in February 2011 that 51 of 59 national administrative agencies and 70 percent of 43 selected city governments failed to pass an administrative transparency evaluation; the National Bureau of Corruption Prevention was among the worst performers. Courts have hesitated to enforce citizens' information requests, and an August 2011 Supreme People's Court ruling—on when courts should accept lawsuits by citizens over rejected requests—left wide discretion for agencies to classify information. China was ranked 75 out of 183 countries surveyed in Transparency International's 2011 Corruption Perceptions Index.

Despite relative freedom in private discussion and citizens' efforts to push the limits of permissible speech, China's media environment remains extremely restrictive, and 2011 featured one of the worst crackdowns on freedom of expression activists in recent memory. Routinely taboo topics include calls for greater autonomy in Tibet and Xinjiang, relations with Taiwan, the persecuted Falun Gong spiritual group, and any criticism of CCP leaders. Specific party directives in 2011 curbed reporting on uprisings in the Middle East, an oil spill, public health issues, labor unrest, and particular human rights activists, journalists, and lawyers. Journalists who fail to comply with official guidance are harassed, fired, or jailed. Chinese leaders also appeared to retreat in 2011 from a policy of allowing greater commercialization and competition in the media sector, and instead strongly emphasized propaganda value over commercial viability and audience demand. Sharp new restrictions were imposed on television entertainment programming, and several periodicals known for investigative journalism faced closure, dismissals, or tighter supervision.

According to international watchdog groups, China jailed 27 journalists in 2011, including many Uighurs and Tibetans. At least 70 online activists remained behind bars at year's end for disseminating proscribed information, though the actual number was likely much higher. One journalist was killed during 2011: Li Xiang, a television reporter in Henan, was stabbed to death in September by unidentified thugs after exposing a food-safety scandal. In a growing trend, other journalists, bloggers, and online activists were subjected to violence and arbitrary detention under harsh conditions. Beginning in February, after calls for a Tunisian-style "Jasmine Revolution" in China appeared online, security forces carried out a campaign of abductions and disappearances targeting dozens of bloggers, activists, and lawyers. The most prominent was artist and blogger Ai Weiwei, who was abducted in April and held incommunicado for over 80 days. In November he was forced to pay 8.7 million yuan (US$1.3 million) as part of an apparently politically motivated tax case against him; the final results of the case were pending at year's end. In custody, many of these detainees were reportedly beaten, deprived of sleep, and forcibly medicated. As a condition of release, they were forced to commit to limiting their public statements and advocacy, particularly via social media. The harsh extralegal crackdown generated a significant chilling effect.

Local officials continue to block, harass, and sometimes assault foreign reporters while intimidating their Chinese sources and assistants. Some international radio and television broadcasts, including the U.S. government–funded Radio Free Asia, remain jammed.

China's population of internet users, estimated at over 500 million in 2011, remained the world's largest. However, the government maintains an elaborate apparatus for censoring and monitoring internet and mobile-telephone communications. The authorities block websites or force deletion of content they deem politically threatening, and detain those who post such information. Although Twitter remains blocked in China and domestic microblogging services engage in government-directed censorship of certain political and social issues, the domestic services have grown rapidly in influence as a source of news and an outlet for public opinion, with the number of Chinese microblog users surpassing 200 million in 2011. In response to several public outcries and online campaigns that outpaced censors, in late 2011, top officials intensified pressure on microblogging services to upgrade existing controls. Deletions and arrests for spreading "rumors" reportedly increased, and in December, authorities in Beijing, Shanghai, and other major cities announced rules requiring microblog users to register with their real names. Also during the year, the authorities temporarily imposed internet blackouts in restive areas—in Inner Mongolia in May, and in the Guangdong Province village of Wukan in December. Despite the government's controls, factors including the technology's flexibility, circumvention tools, and the large volume of online communications have allowed many users to access censored content, expose official corruption, mobilize protests, and circulate banned political texts.

Religious freedom is sharply curtailed, and religious minorities remained a key target of repression during 2011. All religious groups must register with the government, which regulates their activities and guides their theology. Some faiths, such as Falun Gong and certain Buddhist and Christian sects, are forbidden, and their members face harassment, imprisonment, and torture. Other unregistered groups, such as unofficial Protestant and Roman Catholic congregations, operate in a legal gray zone, and state tolerance of them varies from place to place. An apparent escalation in the persecution of unregistered Christians continued in 2011.

Beginning in April, hundreds of members of the Shouwang church in Beijing were briefly detained or placed under house arrest after they sought to gather outside because the owner of their place of worship had reportedly been pressured not to allow them to meet. In May, a vice president of the unregistered Chinese House Church Alliance was sentenced to two years in a labor camp. Meanwhile, the CCP continued a three-year nationwide drive to "transform" Falun Gong adherents, a coercive process aimed at forcing them to renounce their beliefs. In some areas, officials established numerical targets and extralegal detention centers for such transformations. The efforts led to the deaths of several detainees in 2011, according to the Falun Dafa Information Center.

Academic freedom remains restricted with respect to politically sensitive issues. The CCP controls the appointment of university officials, and many scholars practice self-censorship to preserve their positions and personal safety. Political indoctrination is a required component of the curriculum at all levels of education.

Freedoms of assembly and association are severely restricted. In early 2011, hypervigilant security forces swarmed the locations proposed in anonymous, online calls for Tunisian-style prodemocracy protests, and no such demonstrations took place. Local officials face penalties if they fail to limit the flow of petitioners traveling to Beijing to report injustices to the central government. As a result, petitioners are routinely intercepted, harassed, detained in illegal "black jails," or sent to labor camps. Detained petitioners are reportedly subject to beatings, psychological abuse, and sexual violence. Despite such repression, workers, farmers, and others held tens of thousands of protests during 2011, reflecting growing public anger over wrongdoing by officials, especially regarding land confiscation, corruption, pollution, and fatal police beatings. In several instances, violent responses by the authorities and hired thugs drove protesters to attack symbols of authority, such as police cars and government buildings. In other cases, officials tolerated demonstrations or agreed to protesters' demands. In August, after over 10,000 residents of Dalian gathered to protest pollution from a chemical plant, officials announced it would be shuttered. In December, after months of demonstrations over land disputes and the death in custody of a village representative, villagers in Wukan, Guangdong Province, drove out local Communist Party officials. Security forces blockaded the village, but provincial officials eventually intervened and granted villagers' demands to release protest leaders, investigate the death, and hold new village elections.

Nongovernmental organizations (NGOs) are required to register and follow strict regulations, including vague prohibitions on advocating non-CCP rule, "damaging national unity," or "upsetting ethnic harmony." Groups seeking more independence organize informally or register as businesses, though they are vulnerable to closure at any time. In December 2011, authorities banned the unregistered Guizhou Human Rights Forum, which had organized discussions on human rights topics, shortly after detaining 11 members. Forum member Chen Xi was sentenced to 10 years in prison for his activism and online writings. While the number of organizations whose work is not politically sensitive continues to expand, restrictions have tightened on human rights advocacy and even previously tolerated activism on issues like public health. Regulations that took effect in March 2010 increased obstacles for grassroots NGOs to receive foreign donations.

The only legal labor union is the government-controlled All-China Federation of Trade Unions. Collective bargaining is legal but does not occur in practice, and independent labor leaders are harassed and jailed. Nevertheless, workers have increasingly asserted themselves informally via strikes, collective petitioning, and selection of negotiating representatives. In 2011, workers staged a series of strikes over low pay or other grievances, particularly at the factories of foreign companies. Three labor laws that took effect in 2008 were designed to protect workers, counter discrimination, and facilitate complaints against employers, while also empowering CCP-controlled unions. However, implementation has been undermined by the lack of independent arbitration bodies, a growing backlog of complaints, and the authorities' increased use of informal channels of negotiation. In December, new regulations set to take effect in January 2012 required the establishment of mediation committees at all large companies to monitor compliance with labor laws and handle disputes internally, to ease pressure on labor tribunals. Dangerous workplace conditions continue to claim lives, with many tens of thousands of deaths reported each year. Forced labor, including by inmates in "reeducation through labor" camps and juveniles in government-sanctioned "work-study" programs, remains a serious problem.

The CCP controls the judiciary and directs verdicts and sentences, especially in politically sensitive cases. Even in commercial litigation and civil suits involving private individuals, previous minor progress toward the rule of law has stalled or been reversed, particularly since the appointment of a CCP veteran with no formal legal training as chief justice in 2008. Judges have been increasingly pressured to resolve civil disputes through mediation, sometimes forced, rather than actual adjudication. There have been a number of high-profile convictions of people who obtained seemingly ordinary commercial information related to state-owned enterprises that was later labeled a "state secret." In February 2011, a Beijing court upheld an eight-year prison sentence on such charges for U.S. citizen and geologist Xue Feng, who had obtained information related to the oil industry that would be publicly available in most countries.

The government continued its crackdown on civil rights lawyers, law firms, and NGOs offering legal services in 2011. Many of those abducted and abused in the Jasmine Revolution–related crackdown were lawyers, some of whom had previously faced disbarment for taking human rights cases. Prominent lawyer Gao Zhisheng remained "disappeared" and at severe risk of torture following his abduction by security forces in 2009. In December, state media announced that he would be sent to a prison in Xinjiang to serve a three-year term imposed in 2006, but as of year's end, no family members had been allowed to meet him and confirm his whereabouts. Self-trained, blind lawyer Chen Guangcheng remained under strict house arrest after completing a four-year prison term in 2010, having helped victims of forced abortions to file a class-action suit. Throughout 2011, local authorities violently suppressed efforts by fellow activists and foreign journalists to visit Chen. Prominent Beijing activist Hu Jia was released in June from a three-and-a-half-year prison term for speaking out about human rights abuses in the run-up to the 2008 Beijing Olympics; he, too, was placed under strict house arrest, where he remained at year's end.

Trials in China, which often amount to mere sentencing announcements, are frequently closed to the public. Torture remains widespread, coerced confessions are routinely admitted as evidence, and there is impunity for suspicious deaths in custody. Many suspects—including a large proportion of political and religious prisoners—are detained by bureaucratic fiat in "reeducation through labor" camps. The use of various forms of extralegal detention has grown in recent years, including secret jails and psychiatric arrest of petitioners and dissidents. In August 2011, the National People's Congress published proposed legal amendments that, among other changes, would allow the secret detention of suspects in politically sensitive cases for up to six months, essentially legalizing the increasingly common practice of enforced disappearances; at year's end the amendments had not yet been enacted. Overall, detention facilities are estimated to hold three to five million people. Conditions are generally harsh, with reports of inadequate food, regular beatings, and deprivation of medical care; the government generally does not permit visits by independent monitoring groups.

Legal amendments passed in March 2011 reduced the number of capital crimes to 55, including nonviolent offenses, though in recent years few individuals had been executed for the removed offenses. The number of executions each year is a state secret, but in December 2011, a scholar from the Chinese Academy of Social Sciences estimated that the number had been halved since the Supreme People's Court was given authority to review all death penalty cases. The San Francisco–based Duihua Foundation consequently put the number of executions in 2011 at 4,000, though that would still be the world's largest. In 2009, state media reported that executed prisoners "provide the major source of [organ] transplants in China." Some experts have raised concerns and preliminary evidence that those imprisoned for their religious beliefs or ethnic identity have also been used as sources for organs.

Security forces work closely with the CCP at all levels. During 2011, the CCP continued to expand its apparatus for "stability maintenance," a term that encompasses maintaining law and order, suppressing peaceful dissent, and closely monitoring the populace. Key components of this apparatus include state intelligence agencies, such as the Public Security Bureau; paramilitary forces, like the People's Armed Police; and extralegal CCP-based entities, like the 610 Office and stability-maintenance units at the grassroots level. In March 2011, the government announced that it would allocate 624 billion yuan (US$95 billion) that year for internal security forces, an increase of over 13 percent from 2010. The new total surpassed the country's military budget for the first time.

In the Xinjiang Uighur Autonomous Region, tightened restrictions that followed ethnic clashes in July 2009 remained in place for much of 2011, including round-the-clock street patrols and tighter monitoring of ethnic Uighur residents. Many of those abducted in large-scale "disappearances" in 2009 remained unaccounted for, and in January 2011, a court official revealed that 376 related trials for "endangering state security" were held in 2010. Existing political indoctrination programs, curbs on Muslim religious practice, policies marginalizing use of the Uighur language in education, and government efforts to alter the region's demography continued throughout 2011, and in some instances, grew worse. From May to August, under pressure from Beijing, at least 19 Uighur asylum seekers were forcibly repatriated from Kazakhstan, Thailand, Pakistan, and Malaysia despite human rights groups' warnings that they were at risk of torture and imprisonment.

Minorities, the disabled, and people with HIV/AIDS or hepatitis B face widespread societal and official discrimination, including in access to employment and education. A *hukou* (household registration) system remains in place, mostly affecting China's 150 million internal migrants. Some local governments have experimented with reforms, but citizens continue to face restrictions on changing employer or residence, and many migrants are unable to fully access social services, such as education for their children. Among other restrictions on freedom of movement, dissidents, human rights defenders, and certain scholars are prevented from traveling abroad or placed under house arrest. Law enforcement agencies continue to seek out and repatriate North Korean refugees, who face imprisonment or execution upon return.

Property rights protection remains weak in practice, and all land is formally owned by the state. Tens of thousands of forced evictions and illegal land confiscations occurred in 2011. Residents who resist eviction, seek legal redress, or organize protests often face violence at the hands of local police or hired thugs. In January, the government issued new regulations that could offer greater protections against expropriation in urban areas by defining "public interest," requiring compensation at market value, and allowing for administrative review. However, implementation remained uncertain given the lack of independent courts and local governments' incentives to develop land as a key source of operating revenue and a driver of economic growth statistics. The new regulations do not apply to rural land, which lies at the center of most land conflicts.

Despite increasing discussion of potential reforms, China's population controls remain in place. In urban areas, only one child per couple is permitted, while many rural families are limited to two children. Compulsory abortion and sterilization, though less common than in the past, still occur fairly frequently. According to the Congressional-Executive Commission on China, regulations in 18 of 31 provincial-level administrative units explicitly endorse mandatory abortions as an enforcement tool. Officials who fail to meet birth and sterilization quotas risk disciplinary action, and relatives of unsterilized women or couples with unapproved pregnancies were subjected to high fines, job dismissal, and detention in 2011. These controls and a cultural preference for sons have led to sex-selective abortion and a general shortage of females, exacerbating the problem of human trafficking.

Domestic violence affects one-quarter of Chinese women, according to statistics published in October 2011 by the CCP-controlled All-China Women's Federation. That month, the group submitted a draft for a national law that would identify domestic violence as a crime; it is currently addressed inadequately via scattered provisions in other laws. Several laws bar gender discrimination in the workplace, and gender equality has reportedly improved over the past decade, but a March 2011 survey by the New York–based Center for Work-Life Policy found that 48 percent of female respondents had scaled back their career ambitions or considered quitting their jobs because of perceived discrimination.

Colombia

Political Rights: 3
Civil Liberties: 4
Status: Partly Free

Population: 46,871,000
Capital: Bogotá

Ten-Year Ratings Timeline For Year Under Review (Political Rights, Civil Liberties, Status)

2002	2003	2004	2005	2006	2007	2008	2009	2010	2011
4,4PF	4,4PF	4,4PF	3,3PF	3,3PF	3,3PF	3,4PF	3,4PF	3,4PF	3,4PF

Overview: **President Juan Manuel Santos used his congressional majority to pass a set of important laws in 2011, most notably the Victims and Land Restitution Law, which—if properly implemented—would help address the damage caused by Colombia's ongoing internal conflict. However, human rights abuses persisted during the year, with land rights advocates frequently targeted and paramilitary "successor groups" continuing to expand. Regional and local elections held in October were not dominated by any single party, but demonstrated a growing urban-rural divide. In November the military killed guerrilla leader Alfonso Cano even as his Revolutionary Armed Forces of Colombia (FARC) rebel group increased its level of activity.**

Following independence from Spain in 1819, Gran Colombia broke into what became Venezuela, Ecuador, and modern Colombia. The 1903 secession of Panama, engineered by the United States, left Colombia with its present borders. A civil war between Liberals and Conservatives erupted in 1948 and resulted in some 200,000 deaths before subsiding after 1953. From 1958 to 1974, the two parties alternated in the presidency under the terms of a 1957 coalition pact aimed at ending civil strife. Colombia has since been marked by corrupt politics as well as left-wing guerrilla insurgencies, right-wing paramilitary violence, the emergence of vicious drug cartels, and human rights abuses committed by all sides.

A peace process between the government and the leftist Revolutionary Armed Forces of Colombia (FARC) rebel group unraveled in 2001, and Álvaro Uribe, a former provincial governor who ran as an independent, won the 2002 presidential election after pledging to crush the rebels by military means. Right-wing paramilitary death squads, grouped together as the United Self-Defense Forces of Colombia (AUC), also battled the guerrillas, sometimes with the tolerance or covert complicity of government forces.

Although by 2005 the leftist guerrillas had largely ceded control of major cities to the paramilitaries, they held out in remote areas, using the narcotics trade and extortion for financial support. Moreover, social and human rights conditions sometimes deteriorated further where paramilitaries replaced the guerrillas.

The 2005 Justice and Peace Law was designed to demobilize and grant a partial amnesty to the paramilitaries, but human rights groups said it failed to ensure the permanent dismantling of the groups and encouraged impunity. In May 2006, the Constitutional Court struck down certain elements of the law and mandated full confessions, the seizure of illicitly acquired assets, and the provision of reparations to victims. Meanwhile, bolstered by a growing economy and the perception of improved security, Uribe won a second term in that month's presidential election, taking 62 percent of the vote, fully 40 points ahead of his closest rival.

By late 2006, more than 30,000 paramilitaries had formally demobilized. However, human rights groups reported subsequent problems with civilian reintegration, violence against former combatants, a lack of resources for investigations, nonparticipation in the justice and peace process, and delays in reparation payments and physical protection for victims. Moreover, fragmented "successor groups" formed in part by recalcitrant or recidivist paramilitaries continued to engage in drug trafficking, land theft, assassinations of social and human rights activists, and in some cases collaboration with security forces or guerrillas.

In April 2008, 14 paramilitary chiefs were extradited to the United States to face long prison sentences for drug trafficking. However, they ceased cooperation with Colombia's confessions process, which—despite frequent frustration—had yielded valuable information on paramilitary operations and tens of thousands of unsolved murders. Observers also raised concerns that the extraditions removed potential witnesses in the ongoing "parapolitics" scandal, which linked scores of politicians to paramilitaries. By the close of the 2006–2010 Congress, over 90 legislators had been arrested, convicted, or placed under investigation. In August 2009 the Colombian Supreme Court prohibited further extraditions of former paramilitary leaders still involved in the justice and peace process.

Meanwhile, evidence emerged in February 2009 that Colombia's intelligence agency, the Administrative Security Department (DAS), had been spying extensively on targets including journalists, nongovernmental organization (NGO) workers, politicians, and Supreme Court justices since 2003. The revelation led to multiple convictions in 2010 and 2011, including that of former DAS chief Jorge Noguera on murder and conspiracy charges in September 2011. He was sentenced to 25 years in prison. In October 2011 the DAS was formally dissolved, but new information about its spying schemes and involvement in criminal activities continued to come to light.

The DAS scandal added to severe friction between Uribe and the Supreme Court, which was less acquiescent than the Congress regarding his accrual of power. Other factors included the administration's dubious accusations of corruption within the court, the court's rejection of all of Uribe's proposed attorney general candidates, and its probe of his cousin Mario Uribe, who was eventually convicted in February 2011 for ties to paramilitaries. In 2010, the focus shifted to the Constitutional Court, which ruled in March—just weeks before congressional elections—that a prospective third presidential term for Uribe would conflict with constitutional checks and balances, and that multiple regulations and procedural rules had been violated during the effort to collect signatures and win approval for a referendum on the issue.

In the March 2010 congressional elections, putative Uribe allies won a substantial majority in both chambers. Former defense minister Juan Manuel Santos, who benefited from his association with the Uribe administration's security achievements, overcame an ideologically diverse array of opponents in the first round of the presidential poll in May, taking 47 percent of the vote. Former Bogotá mayor

Antanas Mockus, running for the new Green Party, mounted a spirited challenge, winning 22 percent. However, most other candidates endorsed Santos in the June runoff, and he won easily with 69 percent.

The Santos administration adopted a far more conciliatory approach than the previous government, and by mid-2011, Santos had expanded his National Unity coalition to include most parties in Congress. He used this control to enact a series of far-reaching laws, the most ambitious and widely lauded of which was the Victims and Land Restitution Law. It was enacted in June following a prolonged debate, with the most vigorous opposition coming from Uribe and his staunchest supporters. The law recognized the legitimacy of claims by victims of conflict-related abuses, including those committed by government forces. It also established a framework for reparations and resettlement of displaced people; more than 16 million acres of land were estimated to have been stolen during the conflict. However, analysts and rights groups said implementation would pose an enormous challenge given the complexity of adjudicating land titles, the sheer scale of the undertaking, and ongoing collaboration between rural landholders and armed groups. A sharp rise in threats and killings targeting victims' rights advocates in the first part of Santos's term appeared to confirm fears about resistance to the reforms.

In regional and local elections held in October, Santos's Partido de la U, the Liberal Party, and independents won the greatest share of governorships and mayoralties. In Bogotá, left-wing independent Gustavo Petro won after running on an anticorruption platform, while candidates viewed as modernizing also won the mayoralties of Medellín, Cali, and Barranquilla. Although conduct of the elections was generally viewed as an improvement on the previous round in 2007, the campaign period was violent, with 41 candidates killed, mostly in rural municipalities. As in past elections, such interference by armed actors, particularly paramilitary successor groups, partially skewed the overall results. Candidates facing judicial investigation were elected in a number of important regions and municipalities.

In November 2011, the Santos administration registered a dramatic military success when a bombing raid killed the FARC's leader, Alfonso Cano. The killing followed a series of deaths of top FARC commanders—from government attacks, internal disputes, and natural causes—that began in 2008. Later that month, the FARC's reputation among Colombians reached a new low after guerrillas executed four long-term hostages during a rescue attempt. However, despite the group's weakening, it has adapted its tactics in recent years, and the number of attacks rose by approximately 10 percent in 2011, inflicting serious damage on security forces, economic infrastructure, and civilians.

In the international arena, Santos continued a détente with Ecuador and Venezuela, both of which had cut off diplomatic ties after Colombian forces attacked a FARC camp in Ecuador in 2008. Diplomatic and commercial ties were restored in 2010, and Santos met with the leaders of both countries in 2011 over the protests of Uribe and some of his supporters. In October, the United States ratified a free trade agreement long sought by Colombia's business sector, though critics expressed concern that related labor safeguards offered Colombian workers insufficient protection from violence and exploitation.

Political Rights and Civil Liberties: Colombia is an electoral democracy. The 2010 legislative elections, while less violent than previous campaigns, were marred by vote buying, opaque financing, and intimidation in some areas, particularly former paramilitary strongholds. The 2010 presidential election was relatively peaceful. Despite improved legal standards, both the 2010 national elections and the 2011 regional and local contests were characterized by murky campaign-finance practices.

Congress is composed of the Senate and the Chamber of Representatives, with all seats up for election every four years. Of the Senate's 102 members, two are chosen by indigenous communities and 100 by the nation at large using a closed-list system. The Chamber of Representatives consists of 166 members elected by closed-list proportional representation in multimember districts.

The traditional Liberal-Conservative partisan duopoly in Congress has in recent years been supplanted by a rough division between more urban, modernizing forces opposed to former president Álvaro Uribe and pro-Uribe forces representing more conservative, often rural sectors. President Juan Manuel Santos's National Unity coalition has blurred but not completely eliminated this division in the Congress, but the results of the 2011 regional and local elections confirmed the tendency. Party fragmentation remains a problem, and several new parties have formed to serve as vehicles for those implicated in the parapolitics scandal. Such parties achieved some victories in the 2011 subnational elections.

Corruption occurs at multiple levels of public administration. A series of scandals emerged late in the Uribe administration and accelerated in 2010 and 2011. The alleged malfeasance affected an agricultural subsidies program, an agency handling confiscated assets, and the tax agency, among others. The most dramatic case involved contracting abuses in Bogotá and led to the May 2011 removal of Mayor Samuel Moreno from office. Both he and his brother, Senator Iván Moreno, were arrested; their trials were ongoing at year's end. Colombia was ranked 80 out of 183 countries surveyed in Transparency International's 2011 Corruption Perceptions Index.

The constitution guarantees freedom of expression, and opposition views are commonly expressed in the media. However, crime and conflict make it difficult for journalists to work. Dozens of journalists have been murdered since the mid-1990s, many for reporting on drug trafficking and corruption. Most of the cases remain unsolved, and one reporter was killed in 2011. Self-censorship is common, and slander and defamation are criminal offenses, as confirmed by the Supreme Court in June 2011. The government does not restrict access to the internet or censor websites.

The constitution provides for freedom of religion, and the government generally respects this right in practice. The authorities also uphold academic freedom, and university debates are often vigorous, though armed groups maintain a presence on many campuses to generate political support and intimidate opponents. Large-scale student protests during the fall of 2011 prompted the government to withdraw a controversial education reform bill.

Constitutional rights regarding freedoms of assembly and association are restricted in practice by violence. Although the government provides extensive protection to hundreds of threatened human rights workers, trust in the program varies widely, and scores of activists have been murdered in recent years, mostly by paramilitary groups. The Santos administration has emphasized respect for NGOs, unlike the belligerent Uribe, but violations against activists have risen since Santos took office. Victims' and land rights campaigners are especially threatened by former paramilitaries seeking to smother criticism of their ill-gotten assets. At least nine were among the 49 social activists and human rights defenders killed between in 2011, a sharp increase from the 32 deaths in 2010. The June murder of displaced peoples' leader Ana Fabricia Córdoba in Medellín was perhaps the most publicized incident.

Colombia is considered the world's most dangerous country for organized labor. More than 2,600 union activists and leaders have been killed over the last two decades, with attacks coming from all of Colombia's illegal armed groups. Killings have declined from their early-2000s peak, and fell from 51 in 2010 to 29 in 2011. Although a special prosecutorial unit has substantially increased prosecutions for such assassinations since 2007, most have not touched those who ordered the killings, and the impunity rate remains above 90 percent. The Labor Action Plan linked to the U.S. free trade agreement calls for enhanced investigation of rights violations and stepped-up enforcement regarding abusive labor practices.

The justice system remains compromised by corruption and extortion, but the Constitutional Court and Supreme Court have demonstrated their independence from the executive. Lower courts are more susceptible to political and criminal influence, and both judges and prosecutors confront serious risks when investigating powerful figures, as illustrated by the March 2011 killing in Arauca of a judge presiding over the murder trial of a Colombian soldier.

Many soldiers work under limited civilian oversight, though the government has in recent years increased human rights training and investigated a greater number of military personnel for human rights abuses. Collaboration between security forces and illegal armed groups declined following AUC demobilization, but rights groups report toleration of the roughly 8,000-strong paramilitary successor groups in some regions. Primary responsibility for combating them rests with the police, who lack the resources of the military, are frequently accused of colluding with criminal groups, and are largely absent from many rural areas where the groups are active.

The systematic killing of civilians to fraudulently inflate guerrilla death tolls has declined substantially since a 2008 scandal over the practice led to the firing of dozens of senior army officers. More than 2,000 people may have been killed in this way, and thousands of security personnel remained under investigation at the end of 2011. Dozens of convictions were obtained in cases transferred to civilian courts, but far more cases proceeded slowly due to a shortage of prosecutors and delaying tactics by defense lawyers.

Jurisdiction over human rights violations is a sensitive issue. In April 2011, a civilian court imposed a 30-year prison sentence on former army general Jesús Arias Cabrales for the disappearance of 11 suspected rebels following the 1985 siege of the Palace of Justice. Such verdicts have increased tensions between military and civilian justice institutions and prompted a series of proposed bills that would limit security forces' culpability. One government-sponsored bill would amend the constitution to presume that all crimes committed by soldiers were service-related and thus subject to military justice. The measure remained under debate at year's end.

All of the illegal armed groups systematically abuse human rights. While violence has declined since the early 2000s, massacres rose substantially in 2010 and again 2011, and at least 450 police and soldiers were killed during the year. FARC guerrillas regularly extort payments from businesspeople and engage in forced recruitment, including of minors. The use of landmines has added to casualties among both civilians and the military. Impunity for crime in general is rampant.

Colombia's more than 1.7 million indigenous inhabitants live on over 34 million hectares granted to them by the government, often in resource-rich, strategic regions that are increasingly contested by the various armed groups. Indigenous people are frequently targeted by all sides. At least 117 indigenous Colombians were murdered in 2011, and both the Office of the UN High Commissioner for Refugees and the Constitutional Court have warned in recent years that many groups face extinction, often after being displaced by the conflict.

Afro-Colombians, who account for as much as 25 percent of the population, make up the largest sector of Colombia's over 4 million displaced people, and 80 percent of Afro-Colombians fall below the poverty line. The displaced population as a whole suffers from social stigma, arbitrary arrest, and exploitation, as well as generalized poverty. Consultation with Afro-Colombians is constitutionally mandated on issues affecting their communities, but activists expressed dismay over shortcomings in the government's consultation process for the Victims and Land Restitution Law in 2011. In December the president signed the Antidiscrimination Law, which criminalizes discriminatory conduct toward a variety of vulnerable groups.

Child labor is a serious problem in Colombia, as are child recruitment into illegal armed groups and related sexual abuse. Sexual harassment, violence against women, and the trafficking of women for sexual exploitation remain major concerns. Thousands of rapes have occurred as part of the conflict, generally with impunity. The country's abortion-rights movement has challenged restrictive laws, and in 2006 a Constitutional Court ruling allowed abortion in cases of rape or incest, or to protect the mother's life.

Comoros

Political Rights: 3
Civil Liberties: 4
Status: Partly Free

Population: 753,900
Capital: Moroni

Ten-Year Ratings Timeline For Year Under Review (Political Rights, Civil Liberties, Status)

2002	2003	2004	2005	2006	2007	2008	2009	2010	2011
5,4PF	5,4PF	4,4PF	4,4PF	3,4PF	4,4PF	3,4PF	3,4PF	3,4PF	3,4PF

Overview: **Former vice president Ikililou Dhoinine was sworn in as president on May 26, 2011, after winning a December 2010 election. An opposition party in September filed a corruption complaint against Dhoinine's predecessor, Ahmed Abdallah Sambi, for alleged misuse of public funds while in office.**

The Union of the Comoros comprises three islands: Grande Comore, Anjouan, and Mohéli. Mayotte, the fourth island of the archipelago, voted to remain under French rule in 1974. Two mercenary invasions and at least 18 other coups have shaken the Comoros since it gained independence from France in 1975. The 1996 presidential election was considered free and fair by international monitors, but Anjouan and Mohéli fell under the control of separatists the following year. A 1999 coup restored order, installing Colonel Azali Assoumani as leader of the country, and led to the signing of a reconciliation agreement. A 2001 referendum approved a new constitution that increased autonomy for the three islands. Azali won the federal presidency in the 2002 election after his two opponents claimed fraud and withdrew. However, Azali supporters captured only 6 of the 33 seats in the 2004 federal legislative elections, and Ahmed Abdallah Sambi—a moderate Islamist preacher and businessman—won the federal presidency in May 2006.

Mohamed Bacar, the president of the island of Anjouan, organized unauthorized elections in 2007 to extend his rule and claimed to have won with 90 percent of the vote. However, in March 2008, an African Union military force removed him from power, and Moussa Toybou, a Sambi supporter, was elected in June 2008.

In a May 2009 referendum, voters approved constitutional reforms that increased the powers of the federal government at the expense of the individual island governments. The reforms instituted a rotation of the federal presidency among the islands every five (previously four) years, downgraded individual island presidents to the status of governors, limited the size of cabinets, empowered the president to dissolve the federal parliament, and allowed the president to rule by decree with the parliament's approval.

In December 2009 legislative elections, the president's supporters—the Baobab coalition—won 19 of the 24 directly elected seats. Sambi's term of office expired in May 2010, but an election to choose his successor was postponed due to political disputes. This delay provoked tension, especially among residents of Mohéli, which was the next island scheduled to hold the office of federal president.

In December 2010, Sambi's protégé, Vice President Ikililou Dhoinine, won the presidential election with 61 percent of the vote. He became the first president of Comoros from Mohéli. His main rival, Mohamed Said Fazul, claimed fraud. However, the national election monitoring group upheld the legitimacy of the election, and Dhoinine was sworn in on May 26, 2011. Opponents alleged that the long transition period, combined with the delayed election, effectively extended Sambi's term by one year.

Large numbers of Comorans illegally emigrate to Mayotte to settle or to seek entry into metropolitan France, and the economy depends heavily on remittances and foreign aid. In 2009, the global economic downturn contributed to delays and suspensions of public-sector salary payments and a decline in public services. These problems continued in 2011; in June, the legislature took action to try to reduce the government's unsustainably high wage burden by reining in civil service salaries.

Political Rights and Civil Liberties:

Comoros is an electoral democracy. Since 1996, Comorans have voted freely in several parliamentary and presidential elections. The unicameral Assembly of the Union consists of 33 members, with 9 selected by the assemblies of the three islands and 24 by direct popular vote; all members serve five-year terms. Prior to the 2009 reforms, 15 seats had been appointed by the islands' assemblies and 18 had been elected. Each of the three islands also has an individual parliament, which is directly elected. Political parties are mainly defined by their positions regarding the division of power between the federal and local governments.

Corruption remains a major problem. There have been reports of corruption at all levels of the government, judiciary, and civil service, as well as among the police and security forces. In September 2011, the opposition Convention for the Renewal of the Comoros (CRC), led by former president Azali Assoumani, filed a complaint in a Moroni court against former president Ahmed Abdallah Sambi for alleged misuse of public funds while in office; the case was still pending at year's end. Comoros was ranked 143 out of 183 countries surveyed in Transparency International's 2011 Corruption Perceptions Index.

The constitution and laws provide for freedom of speech and of the press, though self-censorship is reportedly widespread. In March 2011, two journalists were charged with "publishing false news" for articles suggesting that the scheduled May 26 inauguration of President-elect Ikililou Dhoinine could be delayed. The public prosecutor considered these reports "of a nature to trouble public order."

Islam is the state religion, and 99 percent of the population is Sunni Muslim. Tensions have occasionally arisen between Sunni and Shiite Muslims, and non-Muslims are reportedly subject to restrictions, detentions, and harassment. Conversion from Islam and non-Muslim proselytizing are illegal. Academic freedom is generally respected.

The government typically upholds freedoms of assembly and association. However, security forces in the past have responded to demonstrations with excessive force. A few human rights and other nongovernmental organizations operate in the country. Workers have the right to bargain collectively and to strike, but collective bargaining is rare. In January 2010, teachers went on strike to protest nonpayment of salaries.

The judicial system is based on both Sharia (Islamic law) and the French legal code, and is subject to influence by the executive branch and other elites. Minor disputes are often settled informally by village elders. Harsh prison conditions include severe overcrowding and inadequate sanitation, medical care, and nutrition.

The law prohibits discrimination based on gender. However, in practice, women enjoy little political representation or economic equality, and they have far fewer opportunities for education and salaried employment than men, especially in rural areas. Sexual violence is believed to be widespread, but rarely reported to authorities.

Congo, Democratic Republic of (Kinshasa)

Political Rights: 6
Civil Liberties: 6
Status: Not Free

Population: 67,823,000
Capital: Kinshasa

Ten-Year Ratings Timeline For Year Under Review (Political Rights, Civil Liberties, Status)

2002	2003	2004	2005	2006	2007	2008	2009	2010	2011
6,6NF	6,6NF	6,6NF	6,6NF	5,6NF	5,6NF	6,6NF	6,6NF	6,6NF	6,6NF

Overview: **In January 2011, the government amended the electoral law to eliminate the requirement for presidential runoff elections, giving undue advantage to incumbent Joseph Kabila. Despite logistical problems, presidential and parliamentary elections went ahead as scheduled on November 28. The polls were deeply flawed, with reports of serious and widespread fraud, as well as a number of violent incidents. Kabila was declared the winner of the presidential race with 49 percent of the vote, while parliamentary results had yet to be announced by year's end. Throughout 2011, all parties in the country's ongoing conflicts continued to carry out killings, rapes, and abductions of civilians.**

In the late 19th century, the king of Belgium claimed a vast area of Central Africa as his private property, and the territory was exploited with extreme brutality. After achieving independence from Belgium in 1960, the then Republic of Congo became an arena for Cold War rivalries, and Colonel Joseph Mobutu seized power with CIA backing in 1965. Mobutu changed the country's name to Zaire in 1971, renamed himself Mobutu Sese Seko, and assumed dictatorial powers.

Following the end of the Cold War, domestic agitation and international pressure for democratization led to a national conference in 1992. President Mobutu was stripped of most of his powers, and a transitional government was formed with a new prime minister, longtime Mobutu opponent Étienne Tshisekedi. However, Mobutu created a rival government, leading to a political standoff. In a compromise that marginalized Tshisekedi, the two governments merged in 1994, with Mobutu remaining head of state and Kengo Wa Dondo becoming prime minister. Presidential and legislative elections were scheduled repeatedly but never took place.

After the 1994 genocide in neighboring Rwanda, the Rwandan and Ugandan governments turned their cross-border pursuit of Rwandan Hutu militia members into an advance on Kinshasa. Rwandan troops, accompanied by representatives of the Alliance of Democratic Forces for the Liberation of Congo-Zaire—a coalition led by former Zairian rebel leader Laurent-Désiré Kabila—reached Kinshasa in May 1997. Mobutu fled to Morocco, where he died months later of cancer. Kabila declared himself president and changed the country's name to the Democratic Republic of Congo (DRC).

Relations between Kabila and his Rwandan and Ugandan backers deteriorated after he ordered all foreign forces to leave the DRC in 1998. Rwanda intervened in support of a newly formed rebel group, the Rally for Congolese Democracy (RCD), but the DRC government was defended by Angolan, Namibian, and Zimbabwean troops. Uganda later backed a rival rebel group, the Movement for the Liberation of the Congo (MLC), establishing control over the northern third of the DRC, while the RCD held much of the eastern Kivu region. The country's vast mineral wealth spurred the involvement of multinational companies, criminal networks, and other foreign governments.

Military stalemate led to the signing of the Lusaka Peace Agreement in 1999. The accord called for a ceasefire, the deployment of UN peacekeepers, the withdrawal of foreign troops, and a transitional government. Kabila drew international criticism for blocking the deployment of UN troops and suppressing internal political activity. He was assassinated in 2001 and succeeded by his son Joseph, who revived the peace process. The 2002 Sun City Agreement led to the creation of a transitional government in 2003 and a formal end to the war.

A new constitution was officially promulgated in 2006. Presidential and legislative elections—the first multiparty polls since independence—followed later that year. Despite daunting logistical challenges, the elections were largely peaceful and drew a turnout of over 70 percent. Kabila's People's Party for Reconstruction and Democracy (PPRD) gained a plurality of seats in the National Assembly, the lower house. In a field of 33 presidential candidates, Kabila won approximately 45 percent of the first-round vote, and went on to defeat MLC leader and transitional vice president Jean-Pierre Bemba in the runoff.

Following the elections, two broad alliances emerged in the 500-seat National Assembly: the Alliance of the Presidential Majority (AMP), comprising 332 seats, and the opposition Union for the Nation (UpN), comprising 116 seats. Eleven provincial assemblies voted in the January 2007 Senate elections, granting the AMP 58 seats and the UpN 21. In March 2007, fighting broke out in Kinshasa between the authorities and Bemba loyalists.

In January 2008, a peace agreement was signed between the government and 22 armed groups operating in the east. Notably, the agreement did not include the Rwandan government or the Democratic Forces for the Liberation of Rwanda (FDLR), an ethnic Hutu–dominated militia led by perpetrators of the 1994 Rwandan genocide who had fled to the DRC. Fighting broke out in August 2008 between government troops and the ethnic Tutsi rebel leader Laurent Nkunda's National Congress for the Defense of the People (CNDP), which allegedly received backing from Rwanda. The clashes resulted in further civilian displacement and an increase in human rights abuses.

In late 2008, the DRC and Rwanda signed an agreement to begin a joint military operation against the FDLR and negotiations with the CNDP. The early 2009 operation coincided with the surprise arrest of Nkunda in Rwanda in January and a settlement with the CNDP in March. The settlement transformed the CNDP into a political party and integrated the leadership into the Armed Forces of the DRC (FARDC). It also included an amnesty for acts of war committed by members of the CNDP. Parliament ultimately expanded the amnesty to cover acts of war and insurrection committed by all armed groups operating in North Kivu and South Kivu between June 2003 and May 2009. In March 2009, Congolese and UN forces began a new military operation against the FDLR. Separately, the FARDC embarked on a joint military operation with Uganda from December 2008 to March 2009 to pursue the Lord's Resistance Army (LRA), a Ugandan rebel group operating in northeastern Congo.

In 2011, FDLR attacks on civilians reportedly increased in some areas, particularly in parts of the Kivus from which the FARDC had withdrawn. LRA incursions into the DRC continued throughout 2010 and 2011, and the DRC joined forces with the Central African Republic, Sudan, and Uganda to pursue the militants. In March 2011, the United Nations reported an increase in LRA violence against civilians in northeastern Congo. In addition, mass rapes continued to be carried out by all parties involved in the conflicts in eastern Congo in 2011. Although impunity for perpetrators of rape remains a major challenge, in February, a military court sentenced Lieutenant Colonel Kibibi Mutware of the FARDC to 20 years in jail, and eight men under his command to between 10 and 20 years, for mass rape and crimes against humanity in connection with an attack on the village of Fizi on New Year's Day.

The impact of years of fighting on civilians has been catastrophic. A mortality survey released by the International Rescue Committee in 2008 reported that 5.4 million people had died since 1998 as a result of conflict and humanitarian crises. In 2010, the Office of the UN High Commissioner for Human Rights issued a report that detailed over 600 of the most serious violations of human rights and humanitarian law that occurred between 1993 and 2003 in the DRC by armed forces and nonstate groups, both foreign and Congolese. In response, the DRC government initiated draft legislation in November 2010 to create a special court to prosecute serious crimes, but the court had yet to be established as of the end of 2011.

In advance of the November 2011 presidential and National Assembly elections, a number of changes to the electoral law were enacted. Most prominently, in January the government amended the law to eliminate the requirement for second-round presidential elections when no candidate wins more than 50 percent of the vote in the first round, despite protests from the opposition. The amendment was seen by opposition parties as an intentional manipulation meant to secure Kabila's reelection.

Opposition politicians and their supporters faced violence and harassment by police in the run-up to the November elections. Police used tear gas, beat protesters with clubs, and fired live rounds into the air to break up a series of demonstrations in September and October by supporters of opposition Union for Democracy and Social Progress (UDPS) leader Tshisekedi, who had emerged as Kabila's main presidential challenger. Twelve people were killed and 41 others were injured on November 26, when security forces fired into the air and into crowds that had gathered to welcome the two presidential candidates at Kinshasa's N'djili Airport. While the November 28 elections were conducted peacefully in most of the country, a number of violent incidents occurred, such as the burning down of at least 12 polling stations by angry protesters, and the reported killing of eight people by masked gunmen who fired on polling stations in Katanga and Lubumbashi.

On December 9, the Independent National Electoral Commission (CENI) announced that Kabila had won with 49 percent of the vote, and Tshisekedi placed second with 32 percent. The U.S.-based Carter Center monitoring group reported that due to insufficient preparation and widespread irregularities throughout the process—including incomplete voter lists, lack of voting materials, missing results from some 3,500 polling stations, and impossibly large voter turnouts in some districts—the presidential election results were not credible. The vote was also criticized by the European Union, the Catholic Church, and the UN peacekeeping mission in the DRC. Nevertheless, the Supreme Court confirmed the results on December 16, and Kabila was sworn in four days later.

Elections for the National Assembly were also held on November 28 and suffered from the same problems. Due to complaints of irregularities, CENI temporarily suspended tabulation of the results on December 21. It began to incrementally publish partial results on December 28, but did not release final results by year's end.

The DRC was ranked lowest in the world on the UN Development Programme's 2011 Human Development Index, as it continued to suffer from instability and the effects of war, economic crisis, and the challenge of strengthening political and social institutions and ensuring their accountability.

Political Rights and Civil Liberties: The DRC is not an electoral democracy. International observers noted that both the 2006 and 2011 elections lacked credibility and transparency, and were marred by fraud, voting irregularities, voter intimidation, and violence. The legitimacy of CENI, established in 2010 to replace a transitional body, has been called into question. Four of its seven members are appointed by the presidential coalition, and it does not include members of civil society, as its predecessor did. The 2011 elections were seen as even less credible than those in 2006 due to a lack of preparation, changes in the structure and function of the electoral commission, absence of a comparable level of international logistical support, and lack of adequate accountability and follow through on reported irregularities. In July 2011, CENI completed a program, begun in 2010, of reregistering all voters. However, the process was criticized as flawed by observers. On October 22, the UDPS, which had been staging weekly demonstrations in front of CENI headquarters to demand transparency of the electoral process, met with CENI and agreed on terms for an audit of the electoral register.

Under the 2006 constitution, the president is elected for up to two five-year terms. The president nominates a prime minister from the leading party or coalition in the 500-seat National Assembly, the lower house of the bicameral legislature, whose members are popularly elected to serve five-year terms. The provincial assemblies elect the upper house, the 108-seat Senate, as well as the provincial governors, for five-year terms. There were 428 political parties registered to participate in the 2011 elections. In March, Kabila's coalition, the AMP, restructured itself into the Presidential Majority (PM), which requires coalition members to have national representation, ensuring that the PPRD will remain in the majority within the coalition. Other major parties include the opposition UDPS and MLC.

The fight against corruption continues to be a challenge for the DRC. A presidential ban on artisanal mining that had been declared in September 2010 to stem the flow of mining revenues to armed groups was lifted in March 2011, when it became clear that it was not helping to curb violence in the east and was in fact making life harder for miners. In an effort to increase transparency, the government announced in May that it would make all contracts involving mineral, oil, timber, and gas concessions public within 60 days of signing them. In September, the International

Monetary Fund (IMF) demanded that two state-owned mining companies explain unannounced asset sales at prices below their market value, as required under the country's IMF loan terms. The country was ranked 178 out of 183 countries in the World Bank's 2011 Doing Business survey, and 168 out of 183 countries surveyed in Transparency International's 2011 Corruption Perceptions Index.

Although guaranteed by the constitution, freedoms of speech and expression are limited. Members of the state security apparatus threaten, detain, and attack journalists whose reporting was critical of government officials. In April 2011, radio host Samy Mbeto was detained on charges of "insulting the authorities" and "defaming politicians." He was released on bail three days later but ordered not to leave Kasai-Occidental province and to report to prosecutors twice a week. Nonstate armed groups have also targeted journalists. In June, a radio host was shot dead near his home in North Kivu. According to UNESCO, he had recently reported on the activities of armed gangs in Kirumba. As elections drew closer, there was an increase in violence against journalists. Radio is the dominant medium in the country due to low literacy rates and limited access to other media. The nongovernmental Centre Résolution Conflits, which works to assist former combatants with disarmament and resettlement, runs more than 70 community radio stations that reach even isolated areas. The government does not monitor online communications or restrict access to the internet, but internet use is limited by lack of infrastructure.

Freedom of religion is guaranteed by the constitution and generally respected in practice. Although religious groups must register with the government in order to be recognized, unregistered groups operate unhindered. Unlike in 2010, there were no reported incidents of religious discrimination in 2011. Academic freedom is restricted by fears of government harassment, which often lead university professors to engage in self-censorship.

The rights to freedom of assembly and association are sometimes limited in practice, and often dangerous to exercise if they involve a political agenda, but the country nevertheless has a vibrant civil society. Groups holding public events must register with local authorities in advance. Nongovernmental organizations are able to operate, but they face pressure from the government and nonstate actors if they offend powerful interests. In June 2011, four national police officers were sentenced to death and one to life in prison for the June 2010 murder of prominent human rights activist Floribert Chebeya Bahizire. However, the head of the national police, John Numbi—who was suspended in June 2010 and was widely suspected of involvement in the murder—had not been charged at year's end.

Under the constitution, Congolese who fulfill a residency requirement of 20 years can form and join trade unions. It is against the law for employers to retaliate against strikers. However, a trend has continued in 2011 in which state authorities and employers encourage the excess proliferation of trade unions, including sham unions, in order to weaken the trade union movement as a whole. Some labor leaders and activists face harassment. In April 2011, the Teachers' Association of the University of Kinshasa ended a 12-day strike after the government agreed to its demands, including academic bonus arrears. In response to a student protest that same month, in which two people were killed, the Teachers' Association sided with the students and deplored the lack of transparency in the determination of academic fees.

Despite constitutional guarantees of independence, the judiciary remains subject to corruption and manipulation, and the court system lacks both trained personnel and resources. Prison conditions are abysmal and life threatening, and long periods of pretrial detention are common. While there are notable exceptions, most government and government-allied forces still enjoy apparent impunity for even the most heinous crimes, and there is little justice for civilian victims of violence and sexual violence.

The International Criminal Court (ICC) continues to pursue cases in the DRC, including those against rebel leaders Mathieu Ngudjolo Chui, Thomas Lubanga, and Germain Katanga, all of whom were on trial at year's end, as well as MLC leader Jean-Pierre Bemba, who was transferred to the ICC in 2008 and remains behind bars. The ICC issued a warrant in 2008 for the arrest of Bosco Ntaganda, but he continued to live openly in Goma as a general in the FARDC in 2011.

Civilian authorities do not maintain effective control of the security forces. Soldiers and police regularly commit serious human rights abuses, including rape. Low pay and inadequate provisions commonly lead soldiers to seize goods from civilians, and demobilized combatants have not been successfully integrated into the civilian economy. Since 2009, Kabila has been overseeing the tenuous process of integrating half of the 330,000 fighters of various militias into the FARDC. However, this process has been problematic, as some former rebels who are now officials in the FARDC are also wanted for serious crimes committed during the war.

Ethnic discrimination continues to be a major problem, particularly against the Mbuti of Ituri and the Congolese Banyamulenge Tutsi of South Kivu. In October 2011, five Banyamulenge aid workers and two other Banyamulenge civilians were killed in an ambush in Fizi, South Kivu, by Mai Mai Yakutumba and allied rebels of Burundi's National Liberation Front. It is widely believed that the seven were targeted based on their ethnicity, as other members of the group in the vehicle who were not Tutsi were released.

Although the law provides for freedom of movement, security forces seeking bribes or travel permits restrict this right in practice, and foreigners must regularly submit to immigration controls when traveling internally. In conflict zones, various armed groups and soldiers have seized private property and destroyed homes, as well as stolen crops and livestock, devastating people's livelihoods. The United Nations reported in June that 1.7 million people remain internally displaced.

Despite constitutional guarantees, women face discrimination in nearly every aspect of their lives, especially in rural areas. Violence against women and girls, including sexual and gender-based violence, has soared since fighting began in 1994, though sex crimes often affect men and boys as well. Mass rapes continued in 2011, and convictions remain rare. Abortion is prohibited, women's access to contraception is extremely low, and maternal mortality is a serious problem. Women are also greatly underrepresented in government, comprising only 10 percent of the National Assembly. According to the U.S. State Department's 2011 Trafficking in Persons Report, the DRC is both a source and destination country for the trafficking of men, women, and children for the purposes of labor and sexual exploitation. In September, the DRC government signed an accord with Benin to combat child trafficking between the two countries.

Congo, Republic of (Brazzaville)

Political Rights: 6
Civil Liberties: 5
Status: Not Free

Population: 4,100,000
Capital: Brazzaville

Ten-Year Ratings Timeline For Year Under Review (Political Rights, Civil Liberties, Status)

2002	2003	2004	2005	2006	2007	2008	2009	2010	2011
6,4PF	5,4PF	5,4PF	5,5PF	6,5NF	6,5NF	6,5NF	6,5NF	6,5NF	6,5NF

Overview: **With legislative elections scheduled for June 2012, the Republic of Congo's ruling Congolese Labor Party convened in July 2011 for its Sixth Extraordinary Congress. Notable developments included the election of a new 51-member Political Bureau, as well as a 471-member Central Committee. Among those elected was Denis Christel Sassou-Nguesso, son of President Denis Sassou-Nguesso, a development that many observers regarded as further evidence of Sassou-Nguesso's aspirations to have his son succeed him.**

Since gaining independence from France in 1960, the Republic of Congo has been marked by conflict and military coups. The current president, Denis Sassou-Nguesso, first came to power in 1979 with military support. Domestic and international pressure finally forced him to hold multiparty presidential elections in 1992. He lost, placing third in the first round. In the runoff, Pascal Lissouba defeated the late veteran oppositionist Bernard Kolélas.

In 1993, disputed parliamentary elections triggered violent clashes between rival militia groups. The fighting ended in 1997, when Sassou-Nguesso ousted Lissouba with the help of Angolan troops and French political support. In 2002, voters adopted a new constitution by referendum, which extended the presidential term from five to seven years. Sassou-Nguesso won the presidential election easily that year after his main challenger, former National Assembly president André Milongo, alleged fraud and withdrew. In the 2002 legislative election, Sassou-Nguesso's Congolese Labor Party (PCT) and its allies captured most of the seats. Although the polls failed to foster genuine reconciliation, most of the country's rebel factions signed a peace agreement in 2003.

After the government ignored calls to create an independent electoral commission, opposition parties boycotted the 2007 legislative election, in which the PCT and its allies won 125 out of 137 seats in the National Assembly. However, the participation of former rebel leader Frédéric Bintsamou's National Republican Council was an important step toward peace. Sassou-Nguesso also included members of Kolélas's Congolese Movement for Democracy and Integral Development in the cabinet for the first time.

In 2008, the PCT and approximately 60 other parties formed a new political coalition, the Rally of the Presidential Majority (RMP), to broaden support for the government ahead of the 2009 presidential election. In August, councilors from seven departments elected members of the national Senate, and the RMP secured 33 out of 42 seats.

The opposition attempted to unify ahead of the July 2009 presidential poll, with 20 parties forming the Front of Congolese Opposition Parties. Six of the original 16 opposition candidates withdrew to protest electoral conditions. The government again refused to establish an independent electoral commission, and the existing commission disqualified four opposition candidates, including Ange Edouard Poungui, leader of the largest opposition party in the National Assembly, the Pan-African Union for Social Democracy. Sassou-Nguesso won another term with 79 percent of the vote; his closest challenger, independent candidate Joseph Kignoumbi Kia Mboungou, took 7 percent of the vote. The government reported voter turnout of 66 percent, while the opposition claimed 10 percent. Following the election, Sassou-Nguesso eliminated the position of prime minister, becoming both head of state and head of government.

Further efforts were made by Sassou-Nguesso in 2011 to strengthen his grip on power. During the PCT's Sixth Extraordinary Congress in July, Sassou-Nguesso's son Denis Christel Sassou-Nguesso became a member of both the party's newly elected 471-member Central Committee and 51-member Political Bureau. Notorious for his lavish lifestyle, Denis Christel's growing prominence within the PCT is seen as yet another example of his father grooming him for eventual succession to the Congolese presidency. On October 9, indirect elections for half of Congo's Senate seats resulted in yet another overwhelming victory for Sassou-Nguesso's political allies.

Congo is one of sub-Saharan Africa's major oil producers, though corruption and decades of instability have contributed to poor humanitarian conditions. Congo was ranked 137 out of 187 countries on the 2011 UN Human Development Index.

Political Rights and Civil Liberties: The Republic of Congo is not an electoral democracy. Irregularities, opposition boycotts and disqualifications, and the absence of an independent electoral commission marred recent elections. The 2002 constitution limits the president to two seven-year terms. However, current president Denis Sassou-Nguesso, who ruled from 1979 to 1992, has held office continuously since seizing power in 1997. The Senate, the upper house of Parliament, consists of 72 members, with councilors from each department electing 6 senators for six-year terms. Half of them come up for election every three years, although 42 seats were at stake in 2008. Members of the 137-seat National Assembly, the lower house, are directly elected for five-year terms. Most of the over 100 registered political parties are personality driven and ethnically based. The ruling RMP coalition faces a weak and fragmented opposition.

Corruption in Congo's extractive industries remains pervasive. A national Anti-Corruption Commission was created in September 2009. However, the government maintains inadequate internal controls, and Sassou-Nguesso and his family have been beset by allegations of graft. In November 2010, a French court ruled that a case centering on how Sassou-Nguesso obtained assets in France could proceed. Congo was ranked 154 out of 183 countries surveyed in Transparency International's 2011 Corruption Perceptions Index.

The government's respect for press freedom is limited. Speech that incites ethnic hatred, violence, or civil war is illegal. Reports of police harassment and violence against journalists circulated during the 2009 election period. Police attacked foreign journalists and confiscated their equipment during a postelection opposition protest. The government monopolizes the broadcast media, which reach a larger audience than print publications. However, approximately 10 private weekly newspapers in Brazzaville often publish articles and editorials critical of the government. There are no government restrictions on internet access.

Religious and academic freedoms are guaranteed and respected.

Freedoms of assembly and association are generally upheld, although security forces have shown little tolerance for political demonstrations. Police halted the political opposition's postelection protest aggressively in 2009. Nongovernmental organizations operate more or less without interference so long as they do not challenge the ruling elite. Workers' rights to join trade unions and to strike are protected, and collective bargaining is practiced freely. Most workers in the formal business sector, including the oil industry, belong to unions, which have also made efforts to organize informal sectors, such as agriculture and retail trade.

Congo's weak judiciary is subject to corruption and political influence. Members of the security forces act with impunity, and there have been reports of suspects being tortured and dying during apprehension or in custody. Prison conditions are life threatening.

Ethnic discrimination persists. Members of Sassou-Nguesso's northern Mbochi ethnic group dominate key government posts. Autochthonous Mbendjele Yaka suffer discrimination, with many held in lifetime servitude through customary ties to ethnic Bantu "patrons." Members of virtually all ethnicities favor their own groups in hiring practices, and urban neighborhoods tend to be segregated. In February 2011, Sassou-Nguesso promulgated a law to protect and promote indigenous rights. Harassment by military personnel and militia groups inhibits travel, though such practices have declined. The judicial system offers few protections for business and property rights.

Despite constitutional safeguards, legal and societal discrimination against women persists. Equal access to education and employment is limited, and civil codes regarding marriage formalize women's inferior status. Violence against women is reportedly widespread. Abortion is prohibited in all cases except to save the life of the mother. Women are also underrepresented in government and decision-making positions, holding just 7 percent of seats in the National Assembly and 14 percent of Senate seats.

Costa Rica

Political Rights: 1
Civil Liberties: 1
Status: Free

Population: 4,726,000
Capital: San José

Ten-Year Ratings Timeline For Year Under Review (Political Rights, Civil Liberties, Status)

2001	2002	2003	2004	2005	2006	2007	2008	2009	2010
1,2F	1,2F	1,1F	1,1F	1,1F	1,1F	1,1F	1,1F	1,1F	1,1F

Overview: **President Laura Chinchilla's first year in office was marked by declining approval ratings and persistent concerns about rising crime. Control of the Legislative Assembly fell to an opposition coalition for the first time in decades, an indication of her waning support. Meanwhile, Chinchilla revealed a 10-year crime plan in February 2011 to combat growing crime and drug trafficking.**

Costa Rica achieved independence from Spain in 1821 and gained full sovereignty in 1838. The country enjoyed relative political stability until 1948, when José "Pepe" Figueres launched a brief civil war to restore power to the rightful winner of that year's presidential election and successfully pushed to disband Costa Rica's military. In 1949, the country adopted a new constitution that ultimately strengthened democratic rule. Figueres later served as president for two separate terms under the National Liberation Party (PLN). Since 1949, power has alternated between the PLN and the Social Christian Unity Party (PUSC).

The PUSC's Abel Pacheco succeeded Miguel Ángel Rodríguez, also of the PUSC, in the 2002 presidential election. Former president Óscar Arias recaptured the presidency for the PLN in 2006.

In February 2010, former vice president Laura Chinchilla of the PLN became Costa Rica's first female president, capturing nearly 47 percent of the vote in the first round, and defeating Ottón Solís of the Citizens' Action Party (PAC) and Otto Guevara of the Libertarian Movement Party (PML). The balloting resulted in a divided Legislative Assembly: the PLN lost two seats, for a total of 24 seats, the PAC won 11, the PML captured 9, the PUSC took 6, and the Accessibility without Exclusion Party (PASE) captured 4 seats, while the remaining 3 seats went to other smaller parties.

In April 2011, a broad coalition of opposition parties forged an alliance to depose the ruling PLN from the directorate of the legislature. A brief crisis ensued when the PLN legislators voted to reelect Luis Gerardo Villanueva as Assembly president without a quorum, as required by the body's procedural rules. Following opposition protests, Villanueva resigned hours later, and the PAC's Juan Carlos Mendoza was elected president of the Assembly. For the first time in 46 years, the president of the Assembly and the ruling party are from different parties.

Chinchilla began her presidency in May 2010 with a strong mandate and clear policy priorities to strengthen environmental protections, security, and family welfare. While she initially enjoyed strong public approval, by July 2011, public opinion polls demonstrated that only about one-quarter of those surveyed had confidence in her administration. Five cabinet ministers resigned during her first 15 months in office.

In February 2011, Chinchilla revealed a 10-year crime plan, which aims to promote interagency coordination to combat growing public insecurity, crime, and narcotics trafficking. However, the plan lacks concrete policy proposals. Chinchilla's proposal for a 15 percent gambling tax to fund security initiatives faltered in March 2011, after intense lobbying efforts against the bill.

While the quality of life in Costa Rica is relatively high for the region, economic growth is hampered by the national debt, inflation, and cost-of-living increases. The global economic crisis has further threatened economic stability in the country, though the economy posted a modest recovery in 2010 and 2011. Chinchilla signed free-trade agreements with China, which went into effect in 2011, and Singapore in April 2010 in an effort to increase foreign investment and reverse the trend of growing poverty.

Political Rights and Civil Liberties:

Costa Rica is an electoral democracy. The 2010 legislative and presidential elections were considered free and fair. The president and members of the 57-seat, unicameral Legislative Assembly are elected for single four-year terms and can seek a nonconsecutive second term. The main political parties are the PLN, the PAC, the PML, and the PUSC. A special chamber of the Supreme Court chooses an independent national election commission. Ahead of the 2010 elections, Costa Rica approved reforms to its electoral law, including revised regulations on political party and campaign financing, and new quotas for women's participation in political parties. Women were elected to 39 percent of the Legislative Assembly seats in the 2010 elections.

Every president since 1990 has been accused of corruption after leaving office, with the exception of Óscar Arias. In 2010, Rodrigo Arias, brother of Óscar Arias, was accused of misusing funds from the Central American Bank of Economic Integration. Although the initial investigation by the government was quickly dropped due to pressure from Arias's allies, the investigation was reopened in 2011; he was ultimately absolved by the Supreme Court. In April 2011, former president Miguel Ángel Rodríguez was sentenced to five years in prison following his conviction on corruption charges. In 2009, former president Rafael Ángel Calderón was convicted on embezzlement charges. Though his conviction was upheld in May 2011, his five-year sentence was reduced. Costa Rica was ranked 50 out of 183 countries surveyed in Transparency International's 2011 Corruption Perceptions Index.

The Costa Rican media are generally free from state interference. A February 2010 Supreme Court ruling removed prison terms for defamation. There are six privately owned dailies, and both public and commercial broadcast outlets are available, including at least four private television stations and more than 100 private radio stations. There have been reports of abuse of government advertising and direct pressure from senior officials to influence media content. Internet access is unrestricted.

The government recognizes freedom of religion. President Arias backed a 2009 bill that sought to declare Costa Rica a "secular state," rather than a Roman Catholic state; however, the bill, which is not supported by current president Laura Chinchilla, had not been adopted by the end of 2011. Academic freedom is respected.

The constitution provides for freedoms of assembly and association, and numerous nongovernmental organizations (NGOs) are active. Although labor unions organize and mount frequent protests with minimal governmental interference, employers often ignore minimum wage and social security laws, and the resulting fines are insignificant.

The judicial branch is independent, with members elected by the legislature. However, there are often substantial delays in the judicial process and long pretrial detention. There have been complaints of police brutality, which are collected by an ombudsman's office. An attempted prison break at a maximum-security facility in May 2011 led to an investigation of prison conditions, which revealed corruption, overcrowding, guard shortages, and guard-initiated abuse.

Growing public insecurity, crime, and narcotics trafficking have been closely tied to the country's Pacific Coast serving as a major drug transshipment route. Organized criminal networks are also suspected of having infiltrated police and political institutions. The U.S. Department of State added Costa Rica to its list of major drug transit and drug trafficking countries in 2010. The country's homicide rate rose dramatically in 2011, to an estimated 11.3 murders per every 100,000 people. During her first year in office, President Laura Chinchilla created a national antidrug commission, hired 1,000 new police officers, earmarked additional funds for the country's judicial investigation agency, and made plans to expand prison capacity. As Costa Rica has no standing army, Chinchilla also agreed in July 2010 to station more than 13,000 U.S. military personnel on Costa Rican territory to lead regional antidrug efforts.

A 2006 law permits security forces to raid any home, business, or vehicle where they suspect undocumented immigrants, who can then be detained indefinitely. Abuse and extortion of migrants by the border guard have also been reported. Reforms made to migration law that went into effect in March 2010 include fines for employers who hire undocumented immigrants and stricter controls over marriages between Costa Ricans and foreigners.

Indigenous rights are not a government priority, and NGOs estimate that about 73 percent of the country's 70,000 indigenous people have little access to health and education services, electricity, or potable water. Costa Ricans of African descent have also faced racial and economic discrimination.

Women still face discrimination in the economic realm. Female domestic workers are subject to exploitation; they lack legal protections, receive the lowest minimum wage, and are excluded from social security programs. Despite the existence of domestic violence legislation, violence against women and children is a major problem. Costa Rica has failed to enforce anti-trafficking legislation and remains a transit and destination country for trafficked persons. The country was downgraded from Tier 1 to Tier 2 in the 2011 US Department of State's Trafficking in Persons Report.

President Chinchilla faced criticism from civil society organizations and gay rights advocates when she supported a referendum put forth by conservative groups against same-sex unions. However, the Constitutional Court ruled in August 2010 that holding a referendum on this issue was unconstitutional. In October 2011, the Supreme Court ruled against sexual orientation as grounds for discrimination by overturning a penitentiary regulation that had prohibited conjugal visits for same-sex prisoners.

Côte d'Ivoire

Political Rights: 6*
Civil Liberties: 6
Status: Not Free

Population: 22,621,000
Capital: Yamoussoukro (official); Abidjan (de facto)

Ratings Change: Côte d'Ivoire's political rights rating improved from 7 to 6 as a result of Alassane Ouattara, the president-elect, finally assuming office in April 2011, after deposing former president Laurent Gbagbo, who refused to relinquish power after losing the presidential election in November 2010.

Ten-Year Ratings Timeline For Year Under Review (Political Rights, Civil Liberties, Status)

2002	2003	2004	2005	2006	2007	2008	2009	2010	2011
6,6NF	6,5NF	6,6NF	6,6NF	7,6NF	7,5NF	6,5NF	6,5NF	7,6NF	6,6NF

Overview: **A long-delayed presidential election was finally held at the end of 2010, but the incumbent, Laurent Gbagbo, refused to relinquish power after losing to opponent Alassane Ouattara, leading to a protracted conflict in 2011 in which both claimed the presidency. The conflict left 3,000 dead and an estimated one million displaced before Ouattara finally assumed power in April 2011 and Gbagbo was arrested. A Truth and Reconciliation Commission was formed to investigate the committed atrocities, but lawlessness and impunity continued to pervade the country. Ouattara's Rally of the Republicans party captured the largest number of seats in the December 2011 parliamentary elections, the first held in over a decade.**

Côte d'Ivoire gained independence from France in 1960, and its first president, Félix Houphouët-Boigny, ruled until his death in 1993, presiding over a period of economic prosperity. Henri Konan Bédié, then the Speaker of the National Assembly, assumed power and won a fraudulent election in 1995. Bédié popularized the interpretation of "Ivoirité," emphasizing that only those from ethnic groups originating from the south of the country were "true" Ivoirians, to disqualify and discredit his opponent, Alassane Ouattara, for his alleged Burkinabe origins.

General Robert Guéï seized power in 1999 and declared himself the winner of an October 2000 presidential election after initial results showed that he was losing to opposition politician Laurent Gbagbo. Guéï was soon toppled by a popular uprising, and Gbagbo, who was eventually declared the winner, refused to call new polls. The postelection violence cost hundreds of civilian lives and deepened the divisions between north and south, as well as between Muslims and Christians. In the December 2000 legislative elections, Gbagbo's Ivorian Popular Front (FPI) won 96 seats, while Bédié's Democratic Party of Côte d'Ivoire–African Democratic Rally (PDCI-RDA) took 94, and smaller parties and independents won the remainder.

Civil war erupted in September 2002, when some 700 soldiers mounted a coup attempt, and government forces killed Guéï under unclear circumstances on the first day of fighting. Rebel forces quickly took control of the north and called for Gbagbo to step down. This call was echoed by other rebels in the west. By December 2002, the rebel factions had united to form the New Forces (FN), led by Guillaume Soro.

Gbagbo's government and the FN signed a French-brokered ceasefire in 2003, but it soon broke down. In April 2005, South African president Thabo Mbeki brokered a new peace accord that set general elections for the end of that year. However, because the requisite disarmament and poll preparations were not completed in time, the African Union postponed the elections, extended Gbagbo's term, and appointed an interim prime minister, economist Charles Konan Banny. Similar delays prevented elections from taking place again in 2006. With the expiration of Gbagbo's extended mandate in October 2006, the UN Security Council passed a resolution transferring all political and military power to the prime minister until the next elections. Gbagbo refused to accept the move and called for the withdrawal of all foreign troops.

In March 2007, Gbagbo and Soro met in Burkina Faso and signed an entirely new peace deal, the Ouagadougou Political Accord (APO), according to which Soro was appointed interim prime minister until elections could be held. The situation began to slowly improve, and the "confidence zone" separating the two parts of the country was officially dismantled.

Despite the more peaceful climate, the elections envisioned in the APO were postponed five times over the next three years. Less than 12,000 of more than 30,000 FN troops and almost none of the pro-Gbagbo militia groups slated for formal disarmament actually went through the process. Some progress was made during this period on voter registration, particularly among previously disenfranchised groups in the north, who were seen as foreigners by the southern ethnic groups who bought into the notion of "Ivoirité." Nonetheless, the registration effort was badly organized, cumbersome, and frequently contested by both sides of the political divide.

The first round of the long-awaited presidential election was finally held on October 31, 2010, and was deemed relatively free and fair by domestic and international observers. Gbagbo led with 38 percent of the vote, and Ouattara of the Rally of the Republicans (RDR) party placed second with 32 percent. Bédié of the PDCI-RDA, who came in third with 25 percent, threw his support behind Ouattara ahead of the November 28 runoff. The day of the runoff itself was relatively peaceful, and UN and European Union observers generally approved of the polling, but violence increased considerably during the period before the results were officially announced, with pro-Gbagbo militiamen directly attacking Ouattara's campaign headquarters on December 1.

On December 2, the Electoral Commission, backed by the United Nations, formally announced that Ouattara had won with 54 percent of the vote. The Constitutional Council, which was filled with Gbagbo loyalists, quickly annulled the results from largely pro-Ouattara northern districts, alleging widespread fraud, and announced that Gbagbo had in fact won with 51 percent. By December 4, both Gbagbo and Ouattara had been sworn in as president in separate, conflicting ceremonies.

This standoff led to a protracted conflict involving former FN rebels and other volunteer pro-Ouattara fighters on one side, and Gbagbo's security forces and

Young Patriots and other militia groups on the other, leading to the death of approximately 3,000 civilians and the displacement of up to one million between December 2010 and April 2011. After months of fighting, Ouattara launched a military offense throughout the country in March, with the support of French and UN troops backed by a Security Council resolution, that ended in the successful seizure of the presidential palace and the arrest of former president Laurent Gbagbo.

According to the United Nations, forces on both sides of the conflict were guilty of committing atrocities during the conflict. However, it is widely believed that pro-Ouattara forces are responsible for the single largest massacre of the period, in which up to 1,000 people are believed to have been murdered in a single day in March in the western town of Duékoué. Ouattara's government has since instituted a Truth and Reconciliation Commission and has agreed to allow the International Criminal Court (ICC) to investigate those most responsible. However, although Gbagbo was transferred to The Hague on four charges of crimes against humanity and appeared before the court for the first time in December 2011, the national courts had yet to press charges against any pro-Ouattara forces by year's end.

While the situation on the ground is slowly stabilizing with significant financial backing from the likes of the International Monetary Fund, the African Development Bank, and the French and U.S. governments, serious problems remain. One of the main problems is Ouattara's security forces, the Republican Forces of Côte d'Ivoire (FRCI), who are largely disorganized and able to roam the country committing crimes with impunity. FRCI troops are currently an amalgamation of former FN rebels and former Gbagbo troops, many of whom still wear different uniforms and have little trust in one another.

UN troops and members of Oattara's security force were enlisted to help ensure a peaceful parliamentary election on December 11, 2011. While international observers judged them to have been carried out in a largely peaceful and fair manner, turnout was significantly lower than for the previous year's presidential election. Gbagbo's party, the FPI, instituted a boycott, accusing the Electoral Commission of bias and Ouattara's security forces of intimidation. Ouattara's RDR party took just over 42 percent of the seats, while the PDCI-RDA captured nearly 29 percent.

Political Rights and Civil Liberties: Côte d'Ivoire is not an electoral democracy. While, December 2011 saw the first largely peaceful and fair parliamentary elections in over a decade, President Alassane Ouattara governed by decree until the legislative elections were held. The constitution provides for the popular election of a president and a 225-seat unicameral National Assembly for five-year terms. In 2011, Ouattara reappointed former rebel leader Guillaume Soro as prime minister, who had resigned in December 2010 in protest of Gbagbo's refusal to step down. Soro and other former rebel leaders, to whom Ouattara is greatly indebted, appear to have significant influence over his policy decisions.

Ouattara's RDR party dominates the political scene, followed by the PDCI-RDA. Gbagbo's FPI party is in ruins and continues to demand a complete overhaul of the Electoral Commission.

Corruption is a serious problem, and perpetrators rarely face prosecution or public exposure. Under Gbagbo, earnings from informal taxes and the sale of cocoa, cotton, and weapons gave many of those in power, including members of the military and rebel forces, an incentive to obstruct peace and political normalization. In August 2011, Ouattara instructed his ministers to sign an antigraft code of ethics in order to eliminate corruption, largely to improve the country's prospects of foreign investment.

Despite constitutional protections, press freedom is generally not respected in practice. Violence against journalists increased in 2011. Both sides of the conflict directly targeted journalists who criticized them or were in any way affiliated with the opposition, forcing many to stop working or to flee the country. After Gbagbo's arrest, media outlets loyal to the former leader were shut down, and the pro-Gbagbo, state-owned Radio-Télévision Ivoirienne was replaced by the pro-Ouattara Télévision Côte d'Ivoire, leading to a monopoly over the flow of information until opposition papers were able to resume printing in May.

Legal guarantees of religious freedom are typically upheld. However, the north-south political divide corresponds roughly with the distribution of the Muslim and Christian populations. While individuals were not targeted during the conflict because of their religion, religious services and houses of worship were used to single people out for attack.

Academic freedom was already severely limited under Gbagbo, with progovernment student organizations, such as the Student Federation of Côte d'Ivoire (FESCI), engaging in systematic intimidation on campuses. In 2011, universities throughout the country were closed and occupied by military forces from both sides that used them for military bases and training grounds. Students either left or joined the militias as volunteer fighters. In May, the militias were ordered to vacate university campuses. Many professors recommended that the 2010-2011 academic year be cancelled entirely.

The constitution protects the right to free assembly, but it is often denied in practice. Under Ouattara, security forces targeted former Gbagbo supporters, or even those who share the same ethnic group as his supporters, forcing them to stay under ground or in exile. While it is unlikely that Ouattara ordered these attacks, they went unpunished. An initial coordinated effort by FPI party members and Gbagbo supporters to demonstrate in October 2011 was prevented by the government for fear of violence, but a second attempt near the end of the month was permitted and was carried out peacefully. Freedom of association improved in 2011, with international nongovernmental organizations (NGOs) able to operate more freely than they were under the Gbagbo administration, particularly as the violence dissipated. Domestic NGOs also began to speak out and operate regularly and were not directly targeted.

The right to organize and join labor unions is constitutionally guaranteed, and workers have the right to bargain collectively. While these rights were not directly attacked in 2011, unions suffered greatly during the crisis, becoming disorganized and largely ineffectual.

The judiciary is not independent. Judges are political appointees without tenure and are highly susceptible to external interference and bribes. While there were hopes that this situation would change under Ouattara, national, regional, and military courts that began to prosecute crimes committed during the crisis targeted Gbagbo supporters exclusively. Nonetheless, the government officially launched a

Truth and Reconciliation Commission in September, and Ouattara agreed to allow the International Criminal Court to begin investigating the most egregious crimes in October.

The security situation markedly deteriorated in 2011. There was a rapid surge in the proliferation of small arms throughout the country, seriously setting back any progress that had been made on disarmament in previous years. The situation was particularly dire in the west, where members of ethnic groups who supported Gbagbo fled to Liberia and are afraid to return for fear of persecution and attack by the FRCI. Untrained civilian youth were also heavily recruited to join the fighting, and many have now been incorporated into the FRCI. The United Nations extended the mandate of its approximately 8,000 peacekeeping troops and sent an additional 2,000 troops in March to support the ousting of former president Gbagbo.

Côte d'Ivoire's cocoa and other industries have historically depended on workers from neighboring countries, particularly in the west, but conflicts between immigrant groups and longer-term residents have played a significant part in the current conflict. Gbagbo's repeated use of xenophobic language, and the reciprocal violence against the ethnic groups that supported Gbagbo, were driving forces behind the 2011 conflict.

Economic freedom and employment also suffered as a result of the conflict, with businesses across the country, including those in the cocoa and chocolate industries, forced to close. Even after the conflict, in an effort to clean up Abidjan, government forces forcibly removed numerous small businesses in Abidjan and bulldozed houses. While many of these were built illegally, others had permits that the government disregarded.

In the past, Côte d'Ivoire has made symbolic efforts to combat child trafficking, but tens of thousands of children from all over the region are believed to be working on Ivorian plantations; virtually no attention was paid to this issue in 2011.

Despite official support for their constitutional rights, women suffer widespread legal and economic discrimination. Rape was reportedly common during the 2002 civil war, and was again a major problem during the 2011 conflict. The law does not specifically criminalize domestic violence, which is a widespread problem. Women are also heavily underrepresented in government and decision-making positions, filling just 11 percent of seats in the National Assembly following the December 2011 elections.

Croatia

Political Rights: 1
Civil Liberties: 2
Status: Free

Population: 4,405,000
Capital: Zagreb

Ten-Year Ratings Timeline For Year Under Review (Political Rights, Civil Liberties, Status)

2002	2003	2004	2005	2006	2007	2008	2009	2010	2011
2,2F	2,2F	2,2F	2,2F	2,2F	2,2F	2,2F	1,2F	1,2F	1,2F

Overview: **Croatia completed European Union (EU) accession negotiations in June 2011, with membership expected in 2013. The government made progress on key EU reforms and continued to cooperate with the International Criminal Tribunal for the former Yugoslavia in a year that saw significant war crimes convictions. The opposition coalition Kukuriku defeated the ruling Croatian Democratic Union in December parliamentary elections.**

Formerly a constituent republic within socialist Yugoslavia, Croatia held its first multiparty elections in 1990, which were won by the former communist general and dissident Franjo Tudman and his Croatian Democratic Union (HDZ). Independence was subsequently declared in June 1991 under Tudman's leadership. From 1991–95, Croatia was consumed by the wars accompanying Yugoslavia's disintegration, both on its own territory, where the indigenous Serb population attempted to secede, and in neighboring Bosnia and Herzegovina.

Tudman's HDZ continued to rule Croatia until his death in December 1999. An erstwhile Tudman ally, Stjepan Mesic, was elected president in January 2000, and parliamentary elections held later that month resulted in a victory for a center-left coalition led by the Social Democratic Party (SDP). Ivica Racan, leader of the SDP, became prime minister.

The HDZ returned to power in 2003 under the leadership of Prime Minister Ivo Sanader and refashioned itself as a conventional European center-right party. The Sanader government's foreign and domestic policies focused on gaining Croatia's acceptance into NATO and the European Union (EU). Croatia formally joined NATO in April 2009.

The HDZ, which won the November 2007 parliamentary elections, formed a governing coalition with the Croatian Peasant Party, the Croatian Social Liberal Party, and seven of the country's eight ethnic minority parliamentary representatives. In July 2009, Sanader unexpectedly resigned, and was replaced by Jadranka Kosor, a deputy prime minister of the HDZ. In January 2010, after two rounds of elections to replace President Mesic, SDP candidate Ivo Josipovic was victorious, capturing 60 percent of a runoff vote.

Government corruption dominated public debate throughout 2010 and remained prominent in 2011. In October, the State Attorney's Office for the Suppression of Corruption and Organized Crime (USKOK) expanded its ongoing investigation into the so-called Fimi media case, which includes indictments of Sanader and other HDZ officials, to include the HDZ as a legal entity. In Croatia's first legal case against a political party, the HDZ is accused of funneling money from public companies to a slush fund from 2003 to 2009. In November, a Croatian court added two other corruption indictments against Sanader.

Croatia made strides in 2011 to cooperate with the International Criminal Tribunal for the former Yugoslavia (ICTY), a pre-condition for EU membership. In April, the court convicted Croatian army generals Ante Gotovina and Mladen Markac of crimes against humanity for participating in Operation Storm, a 1995 campaign to remove ethnic Serbs from the Krajina, a self-proclaimed Serb republic within Croatia that existed from 1991 to 1995.

Though Croatia's EU bid had stalled in recent years over concerns about insufficient cooperation with the ICTY, mixed results at reducing corruption, and a territorial dispute with Slovenia, the country closed the final 4 of 35 accession negotiation chapters required to join the EU in 2011. Noting reform progress in two key chapters—judiciary and fundamental rights and competition policy—the European Commission (EC), the leading body of the EU, cleared Croatia to sign the Accession Treaty, which Josipovic and Kosor did in Brussels on December 9. Croatia should become the 28th EU member state in July 2013, following ratification procedures.

In the December 4 parliamentary elections, the center-left opposition Kukuriku coalition, comprising the SDP and three other parties, placed first with 80 seats. The HDZ and its coalition partners, the Croatian Civic Party and the Democratic Centre, followed with 47 seats. Zoran Milanovic of the SDP succeeded Kosor as prime minister.

Political Rights and Civil Liberties:

Croatia is an electoral democracy. The 151-member unicameral parliament (Sabor) comprises 140 members from 10 geographical districts; in addition, 8 members represent ethnic minorities, with 3 representing Croatians living abroad. Members are elected to four-year terms. The president, who serves as head of state, is elected by popular vote for a maximum of two five-year terms. The prime minister is appointed by the president and requires parliamentary approval.

The largest political parties are the center-right HDZ and center-left SDP. Several smaller parties have also won representation in the parliament.

In 2011, the EC noted that Croatia had made progress on anticorruption efforts, including operational upgrades to USKOK, specifically the hiring of new staff and the resolution of several prominent public misconduct cases. However, most high-profile cases remain unresolved. In addition to the indictments against former prime minister Ivo Sanader, former prime minister Jadranka Kosor was implicated, though not indicted, in the Fimi media case. Croatia was ranked 66 out of 183 countries surveyed in Transparency International's 2011 Corruption Perceptions Index.

The constitution guarantees freedoms of expression and the press. While these rights are generally respected, reporters face political pressure and intimidation. The journalist Drago Hedl reported receiving death threats for his reporting on war crimes and misconduct in the Catholic church. Investigative journalists covering organized crime and corruption are also subject to intimidation and attack. Internet access is unrestricted.

The constitution guarantees freedom of religion. A group needs at least 500 members and five years of registered operation to be recognized as a religious organization. Members of the Serbian Orthodox Church continue to report cases of intimidation and vandalism, although such incidents are declining as memories of the 1991–95 war recede. Little progress has been made in restoring property nationalized by the communists to non-Roman Catholic groups.

Academic freedom is guaranteed by law. The EU is advising Croatia on higher education reform to increase tertiary education rates.

The constitution provides for freedoms of association and assembly. According to Amnesty International (AI), participants in a June 2011 gay pride parade in Split reported that police failed to provide adequate protection after they were attacked by extremists. Police arrested 137 people, whose cases were pending at year's end. A variety of nongovernmental organizations operate in Croatia without governmental interference or harassment. The constitution allows workers to form and join trade unions, and they do so freely. The International Trade Union Confederation has nevertheless criticized the government for endangering the right of collective bargaining as a result of legislation passed in 2009.

The judicial system suffers from excessively long trials, inadequate implementation of court decisions, and murky criteria for the selection of judges. In October 2011, the EC praised Croatia for progress in judicial reform, citing new methods for appointing and evaluating judges and public prosecutors and the opening of the State School for Judicial Officials. While implementation of an integrated case management system in most courts has improved efficiency and helped reduce case backlogs in recent years, the backlog of civil cases older than three years remains a problem. Prison conditions do not fully meet international standards due to overcrowding and poor medical care.

The legacy of the 1991–95 war in Croatia remains a sensitive issue. In December 2010, AI reported that Croatia was processing an average of only 18 war crimes trials annually. The group continues to criticize Croatia for failing to identify the total number of war crimes cases and prosecute them expeditiously. In February 2011, Croatia introduced a new strategy for addressing impunity, though it was not fully implemented by year's end, and it recently concluded several war crimes cases against defendants of different ethnic backgrounds. Although AI praised the 2011 convictions of Ante Gotovina and Mladen MarkaC, it criticized former prime minister Kosor for publicly thanking the generals in August.

Respect for minority rights has improved over the past decade. Although returning Serbs face harassment by local populations, such incidents have declined over the last several years. Despite the 2002 Constitutional Act on the Rights of National Minorities and studies into the underrepresentation of minorities in the public sector, minorities, including Serbs, remain underemployed. Approximately 70,000 Croatian Serbs are registered refugees. The Action Plan on the Housing Care Program to aid returning refugees was fully implemented in October 2011, though further progress is needed on providing housing for returnees. The Roma population also faces discrimination and widespread poverty.

The constitution prohibits gender discrimination. However, women have a higher unemployment rate and earn less than men. Though Croatia's 2008 Gender Equality Act calls for women to be equally represented on candidate lists, the Organization for Security and Cooperation in Europe faults the law as unclear. Only 35 percent of candidates in the December 2011 election were women. Domestic violence against women is believed to be widespread and underreported, though law enforcement is strengthening its capacity to combat such crimes. Croatia remains a transit country for women trafficked to Western Europe for prostitution.

Cuba

Political Rights: 7
Civil Liberties: 6
Status: Not Free

Population: 11,240,000
Capital: Havana

Ten-Year Ratings Timeline For Year Under Review (Political Rights, Civil Liberties, Status)

2002	2003	2004	2005	2006	2007	2008	2009	2010	2011
7,7NF	7,7NF	7,7NF	7,7NF	7,7NF	7,7NF	7,6NF	7,6NF	7,6NF	7,6NF

Overview: **In 2011, the government continued its negotiated release of the 52 remaining political prisoners from a 2003 crackdown on democratic activists. In total, 166 political prisoners were freed under an agreement with the Roman Catholic Church and the Spanish government, though a sharp increase in politically motivated short-term detentions was reported during the year. In April, the ruling Cuban Communist Party held its Sixth Congress, at which President Raúl Castro formally replaced his brother, former president Fidel Castro, as the party's first secretary. In October, as part of the government's incremental relaxation of long-standing economic restrictions on individuals, Cubans obtained greater leeway to buy and sell privately owned cars and houses.**

Cuba achieved independence from Spain in 1898 as a result of the Spanish-American War. The Republic of Cuba was established in 1902 but remained under U.S. tutelage until 1934. In 1959, the U.S.-supported dictatorship of Fulgencio Batista was overthrown by Fidel Castro's July 26th Movement. Castro declared his affiliation with communism shortly thereafter, and the island has been governed as a one-party state ever since.

Following the 1991 collapse of the Soviet Union and the end of roughly $5 billion in annual Soviet subsidies, Castro opened some sectors of the economy to direct foreign investment. The legalization of the U.S. dollar in 1993 created a new source of inequality, as access to dollars from remittances or through the tourist industry enriched some, while the majority continued to live on peso wages averaging less than $10 a month. Meanwhile, the authorities remained highly intolerant of political dissent, enacting harsh new sedition legislation in 1999 and mounting a series of campaigns to undermine the reputations of leading opposition figures by portraying them as agents of the United States.

In 2002, the Varela Project, a referendum initiative seeking broad changes to the socialist system, won significant international recognition. However, the constitutional committee of the National Assembly rejected the referendum proposal, and the government instead held a counterreferendum in which 8.2 million people supposedly declared the socialist system to be "untouchable." The government initiated a crackdown on the prodemocracy opposition in March 2003. Seventy-five people, including 27 independent journalists, 14 independent librarians, and dozens of signature collectors for the Varela Project, were sentenced to an average of 20 years in prison following one-day trials held in April.

In July 2006, Fidel Castro passed power on a provisional basis to his younger brother, defense minister and first vice president Raúl Castro, after internal bleeding forced him to undergo surgery. The 81-year-old Fidel resigned as president in February 2008, and Raúl, 76, formally replaced him. Though officially retired, Fidel remained in the public eye through the release of carefully selected newspaper columns, photographs, and video clips.

The government approved a series of economic reforms in March 2008. These included allowing ordinary Cubans to buy consumer electronic goods and stay in the country's tourist hotels, eliminating salary caps, and raising pensions for the country's more than two million retirees. However, two hurricane strikes and a global economic downturn late in the year sent the Cuban economy into a crisis that halted the tentative reform process.

In 2009, the government began to distribute land leases to agricultural workers, but other key aspects of the reform agenda remained stalled. Cuba's heavy dependence on imports led to a shortage of foreign exchange, forcing layoffs and closures of many state enterprises.

In August 2010, the government approved an initiative that allowed foreign investors to obtain 99-year property leases. A month later, it was announced that up to 1.5 million workers would be laid off from public sector jobs over the next 18 months, while 178 economic activities would be allowed in the private sector, subject to high taxes. However, in March 2011, Raúl Castro stated that a five-year timeline for the public sector layoff process would be more realistic. Eased rules on private home and car sales were announced later in 2011.

From July 2010 to March 2011, as a result of negotiations with the Roman Catholic Church and the Spanish government, Cuban authorities released 166 political prisoners, including the 52 remaining from the 2003 crackdown on independent journalists and dissidents. While most released activists went into exile, 12 remained in Cuba under "extrapenal" license, a form of parole granted to prisoners facing health or other problems that may have arisen during their incarceration. The Damas de Blanco, a group of female relatives of the 2003 political prisoners, continued their protests during 2011 despite repeated episodes of harassment from authorities and regime supporters, and the death of their leader, Laura Pollán, in October.

Even as the long-term political prisoners were released, the government significantly increased the number of short-term detentions, making them the preferred form of repression. Other abuses by the authorities also continued. In May, dissident Juan Wilfredo Soto García died after a police beating in Santa Clara.

U.S. government contractor Alan Gross, who was arrested in December 2009 for distributing communications equipment to Jewish groups in Cuba, was sentenced to 15 years in prison in March 2011, after a court found him guilty of engaging in "subversive" activities aimed at undermining Cuban sovereignty. Meanwhile, the U.S. government eased travel restrictions but maintained its economic sanctions on the island.

Political Rights and Civil Liberties: Cuba is not an electoral democracy. Longtime president Fidel Castro and his brother, current president Raúl Castro, dominate the one-party political system, in which the Communist Party of Cuba (PCC) controls all government institutions. The 1976 constitution provides for a National Assembly, which designates the Council of State. This body in turn appoints the Council of Ministers in consultation with its president, who serves as chief of state and head of government. Raúl Castro is now president of the Council of Ministers and the Council of State, commander in chief of the armed forces, and first secretary of the PCC. In April 2011, the PCC held its Sixth Congress. In addition to electing Raúl Castro as head of the party, congressional delegates appointed a greater number of high-level military officials to the PCC Politburo and Central Committee, and failed to renew these leadership structures by adding younger party members. A National Conference of the PCC, scheduled for January 2012, will discuss organizational and political issues, including Raúl Castro's proposal to impose a limit of two five-year terms on elected public officials.

In the January 2008 National Assembly elections, as in previous elections, voters were asked to either support or reject a single PCC-approved candidate for each of the 614 seats. All candidates received the requisite 50 percent approval, with Raúl Castro winning support from over 99 percent of voters. In April 2010, Cuba held elections for the roughly 15,000 delegates to the country's 169 Popular Municipal Assemblies, or municipal councils, which are elected every two and a half years.

All political organizing outside the PCC is illegal. Political dissent, whether spoken or written, is a punishable offense, and dissidents frequently receive years of imprisonment for seemingly minor infractions. The regime has also called on its neighborhood-watch groups, known as Committees for the Defense of the Revolution, to strengthen vigilance against "antisocial behavior," a euphemism for opposition activity. Dissident leaders have reported an increase in intimidation and harassment by state-sponsored groups as well as short-term detentions by state security forces. The absolute number of politically motivated short-term detentions in Cuba increased from 2,078 in 2010 to 4,123 in 2011. Meanwhile, the total number of longer-term political prisoners decreased from 167 as of July 2010 to an estimated 73 as of December 2011. In December 2011, the Cuban government released 2,999 prisoners who had mostly fulfilled their sentence, but only 7 of those had been imprisoned for political reasons.

Official corruption remains a serious problem, with a culture of illegality shrouding the mixture of private and state-controlled economic activities that are allowed on the island. The Raúl Castro government has made the fight against corruption a central priority. In May 2011, Chilean businessman and former Castro associate Max Marambio was sentenced in absentia to 20 years in prison—along with former Cuban food minister Alejandro Roca, who received a 15- year sentence—after being found guilty of economic distortion and fraud. In June, the Cuban authorities sentenced 10 high-level government officials to three to five years in person after being convicted of corruption tied to the Marambio case. In addition, the authorities closed the offices of Canadian companies Tri-Star Caribbean and the Tokmakjian Group in August, and arrested the deputy sugar industry minister a month later amid a corruption investigation. Cuba was ranked 61 out of 183 countries surveyed in Transparency International's 2011 Corruption Perceptions Index.

The news media are owned and controlled by the state. The government considers the independent press to be illegal and uses Ministry of Interior agents to infiltrate and report on the outlets in question. Independent journalists, particularly those associated with the dozen small news agencies that have been established outside state control, are subject to harassment by state security agents. Foreign news agencies may only hire local reporters through government offices, limiting employment opportunities for independent journalists. Nevertheless, some state media, such as the newspaper *Juventud Rebelde*, have begun to cover previously taboo topics, such as corruption in the health and education sectors.

Access to the internet remains tightly controlled, and it is difficult for most Cubans to connect from their homes. The estimated internet penetration rate is less than 3 percent. Websites are closely monitored, and while there are state-owned internet cafes in major cities, the costs are prohibitively high for most residents. Only selected state employees have workplace access to e-mail and restricted access to websites deemed inappropriate by the Ministry of Communications. There are an estimated 25 independent, journalistic bloggers working on the island. Although they have faced some episodes of harassment, they have avoided close links to dissidents and are not subject to the same type of systematic persecution as other independent journalists. Blogger Yoani Sánchez has gained international acclaim, though few within Cuba can access the ironic and critical musings about life in Cuba on her blog, *Generation Y*.

In 1991, Roman Catholics and other believers were granted permission to join the PCC, and the constitutional reference to official atheism was dropped the following year. The Catholic Church has been playing an increasingly important role in civil society, mediating in the case of the 2,003 political prisoners, enabling discussion of topics of public concern, and offering material assistance to the population, especially in the countryside. In November 2011, the church began offering a master's in business administration (MBA) program that focuses on small and medium-sized enterprises. Nevertheless, official obstacles to religious freedom remain substantial. Churches are not allowed to conduct ordinary educational activities, and many church-based publications are subject to censorship by the Office of Religious Affairs. While Roman Catholicism is the traditionally dominant faith, an estimated 70 percent of the population practices some form of Afro-Cuban religion. And, as in the rest of Latin America, Protestantism is making rapid gains in Cuba.

The government restricts academic freedom. Teaching materials for subjects including mathematics and literature must contain ideological content. Affiliation with PCC structures is generally needed to gain access to educational institutions, and students' report cards carry information regarding their parents' involvement with the party.

Limited rights of assembly and association are permitted under the constitution. However, as with other constitutional rights, they may not be "exercised against the existence and objectives of the Socialist State." The unauthorized assembly of more than three people, even for religious services in private homes, is punishable with up to three months in prison and a fine. This rule is selectively enforced and is often used to imprison human rights advocates. Workers do not have the right to strike or bargain collectively. Members of independent labor unions, which the government considers illegal, are often harassed, dismissed from their jobs, and barred from future employment.

The Council of State, led by Raúl Castro, controls the courts and the judicial process as a whole. Beginning in 1991, the United Nations voted annually to assign a special investigator on human rights to Cuba, which consistently denied the appointee a visa. In 2007, the UN Human Rights Council ended the investigator position for Cuba. However, Raúl Castro authorized Cuban representatives to sign two UN human rights treaties in 2008. Cuba does not grant international humanitarian organizations access to its prisons.

Afro-Cubans have frequently complained about widespread discrimination by government and law enforcement officials. Many Afro-Cubans have only limited access to the dollar-earning sectors of the economy, such as tourism and joint ventures with foreign companies.

Since 2008, Cuba has made important strides to redress discrimination against the lesbian, gay, bisexual, and transgender (LGBT) community, thanks in part to the advocacy work of Mariela Castro, director of the National Center for Sexual Education (CENESEX) and Raúl Castro's daughter. The government has helped to sponsor an annual International Day Against Homophobia, and the Ministry of Public Health has authorized government-provided sex-change surgeries for transsexuals. Nonetheless, a bill proposing the legalization of same-sex marriages has been stalled in the National Assembly since 2008. Moreover, the authorities do not recognize the work of independent, grassroots LGBT rights groups, and their efforts have often been attacked by CENESEX.

Freedom of movement and the right to choose one's residence and place of employment are severely restricted. Attempting to leave the island without permission is a punishable offense. Intercity migration or relocation, particularly to Havana, requires permission from the local Committee for the Defense of the Revolution and other authorities. Recent economic reforms offering a variety of incentives for rural production hint at a possible attempt to stem the historical tide of migration from the countryside to Havana.

Only state enterprises can enter into economic agreements with foreigners as minority partners; ordinary citizens cannot participate. PCC membership is still required to obtain good jobs, suitable housing, and real access to social services, including medical care and educational opportunities.

The government of Raúl Castro continued pressing forward with its incremental relaxation of economic restrictions on individuals in 2011. In September, the authorities approved three additional activities for private employment, and lowered taxes and eased regulations on others, as a way to incentivize growth in the *cuentapropista* (self-employment) sector. The number of self-employment licenses increased from 157,000 in October 2010 to over 338,000 in September 2011. In October, the government authorized Cubans to buy and sell privately owned cars as well as new vehicles, though strict regulations limit the ability of most citizens to participate. Similarly, a decree that took effect in November allowed Cubans to buy and sell houses without prior government approval, opening up the prospect of a real-estate market for the first time in 50 years.

The Cuban constitution establishes full equality of women. About 40 percent of all women work in the official labor force, and they are well represented in most professions. However, the ongoing economic reforms have begun to widen the gender gap in the labor force. As of August 2011, women represented only 22 percent of the licensed self-employed workers.

Cyprus

Political Rights: 1
Civil Liberties: 1
Status: Free

Population: 1,107,000
Capital: Nicosia

Note: The numerical ratings and status listed above do not reflect conditions in Northern Cyprus, which is examined in a separate report.

Ten-Year Ratings Timeline For Year Under Review (Political Rights, Civil Liberties, Status)

2002	2003	2004	2005	2006	2007	2008	2009	2010	2011
1,1F	1,1F	1,1F	1,1F	1,1F	1,1F	1,1F	1,1F	1,1F	1,1F

Overview: **Following May 2011 parliamentary elections, a massive explosion on a Cypriot naval base in July caused major political damage to the new coalition government of President Demetris Christofias. The accident imperiled prospects for unification with Northern Cyprus, as did an outbreak of tensions between Cyprus and Turkey over the exploration and exploitation of natural gas in the island's Exclusive Economic Zone.**

Cyprus gained independence from Britain in 1960 after a five-year guerrilla campaign by partisans demanding union with Greece. In July 1974, Greek Cypriot National Guard members, backed by Greece's military junta, staged an unsuccessful coup aimed at such unification. Five days later, Turkey invaded from the north, seizing control of 37 percent of the island.

Since then, a buffer zone known as the Green Line has divided Cyprus; the Greek and Turkish communities remain almost completely separated in the south and north, respectively. In 1983, Turkish-controlled Cyprus declared its independence, a move recognized only by Turkey. UN resolutions stipulate that Cyprus is a single country of which the northern third is illegally occupied.

In 2004, both parts of the island voted simultaniously on a unification plan prepared by then UN secretary general Kofi Annan. Ultimately, 76 percent of Greek Cypriots voted against the plan, while 65 percent of Turkish Cypriots voted in favor. With the island still divided, only Greek Cyprus joined the European Union (EU) as scheduled in May 2004.

In the 2008 presidential election, Demetris Christofias of the Progressive Party of the Working Republic (AKEL), a communist party, won 53 percent of a runoff vote, making him the only communist head of state in Europe. His cabinet included ministers from the Democratic Party (DIKO) as well as the Movement for Social Democrats (EDEK). Christofias had voiced a commitment toward unification, and met regularly with Northern Cypriot leaders. However, only symbolic progress was made in the years following his election, mostly in the form of UN-sponsored meetings and small border openings. Tripartite talks in January, March, and July 2011 between UN secretary-general Ban Ki-moon and representatives of Cyprus and Northern Cyprus failed to make substantial progress toward unification.

In parliamentary elections held in May 2011, the Democratic Rally (DISY) took 20 seats, AKEL won 19 seats, and DIKO took 9 seats; three small parties captured the remaining 8 seats. In July, a massive explosion of confiscated weaponry occurred on a naval base, killing the commander of the Cyprus Navy and severely threatening Cyprus's economy. The explosion nearly destroyed Cyprus' largest power plant, prompting waves of blackouts that jeopardized tourism and disrupted an already beleaguered financial system. The incident, considered the result of government oversight, resulted in the mass resignation of Christofias's cabinet, the withdrawal of DIKO from the coalition government, and widespread calls for the president's resignation.

The dissolution of Christofias's coalition, one of the most amenable to unification in decades, had a deleterious effect on negotiations with Northern Cyprus. Hope for unification had already been diminished by the election of a nationalist, antiunification Northern Cypriot government in 2010. Tensions were further exacerbated in 2011, when Cyprus became embroiled in a diplomatic dispute involving Turkey, Greece, and Israel over the exploration and extraction of natural resources, particularly natural gas, in the eastern Mediterranean Sea. Nevertheless, the international community has made a renewed push for a unification agreement in light of Cyprus's assumption of the EU presidency in July 2012.

Political Rights and Civil Liberties:

Cyprus is an electoral democracy. The president is elected by popular vote to serve a five-year term. The unicameral House of Representatives has 80 seats filled through proportional representation for five-year terms; 24 seats are reserved for the Turkish Cypriot community, but they have not been occupied since Turkish Cypriot representatives withdrew from the chamber in 1964.

Following a 2004 ruling against Cyprus by the European Court of Human Rights (ECHR), a law was passed allowing Turkish Cypriots living in the south to vote and run for office in Greek Cypriot elections. Turkish Cypriots cannot run for president, as the constitution states that a Greek Cypriot should hold that post and a Turkish Cypriot should be vice president. The Maronites (Levantine Catholics), Armenians, and Latins (Roman Catholics) elect special, nonvoting representatives.

Corruption is not a major problem in Cyprus. Laws passed in 2008 aimed to prevent conflicts of interest for government officials and criminalized the withholding of information on bribery in defense procurement. Cyprus was ranked 30 out of 183 countries surveyed in Transparency International's 2011 Corruption Perceptions Index. Parliamentary hearings on freedom of information in May 2009 indicated that many legal requests for information are not fulfilled, mostly due to lack of resources.

Freedom of speech is constitutionally guaranteed and generally respected. A vibrant independent press frequently criticizes the authorities, and several private television and radio stations compete effectively with public stations. Although Turkish Cypriot journalists can enter the south, Turkish journalists based in the north have reported difficulties crossing the border. In January 2010, Andis Hadjicostis, the owner of Cyprus's largest media group, was shot and killed outside his home. Four people were charged in the case, including a well-known television presenter who allegedly hired assassins after being fired from one of the victim's stations. Access to the internet is unrestricted.

Freedom of religion is guaranteed by the constitution and protected in practice. Nearly all inhabitants of the south are Orthodox Christians, and some discrimination against other religions has been alleged. In September 2009, more than 100 Muslims from rival sects clashed at a mosque in the capital. The police controversially arrested 150 people in a subsequent sweep; 36 were found to be illegal immigrants and faced deportation, while the remainder were released. State schools use textbooks containing negative language about Turkish Cypriots and Turkey.

Freedoms of association and assembly are generally respected, though Cyprus received international criticism in 2011 for putting Doros Polycarpou, director of the local human rights group KISA, on trial for illegal assembly. Polycarpou had organized a multicultural unity festival in the city of Larnaca in December 2010, which had been attacked by members of the far-right nationalist group ELAM; a Turkish Cypropt musician was stabbed during the incident. The trial was ongoing at year's end. Nongovernmental organizations (NGOs) generally operate without government interference. Workers have the right to strike and to form trade unions without employer authorization.

The independent judiciary operates according to the British tradition, upholding due process rights. However, the ECHR ruled against Cyprus in 2009 for failure to provide a timely trial in a case that lasted nearly six years. The problem of indefinite detentions of asylum seekers has improved somewhat since the country's ombudswoman filed complaints on the matter in 2008, but long-term detention of migrants continues. The Council of Europe and other groups have noted cases of police brutality, including targeted beatings of minorities. Prison overcrowding has decreased but remains a problem.

A 1975 agreement between the two sides of the island governs treatment of minorities. Turkish Cypriots are now entitled to Republic of Cyprus passports, and thousands have obtained them. However, Turkish Cypriots in the south have reported difficulty obtaining identity cards and other documents, as well as harassment and discrimination. Asylum seekers face regular discrimination, especially in employment, and KISA has warned of racially motivated attacks.

Since 2004, all citizens have been able to move freely throughout the island using a growing number of border crossings. While the Greek Cypriots have thwarted attempts to lift international trade and travel bans on the north, trade continues to increase between the two sides.

The status of property abandoned by those moving across the Green Line after the 1974 invasion is a point of contention in reunification talks. A 1991 law states that property left by Turkish Cypriots belongs to the state. Under the law in the north, Greek Cypriots can appeal to the Immovable Property Comission (IPC), which in March 2010 was recognized by the ECHR as an adequate local authority for the resolution of property disputes. As of October 2011, the IPC had processed 2,095 applications and settled 181 cases, in which more than $720 million have been dispersed.

Gender discrimination in the workplace, sexual harassment, and violence against women are problems in Cyprus. Women are underrepresented in government, with only three women in the cabinet and six in the parliament. While the government has made genuine progress in preventing human trafficking and launched a new anti-trafficking plan in 2010, Cyprus remains a transit and destination country, and prosecution is weak. In January 2010, the ECHR found Cyprus guilty of failing to protect a 20-year-old Russian woman who fell to her death while trying to escape a cabaret where she was forced to work.

Czech Republic

Political Rights: 1
Civil Liberties: 1
Status: Free

Population: 10,546,000
Capital: Prague

Ten-Year Ratings Timeline For Year Under Review (Political Rights, Civil Liberties, Status)

2002	2003	2004	2005	2006	2007	2008	2009	2010	2011
1,2F	1,2F	1,1F	1,1F	1,1F	1,1F	1,1F	1,1F	1,1F	1,1F

Overview: **In March 2011, the Constitutional Court struck down as unconstitutional austerity measures that the ruling coalition had pushed through Parliament via a legislative state of emergency in November 2010. The lower house of Parliament approved health-care and welfare reforms in June and major pension reforms in September, despite opposition from the Senate, President Václav Klaus, and the general public. Meanwhile, the government continued to face criticism for failing to adequately address the unfair treatment of Roma children in the education system.**

Czechoslovakia was created in 1918 amid the collapse of the Austro-Hungarian Empire. Soviet forces helped establish a communist government after World War II, and in 1968 they crushed the so-called Prague Spring, a period of halting political liberalization under reformist leader Alexander Dubcek.

In December 1989, a series of peaceful anticommunist demonstrations led by dissident Václav Havel and the Civic Forum opposition group resulted in the resignation of the government, in what became known as the Velvet Revolution. Open elections were held the following year. In 1992, a new constitution and the Charter of Fundamental Rights and Freedoms were adopted, and the country began an ambitious program of political and economic reform under Václav Klaus of the center-right Civic Democratic Party (ODS), who became prime minister that year. In 1993, the state dissolved peacefully into separate Czech and Slovak republics.

Close parliamentary elections in 1998 brought the center-left Czech Social

Democratic Party (CSSD) to power, though an "opposition agreement" between the CSSD and the ODS limited meaningful political competition and brought about several years of political gridlock. Klaus was elected president by Parliament in 2003. The Czech Republic joined the European Union (EU) in May 2004.

The 2006 lower house elections produced a chamber that was evenly divided between left- and right-leaning parties, leading to a series of short-lived, ODS-led coalitions and caretaker governments. The caretaker government headed by independent Jan Fischer led the government until May 2010, when parliamentary elections resulted in 56 and 53 seats in the lower house for CSSD and ODS, respectively. The center-right, free-market Tradition Responsibility Prosperity 09 (TOP 09) party placed third with 41 seats, followed by the Communist Party of Bohemia and Moravia (KSCM) with 26 seats, and the right-leaning Public Affairs (VV) party with 24 seats. In June, Klaus appointed ODS leader Petr Necas as prime minister, who formed a center-right coalition government with TOP 09 and VV.

In an effort to trim the budget deficit following a recession in 2009, the new government pledged to cut public sector wages by 10 percent in 2011 and replace seniority-based raises with a system of personal bonuses. The unpopular move allowed the opposition to gain control in the October 2010 Senate elections, giving the CSSD, along with other opposition parties, the power to obstruct legislation passed by the lower house, the Chamber of Deputies. In order to bypass the opposition, the lower house declared a legislative state of emergency at the end of October, allowing it to expedite the passage of several controversial austerity bills.

Throughout 2011, thousands of protestors demonstrated against the government's austerity package. Many claimed that the nation's financial problems were not the result of insufficient funds, but rather that public funds were being unfairly distributed. In April, the Constitutional Court rejected the government's austerity package and declared the fast-tracked legislation procedures unconstitutional. After months of infighting and a veto by the CSSD-controlled Senate, the lower house pushed through healt hcare and welfare reforms in June. In addition to altering pricing schemes, the bill divided health care into a two-tiered system, with basic care covered by public funds, and privately purchased so-called premium care. After a long battle against the opposition, the lower house passed major pension reforms in September that semi-privatize the system. The reforms were largely unpopular with the public.

Political Rights and Civil Liberties: The Czech Republic is an electoral democracy. The Chamber of Deputies, the lower house of Parliament, has 200 members elected for four-year terms by proportional representation. The Senate has 81 members elected for six-year terms, with one-third up for election every two years. The president, elected by Parliament for five-year terms, appoints judges, the prime minister, and other cabinet members, but has few other formal powers.

The two main political parties are the center-left CSSD and the center-right ODS. Two other right-leaning parties, TOP 09 and VV, entered Parliament for the first time in 2010.

Corruption and lack of transparency remain core structural problems, and government reforms have been slow. The authorities have consistently failed to fully investigate and follow through on corruption accusations brought against politicians. The European Commission issued a harsh warning in 2011 concerning the transparency of public tenders, cautioning that the lack of transparency could lead to a reduction in EU funding. A Center for Empirical Studies (STEM) poll released in June 2011 suggests that corruption may be a deeper problem than previously thought, with 83 percent of Czechs believing that most civil servants can be bribed. Several government ministers, including the trade and industry minister, were forced to resign in 2011 over corruption allegations or past dubious business deals. In 2011, former police officer Radka Kadlecova, who was convicted in 2009 of accepting bribes from foreigners applying for residence permits, received a presidential pardon that was allegedly the result of a bribe paid to the administration. President Vaclav Klaus provided no official reason for the pardon, and at Kadlecova reportedly had boasted to a psychologist about purchasing the pardon. The allegations were still under investigation at year's end.

Freedom of expression is respected, though the Charter of Fundamental Rights and Freedoms—included in the Czech constitution—prohibits threats against individual rights, state and public security, public health, and morality. Freedom of expression was called into question when armed military police officers in masks raided the offices of the public television station Czech Television on March 11, 2011, supposedly in search of a classified document that the military said had been shown on the air. The military police came under strong criticism, causing Defense Minister Alexandr Vondra to suspend General Vladimir Ložek, who had ordered the raid.

Most media outlets are owned by private foreign companies and are allegedly not influenced by the state. In June 2011, the Senate approved an amendment to the 2009 "muzzle law," which bans the publication of information obtained through police wiretaps, but allows for an exception in the case of "public interest." The validity of "public interest" claims must be examined by a judge on a case-by-case basis. Journalists had complained that the "Muzzle Law" prevented them from effectively reporting on corruption.

The government generally upholds freedom of religion. Academic freedom is widely respected.

Czechs may assemble peacefully, form associations, and petition the government. Thousands of protestors took to the streets in 2011 against the government's austerity package over concerns that public funds were being unfairly distributed. Trade unions and professional associations function freely but are weak in practice. The 2007 labor code requires unions within a single enterprise to act in concert when conducting collective bargaining.

The independence of the judiciary is largely respected in practice. The rule of law generally prevails in civil and criminal matters, though corruption reportedly is a problem within law enforcement agencies. Prisons suffer from overcrowding and poor sanitation.

The 2009 Antidiscrimination Act provides for equal treatment regardless of sex, race, age, or sexual orientation. However, members of the small Roma community sometimes face threats and violence from right-wing groups. The European Court of Human Rights (ECHR) ruled in 2007 that sending Roma children to special schools violated their rights to a full education. Although the government adopted a National Action Plan for Inclusive Education in March 2010 and a Strategy for the Fight Against Social Exclusion 2011-2015 in September 2011, the exclusion of Roma children from mainstream schools continues. In May 2011, Parliament adopted amendments to two governmental decrees that introduced parental and/or pupil consent for placement in special schools or programs and some support mechanisms for socially disadvantaged pupils, claiming that these measures would lead to the implementation of the ECHR judgment. However, the amendments do not explicitly guarantee mainstream education for socially disadvantaged children, sidestepping the cornerstone of the ECHR ruling. In some regions, Roma children are 27 times more likely than other children to be wrongly placed in special schools for the mentally disabled. Promoting denial of the Holocaust and inciting religious hatred remain illegal.

Gender discrimination is legally prohibited. However, sexual harassment in the workplace appears to be fairly common, and women are underrepresented at the highest levels of government and business. Women nevertheless increased their parliamentary presence in the 2010 elections, capturing 44 seats in the 200-member Chamber of Deputies. Trafficking of women and girls for prostitution remains a problem. In April 2011, the government approved a new National Action Plan for the Prevention of Domestic Violence, which outlines steps for supporting victims and dealing with perpetrators.

Denmark

Political Rights: 1
Civil Liberties: 1
Status: Free

Population: 5,574,000
Capital: Copenhagen

Ten-Year Ratings Timeline For Year Under Review (Political Rights, Civil Liberties, Status)

2002	2003	2004	2005	2006	2007	2008	2009	2010	2011
1,1F	1,1F	1,1F	1,1F	1,1F	1,1F	1,1F	1,1F	1,1F	1,1F

Overview: **Parliamentary elections in September 2011 resulted in Helle Thorning-Schmidt, leader of the Social Democratic Party, becoming Denmark's first female prime minster, ousting Lars Løkke Rasmussen's center-right coalition. Thorning-Schmidt formed a governing coalition with the Social Liberal Party and the Socialist People's Party.**

Denmark has been a monarchy since the Middle Ages, though the monarch's role became largely ceremonial after the promulgation of the first democratic constitution in 1849. The country was occupied by Nazi Germany during World War II despite its attempts to maintain neutrality, and in 1949, it joined NATO. In 1973, Denmark became a member of the European Economic Community, forerunner of the European Union (EU).

Postwar Danish politics have been dominated by the Social Democratic Party.

However, in the 2001 elections, a right-wing coalition led by Anders Fogh Rasmussen's Liberal Party won control by pledging to reduce immigration and lower taxes. The coalition, which also included the Conservative People's Party, was supported by the anti-immigrant and Euroskeptic Danish People's Party. Denmark has had a conflicted relationship with the EU, securing opt-outs from the bloc's 1992 Maastricht Treaty on justice, foreign, and monetary policy, and opting not to adopt the euro in 2000.

The Liberal Party won reelection in 2005, maintaining its coalition with the Conservative People's Party and receiving external support from the Danish People's Party. Prime Minister Rasmussen was returned to office in the 2007 elections, but resigned in April 2009, after being named NATO secretary general; he was replaced by finance minister Lars Løkke Rasmussen (no relation).

Parliamentary elections in September 2011 led to a change of government, with Helle Thorning-Schmidt leading the Social Democratic Party to power after forming a coalition with the Social Liberal Party, the Socialist People's Party, and the Red-Green Party. Although Thorning-Schmidt's coalition was able to narrowly defeat Rasmussen's center-right coalition, the Social Democratic Party itself suffered its worst electoral result since 1903 and won fewer seats in parliament than Rasmussen's Liberal Party. As a result of the election, Thorning-Schmidt became Denmark's first female prime minister. The new government faces internal divisions on issues such as welfare reform and early retirement benefits; it also inherited the weakest economy in Scandinavia.

In 2009, two men were arrested in Chicago in connection with a plot to bomb the offices of the newspaper *Jyllands-Posten*, which had printed controversial cartoons of the prophet Muhammad in 2005. One of those arrested, Pakistani-American David Headley, pleaded guilty in 2010 to planning the attack, as well as participating in the planning of the 2008 terrorist attack in Mumbai, India. In September 2011, his accomplice, Tahawur Rana, was found guilty of planning to attack *Jyllands-Posten*, but had not been sentenced by year's end.

The cartoonist Kurt Westergaard, who had drawn the most contentious of the Muhammad cartoons, was attacked in his home in January 2010 by a Somali assailant wielding an axe and a knife. Westergaard escaped unharmed, and the intruder, Mohamed Geele, was apprehended by police. Geele, who was believed to have ties to the Shabaab, an Islamist militant group based in Somalia, was sentenced in June 2011 to nine years in prison.

In September 2011, a small bomb exploded in a hotel in central Copenhagen, causing little material damage but injuring the alleged bomber. Danish police apprehended the suspect, Chechen national Lors Dukajev, several hours later. He was found guilty of carrying out a terrorist attack and sentenced to 12 years in prison. The intended target was *Jyllands-Posten*, particularly its former editor, Flemming Rose, who commissioned the cartoons.

Political Rights and Civil Liberties: Denmark is an electoral democracy. The current constitution, adopted in 1953, established a single-chamber parliament (the Folketing) and retained a monarch, currently Queen Margrethe II, with mostly ceremonial duties. The parliament's 179 representatives are elected at least once every four years through a system of modified proportional representation. The leader of the majority party or government coalition is usually chosen to be prime minister by the monarch. Danish governments most often control a minority of seats in the parliament, ruling with the aid of one or more supporting parties. Since 1909, no single party has held a majority of seats, helping to create a tradition of compromise.

The territories of Greenland and the Faroe Islands each have two representatives in the Folketing. They also have their own elected institutions, which have power over almost all areas of governance.

Levels of corruption are very low in Denmark, which was ranked 2 out of 183 countries surveyed in Transparency International's 2011 Corruption Perceptions Index.

The constitution guarantees freedom of expression. The media reflect a wide variety of political opinions and are frequently critical of the government. The state finances radio and television broadcasting, but state-owned television companies have independent editorial boards. Independent radio stations are permitted but tightly regulated. After complaints from the Turkish Ambassador to Denmark in March 2010, the Danish attorney general charged the Danish-based, Kurdish-language satellite television station Roj-TV for promoting the Kurdistan Workers' Party, which the EU and United States consider a terrorist organization. A trial, which began in August 2011, continued through year's end. The station was the first Danish media organization to face prosecution for promoting terrorism, and the trial has been criticized across the political spectrum for harming freedom of speech and being unduly influenced by Turkish political pressure on the Danish government. Access to the internet is not restricted, and Denmark's internet penetration rate is among the highest in the world.

Freedom of worship is legally protected. However, the Evangelical Lutheran Church is subsidized by the government as the official state religion. The faith is taught in public schools, though students may withdraw from religious classes with parental consent. At present, about half of all schoolchildren are exempted from the catechism taught in public schools. In 2009, religious and political symbols were banned from judicial attire.

The constitution provides for freedoms of assembly and association. Demonstrations during 2011 were peaceful. Civil society is vibrant, and workers are free to organize. The labor market is mainly regulated by agreements between employers' and employees' organizations.

The judiciary is independent, and citizens enjoy full due process rights. The court system consists of 100 local courts, 2 high courts, and the 15-member Supreme Court, with judges appointed by the monarch on the government's recommendation. Prisons generally meet international standards.

Discrimination is prohibited under the law. However, strict immigration laws introduced in 2002 were tightened further during 2010, adding more obstacles for citizens attempting to bring foreign spouses into the country. The Danish partner is required to pass a solvency test, post a bond of $12,000, and be at least 24 years of age. A new point system aimed at facilitating the reunification of spouses favors visa candidates who are considered attractive to the Danish economy and society. The rules were criticized by the UN Committee on the Elimination of Racial Discrimination for unfairly penalizing vulnerable refugees seeking asylum. Denmark also denies religious worker visas, which restricts access to missionaries entering the country from abroad.

Denmark has closed many of its asylum centers since the introduction of the restrictive 2002 immigration laws. In 2009, the government was criticized by the Office of the UN High Commissioner for Human Rights for deporting 22 Iraqis, even though their home country had been deemed "dangerous." The European Court of Human Rights in 2010 called on Denmark to stop deporting asylum seekers to Greece, their point of entry to the EU, on the grounds that the Greek asylum system no longer functioned effectively and could not process cases. Nevertheless, Denmark continued the policy throughout 2010. A binding decision from the Strasbourg court was pronounced in January 2011, compelling Denmark to stop the practice; Denmark changed its policy accordingly. In June 2011, the Rasmussen-led government imposed border controls with Germany, and EU authorities questioned whether these were in compliance with Denmark's membership of the Schengen free-movement area. The Thorning-Schmidt government abolished the changes in September.

Women enjoy equal rights in Demark and represent half of the workforce. However, disparities have been reported in the Faroe Islands and Greenland. Denmark is a destination and transit point for women and children trafficked for the purpose of sexual exploitation. Following the 2003 adoption of legislation that defined and criminalized such trafficking, the government began working regularly with nongovernmental organizations in their trafficking-prevention campaigns.

↓ Djibouti

Political Rights: 6
Civil Liberties: 5
Status: Not Free

Population: 905,600
Capital: Djibouti

Trend Arrow: Djibouti received a downward trend arrow due to harassment and intimidation of opposition parties that resulted in President Ismail Omar Guelleh winning a third term in office, a crackdown on antigovernment protesters, and a ban on public demonstrations.

Ten-Year Ratings Timeline For Year Under Review (Political Rights, Civil Liberties, Status)

2002	2003	2004	2005	2006	2007	2008	2009	2010	2011
4,5PF	5,5PF	5,5PF	5,5PF	5,5PF	5,5PF	5,5PF	5,5PF	6,5NF	6,5NF

Overview: **Djibouti's president, Ismail Omar Guelleh, won a third term in office in April 2011 following an opposition boycott of the election. Popular disquiet at his decision to run led to street protests, which were met with mass arrests and a crackdown on civil liberties. Meanwhile, Djibouti continued to suffer from the worst drought to hit the Horn of Africa region in six decades.**

Djibouti gained independence from France in 1977. Its people are divided along ethnic and clan lines, with the majority Issa (Somali) and minority Afar peoples traditionally falling into opposing political camps. An Afar rebel group, the Front for the Restoration of Unity and Democracy (FRUD), launched a guerrilla war against Issa domination in 1991. In 1994, the largest FRUD faction agreed to end its insurgency in exchange for inclusion in the government and electoral reforms.

President Hassan Gouled Aptidon controlled a one-party system until 1992, when a new constitution authorized four political parties. In 1993, Gouled won a fourth six-year term in Djibouti's first contested presidential election, which was considered fraudulent by international observers.

Gouled stepped down in 1999, but his nephew, Ismail Omar Guelleh, won the 1999 presidential poll with 74 percent of the vote. It was regarded as Djibouti's first fair election since independence. In 2001, a peace accord was signed with the remaining Afar rebel groups. A four-party coalition, the Union for the Presidential Majority (UMP), ran against a four-party opposition bloc, the Union for a Democratic Alternative (UAD), in the 2003 parliamentary elections, and won all 65 seats.

In 2005, Guelleh won a second six-year term. The only challenger withdrew from the election, citing government control of the media and repression of the opposition. Legislative elections in 2008 were also boycotted by the main opposition parties, which complained of government abuses including the house arrest of opposition leaders and manipulation of the electoral process.

Unresolved grievances among the Afar led to a revival of the FRUD insurgency, with sporadic violence in 2010. In April, Guelleh, a member of the Issa majority, pressured the parliament into passing a constitutional amendment that overturned the two-term limit for presidents; the change cleared the way for him to run for a third term in 2011.

On January 28, 2011, a series of protests by university students against failures in the education system quickly broadened into antigovernment demonstrations. In the largest rally, which started on February 18, several thousand people gathered outside Djibouti's national stadium to protest against Guelleh's decision to stand for the presidency. Cars were burned and stones thrown at the police, who responded with tear gas. At least two people were killed, and at least 100 others were arrested, including the leaders of three political parties.

The presidential election campaign was marred by harassment of opposition candidates and a clampdown on public gatherings. Opposition parties argued that the restrictions made it impossible to fairly contest the election, and chose not to select candidates for the presidential race. As a result, Guelleh faced only one challenger on April 8, independent candidate Mohammed Warsama, although he ultimately gained the support of one of the main opposition coalitions on April 3. Guelleh won with 81 percent of the vote. An African Union election observer mission declared the election process peaceful, fair, and transparent.

Guelleh has used Djibouti's strategic location on the Gulf of Aden to generate millions of dollars in state revenue by renting military bases to his allies. Since 2001, Djibouti has been home to large U.S. and French bases, and Japan opened a naval facility in July 2011.

The fourth consecutive year of drought placed an estimated 150,000 people in need of emergency assistance. Further, Djibouti faced the added burden of an influx of almost 20,000 refugees from famine-struck areas of Somalia.

Political Rights and Civil Liberties: Djibouti is not an electoral democracy. The ruling UMP coalition party has effectively usurped the state. The constitutional amendment passed by the parliament in 2010, in addition to removing the two-term limit for presidents, reduced presidential terms from six years to five, and specified that candidates must be between the ages of 40 and 75. The changes allowed President Ismail Omar Guelleh to stand for a third term in 2011.

The 65 members of the unicameral parliament, the National Assembly, are directly elected for five-year terms. The 2010 constitutional changes provide for the formation of a bicameral parliament comprising the existing National Assembly and a newly created senate, though no steps were taken in 2011 to establish this body. Opposition parties are disadvantaged by the country's first-past-the-post electoral system, as well as the government's abuse of the administrative apparatus. In the last legislative elections contested by the opposition, in 2003, the UMP won 62 percent of the vote but captured all the seats in the National Assembly, because the election law stipulates that the winner of the majority in each of the country's five electoral constituencies is awarded all seats in that district.

Political parties are required to register with the government. In 2008, Guelleh issued a decree that dissolved the opposition Movement for Democratic Renewal and Development OK party, whose leader had reportedly voiced support for that year's Eritrean military incursion.

Efforts to curb corruption have met with little success. Government corruption is a serious problem and public officials are not required to disclose their assets.

Despite constitutional protections, freedom of speech is not upheld in practice. There are no privately owned or independent media, though political parties are allowed to publish a journal or newspaper. The government dominates the domestic media sector and monopolized the airwaves during the 2011 election. The government owns the principal newspaper, *La Nation*, as well as Radio-Television Djibouti, which operates the national radio and television stations. Strict libel laws lead journalists to practice self-censorship. Six radio journalists working for an opposition station, La Voix de Djibouti, were among the demonstrators arrested during antigovernment protests in February. They were charged with insurrection and held for four months before being released in June, pending trial. Two were rearrested in November and reportedly tortured for four days before being conditionally released. Some foreign radio broadcasts are available. The government places few restrictions on internet access, although the Association for Respect of Human Rights in Djibouti claims that its site is regularly blocked.

Islam is the state religion, and 99 percent of the population is Sunni Muslim. Freedom of worship is respected. While academic freedom is generally upheld, higher educational opportunities are limited.

Freedoms of assembly and association are nominally protected under the constitution, but are not respected in practice. A ban was placed on public assembly by the Interior Minister during the February 2011 protests. Local human rights groups do not operate freely. Since 2007, Djiboutian League of Human Rights chairman Jean-Paul Noël Abdi has been arrested at least three times, the latest in February 2011, when he was charged with insurrection for reporting on the arrests of students during demonstrations that month. He was released weeks later, though the charges were still pending.

Workers may join unions and strike. However, the government discourages truly independent unions and has been accused of meddling in their internal elections and harassing union representatives.

The judicial system is based on the French civil code, though Sharia (Islamic law) prevails in family matters. The courts are not independent of the government. A lack of resources often delays legal proceedings. Security forces frequently make arrests without a proper decree from a judicial magistrate, in violation of constitutional requirements. Allegations of politically motivated prosecutions surfaced in 2010, following the conviction in absentia of Djibouti's richest businessman, Abdourahman Boreh, on charges of terrorism. Boreh, who received a 15-year sentence, had been considering a presidential bid in 2011. Following the arrests of more than 100 antigovernment protesters in February, about 80 suspects were brought to court and charged with assault and demonstrating without a permit. According to Human Rights Watch, a judge dismissed 40 cases and was promptly removed by the Justice Minister. His replacement then proceeded to convict and imprison 25 defendants. Prison conditions are harsh, but have improved in recent years. The 2010 constitutional amendments abolished the death penalty.

Minority groups including the Afar people, Yemeni Arabs, and non-Issa Somalis suffer social and economic marginalization.

Women face discrimination under customary practices related to inheritance and other property matters, divorce, and the right to travel. The law prohibits female genital mutilation, but more than 90 percent of women are believed to have undergone the procedure. An estimated 50 percent of girls are now receiving primary education following efforts to increase female enrollment. While the law requires at least 20 percent of upper-level public service positions to be held by women, women still hold just close to 14 percent of legislative seats.

Dominica

Political Rights: 1
Civil Liberties: 1
Status: Free

Population: 73,000
Capital: Roseau

Ten-Year Ratings Timeline For Year Under Review (Political Rights, Civil Liberties, Status)

2002	2003	2004	2005	2006	2007	2008	2009	2010	2011
1,1F	1,1F	1,1F	1,1F	1,1F	1,1F	1,1F	1,1F	1,1F	1,1F

Overview: **Prime Minister Roosevelt Skerrit and Education Minister Petter Saint Jean went on trial in September 2011 for holding dual citizenship at the time of their inauguration in 2009, which violates Dominican law and the validity of their election. The case was pending at year's end.**

Dominica gained independence from Britain in 1978. The centrist Dominica Labour Party (DLP) swept to victory in the January 2000 parliamentary elections, and formed a coalition with the right-wing Dominica Freedom Party (DFP). DLP leader Roosevelt "Rosie" Douglas was named prime minister, but died of a heart attack in October 2000. His replacement, Pierre Charles, died of heart failure in January 2004, and was succeeded by DLP member Roosevelt Skerrit.

Skerrit's government inherited financial troubles and lost public support as it implemented austerity measures. Increased global competition hit the agriculturally based economy hard, and the imposition of an International Monetary Fund stabilization and adjustment program proved unpopular. Despite such difficulties, the DLP easily won the April 2004 by-election.

Skerrit and the DLP secured 12 seats in the 2005 elections, ensuring a majority. Edison James, former prime minister and leader of the United Workers Party (UWP), initially accepted the results but later claimed that five of the DLP seats were obtained through fraud. Meanwhile, the DFP struggled to remain relevant and was not represented in the parliament.

In the December 2009 legislative election, the DLP captured 18 seats, while the UWP took only 3 seats. The elections were deemed generally fair by observer teams from both the Organization of American States and CARICOM. However, opposition members accused the DLP of misconduct during the campaign and filed complaints of election irregularities, including having been denied equal access to state media during the campaign period. They also accused Skerrit and Education Minister Petter Saint Jean of holding dual citizenship at the time of the election, which under Dominican law should have made them ineligible to hold office. The courts rejected all of the complaints in 2010, except for the dual citizenship case, which was brought to trial in September 2011 and was pending at year's end.

Skerrit's administration continued to be plagued by accusations of corruption during the year. In July 2011, the government was accused of theft of public funds due to its purchase of building supplies that were later possessed by an individual with close ties to Trade Minister Dr. Colin McIntyre. In 2009, Dr. McIntyre's brother had profited from the so-called "rubbish bin scandal," in which the government imported 2,700 garbage bins at four times their average retail price. The opposition also accused Skerrit of establishing a network of spies to monitor his opponents during 2011.

Political Rights and Civil Liberties:

Dominica is an electoral democracy. The unicameral House of Assembly consists of 30 members who serve five-year terms; 21 members are directly elected and 9 senators are appointed—5 by the prime minister and four by the opposition leader. The president is elected by the House of Assembly for a five-year term, and the prime minister is appointed by the president. The three main political parties are the ruling DLP, the opposition UWP, and the DFP.

The government generally implements anticorruption laws effectively. However, the independent director of public prosecutions, which prosecutes crimes including corruption, lacks sufficient resources to tackle complex corruption cases. Dominica was ranked 44 out of 182 countries surveyed in Transparency International's 2011 Corruption Perceptions Index.

Although Dominica does not have legislation that guarantees access to information or freedom of expression, the press is free in practice, and there is no government censorship. Four private newspapers and an equal number of political party journals publish without interference. Although the main radio station is state owned, there is also an independent station. Citizens have unimpeded access to cable television and regional radio broadcasts, as well as to the internet.

Freedom of religion is recognized. While the majority of the population is Roman Catholic, there are some Protestant churches. Academic freedom is respected.

The authorities uphold freedoms of assembly and association, and advocacy groups operate freely. Workers have the right to organize, strike, and bargain collectively. Unions are independent of the government, and laws prohibit antiunion discrimination by employers. Approximately 13 percent of the workforce is unionized.

The judiciary is independent, and the rule of law is enhanced by the courts' subordination to the inter-island Eastern Caribbean Supreme Court. Efforts to establish the Caribbean Court of Justice as its final court of appeal, instead of the Privy Council in London, continued in 2011. The judicial system generally operates with efficiency, and its handling of cases compares favorably with other islands in the region, though staffing shortfalls remain a problem.

The Dominica police force, which became responsible for security after the military was disbanded in 1981, operates professionally and with few human rights complaints. However, in 2011, the government was accused of illegally establishing a National Joint Intelligence Committee, comprised of police officers selected by Skerrit, to intercept e-mail and phone messages, as well as monitor the activities of select residences and businesses.

Women are underrepresented in government and hold just four seats in the House of Assembly. There are no laws mandating equal pay for equal work in privatesector jobs, and while there is no specific law that criminalizes domestic abuse, the Protection against Domestic Violence Act allows abused persons to appear before a judge and request a protective order without seeking legal counsel.

Dominican Republic

Political Rights: 2
Civil Liberties: 2
Status: Free

Population: 10,010,000
Capital: Santo Domingo

Ten-Year Ratings Timeline For Year Under Review (Political Rights, Civil Liberties, Status)

2002	2003	2004	2005	2006	2007	2008	2009	2010	2011
2,2F	3,2F	2,2F	2,2F	2,2F	2,2F	2,2F	2,2F	2,2F	2,2F

Overview: **In 2011, President Leonel Fernández's approval ratings suffered as a result of rising electricity prices, higher income tax rates, and inadequate services for the poor. Three demonstrators were killed by police during protests in July against economic austerity measures imposed by the government. Meanwhile, drug trafficking and the mistreatment of Haitian migrants continued to be problems during the year.**

After achieving independence from Spain in 1821 and from Haiti in 1844, the Dominican Republic endured recurrent domestic conflict, foreign occupation, and authoritarian rule. The assassination of General Rafael Trujillo in 1961 ended 30 years of dictatorship, but a 1963 military coup led to civil war and U.S. intervention. Under a new constitution, civilian rule was restored in 1966 with the election of conservative president Joaquín Balaguer. His ouster in the 1978 election marked the first time an incumbent president peacefully handed power to an elected opponent.

Since the mid-1990s, Dominican politics have been defined by competition between the Dominican Liberation Party (PLD) and the Dominican Revolutionary Party (PRD), although Balaguer's Social Christian Reformist Party (PRSC) remained an important factor. Leonel Fernández of the PLD was first elected president in 1996, but term limits prevented him from running in 2000. He was succeeded by the PRD's Rafael Hipólito Mejía Domínguez, a former agriculture minister. In 2001, Mejía successfully enacted a constitutional change to allow a second consecutive presidential term, but decisively lost his 2004 reelection bid to Fernández.

While his 1996–2000 presidential term had featured substantial economic growth, Fernández returned to face serious financial difficulties, including a ballooning foreign debt, high unemployment and inflation rates, and a deep energy crisis. Nonetheless, the country's economy improved dramatically, posting a 9 percent growth rate in 2005. In return for International Monetary Fund (IMF) financing, the government agreed to cut subsidies on fuel and electricity and reduce the bloated government payroll. The PLD captured a majority in both houses of Congress in the 2006 legislative elections, and Fernández secured a third term in the 2008 presidential elections.

Fernández promoted a constitutional reform process that resulted in the promulgation of the country's 38th constitution in January 2010. The new constitution removed restrictions on nonconsecutive presidential reelection, which would allow Fernández to run for president again in 2016. It also changed the electoral calendar so that future presidential, legislative, and local elections will be held on the same date.

Capitalizing on the president's continued successful economic management, the PLD captured 31 of 32 Senate seats in the May 2010 legislative elections. The PRSC took the remaining seat, leaving the PRD shut out of the upper parliamentary chamber. In the Chamber of Deputies, the PLD captured 105 seats, the PRD won 75, and the PRSC took only 3. The PLD also won a majority of the municipal elections. The opposition subsequently presented allegations of electoral fraud to the Organization of American States (OAS), and international observers noted that campaigning resources were not equally distributed between government and opposition candidates. The OAS also noted certain irregularities, including vote-buying, though it certified the results.

The Dominican Republic has faced various economic challenges over the past few years. The country became a conduit for relief and reconstruction efforts in the wake of the 2010 earthquake that devastated neighboring Haiti; the resulting influx of refugees, combined with emergency financial assistance to Haiti, strained the Dominican Republic's economy. Although the Dominican economy has largely withstood the global financial crisis, fuel prices have soared about 30 percent since the beginning of 2011. Increased electricity prices and income tax rates, combined with inadequate services for the poor—particularly in the areas of education and health—have negatively affected President Fernández's overall popularity. In July, demonstrations against fiscal and economic measures, including increases on income tax and electricity tariffs, paralyzed transportation and trade, and three protesters were killed in clashes with police.

Political Rights and Civil Liberties: The Dominican Republic is an electoral democracy. The 2008 presidential election and the 2010 legislative elections were deemed free and fair, though the OAS did note several electoral violations in the 2010 polls, including vote buying. The bicameral National Congress consists of the 32-member Senate and the 183-member Chamber of Deputies, with members of both chambers elected to four-year terms. The three main political parties are the ruling PLD, the opposition PRD, and the smaller PRSC.

Official corruption remains a serious problem, and has not improved markedly during President Fernández's tenure. The Dominican Republic was ranked 129 out of 183 countries surveyed in Transparency International's 2011 Corruption Perceptions Index.

The law provides for freedoms of speech and of the press, and the government generally respects these rights. There are five national daily newspapers and a large number of local publications. The state-owned Radio Television Dominicana operates radio and television services. Private owners operate more than 300 radio stations and over 40 television stations, most of which are small, regional broadcasters. Journalists reporting on possible collusion between drug traffickers and state officials have faced intimidation, and some have been killed. Internet access is unrestricted but not widely available outside of large urban areas; the Fernández government has worked to improve access to technology in rural areas.

Constitutional guarantees regarding religious and academic freedom are generally observed.

Freedom of assembly is generally respected, though three people were killed by police in July 2011 while protesting government austerity measures. Freedom of association is constitutionally guaranteed, but is limited for public servants. The government upholds the right to form civic groups, and civil society organizations in the Dominican Republic are some of the best organized and most effective in Latin America. Labor unions are similarly well organized. Although legally permitted to strike, they are often subject to government crackdowns. In 2010, peasant unions were occasionally targeted by armed groups working for major landowners, and the rights of Haitian workers were routinely violated.

The judiciary, headed by the Supreme Court, is politicized and riddled with corruption, and the legal system offers little recourse to those without money or influence. However, reforms implemented in recent years have included measures aimed at promoting greater efficiency and due process. The 2010 constitution seeks to further modernize the judiciary, with measures such as the creation of a Constitutional Court and Judiciary Branch Council, as well as mandating retirement for Supreme Court magistrates over the age of 75 years. Extrajudicial killings by police remain a problem, and low salaries encourage endemic corruption in law enforcement institutions. According to the Dominican Republic's Office of the Prosecutor General, at least 154 people were killed by police from January to July 2011, compared to 125 people during the same period in 2010. Prisons suffer from severe overcrowding, poor sanitation, and routine violence.

The Dominican Republic is a major transit hub for South American drugs, mostly cocaine, en route to the United States. Local, Puerto Rican, and Colombian drug smugglers use the country as both a command-and-control center and a transshipment point. In September 2011, prosecutors from U.S. federal courts indicated that Colombian drug smugglers had in at least three cases even been able to use Dominican military facilities to transfer narcotics.

The mistreatment of Haitian migrants continues to mar the Dominican Republic's international reputation, but no strategy has been adopted to handle this growing problem. The 2010 constitution removed the possibility of Dominican citizenship for children born of illegal Haitian migrants. Despite important advances in relations with Haiti, especially after the January 2010 earthquake, Dominican authorities continued to illegally deprive Dominicans of Haitian descent of their nationality, leaving them without access to health care, education, employment, or the right to vote. This virtual statelessness increases their chance of being subject to arbitrary detentions and mass expulsion, without judicial review, and in violation of bilateral agreements with Haiti. Mass deportations of Haitians illegally in the Dominican Republic continued in 2011.

The trafficking in women and girls, child prostitution, and child abuse are major concerns. In February 2011, authorities dismantled a network trafficking Haitian children and forcing them to beg in the streets; in July, traffickers of Venezuelan women working as exotic dancers were arrested. The new Dominican constitution includes one of the most restrictive abortion laws in the world, making the practice illegal even in cases of rape, incest, or to protect the life of the mother. The measure was strongly opposed by Amnesty International and domestic women's rights groups, who feared that it would have drastic consequences for women's health. The new constitution also defined marriage as solely between a man and a woman, making the country one of the few in the world to ban gay marriage at the constitutional level.

East Timor

Political Rights: 3
Civil Liberties: 4
Status: Partly Free

Population: 1,186,000
Capital: Dili

Ten-Year Ratings Timeline For Year Under Review (Political Rights, Civil Liberties, Status)

2002	2003	2004	2005	2006	2007	2008	2009	2010	2011
3,3PF	3,3PF	3,3PF	3,3PF	3,4PF	3,4PF	3,4PF	3,4PF	3,4PF	3,4PF

Overview:

While the UN Integrated Mission in Timor-Leste (UNMIT) successfully transferred all policing responsibility

to the national police force in March 2011, leaked internal UNMIT documents criticizing the Timorese government hastened calls for the end of the UN mission. In April, Deputy Minister José Luis Guterres formed a new political party, Frenti-Mudanca, a Fretilin reform party. A new civil code was approved in September, and an increase in the quota law for women's political participation was passed in May, leading up to the 2012 national elections.

Portugal abandoned its colony of East Timor in 1975, and Indonesia invaded within days of the declaration of independence by the leftist Revolutionary Front for an Independent East Timor (Fretilin). Over the next two decades, Fretilin's armed wing, Falintil, waged a low-grade insurgency against the Indonesian army, which committed widespread human rights abuses as it consolidated control. Civil conflict and famine reportedly killed between 100,000 and 250,000 Timorese during Indonesian rule.

International pressure on Indonesia mounted following the 1991 Dili massacre, in which Indonesian soldiers were captured on film killing more than 200 people. In 1999, 78.5 percent of the East Timorese electorate voted for independence in a referendum approved by Indonesian president B. J. Habibie. The Indonesian army's scorched-earth response to the vote killed roughly 1,000 civilians, produced more than 250,000 refugees, and destroyed approximately 80 percent of East Timor's buildings and infrastructure before an Australian-led multinational force restored order.

In 2001, East Timor elected a Constituent Assembly to draft a constitution. Kay Rala Xanana Gusmão—former commander in chief of Falintil and leader of Fretilin until he broke from the party in 1988 to form a wider resistance coalition—won the presidency the following year. Independence was officially granted in May 2002. The Fretilin party, led by Prime Minister Mari Alkatiri, won the country's first local elections in 2004 and 2005.

A political crisis in 2006 erupted into widespread rioting and armed clashes with the police, leading to numerous deaths and the displacement of an estimated 150,000 people. Alkatiri was forced to resign as prime minister in June 2006, and a UN Integrated Mission in Timor-Leste (UNMIT) was established to help restore peace and increase police presence. José Ramos-Horta, who was appointed to replace Alkatiri, won the May 2007 presidential runoff election. Outgoing president Gusmão launched a new party, the National Congress for Timorese Reconstruction (CNRT), to compete in June 2007 parliamentary elections. Fretilin led with 21 of the 65 seats, but the CNRT, which had captured 18, joined smaller parties to form the Alliance of the Parliamentary Majority (AMP), securing a total of 37 seats. Ramos-Horta invited the AMP to form a government, with Gusmão as prime minister.

The ruling AMP coalition continued to face criticism in 2011 due to the stalled implementation of recommendations from the truth commissions that had been established to investigate the violence surrounding East Timor's 1999 referendum, and the human rights violations that occurred during the 25 years of Indonesian occupation. While the UNMIT peacekeeping mission mandate was extended by one year, UNMIT formally transferred all policing responsibility to the national police force (PNTL) in March. However, calls for the end of the UNMIT mission were accelerated following the leak in May of an unofficial, internal UNMIT document that accused Gusmão of consolidating power.

East Timor's weak economy is fueled primarily by oil and gas revenues. In August 2011, the government approved amendments to the Petroleum Fund Law to allow for increased diversification in investments and to increase the rate of return; approximately 90 percent of Timor's budget (outside of foreign aid) is drawn from the Petroleum Fund. Despite an oil fund balance valued at over $9.3 billion, East Timor remained the poorest country in Southeast Asia, with more than 40 percent of the population living below the national poverty line. East Timor applied to join the regional Association of Southeast Asian Nations (ASEAN) in March.

Political Rights and Civil Liberties: East Timor is an electoral democracy. The 2007 presidential and parliamentary elections were generally deemed free and fair. The directly elected president is a largely symbolic figure, with formal powers limited to the right to veto legislation and make certain appointments. The leader of the majority party or coalition in the 65-seat, unicameral Parliament becomes the prime minister. The president and members of Parliament serve five-year terms, with the president eligible for a maximum of two terms. In preparation for the 2012 presidential and parliamentary elections, the National Election Commission approved legislation in December covering issues including campaigning, voting, and vote counting and tabulation.

Fretilin, now in opposition, remains the single largest political party. In April 2011, a former member of Fretilin, current deputy prime minister José Luis Guterres, formed a new party, Frenti-Mudanca, describing it as a Fretilin reform party.

Voter frustration with corruption and nepotism has plagued both Fretilin and AMP governments. An anticorruption commission was created in 2009 with a broad mandate, except for powers of prosecution. In March 2011, the government launched a transparency website of government accounts. In May, Deputy Prime Minister for Social Issues José Luis Guterres was cleared of charges relating to corruption and abuse of power. The anticorruption commission submitted eight high-profile cases related to public officials, including those involving two cabinet ministers, to the attorney general's office for investigation in 2011; the cases were pending at year's end. The country was ranked 143 out of 183 countries surveyed in Transparency International's 2011 Corruption Perceptions Index.

Journalists often practice self-censorship, and authorities regularly deny access to government information. The 2009 penal code decriminalized defamation, but it remains part of the civil code. A 2011 UNMIT study found that most people still rely on community leaders for information, followed by radio and television; an estimated 16 percent of the population did not access any form of media. The free flow of information remains hampered primarily by poor infrastructure and scarce resources. Radio has the greatest reach, with 63 percent of people listening on a monthly basis. The country has three major daily newspapers, some of which are loosely aligned with the ruling or opposition parties. Printing costs and illiteracy rates generally prevent the expansion of print media; only about 35 percent of the population has reported ever having read a newspaper. In 2011, an estimated 0.2 percent of the population had access to the internet.

East Timor is a secular state, though 98 percent of the population is Roman Catholic. Church rules prohibit persons living under religious vows from holding political office. There are no significant threats to religious freedom or clashes involving the country's Muslim and evangelical Christian minorities. Academic freedom is generally respected, though religious education is compulsory in schools.

Freedoms of association and assembly are constitutionally guaranteed. However, a 2004 law regulates political gatherings and prohibits demonstrations aimed at "questioning constitutional order" or disparaging the reputations of the head of state and other government officials. The law requires that demonstrations and public protests be authorized in advance.

Workers, other than police and military personnel, are permitted to form and join labor organizations, bargain collectively, and strike. In April 2011, the government approved a law governing the right of workers to strike, which reduced the time required for written notification prior to a strike from 10 days to 5 days. Unionization rates are low due to high levels of unemployment and informal economic activity.

The country suffers from weak rule of law and a prevailing culture of impunity. The understaffed court system hears cases in four district courts and one court of appeal. There is a considerable backlog, with approximately 4,600 criminal cases pending at the Office of the Prosecutor General at year's end. Due process rights are often restricted or denied, owing largely to a lack of resources and personnel. Alternative methods of dispute resolution and customary law are widely used, though they lack enforcement mechanisms and have other significant shortcomings, including unequal treatment of women. In July 2011, the Dili District Court convicted a former militia member of murder as a crime against humanity for actions taken in Liquica in September of 1999. The defense filed an appeal, but the verdict was upheld. The convicted former militia member was not arrested, however, and remained at large at year's end. In September, the government promulgated a new civil code, which will come into effect in March 2012; the government was criticized for limited public consultation on the code.

While there was a significant improvement in internal security in 2011, gang violence—sometimes directed by rival elites or fueled by land disputes—continued sporadically. As a result of several violent incidences between martial arts groups in late 2011 in Dili, the government in December initiated a one-year prohibition of martial arts groups and criminalized their activities. UNMIT completed the phased transfer of policing responsibility to the national police (PNTL) in March 2011, but the UN Security Council expressed concerns over the credibility of the PNTL. According to a report by the human rights group HAK Association, 99 instances of human rights violations were allegedly committed by PNTL members in 2011, and 9 by members of the Timorese Defense Force. In October, a new commander of the Timorese Armed Forces was sworn in; Lere Anan Timur replaced Taur Matan Ruak, who is expected to run for president during the 2012 elections. A November 2011 International Crisis Group report noted a growing concern in the criteria for the determination of veteran status for those who fought in and worked for the resistance movement, citing expensive compensation programs and the political repercussions of formalizing their political and security roles.

The status and reintegration of the thousands of Timorese refugees who still remain in the Indonesian province of West Timor after fleeing the 1999 violence remained an unresolved issue in 2011. The Timorese government has long encouraged the return of the refugees, but concerns over access to property and other political rights, as well as the status of former militia members, continued to hinder their return.

Community property comprises approximately 90 percent of the land in East Timor. A 2010 report issued by the International Crisis Group warned that land rights are likely to become increasingly contentious in light of ambitious government development plans. In July and November 2011, the government approved laws establishing the legal framework and procedures by which to recognize ownership and grant registration titles for undisputed real estate property.

Equal rights for women are constitutionally guaranteed, but discrimination and gender inequality persists in practice and in traditional/customary law. Women hold approximately 30 percent of the seats in parliament. Amendments to the election laws in May 2011 increased the quota requiring one-third of candidates on party lists for parliamentary elections to be women. While a law against domestic violence was adopted in 2010, gender-based violence and domestic violence remain widespread. The 2009 penal code criminalizes abortion except in cases that endanger the health of the mother. East Timor remains a source and destination country for human trafficking into forced labor and prostitution.

↓ Ecuador

Political Rights: 3
Civil Liberties: 3
Status: Partly Free

Population: 14,666,100
Capital: Quito

Trend Arrow: Ecuador received a downward trend arrow due to the government's intensified campaign against opposition leaders and intimidation of journalists, its excessive use of public resources to influence a national referendum, and the unconstitutional restructuring of the judiciary.

Ten-Year Ratings Timeline For Year Under Review (Political Rights, Civil Liberties, Status)

2002	2003	2004	2005	2006	2007	2008	2009	2010	2011
3,3PF	3,3PF	3,3PF	3,3PF	3,3PF	3,3PF	3,3PF	3,3PF	3,3PF	3,3PF

Overview: **President Rafael Correa led his government to another victory in a national referendum held in May 2011. But controversies raged during the year over the president's ongoing confrontations with the press, his plan to restructure the judiciary, and continuing fallout from a September 2010 police rebellion. The importance of the judicial overhaul was highlighted when Correa won a multimillion-dollar defamation suit that threatened to bankrupt one of the country's leading newspapers. Other legal proceedings were pending against participants in the police rebellion, journalists, and indigenous activists.**

Established in 1830 after the region achieved independence from Spain in 1822, the Republic of Ecuador has endured many interrupted presidencies and military governments. The last military regime gave way to civilian rule after a new constitution was approved by referendum in 1978. However, since 1998, three presidents have been forced from office before the conclusion of their terms as a result of popular protests and congressional action.

Indicating their frustration with political instability and the traditional parties, voters endorsed change in the 2006 presidential election. The winning candidate was Rafael Correa, a charismatic young economist who had served briefly as finance minister. A fiery critic of neoliberal economic policies, Correa promised to spearhead a transformative "Citizens' Revolution" that would include a new constitution. In the election's second round, Correa defeated billionaire businessman Álvaro Noboa with 57 percent of the vote.

After taking office in early 2007, Correa eliminated the legal barriers to a constitutional referendum, using questionable maneuvers to remove opposition legislators and members of the Constitutional Court. In April, 82 percent of the electorate approved the creation of a constituent assembly in a national referendum. Correa's Proud and Sovereign Homeland (PAIS) party and then captured 80 of the assembly's 130 seats in a September election. A year later, voters returned to the polls to endorse the newly written constitution, which garnered 64 percent of the vote.

The 2008 constitution stipulated an array of new rights for groups that included women, indigenous people, and the disabled. It also created a new branch of government called Transparency and Social Control, organized around the Council of Popular Participation and Social Control. The council was endowed with important powers in organizing the appointment processes for the attorney general, the human rights ombudsman, and the Judicial Council charged with selecting National Court of Justice members. Critics argued that the Council of Popular Participation and Social Control was likely to become an instrument of the executive branch rather than an independent watchdog. Executive power was enhanced further by a constitutional provision allowing presidents to serve up to two consecutive terms and the creation of a line-item veto.

Correa won a new four-year term in the April 2009 general elections, taking 52 percent of the vote in the first round. PAIS captured 59 of 124 seats in the new National Assembly. Smaller parties allied with PAIS garnered over a dozen seats, giving it a working majority. However, subsequent defections from PAIS and diminished support from other small parties made it difficult for the government to maintain its majority.

On September 30, 2010, a date known as 30-S, Correa faced the greatest crisis of his presidency. Police and a few military regiments staged a one-day rebellion, protesting a new public service law that altered salaries and benefits. After an angry confrontation with the protesters, Correa was forced to take refuge in a nearby hospital and declared a state of emergency. By the end of the day, he had been rescued in a military operation that left five people dead. The government then alleged that the events constituted an attempted coup by Correa opponents, including former president Lucio Gutiérrez.

The 30-S episode had far-reaching political consequences. In February 2011, Guayaquil's leading newspaper, *El Universo*, published an opinion column suggesting that Correa could be held accountable in the future for the use of lethal force during the rescue operation. In response, Correa lodged a lawsuit against the author, Emilio Palacio, and the owners of the newspaper. The president appeared in court during the proceedings, with a large security escort and throngs of supporters. All four defendants were found guilty of aggravated defamation and sentenced in July to three-year prison sentences and an unprecedented fine of $40 million. International human rights and press freedom organizations, along with the Organization of American States (OAS) and the United Nations, denounced the court decision as a clear effort to intimidate the press.

In a move to reestablish the administration's momentum and confirm Correa's popularity, a national referendum was scheduled for May 2011. The ballot contained nine separate questions on matters ranging from casinos and bullfighting to major reforms affecting the judiciary and the media. Critics, including some high-profile former allies of the president, regarded the referendum question allowing a judicial overhaul as unconstitutional because it violated the system prescribed in 2008. Another controversial question concerned the creation of a government-controlled media oversight body, the Council of Regulation. Correa led the campaign to approve all nine initiatives. After a long tabulation process, the government declared victory, registering over 45 percent approval for every question.

The referendum paved the way for the creation of a new body, the Transitory Council of the Judiciary. It was tasked with reviewing all personnel appointments in the judicial branch, including prosecutors and judges at all levels. The council was empowered to fire, hire, or reappoint. The government justified the measure as the only way to address the acute problem of corruption and the backlog in the judicial system, which was estimated at 1.2 million cases. In September, the government issued Decree 872, which declared the judicial branch to be in a "state of exception," allowing for an estimated $400 million in emergency funds to be allotted to the Transitory Council. The government also announced a plan to have the work of the council reviewed by a panel of foreign experts that included prominent Spanish jurist Baltasar Garzón.

The overhaul of the judicial system came at a time when the courts were poised to rule on numerous cases of interest to the government. These cases included the criminal prosecutions of activists involved in antigovernment protests along with individuals involved in the 30-S events. In September, three police officers were found guilty of the attempted assassination of the president.

Political Rights and Civil Liberties: Ecuador is an electoral democracy. The 2009 elections, the first under the 2008 constitution, were deemed generally free and fair by international observers, although the European Union monitoring team noted some problems with vote tabulation procedures and the abuse of state resources on behalf of progovernment candidates.

The 2011 referendum was monitored by an OAS observer mission. While it found no major irregularities in the voting process itself, the mission recommended enhanced monitoring and legislation to control campaign spending and the unfettered use of public resources. Unregulated campaign spending by the government has also been a focal point of concern among domestic observers.

The new constitution provides for a president elected to serve up to two four-year terms. In practice, this means that President Rafael Correa, who won his first term under the charter in 2009, could serve until 2017. The unicameral, 124-seat National Assembly is elected via open-list proportional representation for four-year terms. The president has the authority to dissolve the legislature once in his term, which triggers new elections for both the assembly and the presidency. The assembly can likewise dismiss the president, though under more stringent rules. The president enjoys line-item veto power over legislation.

For decades, Ecuador's political parties have been largely personality-based, clientelist, and fragile. Correa's PAIS party remains by far the largest in the legislature, though it has suffered defections. The opposition includes the center-right Institutional Renewal Party of National Action (PRIAN), the Social Christian Party–Madera de Guerrero, and the Patriotic Society Party. Pachakutik, a party with four seats in the legislature, is loosely affiliated with the Confederation of Indigenous Nationalities (CONAIE), the leading national organization representing indigenous groups. In 2011, Correa increased his use of national broadcasts to castigate opposition and indigenous leaders, creating a hostile environment for opposition political activity.

Ecuador is racked by corruption. The weak judiciary and lack of investigative capacity in government oversight agencies contribute to an atmosphere of impunity. Corruption investigations fall under the jurisdiction of the Council of Popular Participation, which has an estimated backlog of over 3,000 unresolved cases. Ecuador was ranked 120 out of 183 countries surveyed in Transparency International's 2011 Corruption Perceptions Index.

The environment for freedom of expression deteriorated in 2011, as reflected in the El Universo defamation case. In addition to the verbal attacks that Correa routinely directs at the press in his weekly television and radio broadcasts, the government uses its unlimited access to public service airtime to interrupt news programming on privately owned stations and discredit journalists. The press watchdog Fundamedios reported 156 cases of verbal, physical, or legal harassment against journalists in 2011. The Inter-American Commission on Human Rights held hearings during the year to investigate the status of press freedom in Ecuador, and condemned the government's targeting of journalists who testified.

Freedom of religion is constitutionally guaranteed and generally respected in practice. Academic freedom is not restricted.

The right to organize political parties, civic groups, and unions is unabridged in law. However, domestic and international nongovernmental organizations (NGOs) have come under increasing government scrutiny and regulation. In July 2011, a presidential decree outlined broadly framed regulations for foreign-sponsored NGOs, forbidding activities that are "incompatible with public security and security." Correa has denounced many NGOs as part of a right-wing conspiracy to bring down his government.

Numerous protests occur peacefully. However, national security legislation that predates the Correa administration provides a broad definition of sabotage and terrorism, which includes acts against persons and property by unarmed individuals. The use of such charges against protestors, along with the application of criminal and civil law, has increased under Correa. Marcelo Rivera, a student leader, continued serving a three-year prison term on terrorism charges related to an altercation during a 2008 protest at the Central University. In 2011, the National Prosecutor reported handling 994 sabotage and terrorism cases, with guilty findings rendered in 185 cases. Indigenous organizations in particular complain that the government is "criminalizing" protest by targeting leaders for legal harassment and applying more aggressive police tactics against demonstrators. CONAIE maintained that the Correa government has filed a variety of charges against 204 participants in social protests since taking power in 2007. In January 2011, three Shuar leaders were arrested and charged with sabotage and treason for their involvement in a 2009 protest in the province of Morona Santiago that ended in violent clashes between police and demonstrators. They were released in February, though the charges remained pending at year's end, as did those against other indigenous leaders on crimes related to protests.

The country's labor unions have the right to strike, though the labor code limits public sector strikes. Public employees have questioned the legality of terminations that removed 2,700 workers from their jobs in the last quarter of 2011. Only 1 percent of the workforce is unionized, partly because most people work in the informal sector.

The highest judicial bodies under the new constitution are the 9-member Constitutional Court and the 21-member National Court of Justice; the latter is now subject to the personnel review by the Transitory Council of the Judiciary. Galo Chiriboga's appointment as the new attorney general in April was the subject of political controversy due to a lack of transparency in the system used by the Council of Popular Participation to vet candidates. A similar dispute erupted about the council's selection process for members of the National Electoral Council, which will supervise the 2013 elections.

Judicial processes remain slow, and many inmates reach the time limit for pretrial detention while their cases are still under investigation. Prisons are seriously overcrowded, and torture and ill-treatment of detainees and prisoners remain widespread. Various projects to reform the penal and criminal procedure codes in order to improve efficiency and fairness were undertaken in 2009 and 2010, but rising crime—partly blamed on prisoners who were released to relieve overcrowding—pushed the focus of debate away from comprehensive reform. Voters endorsed more restrictive rules on pretrial detention in the 2011 referendum.

Ecuador has granted 54,500 refugee visas to Colombians fleeing violence in their country, and 25,000 requests are pending. This makes Ecuador the largest recipient of refugees in Latin America. According to the United Nations, 70 percent of the refugees are women, children, and adolescents. The government provides the refugees with access to health facilities, schools, and small-business loans.

Indigenous people continue to suffer discrimination at many levels of society. In the Amazon region, indigenous groups have attempted to win a share of oil revenues and a voice in decisions on natural resources and development. The government has maintained that it will not hand indigenous groups a veto on core matters of national interest.

Women took 40 of 124 assembly seats in the 2009 elections, and the new constitution calls for a significant female presence in public office. The election law requires that women account for 50 percent of the party lists in national legislative elections. Violence against women is common, as is employment discrimination. The 2008 constitution does not provide for same-sex marriage, but civil unions are recognized. Trafficking in persons, generally women and children, remains a problem.

⬆ Egypt

Political Rights: 6
Civil Liberties: 5
Status: Not Free

Population: 82,637,400
Capital: Cairo

Trend Arrow: Egypt received an upward trend arrow due to the development of a robust culture of popular protest, enhanced judicial independence, and an increase in political pluralism in connection with the ouster of longtime president Hosni Mubarak.

Ten-Year Ratings Timeline For Year Under Review (Political Rights, Civil Liberties, Status)

2002	2003	2004	2005	2006	2007	2008	2009	2010	2011
6,6NF	6,6NF	6,5NF	6,5NF	6,5NF	6,5NF	6,5NF	6,5NF	6,5NF	6,5NF

Overview: **President Hosni Mubarak was forced to resign on February 11, 2011, after nearly 30 years in power, as a result of 18 days of popular protests and a harsh government crackdown that caused more than 800 deaths. A military council that took over after Mubarak's ouster was initially welcomed but soon faced criticism for continuing human rights violations, harassment of activists and nongovernmental organizations, and its apparent attempts to postpone a transfer to civilian rule. Three-round parliamentary elections, monitored by the judiciary and featuring previously outlawed political parties, began in late November but were not scheduled to be completed until early January.**

Egypt formally gained independence from Britain in 1922 and acquired full sovereignty following World War II. After leading a coup that overthrew the monarchy in 1952, Colonel Gamal Abdel Nasser ruled until his death in 1970. The constitution adopted in 1971 under his successor, Anwar al-Sadat, established a strong presidential system with nominal guarantees for political and civil rights that were not respected in practice. Sadat signed a peace treaty with Israel in 1979 and built an alliance with the United States, which subsequently provided the Egyptian government with roughly $2 billion in aid annually. U.S. military aid eventually decreased to about $1.3 billion a year as of 2011.

Following Sadat's 1981 assassination, then vice president Hosni Mubarak became president and declared a state of emergency, which has been in force ever since. In the midst of an Islamist insurgency in the 1990s, the authorities jailed thousands of suspected militants without charge and cracked down on dissent. Although the armed infrastructure of Islamist groups was largely eradicated by 1998, the government continued to restrict political and civil liberties and struggled with Egypt's dire socioeconomic problems.

Economic growth in the late 1990s temporarily alleviated these problems, but the country experienced a downturn in 2001. Popular disaffection with the government spread, and antigovernment demonstrations were harshly suppressed by security forces.

The government sought to recast itself as a champion of reform in 2004. Mubarak appointed a new cabinet of young technocrats and introduced market-friendly economic changes. However, associates of the president's son Gamal, a rising star in the ruling National Democratic Party (NDP), received key portfolios, stoking suspicions of an impending hereditary succession.

In December 2004, Kifaya (Enough), an informal movement encompassing a broad spectrum of secular and Islamist activists, held the first-ever demonstration calling for Mubarak to step down. Similar protests by Kifaya and other opposition groups continued in 2005, but met with a heavy-handed response from the authorities.

A Mubarak-initiated constitutional amendment allowing Egypt's first multicandidate presidential election required candidates to be nominated by licensed parties or a substantial bloc of elected officials. All major opposition groups denounced the measure and boycotted the May 2005 referendum that approved it. Mubarak then won 88 percent of the vote in the September presidential election. His main opponent, Al-Ghad (Tomorrow) Party leader Ayman Nour, took just 8 percent and was later sentenced to five years in prison on fraud charges.

The banned Muslim Brotherhood, whose candidates ran as independents, increased its representation in the NDP-dominated lower house sixfold in the 2005 parliamentary elections, securing 88 of 454 seats. Voter turnout was low, and attacks on opposition voters abounded. Judges criticized the government's conduct and refused to certify the results, prompting the authorities to suppress judicial independence in 2006.

After postponing the 2006 municipal elections by two years, the government renewed a crackdown on the Muslim Brotherhood. In 2007, constitutional amendments passed in an opposition-boycotted referendum limited judicial election monitoring and prohibited the formation of religious political parties. The referendum and upper-house elections that June were marred by irregularities, and the Muslim Brotherhood was prevented from campaigning freely or winning any seats. When the postponed municipal elections were finally held in 2008, the Brotherhood was again marginalized, and many senior members were sent to prison.

Political tension rose in 2010 amid rumors of Mubarak's failing health and growing uncertainty over his successor. In February, former International Atomic Energy Agency director general Mohamed ElBaradei and several opposition leaders formed the nonpartisan National Association for Change to advocate for electoral reform, particularly the removal of restrictions on presidential candidates. Popular support for reform and dissatisfaction with the regime swelled after parliamentary elections in November, in which the NDP was officially credited with 420 seats in the lower house. Six small parties won a total of 15 seats, and independents—none of whom were affiliated with the Muslim Brotherhood and all of whom reportedly cooperated with the NDP—took the remainder. The campaign period was seriously marred by an array of state abuses, and the results were seen as blatantly rigged. Increases in state violence, including the brutal police murder of Alexandria-based blogger Khaled Said in June, exacerbated animosity between the population and the authorities.

This tension erupted into protests in January 2011, shortly after longtime Tunisian president Zine el-Abidine Ben Ali was deposed by a popular revolution. An 18-day protest against Mubarak and the NDP began on January 25, with demonstrators occupying Tahrir Square in downtown Cairo and similar public spaces across the country. The Mubarak regime initially responded with brute force, deploying police and hired thugs to assault protesters and shutting down the internet to prevent organizers from communicating with each other and the outside world. However, the protests continued. Mubarak finally stepped down on February 11, and the Supreme Council of the Armed Forces (SCAF), a group of senior army officers, took over, promising an orderly transition to civilian rule. In a referendum held on March 19, voters overwhelmingly approved a set of amendments to the 1971 constitution. The changes included a reduction in the requirements for presidential candidacy, the restoration of judicial supervision of elections, establishment of presidential term limits, and a restriction of the conditions under which a state of emergency can be declared.

The months after Mubarak's ouster were marked by rising sectarian tensions and periodic protests aimed at ending military rule. In October, security forces killed 28 civilians in front of the state television building in Cairo, known as Maspero, following a Coptic Christian protest over a recent church burning. The military leadership, which had already faced criticism for ongoing human rights abuses and the trying of thousands of civilians in military courts, was denounced for using live ammunition and excessive force in the incident, during which two military vehicles appeared to deliberately run over and kill 10 protesters.

Many observers questioned the military's commitment to a transition to civilian rule, as the SCAF postponed elections, renewed the oppressive Emergency Law, and sought to reserve significant power and autonomy for itself in any future civilian government. Delayed parliamentary elections began at the end of November, with the third and final round scheduled to be held in early January. Initial results indicated a strong showing by Islamist parties—most notably the Muslim Brotherhood's Freedom and Justice Party and the Al-Nour Party, which represented ultraconservative Salafi Muslims—even as the military suggested that it would temper parliamentary authority with its own informal veto power. These statements, the security forces' brutal handling of ongoing protests, state harassment of nongovernmental organizations (NGOs) advocating democratic reforms, and a mounting economic crisis all served to increase public discontent with military rule at year's end.

Political Rights and Civil Liberties: Egypt is not an electoral democracy. For most of 2011, the SCAF exercised executive powers, appointing a series of short-lived, interim civilian cabinets. The existing parliament was dissolved in February, and a new legislature was not scheduled to be seated until the completion of parliamentary elections in early 2012.

The 508-seat People's Assembly (Majlis al-Sha'b), the parliament's lower house, has traditionally exercised only limited policy influence, as the executive branch initiated almost all legislation. According to new rules enacted by the SCAF in September, 166 members of the People's Assembly are elected through individual candidacy, 332 are elected through a party-list system, and the remaining 10 are appointed by the president. (The SCAF will make such appointments until a civilian president is elected.) All members serve five-year terms.

The 270-seat upper house, the Consultative Council (Majlis al-Shura), has functioned solely in an advisory capacity. The president (currently the SCAF) appoints

90 of its members, 60 are elected through individual candidacy, and the remaining 120 are elected through party lists. The next Consultative Council elections were scheduled to begin in late January 2012.

The SCAF initiated a series of electoral reforms in 2011, including the restoration of judicial supervision over elections, the lifting of severe restrictions on political parties, and key changes to the voter registry. Early reports on the first rounds of the lower-house elections, which began on November 28, indicated that they broadly met international standards regarding election day conduct.

However, the Supreme Electoral Commission (SEC) lacked comprehensive authority to enforce election laws. Full compliance with such laws appeared to be lacking, as extensive campaigning took place outside polling sites in direct contravention of regulations. In addition, the participation of Al-Nour appeared to violate the ban on explicitly religious parties. Observers noted insufficient preparation and late, ad hoc decisions on ballot distribution and security, staff supervision and instructions, and other key logistical issues.

The open participation of groups like the previously banned Muslim Brotherhood, and the formation of several new parties from across the political spectrum, represented a clear departure from the Mubarak era, in which the legal and electoral framework was designed to ensure solid majorities for the ruling NDP at all levels of government. An April 2011 court ruling dissolved the NDP, though many figures affiliated with the party remained active in politics. A law on political corruption, designed to ban participation of such individuals, was issued by the SCAF in November 2011 but was not yet in effect for the parliamentary elections that started later that month.

Corruption remains pervasive at all levels of government. Egypt was ranked 112 out of 183 countries surveyed in Transparency International's 2011 Corruption Perceptions Index. In April 2011, former president Hosni Mubarak was arrested on charges of corruption and abuse of power, including the use of force against civilians during the protests the led to his downfall. Mubarak's two sons, Alaa and Gamal, were also arrested on corruption charges. The trials of all three were ongoing at year's end.

Freedom of the press improved slightly after Mubarak's ouster in early 2011, particularly through an increase in independent television stations and other media, but it continues to be restricted in law and practice. The September 2011 renewal of the Emergency Law included the criminalization of spreading false news and information. Dozens of journalists were called in for questioning by military prosecutors during the year, and in September, police conducted multiple raids on offices of the Qatar-based satellite television station Al-Jazeera, during which they confiscated equipment. Press freedom groups documented harassment of dozens of journalists and bloggers, particularly those who had criticized military rule. Among other prominent cases, blogger Maikel Nabil Sanad was sentenced in December to two years in prison for criticizing the military; his health was in severe peril due to a hunger strike and authorities' refusal to provide him with heart medication. Blogger Alaa Abd el-Fattah, arrested after criticizing the military's role in the Maspero incident, was initially charged in a military court with inciting violence against the military and stealing automatic weapons from troops during the clashes. After a public outcry over the case, Fattah was transferred to civilian court and released in December.

Censorship, both official and self-imposed, remained widespread during the year. A weekly English-language affiliate of the newspaper *Al-Masry al-Youm* was suspended in December following an internal dispute over the removal of an article on possible dissent within the military. The influence of state media decreased, but they were criticized for imploring "honorable citizens" to defend the army from what they claimed was an attack by Copts during the Maspero incident. There were also multiple reports of state raids on television stations that aired live feeds of the violence at Maspero.

Islam is the state religion. Some reforms were initiated in 2011 to decrease state involvement in religious institutions, but the SCAF said it would continue monitor religious extremism. While most Egyptians are Sunni Muslims, Coptic Christians form a substantial minority, and there are a very small number of Jews, Shiite Muslims, and Baha'is. The Baha'i faith is not recognized, though a 2009 decree allowed adherents to obtain identification papers without claiming to be Muslims or Christians. Separately, a 2008 court ruling found that Christian converts to Islam were free to return to Christianity. Anti-Christian employment discrimination is evident in the public sector, especially the security services and military, and the government frequently denies or delays permission to build and repair churches.

Interreligious bloodshed has been increasing, with Christians suffering the brunt of the violence. The trend continued in 2011, which began with an Alexandria church bombing that killed 23 people. In the Maspero incident in October, members of the Coptic community marched to the state television building to protest the burning of a church. The protesters were then attacked by security forces and armed civilians; ultimately, 28 people were killed and more than 300 were injured.

Academic freedom improved somewhat in 2011. Senior university officials are no longer appointed by the government, and a series of Mubarak-era education officials resigned during the year, sometimes following faculty strikes.

Freedoms of assembly and association are restricted, but Egyptians participated in public demonstrations of unprecedented size and duration in 2011, beginning with the January 25 protests that led to Mubarak's ouster. In March, the SCAF instituted a ban on strikes and demonstrations, and repeatedly used excessive force, including live ammunition, in attempts to disperse protests. Security forces, and in some cases progovernment thugs, engaged in prolonged street battles with demonstrators in June, October, November, and December.

Numerous civil society activists were targeted by the authorities throughout the year, including a well-known founder of the April 6 Youth Movement, Asmaa Mahfouz, who was charged with insulting the armed forces and inciting violence against the military after she criticized the SCAF online and in an interview. Following a public outcry, the charges against Mahfouz were eventually dropped.

The Law of Associations prohibits the establishment of groups "threatening national unity [or] violating public morals," bars NGOs from receiving foreign grants without the approval of the Social Affairs Ministry, and allows the ministry to dissolve NGOs without a judicial order. Using such legislation and the Emergency Law, government officials continued to harass NGOs after Mubarak's fall, despite early and sporadic attempts by the SCAF to show a willingness to consult with civil society. Human rights groups accused the military of conducting a smear campaign against NGOs by characterizing them as representing foreign interests. In December, security forces raided the offices of 17 domestic and international civil society groups, confiscating equipment and temporarily detaining some staff.

The labor movement made important advances during and after the 2011 uprising, as workers and strikes played a significant role in increasing pressure on Mubarak to step down. Workers were granted the right to establish independent unions and formed an independent trade union federation, ending the long-standing monopoly of the state-run federation. However, the government criminalized protests that disrupt the economy, a clear effort to limit the power of strikes, and initial investigations into corruption at the state-dominated labor movement foundered.

The Supreme Judicial Council, a supervisory body of senior judges, nominates and assigns most members of the judiciary. However, the Justice Ministry controls promotions and compensation, giving it undue influence over the courts. In 2011, judicial independence improved as judicial supervision of elections was restored, and prosecutors pursued cases against Mubarak, his sons, and other senior NDP officials for their roles during the January 25 uprising, among other matters. Trials were ongoing at year's end.

Egypt's Emergency Law, in effect since 1981, was renewed again in September 2011, despite the fact that the abolition of the law was one of the protest movement's central demands. Under the Emergency Law, "security" cases are usually referred to executive-controlled exceptional courts that deny defendants many constitutional protections. Special courts issue verdicts that cannot be appealed and are subject to ratification by the president. Although judges in these courts are typically selected from the civilian judiciary, they are appointed directly by the president. Political activists are often tried under the Emergency Law. Individuals can be prosecuted for inciting instability, criticizing the military or government, obstructing traffic, and spreading false or misleading information in the media. In addition to its trial provisions, the Emergency Law restricts many other basic rights, empowering the government to tap telephones, intercept mail, conduct warrantless searches, and indefinitely detain suspects without charge if they are deemed a threat to national security.

Because military judges are appointed by the executive branch to renewable two-year terms, military tribunals lack independence. Verdicts are based on little more than the testimony of security officers and informers, and are reviewed only by a body of military judges and the president. More than 12,000 civilians were tried by military courts under the SCAF in 2011, and at least 13 were sentenced to death. Charges brought in military courts are often vague and trumped up, according to human rights organizations. They can include property damage, insulting the army, and general vandalism.

Prison conditions are very poor; inmates are subject to torture and other abuse, overcrowding, and a lack of sanitation and medical care. Thousands of inmates escaped amid the disorder surrounding Mubarak's resignation; while some were recaptured, many remained at large. The looting of police stations during the uprising also led to the circulation of large numbers of weapons. These factors, combined with sporadic police strikes and other difficulties related to reestablishing central control over police forces, diminished security throughout the country.

The Mubarak regime was heavily criticized for the regular use of torture and other forms of brutality by its security personnel, and the issue was one of main grievances that drove the 2011 protests. Nevertheless, police brutality appeared to continue unabated after Mubarak's ouster. Human rights groups reported on torture of those detained by the military and police, and video footage that surfaced in September showed police and army officials using electrical shocks and beatings during an interrogation. In another prominent case in October, 24-year-old civilian Essam Ali Atta, who had been sentenced to two years in prison by a military tribunal for an apparently minor crime, was allegedly tortured to death by guards after they found him attempting to smuggle a mobile-telephone card.

Although the constitution provides for equality of the sexes, some aspects of the law and many traditional practices discriminate against women. Job discrimination is evident in the civil service. Muslim women are placed at a disadvantage by laws on divorce and other personal status issues, and a Muslim heiress typically receives half the amount of her male counterparts. However, Christians are not subject to such provisions of Islamic law. Domestic violence is common, as is sexual harassment on the street. Spousal rape is not illegal, and the penal code allows for leniency in so-called honor killings. The government has been involved in a major public-information campaign against female genital mutilation, but it is still widely practiced.

The military was criticized throughout 2011 for its harsh and sometimes predatory treatment of female protesters, including the widely publicized stripping and beating of a woman in December, to which thousands of women responded with a march in downtown Cairo. In March, soldiers subjected women arrested at Tahrir Square to "virginity checks," in addition to beating them and photographing them after they were strip-searched. At least one general reportedly argued that the examinations were aimed at preventing the women from making false rape allegations, and claimed that none of the detainees were virgins and, therefore, could not have been the victims of sexual assault in custody. Cairo's administrative court eventually banned the checks in a December ruling.

El Salvador

Political Rights: 2
Civil Liberties: 3
Status: Free

Population: 6,227,500
Capital: San Salvador

Ten-Year Ratings Timeline For Year Under Review (Political Rights, Civil Liberties, Status)

2002	2003	2004	2005	2006	2007	2008	2009	2010	2011
2,3F	2,3F	2,3F	2,3F	2,3F	2,3F	2,3F	2,3F	2,3F	2,3F

Overview: **President Mauricio Funes and several right-wing political parties tried to weaken the Constitutional Court in June 2011 with Decree 743, which required all decisions to be unanimous; the decree was quickly repealed in July in response to protests. The government continued to combat corruption in line with a new transparency and access to information law that was passed in March 2011. El Salvador also faced serious**

economic and social problems during the year, including an escalating murder rate and a weak economy.

El Salvador gained independence from Spain in 1821 and broke away from the Central American Federation in 1841. A republican political system dominated by an oligarchy of landowning elite, and subject to foreign interference, gave way to military rule in the mid-20th century. A 1979-92 civil war pitted El Salvador's Christian Democratic Party (PDC) government, the right-wing oligarchy, and the military, with support from the United States, against the Marxist-Leninist Farabundo Martí National Liberation Front (FMLN) and other leftist groups. The war left more than 75,000 dead and 500,000 displaced. In 1989, the conservative Nationalist Republican Alliance (ARENA) captured the presidency, and the civil war ended in 1992 with the signing of a peace treaty. The ARENA held the presidency for two decades, with ongoing competition from the FMLN party.

In the January 2009 parliamentary elections, the FMLN won 35 seats, while ARENA captured 32 seats. However, shifting political alliances in the months following the election led to the creation of the Grand Alliance for National Unity (GANA) party by former ARENA deputies in January 2010.

In the March 2009 presidential election, FMLN candidate, Mauricio Funes, defeated ARENA's Rodrigo Ávila, 51.3 percent to 48.7 percent. Observers noted that many of the irregularities that had been witnessed during the legislative elections, such as voter cards being issued to residents of other districts, had been rectified. However, calls continued for the Supreme Electoral Tribunal to address well-documented irregularities in the voter registry. In June 2011, President Funes announced his support for electoral reforms that would grant Salvadorans living abroad the right to vote in 2014 elections.

While the FMLN has supported Funes on several issues since taking office, important disagreements have complicated their relationship, causing a rift between the president and his party. Funes was accused by some on the left of moving towards the center after taking office and deviating from the FMLN's original program. While Funes's national approval ratings were still well above 60 percent in late 2011, long-standing party members distanced themselves from Funes in the run-up to the 2012 elections.

Following a Constitutional Court ruling in April 2011, two of the country's longest running political parties, the PDC and PCN, were disbanded due to their failure to have met the minimum required number of votes in the 2004 elections.

Decree 743—which would require the Constitutional Court to reach unanimous decisions before rulings could take effect—was signed it into law in June without public debate. It is widely believed that Funes and right-wing political parties sought to preempt court involvement in determining the constitutionality of the Central America Free Trade Agreement (CAFTA) and the 1993 Amnesty Law that protects those responsible for thousands of killings and disappearances during the country's 12-year armed conflict by passing this decree. In the weeks that followed, protestors from across the political spectrum claimed that the decree violated the principle of an independent judiciary. Congress repealed the decree in July in what was generally regarded as a victory for the rule of law and judicial independence.

The global economic crisis continued to have a significant effect on the country, as the economy is closely linked to that of the United States through trade and remittances. Analysts estimate that the economy grew 1.5 percent in 2011—one of the lowest rates in all of Latin America. However, remittances totaled $3.64 billion dollars in 2011, a 6.4 percent increase over 2010. It is estimated that between 30 and 40 percent of all Salvadorans live in poverty, which has fueled social alienation, as well as organized crime and violence.

Political Rights and Civil Liberties: El Salvador is an electoral democracy. The 2009 elections were deemed free and fair, although several irregularities were reported. The president is elected for a five-year term, and the 84-member, unicameral Legislative Assembly is elected for three years. The two largest political parties are the conservative ARENA and the leftist FMLN. However, ARENA's political influence has declined since a number of deputies abandoned the party in 2009 to establish GANA.

Corruption remains a serious problem at all levels of government. After addressing President Mauricio Funes's concerns, the Legislative Assembly passed a law in March 2011 to facilitate transparency and to combat corruption, which requires public entities to provide information in order to promote accountability and to encourage participation and public oversight. The reforms will go into effect in early 2012. In April 2011, the attorney general's office arrested former ARENA health minister Guillermo Maza and eight others on charges of defrauding the state of more than $3 million in the reconstruction of a hospital damaged by the 2001 earthquakes. Maza was placed under house arrest in November. El Salvador was ranked 80 out of 183 countries surveyed in Transparency International's 2011 Corruption Perceptions Index.

The constitution provides for freedom of the press, and this right is generally respected in practice. A 2010 Supreme Court ruling extended criminal penalties for defamation to journalists, editors, media owners, and managers. However, in September 2011, the Assembly approved reforms to the penal code that would replace jail time with fines in cases involving crimes against public image and privacy. Several journalists reported receiving death threats in 2011, and one journalist, Canal 33 cameraman Alfredo Antonio Hurtado, was murdered in April. The media are privately owned, but ownership is confined to a small group of powerful businesspeople who often impose controls on journalists to protect their political or economic interests. ARENA-aligned Telecorporación Salvadoreña owns three of the five private television networks and dominates the market. There is unrestricted access to the internet, and the government and private organizations have worked to extend internet access to the poor.

The government does not encroach on religious freedom, and academic freedom is respected.

Freedoms of assembly and association are generally upheld. The Assembly passed a controversial law in 2010 criminalizing gang membership. Critics argued that the law threatened freedom of association and would not succeed in addressing gang-related crime. Nationwide transportation strikes, supposedly led by gang leaders, were staged in protest of the law's passage. El Salvador's nongovernmental organizations (NGOs) generally operate freely, but some have reported registration difficulties. Labor unions have long faced obstacles in a legal environment that has traditionally favored business interests.

The judicial system improved its performance in 2011, demonstrating independence on a number of important cases, including corruption investigations against former political officials. However, several judges have spoken out against the corruption and obstructionism that permeates the Supreme Court and the entire judiciary. While very few complaints against judges ever move forward, the Supreme Court investigation unit dismissed two judges and suspended six others in 2011. It also submitted three cases to the OAG for investigation of possible judicial corruption. The OAG investigated 50 complaints against prosecutors for misconduct, eventually dismissing eight prosecutors and suspending 30 others.

Law enforcement officials have been criticized for brutality, corruption, arbitrary arrest, and lengthy pretrial detention. The Office of the Inspector General (OIG) reported that authorities received 964 complaints of alleged police misconduct in 2011. The OIG referred 679 of these cases to the OAG and sanctioned 919 officers in response to complaints filed during the year and in prior years. The OIG also charged eight police officers with homicide. According to the UN Office on Drugs and Crime's 2011 Global Study on Homicide, El Salvador has a homicide rate of 66 per 100,000 people, the second-highest rate in the world after neighboring Honduras. The forced repatriation of hundreds of Salvadoran criminals from the United States has contributed to the violence and reflects the international reach of major gangs like Mara Salvatrucha (MS-13). There are an estimated 20,000 gang members in the country; nearly 10,000 were in detention centers in 2011. In 2010, more than 18,700 Salvadorans were deported from the United States, 7,556 with criminal records.

The Legislative Assembly elects a human rights ombudsman for a three-year term. While abuses have declined since the war's end, civil liberties are still limited by sporadic political violence, repressive police measures, and vigilante groups. In November 2009, Funes authorized a six-month deployment of troops to high-crime communities to address public security issues. In May 2010, Funes extended the program—which granted the military greater power to conduct patrols and searches among civilians—for an additional year, signaling a return to practices initiated under previous ARENA governments.

According to the country's Prison Directorate, as of December 20, 2011, there were 25,294 prisoners, including 2,440 women, held in 21 correctional facilities and 2 secure hospital wards that have a combined capacity of 8,090. The prison population included 18,139 convicted prisoners and 7,155 inmates held in pretrial detention. In an attempt to disrupt organized crime in the penitentiary system, the military also patrols inside prisons.

Salvadoran law, including a 1993 general amnesty, bars prosecution of crimes and human rights violations committed during the civil war, but the authorities have faced criticism from NGOs and the Inter-American Court of Human Rights for failing to adequately investigate such crimes. In hopes of initiating extradition processes, a Spanish court issued an Interpol Red Notice in August 2011 for the provisional arrests of former Salvadoran military officers implicated in the murders of six Jesuit priests—five of whom were Spanish—and their housekeeper and her daughter in 1989. However, the Salvadoran Supreme Court claimed that they had not received an official extradition request from Spain, and, therefore, the government was only responsible for locating the individuals, not arresting them. The Spanish government then formally requested the extradition of 15 military officers in November; the request was pending at year's end.

There are no national laws regarding indigenous rights. According to the U.S. State Department's 2011 human rights report, access to land and credit remain a problem for indigenous people, along with poverty, unemployment, and labor discrimination.

Businesses are subject to regular extortion by organized criminal groups.

While women are granted equal rights under the constitution, they are often discriminated against in practice, including in employment. Violence against women and children is a serious problem, including domestic violence. Despite governmental efforts, El Salvador remains a source, transit, and destination country for the trafficking of women and children for the purposes of prostitution and forced labor.

Equatorial Guinea

Political Rights: 7
Civil Liberties: 7
Status: Not Free

Population: 720,200
Capital: Malabo

Ten-Year Ratings Timeline For Year Under Review (Political Rights, Civil Liberties, Status)

2002	2003	2004	2005	2006	2007	2008	2009	2010	2011
7,6NF	7,6NF	7,6NF	7,6NF	7,6NF	7,6NF	7,7NF	7,7NF	7,7NF	7,7NF

Overview: **The African Union selected Equatorial Guinea to host its 17th summit in 2011, despite the country's reputation as one of the most repressive states in sub-Saharan Africa. The event highlighted the repressive nature of President Teodoro Obiang Nguema Mbasogo's regime, with security forces reportedly detaining hundreds of suspected dissidents during the lead-up to the summit. In a process described by watchdog organizations as flawed, a constitutional referendum approved in November granted the president increased powers.**

Equatorial Guinea achieved independence from Spain in 1968. Current president Teodoro Obiang Nguema Mbasogo seized power in 1979, after deposing and executing his uncle, the country's first president, Francisco Macías Nguema. While international pressure compelled Obiang to establish a multiparty system in 1991, Equatorial Guinea has yet to hold credible elections; the Equatoguinean strongman and his Democratic Party of Equatorial Guinea (PDGE) have remained firmly entrenched in power. The discovery and exploitation of offshore hydrocarbon resources has allowed Obiang to amass a vast personal fortune, bolstering his domestic position and making him largely impervious to calls from abroad to implement meaningful political reforms.

Obiang dissolved the parliament in February 2008 and called legislative and municipal elections for May. A new coalition composed of the PDGE and nine smaller parties won a reported 100 percent of the vote in many districts, taking 99 out of 100 seats in the parliament amid allegations of widespread irregularities. The Convergence for Social Democracy (CPDS), the sole opposition party, was reduced from two seats to one.

In February 2009, a group of unidentified gunmen attacked the presidential palace in Malabo. The government asserted that the assailants were Niger Delta militants working in league with members of the Equatoguinean opposition-in-exile. In the ensuing months, security forces rounded up and expelled hundreds of foreign residents amidst international outcry. Seven Nigerian suspects were convicted and sentenced in April 2010 on charges related to the attack. In August 2010, four former military and government officials were executed within an hour of being sentenced to death by a military court for attempting to assassinate the president during the attacks. According to Amnesty International, Equatoguinean operatives abducted the four individuals in Benin, where they had been living as refugees, and proceeded to hold them incommunicado in Black Beach Prison, where the suspects were reportedly tortured before confessing to the attack.

Obiang swept the November 2009 presidential elections with 95.4 percent of the vote, although as with past balloting, the election was widely regarded as rigged. The president's main opponent, CPDS leader Plácido Micó Abogo, received less than 4 percent of the vote. The new government appointed in January 2010 included nearly all of the previous cabinet members, and the creation of many new junior minister posts increased the total size of the cabinet by 50 percent. Obiang's son and reportedly favored successor, Teodoro (known as Teodorín) Nguema Obiang Mangue, retained the agriculture and forests portfolio, was promoted to minister of state, and became vice president of the PDGE. After the changes, members of the president's family held 11 ministerial posts.

There was a dramatic increase in arbitrary arrests and police raids in the months leading up to the country's hosting of the June 2011 meeting of the 17th African Union Summit. In addition to the detention of approximately 100 students in the city of Bata, police raided neighborhoods with high foreign-born populations. Some observers attributed the crackdown to preemptive government efforts to prevent any manifestations of political unrest during the summit.

On November 13, 2011, a constitutional referendum was approved by 97.7 percent of voter,s according to the government. However, organizations such as Human Rights Watch reported voting fraud, the harassment and intimidation of voters, and other irregularities. While the reforms imposed a term limit for the presidency to two consecutive terms, the age limit for eligibility was lifted, which would allow Obiang to run again for a third term in the future. The referendum also increased presidential powers by allowing the president to appoint a vice president who would assume Obiang's presidency should he retire or die in office. Expectations are that Obiang will appoint his son.

Equatorial Guinea's abundant oil revenues do not reach the majority of its citizens. According to the Centre for Global Development, 77 percent of the population lives on fewer than two dollars a day. As Human Rights Watch noted, the government spent four times as much money building facilities to host the African Union summit in 2011 than it did on education in 2008.

Political Rights and Civil Liberties: Equatorial Guinea is not an electoral democracy. The 2009 presidential election that resulted in President Teodoro Obiang Nguema Mbasogo securing a new, seven-year term reportedly featured intimidation and harassment of the opposition by security forces and restrictions on foreign observers. Power rests firmly in the hands of Obiang and his supporters, the overwhelming majority of whom hail from the Esangui clan, part of the Fang ethnic group. The 100 members of the unicameral House of People's Representatives are elected to five-year terms, but wield little power; all but one of the chamber's seats are held by members of the propresidential coalition. However, the November 2011 referendum approved the creation of a new bicameral parliament to consist of a 100-member Chamber of Deputies and a 70-member Senate. Each body is to be directly elected for five-year terms, but the law will determine how many senators the president may nominate.

The PDGE regime has little tolerance for political dissent. Equatoguinean security agents closely monitor suspected Obiang opponents, including members of the CPDS.

As with politics, Obiang and his inner circle dominate Equatorial Guinea's economic landscape, and graft is rampant. Most major business transactions cannot transpire without involving an individual connected to the regime. Transparency International's 2011 Corruption Index ranked Equatorial Guinea 172 out of 183 countries surveyed.

Although the constitution guarantees media freedom, the 1992 press law authorizes government censorship. Libel remains a criminal offense, and the government requires all journalists to register with state officials. A few private newspapers are published irregularly but face intense financial and political pressure. The government holds a monopoly on broadcast media, with the exception of RTV-Asonga, a private radio and television outlet owned by Obiang's son. In mid-February 2011, the Equatoguinean regime forbade media outlets from reporting on the political unrest in the Arab world, even suspending the host of a French-language radio program, Juan Pedro Mendene, for briefly mentioning Libya during a March broadcast. Mendene was then reportedly assaulted by the bodyguard of the secretary of state for radio and television information while leaving the station. In June, security personnel arrested and then deported three journalists from a German television station who had interviewed CPDS leader Plácido Micó Abogo and recorded some footage of an impoverished Malabo neighborhood.

The constitution protects religious freedom, though in practice, it is sometimes affected by the country's broader political repression. Official preference is given to the Roman Catholic Church and the Reform Church of Equatorial Guinea. Academic freedom is also politically constrained, and self-censorship among faculty is common.

Freedoms of assembly and association are severely restricted, and political gatherings must have official authorization to proceed. The Equatoguinean regime reportedly banned the Popular Union (UP) opposition party from organizing demonstrations on March 23 in Malabo and Bata. The few international nongovernmental organizations that operate in the country promote social and economic improvements rather than political and civil rights. The constitution provides for the right to organize unions, but there are many legal barriers to collective bargaining. While it has ratified key International Labour Organization conventions, the government has refused to register a number of trade unions, including the Workers' Union of Equatorial Guinea and the Organization of Rural Workers. The country's only legal labor union is the Unionized Organization of Small Farmers.

The judiciary is not independent. Civil cases rarely go to trial, and military tribunals handle national security cases. Equatorial Guinea has been condemned internationally for holding detainees in secret, denying them access to lawyers, and jailing them for long periods without charge. UN investigators have also reported systematic torture in the penal system. Prison conditions are deplorable.

Immigrants from neighboring African states and the ethnic Bubi are frequent targets of government harassment. Important contributors to the local economy, foreign workers have frequently been expelled or jailed. Similarly, the Bubi, indigenous inhabitants of the oil-rich island Bioko, have seen their economic rights undermined by successive Fang-dominated regimes.

All citizens are required to obtain exit visas to travel abroad, and some opposition figures have been denied such visas. Those who do travel are sometimes subjected to interrogation upon their return.

Constitutional and legal guarantees of equality for women are largely ignored. Both violence against women and discriminatory traditional practices are reportedly widespread. Women hold just 6 percent of the seats in the House of People's Representatives; however, the 2011 referendum explicitly commits the government to adopting measures to increase women's representation and participation in institutional functions.

Eritrea

Political Rights: 7
Civil Liberties: 7
Status: Not Free

Population: 5,939,000
Capital: Asmara

Ten-Year Ratings Timeline For Year Under Review (Political Rights, Civil Liberties, Status)

2002	2003	2004	2005	2006	2007	2008	2009	2010	2011
7,6NF	7,6NF	7,6NF	7,6NF	7,6NF	7,6NF	7,6NF	7,7NF	7,7NF	7,7NF

Overview: **The Eritrean government's suppression of the basic political rights and civil liberties of its citizens continued in 2011. Plans for national elections remained on permanent hold 18 years after independence, and a ban on independent media and foreign organizations remained in place during the year. Meanwhile, a UN report accused Eritrea of planning a terrorist attack against neighboring Ethiopia.**

Britain ended Italian colonial rule in Eritrea during World War II, and the country was formally incorporated into Ethiopia in 1952. Its independence struggle began in 1962 as a nationalist and Marxist guerrilla war against the Ethiopian government of Emperor Haile Selassie. The seizure of power in Ethiopia by a Marxist junta in

1974 removed the ideological basis of the conflict, and by the time Eritrea finally defeated Ethiopia's northern armies in 1991, the Eritrean People's Liberation Front (EPLF) had discarded Marxism. Formal independence was achieved in May 1993, after a referendum supervised by the United Nations produced a landslide vote for statehood. EPLF leader Isaias Afwerki was chosen by the Transitional National Assembly to fill the position of president until elections could be held; these elections were eventually scheduled to take place in 2001 but were postponed and have yet to take place.

War with Ethiopia broke out again in 1998. In May 2000, an Ethiopian offensive made significant gains. The two sides signed a truce the following month, and a peace treaty was signed that December. Both countries accepted an independent ruling that set the common border, but Ethiopia later reneged on the agreement. The war and the unresolved grievances stemming from the broken peace deal have driven the Eritrean government's fixation with national security and perpetuated the militarization of the state.

In May 2001, a group of 15 senior ruling-party members publicly criticized President Isaias Afwerki and called for "the rule of law and for justice, through peaceful and legal ways and means." Eleven members of the group were arrested for treason in September of that year. The small independent media sector was also shut down, and a number of journalists were imprisoned. Many of the jailed dissidents and journalists were subsequently reported to have died in custody, but the government steadfastly refuses to divulge information about their whereabouts or well-being.

The government clamped down on nongovernmental organizations (NGOs) in 2005, and ordered the U.S. Agency for International Development to end its operations in the country. In 2006, reports emerged that hundreds of followers of various unregistered churches were being detained, harassed, and abused. The government has continued this pattern of suppressing civil society, religious practice, and political dissent. Arbitrary detention remains the authorities' most common method of stifling independent action by citizens.

A border dispute with Djibouti that led to a military confrontation in 2008 was resolved in 2010, when both sides agreed to a negotiated settlement. But tensions with Ethiopia escalated once more when a UN report in July 2011 accused Eritrean officials of masterminding a failed plot to bomb the African Union headquarters in Addis Ababa in January 2011. The report also claimed that Eritrea was continuing to fund and organize Islamist militant groups in Somalia, including Al Shabaab. Eritrea denied the claims and made some efforts to reengage with its neighbors by applying to rejoin the regional organization, the Intergovernmental Authority on Development (IGAD). IGAD members stalled on making a decision and instead pushed for tightening sanctions against Eritrea, including an arms embargo, which were agreed to by the UN Security Council in December.

The worst drought to affect the Horn of Africa in 60 years has affected more than 12 million people throughout the region. However, President Isaias claimed that the drought stopped at his borders, and continued to limit access to food and humanitarian organizations. Meanwhile, approximately 900 Eritreans risked their lives to flee the country each month.

Political Rights and Civil Liberties: Eritrea is not an electoral democracy. Created in 1994 as a successor to the EPLF, the People's Front for Democracy and Justice (PFDJ) is the only legal political party. Instead of moving toward a democratic system, the PFDJ government has become harshly authoritarian since the end of the war with Ethiopia.

A new constitution was ratified in 1997, calling for "conditional" political pluralism and an elected 150-seat National Assembly, which would choose the president from among its members by a majority vote. However, this system has never been implemented, as national elections planned for 2001 have been postponed indefinitely. The Transitional National Assembly is comprised of 75 PFDJ members and 75 elected members. In 2004, regional assembly elections were conducted, but they were carefully orchestrated by the PFDJ and offered no real choice to voters. The PFDJ and the military, both strictly subordinate to President Isaias, are in practice the only institutions of political significance in Eritrea.

Corruption continued to be a problem in 2011. The government's control over foreign exchange effectively gives it sole authority over imports. At the same time, those in favor with the regime are allowed to profit from the smuggling and sale of scarce goods such as building materials, food, and alcohol. According to the International Crisis Group, senior military officials are the chief culprits in this trade. They have also been accused of enriching themselves by charging fees to assist the growing number of Eritreans who wish to flee the country, and using conscript labor for private building projects.

There are no independent media in Eritrea. The government controls all broadcasting outlets and banned privately owned newspapers in its 2001 crackdown. A group of journalists arrested in 2001 remained imprisoned without charge, and as many as half of the original 10 are believed to have died in custody; however, the government refuses to provide any information on their status. In 2009, the entire staff of the Asmara-based broadcaster Radio Bana was detained; at least 11 of them remained in custody without charge at year's end. According to the Committee to Protect Journalists, at least 28 journalists were in prison in 2011. Eritrea's treatment of the media drew a rebuke from the European Union, which in September 2011 passed a resolution condemning its detention of independent journalists and calling for the release of a dual Swedish-Eritrean national who was among those arrested in 2001. The government controls the internet infrastructure and is thought to monitor online communications. Foreign media are available to those few who can afford a satellite dish.

The government places significant limitations on the exercise of religion. Since 2002 it has officially recognized only four faiths: Islam, Orthodox Christianity, Roman Catholicism, and Lutheranism as practiced by the Evangelical Church of Eritrea. Members of Evangelical and Pentecostal churches face persecution, but the most severe treatment is reserved for Jehovah's Witnesses, who are barred from government jobs and refused business permits or identity cards. Abune Antonios, patriarch of the Eritrean Orthodox Church, has been under house arrest since speaking out against state interference in religion in 2006. According to Amnesty International, members of other churches have been jailed and tortured or otherwise ill-treated to make them abandon their faith. As many as 3,000 people from unregistered religious groups are currently in prison because of their beliefs; the majority are Pentecostal or Evangelical Christians. According to Christian news service, Compass Direct, three Christians incarcerated at a military detention center died from mistreatment during 2011. Muslims also complain of discrimination. In 2010, a leading Islamic organization accused the government of marginalizing Muslims, closing traditional Muslim schools, persecuting religious leaders, and appropriating Muslim-owned land.

Academic freedom is constrained. Students in their last year of secondary school are subject to the highly unpopular policy of obligatory military service and are often stationed at bases far from their homes. Academics practice self-censorship, and the government restricts course content. Eritrea's university system has been effectively closed, replaced by regional colleges whose main purposes are military training and political indoctrination. Freedom of expression in private discussions is limited. People are guarded in voicing their opinions for fear of being overheard by government informants.

Freedoms of assembly and association are not recognized. The government maintains a hostile attitude toward civil society, and independent NGOs are not tolerated. A 2005 law requires NGOs to pay taxes on imported materials, submit project reports every three months, renew their licenses annually, and meet government-established target levels of financial resources. International human rights NGOs are barred, and only six international humanitarian NGOs are present in the country. In September 2011, Eritrea accused Amnesty International of infiltrating the country to try to foment a North African-style revolution. Amnesty denied the claims, saying that it has been refused access to Eritrea for more than a decade by the government.

The government controls all union activity. The National Confederation of Eritrean Workers is the country's main union body and has affiliated unions for women, teachers, young people, and general workers.

The judiciary, which was formed by decree in 1993, has never issued rulings significantly at variance with government positions. Constitutional due process guarantees are often ignored in cases related to state security. The International Crisis Group has described Eritrea as a "prison state" for its flagrant disregard of the rule of law and its willingness to detain anyone suspected of opposing the regime, often without charge. According to Amnesty International and Human Rights Watch, torture, arbitrary detentions, and political arrests are common. The police are poorly paid and prone to corruption. Prison conditions are harsh, and outside monitors such as the International Committee of the Red Cross have been denied access to detainees. In some facilities, inmates are held in metal shipping containers or underground cells in extreme temperatures. Prisoners are often denied medical treatment. The government maintains a network of secret detention facilities.

The Kunama people, one of Eritrea's nine ethnic groups, reportedly face severe discrimination. They are viewed with suspicion for having backed a rival group of the EPLF during the war of independence and for resisting attempts to integrate them into national society. Members of the Afar ethnic group have also been targeted. Several hundred Afars were arrested during 2010, according to Human Rights Watch. Sexual minorities face legal and social discrimination due to the criminalization of same-sex sexual conduct.

Freedom of movement is heavily restricted. Eritreans under the age of 50 are rarely given permission to leave the country, and those who try to travel without the correct documents face imprisonment. Eritrean refugees and asylum seekers who are repatriated from other countries are also detained; a number of repatriated Eritreans disappeared while in custody in 2011. These strict penalties, however, fail to deter thousands of people from risking their lives to escape the country each year. In July, one Eritrean refugee died, and another was seriously injured after they jumped off a truck that was forcibly returning them from Sudan.

Government policy is officially supportive of free enterprise, and citizens are in theory able to choose their employment, establish private businesses, and operate them without government harassment. However, few private businesses remain in Eritrea. This is largely because of the conscription system, which ties most able-bodied men and women to an indefinite period of obligatory military service and can also entail compulsory labor for enterprises controlled by the political elite. The official 18-month service period is frequently open-ended in practice, and conscientious-objector status is not recognized. The government imposes collective punishment on the families of deserters, forcing them to pay heavy fines or putting them in prison. The enforced contraction of the labor pool, combined with a lack of investment and rigid state control of private enterprise, has crippled the national economy. The government levies a compulsory 2 percent tax on income earned by citizens living overseas, and those who do not pay place their relatives back home at risk of arrest.

The U.S. State Department describes Eritrea as a source country for human trafficking for the purposes of forced labor and sexual exploitation. It is believed that the Eritrean government has not taken any measures to address this problem.

Women hold some senior government positions, including four ministerial posts. The government has made attempts to promote women's rights, with laws mandating equal educational opportunity, equal pay for equal work, and penalties for domestic violence. However, traditional societal discrimination against women persists in the countryside. While female genital mutilation was banned by the government in 2007, the practice remains widespread in rural areas.

Estonia

Political Rights: 1
Civil Liberties: 1
Status: Free

Population: 1,340,000
Capital: Tallinn

Ten-Year Ratings Timeline For Year Under Review (Political Rights, Civil Liberties, Status)

2002	2003	2004	2005	2006	2007	2008	2009	2010	2011
1,2F	1,2F	1,1F	1,1F	1,1F	1,1F	1,1F	1,1F	1,1F	1,1F

Overview: **Estonia officially joined the euro currency zone on January 1, 2011, and the government continued to implement fiscal austerity measures as the economy slowly improved. Parliamentary elections in March saw the reelection of Andrus Ansip's Reform Party, which**

formed a majority coalition with the Union of Pro Patria and Res Publica. Incumbent president Toomas Hendrik Ilves was reelected in August for another five-year term.

Estonia gained independence from Russia in 1918, but was captured—along with Latvia and Lithuania—by Soviet troops during World War II. Under Soviet rule, approximately one-tenth of Estonia's population was deported, executed, or forced to flee abroad. Subsequent Russian immigration reduced ethnic Estonians to just over 60 percent of the population by 1989. Estonia regained its independence with the disintegration of the Soviet Union in 1991. It adopted a new constitution in July 1992 and held its first legislative elections in September of that year. Russian troops withdrew from Estonia in 1994. The country joined both NATO and the European Union (EU) in 2004.

A series of shifting multiparty coalitions have held power since independence. Following 2007 parliamentary elections, Prime Minister Andrus Ansip's center-right Reform Party formed a coalition with the Union of Pro Patria and Res Publica (IRL) and the Social Democratic Party (SDE). The new government faced a major crisis in April 2007, when plans to relocate a Soviet World War II memorial and exhume the remains of Soviet soldiers buried at the site sparked two days of violent protests, mostly by young ethnic Russians. Meanwhile, large-scale cyberattacks, which were reportedly traced to internet addresses within Russia, took down Estonian commercial and governmental websites. Intermittent tensions with Russia have continued; in 2011, Estonia expressed concern over Russia's growing military operations in its western military district, which borders Estonia, and over increased military spending, including Russia's recent contract for the purchase of two warships that could be stationed in the Baltic Sea.

In the March 6, 2011, parliamentary elections, the incumbent Reform Party won 33 seats, the Center Party took 26 seats, the Union of Pro Patria and IRL captured 23 seats, and the SDE won 19 seats. For the first time, both the Green Party and the Estonian People's Union failed to pass the five percent electoral threshold. The Reform Party and the IRL formed a governing coalition, and Andrus Ansip became the first prime minister since Estonia's independence to win two successive elections. Presidential elections were held on August 29, and incumbent Toomas Hendrik Ilves was reelected by Parliament for a second five-year term. He enjoyed the support of 73 members of Parliament, marking the first time since independence a candidate received the requisite two-thirds majority in the first round of voting. Indrek Tarand, an independent candidate nominated by the Center Party, received 25 votes.

The Estonian economy continued its slow recovery from the international downturn that began in 2008, with real GDP growth for 2011 at 7.6 percent, and an unemployment rate that decreased from 14.4 percent to 11.4 percent between the first and fourth quarters of 2011. While the country's entry into the euro currency zone on January 1, 2011, went smoothly, protests were held in Tallinn in September over Estonia's proposed contribution to the eurozone bailout package. However, the government's commitment to long-term fiscal austerity measures was rewarded, when two international ratings agencies upgraded Estonia's credit rating.

Political Rights and Civil Liberties: Estonia is an electoral democracy. The 1992 constitution established a 101-seat, unicameral Parliament, or Riigikogu, whose members are elected for four-year terms. A prime minister serves as head of government, and is chosen by the president and confirmed by Parliament. The president is elected by parliamentary ballot to a five-year term, filling the largely ceremonial role of head of state. Only citizens may participate in national elections; resident noncitizens may vote in local elections but not run as candidates. There are currently 20 women and 10 minorities serving in the Riigikogu.

Political parties organize freely, though only citizens may be members. Major parties include the Reform Party, the IRL, the SDE, the Center Party, the Greens, and the People's Union.

Corruption is regarded as a relatively minor problem in Estonia, which was ranked 29 out of 183 countries surveyed in Transparency International's 2011 Corruption Perceptions Index. In July, a Ministry of Environment official was charged with corruption in association with the awarding of procurement contracts. In the same month, a Narva city councilmen and a construction contractor were arrested on charges of price-setting and entering into cartel agreements over procurement contracts. In September, Parliament expanded the powers of Estonia's security police (KAPO) to investigate public organizations and state-owned companies in addition to government and municipal corruption. By year's end, a revised, draft anticorruption act was under review in Parliament; the act would increase public sector transparency and make requirements more stringent for politicians to declare their assets. In November, it was discovered that two IRL members, a parliamentary deputy and a Tallinn city councillor, had been selling temporary Estonian residence permits to wealthy foreigners for profit. Both men gave up their positions and membership in the IRL, and a parliamentary investigation will take place in 2012. No actions were taken in 2011 against Tallinn mayor and Center Party leader Edgar Savisaar, who was accused by the KAPO in December 2010 of taking 1.5 million (US$2 million) from the president of Russian Railways for use in his 2011 election campaign. Legal guarantees for public access to government information are respected in practice.

The government respects freedom of the press. In addition to the public broadcaster, Estonian Television, there are a variety of commercial channels as well as independent newspapers and radio stations. In November 2010, lawmakers passed the Sources Protection Act, which allows for fines for outlets that provide an "inappropriate," "inaccurate," or libelous assessment of events, and fines for journalists who refuse to reveal sources under certain circumstances. However, no prosecutions were made under the act in 2011. The government does not restrict access to the internet, and Estonia's 2007 legislative polls were the world's first such elections to employ internet voting.

Religious freedom is respected in law and in practice, as is academic freedom. However, a mandate that public, Russian-language high schools teach 60 percent of their curriculum in the Estonian language went into effect in September 2011, prompting 40 Russian students to protest in October. The law is meant to ensure that the Russian-speaking population is granted equal access to jobs, many of which require command of the Estonian language.

The constitution guarantees freedoms of assembly and association, and the government upholds those rights in practice. Tallinn hosted the June 2011 Baltic Pride parade to celebrate sexual diversity without incident. Civil society is vibrant, and the government involves nongovernmental organizations in the drafting of legislation. Workers may organize freely, strike, and bargain collectively, although public servants at the municipal and state levels may not strike. The Confederation of Estonian Trade Unions has reported private sector violations of union rights, including threatening workers with dismissal or pay cuts if they form unions.

The judiciary is independent and generally free from government interference. Laws prohibiting arbitrary arrest and detention and ensuring the right to a fair trial are largely observed. However, the average length of pretrial detention is seven months, due to judicial extensions of the six-month legal limit. There have been reports of police officers physically or verbally abusing suspects. The country's prison system continues to suffer from overcrowding and poor access to health care. In May 2011, the Minister of Justice announced the creation of a specialized center to review prisoners' complaints, which constituted over 40 percent of the cases in Estonia's administrative court system. Plans were also approved in July for a more updated and efficient prison to be built in Tallinn, and a new minimum-security prison to be constructed in the city of Tartu.

Many ethnic Russians arrived in Estonia during the Soviet era and are now regarded as immigrants who must apply for citizenship through a process that requires knowledge of the Estonian language. Roughly 30 percent of Estonians speak Russian as their first language. In 2011, an estimated 7 percent of the population were of undetermined citizenship. The authorities have adopted policies to assist those seeking Estonian citizenship, including funding Estonian-language courses. The use of Estonian is mandatory in certain work environments, including among public sector employees, medical professionals, and service personnel.

Though women enjoy the same legal rights as men, the World Economic Forum's 2011 Global Gender Gap Report found that Estonian women earn roughly 30 percent less than men for the same job—the largest gap in the EU. Violence against women, including domestic violence, remains a problem, and Estonia is a source, transit point, and destination for women trafficked for the purpose of prostitution. Estonia remains the only EU member without a criminal anti-trafficking law.

↓ Ethiopia

Political Rights: 6
Civil Liberties: 6
Status: Not Free

Population: 87,118,000
Capital: Addis Ababa

Trend Arrow: Ethiopia received a downward trend arrow due to the government's increased use of antiterrorism legislation to target political opponents and a decision by the parliament's lower house to include a leading opposition movement in its list of terrorist organizations.

Ten-Year Ratings Timeline For Year Under Review (Political Rights, Civil Liberties, Status)

2002	2003	2004	2005	2006	2007	2008	2009	2010	2011
5,5PF	5,5P	5,5PF	5,5PF	5,5PF	5,5PF	5,5PF	5,5PF	6,6NF	6,6NF

Overview: **Ethiopia's authoritarian government showed no sign of loosening its grip on power in 2011, using an antiterrorism law to target opponents of the ruling party. More than 100 political activists and journalists were detained, often for several months, before being charged with vaguely defined terrorism offenses. Also during the year, tensions with neighboring Eritrea increased after it was accused by a UN panel of plotting a terrorist attack in Ethiopia.**

Ethiopia, one of the few African countries to avoid decades of European colonization, ended a long tradition of monarchy in 1974, when Emperor Haile Selassie was overthrown in a Marxist military coup. Colonel Mengistu Haile Mariam ruled the country until he was toppled by guerrilla groups led by forces from the northern Tigray region in 1991. The main rebel group, the Ethiopian People's Revolutionary Democratic Front (EPRDF), formed a provisional government with Meles Zenawi as head of state.

The EPRDF introduced democratic institutions and a new constitution, and Meles became prime minister after elections in 1995. However, most of the opposition boycotted the polls, claiming harassment of its supporters. The EPRDF easily won the 2000 elections, and Meles began his second five-year term. Opposition parties and some observers criticized the government's conduct of the vote.

A border dispute with Eritrea, which had gained formal independence from Ethiopia in 1993 after a long guerrilla conflict, triggered a 1998–2000 war between the countries. Ethiopia later rejected the findings of an international commission that awarded the contested area to Eritrea, and the two neighbors have remained at odds ever since.

The EPRDF and its allies led the 2005 parliamentary elections, though the main opposition parties performed well, winning a third of the seats. Claiming that voter fraud had deprived them of outright victory, opposition supporters took to the streets. The authorities responded harshly, killing at least 193 people and arresting more than 4,000, including leading opposition figures. Several prominent detainees received harsh sentences, and though all were pardoned and released in 2007, some were later rearrested.

The opposition boycotted local elections in 2008, accusing the EPRDF of harassment. Opposition activities were further restricted in 2009, when 40 members of an unregistered political party were convicted of trying to topple the government. In contrast to the 2005 elections, the May 2010 federal and regional elections were tightly controlled by the EPRDF. Voters were threatened with losing their jobs, homes, or government services if they did not turn out for the ruling party. Opposition meetings were broken up, and candidates were threatened and detained. Opposition-aligned parties saw their 160-seat presence in Parliament virtually disappear, with the EPRDF and its allies taking all but 2 of the 547 seats in the lower house. The European Union and the United States expressed serious reservations about the outcome, but opposition demands for a rerun were dismissed by the Supreme Court. Meles was sworn in for a third term as prime minister in September 2010.

Shorn of its representation in Parliament and placed under relentless pressure by the authorities, opponents of the EPRDF found it increasingly difficult to operate. A planned antigovernment protest inspired by the uprisings in North Africa fizzled out in May 2011. In June, Parliament's lower house declared five groups to be terrorist entities, including the U.S.-based opposition movement Ginbot 7. The designation meant that any journalist who interviewed party members faced possible arrest on terrorism charges. Scores of activists and journalists were arrested in the following months, including well-known actor Debebe Eshetu, who was charged with planning attacks on behalf of Ginbot 7. Two political leaders from the Oromia region were arrested in August and charged under the same antiterrorism legislation; another four politicians were detained the following month.

Tensions between Ethiopia and Eritrea ratcheted up once more after evidence emerged that Eritrean officials were behind a failed plot to bomb an African Union summit and other high-profile targets in Addis Ababa in January. Eritrea denied involvement, but a panel of UN experts endorsed the allegations in a July report. Meles called for regime change in Eritrea and accused his domestic opponents of acting as agents for Asmara. More than 120 suspected members of a leading rebel movement, the Oromo Liberation Front (OLF), were rounded up. In July, 14 were found guilty of involvement in the bomb plot and received lengthy prison terms. Also during the year, the government claimed successes against the main rebel movement in the Ogaden region. The Ogaden National Liberation Front (ONLF) had split in two, with one faction signing a peace deal in 2010 and winning the release of 400 members from prison in January 2011. Military operations continued against the other faction, which alleged that 100 civilians were killed during a government offensive in May.

A prolonged drought, the worst to hit the Horn of Africa in 60 years, left nearly 5 million Ethiopians in need of assistance at the end of 2011. Over 270,000 refugees fleeing famine in Somalia had crossed into Ethiopia, adding to the crisis. Ethiopians' difficulties were compounded by large rises in the price of food; the annual rate of inflation reached 41 percent in August.

Political Rights and Civil Liberties: Ethiopia is not an electoral democracy. Parliament is made up of a 108-seat upper house, the House of Federation, and a 547-seat lower house, the House of People's Representatives. The lower house is filled through popular elections, while the upper chamber is selected by the state legislatures, with both serving five-year terms. The lower house selects the prime minister, who holds most executive power, and the president, a largely ceremonial figure who serves up to two six-year terms. However, all of these institutions are dominated by the EPRDF, which tightly controlled the 2010 elections. The leader of the EPRDF, Meles Zenawi, has ruled continuously since 1991, first as transitional head of state and then as prime minister. While the 1995 constitution in theory grants the right of secession to ethnically based states, the government acquired powers in 2003 to intervene in states' affairs on issues of public security.

Corruption is a significant problem in Ethiopia. According to the Heritage Foundation's Index of Economic Freedom, EPRDF officials receive preferential access to credit, land leases, and jobs.

The news media are dominated by state-owned broadcasters and government-oriented newspapers. One of the few independent papers in the capital, *Addis Neger*, closed in 2009, claiming harassment by the authorities. Privately owned papers are small in number, tend to steer clear of political issues, and have low circulations. A 2008 media law allows prosecutors to seize material before publication in the name of national security, and makes defamation a criminal offense.

Journalists who reported on opposition activities faced serious harassment in 2011. Two newspaper reporters were detained under the country's antiterrorism law in June. They were formally charged with terrorism offenses during a court hearing in September, at which one of them claimed to have been tortured. A third journalist was charged in absentia. In a separate case, two Swedish journalists were charged on the same day with terrorism offenses for reporting on the activities of the ONLF. In December, they were found guilty of supporting terrorism and were each sentenced to 11 years in prison. Another well-known journalist, Eskinder Nega, who had previously been pardoned for treason relating to the postelection protests in 2005, was detained again in September and accused of terrorism. Because of these risks, many of Ethiopia's journalists work in exile. In September, a reporter fled the country after being asked to reveal the source of a story he wrote that was cited in a U.S. diplomatic cable published by the antisecrecy group WikiLeaks. The authorities routinely block opposition websites, and in 2010, they jammed the Amharic-language broadcasts of Voice of America for eight months.

Constitutionally mandated religious freedom is generally respected, though religious tensions have risen in recent years. The Ethiopian Orthodox Church is influential, particularly in the north. In the east there is a large Muslim community, made up mainly of the Somali, Oromo, and Afar ethnic groups.

Academic freedom is restricted. The government has accused universities of being friendly to the opposition, and prohibits political activities on campuses. There have been reports of students being pressured into joining the EPRDF in order to secure places at universities.

The presence of the EPRDF at all levels of society inhibits free private discussion. Many people are wary of speaking against the government for fear of being overheard by party officials. The EPRDF maintains a network of paid informants, and opposition politicians have accused the government of tapping their telephones.

Freedoms of assembly and association are guaranteed by the constitution but limited in practice. Organizers of large public meetings must request permission from the authorities 48 hours in advance. Applications by opposition groups are routinely denied. During the 2010 election campaign, police routinely broke up political rallies and meetings organized by the opposition.

The 2009 Charities and Societies Proclamation restricts the activities of foreign nongovernmental organizations (NGOs) by prohibiting work on human and political rights. Foreign NGOs are defined as groups receiving more than 10 percent of their funding from abroad, a classification that captures most domestic organizations as well. NGOs have struggled to maintain operations as a result of the law, which also obliged them to reregister with the authorities. According to Justice Ministry figures, there were 3,522 registered NGOs before the law was passed and 1,655 afterward. In 2010, the Ethiopian Human Rights Council and the Ethiopian Women Lawyers' Association had their bank accounts frozen for violating the rules on receiving foreign funds, and the Ethiopian Bar Association had its license suspended for alleged irregularities. It was forced to register under a new name after its identity was assumed by a new organization affiliated with the EPRDF. In August 2011, a visiting delegation from Amnesty International was expelled following a meeting with opposition leaders, who were subsequently arrested.

Trade union rights are tightly restricted. All unions must be registered, and the government retains the authority to cancel registration. Two-thirds of union members belong to organizations affiliated with the Confederation of Ethiopian Trade Unions (CETU), which is under government influence. Independent unions face harassment. There has not been a legal strike since 1993.

The judiciary is officially independent, but its judgments rarely deviate from government policy. The 2009 Antiterrorism Proclamation defines terrorist activity very broadly and gives great discretion to the security forces, allowing the detention of suspects for up to four months without charge. It was used in 2011 to detain more than 100 members of opposition parties; terrorist suspects were denied legal assistance while they awaited trial. Conditions in Ethiopia's prisons are harsh, and detainees frequently report abuse.

The government has tended to favor Tigrayan ethnic interests in economic and political matters. Politics within the EPRDF have been dominated by the Tigrayan People's Liberation Front, one of its constituent groups. Repression of the Oromo and ethnic Somalis, and government attempts to co-opt their parties into subsidiaries of the EPRDF, have fueled nationalism in both Oromia and the Ogaden. Persistent claims that war crimes have been committed by government troops in the Ogaden are difficult to verify, as independent media are barred from the region.

Private business opportunities are limited by rigid state control of economic life and the prevalence of state-owned enterprises. All land must be leased from the state. The government has evicted indigenous groups from areas like the Lower Omo Valley to make way for projects such as hydroelectric dams. It has also leased large tracts of land to foreign governments and investors for agricultural development in opaque deals. Persistent allegations have been made by journalists and groups such as Human Rights Watch that the government has withheld development assistance from villages perceived as being unfriendly to the ruling party.

Women are relatively well represented in Parliament, winning 152 seats in the lower house in the 2010 elections. Legislation protects women's rights, but they are routinely violated in practice. Forced child labor is a significant problem, particularly in the agricultural sector.

Fiji

Political Rights: 6
Civil Liberties: 4
Status: Partly Free

Population: 852,000
Capital: Suva

Ten-Year Ratings Timeline For Year Under Review (Political Rights, Civil Liberties, Status)

2002	2003	2004	2005	2006	2007	2008	2009	2010	2011
4,3PF	4,3PF	4,3PF	4,3PF	6,4PF	6,4PF	6,4PF	6,4PF	6,4PF	6,4PF

Overview: **New antiunion regulations, which took effect in September 2011, seriously limit trade union and collective bargaining rights. Also during the year, the interim government tightened control over the media, and prominent political opponents and critics continued to face harassment, including overseas travel bans, arrests, and serious charges such as sedition.**

Fiji, colonized by Great Britain in 1874, became an independent member of the Commonwealth in 1970. Intense rivalry between indigenous Fijians and Indo-Fijians is the main source of political and social tension in the country. Indians, who were first brought to Fiji in the 19th century to work on sugar plantations, came to control a large share of the economy. Armed coups by indigenous factions in 1987 and 2000 overthrew governments led by Indo-Fijian parties.

Following the 2000 coup, the military installed Laisenia Qarase, an indigenous Fijian of the United Fiji Party (UFP), to lead an interim government. Qarase was elected prime minister in 2001 and won a second term in 2006. That year, differences between Qarase and military chief Frank Bainimarama—another indigenous Fijian—over the fate of the 2000 coup participants resulted in another military coup. In December 2006, Bainimarama ousted Qarase and dissolved Parliament. He soon began silencing his critics, including filing legal suits against opposition leaders, and detaining, arresting, and expelling journalists.

In 2008, a 45-member council—handpicked by Bainimarama—completed the drafting of the People's Charter for Change, Peace, and Progress, a legal document designed to complement the constitution. The charter recommended addressing major sources of ethnic tensions by replacing communal electoral rolls with a one-person-one-vote system, and designating all citizens as Fijians, a term previously reserved only for the indigenous. The charter also officially confirmed the military's role in governing Fiji, paving the way for the replacement of civilians with military personnel in many high-level positions.

In 2009, the court of appeals ruled that the 2006 dismissal of Qarase and his cabinet, the dissolution of Parliament, and the 2007 appointment of Bainimarama as interim prime minister were illegal. The interim president, Josefa Iloilo, was ordered to appoint a caretaker prime minister to dissolve Parliament and call elections. The next day, Iloilo suspended the 1997 constitution, nullified all judicial appointments, reconfirmed himself as president, reappointed Bainimarama as interim prime minister, and imposed Public Emergency Regulations (PER) to ban public protests and tighten government control of the media. In July 2009, Iloilo stepped down, and Vice-President Epeli Nailatikau assumed the role of interim president.

The international community reacted by terminating millions of dollars in development aid and suspending Fiji from the Commonwealth. In spite of international pressure, Bainimarama announced in 2009 that new elections would not be held until September 2014, pending the passage by 2013 of a new constitution that would address the recommendations of the People's Charter. Bainimarama also declared in March 2010 that no politician active since 1987 would be allowed to run in the 2014 elections. In 2010, the interim government granted immunity from prosecution to all those involved in the 2000 and 2006 coups who had not been convicted in court hearings. Beneficiaries included Iloilo, Bainimarama, and members of the military, police, and prison service.

In 2011, the interim government continued to silence its critics. Ratu Tevita Uluilakeba Mara, a former lieutenant colonel and ally of Bainimarama in the 2006 coup, absconded bail and fled to Tonga in May, accused of making seditious comments and inciting a mutiny. Mara's sister, Adi Ateca Ganilau, then lost her position in July as head of the Lau provincial council for allegedly criticizing the interim government. On December 30, Dr. Mere Samisoni, a 74-year-old former parliamentarian who has close ties to Mara's family, was taken into military custody and charged with inciting violence. The interim government also increased its control of organized labor during the year, including limiting collective bargaining rights, refusing to grant permits for union meetings, and harassing union leaders.

Fiji's economy continued to suffer from the global economic downturn and the suspension of development assistance from international donors. The government consequently intensified efforts to attract Chinese investment in casino gaming, hotels, and mining. In 2011, China promised $4.3 million to fund a new hospital and gave $3 million to various development programs. To increase state revenues, the interim government raised the value-added tax in January and cut pensions in September.

Political Rights and Civil Liberties:

Fiji is not an electoral democracy. Under the 1997 constitution, which was suspended in 2009, Parliament consisted of a 32-seat Senate and a 71-seat House of Representatives. The president was appointed to a five-year term by the Great Council of Chiefs; however, this role was suspended in 2007. The prime minister was appointed by the president and was generally the leader of the majority party or coalition in Parliament. Since the suspension of the constitution, the interim government has essentially ruled by decree.

The two main political parties are the UFP, largely supported by indigenous Fijians, and the Fiji Labor Party, which has a largely Indo-Fijian constituency.

Official corruption remains widespread, and reform agendas by multiple governments have not produced significant results.

While the 1997 constitution provided for freedoms of speech and of the press, extensive government censorship has been in place under the PER since 2009. In 2010, the government created the Media Industry Development Authority to enforce more restrictive media laws, including one requiring all media organizations to be 90 percent owned by local entities. The interim authorities continued their crackdown on freedom of expression in 2011. Numerous *Fiji Times* reporters were detained or arrested for material deemed critical of the government or its industries. In May, Mahendra Mohitibai Patel, the owner of *Fiji Times*, was sentenced to a year in prison for abuse of office while he was the managing director of *Post Fiji* for buying a clock for the office building without board approval. In August, the Ministry of Information began to require all media organizations to send news headlines to on-site government censors for approval half an hour before stories are published or broadcast. The interim government arrested five people in October for graffiti it considered seditious, and requested a closed court for their hearing in December. Access to the internet is spreading with increased competition, but remains limited outside the capital due to cost and infrastructure constraints.

Freedom of religion is generally respected, but the interim government appears to target those, including religious leaders, who speak out against the regime. Most indigenous Fijians are Christians, and Indo-Fijians are generally Hindus. Places of worship, especially Hindu temples, have been attacked. In August 2011, the interim government canceled the Methodist Church annual conference for the third consecutive year, citing that the speakers included senior church officials critical of the interim government. Methodist officials were also banned from traveling overseas to attend church meetings and conferences. Hindus are also now required to obtain a permit to hold religious events that involve more than 10 people.

While academic freedom is generally respected, the education system suffers from a lack of resources, and indigenous Fijians are granted special privileges in education.

Freedoms of assembly and association have been restricted since 2009, when the interim government suspended the 1997 constitution and imposed the PER, which gives power to law enforcement authorities to prohibit any public or private assemblies or meetings by three or more people.

The interim government increased its control over organized labor in 2011. In July, the interim government stopped automatically deducting union dues from the salaries of civil servants, claiming that union dues were unnecessary since amendments to the Public Service Act protect the rights of workers. The Essential National Industries Decree limits trade union and collective bargaining rights for those employed in industries that are considered essential to Fiji's economy, including the sugar industry, the airline industry, utility corporations, banks, and telecommunication firms. The decree took effect in September. Previously held collective agreements remained valid only for 60 days, until new agreements could be negotiated, and strikes in essential businesses were banned. Violations carry a penalty of $50,000 or five years in jail. Furthermore, all union officials must be employees of the company whose workers they represent, and bargaining units must have at least 75 members. In October and November, the interim government arrested Daniel Urai and Felix Anthony, leaders of the Fiji Trades Union Congress. Urai was charged with sedition and released after posting bail, while Anthony was interrogated and released without being charged. Also in December, the government refused to grant permits—required under the PER—for union meetings.

Suspension of the constitution in 2009, the related dismissal of judges, and their replacement by appointees of the interim government have raised serious questions about judicial independence. The 2009 dismissals exacerbated an already serious backlog of cases, which continued in 2011. Prisons are seriously overcrowded, with poor sanitary and living conditions.

Race-based discrimination is pervasive. Indigenous Fijians receive preferential treatment in education, housing, land acquisition, and other areas. Discrimination, economic hardship, and political turmoil have prompted many Indo-Fijians to leave Fiji. A December 2011 study reported that an estimated 250,000 Fijians—many of them educated and skilled Indo-Fijians—had left the country in the last 25 years.

Discrimination and violence against women are widespread. Women are also underrepresented in government and leadership positions and do not receive equal wages. Homosexuality was decriminalized in 2010. A decree was passed in January 2011 to officially outlaw discrimination against people with HIV/AIDS. Fiji is a source country for the trafficking of children for sexual exploitation and a destination country for the trafficking of men and women for forced labor and prostitution.

Finland

Political Rights: 1
Civil Liberties: 1
Status: Free

Population: 5,387,000
Capital: Helsinki

Ten-Year Ratings Timeline For Year Under Review (Political Rights, Civil Liberties, Status)

2002	2003	2004	2005	2006	2007	2008	2009	2010	2011
1,1F	1,1F	1,1F	1,1F	1,1F	1,1F	1,1F	1,1F	1,1F	1,1F

Overview: **In April 2011 parliamentary elections, the True Finns—a nationalist, populist party led by Timo Soini—captured an unprecedented 19 percent of the popular vote but was eventually excluded from the six-party coalition government. The elections attracted international attention due to the True Finns' fierce opposition to European Union economic bailouts for Portugal and Greece. Immigration remained a politically sensitive topic during the year, and Finland made its first arrest in an anti-terrorism case in September.**

After centuries of Swedish and then Russian rule, Finland gained independence in 1917. The country has traditionally been neutral, but its army has enjoyed broad popular support since it fended off a Soviet invasion during World War II. Finland joined the European Union (EU) in 1995 and is the only Nordic country to have adopted the euro currency.

In the 2000 presidential election, Tarja Halonen of the Social Democratic Party (SDP) was elected as the country's first female president. She defeated six other candidates—including three women—from across the political spectrum. Halonen won a second term as president in 2006. In the 2007 parliamentary elections, the ruling Center Party held on to its plurality by one seat, while the National Coalition Party (KOK), a moderate conservative party, gained 10 seats; the left-leaning parties received record-low levels of support. Acknowledging the shift to the right, Prime Minister Matti Vanhanen formed a four-party coalition consisting of his Center Party, the KOK, the Greens, and the Swedish People's Party, leaving the SDP in opposition for the first time since 1995.

In February 2010, the National Bureau of Investigation began investigating accusations of malfeasance against Vanhanen over his involvement in the distribution of government funds to a nongovernmental organization that had supported his 2006 campaign. The prime minister announced his resignation in June but cited medical and family issues for his departure. On June 22, the Finnish Parliament appointed Center Party leader Mari Kiviniemi as Vanhanen's replacement until the April 2011 elections. In February 2011, parliament voted to drop the charges of malfeasance against Vanhanen, and decided that he would not have to face a court of impeachment.

The April 2011 parliamentary elections resulted in a dramatic shift in Finnish politics. Most significantly, the populist, nationalist party True Finns, led by Timo Soini, gained an unprecedented 19 percent of the popular vote, increasing their seats from 5 to 39, making them the third-largest party. The ruling Center Party was ousted with a loss of 16 seats (down from 51), representing the biggest loss of any party in postwar Finland. Every other party in parliament but the True Finns experienced either a loss or maintained their number of seats, with left-leaning parties continuing to receive less support. The elections attracted an unusual amount of international attention due to the very vocal opposition to eurozone bailouts from the vehemently, euro-skeptic True Finns. Finland is the only country in the EU that has reserved the right to put any bailout to parliamentary vote.

After two months of tense negotiations, a coalition government was formed in June 2011, comprised of the KOK, led by Prime Minister Jyrki Katainen, along with the SDP, the Left Alliance, the Green League, the Swedish People's Party, and the Christian Democrats. The True Finns withdrew from coalition talks in May, when Parliament approved the bailout package for Portugal.

Political Rights and Civil Liberties: Finland is an electoral democracy. The president, whose role is mainly ceremonial, is directly elected for a six-year term. The president appoints the prime minister and deputy prime minister from the majority party or coalition after elections; the selection must be approved by Parliament. Representatives in the 200-seat unicameral Parliament, or Eduskunta, are elected to four-year terms. The Åland Islands—an autonomous region located off the southwestern coast, whose inhabitants speak Swedish—have their own 30-seat Parliament, as well as a seat in the national legislature. The indigenous Saami of northern Finland also have their own legislature.

Corruption is not a significant problem in Finland. A 2010 law requires candidates and parties to report campaign donations of more than EUR 800 (US$1,072) in local elections or EUR 1,500 (US$2,010) in parliamentary elections. However, the campaign law had no major impact on campaign financing for the 2011 elections.

Finland was ranked 2 out of 183 countries surveyed in Transparency International's 2011 Corruption Perceptions Index.

Finnish law provides for freedom of speech, which is also respected in practice. Finland has a large variety of newspapers and magazines and protects the right to reply to public criticism. Newspapers are privately owned but publicly subsidized, and many are controlled by or support a particular political party. In March 2010, the Finnish police launched an internet tip-off system in an effort to simplify flagging threats of violence and racist slander.

Finns enjoy freedom of religion. The Evangelical Lutheran Church and the Orthodox Church are both state churches and receive public money from the income taxes of members; citizens may exempt themselves from contributing to those funds, but must renounce their membership. Religious communities other than the state churches may also receive state funds. Religious education is part of the curriculum in all secondary public schools, but students may opt out in favor of more general instruction in ethics. In September 2010, Finland's Evangelical Lutheran Church ordained its first female bishop. In April 2011, a Lutheran minister was defrocked and stripped of his priestly livelihood for referring to the Chechen national Dokku Umarov as a "terrorist," Academic freedom is respected.

Freedoms of association and assembly are upheld in law and in practice. Workers have the right to organize, bargain collectively, and strike. Throughout October and November 2011, significant, weeklong strikes took place in the technology, banking, and metal/engineering sectors. However, unlike the harbor strikes of 2010, no exports or production were disrupted. Industry leaders expressed concern that adhering to collective frameworks for wage negotiations crippled Finnish industry; eventually all parties accepted mediations and returned to work. Approximately 70 percent of workers belong to trade unions.

The constitution provides for an independent judiciary, which consists of the Supreme Court, the supreme administrative court, and the lower courts. The president appoints Supreme Court judges, who in turn appoint the lower-court judges. Finland has been criticized by the European Court of Human Rights for slow trial procedures. The Ministry of the Interior controls police and Frontier Guard forces. Ethnic minorities and asylum seekers report occasional police discrimination.

The criminal code covers ethnic agitation and penalizes anyone who threatens a racial, national, ethnic, or religious group. The constitution guarantees the Saami cultural autonomy and the right to pursue their traditional livelihoods, which include fishing and reindeer herding. Their language and culture are also protected through public financial support. However, representatives of the community have complained that they cannot exercise their rights in practice and that they do not have the right to self-determination with respect to land use. While Roma also make up a very small percentage of the population, they are more significantly disadvantaged and marginalized.

Immigration issues remained divisive in 2011, gaining particular prominence with the political ascent of the True Finns. According to a November 2011 poll commissioned by *Helsingin Sanomat*, True Finns supporters were twice as likely to exhibit negative attitudes towards foreigners as non-True Finns voters. The political identity of the True Finns on this particular issue remains a controversial subject, both within and outside the party. Leader Timo Soini has sought to maintain a more moderate stance on immigration, but several high-profile members of Parliament belonging to the nationalist group Suomen Sisu have expressed fierce disagreement with party leadership on this issue. Internet death threats against Minister of Migration and European Affairs Astrid Thors continued in 2011.

Women enjoy equal rights in Finland. Women hold approximately 42 percent of the seats in Parliament, and 9 of 19 cabinet ministers are women. Despite a law stipulating equal pay for equal work, women earn only about 82 percent as much as men with the same qualifications. Domestic violence is an ongoing concern. Finland remains a destination and a transit country for trafficked men, women, and children. Amendments to the Alien Act in 2006 allow trafficked victims to stay in the country and qualify for employment rights.

France

Political Rights: 1
Civil Liberties: 1
Status: Free

Population: 63,305,000
Capital: Paris

Ten-Year Ratings Timeline For Year Under Review (Political Rights, Civil Liberties, Status)

2002	2003	2004	2005	2006	2007	2008	2009	2010	2011
1,1F	1,1F	1,1F	1,1F	1,1F	1,1F	1,1F	1,1F	1,1F	1,1F

Overview: **Control of the Senate was captured by the left in September 2011 elections for the first time since the founding of the Fifth Republic. Reforms regarding police custody were approved in January to grant suspects the right to remain silent and to have an attorney present during questioning. France continued to face criticism for a controversial ban on full facial coverings, which came into effect in April, and restrictions on internet freedom.**

After the French Revolution of 1789, France experienced both republic and monarchist regimes until the creation of the Third Republic in 1871. The Fourth Republic was established after World War II, but eventually fell victim to domestic political turbulence and a series of colonial setbacks. In 1958, Charles de Gaulle, France's wartime leader, created the strong presidential system of the Fifth Republic, which stands today.

Jacques Chirac, a right-leaning Gaullist, was first elected president in 1995. In the first round of the 2002 presidential election, Jean-Marie Le Pen—head of the far-right, xenophobic National Front—unexpectedly received more votes than Lionel Jospin, the prime minister and head of the center-left Socialist Party (PS). However, with Socialist support, Chirac defeated Le Pen overwhelmingly in the second round.

In late 2005, the accidental deaths of two teenagers of North African descent who were fleeing police touched off weeks of violent riots. Most of the rioters were youths descended from immigrants from North and sub-Saharan Africa. Despite their French birth and citizenship, many reported discrimination and harassment by police in anticrime operations. The violence provoked a major discussion about the failure to fully integrate minorities into French society.

The ruling Union for a Popular Movement (UMP) nominated party leader Nicolas Sarkozy as its candidate for the 2007 presidential elections. However, Sarkozy's law-and-order message, pro-American foreign policy views, opposition to Turkish European Union (EU) membership, and other positions made him a controversial candidate. Sarkozy defeated the PS candidate Ségolène Royal in the second round, with 53 percent of the vote, and the UMP renewed its majority in subsequent parliamentary elections.

The government's popularity declined in late 2007, when riots erupted after two teenagers of African descent were killed in a collision with a police car. Unlike in 2005, the riots were better organized, and scores of police were wounded.

By May 2008, Sarkozy's popularity was the lowest of any first-year president in 50 years. His reputation recovered somewhat with a revived foreign and domestic agenda, including economic liberalization, though it declined again with the arrival of the global economic crisis. The economic downturn caused an increase in already high unemployment and incited many protests in 2009.

The government considered a number of reforms in 2010 to decrease the country's debt, the most significant of which was an increase in the retirement age from 60 to 62, which became law in November. The controversial proposals touched off weeks of protests and strikes throughout the summer and fall.

On September 25, 2011, indirect elections for some half the seats in the Senate gave control to parties on the left for the first time in the history of France's Fifth Republic. Jean-Pierre Bel was also elected the country's first Socialist Senate president on October 1, 2011.

During the year, the government imposed a series of controversial legal measures, such as restrictions on internet freedoms, and a ban on full facial coverings. However, measures were taken to improve the rights of suspects in police custody.

Political Rights and Civil Liberties: France is an electoral democracy. The president and members of the lower house of Parliament, the 577-seat National Assembly, are elected to five-year terms. The upper house, the 348-seat Senate, is an indirectly elected body whose members serve six-year terms. The prime minister is appointed by the president. Until 1986, the president and prime minister were always of the same party, and the president was the most powerful figure in the country. However, since 1986, there have been periods lasting several years in which the president and prime minister hailed from rival parties. In such circumstances, the prime minister has the dominant role in domestic affairs, while the president largely guides foreign policy.

Parties organize and compete on a free and fair basis. The center-left PS and the center-right UMP are the largest parties, though the largely unreformed French Communist Party on the left and the far-right National Front party receive significant support. The National Front, led by Jean-Marie Le Pen's daughter Marine, is opposed to immigration and advocates an increasingly eurosceptic position; the party's popularity has risen as President Nicolas Sarkozy's support has declined. Members of the French elite, trained in a small number of prestigious schools, often move between politics and business, increasing opportunities for corruption. In 2010, Labor Minister Éric Woerth was accused of corruption for allegedly accepting illegal donations from L'Oréal heiress Liliane Bettencourt on behalf of Sarkozy's campaign in 2007; however, no direct connection to Sarkozy has been found in investigations that were ongoing at year's end. Formal corruption charges were brought against former president Jacques Chirac in 2009 for events that dated back to when he was mayor of Paris. On December 15, 2011, he was found guilty of diverting public funds and abusing public trust, and received a two-year suspended sentence. Furthermore, in September, a former aide accused Chirac and potential presidential candidate Dominique de Villepin of receiving $20 million in cash from leaders of former African colonies to finance elections. An official inquiry into the allegations was dropped in November, however, due to lack of evidence. Meanwhile, two of Sarkozy's political allies, Thierry Gaubert and Nicolas Bazire, were arrested in September on charges of misuse of public funds in an arms sale to Pakistan in 1994; the investigation was ongoing at year's end. France was ranked 25 out of 183 countries surveyed in Transparency International's 2011 Corruption Perceptions Index.

The media operate freely and represent a wide range of political opinions. Though an 1881 law forbids "offending" various personages, including the president and foreign heads of state, the press remains lively and critical. However, journalists covering events involving the National Front or the Corsican separatist movement have been harassed, and they have also faced difficulty covering unrest in the volatile suburbs. Reporters covering criminal cases or publishing material from confidential court documents have occasionally come under pressure by the courts to reveal sources. In 2010 daily newspaper *Le Monde* filed a complaint against the government after a public prosecutor was ordered to obtain a list of calls made by two of its journalists in connection with the Bettencourt case. In September 2011, the government confirmed that its intelligence agency had requisitioned the reporters' telephone records, claiming that its actions were legal, as they were in defense of national interests. In November, the offices of the magazine *Charlie Hebdo* were burned and its website hacked the day the magazine's cover was due to feature a cartoon depiction of Mohammed.

While internet access is generally unrestricted, a new domestic security law, which came into effect in March 2011, allows the filtering of online content; while this is ostensibly to prevent child pornography, free media advocates call it unnecessary censorship. A separate March decree requires internet companies to provide user data, including passwords, to authorities if requested; several major companies including Google and Microsoft, have protested.

Freedom of religion is protected by the constitution, and strong antidefamation laws prohibit religiously motivated attacks. Denial of the Nazi Holocaust is illegal. France maintains the policy of laïcité, whereby religion and government affairs are strictly separated. A 2004 law bans "ostentatious" religious symbols in schools. In October 2010, the Senate nearly unanimously passed a bill banning clothing that covers the face, including the burqa and niqab, in public spaces. The ban went into effect in April 2011. Violators of the ban can be fined up to 150 Euros (approximately US$215) or ordered to take citizenship lessons, and a man who forces a woman to wear a niqab can be fined 30,000 Euros (approximately US$43,000). The first fine, of 150 Euros, was issued in April to a woman in the northwest of Paris. In addition, a controversial September 2011 directive bans street prayer, affecting thousands of Muslims in Paris who had previously prayed in the street due to a lack of space in local mosques. Academic freedom is respected by French authorities.

Freedoms of assembly and association are respected. Civic organizations and nongovernmental organizations can operate freely. Trade union organizations are weak, and membership has been declining since 1980. Nevertheless, civil service unions remain relatively strong, and strike movements generally gain wide public support.

France has an independent judiciary, and the rule of law is firmly established. The country's antiterrorism campaign has included surveillance of mosques, and terrorism suspects can be detained for up to four days without charge. In response to repeated challenges from the European Court of Human Rights, the National Assembly adopted new rules in January 2011 that extend the right to suspects to remain silent and to have an attorney present during questioning. In February, members of the judiciary went on strike in cities throughout the country to protest executive interference after Sarkozy publicly criticized the handling of a well-publicized murder case. Prisons are overcrowded, and suicides are common.

French law forbids the categorization of people according to ethnic origin, and no official statistics are collected on ethnicity. However, the riots and violence in 2005 and 2007 fueled concerns about Arab and African immigration and the failure of integration policies in France, where minorities are underrepresented in leadership positions in both the private and public sectors. Discrimination against immigrants and religious and ethnic minorities remains a problem.

During 2010, France deported at least 8,000 Roma to Bulgaria and Romania and dismantled over 400 camps on the outskirts of French cities. Although the government claimed that the deportations were part of a larger crackdown on illegal immigration, a leaked memo from the interior ministry revealed that officials had been instructed to prioritize the dismantling of Roma camps, thus constituting illegal discrimination. Deportations continued during 2011, with official statistics reporting nearly 5,000 deportations in the first three months alone. Close to 6,000 were evicted between April and October according to the nongovernmental European Roma Rights Center.

Corsica continues to host a sometimes violent separatist movement. Low-level attacks against property and government targets continue to occur, though people are rarely harmed. In 2001, the government devolved some legislative powers to the island and allowed teaching in the Corsican language in public schools.

Gender equality is protected in France. Constitutional reforms in 2008 institutionalized economic and social equality. However, in the 2011 Global Gender Gap report, France ranked the lowest of 131 countries that responded to a question on wage equality. Some electoral lists require the alternation of candidates by sex. Women hold only 18 percent of seats in the legislature and 22 percent of Senate seats, but have served as key ministers, as well as the prime minister. Discrimination based on sexual orientation is prohibited by law. While a type of civil union for same-sex partners is recognized, the Constitutional Council upheld a ban on same-sex marriage in January 2011.

Gabon

Political Rights: 6
Civil Liberties: 5
Status: Not Free

Population: 1,534,300
Capital: Libreville

Ten-Year Ratings Timeline For Year Under Review (Political Rights, Civil Liberties, Status)

2002	2003	2004	2005	2006	2007	2008	2009	2010	2011
5,4PF	5,4PF	5,4PF	6,4PF	6,4PF	6,4PF	6,4PF	6,5NF	6,5NF	6,5NF

Overview: **Tensions between President Ali Ben Bongo Ondimba and National Union (UN) opposition leader André Mba Obame erupted in January 2011, when Obame declared himself the rightful winner of the 2009 presidential election. The ensuing government crackdown resulted in the dissolution of the UN party, and Obame was charged with treason. An opposition boycott of the December legislative election led to a landslide victory for the ruling Gabonese Democratic Party.**

Gabon gained independence from France in 1960. Omar Bongo Ondimba became president in 1967 and solidified the Gabonese Democratic Party's (PDG) grip on power. In 1990, protests prompted by economic hardship led to multiparty legislative elections. Bongo and the ruling PDG retained power over subsequent years through a series of flawed elections.

In 2006 legislative elections, the PDG and allied parties won some 100 of the 120 seats in the National Assembly, the bicameral parliament's lower house. Observers called the elections credible and an improvement over the 2005 presidential contest, which had led to postelection violence and accusations of irregularities. Regional and municipal councilors voted in the 2009 Senate election in which the PDG captured 75 of 102 seats.

Bongo died in June 2009, after more than 40 years in power, and in keeping with the constitution, Senate president Rose Francine Rogombe became interim head of state. Defense Minister Ali Ben Bongo Ondimba, son of the late president, was nominated as the PDG candidate for a snap presidential election. Several senior PDG figures, including former interior minister André Mba Obame, decided to run as independents. Bongo won the August 2009 election with almost 42 percent of the vote, while Mba Obame and Pierre Mamboundou each received 25 percent. Although the opposition challenged the official results amid violent protests, the Constitutional Court upheld Bongo's victory following a recount in September.

On January 25, 2011, Mba Obame declared himself the legitimate president of Gabon and established a parallel government. Drawing analogies with the successful rebellion against Tunisia's Ben Ali regime, Mba Obame and his supporters tried to ignite a popular uprising. However, aside from a series of demonstrations held on January 29, Mba Obame's pronouncements did not lead to large-scale protests. The Gabonese government charged Mba Obame with treason and outlawed his opposition party, the National Union (UN).

Legislative elections for the 120-seat National Assembly were held on December 17, 2011. Voter turnout was only 34 percent due to a boycott called by the opposition over the Bongo government's failure to implement biometric technology for voter registration. Claiming to respect a June 2011 Constitutional Court ruling that rejected a proposal to delay elections for a year, the Bongo government announced in August that the December legislative elections would be held as planned. Consequently, 13 opposition parties withdrew from Gabon's independent electoral commission in protest. As a result, the PDG captured 114 of the 120 seats. By year's end, 45 objections to the election had been filed, and the Constitutional Court had yet to confirm the results.

Political Rights and Civil Liberties: Gabon is not an electoral democracy. The 2009 presidential election was marred by irregularities, including allegations of vote rigging and intimidation of the press. The 2011 legislative elections were boycotted by the opposition. The president is elected for seven-year terms, and a 2003 constitutional amendment removed the two-term limit imposed in 1991. The president has extensive powers, including the authority to appoint judges and dissolve the parliament. The bicameral legislature consists of a 102-seat Senate and a 120-seat National Assembly. Regional and municipal officials elect senators for six-year terms, while National Assembly members are elected by popular vote for five-year terms. In December 2010, the legislature approved several constitutional amendments, including one that permits the president to prolong his term during a declared national emergency.

Freedom to form and join political parties is generally respected, but civil servants face harassment and discrimination if they affiliate with opposition groups. The PDG has held power continuously since 1968. Of some 50 other registered parties, 40 are part of the PDG's ruling coalition, the Union for the Gabonese Presidential Majority. In late 2009, eight opposition parties formed a new alliance, the Coalition of Groups and Political Parties for Change (CGPPA), with presidential runner-up Mba Obame as a leading member. In 2010, the CGPPA coalesced into the opposition UN party, which received accreditation in April. However, the UN party was dissolved by the Gabonese government in response to Mba Obame appointing himself president in January 2011.

Corruption is widespread, and rampant graft prevents the country's significant natural-resource revenue from benefiting most citizens. In February 2010, the U.S. Senate released a report highlighting money laundering by former president Omar Bongo and his family in the United States. Combating corruption is touted as a priority by the government, which has, among other things, audited government agencies to expunge ghost workers from payrolls. Gabon was ranked 100 out of 183 countries surveyed in Transparency International's 2011 Corruption Perceptions Index.

Press freedom is guaranteed by law but restricted in practice. The state has the power to criminalize civil libel suits, and because legal cases against journalists are relatively common, many reporters practice self-censorship. State-controlled outlets dominate the broadcast media, but there are some private broadcasters, and foreign news sources are available. Opposition-affiliated media continued to face restrictions in 2011, including limited access to broadcasting towers. Access to the internet is not restricted by the government.

Religious freedom is enshrined in the constitution and generally upheld by the authorities. The government does not restrict academic freedom.

The rights of assembly and association are legally guaranteed but not always respected in practice. On January 29, 2011, police used tear gas to break up pro-UN protests. Due to the lack of strong opposition parties, nongovernmental organizations (NGOs) are important vehicles for scrutiny of the government. However, it remains difficult for these groups to operate freely. In 2008 the interior minister suspended 22 NGOs for a week after they issued a public statement criticizing the government. Virtually the entire private sector workforce is unionized, and collective bargaining is allowed by industry, not by firm.

The judiciary is not independent. Judges may deliver summary verdicts in some cases, and prosecutions of former government officials appear to target opposition members. However, rights to legal counsel and a public criminal trial are generally respected. Torture is sometimes used to extract confessions. Prison conditions are poor, and long periods of pretrial detention are common.

Discrimination against African immigrants is widespread, and security forces harass and solicit bribes from African expatriates working in the country. Though equal under the law, most of Gabon's several thousand indigenous Pygmies live in extreme poverty in isolated forest communities and are often exploited as cheap labor.

The law provides for gender equality in education and employment, but women continue to face discrimination, particularly in rural areas. Several women hold high-level positions in the government, including the minister of defense and the minister of justice. Domestic violence legislation is rarely enforced, and the crime continues to be widespread. Rape is seldom prosecuted. Children and young adults are susceptible to ritual killings. Abortion is prohibited.

The Gambia

Political Rights: 5
Civil Liberties: 6*
Status: Not Free

Population: 1,778,000
Capital: Banjul

Ratings Change: The Gambia's civil liberties rating declined from 5 to 6 and its status from Partly Free to Not Free due to President Yayha Jammeh's severe suppression of the opposition, media, and civil society in the run-up to the November presidential election, which was boycotted by ECOWAS monitors because the electoral and political environment was not conducive to free or fair polls.

Ten-Year Ratings Timeline For Year Under Review (Political Rights, Civil Liberties, Status)

2002	2003	2004	2005	2006	2007	2008	2009	2010	2011
4,4PF	4,4PF	4,4PF	5,4PF	5,4PF	5,4PF	5,4PF	5,5PF	5,5PF	5,6NF

Overview: **President Yayha Jammeh secured an extension of his 17-year rule by winning his fourth term in office in the**

November 2011 election. The Economic Community of Western Africa States criticized the electoral environment as not conducive to free and fair elections and refused to send observers. The government continued to intimidate and persecute journalists, the political opposition, and civil society groups throughout the year.

After gaining independence from Britain in 1965, The Gambia functioned for almost 30 years as an electoral democracy under President Dawda Jawara and his People's Progressive Party. A 1981 coup by leftist soldiers was reversed by intervention from Senegal. The two countries formed the Confederation of Senegambia a year later, but it was dissolved in 1989.

Lieutenant Yahya Jammeh deposed Jawara in a 1994 military coup. The junior officers who led the coup quickly issued draconian decrees curtailing civil and political rights. A new constitution, adopted in a closely controlled 1996 referendum, allowed Jammeh to transform his military dictatorship into a nominally civilian administration.

Jammeh defeated human rights lawyer Ousainou Darboe in the 2001 presidential election, and the ruling Alliance for Patriotic Reorientation and Construction (APRC) won all but three seats in the 2002 National Assembly elections, thanks to a widespread boycott by opposition parties.

Jammeh secured a new five-year term in the September 2006 presidential election, which was marred by serious government repression of the media and the opposition. During the 2007 legislative elections, in which the APRC captured 42 of 48 seats, there were reports of intimidation of the opposition by security forces; restrictions on the media; and accusations of unfair voting procedures, including with voter registration and ballot counting.

The government announced in March 2006 that it had foiled an attempted coup, leading to the arrest of dozens of people, including several prominent journalists and senior intelligence and defense personnel. Ten military officers were sentenced to lengthy prison terms in April 2007. Eight individuals, most of whom belonged to the military, were arrested in late 2009 on suspicion of planning another coup to overthrow Jammeh. In July 2010, all of the accused were found guilty of treason and conspiracy and received death sentences.

Jammeh has drawn criticism for his erratic statements and behavior. Between 2007 and 2009 he claimed that he could personally cure HIV/AIDS using traditional herbs, threatened decapitation for any homosexuals who remained in the country, and warned against causing instability through human rights activism. Jammeh threatened to withhold government services to voters who failed to support him in the 2011 presidential election, while declaring that neither coups nor elections could remove him from power as he had been installed by God.

In the run-up to the November 24 presidential poll, the government-controlled Independent Electoral Commission (IEC) installed a new biometric voter registration system, though it stated that 1,897 voters had nonetheless registered at least twice. The IEC failed to share the electoral register with opposition parties, shortened the campaign period from four weeks to eleven days, and barred opposition parties from campaigning via national media or holding political assemblies. Meanwhile, clashes between supporters of the opposition and the APRC during the campaign period resulted in three deaths. Jammeh secured his fourth term as president with 72 percent of the vote; opposition parties rejected the results as fraudulent. In a landmark move, the 15-member state Economic Community of West African States (ECOWAS) refused to send election observers, citing the lack of an environment conducive to holding free and fair elections, including government intimidation of voters and the opposition.

The Gambia has increasingly become a transit point for drug shipments from South and Central America. In 2010, the National Assembly voted to introduce the death penalty for possession of more than 250 grams of cocaine or heroin; however, the law was repealed in April 2011, since the constitution forbids the death penalty for crimes other than aggravated or premeditated murder. In 2011 eight foreign nationals were sentenced to 50 years in prison for trafficking narcotics, and the EU began talks with The Gambia on conducting joint operations to combat drug trafficking.

Political Rights and Civil Liberties: The Gambia is not an electoral democracy. The 2011 presidential election was marred by voter intimidation and government control of the media. The president is elected by popular vote for unlimited five-year terms. Of the 53 members of the unicameral National Assembly, 48 are elected by popular vote, with the remainder appointed by the president; members serve five-year terms.

Official corruption remains a serious problem, although President Yahya Jammeh's recent focus on economic development policies led to increased anticorruption efforts, including the establishment of an Anti-Corruption Commission. In March 2010, the government prosecuted and dismissed several high-ranking security officials for corruption and drug-related charges. In 2011 a former inspector general of police was convicted of corruption and sentenced to life in prison. During the year, lower-level government officials were also accused of corruption, often in the form of soliciting bribes. Gambia was ranked 77 out of 183 countries surveyed in Transparency International's 2011 Corruption Perceptions Index.

The government does not respect freedom of the press. Laws on sedition give the authorities great discretion in silencing dissent, and independent media outlets and journalists are subject to arrests, harassment, and violence. The 2004 assassination of journalist and press freedom activist Deyda Hydara has not been solved, and the whereabouts of *Daily Observer* journalist, Ebrima Manneh, remain unknown since his 2006 arrest for publishing a report critical of Jammeh. The government runs Radio Gambia, as well as the sole television channel and the *Gambia Daily* newspaper. There are several private radio stations and newspapers, and foreign broadcasts are available. While the state generally does not restrict internet usage, some websites, including that of the U.S.-based newspaper *Gambia Echo*, have been blocked. In July 2011, former president of the *Gambia Press Union*, N'dey Tapha Sosseh, was charged with conspiracy. In June, former communication minister Amadou Scattred Janneh and six of his colleagues were put on trial for treason for distributing antigovernment T-shirts; the trial continued at year's end. In the run-up to the 2011 election, journalists practiced self-censorship, and the National Intelligence Agency (NIA) shut down community and independent radio stations. Notably, in August, it ordered Teranga FM, the only independent radio station in the country that had continued to broadcast news, off the air.

Freedom of religion is legally guaranteed and generally upheld by the government. However, in 2009, state forces led mass hunts for those accused of witchcraft. Nearly 1,000 people were kidnapped, with many brought to secret government detention centers, forced to drink hallucinogenic substances, and beaten; two people were reported to have died from the substances. Limitations on freedom of speech are thought to encourage self-censorship among scholars. Open and free private discussion is limited by fears of government surveillance and arrest by the NIA.

Freedoms of assembly and association are legally protected but constrained by state intimidation in practice. Gambians, except for civil servants and members of the security forces, have the right to form unions, strike, and bargain for wages. However, the climate of fear generated by the state and the NIA dissuades workers from taking action.

The constitution provides for an independent judiciary; however, Jammeh has the authority to, and does, handpick and dismiss members. Courts are hampered by corruption and executive influence. The judicial system recognizes customary law and Sharia (Islamic law), primarily with regard to personal status and family matters. In the run up to the 2011 election, local government leaders were pressured to campaign for Jammeh or face dismissal from office.

Impunity for the country's security forces, particularly the NIA, is a problem. A 1995 decree allows the NIA to search, arrest, or seize any person or property without a warrant in the name of state security. In 2011, individuals continued to be arrested without warrants and held incommunicado. Torture of prisoners, including political prisoners, has been reported. Prisons are overcrowded and unsanitary, and inmates suffer from inadequate nutrition and lack of medical attention.

The Gambia's various ethnic groups coexist in relative harmony, though critics have accused Jammeh of giving preferential treatment to members of the Jola ethnic group in the military and government.

The government has encouraged female education by waiving primary school fees for girls, but women enjoy fewer opportunities for higher education and employment than men. While the vice president and several cabinet ministers are women, there are only 4 women in the 53-seat National Assembly. Rape and domestic violence are common. Sharia provisions regarding family law and inheritance restrict women's rights, and female genital mutilation remains legal and widely practiced. The Gambia does not fully comply with the minimum standards for the elimination of trafficking, and it is a source, destination, and transit country for the trafficking of women and children.

Georgia

Political Rights: 4
Civil Liberties: 3
Status: Partly Free

Population: 4,329,000
Capital: Tbilisi

Note: The numerical ratings and status listed above do not reflect conditions in South Ossetia or Abkhazia, which are examined in separate reports.

Ten-Year Ratings Timeline For Year Under Review (Political Rights, Civil Liberties, Status)

2002	2003	2004	2005	2006	2007	2008	2009	2010	2011
4,4PF	4,4PF	3,4PF	3,3PF	3,3PF	4,4PF	4,4PF	4,4PF	4,3PF	4,3PF

Overview: **Georgia's political scene was shaken in 2011 by the emergence of Bidzina Ivanishvili, a billionaire who returned to Georgia after years abroad and announced plans to form his own political party ahead of parliamentary elections in 2012. Separately, Georgia finally relented on its long-standing objections to Russia's entry into the World Trade Organization. More than three years after invading Georgia during an August 2008 war, Russian troops continued to occupy the breakaway republics of Abkhazia and South Ossetia, which are recognized as Georgian territory by all but a handful of countries.**

Georgia gained its independence from Russia in 1918, only to become part of the Soviet Union in 1922. In 1990, shortly before the Soviet Union's collapse, an attempt by the region of South Ossetia to declare independence from Georgia and join Russia's North Ossetia republic sparked a war between the separatists and Georgian forces. Although a ceasefire was signed in 1992, South Ossetia's final political status remained unresolved.

Following a national referendum in April 1991, Georgia declared its independence from the Soviet Union. Nationalist leader and former dissident Zviad Gamsakhurdia was elected president in May. The next year, he was overthrown by opposition militias and replaced with former Georgian Communist Party head and Soviet foreign minister Eduard Shevardnadze. Parliamentary elections held in 1992 resulted in more than 30 parties and blocs winning seats, with none securing a majority.

In 1993, Georgia was shaken by the violent secession of the Abkhazia region and an insurrection by Gamsakhurdia loyalists. Shevardnadze legalized the presence of some 19,000 Russian troops in Georgia in return for Russian support against Gamsakhurdia, who reportedly committed suicide after his defeat. In early 1994, Georgia and Abkhazia agreed to a ceasefire under which Russian-led troops were stationed along the de facto border.

In 1995, Shevardnadze and his Citizens' Union of Georgia (CUG) party won presidential and parliamentary polls. The CUG won again in the 1999 parliamentary elections, and observers from the Organization for Security and Cooperation in Europe (OSCE) concluded that, despite some irregularities, the vote was generally fair. In the 2000 presidential poll, however, Shevardnadze's wide margin of victory led to accusations of fraud that were supported by election monitors.

Shevardnadze faced growing opposition from prominent members of the CUG, including Justice Minister Mikheil Saakashvili, who criticized the president's failure to contain widespread corruption. While Shevardnadze resigned as CUG chairman in 2001, Saakashvili left to form his own party, the National Movement.

Flawed parliamentary elections in November 2003 sparked a campaign of street protests known as the Rose Revolution. OSCE observers reported a variety of electoral violations, Shevardnadze was forced to resign, and the Supreme Court cancelled the election results. Saakashvili won a snap presidential election in January 2004, running virtually unopposed and capturing 96 percent of the vote. Fresh parliamentary elections in March gave two-thirds of the seats to the National Movement and allied parties.

Georgia's relations with Russia soured as Saakashvili quickly reestablished Tbilisi's control over the semiautonomous southwestern region of Ajaria and pledged to reintegrate the separatist enclaves of Abkhazia and South Ossetia, which were tacitly supported by the Kremlin.

Mounting frustration with Saakashvili's dominance of the Georgian political scene culminated in large street protests in late 2007. Demonstrations in November drew between 50,000 and 100,000 people, prompting a violent police crackdown and the imposition of a November 7–16 state of emergency that barred opposition media from the airwaves and restricted freedom of assembly. Responding to opposition demands for elections, Saakashvili scheduled an early presidential vote for January 5, 2008, giving his opponents little time to prepare.

Saakashvili won with roughly 53 percent of the vote, but his main challenger alleged fraud, and OSCE observers noted an array of irregularities. The ruling party and its allies captured 119 of the 150 seats in May parliamentary elections, with the opposition again declaring that the balloting was rigged.

Armed conflict erupted in South Ossetia in early August, and an ensuing Russian invasion pressed deep into Georgian territory. A French-brokered ceasefire took hold after more than a week of fighting, and by fall, Russian forces had largely withdrawn to the confines of South Ossetia and Abkhazia. Russia recognized the territories' independence in the wake of the conflict, but few other countries followed suit. Russia also established a substantial, long-term troop presence in both territories, despite the fact that the ceasefire deal called for a withdrawal of all forces to their positions before the fighting. A European Union (EU) report released in September 2009 assigned blame to both Russia and Georgia for the 2008 hostilities.

Opposition leaders demanded the president's resignation in April 2009, and his refusal led to a series of street protests, beatings, and arrests that lasted into the summer. Some opposition members were accused of plans to foment violence during the year, and a tank battalion allegedly launched an abortive mutiny in early May. Political and security conditions eased considerably in 2010, and the frequent protests that characterized the preceding three-year period were largely absent.

In October 2011, Georgian billionaire Bidzina Ivanishvili announced plans to establish his own opposition political party. However, he had lived abroad for years, acquiring French and Russian citizenship. Within days of his announcement, his Georgian citizenship was revoked on the grounds that he had not obtained the requisite permission for multiple citizenships. Under Georgian law, only citizens may form or finance political parties, or run for elective office. At year's end, Ivanishvili was seeking a remedy in the courts.

Russian troops continued to occupy South Ossetia and Abkhazia, and Georgia's relations with Russia generally remained fraught. Nevertheless, the countries managed to reach an agreement that would allow Russia to join the World Trade Organization, following a protracted period during which Georgia effectively blocked Russia's entry.

Political Rights and Civil Liberties: Georgia is not an electoral democracy. In recent election cycles, including the 2008 presidential and parliamentary elections, OSCE monitors have identified problems, including the abuse of state resources, reports of intimidation aimed at public employees and opposition activists, and apparent voter list inaccuracies. In its report on municipal polls held in 2010, the OSCE noted some progress toward meeting international election standards, but warned that "further efforts in resolutely tackling recurring misconduct are required in order to consolidate the progress and enhance public trust before the next national elections."

Parliament has 150 seats, with half chosen by party list and the other half in single-member districts. According to the constitution, the president appoints the cabinet and serves up to two five-year terms, though current president Mikheil Saakashvili—first elected in 2004—was reelected in 2008 after calling an early vote. The cabinet's membership under Saakashvili has been fairly unstable; in 2009 he named Nikoloz Gilauri to serve as his fifth prime minister. Under a package of constitutional amendments adopted in October 2010, the bulk of executive authority will shift from the president to the prime minister in 2013, and new rules surrounding votes of no confidence will make it difficult for Parliament to remove the prime minister. The opposition claimed that the amendments were designed to allow Saakashvili to remain in power by becoming prime minister after the end of his second presidential term. Saakashvili has not categorically ruled out such a move.

In late December 2011, Parliament approved a new electoral code that aimed to address the shortcomings observed in past elections. While it was seen as an improvement on some fronts, with provisions that could benefit smaller parties, it failed to address key problems identified by the Council of Europe's Venice Commission, including the drastically varying sizes of the single-member parliamentary districts. The full impact of the new code would only become clear during the 2012 parliamentary elections.

Saakashvili's National Movement has been the dominant party since 2004, and although a number of key Saakashvili allies have defected to the opposition in recent years, the fragmented opposition parties have struggled to form a stable alliance that could successfully challenge the president. Bidzina Ivanishvili brought new impetus to the opposition's efforts with his 2011 announcement that he was entering politics.

Corruption remains a challenge in Georgia. While notable progress has been made with respect to lower- and mid-level corruption, particularly in comparison with the country's neighbors, efforts to combat high-level corruption have stalled. The government's achievements have included an overhaul of the police force and university-level education reforms that curbed bribery in admissions and grading. However, implementation of a 2005 plan aimed at improving the transparency and effectiveness of the civil service, in part by strengthening the role of inspectors general within public agencies, has been lacking. Georgia apparently continues to suffer from corruption at elite levels, and the administration's insularity has fostered opportunities for cronyism and insider deals.

The constitution provides guarantees for press freedom, and the print media offer a range of political views. The state television and radio outlets were converted into public service broadcasters in 2005, but critics maintain that the stations show a progovernment bias. The private broadcast media feature a degree of pluralism, though each station tends to favor a specific political camp, and progovernment stations are dominant. To help address the lack of ownership transparency, Parliament in 2011 adopted legal amendments that banned ownership of broadcasters by offshore firms and required stations to reveal their ownership structures. The measure was set to take effect in 2012. The authorities do not restrict access to the internet, but high-speed connections are prohibitively expensive for many citizens.

Freedom of religion is respected for the country's largely Georgian Orthodox Christian population and some traditional minority groups, including Muslims and Jews. However, members of newer groups, including Baptists, Pentecostals, and Jehovah's Witnesses, have faced harassment and intimidation by law enforcement officials and Georgian Orthodox extremists. The government does not restrict academic freedom.

Freedoms of association and assembly were generally respected in 2011, though the year was marred by a high-profile incident in May, when five days of antigovernment protests organized by former Parliament Speaker Nino Burjanadze ended in violent clashes between police and demonstrators. The protesters had refused to disperse or relocate after their permit expired, and some reportedly assaulted police, touching off the violence. Nevertheless, an inquiry by the authorities found that police had used excessive force, and several officers were fired or demoted. At least two people were killed in connection with the protests, allegedly struck by an opposition motorcade that was fleeing the violence. Two other men were found dead, with their hands bound, in the aftermath of the protests, though it was unclear whether their deaths were directly related to the demonstrations.

Nongovernmental organizations (NGOs) are able to register and operate without arbitrary restrictions. They play an active role in public debate, but their influence has been limited by the general unwillingness of the current administration to engage with civil society on a consistent basis. Funding for civil society organizations is a challenge. Local business support for charities has developed over the years, but this tends not to be directed toward organizations that work on government policy and reform issues. A law adopted in 2011 will allow the government to provide financial support for projects administered by NGOs and universities.

The constitution and the Law on Trade Unions allow workers to organize and prohibit antiunion discrimination. The Amalgamated Trade Unions of Georgia, the successor to the Soviet-era union federation, is the principal trade union bloc. It is not affiliated with and receives no funding from the government. While Georgia replaced its Soviet-era labor code with a new framework in 2006, union influence remains marginal in practice.

The judiciary continues to suffer from significant corruption and pressure from the executive branch. The government has taken some measures designed to improve the independence and capacity of the judiciary, such as pay increases for judges and the implementation of jury trials, the first of which began in 2011, but more comprehensive reforms have yet to be enacted. The human rights ombudsman has repeatedly accused the police of abusing and torturing detainees. Prison conditions in Georgia continue to be abhorrent.

The government generally respects the rights of ethnic minorities in areas of the country that are not contested by separatists. Freedom of residence and freedom to travel to and from the country are observed.

Societal violence against women is a problem, and cases of rape and domestic violence are believed to be underreported. A 2006 law on domestic violence allows victims to file immediate protective orders against their abusers, and permits police to issue a temporary restrictive order against suspects. However, these orders are rarely utilized, and the penalties for violating them are relatively mild. Georgia remains primarily a source country for trafficking in persons, but the government's efforts to combat the problem place it in Tier 1 in the U.S. State Department's annual Trafficking in Persons Report.

Germany

Political Rights: 1
Civil Liberties: 1
Status: Free

Population: 81,755,000
Capital: Berlin

Ten-Year Ratings Timeline For Year Under Review (Political Rights, Civil Liberties, Status)

2002	2003	2004	2005	2006	2007	2008	2009	2010	2011
1,1F	1,1F	1,1F	1,1F	1,1F	1,1F	1,1F	1,1F	1,1F	1,1F

Overview: **Chancellor Angela Merkel's Christian Democratic Union (CDU) was defeated in a number of state parliamentary elections held throughout 2011. In Baden-Württemberg, a new Green Party-led coalition came to power, representing the first time a Green Party member has held the presidency of a state's parliament. In Mecklenburg-Vorpommern, the extreme right National Democratic Party was reelected to the state parliament, creating considerable political controversy. Meanwhile, the trial of John Demjanjuk ended in May with a conviction of accessory to murder in 28,060 counts in Holocaust-related war crimes.**

Modern Germany emerged in 1871, when the patchwork of German states united under Prussian leadership following the Franco-Prussian war. After Germany's defeat in World War I, the German Empire was replaced in 1919 by the Weimar Republic, which gave way in 1933 to Nazism and led to World War II. Following its defeat in World War II, Germany was divided into two states—the capitalist and democratic Federal Republic in the west and the communist German Democratic

Republic in the east—during the ensuing Cold War. The Berlin Wall, which had kept East Berliners from fleeing west, was opened in 1989, and East Germany was absorbed into the Federal Republic the following year. Despite nearly two decades of massive subsidies, the federal states of former East Germany remain considerably poorer than the rest of the country. The economic situation has contributed to greater support for extremist political groups in the east.

Chancellor Helmut Kohl and a coalition of his center-right Christian Democratic Union and Christian Social Union (CDU/CSU) and the socially liberal, market-oriented Free Democratic Party (FDP) ruled Germany for 16 years. In 1998, Germans elected the so-called red-green coalition, consisting of the Social Democratic Party (SPD) and the Green Party, with the SPD's Gerhard Schröder as chancellor. The red-green coalition won a narrow victory in the 2002 election, despite sluggish economic growth in its first term.

In 2005, Schröder engineered a no-confidence vote against himself to trigger national elections. Neither the red-green coalition nor the CDU/CSU-FDP opposition was able to garner an outright majority. After unusually protracted coalition negotiations, the CDU/CSU and the SPD were obliged to form a "grand coalition," and the CDU's Angela Merkel became Germany's first female chancellor. Tensions between the two parties of the grand coalition grew during the second half of its term, with each party trying to distinguish itself.

The political scene in 2009 was dominated by the federal parliamentary election. The CDU/CSU won 239 seats, while the FDP took 93 seats. The SPD received its worst result in a federal election since World War II, capturing only 146 seats. Meanwhile, the Left and the Greens both made large gains, receiving the highest share of votes in their histories; however, they could not offset the SPD's losses. As a result, the alliance of the CDU/CSU and FDP received an outright majority of seats and formed a new center-right government, ensuring Angela Merkel a second term as chancellor.

In November 2009, the controversial trial of John Demjanjuk—a Ukrainian-born former U.S. citizen and alleged World War II Nazi concentration camp guard—began in Munich. Demjanjuk, the lowest-ranking official to go on trial for Holocaust-related crimes, was charged with facilitating the murder of thousands of Jews at the Sobibor concentration camp in Nazi-occupied Poland. In May 2011, Demjanjuk, then 91, was convicted of accessory to murder in 28,060 counts at the Sobibor camp, and was sentenced to five years in jail. However, he was released pending appeal and was living in a German nursing home at year's end.

In May 2010, state parliamentary elections were held in Germany's most populous state, North Rhine-Westphalia, and were largely seen as a test of the new federal government's performance. Similar to its federal counterpart, the incumbent government was a CDU-FDP coalition, with the main opposition coming from the SPD. Both major parties, the CDU and the SPD, did poorly, while both the Greens and the Left fared well, the latter winning seats for the first time. The overall result of the election was a hung parliament, with the CDU and SPD each capturing 67 out of 181 available seats. After various coalition options were exhausted, the SPD and the Greens ultimately formed a minority coalition. Some political analysts interpreted the outcome of the election as indicating potential trouble for Merkel's government during the next federal elections.

President Horst Köhler of the CDU resigned in May 2010, after criticism over comments he made that insinuated that military intervention abroad could be justified by economic interests. One month later, CDU candidate Christian Wulff was elected to replace Köhler, but only after three election rounds, which demonstrated dissidence in Merkel's majority coalition.

Marked by ongoing antinuclear sentiment reignited by the nuclear incident in Fukushima, Japan, and the eurozone debt crisis, the 2011 state parliamentary elections, which were held in seven states throughout the year, saw a series of electoral defeats for Merkel's CDU. Except in Rhineland-Palatinate and Berlin, the conservative party lost votes in each state and even lost political majorities in Baden-Württemberg and Mecklenburg-Vorpommern. In Baden-Württemberg, a region ruled by the CDU since 1953, a new coalition came to power led by the Green party, which won 24.2 percent of the vote, and the SPD, which received 23.1 percent. It marked the first time in German political history that a member of the Green Party would preside over a state parliament; the Greens now hold seats in each of the 16 state parliaments. In Mecklenburg-Vorpommern elections, the SPD gained 5 seats for a total of 28, while the CDU received 18 seats. The Free Democratic Party (FDP), CDU allies in the federal government, lost all of their previously held seven seats. The extreme right National Democratic Party (NDP) was reelected with 6 percent of the vote. Other noted results included the election of the Pirate Party, which campaigned for issues including information privacy and internet freedom. The Pirate Party won 15 seats in the Berlin state parliament—the first time it captured seats in a state legislature in Germany.

Political Rights and Civil Liberties: Germany is an electoral democracy. The constitution provides for a lower house of parliament, the 622-seat Bundestag (Federal Assembly), elected at least every four years through a 50-50 mixture of proportional representation and single-member districts; as well as an upper house, the Bundesrat (Federal Council), which represents the states. The country's head of state is a largely ceremonial president, chosen jointly by the Bundestag and a group of state representatives to serve up to two five-year terms. In Germany's federal system, state governments have considerable authority over matters such as education, policing, taxation, and spending. The chancellor, the head of government, is elected by the Bundestag and usually serves for the duration of a four-year legislative session, which can be cut short only if the Bundestag chooses a replacement in a so-called constructive vote of no confidence.

For historical reasons, political pluralism is somewhat constrained. Under electoral laws intended to restrict the far left and far right, a party must receive either 5 percent of the national vote or win at least three directly elected seats to be represented in parliament. The constitutional court outlawed the Socialist Reich Party (a successor to the Nazi Party) in 1952 and the Communist Party of Germany in 1956 on the grounds that their goals disregarded the principles of the constitution. However, the former ruling party of communist East Germany—the Socialist Unity Party, renamed the Party of Democratic Socialism—participated in state governments after reunification. It then merged with Labour and Social Justice The Electorate Alternative, a party of former left-wing SPD members, to form the new Left Party ahead of the 2005 elections. The main extreme right party, the NDP, is hostile to immigration and the European Union, and has been accused of glorifying Adolf Hitler and the Third Reich.

The government is held accountable for its performance through open debates in the parliament, which are covered widely in the media. Germany is free of pervasive corruption and was ranked 14 out of 183 countries surveyed in Transparency International's 2011 Corruption Perceptions Index.

Freedom of expression is enshrined in the constitution, and the media are largely free and independent. However, hate speech is punishable if publicly pronounced against specific segments of the population and in a manner that incites hatred, such as racist agitation and anti-Semitism. It is also illegal to advocate Nazism, deny the Holocaust, or glorify the ideology of Hitler. There are no restrictions on access to the internet.

Freedom of belief is legally protected. However, Germany has taken a strong stance against the Church of Scientology, which it deems an organization pursuing commercial interests rather than a religion. A number of federal states have also denied the Jehovah's Witnesses the official "public law corporation" status, which has been granted to 180 other religious groups in the country. Eight states have passed laws prohibiting female Muslim schoolteachers from wearing the headscarf, while Berlin and the state of Hesse have adopted legislation banning headscarves for all civil servants. Economic uncertainties in the aftermath of the global recession have worsened xenophobic tendencies toward immigrants in general, and Muslims in particular, as evidenced by the reelection of the extreme right NDP party in Mecklenburg-Vorpommern. Academic freedom is generally respected.

The right of peaceful assembly is not infringed upon, except in the case of outlawed groups, such as those advocating Nazism or opposing the democratic order. Civic groups and nongovernmental organizations operate without hindrance. Trade unions, farmers' groups, and business confederations are free to organize.

The judiciary is independent, and the rule of law prevails. Prison conditions are adequate, though the Council of Europe has criticized elements in the practice of preventive detention.

Germany was accused by international human rights organizations in 2011 of repatriating asylum seekers to countries where their safety could be threatened, such as Afghanistan, Iraq, and Kosovo.

Women's rights are well protected under antidiscrimination laws. However, gender wage gaps persisted in 2011, with women's wages and salaries approximately 23 percent less than men's wages for the same work. Women held 6 of the 16 federal cabinet positions and 33 percent of the seats in parliament. Limited same-sex partnership rights are respected.

Ghana

Political Rights: 1
Civil Liberties: 2
Status: Free

Population: 24,966,000
Capital: Accra

Ten-Year Ratings Timeline For Year Under Review (Political Rights, Civil Liberties, Status)

2002	2003	2004	2005	2006	2007	2008	2009	2010	2011
2,3F	2,2F	2,2F	1,2F	1,2F	1,2F	1,2F	1,2F	1,2F	1,2F

Overview: **Mounting tensions within the ruling National Democratic Congress party culminated in a failed attempt by the wife of former president Jerry Rawlings to replace the incumbent, John Atta Mills, as the party's standard-bearer in the 2012 presidential poll. With the NDC's nomination secured, Atta Mills focused his attention on next year's rematch against Nana Akufo-Addo of the main opposition New Patriotic Party. Concerns over electoral violence prompted major Ghanaian political actors to commit to a code of ethics aimed at discouraging inflammatory campaign rhetoric. Meanwhile, legislation to regulate Ghana's incipient oil sector proceeded at a slow pace.**

Ghana achieved independence from British rule in 1957. After the 1966 ouster of its independence leader, Kwame Nkrumah, the country was rocked for 15 years by a series of military coups and experienced successive military and civilian governments.

In May 1979, air force officer Jerry Rawlings led a coup against the ruling military junta; he handed power in September to an elected president, Hilla Limann. However, Limann was overthrown in another coup led by Rawlings in December 1981. Rawlings proved to be brutally repressive, banning political parties and quelling all dissent. While he agreed under economic and political pressure to hold multiparty elections in the late 1980s, the elections were considered neither free nor fair, and Rawlings and his National Democratic Congress (NDC) party remained in power. The 1996 elections were generally respected at home and abroad, but Rawlings and the NDC again retained their positions.

In 2000, free and fair presidential and parliamentary polls led to a peaceful transfer of power from Rawlings—who was forced to step down due to term limits—and the NDC to opposition leader John Kufuor and his New Patriotic Party (NPP). Kufuor secured 57 percent of the vote, while NDC candidate John Atta Mills captured 43 percent. Kufuor was reelected in 2004 with 52 percent of the vote, defeating Atta Mills, who captured 45 percent, as the NDC alleged irregularities. The NPP won 128 seats in concurrent legislative elections, while the NDC took 94. Although there were reports of sporadic violence and a few incidents of intimidation and other irregularities, domestic and international observers judged the elections to be generally free and fair.

In advance of the December 2008 presidential election, the NPP faced internal divisions, as over 20 candidates vied for the party's nomination. Ultimately, former foreign minister Nana Akufo-Addo was chosen over Kufuor's preferred candidate, Alan Kyerematen. Akufo-Addo and many of his supporters belonged to the Akyem ethnic group, while Kufuor and Kyerematen were Ashanti, illustrating how ethnocultural rifts often complicated political divisions. Meanwhile, the NDC chose Atta Mills as its candidate for the third time.

While problems with voter registration and fighting between NDC and NPP supporters were reported before and during the vote, the election was ultimately viewed as a success by domestic and international observers. The January 2009 inauguration of Atta Mills, who narrowly won the runoff with 50.23 percent of the vote, marked the second peaceful, democratic transfer of power in Ghana. The NDC also won concurrent parliamentary elections, taking 114 seats while the NPP secured 107.

During his first three years in office, Atta Mills has faced the difficult task of attempting to fulfill at least some of his campaign pledges while also steering Ghana through the global economic crisis. Some NDC supporters, backed by Rawlings, have complained about the president's inability to make good on his promises or to "support those who supported him"—a reference to the patronage networks underlying Ghanaian politics. During the party's July 2011 party congress, Rawlings's wife, Nana Konadu Agyemang Rawlings, challenged Atta Mills for the right to represent the NDC in the 2012 presidential election. Although Atta Mills survived this challenge, the Rawlings family continued to voice its displeasure with his leadership. In August 2010, the NPP had again nominated Akufo-Addo to serve as its presidential candidate.

Ongoing divisions within the NDC have led many observers to predict that the 2012 presidential and legislative polls will be decided by a razor-thin margin. The ruling party's vulnerability, coupled with growing government revenues from the Jubilee offshore oilfield, ensure that the elections will be fiercely contested and have raised concerns that electoral violence could break out. In an effort to address this potential danger, in August 2011, all major political parties agreed to adhere to a code of ethics that call for them to sharply curtail vitriolic campaign language and to publicly denounce any intimidation or violence that did occur. The establishment of enforcement bodies to deal with transgressors was proposed in an effort to ensure compliance.

While Ghana has been working to move away from donor dependency, Atta Mills's government has been forced to make exceptions to counter the effects of the economic crisis. In 2009, it was awarded $1.2 billion in interest-free loans over three years from the World Bank and $602.6 million from the International Monetary Fund to help tackle "macroeconomic instability." During Atta Mills's visit to Beijing in October 2010, Ghana and China signed agreements totaling $15 billion in support of infrastructure projects in the country. Ghana started producing oil for the first time in December 2010; however, growth has been slowed by the government's inability to quickly establish regulatory frameworks.

Political Rights and Civil Liberties: Ghana is an electoral democracy. The December 2008 presidential and parliamentary elections were considered fair and competitive. The president and vice president are directly elected on the same ticket for up to two four-year terms. Members of the unicameral, 230-seat Parliament are also elected for four-year terms. The political system is dominated by two rival parties, the NPP and the NDC.

One of President John Atta Mills's campaign promises was to fight corruption and improve governance. The NDC administration has used the Bureau of National Investigation to examine corruption allegations against a number of former NPP officials, including former president John Kufuor's health, information, and foreign ministers. While many Ghanaians have supported these anticorruption efforts, NPP officials allege that the cases are politicized. In the summer of 2010, NPP leaders accused the government of corruption when documents regarding a $10 billion housing deal with the company STX Korea were not made available for review by Parliament. Nonetheless, the government signed an agreement to commence construction in December. Observers have voiced concern over the glacial pace of Accra's efforts to set up regulatory institutions to manage Ghanaian hydrocarbon production. Ghana was ranked 69 out of 183 countries surveyed in Transparency International's 2011 Corruption Perceptions Index.

Freedom of expression is constitutionally guaranteed and generally respected. Numerous private radio stations operate, and many independent newspapers and magazines are published in Accra. However, the government occasionally restricts press freedom in practice through harassment, arrests, and criminal charges. Section 208 of the 1960 Criminal Code bans "publishing false news with intent to cause fear or harm to the public or to disturb the public peace." In June 2011, the High Court found the publishers and editors of the *Chronicle*, a privately owned daily newspaper, guilty of defaming a university professor in two 2009 articles and imposed approximately $331,500 in fines and damages. On August 9, the Accra offices of the *Chronicle* were sealed off by police and court officers; it resumed publication later that month.

Religious freedom is protected by law and largely respected in practice. While relations between Ghana's Christian majority and Muslim minority are generally peaceful, Muslims often report feeling politically and socially excluded, and there are few Muslims at the top levels of government. Both domestic and international human rights observers have reported a high incidence of exorcism-related physical abuse at Pentecostal prayer camps. Academic freedom is legally guaranteed and upheld in practice.

The rights to peaceful assembly and association are constitutionally guaranteed, and permits are not required for meetings or demonstrations. However, in March 2011, teachers' union members who were conducting a peaceful march against a new wage policy were subjected to beatings, tear gas, and arrest by police in Accra. Civil society organizations have noted that NDC "foot soldiers"—activists that assist NDC campaigns by distributing literature and generating crowds, among other activities—have become increasingly disgruntled with the government and have reportedly harassed and attacked state officials, with few consequences. In August, police in Ho, capital of the Volta region, broke up a demonstration by NDC supporters who were protesting against alleged incompetence by local party officials. Eight demonstrators were arrested and later released on bail. Nongovernmental organizations were generally able to operate freely.

Under the constitution and 2003 labor laws, which conform to International Labour Organization (ILO) conventions, workers have the right to form and join trade unions. However, the government forbids industrial action in a number of essential industries, including fuel distribution, public transportation, and the prison system.

Ghanaian courts have acted with increased autonomy under the 1992 constitution, but corruption remains a problem. Scarce resources compromise the judicial process, and poorly paid judges are tempted by bribes. The Accra Fast Track High Court is specifically tasked with hearing corruption cases involving former government officials, but many observers raised doubts about its impartiality and respect for due process under the Kufuor administration. In August 2010, the chairman of the NDC urged the chief justice to "purge" the judiciary of corruption or face government intervention, leading critics to condemn the NDC for attempting to infringe upon the judiciary's independence.

Prisons suffer from overcrowding and often life-threatening conditions. In an attempt to reduce overcrowding, a government initiative introduced in 2008 has led to the release of some prisoners who had been on prolonged remand without trial. A 2009 presidential pardon of 1,021 prisoners eased some of the strain on prison infrastructure.

Communal and ethnic violence occasionally flares in Ghana. In March 2010, tensions rose in the Brong Ahafo region between the Tuobodom and Techiman groups, resulting in three deaths. Some argued that the regional police failed to prevent the escalation of violence, though a government investigation into the incident was ongoing at year's end. Other isolated cases of communal and ethnic violence occur periodically, including several ritual killings and lynchings of suspected thieves.

Despite equal rights under the law, women suffer societal discrimination, especially in rural areas where opportunities for education and wage employment are limited. Notwithstanding legal protections, few victims report cases of rape or domestic violence because of persistent social stigmas. However, women's enrollment in universities is increasing, and there are a number of high-ranking women in the current government. Sodomy remains illegal in Ghana; in November 2011, police in the port city Tema arrested three men for allegedly performing homosexual acts.

The country serves as a source, transit point, and destination for the trafficking of women and children for the purposes of labor and sexual exploitation. In 2009, following undercover work conducted by a journalist working for the *New Crusading Guide* newspaper, three Chinese nationals were sentenced to a combined 36 years of hard labor for trafficking fellow Chinese for prostitution in Ghana.

Greece

Political Rights: 2*
Civil Liberties: 2
Status: Free

Population: 11,329,000
Capital: Athens

Ratings Change: Greece's political rights rating declined from 1 to 2 due to the installation of an unelected technocrat as prime minister following anti-austerity riots, and the growing influence of outside entities over the country's fiscal and economic policies.

Ten-Year Ratings Timeline For Year Under Review (Political Rights, Civil Liberties, Status)

2002	2003	2004	2005	2006	2007	2008	2009	2010	2011
1,3F	1,2F	1,2F	1,2F	1,2F	1,2F	1,2F	1,2F	1,2F	1,2F

Overview: **The country's debt crisis continued to worsen in 2011, threatening to spread across Europe and upend the stability of European unity. New rounds of austerity measures passed in June and October led to massive protests and strikes across the country. Prime Minister George Papandreou resigned under pressure in November, and the government appointed Lucas Papademos, former head of the Bank of Greece, to lead a coalition government and tackle the country's economic woes.**

The core of modern Greece gained independence from the Ottoman Empire in 1830. The ensuing century brought additional territorial gains at the Ottomans' expense, as well as domestic political struggles between royalists and republicans. Communist and royalist partisans mounted a strong resistance to Nazi German occupation during World War II, but national solidarity broke down in the early postwar period when royalists won national elections and eventually defeated the Communists in a civil war. In 1967, a group of army officers staged a military coup, suspending elections and arresting hundreds of political activists. A 1974 referendum rejected the restoration of the monarchy, and a new constitution in 1975 declared Greece a parliamentary republic.

The Panhellenic Socialist Movement (PASOK) governed the country from 1981 to 2004, except for a brief period from 1990 to 1993, when the conservative New Democracy (ND) party held power. The ND returned to power in the 2004 elections and won another term in 2007.

Prime Minister Costas Karamanlis called national elections halfway through his four-year mandate in October 2009, partly due to a number of corruption scandals that had rocked his coalition. PASOK led the voting with 160 seats, followed by New Democracy with just 91 seats. The Communist Party of Greece took 21 seats, the Popular Orthodox Rally—a nationalist and xenophobic party—won 15, and the Coalition of the Radical Left took 13. George Papandreou of PASOK was elected as the new prime minister.

A growing economic and debt crisis began at the end of 2009. In early 2010, the government presented a plan to cut the budget deficit and initiated a number of austerity measures, including a freeze on public sector pay, an increase in the retirement age, and a hike of the value-added tax from 19 to 23 percent. These steps were met with a series of national strikes and protests. In May 2010, a euro 110 billion (US$145 billion) rescue plan, including financing from the International Monetary Fund and 15 eurozone countries, was issued to help prevent a Greek debt default. At the end of 2010, the Greek debt was reported to be as high as 145 percent of the country's gross domestic product (GDP).

Another austerity package was passed in June 2011 as a condition for additional bailout funds, resulting in a string of protests across the country. Parliament passed yet another round of austerity reforms in October, despite massive public protests and a general strike. After a failed attempt to hold a referendum on the bailout package and facing pressure from eurozone leaders and bailout creditors to implement the austerity measures or lose further economic assistance, Papandreou stepped down on November 11. Lucas Papademos, former head of the Bank of Greece, was appointed to lead a new coalition government and tasked with negotiating the rest of the bailout deal before elections set for 2012. Journalists covering the protests, which continued throughout the year, complained of acts of aggression by Greek police.

Greece continued to struggle with an influx of close to 100,000 undocumented immigrants during 2011. In October 2010, European Union (EU) Rapid Border Intervention Teams were deployed for the first time to guard Greece's border as a result of an increase in the flow of immigrants—many of whom claimed to be from Afghanistan—from Turkey into Greece. In January 2011, six European countries refused to send refugees back to Greece due to the country's inability to treat asylum seekers humanely. These decisions were made shortly after the European Court of Human Rights ruled that Belgium should not have sent an Afghan asylum seeker back to Greece, where he faced degrading and inhumane treatment.

Political Rights and Civil Liberties: Greece is an electoral democracy. All 300 members of the unicameral Parliament are elected by proportional representation for four-year terms. The largely ceremonial president is elected by a supermajority of Parliament for a five-year term. The prime minister is chosen by the president and is usually the leader of the majority party in Parliament. Lucas Papademos was installed as an unelected leader of the country in November 2011 to head a crisis government after Prime Minister George Papandreou stepped down. The move has been condemned by some in the media as undemocratic and orchestrated by the EU and other powers behind the bailout. The country has generally fair electoral laws, equal campaigning opportunities, and a system of compulsory voting that is weakly enforced. Some representatives of the Romany community complain that certain municipalities have failed to register Roma who did not fulfill basic residency requirements. A 2010 law allows documented immigrants to vote in municipal elections.

Corruption remains a problem, particularly within the police forces. A parliamentary panel ruled in October 2010 that five former New Democracy ministers should stand trial on charges of fraud and breach of duty related to the Vatopedi land-swap scandal, which involved exchanging state-owned land for property of much poorer quality owned by the Vatopedi monastery. The abbot of the prestigious monastery was jailed pending trial on fraud and embezzlement in December 2011. Greece was ranked 80 out of 183 countries surveyed in Transparency International's 2011 Corruption Perceptions Index, the worst ranking of any country in Western Europe.

The constitution includes provisions for freedom of speech and the press, and citizens enjoy access to a broad array of privately owned print and broadcast outlets. There are, however, some limits on speech that incite fear, violence, and public disharmony, as well as on publications that offend religious beliefs, are obscene, or advocate the violent overthrow of the political system. Requirements under a 2007 media law place disproportionate burdens on smaller, minority-owned and community radio stations, such as the use of Greek as the main transmission language, maintaining a certain amount of money in reserve, and hiring a specific number of full-time staff. A number of journalists were physically assaulted by police while attempting to cover the anti-austerity protests in 2011. Internet access is generally not restricted.

Freedom of religion is guaranteed by the constitution, though the Orthodox Church receives government subsidies and is considered the "prevailing" denomination of the country. Members of some minority religions face social discrimination and legal barriers, such as permit requirements to open houses of worship and restrictions on inheriting property. Proselytizing is prohibited, and consequently, Mormons and Jehovah's Witnesses are routinely arrested and have reported abuse by police officers. Anti-Semitism also remains a problem. In September 2011, Parliament approved a long-delayed plan to build a state-funded mega-mosque in Athens. Academic freedom is not restricted.

Freedoms of assembly and association are guaranteed by the constitution and generally protected by the government, though there are some limits on groups representing ethnic minorities. Nongovernmental organizations generally operate without interference from the authorities, and some domestic human rights groups receive government funding and assistance. Workers have the right to join and form unions. Anti-austerity protests broke out throughout the year, with some turning violent. During protests in June, around 270 people were injured; in October, one person was killed in Athens. Many of the protests were unique in their nonpartisan nature and the use of social media sites to organize and spread information.

The judiciary is independent, and the constitution provides for public trials. Prisons suffer from overcrowding. Acts of violence by left- and right-wing extremist groups remain a problem. In September 2011, the far-right group Chrysi Avgi (Golden Dawn) threatened to physically remove a group of Muslims holding open-air prayers in a public square, but was eventually held back by riot police.

Despite government efforts to combat racial intolerance, it is pervasive in society and is often expressed by public figures. In September 2011, a trial began of 39 members of the Coast Guard who were accused of hurling racist slogans at Albanians and Macedonians during a parade in 2010. Only two of the defendants were convicted and the rest acquitted in December. The government does not officially recognize the existence of any non-Muslim ethnic minority groups. Macedonian is not recognized as a language, and using the terms *Tourkos* or *Tourkikos* ("Turk" and "Turkish," respectively) in the title of an association is illegal and may lead to the dissolution of the group. The Romany community continues to face considerable governmental and societal discrimination.

Immigrants are disproportionately affected by institutional problems in the judicial system. Bureaucratic delays force many into a semi-legal status, whereby they are not able to renew their documents, putting them in jeopardy of deportation. A 2010 Amnesty International report noted that asylum seekers are often treated as criminals and face inhuman conditions in detention centers.

Greece passed a law to address domestic violence in 2006; however, the law has been criticized for lacking provisions to give the state power to protect the rights of women. Women continue to face discrimination in the workplace. Women currently hold only 17 percent of the seats in Parliament. The country serves as a transit and destination country for the trafficking of men, women, and children for the purposes of sexual exploitation and forced labor.

Grenada

Political Rights: 1
Civil Liberties: 2
Status: Free

Population: 104,900
Capital: St. George's

Ten-Year Ratings Timeline For Year Under Review (Political Rights, Civil Liberties, Status)

2002	2003	2004	2005	2006	2007	2008	2009	2010	2011
1,2F	1,2F	1,2F	1,2F	1,2F	1,2F	1,2F	1,2F	1,2F	1,2F

Overview: **Grenada's economy, which suffered from the effects of Hurricane Ivan in 2004 and the global economic crisis in 2008, saw modest growth in 2011 due to expansion of the construction and tourism industries. Meanwhile, the country's political opposition charged that a proposed Financial Intelligence Unit Bill would be used by Prime Minister Tillman Thomas' administration to engage in politically motivated investigations of financial crimes.**

Grenada gained independence from Britain in 1974. Maurice Bishop's Marxist New Jewel Movement seized power in 1979, creating the People's Revolutionary Government (PRG). In 1983, Bishop was murdered by New Jewel hard-liners Bernard Coard and Hudson Austin, who took control of the country. However, a joint U.S.-Caribbean military intervention quickly removed the PRG and set the country on a path toward new elections. In 1986 Coard and 18 others were sentenced to death; subsequently, 2 of the 19 were pardoned, and the rest—who became known as the Grenada 17—had their sentences commuted to life imprisonment. Between 2006 and 2009, all of the members of the Grenada 17 had their sentences reduced from life imprisonment to lesser terms after a ruling on the constitutionality of their sentences was handed down by Grenada's highest court, the London-based Privy Council. The last prisoners were released in September 2009.

Prime Minister Keith Mitchell of the New National Party (NNP) ruled Grenada from 1995 to 2008, when his party lost parliamentary elections to the opposition National Democratic Congress (NDC). The NDC captured 11 seats in the 15-member House of Representatives, while the NNP won the remaining 4 seats. Tillman Thomas, the NDC leader, was sworn in as prime minister in July 2008.

While Grenada continues to struggle with the effects of the global financial crisis and the impact of Hurricane Ivan, which devasted the country in 2004, the country enjoys greater economic stability than some of its neighboring countries. The economy enjoyed modest growth in 2011, as a financial stimulus provided incentives for the tourism and construction industries.

Grenada concluded a maritime demarcation treaty with Trinidad in April 2010, which may facilitate private investment in oil exploration. However, Grenada's link with foreign oil exploration investors remains a contentious issue. In August 2010, a state appellate court in the United States cleared former deputy prime minister Gregory Bowen of any wrongdoing in the 2005 cancellation of American investor Jack Grynberg's oil exploration contract. Bowen's legal costs were assumed by Global Petroleum Group (GPG), a Russian company that was granted oil exploration rights in 2005 after the termination of Grynberg's contract. Oil exploration by GPG has stalled as the Thomas administration revisits the GPG deal.

Political Rights and Civil Liberties: Grenada is an electoral democracy. The 2008 parliamentary elections were considered generally free and fair, although there were allegations of voter list manipulation. The bicameral Parliament consists of the directly elected, 15-seat House of Representatives, whose members serve five-year terms, and the 13-seat Senate, to which the prime minister appoints 10 members and the opposition leader appoints 3 members. The prime minister is typically the leader of the majority party in the House of Representatives and is appointed by the governor-general, who represents the British monarch as head of state. Grenada's main political parties are the NDC, the NNP, the Grenada United Labor Party, and the People's Labor Movement.

Despite the adoption of anticorruption legislation in 2007, corruption remains a serious political issue in Grenada. In August 2010, the NDC announced plans to request a special prosecutor to investigate multiple allegations of corruption in the Keith Mitchell administration, including accusations of corruption in relation to the decision to switch Grenada's diplomatic relations from Taiwan to China. In 2011, a Financial Intelligence Unit Bill was introduced that would expand the role of the existing Financial Intelligence Unit (FIU), which investigates financial crimes, move it from a department within the police force to a branch of government, and give legal protection from lawsuits to the director of the unit. Opposition politicians expressed serious concern that the bill would limit the independence of the FIU and be used to engage in politically motivated investigations. The bill had not been adopted by year's end.

The right to free expression is generally respected. The media, including three weekly newspapers and several other publications, are independent and freely criticize the government. A private corporation, with a minority stake owned by the government, operates the principal radio and television stations. There are also nine privately owned radio stations, one privately owned television station, and a privately owned cable company. Access to the internet is unrestricted.

Citizens of Grenada generally enjoy the free exercise of religious beliefs, and there are no official restrictions on academic freedom.

Constitutional guarantees regarding freedoms of assembly and association are respected. Grenada has a robust civil society that participates actively in domestic and international discussions, although limited resources hamper its effectiveness. Workers have the right to strike and to organize and bargain collectively, though employers are not legally bound to recognize a union of their employees if the majority of the workers are not unionized. All unions belong to the government-subsidized Grenada Trades Union Council (GTUC).

The independence and authority of Grenada's judiciary are generally respected by the Royal Grenada Police Force. Grenada is a member of the Organization of Eastern Caribbean States court system and a charter member of the Caribbean Court of Justice, but the country still relies on the Privy Council in London as its final court of appeal. Detainees and defendants are guaranteed a range of legal rights, which the government respects in practice. However, a lack of judges and facilities has led to a backlog of six months to one year for cases involving serious offenses. The Grenada 17 case was repeatedly criticized for perceived political manipulation by the government, and Amnesty International classified the group as political prisoners. Grenada's prisons are significantly overcrowded with occupancy level at 195 percent.

While women are represented in the government, they comprise 23 percent of the Senate and only 13 percent of the lower house following 2008 elections. Women generally earn less than men for equal work. New domestic violence legislation was introduced in 2010; however, most instances of abuse go unreported or are settled out of court. Sexual minorities remain a target of discrimination.

Guatemala

Political Rights: 3*
Civil Liberties: 4
Status: Partly Free

Population: 14,740,000
Capital: Guatemala City

Ratings Change: Guatemala's political rights rating improved from 4 to 3 due to progress made by the UN-backed International Commission against Impunity in Guatemala in investigating corruption, violence, and organized crime within Guatemalan public institutions, political parties, and civil society, and due to the anticorruption efforts of the country's attorney general.

Ten-Year Ratings Timeline For Year Under Review (Political Rights, Civil Liberties, Status)

2002	2003	2004	2005	2006	2007	2008	2009	2010	2011
4,4PF	4,4PF	4,4PF	4,4PF	3,4PF	3,4PF	3,4PF	4,4PF	4,4PF	3,4PF

Overview: **The Patriotic Party and National Unity for Hope parties captured two-thirds of the legislative seats in September 2011 elections. After the governing party's presidential candidate was disqualified from the presidential race, Otto Peréz Molina defeated Manuel Baldízon in a November runoff. High profile killings of 27 farmworkers and Argentine**

folk singer Facundo Cabral, and states of siege in Alta Verapaz and Petén, dominated the headlines, even though the country's murder rate declined for a second consecutive year.

The Republic of Guatemala, which was established in 1839, has endured a history of dictatorship, foreign intervention, military coups, and guerrilla insurgencies. Civilian rule followed the 1985 elections, and a 36-year civil war, which claimed the lives of more than 200,000 people, ended with a 1996 peace agreement. The Guatemalan National Revolutionary Uniy (URNG) guerrilla movement became a political party, and two truth commissions began receiving complaints of human rights violations committed during the conflict. However, voters in 1999 rejected a package of constitutional amendments that had been prepared in accordance with the peace plan.

In 2003, Óscar Berger of the Grand National Alliance (GANA) defeated Álvaro Colom of the National Unity for Hope (UNE) in runoff presidential elections. In 2007, Colom defeated Otto Pérez Molina of the Patriotic Party (PP) in a runoff vote to become president, capturing 53 percent of the vote amid a mere 45 percent turnout. Elections for congressional seats that September saw the UNE party capture 51 seats, followed by GANA with 37 seats, and Pérez's PP with 29 seats.

Guatemalans returned to the polls in September 2011 to elect a president, all 158 members of the parliament, mayors for each of the 333 municipalities, and 20 members of the Central American Parliament. Manuel Baldizón of the Renewed Democratic Liberty (LIDER) party emerged as the main competitor against presidential candidate Otto Pérez of the PP when, after the courts determined that the candidacy of former first lady Sandra Torres of the UNE-GANA coalition would violate Article 186 of the constitution, which prevents close relatives from immediately succeeding the president. As a result, the ruling coalition lacked a candidate in the presidential elections. Pérez defeated Baldizón in a November runoff with an estimated 54 percent of the vote. The PP and UNE parties captured two-thirds of the seats in parliamentary elections; nine other parties took the remaining 54 seats.

The elections were generally considered free and fair despite accompanying violence, repeated campaign violations, and vote irregularities. While not as bloody as the 2007 elections, at least 36 candidates, party activists, and their relatives were killed in campaign-related violence. One high-profile case involved a mayoral candidate from the municipality of San José Pinula who murdered his two competitors. Both the LIDER and the PP violated campaign spending laws, and electoral observers reported irregularities including intimidation, vote-buying, and the burning of ballots and electoral boxes. Five municipal elections had to be repeated due to irregularities. The electoral authority, the Supreme Electoral Tribunal, was criticized for its slow transmission of election results.

The mandate of the UN-backed International Commission against Impunity in Guatemala (CICIG)—tasked with investigating corruption, violence, and organized crime within Guatemalan public institutions, political parties, and civil society—was extended through September 2013. After Attorney General Conrado Reyes was accused of obstructing the CICIG's ability to carry out investigations and having ties to organized crime in 2010, Commissioner Carlos Castresana resigned in protest, citing insufficient support from Guatemalan officials. Reyes denied the accusations, but the Constitutional Court removed him from office. The United Nations selected former Costa Rican attorney general Francisco Dall'Anese to be the CICIG's new commissioner in June 2010, and Colom nominated Claudia Paz y Paz to become the country's first female attorney general in December.

Two states of siege were in effect in 2011. The first was declared in the department of Alta Verapaz from December 2010 to February 2011 in order to fight increased drug trafficking. However, human rights and local community groups expressed skepticism of the government's intentions, as the department is home to many land conflicts, and at least two community activists were arrested during the siege. The declaration of a state of siege grants security forces the right to conduct searches and to detain suspects without warrants, prohibits gun possession, and limits freedom of association and freedom of the press in the name of security. The president declared a second state of siege in the northern province of Petén in May after 27 workers were murdered on a farm by the Mexican-based Zetas drug gang. The siege remained in effect through the end of the year.

Political Rights and Civil Liberties: Guatemala is an electoral democracy. Despite many difficulties, the 2011 elections were regarded by international observers as generally free and fair. The constitution stipulates a four-year presidential term and prohibits reelection. The unicameral Congress of the Republic, consisting of 158 members, is elected for four years. Elections take place within a highly fragmented and fluid multiparty system. The main political parties are the UNE, the Patriotic Party, GANA, the Nationalist Change Union (UCN), LIDER, and the Commitment, Renewal, and Order (CREO) party.

Efforts to combat corruption, such as the introduction of an electronic procurement system for government entities, have made some progress, but serious problems remain. Unregulated campaign financing enables graft and criminal influence on politics. Among other high-profile corruption cases in 2011, former president Alfonso Portillo and his former defense and finance ministers were acquitted by a Guatemalan court in May of having embezzled money from the Ministry of Defense in 2001 during Portillo's presidential term. However, the Guatemalan Constitutional Court ruled in August 2011 that Portillo could be extradited to the United States, where he was indicted in 2010 for allegedly embezzling state funds while in office (2000-2004) and laundering the money through Guatemalan, European, and U.S. banks. Guatemalan courts also failed to prosecute Alejandro Giammattei, a former prison director, who was accused of participating in the killing of seven inmates during a 2007 uprising at Pavon prison and the alleged execution of three inmates who escaped from another prison in 2005. After being released in May 2011, Giammattei immediately entered the 2011 presidential race as the candidate for the Center for Social Action Party. Along with Giammattei and 16 other people, former police chief Erwin Sperisen and former interior minister Carlos Vielmann fought extradition requests from Switzerland and from Spain, respectively, for allegedly executing people inside and outside the prison system. On a positive note, the CICIG won convictions against those accused of the murder of Victor Rivera, a former adviser to the country's Interior Minister, and also played an important role in arresting several suspects in the July murder of Argentine folk singer Facundo Cabral and the

May massacre in Petén. Guatemala was ranked 120 out of 183 countries surveyed in Transparency International's 2011 Corruption Perceptions Index.

The 2009 Law for Free Access to Public Information grants citizens access to information on budgets and salaries. In line with this legislation, the government has taken steps towards developing an institutional framework for transparency, including the creation of a Vice Ministry of Fiscal Transparency and Evaluation and a Public Information Unit responsible for handling requests for public records.

While freedom of speech is protected by the constitution, journalists often face threats and practice self-censorship when covering drug trafficking, corruption, organized crime, and past human rights violations. A number of journalists received death threats, were physically assaulted, and murdered in 2011. Television correspondent Oscar de León received continuous death threats and his vehicle was fired upon in February, following his investigations of police corruption. In May, television reporter Yensi Roberto Ordoñez Galdámez was found stabbed to death in the southern province of Escuintla. Ordoñez had received previous threats related to his reporting and was allegedly being extorted; no arrests had been made by year's end. Journalist Lucía Escobar was threatened and forced to flee for her safety in October after writing a piece for *elPeriódico* that accused a municipal security commission in the city of Panajachel of extralegal activities and the disappearance of a city resident. However, prosecutors arrested the involved assailants. The press and most broadcast outlets are privately owned. Mexican businessman Remigio Ángel González owns a monopoly of broadcast television networks and has significant holdings in radio. Newspaper ownership is concentrated in the hands of moderate business elites, and most papers have centrist or conservative editorial views.

The constitution guarantees religious freedom. However, indigenous communities have faced discrimination for openly practicing the Mayan religion. The government does not interfere with academic freedom, but scholars have received death threats for raising questions about past human rights abuses or continuing injustices.

Freedom of assembly is guaranteed and generally respected in practice, though police have at times used force to end disruptive demonstrations, resulting in the injury and death of some protesters.

The constitution guarantees freedom of association, and a variety of nongovernmental organizations (NGOs) operate without major legal or government obstacles. However, the Unit for the Protection of Human Rights Defenders in Guatemala identified 402 attacks against human rights defenders in 2011, including journalists and advocates of union and environmental rights. International agencies also encountered intimidation and threats during the year. Amid continued protests against the Marlin Mine in Guatemala's western highlands, the Inter-American Commission on Human Rights (IACHR) in May 2010 granted precautionary protective measures to members of 18 indigenous Mayan communities in the Sipacapa and San Miguel Ixtahuacán municipalities. The indigenous inhabitants allege that the Marlin Mine has resulted in grave human rights violations and created serious health hazards for the communities. While activists continued to receive threats throughout 2011, the IACHR withdrew its demand that the government close the Marlin Mine in December after further study indicated that its operations posed no serious threat.

Guatemala is home to a vigorous labor movement, but workers are frequently denied the right to organize and face mass firings and blacklisting, especially in export-processing zones. Trade union members are also subject to intimidation, violence, and murder, particularly in rural areas during land disputes. According to the International Trade Union Confederation, Guatemala is the second-most dangerous country in the world for trade unionists, after Colombia. In 2010, the United States filed a formal complaint against Guatemala under the Dominican Republic-Central American Free Trade Agreement, alleging government failure to protect workers' rights. In August 2011, the U.S. further requested a dispute settlement panel to address its complaint. Two former policemen were sentenced in October 2011 to 40 years in prison for the 1984 forced disappearance of union leader Fernando García. A former chief of police was also arrested in June 2011 for complicity in García's disappearance. He was awaiting trial at year's end.

The judiciary is troubled by corruption, inefficiency, capacity shortages, and the intimidation of judges, prosecutors, and witnesses. Witnesses and judicial-sector workers continued to be threatened and, in some cases, murdered in 2011. In 2010, the CICIG reported irregularities in the selection of judges and accused the public prosecutor's office of impeding its investigations of corruption and organized crime within public institutions. CICIG voiced similar concerns about the court's integrity following the acquittal of former president Alfonso Portillo in 2011.

Prosecutions of perpetrators of past human rights atrocities continued in 2011. In August, four former military officers each received sentences of 6,060 years for their roles in the 1982 massacre of more than 250 people in Dos Erres, El Petén, and for crimes against humanity. Several high-ranking officials were also arrested throughout the year, including former general and de facto president Oscar Mejia, for their roles in implementing mass killings in the 1980s, which targeted government opponents and civilians.

Police continued to be accused of torture, extortion, kidnapping, and extrajudicial killings. A 2010 Law for the National Prevention of Torture and Other Cruel and Unusual Punishments provides for the creation of a monitoring unit to oversee the prevention of torture in prisons. Police officers continue to be charged with drug-related crimes. The government uses the military to maintain internal security, despite restrictions on this practice imposed by the 1996 peace accord.

Prison conditions are harsh, and the facilities are overcrowded and rife with gang- and drug-related violence and corruption. Although the provision of indigenous-language translators in courtrooms is legally mandated, a lack of funding has prevented proper implementation.

Guatemala remains one of the most violent countries in Latin America. Over 5,600 people were murdered during 2011, which actually represents a 5 percent decrease from 2010. Violence related to the shipment of drugs from South America to the United States has spilled over the border from Mexico, with rival drug trafficking organizations battling for territory. These groups have operated with impunity in the northern jungles, which serve as a storage and transit hub for cocaine en route to the United States. The local drug problem has also worsened, as traffickers have paid Guatemalan associates in cocaine rather than cash. The administration of Álvaro Colom reacted to this situation by declaring states of siege in two departments and repositioning police and military.

Indigenous communities suffer from especially high rates of poverty, illiteracy, and infant mortality. Indigenous women are particularly marginalized. Discrimination against the Mayan community continues to be a major concern. The government in recent years has approved the eviction of indigenous groups to make way for mining, hydroelectric, and other development projects. Several large indigenous communities have reportedly been forcibly evicted in the Polochic Valley with killings, beatings, and the burning of houses and crops.

The constitution prohibits discrimination based on gender, though gender inequalities persist in practice. Sexual harassment in the workplace is not penalized. Young women who migrate to the capital for work are especially vulnerable to harassment and inhumane labor conditions. Physical and sexual violence against women and children, including domestic violence, remain widespread, with perpetrators rarely prosecuted. While Guatemala now has its first female attorney general, police reform commissioner, and vice president, women remain underrepresented in politics, and held just 13 percent of the seats in congress following September 2011 elections. Sexual minorities also continued to be targets of violent attacks.

Guatemala has one of the highest rates of child labor in the Americas. According to the U.S. State Department, the government does not fully comply with the minimum standards for eliminating trafficking but is making efforts to do so, including launching a program to provide specialized services for trafficking victims.

Guinea

Political Rights: 5
Civil Liberties: 5
Status: Partly Free

Population: 10,231,800
Capital: Conakry

Ten-Year Ratings Timeline For Year Under Review (Political Rights, Civil Liberties, Status)

2002	2003	2004	2005	2006	2007	2008	2009	2010	2011
6,5NF	6,5NF	6,5NF	6,5NF	6,5NF	6,5NF	7,5NF	7,6NF	5,5PF	5,5PF

Overview: **In July 2011, dissident army officers carried out an unsuccessful assassination attempt on President Alpha Condé. The run-up to December legislative elections—seen as the final step in cementing Guinea's return to civilian rule after a 2008 military coup—was marred by violence and political infighting, including a police crackdown on a September opposition protest in which at least two people were killed. The elections were ultimately postponed due to objections from the opposition.**

Guinea gained independence from France in 1958 and grew increasingly impoverished under the repressive, one-party rule of President Ahmed Sékou Touré. After his death in 1984, a military junta led by Lieutenant Colonel Lansana Conté abolished all political parties and the constitution, and began a program of economic liberalization.

A new constitution was adopted in 1990. Conté won the country's first multiparty presidential election in 1993, but international observers said the poll was deeply flawed. Presidential, legislative, and municipal elections over the next 12 years were similarly marred by serious irregularities; all resulted in victories for Conté and the ruling party.

Security forces killed more than 130 people during nationwide antigovernment demonstrations in 2007, and martial law was declared. Union leaders agreed to suspend a general strike in exchange for Conté's pledge to implement political and economic reforms. Conté died in December 2008, and junior officers quickly mounted a successful military coup, promising to hold elections in two years.

Captain Moussa Dadis Camara, the coup leader, initially enjoyed considerable popularity, especially as he sought to expose corruption among former officials. However, following signs that Camara might renege on his earlier promise not to run in a presidential election set for January 2010, opposition forces mounted a massive rally on September 28, 2009. The gathering was viciously suppressed by security forces, who killed more than 150 people and raped and beat hundreds of others. The international community condemned the crackdown and imposed sanctions on the regime. In December, the commander of the presidential guard shot and seriously injured Camara.

While Camara recuperated in Burkina Faso, his deputy, General Sékouba Konaté, became interim president. In January 2010, Konaté negotiated an accord with Camara that established conditions for the upcoming presidential election. Prodemocracy opposition leader Jean-Marie Doré, who was named interim prime minister later in January, was charged with leading a power-sharing government and facilitating a return to civilian rule. The accord also created a broad-based, 155-member interim parliament, the National Transitional Council. In February, the International Criminal Court (ICC) found that the September 2009 massacre was a crime against humanity, and called on Guinean courts to try the perpetrators or allow the ICC to do so.

The presidential election took place in June 2010, though no candidate garnered more than 50 percent of the vote. In the November runoff election, longtime opposition leader Alpha Condé of the Rally of the Guinean People (RPG) defeated former prime minister Cellou Dalein Diallo of the Union of Democratic Forces of Guinea (UFDG), 52.5 percent to 47.5 percent. The election was deemed legitimate and representative of popular opinion by most domestic and international observers, and Diallo eventually accepted the results. However, violence and voter intimidation in Guinea's eastern region resulted in the displacement of thousands of ethnic Peul supporters of Diallo.

Progress toward consolidating democratic gains in early 2011 was hampered by ongoing ethnic tensions, with Condé facing accusations of awarding government posts to members of his Malinké group. The new president also had a fraught relationship with the military, parts of which had difficulty accepting their diminished status under a civilian government. In July 2011, former army officers led an unsuccessful assassination attempt, firing rocket-propelled grenades into Condé's walled compound and exchanging fire with the presidential guard. Among the some 50 soldiers and civilians arrested for the attack was former army chief Nouhou Thiam and former members of Konaté's presidential guard.

At least two people were killed and scores more injured when police and opposition demonstrators clashed on September 27. The demonstrators, who gathered in several neighborhoods of Conakry, were demanding electoral reforms ahead of December legislative elections, and had planned to meet at the stadium, where the September 28, 2009, massacre had taken place. The government responded by stationing police vehicles and paramilitary forces around the stadium. Security forces arrested 322 people during the demonstrations, according to the government. In mid-December, parliamentary elections scheduled for December 29 were officially postponed, following objections from opposition members that they had not been consulted about the date; Condé agreed to delay the elections and to open dialogue with the opposition.

Political Rights and Civil Liberties: Guinea is not an electoral democracy. The president is elected by popular vote for up to two five-year terms. The legislature was dissolved in 2008, and replaced in 2010 by an appointed 155-member National Transitional Council that acts in its stead. A new date for the delayed legislative elections originally scheduled for December 29, 2011, was not decided by year's end. The 2010 election represented the country's first ever peaceful rotation of power. In May 2010, interim president Sékouba Konaté approved a new constitution that reinforces democratic rights, including explicitly outlining the legal status of the prime minister and establishing a number of bodies such as an independent electoral commission, a national human rights body, and a constitutional court. That constitution remained in place at the end of 2011.

The main political parties are President Alpha Condé's RPG and former prime minister Cellou Dalein Diallo's opposition UFDG. There are more than 130 other registered parties, most of which have clear ethnic or regional bases.

Corruption has been cited as a serious problem by international donors, and many government activities are shrouded in secrecy. Despite its rich natural resources—Guinea is the world's largest bauxite exporter—the majority of the population lives in poverty. A May 2011 Human Rights Watch (HRW) report called for the creation of an anticorruption commission to address misappropriation of the nation's vast mineral wealth. Condé has faced criticism for bringing corrupt officials from Conté's regime into his government. Guinea was ranked 164 out of 183 countries surveyed in Transparency International's 2011 Corruption Perceptions Index.

The 2010 constitution guarantees media freedom. In June 2010, the National Transitional Council passed two new media laws, one of which decriminalized press offenses and more clearly defined defamation provisions, while the other provided for the creation of a new media regulatory body. However, these laws had yet to be implemented under Condé. In 2011, Condé's government harassed, suspended, or arrested journalists at both independent and state-owned media outlets for reporting that was either critical of the government or favorable to the opposition. The regulatory body imposed a brief media blackout after the July assassination attempt. The state controls the national radio station and the only television broadcaster and daily newspaper. Due to the high illiteracy rate, most of the population accesses information via radio. Internet access is limited to urban areas, but has generally not been restricted by the government.

Religious rights are generally respected in practice, though there have been cases of discrimination against non-Muslims in government employment, as well as restrictions on Muslims' freedom to convert to other religions. Academic freedom has been hampered to some degree by government influence over hiring and curriculum content. Free private discussion, which had been limited under previous authoritarian governments and Camara's repressive and erratic rule, continued to improve in 2011.

Respect for freedoms of association and assembly, which had been seriously circumscribed under Conté and the military junta, improved in 2011. However, the crackdown on the September 2011 demonstrations was evidence that these freedoms have yet to be fully guaranteed. Trade unions enjoyed greater freedoms in 2011. There were reports of strike activities in the mining industry, including a violent protest by locals in September at a gold-processing plant owned by Canada's Semafo against the use of expatriate workers.

The judicial system demonstrated a modest degree of independence beginning in 2010; a panel of magistrates was empowered to investigate the September 2009 massacre, though no perpetrators were brought to justice by the end of 2011. HRW's May 2011 report found that the courts are severely underfunded. Informal customary justice mechanisms continue to operate in addition to official courts. Security forces have long engaged in arbitrary arrests, torture of detainees, and extrajudicial execution with impunity. Amnesty International called for an investigation into the security forces' actions during the September 2011 demonstrations, alleging that they resorted to tactics used under past repressive regimes. Prison conditions remain harsh and sometimes life threatening.

While the law prohibits ethnic discrimination, human rights reports have noted societal discrimination in employment, housing, and marriage patterns. Ethnic clashes during the campaign for the second round of the 2010 presidential elections pitted the principally Peul supporters of Diallo against Malinké partisans of Condé.

Societal discrimination against women is common, and while women have legal access to land, credit, and business, inheritance laws and the traditional justice system favor men. Security personnel openly raped dozens of women in the 2007 and 2009 crackdowns. HRW has reported that thousands of young girls serving as unpaid domestic workers in Guinea are subject to beatings or rape by their employers. Location and political instability have made Guinea a source and transit point for many irregular migrants heading to Europe. Advocacy groups are working to eradicate the illegal but nearly ubiquitous practice of female genital mutilation.

Guinea-Bissau

Political Rights: 4
Civil Liberties: 4
Status: Partly Free

Population: 1,610,000
Capital: Bissau

Ten-Year Ratings Timeline For Year Under Review (Political Rights, Civil Liberties, Status)

2002	2003	2004	2005	2006	2007	2008	2009	2010	2011
4,5PF	6,4PF	4,4PF	3,4PF	4,4PF	4,4PF	4,4PF	4,4PF	4,4PF	4,4PF

Overview: **In 2011, Guinea-Bissau—with the support of the international community—attempted to implement security sector reforms in the wake of a 2010 army mutiny. Tensions between Prime Minister Carlos Gomes Júnior and President Malam Bacai Sanhá eased somewhat. However, in late December, Guinea-Bissau was rocked by military clashes that led to the arrest of Admiral Bubo Na Tchuto on charges of plotting a coup d'état.**

Guinea-Bissau declared independence from Portugal in 1973 following a 13-year guerrilla war by the leftist African Party for the Independence of Guinea-Bissau and Cape Verde (PAIGC). Luís Cabral became president in 1974, but disaffection with his repressive rule led to divisions within the PAIGC, and in 1980 prime minister and former military commander João Bernardo "Nino" Vieira toppled him.

Vieira ruled from 1980 to 1984 as head of a Revolutionary Council, and was made head of state by a reconstituted single-party legislature in 1984. International pressure from donors eventually led to economic liberalization, and in 1994, the country's first multiparty legislative and presidential elections, in which Vieira won the presidency.

An army mutiny broke out in 1998 after Vieira fired General Ansumane Mané. Hostilities escalated when Vieira called on troops from neighboring Senegal and Guinea to put down the uprising. The war that ensued displaced hundreds of thousands of people and destroyed the country's infrastructure and economy. Vieira was ousted in 1999 and went into exile in Portugal.

The 1999 presidential and legislative elections resulted in defeat for the PAIGC and the election of Kumba Yalá, leader of the Social Renovation Party (PRS), as president. Mané declared himself head of the armed forces in 2000, inciting violence between the military factions supporting him and those backing Yalá. Mané was subsequently killed. In 2002, Yalá dissolved the parliament and ruled by decree until he was overthrown in a 2003 coup.

The PAIGC returned to power after winning a plurality of seats in the 2004 legislative elections, and Carlos Gomes Júnior became prime minister. Vieira returned from exile to stand in the 2005 presidential election as an independent candidate, and ultimately defeated both Yalá of the PRS and Malam Bacai Sanhá of the PAIGC.

Vieira soon dismissed Carlos Gomes Júnior and appointed former PAIGC ally Aristides Gomes to replace him as prime minister, causing tensions between

Vieira's supporters and the opposition. After months of negotiations, the PAIGC, PRS, and United Social Democrat Party agreed on a national political stability pact in March 2007. Days later, the coalition passed a no-confidence vote against Gomes, leading to his resignation and the appointment of Martinho Ndafa Kabi of the PAIGC to the premiership.

The 2008 legislative elections resulted in a resounding victory for the PAIGC, which took 67 seats in the 100-seat legislature. The PRS took 28, and the Vieira-backed Republican Party for Independence and Development captured 3. Carlos Gomes Júnior of the PAIGC once again became prime minister.

In March 2009, Vieira and the chief of the armed forces, Batista Tagme Na Wai, were assassinated in separate attacks. A new presidential election was held in June despite serious political violence during the campaign, including the fatal shootings of presidential candidate Baciro Dabó and former defense minister Helder Proença. Sanhá of the PAIGC defeated Yalá of the PRS in the July runoff, 63.3 percent to 36.7 percent. International observers reported that the voting itself was peaceful, free, and transparent.

In April 2010, mutinous soldiers led by the deputy chief of the armed forces, Antonio Indjai, detained Gomes as well as the armed forces chief, General José Zamora Induta, and 40 of his subordinates. Gomes was released the following day and remained in office, but Induta and the military intelligence chief, Colonel Samba Diallo, were detained without charges until late December. In June, Sanhá officially appointed Indjai as chief of the armed forces, a decision that drew condemnation from the international community. In October, Sanhá reappointed Rear Admiral José Américo Na Tchuto as chief of the navy, just months after he had been named a drug kingpin by the U.S. Treasury Department.

The year 2011 was marked by some progress in security sector reform, which aimed to create a smaller, more professional army, improve conditions in the barracks, and provide adequate pensions to retiring members of security forces. Guinea-Bissau received technical and financial support to implement these reforms from several international actors, including the UN Integrated Peacebuilding Office in Guinea-Bissau (UNIOGBIS), the Community of Portuguese Speaking Countries, and the governments of Angola and Brazil. In view of the progress in security sector reform, donors such as the European Union gradually resumed the external assistance that is critical for the country's economic stability.

On December 26, armed military personnel attacked military targets, demanding pay increases. The clashes occurred while Sanhá was undergoing medical treatment in France. The days that followed saw a return to violent infighting between different branches of the military, and Admiral Na Tchuto was arrested for plotting a coup d'état.

Political Rights and Civil Liberties: Guinea-Bissau is not an electoral democracy. Military intervention and the influence of the drug trade have undermined the authority of elected officials. The 100 members of the unicameral National People's Assembly are elected by popular vote to serve four-year terms. The president is elected for a five-year term, and there are no term limits. The president appoints the prime minister after consultation with party leaders in the legislature.

Political parties in Guinea-Bissau are competitive but institutionally weak. They routinely suffer from military interference and shifting personal cliques. Party leaders are often unable or unwilling to fully carry out their constitutional functions and policy agendas, as military factions have repeatedly shown a readiness to maintain or expand their own interests through coups, assassinations, and threats. In this context, Guinea-Bissau was ranked 44 out of 53 countries surveyed in the 2011 Ibrahim Index of African Governance.

Corruption is pervasive, driven in large part by the illicit drug trade. With weak institutions and porous borders, Guinea-Bissau has become a major transit point for Latin American drug traffickers moving cocaine to Europe. Powerful segments of the military, police, and government are reportedly complicit in the trade, and the judiciary—either through lack of resources or collusion in the crimes—did not investigate or prosecute corruption cases. UNIOGBIS and the UN Office on Drugs and Crime (UNODC) are helping the government tackle this growing problem as part of an Economic Community of West African States regional action plan. Guinea-Bissau was ranked 154 out of 183 countries surveyed in Transparency International's 2011 Corruption Perceptions Index.

Although the constitution provides for freedoms of speech and of the press, these freedoms are not always respected. Journalists regularly face harassment and intimidation, especially regarding the military's alleged involvement in drug trafficking, and some practice self-censorship. In April 2011, the government threatened to suspend the newspaper *Última Hora* after it ran a front-page article accusing soldiers loyal to then-deputy armed forces chief of staff Antonio Indjai of the 2009 assassination of President João Bernardo "Nino" Vieira; the threat was subsequently dropped. Several journalists have become advisers of politicians, helping them manage their images. There are a number of private and community radio stations in addition to the national broadcasters, and several private newspapers publish sporadically. Internet access is unrestricted.

Religious freedom is legally protected and usually respected in practice. Academic freedom is similarly guaranteed and upheld.

Freedoms of assembly and association are recognized and usually respected, but security forces have occasionally suppressed public demonstrations. Nongovernmental organizations (NGOs) generally operate freely, though members of local human rights organizations have at times been subject to harassment and even physical attack. Workers are allowed to form and join independent trade unions, but few work in the wage-earning formal sector. The right to strike is protected, and government workers frequently exercise this right.

Scant resources and endemic corruption severely challenge judicial independence. The U.S. State Department has reported that there are essentially no resources to conduct criminal investigations, and few formal detention facilities. With support from UNODC, the government rehabilitated the Mansôa and Bafatá prisons. These facilities, currently the only secure prisons in Guinea-Bissau, started receiving their first prisoners in June 2011. Judges and magistrates are poorly trained, irregularly paid, and highly susceptible to corruption and political pressure. A culture of impunity prevails, especially in the military. A commission formed in 2009 to probe that year's assassinations of Vieira and the chief of the armed forces, Batista Tagme Na Wai, did not make any progress in 2011.

Ethnic identity is an important factor in politics, and the country's largest ethnic group, the Balanta, dominates the military.

Women face significant traditional and societal discrimination, despite some legal protections. They generally do not receive equal pay for equal work and have fewer opportunities in education and employment. Women of certain ethnic groups cannot own or manage land or inherit property. Domestic violence, female genital mutilation (FGM), and early marriage are widespread. The National People's Assembly in June 2011 approved a law banning FGM; it provided for penalties of up to five years in prison for violators. Trafficking in persons, especially children, is a significant problem, despite efforts by NGOs to raise awareness, improve law enforcement, and repatriate victims.

Guyana

Political Rights: 2
Civil Liberties: 3
Status: Free

Population: 756,900
Capital: Georgetown

Ten-Year Ratings Timeline For Year Under Review (Political Rights, Civil Liberties, Status)

2002	2003	2004	2005	2006	2007	2008	2009	2010	2011
2,2F	2,2F	2,2F	3,3PF	2,3F	2,3F	2,3F	2,3F	2,3F	2,3F

Overview: **The ruling alliance of the People's Progressive Party and the Civic Party (PPP-C) won reelection in November 2011 over the newly formed opposition group Partnership Through National Unity. The PPP-C's Donald Ramotar became president of Guyana in December.**

Guyana gained independence from Britain in 1966 and was ruled by the autocratic, predominantly Afro-Guyanese People's National Congress (PNC) for the next 26 years. In 1992, Cheddi Jagan of the largely Indo-Guyanese People's Progressive Party (PPP) won the presidency in Guyana's first free and fair elections. He died in 1997, and the office passed to his wife, Janet, who resigned in 1999 for health reasons. She was succeeded by Finance Minister Bharrat Jagdeo of the PPP-C, an alliance of the PPP and the Civic Party. Jagdeo was elected in his own right in 2001.

Guyanese politics are dominated by a tense split between descendants of indentured workers from India, known as Indo-Guyanese, who generally back the PPP-C, and Afro-Guyanese, who largely support the PNC-Reform (PNC-R) party. In 2004, the political climate showed brief signs of improving, when the PPP-C and PNC-R announced that they had reached agreement on a wide variety of issues. However, the emerging harmony was disrupted when a police informant revealed the existence of death squads that enjoyed official sanction and had killed some 64 people. An investigation exposed apparent links to the home affairs minister, Ronald Gajraj, but he was largely exonerated by an official inquiry in 2005.

In the run-up to the 2006 legislative elections, Agriculture Minister Satyadeo

Sawh was brutally slain by masked gunmen, and four newspaper employees were shot dead on the outskirts of the capital. The elections were delayed by several weeks as deep conflicts within the seven-member Guyana Elections Commission undermined the credibility of the process. Nevertheless, the elections took place without incident in August, due in part to the presence of international observers. The PPP-C emerged victorious, with President Jagdeo securing another five-year term.

In November 2011 elections, the PPP-C's reelection bid was led by 61-year-old Donald Ramotar, an economist. Denis Marshall, the chairperson of a Commonwealth Observer Group for the 2011 national and regional elections in Guyana noted that, despite some minor issues, the elections represented progress in strengthening Guyana's democratic processes. The PPP-C captured 32 seats, while the newly established Partnership for National Unity took 26 seats, and the Alliance for Change (AFC) won 7 seats. Ramotar became president in December.

Political Rights and Civil Liberties: Guyana is an electoral democracy. The 1980 constitution provides for a strong president and a 65-seat National Assembly, with members elected every five years. Two additional, nonvoting members are appointed by the president. The leader of the party with a plurality of parliamentary seats becomes president for a five-year term and appoints the prime minister and cabinet.

The 2006 elections strengthened the hand of the ruling PPP-C, but also demonstrated that some Guyanese are beginning to vote across racial lines, as symbolized by the establishment of the multiracial AFC. The main opposition party remains the PNC-R. Other significant political parties or groupings include the Alliance for Guyana, the Guyana Labor Party, the United Force, the Justice for All Party, the Working People's Alliance, and the Guyana Action Party, which enjoys strong support from indigenous communities in the south.

Guyana is home to nine indigenous groups with a total population of about 80,000. Human rights violations against them, particularly with respect to land and resource use, are widespread and pervasive. Indigenous peoples' attempts to seek redress through the courts have been met with unwarranted delays by the judiciary. While racial clashes have diminished in the last decade, long-standing animosity between Afro- and Indo-Guyanese remains a serious concern. A 2002 Racial Hostility Bill increased penalties for race-based crimes.

The country is a transshipment point for South American cocaine destined for North America and Europe, and counternarcotics efforts are undermined by corruption that reaches to high levels of the government. The informal economy is driven primarily by drug proceeds and may be equal to between 40 and 60 percent of formal economic activity. Guyana was ranked 134 out of 183 countries surveyed in Transparency International's 2011 Corruption Perceptions Index.

Although freedom of the press is generally respected, an uneasy tension between the state and the media persists. Several independent newspapers operate freely, including the daily *Stabroek News* and *Kaieteur News*. However, opposition party leaders complain that they lack access to state media. The state owns and operates the country's sole radio station, which broadcasts on three frequencies. In 2009, the Guyana Press Association denounced a government initiative to license media professionals as an attempt to impose control over the profession. Government officials occasionally use libel lawsuits to suppress criticism. The government also closed an internationally funded Media-Monitoring Unit, established in 2006 to monitor media ahead of national elections. Prior to the 2011 elections, President Bharrat Jagdeo had disparaged journalists from Guyana's best known media outlets as "vultures and carrion crows." In October, Guyana Elections Commission Chairman Steve Surujbally expressed concern about such attacks, calling them "self-destructive, nation-wrecking, counterproductive and, quite frankly, inane." There are no government restrictions on the internet.

Guyanese generally enjoy freedom of religion, and the government does not restrict academic freedom.

The government largely respects freedoms of assembly and association. The right to form labor unions is also generally upheld, and unions are well organized. However, employers are not required to recognize unions in former state enterprises. The judicial system is independent, but due process is undermined by shortages of staff and funds. In 2005, Guyana cut all ties to the Privy Council in London, the court of last resort for other former British colonies in the region, and adopted the Trinidad-based Caribbean Court of Justice as its highest appellate court. Prisons are overcrowded, and conditions are poor.

The Guyana Defence Force and the national Guyana Police Force are under civilian control. Racial polarization has seriously eroded law enforcement, with many Indo-Guyanese complaining that they are victimized by Afro-Guyanese criminals and ignored by the predominantly Afro-Guyanese police. Meanwhile, many Afro-Guyanese claim that the police are manipulated by the government for its own purposes. Official inquiries have repeatedly called for improved investigative techniques, more funding, community-oriented policing, better disciplinary procedures, greater accountability, and a better ethnic balance in the police force, but the government has taken few concrete steps to implement the proposed reforms.

Violence against women, including domestic abuse, is widespread. Rape often goes unreported and is rarely prosecuted. The Guyana Human Rights Association has charged that the legal system's treatment of victims of sexual violence is intentionally humiliating. The 2010 Sexual Offenses Act makes rape gender-neutral and expands its definition to include spousal rape and coercion and child abuse; the new law also provides for offenses committed against the mentally disabled. Sodomy is punishable with a maximum sentence of life in prison, and cross-dressing is criminalized for both men and women. In February 2010, the Society against Sexual Orientation Discrimination filed a motion with the Supreme Court, challenging the constitutionality of the law banning cross-dressing; a hearing on the issue is expected by mid-2012.

Haiti

Political Rights: 4
Civil Liberties: 5
Status: Partly Free

Population: 10,123,800
Capital: Port-au-Prince

Ten-Year Ratings Timeline For Year Under Review (Political Rights, Civil Liberties, Status)

2002	2003	2004	2005	2006	2007	2008	2009	2010	2011
6,6NF	6,6NF	7,6NF	7,6NF	4,5PF	4,5PF	4,5PF	4,5PF	4,5PF	4,5PF

Overview: **Michel Martelly won a presidential runoff election in March 2011 and took office in May, but the parliament did not approve his choice for prime minister until October. A major crisis erupted two weeks later, when the president ordered police to take a sitting member of parliament into custody without any formal charges. The incident raised doubts about the president's determination to uphold the rule of law as the country continued to reel from a January 2010 earthquake that killed more 200,000 people and left close to 1.5 million others homeless. A cholera epidemic that broke out in October 2010 continued in 2011, producing an overall death toll of nearly 7,000 people by year's end.**

Since gaining independence from France in 1804 following a slave revolt, the Republic of Haiti has endured a history of poverty, violence, instability, and dictatorship. A 1986 military coup ended 29 years of rule by the Duvalier family, and although the military permitted the implementation of a French-style constitution under international pressure in 1987, army officers continued to dominate political affairs for most of the next eight years.

Jean-Bertrand Aristide, a popular former priest, was elected president in 1990. After only eight months in office, he was deposed and exiled by a military triumvirate. While paramilitary thugs terrorized the populace, the ruling junta engaged in blatant narcotics trafficking. The United Nations ultimately authorized a multinational force to restore the civilian government, and in September 1994, facing an imminent invasion, the military rulers stepped down. U.S. troops took control of the country, and Aristide was reinstated. He dismantled the military before the June 1995 parliamentary elections, but his support began to fracture when international observers questioned the legitimacy of the balloting. Aristide retained the backing of the more radical Lavalas Family (FL) party, which won an overwhelming parliamentary majority.

FL nominee René Préval, who had been Aristide's prime minister in 1991, won the 1995 presidential election and took office in February 1996. The constitution had barred Aristide from seeking a second consecutive term. U.S. forces withdrew from the country in April 1996, while the UN force extended its stay at Préval's urging.

Aristide returned to the presidency in the 2000 election, which was boycotted by all major opposition parties amid widespread civil unrest and voter intimidation. He ran on a populist platform of economic revitalization, though opponents claimed that he was bent on establishing a one-party state. His supporters gained a majority of seats in both the upper and lower houses in that year's parliamentary elections.

Aristide's second term was undermined by cuts in foreign aid, increasing levels of poverty, and conflict with business elites and opposition groups. Faced with an armed revolt by political gangs and former army officers in February 2004, Aristide was flown out of the country in a plane chartered by the United States. He eventually accepted exile in South Africa. A constitutional transition elevated Boniface Alexandre, head of the Supreme Court, to the position of president, and a new prime minister was named in March. Meanwhile, the UN peacekeeping force gradually expanded beyond the capital.

In 2006, Préval returned to power in relatively well-conducted elections, taking 51 percent of the presidential vote. However, his newly organized Front for Hope (Lespwa) party failed to win a majority in either house of parliament. Security improved the following year, after a UN crackdown on gangs in the capital.

The parliament clashed with the government in 2008 and 2009, forcing out two prime ministers, though the replacement for the second was approved in an orderly succession in late 2009.

On January 12, 2010, a powerful earthquake struck near Port-au-Prince, killing more than 200,000 people and injuring as many as 300,000. At year's end, over a million people remained homeless; the figure had fallen to about half a million a year later. The UN headquarters in Port-au-Prince was destroyed in the quake, and the infrastructure of the police force and judiciary were severely damaged, compromising security and leading to lost casework and trial delays for an already overburdened court system. In October 2010, the country suffered an outbreak of cholera, which continued in 2011 and had killed nearly 7,000 people by year's end.

Presidential and parliamentary elections held in November 2010 were marred by widespread reports of fraud, voter intimidation, violations of electoral law, and problems with the composition of the Provisional Electoral Council (CEP). Supporters of popular musician Michel Martelly—who finished third in the presidential first round, according to the initial results—took to the streets, claiming that fraud had prevented him from advancing to the runoff. Under pressure from the international community, Jude Célestin, Préval's chosen successor, was ultimately forced to relinquish his place in the runoff. Martelly went on to defeat first-round leader Mirlande Manigat of the opposition Rally of Progressive National Democrats (RDNP), 68 percent to 32 percent, in the March 2011 second round. Meanwhile, after parliamentary runoff elections, the Inité coalition—founded by Préval in 2010 to replace Lespwa—held 46 seats in the lower house and 6 of the 11 Senate seats at stake. Smaller parties divided the remainder, with none taking more than eight seats in the lower house.

Martelly was sworn in as president in May, but the parliament rejected his first two choices for prime minister. Lawmakers finally granted approval to Gary Conille, a medical doctor and former UN official, in October. A standoff between the executive and legislative branches took shape two weeks later, when police arrested sitting parliament member Arnel Bélizaire, whom the media identified as an escaped prisoner convicted of murder in 2004. Lawmakers objected to the arrest, citing parliamentary immunity. The justice minister and a prosecutor were forced to resign, but the case remained unresolved at year's end.

Separately during 2011, Aristide and former dictator Jean-Claude Duvalier returned to the country as private citizens. Duvalier faced a variety of criminal charges concerning his time in office, which remained pending at year's end, but no charges were filed against Aristide in 2011.

Political Rights and Civil Liberties: Haiti is not an electoral democracy. The first round of the presidential and parliamentary elections, held in November 2010, suffered from a number of critical flaws, including widespread complaints of unfairness and lack of transparency in the approval of candidates by the CEP and massive voter fraud. The results were rejected by the major international election monitoring organizations, and the line-up for the presidential runoff was altered under pressure from the Organization of American States (OAS) and the U.S. State Department. Midterm parliamentary and municipal elections that were scheduled to take place in November 2011 were not held, since the incumbent CEP is under assault by the current government. Several members of the council went into hiding during 2011, and in October, the police went to search the house of the council's president.

The country's 1987 constitution provides for a president elected for a five-year term, a National Assembly composed of the 30-member Senate and the 99-member Chamber of Deputies, and a prime minister appointed by the president. Senators are elected for six-year terms, with one-third coming up for election every two years and deputies for four-year terms. There are no term limits, but a president cannot serve consecutive terms. Lawmakers are sorely short of financial and administrative resources, and the parliament plays a reactive role, opposing or accepting initiatives from the executive branch. Most factions in the country's fragmented party system are based on personal leadership or support from a particular region.

Endemic corruption continues to hobble Haiti's political and economic development. A number of lawmakers elected in 2006 and 2010 have reportedly been involved in drug trafficking and other criminal activities; many seek parliamentary seats primarily to obtain immunity from prosecution. Although the administration of Michel Martelly has raised the issue of corruption as a problem, very few members of his cabinet have complied with the anticorruption agency's demand to provide full disclosure of their financial records. Campaign financing remains unregulated and emerged as a serious problem in the 2010 campaign. Attempts by foreign donors to safeguard the inflows of post-earthquake aid and promote investments have remained a challenge. Haiti was ranked 175 out of 183 countries surveyed in Transparency International's 2011 Corruption Perceptions Index.

Freedom of the press has been constrained by the absence of a viable judicial system and widespread insecurity. Violence against journalists remains a problem, and media outlets tend to practice self-censorship to avoid retribution for critical reporting. After the inauguration of President Martelly in May 2011, various media outlets protested against the president's intimidation and threats against their reporters. The country hosts a number of newspapers from across the political spectrum, though their circulations are fairly small. More than 90 percent of Haitians have access to radio, and more than 290 FM stations operate without a license. There are more than 70 community radio stations, which are often linked to political groups or parties. Television stations are far less common, with about

20 in Port-au-Prince and another 15 in the provinces. The total television audience in Haiti remains below 10 percent due to lack of electricity and resources. Internet access is hampered by similar problems.

The government generally respects religious and academic freedoms. However, the absence of an effective police force has led to poor protection for those who are persecuted for their views.

The 1987 constitution guarantees freedom of assembly and association. However, these rights are often not respected in practice. While Haiti has rich civil society traditions at the local level, many of its formally organized civil society groups have been co-opted by political and economic elites. Unions are too weak to engage in collective bargaining, and their organizing efforts are undermined by the country's high unemployment rate. New labor regulations introduced in 2009 included a stratified minimum wage system for the commercial and industrial sectors, and minimum health and safety standards. Still, the minimum wage increases apply only to a small segment of the population, and enforcement remains weak.

The judicial system is corrupt, inefficient, and dysfunctional. It is burdened by a large backlog of cases, outdated legal codes, and poor facilities. Moreover, official business is conducted in French rather than Creole, rendering large portions of court proceedings only marginally comprehensible to those involved. Prison conditions are harsh, and the ponderous legal system guarantees lengthy pretrial detentions. Some two-thirds of the inmate population are awaiting trial, including many who have been behind bars for over a year. During a prison riot in Les Cayes in January 2010, police shot dead 12 prisoners who had been living in overcrowded and inhumane conditions; in December 2011, 8 officers and 1 inmate were sentenced to between 3 and 13 years in prison for the incident. Police are regularly accused of abusing suspects and detainees.

Widespread violence against women and children worsened considerably in the aftermath of the 2010 earthquake. Rapes were reportedly commonplace and pervasive in the displacement camps, where insufficient police protection and inadequate housing exacerbated the vulnerability of women and children. Trafficking of children out of the country also reportedly increased sharply after the earthquake. More than 7,300 were thought to have been smuggled to the Dominican Republic in 2010, often to work in the sex trade, compared with an estimated 950 in 2009. Up to half a million children in Haiti reportedly serve as *restavec* ("live with," in Creole), a form of unpaid domestic labor with a long history in the country.

Honduras

Political Rights: 4
Civil Liberties: 4
Status: Partly Free

Population: 7,754,700
Capital: Tegucigalpa

Ten-Year Ratings Timeline For Year Under Review (Political Rights, Civil Liberties, Status)

2001	2002	2003	2004	2005	2006	2007	2008	2009	2010
3,3PF	3,3PF	3,3PF	3,3PF	3,3PF	3,3PF	3,3PF	3,3PF	4,4PF	4,4PF

Overview: **Honduras in 2011 took some steps to repair the damage caused by a 2009 coup that removed President José Manuel Zelaya from office. The internationally brokered Cartagena Accords, signed in April, paved the way for Zelaya's return to the country in June, and a Truth and Reconciliation Commission published its report on the coup in July. However, Honduras continued to suffer from human rights violations, impunity, and corruption, and crime rates increased dramatically, making Honduras one of the most violent countries in the world.**

The Republic of Honduras was established in 1839. The country endured decades of military rule and intermittent elected governments, with the last military regime giving way to civilian authorities in 1982. However, the military remained powerful in the subsequent decades; the first president to exercise his constitutional authority to veto the military and choose its leaders did so in 1999.

Under civilian rule, power has alternated between the Liberal Party (PL) and the National Party (PN). In the 2005 presidential election, José Manuel Zelaya of the PL defeated the PN's Porfirio Lobo. The run-up to the balloting had been marred by political violence that left several PL supporters injured and at least two dead.

Under Zelaya's administration, political polarization increased in an environment characterized by poor policy performance and faltering public institutions. The president deepened the country's political divisions, including within his own party, and pitted factions of the political and business elite against one another through increasingly populist posturing. In 2008, he brought Honduras into two Venezuelan-led regional trade initiatives, drawing objections from business organizations, the opposition, and elements within his government. Zelaya's nontransparent use of government resources and Venezuelan aid also caused friction, as did his perceived disregard for institutional checks and balances.

Zelaya was removed from power and forcibly deported in a coup on June 28, 2009, after he attempted to hold a nonbinding referendum to gauge support for an overhaul of the constitution. His opponents interpreted the proposal as a power grab, as it included the elimination of presidential term limits, though the constitutional reform process would have begun only after the end of his nonrenewable four-year term in 2010. Both the Supreme Court and the military participated in the coup. Roberto Micheletti of the PL, the president of Congress, was named acting president after the legislature accepted a forged resignation letter from Zelaya. The international community condemned the coup and continued to recognize Zelaya as the legitimate president.

The de facto government curtailed civil and political liberties in the months following the coup. In September, Micheletti issued an executive decree suspending civil liberties for 45 days. Police were granted new powers of detention, all public meetings were banned, and the security forces were effectively permitted to act without regard for human rights or the rule of law. Nationwide curfews were imposed at times, and public demonstrations supporting Zelaya's reinstatement were violently suppressed, resulting in the death of several protesters. Media outlets and journalists faced harassment, threats, power outages, and blocked transmissions; authorities also temporarily closed radio and television stations. Civil society organizations and human rights defenders similarly encountered harassment, including increased surveillance, threats, and physical assaults. Micheletti reversed his decree under international pressure, though many of the abuses continued.

The international community fostered negotiations aimed at reinstating Zelaya and allowing him to serve out his legal term; many countries warned that they would not recognize the national elections scheduled for November if the coup leaders refused to comply. Nevertheless, the de facto authorities pressed ahead with the elections. Lobo won the presidency with 56 percent of the vote, defeating Zelaya's vice president, Elvin Santos Lozano of the PL. The PN captured 71 seats in Congress, followed by the PL with 45, and three smaller parties with the remainder.

Lobo was inaugurated in January 2010. However, the new government made little progress toward restoring the rule of law. The Inter-American Commission on Human Rights (IACHR) voiced concern over the high rate of violent crime and continued human rights violations, including the harassment and killing of journalists and activists. Four lower-court judges who challenged the legality of the coup in 2009 were dismissed from their posts in May 2010. Also that month, a Truth and Reconciliation Commission charged with leading an impartial investigation into the events surrounding the coup began operating, though it received little institutional support and had difficulties in accessing the key players.

In April 2011, the presidents of Colombia and Venezuela sponsored talks to resolve the political crisis. In May, corruption charges against Zelaya were dropped, and both he and Lobo signed the Cartagena Accords, which guaranteed Zelaya's safety and freedom upon his return to Honduras. The agreement also paved the way for Zelaya's organization, the National Front for Popular Resistance (FRNP), to register as a political party, and reaffirmed the right of citizens to modify the constitution through referendums. In June, the Organization of American States (OAS) voted to readmit Honduras as a member.

The Truth and Reconciliation Commission issued its report in July, finding that Zelaya's removal from office constituted an illegal coup, that Congress had no means by which to remove a sitting president, that the interim government was illegal, and that the military used disproportionate force that resulted in at least a dozen deaths following the coup. The commission also stated that Zelaya shared blame for instigating the crisis with his push for a referendum, and that the international community, and the OAS in particular, failed to stop or reverse the coup. The report contained dozens of recommendations for strengthening the rule of law, including the creation of a constitutional court and the development of clear legal procedures for political trials.

In October 2011, the Supreme Court overwhelmingly ruled against the prosecution of six army generals who had been charged with overthrowing Zelaya and transferring him to Costa Rica. The decision made it unlikely that any coup participants would be charged.

Political Rights and Civil Liberties: Honduras is not an electoral democracy. General elections were held as scheduled in November 2009, and the voting itself was largely considered to have met international standards. However, the elections were overseen by an interim government established after President José Manuel Zelaya was forcibly removed by the military in a June 2009 coup, and they took place in a climate of severely compromised civil liberties and press freedoms.

The president is elected by popular vote for a single four-year term. Members of the 128-seat, unicameral National Congress are also elected for four-year terms. The proportion of the votes received by a party's presidential candidate determines its representation in the National Congress. The PL was the ruling party at the time of the coup, with the PN in opposition and three smaller parties also holding seats. The PL then fractured between Zelaya supporters and opponents, and the PN won a majority in the November elections. The military has long exerted considerable influence on civilian governments.

Official corruption continues to dominate the political scene. Army officers have been found guilty of involvement in drug trafficking and related criminal conflicts. A 2006 transparency law was marred by claims that it contained amendments designed to protect corrupt politicians. However, the Institute for Access to Public Information has made efforts to enforce transparency rules and punish entities that fail to respond properly to information requests. Honduras was ranked 129 out of 183 countries surveyed in Transparency International's 2011 Corruption Perceptions Index.

Since the 2009 coup, authorities have systematically violated the constitution's press freedom guarantees. Numerous radio and television stations reported continued harassment in 2011, including police surveillance as well as assaults, threats, blocked transmissions, and power outages. In February, the National Commission for Telecommunications (CONATEL) suspended licenses for low-frequency FM community radio stations. In March and April, journalists were attacked by police while covering teacher and student protests. Others were threatened as they investigated the whereabouts of detainees. The head of community radio station La Voz de Zacate Grande was shot in March by an ally of Miguel Facussé, a powerful landowner who had previously lodged a criminal complaint against the radio station. In April, the home of the director of the Afro-Honduran community radio station Radio Faluma Bimetu (Radio Coco Dulce) was set on fire, and the director of Radio Uno narrowly escaped an armed ambush. Nery Jeremías Orellana, the manager of Radio Joconguera, was assassinated the night before a meeting of community radio stations in July.

Honduras is considered the second-most dangerous country in the world for journalists, with 19 killed since the 2009 coup, including several known Zelaya supporters. The government's reaction has been inadequate, alternating between remaining silent and dismissing the cases as routine street crime.

Media ownership is concentrated in the hands of a few powerful business interests, and many journalists practice self-censorship, particularly since the coup. Lack of access to public officials and information is also a significant obstacle for reporters. Payments to journalists and manipulation of state advertising are reportedly used to secure favorable coverage or silence criticism. Internet use is generally unrestricted, but access was impaired following the coup by multiple politically motivated power outages and cuts in telephone service.

Freedom of religion is generally respected. Academic freedom is also usually honored, but scholars have faced pressure to support the privatization of the national university.

Constitutional guarantees on the freedoms of assembly and association have not been consistently upheld. In addition to the violent suppression of peaceful demonstrations in 2009, police were accused of using excessive force during confrontations with striking and demonstrating teachers in August 2010 and March 2011.

The 2006 Citizen Participation Law protects the role of civil society groups and individuals in the democratic process. However, human rights defenders and political activists continued to face significant threats following the coup, including harassment, surveillance, and detentions, as well as the murder of a number of coup opponents. Labor unions are well organized and can strike, but labor actions often result in clashes with security forces. Labor, gay and transgender rights, land rights, environmental, and Afro-Honduran activists are regularly victims of threats and repression.

The judicial system is weak and inefficient, and there are significant tensions between the national police, the prosecutor's office, and the Ministry of Justice and Human Rights. Approximately 80 percent of crimes committed in Honduras are never reported, according to the government, and only 3.8 percent of reported crimes are investigated by police. The vast majority of inmates are awaiting trial, prison conditions are harsh, and the facilities are notoriously overcrowded. There is an official human rights ombudsman, but critics claim that the office's work is politicized. The ombudsman not only supported and justified the 2009 coup, but has also publicly declared his opposition to the Truth and Reconciliation Commission.

Honduras had one of highest murder rates in the world in 2011. In October, the UN Office on Drugs and Crime reported a homicide rate of 82.1 per 100,000 inhabitants, a significant increase over the previous year. Most murders are attributed to organized crime, including transnational youth gangs and Mexican drug-trafficking syndicates. The government has made membership in a gang punishable by up to 12 years in prison and uses the military to help maintain order. However, police officers and other vigilantes have committed extrajudicial killings, arbitrary arrests, and illegal searches. Hundreds of juveniles have reportedly been killed in "social cleansing" campaigns.

The country's growing crime wave has increased concerns about further limitations on civil liberties. In 2011, the detention of criminal suspects was extended from 24 to 48 hours, and a new wiretapping bill was passed, both despite protests from Minister of Justice and Human Rights Ana Pineda. President Porfirio Lobo and key military officials have suggested reforms that would abolish the Ministry of Security and place the police under the Defense Ministry, potentially exacerbating the existing overlap between police and military functions.

Indigenous and Afro-Honduran residents have faced various abuses by property developers and their allies in recent years, including corrupt titling processes and acts of violence. In February 2011, a special unit was established in the Attorney General's office to investigate crimes against the gay and transgender communities, and a new Sexual Diversity Unit was established in the police force in September to investigate crimes committed against this population in September.

Women remain vulnerable to exploitation by employers, particularly in the low-wage *maquiladora* (assembly plant) export sector. Child labor is a problem in rural areas and in the informal economy, and school dropout rates are high. The overall population is dominated by young people, with some two-thirds under age 25. The U.S. State Department's 2011 Trafficking in Persons Report found that while Honduras does not fully comply with minimum international standards to combat human trafficking, the government is making efforts to do so. The report also found that criminal gangs' use of forced child labor is a serious concern.

Hungary

Political Rights: 1
Civil Liberties: 2*
Status: Free

Population: 9,972,000
Capital: Budapest

Ratings Change: Hungary's civil liberties rating declined from 1 to 2 due to controversial constitutional and legal changes that threaten to seriously undermine the independence of the judiciary.

Ten-Year Ratings Timeline For Year Under Review (Political Rights, Civil Liberties, Status)

2002	2003	2004	2005	2006	2007	2008	2009	2010	2011
1,2F	1,2F	1,1F	1,1F	1,1F	1,1F	1,1F	1,1F	1,1F	1,2F

Overview: **While Hungary made modest reforms to its new, restrictive media legislation in 2011, human rights organizations continued throughout the year to voice concerns over the law's remaining provisions. In April, the parliament passed a new constitution, which was boycotted by the opposition and was strongly criticized for having been formulated quickly and with little input from civil society.**

Hungary achieved full independence from the Austro-Hungarian Empire following World War I. Soviet occupation after World War II led to communist rule, and Soviet troops crushed a 1956 uprising by Hungarians seeking to liberalize the political and economic system. By the late 1980s, the ruling Hungarian Socialist Workers' Party had come under intense pressure to accept reforms. Free parliamentary elections were held in 1990, and over the next decade, power alternated between conservative and socialist blocs, both of which pursued European integration. Hungary formally entered the European Union (EU) in 2004.

A ruling coalition consisting of the Hungarian Socialist Party (MSzP) and the

Alliance of Free Democrats (SzDSz) won reelection in April 2006. In September, Prime Minister Ferenc Gyurcsány's recorded admission that his government had repeatedly lied to the electorate about its budgetary and economic performance was leaked to the press, sparking major riots and severely damaging public confidence in the government as it struggled to rein in a large budget deficit. The SzDSz withdrew from the coalition in 2008, but after Gyurcsány announced his resignation in March 2009, it joined the larger MSzP in endorsing Economy Minister Gordon Bajnai, an independent, as the new prime minister in April.

In April 2010 parliamentary elections, a conservative opposition bloc consisting of the Alliance of Young Democrats–Hungarian Civic Union (Fidesz) and the much smaller Christian Democratic People's Party (KDNP) captured 263 of 386 National Assembly seats, giving it a two-thirds majority and the ability to amend the constitution. The MSzP won just 59 seats. The far-right Movement for a Better Hungary (Jobbik) entered the parliament for the first time with 47 seats, and the liberal Politics Can Be Different (LMP) party, also new to the legislature, captured 16 seats. An independent took the remaining seat. Fidesz leader Viktor Orbán, who had served as prime minister from 1998 to 2002, reclaimed the post in May. Using its dominance of the legislature, the government installed a Fidesz loyalist as president in August and increased control over a number of institutions during 2010, including the media.

Hungary faced several economic challenges in 2011, including a decrease in exports and currency depreciation. Despite an original outlook of 1.5 percent economic growth in 2012, by the end of 2011 this projection had changed to -0.5 percent.

The Fidesz government passed a new constitution in April, which was boycotted by the opposition. In June, the Venice Commission of the Council of Europe criticized the process by which Hungary adopted the new constitution, as it had been formulated rapidly and with very limited input from the opposition or members of civil society. The new constitution places policies on culture, religion, morality, and the economy, including issues such as public debt and pensions, under the category of "cardinal law." Amendments to cardinal laws will require a two-thirds majority, making changes to such policies virtually impossible unless implemented by Fidesz.

Political Rights and Civil Liberties: Hungary is an electoral democracy. Voters elect representatives every four years to the 386-seat, unicameral National Assembly under a mixed system of proportional and direct representation. The National Assembly elects both the president and the prime minister. The president's duties are mainly ceremonial, but he can influence appointments and return legislation for further consideration before signing it into law. In late December, the parliament passed a government-backed electoral law redrawing parliamentary electoral districts and making changes to the allocation of seats and votes in Hungary's mixed system of single-member districts and party lists. Hungary's political parties have historically been the center-left MSzP and the conservative Fidesz.

Hungary's constitution guarantees the right of ethnic minorities to form self-governing bodies, and all 13 recognized minorities have done so. Despite their large population, Roma hold just four seats in the current National Assembly. The 2011 constitution restricts voting rights for people considered to have "limited mental ability," raising concerns that the mentally disabled will be legally prohibited from participating in politics.

The country lacks a comprehensive anticorruption policy. The independent Fiscal Council, which is responsible for overseeing budgetary policy, was abolished at the end of 2010, after criticizing tax measures implemented by Prime Minister Viktor Orbán's government. The new council, installed in January 2011, comprises just three members—all of whom are Orbán allies—and has the power to dismiss parliament. A special commissioner appointed by Orbán investigated a number of cases of alleged corruption by officials from the previous government. Former prime minister Ferenc Gyurcsány was investigated for allegedly abusing his position in relation to a land development deal, and he has also been under investigation for directly contributing to Hungary's debt crisis while in office; the cases, which were ongoing at year's end, have been criticized for being politically motivated. In September 2011, Gyurcsány requested that his immunity be lifted in order for him to defend himself. At the end of 2011, the Budapest Military Tribunal brought espionage charges against two former chiefs of the national security office under Gyurcsány. In July 2011, the government passed a law establishing a new data protection and freedom of information authority, effective January 1, 2012. The commissioner of the previous data protection body, András Jóri, was removed before the end of his term; his replacement, Attila Peterfalvi, was proposed by Orbán in November and appointed by President Pal Schmitt in December. Hungary was ranked 54 out of 183 countries surveyed in Transparency International's 2011 Corruption Perceptions Index.

New media legislation, which came into effect in 2011, places further restrictions on both private and public media. Media outlets must register with a new, single regulatory body, the National Media and Infocommunications Authority (NMHH), which can revoke licenses for infractions. A new Media Council under the NMHH can close media outlets or impose fines of up to $950,000 for violating vaguely defined content rules. Fidesz, with its parliamentary supermajority, controlled appointments to the Media Council, whose members serve nine-year terms. The Council's president, who is directly appointed by the prime minister, nominates the heads of all public media outlets for approval by a Fidesz-dominated board of trustees. Despite minor amendments to the legislation made in March 2011, the Organization of Security and Cooperation in Europe considered the laws insufficient in protecting media freedom. In April, Frank LaRue, the UN's Special Rapporteur for Freedom of Opinion and Expression, warned that the new legislation could lead to greater self-censorship.

While foreign ownership of Hungarian media is extensive, domestic ownership is highly concentrated in the hands of Fidesz allies. In April 2011, Jobbik cofounder Daniel Papp was awarded the position of editor in chief of the news office at the MTVA media fund, which is responsible for the management of all public media. Since taking office, Papp has laid off a quarter of the organization's approximately 400 news editors. By the end of 2011, Hungary had laid off about 1,000 state media employees. In October, the radio station Klubradio—which is critical of the Fidesz government—had to discontinue broadcasting in four counties after it was precluded from renewing its broadcasting license for five frequencies, which NMHH claimed were being reserved for stations featuring more local news and music. In September, writer Kertész Ákos was pressured into withdrawing his statement in the U.S. newspaper *Amerikai Népszava* that "Hungarians are genetically subservient" after the government threatened to revoke his Kossuth Prize, a prestigious Hungarian award that he had won in 2008.

The constitution guarantees religious freedom and provides for the separation of church and state. While adherents of all religions are generally free to worship, a July 2011 law restricts official recognition to only 14 of the 358 religious groups in Hungary; hundreds of religious organizations will lose their registered status and budgetary allocations for social and charitable services in January 2012. Additionally, recognition of religious groups will be awarded by parliament instead of the courts. Despite criticism of the new law, 98.9 percent of Hungarian believers belong to one of the 14 recognized organizations.

While the state generally does not restrict academic freedom, Orbán's government began investigating writer and philosopher Agnes Heller, as well as some of her contacts, for allegedly embezzling research funds. Heller has publically criticized Orbán's "dictatorial inclinations" and testified against his policies before the European Parliament.

The constitution provides for freedoms of assembly and association, and the government generally respects these rights in practice. Nongovernmental organizations operate without restrictions. The government recognizes workers' rights to form associations, strike, and petition public authorities. Trade unions represent less than 30 percent of the workforce. In 2011, the government passed a law stating that those out of work for 90 days or more will not receive social benefits or membership in the social insurance system.

Hungary has an independent judiciary, though case processing remains slow, and transparency is weak. A judicial reform package pushed through in November 2011, and which will enter into effect in January 2012, grants extensive administrative powers to the National Judicial Office (OBH), a new body whose leader is elected by a two-thirds parliamentary majority for a nine-year term. Among other responsibilities, the new OBH leader will choose candidates to fill the vacancies created by a provision in the April 2011 constitution sending at least 274 judges into early retirement. The OBH head's discretionary powers will include the appointment of the presidents of local and higher-level courts, and the temporary transfer of individual judges to other districts. In December 2011, the parliament appointed new heads to both the OBH and Hungary's Supreme Court, renamed the Curia; the opposition opposed the appointments, claiming they gave too much power to Fidesz. The 2011 constitution introduced the possibility of life without parole, sparking criticism from human rights groups that claimed such sentencing conflicts with the International Covenant of Civil and Political Rights. Prisons are generally approaching Western European standards, though overcrowding, inadequate medical care, and poor sanitation remain problems. Inmates do not have access to independent medical staff to assess abuse allegations.

Hungary has taken a number of steps to improve monitoring of Romany legal rights and treatment, but the community still faces widespread discrimination. Romany children continue to be segregated in schools and improperly placed in schools for students with mental disabilities. In April 2011, three Roma were injured during fighting between right-wing radicals and local Roma in the village of Gyöngyöspa; more than 250 Romany women and children were temporarily evacuated from the area by the Red Cross. In September, the Hungarian Helsinki Committee criticized the government for failing to protect the Roma in Gyöngyöspata.

Women possess the same legal rights as men, but they face hiring discrimination and tend to be underrepresented in high-level business and government positions. The ratio of women to men in Hungarian politics is lower than in any other EU member state, with women holding only 35 of 386 seats in the National Assembly. The right to life from conception is protected under the 2011 constitution, raising concerns that women's right to abortions may be restricted. Hungary remains a transit point, source, and destination for trafficked persons, including women trafficked for prostitution. Same-sex couples can legally register their partnerships. However, the 2011 constitution enshrines the concept that marriage should exist between a man and woman, and fails to directly prohibit discrimination based on sexual orientation.

Iceland

Political Rights: 1
Civil Liberties: 1
Status: Free

Population: 318,900
Capital: Reykjavik

Ten-Year Ratings Timeline For Year Under Review (Political Rights, Civil Liberties, Status)

2002	2003	2004	2005	2006	2007	2008	2009	2010	2011
1,1F	1,1F	1,1F	1,1F	1,1F	1,1F	1,1F	1,1F	1,1F	1,1F

Overview: **In an April 2011 referendum, Icelanders voted against a repayment deal to British depositors at an Icelandic bank, which had collapsed during the country's banking crisis of 2008. Meanwhile, a new draft constitution was presented to parliament in July.**

After gaining independence from Denmark in 1944, Iceland became a founding member of NATO in 1949, despite having no standing army. The country declared itself a nuclear-free zone in 1985. Davíð Oddsson of the center-right Independence Party (IP), first elected prime minister in 1991, finally stepped down in 2004. He was succeeded by Halldór Ásgrímsso of the Progressive Party (PP), the coalition partner of the IP. After a poor government showing in local elections, Ásgrímsso resigned the premiership in favor of the IP's Geir Haarde in June 2006.

The ruling coalition broke up following May 2007 parliamentary elections, in which the IP took 25 seats and the PP captured 7 seats in the 63-seat legislature. The IP then formed a new coalition with the center-left Social Democratic Alliance (SDA), which held 18 seats, and Haarde returned as prime minister. A credit crisis forced the government to nationalize three large banks in 2008, resulting in widespread protests and Haarde's resignation on January 26, 2009.

In February 2009, Jóhanna Sigurðardóttir of the SDA was named interim prime minister. Her center-left coalition, consisting of the SDA and the Left-Green Movement, captured 34 of 63 seats in early parliamentary elections in April 2009, marking the first time leftist parties have held a majority in Iceland. The elections also resulted in the highest number of first-time members and the largest percentage of women in parliament in Iceland's history. A government shakeup in September 2010 reduced the number of cabinet seats from 12 to 10.

While the majority of Icelanders remain opposed to European Union (EU) membership, the country opened EU accession negotiations in July 2009. Negotiations were ongoing at year's end.

The anti-establishment Best Party, led by comedian Jón Gnarr, rode a wave of protest votes to capture 6 of the 15 seats in the May 2010 Reykjavik City Council election, making Gnarr mayor of the Icelandic capital.

In April 2011, voters defeated a referendum on a repayment plan for British and Dutch depositors at Icesave, an online savings account brand owned and operated by the private Landsbanki, which collapsed in 2008. An international court case to resolve the issue was being prepared by year's end. In September 2011, Landsbanki announced that a sale of its assets should fully cover repayment to all British and Dutch depositors. The sale of assets was ongoing at year's end.

In January 2011, the Supreme Court invalidated the November 2010 Constitutional Assembly election due to various irregularities, including a lack of voting secrecy at polling stations. However, parliament subsequently ruled that the 25 officials elected to the assembly could serve on a similar Constitutional Council, which would allow them to continue revising the country's constitution. In July 2011, the Constitutional Council submitted to parliament a draft of a new constitution, which emphasizes transparency of information and respect for natural resources and human rights. A referendum on the new draft was expected in 2012.

Political Rights and Civil Liberties: Iceland is an electoral democracy. Elections are free, fair, and competitive. The constitution, adopted in 1944, vests power in a president, a prime minister, the 63-seat unicameral legislature (the Althingi), and a judiciary. The president, whose duties are mostly ceremonial, is directly elected for a four-year term; Ólafur Ragnar Grímsson was reelected president in the 2008 elections. The legislature is also elected for four years, but it can be dissolved for early elections in certain circumstances. The prime minister is appointed by the president but responsible to the legislature.

The center-right IP dominated politics until May 2009, when Jóhanna Sigurðardóttir's center-left coalition took power. Six major political parties and several smaller parties are represented in the Althingi.

While corruption not a serious problem in Iceland, the country has experienced politically tinged business fraud scandals in recent years. In 2010, Steinunn Valdís Óskarsdóttir of the SDA stepped down after it was revealed that she had accepted large corporate donations for her 2006 campaign. A number of bankers—including former director of Kaupthing Iceland, Ingólfur Helgason—were arrested in 2010 in connection with the Icesave banking crash in 2008. Several members of parliament were also implicated in the crash, including former prime minister Geir Haarde, who faced charges of negligence in the wake of the financial crisis. Some of the charges against Haarde were dismissed because the wording "gross neglect of duty" was considered too vague, while the remaining charges were still being processed by year's end. Iceland was ranked 13 out of 183 countries surveyed in Transparency International's 2011 Corruption Perceptions Index.

The constitution guarantees freedom of speech and of the press. In June 2010, parliament unanimously passed the Icelandic Modern Media Initiative, which mandates the establishment of stringent free speech and press freedom laws with a focus on the protection of investigative journalists and media outlets. Iceland's wide range of print publications includes both independent and party-affiliated newspapers. The autonomous Icelandic National Broadcasting Service competes with private radio and television stations. Private media ownership is concentrated, with the Norðurljós (Northern Lights) Corporation controlling most of the private television and radio outlets and two of the three national newspapers. Internet access is unrestricted.

The constitution provides for freedom of religion. Almost 90 percent of Icelanders belong to the Evangelical Lutheran Church. The state supports the church through a special tax, which citizens can choose to direct to the University of Iceland instead. A 2008 law requires the teaching of theology in grades 1 through 10. Academic freedom is respected, and the education system is free of excessive political involvement.

Freedoms of association and peaceful assembly are generally upheld. Peaceful protests occurred in September and October 2011 against International Monetary Fund (IMF) austerity measures and the government's failure to protect Icelanders from housing foreclosures. Many nongovernmental organizations operate freely and enjoy extensive government cooperation. The labor movement is robust, with over 80 percent of all eligible workers belonging to unions. All unions have the right to strike.

The judiciary is independent. The law does not provide for trial by jury, but many trials and appeals use panels of several judges. The constitution states that all people shall be treated equally before the law, regardless of sex, religion, ethnic origin, race, or other status. Prison conditions generally meet international standards.

The Act on Foreigners was amended in 2004 to allow home searches without warrants in cases of suspected immigration fraud, among other changes. Foreigners can vote in municipal elections if they have been residents for at least five years, or three years for citizens of Scandinavian countries. In September 2010, a father and son of Cuban origin who had held Icelandic citizenship for more than a decade fled the country after intense racially motivated intimidation. Approximately 1,000 people gathered for an antiracism rally in the same month in response to threats received by the family.

Women enjoy equal rights, and more than 80 percent of women participate in the workforce. However, a pay gap exists between men and women despite laws designed to prevent disparities. In 2009, Sigurðardóttir became Iceland's first female prime minister and the world's first openly homosexual head of state. Women hold nearly 43 percent of seats in parliament, the highest number in the country's history, and Iceland topped the World Economic Forum's 2011 ratings on gender equality. The government participates in the Nordic-Baltic Action Group against Human Trafficking. A committee was appointed in 2008 to develop new strategies to combat human trafficking in Iceland, and in April 2009, parliament passed a law criminalizing human trafficking.

India

Political Rights: 2
Civil Liberties: 3
Status: Free

Population: 1,241,275,000
Capital: New Delhi

Note: The numerical ratings and status listed above do not reflect conditions in Indian-controlled Kashmir, which is examined in a separate report.

Ten-Year Ratings Timeline For Year Under Review (Political Rights, Civil Liberties, Status)

2001	2002	2003	2004	2005	2006	2007	2008	2009	2010
2,3F	2,3F	2,3F	2,3F	2,3F	2,3F	2,3F	2,3F	2,3F	2,3F

Overview: **A popular anticorruption movement maintained intense pressure on the Congress Party–led government to take action in 2011, even as new corruption scandals emerged. Discourse in the media and civil society was also instrumental in instigating parliamentary debates on other significant issues. While there were no major incidents of violence during the year, ongoing Maoist and separatist insurgencies, abuse by security forces, and general human rights violations continued to plague "disturbed areas" of the country.**

India achieved independence from Britain in 1947. The secular Congress Party ruled at the federal level for nearly all of the first 50 years of independence, but the Hindu nationalist Bharatiya Janata Party (BJP) became a major factor in Parliament in the 1990s, and led a governing coalition from 1998 to 2004. The 1990s also featured significant economic reforms, with a Congress government initiating a move toward market-oriented policies following a balance-of-payments crisis in 1991. Meanwhile, a pattern of single-party governments gave way to ruling coalitions involving large numbers of parties. The change stemmed in part from the rise of new parties that held power and legislative seats in a single state or region.

After recapturing power from the BJP in the 2004 national elections, the Congress Party formed a ruling coalition with a number of regional parties, and Congress leader Sonia Gandhi handed the premiership to former finance minister Manmohan Singh. The new Congress-led United Progressive Alliance (UPA) government reversed several of its predecessor's policies, including controversial antiterrorism legislation and the introduction of Hindu nationalism into school curriculums. However, the UPA suffered internal pressures from leftist allies over economic issues, such as privatization and labor law reform. The government survived a contentious July 2008 confidence vote in Parliament triggered by leftist objections to a nuclear pact with the United States, though the vote was marred by bribery allegations.

The UPA gained strength in the April–May 2009 parliamentary elections, decisively defeating the BJP-led National Democratic Alliance, its closest rival. Congress itself won 206 of 543 lower-house seats, and the UPA won 260 seats overall. The UPA also made alliances with several independent parties, eventually giving it a significant majority. Congress's electoral victory led to a more stable government, and India's success in weathering the global financial crisis that began in late 2008 weakened calls for additional free-market economic reforms.

In 2010, the government focused on measures designed to bolster existing legal protections and benefits for marginalized groups. The Right of Children to Free and Compulsory Education Act (RTE) took effect in April, making education a fundamental right for every child in India between the ages of 6 and 14. In addition, the RTE reserved 25 percent of the seats in private schools for disadvantaged children.

After a string of high-profile corruption scandals, including a telecommunications bribery scam thought to have cost the public close to $39 billion and allegations of financial malfeasance related to the 2010 Commonwealth Games, anticorruption efforts dominated political debate during 2011. A hunger strike by political and social activist Anna Hazare, backed by large street demonstrations in all major metropolitan cities, was aimed at compelling Parliament to accept changes to pending anticorruption legislation that would empower a Jan Lokpal or Citizens' Ombudsman to investigate and prosecute government corruption. A version of the bill was passed by the lower house of Parliament (Lok Sabha) in December and would be up for debate in the upper house (Rajya Sabha).

Political Rights and Civil Liberties: India is an electoral democracy. Members of the lower house of Parliament, the 545-seat Lok Sabha (House of the People), are directly elected for five-year terms (except for two appointed members representing Indians of European descent). The Lok Sabha determines the leadership and composition of the government. Most members of the less powerful 250-seat upper house, the Rajya Sabha (Council of States), are elected by the state legislatures using a proportional representation system to serve staggered six-year terms; up to 12 members are appointed. Executive power is vested in a prime minister and cabinet. The president, who plays a largely symbolic role, is chosen for a five-year term by state and national lawmakers.

Under the supervision of the Election Commission of India (ECI), elections have generally been free and fair. The 2009 national polls were mostly peaceful, though Maoist militant attacks in parts of the country led to 17 deaths during the first phase of voting. Electronic voting machines, also used in 2004, helped reduce election day irregularities. Violence declined during state-level elections in 2009 and 2010. Assam, Kerala, Tamil Nadu, West Bengal, and Pondicherry held their state-level assembly elections in 2011. The Trinamool Congress party marked a historic win in Bengal, bringing an end to the 34-year rule of the Left Front, led by the Communist Party of India–Marxist (CPM), which had been noted as the longest-serving communist-led government in a democracy. The state also elected its first female chief minister. Badly maintained voter lists and the intimidation of voters in some areas continue to be general matters of concern.

Recent attempts to address political corruption, through legislation and activism, have been driven by domestic and international pressure to counter the negative effect of graft on government efficiency. India was ranked 95 out of 183 countries surveyed in Transparency International's 2011 Corruption Perceptions Index. Though politicians and civil servants are regularly caught accepting bribes or engaging in other corrupt behavior, a great deal of corruption goes unnoticed and unpunished. The federal government has already introduced a number of initiatives to tackle the problem, such as the 2005 Right to Information Act, which has been actively used to improve transparency and expose corrupt activities. While the effects of this legislation have been transformative in the public sphere, over a dozen right to information activists have reportedly been killed since late 2009.

India's private media are vigorous and diverse. Investigations and scrutiny of politicians make the news media one of the most important components of India's democracy. While radio remains dominated by the state and private radio stations are not allowed to air news content, the television and print sectors have expanded considerably in recent years, with many of the new outlets targeting specific regional or linguistic audiences. Despite this vibrant media landscape, journalists, creative writers, and human rights defenders continue to face a number of constraints. The authorities have sometimes used security laws, criminal defamation legislation, hate-speech laws, and contempt of court charges to curb critical voices.

Violence against journalists by both state and nonstate actors has continued to be a problem in India. At least two journalists were killed during 2011. *Nai Dunia* reporter Umesh Rajput was shot dead outside his home in Chhattisgarh in February, though the motive remained unclear. In June, *Midday* reporter Jyotirmoy Dey, who had reported extensively on organized crime in Mumbai, was killed by unidentified gunmen. In an example of the lesser assaults faced by journalists, police in Andhra Pradesh chased and beat a television journalist in June in apparent retaliation for his reporting on student protests at Usmania University.

Internet access is largely unrestricted, although some states have passed legislation that requires internet cafés to register with the state government and maintain user registries. Under Indian internet crime law, the burden is on website operators to demonstrate their innocence. Potentially inflammatory books, films, and internet sites are occasionally banned or censored.

Freedom of religion is constitutionally guaranteed in India and is generally respected. However, legislation in several states criminalizes religious conversions that take place as a result of "force" or "allurement." Hindus make up over 80 percent of the population, but the state is secular. An array of Hindu nationalist organizations and some local media outlets promote antiminority views. In 2010, the Allahabad High Court issued a decision in a high-profile case stemming from the 1992 destruction of a 16th-century mosque in Ayodhya by Hindus who claimed it was built on a Hindu holy site. The court ruled that the land should be divided, with one-third going to a Muslim organization and two-thirds set aside for Hindus. The Supreme Court stayed the order of partition, and several parties filed appeals to the lower court's decision at year's end.

Academic freedom is generally robust, though intimidation of professors and institutions over political and religious issues sometimes occurs. Scholars and activists accused of sympathizing with Maoist insurgents have reportedly faced increased pressure from authorities.

There are some restrictions on freedoms of assembly and association. Section 144 of the criminal procedure code empowers the authorities to restrict free assembly and impose curfews whenever "immediate prevention or speedy remedy" is required. An array of state laws based on this standard are often abused to limit the holding of meetings and assemblies. Nevertheless, protest events take place regularly in practice, and the peaceful demonstrations associated with anticorruption activist Anna Hazare drew tens of thousands of people into the streets during 2011.

Human rights organizations operate freely, but continue to face threats, legal harassment, excessive police force, and occasionally lethal violence. In October 2011, police in Delhi assaulted a human rights lawyer when he went to file a complaint regarding illegal property demolitions in the city. While India is home to a strong civil society sector and academic community, foreign monitors are occasionally denied visas to conduct research trips in the country on human rights and other topics. An American activist and radio broadcaster, David Barsamian, was denied entry by immigration authorities in September 2011, apparently due to his history of critically examining human rights abuses in India.

While workers in the formal economy regularly exercise their rights to bargain collectively and strike, the Essential Services Maintenance Act has enabled the government to ban certain strikes. Article 23 of the constitution bans human trafficking, and bonded labor is illegal, but the practice is fairly common across the country. Estimates of the number of affected workers range from 20 to 50 million. Children are also banned from working in potentially hazardous industries, though in practice the law is routinely flouted.

The judiciary is independent of the executive branch. Judges have displayed considerable activism in response to public-interest litigation matters. However, in recent years judges have initiated several contempt of court cases against activists and journalists who expose judicial corruption or question verdicts. Contempt of court laws were reformed in 2006 to make truth a defense with respect to allegations against judges, provided the information is in the public and national interest. In 2010, lawyer Prashant Bhushan asserted that many of India's Supreme Court chief justices have been corrupt, leading to contempt of court proceedings against him that remained unresolved at the end of 2011.

The lower levels of the judiciary in particular have been rife with corruption, and most citizens have great difficulty securing justice through the courts. The system is severely backlogged and understaffed, with millions of civil and criminal cases pending. This leads to lengthy pretrial detention for a large number of suspects, many of whom remain in jail beyond the duration of any sentence they might receive if convicted. In July 2011, for example, a 19-year-old suspect was convicted of stealing 200 rupees (approximately US$4) after spending a year in detention, despite the fact that his crime would generally carry a sentence of only three months in jail.

The criminal justice system fails to provide equal protection to marginalized groups. Muslims, who make up some 14 percent of the population, are underrepresented in the security forces as well as in the foreign and intelligence services. Particularly in rural India, informal councils often issue edicts concerning social customs. While these bodies play a role in relieving the overburdened official courts, their decisions sometimes result in violence or persecution aimed at those perceived to have transgressed social norms, especially women and members of the lower castes.

Police torture, abuse, and corruption are entrenched in the law enforcement system. The police also suffer from understaffing, as according to a 2009 Human Rights Watch report, there is one officer for every 1,037 civilians, less than a third of the global average. Custodial rape of female detainees continues to be a problem, as does routine abuse of ordinary prisoners, particularly minorities and members of the lower castes. Between 2001 and March 2009, there were 1,184 reported deaths in police custody, nearly all of which were caused by torture, according to the Asian Centre for Human Rights. The group estimated that the actual number of deaths is far greater.

The National Human Rights Commission (NHRC) is headed by a retired Supreme Court judge and handles roughly 80,000 complaints each year. However, while it monitors abuses, initiates investigations, makes independent assessments, and conducts training sessions for the police and others, its recommendations are often not implemented, and it has few enforcement powers. The commission also lacks jurisdiction over the armed forces, one of the principal agents of abuse in several parts of the country, further hampering its effectiveness.

Security forces operating in the context of regional insurgencies continue to be implicated in extrajudicial killings, rape, torture, arbitrary detention, kidnappings, and destruction of homes. The criminal procedure code requires the government to approve the prosecution of security force members, but such approval is rarely granted, leading to impunity for personnel implicated in human rights abuses. The Armed Forces Special Powers Act (AFSPA) grants security forces broad authority to arrest, detain, and use force against suspects in restive areas; civil society organizations and multiple UN human rights bodies have called for the act to be repealed. An activist in the "disturbed area" of Manipur, Sharmila Chanu, has been on a hunger strike for 11 years to demand the revocation of the AFSPA, but has faced continual arrests and forced feeding by the authorities. A number of other security laws allow detention without charge or based on vaguely worded offenses.

The Maoist insurgency in several parts of India has been of serious concern to the government. There were over 600 Maoist-related deaths across nine states in 2011, according to the South Asia Terrorism Portal (SATP), though that represented a sharp decline from the previous year's 1,180. Among other abuses, the rebels have allegedly imposed illegal taxes, seized food and shelter, and engaged in abduction and forced recruitment of children and adults. Local civilians who are perceived to be progovernment have been targeted by the Maoists. Tens of thousands of civilians have been displaced by the violence and live in government-run camps.

Separately, in India's seven northeastern states, more than 40 insurgent factions—seeking either greater autonomy or complete independence for their ethnic or tribal groups—attack security forces and engage in intertribal violence. Such fighters have been implicated in numerous bombings, killings, abductions, and rapes of civilians, and they also operate extensive extortion networks. However, the number of killings of civilians, security personnel, and militants in the northeastern insurgencies have fallen sharply in recent years, reaching 247 in 2011, compared with 852 in 2009, according to the SATP.

The constitution bars discrimination based on caste, and laws set aside quotas in education and government jobs for the so-called scheduled tribes, scheduled castes (Dalits), and other backward classes (OBCs). Women and religious and ethnic minorities are represented in government; as of 2011, the president was a woman, the vice president was a Muslim, the prime minister was a Sikh, and the Speaker of the Lok Sabha was a Dalit woman. A number of states were headed by female chief ministers, including one Dalit. However, members of the lower castes and minorities continue to face routine discrimination and violence. Dalits are often denied access to land and other public amenities, abused by landlords and police, and forced to work in miserable conditions. Indian Muslims are disproportionately more likely to be poor and illiterate, with less access to government employment, medical care, or loans.

Property rights are somewhat tenuous for tribal groups and other marginalized communities, and members of these groups are often denied adequate resettlement opportunities and compensation when their lands are seized for development projects. While many states have laws to prevent land transfers to nontribal groups, the practice is reportedly widespread.

Rape and other violence against women are serious problems, and lower-caste and tribal women are particularly vulnerable. Despite the criminalization of dowry demands and hundreds of convictions each year, the practice continues. According to a recent National Health Survey, on average, one in three married women between 15 and 49 has experienced physical violence. A 2006 law banned dowry-related harassment, widened the definition of domestic violence to include emotional or verbal abuse, and criminalized spousal rape. However, reports indicate that enforcement is poor. The National Crime Records Bureau reports that about 6,000 females are killed every year for dowry-related issues alone. Muslim personal laws and traditional Hindu practices discriminate against women in terms of inheritance, adoption, and property rights. The malign neglect of female children after birth remains a concern, as does the banned but growing use of prenatal sex-determination tests to selectively abort female fetuses.

A landmark court decision in 2009 struck down Section 377 of the Indian penal code, which criminalized homosexual behavior. However, an appeal of the ruling was pending at the Supreme Court at the end of 2011, and widespread discrimination continues. At a May 2011 conference on HIV/AIDS, the health minister referred to homosexuality as "unnatural" and a "disease," adding to the difficulties faced by activists combating harmful social stigmas regarding both issues.

Indonesia

Political Rights: 2
Civil Liberties: 3
Status: Free

Population: 238,181,000
Capital: Jakarta

Ten-Year Ratings Timeline For Year Under Review (Political Rights, Civil Liberties, Status)

2002	2003	2004	2005	2006	2007	2008	2009	2010	2011
3,4PF	3,4PF	3,4PF	2,3F	2,3PF	2,3F	2,3F	2,3F	2,3F	2,3F

Overview: **The reformist credentials of President Susilo Bambang Yudhoyono and his Democratic Party suffered in 2011,**

as the party treasurer was arrested on corruption charges, and several other high-ranking party members faced similar accusations. Also during the year, deadly communal violence erupted between Muslims and Christians, and members of the Ahmadi religious minority faced increasing harassment, including deadly attacks, with perpetrators enjoying relative impunity. Terrorist bombings struck places of worship as well as public figures known to oppose Islamic extremism, though one prominent terrorism suspect was extradited from Pakistan, and a longtime extremist leader was sentenced to prison in June. Separately, in October, security forces opened fire to disperse an assembly of Papuan separatist leaders.

Indonesia declared independence from its Dutch colonial rulers in 1945, though the Netherlands did not recognize its sovereignty until 1949. The republic's first president, Sukarno, assumed authoritarian powers in 1957. The army, led by General Suharto, crushed an apparent Communist Party of Indonesia (PKI) coup attempt in 1965. Mass acts of violence followed, ostensibly against suspected PKI members, resulting in an estimated 500,000 deaths. With military backing, Suharto formally became president in 1968.

Suharto's regime created Golkar, a progovernment party based on bureaucratic and military interests, and embarked on a development program that helped the economy grow by an annual average of 7 percent for three decades. By the 1990s, Suharto's children and cronies were the major beneficiaries of state privatization schemes and in many cases ran business monopolies with little oversight. Soaring inflation and unemployment following the Asian financial crisis of 1997 prompted urban riots in 1998, and Suharto was forced to resign. He was succeeded by then vice president B. J. Habibie, who removed legal constraints on the press, labor unions, and political parties. The province of East Timor voted to separate from Indonesia in a 1999 referendum and gained independence in 2002.

Also in 1999, Indonesia held its first free legislative elections since 1955. The Indonesian Democratic Party–Struggle (PDI-P), led by Sukarno's daughter, Megawati Sukarnoputri, won the largest number of seats, followed by Golkar. The People's Consultative Assembly, made up of elected lawmakers and appointed officials, chose Muslim leader Abdurrahman Wahid as president and Megawati as vice president that year, but Megawati rose to the presidency in 2001, after Wahid was impeached over corruption allegations. Support for the PDI-P dropped in the 2004 legislative elections, and Golkar once again became the largest party. Later that year, Susilo Bambang Yudhoyono (SBY) of the new Democratic Party and his running mate, Jusuf Kalla of Golkar, won the presidency and vice presidency in the country's first direct presidential election.

The Democratic Party won the April 2009 parliamentary elections, raising its share of seats to 148, from 55 in 2004. Golkar garnered 106 seats, and the PDI-P took 94. Religious parties generally fared poorly, though the Prosperous Justice Party (PKS), with its strong anticorruption platform, captured 57 seats. SBY easily secured a second five-year term in the July presidential election, defeating Megawati and Kalla with 61 percent of the vote in the first round. SBY's new running mate, former central bank governor Boediono, became vice president.

Public awareness of the extent of corruption in the legal system and attempts to weaken anticorruption efforts grew in 2010, and new corruption allegations against members of the Democratic Party continued to undermine SBY's reformist credentials during 2011. In August, party treasurer Muhammad Nazaruddin was extradited from Colombia after he fled the country in May, having been accused of masterminding extensive graft surrounding preparations for the 2012 Southeast Asian Games in South Sumatra. Nazaruddin was formally charged with corruption in December. He had made frequent public statements accusing other senior officials of corruption, including Democratic Party chairman Anas Urbaningrum, Democratic lawmaker Angelina Sondakh, and members of the Corruption Eradication Commission (KPK) itself, though they were later cleared of any ethics violations. Two other officials received prison sentences of up to two and a half years in September—and suspended Sports and Youth Affairs Ministry secretary Wafid Muharram received a three-year sentence in December—for paying bribes related to the case.

Religious violence continued in 2011, with a deadly February attack on an Ahmadi community in Cikeusik, West Java. Twelve men were sentenced to between three and six months jail for a collection of minor offenses, but none were charged for the killing of three Ahmadis during the assault. In a widely decried ruling, one Ahmadi victim was sentenced to six months in jail for defying a police order to leave the area during the incident. Three police officers were named as suspects for allegedly failing to protect civilians; their cases had not advanced by year's end. Separately, communal clashes reemerged in Ambon in September, after false rumors were circulated via text message that a Muslim man had been tortured and killed by Christians. The claims led to three days of violence that damaged over 200 buildings and left 7 people dead, 65 injured, and 4,000 displaced. Past violence between the two communities in Ambon had peaked in 1999 and 2000. The Setara Institute for Democracy and Peace recorded a total of 299 violations of religious rights and acts of violence in the name of religion in 2011, 105 of which were committed by state actors, including the military, police, and government officials.

There were a number of terrorist incidents during the year, including small or thwarted bomb attacks that targeted churches and public figures known for their outspoken opposition to Islamic hard-liners. In June, radical Muslim cleric Abu Bakar Bashir was found guilty of supporting a terrorist training camp in Aceh and sentenced to 15 years in prison; the sentence was reduced to 9 years on appeal in October. Umar Patek, a suspect in the 2002 Bali bombing that killed 102 people, was extradited to Indonesia in October after being captured in Pakistan.

In the eastern region of Papua, where the central government's exploitation of natural resources has stirred resentment and separatist sentiment, members of the security forces continued to enjoy relative impunity for abuses against civilians. Three soldiers caught on video torturing two Papuan men were sentenced to between 8 and 10 months in jail for "disobedience" in January, and in August, three soldiers involved in the killing of a Papuan priest were sentenced to between 7 and 15 months for "insubordination." In October, police opened fire on participants in a proindependence Papuan People's Congress and arrested 300 people. Some 96 people were reportedly assaulted by security personnel, and 6 were found dead in the aftermath. All but six detainees were released, and five were on trial for treason at the end of the year. In November, eight security officers were given written warnings for their conduct during the incident.

Corruption has undermined the central government's efforts to improve economic conditions in Papua. In 2011, the Supreme Audit Agency reported the misuse of $2.2 billion in special autonomy funds by the Papuan government, even as the central government increased the 2011 budget for Papua and West Papua by 23 percent. Special autonomy status had been introduced in 2001 to undercut separatist agitation and a low-grade insurgency dating to the early 1950s. It provided for increased economic but not political autonomy. Separately, in August, all 44 members of the West Papua provincial legislature were named as corruption suspects.

Political Rights and Civil Liberties: Indonesia is an electoral democracy. In 2004, for the first time, Indonesians directly elected their president and all members of the House of Representatives (DPR), as well as members of a new legislative body, the House of Regional Representatives (DPD). Previously, presidents had been elected by the People's Consultative Assembly (MPR), then made up of elected lawmakers and appointed officials. The MPR now performs tasks involving the swearing in and dismissal of presidents and the amendment of the constitution, and consists of elected DPR and DPD members. The DPR, with 560 seats, is the main parliamentary chamber. The 132-member DPD is responsible for proposing and monitoring laws related to regional autonomy. Presidents and vice presidents can serve up to two five-year terms, and all legislators also serve five-year terms.

Parties or coalitions must attain 25 percent of the popular vote or 20 percent of the seats in the DPR to nominate candidates for president. Voters for the DPR can select either a party list or an individual candidate, but candidates are seated based on the number of direct votes they receive. The changes, introduced in 2008, were designed to increase lawmakers' accountability to voters and reduce the power of party bosses. The 2009 elections yielded a significant turnover in the DPR's membership, with approximately 75 percent of the chamber consisting of new lawmakers. Several parties protested against the revised Law on Political Parties passed in 2010, charging that it was biased against smaller parties. In September 2011, the parliament revised the Law on Election Organization, removing a mandatory five-year waiting period between resignation from one's political party and application to serve on the General Elections Commission. Critics of the change said it could lead to conflicts of interest.

Staggered, direct elections for regional leaders began in 2005 and have generally been considered free and fair. Independent candidates were allowed to contest local elections for the first time in 2008, although Aceh's 2006 governance law had already allowed independent candidates there as part of an effort to cement a 2005 peace agreement with the separatist Free Aceh Movement (GAM) militant group by integrating former GAM members into the political process.

Corruption remains endemic, including in the parliament and other key institutions. Indonesia was ranked 100 out of 183 countries surveyed in Transparency International's 2011 Corruption Perceptions Index. The KPK's success in a series of high-profile cases has raised public expectations that acts of corruption, even by senior officials, will be punished. In March 2011, former chief detective Susno

Duadji was sentenced to three and a half years in prison for graft and embezzlement. After being implicated, he had made corruption allegations against a number of high-ranking police officers and government officials. In another major case in June, the last of 28 elected officials and party members were sentenced for receiving bribes linked to the election of Miranda Goeltom as deputy governor of the central bank. In December, Nunun Nurbeati, the wife of a PKS member of parliament, was extradited from Thailand after being accused of distributing bribes to lawmakers in the same case. A separate case against former justice minister Yusril Ihza Mahendra over a $46 million embezzlement involving the ministry's website was ongoing at the end of 2011.

Critics have accused entrenched elites of attempting to weaken anticorruption bodies, citing an alleged conspiracy against the KPK that emerged in 2009, as well as a 2009 anticorruption law that diluted the authority and independence of both the KPK and the Anticorruption Court (Tipikor), where cases brought by the KPK are tried. The 2009 law decentralized anticorruption efforts, allowing the opening of regional corruption courts. Seven have since been opened, and the KPK lost its first case ever in the Bandung regional court in October 2011. Tipikor had been established partly to counteract the acquittals commonly issued in regular courts. Even those who are convicted often receive light sentences or benefit from mass pardons on certain holidays.

The alleged conspiracy against the KPK highlighted pervasive corruption in the legal system. A wiretap recording indicated that extortion charges against two deputy commissioners in 2009 were fabricated by elements in the national police and attorney general's office to discredit the anticorruption body. However, the Supreme Court in 2010 rejected an initial attempt by prosecutors to drop the charges against the commissioners, and the case was not put to rest until January 2011, when the attorney general's office formally invoked its authority to set the charges aside in the public interest. Separately, in April 2011, the Judicial Commission announced that district court judges who in 2010 convicted former KPK chairman Antasari Azhar of planning the murder of a businessman may have overlooked important evidence, and that high court and Supreme Court judges may have done the same on appeal.

Indonesia is home to a vibrant and diverse media environment, though press freedom remains hampered by a number of legal and regulatory restrictions. Strict but unevenly enforced licensing rules mean that thousands of television and radio stations operate illegally. Foreign journalists are not authorized to travel to the restive provinces of Papua and West Papua without special permission. Reporters often practice self-censorship to avoid running afoul of civil and criminal libel laws. In addition to legal obstacles, reporters sometimes face violence and intimidation, which in many cases goes unpunished. In January 2011, the police ruled that the December 2010 death of *Pelangi Weekly* editor Alfrets Mirulewan in Maluku had been a homicide; several suspects were arrested, and the case was ongoing at year's end. In East Java in May, four journalists were beaten by police while reporting on a Falun Gong march. In December, a mob destroyed the home of journalist Dance Henukh, resulting in the death of his child. The mob was allegedly incited by a local official whom Henukh was investigating in a corruption case. The Alliance of Independent Journalists documented approximately 49 cases of violence against journalists in 2011, while the Legal Aid Foundation for the Press reported 96 acts of violence against members of the media, with approximately 25 percent committed by police or the armed forces.

Freedom of expression is generally upheld. However, in December 2011, over 60 "punks" were rounded up by police in Aceh for supposedly "insulting Islam." They were then subjected to "reeducation," which included the forcible shaving of their punk-rock hairstyles and a traditional cleansing ceremony. Censorship and self-censorship of books and films is fairly common. In August 2011, after pressure from the extremist Islamic Defenders Front (FPI), a television network decided not to air a film promoting religious tolerance.

The 2008 Law on Electronic Information and Transactions (ITE) extended libel and other restrictions to the internet and online media, criminalizing the distribution or accessibility of information or documents that are "contrary to the moral norms of Indonesia" or related to gambling, blackmail, or defamation. In July 2011, the Supreme Court found Prita Mulyasari guilty of defamation under the ITE law and imposed a six-month suspended jail sentence. She was prosecuted for complaining to friends via e-mail about a hospital where she had been a patient. In 2010 the Supreme Court had overturned a 2009 civil defamation ruling against her, and she had initially been acquitted in the parallel criminal case.

Indonesia officially recognizes Islam, Protestantism, Roman Catholicism, Hinduism, Buddhism, and Confucianism. Members of unrecognized religions have difficulty obtaining national identity cards. Atheism is not accepted, and the criminal code contains provisions against blasphemy, penalizing those who "distort" or "misrepresent" official faiths. The national government has often failed to respond to religious intolerance in recent years, and societal discrimination has increased. A 2006 joint ministerial decree requires religious groups seeking to build houses of worship to obtain the written approval of 60 immediate neighbors. In 2010 the Supreme Court overturned the 2006 revocation of a building permit for GKI Yasmin Church in West Java, but the local administration has continued to prevent the congregation from using the premises. In April 2011, a Buddhist statue in Sumatra was ordered taken down by the Religious Affairs Ministry after complaints from local residents.

Violence against Ahmadiyya, a heterodox Islamic sect with approximately 400,000 Indonesian followers, continued in 2011. In the February mob attack in Cikeusik, West Java, the brutal killing of three Ahmadis was captured on video. Soon afterward, 29 Ahmadis, allegedly under coercion, renounced their faith and converted to mainstream Islam. Allegations of a military role in forcing conversions surfaced in March. Ahmadiyya was banned in West Sumatra and Depok that month, in South Sulawesi in June, and in Bekasi in October. In a December report, the National Commission on Violence against Women listed 26 regencies and municipalities that have passed bylaws restricting or banning Ahmadiyya. Discrimination and violence against the sect have increased since 2008, when the Religious Affairs Ministry recommended that it be banned nationwide, and the government, seeking a compromise, instead barred Ahmadis from proselytizing.

In addition to the Christian-Muslim violence that erupted in Ambon in September, attacks against churches continued in 2011. In February, a mob burned two churches in Temanggung, Central Java, after defendant Antonius Richmond

Bawengan was sentenced to the maximum of five years in prison for blasphemy against Islam. The rioters reportedly called for the death penalty. In June, Muslim cleric Syihabudin was sentenced to one year in jail for inciting the Temanggung mob. Also in February, Murhali Barda, the head of the FPI branch in Bekasi, West Java, was sentenced to less than six months in jail for "unpleasant conduct," having incited a September 2010 attack that included the stabbing and beating of leaders of a Protestant church. Several other defendants received similar sentences for the attack.

Academic freedom in Indonesia is generally respected.

Freedom of assembly is usually upheld, and peaceful protests are commonplace in the capital. However, authorities have restricted the right to assembly in conflict areas. Flag-raising ceremonies and independence rallies in Papua are routinely disbanded—as was the case with the Papuan People's Congress gathering in October 2011—and participants have been prosecuted.

Indonesia hosts a strong and active array of civil society organizations, though some human rights groups are subject to monitoring and interference by the government. Moreover, independence activists in Papua and the Maluku Islands, and labor and political activists in Java and Sulawesi, remain targets for human rights abuses. No high-level official has been convicted for any serious human rights violation since the fall of Suharto. Two Greenpeace activists were deported for visa violations in October 2011; the organization said it was under pressure after antagonizing business interests in the country with its efforts to halt deforestation.

Workers can join independent unions, bargain collectively, and with the exception of civil servants, stage strikes. The labor movement is generally fragmented, and government enforcement of minimum-wage and other labor standards is weak. However, relatively rigid labor laws include generous severance pay and strike provisions. Approximately 10 percent of workers in the formal economy—which accounts for one-sixth of the total economy—belong to unions. Domestic workers are currently excluded from labor law protections. In December, a three-month strike of approximately 8,000 workers ended at the Freeport Indonesia mine in Papua. The dispute, marred by at least nine deaths, was resolved with a pay increase.

The judiciary, particularly the Constitutional Court, has demonstrated its independence in some cases, but the court system remains plagued by corruption and other weaknesses. The Supreme Court has been the slowest to reform among the country's judicial institutions. Low salaries for judicial officials and impunity for illegal activity perpetuate the problems of bribery, forced confessions, and interference in court proceedings by military personnel and government officials at all levels. In June 2011, the parliament passed a bill that limited the powers of the Constitutional Court, removing its authority to revise laws or issue rulings that address issues beyond the petitioners' requests. However, the court annulled the controversial articles in the law in October, effectively restoring its powers. Also in 2011, the Presidential Judicial Mafia Task Force, appointed by the president in 2009 to fight corruption and case brokering in the legal system, reported 51 cases of allegedly corrupt prosecutors to the attorney general's office.

Since 2006, a number of districts have issued local ordinances based on Sharia (Islamic law). Many are unconstitutional, contradict Indonesia's international human rights commitments, or are unclear, leading to enforcement problems. The national government and various parties have failed to take decisive action on the issue, apparently for political reasons. Many of the ordinances seek to impose an Islamic dress code, Koranic literacy requirements, and bans on prostitution. For example, a bylaw passed in 2009 by the West Aceh legislature prohibits women from wearing trousers. Other measures are more extreme. In 2009, the Aceh provincial parliament passed legislation that, among other provisions, allows stoning for adultery and public lashing for homosexual acts. Two people were caned in Aceh in April 2011 for having an extramarital affair, and 14 people were caned for gambling in May. Other local regulations unrelated to Sharia have also been criticized for violating constitutional protections.

Members of the security forces regularly go unpunished or receive light sentences for human rights violations. These include ongoing abuses in conflict zones like Papua, but they are largely related to land disputes and military involvement in illegal activities such as logging and mining. According to the Indonesian Farmers Union, there were 120 land conflicts nationwide in 2011, an increase from 22 in 2010. Such clashes frequently lead to the shooting of protesters by police. In 2010 the national police issued a regulation allowing officers to use live ammunition to quell anarchic violence.

In October 2011, the parliament passed legislation that gave the State Intelligence Agency (BIN) greater authority to gather information on those suspected of terrorism, espionage, or threatening national security. The law also criminalized the leaking of state secrets to the public, which critics warned could lead to abuse of power given the broad definitions of secret information.

Effective police work has proven critical to Indonesia's recent successes in fighting terrorism, but the police force remains rife with corruption and other abuses, and officers have generally avoided criminal penalties. Currently, information garnered through torture is permissible in Indonesian courts, and torture carried out by law enforcement officers is not a criminal offense. The Indonesian Legal Aid Institute found in 2010 that up to 80 percent of detainees suffered from acts of violence in police custody. Detention laws are generally respected, but there are many reports of abuse aimed at female and minority detainees. Student activists are the most prone to arbitrary arrest, followed by farmers and journalists. Poor prison governance is compounded by overcrowding.

Members of Indonesia's ethnic minority groups face considerable discrimination. The problems of mining and logging on communal land and state appropriation of land claimed by indigenous groups are most acute in Kalimantan. Ethnic Chinese, who make up less than 3 percent of the population but are resented for reputedly holding much of the country's wealth, continue to face harassment and occasional violence. Sexual minorities also suffer discrimination, and gay-themed events have encountered resistance from local officials and open hostility from groups like the FPI. Many local bylaws criminalize homosexuality, and a 2008 antipornography law labels homosexuality a "deviant act."

Discrimination against women persists, particularly in the workplace. In the political sphere, a 2008 law states that 30 percent of a political party's candidates and board members must be women. While only 101 women were elected to the 560-seat DPR in 2009, this was an increase over the 63 who served during the previous term. Trafficking of women and children for prostitution, forced labor, and debt bondage continues, despite the passage of new laws and stricter penalties. Abortion is illegal, except to save a woman's life. Sharia-based ordinances in a number of districts infringe on women's constitutional rights; it is estimated that over 150 bylaws discriminate against women and minorities.

The 2008 antipornography law applies not just to published images but to speech and gestures that "incite sexual desire," drawing concerns that it could be used to persecute women. Significantly, the law invites the "public" to participate in the discouragement of pornographic acts, which has led to extrajudicial enforcement. A Constitutional Court ruling in 2010 upheld the law. In January 2011, the lead singer of a popular band was sentenced to three and a half years in prison for making sexually explicit video recordings that circulated on the internet in 2010. However, in a separate case in June, after a review of its own 2009 ruling, the Supreme Court exonerated the editor of the relatively mild Indonesian version of *Playboy* magazine, who had been jailed in 2010 for public indecency.

↓Iran

Political Rights: 6
Civil Liberties: 6
Status: Not Free

Population: 77,891,000
Capital: Tehran

Trend Arrow: Iran received a downward trend arrow due to the imposition of severe restrictions on nongovernmental organizations and the prosecution of an increasing number of civic leaders.

Ten-Year Ratings Timeline For Year Under Review (Political Rights, Civil Liberties, Status)

2002	2003	2004	2005	2006	2007	2008	2009	2010	2011
6,6NF	6,6NF	6,6NF	6,6NF	6,6NF	6,6NF	6,6NF	6,6NF	6,6NF	6,6NF

Overview: **Human rights violations continued to be committed during 2011 against political and social activists, human rights defenders, ethnic and religious minorities, journalists, students, and women. Freedoms of expression and assembly remained curtailed, and a growing number of prisoners, including juvenile offenders, were executed. The authorities placed the two most prominent opposition leaders, Mir Hussein Mousavi and Mehdi Karroubi, under house arrest and refused to allow the newly appointed UN special rapporteur on the human rights situation in Iran to visit the country.**

A popular revolution ousted Iran's monarchy in 1979, bringing together an unwieldy coalition of diverse political interests that opposed the regime's widespread corruption, misguided modernization efforts, and pro-Western foreign policy. Subsequently, the revolution's democratic and secular elements were largely subsumed under the leadership of the formerly exiled Ayatollah Ruhollah Khomeini. Although a newly drafted constitution incorporated democratic institutions and values, Khomeini was named supreme leader based on the religious concept of *velayat-e faqih* (guardianship of the Islamic jurist). He was vested with control over the security and intelligence services, the armed forces, the judiciary, and the state media. With Iran in political turmoil, Iraqi leader Saddam Hussein considered the time ripe to stop the spread of the Islamic revolution and settle a long-running border dispute. The ensuing Iran-Iraq war, which lasted from 1980 to 1988, cost over a million lives.

After Khomeini's death in 1989, the title of supreme leader passed to Ayatollah Ali Khamenei, a compromise candidate who lacked the religious credentials and charisma of his predecessor. The constitution was amended, the office of prime minister was abolished, and Khamenei's power was consolidated, giving him final authority over all matters of foreign and domestic policy.

Beneath its veneer of religious probity, the Islamic Republic gave rise to a new elite that accumulated wealth through opaque and unaccountable means. Basic freedoms were revoked, and women in particular experienced a severe regression in their status and rights. By the mid-1990s, dismal economic conditions and a demographic trend toward a younger population had contributed to significant public dissatisfaction with the regime. A coalition of reformists began to emerge within the leadership, advocating a gradual process of political change, economic liberalization, and normalization of relations with the outside world that was designed to legitimize, but not radically alter, the existing political system.

Representing this coalition, former culture minister Mohammad Khatami was elected president in 1997 with nearly 70 percent of the vote. Under his administration, more than 200 independent newspapers and magazines with a diverse array of viewpoints were established, and the authorities relaxed the enforcement of restrictions on social interaction between the sexes. Reformists won 80 percent of the seats in the country's first nationwide city council elections in 1999 and took the vast majority of seats in parliamentary elections the following year, with student activists playing a major role in their success.

The 2000 parliamentary elections prompted a backlash by hard-line clerics. Over the ensuing four years, the conservative judiciary closed more than 100 reformist newspapers and jailed hundreds of liberal journalists and activists, while security forces cracked down on student protests. Khatami was reelected with 78 percent of the vote in 2001, but popular disaffection stemming from the reformists' limited accomplishments, coupled with the disqualification and exclusion of most reformist politicians by the conservative Guardian Council, allowed hard-liners to triumph in the 2003 city council and 2004 parliamentary elections. These electoral victories paved the way for the triumph of hard-line Tehran mayor Mahmoud Ahmadinejad in the 2005 presidential contest—an election that reflected the public's political apathy and economic dissatisfaction. Although Ahmadinejad had campaigned on promises to fight elite corruption and redistribute Iran's oil wealth to the poor and middle class, his ultraconservative administration oversaw a crackdown on civil liberties and human rights, and harsher enforcement of the regime's strict morality laws.

The new government also adopted a more confrontational tone on foreign policy matters, feeding suspicions that its expanding uranium-enrichment activity, ostensibly devoted to generating electricity, was in fact aimed at weapons production.

Beginning in 2006, in an effort to compel Iran to halt the uranium enrichment, the UN Security Council imposed four rounds of sanctions on Iran. However, Tehran's uncompromising nuclear policy created a stalemate in diplomatic negotiations.

In the December 2006 city council and Assembly of Experts elections, voters signaled their disapproval of the government's performance by supporting more moderate officials. Carefully vetted conservative candidates won nearly 70 percent of the seats in the March 2008 parliamentary elections, but many were considered critics of Ahmadinejad, and particularly of his economic policies.

Despite crackdowns on human and women's rights activists and restrictions on internet freedom in the months prior to the June 2009 presidential election, supporters of all candidates seemed to enjoy a relatively relaxed and politically vibrant atmosphere. The Guardian Council approved only 3 of 475 potential candidates to compete against Ahmadinejad, but all 3 were well-known political personalities with established revolutionary credentials: Mir Hussein Mousavi, a former prime minister; Mohsen Rezai, a conservative former head of the Islamic Revolutionary Guard Corps (IRGC); and Mehdi Karroubi, a reformist former speaker of parliament and cleric. Mousavi emerged as the main challenger, confronting Ahmadinejad in televised debates.

Polls indicated a close race, but Ahmadinejad was declared the winner soon after the election, credited with over 63 percent of the vote. All three challengers lodged claims of fraud. Protests broke out on a massive scale across the country as voters rejected the official results. The security forces violently cracked down on all public expressions of dissent and tightened government control of both online and traditional media. However, protesters continued to mount periodic demonstrations, using mobile-telephone cameras and the internet to document abuses and communicate with the outside world. Over the course of 2010, however, the government effectively crippled the opposition's ability to mount large-scale demonstrations.

The postelection confrontations created a new political landscape, in which basic freedoms deteriorated and political affairs were further militarized. In February 2011, the government moved to put opposition leaders Mousavi and Karroubi under house arrest. With the reformist opposition pushed to the sidelines, a power struggle between Ahmadinejad and Khamenei spilled into public view in May, when the latter reinstated the minister of intelligence who had been fired by the president. Subsequently a dozen associates of Ahmadinejad and his controversial chief of staff, Esfandiar Rahim-Mashaei, were arrested and accused of constituting a "deviant current" within the country's leadership. The president himself was threatened with impeachment and questioning. Deep internal divisions in the conservative camp were expected to intensify in connection with legislative elections set for March 2012.

In response to worsening conditions in the country, the UN Human Rights Council in March 2011 established the mandate for a special rapporteur on the situation of human rights in Iran. Ahmed Shaheed, a former Maldivian foreign minister, was entrusted with the post, but the Iranian government refused to allow him into the country. None of the UN's thematic special rapporteurs have been able to visit Iran since 2005. Shaheed published an interim report in September, expressing concern over flagrant human rights violations, including widespread use of secret and public executions and repression of ethnic and religious minorities.

Political Rights and Civil Liberties: Iran is not an electoral democracy. The most powerful figure in the government is the supreme leader, currently Ayatollah Ali Khamenei. He is chosen by the Assembly of Experts, a body of 86 clerics who are elected to eight-year terms by popular vote, from a list of candidates vetted by the Guardian Council. The supreme leader, who has no fixed term, is the commander in chief of the armed forces and appoints the leaders of the judiciary, the heads of state broadcast media, the Expediency Council, and half of the Guardian Council members. Although the president and the parliament, both with four-year terms, are responsible for designating cabinet ministers, the supreme leader exercises de facto control over appointments to the Ministries of Defense, Interior, Foreign Affairs, and Intelligence.

All candidates for the presidency and the 290-seat, unicameral parliament are vetted by the Guardian Council, which consists of six Islamic theologians appointed by the supreme leader and six jurists nominated by the head of the judiciary and confirmed by the parliament, all for six-year terms. The Guardian Council generally disqualifies about a fourth of parliamentary candidates, though some are able to reverse these rulings on appeal. The Guardian Council also has the power to reject legislation approved by the parliament. Disputes between the two bodies are arbitrated by the Expediency Council, another unelected, conservative-dominated body, headed by former president Ali Akbar Hashemi Rafsanjani.

Opposition politicians and party groupings have faced especially harsh repression since the 2009 presidential election, with many leaders—including former lawmakers and cabinet ministers—facing arrest, prison sentences, and lengthy bans on political activity. Beginning in February 2011, the former presidential candidates and prominent opposition leaders Mir Hussein Mousavi and Mehdi Karroubi, along with their wives Zahra Rahnavard and Fatemeh Karroubi, were kept under strict house arrest without trial. They were still being held incommunicado at year's end, with only limited access to family members.

Corruption is pervasive. The hard-line clerical establishment and the IRGC, to which it has many ties, have grown immensely wealthy through their control of tax-exempt foundations that dominate many sectors of the economy. The administration of President Mahmoud Ahmadinejad has gravely damaged fiscal transparency and accountability through the abolition of independent financial watchdogs and the murky transfer of profitable state companies to the IRGC and other semigovernmental conglomerates. Iran was ranked 120 out of 183 countries surveyed in Transparency International's 2011 Corruption Perceptions Index. A $2.6 billion banking embezzlement case that emerged in 2011 involved at least seven Iranian state-owned and private banks, exacerbating concerns about rampant corruption in Iran.

Freedom of expression is severely limited. The Ministry of Culture must approve publication of all books and inspects foreign books prior to domestic distribution. The government directly controls all television and radio broadcasting. Satellite dishes are popular, despite being illegal, and there have been increasing reports of dish confiscation and steep fines. In September 2011, the U.S. Broadcasting Board of Governors (BBG) and the British Broadcasting Corporation (BBC) jointly called on the UN General Assembly and the International Telecommunication Union to condemn the Iranian government's efforts to jam satellite broadcasts, disrupt and hack websites, and intimidate journalists.

The authorities frequently issue ad hoc orders banning media coverage of specific topics and events. The foreign media are banned from covering demonstrations. Cooperation with Persian-language satellite news channels based abroad is also banned. Shortly after a documentary about Khamenei was aired on BBC Persian television in August 2011, six independent documentary filmmakers were arrested on allegations of collaborating with the network. Since then, the Iranian government has ratcheted up pressure on BBC Persian by arresting, questioning, intimidating, and confiscating the passports of relatives of BBC staff.

The Press Court has extensive power to prosecute journalists for such vaguely worded offenses as "mutiny against Islam," "insulting legal or real persons who are lawfully respected," and "propaganda against the regime." The use of "suspicious sources" or sources that criticize the government is also forbidden. Numerous periodicals were closed for morality or security offenses during 2011, including the independent newspapers *Shahrvand-e Emrooz* and *Roozegar*. According to an August 2011 Human Rights Watch report, at least 40 publications have been shut down since 2009. Iran leads the world in the number of jailed journalists, with 42 behind bars at the close of 2010 and many serving lengthy prison sentences. Several dozen other journalists were arrested, coerced into self-incriminating confessions, and released on exorbitant bail payments. The Committee to Protect Journalists reported in June 2011 that 18 journalists had been forced into exile in the past 12 months.

Internet penetration has skyrocketed in recent years, and web-based citizen journalism flourished after the 2009 presidential election, as many Iranians used mobile-telephone cameras and social-networking sites to provide some of the only independent coverage of the crackdown. However, recognizing the internet's rising influence, the government has forced service providers to block a growing list of "immoral" or politically sensitive sites, and the country has developed one of the most expansive and sophisticated internet surveillance and filtering frameworks in the world. Key international social-media websites like Facebook, Twitter, and YouTube were blocked after the 2009 election, and the number of disabled political sites continued to increase in 2011, hampering the opposition's ability to communicate and organize. A special Iranian police unit was formed in 2011 to counter "cybercrimes."

Iranian filmmakers are subject to tight restrictions, and many have been arrested or harassed since the 2009 election. In October 2011, an appeals court in Tehran upheld the conviction of prominent director Jafar Panahi, who was sentenced to six years in prison and a 20-year ban preventing him from travelling abroad or engaging in any artistic activity.

Religious freedom is limited in Iran, whose population is largely Shiite Muslim but includes Sunni Muslim, Baha'i, Christian, Jewish, and Zoroastrian minorities. The Special Court for the Clergy investigates religious figures for alleged crimes and has generally been used to persecute clerics who stray from the official interpretation of Islam or criticize the supreme leader. Ayatollah Seyed Hussain Kazemeini Boroujerdi, a cleric who advocates the separation of religion and politics, is currently serving 11 years in prison for his beliefs. Ayatollah Ali-Mohammad Dastgheib and Ayatollah Yusuf Saanei, both ardent critics of the postelection crackdown, have been harassed and had their properties attacked by plainclothes security agents.

Sunnis enjoy equal rights under the law but face discrimination in practice; there is no Sunni mosque in Tehran, and few Sunnis hold senior government posts. In August 2011, the chief religious authority of the Sunni community in Iran asked the supreme leader to allow Sunnis to freely observe their religious holidays and Friday prayer ceremonies, and expressed concern over discrimination against Sunni citizens.

Sufi Muslims have also faced persecution by the authorities. Since the leader of the Sufi order Nematollahi Gonabadi was arrested in 2009 and sentenced to four years in prison, the security forces have repeatedly clashed with the members of this order in Gonabad and Kavar, arrested numerous adherents, and shut down their websites.

Iranian Baha'is, thought to number between 300,000 and 350,000, are not recognized as a religious minority in the constitution, enjoy virtually no rights under the law, and are banned from practicing their faith. Baha'i students are barred from attending university and prevented from obtaining their educational records. Under Ahmadinejad, concerted efforts to intimidate, imprison, and physically attack Baha'is have been carried out by security forces, paramilitary groups, and ordinary citizens with impunity. Hundreds of Baha'is have been executed since the Islamic Revolution in 1979, and at least 100 were in prison in 2011, including 7 main Baha'i community leaders who were sentenced in 2010 to 20 years in prison on charges of espionage and "engaging in propaganda against Islam." In May 2011, at least 30 Baha'is were arrested in coordinated raids in Tehran, Karaj, Isfahan, and Shiraz. The imprisoned individuals were involved in an online university initiative that provided higher education to Baha'i students.

The constitution recognizes Zoroastrians, Jews, and Christians as religious minorities, and they are generally allowed to worship without interference, so long as they do not proselytize. Conversion by Muslims to a non-Muslim religion is punishable by death. In 2011, 34-year-old Protestant pastor Yousef Naderkhani, who had converted to Christianity at age 19, was sentenced to execution by hanging, though the sentence was not carried out by year's end. The non-Muslim minorities are barred from election to representative bodies (though five seats have been allocated to the Armenian Christian, Chaldean Christian, Zoroastrian, and Jewish minorities), cannot hold senior government or military positions, and face restrictions in employment, education, and property ownership.

Academic freedom is limited. Scholars are frequently detained, threatened, and forced to retire for expressing political views. Students involved in organizing protests face suspension or expulsion in addition to criminal punishments. Since the 2009 presidential election, the IRGC-led Basij militia has increased its presence on campuses, and vocal critics of the regime face increased persecution and prosecution. In October 2011, Peyman Aref, a political science student at Tehran University, was publicly lashed 74 times for insulting Ahmadinejad, hours after he completed a one-year prison term. Meanwhile, on Khamenei's orders the government announced increased scrutiny over degree programs in the humanities to ensure their commitment to Islamic principles. In September, the country's top humanities university, Allameh Tabatabai, eliminated 13 branches of social sciences, including political science, history, sociology, philosophy, pedagogy, and journalism.

The constitution prohibits public demonstrations that "are detrimental to the fundamental principles of Islam," a vague provision that was regularly invoked to deny permit requests after the 2009 presidential election. Vigilante and paramilitary organizations that are officially or tacitly sanctioned by the government—most notably the Basij and Ansar-i Hezbollah—regularly play a major role in breaking up demonstrations. These forces even deny mourners the right to attend the funerals of political activists. An emblematic case occurred in June 2011, when security forces disrupted the funeral of Ezatollah Sahabi, a nationalist-religious leader. During the violent confrontation between the security forces and the mourners, Haleh Sahabi, the deceased's daughter and a political activist on furlough from a two-year prison term, sustained beatings and suffered a fatal heart attack. In reaction to her death, imprisoned journalist Reza Hoda Saber started a hunger strike that resulted in his death a few days later. Peaceful, nonpolitical demonstrations are increasingly met with brutal violence. In August 2011, environmentalist protests to protect Lake Urmia in northwestern Iran resulted in the arrest of 60 protesters and injuries to 45. In addition, under the pretense of "countering immoral behavior," the government regularly disrupts private gatherings.

The constitution permits the establishment of political parties, professional syndicates, and other civic organizations, provided that they do not violate the principles of "freedom, sovereignty, and national unity" or question the Islamic basis of the republic. Human rights discourse and grassroots activism are integral parts of Iranian society. However, the security services routinely arrest and harass secular activists as part of a wider effort to control nongovernmental organizations (NGOs). Although permits are not required by law, the Interior Ministry has been issuing them and shutting down organizations that do not seek or qualify for them. In 2011, the government began reviewing a new bill on the establishment and supervision of NGOs that could unduly restrict and severely impede their activities; the process continued at year's end.

Iranian law does not allow independent labor unions, though workers' councils are represented in the Workers' House, the only legal labor federation. Workers' public protests and May Day gatherings are regularly suppressed by security forces. Leading workers' rights activist and trade union leader Mansour Ossanlou has become the symbol of the labor rights situation in Iran. Serving a five-year prison sentence since 2007 on charges of "acting against national security," he is reportedly suffering from several health problems in prison.

The judicial system is not independent, as the supreme leader directly appoints the head of the judiciary, who in turn appoints senior judges. Suspects are frequently tried in closed sessions without access to legal counsel. Political and other sensitive cases are tried before revolutionary courts, where due process protections are routinely disregarded, and trials are often summary. Judges deny access to lawyers, commonly accept coerced confessions, and disregard torture or abuse during detention.

Pressuring lawyers to abandon the cases of political and social detainees is another widespread government practice in Iran. If the lawyers persist in fulfilling their duties, they can face harassment, interrogation, and incarceration. Since 2009, at least 42 attorneys have been prosecuted. In one prominent case, human rights lawyer Nasrin Sotoudeh was sentenced in January 2011 to 11 years in prison and a 20-year ban on professional activity and travel. An appellate court in September reduced the prison term to six years and halved the professional and travel ban, but one of the attorneys representing Sotoudeh was jailed. Sotoudeh was reportedly in poor health and had gone on several hunger strikes behind bars.

The country's penal code is based on Sharia (Islamic law) and provides for flogging, amputation, and execution by stoning or hanging for a range of social and political offenses; these punishments are carried out in practice. Iran has the highest number of executions per capita in the world, with hundreds carried out each year. While many are executed for drug-related offenses, a number of political prisoners convicted of *moharebeh* (enmity against God) also receive death sentences. Iran's overall execution rate has increased significantly under Ahmadinejad. In January 2011 alone, it was reported that 83 people, including 3 political prisoners, were executed. By September, there had been more than 200 officially announced executions, including over two dozen public hangings, while at least 146 others were carried out in secret, without the knowledge of the inmates' lawyers or relatives. The total number of executions in 2011 was reportedly as high as 600.

Contrary to Iran's obligations under the Convention on the Rights of the Child, the judiciary continues to execute juvenile offenders. Two minors were publicly hanged in Bandar Abbas in April 2011, and a 17-year-old boy was executed in September. More than 100 juveniles reportedly remained on death row. The government announced in 2008 that it would no longer execute minors, but it later clarified that the death penalty remained an option under the parallel "retribution" system, in which the sentence is imposed by the victim's family rather than the state. This would expose male offenders over the age of 15 and female offenders as young as 9 to capital punishment.

Although the constitution prohibits arbitrary arrest and detention, such abuses are increasingly employed, and family members of detainees are often not notified for days or weeks. Suspected dissidents are frequently held in unofficial, illegal detention centers. Prison conditions in general are notoriously poor, and there are regular allegations of abuse, rape, torture, and death in custody. In a letter to Iranian authorities published in May 2011, 26 prominent political prisoners reported ill-treatment, prolonged solitary confinement, torture, and systemic due process violations during their interrogation and detention.

The constitution and laws call for equal rights for all ethnic groups, but in practice, these rights are restricted by the regime. Minority languages are prohibited in schools and government offices. Minority rights activists are consistently threatened and arrested. Ethnic Kurds, Arabs, Baluchis, and Azeris complain of discrimination. Kurdish opposition groups suspected of separatist aspirations, such as the Democratic Party of Iranian Kurdistan (KDPI), are brutally suppressed. The Free Life Party of Kurdistan (PJAK), a separatist militant group linked to the Kurdistan Workers' Party (PKK) of Turkey, has conducted a number of guerrilla attacks in recent years and was declared a terrorist organization by the United States in 2009. Iranian efforts to combat the PJAK have included raids into Kurdish territory in neighboring Iraq.

Sexual orientation is also a subject of government scrutiny. The penal code criminalizes all sexual relations outside of traditional marriage, and Iran is among the few countries where individuals can be put to death for consensual same-sex conduct.

Women are widely educated; a majority of university students are female. However, women currently hold less than 3 percent of the seats in the parliament, and they are routinely excluded from running for higher office. Female judges may not issue final verdicts, and a woman cannot obtain a passport without the permission of her husband or a male relative. Women do not enjoy equal rights under Sharia-based statutes governing divorce, inheritance, and child custody, though some of these inequalities are accompanied by greater familial and financial obligations for men. A woman's testimony in court is given only half the weight of a man's, and the monetary damages awarded to a female victim's family upon her death is half that owed to the family of a male victim. Women must conform to strict dress codes and are segregated from men in some public places. There has been a crackdown in recent years on women deemed to be dressed immodestly. Women's rights activists, especially members of the One Million Signatures Campaign, continue to face repression. In 2011, two prominent members of the campaign, Bahareh Hedayat and Mahboubeh Karami, were sentenced to nine and a half and three years in prison, respectively.

Iraq

Political Rights: 5
Civil Liberties: 6
Status: Not Free

Population: 32,665,000
Capital: Baghdad

Ten-Year Ratings Timeline For Year Under Review (Political Rights, Civil Liberties, Status)

2002	2003	2004	2005	2006	2007	2008	2009	2010	2011
7,7NF	7,5NF	7,5NF	6,5NF	6,6NF	6,6NF	6,6NF	5,6NF	5,6NF	5,6NF

Overview: **In December 2011, immediately after the U.S. military completed its scheduled withdrawal from the country, tensions arose again between Sunni and Shiite political parties. The Sunni Iraqiya Party boycotted the parliament in response to a perceived power grab by Prime Minister Nouri al-Maliki and the issuing of an arrest warrant for the Sunni vice president. Also during the year, Turkey and Iran launched attacks into northern Iraq to suppress Kurdish guerrilla groups, and ongoing sectarian, terrorist, and political violence targeted government forces, journalists, and ordinary civilians.**

The modern state of Iraq was established after World War I as a League of Nations mandate administered by Britain. The British installed a constitutional monarchy that privileged the Sunni Arab minority at the expense of Kurds and Shiite Arabs. Sunni Arab political dominance continued after independence in 1932 and a military coup that toppled the monarchy in 1958. The Arab nationalist Baath Party seized power in 1968, and the new regime's de facto strongman, Saddam Hussein, assumed the presidency in 1979. Over the next two decades, Iraq endured brutal political repression, a destructive war with Iran from 1980 to 1988, military defeat by a U.S.-led coalition following Hussein's 1990 invasion of Kuwait, and years of onerous postwar trade sanctions.

After the establishment of a U.S.-enforced no-fly zone north of the 36th parallel in 1991, most of the three northern provinces of Erbil, Duhok, and Sulimaniyah came under the control of the Kurdistan Democratic Party (KDP) and the Patriotic Union of Kurdistan (PUK). The two factions fought openly in the mid-1990s, but they eventually reconciled and formed an autonomous Kurdistan Regional Government (KRG).

A U.S.-led coalition invaded Iraq in March 2003 and established a Coalition Provisional Authority (CPA) to administer the country. It disbanded the Iraqi military and prevented members of the Baath Party from serving in government or the new security forces. The resulting security vacuum led to widespread looting, damage to infrastructure, and acute electricity and water shortages.

Exploiting Sunni Arab frustrations with the de-Baathification policy and the impending shift of political power toward the Shiite majority, loose networks of former Baathist officials, Sunni Arab tribe members, and Islamist militants associated with al-Qaeda began organizing and funding an insurgency that rapidly gained strength in late 2003 and 2004.

Intimidation by insurgents ensured that Sunni Arabs boycotted the 2005 elections for a Transitional National Assembly (TNA) and provincial governments, resulting in a landslide victory for Shiite and Kurdish parties. A new constitution was approved by referendum in October 2005, though more than two-thirds of voters in two largely Sunni Arab provinces rejected it.

Meanwhile, Shiite party militias were able to infiltrate the Interior Ministry's police and counterinsurgency forces, and extrajudicial detentions and killings by both the militias and militia-dominated police units became common during 2005 and 2006. Sunni militias responded in kind, and an intense cycle of sectarian conflict ensued. Ethnically cleansed or segregated neighborhoods soon became a fixture in Baghdad and other multiethnic or religiously diverse provinces.

Sunni Arabs participated in the December 2005 elections for a full-term parliament, increasing their political representation. Nouri al-Maliki of the Shiite Da'wa Party was chosen as prime minister. However, further political progress remained elusive; the main Sunni Arab bloc in parliament and a Shiite faction loyal to populist cleric and militia leader Moqtada al-Sadr both began a boycott of the legislature in 2007.

The parliament adopted several symbolic measures in 2008 to bring Sunni Arabs back into the political process. In January, many former Baathists were permitted to return to jobs they lost, and in February, the government granted amnesty to thousands of mainly Sunni Arab prisoners. The largest Sunni bloc returned to government in April after a boycott of almost a year, and six Sunni ministers joined al-Maliki's cabinet. Also in 2008, Iraqi security forces cracked down on al-Sadr's militia network, and local, U.S.-funded Sunni militias that had formed over the previous two years began to successfully suppress the insurgencies in the western provinces.

Under electoral legislation passed in late 2008, voters in the January 2009 provincial elections could choose candidates rather than party lists, the use of religious symbols in campaigning was restricted, a 25 percent quota was set for female council members, and just 6 seats—down from 15 in an earlier draft—were set aside for Christians and other small minorities out of a total of 440 provincial council seats. The voting was largely peaceful, and turnout in most provinces ranged from 50 percent to 75 percent. On the whole, al-Maliki's Da'wa Party emerged as the winner, though it needed to form coalitions to govern in most provinces.

The 2009 provincial elections did not include the autonomous Kurdish region or the contested province of Kirkuk. Separate elections in July 2009 for the Kurdish regional parliament and presidency featured high turnout and a fairly strong showing by a new opposition bloc called Gorran (Change), which took about a quarter of the parliamentary vote. A referendum to determine whether Kirkuk would join the Kurdish region remained delayed through 2011, despite a constitutional provision that had required it before the end of 2007.

Parliamentary elections were held in March 2010, despite having been constitutionally mandated for January 2010. They were governed by a 2009 election law that called for an open-list, proportional-representation voting system, with multimember districts corresponding to the 18 provinces. A total of eight seats were reserved for Christians and other religious minorities.

Despite violence on election day, the polling itself was seen as relatively free and fair. The electoral commission took candidates' complaints seriously and conducted a partial recount, but found no evidence of significant fraud. Voters clearly demonstrated their frustration with the government by returning only 62 of the previous parliament's 275 members, but the elections resulted in political deadlock. Despite a constitutional requirement to form a government within 30 days of the election results' announcement, neither of the rival blocs was able to organize a majority, with foreign powers including Iran, Saudi Arabia, and the United States reportedly playing a role in the lengthy negotiations. The new parliament reelected Kurdish leader Jalal Talabani as president in November 2010, and in December 2010, al-Maliki finally secured parliamentary approval for a unity government that encompassed all major factions, including Iraqiya and al-Sadr's Shiite movement.

The long postelection interregnum featured an escalation in sectarian and antigovernment violence. Insurgents began targeting national institutions, especially the security services, and sites with sectarian significance during the spring. By the summer of 2010, violence had reached heights not seen in years. In the beginning of 2011, U.S. military officials estimated a 20 percent decrease in overall security incidents from 2010. However, al-Qaeda launched retaliatory in Mesopotamia against civilians, politicians, Iraqi security forces, and American troops after the killing of Osama bin Laden by U.S. forces in Pakistan in May. Additionally, as the U.S. military ramped up its efforts to redeploy troops and evacuate Iraq during the summer, various militia groups sought to take advantage of a security vacuum as Iraqi forces proved unable to stem the violence. In total, the violence was estimated to have cost the lives of over 4,000 Iraqi civilians in 2011.

In keeping with a 2008 security agreement between Iraq and the United States, about 50,000 U.S. military personnel remained in Iraq through 2011, though they had withdrawn from Iraqi cities in 2009 and formally ended combat operations in 2010. American and Iraqi political leaders had expected to agree on a reduced presence of up to 5,000 U.S. troops beyond 2011, but such a pact was ultimately precluded by the Iraqi parliament's refusal to grant U.S. personnel immunity from prosecution under Iraqi law. Consequently, the last U.S. troops left the country in December.

Within days of the completion of the U.S. withdrawal, tension arose once again between Sunni and Shiite political parties. In an apparent power grab by Prime Minister Nouri al-Maliki's ruling coalition, an arrest warrant was issued for Vice President Tariq al-Hashmi, a Sunni politician, alleging him of running a "death squad" that targeted police and government officials. Al-Hashmi fled to the northern Kurdish region, but arrests of other Sunni, Baathist, and secular Shiite political figures followed, and al-Hashmi's Sunni Iraqiya Party boycotted the parliament in protest.

In addition to ongoing violence and political strife, Iraq continues to suffer from economic difficulties and insecure borders. The government has remained unable to provide basic public services. While electricity provision, for example, has increased significantly in recent years, it has not kept pace with growing demand, and most Iraqis lack a reliable source of power. Unemployment hovers above 20 percent nationally, and reaches as high as 55 percent in some rural areas. Employment among those aged 15 to 24 is also high at around 23 percent.

In August and October 2011, in response to Kurdish guerrilla attacks, Turkey and Iran launched cross-border assaults on suspected guerrilla targets in northern Iraq. These were the first such attacks since 2008.

Political Rights and Civil Liberties: Iraq is not an electoral democracy. Although it has conducted meaningful elections, political participation and decision-making in the country remain seriously impaired by sectarian and insurgent violence, widespread corruption, and the influence of foreign powers. Under the constitution, the president and two vice presidents are elected by the parliament and appoint the prime minister, who is nominated by the largest parliamentary bloc. Elections are held every four years. The prime minister forms a cabinet and runs the executive functions of the state. The parliament consists of a 325-seat lower house, the Council of Representatives, and a still-unformed upper house, the Federal Council, which would represent provincial interests. The Independent Electoral Commission of Iraq (IECI), whose nine-member board was selected by a UN advisory committee, has sole responsibility for administering elections.

Political parties representing a wide range of viewpoints operate without legal restrictions, but the Baath Party is officially banned. Additionally, after the U.S. troop withdrawal in December, barriers to political participation appeared to be growing for Sunni and secular political actors in light of Prime Minister Nouri al-Maliki's attempts to consolidate power.

Home to one-fifth of the country's population, the autonomous Kurdish region constitutes a distinct polity within Iraq, with its own flag, military units, and language. The 111-seat regional legislature remains dominated by the allied PUK and KDP, despite the presence of the new Gorran opposition bloc following 2009 elections. The Kurdish region's political leaders profess their commitment to remaining part of a federal Iraqi state, but Kurdish security forces maintain a de facto border with the rest of Iraq, Iraqi Arabs are often treated as foreigners, and the regional government frequently acts in its own interest over Baghdad's objections.

Iraq is plagued by pervasive corruption at all levels of government. A national Integrity Commission is tasked with fighting corruption, but it conducts its investigations in secret and does not publish its findings until the courts have issued final decisions. The overwhelming majority of offenders enjoy impunity, largely because of an amnesty law allowing ministers to intervene and dismiss charges. As a result, cases are generally brought against low- and mid-ranking officials. While the Integrity Commission had gained some momentum in recent years, it faced a number of setbacks in 2011. Most prominently, the commission's chairman was forced to resign amid mounting political pressure, and there were numerous reports of government attempts to silence corruption whistle-blowers. Recruits allegedly pay bribes as high as $5,000 to enter the Iraqi security forces, and reports suggest that ordinary citizens must resort to bribery to accomplish simple bureaucratic tasks like obtaining vehicle license plates. Iraq was ranked 175 out of 183 countries surveyed in Transparency International's 2011 Corruption Perceptions Index.

Freedom of expression is protected by the constitution, but in practice it has been seriously impeded by sectarian tensions and fear of violent reprisals. Over a dozen private television stations are in operation, and major Arab satellite stations are easily accessible. Hundreds of print publications have been established since 2003 and are allowed to function without significant government interference. Internet access is not currently restricted. Legislation passed in 2006 criminalized the ridicule of public officials, who often file suits when journalists report on corruption allegations. Iraq's media regulatory body, the Communication and Media Commission, cracked down on journalists in the run-up to the 2010 parliamentary elections.

Violent retribution has hindered journalists' ability to report widely and objectively. There was an increase in intimidation and violence against journalists in 2011, including a series of physical attacks on reporters during the summer months. Most prominently, in September, well-known critical radio personality Hadi al-Mahdi was shot dead in his Baghdad home only days after expressing fears that the government would harm him. The Committee to Protect Journalists (CPJ) estimates that over 140 journalists have been killed since 2003, while Reporters Without Borders (RSF) puts the number closer to 230.

Journalists previously operated more freely in the Kurdish region, but conditions there have deteriorated in the last few years. A 2008 press law imposed fines for creating instability, spreading fear or intimidation, causing harm to people, or violating religious beliefs. Journalists who offend local officials and top party leaders or expose high-level corruption remain subject to physical attacks, arbitrary detention, and harassment. Most notably in 2011, Asos Hardi, editor of *Awene*, an independent Kurdish newspaper, was beaten in August.

The Kurdish Islamic Union (KIU), an opposition political movement, was suspected of involvement in a string of criminal acts in the Kurdish regions in December 2011. As a result, two KIU buildings and five buildings belonging to sympathetic media outlets were ransacked and set ablaze by unidentified arsonists. Twelve journalists from Kurdish media outlets were detained by KRG authorities, and at least 15 Kurdish and Al-Jazeera journalists were victims of physical attacks by plainclothes security officers.

Freedom of religion is guaranteed by the constitution, and religious institutions are allowed to operate with little formal oversight. However, all religious communities in Iraq have been threatened by sectarian violence. An estimated 300,000 to 900,000 Christians have sought safety abroad since 2003. Religious and ethnic minorities in northern Iraq—including Turkmens, Arabs, Christians, and Shabaks—have reported instances of discrimination and harassment by Kurdish authorities, though a number have fled to the Kurdish-controlled region due to its relative security. Formerly mixed areas across Iraq are now much more homogeneous, and terrorist attacks continue to be directed toward sectarian targets.

Academic institutions operate in a highly politicized and insecure environment. Hundreds of professors were killed during the peak of sectarian and insurgent violence, and many more stopped working or fled the country, though there have been some reports of scholars returning to their jobs following security improvements in the last several years.

Rights to freedom of assembly and association are recognized by the constitution, though it guarantees these rights "in a way that does not violate public order and morality." Some isolated protests were held in February and March 2011, inspired by popular uprisings in North Africa. In Baghdad in February, more than 20 protesters were killed by security forces as they tried to disperse the crowds. Domestic and international nongovernmental organizations (NGOs) are able to operate without legal restrictions, although safety concerns severely limit their activities in many areas.

The constitution provides for the right to form and join trade unions. Union activity has flourished in nearly all industries since 2003, and strikes have not been uncommon. However, Iraq's 1987 labor law remains in effect, prohibiting unionization in the public sector, and a 2005 decree gave authorities the power to seize all union funds and prevent their disbursal. Some elements in the government moved to ban labor unions in May 2011, but domestic and international objections forced officials to back away from any concrete plans.

Judicial independence is guaranteed in the constitution. The Higher Judicial Council—headed by the chief judge of the Federal Supreme Court and composed of Iraq's 17 chief appellate judges and several judges from the Federal Court of Cassation—has administrative authority over the court system. In practice, however, judges have come under immense political and sectarian pressure and have been largely unable to pursue cases involving organized crime, corruption, and militia activity, even when presented with overwhelming evidence. Iraqi citizens often turn to local militias and religious groups to dispense justice rather than seeking redress with official law enforcement bodies that are seen as corrupt or ineffective.

The criminal procedure code and the constitution prohibit arbitrary arrest and detention, though both practices are common in security-related cases. The constitution also prohibits all forms of torture and inhumane treatment and affords victims the right to compensation, but there are few effective safeguards in place. A previously unknown detention facility where credible accusations of torture were reported was found to be under the direct control of the prime minister's office in 2010. While KRG laws also prohibit inhumane treatment, it is widely acknowledged that Kurdish security forces practice illegal detention and questionable interrogation tactics. Detainees in U.S. custody have also experienced torture and mistreatment, though by 2011, U.S. forces no longer directly held detainees in Iraq.

About five million Iraqis have been displaced from their homes since 2003. While hundreds of thousands—most of them Sunni Arabs—have fled to Jordan and Syria, nearly three million Iraqis are displaced within Iraq. In regions like Kirkuk, the Saddam Hussein regime forced some 250,000 Kurdish residents to move from their homes in the name of regional "Arabization." Ethnic disputes in the region have resulted in a long-standing political impasse between the majority Kurds and minorities of Arabs, Turkmen, and Assyrian-Chaldean Christians.

The constitution promises women equal rights under the law, though in practice they face various forms of legal and societal discrimination. Women are guaranteed 25 percent of the seats in the legislature, and their participation in public life has increased in recent years. While they still face serious social pressure and restrictions, women have also returned in larger numbers to jobs and universities. Women enjoy somewhat greater legal protections and social freedoms in the Kurdish region, but their political power is limited. Moreover, domestic abuse and so-called honor killings remain serious problems both in the Kurdish region and across the country. The laws applicable outside the Kurdish region offer leniency to the perpetrators of honor killings. In July 2010, Kurdish religious leaders formally declared that female genital mutilation (FGM) was un-Islamic, but advocacy groups claim that more than 50 percent of Kurdish teenage girls are victims of FGM. The U.S. State Department placed Iraq on the Tier 2 Watch List in its 2011 Trafficking in Persons Report, noting problems including the trafficking and sexual exploitation of women and children from impoverished and displaced Iraqi families, and the abuse of foreign men and women who are recruited to work in Iraq.

Ireland

Political Rights: 1
Civil Liberties: 1
Status: Free

Population: 4,584,000
Capital: Dublin

Ten-Year Ratings Timeline For Year Under Review (Political Rights, Civil Liberties, Status)

2002	2003	2004	2005	2006	2007	2008	2009	2010	2011
1,1F	1,1F	1,1F	1,1F	1,1F	1,1F	1,1F	1,1F	1,1F	1,1F

Overview: **In early parliamentary elections in February 2011, the Fianna Fáil party suffered a crushing defeat to the Fine Gael party, which entered into a coalition with the Labour Party. In October, former Labour Party leader Michael D. Higgins was elected Ireland's president. The country continued to struggle with serious economic problems, though Prime Minister Enda Kenny secured an interest rate reduction on Ireland's European Union loans. Meanwhile, tensions between the government and the Catholic Church escalated over the handling of clerical sexual abuse.**

The Irish Free State emerged from the United Kingdom under the Anglo-Irish Treaty of 1921, though six counties in the province of Ulster remained part of the

United Kingdom. A brief civil war followed, ending in 1923. In 1937, the Irish Free State adopted a new constitution and a new name—Ireland, or Éire.

Ireland joined the European Community (now the European Union, or EU) in 1973. Thanks in part to large subsidies from the EU, Ireland enjoyed high rates of economic growth beginning in the mid-1990s.

The Fianna Fáil party dominated Ireland's government since the 1930s, and Prime Minister Patrick "Bertie" Ahern helped Fianna Fáil to defeat Fine Gael in the 2007 general elections. Fianna Fáil formed a governing coalition for the first time with the Green Party and the Progressive Democrats. However, Ahern resigned in September, after evidence of corruption emerged. Finance Minister Brian Cowen took over as prime minister in May 2008.

Support for the ruling Fianna Fáil and Green parties declined significantly in the June 2009 local elections. Following a series of resignations and defections, the number of coalition backers dropped to equal that of the opposition, but the coalition remained in power after agreeing on a governmental program in October that provided for electoral reform.

Frustration with and distrust of the government reached new levels in late 2010 following the acceptance of a $113 billion loan package from the International Monetary Fund and the EU, which would require harsh austerity measures. Fianna Fáil was largely blamed for failing to address the reckless lending that ultimately resulted in a burst of the country's housing bubble, and the party's popularity sank to 15 percent. Under serious pressure, Cowen resigned as party leader in late January 2011, and Micheál Martin took his place. The Green Party subsequently quit the coalition, leaving Fianna Fáil without a majority in Parliament. Cowen called for early elections, pledging to stay on in a caretaker capacity.

After holding power for 61 of the last 79 years, Fianna Fáil suffered its worst defeat in early elections held on February 25, capturing only 20 seats in Parliament's lower house, down from 78 in 2007. Fine Gael won 76 seats, but lacked a majority, and was forced to enter into a coalition with the Labour Party, which took 37 seats. The Greens failed to enter Parliament, while Sinn Féin won 14 seats. The remaining seats went to independents and two smaller parties. Enda Kenny of Fine Gael was elected prime minister. Holding two-thirds of the seats, Kenny's Fine Gael-Labour coalition held the largest parliamentary majority in Ireland's history.

Former Labour member of parliament Michael D. Higgins was elected president on October 29 with 40 percent of the vote, replacing outgoing President Mary McAleese. Higgins successfully defeated second place contender Martin McGuiness, deputy leader of Sinn Féin and former Irish Republican Army commander, and third place Gay Mitchell of Fine Gael.

Ireland has faced severe economic problems in conjunction with the global economic crisis, driven by a rapid decline in property prices. The economy entered a technical depression in 2009, mostly due to government bailouts for the banking system. After three years of austerity measures, during which time household wealth fell by almost a third, the government continued to make painful cuts. In a July 2011 euro-zone summit in Brussels, Kenny successfully reduced the interest rate of Ireland's loans and extended their maturity. However, by the end of 2011, the budget deficit had climbed to 24.9 billion euros (approximately US$30 billion).

Political Rights and Civil Liberties: Ireland is an electoral democracy. The Parliament (Oireachtas) consists of a lower house (the Dáil), whose 166 members are elected by proportional representation for five-year terms, and an upper house (the Seanad, or Senate) with 60 members, 11 appointed and 49 elected by various interest groups. The Senate is mainly a consultative body in which members serve five-year terms. The president, whose functions are largely ceremonial, is directly elected for a seven-year term. The prime minister, or *taoiseach*, is chosen by Parliament.

The political party system is open to the rise and fall of competing groups. The two largest parties—Fianna Fáil and Fine Gael—do not differ widely in ideological orientation but represent the opposing sides of the 1922-23 civil war. The smaller parties include the Labour Party, Sinn Féin, and the Green Party.

Corruption has been a recurring problem, particularly in the form of undue political influence through cronyism, political patronage, favors, and donations. In November 2011, Ireland ratified the United Nations Convention against Corruption. Likely due to the low levels of petty corruption, Ireland was ranked 19 out of 183 countries surveyed in Transparency International's 2011 Corruption Perceptions Index.

The media are free and independent, and internet access is unrestricted. The print media present a variety of viewpoints. Television and radio are dominated by the state broadcaster, but the growth of cable and satellite television is weakening its influence. The state maintains the right to censor material deemed indecent or obscene, which critics charge is an anachronistic practice and possibly a violation of the European Convention on Human Rights. Reforms to Ireland's defamation legislation, which came into effect in January 2010, introduced the offense of blasphemous libel, with penalties of up to 25,000 euros (US$33,500). After taking power in March 2011, the Fine Gael-Labour coalition pledged to remove blasphemy from the constitution; however, no action had been taken by year's end.

Freedom of religion is guaranteed by the constitution, and discrimination on the basis of religion is illegal. Although the country is overwhelmingly Roman Catholic, there is no state religion, and adherents of other faiths face few impediments to religious expression. The Catholic Church operates approximately 90 percent of Ireland's schools, most of which provide religious education. However, parents may exempt their children from religious instruction, and the constitution requires equal funding for students wishing instruction in other faiths. In 2011, the government established a working group charged with wresting control of half the country's primary schools from the Church. Academic freedom is respected.

The right of public assembly and demonstration is not legally infringed. Freedom of association is upheld, and nongovernmental organizations can operate freely. Collective bargaining is legal and unrestricted, and labor unions operate without hindrance.

The legal system is based on common law, and the judiciary is independent. A February 2011 report by the European Committee for the Prevention of Torture and Inhuman or Degrading Treatment or Punishment criticized prison conditions in Ireland as dangerous, unsanitary, and overcrowded, with poor health services and problems of drug abuse, among other issues. The report sparked discussions over reforming the country's penitentiary system.

Despite equal protection for all under the law, the Irish Travellers, a traditionally nomadic group of about 25,000 people, are not recognized as an ethnic minority, and face discrimination in housing, hiring, and other areas.

While discrimination in employment on the basis of sex or sexual orientation is prohibited, gender inequality in wages persists. Although the previous two presidents were female, women continue to be underrepresented in the political sphere. Abortion is legal only when there is "real and substantial risk" to the life of the mother. In December 2010, the European Court of Human Rights ruled that Ireland had violated this constitutional right in denying a pregnant woman with cancer an abortion.

The 2010 Civil Partnership and Certain Rights and Obligations of Cohabitants Act, which came into effect in January 2011, legally recognizes same-sex couples, although it denies them some rights awarded to heterosexual married couples, such as adoption rights.

Reports released in 2009 by the Commission to Inquire into Child Abuse documented decades of widespread physical and emotional abuse against children in state institutions and by Catholic priests, as well as collusion to hide the abuse. The Cloyne report, which was released in July 2011, documented such abuse and subsequent cover-ups in the diocese of Cloyne. In response, Prime Minister Enda Kenny criticized the Vatican and pledged to implement new laws that would require citizens to report information on child abuse. The Vatican reacted by recalling its envoy to Dublin. Further tensions between the government and the Catholic Church stemmed from conflict over whether Ireland's churches should bear more of the financial responsibility in compensating victims of clerical sexual abuse, as the government has already paid some $2 billion in compensation to victims.

↓ Israel

Political Rights: 1
Civil Liberties: 2
Status: Free

Population: 7,600,000 [Note: There are an estimated 311,100 Israeli settlers in the West Bank, about 18,100 in Golan Heights, and nearly 187,000 in East Jerusalem.]
Capital: Jerusalem

Trend Arrow: Israel received a downward trend arrow due to the imposition of the so-called Boycott Law, which allows civil lawsuits against Israeli individuals and groups that call for an economic, cultural, or academic boycott of the State of Israel or the West Bank settlements.

Note: The numerical ratings and status above reflect conditions within Israel itself. Separate reports examine the West Bank and the Gaza Strip.

Ten-Year Ratings Timeline For Year Under Review (Political Rights, Civil Liberties, Status)

2002	2003	2004	2005	2006	2007	2008	2009	2010	2011
1,3F	1,3F	1,3F	1,2F	1,2F	1,2F	1,2F	1,2F	1,2F	1,2F

Overview: **Right-leaning parties in the Knesset (parliament) proposed or successfully passed a range of measures**

in 2011 that appeared to target Arab Israelis or restrict dissent over Israel's policies toward the Palestinians. Among the laws adopted was one that allowed civil suits against those who advocated a boycott against the Israeli state or West Bank settlements. Proposed legislation included a bill that would restrict the funding of certain nongovernmental organizations. Also during 2011, Israel saw wide-scale social protests over economic conditions. The military periodically attacked Gaza-based militants who fired ordnance into Israel, and small-scale terrorist or militant attacks killed several people.

Israel was formed in 1948 from part of the British-ruled mandate of Palestine, which had been created by the League of Nations following World War I. A 1947 UN partition plan dividing Palestine into two states, Jewish and Arab, was rejected by the Arab Higher Committee and the Arab League, and Israel's 1948 declaration of independence led to war with a coalition of Arab countries. While Israel maintained its sovereignty and expanded its borders, Jordan (then known as Transjordan) seized East Jerusalem and the West Bank, and Egypt took control of the Gaza Strip.

After its 1967 war with Egypt, Jordan, and Syria, Israel occupied the Sinai Peninsula, the West Bank, the Gaza Strip, East Jerusalem, and the Golan Heights. While it returned Sinai to Egypt in 1982 as a result of the Camp David Accords, Israel annexed East Jerusalem in 1967 and unilaterally extended Israeli law to the Golan Heights in 1981.

In 1993, following a Palestinian uprising that began in the late 1980s, Israel secured an agreement with the Palestine Liberation Organization (PLO) that provided for a phased Israeli withdrawal from the West Bank and Gaza Strip and a degree of Palestinian autonomy in those areas, in exchange for Palestinian recognition of Israel and a renunciation of terrorism. In 1994, Israel and Jordan agreed to a U.S.-brokered peace agreement. However, Israeli-Palestinian negotiations on a future Palestinian state broke down in 2000, and Palestinian militant violence resumed.

In 2002, the Israel Defense Forces (IDF) reoccupied many of the West Bank areas that the Israeli government had ceded to the Palestinian Authority (PA) in the 1990s. Israel also began construction of a security barrier in the West Bank that roughly followed the 1949 armistice line, though it frequently extended deeper into the occupied territory to incorporate Jewish settlements. Critics accused the Israelis of confiscating Palestinian property and impeding access to land, jobs, and services for those living in the barrier's vicinity. As a result, the barrier has been rerouted six times by order of the Israeli Supreme Court; two of these orders have yet to be implemented.

In 2005, an informal cease-fire between the PA and Israel led to a general decline, but not a halt, in violence, and Israel completed a unilateral withdrawal of Jewish settlers from the Gaza Strip. Because his own right-wing Likud Party opposed the latter move, Prime Minister Ariel Sharon left it and founded the centrist Kadima party. In January 2006, Sharon suffered a stroke that put him in a coma, and Deputy Prime Minister Ehud Olmert became prime minister and Kadima chairman. After the 2006 parliamentary elections, Olmert and Kadima headed a new coalition government that included the center-left Labor Party, the religious Shas party, and other factions.

Israeli-Palestinian relations deteriorated after the Islamist group Hamas won elections to the Palestinian Legislative Council (PLC) in January 2006, outpolling PA President Mahmoud Abbas's Fatah party. Over the next two years, Israel experienced regular rocket and mortar fire from the Gaza Strip, as well as some terrorist attacks; the IDF continued to stage airstrikes against militant leaders and make extensive incursions into Palestinian territory, including an invasion of the Gaza Strip in the summer of 2006. Also that summer, Israel went to war against the Lebanese Islamist militia Hezbollah after the group staged a cross-border attack. By the time a UN-brokered cease-fire took effect in mid-August, about 1,200 Lebanese, including many civilians, had been killed; 116 IDF soldiers and 43 Israeli civilians were also killed.

Olmert resigned in September 2008, after being charged in a corruption case. Foreign Minister Tzipi Livni replaced him, but she was unable to form a new majority coalition in the Knesset (parliament), prompting early elections in February 2009. While Kadima led with 28 seats, Likud (27 seats) ultimately formed a mostly right-wing government with the secular nationalist Yisrael Beiteinu (15 seats), Shas (11 seats), and other parties. The Labor Party (13 seats) also joined the coalition, leaving Kadima in opposition. The new government, headed by Likud leader Benjamin Netanyahu, took office in April 2009.

Meanwhile, unilateral cease-fires in January 2009 ended a weeks-long conflict between Israel and Hamas, which had ruled the Gaza Strip exclusively since driving out Fatah officials in a 2007 PA schism. The exact death toll from the conflict remained in dispute, but well over 1,000 Palestinians were killed, including hundreds of noncombatants. Thirteen Israelis were killed, including three civilians.

In 2010 and 2011, a series of private ships carrying food and goods attempted to break Israel's economic blockade of Gaza, which Israeli authorities had maintained to varying degrees since 2007. In May 2010, Israeli forces intercepted a six-ship flotilla from Turkey and killed nine activists on board one vessel—the Mavi Marmara—in an ensuing confrontation; a total of 632 activists were arrested and detained in Israel. The international community condemned the Israeli government for its conduct, while Israel claimed that its soldiers were acting in self-defense. A UN report concluded that Israel was legally allowed to blockade Gaza, but that it had used excessive force and should not have operated so far from Israeli shores. Israel later eased the Gaza blockade substantially.

In January 2011, the Labor Party quit the coalition government, but Defense Minister Ehud Barak and four other lawmakers resigned from Labor and started a new party, Independence, which remained in the ruling coalition.

Bouts of fighting between Israel and Gaza-based militants broke out regularly in 2011, with rocket and mortar fire into Israel prompting Israeli airstrikes and artillery bombardments (see Gaza Strip report). Two Israelis were killed by rocket fire, and hundreds were wounded. Nine people were killed and several dozen were injured in separate terrorist and militant attacks in Israel during 2011, including an attack by gunmen near the Egyptian border.

In May, thousands of Palestinians marched on Israel's borders from Syria, Lebanon, the West Bank, and Gaza to mark Al-Nakba, the Arab day of mourning, and to protest the creation of Israel. The marchers tried to breach the borders, leading to clashes with Israeli troops, and a dozen protesters were killed. In a similar incident in June, Israeli soldiers clashed with hundreds of Syrian and Palestinian protesters who entered the Golan Heights. According to Syria, Israeli troops killed 23 demonstrators; Israel disputed this account, claiming that some protesters were killed by a Syrian land mine, and that fewer people died overall.

In October 2011, Israel and Hamas negotiated a prisoner exchange whereby Hamas freed IDF soldier Gilad Shalit, who had been held captive since 2006, and Israel freed 1,027 Palestinian prisoners; 447 were released in October—mostly to Gaza, but some to the West Bank and foreign countries—and another 550 in December.

Political Rights and Civil Liberties:

Israel is an electoral democracy. A largely ceremonial president is elected by the 120-seat Knesset for seven-year terms. The prime minister is usually the leader of the largest party or coalition in the Knesset, members of which are elected by party-list proportional representation for four-year terms. At under 3 percent, Israel's vote threshold for a party to win parliamentary representation is the world's lowest, leading to the regular formation of niche parties and unstable coalitions.

Parties or candidates that deny the existence of Israel as a Jewish state, oppose the democratic system, or incite racism are prohibited. In 2009, the Knesset's central election committee voted to ban two Arab parties—Balad and the United Arab List (UAL)–Ta'al—from that year's elections, citing their alleged support for Hamas in the Gaza conflict. The ban was rapidly overturned by the Supreme Court, and the parties won three and four seats, respectively. In 2010, a Knesset plenum voted to strip Balad member Haneen Zoabi of some parliamentary privileges following her participation in the Mavi Marmara flotilla. Zoabi appealed to the High Court, and the case was pending in 2011.

Arabs enjoy equal political rights under the law but face discrimination in practice. Before 2005, Israeli identity cards classified residents by their ethnicity (such as "Jewish," "Arab," "Druze," or "Circassian"). After 2005, Jewish Israelis can often be identified by the inclusion of their Hebrew birth date. Arab Israelis currently hold 13 seats in the Knesset—though they constitute some 20 percent of the population—and no independent Arab party has ever been formally included in a governing coalition. Arabs generally do not serve in senior positions in government. Rising calls on the political right to impose a loyalty oath and to insist that Arab public officials sing the national anthem—which refers explicitly to the Jewish yearning for Israel—have encouraged Arab Israelis' political marginalization, though such measures have been rejected to date.

After Israel annexed East Jerusalem in 1967, the Arab residents were issued Israeli identity cards and given the option of obtaining Israeli citizenship, though most choose not to seek citizenship for political reasons. These noncitizens have the same rights as Israeli citizens, except the right to vote in national elections. They can vote in municipal as well as PA elections, and remain eligible to apply for Israeli citizenship. However, Israeli law strips noncitizens of their Jerusalem residency if they stay outside the city for more than three months.

A 2003 law denies citizenship and residency status to West Bank or Gaza residents married to Israeli citizens. While the measure, which affects about 15,000 couples, was criticized as blatantly discriminatory, supporters cited evidence that 14 percent of suicide bombers acquired Israeli identity cards via family reunification laws. In March 2011, the Knesset passed a law allowing the courts to revoke the citizenship of any Israeli convicted of spying, treason, or aiding the enemy. A number of rights groups and the Shin Bet security service criticized the legislation as unnecessary and overly broad.

Under the 1948 Law of Return, Jewish immigrants and their immediate families are granted Israeli citizenship and residence rights; other immigrants must apply for these rights.

Israel was ranked 36 out of 183 countries surveyed in Transparency International's 2011 Corruption Perceptions Index. Corruption scandals in recent years have implicated several senior officials. Ehud Olmert resigned as prime minister in 2008 amid an investigation into donations and other gifts he had reportedly received from a U.S. businessman over many years, as well as several other alleged misdeeds dating to his previous posts in the cabinet and as mayor of Jerusalem. In 2009, Olmert was indicted in three of these scandals; one trial began in 2010 and continued in 2011. In April 2011, the attorney general announced a pending indictment of Yisrael Beiteinu leader and current foreign minister Avigdor Lieberman on charges of money laundering, fraud, breach of trust, and tampering with a witness, though the indictment was still pending at year's end.

Press freedom is respected in Israel, and the media are vibrant and independent, though a number of threats to free expression arose in 2011 and ownership of private media is concentrated among a small number of media companies. All Israeli newspapers are privately owned and freely criticize government policy. In November 2011, the Knesset advanced legislation that would increase the financial penalty for libel—beyond compensation for actual damages—by 300,000 shekels (US$85,000); the proposed bill was criticized vociferously by press freedom organizations and most media outlets. The Israel Broadcasting Authority operates public radio and television services, and commercial broadcasts are widely available. Most Israelis subscribe to cable or satellite television. In September 2011, the financially troubled Channel 10 television station was allegedly pressured by investors into apologizing for a story on a supporter of Prime Minister Benjamin Netanyahu, American businessman Sheldon Adelson; in addition, both Netanyahu and his wife initiated libel suits against the station in 2011. Internet access is widespread and unrestricted.

Print articles on security matters are subject to a military censor, and while the scope of permissible reporting is generally broad, press freedom advocates have warned of more aggressive censorship in recent years. In 2010, a widely condemned gag order on the case of journalist Anat Kam was lifted, revealing that she had been charged with "serious espionage" for giving Haaretz newspaper reporter Uri Blau over 2,000 classified military documents during her military service. Kam eventually pleaded guilty to a lesser charge of "leaking classified material" and was sentenced to four and a half years in prison in October 2011. The Government Press Office (GPO) has occasionally refused to provide press cards to journalists, especially Palestinians, to restrict them from entering Israel, citing security considerations.

Legislation passed in March 2011 requires the state to fine or withdraw funds from local authorities and other state-funded groups that hold events marking Al-Nakba on Israeli independence day, that support armed resistance or "racism" against Israel, or that desecrate the state flag or national symbols. Both Arab rights and freedom of expression groups criticized the law as an unnecessary and provocative restriction. In July, the Knesset passed the so-called Boycott Law, which exposes Israeli individuals and groups to civil lawsuits if they advocate an economic, cultural, or academic boycott of the State of Israel or West Bank settlements, even without clear proof of financial damage. Petitions filed against the law were pending at year's end.

While Israel's founding documents define it as a "Jewish and democratic state," freedom of religion is respected. Christian, Muslim, and Baha'i communities have jurisdiction over their own members in matters of marriage, divorce, and burial. The Orthodox establishment generally governs these matters among Jews, drawing objections from many non-Orthodox and secular Jews. Marriages between Jews and non-Jews are not recognized by the state unless conducted abroad, and legislation allowing nonreligious civil unions is restricted to two parties with no official religion. In a landmark case in 2011, one Israeli Jew won the right to an identity card that excluded his Hebrew birth date. A 2010 proposal to give the Chief Rabbinate exclusive control over the conversion process prompted significant opposition from non-Orthodox denominations, and the bill remained frozen in 2011. Another conversion bill giving the chief rabbi of the IDF—and not the Chief Rabbinate—ultimate control over soldiers' conversions was also stalled in the Knesset during the year. In June, two prominent rabbis were arrested for endorsing racism after they supported a highly controversial religious book that justifies the killing of non-Jewish civilians in "times of war" in order to save Jews.

Muslim and Christian religious authorities are occasionally discriminated against in resource allocation and upkeep of religious sites, though the state budget officially assigns funds according to need. Citing security concerns, Israel occasionally restricts Muslim worshippers' access to the Temple Mount, or Haram al-Sharif, in Jerusalem. In October 2011, Jewish extremists burned and vandalized a mosque in the northern village of Tuba-Zangariya, leading to protests by hundreds of residents and minor clashes with police.

Primary and secondary education is universal, with instruction for the Arab minority based on the common curriculum used by the Jewish majority, but conducted in Arabic. In 2010, the government mandated the teaching of Arabic in all state schools. School quality is generally worse in mostly Arab municipalities, and Arab children have reportedly had difficulty registering at mostly Jewish schools. Israel's universities are open to all students based on merit, and have long been centers for dissent. University administrators in 2010 generally rebuffed calls by a number of civic organizations to censure or fire faculty for allegedly enforcing "anti-Zionist" curriculums and attitudes in the classroom, a charge echoed by Education Minister Gideon Sa'ar. Periodic road closures and other security measures restrict access to Israeli universities for West Bank and Gaza residents.

Freedoms of assembly and association are respected. Israel hosts an active civil society, and demonstrations are widely permitted, though groups committed to the destruction of Israel are not allowed to demonstrate. Beginning in July 2011, hundreds of thousands of Israelis took part in a series of protests over the cost of living in the country. For nearly 60 days, thousands of protesters in Tel Aviv lived in tents along a central boulevard, while in both August and September, about 400,000 people participated in "social justice" demonstrations across the country.

In 2011, two bills that aimed to cap the contributions of foreign governments to so-called "political" nongovernmental organizations (NGOs) at 20,000 shekels (US$5,700) passed through the government's ministerial committee, drawing protests from both domestic and international rights groups; both measures were later procedurally stalled by Netanyahu. The laws were aimed at a number of left-wing NGOs that have been highly critical of Israeli policies in the West Bank and Gaza Strip.

Workers may join unions of their choice and have the right to strike and bargain collectively. Three-quarters of the workforce either belong to Histadrut, the national labor federation, or are covered by its social programs and bargaining agreements. Both sector-specific and general strikes are common, but typically last fewer than 24 hours. About 100,000 legal foreign workers enjoy wage protections, medical insurance, and guarantees against employer exploitation. However, those who leave their original employers can be stripped of such rights and may face deportation, and a March 2011 amendment to the Israel Entry Law restricts the number of times a foreign worker can change employers and may limit them to working in a specific geographical area or field. Advocacy groups claim that there are at least 100,000 illegal workers in Israel, many of whom are exploited. In 2010, Israel began construction of a barrier along its border with Egypt to prevent undocumented African migrants from entering.

The judiciary is independent and regularly rules against the government. The Supreme Court hears direct petitions from citizens and Palestinian residents of the West Bank and Gaza Strip, and the state generally adheres to court rulings. In November 2011, Netanyahu blocked a bill that subjected candidates for the court to a public hearing and possible veto by the Knesset Constitution Committee. Netanyahu also opposed a November bill that aimed to limit the scope and nature of civic petitions to the Supreme Court. That same month, two bills concerning the appointment of Supreme Court justices—one related to an age threshold and another to the selection of Israeli Bar Association (IBA) representatives on the Judge Selection Commission—passed through the Knesset Justice Committee, but were not voted on by year's end. Later in November, the IBA selected the first Arab member of the commission.

The Emergency Powers (Detention) Law of 1979 provides for indefinite administrative detention without trial. According to the human rights group B'Tselem, by year's end there were 4,772 Palestinians in Israeli jails: 3,753 serving sentences, 131 detainees, 609 being detained until the conclusion of legal proceedings, 278 administrative detainees, and 1 detained under the Illegal Combatants Law. A temporary order in effect since 2006 permits the detention of suspects accused of security offenses for 96 hours without judicial oversight, compared with 24 hours for other detainees. Israel outlawed the use of torture to extract security information in 2000, but milder forms of coercion are permissible when the prisoner is believed to have vital information about impending terrorist attacks. Human rights groups criticize Israel for continuing to engage in what they consider torture. Interrogation methods include binding detainees to a chair in painful positions, slapping, kicking, and threatening violence against detainees and their relatives.

According to the Israeli Prison Service, as of October 2011, there were 164 Palestinian minors (ages 12–17) in Israeli jails. Most are serving two-month sentences—handed down by a Special Court for Minors created in 2009—for throwing stones or other projectiles at Israeli troops in the West Bank; acquittals on such charges are very rare. East Jerusalem Palestinian minors are tried in Israeli civil juvenile courts. In July 2011, a B'Tselem report accused the IDF of unfairly arresting and judging minors; the IDF denied the allegations.

Arab citizens of Israel receive inferior education, housing, and social services relative to the Jewish population. According to a 2010 report by the NGO Mosawa, Arab Israelis own only 3.5 percent of the land in Israel and receive 3 to 5 percent of government spending, figures that were challenged by the government. The government subsequently implemented a $214 million investment plan to improve housing, transportation, and economic infrastructure in 12 Arab communities. Arab Israelis, except for the Druze minority, are not subject to the military draft, though they may volunteer. Those who do not serve are ineligible for the associated benefits, including scholarships and housing loans.

At the end of 2011, the courts were reviewing the constitutionality of a bill, advanced in the first of three readings by the Knesset in March, that would allow many Jewish communities to exclude would-be residents based on vague criteria of "social suitability" or compatibility with the communities' "unique characteristics." The measure was seen by critics as an attempt to legalize restrictions that could be used to bar Arab residents. More explicitly, Zionist residency rules adopted by a number of communities beginning in 2008 had been struck down by the courts in 2009.

There are about 110,000 Bedouin in the Negev region, most of whom live in dozens of towns and villages that are not recognized by the state; there are 14 recognized Bedouin towns. Those in unrecognized villages cannot claim social services and have no official land rights, and the government routinely demolishes their unlicensed structures. International and domestic human rights groups accuse the government of pervasive land and housing discrimination against the historically nomadic Bedouin. In July 2011, the state initiated a lawsuit against a group of Bedouin to cover the costs of repeatedly demolishing homes in the unrecognized village of Al-Araqib, which the state owns but to which the Bedouin claim historic rights.

The state's Israeli Lands Administration owns 93 percent of the land in Israel; 13 percent of that is owned by the Jewish National Fund (JNF). In 2005, the Supreme Court and attorney general ruled that the JNF could no longer market property only to Jews. The Knesset made several unsuccessful attempts to override those rulings. Security measures can lead to delays at checkpoints and in public places. By law, all citizens must carry national identification cards. The West Bank security barrier restricts the movement of some East Jerusalem residents. Formal and informal local rules that prevent driving on Jewish holidays can also hamper freedom of movement.

Women have achieved substantial parity at almost all levels of Israeli society. However, Arab women and religious Jewish women face some discrimination and societal pressures that negatively affect their professional, political, and social lives. In addition, many ultra-Orthodox communities enforce gender separation, impinging on women's rights in nearby public places, including public transportation. The trafficking of women for prostitution has become a problem in recent years; both the United Nations and the U.S. State Department have identified Israel as a top destination for trafficked women. The government has opened shelters for victims, and a 2006 law mandates prison terms of up to 20 years for perpetrators. In what was considered a notable achievement for the rule of law and the punishment of violence against women, former president Moshe Katsav was sentenced in March 2011 to seven years in prison for rape committed while he was tourism minister in the 1990s.

Nonbiological parents in same-sex partnerships are eligible for guardianship rights. Openly gay Israelis are permitted to serve in the armed forces.

Italy

Political Rights: 1
Civil Liberties: 1*
Status: Free

Population: 60,769,000
Capital: Rome

Ratings Change: Italy's civil liberties rating improved from 2 to 1 due to a reduction in the concentration of state and private media outlets following Silvio Berlusconi's resignation as prime minister in November.

Ten-Year Ratings Timeline For Year Under Review (Political Rights, Civil Liberties, Status)

2002	2003	2004	2005	2006	2007	2008	2009	2010	2011
1,1F	1,1F	1,1F	1,1F	1,1F	1,1F	1,2F	1,2F	1,2F	1,1F

Overview: **A technocratic government led by Mario Monti, a former member of the European Commission, took power in November 2011, after the country's economic woes forced Prime Minister Silvio Berlusconi to step down. Opposition to unpopular austerity measures had led to massive protests that turned violent the previous month.**

Italy was unified under the constitutional monarchy of Piedmont and Sardinia in the 19th century. Its liberal period ended in 1922 with the rise Benito Mussolini and his Fascist Party, which eventually led the country to defeat in World War II. A referendum in 1946 replaced the monarchy with a republican form of government. The "clean hands" corruption trials of the early 1990s prompted the collapse of the major political factions that had dominated postwar Italian politics—the Christian Democrats, the Communists, and the Socialists. Since that time, many new parties and coalitions have emerged.

Parliamentary elections in 2006 ushered in a new center-left coalition government led by Romano Prodi, leaving outgoing prime minister Silvio Berlusconi's center-right bloc in opposition for the first time since 2001. Berlusconi's most recent premiership had been marred by abortive attempts to prosecute him on money-laundering, fraud, and tax evasion charges, and by his personal domination of the national media, including state outlets and his extensive private holdings. However, Prodi's new government proved unstable; it lost key votes in Parliament over Italy's troop presence in Afghanistan in 2007, and it finally collapsed after a no-confidence vote in January 2008.

Berlusconi's rightist coalition, People of Freedom (PDL), handily won early parliamentary elections in April 2008, capturing a total of 344 seats in the lower house and 174 in the Senate in combination with two smaller allies. A center-left coalition led by Rome mayor Walter Veltroni's new Democratic Party placed second, with 246 seats in the lower house and 132 seats in the Senate. Berlusconi ran on pledges to crack down on crime and illegal immigration, and the new Parliament passed a number of measures on those issues in 2008 and 2009.

In the month preceding the March 2010 regional elections, which resulted in key losses for the center-left opposition, the state-owned RAI television network suspended political discussion on its three channels, ostensibly due to the difficulty of ensuring "equality of treatment" for all parties. Critics viewed the move as an attempt by Berlusconi's government to limit potentially critical commentary.

The country's major trade unions called a national strike in June 2010 to protest fiscal austerity measures taken by the government in response to a global economic downturn that began in late 2008. In 2011, Italy's growing public debt, at 120 percent of gross domestic product, fueled international concerns about the sustainability of the country's finances. A crucial austerity package was passed by both houses of Parliament in November, allowing the sale of state assets and hikes in the value-added tax, the retirement age, and fuel prices. The increasingly unpopular Berlusconi had pledged to resign once the legislation was approved, and he duly made way for a technocratic government led by the respected economist Mario Monti, a former member of the European Commission. The new government ushered yet another austerity package through Parliament in December.

In the months leading up to his resignation, Berlusconi had faced a series of personal legal difficulties that damaged his political standing and apparently influenced legislative priorities. In February, women across Italy held demonstrations to protest the prime minister's multiple sex scandals, including one in which he allegedly paid an underage girl for sex. In March, Berlusconi appeared in court for the first time since 2003 to face charges of corruption. The lower house approved a bill in April that would cut short the length of some trials and potentially end a bribery case against Berlusconi, though it had yet to pass the Senate at year's end. The prime minister was cleared in a fraud and embezzlement case in October. Also that month, the lower house resumed discussion of a bill passed by the Senate in June 2010 that would limit the use of wiretaps and force news websites to publish corrections automatically. The bill, which was seen primarily as an effort to keep embarrassing information about politicians out of the news, was opposed by all of the major newspapers in Italy.

Political Rights and Civil Liberties: Italy is an electoral democracy. The president, whose role is largely ceremonial but sometimes politically influential, is elected for a seven-year term by Parliament and representatives of the regions. Giorgio Napolitano, a former Communist, was selected for the post in 2006. The president chooses the prime minister, who is often, but not always, the leader of the largest party in the elected, 630-seat lower house, the Chamber of Deputies. The upper house is the Senate, with 315 elected seats. Members of both chambers serve five-year terms. The next national elections are due to be held in April 2013, unless snap elections are held prior to that date.

The president may appoint up to five senators for life, and in November 2011, Napolitano used this mechanism to make Mario Monti a member of Parliament, smoothing his political path to the premiership. Monti's technocratic government received the support of the elected Parliament, but he is not himself an elected officeholder.

A 1993 electoral law replaced the existing system of proportional representation with single-member districts for most of the seats in Parliament. The move was designed to reduce the number of political parties that could obtain seats and ensure a more stable majority for the parties in power; Italians had seen more than 50 governments since 1945. However, in 2005, proportional representation was restored, with a provision awarding at least 54 percent of the seats in the lower house to the winning party or coalition, no matter how small its margin of victory. For the Senate, victory in a given region assures the winning party or coalition a 55 percent majority of that region's allotment of seats. Just 6 parties won seats in the lower house in the 2008 elections, down from 26 in the previous elections.

The Democratic Party has been the main party of the left since it was formed through a merger of multiple smaller parties in 2007, and it remained in opposition during Silvio Berlusconi's premiership. Berlusconi's right-leaning PDL first emerged as a multiparty electoral alliance in 2008. In 2009, it became a single party following a formal merger between Berlusconi's Forza Italia party and the formerly neofascist National Alliance party. The Northern League, though allied with the PDL, decided to remain an independent party. The PDL fractured in July 2010, after Gianfranco Fini—former leader of the National Alliance and the Speaker of the Chamber of Deputies—split with Berlusconi over the latter's legal woes.

Corruption remains a central issue in politics. Italy was ranked 69 out of 183 countries surveyed in Transparency International's 2011 Corruption Perceptions Index, the second-lowest ranking in Western Europe. Berlusconi has faced numerous corruption charges over the years, but has never been convicted. In February 2011, the Constitutional Court lifted Berlusconi's immunity from prosecution under a law passed in March 2010, which had allowed the prime minister to postpone any trial for up to 18 months. Berlusconi had insisted that he could not be called to trial while serving as prime minister because of his government duties. As of the end of 2011, he faced three trials: one for allegedly bribing the British lawyer David Mills, one regarding the corruption of senators, and one for allegedly paying an underage prostitute for sex.

Freedoms of speech and of the press are constitutionally guaranteed. However, while Berlusconi was prime minister, he controlled up to 90 percent of the country's broadcast media through state-owned outlets and his own private media holdings. There are many newspapers and news magazines, most with regional bases. Newspapers are primarily run by political parties or owned by large media groups. Internet access is generally unrestricted.

Religious freedom is constitutionally guaranteed and respected in practice. Although Roman Catholicism is the dominant faith and the state grants some privileges to the Catholic Church, there is no official religion. The state provides support, if requested, to other sects represented in the country. Agreements between the government and a number of religious groups have been signed, but an omnibus religious freedom law has yet to be passed.

In March 2011, the European Court of Human Rights ruled that crucifixes traditionally hung in school classrooms across the country do not violate the rights of non-Catholics. The decision overruled a 2009 decision by the same court that banned such crosses. Academic freedom is respected.

Italians are free to assemble and form social and political associations, and about 35 percent of the workforce is unionized. The constitution recognizes the right to strike, with the exception of those employed in essential services and a number of self-employed professions, such as lawyers, doctors, and truck drivers. Protests that were sparked by proposed budget cuts and inspired by the global Occupy movement turned violent in October. At least 70 people were injured, many of them police officers.

The judicial system is undermined by long trial delays and the influence of organized crime. Despite legal prohibitions against torture, there have been reports of excessive use of force by police, particularly against illegal immigrants. In March 2010, a Genoa court confirmed the convictions of 15 police officers, prison guards, and doctors who had been found guilty of mistreating protesters detained during the 2001 Group of Eight summit. The court also overturned the initial acquittals of 29 others involved in mistreating the detainees. Some prisons continue to suffer from overcrowding.

The country continued to make gains against organized crime in 2011. In April, police arrested the head of an organized crime group in the Puglia region and seized over $300 million in assets from the 'Ndrangheta, a criminal organization based in Calabria. In May, police captured a leader of the Campania-based Camorra organized crime group who had been on the run for nine years.

Italy is a major entry point for undocumented immigrants trying to reach Europe, and the government has been criticized for holding illegal immigrants in overcrowded and unhygienic conditions and denying them access to lawyers and other experts. A government crackdown on illegal immigration that began in 2008 has led to the arrest of hundreds of people. A 2009 immigration law imposes fines on illegal immigrants and grants authorities the power to detain them for up to six months without charge. Political turmoil in Tunisia and Libya during 2011 led to a sharp increase in the number of undocumented immigrants landing on Italy's shores. By August, around 52,000 immigrants had arrived since the beginning of the year.

Women benefit from generous maternity-leave provisions, equality in the workforce, and considerable educational opportunities. However, violence against women continues to be a problem, and female political representation is low for the region. Women hold 21 percent of the seats in the Chamber of Deputies. Italy is a destination country for the trafficking of women and children for sexual and labor exploitation. The government has made efforts to tackle the problem by increasing the prosecution of traffickers; it also finances nongovernmental organizations that work to raise awareness of the problem and support trafficking victims.

Jamaica

Political Rights: 2
Civil Liberties: 3
Status: Free

Population: 2,709,000
Capital: Kingston

Ten-Year Ratings Timeline For Year Under Review (Political Rights, Civil Liberties, Status)

2002	2003	2004	2005	2006	2007	2008	2009	2010	2011
2,3F	2,3F	2,3F	2,3F	2,3F	2,3F	2,3F	2,3F	2,3F	2,3F

Overview: **In August 2011, Jamaican drug lord Christopher "Dudus" Coke pleaded guilty in the United States to drug trafficking charges. The following month, Jamaican prime minister Bruce Golding resigned, likely as a result of public anger over his handling of the Coke situation. Golding was replaced as prime minister and leader of the Jamaica Labour Party (JLP) by Andrew Holness, who called for early elections in December. The People's National Party (PNP) won a strong parliamentary majority, and PNP leader Portia Simpson Miller became prime minister.**

Jamaica achieved independence from Britain in 1962. Since then, power has alternated between the social democratic People's National Party (PNP) and the more conservative Jamaica Labour Party (JLP). In September 2007, the JLP won a majority of seats in the House of Representatives, ending 18 years in power for the PNP. JLP leader Bruce Golding became the new prime minister.

Under Golding, Jamaica struggled with high levels of crime, sluggish economic growth, and a public sector in need of major reform. In 2009, an all-time high of 1,682 homicides were reported. Over half of these were gang related, and only 21 percent were resolved in court. The situation improved slightly in 2011, after police crackdowns on gang violence; according to police statistics, the murder rate during the first three months of the year fell 44 percent from their rate over the same period in 2010. The government also established a commission, the Independent Investigation of Commissions, to investigate incidents of civilian shootings, though local human rights organizations have expressed doubt whether the organization will have the resources it needs to function effectively.

Long-standing relationships between elected representatives and organized crime, in which criminal gangs guaranteed voter turnout in certain neighborhoods in exchange for political favors and protection, received special scrutiny in recent years as the U.S. government pressed for the extradition of alleged drug trafficker Christopher "Dudus" Coke. The gang Coke reputedly led, the Shower Posse, was based in Tivoli Gardens, an area of Kingston that Golding represented in Parliament. In April 2010, the *Washington Post* reported that a JLP government official had signed a $400,000 contract with the U.S. lobbying firm Manatt, Phelps & Phillips to fight Coke's extradition. The public outcry in the United States and Jamaica forced Golding in May 2010 to order Jamaican security forces into Tivoli Gardens to arrest Coke, leading to days of violence in which over 70 civilians and several police personnel were killed. Coke was finally apprehended in late June, reportedly on his way to surrender at the U.S. embassy. In August 2011, after being extradited to the United States, he pleaded guilty to drug trafficking and assault charges, and faced up to 21 years in prison under a plea bargain. Coke had not been sentenced by year's end.

Prime Minister Golding suddenly announced his resignation in September 2011, a move widely interpreted as fallout from the Coke affair, which had caused Golding to lose support within his own party and among the electorate. Observers speculated that the managed transition to a successor was a preemptive political maneuver to keep the JLP as a viable political contender. In October, the JLP elected Minister of Education Andrew Holness to become Golding's successor as party leader and prime minister. The transition to Holness, who was 39 years old, was seen by some as marking a generational shift within the JLP, and possibly within Jamaican party politics in general.

Holness called for early general elections at the end of the year. On December 29, the PNP was overwhelmingly victorious in those elections, winning 41 seats in Parliament, while the JLP took only 22. Portia Simpson Miller became prime minister; she had previously held the position in 2006 and 2007.

Political Rights and Civil Liberties: Jamaica is an electoral democracy. The British monarch is represented as head of state by a governor general, who is nominated by the prime minister and approved by the monarch. Following legislative elections, the leader of the party or coalition holding a majority in the lower house is appointed as prime minister by the governor general. The bicameral Parliament consists of the 60-member House of Representatives, elected for five years, and the 21-member Senate, with 13 senators appointed on the advice of the prime minister and 8 on the advice of the opposition leader.

Powerful criminal gangs in some urban neighborhoods maintain influence over voter turnout in return for political favors, which has called into question the legitimacy of election results in those areas.

Corruption remains a serious problem in Jamaica. Government whistle-blowers who object to official acts of waste, fraud, or abuse of power are not well protected by Jamaican law, as is required under the Inter-American Convention against Corruption. Implementation of the 2002 Corruption Prevention Act has been problematic. Jamaica was ranked 86 out of 183 countries surveyed in Transparency International's 2011 Corruption Perceptions Index.

The constitutional right to free expression is generally respected. While newspapers are independent and free of government control, circulation is generally low. Broadcast media are largely state owned but are open to pluralistic points of view. Journalists occasionally face intimidation in the run-up to elections. The country enacted an access to information law in 2002.

Freedom of religion is constitutionally protected and generally respected in practice. While laws banning Obeah—an Afro-Caribbean shamanistic religion—remain on the books, they are not actively enforced. The government does not hinder academic freedom.

Freedoms of association and assembly are generally respected. Jamaica has a small but robust civil society and active community groups. Approximately 20 percent of the workforce is unionized. Labor unions are politically influential and have the right to strike.

The judicial system is headed by the Supreme Court and includes a court of appeals and several magistrates' courts. The Trinidad-based Caribbean Court of Justice became the highest appellate court for Jamaica in 2005. A growing backlog of cases and a shortage of court staff at all levels continue to undermine the justice system.

Extrajudicial killings by police are a major problem in Jamaica, accounting for 12 percent of murders each year, according to Amnesty International. Since 2006, the government has paid an estimated J$365 million (US$3.8 million) to victims of such violence, and it reportedly owes an additional $400 million (US$4.4 million). Ill-treatment by prison guards has also been reported, and conditions in detention centers and prisons are abysmal.

Kingston's insular "garrison" communities remain the epicenter of most violence and serve as safe havens for gangs. Jamaica is a transit point for cocaine shipped from Colombia to U.S. markets, and much of the island's violence is the result of warfare between drug gangs known as posses. Contributing factors include the deportation of Jamaican-born criminals from the United States and an illegal weapons trade.

Violence against gay, lesbian, and transgendered individuals remains a major concern. Amnesty International has identified homosexuals in Jamaica as a marginalized group, openly targeted for extreme harassment and violence. Same-sex intercourse is punishable by 10 years in prison with hard labor. The continuing existence of such laws is considered a violation against the right to equal protection under the International Covenant for Civil and Political Rights, to which Jamaica is a party. Violence against homosexuals is frequently ignored by the police, who fail to make arrests in such cases. The antigay lyrics of Jamaican entertainers, particularly dancehall singers, remain a source of contention.

Legal protections for women are poorly enforced, and violence and discrimination remain widespread. Women are underrepresented in government, holding just eight seats in the House of Representatives.

Japan

Political Rights: 1
Civil Liberties: 2
Status: Free

Population: 128,100,000
Capital: Tokyo

Ten-Year Ratings Timeline For Year Under Review (Political Rights, Civil Liberties, Status)

2002	2003	2004	2005	2006	2007	2008	2009	2010	2011
1,2F	1,2F	1,2F	1,2F	1,2F	1,2F	1,2F	1,2F	1,2F	1,2F

Overview: **In the midst of a faltering economy, Japan was hit by a massive earthquake and subsequent tsunami in March 2011 that caused widespread devastation and a nuclear meltdown at the Fukushima Daiichi Nuclear Power Plant. Criticism of the government's response to the disaster led to the resignation of Prime Minister Naoto Kan and his**

replacement in August by Yoshihiko Noda. Antinuclear power rallies and efforts to rebuild the affected areas and to support the hundreds of thousands displaced by the disasters continued throughout the year.

Japan has operated as a parliamentary democracy with a largely symbolic monarchy since its defeat in World War II. The Liberal Democratic Party (LDP) presided over Japan's economic ascent while maintaining close security ties with the United States during the Cold War. The so-called "iron triangle"—the close relationship between the LDP, banks, and big-business representatives—was a key factor behind Japan's economic success. The LDP government mandated that corporations, specifically construction firms in charge of major public-works projects, rely on banks for capital, and the banks, in turn, took large equity stakes in the companies. Over time, companies engaged in politically expedient but financially unviable projects in order to reap government rewards, and the iron triangle became a major source of corruption in the government. The economy ran into trouble in the early 1990s, following a collapse in the stock and real estate markets, but slowly recovered in 2002.

Shinzo Abe became prime minister in 2006, though his tenure was marred by repeated scandals and political gaffes. Abe stepped down in September 2007 after the LDP lost control of the legislature's upper chamber in the July elections to the Democratic Party of Japan (DPJ).

Yasuo Fukuda, who succeeded Abe, failed to rally support and govern effectively, and he resigned in September 2008. Former foreign minister Taro Aso, the LDP secretary general, succeeded him later that month. The Aso government focused on rejuvenating the faltering economy, which remained burdened with a government debt equal to almost 200 percent of the country's gross domestic product.

The LDP's nearly 55-year dominance in the legislature's lower chamber ended when the DPJ captured 308 seats in the August 2009 elections, and Yukio Hatoyama became prime minister. The DPJ's platform challenged many of the LDP's long-standing policies, including greater independence from U.S. influence, improved relations with neighboring Asian countries, and a more decentralized and accountable government concerned with social welfare and environmental issues. However, confronted with an economic recession and increased regional tensions, Hatoyama shifted his foreign policy focus back to the United States for security guarantees. The prime minister also failed to implement a number of his campaign promises, including closing the controversial U.S. military base on the island of Okinawa. Hatoyama announced his resignation in June 2010, partly due to a financial scandal involving DPJ secretary general Ichiro Ozawa.

On June 4, Finance Minister Naoto Kan was chosen prime minister, though his approval ratings plummeted after he proposed raising the country's sales tax from 5 percent to 10 percent. Following this unpopular move, the DPJ captured only 44 of the 121 seats at stake in the July elections to the legislature's upper chamber, while a coalition of the LDP and two smaller parties took 61 seats. Kan continued to face significant domestic and international challenges, including continued inflation, a faltering economy, and diplomatic disputes with China and Russia.

On March 11, 2011, Japan was hit by a 9.0 earthquake just off the east coast of Tohoku, which triggered a subsequent tsunami. The majority of buildings and critical infrastructure were damaged or destroyed, and there was a massive toll on human lives. The National Policy Agency of Japan has reported that the known death toll for the earthquake and tsunami is just over 18,000, though the real toll may never be known. The overall costs of the earthquake are estimated at over $300 billion. The Fukushima Daiichi Nuclear Power Plant also suffered severe damage; reactor cooling systems were debilitated, triggering nuclear meltdown. Widespread radioactive contamination led to an evacuation of the surrounding area, displacing several hundred thousand residents.

Amid plunging approval ratings over the government's handling of the crises, Kan resigned in August, and Finance Minister Yoshihiko Noda was elected in DPJ preliminary elections that same month to succeed Kan. Noda will serve as prime minister for the duration of Kan's regular term, until fall 2012, when regular DPJ presidential elections will be held.

Political Rights and Civil Liberties: Japan is an electoral democracy. The prime minister—the leader of the majority party or coalition in the bicameral legislature's (Diet's) lower chamber, the House of Representatives—serves as head of government. Members of the 480-seat House of Representatives serve four-year terms; 300 are elected in single-member constituencies and 180 are elected by party list in 11 regional districts. The 242-seat upper chamber, the House of Councillors, consists of 146 members elected in multiseat constituencies and 96 elected by national party list; members serve six-year terms, with half facing election every three years. Emperor Akihito serves as the ceremonial head of state.

Although several political parties compete for power, the center-right LDP dominated for almost 55 years. The DPJ's victory in the August 2009 elections to the House of Representatives opened the way for the development of a two-party system.

Significant reform efforts have focused on battling corruption stemming from the iron triangle system, mostly by loosening ties between the government and big business. Although Japan is a signatory of the U.N. Convention against Corruption, the Diet has not yet ratified it into law. In January 2011, Ichiro Ozawa, the LDP candidate who lost to Naoto Kan in the 2010 elections, and three of his aides were indicted for under-reporting income and violating campaign finance laws. The case went to trial in October and was expected to last through March 2012. In March, Japan's foreign minister Seiji Maehara resigned after admitting he accepted a political donation from a foreign national, also violating campaign finance laws. Japan was ranked 14 out of 183 countries surveyed in Transparency International's 2011 Corruption Perceptions Index.

Japan's press is private and independent, but the presence of press clubs, or kisha kurabu, even under the more liberal DPJ, continues to be an obstacle to press freedom. Press clubs ensure homogeneity of news coverage by fostering close relationships between the major media and bureaucrats and politicians. Government officials often give club members exclusive access to political information, leading journalists to avoid writing critical stories about the government and reducing the media's ability to pressure politicians for greater transparency and accountability. Internet access is not restricted.

Japanese of all faiths can worship freely. Religious groups are not required to be licensed, but registering with government authorities as a "religious corporation" brings tax benefits and other advantages. There are no restrictions on academic freedom.

The constitution guarantees freedoms of assembly and association, and there are active human rights, social welfare, and environmental groups. After the Fukushima nuclear crisis, several antinuclear power rallies were held in Tokyo. The largest demonstration took place on September 19, with more than 20,000 people calling for the immediate closure of Japan's nuclear reactors and for the creation of a new energy policy centered on renewable energy sources. Prime Minister Yoshihiko Noda responded by acknowledging the need for greater safety standards and a long-term goal to reduce dependency on nuclear energy. In November, Japanese farmers led rallies opposing Japan's participation in the Trans-Pacific Partnership, concerned about potential effects on their livelihoods. Trade unions are independent, and with the exception of public sector employees, all unionized workers have the right to strike.

Japan's judiciary is independent. There are several levels of courts, and suspects are generally given fair public trials by an impartial tribunal within three months of being detained. In 2009, a new *saiban-in* (lay judge) system was instituted for serious criminal cases. The judicial panel is composed of a mix of saiban-in selected from the general public and professional judges, who together determine the guilt and/or sentence of the defendants. The Justice Ministry is scheduled to conduct a full evaluation of the saiban-in system in 2012. While arbitrary arrest and imprisonment are not practiced, there is potential for abuse due to a law that allows the police to detain suspects for up to 23 days without charge in order to extract confessions. Prison conditions comply with international standards, though prison officials have been known to use physical and psychological intimidation to enforce discipline or elicit confessions.

The constitution prohibits discrimination based on race, creed, sex, or social status. However, Japan's estimated three million burakumin—descendants of feudal-era outcasts—and the indigenous Ainu minority suffer from entrenched societal discrimination that prevents them from gaining equal access to housing and employment opportunities. Foreign-born populations, Koreans in particular, suffer similar disadvantages.

Although women in Japan enjoy legal equality, discrimination in employment and sexual harassment on the job are common. Violence against women often goes unreported due to concerns about family reputation and other social mores. Japanese courts continue to hold a no-compensation policy towards comfort women—World War II–era sex slaves—despite international pressure to provide reparations. Japan is a destination, source, and transit country for people trafficked for forced labor and sexual exploitation.

Jordan

Political Rights: 6
Civil Liberties: 5
Status: Not Free

Population: 6,632,000
Capital: Amman

Ten-Year Ratings Timeline For Year Under Review (Political Rights, Civil Liberties, Status)

2002	2003	2004	2005	2006	2007	2008	2009	2010	2011
6,5PF	5,5PF	5,4PF	5,4PF	5,4PF	5,4PF	5,5PF	6,5NF	6,5NF	6,5NF

Overview: **Although demands for political reform grew as the year progressed, Jordan's King Abdullah avoided the major challenges to his rule that characterized other uprisings across the Middle East and North Africa in 2011. Constitutional amendments and a government reshuffle allowed the king to temporarily alleviate popular discontent. However, little improvement was made to Jordan's record on corruption and press freedom by year's end.**

The Hashemite Kingdom of Jordan, then known as Transjordan, was established as a League of Nations mandate under British control in 1921 and won full independence in 1946. The 46-year reign of King Hussein, which began in 1953, featured a massive influx of Palestinian refugees, the occupation of the West Bank by Israel in 1967, and numerous assassinations and coup attempts. Nevertheless, with political and civil liberties tightly restricted, Hussein proved adept at co-opting his political opponents.

When Crown Prince Abdullah II succeeded his father in 1999, the kingdom faced severe economic problems. Jordan's 1994 peace treaty with Israel had failed to improve conditions for most of the population, and Abdullah began major economic reforms. Meanwhile, additional restrictions on the media, public protests, and civil society were imposed after Islamists, leftists, and Jordanians of Palestinian descent staged demonstrations to demand the annulment of the 1994 treaty and express support for the Palestinian uprising (intifada) that began in 2000. The year 2001 began a period of more than two years in which Abdullah ruled by decree and in which due process and personal freedoms were curtailed. The king allowed reasonably free and transparent—though not fair—parliamentary and municipal elections in 2003. In an informal understanding with the palace, dissident leftist and Islamist groups gained limited freedom of expression and political participation in exchange for silencing their critiques of Jordan's pro-U.S. foreign policy.

The relationship between the government and political parties remained strained, however. In 2007, security forces arrested nine members of the Islamic Action Front (IAF), the main opposition party, before that year's municipal and parliamentary elections. Only a handful of IAF candidates won seats in the polls, which were marred by irregularities. A new law in 2008 required parties to have broader membership bases, and the number of registered parties consequently fell to 14, from 37.

The king unexpectedly dismissed parliament in November 2009 and ruled by decree without elections until November 2010. International observers deemed the November 2010 polls to have been technically well conducted, but the IAF boycotted them, citing structural biases that guaranteed the success of the king's traditional supporters.

Jordan largely avoided the widespread political unrest that swept across the Middle East in 2011. Calls for reform did escalate late in the year, though, resulting in the October resignation of Prime Minister Marouf al-Bakhit and all but four Cabinet ministers. The king replaced Bakhit with Awn Khasawneh, a former judge at the International Court of Justice considered friendly to reform. While the king's actions aimed to placate popular demands, they have not yet produced significant change. The IAF has no formal role in the new government. Both the king and the prime minister have promised to grant parliament a direct role in forming governments, as well as to hold a "public debate" over changes to the election law, but the timeline for such shifts remained unclear.

Political Rights and Civil Liberties:

Jordan is not an electoral democracy. King Abdullah II holds broad executive powers, appoints and dismisses the prime minister and cabinet, and may dissolve the bicameral National Assembly at his discretion. The 120 members of the lower house of the National Assembly, the Chamber of Deputies, are elected through universal adult suffrage. The Chamber of Deputies may approve, reject, or amend legislation proposed by the cabinet, but its ability to initiate legislation is limited. It cannot enact laws without the assent of the 55-seat upper house, the Senate, whose members are appointed by the king. Members of both houses serve four-year terms. Regional governors are appointed by the central government.

Voters must choose a single candidate in what are generally multiseat districts. Reformers have long called for a move toward proportional representation, arguing that the existing system encourages voting based on tribal ties rather than political and ideological affiliation. The 2010 election law reinforces these traditional allegiances by creating large electoral zones, each with several subdistricts. Both voters and candidates can choose to vote or run in any subdistrict within their zone, effectively making it easier for well-connected candidates to engineer victories for themselves and their allies. Constitutional amendments approved by the king in September 2011 call for an independent organization to monitor elections, but implementation has lagged. In late October, the government postponed municipal elections originally scheduled for December, in order to extend the voter registration period and to address concerns over the previous government's proposed changes to the election law.

The security forces exercise significant influence over political life by limiting freedoms of speech and assembly. Opposition figures also charge that the General Intelligence Department (GID) has hindered prospects for reform by meddling in the activities of the cabinet.

The Chamber of Deputies remains heavily imbalanced in favor of rural districts, whose residents are generally of Transjordanian (East Bank) origin. Twelve seats are reserved for women, and the Christian and Circassian minorities are guaranteed nine and three seats, respectively. As noncitizen residents, Jordan's roughly 600,000 refugees, overwhelmingly Palestinian, cannot vote.

Efforts to combat corruption in recent years have yielded mixed results, and investigations and arrests rarely lead to serious punishment. Corruption charges against former prime minister Marouf al-Bakhit in connection with a high-profile casino deal were dropped in June 2011, along with those of 13 other cabinet members, leaving only a former tourism minister to face charges. In February, a group of Bedouin tribal figures—traditionally staunch supporters of the king—released an unprecedented statement charging Queen Rania with corruption. Jordan was ranked 56 out of 183 countries surveyed in Transparency International's 2011 Corruption Perceptions Index.

Freedom of expression is restricted, and those who violate unwritten rules, or red lines, regarding reporting on the royal family and certain societal taboos face arrest. While imprisonment was abolished as a penalty for press offenses in 2007, journalists can still be jailed under the penal code. In September 2011, a draft law was approved that would fine journalists up to approximately $85,000 for reporting on corruption without "solid facts." Self-censorship is common in Jordan, and the government regularly gives both warnings and bribes to journalists to keep them from crossing red lines. In July 2011, police assaulted 16 local and international journalists who were covering protests in Amman. Unidentified men charged into the office of the news website *Al-Muharrir* and threatened the editor, Jihad Abu Baidar, after reporting on an anticorruption commission investigating the former chief of staff, General Khaled Jamil al-Saraira.

Most broadcast news outlets remain under state control, but satellite dishes give residents access to foreign media. While there are dozens of private newspapers and magazines, the government has broad powers to close them. Authorities receive tips about potentially offensive articles by informers at printing presses, and editors are urged to remove such material. Websites are subject to similar restrictions, and police have considerable discretion in monitoring and sanctioning online content. Islam is the state religion. Christians are recognized as religious minorities and can worship freely. While Baha'is and Druze are not officially recognized, they are allowed to practice their faiths. The government monitors sermons at mosques, where political activity is banned. Preachers cannot practice without written government permission. Only state-appointed councils may issue religious edicts, and it is illegal to criticize these rulings.

Academic freedom is generally respected, and Jordanians openly discuss political developments within established red lines. However, there have been reports of a heavy intelligence presence on some university campuses.

Freedom of assembly is generally restricted, and provincial governors often deny permission to hold demonstrations. Jordan's limited protests in 2011 primarily targeted the Bakhit government rather than the king or the royal family. While the scale of the protests remained small, some demonstrations did turn violent. In March and July, security forces reportedly used weapons including wooden clubs and water hoses to disperse protests in Amman, injuring a number of demonstrators.

Freedom of association is limited. The Ministry of Social Development has the authority to reject registration and foreign funding requests for nongovernmental organizations (NGOs). Furthermore, NGOs supporting associations with political purposes are prohibited. While widely feared restrictions on foreign funding have not yet materialized, the Ministry of Social Development at times rejects requests for foreign funding approval. State security must approve all NGO board members, and the Ministry of Social Development can shuffle NGO boards and disband organizations it finds objectionable.

Workers have collective bargaining rights but must receive government permission to strike. More than 30 percent of the workforce is organized into 17 unions. Teachers in several cities went on strike in March 2011 to demand the creation of a national teachers' union, though the government has not met their demands. Labor rights organizations have raised concerns about poor working conditions and sexual abuse in Qualifying Industrial Zones (QIZs), where mostly female and foreign factory workers process goods for export.

The judiciary is subject to executive influence through the Justice Ministry and the Higher Judiciary Council, most of whose members are appointed by the king. While most trials in civilian courts are open and procedurally sound, the State Security Court (SSC) may close its proceedings to the public. The prime minister may refer any case to the SSC, and people convicted of misdemeanors by the SSC lack the right of appeal. While recent constitutional amendments would place all crimes except treason, espionage, and terrorism outside the SSC's purview, specific legislation has not been adopted yet to institutionalize this change. Groups like the IAF continue to call for the SSC to be dissolved altogether.

Suspects may be detained for up to 48 hours without a warrant and up to 10 days without formal charges being filed; courts routinely grant prosecutors 15-day extensions of this deadline. Suspects referred to the SSC are often held in lengthy pretrial detention and refused access to legal counsel until just before trial. Provincial governors can also order indefinite administrative detention, and about a fifth of all Jordanian prisoners are held under this provision; there are approximately 10,000 new cases of administrative detention each year. Torture is routinely employed by the GID to obtain confessions in SSC cases. Prison conditions are poor, and inmates reportedly experience severe beatings and other abuse by guards.

Women enjoy equal political rights but face legal discrimination in matters involving inheritance, divorce, and child custody, which fall under the jurisdiction of Sharia (Islamic law) courts. Although women constitute only about 23 percent of the workforce, the government has made efforts to increase the number of women in the civil service. Women are guaranteed 12 seats in the lower house of parliament and 20 percent of municipal council seats. The upper house of parliament currently has seven female senators. Article 98 of the penal code allows for lenient treatment of those who commit a crime in a "state of fit or fury" resulting from an unlawful or dangerous act on the part of the victim—a provision often applied to benefit men who commit "honor crimes" against women. In February 2011, a man was accused of the premeditated murder of his sister—whom he confessed to stabbing 35 times—in order to "cleanse the family's honor." Between 15 and 20 such crimes occur in Jordan each year.

↓ Kazakhstan

Political Rights: 6
Civil Liberties: 5
Status: Not Free

Population: 16,553,000
Capital: Astana

Trend Arrow: Kazakhstan received a downward trend arrow due to new legislation restricting public expression of religious belief and the right to form religious organizations.

Ten-Year Ratings Timeline For Year Under Review (Political Rights, Civil Liberties, Status)

2002	2003	2004	2005	2006	2007	2008	2009	2010	2011
6,5NF	6,5NF	6,5NF	6,5NF	6,5NF	6,5NF	6,5NF	6,5NF	6,5NF	6,5NF

Overview: **President Nursultan Nazarbayev, 71, won a new five-year term in an April 2011 snap election, reportedly receiving 96 percent of the vote. Many potential challengers had been disqualified or boycotted the election, leaving three mostly symbolic opponents. After the country suffered an unusual series of minor attacks that were blamed on religious extremists, the government pushed through a new law in October that stepped up state control over religious groups and restricted public religious expression. The president dissolved Parliament in November and scheduled early legislative elections for January 2012. In December, police fired on striking oil workers in the western city of Zhanaozen and the city erupted in rioting, leaving at least 16 people dead and triggering a state of emergency.**

Kazakh Communist Party leader Nursultan Nazarbayev won an uncontested presidential election in December 1991, two weeks before Kazakhstan gained its independence from the Soviet Union. In April 1995, Nazarbayev called a referendum on extending his five-year term, due to expire in 1996, until December 2000. A reported 95 percent of voters endorsed the move. An August 1995 referendum, which was boycotted by the opposition, approved a new constitution designed to strengthen the presidency. Nazarbayev's supporters captured most of the seats in December 1995 elections for a new bicameral Parliament.

In October 1998, Parliament amended the constitution to increase the presidential term from five to seven years and moved the presidential election forward from December 2000 to January 1999. The main challenger was disqualified on a technicality, and Nazarbayev was reelected with a reported 80 percent of the vote.

Progovernment parties captured all but one seat in 2004 elections for the lower house of Parliament. International monitors from the Organization for Security and Cooperation in Europe (OSCE) found some improvements over previous polls, but criticized the lack of political balance on election commissions, media bias in favor of propresidential candidates, and the politically motivated exclusion of other candidates.

The president again secured reelection in 2005, with 91 percent of the vote amid opposition allegations of fraud. An international monitoring report found intimidation and media bias in favor of the incumbent.

Political violence flared in 2005–2006, with the suspicious suicide of opposition leader Zamanbek Nurkadilov in December 2005 and the murder of Altynbek Sarsenbayev, a leading member of the opposition coalition For a Just Kazakhstan, in February 2006. The investigation of Sarsenbayev's killing pointed to the involvement of state security officers but left many questions unanswered.

Constitutional changes in May 2007 removed term limits for Nazarbayev, reduced the terms to five years, and eliminated individual district races for the lower house of Parliament, leaving only party-slate seats filled by nationwide proportional representation. Elections under the new rules in August produced a one-party legislature, with the propresidential Nur Otan party taking 88 percent of the vote and no opposition parties clearing the 7 percent threshold for representation. Opposition protests foundered, and the government ignored a critical OSCE report. No opposition candidates participated in the October 2008 indirect elections for the upper house of Parliament.

Although Nazarbayev rejected a proposal to hand him the presidency for life in 2009, a constitutional amendment in 2010 gave him immunity from prosecution and made his family's property effectively inviolable. In January 2011, at Nazarbayev's request, the Constitutional Council blocked parliamentary proposals for a referendum that would have extended his current term through 2020. A snap election was called instead, with the necessary constitutional changes rushed through in February. After Nazarbayev's only genuine opponents were disqualified or decided to boycott the race, he was left with three little-known competitors, all of whom publicly expressed support for him. Nazarbayev ultimately won 96 percent of the April vote. OSCE observers found that the election failed to meet democratic standards.

Also during the first half of 2011, the country was shaken by a number of minor bomb attacks that were blamed on religious extremists. The government responded in October by enacting new legislation that broadly restricted religious freedoms. Later during the year, an extended strike by oil workers in the city of Zhanaozen turned violent in December, resulting in at least 16 deaths and prompting Astana to declare a state of emergency. Meanwhile, Nazarbayev dissolved Parliament in November and scheduled early legislative elections for January 2012.

Throughout the year, Astana maintained good relations with China, Russia, and the United States, which continued to ship supplies for its operations in Afghanistan through Kazakh territory.

Political Rights and Civil Liberties: Kazakhstan is not an electoral democracy. The constitution grants the president considerable control over the legislature, the judiciary, and local governments. Under the current constitutional rules, President Nursultan Nazarbayev may serve an indefinite number of five-year terms.

The upper house of the bicameral Parliament is the 47-member Senate, with 32 members chosen by directly elected regional councils and 15 appointed by the president. The senators serve six-year terms, with half of the 32 elected members up for election every three years. The lower house (Mazhilis) has 107 deputies, with 98 elected by proportional representation on party slates and 9 appointed by the Assembly of Peoples of Kazakhstan, which represents the country's various ethnic groups. Members serve five-year terms.

Parties must clear a 7 percent vote threshold to enter the Mazhilis, and once elected, deputies must vote with their party. A June 2007 law prohibited parties from forming electoral blocs. These rules effectively prevented opposition parties from winning seats in the August 2007 parliamentary elections and 2008 Senate elections, producing a legislature with no opposition representation. The ruling party, Nur Otan, is headed by the president, and his nephew was named party secretary in 2010. A 2009 electoral law amendment guarantees the second-ranked party at least two seats in the Mazhilis if only one party passes the 7 percent threshold. However, Ak Zhol, the opposition party thought to have the best chances in the next parliamentary elections, was taken over in 2011 by a prominent member of Nur Otan who had resigned his membership in the ruling party only the day before.

The country's broader law on political parties prohibits parties based on ethnic origin, religion, or gender. A 2002 law raised the number of members that a party must have to register from 3,000 to 50,000; modest amendments in 2009 lowered the number to 40,000.

Corruption is widespread at all levels of government. Rakhat Aliyev, Nazarbayev's former son-in-law, issued allegations of corruption among top officials after falling out of favor with the regime in 2007. His claims were accompanied by some documentary evidence and matched reports from numerous other sources. Kazakhstan was ranked 120 out of 183 countries surveyed in Transparency International's 2011 Corruption Perceptions Index.

While the constitution provides for freedom of the press, the government has repeatedly harassed or shut down independent media outlets. Libel is a criminal offense, and the criminal code prohibits insulting the president; self-censorship is common. Most media outlets, including publishing houses, are controlled or influenced by members of the president's family and other powerful groups.

As in previous years, independent media suffered attacks, arrests and pressure from authorities in 2011. The proposal to extend Nazarbayev's term until 2020 sparked a wave of critical coverage from independent media that was quickly put down by local authorities. In January, thousands of copies of the weekly paper Golos *Respublikii* were seized by police on charges of carrying "illegal content." In Uralsk, six journalists were arrested for protesting the planned referendum and fined up to 15 months' salary. Separately, journalists from the popular news site Stan TV were repeatedly harassed by authorities during coverage of the extended oil workers' strike in the western region of Mangystau. In October, cameraman Asan Amilov and reporter Orken Bisenov were brutally attacked by unknown assailants using bats and rubber bullets as they traveled to cover the strike. As the strikes erupted into violence in December and protests spread to neighboring cities, police used special powers granted under the state of emergency to arrest or detain journalists attempting to cover the protests. The government shut down access to social media outlets, local internet service providers in the affected areas, and some web-based independent news outlets in an attempt to prevent the spread of news about the violence and demonstrations.

The government has a record of blocking websites that are critical of the regime. In August 2011, the popular blogging sites LiveJournal and LiveInternet.ru were blocked along with some 20 other sites on the grounds that they contributed to "terrorism." In July, a new independent news site, Guljan.org, reported suffering a complex denial-of-service cyberattack shortly after it opened.

The constitution guarantees freedom of worship, and many religious communities practice without state interference. However, laws passed in 2005 banned all activities by unregistered religious groups and gave the government great discretion in outlawing organizations it designated as "extremist." Local officials have harassed groups defined as "nontraditional," such as Hare Krishnas, Protestant Christians, and Jehovah's Witnesses. Legislation enacted in October 2011 required reregistration of all religious groups, gave the government unprecedented authority to regulate the activities and organization of religious communities, and forbade prayer or religious expression in government institutions.

The government reportedly permits academic freedom, except with respect to criticism of the president and his family. Corruption in the education system is widespread, and students frequently bribe professors for passing grades.

Despite constitutional guarantees, the government imposes restrictions on freedom of association and assembly. Unsanctioned opposition gatherings are frequently broken up by police. Nongovernmental organizations continue to operate despite government harassment surrounding politically sensitive issues. Workers can form and join trade unions and participate in collective bargaining, although co-opted unions and close links between the authorities and big business make for an uneven playing field.

Beginning in May 2011, oil workers in Aktau and Zhanaozen held months-long strikes involving as many as 15,000 people to protest low pay and other grievances. Although the strikes were allowed to continue, hundreds of workers were fired in retaliation; several strikers or their close relatives allegedly committed suicide or were murdered; and journalists, lawyers, and politicians faced government harassment and other repercussions for reporting on, representing, or meeting with the strikers. On December 16, police fired into a crowd of protestors, killing at least 14 people. At least two more civilians died and dozens were injured as protests spread to neighboring towns.

The constitution makes the judiciary subservient to the executive branch. Judges are subject to political bias, and corruption is evident throughout the judicial system. Conditions in pretrial facilities and prisons are harsh. Police at times abuse detainees and threaten their families, often to obtain confessions, and arbitrary arrest and detention remain problems. In August 2011, control of prisons was transferred from the Penitentiary Committee to the Interior Ministry, which oversees police forces and conducts criminal investigations. This move transfers funding for prisons to the same agency that makes arrests, potentially creating conflicts of interest and eliminating important external oversight in the criminal justice system.

In June 2011, at least 28 ethnic Uzbeks and Tajiks who had been denied asylum were repatriated to Uzbekistan despite warnings from human rights organizations that they could face unfair trials and torture.

Members of the sizable Russian-speaking minority have complained of discrimination in employment and education. The Russian and Kazakh languages officially have equal status, but in 2011, newly rigorous Kazakh language testing for candidacy in the snap presidential election eliminated many opposition candidates, several of whom noted that the early vote left them unable to prepare adequately. The standards for the tests were unclear, and the scoring methodology was reportedly subjective and opaque.

While the rights of entrepreneurship and private property are formally protected, equality of opportunity is limited by bureaucratic hurdles and the control of large segments of the economy by clannish elites and government officials. Astana residents whose homes have been demolished to make way for large construction projects have said they were denied legally guaranteed compensation.

Traditional cultural practices and the country's economic imbalances limit professional opportunities for women. The current Mazhilis includes only 17 female deputies. Domestic violence often goes unpunished, as police are reluctant to intervene in what are regarded as internal family matters. Despite legal prohibitions, the trafficking of women for the purpose of prostitution remains a serious problem. The country's relative prosperity has drawn migrant workers from neighboring countries, who often face poor working conditions and a lack of legal protections. A 2010 Human Rights Watch report detailed the exploitation of migrant workers and the use of child labor in the Kazakh tobacco industry.

Kenya

Political Rights: 4
Civil Liberties: 3
Status: Partly Free

Population: 41,610,000
Capital: Nairobi

Ten-Year Ratings Timeline For Year Under Review (Political Rights, Civil Liberties, Status)

2002	2003	2004	2005	2006	2007	2008	2009	2010	2011
4,4PF	3,3PF	3,3PF	3,3PF	3,3PF	4,3PF	4,3PF	4,4PF	4,3PF	4,3PF

Overview: **The Kenyan government and civil society groups worked throughout 2011 to implement wide-ranging reforms stipulated in a new constitution approved in August 2010. In April 2011, six prominent Kenyans—including Deputy Prime Minster Uhuru Kenyatta—appeared before the International Criminal Court in connection with its probe of Kenya's postelection violence in late 2007 and early 2008. In October, Kenyan forces moved into Somalia in response to abductions by Somali Islamist group Al-Shabaab in Kenyan territory, and a week later retaliatory grenade attacks in Nairobi killed one person.**

Kenya achieved independence from Britain in 1963. Nationalist leader Jomo Kenyatta served as president until his death in 1978, when Vice President Daniel arap Moi succeeded him. While the Kenyan African National Union (KANU) party remained in power, Moi diminished the influence of the previously dominant Kikuyu ethnic group, favoring his own Kalenjin group.

In 1992, after a lengthy period of single-party rule, domestic unrest and pressure from international donors forced Moi to hold multiparty elections. However, he and KANU continued to win elections by using political repression, state patronage, media control, and dubious electoral procedures.

Government corruption remained common, as did police abuses, political influence in the judiciary, and state efforts to undermine independent civil society activity. Political polarization increased amid government-sponsored ethnic violence, perpetrated in most cases by Kalenjin or Maasai KANU supporters against members of the Kikuyu and Luhya ethnic groups, who were believed to support opposition parties. Despite these problems, political space for opposition views continued to open, and many of the core elements necessary for a democratic political system developed.

The opposition united to contest the 2002 elections as the National Rainbow Coalition. The bloc won a majority in the National Assembly, and its presidential candidate, Mwai Kibaki, emerged victorious. The new leadership's ambitious reform program achieved some successes, but the effort was blunted by factors including the fragility of the governing coalition, a complex bid to overhaul the constitution, significant fiscal constraints, and the threat of terrorism.

The lively press and public investigative commissions became increasingly critical of the substance and slow pace of the government's reform agenda, and in November 2005 referendum voters soundly rejected a draft constitution that failed to shift power away from the presidency.

In January 2006, John Githongo—who in 2005 as Kibaki's anticorruption chief had resigned and fled the country after receiving threats arising from his investigation of top officials—issued an authoritative report indicating that corruption had reached the highest ranks of the government. The findings implicated the vice president and prompted the resignation of several cabinet ministers.

Kenya's democratic and economic development suffered a sharp reversal as a result of apparent manipulation of the December 2007 presidential election, causing existing public discontent to lead to violence. While the concurrent parliamentary polls showed major gains for the opposition Orange Democratic Movement (ODM), Kibaki was declared the winner of the presidential vote amid credible allegations of fraud. He had long been accused of favoring his Kikuyu ethnic group, and the presidential results sparked weeks of violence between the Kikuyu, the Luo, and other groups. Approximately 1,500 people were killed, and over 300,000 were displaced, though many eventually returned or were resettled by the government. In late February 2008, Kibaki and ODM presidential candidate Raila Odinga, a Luo, negotiated a compromise agreement under intense foreign pressure in which Odinga received the newly created post of prime minister, and the ODM joined Kibaki's Party of National Unity in a coalition cabinet.

A Commission of Inquiry into Post-Election Violence, also known as the Waki Commission, issued a report in October 2008 that identified systemic failures in Kenya's security institutions, governmental impunity, and popular anger as the primary instigating factors in the crisis. The report called for the creation of a special tribunal to prosecute crimes committed during the postelection violence, and stated that in the absence of such a tribunal, the names of organizers of the violence should be sent to the International Criminal Court (ICC) for possible prosecution.

In 2009, the government and legislature made little progress in addressing the postelection violence, prompting former UN secretary general Kofi Annan—who had overseen negotiations for the 2008 power-sharing deal—to provide the ICC with a list of alleged perpetrators, though the names were not made public. In March 2010, the ICC, having determined that Kenya was unable to bring the alleged perpetrators to justice, initiated an investigation into crimes against humanity. In December, ICC prosecutor Luis Moreno-Ocampo named six high-profile Kenyans, including Deputy Prime Minister Uhuru Kenyatta, as the chief organizers of the violence. Summonses for all six were issued in March 2011, and they appeared at The Hague in April. The Kenyan government and the African Union have been lobbying for the charges to be dropped.

In a peaceful and well-organized August 2010 referendum, Kenyan voters overwhelmingly approved a new constitution that delineated and checked the roles and powers of the executive, legislative, and judicial branches of government. The new arrangement particularly limited previously expansive presidential and other executive powers, and shifted some authority from the central government to local officials.

In 2011, numerous legislative bodies, government commissions, and civil society groups worked to implement the far-reaching reforms called for in the new constitution. These included the creation of the Independent Electoral and Boundaries Commission (IBEC), which became fully functional in late 2011. The IBEC is tasked with organizing the first presidential and parliamentary elections since the flawed 2007 polls; these elections are scheduled for late 2012 or early 2013.

Political Rights and Civil Liberties: Kenya is not an electoral democracy. While there were few claims of irregularities in the December 2007 parliamentary vote, the flawed presidential poll featured apparent vote rigging and other administrative manipulations that favored the incumbent, Mwai Kibaki. In September 2008, an international commission found that the legitimacy of the election results had been undermined by several factors, including a defective voter registry and widespread fraud. The panel's recommended electoral reforms have yet to be fully implemented. However, the conduct of the constitutional referendum held in August 2010 was considered legitimate and competitive, indicating an improvement in electoral transparency.

Under the new constitution, which entered into force in August 2010, the president is still elected for up to two five-year terms. However, following the next elections, the post of prime minister—created as part of the 2008 compromise—will be abolished, and a new position of deputy president will be established. The unicameral National Assembly, which consists of 210 members elected for five-year terms, 12 members appointed by the president based on each party's share of the popular vote, and 2 ex-officio members, is set to be replaced by a bicameral legislature. The upper house, the Senate, will have at least 60 members, while the lower house is expected to number about 290 members. Ministers may not serve in the parliament, which will have the authority to approve or reject cabinet appointments. Local authorities are to be granted heightened powers. The country will be divided into 47 counties, each of which will have a directly elected governor and assembly.

Political parties representing a range of ideological, regional, and ethnic interests are active and vocal, and there are no significant impediments to party formation. Corruption remains a very serious problem. Political parties, nongovernmental organizations, and the press, as well as some official bodies, have exposed many examples of corruption and malfeasance at all levels of government. However, official probes and prosecutions have yielded meager results. National and international watchdog bodies have identified the police, the judiciary, and the Ministry of Defense as some of the most corrupt institutions in the country. In September 2011, the Ethics and Anti-Corruption Commission (EACC)—created under the new constitution—replaced the ineffective Kenya Anti-Corruption Commission. Although the EACC had an expanded investigative mandate, like its predecessor, it lacks prosecutorial authority. Transparency International's 2011 Corruption Perceptions Index ranked Kenya 154 out of 183 countries surveyed.

The constitution provides for freedoms of speech and of the press, and these rights were strengthened in the new constitution. However, the government occasionally attempts to restrict these rights in practice. There were several cases in 2011 of government officials bringing libel and defamation cases against journalists or media outlets for reporting on alleged corruption. There were also reports of harassment and threats against media workers by the security forces, allegedly for reporting on issues such as corruption and the 2007–2008 postelection violence. Most Kenyans rely on the broadcast media, particularly radio, for news. A number of private television and radio stations operate, though their reach is limited. The government-owned Kenya Broadcasting Corporation continues to dominate the broadcast sector, particularly outside urban centers. The government does not restrict access to the internet.

The authorities generally uphold freedom of religion. The Islamic (Kadhi) court is a subordinate body to the superior courts of Kenya. The Kadhi court system adjudicates cases related to personal status, marriage, divorce, or inheritance for people who profess the Muslim religion and who voluntarily submit to the Kadhi courts' jurisdiction authority. Religious groups are required to register with the government, which permits them to apply for tax-exempt status. Religious tension has risen since terrorist attacks in Kenya in 1998 and 2002 that were associated with Islamic extremism, but religion was not a major factor in the political and ethnic unrest of early 2008.

Academic freedom is the norm in Kenya, though the education system suffers from structural, funding, and other problems. The 2008 postelection violence had at least a temporary chilling effect on freedom of private discussion, as many individuals became hesitant to openly discuss ethnic issues. This effect had eased significantly.

The constitution guarantees freedom of assembly. This right is generally respected, but there have been cases of unnecessary use of force at demonstrations, and public gatherings were curtailed during the 2008 postelection violence. Kenya's civil society sector has remained robust even in recent periods of political polarization.

There are some 40 trade unions in the country, representing about 900,000 workers. Most of the unions are affiliated with the sole approved national federation, the Central Organization of Trade Unions. The 2007 Labour Relations Act establishes broad criteria for union registration, leaving authorities with limited grounds for suspending or refusing to register a union. However, there are restrictions on the right to strike, and the relevant government bodies have been accused of failing to adequately enforce labor laws and protections.

The judiciary's actions have reflected the primacy of the executive branch for much of the period since independence, and judicial corruption remains an impediment to the rule of law. The courts are understaffed and underfinanced, leading to long trial delays that violate defendants' right to due process. The new constitution includes provisions designed to enhance judicial independence, including the establishment of an Independent Judiciary Service Commission to handle the appointment of judges. The Truth, Justice, and Reconciliation Commission (TJRC) was established in 2008 to investigate gross human rights abuses and historical injustices between independence at the end of 1963 and 2008. The TJRC started holding hearings in 2011.

Legal checks on arbitrary arrest are not uniformly respected, and police still use force to extract information from suspects and deny them access to legal representation. Security forces engaged in extrajudicial killings during the 2008 postelection violence. Philip Alston, the UN special rapporteur on extrajudicial executions, visited Kenya in 2009 and found evidence of "a systematic, widespread and clearly planned strategy to execute individuals carried out on a regular basis by the Kenya police." In January 2011, plainclothes police officers were photographed executing three alleged criminals on a public road, prompting an outcry. Such condemnations, however, have not resulted in prosecutions. In 2011, the inmate population in Kenyan prisons was determined to be more than double the intended capacity.

Kenya's population comprises more than 40 ethnic groups, and friction between them has led to frequent allegations of discrimination and periodic episodes of violence. Land disputes frequently underlie ethnic clashes, and long-awaited land reforms have languished. The Mungiki sect of mainly Kikuyu youth has been linked to postelection and other criminal violence. In addition, the continued presence of refugees from Somalia, and associated criminal activity, have exacerbated the problems faced by Kenya's own Somali minority. The Somali Islamist organization Al-Shabaab has recently threatened Kenya with attacks, and it has been accused by the Kenyan government of several kidnappings in Kenyan territory, including four in 2011. In response, Kenya in October sent forces into southern Somalia to pursue Al-Shabaab. A week later, two grenade attacks in Nairobi killed one person and injured more than twenty others. At the end of the month, a 28-year-old man who identified himself as a member of Al-Shabaab was convicted of the attacks and given a life sentence; the trial of two alleged accomplices was ongoing at year's end. Other factors contributing to ethnic tension include widespread firearms possession, the commercialization of traditional cattle herding, poor economic conditions, drought, and ineffective security forces.

The Waki Commission's report cited specific cases of both state- and opposition-sponsored violence and massive internal population displacements during the 2008 postelection crisis. The population movements led in some cases to expropriation of property and belongings. Resettlement of internally displaced people (IDPs) has proceeded slowly. In August 2010, Kibaki ordered that all remaining displaced people be expeditiously resettled, but by mid-2011, government statistics indicated that 6,713 families were still displaced. That figure likely understated the scale of the problem, as anyone who had fled without an identity card would not have been registered as an IDP. Kenya has also neglected IDPs who were evicted from the Mau forest in 2009, as part of an environmental initiative to restore this vital water tower; about 6,500 families were moved, but the promise of resettlement in three months has yet to be fulfilled.

Women in Kenya continue to face serious discrimination. Rape and domestic violence are widespread but rarely prosecuted; due to poor police investigative procedures and societal stigma, an estimated 95 percent of sexual offenses were not reported. Traditional attitudes also limit the role of women in politics. However, noticeable progress has been made. The 2007 elections increased the number of women in the National Assembly to 20, or about 8 percent, and the new constitution guarantees women at least one-third representation in all elected bodies and state commissions. It also voids any customary law inconsistent with constitution, eliminates gender differentiation regarding the right to pass on Kenyan citizenship to spouses and offspring, and guarantees women equal inheritance rights for the first time. A 2011 World Bank report, Women, Business and the Law, found that Kenya showed the greatest improvements among the countries studied—due primarily to the reforms in the new constitution—with significant gains in women entering institutions, utilizing property, and accessing the courts.

Kiribati

Political Rights: 1
Civil Liberties: 1
Status: Free

Population: 103,000
Capital: Tarawa

Ten-Year Ratings Timeline For Year Under Review (Political Rights, Civil Liberties, Status)

2002	2003	2004	2005	2006	2007	2008	2009	2010	2011
1,1F	1,1F	1,1F	1,1F	1,1F	1,1F	1,1F	1,1F	1,1F	1,1F

Overview: **The ruling Pillars of Truth Party secured the most seats in the October 2011 parliamentary elections. The Kiribati government continued throughout the year to seek access to overseas settlements for citizens threatened by rising sea levels, as well as more foreign assistance with training and employment for its people.**

Kiribati gained independence from Britain in 1979. The country consists of 33 atolls scattered across nearly 1.5 million square miles of the central Pacific Ocean, as well as Banaba Island in the western Pacific.

Chinese military ambitions in the Pacific and competing offers of development assistance from China and Taiwan have been major issues in Kiribati politics. President Teburoro Tito's refusal to release details about a 15-year land lease to China for a satellite-tracking facility led to the collapse of his government in 2003. Opposition leader Anote Tong, who was elected president in 2004, immediately terminated the Chinese lease and restored diplomatic ties with Taiwan. Tong won a second four-year term in the 2007 presidential election. In the August 2007 parliamentary elections, independents took 19 seats, followed by Tong's Pillars of Truth Party (BTK) with 18 seats and Tito's Protect the Maneaba party with 7 seats.

Tong has vigorously called for international attention to the growing threats Kiribati faces from rising sea levels and dwindling fresh-water supplies. He has warned that relocation of the entire population might be necessary if ongoing climate change makes inundation inevitable. New Zealand has pledged to accept environmental refugees from Kiribati, and some have already moved there. In March 2011, Tong declared that more coastal villages need resettlement because the sea walls are no longer sufficient to protect them, and that those who move overseas need resettlement assistance.

The government is the main employer in Kiribati, and many residents practice subsistence agriculture. The economy depends considerably on interest from a trust fund built on royalties from phosphate mining, overseas worker remittances, and foreign assistance. In 2011, New Zealand committed $23 million to help Kiribati develop its fishing industry, while Australia announced a Seasonal Worker Program to begin in July 2012 open to horticulture workers from many Pacific Islands, including Kiribati.

Parliamentary elections took place in 2011 over two rounds, on October 21 and 28. Thirty incumbents were reelected; the ruling BTK won 15 seats, with the opposition Karikirakean Tei-Kiribati (KTK) and Maurin Kiribati (MKP) parties taking 10 seats and 3 seats, respectively. Independents won the remaining seats. In November, Parliament nominated three candidates for the upcoming presidential elections, including the BTK's Tong, Tetaua Taitai of the KTK, and Rimeta Beniamina of the MKP. Although the elections were initially scheduled for December 30, they were postponed until January 2012 to avoid low voter turnout during the holiday season.

Political Rights and Civil Liberties: Kiribati is an electoral democracy. The president is popularly elected in a two-step process whereby Parliament nominates candidates from its own ranks and voters then choose one to be president. Forty-four representatives are popularly elected to the unicameral House of Parliament for four-year terms. The attorney general holds a seat ex officio, and the Rabi Island Council nominates one additional member. (Although Rabi Island is part of Fiji, many of its residents were originally from Kiribati's Banaba Island; British authorities forced them to move to Rabi when phosphate mining made Banaba uninhabitable.) The president, vested with executive authority by the constitution, is limited to three four-year terms.

Political parties are loosely organized and generally lack fixed ideologies or formal platforms. Geography, tribal ties, and personal loyalties influence political affiliations.

Official corruption and abuse are serious problems. The number of Chinese-owned businesses has sharply increased in recent years, raising concerns over possible corruption in granting immigration status to Chinese investors and other legal wrongdoing in overseeing foreign investments. Kiribati was ranked 95 out of 183 countries surveyed in Transparency International's 2011 Corruption Perceptions Index.

Freedom of speech is generally respected. There are two weekly newspapers: the state-owned *Te Uekara* and the privately owned *Kiribati Newstar*, and churches publish newsletters and periodicals. There are two radio stations and one television channel, all owned by the state. Internet access is limited outside the capital due to costs—the highest in the Pacific—and lack of infrastructure.

There have been no reports of religious oppression or restrictions on academic freedom. The expansion of access to and quality of education at all levels, however, is seriously restricted by a lack of resources. Secondary education is not available on all islands, and there is a shortage of qualified teachers.

Freedoms of assembly and association are generally respected. A number of nongovernmental organizations are involved in development assistance, education, health, and advocacy for women and children. Workers have the right to organize unions, strike, and bargain collectively, though only about 10 percent of the workforce is unionized. The largest union, the Kiribati Trade Union Congress, has approximately 2,500 members.

The judicial system is modeled on English common law and provides adequate due process rights. There is a high court, a court of appeal, and magistrates' courts; final appeals go to the Privy Council in London. The president makes all judicial appointments. Traditional customs permit corporal punishment. Councils on some outer islands are used to adjudicate petty theft and other minor offenses.

A 260-person police force performs law enforcement and paramilitary functions. Kiribati has no military; Australia and New Zealand provide defense assistance under bilateral agreements.

Citizens enjoy freedom of movement, though village councils have used exile as a punishment.

Discrimination against women is common in the traditional, male-dominated culture. Sexual harassment is illegal and not reported to be widespread. Spousal abuse and other forms of violence against women and children are often associated with alcohol abuse. In response to growing domestic and international criticism for the low level of female participation in politics, the government selected 30 women to receive parliamentary training in advance of the October 2011 elections; 4 women won seats in Parliament in the elections.

Kosovo

Political Rights: 5
Civil Liberties: 4
Status: Partly Free

Population: 2,284,000
Capital: Pristina

Ten-Year Ratings Timeline For Year Under Review (Political Rights, Civil Liberties, Status)

2002	2003	2004	2005	2006	2007	2008	2009	2010	2011
5,5PF	5,5PF	6,5NF	6,5NF	6,5NF	6,5NF	6,5NF	5,4PF	5,4PF	5,4PF

Overview: **In January 2011, Kosovo held repeat voting in certain municipalities following evidence of fraud during the December 2010 general elections. Hashim Thaçi's PDK was victorious in those elections, and parliament reelected him prime minister. In April 2011, law enforcement official Atifete Jahjaga became Kosovo's first female president**

after the Constitutional Court overturned the election of the previous president, Behgjet Pacolli. Meanwhile, ongoing talks between Kosovo and Serbia were disrupted by a border conflict in northern Kosovo.

Ethnic Albanians and Serbs competed for control over Kosovo throughout the 20th century. In the late 1980s, the Serbian government began revoking much of Kosovo's provincial autonomy, but the Kosovo Albanians, under longtime leader Ibrahim Rugova, developed their own quasi-governmental institutions during the 1990s.

An ethnic Albanian guerrilla movement, the Kosovo Liberation Army (KLA), began attacking Serbs and suspected ethnic Albanian collaborators in late 1997, provoking harsh responses by government forces. In March 1999, after internationally sponsored negotiations failed to halt the violence, NATO launched a 78-day bombing campaign that compelled Serbia to relinquish control over the province. After the fighting ended, hundreds of thousands of ethnic Albanians who had been expelled by government forces returned. NATO and the United Nations took responsibility for Kosovo's security and civilian administration, though Serbian rule remained legally intact.

After the international takeover, tens of thousands of non-Albanians were forced to flee the province. Currently, ethnic Albanians comprise about 90 percent of the population, with Serbs making up most of the remainder. The largest Serb enclave is north of the Ibar River, anchored by the divided city of Mitrovica, while smaller Serb areas are scattered throughout the province. In March 2004, two days of rioting against non-Albanian ethnic groups left 20 people dead and 800 homes and 30 churches destroyed.

The October 2004 parliamentary elections resulted in a governing coalition between Rugova's Democratic League of Kosovo (LDK) and the Alliance for the Future of Kosovo (AAK). The Democratic Party of Kosovo (PDK), led by former KLA political leader Hashim Thaçi, won the 2007 parliamentary elections, raising Thaçi to the premiership.

The 2004 riots accelerated talks on Kosovo's final status. While ethnic Albanian negotiators demanded full independence, Serbian officials offered only autonomy. In late 2007, Finnish mediator Martti Ahtisaari recommended that the UN Security Council grant Kosovo a form of internationally supervised independence. Russia continued to support Serbia's position, however, and the international community was unable to reach consensus.

Kosovo's Assembly formally declared independence from Serbia on February 17, 2008, and the United States and most European Union (EU) members quickly recognized the new country. In June 2008, Kosovo's Serb municipalities formed a separate assembly that refused to recognize Pristina's independence and affirmed its allegiance to Belgrade. The legal situation was further complicated by the ongoing supervision of international entities in Pristina, including the UN Interim Mission in Kosovo (UNMIK), an EU mission known as EULEX, and the NATO peacekeeping force.

In August 2008, Serbia submitted a resolution to the United Nations requesting an advisory opinion from the International Court of Justice (ICJ) on whether Kosovo's declaration of independence violated international law; in July 2010, the

ICJ found that it did not. While the country became a member of the International Monetary Fund (IMF) and the World Bank in 2009, continued resistance from Russia and China blocked membership to the United Nations and other international organizations. As of December 2011, 81 countries recognized Kosovo.

In September 2010, Kosovo's Constitutional Court ruled that President Fatmir Sejdiu had violated the constitution by simultaneously serving as Kosovo's president and leader of the LDK. Sejdiu resigned as president, and the LDK withdrew from Thaçi's governing coalition. The weakened government lost a confidence vote in November, triggering early elections on December 12. Significant fraud in parts of Kosovo—especially in Thaçi's stronghold in the Drenica region—necessitated reruns in several municipalities in January 2011. In February 2011, the Central Election Commission announced that the PDK won 30 percent of the vote and 34 seats, while the LDK took 24 percent and 27 seats. The Vetëvendosje (Self-Determination) opposition movement finished a strong third with 12 percent and 12 seats.

A December 2010 report by Council of Europe rapporteur Dick Marty accused high-level Kosovo officials, including Thaçi, of involvement in an organized crime network that was active during and after the 1999 conflict. Most controversially, the report alleged that the group harvested organs from KLA prisoners. Despite these allegations, on February 22, 2011, Kosovo's parliament elected Thaçi to a second term as prime minister after lengthy coalition talks. The legislature also elected businessman Behgjet Pacolli of the New Alliance for Kosovo (AKR) as president, though the opposition contested his election on the grounds that he had not received enough votes in the Assembly in accordance with the constitution. The Constitutional Court sided with the opposition and overturned Pacolli's election in March. Atifete Jahjaga, deputy director of the Kosovo police, succeeded Pacolli in April under controversial circumstances. Jahjaga had no party affiliation, which was cited as a major reason for the legislature agreeing on her candidacy. Shortly after Jahjaga's election, Pacolli announced that she had been chosen for the position during a meeting attended by himself, Thaçi, LDK leader Isa Mustafa, and U.S. ambassador Christopher Dell.

In March, Kosovo and Serbia began bilateral talks on technical issues regarding trade and other areas. The ongoing negotiations were repeatedly disrupted by a border conflict in northern Kosovo, the majority-Serb contested territory where Serbia funds "parallel" public services, including education and health care, and Pristina has scant influence. Hostilities had erupted there in July after Thaçi sent police forces to the border to enforce an effective embargo of Serbian goods in retaliation for a 2008 Serb ban on Kosovo imports. Local Serbs responded by burning checkpoints, blocking roads, and mobilizing demonstrations. A Kosovo policeman was killed in the hostilities. NATO forces helped restore peace, and the two countries resumed their dialogue following a NATO-brokered interim agreement that allowed most traffic to pass through the border. However, the implementation of a separate customs agreement reached during the dialogue on September 2 led to further protests from the northern Kosovo Serbs.

Political Rights and Civil Liberties: Kosovo is not an electoral democracy. Members of the unicameral, 120-seat Assembly are elected to four-year terms, and 20 seats are reserved for ethnic minorities. The Assembly elects the president, who serves a five-year term. The prime minister, who is nominated by the president, requires Assembly approval. According to the constitution, the president and the Assembly have governing authority, though the International Civilian Representative (ICR) retains the right to override legislation and decisions deemed to be at odds with the human rights and minority protection provisions of the Ahtisaari Plan.

Kosovo's December 2010 parliamentary elections were the most problematic of any held after 1999. Reported irregularities included vote buying; limited freedom of movement for ethnic minorities; and limitations imposed on women in rural areas. More than 500 people have been indicted for electoral fraud. While most Serbs north of the Ibar boycotted the vote, up to 40 percent of the roughly 55,000 Serbs in the enclaves south of the Ibar reportedly participated.

Corruption is a serious problem. Misconduct is widespread in many areas, including the judiciary and law enforcement. In October 2011, EULEX arrested six officials in an investigation of weapons procurement fraud in the police. Overall, implementation of anticorruption legislation is weak, and better cooperation is needed between the Anti-Corruption Agency, police, and courts, according to the European Commission's (EC) Kosovo 2011 Progress Report, released in October. Kosovo was ranked 112 of 183 countries surveyed in Transparency International's 2011 Corruption Perceptions Index.

The constitution protects freedoms of expression and the press, with exceptions for speech that provokes ethnic hostility. Despite a wide variety of technically free media, journalists report frequent harassment. Freedom of expression is also limited in practice by a lack of security, especially for ethnic minorities. In July 2011, Kosovo's media watchdog demanded a retraction from the public broadcaster RTK for effectively slandering Krenar Gashi, then the director of a prominent Pristina think tank, following publication of Freedom House's 2011 *Nations in Transit* report, which Gashi had coauthored; the report faulted the politicization of RTK. International officials in Kosovo have been accused of occasionally restricting media independence.

The constitution guarantees religious freedom. The predominantly Muslim ethnic Albanians enjoy this right in practice, but the Muslim community increasingly complains of discrimination. An October 2011 Constitutional Court ruling upholding the government's effective ban on girls wearing the Islamic headscarf in public schools sparked protests and condemnation from Muslim leaders. Several cases of vandalism at Serbian Orthodox cemeteries were reported in 2010 and 2011, and vandals attacked an Orthodox Church in Samodreža in October 2011. Overall, however, attacks on minority religious sites have declined since 2004.

Academic freedom is not formally restricted, but appointments at the University of Pristina are politicized. In October 2011, Pristina education director Remzi Salihu was murdered by a teacher who was allegedly denied promotion for political reasons. Kosovo's education system is largely segregated along ethnic lines.

Freedom of assembly has occasionally been restricted for security reasons, and the constitution includes safeguards for public order and national security. Islamic groups organized several peaceful demonstrations in 2011, though protests during the northern conflict with Serb demonstrators were marked by violence. Nongovernmental organizations generally function freely. The courts can ban groups that infringe on the constitutional order or encourage ethnic hatred. The constitution protects the right to establish and join trade unions.

Kosovo made progress on the judiciary in 2011. The Constitutional Court issued several important decisions, including on the presidency, to reinforce rule of law. Authorities continued to implement reform measures such as the laws on the Judicial and Prosecutorial Councils, and salaries for judges and prosecutors were increased to promote independence. The number of backlogged cases fell 26 percent in six months following the January 1, 2011, implementation of a reduction strategy. Nevertheless, courts are subject to political influence and intimidation, and enforcement of legal decisions remains weak. Moreover, the absence of municipal courts in northern Kosovo undermines rule of law there.

Ethnic Albanian officials rarely prosecute cases involving Albanian attacks on non-Albanians. Despite several convictions and indictments in war crimes trials in 2011, impunity is a problem. In September 2011, the key witness in the war crimes trial of former KLA commander Fatmir Limaj was found dead of an apparent suicide. The circumstances were suspicious, however, as were those of several witnesses in the 2008 war crimes trial of former prime minister Ramush Haradinaj. Prison conditions are generally in line with international standards, though overcrowding and the abuse of prisoners remain problems.

Freedom of movement for ethnic minorities is a significant problem, and returnees to Kosovo still face hostility. In October 2011, the OSCE admonished local institutions regarding returnee security after a spate of harassment at returns sites in Ferizaj. Blockades during the northern border conflict restricted freedom of movement, and the EC called for an urgent resolution in October. Kosovo's Roma, Ashkali, Gorani, and other minority populations face difficult socioeconomic conditions. Property reclamation by displaced persons remains problematic.

Kosovo is a principal transit point along the heroin-trafficking route between Central Asia and Western Europe. Organized crime is endemic, especially in northern Kosovo. Kosovo authorities are cooperating with the EULEX investigation into the allegations in Dick Marty's 2010 report.

Patriarchal attitudes often limit women's ability to gain an education or secure employment. Women are underrepresented in politics, despite rules that they must occupy every third spot on each party's candidate list. Women in rural areas remain effectively disenfranchised through family voting—in which the male head of a household casts ballots for the entire family—though attitudes toward women's rights are becoming more open in urban areas. Domestic violence is a serious problem, as is discrimination against sexual minorities. Kosovo is a source, transit point, and destination for human trafficking. In 2011, the government adopted an antitrafficking action plan, but the implementation of such legislation tends to be weak.

Kuwait

Political Rights: 4
Civil Liberties: 5
Status: Partly Free

Population: 2,818,000
Capital: Kuwait City

Ten-Year Ratings Timeline For Year Under Review (Political Rights, Civil Liberties, Status)

2002	2003	2004	2005	2006	2007	2008	2009	2010	2011
4,5PF	4,5PF	4,5PF	4,5PF	4,4PF	4,4PF	4,4PF	4,4PF	4,5PF	4,5PF

Overview: **Allegations of corruption by the National Assembly, combined with popular protests against the prime minister and the cabinet, led to the resignation of the cabinet twice, the prime minister once, and the Emir's dissolution of the National Assembly by the end of 2011. In January, police detained and fatally tortured a Kuwaiti citizen, Mohammed al-Mutairi, leading to the resignation of the interior minister and the arrest of 16 police officers. Members of Kuwait's stateless bidoon community staged demonstrations demanding expanded rights.**

For more than 200 years, the al-Sabah dynasty has played a role in ruling Kuwait. A year after the country gained its independence from Britain in 1961, a new constitution gave broad powers to the emir and created the National Assembly. Iraqi forces invaded in August 1990, but a military coalition led by the United States liberated the country in February 1991.

Emirs have suspended the National Assembly two times, from 1976 to 1981 and from 1986 to 1992. After its restoration in 1992, the parliament played an active role in monitoring the emir and the government, often forcing cabinet ministers out of office and blocking legislation proposed by the ruling family. However, the legislature has also served as an impediment to progressive political change by rejecting measures on women's rights and economic reform.

After 28 years of rule, Sheikh Jaber al-Ahmad al-Sabah died in 2006. The cabinet and parliament removed his heir for health reasons and elevated Sheikh Sabah al-Ahmad al-Sabah, the half-brother of the previous emir, as the new emir. In parliamentary elections that year, a coalition of liberals, Islamists, and nationalists campaigning against corruption captured a majority of seats.

The emir dissolved parliament in March 2008, leading to early elections in May. In November, Prime Minister Nasser Mohammed al-Ahmed al-Sabah—the emir's nephew—and the cabinet resigned to avoid questioning by the parliament regarding corruption allegations. In December, the emir accepted the cabinet's resignation but immediately reappointed his nephew as prime minister to demonstrate his displeasure with the legislature.

A new cabinet was finalized in January 2009 and opposition members of the parliament quickly renewed calls to question cabinet members over the misuse of public funds. The government again resigned in March 2009, prompting the emir to dissolve the parliament two days later. For the third time in three years, parliamentary elections were held in May with Sunni Islamists, Shiites, liberals, and tribal representatives all winning seats. The prime minister went before the parliament in December to answer to allegations of corruption and survived the subsequent vote of confidence.

In January 2011, the prime minister narrowly survived another no-confidence vote over corruption charges. Opposition members also accused the prime minister of rolling back the country's political freedoms after his harsh response to a December 2010 public rally. Tensions between the government and the public persisted throughout 2011, sparking regular protests in the country's capital demanding the prime minister's resignation and the eradication of systemic corruption. The cabinet resigned in March rather than have three of its members appear before the National Assembly for questioning about corruption and for their support of the Cooperation Council of the Arabs States of the Gulf intervention in Bahrain. The Emir appointed a new cabinet in May, but retained the controversial Nasser Mohammed al-Ahmed al-Sabah in his post as prime minister. Over 10,000 Kuwaitis demonstrated in opposition to the prime minister and state corruption in October.

Protests at Kuwait's parliament continued into November, leading to two dozen arrests as well as the cabinet's resignation later that month. The emir swore in a new cabinet in December headed by former Minister of Defense Jaber Al Mubarak Al Sabah, although he reappointed most of those who had resigned the previous month. The emir also dissolved parliament in December, setting the date for new elections in February 2013.

Political Rights and Civil Liberties: Kuwait is not an electoral democracy. The ruling family sets the policy agenda and dominates political life. The emir has overriding power in the government system and appoints the prime minister and cabinet. Under the constitution, the emir shares legislative power with the 50-member National Assembly, which is elected to four-year terms by popular vote. The electorate consists of men and women over 21 years of age who have been citizens for at least 20 years; members of most security forces are barred from voting. A 2006 law reduced the number of multimember electoral districts from 25 to 5 in an effort to curb corruption. The emir has the authority to dissolve the National Assembly at will but must call elections within 60 days. The parliament can overturn decrees issued by the emir while it is not in session. It can also veto the appointment of the country's prime minister, but then it must choose from three alternates put forward by the emir. The parliament also has the power to remove government ministers with a majority vote.

Formal political parties are banned. While political groupings, such as parliamentary blocs, have been allowed to emerge, the government has impeded their activities through harassment and arrests.

Corruption remains a dominant political issue, and lawmakers continue to pressure the government to address this problem. In August 2011, allegations emerged that up to 18 members of parliament received large cash deposits into their personal bank accounts. The transactions, disclosed by the National Bank of Kuwait and Kuwait Finance House, have widely been interpreted as evidence of government bribery. The allegations fuelled protests in the fall and have led to demands for all members of parliament and their families to disclose their financial assets; the corruption probe was ongoing at year's end. Kuwait was ranked 54 out of 183 countries surveyed in Transparency International's 2011 Corruption Perceptions Index.

Kuwaiti authorities continue to limit criticism and political debate in the press. While press offenses have been decriminalized, offenders still face steep fines. Kuwaiti law also prohibits and demands prison sentences for the publication of material that insults Islam, criticizes the emir, discloses secret or private information, or calls for the regime's overthrow. In January 2011, Kuwait's Supreme Court overturned the 2010 conviction of Muhammad Abd al-Qader al-Jassem for criticizing the prime minister, freeing him after had had served 62 days of a three-month prison sentence. In June, authorities arrested the political activist Nasser Abul for criticizing the leaders of Saudi Arabia and Bahrain as well as Salafists on his personal twitter feed. He was accused of threatening state security, damaging relations with Kuwait's foreign allies, and for contempt of religion. He was subsequently acquitted of the state security charges, but was convicted of contempt of religion. He spent 111 days in prison.

Kuwait has more than 10 daily and weekly Arabic newspapers and 2 English-language dailies. The state owns four television stations and nine radio stations, but there are also a number of private outlets, including the satellite television station Al-Rai. Foreign media outlets have generally operated relatively freely in Kuwait. However, in December 2010, the government shut down the bureau of Al-Jazeera for its coverage of a police crackdown on a political demonstration in the same month. Kuwaitis enjoy access to the internet, though the government has instructed internet service providers to block certain sites for political or moral reasons.

Islam is the state religion, but religious minorities are generally permitted to practice their faiths in private. Shiite Muslims, who make up around a third of the population, enjoy full political rights but are subject to discrimination and harassment.

Academic freedom is generally respected. Kuwait allows relatively open and free private discussion, often conducted in traditional gatherings (*diwaniyat*) that typically include only men.

Freedoms of assembly and association are guaranteed by law, though the government constrains these rights in practice. Kuwaitis must notify authorities of a public meeting or protest, but do not need a permit. Peaceful demonstrations held throughout 2011, mostly in response to charges of government corruption, have tested the limits of the state's tolerance for public protest. In February, hundreds of members of Kuwait's more than 100,000 stateless residents, known as bidoon, protested for greater rights; they are considered illegal residents, do not have full citizenship rights, and often live in wretched conditions. Riot police responded harshly, arresting scores of people and injuring others. Detainees complained of torture while in state detention; at least 50 of the bidoon protestors went on trial in December for assaulting police and demonstrating without permission.

The government routinely restricts the registration and licensing of associations and nongovernmental organizations (NGOs), forcing dozens of groups to operate without legal standing or state assistance. Representatives of licensed NGOs must obtain government permission to attend foreign conferences on behalf of their organizations. Workers have the right to join labor unions, but Kuwait's labor law mandates that there be only one union per occupational trade. Migrant workers enjoy limited legal protections against mistreatment or abuse by employers.

Kuwait lacks an independent judiciary. The emir appoints all judges, and the executive branch approves judicial promotions. Authorities may detain suspects for four days without charge. The Interior Ministry supervises the main internal security forces, including the national police, the Criminal Investigation Division, and Kuwait State Security. In January 2011, police arrested a Kuwaiti citizen, Mohammed al-Mutairi, for alcohol possession, which is illegal in Kuwait. A parliamentary investigation revealed that authorities tortured al-Mutairi for six days before killing him and then engaged in a cover-up. Controversy surrounding the case forced the resignation of Minister of the Interior Sheikh Jaber al-Khaled al-Sabah in February, and 16 police officers were brought up on charges, though they had not been tried or sentenced by year's end. The government permits visits by human rights activists to prisons, where overcrowding remains a problem. In 2010, Kuwait enacted a disability rights act ensuring health-care, education, and employment rights for the disabled.

The 1962 constitution provides men and women with equal rights. Kuwaiti women have the right to vote and run as candidates in parliamentary and local elections. For the first time in Kuwait's history, four women won seats in the 2009 parliamentary elections. Women also comprise more than 60 percent of the student body at several leading Kuwaiti universities. Nevertheless, women face discrimination in several areas of law and society and remain underrepresented in the workforce. The country's public schools have remained segregated since 2001. Women are offered some legal protections from abuse and discrimination, but they are only permitted to seek a divorce in cases where they have been deserted or subject to domestic violence. Women must have a male guardian in order to marry and are eligible for only one-half of their brother's inheritance. As of 2009, married women have the right to obtain passports and to travel without their husband's permission. Domestic abuse and sexual harassment are not specifically prohibited by law, and foreign domestic servants remain particularly vulnerable to abuse and sexual assault.

Kyrgyzstan

Political Rights: 5
Civil Liberties: 5
Status: Partly Free

Population: 5,600,000
Capital: Bishkek

Ten-Year Ratings Timeline For Year Under Review (Political Rights, Civil Liberties, Status)

2002	2003	2004	2005	2006	2007	2008	2009	2010	2011
6,5NF	6,5NF	6,5NF	5,4PF	5,4PF	5,4PF	5,4PF	6,5NF	5,5PF	5,5PF

Overview: **A three-party coalition that governed for most of the year brought greater stability to Kyrgyzstan in 2011, and a competitive presidential election in October led to Central Asia's first voluntary transfer of power, with interim president Roza Otunbayeva standing down as scheduled. Despite greater openness and political competition, however, serious flaws remained in the treatment of national minorities, due process, prevention of and accountability for torture, and judicial independence.**

Shortly after Kyrgyzstan gained independence from the Soviet Union in 1991, Askar Akayev, a respected physicist, was elected president. He easily won reelection in 1995, and constitutional amendments the following year substantially increased the powers of the presidency. International observers noted serious irregularities in the 2000 parliamentary and presidential elections, which yielded another term for Akayev.

Long-standing frustrations in the economically depressed and politically marginalized south culminated in public protests in 2002. Six protesters were killed when police fired into a crowd in the village of Aksy. Although several prosecutors and police officials were eventually convicted and sentenced to prison, opposition critics continued to argue that senior officials who authorized the use of force were never brought to justice.

After flawed February 2005 parliamentary elections, thousands of demonstrators protested irregularities and ultimately called for Akayev's resignation. On March 24, protesters and opposition supporters stormed the presidential headquarters in Bishkek. Akayev fled abroad and later resigned.

In the July 2005 presidential poll, former prime minister and opposition leader Kurmanbek Bakiyev captured 89 percent of the vote. His victory was regarded as nearly inevitable after Feliks Kulov, his most serious rival, withdrew his presidential candidacy in exchange for the post of prime minister. Observers from the Organization for Security and Cooperation in Europe (OSCE) nevertheless concluded that the election represented an improvement over previous votes.

After violently dispersing opposition protests in April 2007, the government enacted constitutional revisions in an October referendum, expanding the parliament from 75 to 90 seats and introducing party-slate balloting. Parliamentary elections in December resulted in a legislature dominated by the newly formed progovernment party Ak Zhol and devoid of opposition representation.

The president consolidated his power in 2008 and 2009, sidelining the country's remaining well-known opposition figures. In March 2009, Medet Sadyrkulov, Bakiyev's former chief of staff, was found dead in a burned-out car near Bishkek. Opposition representatives charged that he had been assassinated because he was planning to join them. Bakiyev won another five-year term in the July 2009 presidential election, taking 75 percent of the vote. OSCE observers concluded that the poll failed to meet international standards, citing evidence of fraud, intimidation of opposition supporters, and the misuse of administrative resources, among other problems.

In April 2010, Bakiyev fled the country amid antigovernment protests in Bishkek, leading to the formation of an interim government. A reported 86 people were killed in the street confrontations, with most victims apparently shot by security forces. In the first half of June, ethnic rioting swept the southern cities of Osh and Jalalabad, leaving hundreds dead. Ethnic Uzbeks suffered the brunt of the violence, and local security forces were accused of abetting attacks on Uzbek communities. Later the same month, a referendum that international observers deemed generally fair confirmed longtime opposition figure Roza Otunbayeva as interim president through December 2011 and approved a new constitution that shifted power from the presidency to the parliament.

Parliamentary elections held in October 2010 were deemed an improvement over Bakiyev-era balloting. Five parties representing different constituencies and ideologies won seats. The new Ata-Jurt party led with 28 of 120 seats, followed by Otunbayeva's Social Democratic Party of Kyrgyzstan (SDPK) with 26, Ar-Namys with 25, Respublika with 23, and Ata-Meken with 18. Ata-Jurt, the SDPK, and Respublika formed a coalition government in December, leaving Ar-Namys and Ata-Meken in opposition. Almazbek Atambayev of the SDPK became prime minister. The coalition remained stable and governed effectively until after the October 2011 presidential election.

The presidential poll was seen by OSCE observers as free and competitive, though marred by significant irregularities on election day. Atambayev, who had suspended his role as prime minister ahead of the election, defeated 15 other candidates and took 63 percent of the vote. In December, a new coalition composed of the SDPK, Respublika, Ata-Meken, and Ar-Namys was formed, with Omurbek Babanov of Respublika as prime minister.

In 2011, Kyrgyzstan made efforts to balance its relations with Russia and the United States, and improved ties with its Central Asian neighbors as well. When it became clear that Kyrgyzstan's ethnic violence of June 2010 did not threaten regional security, the other countries eased their border restrictions.

Political Rights and Civil Liberties:

Kyrgyzstan is not an electoral democracy, though the parliamentary and presidential elections of 2010 and 2011 were considered improvements over the deeply flawed 2007 parliamentary and 2009 presidential votes. OSCE observers praised the 2010 parliamentary campaign's pluralism and other positive features, but were more critical of the 2011 presidential vote, citing widespread problems with voter lists and numerous faults in the tabulation process.

Constitutional changes adopted in the June 2010 referendum expanded the unicameral parliament from 90 to 120 deputies, with no party allowed to hold more than 65 seats. Parliamentary elections are to be held every five years. The president serves a single six-year term with no possibility of reelection, but retains the power to veto legislation.

The overall aim of the reforms was to establish checks and balances that will ensure political pluralism and prevent the reemergence of an authoritarian, superpresidential system. It remains to be seen whether the country's newly elected leaders will seek to reverse these achievements.

Corruption is pervasive in Kyrgyz society. The nepotistic practices of former president Kurmanbek Bakiyev, whose sons and brothers were prominent in business and government, were a significant source of popular dissatisfaction prior to his ouster. The interim government charged some members of the Bakiyev regime with corruption, but the results in the largely unreformed courts have been inconclusive. In a worrying sign, recordings leaked in May 2011 purported to reveal members of the interim government discussing lucrative backroom deals; no investigation ensued. Kyrgyzstan was ranked 164 out of 183 countries surveyed in Transparency International's 2011 Corruption Perceptions Index.

Kyrgyz-language media experienced less politically motivated harassment after the fall of the Bakiyev government. However, Uzbek-language media virtually ceased to exist in southern Kyrgyzstan after the June 2010 ethnic violence, when several Uzbek television and radio outlets were closed down. Meanwhile, in April 2010, the interim government transformed the state-run television station into a public broadcaster with an independent oversight board.

The media landscape remained bifurcated along ethnic lines in 2011, with significantly improved conditions for Kyrgyz-language media and vastly worse conditions for Uzbek-language outlets. In May, the authorities said they were searching for the authors of two potentially inflammatory books that described the June 2010 violence as an anti-Uzbek genocide. The electoral law that governed the presidential election effectively barred the broadcasting of foreign media reporting on the campaign. The law's sponsors cited the role of Russian media in smearing certain candidates in the 2010 parliamentary campaign. Although all foreign news broadcast media, including CNN and Euronews, were barred from broadcasting on Kyrgyz channels during the elections period, domestic news providers were not hampered in their electoral reporting. The presidential candidates held lively televised debates, and all candidates had access to the media. Also during 2011, several journalists were physically assaulted by unidentified assailants, in some cases sustaining severe injuries that required hospitalization.

The government has generally permitted a broad range of religious practices, but all religious organizations must register with the authorities, a process that is often cumbersome and arbitrary. A January 2009 law banned proselytizing and private religious education, and the wearing of headscarves in schools was banned two months later. The government monitors and restricts Islamist groups that it regards as a threat to national security, particularly Hizb ut-Tahrir, an ostensibly nonviolent international movement calling for the creation of a caliphate.

Tight official restrictions on freedom of assembly have not been altered since the Bakiyev era, but enforcement has been eased considerably in practice, and numerous rallies have been held.

Freedom of association is typically upheld, and nongovernmental organizations

(NGOs) participate actively in civic and political life. In 2011, new public advisory councils were established in the parliament and in most ministries, permitting improved monitoring and advocacy by NGOs. However, rising nationalism has affected both ethnic Kyrgyz and ethnic Uzbek NGO activists. Human rights activists who work on defending Uzbek victims have faced threats, harassment, and physical attacks. In December 2011, the Supreme Court upheld a life sentence against ethnic Uzbek human rights activist Azimjan Askarov, who had been convicted in September 2010 of involvement in the murder of a Kyrgyz police official during the June 2010 violence. Rights organizations and foreign diplomats had called for his release, citing an array of critical flaws in the case against him, including evidence that he was tortured in detention.

The law provides for the formation of trade unions, and unions are generally able to operate without obstruction. However, strikes are prohibited in many sectors. Legal enforcement of union rights is weak, and collective bargaining agreements are not always respected by employers.

The judiciary is not independent and remains dominated by the executive branch. Corruption among judges, who are underpaid, is widespread. In June 2011, civic activists protested the new parliament's judicial appointments, accusing the nominees of past wrongdoing. Defendants' rights, including the presumption of innocence, are not always respected, and there are credible reports of torture against suspects during arrest and interrogation. After a visit to Kyrgyzstan in December 2011, the UN special rapporteur on torture called it a "widespread phenomenon" that was "exacerbated by the reliance placed on confessions in the judicial system." He expressed concern about the lack of effective investigations and convictions of abusers.

The interim government investigated the crimes of Bakiyev-era officials, and a state commission found in April 2011 that there had been 30 prominent contract killings during Bakiyev's tenure. However, the handling of several high-profile cases during the election year demonstrated the politicization and other flaws of the judicial system. The ongoing trials of the Bakiyev family and their accomplices, including a case against 28 former government officials and special forces members for the alleged killing of 86 demonstrators in April 2010, were marred by numerous procedural violations, such as threats against lawyers in the courtroom. Human Rights Watch documented systematic rights violations at numerous trials of ethnic Uzbeks in 2010 and 2011, with defendants attacked in courtrooms, tortured in detention, and convicted on flimsy or fabricated evidence.

The widespread and extensively documented violence against the Uzbek community in southern Kyrgyzstan in 2010 cast a harsh light on the plight of ethnic minorities. Uzbeks, who make up nearly half of the population in Osh, had long demanded more political and cultural rights, including greater representation in government, more Uzbek-language schools, and official status for the Uzbek language. The Kyrgyzstan Inquiry Commission (KIC), an independent international body, put the death toll from the worst outbreak of ethnic violence in June at 470, noting that "the majority of victims were ethnic Uzbeks." Government forces were ineffective at stopping ethnic violence, and may have been complicit in it. The report named specific officials in the interim government as having failed in their duties to impartially enforce the law during the clashes. After the violence ebbed, arrests and sweep operations targeted Uzbek neighborhoods and activists. The KIC report was denounced by all segments of the political spectrum, and the parliament voted unanimously to declare the head of the commission, Finnish diplomat Kimmo Kiljunen, persona non grata.

The government generally respects the right of unrestricted travel to and from Kyrgyzstan. However, barriers to internal migration include a requirement that citizens obtain permits to work and settle in particular areas of the country.

Personal connections, corruption, organized crime, and widespread poverty limit business competition and equality of opportunity. Companies that had belonged to the Bakiyev family were nationalized in 2010 pending a new process of privatization. That year's ethnic violence affected property rights in the south, as a large number of businesses, mainly owned by ethnic Uzbeks, were either destroyed or seized during and after the unrest.

Cultural traditions and apathy among law enforcement officials discourage victims of domestic violence and rape from contacting the authorities. Rumors of rapes accompanied the ethnic violence of June 2010, but they frequently remained unconfirmed. The KIC noted that the government response to the few cases of rape that were actually reported was "inadequate if not obstructive." The trafficking of women and girls into forced prostitution abroad is a serious problem, and some victims report that the authorities are involved in trafficking. The practice of bride abduction persists despite being illegal, and few perpetrators are prosecuted.

Laos

Political Rights: 7
Civil Liberties: 6
Status: Not Free

Population: 6,259,000
Capital: Vientiane

Ten-Year Ratings Timeline For Year Under Review (Political Rights, Civil Liberties, Status)

2002	2003	2004	2005	2006	2007	2008	2009	2010	2011
7,6NF	7,6NF	7,6NF	7,6NF	7,6NF	7,6NF	7,6NF	7,6NF	7,6NF	7,6NF

Overview: **Laos held elections in 2011 for its one-party legislature, which reelected Choummaly Sayasone for a second term as the country's president. Popular anger over plans for a major dam on the Mekong River in Laos led a four-country regional body to postpone approval for the project, but construction activity reportedly continued during the year. Meanwhile, a group of ethnic Hmong refugees who were repatriated from Thailand in 2009 and 2010 remained missing despite inquiries by foreign diplomats.**

Laos won independence in 1953 after six decades of French rule and Japanese occupation during World War II. The constitutional monarchy soon fell into a civil war with Pathet Lao guerrillas, who were backed by the Vietnamese Communist Party. As the conflict raged on, Laos was drawn into the Vietnam War in 1964.

The Pathet Lao seized power in 1975, and the Lao People's Revolutionary Party (LPRP) has ruled the country ever since. By the 1980s, the economy was in tatters after years of civil war and state mismanagement. The LPRP relaxed controls on prices, encouraged foreign investment, and privatized farms and some state-owned enterprises.

The party's policy of maintaining tight political control while spurring economic development continued over the subsequent decades, and the country consistently reported high macroeconomic growth rates. However, the rapid expansion of extractive industries and the influx of thousands of Chinese businesses, particularly in northern Laos, increased economic inequality and fostered greater corruption. The seizure of land from subsistence farmers and tribal communities for leasing to foreign-owned agribusinesses also triggered occasional protests and violence, and resulted in environmental destruction.

In April 2011, the four-country Mekong River Commission delayed a decision on whether to approve Laos's plans for a major dam near the town of Xayaburi. The project had raised environmental and resettlement concerns and stirred popular anger in Laos and downstream countries. The commission postponed its decision again in December, citing the need for further environmental studies, but construction at the site reportedly continued during the year.

Also in April, elections were held for the rubber-stamp National Assembly. The LPRP took 128 of the 132 seats, with the remainder going to nominal independents. All but five of the candidates belonged to the ruling party. The highly circumscribed vote resulted in an infusion of somewhat younger members, though the senior leadership remained in place. The new legislature reelected LPRP general secretary Choummaly Sayasone for a second term as the country's president. Thongsing Thammavong, the prime minister since late 2010, was similarly confirmed in office.

Political Rights and Civil Liberties: Laos is not an electoral democracy. The 1991 constitution makes the LPRP the sole legal political party and grants it a leading role at all levels of government. The party's Central Committee and Politburo dominate decision making. The LPRP vets all candidates for election to the National Assembly, whose members elect the president. In 2011, the legislature was increased in size from 115 members to 132, supposedly to make it more inclusive. Although the system's opacity left much to speculation, some analysts argued that the National Assembly elected in April reflected a shift in influence from the military to the party. Observers also suggested that many new legislators were more technocratic and focused on development rather than political matters. The assembly featured somewhat more open debate than in previous years, but it continued to hold little real power.

Corruption by government officials is widespread. Laws aimed at curbing graft are rarely enforced, and government regulation of virtually every facet of life provides many opportunities for bribery. Senior officials in government and the military are frequently involved in commercial logging, mining, and other extractive enterprises. Laos was ranked 154 out of 183 countries surveyed in Transparency International's 2011 Corruption Perceptions Index. Both Vietnam and China have significant influence in Laos, and their militaries have allegedly participated in widespread smuggling of Lao resources. In 2011, the London-based Environmental Investigation Agency reported that Vietnam's army plays a central role in timber smuggling in Laos. Lao activists also claim that Chinese companies involved in the rubber business have bribed many local officials for access to land.

Freedom of the press is severely restricted. Any journalist who criticizes the government or discusses controversial political topics faces legal punishment. The state owns all media. Residents within frequency range of Radio Free Asia and other foreign broadcasts from Thailand can access these alternative media sources. While very few Lao have access to the internet, its content is not heavily censored, partly because the government lacks the capability to monitor and block most Web traffic. Many educated Lao obtain news about Laos through Thai online newspapers.

Religious freedom is constrained. The religious practice of the majority Buddhist population is somewhat restricted through the LPRP's control of clergy training and supervision of temples. Lao officials reportedly continue to jail Christians or expel them from their villages for proselytizing. Several Christian pastors were arrested in Khammouan Province in early 2011; their whereabouts were unknown at the end of the year. In April, advocacy groups claimed that Lao and Vietnamese troops had killed four ethnic Hmong Christians living near the border.

Academic freedom is not respected. University professors cannot teach or write about democracy or other politically sensitive topics, though Laos has invited select foreign academics to teach courses in the country, and some young people go overseas for university education. Government surveillance of the population has been scaled back in recent years, but searches without warrants still occur.

The government severely restricts freedom of assembly. Laws prohibit participation in organizations that engage in demonstrations or public protests, or that in any other way cause "turmoil or social instability." Violators can receive sentences of up to five years in prison. Groups of demonstrators have sometimes disappeared. After signing the International Covenant on Civil and Political Rights in 2009, Laos created a legal framework for nongovernmental organizations (NGOs), allowing such groups to be licensed; this has affected primarily foreign NGOs, which have proliferated in the country in recent years. There are some domestic nongovernmental welfare and professional groups, but they are prohibited from pursuing political agendas and are subject to strict state control.

All unions must belong to the official Federation of Lao Trade Unions. Strikes are not expressly prohibited, but workers rarely stage walkouts, and they do not have the right to bargain collectively.

The courts are corrupt and controlled by the LPRP. Long procedural delays are common, particularly for cases dealing with public grievances. Security forces often illegally detain suspects. Prisoners are frequently tortured and must bribe officials to obtain better food, medicine, family visits, and more humane treatment.

Discrimination against members of ethnic minority tribes is common. The Hmong, who fielded a guerrilla army allied with U.S. forces during the Vietnam War, are particularly distrusted by the government and face harsh treatment. Although some Hmong who are loyal to the LPRP have been elected to the national legislature, poorer and more rural Hmong have been forced off their land to make way for extractive industries. Some Hmong refugees who returned to the country from Thailand in late 2009 and early 2010 appear to have vanished, and efforts by their families, foreign diplomats, and members of the U.S. Congress to obtain information on their whereabouts in 2011 were largely unsuccessful. Separately, Hmong NGOs claim that three Hmong Americans have been imprisoned in Laos since visiting the country in 2007.

All land is owned by the state, though citizens have rights to use it. On some occasions, the government has awarded land to citizens with government connections, money, or links to foreign companies. Traditional land rights still exist in some areas, adding to confusion and conflict over access. With no fair or robust system to protect land rights or ensure compensation for displacement, development projects often spur public resentment. In May, an unidentified gunman fired on the security vehicles of an Australian-owned mining operation. The 2011 decision to delay approval for the Xayaburi dam was considered a milestone for environmental protection and resettlement rights in Laos, but it had little practical effect as work reportedly continued on the project.

Although laws guarantee women many of the same rights as men, gender-based discrimination and abuse are widespread. Tradition and religious practices have contributed to women's inferior access to education, employment opportunities, and worker benefits. An estimated 15,000 to 20,000 women and girls from the Mekong region, including Laos, are trafficked each year for prostitution, and the construction of new highways linking China to Thailand and Vietnam via Laos has raised concerns over likely increases in prostitution, drug trafficking, and the prevalence of HIV/AIDS. However, the government has made some improvements in combating trafficking over the last five years, including closer cooperation with neighboring governments. A record 33 women were elected to the National Assembly in 2011.

Latvia

Political Rights: 2
Civil Liberties: 2
Status: Free

Population: 2,217,000
Capital: Riga

Ten-Year Ratings Timeline For Year Under Review (Political Rights, Civil Liberties, Status)

2002	2003	2004	2005	2006	2007	2008	2009	2010	2011
1,2F	1,2F	1,2F	1,1F	1,1F	2,1F	2,1F	2,1F	2,2F	2,2F

Overview: **Following a series of high-level government corruption scandals, Latvians voted for the first time to dissolve Parliament in a July 2011 referendum, triggering a snap parliamentary election on September 17. A center-right governing coalition emerged, with incumbent prime minister Valdis Dombrovskis remaining in office. Andris Berzins defeated incumbent Valdis Zatlers in the June 2 presidential election.**

After centuries of foreign domination, Latvia gained its independence in 1918, only to be annexed by the Soviet Union during World War II. The long Soviet occupation featured a massive influx of Russians and the deportation, execution, and emigration of tens of thousands of ethnic Latvians. In 1991, Latvia regained its independence as the Soviet Union disintegrated, and a multiparty system took root during the 1990s. The country joined both the European Union (EU) and NATO in 2004.

In the face of a deepening economic crisis, thousands of Latvians marched on the Parliament building in January 2009, and their peaceful demands for the government's resignation escalated into violent protests. The ruling coalition collapsed in February, and a new government was formed, with Valdis Dombrovskis of the New Era Party becoming prime minister. The government spent the rest of the year enacting spending cuts as Latvia suffered a deep economic recession.

In October 2010 parliamentary elections, Unity—a center-right electoral bloc composed of New Era, Civic Union, and the Society for Political Change—won 33 seats. Unity subsequently formed an unstable 55-seat coalition with the Union of Greens and Farmers (ZZS), a party led by powerful businessman and Ventspils mayor Aivars Lembergs and beset by allegations of corruption and subservience to business interests.

In early 2011, the new governing coalition was strained by a lack of agreement on fiscal measures. By May, corruption had become a dominant political issue; that month, Parliament blocked the lifting of immunity for member of parliament Ainars Slesers, thereby preventing the Bureau for the Prevention and Combating of Corruption (KNAB) from searching his home in connection with a major corruption investigation. President Valdis Zatlers responded by calling for the dissolution of Parliament for the first time in Latvia's independent history. A July 23 referendum on the issue passed with 94 percent of the vote.

In the run-up to the snap September 17 elections, which focused largely on corruption issues, Zatlers formed the center-right, pro-transparency Zatlers Reform Party (ZRP). Two right-wing nationalist parties, For Fatherland and Freedom/LNNK and All for Latvia, officially merged into the National Alliance party. Harmony Center, a party largely backed by ethnic Russians, captured the greatest share of votes for the first time, winning 31 seats. The newly formed ZRP won 22 seats, Unity secured 20 seats, the National Alliance won 14 seats, and the ZZS captured 13 seats. Slesers' Latvia's First Party-Latvian Way, which was renamed the Slesers Reform Party, failed to cross the electoral threshold. Despite its first-place finish, Harmony Center was not included in the new government. Instead, ZRP, Unity, and the National Alliance formed a 56-seat governing coalition, with Dombrovskis returning as prime minister.

Political Rights and Civil Liberties: Latvia is an electoral democracy. The constitution provides for a unicameral, 100-seat Parliament (Saeima), whose members are elected for four-year terms. Parliament elects the president, who serves up to two four-year terms. Incumbent Valdis Zatlers, who took office in 2007, lost reelection to ZZS candidate Andris Berzins on June 2. The prime minister is nominated by the president and must be approved by Parliament. Noncitizen residents may organize political parties, but only if the party counts an equal number of Latvian citizens as members. The political landscape remained fractured and party alliances proved largely unstable in 2011. During the year, former prime minister Andris Skele announced his retirement from politics and dissolved his People's Party, which had been the leader of three governments in the 2000s. In June, the Parliament passed legislation capping political parties' election spending at half of its 2010 limit.

Corruption continued to be a major issue in Latvia in 2011. In 2010, KNAB director Normunds Vilnitis had proposed a sweeping reorganization that many, including KNAB employees, argued would reduce the institution's effectiveness. While Vilnitis was abroad on holiday in May 2011, KNAB launched a major case on bribery, money laundering, and misuse of power involving Ainars Slesers, Andris Skele, and Aivars Lembergs. In June, Vilnitis was dismissed by Parliament after the release of a government commission report critical of his job performance. In November, Parliament unanimously supported the election of Jaroslavs Strelcenoks to head KNAB. In June, a Riga district court recognized an English court decision to freeze $135 million of Lembergs's assets in connection to a case involving the embezzlement of funds from Ventspils Nafta, a major petroleum shipment company; the case was ongoing at year's end. In March, three former Riga City Council officials were sentenced to between three and eight years in prison for bribery. Parliament passed an anticorruption law in December—nearly 15 years after the bill was first debated in the legislature—requiring citizens to declare assets worth more than US$19,000.

The government generally respects freedom of the press. Private television and radio stations broadcast programs in both Latvian and Russian. While newspapers publish a wide range of political viewpoints, there has been evidence of increasing business and political influence on the media. Observers of the 2010 and 2011 elections noted that political parties often made payments to news outlets for favorable coverage. In 2009, the highly respected independent newspaper *Diena* was sold to an undisclosed foreign owner; many of the paper's leading journalists and editors resigned in protest. In 2010, two former public relations experts with political ties to Slesers and Skele were appointed as editor in chief and deputy editor. Viesturs Koziols, a wealthy businessman with similar ties bought a controlling stake in the Diena Media Group in August 2010. In 2011 KNAB revealed that it believed Slesers, Skele, Lembergs, and another business partner to be *Diena's* true owners. In a move to promote media transparency and editorial independence, the Law on the Press and other Mass Media was amended on September 22 to require mass media outlets to reveal their beneficial owners. The government does not restrict access to the internet.

Freedom of religion is generally respected. However, so-called traditional religious groups enjoy certain privileges, such as the ability to provide religious instruction to public school students, which are unavailable to newer groups. There are no government restrictions on academic freedom.

Freedoms of assembly and association are protected by law and in practice. In June 2011, nearly 8,000 people attended an "Oligarch Funeral" protest to denounce political corruption and the perceived concentration of power in the hands of Latvia's supposed oligarchs. The government does not restrict the activities of nongovernmental organizations. Workers enjoy the right to establish trade unions, strike, and engage in collective bargaining. Union members comprise roughly 15 percent of the workforce.

While judicial independence is generally respected, inefficiency, politicization, and corruption continue to be problems. In October 2011, Constitutional Court judge Vineta Muizniece's immunity was lifted so that charges could be brought against her in December for the 2009 falsification of the minutes of Parliament's Legal Affairs Committee. A January 2011 shootout between police officers and a gang robbing a casino left one officer dead and others injured; four out of the five gang members were former or serving policemen, and two of them were members of the elite "Alfa" force. The Alfa members had only recently rejoined the squad following allegations of bribery and extortion. Interior Minister Linda Murniece resigned over the matter, and only days later another elite police officer was arrested on drug dealing charges. Lengthy pretrial detention remains a concern, and law enforcement officials have allegedly abused persons in custody. Prisons continue to suffer from overcrowding and poor access to health care.

Approximately 15 percent of Latvia's residents are noncitizens. Those who immigrated during the Soviet period, the majority of whom are ethnic Russians, must apply for citizenship and pass a Latvian language test. In April, dueling signature drives were held by Latvian and ethnic Russian nationalist groups with the goal of putting linguistic issues to a referendum; the former group aimed to eliminate all instruction in languages other than Latvian in publicly funded schools, while the latter advocated granting Russian official second language status. Both initiatives failed, but another signature drive was held in November, again with the goal of putting the question of Russian as an official language to referendum. On December 19, the Central Election Commission announced that enough signatures had been collected to hold a referendum on making Russian an official second language; the referendum was scheduled for February 2012.

Women enjoy the same legal rights as men, but they often face employment and wage discrimination. There are 23 women in the newly elected Parliament and 4 in the 14-member cabinet. Domestic violence continues to be a serious problem. Latvia continues to be a source for women trafficked for the purpose of prostitution, mostly to Western Europe.

Lebanon

Political Rights: 5
Civil Liberties: 4*
Status: Partly Free

Population: 4,264,000
Capital: Beirut

Ratings Change: Lebanon's civil liberties rating declined from 3 to 4 due to a violent government response to protests against Najib Miqati's appointment as prime minister in January, as well as the imposition of restrictions on those calling for democracy in Syria, which resulted in a number of detentions by military intelligence officials.

Ten-Year Ratings Timeline For Year Under Review (Political Rights, Civil Liberties, Status)

2002	2003	2004	2005	2006	2007	2008	2009	2010	2011
6,5NF	6,5NF	6,5NF	5,4PF	5,4PF	5,4PF	5,4PF	5,3PF	5,3PF	5,4PF

Overview: **After 11 ministers stepped down in January 2011 to protest a UN tribunal's indictment of five Hezbollah members for the 2005 assassination of former prime minister Rafiq Hariri, Najib Miqati was named as the new prime minister. The nomination, backed by Hezbollah, triggered protests and related violence, but Miqati eventually formed a cabinet in June. Also during the year, a civil conflict in neighboring Syria led refugees and defecting soldiers to cross into Lebanon. The government arbitrarily detained a number of Syrian refugees, worked to silence those calling for democracy in Syria, and intimidated human rights activists who criticized the security agencies.**

Lebanon was established as a League of Nations mandate under French control in 1920. After winning its independence in 1943, the new state maintained a precarious electoral system based on the division of power among the country's then 18 officially recognized sectarian communities. As the population's slight Christian majority waned into a minority, Muslim leaders demanded reform of the fixed 6-to-5 ratio of Christian-to-Muslim parliamentary seats and an end to exclusive Maronite Christian control of the presidency. In 1975, war erupted between a coalition of Lebanese Muslim and leftist militias aligned with Palestinian guerrilla groups on one side, and an array of Christian militias bent on preserving the political status quo on the other. Complicating the conflict further, Syrian and Israeli troops entered Lebanon in 1976 and 1978.

In 1989, the surviving members of Lebanon's 1972 parliament convened in Taif, Saudi Arabia, and agreed to an Arab League plan that would weaken the presidency, establish equal Christian and Muslim parliamentary representation, and mandate close security cooperation with occupying Syrian troops. A new Syrian-backed government then extended its writ to most of the country, with southern Lebanon remaining under Israeli occupation until 2000. By the end of the 1990s, Lebanon's economy was in deep recession, and growing public disaffection with the postwar establishment spurred demonstrations against Syrian domination.

In 2004 the United States joined with France and most other European governments in calling for an end to Syria's power over Lebanon. Damascus moved to defend its position by forcing the Lebanese parliament to approve a constitutional amendment that extended the six-year tenure of President Emile Lahoud, a staunch Syrian ally and a rival of Prime Minister Rafiq Hariri. On the eve of the parliamentary vote, the UN Security Council issued a resolution calling for a presidential election, the withdrawal of all foreign forces, and the disarmament of militias. The amendment nevertheless passed, provoking an international outcry.

Encouraged by the international climate, Hariri and other politicians who had been loyal to Syria began defecting to the opposition. In February 2005, four months after resigning as prime minister, Hariri was killed along with 22 others in a car bombing. Widespread suspicions of Syrian involvement led to international pressure for an immediate Syrian withdrawal and to extensive anti-Syrian demonstrations in Beirut. An interim government was formed to oversee legislative elections. Syrian troops pulled out of the country in April 2005, and in the May and June balloting, allies of the late Hariri—calling themselves the March 14 Coalition—expanded their parliamentary bloc to 72 out of 128 seats. The coalition, consisting mainly of Sunni Muslims and certain Christian and Druze factions, and with international support from the United States, Saudi Arabia, and others, went on to form a new government led by Prime Minister Fouad Siniora.

The March 14 Coalition lacked the two-thirds parliamentary majority needed to overturn Lahoud's term extension and elect a new president, leaving Lahoud in office and paralyzing the government. Meanwhile, a series of assassinations and bombings that began in the months after the Syrian withdrawal targeted key anti-Syrian politicians.

In July 2006, the militia of the Shiite Islamist movement Hezbollah attacked Israeli forces in a cross-border raid, sparking a six-week war that severely damaged Lebanon's infrastructure and killed some 1,500 people, most of them Lebanese civilians. After a UN-brokered ceasefire, Lebanese politicians struggled to stabilize the government. The March 8 Coalition—a largely Shiite and Christian bloc that included Hezbollah and was aligned with Syria and Iran—left the national unity government in November, demanding a reorganized cabinet in which it would hold veto power.

In 2007, the army waged a four-month campaign against Fatah al-Islam, a Sunni Islamist militant group based in Nahr el-Bared, a Palestinian refugee camp. The fighting killed some 400 people and displaced more than 30,000 others, and the camp was completely destroyed. Subsequent reconstruction proceeded slowly.

In May 2008, responding to a pair of government decisions they viewed as a threat, Hezbollah and its allies seized West Beirut by force. Battles between opposition and government supporters raged across Lebanon for almost a week, leaving nearly 100 people dead. A power-sharing agreement brokered by Qatar then cleared the way for the delayed election of politically neutral army commander Michel Suleiman as president, the formation of a new national unity government, and the passage of a revised election law in September. In June 2009 parliamentary elections, the March 14 and March 8 coalitions won 71 and 57 seats, respectively, and Saad Hariri—the son of Rafiq Hariri—was named prime minister.

The regional and international climate produced a rapprochement between

Hariri's unity government and both Syria and Iran in late 2009 and 2010. Political leaders of all persuasions tried to calm the public mood after it became clear that the UN Special Tribunal for Lebanon (STL) was investigating Hezbollah members suspected of involvement in the 2005 assassination of Rafiq Hariri, threatening the tenuous 2009 power-sharing agreement. Hezbollah leader Hassan Nasrallah pledged to resist the STL, accused Israel of Hariri's murder, and effectively prevented security forces from executing an arrest warrant for a general previously accused in the case. To avoid political and sectarian fighting, political leaders chose which candidates would run in the 2010 municipal elections, effectively deciding the outcome well in advance of the balloting.

Eleven ministers allied with Hezbollah resigned in January 2011 to protest the STL's indictment of Hezbollah members in the Hariri case and Saad Hariri's refusal to end the government's cooperation with the tribunal. The government collapsed, and Najib Miqati, backed by Hezbollah, was named as the new prime minister. The move spurred protests across the country, which continued periodically until June. The protests in May and June in particular included violent interfactional clashes between pro- and anti-Syrian demonstrators. The Lebanese military response to these protests included door-to-door raids in search of those they suspected of firing shots. Miqati did not announce a new cabinet until June, and the result was a deeply divided governing body. Despite his apparently close ties to Hezbollah, Miqati affirmed in November that his government would contribute its share of the funding for the STL.

Tensions with Israel increased in 2011 due to a maritime border dispute in which the rights to offshore natural gas reserves were at stake. Meanwhile, the internal conflict in Syria spilled over into Lebanon late in the year. Syrian forces allegedly crossed the border to capture or kill fleeing military defectors and refugees on a number of occasions, and there were reports of landmines being placed along the border.

Political Rights and Civil Liberties: Lebanon is not an electoral democracy. Although the 2009 parliamentary elections were conducted peacefully and judged to be free and fair in some respects, vote-buying was reported to be rampant, and the electoral framework retained a number of fundamental structural flaws linked to the country's sectarian political system.

The president is selected every six years by the 128-member National Assembly, which in turn is elected for four-year terms. The president and parliament nominate the prime minister, who, along with the president, chooses the cabinet, subject to parliamentary approval. The unwritten National Pact of 1943 stipulates that the president must be a Maronite Christian, the prime minister a Sunni Muslim, and the speaker of the National Assembly a Shiite Muslim. Parliamentary seats are divided among major sects under a constitutional formula that does not reflect their current demographic weight. Shiites comprise at least a third of the population, but they are allotted only 21 percent of parliamentary seats. The sectarian political balance has been periodically reaffirmed and occasionally modified by foreign-brokered agreements like the 1989 Taif Accords and the 2008 Doha Agreement.

The 2009 parliamentary elections were conducted under the 2008 election law, which stemmed from the Doha Agreement. It condensed nationwide voting into a single day, introduced some curbs on campaign finance and advertising, and created smaller, more religiously homogeneous districts. However, recently proposed reforms—including the reduction of the voting age to 18 from 21, a system allowing expatriates to vote abroad, the provision of preprinted ballots, quotas for women, and institutional reforms to strengthen political parties—have not yet gone in to effect due to sectarian and partisan concerns. While recent elections have been generally free of violence and other irregularities, they have only been competitive in certain Christian districts, as party leaders have sought to avoid divisive campaigning.

The sectarian political system and the powerful role of foreign patrons effectively limit the accountability of elected officials to the public at large. Political and bureaucratic corruption is widespread, businesses routinely pay bribes and cultivate ties with politicians to win contracts, and anticorruption laws are loosely enforced. Lebanon was ranked 134 out of 183 countries surveyed in Transparency International's 2011 Corruption Perceptions Index.

Lebanon has a long tradition of press freedom, though nearly all media outlets have ties to political groups. There are seven privately owned television stations and dozens of privately owned radio and print outlets that reflect a range of views. Internet access is not restricted. However, vaguely worded laws that could be used to ban critical reporting on Syria, foreign leaders, the military, the judiciary, and the presidency remain in effect. While officials generally choose not to enforce such restrictions, they have been applied in isolated cases in the last few years. During the protests in January 2011, targeted attacks on journalists were reported in Beirut, Tripoli, and Sidon.

Freedom of religion is guaranteed in the constitution and protected in practice. However, informal religious discrimination is common. In 2009, the Interior Ministry allowed citizens not to list their religion on their national identity cards or national registration. The reform has had little practical effect, however, since the country's political system is based on sectarian quotas. Those who delete their religion from their national registration therefore seriously limit their ability to hold government positions or run for political office. Academic freedom is firmly established.

Rights to freedom of association and assembly have been generally unrestricted in the past, as hundreds of thousands of Lebanese have rallied in favor of or in opposition to the government. However, there have been reports of detentions of protest organizers who call for democratic change in Syria. In February 2011, for example, six members of a Syrian family were detained after distributing flyers that urged people to protest against the Syrian regime.

In the past, Lebanon's civil society was vibrant, and nongovernmental organizations (NGOs), including human rights groups, operated openly. While this remains the case for many groups, constraints have increased in recent years. By law, the government only requires notification of an NGO's formation, but the Interior Ministry has at times transformed this into an approval process and has been known to conduct inquiries into an organization's founding members. NGOs must invite ministry representatives to votes on bylaws or boards of directors. In July 2011, Saadeddine Shatila of the NGO Alkarama was twice questioned by military intelligence agents about his investigations into torture and human rights violations. International and domestic human rights groups described the case as part of a pattern of systematic intimidation of activists who question the practices of Lebanese security agencies.

All workers except those in government may establish unions, which have the right to strike and bargain collectively. In recent years, unions have been closely affiliated with political groupings, and labor concerns have thus taken a back seat to union-based political activity.

The judiciary is ostensibly independent, but it is subject to heavy political influence in practice. The Judicial Council nominates judges, who are then approved by the Justice Ministry. Both government and opposition parties vet judicial appointments. International standards of criminal procedure are generally observed in the regular judiciary, but not in the military courts, which consist largely of military officers with no legal training. Though civilian oversight is guaranteed in theory, it is very difficult for civilians to observe the trials in practice, and in some cases defendants have no right to appeal. The military courts are tasked with trying those accused of spying for Israel, as well as Fatah al-Islam militants, human rights workers, and individuals perceived to be inciting sectarian conflict.

The security forces' practice of arbitrary detention had declined until the last few years. While the government has made some progress toward ending torture, regulations on the issue are often not enforced, and the use of torture remains widespread in security-related cases. Prison conditions are poor. In 2011, a number of Syrian refugees were detained, with the threat of repatriation to Syria. As of December 2011, there were about 4,500 registered Syrian refugees in Lebanon, but many Syrians have entered illegally and are therefore not registered with the United Nations.

About 400,000 Palestinian refugees living in Lebanon are denied citizenship rights and face employment and property restrictions. A 2010 law allowed them access to social security benefits, end-of-service compensation, and the right to bring complaints before labor courts. However, the law effectively closed off several highly skilled professions to Palestinians, retained very high bars to their entering other skilled professions, and did not remove restrictions on property ownership.

The estimated 50,000 Iraqi refugees in Lebanon also face employment and property restrictions, and there is a substantial Sudanese refugee population. Most of them do not enjoy official refugee status and thus face arbitrary detention, deportation, harassment, and abuse. Human rights groups estimate that at any given time, there are about 100 refugees jailed on immigration or work-violation charges in Lebanon. Some of these refugees are being "voluntarily" detained to avoid repatriation.

Women enjoy many of the same rights as men, but they experience some social and legal discrimination. Since personal status matters are adjudicated by each sect's religious authorities, women are subject to discriminatory rules governing marriage, divorce, inheritance, and child custody. Women are underrepresented in politics, holding only four parliamentary seats, and do not receive equal social security provisions. Men convicted of so-called honor crimes against women usually receive lenient sentences. Foreign female household workers are especially vulnerable to exploitation and abuse. According to the U.S. State Department's 2011 Trafficking in Persons Report, foreign workers from Africa and East Asia are often victims of forced labor, withheld wages, restricted movement, sexual exploitation, and verbal and physical abuse. The Lebanese government has done little to stop this abuse and neglect.

Lesotho

Political Rights: 3
Civil Liberties: 3
Status: Partly Free

Population: 2,193,800
Capital: Maseru

Ten-Year Ratings Timeline For Year Under Review (Political Rights, Civil Liberties, Status)

2002	2003	2004	2005	2006	2007	2008	2009	2010	2011
2,3PF	2,3F	2,3F	2,3F	2,3F	2,3F	2,3F	3,3PF	3,3PF	3,3PF

Overview: **In August 2011, unions, political groups, and civil society organizations staged a series of large demonstrations to protest a variety of economic and governance issues. The ruling Lesotho Congress for Democracy dominated local elections held in October and December.**

Lesotho gained independence from Britain in 1966, and the following 30 years featured a number of military coups, annulled elections, and suspensions of constitutional rule. Parliamentary elections in 1998, although judged free and fair by international observers, set off violent protests after the results gave the ruling Lesotho Congress for Democracy (LCD) party 79 out of 80 constituency seats with just 60.5 percent of the vote. Troops from South Africa and Botswana—under the mandate of the 14-country Southern African Development Community (SADC)—were summoned to restore order. Following an evaluation of the country's electoral process, an Interim Political Authority decided that future elections would be supervised by an independent commission and 40 proportionally determined seats would be added to the National Assembly. In the 2002 elections, the LCD captured 77 constituency seats, while the opposition Basotho National Party (BNP) won 21 of the new proportional-representation seats.

In late 2006, Prime Minister Pakalitha Mosisili called snap elections after 18 members of the LCD joined a new opposition party, the All Basotho Congress (ABC). In the February 2007 voting, the LCD won 61 seats, while the ABC captured 17. Lesotho's Independent Electoral Commission (IEC) allocated 21 of the 40 proportional-representation seats to the LCD-allied National Independent Party (NIP) and 10 to the ABC's ally, the Lesotho Workers' Party (LWP). Six other parties were also awarded seats. The elections were declared free and fair by domestic and international observers.

Opposition parties disputed the allocations, accusing the government of poll-rigging and gerrymandering, and called a general strike. The strike was halted after the SADC agreed to mediate, but the talks failed to formally resolve the dispute. In 2008, 43 by-elections were held, the results of which were also contested by the opposition. ABC supporters protested outside the office of the IEC, holding several workers hostage until the protest was broken up by police. In 2009, gunmen opened fire on Prime Minister Mosisili's house, but he escaped unharmed. Government officials and some journalists linked the assassination attempt to the ongoing election dispute, calling it a failed coup. The same year, the head SADC mediator, former Botswana president Sir Ketumile Masire, ended his mission in Lesotho, accusing the government of avoiding direct talks with the opposition. The Christian Council of Lesotho took over SADC's facilitation of the dialogue, but the disputes remained unresolved at the end of 2011. In local elections held in October and December 2011, the LCD captured 79 of 87 contested councils.

In May 2011, the LCD and ABC youth leagues joined factory and taxi workers to stage a protest in Maseru over economic grievances, including opposition to a government job freeze. After the prime minister rejected the protestors' demands, unions, opposition parties, business organizations, and civil society groups organized a series of much larger demonstrations in August to protest issues including unemployment and corruption. Factory and taxi workers organized a three-day work stay-away to coincide with the demonstrations.

Drought has plagued the country since 2001, leading to food shortages and the dependence of some 450,000 people on food aid. Lesotho suffers an adult HIV/AIDS prevalence rate of approximately 23 percent, one of the world's highest. The government announced in 2005 that it would offer free HIV testing to all citizens, the first such program in the world. Roughly 25 percent of the country's infected citizens receive antiretroviral treatment.

Political Rights and Civil Liberties: Lesotho is an electoral democracy. King Letsie III serves as ceremonial head of state. The lower house of Parliament, the National Assembly, is comprised of 120 seats; 80 seats are filled through first past-the-post constituency votes and 40 through proportional representation. Members serve five-year terms, and the leader of the majority party becomes the prime minister. The Senate, the upper house of Parliament, consists of Lesotho's 22 traditional principal chiefs, who wield considerable authority in rural areas, and 11 other members appointed on the advice of the prime minister.

While the government has aggressively prosecuted cases of graft, political corruption remains a problem. A 2010 report by the African Peer Review Mechanism stated that corruption was rife in all sectors of government and public services, and that cronyism was prevalent in state bidding procedures. In December 2011, the Public Accounts Committee reported a significant increase in corruption and theft by civil servants, most of which go unprosecuted. Lesotho was ranked 77 out of 183 countries surveyed in Transparency International's 2011 Corruption Perceptions Index.

Freedoms of speech and the press are generally respected. Independent newspapers and radio stations routinely criticize the government. However, state-owned print and broadcast media tend to reflect the views of the ruling party, and the state controls the country's largest radio station and its only television station. Critical media outlets and journalists face severe libel and defamation penalties, and reporters are occasionally harassed, threatened, and attacked. In March 2011, the private radio station Harvest FM was served with a M1million (US$145k) defamation suit by Assistant Police Commissioner Thakane Theko over a 2010 story alleging she engaged in accepting bribes and other corrupt activities. In September, High Court Judge 'Maseforo Mahase also initiated an M8 million (US$1.1 million) defamation lawsuit against Harvest FM over comments on a talk show accusing him of corruption. A proposed media reform bill that would create a public service broadcaster, eliminate repressive national security statutes, and place the burden of proof on the plaintiff in cases involving slander and libel, has been under review for 13 years. The government does not restrict internet access.

Freedom of religion in this predominantly Christian country is widely observed. The government does not restrict academic freedom.

Freedoms of assembly and association are generally respected, though demonstrations are sometimes broken up violently. According to the Media Institute of Southern Africa-Lesotho, several people were shot during the August 2011 protests when police opened fire on demonstrators. In 2010, an LCD-proposed bill requiring prior authorization from government officials to hold public meetings passed through the law and public safety committee in Parliament. Following protests from the opposition and civic groups, 21 amendments were made to the bill before it became law, including less onerous requirements for gatherings in rural areas and more discretion for judges in fining violators. While labor rights are constitutionally guaranteed, the union movement is weak and fragmented, and many employers in the textile sector do not allow union activity.

Courts are nominally independent, but higher courts are subject to outside influence. The large backlog of cases often leads to trial delays and lengthy pretrial detention. Mistreatment of civilians by security forces reportedly continues. Prisons are dilapidated, severely overcrowded, and lack essential health services; instances of torture and use of excessive force have been reported. An independent ombudsman's office is tasked with protecting citizens' rights, but its enforcement powers are weak.

Tensions between the Basotho and the small Chinese business community have led to minor incidents of violence in recent years.

The constitution bars gender-based discrimination, but customary practice and law still restrict women's rights in the areas of property and inheritance. While their husbands are alive, women married under customary law have the status of minors in civil courts and may not enter into binding contracts. Domestic violence is reportedly widespread. Women are prevalent in senior political and economic positions in Lesotho: about one in five government ministers are women, and women make up some 52 percent of national legislators and senior managers. In 2011, Lesotho ranked 8th in the World Economic Forum Global Gender gap ranking.

Liberia

Political Rights: 3
Civil Liberties: 4
Status: Partly Free

Population: 4,132,700
Capital: Monrovia

Ten-Year Ratings Timeline For Year Under Review (Political Rights, Civil Liberties, Status)

2002	2003	2004	2005	2006	2007	2008	2009	2010	2011
6,6NF	6,6NF	5,4PF	4,4PF	3,4PF	3,4PF	3,4PF	3,4PF	3,4PF	3,4PF

Overview: **The Unity Party (UP) captured the largest number of seats in October 2011 parliamentary elections, while President Ellen Johnson-Sirleaf of the UP secured a second term in office following a November runoff vote. A national referendum in August on four proposed constitutional amendments led to the eventual adoption of an amendment that allowed for the election of most officials by a simple rather than a majority vote. Meanwhile, little progress was made in advancing national reconciliation and implementing Truth and Reconciliation Commission recommendations, while the political crisis in neighboring Côte d'Ivoire created significant security and humanitarian challenges for Liberia.**

Liberia was settled in 1822 by freed slaves from the United States and became an independent republic in 1847. Americo-Liberians, descendants of the freed slaves, dominated the political landscape for more than a century. During the 1970s, a number of groups agitated for multiparty democracy and an end to the marginalization of indigenous Liberians. In 1980, fighters loyal to Army Master Sergeant Samuel Doe murdered President William Tolbert in a coup. Doe subsequently assumed leadership of the country; his regime concentrated power among members of his Krahn ethnic group and suppressed others. In 1989, Charles Taylor, a former minister in Doe's government, recruited fighters from among the Gio and Mano ethnic groups and launched a guerrilla insurgency against Doe from neighboring Côte d'Ivoire. A year later, an armed intervention led by Nigeria—under the aegis of the Economic Community of West African States (ECOWAS)—prevented Taylor from seizing Monrovia, the capital. However, it failed to protect Doe, who was murdered by a splinter rebel group led by Prince Johnson.

After years of endemic violence and numerous failed transitional arrangements, a peace accord was signed in 1995. Taylor won national elections in 1997, but subsequently made little effort to seek genuine reconciliation or implement security and economic reforms. Violence erupted again in 1999, as the rebel group Liberians United for Reconciliation and Democracy (LURD) sought to overthrow Taylor, purportedly with backing from Sierra Leone and Guinea. Meanwhile, the United Nations in 2001 imposed an arms embargo and diamond sanctions on Liberia in response to its alleged involvement in the conflict in Sierra Leone. By 2003, LURD controlled most of northern Liberia, while another rebel group, the Movement for Democracy in Liberia (MODEL), squeezed Taylor's government from the southeast. In June of that year, a UN-backed war crimes tribunal charged Taylor with supporting militants in Sierra Leone. With the capital threatened and calls from the United States for his resignation, Taylor stepped down in August 2003 and accepted Nigeria's offer of asylum.

Taylor's departure ended 14 years of intermittent civil war that killed some 200,000 Liberians. The ECOWAS helped negotiate an end to the fighting, and West African peacekeepers became part of a 15,000-strong UN peacekeeping force. In accordance with the 2003 Comprehensive Peace Agreement, members of Taylor's government, LURD, MODEL, and civil society representatives formed the National Transitional Government of Liberia (NTGL). Under the chairmanship of businessman Charles Gyude Bryant, the NTGL governed the country until the 2005 elections. Taylor was apprehended in 2006, and his trial before a UN-backed special court opened in 2008 and continued through 2011.

Unity Party (UP) candidate Ellen Johnson-Sirleaf won the 2005 presidential runoff vote, while the CDC placed first in concurrent legislative polls, followed by the UP.

Initial results of an August 2011 national referendum on proposed constitutional amendments indicated that voters had rejected all four proposed amendments. However, the Supreme Court handed down a judgment in September, stating that the National Election Commission had incorrectly calculated the results, and that one of the amendments—which allowed for the election of all public officials, except for the president and vice president, by a simple rather than an absolute majority—had actually passed. Meanwhile, in August, violence in advance of the presidential and parliamentary elections included attacks on a senator's convoy, against senior CDC leaders amidst allegations of fraud in the party's primaries, and on UP party officials; however, no deaths were reported.

In the October 11 presidential poll, Johnson-Sirleaf captured 43.9 percent of the vote, while the CDC's Winston Tubman took 32.7 percent, and Prince Johnson of the National Union for Democratic Progress (NUDP) secured 11.6 percent. Although opposition members alleged fraud and corruption, international and local observers found that the elections had been generally free and fair. One day prior to the November 8 runoff vote, police clashed with demonstrators during a CDC protest, resulting in at least two deaths and numerous injuries. Radio and television stations with perceived pro-CDC biases were shut down by the government. Johnson-Sirleaf won 90.7 percent of the vote in the runoff, while Tubman took 9.3 percent. Johnson-Sirleaf called for greater national reconciliation and appointed fellow Nobel Peace Prize winner Leymah Gbowee to lead the initiative.

In concurrent parliamentary elections, the UP secured the most seats, with 33 percent in each legislative house. In the lower house, the UP took 24 seats, followed by the CDC with 11 seats, the Liberty Party with 7 seats, and the NUDP with 6 seats. Seven other parties and nine independent candidates captured the remaining seats. Following elections to the upper house, in which half of the Senate seats were up for election, the UP held 11 seats, the National Patriotic Party held 6, the CDC held 3, and the NUDP held 2 seats. Five other parties and two independent candidates held the remaining seats.

The first half of 2011 saw an influx of some 180,000 combatants and refugees from political crises in Côte d'Ivoire and, to a lesser extent, Guinea. In April, the Liberian government arrested a known former warlord and other combatants for fighting in Côte d'Ivoire. Although the Johnson-Sirleaf administration made clear its determination to prosecute any Liberian mercenaries, many of those arrested were later released due to a lack of evidence. In June, 88 suspected Ivorian combatants were interned in special facilities in Liberia. Violent ethnic clashes along Liberia's border with Guinea resulted in an influx of some 3,000 Guinean refugees by August. However, by the end of 2011, registered refugee numbers had decreased slightly, to approximately 128,000.

Political Rights and Civil Liberties: Liberia is an electoral democracy. The 2011 presidential and legislative elections were generally considered by international and local observers to have been free and fair. The National Elections Commission (NEC) successfully conducted the August 2011 national referendum, and when the referendum results were challenged in court, the NEC upheld and implemented the court's decisions. The bicameral legislature consists of a 30-member Senate and a 73-member House of Representatives; senators are elected to nine-year terms, and representatives to six-year terms. However, in 2005, as part of the peace agreement, half of the senators were elected to six-year terms only, allowing for staggered senatorial elections to be introduced in 2011. The president can serve up to two six-year terms.

The organizational and policy capacity of most parties remains weak, and politics continues to be largely personality-driven, with strong underlying ethnic and regional loyalties. Political organization remained fluid yet fragmented in 2011, with a high degree of coalition-building in the lead-up to the elections. The Liberia Action Party and Liberia Unification Party merged with the UP; while the CDC, Liberty Party, and Prince Johnson's NUDP are the most prominent opposition parties. The Democratic Alliance and Alliance for Peace and Democracy constitute opposition coalitions.

Anticorruption efforts lagged in 2011. Insufficient follow-up on recommendations made in General Auditing Commission reports persisted. The completion of a civil servants' code of conduct was still pending at year's end. Since March 2009, the Liberian Anti-Corruption Commission (LACC) has referred only 25 cases to the Ministry of Justice for prosecution. No high-profile officials from the Johnson-Sirleaf administration have been convicted of corruption. In 2011 the LACC Chairwoman Frances Johnson-Allison called for the commission to have direct subpoena and prosecutorial powers, but lawmakers failed to act. Additionally, a 2010 corruption-related freeze on county development funds remained in place in 2011. Liberia was ranked 91 out of 183 countries surveyed in Transparency International's 2011 Corruption Perceptions Index.

Liberian media have enjoyed unprecedented freedom following the departure of Charles Taylor, exposing corruption and participating in critical public debates. The 2010 Freedom of Information Act promotes unhindered access to public information and is considered a model for the region. The country hosts a variety of newspapers, which publish mainly in the capital; numerous radio stations also operate across the country. The Press Union of Liberia (PUL) and international partners facilitated workshops on conflict-sensitive election reporting, and the media environment during elections was open. However, following violence that accompanied the November presidential runoff vote, the government shut down four radio and three television stations aligned with prominent opposition figures. The PUL and numerous other international and local media watchdogs condemned the shutdown, and following a court order, the stations reopened by year's end. The government does not restrict internet access, but poor infrastructure and high costs limit usage to a small fraction of the population.

Religious freedom is affirmed in the constitution, and legally there is no official religion. However, Liberia is a de facto Christian state, and the Muslim minority reports discrimination. The government does not restrict academic freedom, though educational infrastructure remains insufficient.

Freedoms of assembly and association are guaranteed and respected. Numerous civil society groups, including human rights organizations, operate in the country. The right of workers to strike, organize, and bargain collectively is recognized, but labor laws remain in need of reform. Labor disputes often turn violent, particularly at the various rubber plantations throughout the country. In May 2011, two plantation buildings were torched and a worker shot at the Cavalla Rubber Company in Maryland County.

Despite constitutional provisions for an independent judiciary, judges are subject to executive influence and corruption. Case backlogs, prolonged pretrial detention, prison overcrowding, and poor security at correctional facilities continue to impede judicial effectiveness. Prisons suffer from inadequate medical care, food, and sanitation, and conditions are often life-threatening. Numerous prison breaks were reported throughout the year. In an effort to improve judicial efficiency, the Judicial Training Institute graduated 61 non-lawyer magistrates in June 2011; however, they had not been assigned to postings by year's end.

Harmonization of formal and customary justice systems remains an ongoing challenge as ritual killings, mob violence, and vigilantism continue largely unhindered. At least six cases of mob violence against the police were reported in 2011. Poor discipline, high levels of absenteeism, and corruption continue to plague the police and armed forces, and relations between the military and the police remain strained.

Communal tensions over land access and ownership remain a potential threat to peace. In March 2011, villages were attacked and houses burned down as land tensions escalated along the border between Maryland and Grand Kru counties, necessitating the dispatch of the national police's emergency response unit. However, the Land Commission, which was established in 2009, in 2011 completed an inventory of land dispute cases in several counties, vetted public land sale deeds, and created a dispute-resolution task force.

Drug and human trafficking continue to pose a threat to peace consolidation in Liberia and the greater Mano River area. The Liberian Transnational Crime Unit became operational in July 2011.

Since being established in October 2010, the Independent National Human Rights Commission has made little progress in pursuing national reconciliation and implementing Truth and Reconciliation Commission (TRC) recommendations. Funding shortfalls, operational deficiencies, and a lack of political determination to break with cycles of impunity has hampered progress. In January 2011, the Supreme Court found that the TRC's recommendation of a 30-year public ban for numerous officials, including Johnson-Sirleaf, was unconstitutional and inconsistent with the right to due process. Although recommended by the TRC, no war crimes tribunal has been established and no prosecutions pursued. Johnson-Sirleaf has focused instead on implementing the Palava Hut program, which would use customary reconciliation processes to promote forgiveness. However, no steps were made to render the program operational by year's end.

While female representation in the legislature remains limited, numerous cabinet ministers and senior officials are women. In October 2011, Johnson-Sirleaf, Liberian women's rights activist Leymah Gbowee, and a Yemeni activist were awarded the Nobel Peace Prize in recognition of their contribution toward women's rights and their participation in peacebuilding. Violence against women and children, particularly rape, remains a grave problem. A specialized prosecution unit and a court with exclusive jurisdiction over sexual and gender-based violence are unable to effectively process the large number of cases brought before them. In 2011, a one-year tracking project found that, in its current capacity, the special unit would take at least 10 years to clear its case backlog.

Libya

Political Rights: 7
Civil Liberties: 6*
Status: Not Free

Population: 6,422,800
Capital: Tripoli

Ratings Change: Libya's civil liberties rating improved from 7 to 6 due to increased academic and media freedom, as well as greater freedom of assembly and private discussion, following the rollback and collapse of the highly oppressive Qadhafi regime.

Ten-Year Ratings Timeline For Year Under Review (Political Rights, Civil Liberties, Status)

2002	2003	2004	2005	2006	2007	2008	2009	2010	2011
7,7NF	7,7NF	7,7NF	7,7NF	7,7NF	7,7NF	7,7NF	7,7NF	7,7NF	7,6NF

Overview: **Influenced by uprisings in neighboring Tunisia and Egypt and spurred by the arrest of a human rights activist in Benghazi, citizens in several Libyan cities took to the streets in February 2011 to protest the 42-year rule of Mu'ammar al-Qadhafi. The protesters soon faced violence from regime loyalists and security forces, and a civil war began in the country within days. By March, a NATO-led campaign of airstrikes was under way to aid civilian protesters and rebel militias in their battles against al-Qadhafi's military. Rebels captured Tripoli in August, and al-Qadhafi, having fled the capital, was eventually killed near his hometown of Sirte in October. A National Transitional Council that had formed in rebel-held Benghazi in February moved to Tripoli toward the end of the year, but it had little effective control over the country's array of locally organized militias.**

Libya comprised three provinces of the Ottoman Empire until the Italian conquest and occupation of the area in 1911. It became an independent country in 1951, after a brief period of UN trusteeship in the wake of World War II. Libya was then ruled by King Idris, a relatively pro-Western monarch, until 1969, when a group of young army officers, led by 27-year-old captain Mu'ammar al-Qadhafi, overthrew the king's government.

Al-Qadhafi argued that foreign oil companies were profiting from the country's resources at the expense of the Libyan people, and he moved to nationalize oil assets, claiming that the revenues would be shared among the population. In the early years of his rule, al-Qadhafi published a multivolume treatise, the *Green Book*, in which he expounded his political philosophy—a fusion of Arab nationalism, socialism, and Islam. He was Libya's undisputed leader from 1969 until 2011, but he held no official title and was referred to as Brother Leader or the Guide of the Revolution.

Al-Qadhafi adopted decidedly anti-Western policies in the 1970s, and after his regime was implicated in several international terrorist attacks, the United States imposed sanctions on Libya in 1981. Relations between the two countries continued to worsen, and in 1986 the United States bombed targets in Libya, including al-Qadhafi's home. In 1988, a U.S. airliner exploded over Lockerbie, Scotland, killing all 259 people aboard as well as 11 residents of the town. After an exhaustive investigation, Scottish police issued arrest warrants for two Libyans, including an intelligence agent. The UN Security Council imposed trade sanctions on the country, and over the next several years, Libya became more economically and diplomatically isolated.

In 1999, al-Qadhafi moved to mend his international image and surrendered the two Lockerbie bombing suspects for trial. He accepted responsibility for past acts of terrorism and offered compensation packages to the families of victims. The United Nations suspended its sanctions, and the European Union (EU) reestablished diplomatic and trade relations with Tripoli. In 2001, a special Scottish court sitting in the Netherlands found one of the Lockerbie suspects guilty of masterminding the attack. Libya agreed to pay a $10 million compensation package to the family of each of the 270 victims in 2003. In light of more normalized relations with Europe, Libya purchased hundreds of millions of dollars in European weapons systems in 2007. The regime also improved its relations with the United States. In 2004, a year after al-Qadhafi's government announced that it had scrapped its nonconventional weapons program, the United States established a liaison office in Tripoli. The U.S. government eventually removed Libya from its list of state sponsors of terrorism, reestablishing a full embassy in Tripoli in 2006. Despite frequent promises, however, observance of political rights and civil liberties in Libya remained abysmal in the wake of these diplomatic and economic shifts, and the Qadhafi regime was consistently hostile to foreign and domestic criticism.

In February 2011, Libyans in several cities took to the streets to protest al-Qadhafi's 42-year rule. They were influenced by the uprisings in neighboring Tunisia and Egypt, but the proximate cause was the arrest of a human rights activist in Benghazi. Security forces violently attacked the protesters, setting off clashes between Qadhafi loyalists and a combination of civilians and defectors from the police and military. The rebels in some areas—particularly in eastern Libya—were able to clear loyalist forces from their territory, leading to a months-long civil war with multiple, shifting battlefronts.

In March, NATO launched an air campaign—led primarily by the United States, Britain, and France—to enforce a no-fly zone over the country, protect civilian protesters, and aid rebel militias in their battles against al-Qadhafi's military. As the fighting continued through the summer, the rebels made slow progress toward Tripoli from both the east and the west.

The rebel militias finally captured Tripoli in August, and al-Qadhafi, his family, and senior members of his regime were forced to flee the city. Efforts to capture the remaining loyalist strongholds and leaders continued into the fall. Al-Qadhafi himself was seized and killed by militia members near his hometown of Sirte on October 20. Saif al-Islam al-Qadhafi, the ousted leader's son and onetime heir apparent, was detained in the southern desert in November, and remained in the custody of a regional militia at year's end.

A National Transitional Council (NTC) that had formed in Benghazi in February to represent the rebel movement eventually relocated to Tripoli, and by year's end it was operating as a de facto national government, though its control over territory and armed groups in the country remained tenuous. The council, led by chairman Mustafa Abdel-Jalil, appointed Abdel Rahim al-Keeb as interim prime minister in October. After weeks of mounting pressure, the executive board of the NTC resigned on November 22, as per the interim constitution, and al-Keeb named an interim cabinet that aimed to incorporate members of competing regional and tribal militias, as well as members of the business community.

Political Rights and Civil Liberties: Libya is not an electoral democracy. Severe repression under Mu'ammar al-Qadhafi has given way to an absence of formal governance institutions and frequent skirmishes among autonomous militias. The NTC, an unelected body of about 50 members, nominally controls all aspects of the national government. Until November 2011, an NTC executive board held a majority of the governing power. After that point, a cabinet was announced by interim prime minister Abdel Rahim al-Keeb. The cabinet is responsible for maintaining order and stability throughout the country in preparation for elections in mid-2012 and the drafting of a constitution.

The 2011 uprising created somewhat more space for free political association and participation in Libya. Under the Qadhafi regime, political parties were illegal, and all political activity was strictly monitored. The NTC has made an effort to include representatives from across the country and from different backgrounds. However, only a handful of political parties have organized, including the Democratic Party of Libya and the New Libya Party.

Corruption has been pervasive in both the private sector and the government in Libya, which was ranked 168 out of 183 countries surveyed in Transparency International's 2011 Corruption Perceptions Index. The fall of the Qadhafi regime has raised some hopes that the level of corruption will decline, but there is concern about the undue influence of oil interests, foreign governments, and armed militias, and opportunities for graft continue to abound in the absence of effective fiscal, judicial, and other institutions.

Under the Qadhafi regime, there was no independent press. State-owned media largely operated as mouthpieces for the authorities, and journalists worked in a climate of fear and self-censorship. To the extent possible, the regime shut off the country's access to the internet and international media outlets during the fighting of 2011, and strict controls were imposed on foreign and domestic journalists working in the country. Qadhafi loyalist forces were responsible for the deaths of at least four foreign journalists, the detention of at least 32 journalists for reporting from the rebel-held eastern part of the country, and the disappearance of three Libyan journalists, who were still missing at year's end. A July NATO attack on a state television outlet in Tripoli resulted in the deaths of three additional journalists.

The media environment in rebel-held areas was decidedly different, especially in the eastern cities. Some 130 print outlets representing a wide range of viewpoints had been registered with the NTC by July, and several radio and television stations had been established. In addition, many individual Libyans utilized the internet and social-networking platforms during the year to share their experiences and other information.

Nearly all Libyans are Muslims. The Qadhafi regime closely monitored mosques for signs of religious extremism and Islamist political activity, but Muslims of various religious and political strains have been much more free to organize and debate their points of view since his fall. In some cases this has led to verbal and armed clashes. Salafi Muslim groups, whose fundamentalist beliefs preclude the veneration of saints, have begun to unilaterally remove bodies from Sufi Muslim shrines and rebury them in ordinary cemeteries. The few non-Muslims in Libya have been permitted to practice their faiths with relative freedom, and human rights organizations have called for this freedom to be upheld in post-Qadhafi Libya.

Academic freedom was tightly restricted under al-Qadhafi. Close state supervision has been lifted since his ouster, and the Green Book has been removed from school curriculums. However, no laws have been drafted to guarantee academic independence, and the education system has yet to resume normal operations in all parts of the country in the wake of the civil war.

Freedom of assembly has dramatically increased in light of the events of 2011. However, like many other freedoms, it came to the relatively secure, rebel-held eastern cities long before it was enjoyed in places like Tripoli. Even after the capture of the last loyalist strongholds late in the year, the ongoing presence of militia groups and the proliferation of firearms in the country limited peaceful assemblies and the public expression of dissenting views in certain areas.

Domestic nongovernmental organizations have been allowed significantly more freedom to act within Libya since the collapse of the Qadhafi regime in October. Human Rights Watch has reported that women's rights groups have organized conferences in Tripoli to discuss the role that women will play in a new Libyan government and political environment, though there have been few concrete achievements, and women only hold two seats in the transitional cabinet. Trade unions were outlawed under the Gadhafi regime; a few have made some small strides, though they are in their organizational infancy.

The role of the judiciary under the NTC remains unclear. The council named a new justice minister in November, but there are several significant legal issues to address. These include the trials of Saif al-Islam al-Qadhafi and Ali Senoussi, the former Qadhafi intelligence minister, and investigations into a large number of suspected extrajudicial executions before and during the civil conflict, including that of Mu'ammar al-Qadhafi. However, no legal framework or fully functioning courts had been established by year's end.

A large number of migrants from sub-Saharan Africa worked in Libya during al-Qadhafi's rule, and many of them were subjected to human rights abuses even before the civil conflict. There were widespread reports of mistreatment at the hands of militia groups during the fighting, and many foreign workers fled the country under perilous conditions.

Women enjoyed many of the same legal protections as men under the Qadhafi regime, but certain laws and social norms perpetuated discrimination, particularly in areas such as marriage, divorce, and inheritance. The NTC has made some limited efforts to address these issues, but the messages have been mixed. Late in the year, NTC chairman Mustafa Abdel-Jalil made comments suggesting that polygamy would be legalized, which drew international condemnation. He subsequently pledged that women would play an important role in determining Libya's future course.

Liechtenstein

Political Rights: 1
Civil Liberties: 1
Status: Free

Population: 36,200
Capital: Vaduz

Ten-Year Ratings Timeline For Year Under Review (Political Rights, Civil Liberties, Status)

2002	2003	2004	2005	2006	2007	2008	2009	2010	2011
1,1F	1,1F	1,1F	1,1F	1,1F	1,1F	1,1F	1,1F	1,1F	1,1F

Overview: **Following two successive referenda in 2011, Liechtenstein rejected full legalization of abortion, which remains a criminal act, and rebuffed a same-sex registered partnership bill passed by Parliament in March.**

Liechtenstein was established as a principality in 1719 and gained its sovereignty in 1806. Since 1995, the country has been a member of the European Economic Area, a free-trade area that links the non-European Union (EU) members of Norway, Iceland, and Liechtenstein with the EU. From 1938 to 1997, it was governed by a coalition of the Progressive Citizens' Party (FBP) and the Fatherland Union, now the Patriotic Union (VU). The latter party then ruled alone until the FBP won the 2001 elections.

In a 2003 referendum, voters approved a constitutional amendment that granted significantly more power to the hereditary monarch, Prince Hans-Adam II. In 2004, Hans-Adam handed his constitutional powers to his son, Prince Alois, though the elder prince retained his title as head of state. Following the 2005 parliamentary elections, the conservative FBP and the liberal VU formed a grand coalition, and FBP leader Otmar Hasler retained his post as prime minister.

In the February 2009 parliamentary elections, the VU won 13 seats and the FBP captured 11, while a small third party, the social-democrat Free List, took the remaining seat. The VU's Klaus Tschütscher, who replaced Hasler as prime minister in March, maintained the coalition government with the FBP.

Liechtenstein, a leading offshore tax haven, has traditionally maintained tight bank secrecy laws. However, in 2009, the principality signed agreements with several countries and agreed to comply with transparency and tax information-sharing standards, as outlined by the Organization for Economic Cooperation and Development (OECD). Following a 2009 agreement with the United Kingdom, Liechtenstein passed laws in July 2010 that will oblige those holding offshore accounts in the country to declare their assets to tax authorities and pay as much as 10 percent in taxes evaded over the past 10 years.

Political Rights and Civil Liberties: Liechtenstein is an electoral democracy. However, the unelected monarch is the most politically powerful in Europe. The prince, as the hereditary head of state, appoints the prime minister on the recommendation of Parliament and possesses the power to veto legislation and dismiss the government. At the same time, freely elected representatives determine the policies of the government, and the unicameral Parliament (Landtag) consists of 25 deputies chosen by proportional representation every four years. Voting is compulsory.

Political parties are able to freely organize. The VU and the FBP have dominated politics over the last half-century.

Liechtenstein's politics and society are largely free of corruption, and the country continues to work to build sufficient mechanisms to fight money laundering in its banking system. Due to recent commitments, the OECD removed Liechtenstein from its list of uncooperative tax havens in 2009. Government officials are not legally obligated to disclose their financial assets.

The constitution guarantees freedoms of expression, though the law prohibits public insults directed against a race or ethnic group. Freedom of the press is also guaranteed. Liechtenstein has one private television station, one privately held radio station and two main newspapers, which are roughly aligned with the major political parties. Foreign newspapers and magazines are widely available to the population, as are television and radio broadcasts from outside the country. Internet access is not restricted.

The constitution protects religious freedom, and the criminal code prohibits any form of discrimination against any religion or its adherents. However, the constitution establishes Roman Catholicism as the state national religion. Catholic or Protestant religious education is mandatory in all primary schools, but exemptions are routinely granted. Islamic religious classes have been introduced in some primary schools since 2008. All religious groups are tax-exempt. The government respects academic freedom.

Freedoms of assembly and association are protected, and the principality has one small trade union. A 2008 law provides civil servants with the right to strike.

The judiciary is independent and impartial despite the appointment of judges by the hereditary monarch. Due process is respected, and prison conditions meet international standards. Most detainees are asylum seekers who entered the country illegally and are being detained prior to their deportation. Switzerland is responsible for Liechtenstein's customs and defense.

A third of the population is foreign born. Some native citizens have expressed concern over the growing number of immigrants from non-German-speaking countries, such as Turkey and Bosnia-Herzegovina. The government has responded by seeking to teach recent immigrants the language and culture of Liechtenstein in formal integration programs. Foreigners have occasionally been the target of violence by right-wing groups. The laws in Liechtenstein provide for the granting of asylum or refugee status, though in 2010 the UN Committee against Torture (CAT) voiced concern that asylum seekers' claims do not always receive adequate attention. In August 2011, the CAT released a report amending its position on Liechtenstein's treatment of refugees and asylum seekers, noting that some of its previous criticisms against the country had not been justified, and some of its recommendations had been implemented.

Women enjoy the same legal rights as men. Nonetheless, gender discrimination has continued to limit opportunities for women in fields traditionally dominated by men, and a gender salary gap still exists, with women earning on average only 80 percent of men's pay for equal work. Following a 2005 reform, abortion has been legal in the first 12 weeks of pregnancy, but only in cases where the mother's life is in danger or the woman was under 14 at the time she got pregnant. A referendum on allowing the full legalization of abortion in the country was held on September 18, 2011, but was rejected by more than 52 percent of voters. Prince Alois had already signaled his intention to veto the referendum had it passed. In March, Parliament passed a law allowing same-sex registered partnerships, though it was overturned in a June referendum by nearly 70 percent of voters.

Lithuania

Political Rights: 1
Civil Liberties: 1
Status: Free

Population: 3,211,000
Capital: Vilnius

Ten-Year Ratings Timeline For Year Under Review (Political Rights, Civil Liberties, Status)

2002	2003	2004	2005	2006	2007	2008	2009	2010	2011
1,2F	1,2F	1,2F	1,1F	1,1F	1,1F	1,1F	1,1F	1,1F	1,1F

Overview: **Lithuania's minority government survived in 2011 due to a lack of cohesion within the opposition, while the results of February's local elections underscored the fractured nature of the country's political landscape. Meanwhile, amendments to an education law, which requires certain subjects to be taught in Lithuanian in minority-language schools, led to strained relations with Poland throughout the year.**

Lithuania became independent at the end of World War I but was annexed by the Soviet Union during World War II. The country declared its independence from the Soviet Union on March 11, 1990, and the move was eventually recognized by Soviet authorities in 1991. Lithuania joined NATO and the European Union (EU) in 2004. Lithuania held the 2011 chairmanship of the Organization for Security and Cooperation in Europe (OSCE).

Lithuanian politics have been characterized by shifting coalitions among several different parties, and in the run-up to the most recent parliamentary elections, the creation of new parties further fragmented the country's political scene. The Homeland Union–Lithuanian Christian Democrats (TS-LKD), an alliance of right-wing parties, was formed in May 2008, as was the National Resurrection Party (TPP). In the October 2008 balloting, the TS-LKD took the lead with 45 seats, followed by the Lithuanian Social Democratic Party (LSDP) with 25, the TPP with 16, Order and Justice with 15, the Liberal Union (LRLS) with 11, the Labor Party with 10, and the Liberal and Center Union (LCS) with 8 seats. Smaller parties and independent candidates won the remaining 11 seats. A four-party, center-right majority coalition was formed in late 2008, consisting of the TS-LKD, TPP, LRLS, and LCS. Andrius Kubilius of the TS-LKD, who had previously served as prime minister in 1999–2000, headed the new government. In May 2009, independent candidate Dalia Grybauskait was elected president with nearly 70 percent of the vote, becoming the first woman to hold the post.

A split in the TPP in mid-2009 resulted in some members of the party withdrawing from the ruling coalition, leaving it with 71 out of 141 seats as of early 2010. Additional defections in the first six months of 2010 reduced the ruling bloc to just 69 seats, forcing Kubilius to secure an informal alliance with the Lithuanian Peasant Popular Union (LVLS), which held 3 seats. Despite continuing divisions within the ruling TS-LKD—mainly between original members and newer, more conservative members—the fragile government was likely to survive until the October 2012 parliamentary elections due to a fragmented opposition. In September 2011, LCS and TPP officially unified under the LCS name.

The fractured nature of Lithuania's political landscape was underscored by the results of the February 27 local elections, in which no party gained more than 21.4 percent of the vote. The LSDP won the greatest share of seats, followed by the TS-LKD.

The economy continued to recover slowly in 2011, as unemployment declined from 17.2 percent in the first quarter to 13.9 percent in the fourth quarter. After a year of disputes over natural gas supplies in 2010, energy issues were once again a source of tension between Russia and Lithuania, when Russia announced that it was planning to build two nuclear reactors—one in Kaliningrad and one in Belarus—near the Lithuanian border. Lithuania's revised education law affecting minority languages in schools strained relations with Poland throughout the year.

Political Rights and Civil Liberties:

Lithuania is an electoral democracy. The 1992 constitution established a unicameral, 141-seat Parliament (Seimas), with 71 members elected in single-mandate constituencies and 70 chosen by proportional representation, all for four-year terms. The prime minister is selected by Parliament, and the president is directly elected for a five-year term. The most recent parliamentary elections, in 2008, were largely free and fair, though there were some reports of irregularities, including alleged bribery and forged ballots. Lithuania's many political parties operate freely, but the Communist Party is banned. In December 2011, Parliament amended party financing legislation, banning donations to political parties from legal entities, and cutting in half the amount individuals can donate to a political party. The changes will go into effect in early 2012, ahead of the next parliamentary election.

Corruption remains a problem in Lithuania, although no major corruption cases broke in 2011. Following pressure from the president and opposition, economy minister Dainius Kreivys resigned in March 2011 over suspected preferential allocation of procurement contracts, though no charges were filed against him. Former economy minister and Labor Party leader Viktor Uspaskich was set to stand trial in Lithuania on fraud charges; the case remained ongoing throughout 2011. In December, the European Parliament rejected a request to have Uspaskich's parliamentary immunity reinstated. In an effort to reduce corruption, Parliament updated freedom of information legislation in April 2011; significantly more public figures are subject to have information on them released publicly. A revised anticorruption program, which was unveiled in June, is set to be implemented between 2011 and 2014. The president also promulgated a revised law on public procurements in October, establishing a Public Procurement Council separate from the Economy Ministry; the head of the Council will be appointed by the president. Lithuania was ranked 50 out of 183 countries surveyed in Transparency International's 2011 Corruption Perceptions Index.

The government generally respects freedom of the press. Privately owned newspapers and independent broadcasters express a wide variety of views and criticize the government freely. However, the press suffers from inadequate standards for transparency of ownership. In 2010 the Law on the Protection of Minors came into effect, prohibiting online and broadcast media from providing "detrimental" material to minors, including material with sexual content or that "denigrates family values," including condoning same-sex marriage. International organizations have expressed concern that the law could be used to restrict freedom of expression for the LGBT community. No prosecutions under the law were reported in 2011. In January 2011, journalist Gintaras Visockas was found guilty of libel for linking a former presidential candidate to the KGB. Unable to pay the large fine imposed, he instead served 40 days in jail. In October, the OSCE Representative on Freedom in the Media called for Lithuania to decriminalize defamation after Lithuanian Union of Journalists' chairman Dainius Radzevicius went to trial on charges brought against him by the owner of the *Respublika* newspaper. Radzevicius had commented on leaked U.S. diplomatic cables that claimed some Lithuanian newspapers coerced advertisers into buying advertisements. The government does not restrict access to the internet.

Freedom of religion is guaranteed by law and largely upheld in practice. However, so-called traditional religious communities enjoy certain government benefits, including annual subsidies, which are not granted to other groups. There were no reports of religiously motivated violence in 2011, although several acts of anti-Semitic vandalism were committed. In June, Parliament decided to award Lithuanian Jews 128 million litas (US$48 million) over 10 years as compensation for loss of property and damages during the Nazi and Soviet eras. Academic freedom is respected.

Freedoms of assembly and association are generally observed. There are no serious obstacles to the registration of nongovernmental organizations, and human rights groups operate without restrictions. Workers have the right to form and join trade unions, to strike, and to engage in collective bargaining, though there have been reports of employees being punished for attempting to organize. Slightly less than 10 percent of the country's workforce is unionized.

The constitution guarantees judicial independence, which is respected in practice. Defendants generally enjoy due process rights, including the presumption of innocence and freedom from arbitrary arrest and detention, but detained suspects are not always granted timely access to an attorney. Lengthy pretrial detention remains a problem. Police abuse of detainees continues to be reported, and judges and prosecutors have failed to respond adequately to claims of such mistreatment. Prisons suffer from overcrowding, and inmates have poor access to health care.

The rights of ethnic minorities, who make up 16 percent of the population, are legally protected. However, roughly a quarter of all ethnic minorities report job discrimination. The small Romany population faces the greatest discrimination, including in access to social services and employment, and in relations with police. Unlike Latvia and Estonia, which continue to have large noncitizen populations, Lithuania made it relatively easy for all existing residents to gain citizenship after independence. In March 2011, Lithuania amended its education law to require that certain subjects in schools for ethnic minorities be taught in Lithuanian starting on September 1. Additionally, graduates from minority-language schools will have to take the same Lithuanian language-exam as students from Lithuanian language schools beginning in 2013. These amendments sparked a number of protests from the Polish-speaking population throughout the year, the largest of which saw 1,500 people demonstrated in front of Parliament on September 23. There are roughly 213,000 ethnic Poles and 175,000 ethnic Russians in Lithuania.

Although men and women enjoy the same legal rights, women earn 17 percent less on average than men in comparable jobs. Twenty-six members of the 141-seat parliament are women, and the first female president and Speaker of Parliament were elected in 2009. Domestic violence, including both spousal and child abuse, remains a serious problem. In May 2011, Parliament passed the Law on Protection from Domestic Violence, which legally defines domestic violence, provides for lines of action, and requires sequestration of the perpetrator. Lithuania continues to be a source, transit point, and destination for the trafficking of women and girls for the purpose of prostitution.

Luxembourg

Political Rights: 1
Civil Liberties: 1
Status: Free

Population: 517,000
Capital: Luxembourg

Ten-Year Ratings Timeline For Year Under Review (Political Rights, Civil Liberties, Status)

2002	2003	2004	2005	2006	2007	2008	2009	2010	2011
1,1F	1,1F	1,1F	1,1F	1,1F	1,1F	1,1F	1,1F	1,1F	1,1F

Overview:

Luxembourg's governing coalition agreed in June 2011 to loosen provisions of the country's strict abortion laws, a measure that was being finalized at year's end. Meanwhile, the country struggled to adequately process and house a growing number of asylum applicants.

The Grand Duchy of Luxembourg was established in 1815 after the Napoleonic wars. Following a brief merger with Belgium, it acquired its current borders in 1839. The country was occupied by Germany during both world wars, and it abandoned neutrality to join NATO in 1949. Luxembourg became a founding member of the European Coal and Steel Community in 1952, a precursor to the European Union (EU); it adopted the euro currency in 1999.

The center-right Democratic Party (DP) performed poorly in June 2004 general elections, allowing the opposition Socialist Workers' Party of Luxembourg (LSAP) to replace the DP as the junior coalition partner of Prime Minister Jean-Claude Juncker's Christian Social Party (CSV).

In the June 2009 parliamentary elections, the CSV captured 26 seats, while the LSAP took 13 seats, and the DP won 9 seats; three other parties won the remaining 12 seats. Juncker remained prime minister for the 15th consecutive year—the longest tenure of any EU head of government—and formed a coalition government with the LSAP in July.

Luxembourg has been criticized for its bank secrecy rules and was placed on the Organization for Economic Cooperation's (OECD) tax-haven gray list in 2009. Luxembourg signed several agreements regarding the sharing of tax information and was removed from the list by the end of the year.

The budget deficit rose from just 0.7 percent of GDP in 2009 to a high of 2.2 percent in 2010. Proposed austerity measures generated tension within the governing coalition and sparked strikes in the publically funded health-care system in 2010. In 2011, the government introduced austerity measures intended to increase competitiveness. In December, after failed negotiations with unions, the government unilaterally reduced the frequency of automatic inflation-based wage increases, a controversial move that contradicted previous practices of consensus-building. Further reforms were planned for 2012.

Political Rights and Civil Liberties:

Luxembourg is an electoral democracy. The head of state is the unelected Grand Duke Henri, whose powers are largely ceremonial. The unicameral legislature, the Chamber of Deputies, consists of 60 members elected by proportional representation to five-year terms. The legislature chooses the prime minister. Voting is compulsory for Luxembourg's citizens. Citizens of EU countries may vote in local and European elections in Luxembourg after six years' residency but are not required to do so; residents from non-EU countries may not vote. Foreigners constitute over a third of Luxembourg's population.

The political system is open to the rise of new parties. There are three traditionally strong parties: the CSV, historically aligned with the Catholic Church; the LSAP, a formerly radical but now center-left party representing the working class; and the DP, which favors free-market economic policies.

The government is largely free from corruption. In February 2011, Luxembourg adopted regulations implementing the OECD Anti-Corruption Convention; in June, the OECD called on Luxembourg to strengthen its enforcement of the new laws. Luxembourg was ranked 11 out of 183 countries surveyed in Transparency International's 2011 Corruption Perceptions Index.

Freedom of expression is guaranteed by the constitution, and Luxembourg maintains a vibrant media environment. A single conglomerate, Radio Télévision Luxembourg, dominates broadcast radio and television. Newspapers generally represent a broad range of opinion. Internet access is not restricted.

Although Roman Catholicism is the dominant religion, there is no state religion, and the state pays the salaries of clergy from a variety of Christian sects; Islamic clergy are not supported. In June 2011, the parliament debated cutting or reducing funding for clergy, removing religious celebrations from Luxembourg's national holidays, and inserting ethics education in schools in place of religion. Schoolchildren may choose to study either the Roman Catholic religion or ethics; most choose the former. Academic freedom is respected.

Freedoms of assembly and association are protected, and nongovernmental organizations operate freely. Luxembourgers may organize in trade unions, and approximately 40 percent of the workforce is unionized. The right to strike is constitutionally guaranteed. Several unions held protests in September 2010, after the government announced austerity reforms to the child and educational subsidy policy.

The judiciary is independent, though judges are still appointed by the grand duke. Detainees are treated humanely in police stations and prisons. However, in January 2011, prosecutors filed a complaint against prison staff at Schrassig prison, alleging that searches of prisoners and visitors were degrading and invasive. Overcrowding has been reported at Schrassig prison, and an April 2011 inspection was critical of prison conditions and the treatment of prisoners. Two minors were held at Schrassig prison for two weeks in November, prompting debate on the treatment of child offenders.

Luxembourg's Muslim minority, mainly of Bosnian origin, faces no official hostility. The government passed a law in January 2011 that increased penalties for hate speech. Asylum claims in Luxembourg have more than doubled since 2010, overburdening government agencies and fostering resentment in some communities; a new detention center for rejected asylum seekers opened in August 2011. In September 2011, 30 Iraqi asylum seekers went on a hunger strike protesting processing times for asylum applications that average 18 months.

Women comprise nearly 50 percent of the labor force, and the gap between men's and women's wages is about 15 percent. Women are underrepresented at the highest levels of government; 12 women currently serve in the 60-member parliament, and only 4 hold seats in the 15-member cabinet.

While the law does not technically allow for abortion on demand, women can legally have abortions if in "distress." In June 2011, the coalition parties broadly agreed on legislation that would allow abortions in a greater number of cases while maintaining current penalties for unapproved abortions; finalization of the measure was ongoing at year's end. Luxembourg's Consultative Committee on Human Rights has expressed concerns regarding several provisions, including a residency restriction requiring women to have lived in Luxembourg for at least three months before obtaining an abortion.

In March 2011, two Romanian men were arrested for human trafficking and involvement in prostitution, and in July, four individuals were arrested and charged with running a human trafficking and prostitution ring in Luxembourg from Eastern Europe since 2007.

Macedonia

Political Rights: 3
Civil Liberties: 3
Status: Partly Free

Population: 2,059,000
Capital: Skopje

Ten-Year Ratings Timeline For Year Under Review (Political Rights, Civil Liberties, Status)

2002	2003	2004	2005	2006	2007	2008	2009	2010	2011
3,3PF	3,3PF	3,3PF	3,3PF	3,3PF	3,3PF	3,3PF	3,3PF	3,3PF	3,3PF

Overview: **In early elections held in June 2011, the center-right ruling coalition led by Nikola Gruevski won its third consecutive victory. The year also saw the closure of the opposition-oriented A1 Television amid growing concerns of political pressure on Macedonia's independent media. In September, the ongoing dispute with Greece was agitated, after Macedonia erected a statue of Greek hero Alexander the Great to mark the 20th anniversary of its independence.**

Macedonia, a republic in the communist-era Yugoslav federation, gained independence in 1991 as the federation dissolved. The country's legitimacy has since been threatened on several levels. Greece objects to the name "Macedonia," arguing that it implies a territorial and cultural claim to the Greek region of the same name. Bulgaria contends that the Macedonian language is a dialect of Bulgarian. The Serbian Orthodox Church does not recognize the separation of the self-proclaimed Macedonian Orthodox Church. Internally, poor relations between the Macedonian Slav majority and the ethnic Albanian minority have raised doubts about the country's long-term viability.

Since independence, power has alternated between center-left and center-right governments, though an ethnic Albanian party has sat in each ruling coalition. In 2000–2001, Albanians mounted an armed insurgency, demanding better political representation. Unofficially, however, the insurgents also wanted control of lucrative smuggling routes in northwestern Macedonia. The August 2001 negotiations known as the Ohrid Accords prevented civil war, but violent incidents continued to erupt periodically.

Parliamentary elections in 2002 returned the Social Democratic Party of Macedonia (SDSM) to power after a period of rule by the center-right Internal Macedonian Revolutionary Organization–Democratic Party for Macedonian National Unity (VMRO-DPMNE). The ethnic Albanian Democratic Union for Integration (DUI) joined the SDSM governing coalition.

VMRO-DPMNE won parliamentary elections in July 2006, with Nikola Gruevski becoming prime minister. The polls were marred by preelection violence and significant irregularities on election day. DUI supporters protested the VMRO-DPMNE's decision to form a coalition with a rival group, the Democratic Party of Albanians (DPA). The DUI subsequently organized intermittent parliamentary boycotts, sometimes blocking key legislation related to the Ohrid Accords and Macedonia's European Union (EU) candidacy.

The VMRO-DPMNE won a majority of seats in early parliamentary elections held in 2008; the polls were widely seen as the worst since independence. Irregularities—mainly in Albanian areas—included attacks on party offices and ballot box stuffing.

University professor Gjorge Ivanov, running for the VMRO-DPMNE, won a 2009 presidential runoff against the SDSM's Ljubomir Frckoski. International observers noted an improvement over the 2008 polls. The VMRO-DPMNE also performed well in the concurrent municipal elections, capturing 55 of the 84 municipalities outright.

In November 2010, police raided the headquarters of the opposition-oriented A1 Television to investigate alleged financial irregularities at companies controlled by the station's owner, Velija Ramkovski. In late December, Ramkovski and more than a dozen associates were charged with crimes including money laundering and tax evasion.

The opposition SDSM subsequently boycotted the parliament in January 2011. Parliament was dissolved in April, and early elections held in June led to a third consecutive victory for the VMRO-DPMNE-led coalition, which took 56 seats. The SDSM-led coalition followed with 42 seats; the DUI took 15 seats, the DPA captured 8, and the National Democratic Revival (NDR) won 2. Gruevski secured a third term as prime minister. International observers called the polls competitive and transparent but noted some problems, including a progovernment bias from the public broadcaster.

August 2011 marked the 10th anniversary of the Ohrid Accords, which the International Crisis Group said were being well implemented despite lingering interethnic tensions. A month later, Macedonia celebrated the 20th anniversary of its declaration of independence, which the government marked by inaugurating a massive statue of Alexander the Great in downtown Skopje as part of the Skopje 2014 urban development plan. The statue exacerbated tension with Greece, where Alexander is seen as a national hero. The dispute between the two countries over

Macedonia's name remained unresolved in 2011, obstructing Macedonia's efforts to join NATO and the EU. In 2008, Greece blocked an invitation for Macedonia to join NATO.

Political Rights and Civil Liberties: Macedonia is an electoral democracy. Most postindependence elections have been deemed satisfactory by international standards, though the 2008 polls were marked by irregularities. Members of the unicameral, 123-seat Sobranie (Assembly) are elected to four-year terms by proportional representation. Parliament added three seats in 2011 for representatives of Macedonians living abroad. The president is elected to a five-year term through a direct popular vote, but the prime minister holds most executive power. Certain types of legislation must pass by a "double majority," or a majority of legislators from both main ethnic groups.

Corruption remains a serious problem. Despite some legislative progress in 2011, including measures to clarify party funding sources, the transparency of general public expenditures is weak. In the 2011 elections, the governing coalition parties' expenditures exceeded their declared incomes. The judiciary lacks a track record of handling high-level corruption cases, and greater cooperation is needed between the Ministry of Justice, the State Commission for the Prevention of Corruption, and law enforcement, according to the European Commission's (EC) 2011 Progress Report. Macedonia ranked 69 out of 173 countries surveyed in Transparency International's 2011 Corruption Perceptions Index.

The constitution provides for freedom of the press, but political tensions have increased pressure on the media. The A1 Television investigation saw the station and three of its newspapers–*Vreme*, *Spic*, and *Koha e Re*—close in 2011. All had criticized the government, and Amnesty International called the closures politically motivated. Moreover, many journalism watchdogs argue that the government—which is among Macedonia's largest advertisers—has shifted ad dollars to friendly outlets to stifle the country's independent press. Though 2011 saw the creation of a new independent media union, amendments made to the Law on the Broadcasting Council increased seats for government-related appointees, further raising concerns about declining independence. Increasingly, journalists face political pressure and harassment, resulting in self-censorship. The public broadcaster, Macedonian Radio and Television, lacks sustainable funding. Macedonian media outlets, like society at large, are strongly divided along ethnic lines. Internet access is unrestricted.

The constitution guarantees freedom of religion. A long-standing dispute between the breakaway Macedonian Orthodox Church and the canonically recognized Serbian Orthodox Church remained unresolved in 2011. In February, the predominantly Muslim Albanians protested construction of a church-shaped museum in Skopje's Kale Fortress, located in an Albanian neighborhood. Hard-line Islamists reportedly control several mosques with financing from Middle Eastern countries.

Academic freedom is generally not restricted, and the government continued education reforms in 2011, including the new Integrated Education Strategy to introduce native language instruction for ethnic minorities. Nevertheless, the country's ethnic divisions affect education, and schools are becoming increasingly segregated.

Constitutional guarantees of freedoms of assembly and association are generally respected. In 2011, Macedonians protested after a police officer killed a youth at a June postelection rally. Nongovernmental organizations play an increasingly important role in policy formulation. Workers may organize and bargain collectively, though the International Trade Union Confederation's 2010 report for Macedonia stated that strikes are difficult to organize, union activities can be easily terminated, and antiunion dismissals are common. Over 50 percent of the legal workforce is unionized, but unions lack stable finances and management capacity.

The EC noted progress on Macedonia's judiciary in 2011. The Minister of Justice's voting rights on the Judicial Council were removed to increase independence. To improve efficiency, the High Administrative Court became operational in July; it hears appeals of Administrative Court decisions that were formerly transferred to the Supreme Court. The EC noted weaknesses in the evaluation of judges, however, and called for tougher recruitment requirements. It also emphasized that more graduates of the Academy for Training of Judges and Prosecutors should be recruited for professional postings. Though the judicial budget is increasing, courts remain underfunded, and more progress is needed on reducing court backlogs and processing cases expeditiously. Prison conditions are generally unsatisfactory, with overcrowding and poor health care.

An April 2010 law prohibits discrimination on various grounds, though not on the basis of sexual orientation. Along with Roma and other vulnerable groups, homosexuals face discrimination. Macedonia's ethnic Albanians also complain of discrimination. The Skopje 2014 project has heightened interethnic tensions, with minority groups saying the plans ignore their heritage. The Kale Fortress dispute culminated with an interethnic clash between ethnic Macedonians and Albanians. In October, a census was cancelled following months of infighting between the Macedonian and Albanian members of the National Census Commission on how to conduct the headcount.

While women in Macedonia enjoy the same legal rights as men, societal attitudes limit women's participation in nontraditional roles, and women rarely participate in local politics. In Albanian Muslim areas, many women are subjected to proxy voting by male relatives and are frequently denied access to education. Of the 1,679 candidates in the 2011 elections, 34 percent were women. Despite the ongoing implementation of a strategy against domestic violence, it remains a serious problem, as is the trafficking of women for forced labor and prostitution.

Madagascar

Political Rights: 6
Civil Liberties: 4
Status: Partly Free

Population: 21,315,000
Capital: Antananarivo

Ten-Year Ratings Timeline For Year Under Review (Political Rights, Civil Liberties, Status)

2002	2003	2004	2005	2006	2007	2008	2009	2010	2011
3,4PF	3,3PF	3,3PF	3,3PF	4,3PF	4,3PF	4,3PF	6,4PF	6,4PF	6,4PF

Overview: **Madagascar's protracted political crisis appeared to draw closer to a resolution in September 2011, when all but one of the main political stakeholders signed an amended "road map" to elections within one year. The agreement called for de facto president Andry Rajoelina—who had taken power after a 2009 military coup—to lead a transitional government until the elections. It also stipulated that former president Marc Ravalomanana, who had been living in exile under threat of arrest, be permitted to return to Madagascar "unconditionally," though he had yet to return to the country at year's end.**

After 70 years of French colonial rule and episodes of severe repression, Madagascar gained independence in 1960. A member of the leftist military junta that seized power in 1972, Admiral Didier Ratsiraka, emerged as leader in 1975 and retained power until his increasingly authoritarian regime bowed to social unrest and nonviolent mass demonstrations in 1991.

Under a new constitution, opposition leader Albert Zafy won the 1992 presidential election. Following Zafy's impeachment by the National Assembly in 1996, Ratsiraka won that year's presidential runoff election, which was deemed generally legitimate by international and domestic observers.

A decentralization plan was narrowly approved in a 1998 referendum amid a boycott by the country's increasingly fractious opposition. In the 2001 presidential election, opposition candidate and Antananarivo mayor Marc Ravalomanana claimed that he had been denied an outright victory in the first round due to polling irregularities. He declared himself president in February 2002, having refused to take part in a postponed runoff against Ratsiraka. After considerable violence between supporters of the two candidates, the High Constitutional Court announced that Ravalomanana had indeed won in the first round, but Ratsiraka refused to acknowledge the result. Sporadic clashes continued until July 2002, when Ratsiraka left the country. The crisis seriously damaged the Malagasy economy.

Ravalomanana's party, I Love Madagascar (TIM), won a large majority in the 2002 parliamentary elections. Observers from the European Union (EU) said the conduct of the polls was generally positive. Political tensions increased in the run-up to the 2006 presidential election, in which Ravalomanana secured a second term. While most observers agreed that the vote reflected the will of the people, the campaign was marred by opposition claims of a biased administration and electoral irregularities.

A constitutional referendum in April 2007 increased presidential powers, and Ravalomanana's authority was bolstered again in the September parliamentary elections, in which TIM won 106 of the 127 seats. Andry Rajoelina, a young and charismatic opposition candidate, won the mayoral race in the capital, Antananarivo, in December.

In December 2008, the government closed a television station run by Rajoelina, triggering months of violent protests in Antananarivo. Well over 100 people were killed as protesters destroyed property and marched on government sites, and police responded with gunfire. Rajoelina called on Ravalomanana to resign and declared himself president. The political crisis deepened in early 2009, with some army officers announcing their support for the opposition. In March, Ravalomanana handed power to the military, which quickly transferred it to Rajoelina.

Rajoelina proceeded to suspend the parliament, suppress opposition protests, and limit press freedom. These actions, combined with his unconstitutional accession to power and erratic leadership, resulted in prolonged political uncertainty. In August 2009, the various political factions backing Rajoelina reached a tentative power-sharing deal—brokered by the Southern African Development Community (SADC) and known as the Maputo Declaration—with former presidents Ravalomanana, Zafy, and Ratsiraka. However, Rajoelina later refused to agree to the formation of a transitional coalition government of national unity, as called for in the pact. Subsequent internationally mediated deals were reached but also collapsed.

In August 2010, Rajoelina announced that he was abandoning the power-sharing agreement. He instead concluded an accord with 99 minor parties and set the presidential poll for May 2011. While Rajoelina stated that he would not stand for the presidency, the main opposition parties and SADC refused to endorse his plan, citing the Maputo Declaration's call for a coalition government to oversee the electoral process. The political climate became further polarized after Ravalomanana, who was living in exile in South Africa, was sentenced in absentia in August to life with hard labor for ordering the killing of at least 30 opposition protesters in February 2009. A national conference sponsored by Rajoelina that was designed to provide an internal solution to the crisis took place in September 2010. It was boycotted by the major opposition parties and did not have the support of the international community. Rajoelina appointed a transitional parliament in October, with some members of the opposition included. In a November referendum boycotted by the opposition, voters approved constitutional changes sought by Rajoelina, including a lowering of the minimum age for the president from 40 to 35. (Rajoelina turned 37 in May 2011.) Continuing unrest within the military led to an unsuccessful coup attempt in November, triggered by the constitutional referendum.

Nevertheless, internationally mediated talks continued, and by March 2011, SADC had shifted its stance, backing a plan that allowed Rajoelina to be recognized as Madagascar's interim president until elections, as long as the opposition was fairly represented in the transitional administration. However, the main opposition parties rejected the plan when Rajoelina reappointed his ally, General Camille Vital, as prime minster, and continued to prevent Ravalomanana from returning from exile. After sustained pressure by SADC and the EU, an amended road map was initialed in September by all the main parties except Ratsiraka. The deal legitimized Rajoelina as Madagascar's interim president, provided for the unconditional return of Ravalomanana, called for elections to be held within one year and a transitional administration that included all parties to lead the country to the elections, and urged the passage of an amnesty law for those accused of political crimes. Rajoelina named Omer Beriziky consensus prime minister in late October, and supporters of Ravalomanana and Zafy in November agreed to join a 35-member unity cabinet. In December, Rajoelina appointed a transitional parliament that included supporters of all signatories of the road map. However, Ravalomanana had yet to return by the end of 2011; some Rajoelina supporters threatened to arrest him if he did, while others pledged to respect the road map.

The 2009 coup and ensuing political crisis seriously damaged Madagascar's economy. Following Rajoelina's takeover, the international community—including the EU and the African Union—levied severe sanctions on the country, but continued to provide humanitarian aid. The September 2011 agreement, if implemented in full, could allow for the lifting of sanctions and the renewal of EU aid.

Political Rights and Civil Liberties: Madagascar is not an electoral democracy. The undemocratic and unconstitutional manner in which Andry Rajoelina assumed the presidency in March 2009 demonstrated that the political culture has so far failed to incorporate a rules-based system and the practice of peaceful democratic succession. The 2007 constitutional referendum had continued a trend of steadily increasing presidential power. Among other provisions, it allowed the president to rule by decree during a state of emergency and abolished autonomous provinces. The elected bicameral parliament was suspended in March 2009. The transitional parliament appointed by Rajoelina in December 2011 was intended to remain in place until elections could be held.

Approximately 150 parties are registered, although only a few have a national presence. Parties tend to suffer from internal divisions, shifting alliances, and a lack of resources and clear ideology. Prior to the suspension of the parliament in 2009, ousted president Marc Ravalomanana's TIM party had an overwhelming majority in both houses. Since Rajoelina's accession to power, opposition political activity has been circumscribed through arbitrary and periodic bans on meetings and protests, killings of opposition supporters, and unsubstantiated government allegations of opposition party involvement in a series of explosions in Antananarivo in mid-2009. As part of the road map, members of the opposition participated in the transitional parliament. Prior to the September 2011 agreement, Rajoelina had consistently broken promises to include opposition members in the transitional cabinet.

Corruption remains a major concern in Madagascar. In spite of an April 2010 decree that prohibited the logging, transport, trading, and export of precious woods, the illegal trade continues. In May 2011, the Ministry of Environment announced that it had concluded a 30-day crackdown on illegal logging, seizing more than 1,000 rosewood logs and arresting seven members of a "logging mafia." The World Bank in June approved $52 million for conservation projects in Madagascar, although the funds would be channeled through independent organizations, rather than Rajoelina's government. Madagascar was ranked 100 out of 183 countries surveyed in Transparency International's 2011 Corruption Perceptions Index.

The constitution provides for freedom of the press. A 1990 law on press freedom was followed by the introduction of privately owned FM radio stations and more critical political reporting by the print media. However, Rajoelina's transitional government has largely ignored these protections. During the early 2009 unrest, media outlets associated with each side were raided by security forces or ransacked by armed civilians, and a Ravalomanana-owned radio station was shut down by the authorities in April. The independent outlets that have remained in operation are subject to censorship, harassment, and intimidation by Rajoelina's government and practice varying levels of self-censorship. Ten employees of the independent Radio Fahazavana were arrested in 2010 on charges of inciting revolt. They were released after four months in jail, but on the same day the authorities banned broadcasts by another independent radio station. There were no reports of journalists being attacked, arrested, or imprisoned in 2011.

The Malagasy people have traditionally enjoyed religious freedom though religious organizations are required to register with the Ministry of the Interior. There are no limitations on academic freedom.

Freedom of association is generally respected, and hundreds of nongovernmental organizations, including human rights groups, are active. Freedom of assembly was severely affected by the unrest in early 2009, as protests degenerated into riots and looting, and security forces opened fire on demonstrators. In March 2011, Ravalomanana accused Rajoelina's security forces of arbitrary arrests of his supporters, as well as torture and detention without trial.

Workers' rights to join unions and strike are largely respected. The Ravalomanana administration endured a series of demonstrations and work stoppages, mainly over the high rate of inflation. Strikes, often politically motivated, have continued under the Rajoelina regime. Some of the country's labor organizations are affiliated with political groups. More than 80 percent of workers are engaged in agriculture, fishing, and forestry at a subsistence level.

The judiciary remains susceptible to corruption and executive influence. Its acquiescence in the face of Rajoelina's unconstitutional rise to power highlighted its weakness as an institution, and subsequent judicial decisions were tainted by frequent intimidation. A lack of training, resources, and personnel hampers judicial effectiveness, and case backlogs are prodigious. More than half of the approximately 20,000 people held in the country's prisons are pretrial detainees, and prisoners suffer from extremely harsh and sometimes life-threatening conditions. Customary-law courts in rural areas continue to lack due process guarantees and regularly issue summary and severe punishments. In the demonstrations and chaos surrounding the change in government in 2009, security forces often engaged in abusive behavior with impunity.

A political cleavage has traditionally existed between the coastal côtier and the highland Merina peoples, of continental African and Southeast Asian origins, respectively. Due to past military conquest and long-standing political dominance, the status of the Merina tends to be higher than that of the côtier. Ethnicity, caste, and regional solidarity are often factors that lead to discrimination.

Malagasy women hold significantly more government and managerial positions than women in many continental African countries. However, they still face societal discrimination and enjoy fewer opportunities than men for higher education and employment. Domestic violence remains common. The U.S. State Department's 2011 Trafficking in Persons Report alleged that weakened rule of law under Rajoelina's government has led to an increase in the number of Malagasy women and children trafficked to the Middle East for forced labor and sex work.

Malawi

Political Rights: 3
Civil Liberties: 4
Status: Partly Free

Population: 15,879,000
Capital: Lilongwe

Trend Arrow: Malawi received a downward trend arrow due to the government's violent suppression of public protests, intimidation of journalists, and threats to academic freedom.

Ten-Year Ratings Timeline For Year Under Review (Political Rights, Civil Liberties, Status)

2002	2003	2004	2005	2006	2007	2008	2009	2010	2011
4,4PF	3,4PF	4,4PF	4,4PF	4,3PF	4,4PF	4,4PF	3,4PF	3,4PF	3,4PF

Overview: **The administration of President Bingu wa Mutharika responded with violence to antigovernment protests in July 2011, killing 18 people. International donors reacted by suspending hundreds of millions of aid dollars to Malawi. The government's heavy-handedness toward critics was also increasingly evident in its threats to media independence, including the introduction of a harsh new press law, and academic freedom.**

Following Malawi's independence from Britain in 1963, President Hastings Kamuzu Banda ruled the country for nearly three decades, exercising dictatorial power through the Malawi Congress Party (MCP) and its paramilitary youth wing. Facing an economic crisis and strong domestic and international pressure, Banda accepted a 1993 referendum that approved multiparty rule. Bakili Muluzi of the United Democratic Front (UDF) won the 1994 presidential election, which was generally perceived as free and fair. He was reelected in 1999.

Muluzi handpicked Bingu wa Mutharika, a relative political outsider, as his successor ahead of the 2004 presidential election. While Mutharika defeated his MCP opponent, the MCP led concurrent parliamentary elections. In early 2005, a rift between Mutharika and Muluzi, who remained the UDF chairman, worsened after several powerful UDF figures were arrested as part of Mutharika's new anticorruption campaign. Mutharika resigned from the UDF and formed the Democratic Progressive Party (DPP), which many lawmakers subsequently joined. With the UDF and the MCP forming an opposition alliance against the president, the remainder of Mutharika's first term was characterized by acute tension between the executive and legislative branches, sometimes leading to the paralysis of governing institutions.

Despite predictions that Muluzi would challenge Mutharika in the May 2009 presidential contest, the constitutional two-term limit prevented him from standing again. Instead, Muluzi and the UDF formed an alliance with the head of the MCP, John Tembo, and backed his candidacy for the presidency. Mutharika ran a highly effective campaign and defeated Tembo with approximately 66 percent of the vote. In concurrent parliamentary elections, Mutharika's DPP won a total of 112 seats in the 193-seat legislature; the MCP took 26, and the UDF captured 17, leaving independent candidates and smaller parties with the remaining seats. According to international and domestic election observers, the 2009 polls were more free and competitive than in previous years. However, incumbents enjoyed a clear advantage due to the use of state resources during the campaign period and a clear bias from government-controlled media outlets.

In late 2010, Mutharika attempted to fire Joyce Banda, who had become Malawi's first female vice president in the 2009 elections. Banda's dismissal sparked a crisis, because the vice presidency is an elected position that cannot be appointed or removed by the president. Although Mutharika claimed he had attempted to fire Banda for missing cabinet meetings, opponents asserted that the president was merely attempting to clear the way for his brother and heir apparent, Peter Mutharika, to assume the vice presidency. Banda refused to resign.

With Mutharika and his party enjoying dominance in the legislature, a new autocratic and repressive style of governance emerged. In January 2011, the president promulgated a harsh new press law, passed in November 2010, that empowered the information minister to prohibit any news story deemed contrary to the public interest. In February 2011, a lecturer at Chancellor College was questioned by police after comparing Malawi with Tunisia and Egypt, which were undergoing profound political upheaval at the time. The teachers union cancelled lectures in protest, and four lecturers were fired. The president intervened, condemning the lecturers for encouraging rebellion and closing the university via his role as its chancellor. In April, the British ambassador to Malawi was expelled from the country after a leaked diplomatic cable quoted him as criticizing the president.

In July 2011, discontent over recent economic turmoil and increasingly authoritarian governance led to public protests. Police shot unarmed demonstrators, killing 18 people in Lilongwe; the government forces insisted that the protesters had been looting. Journalists were targeted for beatings, and all radio stations were shut down. Mutharika declared that the protesters were "led by Satan" and promised to hunt down anyone participating in the demonstrations. Further protests were scheduled in August, but were abandoned when the government agreed to talks with civil society representatives facilitated by the United Nations. Activists quit these talks in September and held further protests. In August, the president dismissed his entire cabinet, temporarily assuming all portfolios himself, and in September, he appointed a new cabinet that included his wife. Mutharika also appointed his brother minister of foreign affairs.

International donors, after years of applauding economic management under the Mutharika administration, responded swiftly to the 2011 crackdown. In July, the U.S. Millennium Challenge Corporation announced that it was suspending its sole project in Malawi, a $350 million investment in the energy sector, which had only been announced in April. The British government, Malawi's largest donor, suspended all its aid, as did the World Bank, European Union (EU), Norway, Germany, and the African Development Bank.

Political Rights and Civil Liberties:

Malawi is an electoral democracy. The president is directly elected for five-year terms and exercises considerable executive authority. The unicameral National Assembly is composed of 193 members elected by popular vote to serve five-year terms. The 2009 presidential and parliamentary elections, though characterized by an uneven playing field in favor of incumbents, were the most fair and competitive since the first multiparty elections in 1994.

While opposition groups had questioned the impartiality and legitimacy of the Malawi Electoral Commission (MEC) in previous years, key observers concluded that it operated with sufficient transparency during the 2009 elections. Concerns have arisen over delayed local government elections, which have not been held since district-level assemblies were dissolved in 2005. In apparent contravention of a court order, the president suspended and closed the MEC in December 2010 after an audit report revealed that large sums of money allocated to run the 2009 elections were unaccounted for. This once again delayed local elections, which had already been postponed to April 2011 and are now scheduled to run concurrently with presidential elections in 2014.

The main political parties are the ruling DPP, the opposition MCP, and the UDF. The opposition was able to organize and campaign freely during the 2009 elections.

While President Bingu wa Mutharika has pledged to fight corruption, opposition and civil society groups have charged that the effort has been directed primarily at his political opponents. The new National Anti-Corruption Strategy launched in 2009 included a plan to establish "integrity committees" in public institutions. However, a February 2010 report by Global Integrity indicated that the Anti-Corruption Bureau has largely focused on low-level civil servants while avoiding high-ranking officials under political pressure. After years of investigation and two prior arrests, former president Bakili Muluzi was arrested in 2009 and charged with 86 counts related to his alleged theft of public resources during his time in office. His trial remained ongoing in 2011, amid delays for medical reasons. Malawi was ranked 100 out of 183 countries surveyed in Transparency International's 2011 Corruption Perceptions Index.

Freedom of the press is legally guaranteed but has come increasingly under threat; journalists were beaten and detained during the July 2011 protests, and radio stations were closed. Despite government pressures, Malawi's dozen or so newspapers present a diversity of opinion. There are approximately 20 radio stations and 2 television stations in the country. However, the government-controlled Malawi Broadcasting Corporation and TV Malawi—the historically dominant outlets in the country—display a significant bias in favor of the government. Independent broadcast outlets have been playing an increasingly important role, though broadcast and print media have been targets of government harassment. In January 2010, the government placed a ban on advertising at the largest independent daily in response to unflattering articles about the president's family. In November 2010, parliament passed a harsh new media law, of doubtful constitutionality, granting the minister of information power to ban publications deemed contrary to the public interest. It remained in force at the end of 2011.

Religious freedom is generally respected. Academic freedom has come under attack, with the ongoing dispute over Chancellor College demonstrating the government's unwillingness to tolerate critical opinions. Additionally, on September 24, a student democracy activist, Robert Chasowa, was found dead; the police verdict that he had committed suicide was discredited by the fact that the suicide note misstated his father's name.

Freedoms of assembly and association have come under pressure in recent years, especially in light of the crackdown on the 2011 protests. Civil society activists have faced harassment, intimidation, death threats, and violent treatment from government forces and the ruling party's own militia, known as the Cadets. The right to organize labor unions and to strike is legally protected, with notice and mediation requirements for workers in essential services. Unions are active, and collective bargaining is practiced, but workers face harassment and occasional violence during strikes. Since only a small percentage of the workforce is formally employed, union membership is low.

During Mutharika's first term, the generally independent judiciary became involved in political disputes and faced government hostility; the courts have rendered several significant decisions against the government in recent years. However, due process is not always respected by the overburdened court system, which lacks resources, personnel, and training. Police brutality is reportedly common, as are arbitrary arrests and detentions. Prison conditions are appalling, with many inmates dying from AIDS and other diseases.

Consensual sexual activity between same-sex couples is illegal and is punishable with prison terms. Malawi faced international attention and outcry in December 2009, when a gay couple who had become engaged through a traditional ceremony was charged with gross public indecency. In May 2010, the couple was found guilty of engaging in unnatural acts, among other violations, and was sentenced to 14 years in prison. However, they were pardoned by Mutharika later that month.

Despite constitutional guarantees of equal protection, customary practices perpetuate discrimination against women in education, employment, business, and inheritance and property rights. Violence against women and children remains a serious concern, though in recent years there has been greater media attention on and criminal penalties for abuse and rape. Forced marriages and the secret initiation of girls into their future adult roles through forced sex with older men remain widespread. The practice of kupimbira, in which young girls are sold by families to pay off debts, still exists in some areas. However, Malawian women recorded significant gains in the 2009 elections, winning 22 percent of the seats, and Banda became the first female vice president in the country's history.

Trafficking in women and children, both locally and to locations abroad, is a problem. Penalties for the few successfully prosecuted traffickers have been criticized as too lenient. A 2010 Child Care, Protection, and Justice Bill details the responsibilities of parents for raising and protecting their children and outlines the duties of local authorities to protect children from harmful, exploitative, or undesirable practices.

Malaysia

Political Rights: 4
Civil Liberties: 4
Status: Partly Free

Population: 28,885,000
Capital: Kuala Lumpur

Ten-Year Ratings Timeline For Year Under Review (Political Rights, Civil Liberties, Status)

2002	2003	2004	2005	2006	2007	2008	2009	2010	2011
5,5PF	5,4PF	5,4PF	4,4PF	4,4PF	4,4PF	4,4PF	4,4PF	4,4PF	4,4PF

Overview: **In July 2011, police in the capital dispersed a peaceful demonstration in favor of electoral reforms, arresting some 1,700 people and firing tear gas into the crowds. Prime Minister Najib Razak in September promised changes to restrictive laws on security, assembly, and the media. However, hopes for reform were undercut by crackdowns on academic freedom, violations of religious rights, and the passage of harsh new legislation on assembly late in the year.**

Malaya gained independence from Britain in 1957 and merged with the British colonies of Sarawak and Sabah to become the Federation of Malaysia in 1963. The ruling Barisan Nasional (National Front, or BN, known as the Alliance before 1969) won at least a two-thirds majority in 10 of the first 11 general elections after independence, the exception being the 1969 elections, which were nullified following largely anti-Chinese race riots. The BN consists of mainly ethnic parties, dominated by the conservative, Malay-based United Malays National Organization (UMNO).

Mahathir Mohamed served as prime minister from 1981 to 2003. His development policies transformed Malaysia into a hub for multinational corporations and high-technology exports. At the same time, he stunted democratic institutions, weakened the rule of law by curtailing the press and political opponents, and drew allegations of cronyism with his state-led industrial development.

In 2003, Mahathir stepped down and handed power to his deputy, Abdullah Ahmad Badawi. The BN won 198 of the 219 seats in the lower house of Parliament in the 2004 elections, though opposition allegations of vote buying and problems with the electoral roll were substantiated. Abdullah's government achieved little in the way of substantive reform. A series of court rulings during 2006 denied certain religious and legal rights for non-Muslims, sparking a national debate on constitutional guarantees and the role of Islam in Malaysia. The government took action to suppress press coverage, public discussion, and related activism on ethnic issues by non-Malay groups, citing the need to prevent national unrest.

During 2007, public frustration skyrocketed in response to government suppression of peaceful protests, high-level political corruption cases, a related crackdown on online media, and a crisis involving alleged politicization of the judiciary. Demands for electoral reform in advance of the 2008 general elections—coupled with perceptions of rising crime, corruption, and inflation—triggered the largest antigovernment demonstrations in nearly a decade.

In the March 2008 elections, the BN lost its two-thirds majority in the lower house of Parliament for the first time since 1969, meaning it could no longer amend the constitution unilaterally. The BN secured just 140 of the 222 lower-house seats, and Abdullah faced calls for his resignation. The opposition People's Justice Party (PKR) captured 31 seats, followed by the Democratic Action Party (DAP) with 28 and the Islamic Party of Malaysia (PAS) with 23. These opposition parties also won control of 5 of Malaysia's 13 states, and formed a coalition called the People's Alliance (PR). However, the PR later suffered from defections and infighting, and lost control of the state of Perak in 2009 after a handful of crucial defections in the state assembly. Meanwhile, Abdullah stepped down as UMNO leader and prime minister, and was succeeded in April 2009 by his deputy, Najib Razak.

In December 2010, PKR leader Anwar Ibrahim was suspended from Parliament for six months after he compared Najib's 1Malaysia program—designed to promote racial and religious unity—to a similar program in Israel. Three of his PKR colleagues received similar punishment for vocally objecting to the suspension. Anwar was also dogged by claims that he sodomized a young male aide in June 2008, a charge he said was a politically motivated fabrication. The trial proceeded slowly in 2011, and a verdict was pending at year's end.

In another case that the opposition characterized as politically motivated harassment, PAS deputy president Mohamad Sabu was charged with criminal defamation in September 2011 for supposedly defaming police and soldiers who defended a police station from an attack by communist guerrillas in 1950. He faced two years in prison and a fine if convicted. By the end of 2011, Mohamad's lawyers had applied for a declaration that the defamation charge was invalid.

A mass demonstration calling for electoral reform was forcibly dispersed by police in July 2011, prompting domestic and international criticism. In September, the government announced plans to repeal the draconian Internal Security Act (ISA), amend the Police Act to expand protections for freedom of assembly, and ease media restrictions in the Printing Presses and Publications Act. However, by year's end it appeared that the ISA would be replaced by similar legislation that was still under consideration, and freedom of assembly would be further curtailed by the Peaceful Assembly Act, passed by both chambers of Parliament in November and December.

Political Rights and Civil Liberties:

Malaysia is not an electoral democracy. The leader of the party that wins a plurality of seats in legislative elections becomes prime minister. Executive power is vested in the prime minister and cabinet. The paramount ruler, the titular head of state, is elected for five-year terms by fellow hereditary rulers in 9 of Malaysia's 13 states. Tuanku Abdul Halim Mu'adzam Shah was elected to the post in December 2011. The upper house of the bicameral Parliament consists of 44 appointed members and 26 members elected by the state legislatures, serving three-year terms. The lower house, with 222 seats, is popularly elected at least every five years.

The ruling BN is a coalition of 13 parties, most with an ethnic or regional base, including the dominant UMNO as well as the Malaysian Chinese Association (MCA) and the Malaysian Indian Congress (MIC). The 2008 electoral gains of the three main opposition parties—the DAP, PAS, and PKR—came despite serious obstacles, such as unequal access to the media and restrictions on campaigning and freedom of assembly, which left them unable to compete on equal terms with the BN. The first-past-the-post voting system also increases the power of the largest grouping, and national electoral outcomes have been affected by the malapportionment of constituencies in favor of East Malaysia. In 2008, the BN won just 51 percent of the vote but secured 140 of 222 lower house seats.

The Election Commission (EC) is frequently accused of manipulating electoral rolls and gerrymandering districts to aid the ruling coalition, and the Registrar of Societies arbitrarily decides which parties can participate in politics.

Government and law enforcement bodies have suffered a series of corruption scandals. The Malaysian Anti-Corruption Commission (MACC) came under scrutiny itself in 2009, when DAP official Teoh Beng Hock was found to have fallen to his death from the window of an MACC building while being questioned about an investigation into the disbursement of state funds. An inquest ruled the death a suicide brought on by aggressive interrogation. Similarly, customs officer Ahmad Sarbani Mohamed was found dead after falling from the third floor of an MACC office in Kuala Lumpur in April 2011. He was allegedly tied to a corruption investigation involving 62 customs officers; an inquest ruled his death an accident in September. Also during 2011, Shahrizat Abdul Jalil, the minister for women, family, and community development, became embroiled in a corruption scandal along with her husband, Mohamad Salleh Ismail, the executive chairman of National Feedlot Corporation. They were accused of using an $82 million loan to the company to buy personal real estate. Malaysia was ranked 60 out of 183 countries surveyed in Transparency International's 2011 Corruption Perceptions Index. A Whistleblower Protection Act took effect in December 2010, but it did not appear to significantly improve transparency in 2011.

Freedom of expression is constitutionally guaranteed but restricted in practice. The 1984 Printing Presses and Publications Act gives the government the authority to revoke licenses without judicial review. It also requires that publications and printers obtain annual operating permits, encouraging self-censorship and limiting investigative journalism. Privately owned television stations have close ties to the BN and generally censor programming according to government guidelines. State outlets also reflect government views. Books and films are directly censored or banned for profanity, violence, and political and religious material.

The internet has emerged as a primary outlet for free discussion and for exposing cases of political corruption. The government has responded in recent years by engaging in legal harassment of critical bloggers, charging them under defamation laws, the ISA, the Official Secrets Act, and the Sedition Act, all of which can draw several years in prison. The Malaysian Communication and Multimedia Commission (MCMC), an agency responsible in part for regulating the internet, has been known to monitor online content and order outlets or bloggers to remove material it views as provocative or subversive.

While the BN government continues to articulate the need for a tolerant and inclusive form of Islam, religious freedom is restricted in Malaysia. Ethnic Malays are defined by the constitution as Muslims, and practicing a version of Islam other than Sunni Islam is prohibited. Muslim children and civil servants are required to receive religious education using government-approved curriculums and instructors. Proselytizing among Muslims by other religious groups is prohibited, and a

2007 ruling by the country's highest court effectively made it impossible for Muslims to have their conversions to other faiths recognized by the state; in very rare exceptions, a small number of non-Malays have been allowed to revert to their previous faiths after converting to Islam for marriage. Non-Muslims are not able to build houses of worship as easily as Muslims, and the state retains the right to demolish unregistered religious statues and houses of worship.

A court ruling in late 2009 overturned a government ban prohibiting non-Muslims from using the word "Allah" to refer to God, touching off a wave of January 2010 arson attacks and vandalism that struck Christian churches as well as some Muslim and Sikh places of worship. Appeals in the case seemed to be in stasis by 2011, and the 2009 ruling had yet to be enforced. However, acts of anti-Christian persecution continued during the year. In August, authorities in Selangor raided a multiracial dinner at a Methodist church, alleging that Christians were proselytizing to Muslim guests. The sultan of Selangor later ruled that neither the Christians nor the Muslim religious officers breached any laws. At the end of 2011, an evangelical Christian leader faced charges of sedition for questioning the monarch's responsibility to safeguard the special position of the Malay community.

The government restricts academic freedom; teachers or students espousing antigovernment views or engaging in political activity are subject to disciplinary action under the Universities and University Colleges Act (UUCA) of 1971. In July 2011, the Court of Appeal ruled that the National University of Malaysia had breached Article 10 of the constitution when it disciplined four students involved in a political campaign in 2010. The prime minister announced in November that the UUCA would be amended, but he stressed that his administration would still appeal the court ruling, and that political activity on campuses remained strictly prohibited. This led to protests by student activists who called for the act to be repealed. On December 17, about 100 undergraduates marched to UMNO's headquarters. Up to 17 were arrested, and several were beaten.

Freedoms of assembly and association are limited on the grounds of maintaining security and public order. A police permit is required for all public assemblies except picket lines, and the granting of permits is sometimes politically influenced. Demonstrators can be detained under laws including the Sedition Act, the Police Act, and the ISA. On July 9, 2011, the Coalition for Free and Fair Elections (Bersih)—an alliance of civil society organizations working for electoral reforms, transparency in government, and an end to corruption—attempted to hold a rally of 20,000 or more participants in Kuala Lumpur. The authorities responded with water hoses, tear gas, and batons, and arrested almost 1,700 people, drawing domestic and international condemnation for their harsh tactics. In an attempt to block further demonstrations by Bersih, a curfew was imposed in the capital, along with roadblocks and police checks for residency papers. Despite the September 2011 announcement of possible legal reforms, the Peaceful Assembly Act passed at the end of the year was seen as a bid to restrict rather than safeguard freedom of assembly. There were protests against the bill before its passage, and opposition politicians walked out of Parliament to express their disapproval.

The Societies Act of 1996 defines a society as any association of seven or more people, excluding schools, businesses, and trade unions. Societies must be approved and registered by the government, which has refused or revoked registrations for political reasons. Numerous nongovernmental organizations operate in Malaysia, but some international human rights organizations are forbidden from forming Malaysian branches.

Most Malaysian workers—excluding migrant workers—can join trade unions, but the law contravenes international guidelines by restricting unions to representing workers in a single or similar trade. The Director General of Trade Unions can refuse or withdraw registration arbitrarily, and the union recognition process can take from 18 to 36 months. Collective bargaining is limited. Unions in essential services must give advance notice of strikes; various other legal conditions effectively render strikes impossible. Amendments in November 2011 to the Employment Act further weakened workers' rights by removing responsibility from employers and allowing greater use of subcontracting arrangements. The changes triggered protests in the capital and in Penang.

Judicial independence has been compromised by extensive executive influence. Arbitrary or politically motivated verdicts are not uncommon, with the most prominent example being the convictions of opposition leader Anwar Ibrahim in 1999 and 2000 for corruption and sodomy. The 1999 sodomy conviction was overturned in 2004, and Anwar was released from prison, but the corruption charge was upheld, delaying his return to elected office until 2008. The second, current sodomy case against him began that year.

Malaysia's secular legal system is based on English common law. However, Muslims are subject to Sharia (Islamic law), the interpretation of which varies regionally, and the constitution's Article 121 stipulates that all matters related to Islam should be dealt with in Sharia courts. This results in vastly different treatment of Muslims and non-Muslims regarding "moral" and family law issues.

Individuals may be arrested without a warrant for some offenses and held for 24 hours without being charged. The ISA, in force since 1960, gives the police sweeping powers to hold any person acting "in a manner prejudicial to the security of Malaysia" for up to 60 days, extendable to two years without trial. The law has been used to jail mainstream politicians, alleged Islamist militants, trade unionists, suspected communist activists, ordinary criminal suspects, and members of "deviant" Muslim sects, among others. Detainees have reported cases of torture while in custody, but official documentation of these claims is rare. More than 40 people remained in detention under the ISA at the close of 2011, as lawmakers considered a replacement law that would focus on combating terrorism.

Although the constitution provides for equal treatment of all citizens, the government maintains an affirmative-action program intended to boost the economic status of ethnic Malays and other indigenous people, known collectively as bumiputera. Bumiputera receive preferential treatment in areas including property ownership, higher education, civil service jobs, and business affairs, and bumiputera-owned companies receive the lion's share of large government contracts.

Foreign household workers are often subject to exploitation and abuse by employers. Indonesia lifted a 2009 ban on sending such workers to Malaysia in December 2011, after the two governments agreed on a minimum wage and other rudimentary worker protections, but Cambodia imposed a similar ban in October. An estimated two million foreigners work in Malaysia illegally. If arrested and found guilty, they can be caned and detained indefinitely pending deportation.

Women are still underrepresented in politics, the professions, and the civil service. Violence against women remains a serious problem. Muslim women are legally disadvantaged because their family grievances are heard in Sharia courts, where men are favored in matters such as inheritance and divorce and women's testimony is not given equal weight. Despite some progress in investigating and punishing sex-trafficking offenses, efforts to combat trafficking are criticized as inadequate.

Maldives

Political Rights: 3
Civil Liberties: 4
Status: Partly Free

Population: 325,000
Capital: Malé

Ten-Year Ratings Timeline For Year Under Review (Political Rights, Civil Liberties, Status)

2002	2003	2004	2005	2006	2007	2008	2009	2010	2011
6,5NF	6,5NF	6,5NF	6,5NF	6,5NF	6,5NF	4,4PF	3,4PF	3,4PF	3,4PF

Overview: **The opposition Maldivian People's Party (DRP) won the largest number of seats in February 2011 local council elections. In May, the DRP accused the government of using violence against demonstrators in Malé, the capital, who were protesting against rising prices. Antigovernment demonstrations erupted again in December, with tens of thousands taking to the streets of the capital.**

The Maldives achieved independence in 1965 after 78 years as a British protectorate, and a 1968 referendum replaced the centuries-old sultanate with a republican system. The first president, Amir Ibrahim Nasir, held office for 10 years. He was succeeded by Maumoon Abdul Gayoom, who served six five-year terms. Gayoom repeatedly renewed his mandate through a tightly controlled system of presidential referendums rather than competitive elections.

Gayoom initiated political reforms after the beating death of a prison inmate sparked riots in 2003. A People's Special Majlis (PSM), composed of lawmakers and other elected and appointed delegates, was tasked with amending the constitution in 2004. The next several years brought incremental improvements to the legislative, judicial, and media frameworks, interspersed with bouts of unrest, crackdowns on the opposition Maldivian Democratic Party (MDP), and restrictions on freedom of expression.

In June 2008, the PSM approved a new constitution. Under pressure from opposition demonstrators, the president in August ratified the new charter, which included protection for a range of civil liberties while maintaining restrictions on religious freedom. The country's first multiparty presidential election was held in October. Gayoom outpolled five challengers in the first round, taking 41 percent of the vote, but MDP leader and former political prisoner Mohamed Nasheed won the runoff with 54 percent. The poll was deemed relatively free and fair, though observers reported flaws including some preelection violence and voter registration problems.

Nasheed's immediate priorities included anticorruption measures, government decentralization, and press freedom. The government in 2009 abolished the Atolls Ministry, appointed seven provincial state ministers, and published a draft decentralization bill. The president also abolished the Information Ministry, and introduced draft bills guaranteeing freedom of expression and press freedom that remained under consideration by the parliament at the end of 2010. These plans for reform remained largely hindered by the opposition in 2011.

In the May 2009 parliamentary elections, Gayoom's Maldivian People's Party (DRP) won 28 of 77 seats, while the MDP captured 26, the DRP-allied People's Alliance (PA) took 7, and independents garnered 13. A Commonwealth observer team characterized the voting as largely transparent and competitive, despite minor problems related to the compilation of the voter list and some other irregularities. Nasheed's cabinet resigned in June 2010, citing frustration over continued efforts by the opposition-controlled legislature to block the reforms supported by the president. Nasheed reappointed the cabinet a week later, though the parliament refused to ratify the appointments. In December 2010, the Supreme Court ruled that seven cabinet members who had not been approved by the opposition-led parliament had to step down from office. Following the court decision, the president appointed new ministers and acting ministers.

In February 2011 local council elections, the DRP won a majority of seats, particularly in major population centers.

In May 2011, protesters marched in Malé, the capital, to express their frustration with rising food prices and unemployment. The DRP blamed the price increases on the government's devaluation of the nation's currency; the government, however, said the increases were the result of rising global commodity prices. Riot police used tear gas and batons to break up the protests, and the government accused the protesters of initiating the violence during the demonstrations. During several nights of protests, police arrested many activists including opposition member Umar Naseer. In December, an opposition alliance was formed against Nasheed, culminating in a December 23 mass rally attended by tens of thousands of demonstrators who alleged that Nasheed's government had failed to protect Islamic values.

Political Rights and Civil Liberties:

The Republic of Maldives is an electoral democracy. Under the 2008 constitution, the president is directly elected for up to two five-year terms. The 2009 Parliamentary Constituencies Act increased the size of the unicameral People's Majlis to 77 seats, with members elected from individual districts to serve five-year terms. The president, parliament members, and other key officials are required to be Sunni Muslims. Since political parties were legalized in 2005, more than a dozen have registered. Under former president Maumoon Abdul Gayoom, government accountability was limited by the executive branch's almost complete control over the legislature and judiciary. However, a new, independent auditor general and the revised constitution have provided greater transparency, shedding light on pervasive corruption. An Anti-Corruption Commission (ACC) was established in 2008 and opened dozens of cases in 2009; however, none of these cases had been resolved as of the end of 2011. In August 2011, the ACC conducted a search of the parliament building to seize the financial statements of members of parliament who had not disclosed their financial records; the constitution requires all members of parliament to report financial information. The Maldives was ranked 134 out of 183 countries surveyed in Transparency International's 2011 Corruption Perceptions Index.

The constitution guarantees freedoms of expression and the press. While restrictions on speech deemed "contrary to the tenets of Islam" remain in place, defamation was decriminalized in 2009. Private print media have expanded and present a diversity of viewpoints, though some publications are still owned by Gayoom allies. The number of private radio stations has also increased, and the country's first private television channels began operating in 2008, though their legal protections remain limited. The 2010 Broadcasting Act established a commission to oversee the licensing and regulatory process. Legislation to transform the state broadcaster into the Maldives Broadcasting Corporation, an independent public-service entity, was passed in April 2010, but the government delayed implementing the handover until 2011. In May 2011, the International Federation of Journalists expressed concern that government authorities had injured a number of journalists covering the protests in Malé. The blocking of Christian websites by the Ministry of Islamic Affairs (MIA) remains an issue.

Freedom of religion remains severely restricted. Islam is the state religion, and all citizens are required to be Sunni Muslims. Imams must use government-approved sermons. The MIA has sole authority to grant licenses to preachers; a number of members of the Islamist Adhaalath Party hold senior positions in the ministry. In May 2010, the MIA introduced new regulations under the 1994 Religious Unity Act that allow the ministry to oversee the curriculum for religious education in schools, create new criteria for preaching licenses for imams, and deport those who openly preach a faith other than Islam. Non-Muslim foreigners, including approximately 70,000 guest workers on long-term visas, are allowed to observe their religions only in private. There were no reported limitations on academic freedom, but many scholars self-censor.

The constitution guarantees freedom of assembly. The DRP accused police of using excessive force against demonstrators during the May 2011 protests, alleging that hundreds of civilians were injured during the clashes. Nongovernmental organizations are allowed to form in the Maldives, but struggle with funding and issues of long-term viability in a weak civil society environment. The constitution and the 2008 Employment Act allow workers to form trade unions and to strike. In response to a series of strikes, the country's first labor tribunal was established in December 2008 to enforce the Employment Act. In 2009, the Maldives joined the International Labour Organization.

The constitution provides for an independent judiciary, and judges were sworn into the first Supreme Court and final court of appeals in 2008. Courts have subsequently shown signs of increased independence from the executive. To further separate the two branches, the president established the Judicial Services Commission in 2009, although concerns remain about its composition. Civil law is used in most cases, but it is subordinate to Sharia (Islamic law), which is applied in matters not covered by civil law and in cases involving divorce or adultery. As a result, the testimony of two women is equal to that of one man, and punishments such as internal exile continue to be carried out.

The constitution bans arbitrary arrest, torture, and prolonged detention without adequate judicial review. The current administration has initiated police reform and established a parole board to recommend sentence reductions for unjustly detained inmates. However, progress on improving prison conditions has been slow, and abuses continue. In September 2011, the UN Development Programme (UNDP) issued a report providing policy recommendations to help reduce the number of offenders in the penal system.

Women are increasingly entering the civil service and receiving pay equal to that of men, though opportunities are sometimes limited by traditional norms. Women hold few senior government positions, though the president appointed several women to high-ranking posts in 2009 and 2010. The new constitution allows a woman to become president. International human rights groups have urged reform of severe legal punishments that primarily affect women, including the sentence of flogging for extramarital sex. The UNDP initiated a training program to help women run in the 2011 local council elections; there were 224 female candidates, and 54 were elected. Homosexual activity is against the law.

Mali

Political Rights: 2
Civil Liberties: 3
Status: Free

Population: 15,394,000
Capital: Bamako

Ten-Year Ratings Timeline For Year Under Review (Political Rights, Civil Liberties, Status)

2002	2003	2004	2005	2006	2007	2008	2009	2010	2011
2,3F	2,3F	2,2F	2,2F	2,2F	2,2F	2,3F	2,3F	2,3F	2,3F

Overview: **In 2011, Mali began preparations for the 2012 presidential and parliamentary elections, which will bring an end to President Amadou Toumani Touré's 10 years in power, and the political atmosphere intensified as parties began to put forth potential candidates. The potential for terrorist attacks remained high throughout 2011, and at the end of the year, three European aid workers kidnapped in Algeria were still being held in Mali by a group affiliated with the terrorist organization Al-Qaeda in the Islamic Maghreb.**

Mali was ruled by military and one-party regimes for more than 30 years following independence from France in 1960. After soldiers killed more than 100 demonstrators demanding a multiparty system in 1991, President Moussa Traoré was overthrown by the military. Alpha Oumar Konaré of the Alliance for Democracy in Mali (ADEMA) won the presidency in the 1992 elections, which were deemed credible by most observers. He secured a second and final term in 1997 amid an opposition boycott. Several opposition parties also boycotted that year's National Assembly elections, in which ADEMA captured a majority of seats.

In the 2002 presidential election, independent candidate Amadou Toumani Touré, a popular former military officer who had led Mali during the post-Traoré transition period, defeated his ADEMA opponent. During legislative elections that year, the opposition Hope 2002 coalition, led by the Rally for Mali party, emerged victorious over an ADEMA-led coalition.

In the April 2007 presidential poll, Touré was reelected with 71 percent in the first round of voting; he had run as an independent candidate, but with support from the Alliance of Democracy and Progress (ADP) coalition, led by ADEMA. In July 2007 elections to the National Assembly, the ADP secured a total of 113 seats, with 51 going to ADEMA. The main opposition coalition, the Front for Democracy and the Republic, captured 15 seats, while a smaller party and a number of independents secured the remaining 19 seats. Meanwhile, ADEMA captured more votes than any other party in the 2009 municipal elections.

While violence between government forces and the marginalized ethnic Tuareg minority flared in the late 2000s, clashes died down somewhat following a 2009 offensive by the Malian army and a subsequent peace agreement between government and Tuareg forces. By 2010, the North Mali Tuareg Alliance for Change, a former rebel faction, was working cooperatively with government troops to police drug-smuggling routes. In 2010, the government announced that a joint operation with Mauritanian forces had resulted in the capture of key members of one of the largest drug-trafficking networks in the Sahel.

A number of international aid workers and European tourists have been kidnapped since 2008, and several have been killed. The terrorist organization Al-Qaeda in the Islamic Maghreb (AQIM) continued to threaten security in the north throughout 2010 and 2011. In February 2010, Mali liberated four AQIM fighters to secure the release of a French hostage in AQIM custody, prompting Algeria and Mauritania to recall their ambassadors from Bamako. Nonetheless, regional cooperation improved following a September 2010 meeting at which military representatives from Mali, Mauritania, Algeria, and Niger signed an agreement on the creation of a shared intelligence command. In October 2011, Islamist rebels kidnapped three aid workers in Algeria, and held them in Mali; Malian officials said the rebels belonged to an AQIM faction.

In October 2011, Mali set April 29, 2012, as the official date for the first round of much-anticipated 2012 presidential elections. In preparation, Mali established a nonpermanent National Independent Electoral Commission. While presidential candidates are technically allowed to formally register only 45 days before polling, some political parties in 2011 were already nominating candidates. Touré is constitutionally barred from running again. Mali will also hold legislative elections in 2012 with the first and second rounds in July. In 2011, the government worked to propose changes to the constitution, including the creation of a Senate and an independent regulatory body for broadcasting, and set the date for a constitutional referendum in 2012.

Although it is one of the world's least developed countries, Mali has undertaken significant political and economic reforms since the early 1990s, including a decentralization program that gave greater autonomy to local communities. Mali has benefited from international debt relief, and is currently working with the International Monetary Fund (IMF) to enact economic reforms and promote foreign investment.

Political Rights and Civil Liberties: Mali is an electoral democracy. The 2007 presidential election was peaceful, and the results were deemed valid by domestic and international observers. The president, who appoints the prime minister, is elected by popular vote and can serve up to two five-year terms. In 2011, Mali saw its first woman prime minister rise to power, Cissé Mariam Kaïdama Sidibé. Members of the 160-seat unicameral National Assembly serve five-year terms, with 13 seats reserved to represent Malians living abroad.

In 2011 a wide variety of political parties and coalitions—often organized around leading personalities—operated in fluid and frequently shifting electoral coalitions. The largest party, ADEMA, participated in the ADP coalition to back President Amadou Toumani Touré during the 2007 elections. A new political party, the Project for Economic and Social Development (PDES), was formed in July 2010 in preparation for the 2012 presidential election; PDES was established as a successor to the Citizen Movement, Touré's nonpartisan political association.

A number of anticorruption initiatives have been launched under Touré's administration, including the creation of a general auditor's office. However, corruption remains a problem in government, public procurement, and both public and private contracting. Between 2010 and 2011, the Global Fund to Fight AIDS, Tuberculosis, and Malaria suspended and terminated several grants to Mali worth millions of dollars due to government embezzlement and fraud. Mali was ranked 118 out of 183 countries surveyed in Transparency International's 2011 Corruption Perceptions Index.

Mali's media is considered among the freest in Africa. Criminal libel laws have not been invoked by authorities since 2007, and there were no reports of harassment or intimidation of journalists in 2011. Throughout the year, various workshops were held to strengthen the media's capacity before the 2012 elections. The government does not restrict internet access, although less than 1 percent of the population had access in 2011.

While Mali's population is predominantly Muslim, and the High Islamic Council has significant influence over politics, the state is secular, and minority religious rights are protected by law. Academic freedom is respected.

Freedoms of assembly and association are respected. Many civic groups and nongovernmental organizations operate actively without interference. The constitution guarantees workers the right to form unions and to strike. However, some workers who perform services deemed essential are required to provide limited services during strikes, and in some cases the labor minister can force strikers into arbitration.

The judiciary, whose members are appointed by the executive, is not independent. Traditional authorities decide the majority of disputes in rural areas. A 2010 law calls for the establishment of Centers for Access to Rights and Justice, which would provide citizens with information about their legal rights and judicial procedures. The centers were not yet operational at year's end. Detainees are not always charged within the 48-hour period set by law, and there are lengthy delays in bringing defendants to trial. Police brutality has been reported, though courts have convicted some perpetrators. Prison conditions are harsh, and while human rights monitors are permitted to visit prisons, cumbersome administrative procedures reportedly make investigations difficult.

No ethnic group predominates in the government or security forces. Long-standing tensions between the more populous nonpastoralist ethnic groups and the Moor and Tuareg pastoralist groups have fueled intermittent instability.

Women are underrepresented in high political posts, and only a few cabinet ministers are women. Domestic violence against women is widespread, and cultural traditions have hindered reform. Despite the creation of the National Coordinating Committee for the Fight Against Trafficking and Related Activities in 2011, adult trafficking has not been criminalized, and Mali remains a source, destination and transit country for women and children trafficked for the purposes of sexual exploitation and forced labor. Prosecution of suspected traffickers is infrequent, with only two trafficking convictions in 2011. Traditional forms of slavery and debt bondage persist, particularly in the north, with thousands of people estimated to be living in conditions of servitude.

Malta

Political Rights: 1
Civil Liberties: 1
Status: Free

Population: 412,000
Capital: Valletta

Ten-Year Ratings Timeline For Year Under Review (Political Rights, Civil Liberties, Status)

2002	2003	2004	2005	2006	2007	2008	2009	2010	2011
1,1F	1,1F	1,1F	1,1F	1,1F	1,1F	1,1F	1,1F	1,1F	1,1F

Overview: **Malta continued to face numerous challenges related to immigration in 2011, including xenophobia, poor conditions in detention and open centers, and rioting. Meanwhile, a law legalizing divorce was adopted in July, and the government continued to take steps to address corruption.**

After gaining independence from Britain in 1964, Malta joined the Commonwealth and became a republic in 1974. Power has alternated between the pro-Western, center-right Nationalist Party (PN) and the nonaligned, leftist Malta Labour Party (MLP). The PN pursued membership in the European Union (EU), which the country finally achieved in 2004.

Former prime minister and veteran PN leader Edward Fenech Adami was elected president of the republic in 2004. Lawrence Gonzi, the deputy prime minister, took over the premiership.

In the March 2008 elections, Gonzi led the PN to a narrow victory over the Labour Party (PL), the renamed MLP; the PN won 49.3 percent of the vote, while the PL captured 48.9 percent. However, results in the country's 13 multimember electoral constituencies gave the PL 34 seats and the PN 31, triggering a constitutional provision that allows extra seats to be added to ensure a legislative majority for the party winning the popular vote. The PN consequently received four additional seats. Voter turnout was 93 percent, the lowest the country had seen since 1971.

Former PL leader George Abela was sworn in as president in April 2009. Abela, who was very popular with voters from both parties, was the first president to be nominated by a political party not in power and the first since 1974 to be backed by both sides of the House of Representatives.

Given Malta's central location in the Mediterranean, Malta has received an increasing number of immigrants, refugees, and asylum-seekers, over the last decade, mostly from sub-Saharan Africa, who subsequently settle in the country or proceed to migrate to other EU countries. A 2008 agreement between Italy and Libya succeeded in curbing immigration to the EU, and by 2010, unauthorized immigration to Malta had significantly declined. A 2010 pilot intra-EU Relocation of Refugees from Malta program also helped to reduce the number of immigrants that Malta would need to accept. However, in 2011, immigration to Malta began to increase again due to the armed conflict in Libya.

Incoming refugees and asylum seekers still face mandatory detention of up to 18 months under Maltese law. In March 2011, the Commissioner for Human Rights of the Council of Europe released a report on the reception of immigrants and asylum seekers in Malta, which concluded that the Maltese policy on forced detention for asylum seekers violates the European Convention of Human Rights. The report also documented inadequate conditions in certain open centers, and reported that a majority of immigrants faced xenophobia and discrimination in housing, employment, and services. Malta's media and political discourse were also criticized for contributing to an atmosphere of hostility and intolerance toward immigrants. Riots occurred at the Safi Detention Centre in May and in August, sparked by limited food supplies and the rejection of asylum applications.

Political Rights and Civil Liberties: Malta is an electoral democracy. Members of the 69-seat unicameral legislature, the House of Representatives, are elected for five-year terms. Lawmakers elect the president, who also serves for five years. The president names the prime minister, usually the leader of the majority party or coalition.

The ruling PN and opposition PL dominate national politics. The smaller Democratic Alternative party also competes, but is not currently represented in the parliament.

Malta continued to fight corruption with new legislation in 2011. The Permanent Commission Against Corruption Bill was amended in March to allow for the appointment of a special prosecutor and to broaden the definition of corruption. However, an October EU report claimed that Malta has one of the worst "black economies" in the eurozone, and that at least a quarter of Malta's annual gross domestic product is not being reported.

The constitution guarantees freedom of speech and of the press, though incitement to racial hatred is punishable by a jail term of six to eight months. Blasphemy is also illegal, and censorship remains an ongoing issue. There are several daily newspapers and weekly publications in Maltese and English, as well as radio and television stations. Residents also have access to Italian television broadcasts. The government does not restrict internet access.

The constitution establishes Roman Catholicism as the state religion, and the state grants subsidies only to Catholic schools. While the population is overwhelmingly Roman Catholic, small communities of Muslims, Jews, and Protestants are tolerated and respected. There is one Muslim private school. Academic freedom is respected.

The constitution provides for freedoms of assembly and association, and the government generally respects these rights in practice. Nongovernmental organizations investigating human rights issues are able to operate without state interference. The law recognizes the right to form and join trade unions, and limits on the right to strike were eased in 2002. A compulsory arbitration clause in the country's labor law allows the government to force a settlement on striking workers; however, this clause is not often used.

The judiciary is independent, and the rule of law prevails in civil and criminal matters. Prison conditions generally meet international standards, though the Council of Europe's Commission for Human Rights has criticized poor detention conditions for irregular migrants and asylum seekers. Migrant workers are reportedly often exploited and subjected to substandard working conditions.

The constitution prohibits discrimination based on gender. However, women are underrepresented in government, occupying only about 9 percent of seats in the parliament. A law legalizing divorce was adopted in July 2011 and came into effect in October. Violence against women remains a problem. Abortion is strictly prohibited, even in cases of rape or incest. Malta is a source and destination country for human trafficking for the purposes of forced labor and sexual exploitation. While the government created a trafficking coordinator and monitoring board in 2011, the U.S. Trafficking in Persons Report criticized Malta for not meeting the minimum standards for the elimination of human trafficking.

Marshall Islands

Political Rights: 1
Civil Liberties: 1
Status: Free

Population: 55,000
Capital: Majuro

Ten-Year Ratings Timeline For Year Under Review (Political Rights, Civil Liberties, Status)

2002	2003	2004	2005	2006	2007	2008	2009	2010	2011
1,1F	1,1F	1,1F	1,1F	1,1F	1,1F	1,1F	1,1F	1,1F	1,1F

Overview: **The Marshall Islands held parliamentary elections in November 2011, in which the Aelon Kein Ad party captured the largest number of seats. Numerous officials, including a cabinet minister, faced charges stemming from a scheme to defraud the government, and Kwajalein landowners agreed to lease their land to the United States for $32 million a year through 2066.**

The atolls and islands that make up the Republic of the Marshall Islands were claimed by Germany in 1885 and occupied by Japan during World War I. The islands came under U.S. control during World War II, and the United States administered them under United Nations trusteeship in 1947. The Marshall Islands became an independent state in 1986.

In the 2007 legislative elections, the Aelon Kein Ad (AKA) party captured 18 seats, while the United Democratic Party (UDP) took 15 seats. In 2008, lawmakers elected Litokwa Tomeing as president. A no-confidence vote in October 2009 ousted Tomeing, and Jurelang Zedkaia, the Speaker of the legislature, was chosen to succeed him later that month.

The Marshall Islands maintains close relations with the United States under a Compact of Free Association. The first compact, which came into force in 1986, allows the United States to maintain military facilities in the Marshall Islands in exchange for defense guarantees, development assistance, and visa-free access for Marshallese to live, work, study, and obtain health care and social services in the United States. The Marshall Islands relies on compact funds for almost 70 percent of its annual budget.

An amended compact with new funding and accountability requirements took effect in 2004 and will run through 2023. The deal authorized the Marshall Islands to receive annual transfers of $57 million from the United States until 2013 and $62 million from 2014 to 2023. In exchange, the United States will have use of the Kwajalein missile-testing site—the primary U.S. testing ground for long-range nuclear missiles—through 2066. Local populations have expressed concern about the about potential health and environmental hazards posed by the testing facility; Bikini Atoll remains uninhabitable, and Enewetak Atoll is partly contaminated. A $150 million Nuclear Claims Fund provides compensation for past, present, and future Marshallese victims, though some critics charge that the fund is inadequate. The U.S. government has rejected additional compensation on the basis that it has already paid $1.5 billion in personal injury and property damages under the original compact. In May 2011, after years of negotiations, a group of Kwajalein landowners agreed to lease their land to the United States for a total of $32 million through 2066.

With limited education and employment opportunities, about one-third of the country's citizens live overseas, mostly in the United States. The government adopted new austerity measures in its 2011 budget in order to counter the impact of the global economic downturn; the economy was also damaged by lower returns on investments in its trust fund and a 20-year low in tourism. The government initiated a large-scale audit of government spending from 2007 to 2011, after law enforcement discovered that more than $500,000 in U.S. grants to the Ministry of Health had been stolen.

Parliamentary elections held on November 21 saw a high voter turnout, with no reports of fraud or violence. Absentee ballots from overseas voters were allowed through December 5. Official election results published in early December did not give a clear majority to either the AKA or UDP. However, the AKA eventually controlled 20 seats after victorious independent candidates joined the party. The parliament had not selected a new president by year's end.

Political Rights and Civil Liberties: The Marshall Islands is an electoral democracy. The president is chosen for a four-year term by the unicameral parliament (Nitijela), from among its 33 members, who are directly elected to four-year terms. An advisory body, the Council of Chiefs (Iroij), consists of 12 traditional leaders who are consulted on customary law. The two main political parties are the AKA and the UDP.

Corruption is a serious problem. In January 2011, the government launched an extensive probe into a scheme to defraud the Marshall Islands. By July, 12 people were charged, including transportation and communication minister Kenneth Tedi, marking the first time in the country's history that a cabinet minister faced criminal charges. Tedi entered a no-contest plea and received a 30-day suspended jail sentence and a fine of $1,000; critics argued that the penalty was too light.

The government generally respects freedom of speech and of the press. A privately owned newspaper, the *Marshall Islands Journal*, publishes articles in English and Marshallese. The government's *Marshall Islands Gazette* provides official news but avoids political coverage. Broadcast outlets include both government- and church-owned radio stations, and cable television offers a variety of international news and entertainment programs. Residents in some parts of the country can also access U.S. armed forces radio and television. The government does not restrict internet access, but penetration rates are low due to cost and technical difficulties.

Religious and academic freedoms are respected in practice. The quality of secondary education remains low and four-year college education is rare.

Citizen groups operate freely in the country. Many are sponsored by or affiliated with church organizations and provide social services. The government broadly interprets constitutional guarantees of freedom of assembly and association to cover trade unions.

The constitution provides for an independent judiciary. Nearly all judges and attorneys are recruited from overseas. To ease the increasing backlog of land dispute cases, the government revived use of Traditional Rights Courts (TRC) in May 2010 to make advisory rulings to the High Court. Police brutality is generally not a problem, and detention centers and prisons meet minimum international standards. The Marshall Islands has a tradition of matrilineal inheritance in tribal rank and personal property, but social and economic discrimination against women is widespread. Women's rights groups say that few women obtain jobs outside the home or hold positions in government. Tensions between the local population and Chinese migrants are increasing, as Chinese businesses control much of the retail sector.

Mauritania

Political Rights: 6
Civil Liberties: 5
Status: Not Free

Population: 3,542,000
Capital: Nouakchott

Ten-Year Ratings Timeline For Year Under Review (Political Rights, Civil Liberties, Status)

2002	2003	2004	2005	2006	2007	2008	2009	2010	2011
5,5PF	6,5NF	6,5NF	6,4PF	6,4PF	4,4PF	6,5NF	6,5NF	6,5NF	6,5NF

Overview:

In August 2011, municipal and legislative elections planned for October were postponed indefinitely. Anti-government protests by several groups took place during the year. A September demonstration against the new national census, which black Mauritanians alleged was discriminatory, resulted in the death of at least one protester.

Following independence from France in 1960, Mauritania was ruled by a series of civilian and military authoritarian regimes. In 1984, Colonel Maaouya Ould Sidi Ahmed Taya ousted President Mohamed Khouna Ould Haidallah. Although Taya introduced a multiparty system in 1991, he repeatedly secured poll victories for himself and his Democratic and Social Republican Party (PRDS) through the misuse of state resources, suppression of the opposition, and manipulation of the media and electoral institutions.

In August 2005, soldiers led by Colonel Ely Ould Mohamed Vall overthrew Taya's government in a move that received strong public support. Soon after taking power, the Military Council for Justice and Democracy (CMJD) pardoned and released hundreds of political prisoners, and dozens of political activists returned from exile. The CMJD established an independent electoral commission to administer elections. Legislative and municipal elections were held in November and December 2006, with independent candidates, mostly former PRDS members, securing a majority of the seats. Independents also won a majority of seats in January and February 2007 Senate elections, while Sidi Ould Cheikh Abdellahi, an independent, won the presidency in March. This series of elections were the first in Mauritania's history to be broadly viewed as generally free and fair.

Abdellahi drew criticism from military leaders and members of the National Party for Democracy and Development (PNDD) for inviting hard-line Islamists and former members of Taya's regime into the cabinet. The government resigned in July 2008 under the threat of a parliamentary no-confidence vote, and Abdellahi formed a new cabinet that included only PNDD members. However, this failed to restore lawmakers' confidence, and 48 PNDD parliamentarians quit the party on August 4. On August 6, Abdellahi fired four top military officers. One of them, General Mohamed Ould Abdel Aziz, mounted a coup the same day.

Aziz and his allies announced that an 11-member junta, the High State Council (HSC), would run the country until new elections were held. While the international community strongly condemned the coup and key donors suspended non-humanitarian aid, the domestic reaction was mixed. A majority of lawmakers and mayors expressed support, but a coalition of four pro-Abdellahi parties formed the National Front for the Defense of Democracy and refused to participate in the junta-led government.

In April 2009, Aziz announced that he would resign from the military in order to run for president. Despite initial resistance, opposition parties agreed to participate in the presidential vote after six days of negotiations. Under international pressure, the HSC handed power in June to a transitional government to supervise an election set for July.

Aziz won the election in the first round with 52.6 percent of the vote. Four opposition parties claimed that the results were predetermined, electoral lists had been tampered with, and fraudulent voters had used fake ballot papers and identity cards. The parties lodged a formal appeal with the Constitutional Council that was ultimately rejected, and the head of the electoral commission resigned over doubts about the election's conduct. While some opposition parties continued to protest the outcome, the Rally for Democratic Forces (RDF) recognized Aziz's presidency in September 2010, citing the need for unity in the face of increased terrorist attacks by Islamist militants.

In May 2011, Aziz initiated a new census, the finalization of voter lists, and the automation of national identity cards. Nevertheless, municipal and legislative elections planned for October were postponed indefinitely in August. Two leading opposition parties had requested this delay, claiming that a promised dialogue with Aziz on wide-ranging political and electoral reforms had yet to occur. A national dialogue took place from September to October to address those issues, as well as opposition complaints about lack of access to the media; however, the elections had yet to be rescheduled as of the end of 2011. Protests by several sectors of society took place in 2011, including by the youth-led February 25 movement—inspired by the popular uprisings in the Arab world—as well as antislavery activists and black Mauritanians alleging bias in the new census.

Political Rights and Civil Liberties: Mauritania is not an electoral democracy. The constitutional government created after the 2006 and 2007 elections was ousted by the August 2008 military coup. The legitimacy of the 2009 presidential election, which installed coup leader Mohamed Ould Abdel Aziz as the civilian president, was challenged by the opposition but declared generally free and fair by international observers. Legislative elections scheduled for October 2011 were postponed indefinitely.

Under the 1991 constitution, the president is responsible for appointing and dismissing the prime minister and cabinet, and a 2006 amendment imposed a limit of two five-year presidential terms. The bicameral legislature consists of the 95-seat National Assembly, elected by popular vote, and the 56-seat Senate, with 53 members elected by mayors and municipal councils and 3 members chosen by the chamber to represent Mauritanians living abroad. Mauritania's party system is poorly developed, and clan and ethnic loyalties strongly influence the country's politics.

Corruption is a serious problem, and political instability has prevented fiscal transparency. The Aziz government's anticorruption campaign has resulted in notable arrests, including the former human rights commissioner in September 2010. However, the opposition has criticized the government's efforts as ineffective and politicized. Mauritania was ranked 143 out of 183 countries surveyed in Transparency International's 2011 Corruption Perceptions Index.

Despite constitutional guarantees for press freedom, some journalists practice self-censorship, and private newspapers face closure for publishing material considered offensive to Islam or threatening to the state. In September 2011, the government ended a 51-year monopoly on broadcast media with a call for applications for licenses from private outlets. In November, the High Press and Audiovisual Authority announced that two independent television stations and five independent radio stations had been awarded licenses, though some opposition members alleged that the licenses favored progovernment stations. In October, the legislature adopted amendments to a 2006 press law that eliminated prison terms for slander and defamation, though fines can still be levied. Two journalists were beaten and detained for their coverage of clashes between police and protesters in September. There were no reports of government restrictions on the internet.

Mauritania was declared an Islamic republic under the 1991 constitution, and proselytizing by non-Muslims is banned in practice. Non-Muslims cannot be citizens, and those who convert from Islam lose their citizenship. In practice, however, non-Muslim communities have not been targeted for persecution. Academic freedom is respected.

The 1991 constitution guaranteed freedoms of association and assembly, though organizers are required to obtain consent from the authorities for large gatherings. In 2011, security forces violently dispersed several allegedly unauthorized demonstrations staged by a wide range of groups. In April, police used tear gas to disperse an antigovernment protest in the capital by the February 25 movement—called a "day of rage" in solidarity with the Arab uprisings. Beginning in June, black Mauritanians constituting the Do Not Touch My Nationality movement protested against the national census, which they claim discriminates against them. A September demonstration in the southern city of Maghama against the census prompted the police to fire live rounds and tear gas, killing at least one protester.

Workers have the legal right to unionize, but unions must be approved by the public prosecutor and encounter hostility from employers. Although only about a quarter of Mauritanians are formally employed, the vast majority of workers in the industrial and commercial sectors are unionized. The right to strike is limited by notice requirements and bans on certain forms of strike action. The authorities repressed a number of strikes throughout 2011, though they did not dissolve any unions. In May, riot police used violence against protesting dockworkers, with several injured.

The judicial system is heavily influenced by the government. The Mauritanian Lawyers Association (ONA) condemned the 2011 arrests of several judges on drug trafficking charges as politically motivated. Many judicial decisions are shaped by Sharia (Islamic law), especially in family and civil matters. Prison conditions are harsh, suspects are routinely held for long periods of pretrial detention, and security forces suspected of human rights abuses operate with impunity. There are reports that prisoners, particularly terrorism suspects, are subject to torture by authorities. Islamist militants, members of Al-Qaeda in the Islamic Maghreb (AQIM), have carried out a number of attacks in Mauritania in recent years. A new antiterrorism law was passed in July 2010. During 2010, numerous AQIM members were killed, and security forces killed 15 in a single incident in February 2011. In May, the governments of Mauritania, Mali, Niger, and Algeria agreed on a joint force to combat AQIM. Meanwhile, the Mauritanian Islamic Affairs Ministry launched workshops in June to train imams to mount an ideological counteroffensive against AQIM. In March, a court convicted three AQIM operatives in the 2009 killing of an American aid worker, and sentenced one to death.

Racial and ethnic discrimination persists in all spheres of political and economic life. The country's three main ethnic groups are the politically and economically dominant White Moors of Arab and Berber descent; the black descendants of slaves, also known as Haratins or Black Moors; and black Africans who are closer in ethnic heritage to the peoples of neighboring Senegal and Mali. In April 2011, a riot between Afro-Mauritanian and Moor students broke out at the University of Nouakchott over allegations of fraud during a student union vote that was split among the two groups.

Despite a 1981 law banning slavery in Mauritania, an estimated half a million black Mauritanians are believed to live in conditions of servitude. A 2007 law set penalties of 5 to 10 years in prison for all forms of slavery, but the law is hampered by a requirement that slaves themselves file a legal complaint before any prosecution can occur. In November 2011, six individuals were successfully prosecuted for enslavement and sentenced to jail, to pay a fine, and to make financial restitution to the victims. In January 2011, Biram Dah Abeid, the head of the Initiative for the Resurgence of the Abolitionist Movement (IRA) antislavery group, was arrested along with seven other activists. In August, four IRA activists were arrested for taking part in an antislavery protest, which was violently dispersed; the activists were later handed six-month suspended sentences.

The Aziz government is continuing an initiative to facilitate the return of the some 30,000 black Mauritanians who still reside in Senegal and Mali after being expelled following communal violence in 1989. For the first time, the government in 2009 publicly acknowledged its involvement in the expulsion of Afro-Mauritanians between 1989 and 1991 and agreed to provide compensation to 244 widows of those killed during the ordeal. At the end of 2011, most refugees had returned. While returnees have faced difficulty in recovering confiscated land, the government has provided them with housing assistance.

Under a 2005 law, party lists for the National Assembly elections must include district-based quotas of female candidates. Women currently hold 21 seats in the National Assembly and 8 Senate seats; also, 20 percent of all municipal council seats are reserved for women. Nevertheless, discrimination against women persists. Under Sharia, a woman's testimony is given only half the weight of a man's. Legal protections regarding property and pay equity are rarely respected in practice. Female genital mutilation (FGM) is illegal but widely practiced. In January 2010, 34 Islamic scholars issued a religious edict banning FGM. Abortion is legal only when the life of the mother is in danger. Human trafficking remains a serious problem, as the country remains a source and destination for women, men, and children trafficked for the purposes of forced labor and sexual exploitation.

Mauritius

Political Rights: 1
Civil Liberties: 2
Status: Free

Population: 1,286,000
Capital: Port Louis

Ten-Year Ratings Timeline For Year Under Review (Political Rights, Civil Liberties, Status)

2002	2003	2004	2005	2006	2007	2008	2009	2010	2011
1,2F	1,2F	1,1F	1,1F	1,2F	1,2F	1,2F	1,2F	1,2F	1,2F

Overview: **Mauritius experienced rare political upheaval in 2011, when the Mauritian Socialist Movement (MSM) pulled out of Prime Minister Navinchandra Ramgoolam's governing coalition in July. The moved was sparked by the filing of corruption charges against the health minister, a member of the MSM. The political turmoil deepened in September when MSM leader and former finance minister Pravind Jugnauth, the son of Mauritius's president, was also charged with corruption.**

Mauritius's ethnically mixed population is primarily descended from immigrants brought as laborers from the Indian subcontinent during the island's 360 years of Dutch, French, and British colonial rule. Since gaining independence from Britain in 1968, Mauritius has maintained one of the developing world's most successful democracies.

Navinchandra Ramgoolam served as prime minister from 1995 until 2000, when President Cassam Uteem called early elections, partly in response to a series of corruption scandals. The opposition alliance, led by the Mauritian Socialist Movement (MSM), won the vote, and its leader, former prime minister Anerood Jugnauth, returned to the premiership. In a planned power shift, Paul Bérenger—the leader of the Mauritian Militant Movement (MMM), which was allied with the MSM—took over as prime minister in September 2003, becoming the first person from outside the island's Indian-origin majority to hold the post. Jugnauth was then elected president.

In the 2005 parliamentary elections, frustration with rising unemployment and inflation following the loss of preferential trade deals resulted in a victory for the opposition Social Alliance, and Ramgoolam returned to power. However, rising prices and increasing levels of crime quickly diminished the popularity of the new government.

In the May 2010 National Assembly elections, Ramgoolam's Alliance for the Future (AF)—which included his Labour Party, the Mauritian Social Democratic Party (PMSD), and the MSM—captured 45 seats, while Bérenger's Alliance of the Heart (AH)—a coalition between the MMM, the National Union, and the Mauritanian Socialist Democratic Movement—took 20. Outside observers judged the elections to be free and fair, and Ramgoolam retained the premiership.

In July 2011, the Independent Commission Against Corruption (ICAC), the antigraft watchdog, arrested Health Minister Santi Bai Hanoomanjee of the MSM on charges of inflating the government's bid to purchase a private hospital. In response, all six MSM cabinet ministers—including party leader Pravind Jugnauth, the finance minster and son of Anerood Jugnauth—resigned. On August 7, the MSM pulled out of the governing coalition, leaving Ramgoolam with just a 36 to 33 seat parliamentary majority. Ramgoolam the previous day had named PMSD leader Charles Gaëtan Xavier-Luc Duval finance minister. Further turmoil came in September, when Pravind Jugnauth was arrested by the ICAC on conflict of interest charges related to the hospital bid.

Political Rights and Civil Liberties: Mauritius is an electoral democracy. Since independence, voters have regularly chosen their representatives in free, fair, and competitive elections. The head of state is a largely ceremonial president elected by the unicameral National Assembly for a five-year term. Executive power resides with the prime minister, who is appointed by the president from the party or coalition with the most seats in the legislature. Of the National Assembly's 70 members, 62 are directly elected and 8 are appointed from among unsuccessful candidates who gained the largest number of votes; all members serve five-year terms. Decentralized structures govern the country's small island dependencies. The largest dependency, Rodrigues Island, has its own government and local councils, and two seats in the National Assembly.

The country enjoys a generally positive reputation for transparency and accountability. However, the arrest in 2011 of the two MSM ministers on graft charges has sullied this image somewhat, as have allegations by the MSM that the ICAC is being used as a political tool by the ruling party. A leaked 2008 diplomatic cable from the U.S. Embassy in Port Louis, made public in September 2011 by the activist organization WikiLeaks, described corruption in Mauritius as "an often overlooked issue," and stated that "the country still suffers from a pervasive and ingrained problem" with graft. In a rare display of public discontent, about 3,000 demonstrators took to the streets of Port Louis in early September to protest against corruption and economic inequality. Mauritius was ranked 46 out of 183 countries surveyed in Transparency International's 2011 Corruption Perceptions Index, and the country has been ranked first in the Ibrahim Index of African Governance since its inception in 2007.

The constitution guarantees freedom of expression. Several private daily and weekly publications criticize both government and opposition politicians and their policies. The state-owned Mauritius Broadcasting Corporation operates radio and television services that generally reflect government viewpoints. A small number of private radio stations have been authorized, but the state-run media hold a monopoly in broadcasting local news. In October 2011, a Supreme Court judge found Dharmanand Dooharika, editor of the private news weekly *Samedi Plus*, guilty of contempt of court as a result of several articles he had written in 2010 about allegations of bias made by a local businessman against the Supreme Court's chief justice. Dooharika was sentenced to three months in prison. The court also levied heavy fines against two other news outlets. Internet use is widespread and unrestricted.

Religious and academic freedoms are respected.

Freedoms of assembly and association are honored, though police in past years occasionally used excessive force in response to riots. There are more than 300 unions in Mauritius. Tens of thousands of foreign workers employed in export-processing zones suffer from poor living and working conditions, and employers in the zones are reportedly hostile to unions.

The generally independent judiciary, headed by the Supreme Court, administers a legal system that is an amalgam of French and British traditions. Civil rights are for the most part well respected, though individual cases of police brutality have been reported.

Various ethnic cultures and traditions coexist peacefully, and constitutional prohibitions against discrimination are generally upheld. However, Mauritian Creoles, descendants of African slaves who comprise about a third of the population, live in poverty and are culturally and economically marginalized. Tensions between the Hindu majority and Muslim minority persist, constituting one of the country's few potential ethnic flashpoints. In November 2011, the Truth and Justice Commission—established to examine the country's history of slavery and indentured labor—released its report. The report recommended steps to encourage national reconciliation, including a slavery memorial and the promotion of a more equitable society through increased economic and political participation by non-Hindu Mauritians. Chagos Islanders—resettled in Mauritius after being evicted by the British in the 1960s to make room for a military base—have not been integrated into society and suffer from high levels of unemployment.

Women comprise about 36 percent of the labor force, but they receive less compensation than men for similar work and generally occupy a subordinate role in society. However, they enjoy equal access to public services and education, and currently hold 13 seats in the National Assembly. Rape and domestic violence against women are major concerns.

Mexico

Political Rights: 3
Civil Liberties: 3
Status: Partly Free

Population: 114,793,300
Capital: Mexico City

Ten-Year Ratings Timeline For Year Under Review (Political Rights, Civil Liberties, Status)

2002	2003	2004	2005	2006	2007	2008	2009	2010	2011
2,2F	2,2F	2,2F	2,2F	2,3F	2,3F	2,3F	2,3F	3,3F	3,3PF

Overview: **Violence between security forces and organized criminal groups, and among the criminal groups themselves, continued to increase in 2011. Over 16,000 people were killed as the crime syndicates fought over territory and control of various illicit activities. The government maintained troop deployments in the regions most affected by violence, but a series of massacres and the discovery of mass graves belied official claims of progress. Civil society groups took a more vocal role in demanding changes in the government's approach. Some improved human rights standards were incorporated into the constitution, even as allegations of severe rights abuses continued to plague the security forces.**

Mexico achieved independence from Spain in 1810 and became a republic in 1822. Seven years after the Revolution of 1910, a new constitution established the United Mexican States as a federal republic. From its founding in 1929 until 2000, the Institutional Revolutionary Party (PRI) dominated the country through patronage, corruption, and repression. The formal business of government often took place in secret, and the rule of law was frequently compromised by arbitrary power.

In the landmark 2000 presidential election, Vicente Fox Quesada of the National Action Party (PAN) defeated the candidates of the PRI and the leftist Party of the Democratic Revolution (PRD), capturing 42.5 percent of the vote. Fox presided over the provision of more open and accountable government and the arrests of some leaders of the country's vicious drug-trafficking groups. However, solutions to the problems of poverty, corruption, crime, and unemployment proved elusive. Elections held in July 2003 confirmed the PRI as the most powerful party in Congress and in many state governments.

In the 2006 presidential election, PAN candidate Felipe Calderón defeated Mexico City mayor Andrés Manuel López Obrador of the PRD by a mere 244,000 votes in the initial count. López Obrador rejected the result and for several months led protests that paralyzed parts of Mexico City, but many Mexicans—and most international observers—were not convinced by the PRD's evidence of fraud. In September, after a partial recount, the Federal Electoral Tribunal formally declared Calderón the winner. Though the PAN won the most seats in the concurrent congressional elections, the PRD's share of deputies exceeded the PRI's for the first time.

In 2007, Calderón managed to forge coalitions with opposition lawmakers to pass modest pension, tax, electoral, and judicial reforms, but the PRI emerged from the July 2009 congressional elections with control of the Chamber of Deputies, taking 237 seats and forming a majority with the 21 seats of the allied Green Party. The PAN's share fell to 143 seats, and the PRD declined to a distant third, with 71. The PRI continued its comeback in 2009 by again outperforming its rivals in state and local elections, which were held in six states. Balloting was held in nine states in 2010, with PRI candidates winning the gubernatorial contests in six. Nonetheless, alliances between the PAN and the PRD led to the election of non-PRI governors in Oaxaca, Sinaloa, and Puebla. Although 2011 opened with wins for the PRD and PAN in Guerrero and Baja California Sur, respectively, the PRI swept the year's four subsequent elections, including in the populous and important state of Mexico.

Intermittent legislative actions and talks among the three major parties failed to yield concrete gains on a major political reform proposed by Calderón in December 2009. The package would, among other changes, allow limited reelection for many elected officials, permit candidates to run as independents, provide for a second round of voting in presidential elections, and reduce the size of Congress. Although the Senate approved a version of the reform in April 2011, the bill remained under consideration in the Chamber of Deputies at year's end.

Also in 2011, over 16,000 people were killed in violence associated with organized crime syndicates, which had increased each year since 2006 and become the dominant concern in Mexican politics. The violence had claimed approximately 50,000 lives during Calderón's presidency, despite—or to some observers, because of—his decision to deploy the military to the worst-affected areas soon after taking office. While a majority of Mexicans continued to support the government's offensive against organized crime, opinion polls also registered skepticism about official claims that the campaign was making progress, as well as a strong and increasing perception of generalized insecurity. In addition, mounting allegations of severe human rights violations have surrounded the security operations conducted by more than 45,000 soldiers in various parts of Mexico. While the rate of increase in the annual death toll declined in 2011, and there was an absolute fall in homicides in the notoriously violent Ciudad Juárez, other cities—notably Monterrey, the country's second-most important economic center—experienced a sharp increase in violence. Moreover, the discovery of mass graves holding over 200 people in both Durango and Tamaulipas, and a series of massacres punctuated by an intentionally set fire that killed 52 people at a Monterrey casino in August, kept violence on the front pages throughout the year.

As a reaction to the onslaught, a new civil society initiative, the Movement for Peace with Justice and Dignity (MPJD), coalesced around Javier Sicilia, a well-known poet whose son was murdered in March in Cuernavaca. Sicilia and other prominent activists embarked on bus caravans in June and September, leading rallies along the way to demand a halt to the violence. Despite several meetings with Calderón, the MPJD's call for a "truce" between the government and the criminal groups went unheeded.

Political Rights and Civil Liberties:

Mexico is an electoral democracy. The president is elected to a six-year term and cannot be reelected. The bicameral Congress consists of the 128-member Senate, elected for six years through a mix of direct voting and proportional representation, with at least two parties represented in each state's delegation, and the 500-member Chamber of Deputies, with 300 elected directly and 200 through proportional representation, all for three-year terms. Members of Congress are also barred from reelection. Each state has an elected governor and legislature.

The Federal Electoral Institute (IFE), which supervises elections and enforces political party laws, has come to be viewed as a model for other countries. The 2006 elections were considered generally free and fair, but there were many complaints, especially by the opposition PRD, concerning negative advertising and the use of administrative resources on behalf of the presidential victor, Felipe Calderón of the ruling PAN. In response, an electoral reform was passed in 2007 to strictly regulate campaign financing and the content of political advertising. Opinion has been mixed regarding the efficacy and fairness of the reform. At the state level, allegations of abuse of public resources to favor specific gubernatorial candidates have increased in recent years, and the closely fought November 2011 race for the mayoralty of Morelia, the capital of Michoacán, was invalidated after the electoral tribunal determined that the PRI had violated the law through unauthorized promotions of the party and its candidate.

Signs of the vulnerability of politicians and municipal governments to pressure from organized crime have increased in recent years. Thirteen small-town mayors and the PRI candidate for governor of Tamaulipas were murdered in 2010, while in 2011 President Calderón decried the suspected influence of drug traffickers on the elections in Michoacán—where his sister narrowly lost the gubernatorial race—after several dozen candidates dropped out and one mayor was assassinated in the run-up to the balloting. In the most violence-plagued regions, provision of public services has become more difficult, and public sector employees such as teachers are subject to extortion. A federal lawmaker was killed in Guerrero in September, and no suspected organizer of the crime had been captured by year's end.

Official corruption remains a serious problem. Billions of dollars in illegal drug money is believed to enter the country each year from the United States, and there is a perception that such funds affect politics, particularly on the state and local levels. However, attempts to prosecute officials for alleged involvement in corrupt or criminal activity have generally failed due to the weakness of the state's cases. Although no senior politicians have been convicted of corruption in recent years, many officials have been dismissed or charged with links to drug traffickers. Two major arson incidents, a 2009 fire in a Sonora day-care center and the 2011 casino blaze in Monterrey, have drawn attention to corruption among permit issuers and safety inspectors, but punishment has been limited. Mexico was ranked 100 out of 183 countries surveyed in Transparency International's 2011 Corruption Perceptions Index. A 2002 freedom of information law, despite some limitations, has been considered successful at strengthening transparency at the federal level, though momentum has slowed and many states lag far behind.

Legal and constitutional guarantees of free speech have been gradually improving, but the security environment for journalists has deteriorated markedly. Some major media outlets are no longer dependent on the government for advertising and subsidies, and the competitive press has taken the lead in denouncing official corruption, though serious investigative reporting is scarce, particularly at the local level. Broadcast media are dominated by two corporations that control over 90 percent of the market.

Since a sharp increase in violence in 2006, reporters probing police issues, drug trafficking, and official corruption have faced a high risk of physical harm. The press freedom organization Article 19 reported nine journalists killed in 2011, making Mexico one of the world's most dangerous countries for media workers. Self-censorship has increased, and many newspapers in high-violence zones no longer publish stories involving in-depth reporting on organized crime. A special prosecutor's office devoted to investigating crimes against journalists has made only slow progress since opening in 2006, and a bill sought by journalists that would federalize crimes against reporters stalled in 2011.

The government does not restrict internet access, but criminals have extended their reach to citizens attempting to report on crime via online outlets. Three individuals killed in Nuevo Laredo in September 2011 were found with notes from the Zetas gang that tied their deaths to their online crime-reporting activities, though only one victim's involvement with such reporting was confirmed. Authorities in Veracruz jailed two citizens in August on terrorism charges for using the Twitter microblogging platform to issue an alert about a possible attack at a school. They were released in September, but the state passed a law criminalizing the "perturbation of public order" through the use of any medium. In October, the Mexican Supreme Court agreed to evaluate the law's constitutionality.

Religious freedom is constitutionally protected and generally respected in practice. However, it is limited in some regions. Political battles over issues such as abortion and homosexual rights have led to an increase in religious discourse in the public sphere in recent years. The government does not restrict academic freedom.

Constitutional guarantees regarding free assembly and association are largely upheld, but political and civic expression is restricted in some regions. In December 2011, two student protesters were shot dead by police in Guerrero; the incident remained under investigation by the National Human Rights Commission (CNDH) at year's end. Nongovernmental organizations, though highly active, sometimes face violent resistance, including threats and murders. Three activists associated with the MPJD were killed in the last few months of 2011, and two more disappeared, leading to demands for greater protection by the authorities.

Although trade unions' role as a pillar of the PRI has diminished significantly, independent unions have long faced government and management interference. Informal, nontransparent negotiations between employers and politically connected union leaders often result in "protection contracts" that govern employee rights but are never seen by workers. Those attempting to form independent unions are frequently fired. Several large unions, particularly the teachers' union, are considered by many observers and citizens to pose obstacles to necessary policy reforms.

The justice system remains plagued by delays and unpredictability. A 2008 constitutional reform replaced the civil-inquisitorial trial system with an oral-adversarial one. An explicit presumption of innocence and stricter rules regarding evidence were also introduced, and the overhaul was widely expected to strengthen due process and increase efficiency and fairness. Nonetheless, human rights groups raised concerns about the vague definition of organized crime and weaker protections afforded to organized crime suspects. Implementation of the new system was expected to take eight years, and application of the reformed procedures continued slowly in 2011.

In many areas, coordination between federal authorities and the state and local police is problematic. In crime-plagued zones, local police have been purged and temporarily replaced by federal troops. A 2009 law requires all members of the police to be vetted, but the process moved slowly at the state and municipal levels in 2011, leading to tension between Calderón and some state governors. A bill sent to Congress in 2010 that mandates the merger of state and municipal police forces again failed to pass in 2011.

Lower courts and law enforcement in general are undermined by widespread bribery. A significant majority of crimes go unreported because the underpaid police are viewed as either inept or in league with criminals, and conviction rates are less than 10 percent even when investigations are opened. In 2011, new attorney general Marisela Morales initiated a purge of the prosecutorial service, with hundreds of officials dismissed on suspicions of corruption. Prisons are violent and overcrowded, and several prison riots in 2011 resulted in the deaths of scores of prisoners, while scores of others escaped during the year.

Presidential authority over the armed forces is extensive, but the military has historically operated beyond public scrutiny, and human rights advocates have warned that its strengthened counternarcotics role has not been accompanied by increased oversight of its conduct. Complaints of abuse have risen dramatically in recent years, and a November 2011 Human Rights Watch report alleged violations including torture, forced disappearances, and extrajudicial executions. Military personnel are generally tried in military courts, but in July the Supreme Court ruled that Mexico must comply with a series of Inter-American Court of Human Rights decisions obliging the country to try cases of human rights violations in civilian courts. The ruling was facilitated by the June entry into force of constitutional amendments that granted new powers to the CNDH and explicitly incorporated international treaty obligations into the charter.

The number of deaths attributed to organized crime has risen sharply each year since 2007. An official figure of over 12,900 deaths in the first nine months of 2011 signaled deceleration in the pace of increase, but expert extrapolations indicated over 16,000 deaths for the year, a rise of roughly 10 percent from 2010. The carnage remained most acute in northern Mexico, although homicides declined by roughly one-third in the previous epicenter of violence, Ciudad Juárez. Nonetheless, Juárez remained one of the world's deadliest cities, and violence spiked in several other key cities, including Acapulco, Veracruz, and Monterrey. The murders often featured extreme brutality designed to maximize the psychological impact on civilians, authorities, and rival groups. The number, severity, and geographic range of massacres also rose, including two massacres of over 30 people in Veracruz in September and October and the public dumping of 26 bodies in Guadalajara in November.

In addition to homicides, organized criminals have increased kidnappings, extortion, oil theft, and other offenses. The government has taken a number of steps in recent years to curb the violence and ease popular frustration, including consultations with civic leaders, the signing of a $1.5 billion counternarcotics aid agreement with the United States, the continued deployment of troops, the reformation of the federal police, and the decriminalization of possession of small quantities of drugs. The government has pointed to the killing or arrest of several dozen criminal kingpins in recent years and the decline of violence in hotspots such as Tijuana and Ciudad Juárez as evidence of increased pressure on the syndicates, although few top criminal figures were arrested in 2011.

Mexican law bans all forms of discrimination, including those based on ethnic origin, gender, age, and religion. Nevertheless, social and economic discrimination has marginalized indigenous peoples, with many relegated to extreme poverty in rural villages that lack essential services. The government has attempted to improve indigenous-language services in the justice system, an area of major concern. Indigenous groups, particularly in Chihuahua and southern states, have been harmed by the criminal violence in recent years. In addition, disputes over land issues within indigenous groups at times become violent.

Rights groups frequently detail the persecution and criminal predation faced by migrants from Central America, many of whom are bound for the United States. Mass graves containing hundreds of bodies found in Tamaulipas in 2011 included many migrants. In October, Calderón stated that 200 officials in the National Migration Institute had been removed for corruption or arbitrary conduct.

In several states in 2011, criminals impeded free movement by blocking major roads, and particularly in Tamaulipas, by boarding buses and removing passengers, who often disappeared or were later found dead.

Domestic violence and sexual abuse are common, and perpetrators are rarely punished. Implementation of a 2007 law designed to protect women from such crimes remains halting, particularly at the state level, and impunity is the norm for the hundreds of women killed each year. Mexico is both a major source and a transit country for trafficked persons. Abortion has been a contentious issue in recent years, with many states reacting to Mexico City's 2007 liberalization of abortion laws by strengthening their own criminal bans on the procedure. Such bans in two states were upheld by Supreme Court rulings in September 2011; although a majority of justices voted to overturn the laws, the bloc fell shy of the supermajority needed to do so.

Micronesia

Political Rights: 1
Civil Liberties: 1
Status: Free

Population: 102,000
Capital: Palikir

Ten-Year Ratings Timeline For Year Under Review (Political Rights, Civil Liberties, Status)

2002	2003	2004	2005	2006	2007	2008	2009	2010	2011
1,2F	1,1F	1,1F	1,1F	1,1F	1,1F	1,1F	1,1F	1,1F	1,1F

Overview: **Parliamentary elections held in March 2011 were deemed free and fair. The new Congress reelected President Emanuel Mori and Vice President Alik L. Alik in May. Meanwhile, the Federated States of Micronesia continued to expand its financial ties with China.**

The U.S. administered Micronesia, which included the Marshall Islands and other Pacific island groups, between 1947 and 1979 as a United Nations Trust Territory. In 1970, the Northern Marianas, Marshall Islands, and Palau demanded separate status from Kosrae, Pohnpei, Chuuk, and Yap; the latter four territories, representing 607 islands, became the Federated States of Micronesia (FSM). The FSM adopted a constitution and became an independent country in 1979.

In 1986, the FSM signed its first Compact of Free Association with the United States, which provides the FSM with economic and defense assistance in exchange for allowing U.S. military bases on the islands. FSM citizens also receive visa-free entry to the United States for health services, education, and employment.

Compact funds represent about one-third of the FSM's national income. An amended compact came into effect in 2003 to extend this core commitment for another 20 years. The federal Congress agreed in 2005 to distribute larger shares of compact funds to each of the FSM's four states. A new system to track funded projects was adopted in 2009 to demonstrate improved transparency and accountability in the use of compact funds.

The March 8, 2011, legislative elections, in which all candidates were independents, were deemed free and fair. In May, the new Congress reelected President Emanuel Mori and Vice President Alik L. Alik.

In November 2011, state delegates to the national legislative conference agreed to address human trafficking. They also agreed to form a task force to evaluate the impact of the Compact of Free Association on FSM citizens living in the United States, for whom the compact provides broad access to education, health, and social services.

In December, the national government returned fiscal power to the Chuuk and Kosrae state governments. Memoranda of understanding between the federal and two state governments signed in April 2007 allowed federal administration of the states' discretionary funds and disbursement from compact transfers after they experienced severe fiscal difficulties.

The FSM has been expanding its ties with China, which is one of only four countries in which the FSM has a permanent embassy. In 2010 the FSM named China as the preferred candidate to receive exclusive fishing rights in FSM waters. Chinese aid to the FSM includes financing expansion of the Chuuk airport terminal and providing scholarships for FSM students to study in China.

Political Rights and Civil Liberties: The FSM is an electoral democracy. The 2011 national legislative elections were deemed largely free and fair. The unicameral, 14-member Congress has one directly elected representative from each of the four constituent states, who serve four-year terms. The other 10 representatives are directly elected for two-year terms from single-member districts. Chuuk state, home to nearly half of the FSM's population, holds the largest number of congressional seats, which has been a source of resentment among the three smaller states. The president and vice president are chosen by Congress from among the four state representatives to serve four-year terms. By informal agreement, the two posts are rotated among the representatives of the four states. Each state has its own constitution, elected legislature, and governor; the state governments have considerable power, particularly in budgetary matters. Traditional leaders and institutions exercise significant influence in society, especially at the village level.

There are no formal political parties, but there are no restrictions on their formation. Political loyalties are based mainly on geography, clan relations, and personality.

Official corruption and abuses, including allegations of improper use of travel funds by government officials, are widespread and a major source of public discontent.

The news media operate freely. Print outlets include government-published newsletters and several small, privately owned, weekly and monthly newspapers. Each state government runs its own radio station, and the Baptist church runs a fifth station. Television stations operate in three of the four states. Cable television is available in Pohnpei and Chuuk, and satellite television is increasingly common. Use of the internet is growing, but low income and small populations make it difficult for service providers to expand coverage.

Religious freedom is respected in this mainly Christian country. There are no reports of restrictions on academic freedom, but lack of funds negatively affects the quality of and access to education.

Freedom of assembly is respected, and citizens are free to organize civic groups.

A small number of student and women's organizations are active. No labor unions exist, though there are no laws against their formation. No specific laws regulate work hours or set workplace health and safety standards. The right to strike and bargain collectively is not legally recognized. The economy is dependent on fishing, tourism, subsistence agriculture, and U.S. assistance.

The judiciary is independent, but it lacks funds to improve the functioning of the courts. There is also cultural resistance to using the court system, particularly for sex crimes. The small national police force is responsible for local law enforcement matters, while the United States provides the FSM's national defense. There were no reports of abuses or inhumane treatment by police or prison officials.

Women enjoy equal rights under the law, including those regarding property ownership and employment. Women generally receive equal pay for equal work and are well represented in the lower and middle ranks of the state and federal governments. However, there are no women in Congress, and social and economic discrimination against women persists in this male-dominated culture. Domestic violence is a problem, and cases often go unreported because of family pressure or an expectation of inaction by the authorities. Offenders rarely face trial, and those found guilty usually receive light sentences. In June 2011, the U.S. State Department's Trafficking in Persons Report downgraded FSM to Tier 3, meaning that the country could become ineligible for U.S. development assistance if it is found to be unresponsive in fighting human trafficking.

Moldova

Political Rights: 3
Civil Liberties: 3
Status: Partly Free

Population: 4,109,000
Capital: Chisinau

Note: The numerical ratings and status listed above do not reflect conditions in Transnistria, which is examined in a separate report.

Ten-Year Ratings Timeline For Year Under Review (Political Rights, Civil Liberties, Status)

2002	2003	2004	2005	2006	2007	2008	2009	2010	2011
3,4PF	3,4PF	3,4PF	3,4PF	3,4PF	3,4PF	4,4PF	3,4PF	3,3PF	3,3PF

Overview: **The ruling Alliance for European Integration (AIE) remained unable to elect a president during 2011, raising the possibility of a fourth round of parliamentary elections since 2009. While crucial defections from the opposition Communist Party in early November potentially gave the AIE the three-fifths parliamentary majority needed to elect a president, the factions involved were unable to immediately agree on a candidate, forcing the cancellation of a planned election bid in mid-November. After a vote held in December failed to reach the required threshold, another attempt was scheduled for January 2012. Also during the year, the Justice Ministry officially registered a Muslim religious organization for the first time**

despite strong objections from the Orthodox Church, and the government was forced to withdraw an antidiscrimination bill after Orthodox and other opponents decried its protection of homosexuals.

Moldova gained independence from the Soviet Union in 1991, and free and fair elections followed in 1994. Centrist parties governed until 2001, when the Party of Communists of the Republic of Moldova (PCRM) won a landslide victory, promising a return to Soviet-era living standards. Communist leader Vladimir Voronin was elected president by Parliament.

The PCRM took 56 of 101 seats in the 2005 parliamentary elections and built a coalition to obtain the 61 votes needed to reelect Voronin. Election monitors noted police harassment of the opposition, manipulation of the state media, and abuse of state funds by the PCRM, among other flaws.

After charting a foreign policy course away from Russia and toward the European Union (EU) in the period surrounding the elections, Voronin steered the country back toward Russia in 2007 and 2008. The Kremlin's cooperation was seen as essential in resolving the status of Transnistria, a separatist region that has maintained de facto independence from Moldova since 1992.

The PCRM won 60 seats in April 2009 parliamentary elections, though international monitors documented problems including flaws in the voter lists, intimidation and harassment of opposition parties, and media bias. Three opposition parties won the remainder. The results triggered youth-led protests in Chisinau, and the demonstrations turned violent on the second day, with some protesters ransacking government buildings. Police responded with beatings, hundreds of arrests, and serious abuse of detainees in custody.

The PCRM failed twice to elect its choice to replace the term-limited Voronin as president, triggering fresh parliamentary elections in July. Although similar electoral flaws were reported by observers, the defection of former PCRM Parliament speaker Marian Lupu to the opposition Democratic Party (PD) helped it and three other opposition parties to secure a simple majority. The new coalition, called the Alliance for European Integration (AIE), elected Liberal Democratic Party (PLD) leader Vlad Filat as prime minister, and Liberal Party (PL) leader Mihai Ghimpu as Parliament speaker and acting president. With just 53 seats, the coalition failed twice—in November and December—to secure Lupu's election as president.

A third round of parliamentary elections was held in November 2010, after a PCRM boycott helped to thwart a September constitutional referendum that would have introduced direct presidential elections. The new balloting, which was praised by observers, strengthened the AIE parties' position overall, though they still lacked the supermajority needed to elect a president. The PCRM took 42 seats, followed by the PLD with 32, the PD with 15, and the PL with 12. Lupu was elected Parliament Speaker and acting president in late December, and Filat resumed his role as prime minister in January 2011.

Internal AIE feuding intensified during 2011, but further factional rifts within the PCRM also emerged. Three key Parliament members—including former prime minister and presidential candidate Zinaida Greceanîi and Chisinau mayoral candidate Igor Dodon—defected from the PCRM caucus in early November, potentially giving the AIE the three-fifths majority needed to elect a president. However, with negotiations on a candidate ongoing, none registered for a planned November 18 vote, and it was consequently canceled. Lupu was the sole candidate in a presidential vote held on December 16, but he secured only 58 ballots, with the three PCRM defectors voting against him and one ballot declared void. A second attempt was scheduled for January 2012.

Political Rights and Civil Liberties: Moldova is an electoral democracy. Voters elect the 101-seat unicameral Parliament by proportional representation for four-year terms. Since 2000, Parliament has elected the president, who serves up to two four-year terms. The prime minister, who holds most executive power, must be approved by Parliament.

Domestic and international observers hailed the November 2010 parliamentary elections as a substantial improvement over the 2009 balloting, citing a more open and diverse media environment, impartial and transparent administration by the Central Election Commission, and a lack of restrictions on campaign activities. Some problems were reported, including flaws in the voter list, unbalanced distribution of overseas polling sites, and isolated cases of intimidation. Local elections in June 2011, in which AIE parties won a majority of positions, were also assessed positively, though observers called for improvements in voter registration and campaign finance regulation.

Corruption remains a major problem. In 2011, Prime Minister Vlad Filat of the PLD repeatedly alleged that the prosecutor general's office and other key institutions were under the control of the PD and its financial backers, leading to politicized decisions in corruption cases. Filat himself has been accused of corruption by his opponents. A number of corruption and fraud allegations were pursued during the year, but convictions in major cases have been lacking. In July, Parliament passed legislation to establish an independent commission tasked with auditing public officials' annual income and asset declarations, which would be published online, though the law had not entered into force by year's end. Moldova was ranked 112 out of 183 countries surveyed in Transparency International's 2011 Corruption Perceptions Index.

The media environment improved following the 2009 change in government. In 2010, the public broadcaster, Teleradio-Moldova, grew more impartial under new management, and two new private satellite television channels added to the diversity of national news coverage. However, several media outlets are perceived as party affiliates; PCRM-allied television and print outlets have been cited by nongovernmental observers and regulators for having an especially strong bias. Reporters sometimes face physical abuse or selective exclusion from events of public interest. In June 2011, Russian blogger Eduard Bagirov was arrested for his alleged role in fomenting the April 2009 violence, with prosecutors accusing him of participating in attacks on government buildings in order to discredit the opposition and justify a crackdown. Bagirov, who maintained that the case against him was politically motivated, fled to Russia after being placed under house arrest in October. In August 2011, a court imposed a roughly $40,000 fine on the weekly Ziarul de Garda after two prosecutors sued it for reporting on corruption claims against them. An appellate court later reduced the fine to about $1,700, and a further appeal was pending at year's end.

Although the constitution guarantees religious freedom, a 2007 law banned "abusive proselytism" and acknowledged the "special significance and primary role" of the Orthodox Church. The AIE government has moved away from the PCRM's clear support for the Russian-backed Moldovan Orthodox Church over the smaller, Romanian-backed Bessarabian Orthodox Church. In March 2011, the government for the first time accepted the registration of a religious organization from Moldova's tiny Muslim population, prompting vocal denunciations and protests by the Moldovan Orthodox Church. Senior officials nevertheless spoke out in defense of the move. While other minority groups have also had difficulty registering and in some cases face harassment, foreign missionaries have reported less bureaucratic obstruction in recent years. Moldovan officials do not restrict academic freedom, though the PCRM claimed that university students were pressured to support the AIE parties ahead of the November 2010 elections.

Organizers of demonstrations must only give notice rather than seek permission from authorities, and the current government has generally upheld freedom of assembly in practice. However, a gay pride parade in the capital was canceled for the third straight year in 2011 due to concerns about violent counterprotesters. State relations with civil society groups have improved under the AIE, though some leading politicians have displayed wariness or hostility toward nongovernmental organizations (NGOs). Domestic NGOs actively monitored the 2010 and 2011 election campaigns. Enforcement of union rights and labor standards is weak, with employers rarely punished for violations. Workers in illegal strikes face possible fines or prison time.

Although the constitution provides for an independent judiciary, reform efforts suffer from lack of funds, and there has been evidence of bribery and political influence among judicial and law enforcement officials. Long-standing concerns about abuse and ill-treatment in police custody were renewed in the aftermath of the April 2009 protests; a small number of officers have received probation and suspended prison sentences for their role in the 2009 abuses. Prison conditions in general are exceptionally poor. Quasi-disciplinary violence in the military remains a problem, with several suspicious deaths reported during 2011. Such incidents were cited as part of the justification for the September dismissal of the chief of the armed forces.

Roma suffer the harshest treatment of the various minority groups in Moldova. They face discrimination in housing and employment, and are targets of police violence. Gay men are also reportedly subject to police harassment. The government was forced to withdraw an EU-backed antidiscrimination bill in March 2011 due to objections by the Orthodox Church and others over its protection of homosexuals.

Women are underrepresented in public life. Nineteen women were elected to Parliament in November 2010. Moldova is a significant source for women and girls trafficked abroad for forced prostitution. The U.S. State Department reported in 2011 that although victims' services and government cooperation with NGOs had improved in the past year, law enforcement efforts declined, and alleged complicity by officials remained largely unchecked. Some cases of forced agricultural labor have been reported.

Monaco

Political Rights: 2
Civil Liberties: 1
Status: Free

Population: 36,200
Capital: Monaco

Ten-Year Ratings Timeline For Year Under Review (Political Rights, Civil Liberties, Status)

2002	2003	2004	2005	2006	2007	2008	2009	2010	2011
2,1F	2,1F	2,1F	2,1F	2,1F	2,1F	2,1F	2,1F	2,1F	2,1F

Overview:

In January 2011, Prince Albert II reshuffled his government in an attempt to attract foreign investors. In July, Albert wed Charlene Wittstock, a South African Olympic swimmer. Issues of free speech arose during the year, when at least two people faced legal penalties for insulting the monarchy.

The Grimaldi family has ruled the Principality of Monaco for more than 700 years, except for a period of French occupation between 1793 and 1814. Under a treaty ratified in 1919, France pledged to protect the territorial integrity, sovereignty, and independence of the country in return for a guarantee that Monégasque policy would conform to French political, military, and economic interests.

Prince Rainier III, who ruled from 1949 until his death in 2005, is often credited with engineering Monaco's impressive economic growth. During his reign, the country ended its dependence on gambling and nurtured other sources of revenue—principally tourism and financial services. Monaco adopted the euro currency in 2002, but remains outside of the European Union (EU). In April 2005, Rainier was succeeded by Prince Albert II, who has made global environmental awareness a priority of his reign.

In the 2008 legislative elections, the Union of Monaco (UPM) won 21 of the 24 seats in the Conseil National, or parliament. The conservative opposition party, Rally and Issues for Monaco (REM), captured the remaining three seats.

In January 2011, Albert performed a long-rumored cabinet reshuffle in an attempt to create a government that would be more attractive to foreign investors. He appointed a new economy minister, foreign minister, and minister for public works, the environment, and urban planning.

On July 1, Albert wed Charlene Wittstock of South Africa, a former Olympic swimmer, in a small civil ceremony at the Palace of Monaco; thousands of people watched the ceremony on screens set up outside the palace. The following day a more elaborate ceremony took place, attended by numerous international celebrities and royal figures. The wedding dominated much of Monegasque news in the first part of 2011.

Political Rights and Civil Liberties:

Monaco is an electoral democracy. However, the prince, who serves as head of state, has the sole authority to initiate legislation and change the government. The 24 members of the unicameral Conseil National are elected for five-year terms; 16 are chosen through a majority electoral system and 8 by proportional representation.

The head of government, known as the minister of state, is traditionally appointed by the monarch from a candidate list of three French nationals submitted by the French government. The current minister of state, Michel Roger, has held the post since March 2010. The monarch also appoints five other ministers who make up the cabinet. All legislation and the budget require the approval of the Conseil National, which is currently dominated by the UPM. The only other party represented is the REM.

Inadequate financial record keeping has traditionally made the country's level of corruption difficult to measure. However, the principality in 2009 started providing foreign tax authorities with information on accounts held by noncitizens, and by October of that year, the Organization for Economic Cooperation and Development (OECD) had removed Monaco from its list of uncooperative tax havens. Monaco took further steps toward improving financial transparency by signing tax information exchange agreements with 24 countries between 2009 and 2010, including with a number of OECD countries. The agreements ensure that Monaco will hand over relevant tax documents requested by the signatories.

The constitution provides for freedoms of speech and of the press, although the penal code prohibits criticism of the ruling family. In June 2011, Robert Eringer, a California-based blogger and former employee of Prince Albert, was ordered to pay 20,000 euros in damages plus 7,000 euros in legal fees to Albert after a court in Paris found him guilty of publishing false information about key figures in Monaco and about the country itself; the suit had been brought by Albert over statements Eringer had published on his website that were critical of the monarchy. In October 2011, a man was imprisoned for six days for insulting the prince.

The constitution guarantees freedom of religion, though Roman Catholicism is the state religion. There are no laws against proselytizing by formally registered religious organizations, but proselytizing in public is strongly discouraged by the authorities. Academic freedom is not restricted. The country's only institution of higher education, the private International University of Monaco, offers graduate and undergraduate programs in business administration, finance, and related fields. Monégasque students are permitted to attend French colleges and universities under various agreements between the two countries.

The constitution provides for freedom of assembly, which is generally respected in practice. No restrictions are imposed on the formation of civic and human rights groups. Workers have the legal right to organize and bargain collectively, although they rarely do so. All workers except state employees have the right to strike. In September 2011, the Union des Retraités de Monaco took to the streets to call on the government to raise pensions in light of rising inflation rates.

The legal rights to a fair public trial and an independent judiciary are generally respected. The justice system is based on the French legal code, and under the constitution, the prince delegates his judicial powers to the courts. The prince names five full members and two judicial assistants to the Supreme Court after the Conseil National and other government bodies submit judicial nominations. Jail facilities generally meet international standards. Once criminal defendants receive definitive sentences, they are transferred to a French prison.

The constitution differentiates between the rights of Monégasque nationals and those of noncitizens. Of the estimated 36,000 residents in the principality, only about 5,000 are citizens, and they alone may participate in the election of the Conseil National. Citizens also benefit from free education, unemployment assistance, and the ability to hold elective office. As long as they secure a residence permit, noncitizens are free to purchase real estate and open businesses.

Women generally receive equal pay for equal work. Women who become naturalized citizens by marriage cannot vote or run as candidates in elections until five years after the marriage. There are six women in the Conseil National. Abortion is legal only under special circumstances, including rape.

Mongolia

Political Rights: 2
Civil Liberties: 2
Status: Free

Population: 2,814,000
Capital: Ulaanbaatar

Ten-Year Ratings Timeline For Year Under Review (Political Rights, Civil Liberties, Status)

2002	2003	2004	2005	2006	2007	2008	2009	2010	2011
2,3F	2,2F	2,2F	2,2F	2,2F	2,2F	2,2F	2,2F	2,2F	2,2F

Overview: **Recent contracts awarded in 2011 to Australian and German companies for the operation of the Tavan Tolgoi coal mine signaled the continuing trend of heavy foreign involvement in Mongolia's extractive resource industry, while the commitment to distribute mining royalties to all citizens has not yet been fulfilled. Meanwhile, a clothing factory outside the capital was discovered to be employing North Korean workers, whose wages were sent directly to the North Korean government.**

Once the center of Genghis Khan's sprawling empire, Mongolia was ruled by China's Manchu Qing Empire for nearly 270 years. Mongolia declared its independence in 1911. After Chinese troops entered the country in 1919, Mongolia invited Russian Soviet forces to help secure control. Mongolia founded a people's republic in 1924, with the Mongolian People's Revolutionary Party (MPRP) governing the country as a one-party communist state. In response to persistent antigovernment protests, the MPRP legalized opposition parties in 1990. However, facing a poorly prepared and underfunded opposition, the MPRP easily won the first multiparty parliamentary elections that year and again in 1992.

The MPRP lost the 1996 parliamentary elections, and power was transferred peacefully to the opposition Democratic Union Coalition. After an economic downturn the following year, the MPRP won both the 1997 presidential election and the 2000 parliamentary vote. The 2004 parliamentary elections were marred by irregularities and gave neither side a majority. The MPRP consequently agreed to a power-sharing government with the opposition Motherland Democracy Coalition (MDC).

The MPRP's Nambaryn Enkhbayar, the parliament speaker and a former prime minister, won the 2005 presidential election, despite street demonstrations by protesters who accused him of corruption. In January 2006, the MDC-MPRP coalition government collapsed, and the MPRP formed a new government with several small parties and MDC defectors. Miyeegombo Enkhbold of the MPRP became prime minister, but he was replaced in November 2007 by Sanjaa Bayar after being accused of excessive political favoritism and corruption.

The initial results of the June 2008 parliamentary elections handed the MPRP a solid majority, but the opposition Democratic Party (DP) and others challenged the outcome. Small-scale protests escalated into large, violent demonstrations in the capital. Five people were killed, scores were injured, and over 700 others were arrested. The government declared a four-day state of emergency on July 2. The final vote tally released in August gave the MPRP 46 seats and the DP 27, and Bayar remained prime minister.

Former Prime Minister Tsakhiagiin Elbegdorj of the opposition DP took 51 percent of the vote in the May 2009 presidential election, which international observers deemed generally free and fair. In October, Bayar resigned as prime minister for health reasons and was replaced by Foreign Minister Sukhbaatar Batbold.

The global economic downturn, combined with an extremely harsh winter, exacerbated Mongolia's high poverty and unemployment rates in 2009. In October, after years of negotiations, a $5 billion contract was signed with the international mining companies Ivanhoe Mines and Rio Tinto to develop a copper and gold mine in Oyu Tolgoi. Some expressed concerns over ongoing corruption and a lack of transparency surrounding the contract's negotiations. In response, the government set up a Human Development Fund (HDF) in 2009 to distribute mining royalties to citizens. However, the HDF has been controversial; President Elbegdorj wants to end most of the program, directing its funds toward children's services and university tuition.

In April 2010, a series of large-scale protests erupted over the government's failure to fulfill a campaign promise to distribute aid from mining royalties. In the largest demonstration, approximately 10,000 people convened in Ulaanbaatar, calling for the dissolution of the parliament. An agreement to officially end the protests was concluded on April 22, outlining constitutional modifications, government reporting requirements, and pledges to disburse funds to citizens in 2012 in the form of tuition fees, health coverage, and cash handouts.

Following German chancellor Angela Merkel's visit to Mongolia in October 2011, the contract to operate the Tavan Tolgoi coal mine was awarded to a joint venture between the German company Operta GmbH and the Australian company Mcmahon Holdings. Disputes over mining continued to dominate public debate in 2011, including concerns over water resources, labor rights, and protectionism.

Political Rights and Civil Liberties:

Mongolia is an electoral democracy. Parliamentary balloting has varied over the years between multimember and single-member districts, and there is concern that these frequent changes make it difficult to instill confidence in democratic governance. The prime minister, who holds most executive power, is nominated by the party or coalition with the most seats in the 76-member parliament (the State Great Hural) and approved by the parliament with the agreement of the president. There is no requirement that the prime minister be an elected member of parliament. The president is head of state and of the armed forces, and can veto legislation, subject to a two-thirds parliamentary override. Both the president and the parliament are directly elected for four-year terms.

The MPRP renamed itself the Mongolian People's Party (MPP) in November 2010 and elected Enkhbayar chairman in January 2011. The MPP continues to be the most powerful party, but a number of smaller opposition groups are competitive.

Corruption remains a serious problem in Mongolia. The Independent Authority Against Corruption (IAAC) has been actively investigating corruption allegations since 2007. In March 2011, the head of the IAAC, Chimgee Sangaragchaa, was sentenced to two years in prison for leaking state secrets and other charges. Sangaragchaa was released from prison on bail in October by order of the State Supreme Court, although his convictions were not overturned.

Although the government operates with limited transparency, the first Citizens' Hall was established in Ulaanbaatar in 2009 to encourage civic participation in the legislative processes. Citizens have the opportunity to provide feedback on draft laws and government services by attending such hearings or submitting their views via letter, fax, e-mail, or telephone. Transparency International ranked Mongolia 120 out of 183 countries surveyed in its 2011 Corruption Perceptions Index.

While the government generally respects press freedom, many journalists and independent publications practice a degree of self-censorship to avoid legal action under the State Secrets Law or libel laws that place the burden of proof on the defendant. The nongovernmental organization Globe International released several statements in 2011 about journalists charged in defamation suits by ministers of parliament and businesspeople; in many cases, the charges were dropped.

There are hundreds of privately owned print and broadcast outlets, but the main source of news in the vast countryside is the state-owned Mongolian National Broadcaster. Foreign content from satellite television and radio services like the British Broadcasting Corporation and Voice of America is also increasingly available. The government does not interfere with internet access.

Freedom of religion is guaranteed by the constitution. The fall of communism led to an influx of Christian missionaries to Mongolia and a revival of Mongolia's traditional Buddhism and shamanism. Religious groups are required to register with the government and renew their status annually. While most registration requests are approved, authorities in Töv Aimag province have routinely denied registration to Christian churches. The Kazakh Muslim minority generally enjoys freedom of religion. Academic freedom is respected.

Freedoms of assembly and association are observed in law and in practice. A number of environmental, human rights, and social welfare groups—while largely reliant on foreign donors—operate without government restriction. However, some journalists and nonprofit personnel have alleged government monitoring of e-mail accounts and wiretapping. Trade unions are independent and active, and the government has generally protected their rights in recent years, though the downsizing or sale of many state factories has contributed to a sharp drop in union membership. Collective bargaining is legal, but in Mongolia's poor economy, employers are often able to set wages unilaterally.

The judiciary is independent, but corruption among judges persists. The police force has been known to make arbitrary arrests and traffic stops, hold detainees for long periods, and beat prisoners. Deaths in prisons continue to be reported, as insufficient nutrition, heat, and medical care remain problems. Ejbegdorj issued a moratorium on the death penalty in January 2010, and talks on abolishing capital punishment permanently are ongoing.

A unit to investigate human trafficking cases was created within the Special Investigation Department of the Police in July 2010. According to the U.S. State Department's 2011 Trafficking in Persons report, 13 cases have been filed since then, leading to nine prosecutions. The report also stated that about 525 North Koreans are used as contract laborers in Mongolia, without access to most of their wages or freedom of movement. Additionally, an October 2011 BBC investigation revealed that most of the wages of North Korean workers at the Eermel garment factory are sent directly to the North Korean government.

While women comprise 60 percent of all university students as well as 60 percent of all judges, they hold only 5 parliamentary seats. Spousal abuse is prohibited by law, but social and cultural norms continue to discourage victims from reporting such crimes.

Montenegro

Political Rights: 3
Civil Liberties: 2
Status: Free

Population: 637,000
Capital: Podgorica

Note: The ratings through 2002 are for the Federal Republic of Yugoslavia, of which Montenegro was a part, and those from 2003 through 2005 are for the State Union of Serbia and Montenegro.

Ten-Year Ratings Timeline For Year Under Review (Political Rights, Civil Liberties, Status)

2002	2003	2004	2005	2006	2007	2008	2009	2010	2011
3,2PF	3,2F	3,2F	3,2F	3,3F	3,3PF	3,3PF	3,2PF	3,2F	3,2F

Overview: **In October 2011, the European Union (EU) cleared Montenegro to begin accession negotiations following progress on seven priorities, including the September passage of a new election reform law. However, the EU noted that further efforts were needed in the areas of anticorruption and antidiscrimination legislation, as well as judicial reforms.**

Montenegro was first recognized as an independent state in 1878. In 1918, it joined the newly formed Kingdom of Serbs, Croats, and Slovenes, which after World War II became the Socialist Federal Republic of Yugoslavia. As that state collapsed in the early 1990s, Montenegro maintained its ties to Serbia in the truncated Federal Republic of Yugoslavia (FRY), dominated by Serbian leader Slobodan Miloševic. In 1997, however, a group of former Miloševic cohorts in Montenegro, led by Prime Minister Milo Đukanovic, decided to break with Miloševic and pursue Montenegrin independence.

Miloševic's fall from power in 2000 did not improve relations between Montenegro and its larger federal partner, and the two republics signed an agreement in 2002 that loosened their bond, replacing the FRY with the State Union of Serbia and Montenegro. The deal allowed either republic to hold an independence referendum after three years, and Đukanovic exercised that option in May 2006. Referendum voters approved the final break with Serbia, and the parliament declared independence in July.

The September 2006 parliamentary elections confirmed voter support for the ruling proindependence coalition. Đukanovic retired in October but returned as prime minister in April 2008, allegedly after a brief attempt to control the country from behind the scenes. Also in April, President Filip Vujanovic of Đukanovic's Democratic Party of Socialists (DPS) was elected to a second five-year term.

In January 2009, Vujanovic called snap parliamentary elections, reportedly because of fears that the global economic crisis could erode voter support before the legislature's full term ended. The March polls saw the DPS-led coalition win a comfortable majority of 48 seats in the 81-seat parliament. The opposition Socialist People's Party took 16 seats, followed by the New Serb Democracy with 8, the Movement for Change with 5, and four small ethnic Albanian parties with 1 seat each. Local elections in several municipalities in May 2010 confirmed the DPS's political dominance.

Since gaining independence, Montenegro has sought to join NATO and the European Union (EU), and in December 2010, the EU granted the country candidate status. A few days later, Đukanovic resigned as prime minister for a second time, asserting that he had successfully guided the country toward European integration. However, there were indications that his continued tenure could have obstructed Montenegro's EU candidacy as a result of allegations that he had been involved in cigarette smuggling in the 1990s. Đukanovic remained chairman of the DPS, and Finance Minister Igor Lukšic, also a DPS member, succeeded him as prime minister.

In September 2011, the parliament broke a four-year impasse to pass a landmark new election law that ensures the representation of minorities and improves technical voting issues. The law's passage had been delayed as a result of a controversy over the languages officially recognized in the country. In 2010, Montenegrin had become the official language of the state broadcaster, and a Montenegrin grammar text was introduced in schools. Critics of those moves argued that the government was promoting an artificial language derived from standard Serbian, and the opposition had vowed that it would not support the election law until the Serbian language was given equal status to Montenegrin in the education system. The law was passed after lawmakers agreed on a class to be taught in the schools called "Montenegrin-Serbian, Bosnian, Croatian language and literature."

In October, the European Commission (EC) noted progress on the seven priorities for EU membership, especially the passage of the election law, and cleared Montenegro to begin accession negotiations. The EC emphasized, however, that efforts needed to continue on key reforms, especially regarding corruption and antidiscrimination legislation.

Despite its NATO and EU ambitions, Montenegro has extensive economic ties with Russia. Some accounts suggest that as much as $13 billion in Russian capital has entered Montenegro since the 1990s, allegedly making it the largest recipient of foreign investment per capita in Europe in recent years.

Political Rights and Civil Liberties: Montenegro is an electoral democracy. International observers deemed the 2006 and 2009 parliamentary elections and the 2008 presidential vote to have been free and fair, despite some irregularities. Members of the unicameral, 81-seat Assembly (Skupština) are elected for four-year terms. The president, directly elected for up to two five-year terms, nominates the prime minister, who requires legislative approval.

Numerous political parties compete for power, though the opposition remains relatively weak. The current coalition government consists of the DPS, the Social Democratic Party, and two smaller parties representing the Bosniak and Croat minorities. Other parties in the parliament represent ethnic Serbs and Albanians, and the Movement for Change advocates liberal policies and European integration. Serbs, who comprise an estimated 35 percent of the population, were generally opposed to independence prior to 2006, but their adjustment to the new reality has eased political tensions.

Corruption, which remains a serious problem, is partly a legacy of the struggle against the Miloševic regime in the 1990s, when the small republic turned to various forms of smuggling to finance government operations. Prime Minister Lukši has prioritized the government's anticorruption campaign, and the EC reported in October 2011 that key legislative frameworks were being implemented to improve party financing transparency and eliminate conflicts of interest. Nevertheless, implementation has been uneven, convictions in high-profile corruption cases remain low, and interagency cooperation needs improvement, especially between prosecutors and police. From October 2010 to September 2011, 28 officials were charged with abuse of office and bribery. Montenegro was ranked 66 out of 183 countries surveyed in Transparency International's 2011 Corruption Perceptions Index.

Freedom of the press is generally respected, and a variety of independent media operate. In July 2011, the government enhanced press freedom by removing provisions on defamation and insult from the Criminal Code, among other measures. However, several old cases of violence against journalists remain unresolved, and reporters still face harassment. The public broadcaster is not fully independent. Internet access is unrestricted.

The constitution guarantees freedom of religious belief. However, the canonically recognized Serbian Orthodox Church and a self-proclaimed Montenegrin Orthodox Church have repeatedly clashed over ownership of church properties and other issues.

Academic freedom is guaranteed by law, but political debates about the nature of Montenegrin identity and history have spilled over into the educational realm, as was the case when controversy over the Montenegrin language almost blocked the adoption of the new election law.

Citizens enjoy freedoms of association and assembly. Nongovernmental organizations are generally able to operate without state interference, and the EC noted improving cooperation between civil society and government institutions in 2011. Most formally employed workers belong to unions, and the right to strike is generally protected. Workers at Montenegro's oldest daily newspaper, *Victory*, organized strikes in October 2011 to protest unpaid wages.

The EC's 2011 report on Montenegro cited improvements in judicial reform, especially regarding the independence and efficiency of judges and prosecutors. However, the report noted concerns about the recruitment and training of new judges and prosecutors, as well as inefficiency in the court system. Despite efforts to improve prison conditions, most facilities are antiquated, overcrowded, and often unhygienic.

Ethnic Albanians, who comprise approximately 7 percent of the population, maintain that they are underrepresented in the civil service, particularly in the police and the judiciary. Members of various other minority groups, such as Roma, Ashkali, Egyptians, and homosexuals, often face discrimination. The EC noted in its 2011 report that, despite some improvements, antidiscrimination laws are unevenly implemented.

Women in Montenegro are legally entitled to equal pay for equal work, but traditional patriarchal attitudes often limit their salary levels and educational opportunities. Women are underrepresented in higher levels of government. In June 2011, the government adopted a five-year strategy to combat domestic violence. Trafficking in persons for the purposes of prostitution and forced labor remains a problem. In 2011 the government investigated only three trafficking cases and did not prosecute a single new case, according to the U.S. Department of State's Trafficking in Persons Report 2012. However, 14 traffickers were convicted in 2011 from earlier cases, compared with 12 trafficking convictions in 2010.

Morocco

Political Rights: 5
Civil Liberties: 4
Status: Partly Free

Population: 32,273,000
Capital: Rabat

Note: The numerical ratings and status listed above do not reflect conditions in Western Sahara, which is examined in a separate report.

Ten-Year Ratings Timeline For Year Under Review (Political Rights, Civil Liberties, Status)

2002	2003	2004	2005	2006	2007	2008	2009	2010	2011
5,5PF	5,5PF	5,4PF	5,4PF	5,4PF	5,4PF	5,4PF	5,4PF	5,4PF	5,4PF

Overview: **Large demonstrations were held on February 20 to demand democratic political reforms. Although the king responded with a revised constitution that won approval in a July referendum, the protest movement continued to press for more substantive curbs on the monarch's power. Parliamentary elections held on November 25 resulted in a victory for the Islamist opposition Justice and Development Party, with Abdelilah Benkirane named prime minister. Meanwhile a bomb attack in a Marrakesh café in April killed 17 people and wounded some two dozen.**

Morocco gained independence in 1956, after more than four decades of French rule. The first ruler after independence, King Mohamed V, reigned until his death in 1961. His son, Hassan II, then ruled the country until his death in July 1999. Thousands of his political opponents were arrested, tortured, and killed, while many simply disappeared. In 1975, Morocco and Mauritania occupied Western Sahara; after three years of fighting the Algerian-backed Polisario Front, a Sahrawi nationalist guerrilla movement, Mauritania withdrew from the portion it claimed. Morocco then annexed the territory in full. A planned referendum on Western Sahara's future—attached to a UN-monitored ceasefire agreement in 1991—never took place. In the last few years of his life, Hassan initiated a political opening. Several political prisoners were released, independent newspapers began publishing, and a new bicameral parliament was established in 1997.

King Mohamed VI inherited the throne in 1999. He declined to expand political freedom much further in the first years of his reign, apparently aiming to check the increased influence of Islamist political parties. However, he removed longtime interior minister Driss Basri, who had led much of the repression under King Hassan, and allowed exiled dissidents to return to the country.

Parliamentary elections held in 2002 were recognized as generally open. Over a dozen political parties participated, though independent journalists and other critics of the king were harassed and detained.

In May 2003, local Islamist militants with purported links to al-Qaeda mounted a series of deadly suicide bombings, targeting symbols of Morocco's Jewish community in Casablanca. The government responded by enacting a harsh antiterrorism law, but it was subsequently used to prosecute nonviolent opponents of the king. An anti-immigration law was also passed, ostensibly to fight illegal immigration from sub-Saharan Africa.

In 2004, King Mohamed inaugurated the Equity and Reconciliation Commission (IER), tasked with addressing the human rights abuses perpetrated by the authorities from 1956 to 1999 and providing the victims with reparations. The commission was headed by a former political prisoner and allowed victims to testify in public hearings. It submitted its final report in 2006, including a series of recommendations for legal and institutional reforms designed to prevent future abuses. Critics of the IER complained that it did not hold perpetrators to account for their actions, and that its recommendations did not lead to major structural changes. Human rights abuses continued to occur on a regular basis, albeit on a smaller scale; political Islamism remained especially circumscribed. Moreover, the authorities were intolerant of further discussion of past abuses. In June 2008, a court in Rabat ordered the private daily Al-Jarida al-Oula to stop publishing IER testimony.

The 2007 elections for the Chamber of Representatives, the lower house of Parliament, drew 37 percent of the eligible electorate, the lowest turnout in Moroccan history. The Socialist Union of People's Forces (USFP), previously the lead party in the governing coalition, fell to 38 seats. Its chief ally, the conservative Independence Party (Istiqlal), won a plurality of 52 seats. Opposition parties, which had criticized the elections as unfair, gained fewer seats than expected. The largest, the Islamist Justice and Development Party (PJD), placed second with 46 seats. Istiqlal leader Abbas el-Fassi was appointed prime minister.

El-Fassi appeared to have fallen out of favor by 2008, as former deputy interior minister Fouad Ali el-Himma, a close associate of the king, organized the Modernity and Authenticity Party (PAM) to contest local elections in June 2009. The new party led the voting with more than 20 percent of local council seats, followed by Istiqlal with about 19 percent. Widespread vote-buying, bribery, intimidation, and other forms of manipulation were reported, and analysts regarded the official turnout figure of 52 percent with some skepticism. Despite the challenges to Istiqlal's leadership, el-Fassi remained prime minister after a cabinet shuffle in January 2010.

In 2011 the political environment was shaken by protests inspired by popular uprisings elsewhere in the Middle East and North Africa. Demonstrations demanding democratic political reforms were held across the country on February 20, and the resulting protest movement, named for this date and comprised of students and activists, continued to press for change throughout the year.

After naming a commission to draft a new constitution in response to the protests, the king presented the proposed document in June. It preserved most of the monarch's existing powers, particularly in the areas of religion and security, and he retained authority over key cabinet positions. But he would now be required to choose the prime minister from the party that wins the most seats in parliamentary elections, and consult the prime minister before dissolving Parliament. Among other provisions, the draft constitution also gave official status to the Berber language, called for gender equality, and emphasized respect for human rights. Although the February 20 movement rejected the changes as insufficient, the main political parties encouraged voters to approve the document in a July referendum, and it reportedly passed with over 98 percent of the vote.

Parliamentary elections were held under the new charter in November, resulting in a victory for the opposition PJD, which took 107 of the 395 seats in the lower house. Istiqlal placed second with 60 seats, followed by the National Rally of Independents with 52, the PAM with 47, the USFP with 39, the Popular Movement with 32, the Constitutional Union with 23, and the Progress and Socialism Party with 18. Ten smaller parties divided the remainder. The February 20 movement and some Islamist and leftist groups had called for a boycott of the vote, but turnout was 45 percent, an increase from the low figure reported in 2007. Abdelilah Benkirane of the PJD was named prime minister, and he formed a coalition government with Istiqlal, the Popular Movement (a party of rural notables), and the Party of Progress and Socialism (the former communist party).

Political Rights and Civil Liberties: Morocco is not an electoral democracy. Most power is held by the king and his close advisers. Even under the 2011 constitution, the monarch can dissolve Parliament, rule by decree, and dismiss or appoint cabinet members. He sets national and foreign policy, commands the armed forces and intelligence services, and presides over the judicial system. One of the king's constitutional titles is "commander of the faithful," giving his authority a claim to religious legitimacy. The king is also the majority stakeholder in a vast array of private and public sector firms.

The lower house of Parliament, the Chamber of Representatives, has 395 directly elected members who serve for five-year terms. Sixty of these seats are reserved for women, and 30 for men under age 40. Members of the 270-seat upper house, the Chamber of Counselors, are chosen by an electoral college to serve nine-year terms. Under a rule that took effect in 2009, women are guaranteed 12 percent of the seats in local elections.

Given the concentration of power in the monarchy, the country's fragmented political parties and even the cabinet are generally unable to assert themselves. The PJD, which won the 2011 parliamentary vote, has long been a vocal opposition party, even as it remained respectful of the monarchy. By contrast, the popular Justice and Charity Movement, also Islamist in its political orientation, is illegal, though it is generally tolerated by the authorities. Other Islamist groups further to the political right are harassed by authorities and not permitted to participate in the political process.

Despite the government's rhetoric on combating widespread corruption, it remains a structural problem, both in public life and in the business world. Morocco was ranked 80 out of 183 countries surveyed in Transparency International's 2011 Corruption Perceptions Index.

Although the independent press enjoys a significant degree of freedom when reporting on economic and social policies, the authorities use restrictive press laws and an array of financial and other, more subtle mechanisms to punish critical journalists, particularly those who focus on the king, his family, the status of the Western Sahara, or Islam. Rachid Nini, editor of the daily *Al-Massae*, was detained in April after the newspaper published articles on alleged corruption involving the royal palace and PAM leader Fouad Ali el-Himma. The paper had also called for the repeal of the 2003 antiterrorism law. Nini was sentenced in June to a year in prison for disinformation and attacking the "security and integrity of the nation and citizens," and an appellate court upheld the sentence in October.

The state dominates the broadcast media, but residents have access to foreign satellite television channels. It was reported in June 2011 that Information Minister Khalid Naciri obtained the dismissal of both the chief editor and the Morocco correspondent for Dubai TV after the station reported on calls to boycott the July constitutional referendum. The authorities occasionally disrupt websites and internet platforms, while bloggers and other internet users are sometimes arrested for posting content that offends the monarchy.

Nearly all Moroccans are Muslims. While the small Jewish community is permitted to practice its faith without government interference, Moroccan authorities are growing increasingly intolerant of social and religious diversity, as reflected in arrest campaigns against Shiites, Muslim converts to Christianity, and those opposed to a law enforcing the Ramadan fast.

While university campuses generally provide a space for open discussion, professors practice self-censorship when dealing with sensitive topics like Western Sahara, the monarchy, and Islam.

Freedom of assembly is not well respected. The February 20 movement remained salient throughout 2011, holding weekly demonstrations to protest the constitutional reforms and often drawing thousands of participants. Detentions and violence by police were reported, including disburse a protest in Rabat in May.

Civil society and independent nongovernmental organizations (NGOs) are quite active and operate with more freedom than in many states in the region, but the authorities monitor Islamist groups, arrest suspected extremists, and harass other groups that offend the government. Moroccan workers are permitted to form and join independent trade unions, and the 2004 labor law prevents employers from punishing workers who do so. However, the authorities have forcibly broken up labor actions that entail criticism of the government, and child laborers, especially girls working as domestic helpers, are denied basic rights.

The judiciary is not independent, and the courts are regularly used to punish opponents of the government. Among the prisoners pardoned during 2011 were several from the so-called Belliraj case, whose terrorism convictions in 2009 were widely seen as political fabrications. In April 2011, a bomb exploded in a Marrakesh café filled with tourists, killing 17 and injuring two dozen. Morocco blamed al Qaeda in the Islamic Maghreb. On October 28, Adel al-Othmani was convicted of planting the bomb and received the death sentence; five other accomplices were given harsh sentences. Arbitrary arrest and torture still occur, though they are less common than under King Hassan. The security forces are given greater leeway with detainees advocating independence for Western Sahara, leading to frequent reports of abuse and lack of due process.

Many Moroccans have a mixed Arab-Berber ancestry, and the government has officially recognized the language and culture of the Berbers.

Women continue to face a great deal of discrimination at the societal level. However, Moroccan authorities have a relatively progressive view on gender equality, which is recognized in the 2011 constitution. The 2004 family code has been lauded for granting women increased rights in the areas of marriage, divorce, and child custody, and various other laws aim to protect women's interests.

Mozambique

Political Rights: 4
Civil Liberties: 3
Status: Partly Free

Population: 23,050,000
Capital: Maputo

Ten-Year Ratings Timeline For Year Under Review (Political Rights, Civil Liberties, Status)

2002	2003	2004	2005	2006	2007	2008	2009	2010	2011
3,4PF	3,4PF	3,4PF	3,4PF	3,4PF	3,4PF	3,3PF	3,3PF	4,3PF	4,3PF

Overview: **Mozambique's economy continued to grow at an impressive rate in 2011, though the country still suffered from double-digit inflation and high unemployment. In May, the government introduced a new plan aimed at making significant reductions in poverty by 2014.**

Mozambique achieved independence from Portugal in 1975. The Front for the Liberation of Mozambique (FRELIMO), a guerrilla group that had long fought to oust the Portuguese, installed itself as the sole legal political party in a Marxist-style state. A 16-year civil war followed, pitting the Soviet-allied FRELIMO against the Mozambique National Resistance (RENAMO), a force sponsored by the white-minority governments of Rhodesia (Zimbabwe) and South Africa. The war resulted in nearly a million deaths and the displacement of several million others. President Samora Machel, the FRELIMO leader, was killed in a suspicious plane crash in 1986; he was succeeded by Joaquim Chissano, a reform-minded FRELIMO moderate. A new constitution was enacted, calling for a multiparty political system, a market-based economy, and free elections. A peace accord signed in 1992 brought an end to the war, and a 7,500-strong UN peacekeeping force oversaw a disarmament and demobilization program and a transition to democratic government.

Mozambique held its first democratic elections in 1994. Chissano retained the presidency, and FRELIMO secured a majority of seats in the National Assembly. RENAMO accepted the outcome, transforming itself into a peaceful opposition political movement. Chissano and FRELIMO were again victorious in 1999 elections, which were deemed credible by the international community, despite technical difficulties and irregularities in the tabulation process. However, RENAMO accused the government of fraud and at one point threatened to form its own government in the six northern and central provinces it controlled.

Chissano announced that he would step down as president upon completion of his second elected term. In 2002, FRELIMO leaders chose Armando Guebuza, a hard-liner, to lead the party. Pledging to address corruption, crime, and poverty, Guebuza and FRELIMO won presidential and legislative elections in 2004 with a wide margin of victory, but RENAMO cited evidence of fraud. The National Electoral Commission (CNE) later admitted that 1,400 vote-summary sheets favoring RENAMO had been stolen—accounting for 5 percent of the total vote—and transferred one parliamentary seat from FRELIMO to RENAMO as compensation. International election observers expressed concerns about the CNE's conduct during the tabulation process, but ultimately determined that the abuses had not altered the overall outcome.

Mozambique held presidential, legislative, and—for the first time—provincial elections in October 2009. Guebuza was reelected by a landslide, securing 75 percent of the vote. His opponents, Afonso Dhlakama of RENAMO and Daviz Simango of the newly formed Democratic Movement of Mozambique (MDM), received 16.4 percent and 8.6 percent, respectively. In the parliamentary contest, FRELIMO captured 191 of 250 seats, while RENAMO won 51, and the MDM took 8. FRELIMO also won absolute majorities in all 10 of the country's provincial assemblies. RENAMO and the MDM both alleged fraud, and international observer groups were highly critical of many preelection processes. Observers also documented irregularities that indicated ballot stuffing and tabulation fraud at some polling stations, though they concluded that the distortions were not significant enough to have impacted the overall result of the election.

Guebuza's government has largely continued the liberal economic reforms and poverty-reduction policies of his predecessor. However, he has been criticized for his heavy-handed management of FRELIMO and his confrontational stance toward opposition parties. His government suffered an embarrassing blow in September 2010, when riots erupted in the capital, Maputo, and in the northern city of Chimoio in response to rising food, transport, and utility prices.

In December 2010, Mozambique's legislature created an ad hoc commission to draft constitutional amendments, though RENAMO has refused to take part in the revision. FRELIMO has said it will push forward with the constitutional review with or without RENAMO's participation; the review is scheduled to be completed by May 2013.

Economic growth in Mozambique remains among the highest in sub-Saharan Africa; the economy grew by 6.5 percent in 2010 and accelerated to 7.2 percent in 2011. Rising commodity prices, as well as well as an increase in public investment and the commencement of new projects in the mining and energy sectors, are expected to bring Mozambique back to the average 8 percent annual growth rate it enjoyed before the global economic downturn of 2009.

Nevertheless, most of the population lives in severe poverty. Mozambique was rated 184 out of 187 countries on the UN Development Programme's 2011 Human Development Index. Inflation reached 13 percent in April 2011, and rising international food and fuel prices, combined with high levels of unemployment, have threatened social stability. In May, the government launched a new Poverty Reduction Strategy to cut poverty from its 2009 level of 55 percent to 42 percent in 2014. This strategy promotes poverty alleviation through equitable economic growth. To encourage such growth, the strategy calls for the government to increase agricultural and fishing productivity, promote job creation, support human and social development, and encourage good governance and solid budget, macroeconomic, and fiscal management.

Following the discovery of large quantities of natural gas by U.S.-based Anadarko and Italy's ENI, Mozambique in November 2011 held a tender for the acquisition of seismic, gravity, and magnetic data of Mozambique's onshore and offshore basins. A new licensing round for offshore blocks in the Rovuma basin is planned for late 2012. Analysts believe the country has the potential to become a large natural gas exporter, as it is particularly well-suited to supply gas to Asian countries due to its location and large port.

Mozambique has long enjoyed close relations with donors, whose support has accounted for roughly half of its budget in recent years. However, in an effort to communicate disapproval of FRELIMO's problematic handling of the 2009 elections and its increasing dominance over the state and economy, Western donors withheld aid in 2010 until late March of that year, when the government agreed to reform the electoral system and introduce new legislation to address rampant corruption. Mozambique has been able to secure the support of other donors, including the African Development Bank, which announced in October 2011 that it would disburse $90 million to support Mozambique's budget between 2011 and 2013.

Political Rights and Civil Liberties:

Mozambique is not an electoral democracy. While international observers have deemed that the overall outcomes of Mozambique's national elections reflected the will of the people, electoral processes have repeatedly been riddled with problems. The 2009 elections were particularly criticized for the widespread rejection of party lists and for irregularities in the tabulation of results.

The president, who appoints the prime minister, is elected by popular vote for up to two five-year terms. Members of the 250-seat, unicameral Assembly of the Republic are also elected for five-year terms. The national government appoints the governors of the 10 provinces and the capital city, Maputo. Despite the introduction of elected provincial assemblies and municipal governments, power remains highly centralized, particularly in the hands of the president. In December 2011, Mozambique held by-elections in three municipalities. FRELIMO candidates won mayoral races in Pemba and Cuamba, while an MDM candidate won the mayorship of Quelimane. RENAMO boycotted the elections, alleging electoral manipulation by FRELIMO.

Political parties are governed by a law that expressly prohibits them from identifying exclusively with any religious or ethnic group. Although RENAMO and the MDM have won representation as opposition parties in the parliament, FRELIMO is the only party to have held power nationally, and its unbroken incumbency has allowed it to acquire significant control over state institutions. In the lead-up to the 2009 elections, the government was heavily criticized for the CNE's disqualification of MDM candidates in 7 of the country's 11 parliamentary constituencies. Elements within FRELIMO are also believed to have instigated several violent attacks against opposition candidates and their supporters during the campaign. In 2011, RENAMO leaders appealed to the population for a revolution reminiscent of the popular uprisings in the Arab world to topple the government without returning the country to a state of civil war.

Corruption in government and business remains pervasive. In May 2011, the country's attorney general, Augusto Paulino, declared that the real estate boom in Maputo was being fueled by money laundering. Local journalists and nongovernmental organizations (NGOs), such as the Center for Public Integrity, have played a crucial monitoring role by investigating and exposing high-profile corruption cases. In June 2010, the U.S. Treasury named prominent businessman Mohamed Bachir Suleman, who is known to have close ties with FRELIMO, a drug kingpin. In June 2011, Paulino voiced concern about the lack of success in determining the groups behind the sharp increase in drug trafficking in the country. Mozambique was ranked 120 out of 183 countries in Transparency International's 2011 Corruption Perceptions Index.

While press freedoms are legally protected, journalists are sometimes harassed or threatened and often practice self-censorship. Mozambique has a government-run daily, *Noticias*, and the privately owned *Diario de Moçambique*. There is also a state news agency and a state radio and television broadcaster. Independent media include several weeklies and the daily *O País*, a number of radio stations, and, more recently, news websites. These sources, however, face sustainability issues as a result of the state's dominance over advertising. Although there are no official government restrictions on internet use, opposition leaders have claimed that government intelligence services monitor e-mail. The government suspended text messaging services for mobile phone users during the September 2010 riots.

Religious freedoms are well respected, and academic freedoms are generally upheld. However, there have been reports of teachers encountering pressure to support FRELIMO and being refused promotions if not party members.

Associational and organizational rights are broadly guaranteed, but with substantial regulations. By law, the right to assembly is subject to notification and timing restrictions, and in practice, it is also subject to governmental discretion. In several instances, campaign rallies in the lead-up to the 2009 elections were violently disrupted by rival party activists, though most events proceeded peacefully.

Security forces have at times broken up protests using disproportionate force. In September 2010, security forces opened fire on rioters in Maputo, killing 12 people, including 2 children, and injuring more than 400. NGOs operate openly but face bureaucratic hurdles in registering with the government, as required by law. Workers have the right to form and join unions and to strike. In November 2011, 700 workers in the Xinavane sugar mill went on strike to demand a wage increase. The provincial government intervened but only as an intermediary. The Organization of Mozambican Workers is the country's leading trade union confederation.

Judicial independence is undermined by corruption, scarce resources, and poor training. The judicial system is further challenged by a dearth of qualified judges and a backlog of cases. In March 2011, police officers killed a man in Nampula in what appeared to be an extrajudicial execution. Responding to international criticism, particularly from Amnesty International, the government in 2011 said it was committed to investigating all cases of arbitrary detention, ill-treatment and torture of prisoners, and excessive force by the police. Prison conditions are abysmal.

Women are fairly well represented politically, holding the premiership from 2004 to 2010 and comprising some 39 percent of the parliament. However, they continue to face societal discrimination and violence. Legal protections for women and children are rarely enforced. Human trafficking has been on the rise, with Mozambicans and Asian immigrants taken to South Africa and sexually exploited.

Namibia

Political Rights: 2
Civil Liberties: 2
Status: Free

Population: 2,324,000
Capital: Windhoek

Ten-Year Ratings Timeline For Year Under Review (Political Rights, Civil Liberties, Status)

2002	2003	2004	2005	2006	2007	2008	2009	2010	2011
2,3F	2,3F	2,3F	2,2F	2,2F	2,2F	2,2F	2,2F	2,2F	2,2F

Overview: **The ruling party, SWAPO, continued to dominate Namibian politics in 2011 despite internal party division, in particular over the choice of a 2014 presidential candidate. Opposition party challenges to the 2009 elections continued in the Supreme Court. A police investigation into the scandal that erupted in July 2010 over the looting of a government pension fund was finally opened in October 2011 and continued at year's end.**

Namibia, formerly known as South West Africa, was claimed by German imperial forces in the late 19th century and became a South African protectorate after World War I. In 1966, South Africa's mandate was revoked by the United Nations, and the South West Africa People's Organization (SWAPO) began a guerrilla campaign for independence. After years of war, a UN-supervised transition led to independence in 1990, and SWAPO leader Sam Nujoma was chosen as president.

Secessionist fighting in Namibia's Caprivi region between 1998 and 1999 led some 2,400 refugees to flee to neighboring Botswana. Treason trials for the alleged perpetrators resulted in guilty verdicts in 2007. Appeals continued in 2011, with final decisions expected in the Supreme Court in 2012.

Nujoma and SWAPO retained control of the presidency and legislature in the 1994 and 1999 elections. In 2004, after a bitter succession contest within the party, Nujoma's longtime ally, Hifikepunye Pohamba, was chosen as the party's presidential candidate and went on to win the elections. He was reelected in November 2009 with 75 percent of the vote, while the candidate of the Rally for Democracy and Progress (RDP), an opposition party formed in 2007 mainly by SWAPO defectors, obtained just 11 percent.

In concurrent parliamentary elections, SWAPO won 54 seats in the 72-member legislature, while RDP took 8 seats. The elections were praised as free and fair by domestic and international observers, although the latter raised some concerns about pro-SWAPO bias on the government-run Namibian Broadcast Corporation (NBC), delays in the counting process, and organizational mishaps during the polling process. Following the contests, nine opposition parties filed a legal challenge calling for the nullification of the parliamentary elections because of "gross irregularities." Key allegations included claims that some areas registered turnouts of over 100 percent and concerns that polling centers failed to post results as they were tallied, as is required by law. The case reached the Supreme Court in October 2011, and a judgment was pending at year's end. Opposition parties have expressed unhappiness with the Electoral Commission on several other occasions, most recently when they accused a commissioner, Rodney Guiseb, of having faked his academic qualifications.

Throughout the year, individuals began positioning themselves for the upcoming contest over who would succeed Pohamba as party president and candidate for the 2014 elections.

The small white minority owns just under half of Namibia's arable land, and redistribution of property has been slow despite efforts to accelerate the process. In December 2010, President Pohamba warned that this could become a threat to political stability.

Namibia's economy has been among the strongest in the region, and the country has consistently been rated positively in terms of competitiveness and ease of doing business. While the economy contracted 0.7 percent in 2009, it grew 6.6 percent in 2010 and about 3.5 to 4.0 percent in 2011.

Political Rights and Civil Liberties: Namibia is an electoral democracy. The bicameral legislature consists of the 26-seat National Council, whose members are appointed by regional councils for six-year terms, and the 72-seat National Assembly, whose members are popularly elected for five-year terms using party-list proportional representation. The president, who is directly elected for five-year terms, appoints the prime minister and cabinet.

The ruling SWAPO party has dominated since independence. Significant opposition parties include the recently formed RDP, the Congress of Democrats, the Democratic Turnhalle Alliance, and the United Democratic Front. Since its formation, RDP supporters have been subject to harassment and intimidation by SWAPO members, who occasionally disrupt RDP rallies despite calls by police to disperse. While these problems have subsided somewhat in recent years, the RDP experienced some difficulty in holding rallies before the 2009 elections and faced isolated bans and disruptions of demonstrations in 2010. The RDP also boycotted parliament for most of 2010 to protest the failure of the high court to decide their election petition on substantive grounds, and the delays in the resolution of their appeal in the Supreme Court.

Although President Hifikepunye Pohamba has made anticorruption efforts a major theme of his presidency, official corruption remains a significant problem, and investigations of major cases proceed slowly. The Anti-Corruption Commission has considerable autonomy, as it reports only to the National Assembly, though it lacks prosecutorial authority. In two separate cases in 2010, a former minister and the former head of the NBC were found guilty of corruption-related charges. A major scandal surfaced in July 2010 over a scam that cost the Government Institutions Pension Fund N$660 million (approximately US$90 million) between 1994 and 2002. Following a forensic audit by the Office of the Auditor General, the full details of which have not yet been made public, the Namibian Police finally started an investigation in October 2011. The investigation is expected to conclude in the second half of 2012. Namibia was ranked 57 out of 183 countries surveyed in Transparency International's 2011 Corruption Perceptions Index.

The constitution guarantees free speech, and Namibia's media have generally enjoyed a relatively open environment. Private broadcasters and independent newspapers usually operate without official interference. However, government and party leaders at times issue harsh criticism and even threats against the independent press, usually in the wake of unflattering stories. While many insist that the state-owned NBC has been free to criticize the government, concerns have increased about excessive government influence over programming and personnel. While many publications and organizations have websites that are critical of the government, the 2009 Communications Act has raised concerns about privacy rights. The new legislation, which allows the government to tap into private communications without a warrant and monitor e-mail and internet usage, threatens to limit private discussion.

Freedom of religion is guaranteed and respected in practice. In 2010, the government was accused of pressuring academics to withhold criticism of the ruling party, though there were no such reports in 2011.

Freedoms of assembly and association are guaranteed by law and permitted in practice, except in situations of national emergency. In August 2010, police attempts to temporarily ban public demonstrations by the opposition RDP and nongovernmental organizations (NGOs) during the South African Development Community Heads of State summit were declared illegal by the high court. The government used informal pressure, such as declining requests for time off from work, to prevent civil servant participation in planned November 2010 protests over the government's tepid response to the pension fund scandal. Although human rights groups generally have operated without interference, government ministers have threatened and harassed NGOs and their leadership in the past. Constitutionally guaranteed union rights are respected. However, essential public sector workers do not have the right to strike. Collective bargaining is not widely practiced outside the mining, construction, agriculture and public service industries.

The constitution provides for an independent judiciary, and the separation of powers is observed in practice. Access to justice, however, is obstructed by economic and geographic barriers, a shortage of public defenders, and delays caused by a lack of capacity in the court system, especially at lower levels. Traditional courts in rural areas have often ignored constitutional procedures. However, legislation to create greater uniformity in traditional court operations and better connect them to the formal judicial system was implemented in 2009. Allegations of police brutality persist, and conditions in prisons and military detention facilities are quite harsh.

Minority ethnic groups have claimed that the government favors the majority Ovambo in allocating funding and services.

Women continue to face discrimination in customary law and other traditional societal practices. Widows and orphans have been stripped of their land, livestock, and other assets in rural areas. Lack of awareness of legal rights as well as informal practices have undermined the success of legal changes, such as the 2002 Communal Land Reform Act. Violence against women is reportedly widespread, and rights groups have criticized the government's failure to enforce the country's progressive domestic violence laws. Namibia serves as a source, transit and destination country for human trafficking for forced labor and prostitution.

Nauru

Political Rights: 1
Civil Liberties: 1
Status: Free

Population: 10,200
Capital: Yaren

Ten-Year Ratings Timeline For Year Under Review (Political Rights, Civil Liberties, Status)

2002	2003	2004	2005	2006	2007	2008	2009	2010	2011
1,2PF	1,1F	1,1F	1,1F	1,1F	1,1F	1,1F	1,1F	1,1F	1,1F

Overview: **Nauru experienced political upheaval in 2011, with shifting alliances among lawmakers and allegations of corruption resulting in the country having three presidents in the course of one week. Former telecommunications minister Sprent Dabwido was elected president in November and held the position through the end of the year.**

Nauru, an eight-square-mile island in the South Pacific, is the world's smallest republic. It was a German protectorate from 1888 until Australian troops seized it during World War I. The League of Nations granted a joint mandate to Australia, Britain, and New Zealand to govern the island in 1919. Japan occupied Nauru during World War II, and in 1947, the United Nations designated it as a trust territory under Australia. Nauru gained independence in 1968 and joined the United Nations in 1999.

Nauru's once-plentiful supply of phosphate, mined by Australia for use as fertilizer, is almost exhausted. Mining has made more than 80 percent of the island uninhabitable, and the government has squandered much of its accumulated wealth through financial mismanagement. The country currently carries a large foreign debt, and rising sea levels threaten its survival.

With few viable methods of generating income, Nauru relies heavily on foreign development assistance. In May 2011, Nauru engaged in talks with aid donors, including the Asian Development Bank, Australia, and New Zealand, about the creation of a new trust fund, with stricter rules on how funds may be accessed, to better secure the long-term needs of its citizens. Nauru has secured considerable aid from China and Taiwan by switching diplomatic recognition between the two rivals.

Between 2001 and 2008, Nauru served as a refugee detention and processing center for Australia in exchange for rent and aid; the center had been criticized for detaining refugees for years while they waited for processing, adjudication, and settlement. Its closure in 2009 cost Nauru approximately one-fifth of the country's gross domestic product. In May 2011, Nauru offered Australia renewed access to the center, though Australia declined, citing Nauru's failure to sign the United Nations Refugee Convention. In June, Nauru signed the convention in hopes of motivating Australia to reopen the detention camp, though the facility remained closed at year's end.

Intense political rivalries and the use of no-confidence votes have been a source of political instability. In August 2007, Ludwig Scotty was reelected president; he was replaced by Marcus Stephen just months later, in December, following a no-confidence vote. Stephen secured a second term as president in a snap election in April 2008. After Stephen survived a no-confidence vote in February 2010, parliamentary elections were held twice, in April and June. With supporters and opponents of the government tied both times at nine seats each, resulting in a hung Parliament, Stephen declared a state of emergency on June 11 and dissolved Parliament. On November 1, the state of emergency was lifted after Stephen was reelected and former president Ludwig Scotty was chosen to be Speaker of Parliament, giving the government a legislative majority. On November 10, 2011, Stephen resigned as president amid corruption allegations, and Frederick Pitcher was chosen as his successor. However, a no-confidence vote on November 15 ended Pitcher's presidency, and former telecommunications minister Sprent Dabwido was elected Nauru's third president in the course of one week.

Political Rights and Civil Liberties: Nauru is an electoral democracy. The 18-member unicameral Parliament is popularly elected from 14 constituencies for three-year terms. Parliament chooses the president and vice president from among its members. Political parties include the Nauru First Party, the Democratic Party, and the Center Party, but many politicians are independents.

Corruption is a serious problem in Nauru. In 2011, President Marcus Stephen resigned amid allegations that he had accepted bribes from the Australian phosphate company, Getax, in an attempt to gain exclusive control of the phosphate reserves remaining on the island.

The government does not restrict or censor the news media. There are several local weekly and monthly publications; foreign dailies, mostly in English, are widely available. The government publishes occasional bulletins, and the opposition publishes its own newsletters. Radio Nauru and Nauru TV, which are government owned and operated, broadcast content from Australia, New Zealand, and other international sources. There are no formal restrictions on internet usage.

The constitution provides for freedom of religion, which the government generally respects in practice. There have been no reports of government suppression of academic freedom.

The government respects freedoms of assembly and association. There are several advocacy groups for women, as well as development-focused and religious organizations. There are no trade unions or labor protection laws, partly because there is little large-scale, private employment.

The judiciary is independent, and defendants generally receive fair trials and representation. The Supreme Court is the highest authority on constitutional issues, and Parliament cannot overturn court decisions. Appeals in civil and criminal cases can be lodged with the high court of Australia. Traditional reconciliation mechanisms, rather than the formal legal process, are frequently used, typically by choice but sometimes under communal pressure. A civilian official controls the 100-person police force, and there have been few reported cases of abuse. Nauru has no armed forces; Australia provides defense assistance under an informal agreement.

Societal pressures limit the ability of women to exercise their legal rights. Sexual harassment is a crime, but spousal rape is not. Domestic violence is frequently associated with alcohol abuse. There are currently no women serving in Parliament. In October 2011, Nauru pledged to decriminalize homosexuality following an audit of their human rights by the United Nations; however, no relevant legislation was adopted by year's end.

Nepal

Political Rights: 4
Civil Liberties: 4
Status: Partly Free

Population: 30,486,000
Capital: Kathmandu

Ten-Year Ratings Timeline For Year Under Review (Political Rights, Civil Liberties, Status)

2002	2003	2004	2005	2006	2007	2008	2009	2010	2011
4,4PF	5,4PF	5,5PF	6,5PF	5,4PF	5,4PF	4,4PF	4,4PF	4,4PF	4,4PF

Overview: **After a delay of roughly seven months, the Constituent Assembly in February 2011 chose Nepal's fourth prime minister in three years. However, political instability and violence continued, and the temporary legislature missed its latest deadline to adopt a permanent constitution. The new prime minister, Jhalanath Khanal, consequently resigned in August, and was replaced by Maoist candidate Baburam Bhattarai. Meanwhile, in addition to more recent abuses, human rights groups criticized the ongoing impunity for crimes committed during the civil war.**

King Prithvi Narayan Shah unified the Himalayan state of Nepal in 1769. Following two centuries of palace rule, the left-leaning Nepali Congress (NC) party won the country's first elections in 1959. King Mahendra abruptly dissolved Parliament and banned political parties in 1960, and in 1962 he began ruling through a repressive panchayat (village council) system. Many parties went underground until early 1990, when the Jan Andolan (Peoples' Movement) organized prodemocracy rallies that led King Birendra to establish parliamentary democracy.

In Nepal's first multiparty elections in 32 years, Girija Prasad Koirala, a veteran dissident, led the NC to victory and formed a government in 1991. Torn by intraparty conflicts, the NC was forced in 1994 to call early elections, which it lost to the Communist Party of Nepal/United Marxist-Leninist, or CPN-UML. The Communists, however, failed to secure a majority in Parliament. Separately, the more militant Communist Party of Nepal (Maoist) launched a guerrilla insurgency in 1996, leading to a decade-long civil conflict that ultimately claimed some 12,800 lives. Hopes for a more stable government rose after the NC won a majority in 1999 elections.

In June 2001, King Birendra's brother Gyanendra took the throne after a bizarre palace incident in which the crown prince apparently shot and killed Birendra and nine other members of the royal family before killing himself. Gyanendra declared a state of emergency in November, and for the next several years, he ruled without Parliament. Moreover, he presided over a sharp escalation in the civil conflict.

By 2005, Gyanendra's government was cracking down on political dissent and shuttering numerous media outlets and other means of communication. A seven-party alliance (SPA) of mainstream political factions entered into talks with the Maoists, yielding an agreement that called for the restoration of democracy. Facing prodemocracy protests by hundreds of thousands of people, Gyanendra in April 2006 agreed to the provisions of the SPA-Maoist pact. The restored Parliament quickly removed most of the king's powers, and the SPA announced plans to elect a Constituent Assembly (CA) that would write a new constitution.

The SPA and Maoists concluded a Comprehensive Peace Agreement (CPA) in November 2006, stipulating that the Maoists would place their weapons under UN monitoring, confine their fighters to camps, disband their parallel government, and join a new interim government alongside members of the existing Parliament. In January 2007, an interim constitution was promulgated.

After a series of delays, CA elections were finally held in April 2008, and international observers deemed them generally free and fair, with few incidents of violence on election day. However, the campaign period was marred by regular attacks on candidates and campaign workers. The Maoists captured 220 of the 601 seats. Its nearest rival was the NC (110 seats), followed by the CPN-UML (103 seats), the Madhesi People's Rights Forum (52 seats), and a range of smaller parties and independents. The CA quickly voted to replace the monarchy with a republican system, and in July it chose the NC's Ram Baran Yadav as president. Maoist leader Prachanda was elected prime minister in August, and the Maoists formed a coalition government.

Frustrated by the military's resistance to integration with former Maoist fighters, Prachanda in May 2009 ordered the firing of army chief Rookmangud Katawal. However, the move drew objections from other parties, and the president, who technically controlled such decisions, ultimately rejected the dismissal. Prachanda resigned, and a new government led by the CPN-UML was formed. The Maoists subsequently mounted frequent protests and physically blockaded the CA for a time.

Ongoing Maoist obstruction contributed to Prime Minister Madhav Kumar Nepal's decision to resign in June 2010. After months of disagreement, the CA finally chose Jhalanath Khanal of the CPN-UML as the new prime minister in February 2011. He, too, was forced from office in August as the major parties failed to make any progress in drafting a permanent constitution. Maoist candidate Baburam Bhattarai was chosen to lead a new coalition government, but his pledges to promote interparty reconciliation and pass a constitution had yet to bear fruit at year's end.

Political Rights and Civil Liberties: Nepal is not an electoral democracy. The CA elections held in April 2008 were found to be "generally organized in a professional and transparent manner" by a European Union observation team. However, the observers noted that they did not fully meet international standards due to restrictions on freedoms of assembly, movement, and expression.

The government is operating under a 2007 interim constitution. In addition to its task of writing a permanent constitution, the 601-seat CA serves as the interim legislature. Members were selected through a mixed system of first-past-the-post constituency races (240 seats), proportional representation (335 seats), and appointments by the cabinet (26 seats). Both the president and the prime minister are elected by a majority of the CA.

In May 2010, the CA amended the constitution to extend its tenure for an additional year, but by the end of 2011, the legislature had still not passed a permanent constitution. It has also made little progress on finalizing the peace process and reintegrating former fighters into society. These and other unresolved problems have led to considerable political instability. Since 2008, Nepal has had five different prime ministers.

Unlike the 1990 constitution, the interim constitution has no limitation on parties formed along ethnic lines. A third of the seats in the CA are reserved for women, and substantial allocations were also made for Madhesis, Dalits, and other minority groups. A 2007 civil service law reserves 45 percent of posts for women, minorities, and Dalits, but their representation in state institutions remains inadequate.

Corruption is endemic in Nepali politics and government. While the Commission for the Investigation of Abuse of Authority is active, high-level officials are rarely prosecuted. Many members of the legislature have been accused or convicted of corruption in the past. Graft is particularly prevalent in the judiciary, with frequent payoffs to judges for favorable rulings, and in the police force, which has been accused of extensive involvement in organized crime. Nepal was ranked 154 out of 183 countries surveyed in Transparency International's 2011 Corruption Perceptions Index.

The interim constitution provides for press freedom and specifically prohibits censorship, although these rules can be suspended during an emergency. Many restrictions on the press were lifted after Parliament was restored in 2006. However, media workers frequently face physical attacks, death threats, and harassment by armed groups, security personnel, and political cadres, and the perpetrators typically go unpunished. Throughout 2011, supporters of several political parties attacked journalists who wrote critical pieces about their organizations and leaders. The government maintains control of both the influential Radio Nepal, whose coverage is supportive of official policies, and the country's main television station. However, there is a variety of independent radio and print outlets. Some have come to show a strong bias toward the Maoists, partly due to intimidation, but other outlets are critical of the Maoists.

The constitution identifies Nepal as a secular state, signaling a break with the Hindu monarchy. Religious tolerance is broadly practiced, but proselytizing is prohibited, and members of some religious minorities occasionally report official harassment. Christian groups have considerable difficulty registering as religious organizations, leaving them unable to own land.

The government does not restrict academic freedom. However, Maoist strikes have repeatedly threatened the school system, and a 2011 report by Human Rights Watch charged that Nepal had largely ignored the right to education of poor and disabled children.

Freedom of assembly is guaranteed under the interim constitution. While security forces have allowed large protests by Maoists and other political parties, Tibetan protests have been violently suppressed in recent years. In certain cases, authorities have detained Tibetan and Nepali monks and pressured them to sign pledges not to participate in future protests.

Nongovernmental organizations (NGOs) played an active role in the movement to restore democracy in 2006, and restrictions on NGO activity imposed by the king in 2005 were lifted under the interim regime. Maoist cadres and the affiliated Young Communist League (YCL) have at times threatened or disrupted the activities of NGOs. Groups working on Tibetan issues in Nepal report increasing intimidation by security forces, allegedly due to pressure from China, a major donor of both military and nonmilitary aid to Nepal.

Labor laws provide for the freedom to bargain collectively, and unions generally operate without state interference. A draconian labor ordinance put in place by the king's government was repealed in 2006, and restrictions on civil service members forming unions were lifted. Workers in a broad range of "essential" industries cannot stage strikes, and 60 percent of a union's membership must vote in favor of a strike for it to be legal. Bonded labor is illegal but remains a problem. Similarly, the legal minimum age for employment is 14 years, but over two million children are believed to be engaged in various forms of labor, often under hazardous conditions.

The constitution provides for an independent judiciary, but most courts suffer from endemic corruption, and many Nepalese have only limited access to justice. Because of heavy case backlogs and a slow appeals process, suspects are frequently kept in pretrial detention for periods longer than any sentences they would face if tried and convicted. Prison conditions are poor, with overcrowding and inadequate sanitation and medical care. The government generally has refused to conduct thorough investigations or take serious disciplinary measures against police officers accused of brutality or torture.

Human rights groups argued in 2011 that no one had been punished for abuses during the decade-long civil war, in part because of the weakness of the judiciary and a prevailing climate of impunity. Several political parties, including the Maoists, concluded an agreement during the summer stating that anyone who committed abuses during the civil war would receive an amnesty, though no such legislation was passed by year's end.

Members of the Hindu upper castes dominate government and business, and low-caste Hindus, ethnic minorities, and Christians face discrimination in the civil service and courts. Despite constitutional provisions banning caste-based discrimination, Dalits continue to be subjected to exploitation, violence, and social exclusion. Separately, Nepal has provided asylum to tens of thousands of Bhutanese refugees since the early 1990s. In recent years, due to pressure from China, Tibetans fleeing to Nepal on their way to India have been detained and in some cases pushed back across the border by Nepali police, though such actions do not reflect official Nepali policy.

Madhesis, plains-dwelling people with close connections to groups across the border in India, comprise 35 to 50 percent of Nepal's population, but they are underrepresented in politics, receive comparatively little economic support from the government, and—until an amendment to the citizenship law in 2006—had difficulty acquiring formal citizenship due to Nepali language requirements. In recent years, the Madhesi People's Rights Forum has organized armed cadres and mounted general strikes and protests to bolster their demands for regional autonomy and other goals, especially in the context of the drafting of the permanent constitution. Combined with attacks by more radical Madhesi groups, such activities have triggered curfews and increased violence from the state.

In 2007, the Supreme Court ordered the government to abolish all laws that discriminate against homosexuals, and in 2008 it gave its consent to same-sex marriage. The government has yet to implement these rulings, though citizens can now obtain third-gender identity documents. Homosexuals reportedly face harassment by the authorities and other citizens, particularly in rural areas.

Women rarely receive the same educational and employment opportunities as men, and domestic violence against women continues to be a major problem. The 2009 Domestic Violence Act provides for monetary compensation and psychological treatment for victims, but authorities generally do not prosecute domestic violence cases. Trafficking of young women from Nepal for prostitution in India is common. According to Human Rights Watch, kidnapping gangs have become rampant in recent years, abducting children to obtain small ransoms. Police rarely intervene in the kidnappings.

Netherlands

Political Rights: 1 **Population:** 16,694,000
Civil Liberties: 1 **Capital:** Amsterdam
Status: Free

Ten-Year Ratings Timeline For Year Under Review (Political Rights, Civil Liberties, Status)

2002	2003	2004	2005	2006	2007	2008	2009	2010	2011
1,1F	1,1F	1,1F	1,1F	1,1F	1,1F	1,1F	1,1F	1,1F	1,1F

Overview: **The coalition government proposed or adopted anti-immigrant measures during 2011, including tighter restrictions on naturalization. In March, the parties of the governing coalition lost support in provincial elections, leading to the loss of their majority in the upper house of parliament. Meanwhile, right-wing politician Geert Wilders was acquitted of charges of inciting hatred and discrimination against Muslims.**

After the Dutch won their independence from Spain in the 16th century, the princely House of Orange assumed the leadership of the Dutch Republic, which later became the Republic of the United Netherlands. Following a brief period of rule by Napoleonic France, the Kingdom of the Netherlands emerged in the 19th century as a constitutional monarchy with a representative government. The Netherlands remained neutral in both world wars, though the 1940 invasion of Nazi Germany influenced the country to join NATO in 1949. In 1952, it became a founding member of the European Coal and Steel Community, a precursor to the European Union (EU).

In May 2002, right-wing politician Pim Fortuyn was murdered a few days before general elections. His newly formed party, the Pim Fortuyn List (LPF), had been running on an anti-immigrant platform, returning issues of immigrant integration to the forefront of Dutch politics. Following the elections, a new coalition—consisting of the center-right Christian Democratic Appeal party (CDA), the far-right populist LPF, and the right-of-centre People's Party for Freedom and Democracy (VVD)—took office in July, only to collapse that October due to party infighting. The CDA narrowly won ensuing elections in January 2003, and subsequently formed a center-right coalition government with the VVD and the smaller Democrats-66 (D66) party.

In May 2006, immigration and integration minister Rita Verdonk moved to annul the citizenship of a fellow VVD member of parliament, the Somali-born Ayaan Hirsi Ali, after it was discovered that she had lied in her 1992 asylum application. Hirsi Ali had received death threats for being an outspoken critic of Islam and for a film made in collaboration with controversial filmmaker Theo Van Gogh, who was killed by a radical Islamist in 2004. D66 quit the government over the handling of the incident, causing the coalition to collapse in June 2006.

The CDA led the voting in the November 2006 elections and formed a centrist coalition government with the Labor Party (PvdA) and the Christian Union party in February 2007. The CDA's Jan-Peter Balkenende continued as prime minister.

The coalition government included the country's first Muslim cabinet ministers and marked the conservative Christian Union's debut in government. The LPF gained no seats and has since disbanded.

Elections were held again in June 2010, following the collapse of the CDA-led government in February. The VVD made major gains, winning a total of 31 seats. The PvdA followed with 30 seats, and the CDA took 21 seats. Geert Wilder's right-wing Party for Freedom (PVV) won 24 seats, nearly tripling the number of votes it received in 2006. The VVD and the CDA entered into a coalition agreement in September, but did not hold a majority of seats. The two parties agreed to include the PVV in the coalition government. The new government's policy statement included several anti-immigration initiatives endorsed by the PVV, such as reducing family migration, eliminating financial support for integration classes, withdrawing residence permits upon failure of an integration exam, and banning clothing that covers the face. Mark Rutte of the VVD became the country's prime minister, with his party leading the government for the first time.

In the March 2011 provincial elections, the VVD captured 20 percent of the national vote, while the CDA took only 14 percent, and the PVV received only 12 percent. The ruling coalition fell one vote short of a majority in the upper house of parliament after the new provincial councils elected members of the upper house in May.

Political Rights and Civil Liberties: The Netherlands is an electoral democracy. The 150-member lower house of parliament, or Second Chamber, is elected every four years by proportional representation. The 75-member upper house, or First Chamber, is elected for four-year terms by the country's provincial councils. Foreigners residing in the country for five years or more are eligible to vote in local elections. The Netherlands extended voting rights to Aruba and the Netherlands Antilles for the first time in the June 2009 European Parliament elections.

The leader of the majority party or coalition is usually appointed prime minister by the monarch, currently Queen Beatrix. Mayors are appointed from a list of candidates submitted by the municipal councils. The monarch appoints the Council of Ministers (cabinet) and the governor of each province on the recommendation of the majority in parliament.

The country has few problems with political corruption. The Netherlands was ranked 7 out of 183 countries surveyed in Transparency International's 2011 Corruption Perceptions Index.

The news media are free and independent. The 1881 *lèse majesté* laws restricting defamation of the monarch are rarely enforced. In June 2011, PVV leader Geert Wilders was acquitted on charges of discrimination and inciting hatred of Muslims through his editorials and his film *Fitna*; the court ruled that Wilders's comments were part of public debate and were not a direct call for violence. In August, the Netherlands Organization of Journalists complained that the PVV was collecting unauthorized personal data on journalists who attended party press briefings. The PVV and the Dutch national police maintained that the information was necessary for security purposes.

The constitution guarantees freedom of religion. Religious organizations that provide educational facilities can receive subsidies from the government. Members of the country's Muslim community have encountered increased hostility in recent years, including harassment and verbal abuse, as well as vandalism and arson attacks on mosques. The government requires all imams and other spiritual leaders recruited from Muslim countries to take a one-year integration course before practicing in the Netherlands. In September 2011, the cabinet introduced a ban on clothing that covers the face, imposing a maximum fine of 380 (US$460) for the first violation. By year's end, the measure, which is generally considered a ban on the burqa, had not come before the parliament, where it has majority support. The government does not restrict academic freedom.

Freedoms of assembly and association are respected in law and in practice. National and international human rights organizations operate freely without government intervention. Police arrested several students during protests in January 2011 against a measure that would impose a 3000 euro (US$3,600) fine for each year of study beyond the officially prescribed length. The "Occupy" movement spread to the Netherlands in October, leading police to clear protestors' tents from Amsterdam at the end of the month. Police arrested 14 demonstrators in December, after protestors failed to heed orders to reduce their presence at another location. Workers have the right to organize, bargain collectively, and strike. In April 2010, sanitation workers ended a nine-week strike, the longest in the Netherlands since 1933. Employees at several government agencies, including public transit workers and members of the military, held strikes in 2011 to protest planned austerity measures that would cut jobs and partially privatize public transportation.

The judiciary is independent, and the rule of law prevails in civil and criminal matters. The police are under civilian control, and prison conditions meet international standards. The population is generally treated equally under the law, although human rights groups have criticized the country's asylum policies for being unduly harsh and violating international standards. Following two highly publicized cases involving the deportation of young asylum applicants, the CDA proposed a bill in October 2011 that would allow underage asylum seekers to receive residence permits if they have been in the country for eight years or more due to delays in their applications; the bill had not been adopted by year's end. However, the government has also proposed harsh measures to encourage failed asylum applicants to return home, such as confiscating their passports during asylum proceedings. Requirements for passing the integration exam became more stringent in 2011, while failure to pass would result in revocation of one's residence permit. In November, a Dutch court ruled in favor of a gay teacher who had been fired by a Christian school because he was living with another man, clarifying a law that schools may not dismiss teachers on the basis of their sexuality.

In April 2010, the Dutch high court ruled that the Calvinist political party, which holds two seats in parliament, must allow women to run on the party's ballot; the party has previously fielded only male candidates. However, implementation is on hold pending an appeal to the European Court of Human Rights. The Netherlands is a destination and transit point for human trafficking, particularly in women and girls for sexual exploitation. A 2005 law expanded the legal definition of trafficking to include forced labor and increased the maximum penalty for convicted offenders. Prostitution is legal and regulated in the Netherlands, although links between prostitution and organized crime have been reported. In November 2011, Dutch police arrested three members of an Iranian human trafficking ring in Amsterdam who used the Netherlands as a transit point before moving victims on to other countries.

New Zealand

Political Rights: 1
Civil Liberties: 1
Status: Free

Population: 4,417,000
Capital: Wellington

Ten-Year Ratings Timeline For Year Under Review (Political Rights, Civil Liberties, Status)

2002	2003	2004	2005	2006	2007	2008	2009	2010	2011
1,1F	1,1F	1,1F	1,1F	1,1F	1,1F	1,1F	1,1F	1,1F	1,1F

Overview: **Prime Minister John Key was elected to a second term as a result of general elections in November 2011 that saw his National Party maintain its parliamentary majority. A massive earthquake in Christchurch in February 2011 killed more than 180 people and left thousands injured and homeless. In October, a cargo ship ran aground on a reef in Tauranga, spilling oil and other hazardous materials.**

British sovereignty in New Zealand was established in 1840 under the Treaty of Waitangi, a pact between the British government and Maori chiefs that also guaranteed Maori land rights. New Zealand gained full independence from Britain in 1947, though the British monarch remained head of state.

In October 2008, Prime Minister Helen Clark dissolved Parliament and called snap elections in November. John Key's National Party, which took 58 seats, also garnered support from the Maori Party (5 seats), the ACT New Zealand Party (5 seats), and the United Future Party (1 seat). The Labour Party—which had been in office since 1999—captured 43 seats of the legislature's 122 seats. Key became prime minister.

The rights and welfare of the Maori population have been major issues in New Zealand. In the first official designation of intellectual property protection for the Maori, the government in 2009 officially acknowledged that the war dance (*haka*) performed by the national rugby team belonged to the Ngati Toa tribe. Although the tribe will not be awarded royalty claims, it can address grievances over inappropriate use of the haka. In addition, the government agreed to pay $111 million in compensation—including both rent payments from state-owned forests and greenhouse gas emission credits—to eight tribes as a comprehensive settlement for grievances over land seizures and other breaches of the Treaty of Waitangi. In June 2010, the government signed a new agreement with the Maori over contentious foreshore and seabed rights, replacing a 2006 deal that had ended Maori rights to claim customary title in courts of law. Tribes can now claim customary title to areas proven to have been under continuous indigenous occupation since 1840. In March 2011,

Jerry Mateparae, a former military chief and head of the intelligence agency, was named governor-general, becoming the second Maori to hold this ceremonial post. In November 2010, New Zealand signed the Wellington Declaration with the United States, which restored bilateral defense ties and marked a significant change in New Zealand's defense and security policies. The United States had ended its previous treaty obligations with New Zealand in 1986, after nuclear weapons were barred from entering New Zealand's ports.

Two disasters struck New Zealand in 2011. In February, a major earthquake hit Christchurch, killing more than 180 people and leaving thousands injured and homeless. Rescue and recovery costs prompted the government to impose major spending cuts to limit an expected budget deficit. The government committed in May to buy more than 5,000 homes destroyed by the earthquake as a way to compensate victims and facilitate reconstruction. Meanwhile, in October, a cargo ship ran aground on a coral reef near the North Island port of Tauranga, spilling at least 70 containers of oil and hazardous materials into the water. The ship's captain was arrested and faced criminal charges for his role in the incident.

In general elections held in November 2011, the National Party took 59 parliamentary seats, and Key secured a second term in office. The National Party formed a coalition government with the ACT New Zealand Party and the United Future Party, both of which won one seat each. Economic issues had dominated the election campaigns, with Key pledging to sell more state assets. The election results caused the number of seats in Parliament to decrease from 122 to 121 as a result of New Zealand's proportional representative system; voters decided to retain that system in a referendum also held in November.

Political Rights and Civil Liberties: New Zealand is an electoral democracy. A mixed-member electoral system combines voting in geographic districts with proportional representation balloting. As a member of the Commonwealth, a governor-general represents Britain's Queen Elizabeth II as the ceremonial head of state. The prime minister, the head of government, is the leader of the majority party or coalition and is appointed by the governor-general. The unicameral Parliament, or House of Representatives, has 121 members who are elected to three-year terms.

The two main political parties are the center-left Labour Party and the center-right National Party. Smaller parties include the Maori Party, the ACT New Zealand Party, and the United Future Party. Seven of the Parliament's constituency seats are reserved for the native Maori population. Approximately 15 percent of the country's 4.4 million people identify themselves as Maori. The Maori Party, the country's first ethnic party, was formed in 2004 to advance Maori rights and interests. In June 2011, a Maori lawmaker was ejected from Parliament for swearing allegiance to the Treaty of Waitangi rather than to Queen Elizabeth II, the titular head of state.

New Zealand is one of the least corrupt countries in the world. It was ranked first out of 183 countries surveyed in Transparency International's 2011 Corruption Perceptions Index.

The media are free and competitive. Newspapers are published nationally and locally in English and in other languages for the growing immigrant population. Television outlets include the state-run Television New Zealand, three private channels, and a Maori-language public network. There is also a Maori-language radio station. The New Zealand Press Association (NZPA), a 131-year-old news service that once dominated the distribution of domestic and world news to New Zealand media outlets, closed in August 2011. The NZPA had struggled in recent years due to increased competition from internet-based news sources and the dominance of Australian newspaper chains, which did not use the NZPA's services. The government does not control or censor internet access, and competitive pricing promotes large-scale diffusion.

Freedom of religion is provided by law and respected in practice. Only religious organizations that collect donations need to register with the government. Although New Zealand is a secular state, the government has fined businesses for operating on the official holidays of Christmas Day, Good Friday, and Easter Sunday. A 2001 law grants exemptions to several categories of stores in response to demands from non-Christian populations. Academic freedom is enjoyed at all levels of instruction.

The government respects freedoms of assembly and association. Nongovernmental organizations are active throughout the country, and many receive considerable financial support from the government. In April 2011, protesters disrupted oil and gas exploration conducted by Brazil's state-owned energy company Petrobas off the North Island. The demonstrators argued that the development would threaten marine wildlife and coastal environments. Elvis Teddy, a local fisherman, was charged with breaching an exclusive zone set up around a Petrobas survey ship and resisting arrest; no verdict was reached by year's end. The New Zealand Council of Trade Unions is the main labor federation. Fewer than 20 percent of the country's wage earners are union members. Under the 2001 Employment Relations Act, workers can organize, strike, and collectively bargain, with the exception of uniformed personnel.

The judiciary is independent, and defendants can appeal to the Privy Council in London. Prison conditions generally meet international standards, though there have been allegations of discrimination against the Maori, who make up more than half of the prison population. Over the past decade, the police have introduced training to better deal with an increasingly racially and culturally diverse population.

Although no laws explicitly discriminate against the Maori and their living standards have generally improved, most Maori and Pacific Islanders continue to lag behind the European-descended majority in social and economic status. The Maori population has become more assertive in its claims for land, resources, and compensation from the government. A government-sponsored study released in August 2011 attributes higher infant mortality among Pacific Islanders in part to poverty and high rate of adult obesity. A special permanent commission hears Maori tribal claims tied to the Treaty of Waitangi.

Violence against women and children remains a significant problem, particularly among the Maori and Pacific Islander populations. Many governmental and nongovernmental programs work to prevent domestic violence and support victims, with special programs for the Maori community. A 2007 law banning the spanking of children remains controversial because it gives police the authority to determine whether a parent should be charged with abuse. A majority of voters rejected the law in a nonbinding referendum in 2009, but the Key government has kept it in place. The 2005 Civil Union Bill grants same-sex partnerships recognition and legal rights similar to those of married couples.

Nicaragua

Political Rights: 5*
Civil Liberties: 4
Status: Partly Free

Population: 5,869,000
Capital: Managua

Ratings Change: Nicaragua's political rights rating declined from 4 to 5 due to shortcomings regarding the constitutionality of Daniel Ortega's presidential candidacy, reported irregularities, and the absence of transparency throughout the electoral process, and the Supreme electoral Tribunal's apparent lack of neutrality.

Ten-Year Ratings Timeline For Year Under Review (Political Rights, Civil Liberties, Status)

2002	2003	2004	2005	2006	2007	2008	2009	2010	2011
3,3PF	3,3PF	3,3PF	3,3PF	3,3PF	3,3PF	4,3PF	4,4PF	4,4PF	5,4PF

Overview: **In November 2011, President Daniel Ortega was re-elected by an overwhelming margin and his party, the Sandanista National Liberation Front, won a two-thirds majority in the National Assembly. There were concerns about the legality of Ortega's candidacy, as well as transparency issues and other irregularities during the election. Although international observers found no evidence of widespread fraud, serious concerns remained about the politicization of institutions and the rule of law.**

The independent Republic of Nicaragua was established in 1838, 17 years after the end of Spanish rule. Its subsequent history has been marked by internal strife and dictatorship. The Sandinista National Liberation Front (FSLN), a leftist rebel group, overthrew the authoritarian regime of the Somoza family in 1979. The FSLN then moved to establish a left-wing government, leading to a civil war. The United States intervened, in part by supporting irregular rebel forces known as the contras.

In 1990, National Opposition Union presidential candidate Violeta Chamorro defeated the FSLN's Daniel Ortega in free and open elections, leading to a peaceful transfer of power. Before leaving office, however, the Sandinistas revised laws and sold off state property to party leaders, ensuring that they would retain political and economic clout.

Former Managua mayor Arnoldo Alemán of the Liberal Constitutionalist Party (PLC) defeated Ortega in the 1996 presidential election, but he was accused of corruption throughout his ensuing presidency. In 1999, the PLC and FSLN agreed to a governing pact that guaranteed Alemán a seat in both the Nicaraguan and the Central American parliaments, ensuring him immunity from prosecution. It also included reforms that lowered the vote threshold for winning an election without a runoff from 45 to 40 percent (or 35 percent if the winner had a lead of 5 percentage points). Using their combined bloc in the legislature, the two parties solidified their control over the Supreme Court and the electoral tribunal, among other institutions.

In the 2001 election, PLC presidential candidate Enrique Bolaños, a respected conservative businessman and former vice president to Alemán, defeated Ortega. He vowed to prosecute Alemán and his aides for corruption, causing a break with the PLC; Bolaños later formed the Alliance for the Republic (APRE) party. The protracted effort to convict Alemán eventually led to a 20-year prison sentence for money laundering in 2003. However, the former leader used his alliance with Ortega to secure his release from parole conditions in March 2007, so long as he did not leave the country.

Ortega won the 2006 presidential election with 38 percent of the vote in the first round. Eduardo Montealegre of the Nicaraguan Liberal Alliance (ALN), who had served as finance minister under Bolaños, took 29 percent.

In 2007, Ortega consolidated his power over the central bank, the police, and the military through a series of legislative changes. His administration also established a system of Citizens' Power Councils (CPCs), from the neighborhood to the federal level, to promote direct democracy and participation in the government's Zero Hunger food-production project. Critics argued that the bodies would blur the lines between state and party institutions. In June 2008, Ortega appointed his wife to serve as head of the Social Cabinet, which put her in charge of programs like Zero Hunger as well as the National Social Welfare System.

Prior to the November 2008 municipal elections, the Supreme Electoral Council (CSE) took a number of steps that appeared designed to ensure FSLN victories, including postponing elections in several municipalities in the Northern Atlantic Autonomous Region (RAAN), where anti-FSLN sentiment was high, and preventing two opposition parties from contesting the elections. The CSE also refused accreditations to local and several credible international electoral observers for the first time since 1990.

After the balloting, the CSE announced that the FSLN had won 105 of 146 municipalities, including Managua. However, independent observers documented fraud in at least 40 municipalities, and the international community condemned the election results, leading to the suspension of more than $150 million in U.S. and European Union (EU) aid in 2009. Civil society groups led nationwide protests against electoral fraud in February 2009, and were met with violence by progovernment groups in some areas.

In July 2009, Ortega publicly stated that the constitutional ban on consecutive presidential terms should be eliminated. The National Assembly opposed his initiative, and Ortega lacked the support to pass a constitutional amendment on the issue. Ortega and more than 100 FLSN mayors subsequently filed a petition with the Constitutional Chamber of the Supreme Court claiming that the ban on consecutive terms violated their rights to participate in the political process. In October 2009, the Supreme Court found in favor of Ortega and the mayors, lifting the ban on consecutive terms; the ruling, however, did not amend the constitution.

In January 2010, Ortega decreed that appointed officials could remain in their posts until the National Assembly selected replacements, even if that occurred after the end of their terms. The decree affected 25 high-level posts, including the presidency and magistrates of the CSE, who had supported allowing Ortega to run for a second consecutive presidential term in 2011. The struggle over these appointments sent Nicaragua into a political crisis in 2010, as members of the National Assembly were unable to achieve the majority necessary to select replacements. In keeping with Ortega's decree, many officials remained in their posts after their terms expired in June, including the CSE president and members of the Supreme Court, which moved ahead with preparations for the 2011 elections.

Ortega's candidacy for another term was officially approved by the CSE in April 2011, effectively ending legal challenges to his candidacy. Fabio Gadea Mantilla's Nicaraguan Unity for Hope (UNE) attempted to unite the opposition against Ortega, but former president Alemán refused to abandon his candidacy. Instead, Gadea became the candidate for the Liberal Independent Party (PLI) coalition, which united parties from Montealegre's ALN and the MRS. Alemán was selected as the presidential candidate for the PLC-Conservative Party alliance.

The CSE delayed issuing invitations to international observer teams until August 2011, significantly reducing the time available for observers to conduct their work. As with the 2008 municipal elections, several domestic observer groups with significant experience in electoral observation did not receive accreditation, though several international observer missions that were excluded in 2008—including the EU, the Organization of American States, and the Carter Center—were invited to observe. There was some controversy over the rules for accompaniment issued by the CSE, which some observer teams feared would limit their capacity to effectively observe the electoral process.

Ortega won the election in November 2011 with almost 63 percent of the vote, followed by Gadea with 31 percent and Alemán with almost 6 percent. The FSLN won 63 seats in the National Assembly, followed by the PLI with 27 and the PLC with 2. Though international observation teams noted irregularities and lamented a lack of transparency, there was no conclusive evidence of fraud. Observers did, however, report issues with the distribution of voting cards, the voter registry, difficulty accessing polling places, and concerns about the composition of electoral boards. Both Gadea and Alemán denounced the outcome and refused to recognize the results. Several protestors were killed and dozens of police officers were injured in postelection violence between supporters of the government and the opposition.

Political Rights and Civil Liberties:

Nicaragua is an electoral democracy. The constitution provides for a directly elected president and a 92-member unicameral National Assembly. Two seats in the legislature are reserved for the previous president and the runner-up in the most recent presidential election. Both presidential and legislative elections are held every five years. While the president is limited to two nonconsecutive terms under the constitution, the Supreme Court lifted the restriction in October 2009 following a petition by Ortega.

Corruption cases against opposition figures are often criticized for being politically motivated. The 2007 Law on Access to Public Information requires public entities and private companies doing business with the state to disclose certain information. However, it preserved the government's right to protect information related to state security.

In February 2010, the Office of the Comptroller General announced that it would carry out an audit of ALBANISA, a privately managed Nicaraguan company tasked with investing business profits in social programs. ALBANISA had been created to handle money earned from businesses created under the auspices of the Bolivarian Alliance for the Americas (ALBA)—a regional economic association—but had been accused of corruption and the misuse of its funds. Although the Comptroller General's office stated in 2011 that it did not have the necessary funding to complete the audit, the Nicaraguan Central Bank did disclose financial information on ALBANISA's earnings and expenditures to the International Monetary Fund (IMF) in April. According to observers, the information revealed to the IMF was vague about the uses of aid money received by Nicaragua from Venezuela each year. Nicaragua purchases 10 million barrels of oil annually from the Venezuelan government; the funds generated from the resale of that oil are dedicated to social projects but are administered directly by Ortega's office and are outside of the national budget, raising concerns that the money could be allocated in a corrupt or politicized manner.

The constitution calls for a free press but allows some censorship. Radio remains the main source of information. Before leaving office in 1990, the Sandinistas privatized some radio stations and handed them to party loyalists. There are six television networks based in the capital, including a state-owned network, and many favor particular political factions. Three national newspapers cover the news from a variety of political viewpoints. The Communications and Citizenry Council, which oversees the government's press relations and is directed by First Lady Rosario Murillo, has been accused of limiting access to information and censoring the opposition. Access to the internet is unrestricted.

The press has faced increased political and judicial harassment since 2007, as the Ortega administration engages in systematic efforts to obstruct and discredit media critics. Journalists have received death threats, and some have been killed in recent years, with a number of attacks attributed to FSLN sympathizers. Luis Galeano, a reporter for *El Nuevo Diario*, received death threats in February 2011, following a series of articles on government corruption that included allegations against CSE president Roberto Rivas Reyes. Another *El Nuevo Diario* reporter, Silvia González, reported receiving death threats following a series of articles on corruption and the mysterious death of a former Contra leader. Though the Ortega administration condemned the attacks, González ultimately fled the country. In addition, members of the ruling elite have acquired stakes in media outlets and used their ownership influence to sideline independent journalists.

Religious and academic freedoms are generally respected.

Freedoms of assembly and association are recognized by law, but their observance in practice has come under mounting pressure. While public demonstrations are generally allowed, opposition members have accused the police of partisan behavior and failing to protect demonstrators. Although nongovernmental organizations are active and operate freely, they have faced harassment in recent years, and the emergence of the CPCs has weakened their influence. The FSLN controls many of the country's labor unions, and the legal rights of non-FSLN unions are not fully guaranteed. Although the law recognizes the right to strike, unions must clear a number of hurdles, and approval from the Ministry of Labor is almost never granted. Employers sometimes form their own unions to avoid recognizing legitimate organizations. Employees have reportedly been dismissed for union activities, and citizens have no effective recourse when labor laws are violated by those in power. Child labor and other abuses in export-processing zones remain problems, though child labor occurs most often in the agricultural sector.

The judiciary remains dominated by FSLN and PLC appointees, and the Supreme Court is a largely politicized body controlled by Sandinista judges. The court system also suffers from corruption, long delays, a large backlog of cases, and a severe shortage of public defenders. Access to justice is especially deficient in rural areas and on the Caribbean coast.

Despite long-term improvements, the security forces remain understaffed and poorly funded, and human rights abuses still occur. Forced confessions are also a problem, as are arbitrary arrests. Prison conditions are poor. Though Nicaragua has generally been spared the high rates of crime and gang violence that plague its neighbors to its north, the country—specifically the Atlantic coast—is an important transshipment point for South American drugs. The police have been active in combating trafficking and organized crime.

The constitution and laws nominally recognize the rights of indigenous communities, but those rights have not been respected in practice. Approximately 5 percent of the population is indigenous and lives mostly in the RAAN and the Southern Atlantic Autonomous Region (RAAS). In 2009, the Miskito Council of Elders in the RAAS announced the creation of a separatist movement demanding independence, citing government neglect and grievances related to the exploitation of natural resources.

Violence against women and children, including sexual and domestic abuse, remains widespread and underreported; few cases are ever prosecuted. Additionally, the murder rate among females increased significantly in 2011. A draft bill prohibiting violence against women and instituting stronger penalties for violations was introduced in May 2011; although the National Assembly reached general consensus to approve the law, the legislation was still awaiting a vote at year's end. Abortion is illegal and punishable by imprisonment, even when performed to save the mother's life or in cases of rape or incest. Scores of deaths stemming from the ban have been reported in recent years. In March 2010, opposition parties introduced a bill in the National Assembly to decriminalize therapeutic abortions; the ban remained in effect in 2011.

Nicaragua is a source country for women and children trafficked for prostitution. In September 2010, the government passed a law that classifies human trafficking as a form of organized crime. The U.S. State Department's 2011 Trafficking in Persons Report noted improvements in Nicaragua's efforts to combat trafficking, including the creation of an anti-trafficking unit within the police force, new public awareness campaigns, and a slight increase in prosecutions, though it criticized the lack of protection and services available to victims.

Niger

Political Rights: 3*
Civil Liberties: 4
Status: Partly Free

Population: 16,069,000
Capital: Niamey

Ratings Change: Niger's political rights rating improved from 5 to 3 due to the holding of successful presidential, legislative, and local elections following the 2010 ouster of former president Mamadou Tandja and a subsequent period of military rule.

Ten-Year Ratings Timeline For Year Under Review (Political Rights, Civil Liberties, Status)

2002	2003	2004	2005	2006	2007	2008	2009	2010	2011
4,4PF	4,4PF	3,3PF	3,3PF	3,3PF	3,4PF	3,4PF	5,4PF	5,4PF	3,4PF

Overview: **In early 2011, Niger held successful legislative and presidential elections that brought longtime opposition leader Mahamadou Issoufou and his Nigerien Party for Democracy and Socialism to power. The international community declared the elections free and fair, and Niger experienced a significant democratic transition after a military coup had overthrown former president Mamadou Tandja in February 2010.**

After gaining independence from France in 1960, Niger was governed by a series of one-party and military regimes. General Ali Seibou took power in 1987, but his one-party regime yielded to international pressure and prodemocracy demonstrations, and a new constitution was adopted by popular referendum in 1992. Mahamane Ousmane of the Alliance of Forces for Change was elected president in 1993, but overthrown in January 1996 by Colonel Ibrahim Baré Maïnassara, who became president in a sham election six months later.

After members of the presidential guard assassinated Maïnassara in April 1999, the guard commander led a transitional government that organized a constitutional referendum in July and competitive elections in November. Retired lieutenant colonel Mamadou Tandja—supported by the National Movement for a Developing Society (MNSD) and the Democratic and Social Convention (CDS) parties—won the presidency in the generally free and fair balloting, and the MNSD and CDS took a majority of seats in the National Assembly. Tandja was reelected in 2004, and in concurrent legislative elections, four parties joined the MNSD and CDS to again secure a majority.

The next few years saw increased tension within the MNSD. Prime Minister Hama Amadou's government lost a vote of confidence in 2007, and he was arrested in 2008 on embezzlement charges. In May 2009, Tandja dissolved the National Assembly after lawmakers refused to approve a constitutional referendum that would delay the next presidential election until 2012, expand executive powers, and eliminate executive term limits. Tandja then dissolved the Constitutional Court—after it ruled against the referendum—and announced that he would rule by decree under emergency powers. The controversial constitutional changes were adopted by referendum in August, but observers rejected the results as fraudulent. Later that month, Tandja lifted emergency rule and announced that legislative elections to replace the dissolved National Assembly would be held in October. Key opposition parties boycotted the vote, allowing Tandja's MNSD to capture a majority. The elections were denounced by the international community, and the Economic Community of West African States (ECOWAS) suspended Niger.

In February 2010, the Supreme Council for the Restoration of Democracy (CSRD), a military junta led by Major Salou Djibo, placed Tandja under house arrest, suspended the constitution, and dissolved all government institutions. The junta appointed a transitional government, which created the National Consultative Council, a 131-member body tasked with drafting a new constitution and electoral code, and a Transition Constitutional Council to replace the Constitutional Court. Despite these institutional advances and the designation of a civilian prime minister, Djibo remained the de facto head of state without any genuine checks on his power. In a referendum held in October 2010, 90 percent of participating voters approved the new constitution, amid a turnout of approximately 52 percent.

Presidential, legislative, and municipal elections were held on January 31, 2011. The junta had forbidden its members and representatives of the transitional government from running for office. In the 113-seat National Assembly, the Nigerien Party for Democracy and Socialism (PNDS), led by longtime opposition leader Mahamadou Issoufou, took the most seats, with 37. The MNSD—led by former prime minister Seini Oumarou—placed second with 26 seats, while Amadou's Nigerien Democratic Movement for an African Federation (MDN) took 25.

In the first round of the presidential election, Issoufou and Oumarou emerged as the top two candidates, winning 36 percent and 23 percent, respectively. Amadou, who placed third with 20 percent, later declared his support for Issoufou. Issoufou claimed victory with 58 percent of the vote in a March runoff election. Both the presidential and legislative elections were declared free and fair by international observers, despite minor administrative problems. In the local elections, the PNDS and MNSD won the majority of positions across the country. In May, the Niamey Court of Appeals ordered that Tandja be released from prison.

Already one of the world's poorest and least developed countries, Niger has been ravaged by extreme food shortages since the 2009–10 drought. In January 2011, the United Nations warned of an impending food crisis in Niger, where acute malnutrition is already rampant. By the end of the year, the United Nations reported that over half of all villages in Niger were in a food crisis, while the World Food Programme urged greater international assistance for the approximately 1 million people at risk. As of 2011, the United States and other donors were supplying humanitarian and nonhumanitarian assistance to Niger, the latter having been suspended since 2009.

Political Rights and Civil Liberties:

Niger is an electoral democracy. In 2011, the transitional government fulfilled its promise to restore democratic civilian rule by holding successful legislative and presidential elections. After the 2010 military coup, former prime minister and presidential hopeful Hama Amadou returned from exile, three former legislators were released from jail, and there was a decrease in harassment of opposition politicians. The

2010 constitution, written in broad consultation with civil society, reinstated executive term limits, curbed executive power, and provided amnesty for members of the CSRD. Under the constitution, the president is elected by popular vote for up to two five-year terms, and members of the 113-seat, unicameral National Assembly serve five-year terms. Since assuming power, President Mahamadou Issoufou has appointed former opponents and members of civil society to high positions in government to foster inclusivity.

Corruption is a serious problem in Niger, and observers have raised transparency concerns regarding uranium mining contracts. However, the 2010 constitution contains provisions for greater transparency in government reporting of revenues from the extractive industries, as well as the declaration of personal assets by government officials, including the president. The transitional government created various institutions to prosecute corruption, including the State Audit Court and the Commission on Economic, Financial, and Fiscal Crime. In July 2011, the government created the High Authority to Combat Corruption, and it opened an anticorruption hotline in August. In addition, key officials from the previous administration were indicted for fraud and corruption during the year. In July, Issoufou was the target of a foiled assassination attempt thought to be motivated by his crackdowns on corruption in the military. Niger was ranked 134 out of 183 countries surveyed in Transparency International's 2011 Corruption Perceptions Index.

In 2010, the transitional government made significant efforts to restore freedoms of speech and of the press. In June, the National Assembly adopted a new press law that eliminated prison terms for journalists, and removed the threat of libel cases that journalists had faced under Tandja. In 2011, the media were praised for their positive role in the elections, and both state and private media were largely allowed to freely publish both political facts and critiques. Under Issoufou, the Niger Independent Monitoring Centre for Media Ethics and Conduct, a self-regulatory body, is active. In November, Issoufou became the first head of state to sign the Table Mountain Declaration, which calls on African governments to promote press freedom. The government does not restrict internet use, though less than 1 percent of the population has access.

Freedom of religion is generally respected in this overwhelmingly Muslim country. In the aftermath of the coup, both Muslim and Christian leaders worked with the CSRD to restore peace and democracy. Academic freedom is guaranteed in principle but not always observed in practice.

Constitutional guarantees of freedoms of assembly and association are largely upheld. The government generally does not restrict the operations of nongovernmental organizations (NGOs), although a lack of security in the north prevents NGOs from adequately assessing human rights conditions there. The constitution and other laws guarantee workers the right to join unions and bargain for wages, although over 95 percent of the workforce is employed in subsistence agriculture and small trading.

The constitution provides for an independent judiciary, and courts have shown some autonomy in the past, though the overburdened judicial system has been at times been subject to executive interference. The Ministry of Justice supervises public prosecutors, and the president has the power to appoint judges. Judicial corruption is fueled partly by low salaries and inadequate training. Prolonged pretrial detention is common, and police forces are underfunded and poorly trained. Prisons are characterized by overcrowding and poor health conditions.

Insecurity continues to plague the northwest of the country along the Malian border. In January 2011, two French nationals were abducted from Niamey and killed along the Malian border; al-Qaeda in the Islamic Maghreb claimed responsibility.

Constitutional protections provide for a quota of eight seats in the National Assembly for the nomadic population and minorities. Nomadic peoples continue to have poor access to government services.

Under a 2002 quota system, political parties must allocate 10 percent of their elected positions to women, which has increased their representation. Although the 2010 constitution prohibits gender discrimination, women continue to suffer discrimination in practice, especially in rural areas. Family law gives women inferior status in property disputes, inheritance rights, and divorce. Sexual and domestic violence are reportedly widespread. Female genital mutilation was criminalized in 2003 but still continues.

While slavery was criminalized in 2003 and banned in the 2010 constitution, an estimated 115,000 adults and children still live in conditions of forced labor. Niger remains a source, transit point, and destination for human trafficking. In December 2010, the country adopted its first anti-trafficking law and developed a five-year anti-trafficking plan, but investigation and prosecution efforts remained weak in 2011.

Nigeria

Political Rights: 4
Civil Liberties: 4
Status: Partly Free

Population: 158,300,000
Capital: Abuja

Ten-Year Ratings Timeline For Year Under Review (Political Rights, Civil Liberties, Status)

2002	2003	2004	2005	2006	2007	2008	2009	2010	2011
4,5PF	4,4PF	4,4PF	4,4PF	4,4PF	4,4PF	5,4PF	5,4PF	4,4PF	4,4PF

Overview: **The ruling People's Democratic Party retained control of the presidency, the National Assembly, and the majority of governorships in April 2011 elections. Hailed by many observers as a marked improvement from the 2007 elections, the polls were nevertheless marred by violence and suspected voter fraud. The worst bloodshed occurred in the north, where rioting by disaffected opposition supporters ignited a wave of clashes that left more than 800 people dead and at least 65,000 displaced. Since President Goodluck Jonathan's inauguration in May, Nigeria has suffered a series of high-profile attacks by the extremist movement Boko Haram, prompting a brutal crackdown by the security forces.**

The armed forces ruled Nigeria for much of the period after independence from Great Britain in 1960. Beginning with the first coup in January 1966, military officers consistently claimed that only they could manage a diverse Nigerian polity beset by simmering tensions among the country's 250 ethnic groups, as well as between religious communities. Muslims, who constitute a majority in the north, make up about 50 percent of the overall population, while Christians, who dominate in the south, account for most of the remaining 50 percent. Ethnic and regional tensions led to the attempted secession of Nigeria's oil-rich southeast as the Republic of Biafra in 1967, which touched off a three-year civil war and a devastating famine that together caused more than one million deaths.

A military-supervised political transition led to the inauguration of a civilian government in 1979, but the new democratic regime was burdened by factionalism, corruption, and communal polarization. Economic mismanagement and deeply flawed elections triggered another military intervention in 1983, followed by 16 more years of military rule.

After several years under the leadership of General Ibrahim Babangida, the country held a presidential election in June 1993. Moshood Abiola, a Muslim Yoruba from the south, was widely considered the winner, but Babangida annulled the election. A civilian caretaker administration governed briefly until General Sani Abacha, a principal architect of previous coups, took power in November 1993. Abacha's dictatorial regime dissolved all democratic structures and banned political parties, governing through a predominantly military Provisional Ruling Council. Abiola was jailed in 1994 and ultimately died in detention, just weeks after Abacha's unexpected demise in 1998.

General Abdulsalami Abubakar emerged as the new military leader and presided over a transition to civilian rule. In 1999, Olusegun Obasanjo—a former general who had led a military regime from 1976 to 1979 and spent a number of years in prison under Abacha—won the presidential election on the ticket of the People's Democratic Party (PDP), which also captured the most seats in the National Assembly. While hailed throughout the international community for bringing an end to almost two decades of military dictatorship, the 1999 elections featured numerous instances of voter intimidation and fraud.

Obasanjo's reelection in 2003 also featured widespread irregularities. The elections were preceded by violence, and observers documented widespread irregularities and fraud. Obasanjo's runner-up, former general Muhammadu Buhari, a northern Muslim and member of the All Nigeria People's Party (ANPP), filed a petition to nullify the election results. However, the Supreme Court in 2005 unanimously rejected the challenge.

The April 2007 elections were marred by bloodshed and reports of massive vote-rigging and fraud. International and local election monitors were highly critical of the vote, and opposition parties refused to accept the results, which gave Umaru Yar'Adua, the PDP candidate and Obasanjo's handpicked successor, 70 percent of the presidential ballots. In the parliamentary vote, the PDP won 85 of 109 Senate seats and 262 of 360 seats in the House of Representatives. The PDP also captured 29 out of 36 governorships. The official results drew a raft of legal challenges that were adjudicated by election officials as well as the court system. In December 2008, the Supreme Court upheld Yar'Adua's victory.

In November 2009, an ailing Yar'Adua left the country to seek medical treatment in Saudi Arabia. The National Assembly in February 2010 provisionally handed power to Vice President Goodluck Jonathan. Yar'Adua died in May, allowing Jonathan to formally assume the presidency. In September, Jonathan replaced leaders within the security forces and appointed the widely respected Attahiru Jega to head the Independent National Electoral Commission (INEC). Although presidential, gubernatorial, and legislative elections were initially scheduled for January 2011, INEC faced significant difficulties in creating an accurate and valid registry of the approximately 70 million eligible voters, and in November 2010, the polls were postponed until April.

Jonathan's decision to run in the 2011 presidential election challenged an informal power-sharing arrangement between the north and south initiated by the PDP in 1999. Under the agreement—which called for the presidency to alternate between a northerner and a southerner—the next presidential nominee should have originated from the north, since Yar'Adua, a northerner, did not finish his term. Despite northern opposition, Jonathan succeeded in winning the PDP nomination in January 2011 through an alleged combination of bribery and extravagant political promises.

Jonathan was declared the winner of the April 16 presidential contest, defeating Buhari, the Congress for Progressive Change (CPC) candidate, 58.9 percent to 32 percent. The vote divided the country along ethnic and sectarian lines, with Buhari winning the northern states and Jonathan taking the south. Protests by Buhari's supporters in parts of 12 northern and so-called Middle Belt states led to sectarian riots and retaliatory killings that resulted in over 800 deaths and forced some 65,000 people to flee their homes.

PDP candidates won a reduced majority of legislative seats in voting April 9 and 26. In the House of Representatives, the PDP claimed 202 of 360 seats, while the Action Congress of Nigeria (ACN) won 66, the CPC, 35, and the ANPP, 25. In the Senate, the PDP lost its two-thirds majority, winning 71 of 109 seats; the ACN took 18 seats, and the CPC and ANPP took 7 each. The PDP captured 18 of the 26 contested governorships. Despite the election-related violence and high number of dubious official results, most observers deemed 2011's elections an improvement from those in 2007, citing the existence of more orderly polling stations and competent INEC personnel.

The year 2011 also saw a rise in activity by the radical Islamist movement Boko Haram, based in northeastern Borno State, with at least 550 people killed in 115 attacks, according to Human Rights Watch (HRW). In August, Boko Haram claimed responsibility for a suicide car bombing that killed 24 people at the United Nations' local headquarters in Abuja. In December, a Christmas Day attack on a Catholic church killed 40 people in Niger State. These attacks—along with more frequent, smaller attacks in Borno and other northern states, mainly on government personnel—drew a harsh response from the security forces, reportedly including random killings and arrests, intimidation, and arbitrary and illegal detentions.

Nigeria's economy is dominated by hydrocarbons, which account for 95 percent of export revenues and most foreign investment. It is estimated that nearly $400 billion in oil revenue has been stolen or squandered since independence. Wealth and political power are concentrated in the hands of a narrow elite, and much of the regular violence in the oil-rich yet impoverished Niger Delta region stems from unequal distribution of oil revenue.

Political Rights and Civil Liberties:

Nigeria is not an electoral democracy. According to the constitution, the president is elected by popular vote for no more than two four-year terms. Members of the bicameral National Assembly, consisting of the 109-seat Senate and the 360-seat House of Representatives, are elected for four-year terms. However, since the return of civilian rule in 1999, elections have by and large been chaotic affairs often marked by vote-rigging, and violence. This has been particularly the case in the Niger Delta, where many prominent politicians reportedly sponsor criminal gangs to target opponents.

As of 2011, the ruling PDP, the ACN, and the CPC formed the largest political parties in Nigeria. The ACN and CPC derive much of their support from regional-based constituencies (the Yoruba-speaking southwest and Muslim north, respectively), while the PDP enjoys the backing of opaque patronage networks consisting of elites from every section of Nigeria. Other prominent parties include the ANPP and the All-Progressive Grand Alliance. Although the PDP has dominated Nigeria's political landscape since 1999, it saw its grip on power weakened following the April 2011 elections. INEC chief Jega has won praise for addressing opposition complaints that the commission functioned as an appendage of the PDP.

Corruption remains pervasive, with government efforts to improve transparency and reduce graft proving cosmetic in nature. An August 2011 report by HRW found that the Economic and Financial Crimes Commission, Nigeria's main anti-corruption agency, had arraigned 30 prominent politicians on corruption charges since it began work in 2002. However, it had won only four convictions, resulting in little or no jail time. The body has been hampered by political interference, an inefficient judiciary, and its own institutional weaknesses, and was subject to criticisms that it targeted those who had lost favor with the government. Nigeria was ranked 143 out of 183 countries surveyed in Transparency International's 2011 Corruption Perceptions Index.

Freedom of speech and expression is constitutionally guaranteed, and Nigeria has a lively independent media sector. However, state security agents occasionally arrest journalists, confiscate newspapers, and harass vendors, notably when journalists are covering corruption or separatist and communal violence. Local authorities frequently condemn those who criticize them, and cases of violence against journalists often go unsolved. Sharia (Islamic law) statutes in 12 northern states impose severe penalties for alleged press offenses. In October 2011, Boko Haram shot and killed Zakariya Isa, a cameraman for the state-owned Nigerian Television Authority; the group alleged that he was an informant for the security services. In a positive development, President Goodluck Jonathan in May signed into law a Freedom of Information Act. The government does not restrict internet access.

Religious freedom is guaranteed by the constitution, though many Nigerians, including government officials, discriminate against adherents of other religions. Religious violence frequently reflects regional and ethnic differences and accompanying competition for resources. In recent years, sectarian clashes have erupted in and around the city of Jos, leaving hundreds dead and displacing thousands more. Christians have also been targeted by Boko Haram.

Academic freedom is generally honored, although government officials frequently pressure university administrators and faculty to ensure special treatment for their relatives and associates. At the state level, policies related to the admission of students and the hiring of teaching staff are subject to ethnic politics. Nigeria's public education system remains dismal; more than a third of the population is illiterate.

Freedoms of assembly and association are generally respected in practice. However, protests are often suppressed by state and private security forces, especially demonstrations organized by youth groups or in the Niger Delta. Human rights groups report that dozens of activists have been killed in recent years and hundreds have been detained. Workers, except those in the military or "essential services," may join trade unions and have the right to bargain collectively. Public health workers strike frequently.

The higher courts are relatively competent and independent, but they remain subject to political influence, corruption, and lack of funding, equipment, and training. Certain departments, particularly the Court of Appeals, have often overturned decisions on election challenges or allegations of corruption against powerful elites, raising doubts about their independence.

Ordinary defendants in Nigerian courts frequently lack legal representation and are often ill-informed about court procedures and their rights. Human rights groups have alleged that Islamic courts in the 12 northern states with Sharia statutes fail to respect due process rights and discriminate against non-Muslims. Pretrial detainees, many of whom are held for several years, account for 70 percent of the country's inmates, and few have had access to a lawyer. Children and the mentally disabled are often held with the general prison population. Prison facilities are rife with disease, as they commonly lack water, adequate sewage facilities, and adequate medical services.

Security forces commit abuses with near impunity, and corruption pervades their ranks. Amnesty International (AI) has accused military forces currently deployed to quell the terrorist activities of Boko Haram in Borno State of randomly targeting unarmed civilians. Extrajudicial killings of prisoners have been reported, and torture and general ill-treatment of suspects are widespread. A report issued by Nigerian and U.S. watchdog groups in May 2010 noted that police kill, torture, and rape suspects to force confessions and extort bribes. Police officers who routinely abuse their power are often supported by a chain of command that encourages and institutionalizes graft. Violent crime in certain cities and areas remains a serious problem, and the trafficking of drugs and small arms is reportedly on the rise.

The constitution prohibits ethnic discrimination by the government and requires government offices to reflect the country's ethnic diversity, but societal discrimination is widely practiced, and ethnic clashes frequently erupt. Ethnocultural groups in the Niger Delta feel particular discrimination, primarily with regard to distribution of the country's oil wealth, and their grievances have fueled militant violence. The government launched an amnesty program in 2009, and some militant factions accepted the offer. Despite the Niger Delta–born Jonathan's ascendancy to the presidency, many locals continue to voice their intense displeasure with Abuja.

The authorities often engage in forcible evictions to pave the way for development projects. AI estimated that more than two million Nigerians had been evicted between 2000 and 2009. In 2011, authorities in Abuja threatened to evict about 50,000 people, claiming their dwellings violated the city plan or lacked proper permits; they reportedly set fire to buildings in certain districts.

Nigerian women face societal discrimination, although their educational opportunities have improved, and women hold several key governmental positions. Women throughout the country experience discrimination in employment and are often relegated to inferior positions. In the northern states governed under Sharia statutes, women's rights have suffered particularly serious setbacks. Rape and spousal rape are considered separate offenses, though both have low rates of reporting and prosecution. Domestic violence is common and accepted in most parts of society. Women in some ethnic groups are denied equal rights to inherit property, and various forms of gender-based violence are not considered crimes. Although the federal government publicly opposes female genital mutilation, it has taken no action to ban the practice. While illegal, human trafficking to, from, and within the country for the purposes of labor and prostitution is reported to be on the rise. Forced labor is illegal but common, especially bonded labor and domestic servitude, and the government makes very little effort to combat the practice. Several organizations have reported on an illegal trade in which pregnant teenagers are promised abortions, only to be held until their babies are delivered and sold. No laws prohibit discrimination against the physically and mentally disabled, and people with disabilities face social stigma, exploitation, and discrimination. Homosexual activity is illegal and punishable by up to 14 years in prison.

North Korea

Political Rights: 7
Civil Liberties: 7
Status: Not Free

Population: 24,457,000
Capital: Pyongyang

Ten-Year Ratings Timeline For Year Under Review (Political Rights, Civil Liberties, Status)

2002	2003	2004	2005	2006	2007	2008	2009	2010	2011
7,7NF	7,7NF	7,7NF	7,7NF	7,7NF	7,7NF	7,7NF	7,7NF	7,7NF	7,7NF

Overview: **North Korea's longtime leader, Kim Jong-il, died in December 2011 and was succeeded by his son and heir apparent, Kim Jong-un. The new leader's relative youth and political inexperience led to speculation about the country's future stability and direction of its foreign and nuclear policies. At the beginning of 2011, relations with South Korea were near an all-time low, though North Korea made deliberate efforts to improve its relations with China, Russia and the United States throughout the year.**

The Democratic People's Republic of Korea (DPRK, or North Korea) was established in 1948 after three years of post–World War II Soviet occupation. The Soviet Union installed Kim Il-sung, an anti-Japanese resistance fighter, as the new country's leader. In 1950, North Korea invaded South Korea in an attempt to reunify the peninsula under communist rule. Drawing in the United States and then China, the three-year conflict resulted in the deaths of at least 2.5 million people and ended with a ceasefire rather than a full peace treaty. Since then, the two Koreas have been on a continuous war footing, and the border remains one of the most heavily militarized places in the world.

Kim Il-sung solidified his control after the war, purging rivals, consigning thousands of political prisoners to labor camps, and fostering an extreme personality cult that promoted him as North Korea's "Great Leader." Marxism was replaced by the *Juche* (translated as "self-reliance") ideology, which combines extreme nationalism, xenophobia, and the use of state terror. After Kim Il-sung died in 1994, he was proclaimed "Eternal President," but power passed to his son, Kim Jong-il.

The end of the Cold War and associated subsidies from the Soviet Union and China led to the collapse of North Korea's command economy. Decades of severe economic mismanagement were exacerbated by harsh floods in 1995 and 1996, resulting in a famine that killed at least a million people. As many as 300,000 North Koreans fled to China in search of food, despite a legal ban on leaving the country. In 1995, North Korea allowed the United Nations and private humanitarian aid organizations to undertake one of the world's largest famine-relief operations. The DPRK continues to force the international community to bear the burden of feeding its citizens while it devotes resources to its military.

The emergence of black markets helped to deal with extreme shortages of food and other goods, and illicit traders smuggled in items of all kinds from China. The regime instituted halting economic reforms in 2002, easing price controls, raising wages, devaluing the currency, and giving factory managers more autonomy. China and South Korea also continued to provide aid, fearing that state collapse could lead to massive refugee outflows, military disorder, the emergence of criminal gangs and regional warlords, and a loss of state control over nuclear weapons.

The DPRK withdrew from the Nuclear Non-Proliferation Treaty in 2003 and proceeded to test ballistic missiles and a nuclear device in 2006. In early 2007, the regime agreed to denuclearize in exchange for fuel aid and other concessions from its four neighbors—China, South Korea, Japan, and Russia—and the United States, but further negotiations and implementation of the deal proceeded haltingly. In 2008, Pyongyang handed over its declaration of nuclear assets and disabled its Yongbyon nuclear plant, and the United States removed North Korea from its list of state sponsors of terrorism. The Six-Party Talks then broke down in December over the issue of verification.

In April 2009, the DPRK tested a long-range missile and announced its withdrawal from the Six-Party Talks. In response, the UN Security Council unanimously passed Resolution 1874, which tightened weapons-related financial sanctions and called on all governments to search North Korean shipments for illicit weapons.

In late November, the government announced a currency revaluation and other measures designed to curb private trading and reassert state control over the economy. With the crippled black market unable to meet demand, prices rose sharply. The economy was disrupted further in early 2010, when the government banned the use of foreign currency. In February 2010, the government backtracked on the currency revaluation, issuing a rare formal apology and allowing markets to reopen.

In March 2010, a South Korean naval vessel, the *Cheonan*, was sunk in the West Sea, killing 46 crew members. While North Korea was widely believed to have perpetrated the attack, it never claimed responsibility. In May, an international group of experts concluded that the ship had been sunk by a North Korean torpedo. The findings triggered a series of escalatory provocations between the two Koreas.

While inter-Korean relations had begun to thaw only a few months after the Cheonan incident, North Korea responded to joint U.S.-South Korean live fire military exercises in the West Sea with a surprise attack on South Korea's Yeonpyeong Island on November 23. South Korea launched a counterattack, and the exchange lasted an hour; the shelling resulted in a number of South Korean casualties, including the first civilian deaths since the Korean War.

North Korean authorities also revealed to the international community that it had built a modern uranium enrichment facility, heightening fears that it would produce weapons grade uranium. This revelation sparked public debate in South Korea over whether it should pursue a nuclear weapons program of its own.

With inter-Korean tensions high, South Korea denounced North Korean requests for food aid in the beginning of 2011, and the United States followed suit. All inter-Korean cooperative activities were stalled except for the operation of the Gaeseong Industrial Complex, the joint North-South Korean economic venture.

In February 2011, a group of five nongovernmental organizations from the United States—Christian Friends of Korea, Global Resource Services, Mercy Corps, Samartian's Purse, and World Vision—found insufficient access to food and chronic malnutrition in North Korea; an assessment from the World Food Programme in March confirmed those findings. Both groups also reported the likely potential for food shortages during the lean months, which would put several millions of people at risk. In May, the United States Agency for International Development and U.S. Special Envoy for North Korean Human Rights Robert King led another food assessment team into North Korea to get a better sense of the severity of the food situation. King's visit marked the first time a designated human rights envoy had been allowed in the country, though he was not there for formal negotiations.

In June, the EU pledged $14.5 million in food aid to North Korea. Later in the year, South Korea approved private sector humanitarian efforts, and although refusing to grant direct aid to the North, approved government provision of food aid through third party organizations. The United States, however, had yet to come to a decision over whether it would provide assistance by the end of the year.

In August, Kim Jong-il travelled to Russia to meet with President Dmitry Medvedev. The two leaders agreed to establish a commission to explore the construction of a gas pipeline from Siberia through North Korea to South Korea. Though all three parties stand to gain from such a pipeline, there is great skepticism as to the North's credibility as a business partner.

In October, U.S. and North Korean officials met again, this time in Geneva, to move the two countries towards renewing dialogue on nuclear disarmament and improving relations. Prospects for resuming multilateral nuclear negotiations seemed high until December 17, when Kim Jong-il reportedly died of a heart attack at the age of 69. Kim Jong-un, Kim Jong-il's son and heir apparent, succeeded his father as the country's leader without a major power struggle, though it was unclear how much he had consolidated his hold on power. At year's end, questions remained over the country's future stability and foreign and nuclear policies under the new leadership of Kim Jong-un, who is in his late twenties and relatively politically inexperienced.

Political Rights and Civil Liberties: North Korea is not an electoral democracy. Kim Jong-il led the DPRK following the 1994 death of his father, Kim Il-sung, to whom the office of president was permanently dedicated in a 1998 constitutional revision. Kim Jong-un, Kim Jong-il's youngest son, became the country's new leader after his father's death in December 2011. Kim Jong-un, about whom little was known outside of North Korea, had been appointed to a number of senior government positions in 2010 and was being groomed as his father's heir apparent. North Korea's parliament, the Supreme People's Assembly (SPA), is a rubber-stamp institution elected to five-year terms. All candidates for office, who run unopposed, are preselected by the ruling Korean Workers' Party and two subordinate minor parties.

Corruption is believed to be endemic at every level of the state and economy. North Korea was ranked 182 out of 183 countries surveyed in Transparency International's 2011 Corruption Perceptions Index.

All media outlets are run by the state. Televisions and radios are permanently fixed to state channels, and all publications are subject to strict supervision and censorship. Internet access is restricted to a few thousand people, and foreign websites are blocked. Still, the black market provides alternative information sources, including cellular telephones, pirated recordings of South Korean dramas, and radios capable of receiving foreign programs.

Although freedom of religion is guaranteed by the constitution, it does not exist in practice. State-sanctioned churches maintain a token presence in Pyongyang, and some North Koreans who live near the Chinese border are known to practice their faiths furtively. However, intense state indoctrination and repression preclude free exercise of religion as well as academic freedom. Nearly all forms of private communication are monitored by a huge network of informers.

Freedom of assembly is not recognized, and there are no known associations or organizations other than those created by the state. Strikes, collective bargaining, and other organized labor activities are illegal.

North Korea does not have an independent judiciary. The UN General Assembly has recognized and condemned severe DPRK human rights violations, including torture, public executions, extrajudicial and arbitrary detention, and forced labor; the absence of due process and the rule of law; and death sentences for political offenses. South Korean reports suggest that up to 154,000 political prisoners are held in six detention camps. Inmates face brutal conditions, and collective or familial punishment for suspected dissent by an individual is a common practice.

The government operates a semihereditary system of social discrimination whereby all citizens are classified into 53 subgroups under overall security ratings—"core," "wavering," and "hostile"—based on their family's perceived loyalty to the regime. This rating determines virtually every facet of a person's life, including employment and educational opportunities, place of residence, access to medical facilities, and even access to stores.

There is no freedom of movement, and forced internal resettlement is routine. Access to Pyongyang, where the availability of food, housing, and health care is somewhat better than in the rest of the country, is tightly restricted. Emigration is illegal, but many North Koreans have escaped to China or engaged in cross-border trade. Ignoring international objections, the Chinese government continues to return refugees and defectors to North Korea, where they are subject to torture, harsh imprisonment, or execution.

The economy remains both centrally planned and grossly mismanaged. Development is also hobbled by a lack of infrastructure, a scarcity of energy and raw materials, an inability to borrow on world markets or from multilateral banks because of sanctions, lingering foreign debt, and ideological isolationism. However, the growth of the black market has provided many North Koreans with a field of activity that is largely free from government control. In 2011, the government announced new policies to attract greater foreign investment, and there were growing indications of a rising middle class in Pyongyang, including the opening of new shopping and entertainment venues and a surge in mobile phone subscriptions.

There have been widespread reports of trafficked women and girls among the tens of thousands of North Koreans who have recently crossed into China. UN bodies have noted the use of forced abortions and infanticide against pregnant women who are forcibly repatriated from China.

Norway

Political Rights: 1
Civil Liberties: 1
Status: Free

Population: 4,952,000
Capital: Oslo

Ten-Year Ratings Timeline For Year Under Review (Political Rights, Civil Liberties, Status)

2002	2003	2004	2005	2006	2007	2008	2009	2010	2011
1,1F	1,1F	1,1F	1,1F	1,1F	1,1F	1,1F	1,1F	1,1F	1,1F

Overview: **The July terrorist attacks in Oslo and Uttoya by Norwegian national Anders Breivik shook Norway in 2011. Breivik detonated a bomb in Oslo near government buildings and attacked participants of a political summer camp on the island of Uttoya with a machine gun, killing 77 people. Widespread criticism of the police's handling of the crisis lead to the resignation of Minister of Justice Knut Storberget in November. Meanwhile, asylum seekers continued to be rejected and repatriated in the midst of calls and marches for increased tolerance and multiculturalism.**

Norway's constitution, the Eidsvoll Convention, was first adopted in 1814, during a brief period of independence after nearly four centuries of Danish rule. Subsequently, Norway became part of a Swedish-headed monarchy. The country gained independence in 1905 and has since functioned as a constitutional monarchy with a multiparty parliamentary structure. Norway became a founding member of NATO in 1949.

Norwegian citizens narrowly rejected membership in the European Union (EU) in 1972 and 1994, despite government support for joining. Norwegians wanted to preserve their sovereignty and feared that membership would threaten the country's energy, agriculture, and fishing industries. As part of the European Economic Area (EEA), Norway has nearly full access to EU markets, and 71 percent of Norwegian exports go to EU countries. While Norway has adopted almost all EU directives, it has little power to influence EU decisions.

In the September 2005 legislative elections, the center-left Red-Green coalition—led by the Labor Party and including the Socialist Left Party and the Center Party (Agrarians)—won 47.9 percent of the vote and 87 of 169 seats. The previous governing bloc—a center-right coalition consisting of the Conservative Party, the Christian People's Party, and the Liberal Party—captured only 26.8 percent of the vote and 44 seats. Prime Minister Jens Stoltenberg reshuffled members of his coalition government in October 2007, resulting in a historic female-majority cabinet, with 10 female and 9 male ministers.

Stoltenberg's coalition was reelected in the September 2009 parliamentary elections, making it the first government to win reelection in the last 16 years. The coalition's Labor Party won 64 seats, while the Socialist Left Party and the Center Party captured 11 seats each. The Progress Party secured 41 seats; the Christian Democrats, 10 seats; and the Liberal Left, 2 seats. In concurrent elections for the Sami Assembly, the Norwegian Labor Party captured 14 seats, the Norwegian Sami Association (NSR) received 11, and various other Sami parties won a total of 14 seats.

On July 22, 2011, Norwegian national and right-wing fundamentalist Anders Breivik detonated a powerful bomb in the center of Oslo, near several government buildings, killing eight people and inflicting widespread material damage. Breivik then proceeded to shoot and kill 69 people attending a Labor Party summer youth camp on the island of Uttoya. The attacks, which were the deadliest in Scandinavia since World War II, inspired a national and regional discussion of the origins of Breivik's ideology, which seemed to be based in the extreme right. It included anti-immigrant sentiments, particularly against Muslim immigration, and a radical resistance and hostility to Norway's multicultural agenda and its native Norwegian supporters. Breivik is scheduled to go to trial in April 2012.

Minister of Justice Knut Storberget resigned in November 2011, citing personal reasons, but tacitly acknowledging the intense critique he received over the poor police response to the July Breivik massacre as significant to his decision; it took police more than an hour and a half to reach the island of Uttoya and arrest Breivik after he opened fire.

Municipal and county elections in September 2011 saw a loss of votes for the anti-immigration Progress Party, but gains for the Conservatives, Liberals, and Labour parties.

Immigration to Norway has increased fivefold since the 1970s, including recent asylum seekers predominantly from Afghanistan, Iraq, Somalia, and Eritrea. More than 10 percent of Norway's population was foreign-born in 2011. However, according to the United Nations High Commissioner for Refugees, there was a 42 percent drop in the number of people seeking asylum in Norway in 2010, but a dramatic increase in the number of rejected asylum claims and voluntary and forced repatriations. In July 2010, residents vandalized and set fire to asylum "waiting centers" near Nannestad and Drammen. Officials alleged that the fire was intentionally set by asylum seekers whose applications had been denied. Residents have reported poor living conditions in the centers, including a lack of food and mental health care, though the authorities have denied such claims. Plans proposed in 2010 to create "return facilities" for those denied asylum in order to expedite deportation and reduce overcrowding were rejected in September 2011 due to costs. However, the national debate on immigration was affected by the Breivik attacks in July, resulting in numerous marches and calls for strengthening Norway's tolerance and multiculturalism.

The trial of three terrorist suspects arrested in 2010 commenced in September 2011. The three were charged with conspiracy to commit terrorism based on their plans to attack the headquarters of *Jyllands-Posten*, the Danish newspaper that published cartoons featuring the prophet Muhammad in 2005. The trial was ongoing at year's end.

Political Rights and Civil Liberties: Norway is an electoral democracy. The unicameral Parliament, called the Storting, currently has 169 members who are directly elected for four-year terms through a system of proportional representation. The leader of the majority party or coalition in the Storting is appointed prime minister by the constitutional monarch, currently King Harald V. While the monarch is officially the head of state and commander in chief of the armed forces, his duties are largely ceremonial.

The indigenous Sami population, in addition to participating in the national political process, has its own Consultative Constituent Assembly, or Sameting, which has worked to protect the group's language and cultural rights and to influence the national government's decisions about Sami land and its resources. The Sameting is comprised of 39 representatives, who are elected for four-year periods. The government supports Sami-language instruction, broadcast programs, and subsidized newspapers in Sami regions. A deputy minister in the national government deals specifically with Sami issues.

Norway remains one of the least corrupt countries in the world. However, isolated incidents of bribery and misconduct have occurred, and Norway's role in the international energy and mining industries has received particular scrutiny. Norway was ranked 6 out of 183 countries surveyed in Transparency International's 2011 Corruption Perceptions Index.

Freedom of the press is constitutionally guaranteed. In an effort to promote political pluralism, the state subsidizes many newspapers, the majority of which are privately owned and openly partisan. Internet access is not impeded by the government.

Freedom of religion is protected by the constitution and respected in practice. The monarch is the constitutional head of the official Evangelical Lutheran Church of Norway, and at least half of the cabinet must belong to the church. Other denominations must register with the state to receive financial support, which is determined by size of membership. A course on religion and ethics focusing on Christianity is mandatory for students, but is considered to be in violation of international human rights conventions. Contrary to a decision reached in 2009, an administrative court in August 2010 issued a nonbinding opinion that banning female police officers from wearing the hijab (headscarf) violates Norway's freedom of religion and antidiscrimination laws.

The constitution guarantees freedoms of assembly and association. Norwegians are very active in nongovernmental organizations. Labor unions play an important role in consulting with the government on social and economic issues, and approximately 53 percent of the workforce is unionized. The right to strike is legally guaranteed, except for military and senior civil servants, and is practiced without restrictions. All workers also have the right to collective bargaining.

The judiciary is independent, and the court system, headed by the Supreme Court, operates fairly at the local and national levels. The king appoints judges on the advice of the Ministry of Justice. The police are under civilian control, and human rights abuses by domestic law enforcement authorities are rare. Prison conditions generally meet international standards, though problems with overcrowding continued in 2011.

The mandate of the Office of the Ombudsman was expanded in 2006 to include all forms of discrimination, and is responsible for enforcing the country's Gender Equality Act, the Discrimination Act, and the Worker Protection and Working Environment Act. While citizens within the EEA no longer need a residence permit to work in Norway, the agreement excludes Romanians and Bulgarians.

The Gender Equality Act provides equal rights for men and women. In 2009, nearly 40 percent of the seats in Parliament were won by women, a slight increase over the previous elections. Norway is a destination country for human trafficking for the purposes of labor and sexual exploitation. The country, however, remains a leader in anti-trafficking efforts, according to the U.S. State Department's 2011 Trafficking in Persons Report.

Oman

Political Rights: 6
Civil Liberties: 5
Status: Not Free

Population: 2,997,000
Capital: Muscat

Ten-Year Ratings Timeline For Year Under Review (Political Rights, Civil Liberties, Status)

2002	2003	2004	2005	2006	2007	2008	2009	2010	2011
6,5NF	6,5NF	6,5NF	6,5NF	6,5NF	6,5NF	6,5NF	6,5NF	6,5NF	6,5NF

Overview: **Thousands of Omanis demonstrated across the country in 2011, demanding economic and political reform. Several protests turned violent, leading to the detention of hundreds and at least two deaths. In September, two newspaper editors were sentenced to five months in prison and their website shut down for a month for alleging corruption at the ministry of justice, while an October royal decree further restricted freedom of expression.**

Except for a brief period of Persian rule, Oman has been an independent state since a native dynasty expelled the Portuguese from Muscat in 1650. The sultan subsequently conquered neighboring territories and built a small empire that included parts of the eastern coast of Africa and the southern Arabian Peninsula. The overseas possessions were gradually lost beginning in the mid-19th century.

During the 1950s and 1960s, Oman experienced a period of civil unrest centered mostly in the interior regions of the country. In 1964, a group of separatists supported by Marxist governments, including that of the neighboring People's Democratic Republic of Yemen (South Yemen), started a revolt in Oman's Dhofar province. The insurgency was not completely quelled until the mid-1970s. Sultan Qaboos bin Said al-Said seized power in 1970 by overthrowing his father, Sultan Said bin Taimur, who had ruled for nearly four decades. The new sultan launched a program to modernize Oman's infrastructure, educational system, government, and economy.

In 1991, Qaboos replaced the appointed State Consultative Council, established in 1981, with a partially elected Consultative Council (Majlis al-Shura) designed to provide the sultan with a wider range of opinions on ruling the country. A limited number of women gained the right to vote and run as candidates in 1994. The 1996 basic law, promulgated by royal decree, created a bicameral parliament consisting of an appointed Council of State (Majlis al-Dawla) and a wholly elected Consultative Council. Only a limited number of citizens selected by tribal leaders were allowed to vote in the first elections. The basic law granted certain civil liberties; banned discrimination on the basis of sex, religion, ethnicity, and social class; and clarified the process for royal succession.

This limited political reform in the 1990s was overshadowed by a stronger effort, spearheaded by Qaboos in 1995, to liberalize and diversify Oman's oil-dependent economy. In preparation for Oman's accession to the World Trade Organization in 2000, the government lifted restrictions on foreign investment and ownership of enterprises in the country.

In 2003 the sultan decreed universal suffrage for all Omanis over the age of 21. Parliamentary elections have been held twice since, once in 2007 and again in 2011. In October 2011, Omanis elected 84 members of the new Majlis al-Shura from over 1,100 candidates. Out of 77 female candidates, 1 was elected. The elections were overshadowed by ongoing public protests that roiled the country earlier in the year, as thousands of Omanis across the country mounted regular demonstrations calling for economic and political reform.

Political Rights and Civil Liberties: Oman is not an electoral democracy. Citizens elect the 84-member Consultative Council for four-year terms, but the chamber has no legislative powers and can only recommend changes to new laws. The Consultative Council is part of a bicameral body known as the Council of Oman. The other chamber, the 59-member State Council, is appointed by the sultan, who has absolute power and issues laws by decree. The sultan serves as the country's prime minister; heads the ministries of Defense, Foreign Affairs, and Finance; and is the governor of Oman's central bank.

Political parties are not permitted, and no meaningful organized political opposition exists. However, mechanisms exist for citizens to petition the government through local officials, and certain citizens are afforded limited opportunities to petition the sultan in direct meetings.

Although corruption has not been perceived to be a serious problem, the issue was an important factor in mobilizing protest in 2011. The legal code does not include freedom of information provisions. Oman was ranked 50 out of 183 countries surveyed in Transparency International's 2011 Corruption Perceptions Index.

Freedom of expression is limited, and criticism of the sultan is prohibited. The 2004 Private Radio and Television Companies Law allows for the establishment of private broadcast media outlets. The government permits private print publications, but many of these accept government subsidies, practice self-censorship, or face punishment for crossing political redlines. In August 2011, Oman's public prosecutor brought charges against Youssef al-Haj and Ibrahim Ma'mari of the newspaper *Al-Zaman* for allegations the former made in May about corruption in the Ministry of Justice. In September, both were convicted of "insulting" the Minister of Justice and sentenced to five months in prison. The judge also ordered Al-Zaman to be closed for one month. The men were released on bail pending an appeals hearing. In October, Oman further restricted freedom of the press and expression by vaguely outlawing discussion critical of state security, the military, or other government officials.

Omanis have access to the internet through the national telecommunications company, and the government censors politically sensitive and pornographic content. The sultan issued a decree in 2008 expanding government oversight and regulation of electronic communications, including communication on personal blogs. In April 2011, authorities blocked the website alhara.net, due to vague complaints from citizens that they had been unfairly criticized on the site.

Islam is the state religion. Non-Muslims have the right to worship, although they are banned from proselytizing. Non-Muslim religious organizations must register with the government. The Ministry of Awqaf (Religious Charitable Bequests) and Religious Affairs distributes standardized texts for mosque sermons and expects imams to stay within the outlines of these texts. The government restricts academic freedom by preventing the publication of material on politically sensitive topics.

The right to peaceful assembly within limits is provided for by the basic law. However, all public gatherings require official permission, and the government has the authority to prevent organized public meetings without any appeal process. During the ongoing protests in 2011, demonstrators carefully avoided calling for the downfall of the regime, and most protests remained peaceful. However, several turned violent, with authorities killing at least two people in separate incidents in February and April. In late February, demonstrators in the northern city of Sohar launched a sustained protest campaign calling for better jobs, improved wages, an end to state corruption, and political reforms. Throughout the spring and summer, authorities cracked down on the protests, detaining hundreds. Dozens convicted of inciting violence were sentenced to prison terms ranging from one month to five years, while hundreds of others were released, never charged, or pardoned. Sultan Qaboos addressed the protestors' grievances by replacing ten cabinet members and pledging sweeping financial reforms, including raising the minimum wage, bolstering the country's pension plan, taking measures to create 50,000 new jobs, and providing support for the unemployed.

The basic law allows the formation of nongovernmental organizations, but civic and associational life remains limited. The government has not permitted the establishment of independent human rights organizations and generally uses the registration and licensing process to block the formation of groups that are seen as a threat to stability.

Oman's 2003 labor law allows workers to select a committee to represent their interests but prevents them from organizing unions. Additional labor reforms enacted in 2006 brought a number of improvements, including protections for union activity, collective bargaining, and strikes. However, legal provisions covering migrant workers remain inadequate, and domestic servants are particularly vulnerable to abuse. Employers using child labor face increased penalties, including prison terms, under the law.

The judiciary is not independent and remains subordinate to the sultan and the Ministry of Justice. Sharia (Islamic law) is the source of all legislation, and Sharia Court Departments within the civil court system are responsible for family-law matters, such as divorce and inheritance. In less populated areas, tribal laws and customs are frequently used to adjudicate disputes. Although government authorities must obtain court orders to hold suspects in pretrial detention, they do not regularly follow these procedures. Prisons are not accessible to independent monitors, but former prisoners report overcrowding. The penal code contains vague provisions for offenses against national security, and such charges are prosecuted before the State Security Court, which usually holds proceedings that are closed to the public.

Omani law does not protect noncitizens from discrimination. Foreign workers risk deportation if they abandon their contracts without documentation releasing them from their previous employment agreement. Under these regulations, employers can effectively keep workers from switching jobs and hold them in conditions susceptible to exploitation.

Although the basic law prohibits discrimination on the basis of sex, women suffer from legal and social discrimination. Oman's personal status law, based on Sharia, favors the rights of men over those of women in marriage, divorce, inheritance, and child custody. According to official statistics, women constitute a very small percentage of the total labor force in Oman. Despite a 2008 antitrafficking law, Oman remains a destination and transit country for the trafficking of women and men.

↓ Pakistan

Political Rights: 4
Civil Liberties: 5
Status: Partly Free

Population: 176,940,000
Capital: Islamabad

Trend Arrow: Pakistan received a downward trend arrow due to greater self-censorship on the issue of blasphemy laws in the wake of the murder of Punjab governor Salman Taseer in January, as well as an increase in official attempts to censor internet-based content during the year.

Note: The numerical ratings and status listed above do not reflect conditions in Pakistani-controlled Kashmir, which is examined in a separate report.

Ten-Year Ratings Timeline For Year Under Review (Political Rights, Civil Liberties, Status)

2002	2003	2004	2005	2006	2007	2008	2009	2010	2011
6,5NF	6,5NF	6,5NF	6,5NF	6,5NF	6,5NF	4,5F	4,5PF	4,5PF	4,5PF

Overview: **In 2011, tensions between the civilian government, the military and intelligence agencies, and the judiciary—and attempts by all three groups to exert greater control over policy formulation—continued to threaten the government's stability and the consolidation of democracy in Pakistan. Societal discrimination and attacks against religious minorities and women, as well as weak rule of law and impunity, remained issues of concern. Journalists and human rights defenders came under increased threat during the year, particularly those who spoke out on Pakistan's blasphemy laws or abuses by security and intelligence agencies. Freedom of expression also suffered due to official attempts to censor online media content and greater self-censorship on sensitive issues. The army's campaigns against Islamist militants in the tribal areas led to a range of human rights abuses, displacement of civilians, and retaliatory terrorist attacks across the country, while violence in Balochistan and the city of Karachi worsened.**

Pakistan was created as a Muslim homeland during the partition of British India in 1947, and the military has directly or indirectly ruled the country for much of its independent history. As part of his effort to consolidate power, military dictator Mohammad Zia ul-Haq amended the constitution in 1985 to allow the president to dismiss elected governments. After Zia's death in 1988, successive civilian presidents cited corruption and abuse of power in sacking elected governments headed by prime ministers Benazir Bhutto of the Pakistan People's Party (PPP) in 1990 and 1996, and Nawaz Sharif of the Pakistan Muslim League (PML) in 1993.

Sharif, who returned to power in the 1997 elections, was deposed in a military coup after he attempted to fire the army chief, General Pervez Musharraf, in 1999. Musharraf appointed himself "chief executive" (and later president), declared a state of emergency, and suspended democratic institutions. The 2002 Legal Framework Order (LFO) gave Musharraf effective control over Parliament and changed the electoral rules to the detriment of opposition parties. The regime also openly promoted progovernment parties, such as the newly formed Pakistan Muslim League Quaid-i-Azam (PML-Q), which captured the largest share of seats in the 2002 parliamentary elections and led the new government.

While he managed to contain the secular opposition over the next several years, Musharraf was less willing to rein in radical Islamist groups, with which the military traditionally had a close relationship. These groups gradually extended their influence from outlying regions like the Federally Administered Tribal Areas (FATA) to major urban centers, carrying out attacks on both military and civilian targets.

Tensions between Musharraf and the increasingly activist judiciary came to a head in 2007 when he suspended Iftikhar Chaudhry, the chief justice of the Supreme Court, sparking mass protests by lawyers and wider political unrest. When the court attempted to rule on the validity of Musharraf's victory in the October presidential election, he again took preemptive action and imposed martial law on November 3, suspending the constitution, replacing much of the higher judiciary, and arresting more than 6,000 civil society activists, political leaders, and lawyers. The state of emergency was lifted in mid-December and an amended version of the constitution was restored, but some restrictions on the press and freedom of assembly remained in place, as did the emasculated judiciary. Following the December 27 assassination of former prime minister Bhutto, parliamentary elections planned for early January 2008 were postponed until February, and Bhutto's widower, Asif Ali Zardari, assumed de facto leadership of the PPP.

The PPP led the February voting with 97 out of 272 directly elected seats in the National Assembly, followed by Nawaz Sharif's PML-N with 71. The ruling PML-Q was routed, taking only 42 seats, and the Muttahida Majlis-i-Amal (MMA), an alliance of Islamic parties, was also severely weakened. At the provincial level, the PML-N triumphed in its traditional stronghold of Punjab, the PPP dominated in Sindh, and the Awami National Party (ANP), a secular and ethnic Pashtun group, won the most seats in North-West Frontier Province (NWFP).

The PPP and PML-N initially agreed to share power in a coalition government. However, less than a week after Musharraf resigned as president in the face of impeachment efforts in August, the PML-N withdrew from the coalition, accusing the PPP of breaking a promise to immediately reinstate all of the ousted judges following Musharraf's exit. In September, Zardari won an indirect presidential election with 481 of the 702 votes cast; 368 national and provincial lawmakers abstained or boycotted the vote. In addition, the PPP and its allies gained a plurality in the March 2009 Senate elections. After Chaudhry was reinstated as chief justice, also in March, the Supreme Court began dismantling the actions taken by Musharraf, declaring them illegal and calling on Parliament to "regularize" them through ordinary legislation.

During 2010, tensions between the civilian government, the judiciary, and the military persisted. The government faced pressure from the military to replace Zardari, and the judiciary repeated its calls for Zardari's old corruption cases to be reopened. The military and intelligence agencies also attempted to undercut the government's policies and decision making. In a step intended to strengthen the democratic process, Parliament in April unanimously passed the 18th Amendment to the constitution, which among other provisions, rescinded the power of the president to dismiss Parliament and reduced executive power over appointments to the judiciary, the electoral commission, and the military leadership. At the end of the year, both houses of Parliament also passed the 19th Amendment, strengthening the role of the senior judiciary in making appointments to superior courts and thus neutralizing a potential source of conflict between the executive and judiciary.

The government's hold on power became tenuous in early 2011, following the withdrawal of the MQM from the ruling coalition, which left the PPP with a minority in Parliament. In addition, the government, the military, and the judiciary continued to grapple with one another for control over policy formulation. However, the PPP-led government remained in place at year's end, and predictions that it would be forced to call early elections failed to materialize, amid a careful balancing act by politicians to keep power in civilian hands.

Armed conflict between the military and Islamist militants affiliated with the Tehrik-i-Taliban Pakistan (TTP, or Pakistani Taliban) network persisted during 2011, as did regular missile attacks by U.S. drone aircraft that killed militant leaders but also caused civilian casualties and stoked resentment among many Pakistanis. Meanwhile, a range of Islamist militant groups continued to stage bombing and other attacks against official buildings, prominent politicians and military personnel, and religious ceremonies and places of worship. These included an audacious assault on the Mehran naval base in Karachi in May. While the number of killings overall declined from 2010, spreading radicalization led to high-profile murders such as that of Punjab governor Salman Taseer in January, contributing to a climate of fear and widespread self-censorship on sensitive issues such as blasphemy.

Pakistan's relations with the United States deteriorated during 2011 amid a series of high-profile scandals over matters including a January shooting involving a CIA contractor, a secret May raid by U.S. commandos that killed international terrorist leader Osama bin Laden in the northwestern city of Abbottabad, and a November NATO attack that killed two dozen Pakistani soldiers near the Afghan border. After the soldiers' deaths, Pakistan cut off shipments of NATO supplies to Afghanistan through its territory, and the dispute remained unresolved at year's end.

Political Rights and Civil Liberties:

Pakistan is not an electoral democracy. A civilian government and president were elected in 2008, ending years of military rule, but the military continues to exercise de facto control over many areas of government policy. The political environment is also troubled by corruption, partisan clashes, and Islamist militancy, among other problems.

The lower house of the bicameral Parliament is the 342-seat National Assembly, which has 272 directly elected members and additional seats reserved for women (60 seats) and non-Muslim minorities (10 seats), all with five-year terms. The upper house is the 100-seat Senate, most of whose members are elected by the four provincial assemblies for six-year terms, with half up for election every three years. The president is elected for a five-year term by an electoral college consisting of the national and provincial legislatures. The Constitution (18th Amendment) Act of 2010 rescinded the president's right (granted by the 2002 LFO) to unilaterally dismiss the prime minister and the national and provincial legislatures and to impose a provincial state of emergency. The president also lost the power to appoint the head of the army and the chief election commissioner. The reforms were intended to strengthen the premiership and Parliament.

The 2008 parliamentary elections were not completely free and fair. A European Union observer mission noted the abuse of state resources and media, inaccuracies in the voter rolls, and rigging of the vote tallies in some areas. Opposition party workers faced police harassment, and more than 100 people were killed in political violence during the campaign period. However, private media and civil society groups played a significant watchdog role, and despite the irregularities, the balloting led to an orderly rotation of power that reflected the will of the people. An amendment to the Election Law passed in April 2011 was designed to strengthen the independence of the Election Commission and improve procedures for voter registration while limiting the scope for rigging.

The institutional capacity and internal democratic structures of political parties—some of which are based more on personalities than ideologies or platforms—remain weak. Some political parties also have armed or militant wings, which raised concern in 2011 as turf battles among various factions worsened in Karachi.

A certain number of legislative seats are reserved for women and religious minorities at the national, provincial, and local levels. In some parts of the country, women have difficulty voting and running for office due to objections from social and religious conservatives, though women won an additional unreserved 16 National Assembly seats in the 2008 elections. At least 17 seats in the Senate are reserved for women, and religious minorities were allotted four seats in the Senate as part of the 18th Amendment. Members of the heterodox Ahmadiyya sect, who consider themselves Muslims but are deemed a non-Muslim minority by the constitution, largely boycotted the 2008 elections to protest this official designation.

The FATA are governed by the president through unelected civil servants. Elected councils set up in 2007 have not altered the established decision-making structures. In April 2011, President Asif Ali Zardari issued a decree that allowed political parties in the tribal areas and reformed several regressive aspects of the FATA justice system.

Pakistan's government operates with limited transparency and accountability, though this has improved with the resumption of civilian rule. The military has a stake in continuing to influence both commercial and political decision-making processes, in addition to its traditional dominance of foreign policy and security issues. Serving and retired officers have received top jobs in ministries, state-run corporations, and universities, and they enjoy a range of other privileges. Although several thousand active-duty officers were withdrawn from civilian posts in 2008, a tenth of all civilian jobs remain reserved for officers.

Corruption is pervasive at all levels of politics and the bureaucracy, and oversight mechanisms to ensure transparency remain weak. Hundreds of politicians, diplomats, and officials, including Zardari, were granted immunity in ongoing corruption cases under the 2007 National Reconciliation Ordinance (NRO). Though the Supreme Court revoked the NRO in December 2009 and upheld this decision in a November 2011 ruling, prosecution of reopened cases remains uneven and ineffective. The National Accountability Bureau (NAB), established in 1999 to combat corruption, has been criticized for failing to act on the judiciary's calls for it to reopen hundreds of cases. In late 2011, the opposition denounced Zardari's nomination of an admiral to the post of NAB chairman. Pakistan was ranked 134 out of 183 countries surveyed in Transparency International's 2011 Corruption Perceptions Index. Transparency International–Pakistan, under official pressure, decided not to produce its annual corruption survey in 2011; the organization also faced harassment and threats over its efforts to highlight an increase in corrupt practices under the Zardari administration. In general, Pakistan has an extremely low level of tax collection, as many of the country's wealthiest citizens, including members of Parliament, use legal loopholes to avoid paying taxes.

Pakistan's outspoken newspapers and private television stations present a diverse range of news and opinion. However, powerful figures, including military officials and members of the higher judiciary, attempt to silence critical reporting, and there is a high level of violence against journalists. The constitution and other laws authorize the government to curb speech on subjects including the armed forces, the judiciary, and religion. Blasphemy laws are occasionally used against the media, and since 2010 broadly defined contempt laws have increasingly been employed to restrict reporting on particular court cases or judges. The government in 2011 continued to engage in sporadic efforts to temporarily suspend certain broadcasts or programs under other media regulations or on an ad hoc basis surrounding sensitive events, such as the killing of Osama bin Laden.

According to the Committee to Protect Journalists, at least seven journalists were murdered because of their work in 2011, making Pakistan the world's deadliest country for members of the press. In late May, investigative reporter Syed Saleem Shahzad was abducted, tortured, and killed, allegedly by the military's powerful Directorate for Inter-Services Intelligence (ISI); Shahzad had previously received threats from the agency. Amid an outcry over his death, an official commission was established to investigate the murder, but had not released a report by year's end. Intimidation by the security forces—including physical attacks and arbitrary, incommunicado detention—continues to occur, as do harassment and attacks by Islamic fundamentalists and hired thugs working for feudal landlords or local politicians. A number of reporters covering the conflict between the military and Islamist militants in Khyber-Pakhtunkhwa (or KP, as NWFP was renamed in 2010) and the FATA were detained, threatened, expelled, or otherwise obstructed in 2011, by either government forces or militants. Conditions for journalists in Balochistan also deteriorated sharply.

While websites addressing sensitive subjects, particularly Balochi separatism, have routinely been blocked by the authorities, in 2010 the government moved more aggressively to block "blasphemous" material. This trend continued in 2011, affecting websites as well as mobile-telephone content. For example, a September 2011 decision by the Lahore High Court ordered officials to block access to a number of websites, including the U.S.-based social-networking site Facebook.

Pakistan is an Islamic republic, and there are numerous legal restrictions on religious freedom. Violations of blasphemy laws draw harsh sentences, including the death penalty, and injuring the "religious feelings" of individual citizens is prohibited. Incidents in which police take bribes to file false blasphemy charges against

Ahmadis, Christians, Hindus, and occasionally Muslims continue to occur, with several dozen cases reported each year. No executions on blasphemy charges have been carried out to date, but the charges alone can lead to years of imprisonment, ill-treatment in custody, and extralegal persecution by religious extremists. Aasia Bibi, a Christian woman sentenced to death for blasphemy in 2010, remained in jail throughout 2011 pending an appeal.

Religious hard-liners have argued that even advocacy of reforming the blasphemy laws constitutes an act of blasphemy. In January 2011, Punjab governor Salman Taseer was assassinated by his own bodyguard after he publicly defended Aasia Bibi and spoke out against abuse of the blasphemy laws. Shahbaz Bhatti, the minister for minorities affairs and a Christian, was murdered by Islamist extremists in March, also in response to his stance on the blasphemy laws. Others who shared the views of Taseer and Bhatti faced death threats and legal harassment, and many more were reluctant to denounce the murders or even attend memorial events, particularly as religious leaders and media commentators openly defended the killings. In September, the guard who murdered Taseer was sentenced to death, though the judge reportedly received death threats from both lawyers and Islamist groups and briefly left the country following the verdict.

The penal code severely restricts the religious practice of Ahmadis, who comprise a small percentage of the population, and they must effectively renounce their beliefs to vote or gain admission to educational institutions. Authorities occasionally confiscate or close Ahmadiyya publications and harass their staff, and dozens of Ahmadis faced criminal charges under blasphemy or other discriminatory laws during 2011.

Religious minorities also face unofficial economic and social discrimination, and they are occasionally subject to violence and harassment. In a growing trend, particularly in Sindh Province, Hindu girls are kidnapped, forcibly converted to Islam, and compelled to marry their kidnappers. Terrorist and other attacks on places of worship and religious gatherings occur frequently, leading to the deaths of dozens of people every year. There has been a notable upsurge in violence between members of the Sunni Muslim majority and the Shiite Muslim minority since 2009, with largely Shiite ethnic Hazaras in Balochistan facing particular threats during 2011. Recent waves of attacks on Christians have also been attributed to the spread of Sunni extremist ideology.

The government generally does not restrict academic freedom. However, the university cadres of political parties and Islamist groups intimidate students, teachers, and administrators; aim to impose "Islamic" moral codes by blocking certain types of classes or behavior; and try to influence university policies. In several cases noted during 2011, professors were reportedly attacked or murdered. Schools and female teachers, particularly in the FATA and KP, continue to face threats and attacks by Islamist militants.

The rights to freedom of assembly and association are selectively upheld. Authorities sometimes restrict public gatherings, disperse protests with excessive force, and use preventive detention to forestall planned demonstrations. However, such tactics were employed less in 2011 than in previous years.

Authorities generally tolerate the work of nongovernmental organizations (NGOs) and allow them to publish critical material. However, NGOs that focus on female education and empowerment, and female NGO staff in general, have faced threats, attacks, and a number of murders by radical Islamists, particularly in the FATA and KP. Citing security concerns, the government has at times prevented aid groups from operating in Balochistan, exacerbating the province's humanitarian situation, and access to KP and the FATA remains challenging. Working or commenting on issues concerning blasphemy or the intelligence services became more risky in 2011, for both local and international activists. Attacks on human rights defenders appeared to be on the rise. Pakistan is home to a large number of charitable or cultural organizations, such as the Jamaat-ud-Dawa (JD), that have links to Islamist militant groups.

An April 2010 constitutional amendment placed labor law and policy under the purview of the provinces. Provincial labor laws allow workers to form and join trade unions, but place restrictions on union membership, the right to strike, and collective bargaining, particular in industries deemed essential. Although protests and strikes occur regularly, many workers have been fired for union activity, and union leaders have faced harassment. An antiterrorism court sentenced six leaders from the Labour Qaumi Movement to a collective 490 years in prison in November 2011, after they attempted to organize strikes in 2010. Illegal bonded labor is widespread, though the authorities in 2011 continued efforts to combat the practice in the brick-kiln industry. Enforcement of child labor laws remains inadequate; recent surveys have indicated that there are at least 10 million child workers in Pakistan.

The judiciary consists of civil and criminal courts and a special Sharia (Islamic law) court for certain offenses. Lower courts remain plagued by corruption, intimidation, and a backlog of more than a million cases that results in lengthy pretrial detention. The 2009 National Judicial Policy aimed to tackle all three problems, and appears to have had some positive effects, with backlogs dramatically reduced in certain provinces.

Provisions of the 18th Amendment granted power over judicial appointments to a judicial commission rather than the president, and the 19th Amendment further strengthened the role of the chief justice and other senior judges in the commission and appointments process. However, tensions between the judiciary and the executive persisted in 2011. The Supreme Court continued to push for the revival of corruption cases against Zardari and engaged in activism in politically popular cases concerning blasphemy and economic policy. Observers voiced concern that the judiciary was becoming increasingly close to the army, supporting its agenda while trying to undermine the executive.

Other parts of the judicial system, such as the antiterrorism courts, operate with limited due process rights. The Sharia court enforces the 1979 Hudood Ordinances, which criminalize extramarital sex and several alcohol, gambling, and property offenses. They provide for Koranic punishments, including death by stoning for adultery, as well as jail terms and fines. In part because of strict evidentiary standards, authorities have never carried out the Koranic punishments. The justice system in the FATA is governed by the Frontier Crimes Regulation, which allows collective punishment for individual crimes and preventive detention of up to three years. It also authorizes tribal leaders to administer justice according to Sharia and tribal custom. In designated parts of the Provincially Administered Tribal Areas and KP, Sharia is imposed under the 2009 Nizam-e-Adl regulation, and judges are assisted by Islamic scholars.

Feudal landlords and tribal elders throughout Pakistan adjudicate some disputes and impose punishments—including the death penalty and the forced exchange of brides between tribes—in unsanctioned parallel courts called jirgas. Human rights groups have noted that such jirgas impose hundreds of death sentences each year, the majority on women. Militants in the tribal areas and parts of KP have reportedly set up their own courts, enforcing a strict interpretation of Islamic law and dispensing harsh penalties with little regard for due process.

Police and other security services routinely engage in excessive force, torture, extortion, arbitrary detention, rape of female detainees, and extrajudicial killings. Outrage over extrajudicial executions resurfaced in June 2011, when the killing of an unarmed student by paramilitary police was captured on video in Karachi. Conditions in the overcrowded prisons are extremely poor, and case backlogs mean that the majority of inmates are awaiting trial. Feudal landlords, tribal groups, and some militant groups operate private jails where detainees are regularly maltreated. Progress on creating an official human rights body empowered to investigate cases and redress grievances has been slow, and while a number of cases are investigated and some prosecutions do occur, impunity for human rights abuses remains the norm.

In 2010 the Human Rights Commission of Pakistan (HRCP)—an NGO—estimated that at least 1,100 people were being illegally detained by state agencies, while the Interior Ministry acknowledged 965 cases of disappearance; other estimates range from 200 to 7,000 cases. Some victims were suspected of links to radical Islamist groups, but such detentions have also affected Balochi and Sindhi nationalists, journalists, researchers, and social workers. The ISI, which operates largely outside the control of civilian leaders and the courts, has faced intermittent pressure from the Supreme Court to end the practice of secret detentions, but the court's ability to resolve cases has been limited, according to a September 2011 Amnesty International report. While official commissions of inquiry established by the government in March 2010 and March 2011 to trace individual cases have had some success, new cases continued to be reported in 2011, particularly in Balochistan.

Tens of thousands of armed militants belonging to radical Sunni Islamist groups have varying agendas and carry out terrorist attacks against foreign, government, and religious minority targets, killing hundreds of civilians each year. Sunni and Shiite groups engage in tit-for-tat sectarian violence, mostly bomb attacks against places of worship and religious gatherings. The New Delhi–based South Asia Terrorism Portal (SATP) reported that 203 people were killed and 297 were injured in sectarian violence in 2011, a substantial decrease from the previous year.

The military's campaigns against Islamist fighters in the tribal areas since 2002 have been accompanied by human rights abuses, and missile strikes attributed to U.S. drone aircraft have reportedly killed or injured civilians along with their intended targets. In total, more than 550 people were killed by alleged drone attacks in 2011. The authorities are sponsoring tribal militias, or lashkars, to help control the FATA, creating yet another unaccountable armed force. Islamist militants' expanding influence over territory in KP and the FATA has led to severe practical restrictions on local inhabitants' dress, social behavior, educational opportunities, and legal rights. The militant groups also target political leaders (particularly from the ANP), tribal elders, teachers, and aid workers in their quest for control over local populations. In January 2011, militants killed a female police officer and several members of her family; she had received threats urging her to quit her profession. On a positive note, many of the internally displaced civilians in KP returned to their homes in 2011, although hundreds of thousands remained displaced in the FATA. The SATP reported that 6,303 people were killed nationwide in terrorist- or insurgent-related violence in 2011, including 2,738 civilians, 765 security force personnel, and 2,800 militants, an overall decrease from the previous year but an increase in the number of civilians affected.

A simmering insurgency continued in Balochistan in 2011, with ethnic Balochi activists demanding either enhanced political autonomy or outright independence as well as more local control over the province's natural resources. Armed militants carried out a growing number of attacks on infrastructure, security forces, and non-Balochi teachers and educational institutions during the year. The army's counterinsurgency operations have led to increasing human rights violations and the displacement of civilians. Thousands of activists, political leaders, and other locals with suspected separatist sympathies have been detained, according to the International Crisis Group, with scores killed in apparent extrajudicial executions. Sunni militants, seen to operate under the protection of the security forces, carried out a campaign against mostly ethnic Hazara Shiites in Balochistan, killing dozens of Hazaras in a series of targeted attacks during the year.

Ethnic violence in Karachi escalated in 2011, killing more than 1,000 people, mostly ordinary civilians. The turf battles are exacerbated by the fact that each faction has the support of a political party, including the traditionally dominant Muttahida Qaumi Movement (MQM), which represents refugees from India who settled in Karachi in 1947; the ANP, representing ethnic Pashtun migrants from other areas of Pakistan; and the PPP, which is allied with Balochi gangs. The criminal gangs that carry out much of the violence also regularly extort money from businesses in Karachi, a crucial economic hub.

Pakistan hosts approximately 1.7 million registered Afghan refugees and more than a million undocumented Afghans, with the majority living in urban areas rather than refugee settlements on the border. They face societal and official discrimination as well as economic exploitation, since even registered refugees are not allowed to work legally.

Traditional norms, discriminatory laws, and weak policing contribute to a high incidence of rape, domestic abuse, and other forms of violence—including acid attacks—against women. According to the HRCP, up to 80 percent of women are victims of such abuse during their lifetimes. Female victims of sexual crimes are often pressured by police not to file charges, and they are sometimes urged by their families to commit suicide. Gang rapes sanctioned by village councils to punish the targeted woman's relatives continue to be reported, even though perpetrators in some cases have received harsh sentences. In April 2011, the Supreme Court upheld the acquittals of five of the six accused in the 2002 gang rape of Mukhtar Mai, whose case garnered international attention. The 2006 Women's Protection Act (WPA) requires judges to try rape cases under criminal law rather than Sharia. However, extramarital sex is still criminalized, and spousal rape is not recognized as a crime. In late 2010, a Federal Shariat Court decision declared four provisions of the WPA to be unconstitutional; an appeal of the ruling by a consortium of women's rights groups was pending before the Supreme Court at the end of 2011.

According to the HRCP, at least 943 women were killed by family members in so-called honor killings in 2011, a significant increase from the previous year, but many such crimes may go unreported. Activists have cast doubt on the authorities' willingness to enforce a 2005 law that introduced stiffer sentences and the possibility of the death penalty for honor killings. Illegal forms of child and forced marriage remain problems. Most interfaith marriages are considered illegal, and the children of such unions would be illegitimate.

Pakistani inheritance law discriminates against women, who also face unofficial discrimination in educational and employment opportunities. Two laws were enacted in 2010 to criminalize sexual harassment in the workplace and establish related codes of conduct and mechanisms for complaints. The trafficking of women and children remains a serious concern, with female victims used for forced labor or sexual exploitation.

Societal discrimination against gay men and lesbians is pervasive, and most individuals do not identify themselves as such openly. In 2009 the Supreme Court ordered that *hijras* (a term covering transvestites, hermaphrodites, and eunuchs) be considered equal citizens and allowed to classify themselves as a distinct gender on national identity cards.

Palau

Political Rights: 1
Civil Liberties: 1
Status: Free

Population: 20,600
Capital: Melekeok

Ten-Year Ratings Timeline For Year Under Review (Political Rights, Civil Liberties, Status)

2002	2003	2004	2005	2006	2007	2008	2009	2010	2011
1,2F	1,1F	1,1F	1,1F	1,1F	1,1F	1,1F	1,1F	1,1F	1,1F

Overview: **In 2011, President Johnson Toribiong appointed a new special prosecutor to investigate white-collar crime as well as a new public auditor, though neither appointment had been approved by the legislature by year's end. Meanwhile, a fire at a power plant in November led to power outages, rationing, and the declaration of a state of emergency.**

The United States administered Palau, which consists of 8 main islands and more than 250 smaller islands, as a UN Trust Territory from 1947 until 1981, when it became a self-governing territory. Palau gained full independence in 1994 under a Compact of Free Association with the United States; the compact granted Palau $442 million in U.S. economic aid between 1994 and 2009 and allowed Palauan citizens to reside, work, study, and access federal government programs in the United States in exchange for U.S. military access to the archipelago until 2044. A new financial agreement signed in September 2010 under the compact promises more than $250 million in total assistance through 2024, though the U.S. Congress had not ratified the deal by the end of 2011. Development assistance from Taiwan and other donors is a significant source of revenue for Palau.

Johnson Toribiong was elected president in November 2008. Parliamentary elections were held the same month, with all candidates running as independents.

In February 2011, the Supreme Court struck down a law that had been in effect since June 2010 that required all foreign nationals—except diplomats, their dependents, and tourists—to register with the state within their first seven days of arrival and pay a registration fee of $25. The government had said the measure was necessary to help fight illegal immigration and that the fee was required to cover administrative expenses.

In June, voters rejected a proposal to legalize casino gambling. The referendum was held in accordance with a law signed by Toribiong in December 2010 that would have created a casino gaming commissioner had the referendum passed, and barred the legislature from reconsidering the issue in the event of the referendum's failure.

A power plant fire in November 2011 prompted the government to declare a state of emergency for two weeks that month to ration electricity. Power shortages lasted through the end of the year, and rationing took place throughout the islands; hospitals, the sewage system, schools, and public services were all affected. The incident demonstrated the vulnerability of the nation's infrastructure.

Political Rights and Civil Liberties: Palau is an electoral democracy. The bicameral legislature, the Olbiil Era Kelulau, consists of the 9-member Senate and the 16-member House of Delegates. Legislators are elected to four-year terms by popular vote, as are the president and vice president. The president can serve only two consecutive terms. Palau is organized into 16 states. Each is headed by a governor and has a seat in the House of Delegates. Every state is also allowed its own constitutional convention and to elect a legislature and head of state.

There are no political parties, though no laws prevent their formation. The current system of loose political alliances that can quickly form and dismantle has had a destabilizing effect on governance.

Official corruption and abuse are serious problems, with several high-ranking public officials having faced charges in recent years. Although anti-money-laundering measures were introduced in 2007, evaluations have found significant deficiencies in due diligence, record keeping, and monitoring, and the attorney general's office generally lacks the resources to oversee implementation of these measures. As part of Palau's continuing effort to improve accountability and continue receipt of U.S. assistance, in January 2011, President Johnson Toribiong named a new special prosecutor to investigate white-collar crime and wrongdoing by government officials. In December, he appointed a public auditor, a position that had been empty for six years. Neither appointee had been confirmed by the legislature by year's end.

Freedoms of speech and the press are respected. There are several print publications, five privately owned radio stations, and one privately owned television station. Cable television rebroadcasts U.S. and other foreign programs. The government does not impede internet access, but high costs and a lack of connectivity outside the main islands limit diffusion. Palau is seeking assistance from multilateral development banks to finance an underwater cable that would expand internet access.

Citizens of Palau enjoy freedom of religion. Although religious organizations are required to register with the government, applications have never been denied. There have been no reports of restrictions on academic freedom, and the government provides well-funded basic education for all.

Freedoms of assembly and association are respected. Many nongovernmental groups represent youth, health, and women's issues. Workers can freely organize unions and bargain collectively, though the economy is largely based on subsistence agriculture and is heavily dependent on U.S. aid, as well as rent payments and remittances from Palauans working overseas.

The judiciary is independent, and trials are generally fair. A 300-member police and first-response force maintains internal order. Palau has no military. There have been no reports of prisoner abuse, though overcrowding is a problem in the country's only prison.

Foreign workers account for about one-third of the population and 75 percent of the workforce. There have been reports of discrimination against and abuse of foreign workers, who cannot legally change employers once they arrive in Palau. In response to social tensions and a slower economy, the government in 2009 decided to limit the total number of foreign workers in the country at any time to 6,000.

Women are highly regarded in this matrilineal society; land rights and familial descent are traced through women. Many women are active in traditional and modern economic sectors and in politics, though there are no women in the current legislature. The number of domestic violence and child abuse cases is small. Sexual harassment and rape, including spousal rape, are illegal. The U.S. State Department reports that Palau is a destination for women trafficked for prostitution. In October 2011, Palau pledged to end discrimination against homosexuals following a UN audit of human rights in the island state.

Panama

Political Rights: 1
Civil Liberties: 2
Status: Free

Population: 3,571,000
Capital: Panama City

Ten-Year Ratings Timeline For Year Under Review (Political Rights, Civil Liberties, Status)

2002	2003	2004	2005	2006	2007	2008	2009	2010	2011
1,2F	1,2F	1,2F	1,2F	1,2F	1,2F	1,2F	1,2F	1,2F	1,2F

Overview: **The governing Alliance for Change coalition collapsed in September 2011 when the Panameñista Party withdrew in protest over President Ricardo Martinelli's plan to hold a referendum on electoral reforms that could allow him to run for a second consecutive term. Juan Carlos Varela, head of the Panameñista Party, was subsequently dismissed from his position as foreign minister. Freedom of the press continued to be infringed upon in 2011.**

Panama was part of Colombia until 1903, when a U.S.-supported revolt resulted in the proclamation of an independent republic. A period of weak civilian rule ended with a 1968 military coup that brought General Omar Torrijos to power. After signing the 1977 Panama Canal Treaty with the United States, under which the canal was gradually transferred to Panamanian control by 1999, Torrijos promised democratization.

After Torrijos's death in 1981, General Manuel Noriega emerged as Panamanian Defense Force (PDF) chief. He rigged the 1984 elections to bring the Democratic Revolutionary Party (PRD), then the PDF's political arm, to power. The Democratic Alliance of Civic Opposition (ADOC) won the 1989 elections, but Noriega annulled the vote and declared himself head of state. He was removed during a U.S. military invasion later that year, and ADOC's Guillermo Endara became president. Both the PRD and the Arnulfista Party won elections in the 1990s. Presidential and legislative elections in 2004 returned the PRD to power, with Martín Torrijos, son of the former strongman, winning the presidency.

In the 2009 elections, Ricardo Martinelli of the center-right, business-oriented Democratic Change (CD) party won the presidency as part of the Alliance for Change coalition with the Panameñista Party (PP), capturing 60 percent of the vote. Balbina Herrera of the PRD, who had served as housing minister under the outgoing administration, placed second with 38 percent. The PRD won 26 of 71 congressional seats, followed by the PP with 22 seats, the CD with 14 seats, and smaller parties and independents each taking fewer than 5 seats.

Martinelli made several controversial decisions in 2010, including the passage of Law 30, which weakened labor unions, relaxed environmental laws, and reduced penalties for police officers who break the law while on duty. In October, Martinelli agreed to repeal the controversial measures contained in the original legislation following public protests.

The CD's congressional representation increased from 17 to 35 members by the end of 2011 due to changes in party affiliation by several deputies. The CD's alliance with the PP collapsed in August 2011, when Martinelli announced plans to hold a referendum on proposed electoral reforms, including abolishing the requirement that presidents may not seek consecutive terms in office. The PP's opposition to the proposal also led to Martinelli dismissing Juan Carlos Varela—the president of the PP and the country's vice president—as foreign minister. The finance minister and several other PP ministers, who had been widely credited with Panama's economic growth, tendered their resignations shortly thereafter. Martinelli's approval ratings declined from 64 percent in May to 48 percent in November. Proposals to reform the constitution were continuing at year's end.

Political Rights and Civil Liberties:

Panama is an electoral democracy. The 2009 national elections were considered free and fair by international observers. The president and deputies of the 71-seat unicameral National Assembly are elected by popular vote for five-year terms. Presidents may not seek consecutive terms and must wait two terms before running again.

Anonymous campaign contributions were banned in 1999 in an effort to stem the infiltration of drug money into the political process. Nevertheless, corruption remains widespread, and electoral reforms have been criticized for failing to improve the transparency of campaign financing. Panama and the UN Office on Drugs and Crime signed an agreement in June 2011 to establish a regional anticorruption academy. After serving 20 years in a U.S. jail for drug trafficking, racketeering, and money laundering, former dictator Manuel Noriega was extradited to France in April 2010 to complete a seven-year prison term on money laundering charges. However, in December 2011, France extradited Noriega to Panama to serve a 20-year sentence related to human rights violations. Panama was ranked 86 out of 183 countries surveyed in Transparency International's 2011 Corruption Perceptions Index.

The country's media outlets are privately owned, with the exceptions of the state-owned television network and a network operated by the Roman Catholic Church. However, media ownership is generally concentrated among relatives and associates of former president Ernesto Pérez Balladares (1994–99) of the PRD. Panama maintains a harsh legal environment for journalists. Ebrahim Asvat, president of *El Siglo* and *La Estrella* newspapers, resigned in January 2011 after President Ricardo Martinelli allegedly pressured the papers' owners to have him removed. The legislature considered a bill to make it illegal to criticize the country's president and other top officials, but it abandoned the proposal in January amid international and national pressure. Darío Fernández Jaén, owner of radio station Radio Mi Favorita and an outspoken critic of Martinelli, was murdered in November; one of the suspects arrested allegedly confessed to being hired to commit the crime. Internet access is unrestricted.

Freedom of religion is respected, and academic freedom is generally honored.

Freedom of assembly is recognized, and nongovernmental organizations are free to operate. Although only about 10 percent of the labor force is organized, unions are cohesive and powerful. In July 2010, opposition to Law 30 erupted into violence during a strike led by 5,000 banana plantation workers in Bocas del Toro. After the demonstration was violently suppressed by security forces, the Inter-American Commission on Human Rights condemned the violence and expressed concern over the government's restrictions on freedom of association. That same month, authorities violently dispersed a similar protest organized by Panama Canal construction workers, which resulted in the arrest of several union leaders. In March 2011, public protests forced the government to repeal Law 8, which had imposed controversial reforms to the Mining Code; this was regarded as a victory for environmental and indigenous groups.

The judicial system remains overburdened, inefficient, politicized, and prone to corruption. Criminal code reforms that took effect in 2008 increased sentences for a number of offenses. The prison system is marked by violent disturbances in decrepit, overcrowded facilities. As of August 2011, the prison system held 13,069 prisoners in a system designed to hold 7,342. In January, juvenile offenders at a prison in Tocumen rioted over a lack of clean drinking water. Several young men were badly injured, five of them fatally.

The police and other security forces are poorly disciplined and corrupt. Security decrees issued by the Torrijos government in 2008 included the creation of a national aero-naval service, a border service, a council for public security and national defense, and a national intelligence service. Opponents warned of a return to Panama's military past and said the changes lacked safeguards against abuse of power. Panama's growing importance as a regional transport center makes it appealing to drug traffickers and money launderers. The quantity of cocaine seizures declined from 50 metric tons in 2010 to 34 metric tons in 2011.

Refugees from Colombia have faced difficulty obtaining work permits and other forms of legal recognition. The Martinelli administration had suggested measures to normalize the status of thousands of undocumented Colombians living in Panama without official refugee status, but minimal progress had been made on these measures. New immigration rules that took effect in 2008 tightened controls on foreigners, but other legislation grants recognized refugees who have lived in Panama for more than 10 years the right to apply for permanent residency. Of the approximately 2,500 refugee and asylum seekers living in Panama at the end of 2010, 41 were granted refugee status in 2011.

Discrimination against darker-skinned Panamanians is widespread. The country's Asian, Middle Eastern, and indigenous populations are similarly singled out. Indigenous communities enjoy a degree of autonomy and self-government, but some 90 percent of the indigenous population lives in extreme poverty. Since 1993, indigenous groups have protested the encroachment of illegal settlers on their lands and government delays in formal land demarcations. In July 2011, authorities used tear gas to break up a protest by the Ngabe-Bugle indigenous people against mining and hydroelectric projects. The indigenous Embera-Wounaan community continued to protest illegal settlements on its land in 2011, leading to violent confrontations in August, but government negotiations eventually defused tensions.

Violence against women and children is widespread and common. Panama is a source, destination, and transit country for human trafficking. The government has worked with the International Labour Organization on information campaigns addressing the issue, and it has created a special unit to investigate cases of trafficking for the purpose of prostitution. However, law enforcement is weak, the penal code does not prohibit trafficking for forced labor, and the government provides inadequate assistance to victims.

Papua New Guinea

Political Rights: 4
Civil Liberties: 3
Status: Partly Free

Population: 6,888,000
Capital: Port Moresby

Ten-Year Ratings Timeline For Year Under Review (Political Rights, Civil Liberties, Status)

2002	2003	2004	2005	2006	2007	2008	2009	2010	2011
2,3F	3,3F	3,3PF	3,3PF	3,3PF	3,3PF	4,3PF	4,3PF	4,3PF	4,3PF

Overview: **In August 2011, Peter O'Neill became prime minister after Michael Somare stepped down amid corruption charges and health problems. In October, Somare claimed that he had never formally left office. Although the Supreme Court in December ruled that O'Neill's election was unconstitutional and Somare should be reinstated, the Speaker of Parliament continued to recognize O'Neill as prime minister, in defiance of the court's ruling.**

Papua New Guinea (PNG) gained independence from Australia in 1975. In 1988 miners and landowners on Bougainville Island began guerrilla attacks on a major Australian-owned copper mine, and by 1990, the islanders' demands for compensation and profit-sharing became a low-grade secessionist war. Australia and New Zealand brokered a ceasefire in 1998 and a peace treaty in 2001, which called for elections for an autonomous Bougainville government (ABG) and a referendum on independence in 10 to 15 years. The first election for an ABG was held in May and June 2005.

Prime Minister Michael Somare's ruling National Alliance (NA) won 27 of the 109 Parliament seats in July 2007 elections, and the 71-year-old Somare was chosen for a second five-year term. The elections were marred by many reports of fraud, lost ballots, and attacks on journalists and candidates.

Natural-resource exploitation, including mining and logging, provide the bulk of government revenue, though strong economic growth has been overshadowed by increasing levels of violence and poverty, while public health, education, and infrastructure has also suffered. Gun battles, youth violence, clan wars, sorcery-related violence, rape and domestic abuse are not uncommon. In October 2011, a lawmaker was formally charged with the 2010 rape of a 14-year old girl. In November, two days of youth rioting and ethnic violence in Lae, PNG's second biggest city, left more than a thousand people homeless.

In December 2010, Somare stepped down to face a leadership tribunal for allegedly failing to file complete financial statements between 1993 and 2004. Although legally he remained prime minister, he appointed Deputy Prime Minister Sam Abal as acting prime minister for the duration of the investigation. In March 2011, Somare was found guilty on 13 charges of misconduct; he was sentenced to two weeks of suspension from office without pay, beginning on April 4, but was allowed to keep his position as a member of Parliament. In mid-April, Somare traveled to Singapore to seek medical treatment, and his family in late June announced his retirement as prime minister due to poor health. Abal attempted to stay in power, but faced internal party challenges. On August 2, Parliament elected Peter O'Neill prime minister. In October, Somare claimed that he had never formally left office and sued to regain his position. On December 11, the Supreme Court ruled that O'Neill's election by Parliament had been unconstitutional, and Somare should be reinstated. However, the Speaker of Parliament continued to recognize O'Neill as prime minister at year's end, in defiance of the court's ruling. In an attempt to prevent Somare from continuing his court challenge or competing in future elections, Parliament voted 68 to 3 on December 21 to restrict anyone aged 72 or older from becoming or remaining prime minister; the law was made retroactive to August 1, 2011.

Political Rights and Civil Liberties:

PNG is an electoral democracy. Voters elect a unicameral, 109-member National Parliament to serve five-year terms. A limited preferential voting system allows voters to choose up to three preferred candidates on their ballots. The prime minister, the leader of the majority party or coalition, is formally appointed by the governor general, who represents Britain's Queen Elizabeth II as head of state.

Major parties include the NA, the United Resources Party, the Papua New Guinea Party, and the People's Progressive Party. Political loyalties are driven more by tribal, linguistic, geographic, and personal ties than party affiliation. Many candidates run as independents and align with parties after they are elected.

Official abuse and corruption are serious problems. In April 2010, in response to allegations of corruption involving lawmakers and senior officials, legislators voted unanimously to grant themselves immunity from any charges brought by the ombudsman's office. PNG's high commissioner to Australia reported in March 2011 that half of the $450 million in annual Australian assistance is lost to systemic fraud. That same month, the Public Accounts Committee found that only 10 of about 1,140 government entities maintain records sufficient to account for their expenditures.

Prime Minister Peter O'Neill, who has pledged to fight corruption, created an elite anticorruption investigative team in August 2011 with a budget that stood at $4.2 million by year's end. One of its first tasks was to investigate the alleged misappropriation of $849 million in public funds within the National Planning and Monitoring Department. The government also dismissed the director of the Independent Public Business Corporation in August for making unapproved and illegal payments and investments. Transparency International's 2011 Corruption Perceptions Index ranked PNG 154 out of 183 countries surveyed.

Freedom of speech is generally respected, and the media provide independent coverage of controversial issues such as alleged police abuse, official corruption, and opposition views. However, the government and politicians have occasionally used media laws and libel and defamation lawsuits to limit critical reporting. There are several private and state-owned local and national radio stations and television stations. Internet use is growing, but cost and lack of infrastructure limits its spread outside urban centers.

The government upholds freedom of religion. Academic freedom is generally respected, but the government does not always tolerate criticism.

The constitution provides for freedoms of assembly and association, and the government generally observes these rights in practice. Many civil society groups provide social services and advocate for women's rights, the environment and other causes. The government recognizes workers' rights to strike, organize, and engage in collective bargaining. Marches and demonstrations require 14 days' notice and police approval.

The judiciary is independent. The legal system is based on English common law. The Supreme Court is the final court of appeal and has jurisdiction on constitutional matters. Laypeople sit on village courts to adjudicate minor offenses under customary and statutory law. Suspects often suffer lengthy detentions and trial delays because of a shortage of trained judicial personnel.

Law enforcement officials have been accused of corruption, unlawful killings, extortion, rape, theft, the sale of firearms, and the use of excessive force in the arrest and interrogation of suspects. The correctional service is understaffed, prison conditions are poor, and prisoners have reported torture while in detention. In April 2011, two police officers were charged with the murder of a detainee; the cases were pending at year's end. Prison breaks are frequent, and incidents of street and violent crimes continued to increase in 2011. In May, 91 violent prisoners escaped with high-power weapons from the jail armory in the Southern Highlands. Weak governance and law enforcement have allegedly made PNG a base for organized Asian criminal groups.

Native tribal feuds over land, titles, religious beliefs, and perceived insults frequently lead to violence and deaths. Inadequate law enforcement and the increased availability of guns have exacerbated the problem.

Discrimination and violence against women and children are widespread. Although domestic violence is punishable by law, prosecutions are rare, as police commonly treat it as a private matter, and family pressure and fear of reprisal discourage victims from pressing charges. Women are frequently barred from voting by their husbands. Only one woman sits in Parliament. In December 2011, lawmakers adopted constitutional amendments that would create 22 seats reserved for women in Parliament. However, two pieces of enabling legislation defining the size of the new electorate, which are required for the amendment to go into effect in time for the 2012 elections, had not been passed by year's end. In October 2011, the government rejected a call by the United Nations to decriminalize homosexuality.

Paraguay

Political Rights: 3
Civil Liberties: 3
Status: Partly Free

Population: 6,568,300
Capital: Asuncion

Ten-Year Ratings Timeline For Year Under Review (Political Rights, Civil Liberties, Status)

2002	2003	2004	2005	2006	2007	2008	2009	2010	2011
4,3PF	3,3PF	3,3PF	3,3PF	3,3PF	3,3PF	3,3PF	3,3PF	3,3PF	3,3PF

Overview: **President Fernando Lugo struggled to advance reforms in 2011 due to divisions within his Patriotic Alliance for Change coalition and an opposition-controlled Congress. The passage of the long-awaited Itaipú agreement with Brazil in September fulfilled a campaign promise for the president, but disagreement regarding the use of increased revenue shadowed the political victory. Continued violence by the Paraguayan People's Army, a radical socialist guerrilla group, prompted the deployment of troops to northern Concepción state.**

Paraguay, which achieved independence from Spain in 1811, was wracked by a series of crises following the 1989 ouster of authoritarian president Alfredo Stroessner of the right-wing Colorado Party after 35 years in power. The fragility of the country's emerging democratic institutions resulted in nearly 15 years of popular uprisings, military mutinies, antigovernment demonstrations, bitter political rivalries, and continued rule by the Colorados.

Senate leader Luis González Macchi assumed the presidency in 1999 after the incumbent fled the country amid murder charges. In 2002, González Macchi offered to leave office early to avoid pending impeachment hearings against him for embezzlement. Former education minister Nicanor Duarte Frutos of the Colorado Party emerged victorious in the 2003 national elections. After taking office, Duarte moved to take control of the tax, port, and customs authorities to combat rampant tax evasion and smuggling.

Fernando Lugo, leader of the Patriotic Alliance for Change (APC) coalition—a heterogeneous grouping of 20 parties, including Christian Democrats, socialists, communists, and peasant organizations—was elected president in April 2008. Lugo's election reflected widespread disappointment in the Colorado Party and also raised expectations that the standard of living for Paraguay's poor majority would improve. Reform necessary to address Paraguay's highly skewed land distribution remains one of the administration's principal goals. In the UN Development Programme's 2011 Human Development Report, Paraguay was ranked 107 out of 179 countries—worse than nearby Ecuador, Peru, and Brazil. Prospects for Lugo's reforms were dealt a blow in July 2009 when the coalition's largest member—the conservative Authentic Liberal Radical Party (PLRA)—dropped out, leaving the Colorados, who strongly oppose Lugo's reformist agenda, in control of the legislature.

Lugo's party experienced considerable losses in the November 2010 municipal elections; the Colorado Party won back 132 of Paraguay's 238 municipalities, bolstering its prospects for the 2013 general election.

The rise of the Paraguayan People's Army (EPP)—an armed leftist guerrilla group—forced Lugo to declare a month-long state of emergency in half of the country in April 2010. The administration mobilized 3,300 police and troops to combat the group. After a lull, the group reemerged in January 2011 with a series of bombings across the country; one of the targets was the Asunción headquarters of a privately owned television station. The federal government responded by increasing cash rewards for information leading to the apprehension of high-level combatants. The EPP killed two policemen in the northern state of Concepción in September, and Congress voted in October to send armored troops to the region to support police forces. Several senior EPP members have been captured, but the group continued to function as of the end of 2011.

In July 2011, the opposition-controlled Congress rejected a constitutional reform that would have let Lugo run for reelection in 2013. Lugo's increasingly hostile relationship with Vice President Federico Franco, a political rival, further undermined any semblance of a unified government in 2011. There were also tensions between the president and the military; since the start of his presidency, Lugo has initiated three major purges of military leadership, with the third occurring in mid-2011.

In September 2011, Congress ratified a 2009 agreement with Brazil that settled a decades-long dispute over payments for energy produced by the Itaipú hydroelectric dam. As a result, Paraguay's income from the dam will triple. The Lugo government had promised that increased revenue would finance land reform, but this looked unlikely to pass the Colorado-dominated Congress.

Lugo has maintained a conventional economic program. Supportive macroeconomic policies contributed to robust economic growth in 2011. However, the economy suffered a blow due to an outbreak of foot-and-mouth disease in mid-September 2011, which forced farmers to kill over 800 cattle and to temporarily halt all beef exports.

Political Rights and Civil Liberties: Paraguay is an electoral democracy. The 2008 national elections were considered to be free and fair. The 1992 constitution provides for a president, a vice president, and a bicameral Congress consisting of a 45-member Senate and an 80-member Chamber of Deputies, all elected for five-year terms. The president is elected by a simple majority vote to a five-year term, and reelection is prohibited. The constitution bans the active-duty military from engaging in politics.

Before President Fernando Lugo and the APC came to power in 2008, the Colorado Party had ruled Paraguay for over 60 years. The other major political groupings include the PLRA, the Beloved Fatherland Party, the National Union of Ethical Citizens, and the National Agreement Party.

Corruption cases languish for years in the courts without resolution, and corruption often goes unpunished, as judges favor the powerful and wealthy. The Lugo administration pledged to increase overall transparency in government and reduce corruption, specifically in the judiciary. However, the president has been unable to depoliticize Paraguay's corrupt Supreme Court. Paraguay was ranked 154 out of 183 countries surveyed in Transparency International's 2011 Corruption Perceptions Index, lagging behind all other countries in the Americas save Venezuela and Haiti.

The constitution provides for freedoms of expression and the press, and the government generally respects these rights in practice. There are a number of private television and radio stations and independent newspapers, but only one state-owned media outlet, Radio Nacional, which has a limited audience. In 2011, journalists investigating corruption, organized crime, or drug trafficking continued to suffer threats and violent attacks. Direct pressure by criminal groups and corrupt authorities led to self-censorship by journalists, especially in remote border areas. The government does not restrict use of the internet, nor does it censor its content.

The government generally respects freedom of religion. All religious groups are required to register with the Ministry of Education and Culture, but no controls are imposed on these groups, and many informal churches exist. The government does not restrict academic freedom.

The constitution guarantees freedoms of association and assembly, and these rights are respected in practice. There are a number of trade unions, but they are weak and riddled with corruption. The labor code provides for the right to strike and prohibits retribution against strikers, though the government has generally failed to address or prevent retaliation by employers. Strikers and union leaders are often illegally dismissed and harassed by employers.

The judiciary is highly corrupt. Courts are inefficient and political interference in the judiciary is a serious problem, as politicians routinely pressure judges and block investigations. While the judiciary is nominally independent, more than 60 percent of judges are members of the Colorado Party. The constitution permits detention without trial until the accused has completed the minimum sentence for the alleged crime. Illegal detention by police and torture during incarceration still occur, particularly in rural areas. Poorly paid and corrupt police officials remain in key posts. Overcrowding, unsanitary conditions, and mistreatment of inmates are serious problems in the country's prisons.

The lack of security in border areas, particularly in the tri-border region adjacent to Brazil and Argentina, has allowed organized crime groups to engage in money laundering and the smuggling of weapons and narcotics. The Shiite Islamist movement Hezbollah has long been involved in narcotics and human trafficking in the largely ungoverned tri-border area. In recent years, Hezbollah has developed ties with Mexican drug cartels.

The constitution provides Paraguay's estimated 108,000 indigenous people with the right to participate in the economic, social, and political life of the country. In practice, however, the indigenous population is unassimilated and neglected. Peasant organizations sometimes occupy land illegally, and landowners often respond with death threats and forced evictions by hired vigilante groups. Violence between landless peasants and landowners practicing large-scale farming continued in 2011; tensions are exacerbated by Paraguay's grossly unequal land distribution in which 1 percent of the population owns 77 percent of arable land. On a positive note, the government made some progress in 2011 in returning ancestral land to indigenous groups. After two decades of legal battles, Paraguayan authorities, local companies, and Sawhoyamaxa indigenous leaders signed an agreement in September 2011 outlining the purchase of land by a government agency to eventually return to the indigenous community.

Employment discrimination against women is pervasive. Sexual and domestic abuse of women continues to be a serious problem. Although the government generally prosecutes rape allegations and often obtains convictions, many rapes go unreported, because victims fear their attackers or are concerned that the law will not respect their privacy. Trafficking in persons is proscribed by the constitution and criminalized in the penal code, but there have been occasional reports of trafficking for sexual purposes and domestic servitude.

Peru

Political Rights: 2
Civil Liberties: 3
Status: Free

Population: 29,399,800
Capital: Lima

Ten-Year Ratings Timeline For Year Under Review (Political Rights, Civil Liberties, Status)

2002	2003	2004	2005	2006	2007	2008	2009	2010	2011
2,3F	2,3F	2,3F	2,3F	2,3F	2,3F	2,3F	2,3F	2,3F	2,3F

Overview: **Leftist candidate Ollanta Humala was elected president in June 2011. He defeated Keiko Fujimori, the daughter of former authoritarian president Alberto Fujimori, in a contest characterized by stark polarization. Humala enjoyed a brief honeymoon, but by year's end, he had been challenged by strong antimining protests that led to a state of emergency in the Cajamarca department in December.**

After achieving independence from Spain in 1821, Peru experienced alternating periods of civilian and military rule. Civilians have held office since a 12-year dictatorship ended in 1980. However, that year, a Maoist guerrilla group known as the Shining Path launched a vicious two-decade insurgency. The conflict led to the deaths of some 69,000 people, nearly three-fourths of whom were residents of poor highland villages.

Alberto Fujimori, a university rector and engineer, was elected president in

1990. In 1992, backed by the military, he suspended the constitution, took over the judiciary, and dissolved Congress. A new constitution featuring a stronger presidency and a unicameral Congress was approved in a state-controlled 1993 referendum. Congress passed a law in 1996 that allowed Fujimori to run for a third term, despite a constitutional two-term limit.

According to official results, Fujimori outpolled Alejandro Toledo—a U.S.-educated economist who had been raised in one of Peru's urban squatter settlements—in the first round of the 2000 presidential election. Toledo boycotted the runoff, pointing to widespread doubts about the vote count and a variety of underhanded tactics by the Fujimori camp.

Beginning in September 2000, a series of videotapes emerged showing intelligence chief Vladimiro Montesinos bribing congressmen and other figures. As a result, in late November, opposition forces assumed control of Congress, Fujimori fled to Japan and resigned, and respected opposition leader Valentín Paniagua was chosen as interim president. Toledo's Perú Posible party led the April 2001 congressional elections, and he bested former president Alan García (1985–90) in a runoff presidential election in June.

In 2004, a special anticorruption court convicted Montesinos in the first of many cases against him, sentencing him to 15 years in prison. Fujimori flew to Chile from Japan in 2005 in the hopes of mounting a 2006 presidential bid in Peru, but he was immediately detained as Peru requested his extradition.

Ollanta Humala of the Peruvian Nationalist Party (PNP) won the first round of the presidential election in April 2006, with García placing second. The PNP and its allies led the congressional elections, followed by García's Peruvian Aprista Party (APRA) and other right-of-center groups. García won the June presidential runoff with 52.5 percent of the vote. Once in office, he focused on macroeconomic growth and stability for foreign investors.

Fujimori was extradited from Chile in 2007, and in April 2009, he was sentenced to 25 years in prison for overseeing death-squad killings and two kidnappings. International observers and local rights groups hailed the verdict as an unprecedented example of a democratically elected head of state convicted of human rights violations in his home country.

In June 2009, a violent confrontation in the town of Bagua between police and a group of mainly indigenous protesters left 10 protesters and 23 police officers dead and over 200 people injured. The protesters had objected to June 2008 government decrees that they said violated their land rights. The disputed decrees were rescinded, and the government acknowledged its failure to consult with locals, though it blamed outside agitators for raising tensions. A commission appointed to produce an official report on the incident was unable to reach consensus.

With three other candidates dividing the center and center-right vote, the leftist Humala and right-wing Keiko Fujimori, daughter of the former president, led the April first round of the 2011 presidential election, taking 32 percent and 23 percent, respectively. In concurrent legislative elections, an alliance led by Humala's PNP captured 47 of the 130 seats, followed by Fujimori's Force 2011 party with 38 seats and Toledo's Perú Posible with 21 seats. APRA largely collapsed, capturing just four seats.

The run-up to the presidential second round in June was characterized by sharp polarization. Fujimori portrayed Humala as a clone of Venezuela's populist president Hugo Chávez, though Humala sought to align himself with the more moderate former Brazilian president Luiz Inácio Lula da Silva. Meanwhile, Fujimori backers hoped for a continuation of García's business-friendly economic growth formula, even as opponents tied her to her father's authoritarianism. Many of the country's major print and broadcast media outlets clearly favored Fujimori. Several journalists were dismissed for failing to toe their outlets' pro-Fujimori line, though there were also some reports of Humala backers harassing critical journalists. Humala ultimately won by a margin of three percentage points.

The new president's Peru Wins alliance forged a congressional majority with Perú Posible. The administration's early successes included a new pension for senior citizens, an increase in the state's share of mining revenues, and unanimous passage of the Law of Prior Consultation, which holds that native communities must be consulted on development projects in their areas. However, social conflict reemerged, as opposition to a proposed gold mine in the northern region of Cajamarca led to large-scale protests and scores of injuries. Humala suspended the project but insisted on the importance of mining investments. In early December he reversed course, declaring a state of emergency in several of the affected areas and breaking off talks. He also oversaw a cabinet shuffle that included the resignation of Prime Minister Salomón Lerner. In a marked shift to the right, he was replaced by former army officer Oscar Valdés, adding to suspicions among some initial Humala supporters—not shared by other observers—that the government was undergoing a process of militarization.

Political Rights and Civil Liberties:

Peru is an electoral democracy. The 2011 elections were generally free and fair, according to international observers. However, shortcomings included lack of enforcement of campaign finance norms and pressure on media outlets by powerful economic interests in support of losing candidate Keiko Fujimori.

The president and the 130-member, unicameral Congress are elected for five-year terms. Congressional balloting employs an open-list, region-based system of proportional representation with a 5 percent vote hurdle for a party to enter the legislature. A lack of programmatic coherence among parties and occasional party-switching by politicians have reinforced a broader trend toward political fragmentation. However, regional presidents have become important actors, and the regional and local elections in October 2010 resulted in a moderately increased consolidation of regional political movements, which generally remain separate from the congressional parties.

Corruption is a serious problem. Checks on campaign financing are particularly weak at the local level, where drug traffickers' influence is perceived to have grown in recent years. Peruvians rated corruption as the most negative aspect of outgoing president Alan García's administration, with Congress considered the most corrupt institution. The new legislature in 2011 appointed a commission to investigate corruption among García officials, though nearly a dozen new members of Congress also faced investigations for various alleged crimes. Two members had been suspended by year's end, along with Vice President Omar Chehade, who was accused of influence trafficking on behalf of a supermarket chain. Peru was ranked 80 out of 183 countries surveyed in Transparency International's 2011 Corruption Perceptions Index.

The lively press is for the most part privately owned. Officials and private actors sometimes intimidate or even attack journalists in response to negative coverage. In addition to pressure by outlet owners, low pay leaves reporters susceptible to bribery, and media outlets remain dependent on advertising by large retailers. A congressionally approved measure to decriminalize defamation was not enacted in 2011, and several journalists were convicted during the year. Most received fines and suspended sentences, but journalist Paul Garay spent six months in jail before being acquitted on appeal and freed in October. In addition, two journalists were murdered in unrelated incidents in Ancash and Ica in September. The government does not limit access to the internet.

The constitution provides for freedom of religion, and the government generally respects it in practice. However, the Roman Catholic Church receives preferential treatment from the state. The government does not restrict academic freedom.

The constitution provides for the right to peaceful assembly, and the authorities uphold this right for the most part. However, the executive branch has issued several decrees in recent years that limit police and military responsibility in the event of injury or death during demonstrations. According to the government, 191 Peruvians died in episodes of social conflict during the García administration, including 38 police and soldiers; several thousand others faced charges for protest-related incidents. Analysts frequently observe that the government's approach to local grievances, which often involve environmental issues, typically relies on reaction rather than mediation and early intervention.

Freedom of association is generally respected, but García and other APRA leaders often alleged that nongovernmental organizations (NGOs) hinder economic development, and in September 2011 Defense Minister Daniel Mora accused two prominent NGOs of coordinating human rights accusations in an attempt to "make the armed forces disappear." Anti-mining activists have faced questionable legal charges in recent years; soon after the December emergency declaration, Cajamarca activist Wilfredo Saavedra was arbitrarily detained in Lima for 10 hours before being released.

Peruvian law recognizes the right of workers to organize and bargain collectively. Workers must notify the Ministry of Labor in advance of a strike, with the result that nearly all strikes are categorized as illegal in practice. Less than 10 percent of the formal-sector workforce is unionized. Parallel unionism and criminal infiltration of the construction sector in Lima have led to a series of disputes and murders.

The judiciary is widely distrusted and prone to corruption scandals. While the Constitutional Court is relatively independent, its autonomy has undergone a mix of setbacks and advances in recent years. A 2008 Judicial Career Law improved the entry, promotion, and evaluation system for judges, and the judiciary's internal disciplinary body has been highly active. At least 43 judges, including some high-profile jurists, were dismissed as unsuitable or corrupt in 2011.

A significant majority of inmates are in pretrial detention, and the inmate population is far above the system's intended capacity. Since 2006, an adversarial justice system designed to improve the speed and fairness of judicial proceedings has slowly been implemented. Access to justice, particularly for poor Peruvians, remains problematic, and crime has risen. In a June 2011 poll, 42 percent of Lima residents reported being the victim of a crime in the previous year. The Humala administration initiated an overhaul of the police in October, forcing 30 generals into retirement.

The military has improved its human rights training, but it continues to place numerous obstacles in the path of investigators regarding past violations. The García government made almost no efforts to prioritize justice for cases of human rights abuses by state actors during the 1980s and 1990s. In September 2010, the government announced a decree that would have applied a statute of limitations to grave human rights abuses committed during the internal conflict. After it faced immediate domestic and international objections, Congress, at García's request, rescinded the measure later that month. In March 2011, the Constitutional Court officially declared the decree unconstitutional. Other decrees announced in September 2010, expanding the military's internal role and extending the reach of the military justice system, remained in force. Also in 2011, Fujimori supporters periodically called for a presidential pardon for the former leader, and political backing for such a move appeared to have grown by year's end.

Remnants of the Shining Path, which are involved in the drug trade, continue to clash with security forces in the Apurimac-Ene River Valley (VRAE) and Upper Huallaga zones. The García government's coca-eradication efforts and economic development programs in other regions failed to reverse a trend toward increased coca production. Humala appointed a noted eradication skeptic as head of the antidrug agency in 2011, but the degree of change in antidrug policy remained unclear at year's end.

Discrimination against the indigenous population remains pervasive, as demonstrated by the racist anti-Humala language that frequently appeared in online social media during the 2011 presidential campaign. The Law of Prior Consultation, passed after Humala's victory, was still awaiting implementing regulations at year's end, and the spike in violent protests and state of emergency late in the year fueled worries that the government's need for mining revenue would continue to take precedence over indigenous people's environmental concerns.

In recent years, women have advanced into leadership roles in various companies and government agencies. Although legal protections have improved, domestic violence is epidemic, with over half of Peruvian women reporting instances of physical or emotional abuse. In December 2011, Congress passed a law increasing penalties for the crime of femicide. Forced labor, including child labor, persists in the gold-mining region of the Amazon.

Philippines

Political Rights: 3
Civil Liberties: 3
Status: Partly Free

Population: 95,739,000
Capital: Manila

Ten-Year Ratings Timeline For Year Under Review (Political Rights, Civil Liberties, Status)

2002	2003	2004	2005	2006	2007	2008	2009	2010	2011
2,3F	2,3F	2,3F	3,3PF	3,3PF	4,3PF	4,3PF	4,3PF	3,3PF	3,3PF

Overview: **The government of President Benigno Aquino continued its anticorruption drive in 2011, which yielded progress against military graft as well as the landmark arrest of former president Gloria Macapagal-Arroyo for alleged election fraud in November. Although political violence increased during the year, the government returned to negotiations with the Moro Islamic Liberation Front (MILF) for the first time in two years.**

After centuries of Spanish rule, the Philippines came under U.S. control in 1898 and won independence in 1946. The country has been plagued by insurgencies, economic mismanagement, and widespread corruption since the 1960s. In 1986, a popular protest movement ended the 14-year dictatorship of President Ferdinand Marcos and replaced him with Corazon Aquino, whom the regime had cheated out of an electoral victory weeks earlier.

Aquino's administration ultimately failed to implement substantial reforms and was unable to dislodge entrenched social and economic elites. Fidel Ramos, a key figure in the 1986 protests, won the 1992 presidential election. The country was relatively stable and experienced significant if uneven economic growth under his administration. Ramos's vice president, Joseph Estrada, won the 1998 presidential election by promising concrete socioeconomic reform, but his administration was dogged by allegations of corruption. Massive street protests forced him from office in 2001 after a formal impeachment process failed.

Gloria Macapagal-Arroyo, Estrada's vice president, assumed the presidency, and her political coalition won the May 2001 legislative elections. In the 2004 presidential election, Arroyo initially seemed to have defeated her challenger by some 1.1 million votes. However, claims of massive fraud triggered demonstrations and were verified by some members of the administration. When an audiotape of a conversation between the president and election officials surfaced in June 2005, supporting the previous year's vote rigging allegations, many cabinet officials resigned to join a new opposition movement. An ultimately unsuccessful impeachment bid was launched, and the first of years of frequent protests called for the president's resignation.

The administration mounted several efforts to undercut the opposition movement, including punitive prosecutions and executive orders in 2005 and a week-long state of emergency in 2006 in response to an alleged coup attempt. The congressional opposition initiated a second unsuccessful impeachment bid that June.

Although the president's coalition increased its lower house majority in May 2007 legislative elections, the opposition bolstered its control of the Senate. Later that year, Arroyo was implicated in a major corruption scandal involving a national broadband contract with the Chinese company ZTE that had been approved in April. Separately, Arroyo pardoned Estrada in October, a month after the country's antigraft court sentenced him to life in prison. His conviction had been the first of a former president, and the pardon was widely perceived as a bid to set a favorable precedent for Arroyo's own treatment after leaving office. Leaders of an unsuccessful coup attempt in November called for Arroyo's removal on the grounds of electoral fraud and corruption, and yet another failed impeachment bid was launched in October 2008.

In November 2009, the wife of a local vice-mayor was ambushed by 100 armed men as she traveled with other family members and supporters to file her husband's candidacy for the Maguindanao provincial governorship. A total of 57 people were massacred in the incident, including 29 journalists and three other media workers who were accompanying the unarmed group. Evidence soon emerged to implicate the Ampatuan clan, which dominated the province's politics and was closely allied with the Arroyo administration.

Arroyo responded in early December by declaring martial law for the first time in nearly 30 years, as well as a state of emergency, which remained in place in three provinces even after martial law was lifted in mid-December. At least 62 people were arrested, including Maguindanao governor Andal Ampatuan Sr., and the authorities dug up arms caches amid an effort to weaken local clans. Nevertheless, the Arroyo administration was widely criticized for its longtime policy of tolerating local warlords and supporting clan patronage as part of its counterinsurgency strategy.

National elections held in May 2010 included contests for the presidency and both houses of Congress. A campaign to lift the one-term limit on the presidency had failed, leaving an open field for the presidential contest. The reformist Liberal Party (LP) candidate Benigno "Noynoy" Aquino—the son of former president Corazon Aquino—ultimately prevailed with 42 percent of the vote. As in past elections, the campaign centered more on personality and family connections than policy or party affiliation, with Aquino benefiting from his mother's prodemocracy, anticorruption legacy. His considerable margin of victory protected him from accusations of electoral fraud.

With 12 out of 24 Senate seats up for election, three went to LP candidates; two each to Arroyo's Lakas-Kampi CMD party, the Force of the Filipino Masses, and the Nationalist Party; and one each to the National People's Coalition, the People's Reform Party, and an independent. In the 250-member lower house, the LP ultimately won 119 seats, while Lakas-Kampi CMD took 46 and other parties split the remainder. In keeping with a long-standing pattern, the LP's predominance resulted from a number of lawmakers defecting to join the new president's party.

Soon after taking office, Aquino established a Truth Commission to investigate the corruption and electoral fraud allegations against Arroyo. The former president was arrested on related charges in November 2011, and court proceedings were pending at year's end.

Efforts to end a Muslim insurgency that had plagued the southern provinces since the early 1970s continued in 2011. In February, a government delegation held talks with the Moro Islamic Liberation Front (MILF) leadership for the first time in two years, agreeing to meet again for further negotiations. The government postponed elections set to take place in the Autonomous Region of Muslim Mindanao (ARMM) in 2011 until 2013, citing ongoing disorder and the need to implement governance and electoral reforms. Bombings became more common throughout Mindanao, with attacks in Zamboanga in December claimed by the terrorist group Abu Sayyaf. Other attacks throughout the region are attributed the violence to the terrorist group Jemaah Islamiyah (JI) or carried out by political interests to ensure the delay of the ARMM elections.

Political Rights and Civil Liberties: The Republic of the Philippines is an electoral democracy. The May 2010 elections marked a significant improvement over previous polls marred by fraud, intimidation, and political violence. The country has a presidential system of government, with the directly elected president limited to a single six-year term. The national legislature, Congress, is bicameral. The 24 members of the Senate are elected on a nationwide ballot and serve six-year terms, with half of the seats up for election every three years. The 280 members of the House of Representatives serve three-year terms, with 228 elected in single-member constituencies and the remainder elected by party list to represent ethnic minorities. Legislative coalitions are exceptionally fluid, and members of Congress often change party affiliation.

The Commission on Elections (Comelec) is appointed by the president, and with the president's permission it has the authority to unseat military, police, and government officials. Comelec was widely discredited by the 2005 audiotape scandal regarding cheating in the 2004 elections, and the 2007 legislative elections were overseen by the same tainted officials. However, during the 2010 balloting, the commission was led by the respected lawyer Jose Melo, and its push for a fully automated election system was seen as an effort to restore the commission's reputation. According to international observers, polling stations encountered some problems with the new voting machines, resulting in delays and long lines. Other complications included inaccurate voter lists, some campaigning in polling stations, and security concerns, particularly in the southern provinces. Media bias tended to favor wealthier candidates, and vote buying was noted among the most serious and persistent problems. In a positive step for human rights, detainees were permitted to vote for the first time.

One of the most significant areas of improvement in the 2010 elections was the reduction in political violence, aided by restrictions on firearms during the campaign. Such bloodshed is typically tied to local rivalries and clan competition. Under outgoing president Gloria Macapagal-Arroyo's administration, violence had increasingly targeted leaders of legitimate left-wing parties that were perceived to be associated with leftist guerrillas. Despite the clear 2010 improvements, widespread intimidation, bombing incidents, and low-level violence remained prevalent in the ARMM.

Corruption and cronyism are rife in business and government. A few dozen leading families continue to hold an outsized share of land, corporate wealth, and political power. Local bosses often control their respective areas, limiting accountability and encouraging abuses of power. High-level corruption also abounds. Upon entering office in 2010, President Benigno Aquino ordered the establishment of a Truth Commission, headed by former Supreme Court justice Hilario Davide, to look into Arroyo's corruption record. Arroyo was arrested on charges of corruption and election fraud in November 2011, and court proceedings were pending at year's end. Additionally, Renato Corona, the Chief Justice of the Supreme Court, an Arroyo appointee, was impeached on December 14, 2011. The trial is set to begin in early 2012. Separately, the military faced a widespread corruption scandal when it was uncovered that senior and retired military officials had been siphoning off military funds to personal accounts.

A culture of impunity, stemming in part from a case backlog in the judicial system, hampers the fight against corruption. More high-profile cases have been filed in recent years, and several civic organizations have emerged to combat corruption, but cases take an average of six to seven years to be resolved in the Sandiganbayan anticorruption court. The country's official anticorruption agencies, the Office of the Ombudsman and the Presidential Anti-Graft Commission (PAGC), have mixed records. Many observers maintain that the former was compromised under the Arroyo administration, as convictions declined, while the PAGC lacks enforcement capabilities. In May 2011, the Arroyo-era ombudsman, Merciditas Gutierrez, was forced from office after Aquino's congressional allies voted to impeach her. The Philippines was ranked 129 out of 183 countries surveyed in Transparency International's 2011 Corruption Perceptions Index.

The constitution provides for freedoms of expression and the press. The private media are vibrant and outspoken, although newspaper reports often consist more of innuendo and sensationalism than substantive investigative reporting. The country's many state-owned television and radio stations cover controversial topics and are willing to criticize the government, but they too lack strict journalistic ethics. While the censorship board has broad powers to edit or ban content, government censorship is generally not a serious problem. The internet is widely available and uncensored.

Potential legal obstacles to press freedom include Executive Order 608, which established a National Security Clearance System to protect classified information, and the Human Security Act, which allows journalists to be wiretapped based on mere suspicion of involvement in terrorism. Libel is a criminal offense, and libel suits have been used frequently to quiet criticism of public officials. Despite persistent lobbying by press freedom groups, Congress has yet to pass a draft Freedom of Information Act, and Aquino has not made it a priority.

The Philippines remains one of the most dangerous places in the world for journalists to work, and impunity for crimes against them is the norm. The Maguindanao massacre trial, widely seen as a major test for the country's judicial system, was transferred to Manila to prevent local interference. Although the case has moved forward with unusual speed, a number of complications have been noted, including witness intimidation, flawed forensic investigations, and the fact that only 19 of the 196 suspects were on trial. As of 2011, the trial was not yet complete. A total of five journalists were killed during 2011, according to the Committee to Protect Journalists, which found that at least two were targeted because of their work.

Freedom of religion is guaranteed under the constitution and generally respected in practice. While church and state are separate, the population is mostly Christian, with a Roman Catholic majority. The Muslim minority is concentrated on the southern island of Mindanao and, according to the most recent census, represents 5 to 9 percent of the total population. Perceptions of relative socioeconomic deprivation and political disenfranchisement, and resentment toward Christian settlement in traditionally Muslim areas, have played a central role in the Muslim separatist movement.

Academic freedom is generally respected in the Philippines; professors and other teachers can lecture and publish freely.

Citizen activism is robust, and demonstrations are common. However, permits are required for rallies, and antigovernment protests are often dispersed. The Philippines has many active human rights, social welfare, and other nongovernmental groups, as well as lawyers' and business associations. Various labor and farmers' organizations that are dedicated to ending extrajudicial killings and helping families of the disappeared face serious threats, and their offices are occasionally raided.

Trade unions are independent and may align with international groups. However, in order to register, a union must represent at least 20 percent of a given bargaining unit. Moreover, large firms are stepping up the use of contract workers, who are prohibited from joining unions. Only about 5 percent of the labor force is unionized. Collective bargaining is common, and strikes may be called, though unions must provide notice and obtain majority approval from their members. Violence against labor leaders remains a problem and has been part of the broader trend of extrajudicial killings in recent years.

Judicial independence has traditionally been strong, particularly with respect to the Supreme Court. However, by early 2010 all members of the Supreme Court except outgoing chief justice Reynato Puno were Arroyo appointees. When Arroyo moved to appoint an ally, Associate Justice Renato Corona, as the new chief justice just after the May elections, despite a constitutional ban on such late appointments by outgoing presidents, the court ruled in favor of maintaining the nomination, and Corona took office.

Rule of law in the country is generally weak. A backlog of more than 800,000 cases in the court system contributes to impunity, and low pay encourages rampant corruption. The judiciary receives less than 1 percent of the national budget, and judges and lawyers often depend on local power holders for basic resources and salaries, leading to compromised verdicts. At least 12 judges have been killed since 1999, but there have been no convictions for the attacks.

Arbitrary detention, disappearances, kidnappings, and abuse of suspects continue to be reported. Mounting evidence has confirmed the military's responsibility for many of the numerous killings of leftist journalists, labor leaders, and senior members of legal left-wing political parties in the context of the Arroyo administration's counterinsurgency against the New People's Army (NPA), a communist rebel group. Military officers maintain that such killings are the result of purges within the communist movement. The lack of effective witness protection has been a key obstacle to investigations. About 90 percent of extrajudicial killing and abduction cases have no cooperative witnesses. Especially problematic is the fact that the Department of Justice oversees both the witness-protection program and the entity that serves as counsel to the military. Similarly, the Philippine National Police, tasked with investigating journalist murders, falls under the jurisdiction of the military.

Convictions for extrajudicial killings are extremely rare, and not a single member of the military was found guilty during Arroyo's presidency. Overall numbers of extrajudicial killings have declined from an annual peak of 220 in 2006. However, there was a significant spike in death-squad killings at the local level in 2008 and 2009, especially in Davao. A study conducted by attorney Al Parreño found that 305 extrajudicial killings were committed from 2001 to August 2010, though the actual number is believed to be higher. Since Aquino took office there have been seven extrajudicial killings and at least three forced disappearances, but none of these have been investigated.

Local officials are believed to keep lists of suspected criminals who are abducted or killed if they fail to heed warnings to reform or leave the area. The death squads responsible reportedly collect about 5,000 pesos (US$100) for each job. The Commission on Human Rights launched independent investigations into the death squads in March 2009, but Human Rights Watch has reported that local authorities, powers, and courts are inhibiting the process. There has also been a recent rise in kidnappings for ransom; authorities killed at least 47 suspected kidnappers during 2009, while 60 others were arrested in a government crackdown. In 2011, several foreigners were kidnapped in separate instances by members of the Abu Sayyaf group. Kidnappings are particularly prevalent in Mindanao.

The Muslim separatist conflict has caused severe hardship for many of the 15 million inhabitants of Mindanao and nearby islands, and has resulted in more than 120,000 deaths since it erupted in 1972. Both government and rebel forces have committed summary killings and other human rights abuses. The resumption of violence in 2011 displaced up to 3,500 additional people, bringing the total number to 15,000, mostly in the Maguindano province. Clan violence has been on the rise since 2009 and is now believed to be the greatest source of displacement. Citizens may travel freely outside conflict zones, and there are no restrictions on employment or place of residence. The poor security situation inhibits individuals' ability to operate businesses.

Women have made many social and economic gains in recent years. The UN Development Programme notes that the Philippines is one of the few countries in Asia to have significantly closed the gender gap in the areas of health and education. Although more women than men now enter high school and university, women face some discrimination in private sector employment, and those in Mindanao enjoy considerably fewer rights in practice. Divorce is illegal in the Philippines, though annulments are allowed under specified circumstances. A 2009 law known informally as the Magna Carta of Women included provisions calling for women to fill half of third-level government positions, requiring that each barangay (local administrative unit) have a "violence against women desk" and recognize women's rights as human rights. Despite these measures, enforcement has been uneven. The trafficking of women and girls abroad and internally for forced labor and prostitution remains a major problem, despite antitrafficking efforts by the government and civil society. There are reports of bonded labor, especially by children, in black-market trades such as prostitution and drug trafficking. The country's various insurgent groups have been accused of using child soldiers.

Poland

Political Rights: 1
Civil Liberties: 1
Status: Free

Population: 38,222,000
Capital: Warsaw

Ten-Year Ratings Timeline For Year Under Review (Political Rights, Civil Liberties, Status)

2002	2003	2004	2005	2006	2007	2008	2009	2010	2011
1,2F	1,2F	1,1F	1,1F	1,1F	1,1F	1,1F	1,1F	1,1F	1,1F

Overview: **Parliamentary elections in October 2011 yielded an unprecedented second term for Prime Minister Donald Tusk of the center-right Civic Platform party. The Palikot Movement, an outspoken liberal party founded in 2010, won a surprising 10 percent of the popular vote, bringing homosexual and transgender candidates into the lower house of parliament for the first time.**

After being dismantled by neighboring empires in a series of 18th-century partitions, Poland enjoyed a window of independence from 1918 to 1939, only to be invaded by Germany and the Soviet Union at the opening of World War II. The country then endured decades of exploitation as a Soviet satellite state until the Solidarity trade union movement forced the government to accept democratic elections in 1989.

Fundamental democratic and free-market reforms were introduced between 1989 and 1991, and additional changes came as Poland prepared its bid for European Union (EU) membership. In the 1990s, power shifted between political parties rooted in the Solidarity movement and those with communist origins. Former communist party member Alexander Kwasniewski of the Democratic Left Alliance (SLD) replaced Solidarity's Lech Wałesa as president in 1995 and was reelected by a large margin in 2000. A government led by the SLD oversaw Poland's final reforms ahead of EU accession, which took place in 2004.

Promising to eliminate corruption and protect Polish values from erosion under EU pressure, the conservative Law and Justice (PiS) party, headed by twin brothers Lech and Jarosław Kaczynski, won the September 2005 parliamentary elections. Lech Kaczy ski won the presidential contest in October, and Jarosław Kaczy ski later became prime minister. PiS formed a fragile majority coalition with the leftist-populist, agrarian Self-Defense Party (Samoobrona) and the socially conservative, Catholic-oriented League of Polish Families (LPR). The coalition finally collapsed in 2007, prompting legislative elections in October.

The elections yielded a government led by Prime Minister Donald Tusk of the center-right Civic Platform (PO) party, in coalition with the Polish People's Party (PSL). The relationship between Tusk and President Lech Kaczynski remained tense in 2008 and 2009, as the president resisted the government's generally pro-EU policy initiatives and its less antagonistic stance toward Russia.

In April 2010, President Kaczy ski and a delegation of Poland's political, academic, and military elite flew to Russia to commemorate the 70th anniversary of the Soviet massacre of Polish officers in Katyn Forest. Their plane crashed during a landing attempt in Smolensk, leaving no survivors. The deceased officials were replaced in accordance with the constitution, and Sejm speaker Bronisław Komorowski of PO served as interim president until elections could be held in June. Jarosław Kaczynski took his brother's place as the PiS candidate, but lost to Komorowski, who took 53 percent in the second round of voting.

The first year of Komorowski's presidency featured increased polarization between supporters of PiS and PO, with competing narratives of the Smolensk tragedy remaining a central theme. However, voters ultimately endorsed the ruling coalition in October 2011 parliamentary elections. In the lower house (Sejm), PO won 207 seats, followed by PiS with 157 and a surprising 40 seats for the liberal Palikot Movement (RP), founded the year before by political provocateur Janusz Palikot. The PSL received 28 seats, and the SLD won 27. A representative of the ethnic German minority held the remaining seat. In the Senate, PO took 63 seats, PiS won 31, the PSL received two seats, and the remainder went to independents. The elections marked the first time in Poland's postcommunist history that a prime minister won a second consecutive term.

From July to December, Poland held the rotating presidency of the EU, where it remained the fastest-growing national economy. However, its budget deficit stood at nearly 8 percent of gross domestic product throughout the year.

Political Rights and Civil Liberties: Poland is an electoral democracy. Voters elect the president for up to two five-year terms and members of the bicameral National Assembly for four-year terms. The president's appointment of the prime minister is subject to confirmation by the 460-seat Sejm, the National Assembly's lower house, which is elected by proportional representation. While the prime minister is responsible for most government policy, the president's position also carries significant influence, particularly relating to defense and foreign policy. The 100-member Senate, whose members are elected in individual districts, can delay and amend legislation but has few other powers.

Corruption remains a problem and often goes unpunished. In September 2010, Mariusz Kaminski, the former head of the Central Anticorruption Bureau, was charged with abuse of power after being suspended from his position in 2009 for allegedly encouraging his agents to engage in bribery and forgery. He was elected to the new parliament on the PiS party list in October 2011, potentially allowing him to avoid prosecution through parliamentary immunity. Poland was ranked 41 out of 183 countries surveyed in Transparency International's 2011 Corruption Perceptions Index.

The 1997 constitution guarantees freedom of expression and forbids censorship. Libel remains a criminal offense, though a 2009 amendment to the criminal code eased the possible penalties. Infringements on media freedom include gag orders and arbitrary judicial decisions concerning media investigations of individuals affiliated with parties in power. Poland's print media are diverse, and most are privately owned. The state-owned Polish Television (TVP) and Polish Radio are dominant in their media, but they face growing competition from private domestic and foreign outlets. The government does not restrict internet access and seeks to enhance access in poorer areas. In September 2011, the parliament enacted changes to the law on freedom of information that limited access in cases where information concerning public figures might weaken the negotiating position or economic interests of the country.

The state respects freedom of religion. Religious groups are not required to register with the authorities but receive tax benefits if they do. A case against pop star Dorota "Doda" Rabczewska, accused of violating Poland's controversial blasphemy laws in a 2009 interview, was still unresolved at the end of 2011. In August, death-metal singer Adam Darski was acquitted of offending religious feelings during a 2007 concert, with the presiding judge finding that the act of tearing up a Bible was a form of artistic expression. Academic freedom in Poland is generally respected.

Polish citizens are free to petition the government, assemble legally, organize professional and other associations, and engage in collective bargaining. However, complicated legal procedures and slow courts hinder workers' ability to strike. Public demonstrations require permits from local authorities. Poland has a robust labor movement, though certain groups—including the self-employed and those working under individual contracts—are barred from joining a union. Labor leaders have complained of harassment by employers.

Poland has an independent judiciary, but the courts are notorious for delays in adjudicating cases. Prosecutors have proceeded slowly on corruption investigations, contributing to concerns that they are subject to political pressure. Prison conditions are fairly poor by European standards, and pretrial detention periods can be lengthy.

Ethnic minorities generally enjoy generous protections and rights under Polish law, including funding for bilingual education and publications. They also receive privileged representation in the parliament, as their political parties are not subject to the minimum vote threshold of 5 percent to achieve representation. Some groups, particularly the Roma, are subject to discrimination in employment and housing, racially motivated insults, and, less frequently, physical attacks.

Sexual minorities continue to face discrimination, though the first openly homosexual and transgender lawmakers—Robert Biedro and Anna Grodzka, respectively—entered the Sejm in November 2011. Both belong to the Palikot Movement, which champions a variety of liberal and secularist causes, including access to abortion, civil unions for homosexual couples, and the elimination of religious education from public schools.

Women have made inroads in the professional sphere and are employed in a wide variety of occupations; several hold high positions in government and the private sector. The 2011 Sejm elections featured a new 35 percent minimum for female candidates on party lists. Female lawmakers now hold 24 percent of the seats in the Sejm, up from 20 in the previous chamber. In August 2011, the parliament narrowly defeated a bill that would have banned all abortions—eliminating current exceptions for cases of rape or serious health problems. Women who undergo illegal abortions do not face criminal charges, but any person who assists in such actions—including medical staff—can face up to three years in prison. Domestic violence against women remains a serious concern, as does trafficking in women and girls for the purpose of prostitution.

Portugal

Political Rights: 1
Civil Liberties: 1
Status: Free

Population: 10,653,000
Capital: Lisbon

Ten-Year Ratings Timeline For Year Under Review (Political Rights, Civil Liberties, Status)

2002	2003	2004	2005	2006	2007	2008	2009	2010	2011
1,1F	1,1F	1,1F	1,1F	1,1F	1,1F	1,1F	1,1F	1,1F	1,1F

Overview: **In March 2011, Prime Minister Jose Socrates stepped down after failing to pass his government's fourth austerity budget proposal. Early elections in June saw the victory of the centre-right Social Democratic Party headed by Pedro Passos Coelho. Massive protests swept the country throughout the year due to the dire financial situation that has troubled the country since 2008.**

Portugal was proclaimed a republic in 1910, after King Manuel II abdicated during a bloodless revolution. António de Oliveira Salazar became prime minister in 1932 and ruled the country as a fascist dictatorship until 1968, when his lieutenant, Marcello Caetano, replaced him. During the "Marcello Spring," repression and censorship were relaxed somewhat, and a liberal wing developed inside the one-party National Assembly. In 1974, a bloodless coup by the Armed Forces Movement, which opposed the ongoing colonial wars in Mozambique and Angola, overthrew Caetano.

A transition to democracy began with the election of a Constitutional Assembly that adopted a democratic constitution in 1976. A civilian government was formally established in 1982, after a revision to the constitution brought the military under civilian control, curbed the president's powers, and abolished the unelected Revolutionary Council. Portugal became a member of the European Economic Community (later the European Union, or EU) in 1986, and formally adopted the euro currency in 2002. The country handed over its last colonial territory, Macao, to the People's Republic of China in 1999.

Aníbal Cavaco Silva, a center-right candidate who had served as prime minister from 1985 to 1995, won the 2006 presidential election. He was reelected in a January 2011 presidential poll.

While holding the rotating EU presidency during the second half of 2007, Portugal oversaw the drafting of the Lisbon Treaty, an agreeement that outlined the constitutional framework of the EU. Ratification of the treaty by the 27-country bloc was completed in November 2009.

In March 2011, Jose Socrates of the Socialist Party stepped down as prime minister after his government's fourth austerity budget proposal was rejected by all five opposition parties. Early elections were held in June and saw the victory of the Social Democratic Party (PSD) with 39 percent of the vote, compared to the Socialist Party's 28 percent. PSD leader Pedro Passos Coelho immediately formed a coalition government with the Popular Party.

A series of protests swept the nation in 2011 in response to the financial crisis that has gripped the country for several years. Tens of thousands of people took to the streets in March to protest against a proposed austerity budget, which the parliament ultimately rejected. Another mass protest took place in Lisbon in October, in response to the government's plan to lay off more than 1,700 government workers, raise taxes, and reduce severance pay in the wake of its acceptance of a 78 billion euro (US$96 billion) bailout package from the International Monetary Fund and EU. In October, two of Portugal's largest trade unions, the General Confederation of Portuguese Workers and the General Workers' Union, announced that they would organize a massive strike in November to protest the worsening economy. The ensuing marches were peaceful, and no clashes or arrests were reported.

Political Rights and Civil Liberties: Portugal is an electoral democracy. The 230 members of the unicameral legislature, the Assembly of the Republic, are elected every four years using a system of proportional representation. The president can serve up to two five-year terms; while the position is largely ceremonial, the president can delay legislation through a veto, dissolve the assembly to trigger early elections, and is the commander in chief of the armed forces and has the power to declare war. The prime minister is nominated by the Assembly, and is then confirmed by the president. The constitution was amended in 1997 to allow Portuguese citizens living abroad to vote in presidential and legislative elections as well as national referendums.

The main political parties are the Socialist Party, the PSD, and the Social Centre/People's Party. The autonomous regions of Azores and Madeira—two island groups in the Atlantic—have their own political structures with legislative and executive powers.

Portugal continued to struggle with corruption issues throughout 2011. Portuguese police had carried out a widespread operation in November 2009 to expose companies engaged in illicitly obtaining industrial waste contracts. A number of officials linked to Socialist Prime Minister Jose Socrates were implicated in the scandal, known as "Hidden Face." While Socrates was not implicated, the scandal damaged his government's credibility. Over 30 people were implicated in the scandal, and their trials for graft, money laundering, and influence peddling opened in November 2011. In May 2011, Transparency International released a report recommending that Portugal improve its training for prosecutors, investigators, and judges in corruption cases; that it increase public awareness about foreign bribery in the private sector; and that it encourage companies to offer whistle-blower protection in an effort to lower Portugal's high corruption rate.

Freedom of the press is constitutionally guaranteed, and laws against insulting the government or armed forces are rarely enforced. The poorly funded public broadcasting channels face serious competition from commercial television outlets. Internet access in Portugal is generally not restricted.

Although the country is overwhelmingly Roman Catholic, the constitution guarantees freedom of religion and forbids religious discrimination. The Religious Freedom Act provides religions that have been established in the country for at least 30 years (or recognized internationally for at least 60 years) with a number of benefits formerly reserved only for the Catholic Church, such as tax exemptions, legal recognition of marriage and other rites, and respect for traditional holidays. Academic freedom is respected.

Freedoms of assembly and association are honored, and national and international nongovernmental organizations, including human rights groups, operate in the country without interference. Workers enjoy the right to organize, bargain collectively, and strike for any reason, including a political motive. However, a 2003 labor law mandated that workers assess a proposed strike's impact on citizens, and provide minimal services during such an event. Thousands of people in 2011 participated in public protests and strikes amid high unemployment and other economic struggles, including a massive November 2011 strike against the government's austerity budget. Only 19 percent of the workforce is unionized.

The constitution provides for an independent judiciary, though staff shortages and inefficiency have contributed to a considerable backlog of pending trials. Human rights groups have expressed concern over unlawful police shootings and deaths in custody. Criticism also continues over poor prison conditions, including overcrowding, poor sanitary conditions, mistreatment of prisoners by police and prison guards, and relatively high rates of HIV/AIDS among inmates.

The constitution guarantees equal treatment under the law. The government has taken a number of steps to combat racism, including passing antidiscrimination laws and launching initiatives to promote the integration of immigrants and Roma. A 2007 immigration law facilitates family reunification and legalization for immigrants in specific circumstances. According to a 2008 study by the Observatory for Immigration, immigrants pay excessively high taxes, though little revenue is channeled to projects that beneft them directly.

Domestic violence against women and children remains a problem, and few domestic violence cases are prosecuted. Portugal is a destination and transit point for trafficked persons, particularly women from Eastern Europe and former Portuguese colonies in South America and Africa. In May 2010, Portugal became the sixth European nation to legalize same-sex marriage.

Qatar

Political Rights: 6
Civil Liberties: 5
Status: Not Free

Population: 1,732,000
Capital: Doha

Ten-Year Ratings Timeline For Year Under Review (Political Rights, Civil Liberties, Status)

2002	2003	2004	2005	2006	2007	2008	2009	2010	2011
6,6NF	6,6NF	6,5NF	6,5NF	6,5NF	6,5NF	6,5NF	6,5NF	6,5NF	6,5NF

Overview: **For the seventh consecutive year, Qatar failed to hold promised parliamentary elections in 2011. In March, authorities detained human rights activist and blogger Sultan al-Khalaifi and released him in April without charge. Twenty-nine citizens were elected, including one woman, in municipal council elections in May.**

Qatar gained independence from Britain in 1971. The following year, Khalifa bin Hamad al-Thani deposed his cousin, Emir Ahmad bin Ali al-Thani, and ruled for 23 years as an absolute monarch. In 1995, the emir was deposed by his son, Hamad bin Khalifa al-Thani, who began a program of gradual political, social, and economic reforms. Hamad dissolved the Ministry of Information shortly after taking power, an action designed to demonstrate his commitment to expanding press freedom.

In 1996, Hamad permitted the creation of Al-Jazeera, which has become one of the most popular Arabic-language satellite television channels in the Middle East. However, Al-Jazeera generally does not cover Qatari politics and focuses instead on regional issues.

The country held its first elections in 1999 for a 29-member Central Municipal Council, a body designed to advise the minister on municipal affairs and agriculture. The poll made Qatar the first state of the Gulf Cooperation Council to introduce widespread voting rights for men and women over 18 years of age. Hamad also accelerated a program to strengthen Qatar's educational institutions, inviting foreign universities to establish branches in the country.

In addition to Central Municipal Council elections in 2003, Qataris voted in a referendum that overwhelmingly approved its first constitution, which came into force in 2005. The new constitution slightly broadened the scope of political participation without eliminating the ruling family's monopoly on power. However, most rights in the new constitution do not apply to noncitizen residents, who form a majority of the population.

Voter turnout for the 2007 Central Municipal Council reached 51 percent, a considerable improvement over 2003, when just 30 percent of the eligible electorate voted. The most recent Municipal Council elections were held in May 2011. Four of the 101 candidates were women; the only woman who had previously served on the Council was reelected. Voter turnout was 43 percent, with just 13,606 registered voters participating.

Qatar has hosted U.S. military forces for a number of years, and the U.S. presence grew significantly after 2001. The country has faced severe criticism in the region for its ties to the United States and its tentative links with Israel. Qatar was deeply involved in regional politics. It provided military and political support for the revolution in Libya and played a diplomatic role in the Israel-Palestine prisoner swap in October.

Political Rights and Civil Liberties:

Qatar is not an electoral democracy. The head of state is the emir, whose family holds a monopoly on political power. The 2005 constitution states that the emir appoints an heir apparent after consulting with the ruling family and other notables. The emir is also responsible for appointing a prime minister and cabinet. The constitution stipulates the formation of a new elected parliament, the Advisory Council (Majlis Al-Shura). Elections are to be held for 30 of the 45 seats for four-year terms, while the emir has the power to appoint the other 15 members. Although elections for this body were scheduled for 2010, Emir Hamad bin Khalifa al-Thani extended the existing 35-member Council's current session until 2013; its members are entirely appointed. Since 1999, voters have elected local government representatives with limited powers to the 29-member Central Municipal Council; these representatives serve four-year terms and report to the appointed minister of municipal affairs and agriculture.

Only a small percentage of the country's population is permitted to vote or hold office. The government does not permit the existence of political parties.

Critics continue to complain of a lack of transparency in government procurement. However, Qatar was ranked 22 out of 183 countries surveyed in Transparency International's 2011 Corruption Perceptions Index, making it the best performer in the Middle East.

Although the constitution guarantees freedom of expression, both print and broadcast media content are influenced by leading families. Journalists practice a high degree of self-censorship and face possible jail sentences for slander. In March 2011, state security forces detained human rights activist and regime critic Sultan al-Khalaifi for unknown reasons. Allegations swirled that he was arrested for blogging and for his efforts to have three allegedly detained Qatari citizens released. Authorities released al-Khalaifi in April without charge. In June, Qatar's cabinet approved the draft of a new media law that will prevent journalists from being detained by authorities without a court order, and allow them to protect their sources unless required to do so by a court. Criticism of the royal family and "friendly countries," as well as discussion of national security, will remain off limits. While the law claims that state censorship is forbidden, journalists will be required to obtain licenses and will be monitored by the Ministry of Arts, Heritage and Culture. The law was not ratified by year's end.

The top five daily newspapers are privately owned, but their owners and boards include members of the ruling family. Although the satellite television channel Al-Jazeera is privately held, the government has reportedly paid for the channel's operating costs since its inception. As a result, Al-Jazeera rarely criticizes the ruling family. Qataris have access to the internet, but the government censors content and blocks access to sites that are deemed pornographic or politically sensitive.

Islam is Qatar's official religion, though the constitution explicitly provides for freedom of worship. The Ministry of Islamic Affairs regulates clerical matters and the construction of mosques. The first two churches to be built for Qatar's Christian community were opened in Doha in 2008 and 2009, while another three remained in the planning or construction phase at the end of 2011. The constitution guarantees freedom of opinion and academic research, but scholars often practice self-censorship on politically sensitive topics.

While the constitution grants freedoms of assembly and association, these rights are limited in practice. Protests are rare, with the government restricting the public's ability to organize demonstrations. In spite of early 2011 Facebook campaign efforts to mobilize protests in Qatar, the country did not experience the "Arab Spring" unrest that took place in other countries in the region during the year. All nongovernmental organizations need state permission to operate, and the government closely monitors the activities of these groups. After hosting the 2007 Conference on Democracy and Reform in Doha, the Ministry of Foreign Affairs established the Arab Foundation for Democracy to monitor progress on reform in the region; Sheikh Hamad has contributed $10 million to the foundation. There are no independent human rights organizations, but a government-appointed National

Human Rights Committee, which includes members of civil society and government ministries, investigates alleged abuses.

A 2005 labor law expanded some protections for citizens, but restricts the right to form unions and to strike. The only trade union allowed to operate in the country is the General Union of Workers of Qatar, which prohibits the membership of noncitizens or government sector employees. Foreign nationals comprise most of the workforce, but fear of job loss and deportation often prevents them from exercising their limited rights. Many foreign workers face economic abuses, including the withholding of salaries or contract manipulation, while others endure poor living conditions and excessive work hours. Female domestic workers are particularly vulnerable to abuse and exploitation.

Despite constitutional guarantees, the judiciary is not independent in practice. The majority of Qatar's judges are foreign nationals who are appointed and removed by the emir. The judicial system consists of Sharia (Islamic law) courts, which have jurisdiction over a narrow range of issues including family law, and civil law courts, which have jurisdiction over criminal, commercial, and civil cases. The Supreme Judiciary Council regulates the judiciary. Although the constitution protects individuals from arbitrary arrest and detention and bans torture, a 2002 law allows the suspension of these guarantees for the "protection of society." The law empowers the minister of the interior to detain a defendant for crimes related to national security on the recommendation of the director-general of public security.

While the constitution prohibits discrimination based on nationality, the government discriminates against noncitizens in the areas of education, housing, healthcare, and other services that are offered free of charge to citizens.

The constitution treats women as full and equal persons, and discrimination based on gender, country of origin, language, or religion is banned. In March 2010, Qatar swore in Sheikha Maha Mansour Salman Jassim al-Thani as its first woman judge. In 2006, Qatar implemented a codified family law, which regulates issues such as inheritance, child custody, marriage, and divorce. While this law offers more protections for women than they previously enjoyed, they continue to face some disadvantages, including societal discrimination, and few effective legal mechanisms are available for them to contest incidents of bias. Qatar is a destination for the trafficking of men and women, particularly for forced labor and prostitution.

Romania

Political Rights: 2
Civil Liberties: 2
Status: Free

Population: 21,408,000
Capital: Bucharest

Ten-Year Ratings Timeline For Year Under Review (Political Rights, Civil Liberties, Status)

2002	2003	2004	2005	2006	2007	2008	2009	2010	2011
2,2F	2,2F	3,2F	2,2F	2,2F	2,2F	2,2F	2,2F	2,2F	2,2F

Overview: **The center-right ruling coalition led by Prime Minister Emil Boc continued to implement unpopular fiscal austerity measures in 2011. The government also attempted to crack down on widespread corruption during the year, but Romania failed to win entry to the European Union's passport-free travel zone amid ongoing concerns about graft and smuggling.**

In 1989, longtime dictator Nicolae Ceausescu was overthrown and executed by disgruntled Communists. A provisional government was formed, and regular multiparty elections soon followed, with power changing hands between right-leaning parties and the former Communist Party, renamed the Social Democratic Party (PSD), during the 1990s. The PSD returned to power in the 2000 parliamentary elections, with Adrian Nastase as prime minister.

In 2004, Traian Basescu of the Alliance for Truth and Justice (comprising the National Liberal Party, or PNL, and the Democratic Party, or PD) defeated Nastase in a presidential runoff. The PNL and PD then formed a coalition government with the Humanist Party (later renamed the Conservative Party, or PC) and the Democratic Union of Hungarians in Romania (UDMR). Calin Popescu-Tariceanu of the PNL became prime minister.

The ruling coalition proved rather unstable, and after Romania's accession to the European Union (EU) in January 2007, Popescu-Tariceanu ousted the Basescu-allied PD from the cabinet in April. At the PSD's urging, Parliament voted to suspend Basescu and organize a referendum on his removal, but he easily won the vote in May.

The new Democratic Liberal Party (PDL), a union of the PD and a PNL splinter faction, won parliamentary elections in November 2008, narrowly defeating a PSD-PC alliance in the lower house, 115 seats to 114, and in the Senate, 51 seats to 49. The rivals then formed a grand coalition in December. Meanwhile, the PNL was left with 65 seats in the lower-house and 28 seats in the Senate, followed by the UDMR with 22 and 9. The remaining 18 lower house seats were set aside for ethnic minorities. Voter turnout was less than 40 percent; unlike in previous years, no major fraud allegations were reported. PDL leader Emil Boc was confirmed by Parliament as the new prime minister.

The grand coalition broke down in October 2009, when the PSD withdrew and Boc's resulting minority government was toppled in a no-confidence vote, though it remained in place in a caretaker capacity as the presidential election campaign began.

Basescu and his PSD challenger, Mircea Geoana, led the first round in November with 32 percent and 31 percent, respectively. Although the PNL and UDMR then endorsed Geoana, Basescu won the December runoff by some 70,000 votes amid 58 percent turnout, and the Constitutional Court confirmed the results after the PSD forced a partial recount. Parliament subsequently approved a new PDL-UDMR coalition government led by Boc.

The government struggled throughout 2010 and 2011 to implement a harsh fiscal austerity package as part of a 2009 emergency loan agreement with the International Monetary Fund. The budgetary measures and labor reforms drew repeated protests by workers and criticism from opposition parties, but Boc survived a series of confidence votes. Although the government also pressed ahead in 2011 with a crackdown on corruption, the EU declined to accept Romania into its passport-free travel zone. An EU progress report issued in July found ongoing problems with the judiciary and its handling of high-level corruption cases.

Political Rights and Civil Liberties: Romania is an electoral democracy. Elections since 1991 have been considered generally free and fair. The president is directly elected for up to two five-year terms and appoints the prime minister with the approval of Parliament. Members of the bicameral Parliament, consisting of the 137-seat Senate and 334-seat Chamber of Deputies, are elected for four-year terms. New rules governing the 2008 parliamentary elections replaced the old party-list voting system with single-member districts, although all districts with no majority winner were allotted based on collective proportional representation.

The constitution grants one lower-house seat to each national minority whose representative party or organization fails to win any seats under the normal rules, and 18 such seats were allotted in 2008. The UDMR has long represented the ethnic Hungarian minority, though a new Hungarian party was formed in September 2011 to compete with the UDMR. Political participation and representation of Roma are very weak.

Romania has struggled to meet EU anticorruption requirements since joining the bloc in 2007. The latest EU progress report in July 2011 praised the performance of the National Anticorruption Directorate (DNA) and the newly reestablished National Integrity Agency (ANI) in investigating corruption cases, but cited ongoing problems with follow-up by administrative and judicial bodies. It found that while 70 percent of DNA cases were fully resolved in less than three years of court proceedings, much of the remaining 30 percent, which included many high-level cases, had not even reached an initial verdict in that period. The delays sometimes resulted in dismissals due to statute of limitation rules. Meanwhile, ANI auditing of asset declarations had led to few final sanctions and no final confiscations. The new ANI law, passed in August 2010, stipulated that an investigation must be completed within three years of the end of an official's term in office, leading to the closure of numerous cases. The EU report also cited parliamentary resistance to investigations in some high-level cases.

Several high-ranking officials faced new investigations for alleged bribery or conflicts of interest in 2011, including a member of the European Parliament, two cabinet ministers, an important PDL mayor, and a Supreme Court judge. In a rare instance of a former minister being jailed for corruption, former agriculture minister Ioan Avram Muresan was sentenced in April to seven years in prison for embezzling U.S. aid funds, though his case had proceeded slowly: he served from 1998 to 2000, was charged in 2003, and went on trial in 2008. Also during the year, scores of customs agents and border police were arrested—and the head of the customs service was dismissed—in a crackdown on bribery and smuggling that appeared linked to Romania's efforts to win entry to the EU passport-free travel zone. As part of its fiscal austerity drive, the government sought to eliminate fraudulent claims among the country's unusually large number of disability pensions. Romania was ranked 75 out of 183 countries surveyed in Transparency International's 2011 Corruption Perceptions Index, making it one of the worst performers in the EU.

The constitution protects freedom of the press, and the media have been characterized by considerable pluralism. However, a weakening advertising market led some foreign media companies to sell their Romanian outlets in 2010, and more sought to do so during 2011. This process has left a larger share of important outlets in the hands of wealthy Romanian businessmen, who often use them to advance their own political and economic interests. State-owned media remain vulnerable to political influence. The government does not restrict access to the internet, and penetration is estimated at 35 percent.

Religious freedom is generally respected, but "nontraditional" religious organizations encounter both difficulties in registering with the state and discrimination by some local officials and Orthodox priests. The government formally recognizes 18 religions, each of which is eligible for proportional state support. The Romanian Orthodox Church remains dominant and politically powerful. The government does not restrict academic freedom, but the education system is weakened by rampant corruption. Anticheating measures implemented in 2011 led to a sharp drop in the pass rate of high school graduation exams, from 69 percent in 2010 to just 44 percent. The lack of eligible freshmen triggered a funding crisis at universities.

The constitution guarantees freedoms of assembly and association, and the government respects these rights in practice. Workers have the right to form unions and a limited right to strike, but in practice, many employers work against unions, and enforcement of union and labor protections is weak. Unions continued to demonstrate against the government's austerity and labor code reforms in 2011, and objected to a provision of the new ANI law that forces union leaders, like public officials, to submit asset declarations. One union leader was detained for alleged corruption in March.

The judiciary is one of the most problematic institutions in Romania. The 2011 EU progress report welcomed the removal of certain procedural obstacles that had contributed to lengthy trial delays, but noted that the courts continue to suffer from serious staffing shortages, inefficient resource allocation, and a weak judicial disciplinary system. Conditions in Romanian prisons remain poor.

Roma, homosexuals, people with disabilities, and HIV-positive children and adults face discrimination in education, employment, and other areas. Romania is home to the EU's largest population of Roma, but has struggled to obtain and spend EU funding dedicated to improving their living conditions. A Romany rights group sued the municipality of Baia Mare in late 2011, after local authorities constructed a concrete wall around a Romany neighborhood, citing problems with crime and disorder.

The constitution guarantees women equal rights, but gender discrimination is a problem. Only about 10 percent of the seats in Parliament are held by women. Trafficking of women and girls for forced prostitution remains a major concern, as does trafficking of children for forced begging. The criminal code does not provide for restraining orders in domestic violence cases.

Russia

Political Rights: 6
Civil Liberties: 5
Status: Not Free

Population: 142,800,000
Capital: Moscow

Ten-Year Ratings Timeline For Year Under Review (Political Rights, Civil Liberties, Status)

2002	2003	2004	2005	2006	2007	2008	2009	2010	2011
5,5PF	5,5PF	6,5NF	6,5NF	6,5NF	6,5NF	6,5NF	6,5NF	6,5NF	6,5NF

Overview: **President Dmitry Medvedev announced in September 2011 that he would not seek reelection in 2012 so that Prime Minister Vladimir Putin could return to the presidency. Putin had changed titles in 2008 to avoid violating the constitutional ban on serving more than two consecutive terms as president. Heavy manipulation of State Duma elections in early December barely preserved United Russia's majority in the lower house of parliament, as voters apparently sought to punish the ruling party by casting ballots for three Kremlin-approved opposition groups. In the weeks following the vote, tens of thousands of antigovernment demonstrators turned out to protest electoral fraud and official corruption in an unprecedented Putin-era display of peaceful dissent. Also during the year, insurgent and other violence originating in the North Caucasus continued, with a high-profile attack on Moscow's Domodedovo airport in January.**

With the collapse of the Soviet Union in December 1991, the Russian Federation emerged as an independent state under the leadership of President Boris Yeltsin. In 1993, Yeltsin used force to thwart an attempted coup by parliamentary opponents of radical reform, after which voters approved a new constitution establishing a powerful presidency and a bicameral national legislature, the Federal Assembly. The 1995 parliamentary elections featured strong support for the Communist Party and ultranationalist forces. Nevertheless, in the 1996 presidential poll, which suffered from electoral manipulation by all sides, Yeltsin defeated Communist leader Gennady Zyuganov with the financial backing of powerful business magnates, who used the media empires they controlled to ensure victory. In 1999, Yeltsin appointed Vladimir Putin, then the head of the Federal Security Service (FSB).

Conflict with the separatist republic of Chechnya, which had secured de facto independence from Moscow after a brutal 1994–96 war, resumed in 1999.

Government forces reinvaded the breakaway region after Chechen rebels led an incursion into the neighboring Russian republic of Dagestan in August and a series of deadly apartment bombings—which the Kremlin blamed on Chechen militants and some of Putin's critics blamed on him—struck Russian cities in September. The second Chechen war dramatically increased Putin's popularity, and after the December 1999 elections to the State Duma, the lower house of the Federal Assembly, progovernment parties were able to form a majority coalition.

An ailing and unpopular Yeltsin, who was constitutionally barred from a third presidential term, resigned several months early, on December 31, 1999, transferring power to Putin—allegedly in exchange for immunity from prosecution for corruption. The new acting president subsequently secured a first-round victory over Zyuganov, 53 percent to 29 percent, in the March 2000 presidential election. After taking office, Putin moved quickly to reduce the influence of the legislature, tame the business community and the news media, and strengthen the FSB. He considerably altered the composition of the ruling elite through an influx of personnel from the security and military services. Overall, Putin garnered enormous personal popularity by overseeing a gradual increase in the standard of living for most of the population; the improvements were driven largely by an oil and gas boom and economic reforms that had followed a 1998 financial crisis.

In the December 2003 Duma elections, the Kremlin-controlled United Russia party captured 306 out of 450 seats. With the national broadcast media and most print outlets favoring the incumbent, no opponent was able to mount a significant challenge in the March 2004 presidential election. Putin, who refused to debate the other candidates, received 71.4 percent of the vote in a first-round victory, compared with 13.7 percent for his closest rival, the Communist-backed Nikolai Kharitonov.

Putin introduced legislative changes in 2004 that eliminated direct gubernatorial elections in favor of presidential appointments, citing a need to unify the country in the face of terrorist violence. The government also began a crackdown on democracy-promotion groups and other nongovernmental organizations (NGOs), especially those receiving foreign funding. The authorities removed another possible threat in 2005, when a court sentenced billionaire energy magnate Mikhail Khodorkovsky, founder of the oil firm Yukos, to eight years in prison for fraud and tax evasion. A parallel tax case against Yukos itself led to the transfer of most of its assets to the state-owned Rosneft. Khodorkovsky had antagonized the Kremlin by bankrolling opposition political activities; his prosecution was widely interpreted as a signal to other business magnates to toe the government line.

A law enacted in 2006 handed bureaucrats wide discretion in monitoring and shutting down NGOs, which the authorities used to target organizations critical of official policy. In another sign that safe avenues for dissent were disappearing, an assassin murdered investigative journalist Anna Politkovskaya in October of that year. She had frequently criticized the Kremlin's ongoing military campaign in Chechnya and the excesses of Russian troops in the region.

The heavily manipulated December 2007 parliamentary elections gave the ruling United Russia party 315 of the 450 Duma seats, while two other parties that generally support the Kremlin, Just Russia and the nationalist Liberal Democratic Party, took 38 and 40 seats, respectively. The opposition Communists won 57 seats in the effectively toothless legislature.

Constitutionally barred from a third consecutive term, Putin handpicked his successor, First Deputy Prime Minister Dmitry Medvedev, who won the March 2008 presidential election with 70.3 percent of the vote. Medvedev appointed Putin as his prime minister, and the former president continued to play the dominant role in government. At the end of 2008, the leadership amended the constitution for the first time since it was adopted in 1993, extending future presidential terms from four to six years. Although Medvedev discussed a variety of liberal ideas over the next few years, in practice he did not make any significant changes to the system Putin had developed as president. Despite this political stagnation and ongoing violence against the regime's most serious critics, civil society became more active in 2010 on issues including corruption and environmental protection.

In September 2011, just as the campaign for the December State Duma elections was heating up, Medvedev announced that he would step aside so that Putin could run for the presidency in March 2012. The move raised the prospect that Putin would serve two, six-year terms as president, remaining in office until 2024. Putin immediately said he would appoint Medvedev as his prime minister. The two claimed that Putin's return had been long planned, though there had been intense speculation during Medvedev's presidency that he might stay on for another term. Putin announced his plans at a time when his popularity was declining, largely as a result of Russia's extensive corruption and a plateau in the improvement of living standards.

Although the authorities made extensive use of their incumbency in the December 4 elections, United Russia captured 238 seats, down from 314 seats in the 2007 elections. The Communist Party took 92 seats, followed by A Just Russia with 64 seats, and the Liberal Democratic Party of Russia with 56 seats. The Organization for Security and Cooperation in Europe reported irregularities during the election, including media bias, interference by state authorities, and a lack of independence by the election administration.

In the weeks following the election, large antigovernment demonstrations—the largest since Putin came to power—were held in Moscow, with smaller protests taking place in other cities in Russia. The demonstrations, which began as a reaction to the flawed legislative elections, included demands for annulment of the election results, an investigation into vote fraud, and freedom for political prisoners. Hundreds of people were arrested, and several protest leaders were imprisoned, including prominent blogger and anticorruption activist Alexey Navalny, who was released from jail after two weeks in custody. By the end of the year, public support for the protests was growing, along with questions about Putin's legitimacy and the country's future stability.

Political Rights and Civil Liberties: Russia is not an electoral democracy. The deeply flawed 2011 Duma elections were marked by a "convergence of the state and the governing party, limited political competition and a lack of fairness," according to the Organization for Security and Cooperation in Europe (OSCE), but many voters used them to express a protest against the status quo. In the 2008 presidential election, state dominance of the media was on full display, debate was absent, and incumbent Vladimir Putin was able to pass the office to his handpicked successor, Dmitry Medvedev.

The 1993 constitution established a strong presidency with the power to dismiss and appoint, pending parliamentary confirmation, the prime minister. However, under the current de facto political arrangement, Prime Minister Putin's personal authority and power base among the security services make him the dominant figure in the executive branch. Putin's announced decision to return to the presidency in 2012 will formalize his status as paramount leader. The Federal Assembly consists of the 450-seat State Duma and an upper chamber, the 166-seat Federation Council. Under constitutional amendments adopted in 2008, future presidential terms will be six years rather than the current four, though the limit of two consecutive terms will remain in place. The terms for the Duma increased from four years to five.

Beginning with the 2007 elections, all Duma seats were elected on the basis of party-list proportional representation. Parties must gain at least 7 percent of the vote to enter the Duma. Furthermore, parties cannot form electoral coalitions, and would-be parties must have at least 40,000 members (as of January 2010—a symbolic reduction from 50,000) and organizations in half of the federation's 83 administrative units to register. These changes, along with the tightly controlled media environment and the misuse of administrative resources, including the courts, make it extremely difficult for genuine opposition parties to win representation.

Half the members of the upper chamber are appointed by governors (who are themselves appointed by the president under a 2004 reform) and half by regional legislatures, usually with strong federal input in all cases. As of January 2011, only locally elected politicians are eligible to serve in the Federation Council; the change was expected to benefit United Russia, as most local officeholders are party members. In mid-2011, longtime Federation Council Speaker Sergei Mironov of the Just Russia party, who had grown increasingly critical of United Russia, was replaced with Putin ally Valentina Matviyenko, the unpopular governor of St. Petersburg. She had to win a seat on a local council to qualify, and did so only after the registration process was manipulated to thwart potential challengers.

Corruption in the government and business world is pervasive. A growing lack of accountability enables bureaucrats to act with impunity. In April 2011, Medvedev ordered all government officials to leave any positions they held on the boards of state-owned companies. Despite the formal change, however, the state still has extensive control over these important and lucrative firms. In May, the president signed new laws raising the fines for bribe taking to as much as 100 times the amount of the bribe, but such anticorruption laws are selectively enforced and have had little impact.

Although the constitution provides for freedom of speech, since 2003, the government has controlled, directly or through state-owned companies, all of the national television networks. Only a handful of radio stations and publications with limited audiences offer a wide range of viewpoints. At least 19 journalists have been killed since Putin came to power, including 3 in 2009, and in no cases have the organizers of the murders been prosecuted. The authorities have further limited free expression by passing vague laws on extremism that make it possible to crack down on any speech, organization, or activity that lacks official support. Discussion on the internet is ostensibly free, but the government devotes extensive resources to manipulating online information and analysis. As the 2011 Duma elections approached, businessmen close to Putin purchased additional television, radio, and newspaper assets. Hackers attacked the website of Golos, Russia's only independent election monitoring group, on election day, bringing down a site displaying a map of campaign and voting violations. However, after initially ignoring the December postelection demonstrations, the main state-controlled television channels broke with recent practice and began covering the protests in their broadcasts.

Freedom of religion is respected unevenly. A 1997 law on religion gives the state extensive control and makes it difficult for new or independent groups to operate. Orthodox Christianity has a privileged position, and in 2009 the president authorized religious instruction in the public schools. Regional authorities continue to harass nontraditional groups, such as Jehovah's Witnesses and Mormons.

Academic freedom is generally respected, though the education system is marred by corruption and low salaries. The arrest and prosecution of scientists and researchers on charges of treason, usually for discussing sensitive technology with foreigners, has effectively restricted international contacts in recent years. Historians who seek to examine controversial aspects of Russian history, such as the fate of ethnic Germans deported from the Volga and Crimea during WWII who were labeled "enemies of the people," face severe pressure from the authorities.

The government has consistently reduced the space for freedoms of assembly and association. Overwhelming police responses, the use of force, and routine arrests have discouraged unsanctioned protests, though pro-Kremlin groups are able to demonstrate freely. In the wake of the 2011 elections, the authorities allowed two sanctioned demonstrations in Moscow that attracted tens of thousands of protesters, while smaller rallies took place across the country. A 2006 law imposed onerous new reporting requirements on NGOs, giving bureaucrats extensive discretion in deciding which groups could register and hampering activities in subject areas that the state deemed objectionable. The law also places tight controls on the use of foreign funds, and in July 2008, Putin lifted exemptions from tax obligations on grants from most foreign foundations and NGOs. The state has sought to provide alternative sources of funding to local NGOs, including a handful of organizations that are critical of government policy, though such support generally limits the scope of the recipient groups' activities. A few days before the 2011 elections, Putin described the election monitoring group Golos as a "Judas," while the authorities exerted heavy pressure to limit its activities.

While trade union rights are legally protected, they are limited in practice. Strikes and worker protests have occurred in prominent industries, such as automobile manufacturing, but antiunion discrimination and reprisals for strikes are not uncommon, and employers often ignore collective-bargaining rights. With the economy continuing to change rapidly after emerging from Soviet-era state controls, unions have been unable to establish a significant presence in much of the private sector. The largest labor federation works in close cooperation with the Kremlin.

The judiciary lacks independence from the executive branch, and career advancement is effectively tied to compliance with Kremlin preferences. The justice system has been tarnished by politically fraught cases, such as that of jailed former oil magnate Mikhail Khodorkovsky, whose prison term was extended until 2017 after a conviction on dubious new charges in December 2010. A press officer at Moscow's Khamovnichesky Court claimed in early 2011 that the judge in the Khodorkovsky case issued a conviction on the instructions of superiors at the Moscow City Court. After judicial reforms in 2002, the government has made gains in implementing due process and holding timely trials. Since 2003, the criminal procedure code allows jury trials for serious cases, though they occur rarely in practice. While juries are more likely than judges to acquit defendants, such verdicts are frequently overturned by higher courts, which can order retrials until the desired outcome is achieved. Russia ended the use of jury trials in terrorism cases in 2008. Russian citizens often feel that domestic courts do not provide a fair hearing and have increasingly turned to the European Court of Human Rights.

Critics charge that Russia has failed to address ongoing criminal justice problems, such as poor prison conditions and the widespread use of illegal detention and torture to extract confessions. The circumstances surrounding the 2009 death of lawyer Sergei Magnitsky in pretrial detention, after he accused government employees of embezzling millions of dollars, suggested that the authorities had deliberately denied him medical treatment. As many as 50 to 60 people die each year in investigative isolation wards (SIZOs), according to the Moscow Helsinki Group. In some cases, there has also been a return to the Soviet-era practice of punitive psychiatric treatment.

Parts of the country, especially the North Caucasus area, suffer from high levels of violence. Chechen president Ramzan Kadyrov's relative success in suppressing major rebel activity in his domain has been accompanied by numerous reports of extrajudicial killings and collective punishment. Moreover, related rebel movements have appeared in surrounding Russian republics, including Ingushetia, Dagestan, and Kabardino-Balkaria. Hundreds of officials, insurgents, and civilians die each year in bombings, gun battles, and assassinations. The January 2011 bombing of Moscow's Domodedovo airport, which killed at least 37 people, made clear that the Kremlin had yet to contain the violence. During the first nine months of 2011 in the North Caucasus, there were 444 insurgent and terrorist attacks, slightly less than during the same period the previous year.

Immigrants and ethnic minorities—particularly those who appear to be from the Caucasus or Central Asia—face governmental and societal discrimination and harassment. Institutions representing Russia's large Ukrainian minority have also come under selective government pressure. While racially motivated violence had increased through 2008, the number of attacks continued to decline from 2009 through 2011, according to Sova, a group that tracks ultranationalist activity in the country. Sexual minorities also encounter discrimination and abuse, and gay rights demonstrations are often attacked by counterdemonstrators or suppressed by the authorities.

The government places some restrictions on freedom of movement and residence. Adults must carry internal passports while traveling and to obtain many government services. Some regional authorities impose registration rules that limit the right of citizens to choose their place of residence. In the majority of cases, the targets are ethnic minorities and migrants from the Caucasus and Central Asia.

State takeovers of key industries and large tax penalties imposed on select companies have illustrated the precarious nature of property rights in the country, especially when political interests are involved.

Women have particular difficulty achieving political power. They hold 13 percent of the Duma's seats (down from 14 percent in the previous term) and less than 5 percent of the Federation Council's. Only 3 of 26 cabinet members are women. Domestic violence continues to be a serious problem, and police are often reluctant to intervene in what they regard as internal family matters. Economic hardships contribute to widespread trafficking of women abroad for prostitution.

Rwanda

Political Rights: 6
Civil Liberties: 5
Status: Not Free

Population: 10,932,000
Capital: Kigali

Ten-Year Ratings Timeline For Year Under Review (Political Rights, Civil Liberties, Status)

2002	2003	2004	2005	2006	2007	2008	2009	2010	2011
7,5NF	6,5NF	6,5NF	6,5NF	6,5NF	6,5NF	6,5NF	6,5NF	6,5NF	6,5NF

Overview: **Despite hopes for an improvement in conditions following August 2010 presidential elections, the Rwandan Patriotic Front maintained strict controls on civic and political life in 2011. The prosecution of journalists and opposition politicians continued during the year, with harsh sentences delivered in several cases.**

Belgian colonial rule in Rwanda, which began after World War I, exacerbated and magnified tensions between the minority Tutsi ethnic group and the majority Hutu. A Hutu rebellion beginning in 1959 overthrew the Tutsi monarchy, and independence from Belgium followed in 1962. Hundreds of thousands of Tutsi were killed or fled the country in recurring violence over the subsequent decades. In 1990, the Tutsi-dominated Rwandan Patriotic Front (RPF) launched a guerrilla war from Uganda to force the Hutu regime, led by President Juvénal Habyarimana, to accept power sharing and the return of Tutsi refugees.

Habyarimana was killed when his plane was shot down near Kigali in April 1994. Hutu extremists immediately pursued the complete elimination of the Tutsi. During the genocide, which lasted approximately three and a half months, as many as a million Tutsi and moderate Hutu were killed. By July, however, the RPF had succeeded in taking control of Kigali and establishing an interim government of national unity.

The Hutu-dominated army and militia, along with as many as two million Hutu refugees, fled into neighboring countries, especially the Democratic Republic of Congo (DRC). These forces were able to retrain and rearm in the midst of international relief efforts to assist the refugees. The RPF responded by attacking refugee camps in the DRC in 1996. A 2010 UN report provided strong evidence of war crimes committed by RPF forces in incursions in the DRC from 1996 to 1997 and from 1998 to 2003.

Nearly three million refugees returned to Rwanda between 1996 and 1998 and were reintegrated into society. Security improved considerably after 1997, although isolated killings and disappearances continued. The RPF-led government closely directed the country's political life. In 2000 President Pasteur Bizimungu, a moderate Hutu installed by the RPF, resigned and was replaced by Vice President Paul Kagame, a Tutsi.

Rwanda's extended postgenocide political transition officially ended in 2003 with a new constitution and national elections. The RPF's preeminent position—combined with a short campaign period, the RPF's ability to suppress opposition, and a pliant political culture traumatized by the effects of the genocide—ensured victory for Kagame in the presidential vote and for the RPF and its allies in subsequent parliamentary elections. The largest opposition party, the Hutu-based Democratic Republican Movement (MDR), was declared illegal by the authorities before the elections for allegedly promoting ethnic hatred, as was a new party created by Bizimungu in 2001.

A series of four parliamentary commissions between 2003 and 2008 investigated allegations of "genocide ideology" and "divisionism" in domestic and international nongovernmental organizations (NGOs), opposition political parties, the media, and schools. These commissions equated criticism of the RPF-led government with denial of the genocide, and made accusations against numerous individuals and organizations without recourse to due process, driving a number of government critics into exile and pushing some NGOs and political parties to curtail their activities.

The RPF-led coalition handily won the 2008 parliamentary elections, taking 42 out of 53 elected seats in the lower house. Monitoring by a European Union observer team indicated that the actual RPF share of the vote was higher than reported, suggesting a manipulation of results to make the elections appear more democratic.

In advance of the August 2010 presidential election, the government prevented new political parties from registering and arrested the leaders of several parties, effectively preventing them from fielding candidates. The most credible opposition candidate, Victoire Ingabire, the leader of the United Democratic Forces–Inkingi (FDU-Inkingi), was arrested and released in April on charges of denying the genocide and collaborating with a terrorist group. The Social Party–Imberakuri (PS-Imberakuri) was allowed to register, but its presidential candidate, Bernard Ntaganda, was also arrested in June. André Kagwa Rwisereka, the vice president of the Democratic Green Party of Rwanda, was assassinated in July. With no serious challengers on the ballot, Kagame won reelection with 93 percent of the vote.

Ingabire was arrested again in October 2010, accused of engaging in terrorist activities. In February 2011, Ntaganda of PS-Imberakuri was sentenced to four years in prison for breaching state security and "divisionism" based on his 2010 election campaign speeches, as well as planning unauthorized demonstrations. Three members of FDU-Inkingi were also given heavy fines in February for supporting "divisionism" by conspiring to participate in unauthorized demonstrations in June 2010. Ingabire's trial, which began in September 2011, continued at year's end.

A limited number of special genocide courts continued to operate in 2011, trying those accused of more serious crimes that fell outside the jurisdiction of community-based gacaca courts. The gacaca courts themselves moved to complete their work, as a revision of the gacaca law charged them with trying cases of rape and other serious crimes previously reserved for the special genocide courts. By the end of 2011, the International Criminal Tribunal for Rwanda (ICTR) had arrested 83 individuals and completed cases against 70, with trials of 5 individuals ongoing, and only 1 detainee awaiting trial. Meanwhile, RPF officials facing charges leveled by a Spanish judge for war crimes allegedly committed during the genocide were expelled from or denied entry to a number of countries in 2011.

Political Rights and Civil Liberties:

Rwanda is not an electoral democracy. International observers noted that the 2010 presidential and 2008 parliamentary elections, while administratively acceptable, presented Rwandans with only a limited degree of political choice. The 2003 constitution grants broad powers to the president, who can serve up to two seven-year terms and has the authority to appoint the prime minister and dissolve the bicameral Parliament. The 26-seat upper house, the Senate, consists of 12 members elected by regional councils, 8 appointed by the president, 4 chosen by a forum of political parties, and 2 representatives of universities, all serving eight-year terms. The Chamber of Deputies, or lower house, includes 53 directly elected members, 24 women chosen by local councils, 2 from the National Youth Council, and 1 from the Federation of Associations of the Disabled; all serve five-year terms.

The constitution officially permits political parties to exist, but only under strict controls. The charter's emphasis on "national unity" effectively limits political pluralism. The RPF dominates the political arena, and parties closely identified with the 1994 genocide are banned, as are parties based on ethnicity or religion. These restrictions have been used to ban other political parties that might pose a challenge to RPF rule. The constitutionally mandated Political Party Forum vets proposed policies and draft legislation before they are introduced in Parliament. All parties must belong to the forum, which operates on the principle of consensus, though in practice the RPF guides its deliberations. Parliament generally lacks independence, merely endorsing government initiatives. However, parliamentary committees have begun to question ministers and other executive branch officers more energetically, and some of these deliberations are reported in the local press.

Government countermeasures have helped limit corruption, though graft remains a problem. A number of senior government officials in recent years have been fired and faced prosecution for alleged corruption, embezzlement, and abuse of power, including the director of the National Institute of Statistics and permanent secretaries in the Ministries of Infrastructure and Education. Government institutions focused on combating corruption include the Office of the Ombudsman, the auditor general, and the National Tender Board. Rwanda was ranked 49 out of 183 countries surveyed in Transparency International's 2011 Corruption Perceptions Index.

The RPF has imposed numerous legal restrictions and informal controls on the media, and press freedom groups have accused the government of intimidating independent journalists. Prior to the 2010 elections, the government banned numerous newspapers, journals, and radio stations, many of which did not reopen in 2011. In February 2011, Umurabyo newspaper journalists Agnès Uwimana Nkusi and Saïdati Mukakibibi were sentenced to 17 and 7 years, respectively, for denying the genocide, inciting civil disobedience, and defaming public officials based on an article published in 2009 criticizing President Paul Kagame. In August, the bimonthly *Ishema* temporarily suspended publication after receiving threats for printing an opinion piece that referred to Kagame as a "sociopath." Fidèle Gakire, *Ishema's* publisher, along with the board of the newspaper jointly decided to cease publication for a month. *Ishema* also printed a special edition apologizing to the president, and Gakire apologized to Rwanda's High Media Council, which had ruled that the opinion piece was libelous. Nevertheless, Gakire remained the target of multiple threats, and the Forum of Private Newspapers, a council created to ensure that publications self-regulate, suspended his membership for six months. On November 30, Charles Ingabire, editor of the Uganda-based online publication *Inyenyeri News* and an outspoken critic of the Kagame regime who had fled Rwanda in 2007 due to threats, was shot dead in Uganda. There were reports that the government blocked three critical websites in 2011, and that it monitored e-mail and internet chat rooms. Religious freedom is generally respected, though relations between religious leaders and the government are sometimes tense, in part because of the involvement of clergy in the 1994 genocide. In July, a court in Rwamagana sentenced priest Emile Nsengiyumva to a year and a half in prison for threatening state security because of a sermon he gave criticizing a government housing program and family planning policies.

Fear among teachers and students of being labeled “divisionist” restrains academic freedom. Following the 2004 and 2008 parliamentary commission reports on “divisionism,” numerous students and teachers have been expelled or dismissed without due process. A 2010 Amnesty International report indicated that the 2008 law against “genocide ideology” continued to stifle academic freedom. The crackdown ahead of the 2010 presidential election that severely stifled general free discussion—with the Department of Military Intelligence closely monitoring the population—did not ease in 2011.

Although the constitution codifies freedoms of association and assembly, in reality these rights are limited. Some NGOs have complained that registration and reporting procedures are excessively onerous, and activities that the government defines as “divisive” are prohibited. Several organizations have been banned in recent years, leading others to refrain from criticizing the RPF. In August 2011, leaders of the League for Human Rights in the Great Lakes Region, one of the remaining independent human rights groups in Rwanda, were detained and prevented from traveling. However, most civil society organizations that are not focused on sensitive subjects, such as democracy and human rights, function without direct government interference.

The constitution provides for the rights to form trade unions, engage in collective bargaining, and strike. Public workers are not allowed to unionize, however, and the list of “essential services” in which strikes are not allowed is excessively long. The International Trade Union Confederation reported that although a new 2009 labor code improved workers’ rights, the government continues to pressure unions in subtle and indirect ways. In January and May 2011, respectively, trade unionists were dismissed from the textile factories UTEXRWA and ECOBANK-Rwanda, with no government response.

Recent improvements in the judicial system include an increased presence of defense lawyers at trials, improved training for court staff, and revisions to the legal code, but the judiciary has yet to secure full independence from the executive. The gacaca courts faced criticism from legal experts not only because of their failure to address genocide-era crimes allegedly committed by the RPF, but also because they routinely tried politically motivated cases. Individual police officers sometimes use excessive force, and local officials periodically ignore due process protections. The construction of new prisons during the past decade has improved prison conditions, even as gacaca trials have once again increased the prison population.

Equal treatment for all citizens under the law is guaranteed, and legal protections against discrimination have increased in recent years. A national identity card is required when Rwandans wish to move within the country, but these are issued regularly, and no longer indicate ethnicity.

The 2003 constitution requires women to occupy at least 30 percent of the seats in each chamber of Parliament, and women filled 10 of the 26 Senate seats following the 2011 elections. Legislation has strengthened women's rights to inherit land. Despite these improvements, de facto discrimination against women continues. Domestic violence is illegal, but remains widespread.

Saint Kitts and Nevis

Political Rights: 1
Civil Liberties: 1
Status: Free

Population: 50,000
Capital: Basseterre

Ten-Year Ratings Timeline For Year Under Review (Political Rights, Civil Liberties, Status)

2002	2003	2004	2005	2006	2007	2008	2009	2010	2011
1,2F	1,2F	1,2F	1,1F	1,1F	1,1F	1,1F	1,1F	1,1F	1,1F

Overview: **Nevis Island Assembly elections held in July 2011 resulted in controversy when the Concerned Citizen's Movement alleged the illegal purging of voters from the rolls after it lost a closely contested seat to the Nevis Reformation Party. Meanwhile, a rise in the country's murder rate prompted Prime Minister Denzil Douglas to form an elite police unit to concentrate on crime prevention.**

Saint Kitts and Nevis gained independence from Britain in 1983 but remains a member of the Commonwealth. Denzil Douglas of the ruling Saint Kitts and Nevis Labour Party (SKNLP) has been prime minister since 1995. In the 2002 elections, the SKNLP won all eight Saint Kitts seats in the National Assembly, shutting out the opposition People's Action Movement (PAM). In early elections held in 2004, the SKNLP captured seven Saint Kitts seats, and the PAM took one seat. The Concerned Citizens Movement (CCM), a proindependence party, retained two of Nevis's three parliamentary seats, while the third was captured by the Nevis Reformation Party (NRP).

The most recent parliamentary elections took place in January 2010, despite multiple challenges from the PAM over an SKNLP attempt to redraw district lines shortly before the election and allegations that the SKNP padded votes and registered voters outside their legal districts. These were also the first elections to take place under a new electoral law that had created a voter identification system requiring all existing voters to reregister. International monitors found the elections to be generally free and fair, but noted that several important issues, including campaign finance, media access, and civil society participation, had not been addressed in the reformed electoral law and thus required improvements. Douglas won a fourth term as prime minister as the SKNLP won six seats, while the PAM gained an additional Saint Kitts seat for a total of two. The CCM and NRP retained two and one Nevis seats, respectively.

Since the 2010 election, the Douglas administration has been focused on economic development, the reduction of public debt, and crime prevention. In 2011, Saint Kitts successfully met International Monetary Fund targets for debt reduction. In July 2011 elections for the Nevis Island Assembly, the NRP captured three seats, and the CCM took two seats. The CCM challenged the results in the second constituency, where it lost the seat by 14 votes and alleged the unlawful disenfranchisement of over 200 voters who they said were purged from the rolls two days before the election. Despite considering the overall election free and fair, observers from the Caribbean Community (CARICOM) documented irregularities and voiced concern over the expunging of voters from registration lists. A court hearing in the British Virgin Island courts was set for January 2012.

Political Rights and Civil Liberties: Saint Kitts and Nevis is an electoral democracy. The federal government consists of the prime minister, the cabinet, and the unicameral National Assembly. A governor-general represents Britain's Queen Elizabeth II as ceremonial head of state. Elected National Assembly members—eight from Saint Kitts and three from Nevis—serve five-year terms. Senators are appointed to the body, and their number may not exceed two-thirds of the elected members, with one chosen by the leader of the parliamentary opposition for every two chosen by the prime minister.

Saint Kitts's main political parties are the SKNLP and the PAM. On Nevis, the two main parties are the CCM and the NRP. The Nevis Island Assembly is composed of five elected and three appointed members, and the local government pays for all of its own services except for those involving police and foreign relations. Saint Kitts has no similar body.

The constitution grants Nevis the option to secede if two-thirds of the elected legislators in Nevis's assembly and two-thirds of Nevisian referendum voters approve. Though a 1998 referendum on independence failed, Nevisians continue to feel neglected by the central government.

Saint Kitts and Nevis has generally implemented its anticorruption laws effectively, though government officials are not required to disclose financial assets.

Constitutional guarantees of free expression are generally respected. The sole local television station is owned by the government, but managed by a Trinidadian company. There are some restrictions on opposition access to the medium. In September 2011, Deputy Prime Minister Sam Condor alleged that he was denied access to the local television station when he tried to make a statement about a cabinet reshuffle that lost him control of the police and defense forces. The country has 15 radio stations, which are operated by state and private broadcasters; there is one weekly newspaper, and one daily, both of which are privately owned. Internet access is not restricted.

Freedom of religion is constitutionally protected, and academic freedom is generally honored.

The right to form civic organizations is generally respected, as is freedom of assembly. The right to strike, while not specified by law, is recognized and generally respected in practice. The main labor union, the Saint Kitts Trades and Labour Union, is associated with the ruling SKNLP. An estimated 10 percent of the workforce is unionized.

The judiciary is largely independent, and legal provisions for a fair and speedy trial are generally observed. The highest court is the Eastern Caribbean Supreme Court on Saint Lucia, but under certain circumstances, there is a right of appeal to the Trinidad-based Caribbean Court of Justice. Additionally, an appeal may be made to the Privy Council in Britain.

The islands' traditionally strong rule of law continues to be tested by the prevalence of drug-related crime and corruption. The intimidation of witnesses and jurors also remains a problem. In 2011, the murder rate in Saint Kitts rose 55 percent over its 2010 level, prompting the Denzil Douglas administration to reshuffle its cabinet and create a special stop-and-search police unit known as the Delta Squad. The administration reported that crime had dropped by 48 percent from August to September, and an additional 23 percent from September to October. The national prison is overcrowded, housing over 270 prisoners in a space intended for 150.

While domestic violence was criminalized in 2000, violence against women remains a problem, and there are no laws against sexual harassment or spousal rape. Legislation passed in 2008 increased the age of consent for sexual activity from 16 to 18. Only one woman serves in the National Assembly.

Saint Lucia

Political Rights: 1
Civil Liberties: 1
Status: Free

Population: 176,000
Capital: Castries

Ten-Year Ratings Timeline For Year Under Review (Political Rights, Civil Liberties, Status)

2002	2003	2004	2005	2006	2007	2008	2009	2010	2011
1,2F	1,2F	1,2F	1,1F	1,1F	1,1F	1,1F	1,1F	1,1F	1,1F

Overview: **In November 2011 legislative elections, the Saint Lucia Labour Party (SLP) captured 11 of 17 seats, while the United Worker's Party took the remaining 6 seats. Former prime minister Kenny Anthony of the SLP was returned to power.**

Saint Lucia, a member of the Commonwealth, achieved independence from Britain in 1979. Kenny Anthony led the Saint Lucia Labour Party (SLP) to victory in the 1997 legislative elections, defeating the United Workers' Party (UWP). As prime minister, Anthony began to address the concerns of an electorate that was weary of economic distress and reports of official corruption. In the 2001 general elections, the SLP retained a majority of seats in the House of Assembly, and Anthony returned to the premiership.

John Compton, Saint Lucia's first prime minister after independence, came out of retirement to lead the UWP to an unexpected victory in the December 2006 elections by winning 11 seats in the House of Assembly. He was sworn in again as prime minister at the age of 81. Compton was soon sidelined by illness and died in September 2007. He was replaced by Stephenson King, a UWP cabinet member who had served as acting prime minister for several months before Compton's death.

During 2008, the opposition SLP repeatedly threatened to mount public demonstrations and called for King's resignation. The SLP was particularly critical of the government's intention to ratify the Rome Statute of the International Criminal Court, while opting out of a drug interdiction agreement with Britain. The Rome Statute was eventually ratified in August 2010.

In 2009, King reshuffled his cabinet for the second time since taking office in an effort to regain political momentum in the face of a deteriorating economic situation. Damage inflicted by Hurricane Tomas in 2010 adversely affected revenues in agriculture and tourism and contributed to Saint Lucia's budget deficit. Weak economic growth, an unemployment rate of 20 percent, and a substantial rise in violent crime emboldened opposition leaders as the country prepared for the 2011 general elections.

In elections held on November 28, 2011, the SLP unseated the UWP, giving it an 11 to 6 seat majority in the House of Assembly. As a result of the elections, Kenny Anthony was returned to the position of prime minister in late November.

Political Rights and Civil Liberties: Saint Lucia is an electoral democracy. The 2011 legislative elections were deemed free and fair by observers. A governor-general represents the British monarch as head of state. Under the 1979 constitution, the bicameral Parliament consists of the 17-member House of Assembly, elected for five years, and an 11-member Senate. The prime minister is chosen by the majority party in the House of Assembly. Six members of the Senate are chosen by the prime minister, three by the leader of the parliamentary opposition, and two in consultation with civic and religious organizations. The island is divided into 11 regions, each with its own elected council and administrative services. Political parties are free to organize, but two parties—the UWP and the SLP—dominate politics.

Saint Lucia is generally said to have low levels of corruption and was ranked 25 out of 183 countries surveyed in Transparency International's 2011 Corruption Perceptions Index. Government officials are required by law to present their financial assets annually.

The constitution guarantees freedom of speech, which is respected in practice. Libel offenses were removed from the criminal code in 2006. The media carry a wide spectrum of views and are largely independent of the government. There are five privately owned newspapers, three privately held radio stations, and one government-funded radio station. Three privately owned television stations and one government-owned television station also operate. Internet access is not restricted. The constitution guarantees freedom of religion, and that right is respected in practice. Academic freedom is generally honored.

Constitutional guarantees regarding freedoms of assembly and association are largely upheld. Civic groups are well organized and politically active, as are labor unions, which represent the majority of wage earners.

The judicial system is independent and includes a high court under the Saint Lucia-based Eastern Caribbean Supreme Court. In recent years, the record of Saint Lucia's police and judicial system has been blemished by a series of high-profile incidents, including severe beatings of inmates by police and cases of police assault. Amid other high-profile crimes in 2011, the gang-rape of two British women in

May was still under investigation as the six men originally arrested for the crime were released after not being charged due to lack of evidence.

Citizens have traditionally enjoyed a high degree of personal security, though rising levels of crime have caused widespread concern. Saint Lucia has become a transit point for drugs destined for Britain. In 2011 the island experienced 50 murders, making it the bloodiest year on record. The violence was largely the result of gang-related crimes such as drug trafficking, drive-by shootings, and armed robbery. Prison overcrowding remains a problem, with major backlogs in the judicial system leading to prolonged pretrial detentions.

Women are underrepresented in politics and other professions; there are currently three women serving in Parliament. Domestic violence is a serious concern, especially among women from low-income groups. Homosexuals are occasionally the target of hate crimes.

Saint Vincent and the Grenadines

Political Rights: 1
Civil Liberties: 1
Status: Free

Population: 109,400
Capital: Kingstown

Ten-Year Ratings Timeline For Year Under Review (Political Rights, Civil Liberties, Status)

2002	2003	2004	2005	2006	2007	2008	2009	2010	2011
2,1F	2,1F	2,1F	2,1F	2,1F	2,1F	2,1F	2,1F	1,1F	1,1F

Overview: **In April 2011, torrential rain led to flash flooding and landslides that destroyed banana cultivation and severely impacted the Saint Vincent and the Grenadines' economy; the country had already been reeling from the impact of Hurricane Tomas in October 2010. The government spent the year focused mainly on economic development and the country's recovery from the two disasters.**

Saint Vincent and the Grenadines achieved independence from Britain in 1979, with jurisdiction over the northern Grenadine islands of Bequia, Canouan, Mayreau, Mustique, Prune Island, Petit Saint Vincent, and Union Island.

In the 2001 elections, the social-democratic Unity Labour Party (ULP) captured 12 of the 15 contested legislative seats, and Ralph Gonsalves became prime minister. The incumbent, conservative New Democratic Party (NDP) was reduced to three seats. In the 2005 polls, Gonsalves led the ULP to reelection, again taking 12 seats, while the NDP took the remaining 3 seats.

In 2009, the country was polarized over a November national referendum to replace its 1979 constitution with one produced by a government-appointed Constitution Review Commission. Among other changes, the proposed constitution would make the country a republic, open national elections to members of the clergy and dual citizens, and permit marriage only between a biological man and a biological woman. The opposition strongly opposed the new constitution for falling short of fully reforming the government. Needing two-thirds majority, the measure failed to pass, receiving support from only 43 percent of voters.

In the December 2010 general elections, the ULP, still reeling from the defeat of the proposed constitutional reform referendum, won a slim majority of eight seats, and Gonsalves retained the post of prime minister. Meanwhile, the NDP more than doubled its representation, taking seven seats. Despite threats of legal challenges from NDP leaders, the elections were deemed free and fair by observers from the Caribbean Community, the Organization of American States, and the National Monitoring and Consultative Mechanism.

The focus of the Gonsalves administration during 2011 was on economic development and the recovery from natural disasters. Torrential rains in April 2011 led to flash flooding and landslides that wiped out the country's banana industry—which accounts for a third of Saint Vincent's exports—and resulted in approximately $100 million in damage. The rains compounded the destruction caused in 2010 by Hurricane Tomas, which displaced some 1,200 people and resulted in approximately $25 million in damages to the agriculture sector. Part of Gonsalves's economic plan is to bolster the tourism industry by constructing a modern international airport that would create easier access to Saint Vincent. Construction of the airport began in late 2011, after years of delays.

Political Rights and Civil Liberties:

Saint Vincent and the Grenadines is an electoral democracy. The constitution provides for the election of 15 representatives to the unicameral House of Assembly. Six senators are also appointed to the chamber, four chosen by the government and two by the opposition; all serve five-year terms. The prime minister is the leader of the majority party. A governor-general represents the British monarch as head of state.

In recent years, there have been allegations of money laundering through Saint Vincent banks and drug-related corruption within the government and the police force. Saint Vincent was ranked 36 out of 183 countries surveyed in Transparency International's 2011 Corruption Perceptions Index.

The press is independent. There are two privately owned, independent weeklies and several smaller, partisan papers. The only television station is privately owned and free from government interference. Satellite dishes and cable television are available. The main news radio station is government owned, and call-in programs are prohibited. Equal access to radio is mandated during electoral campaigns, but there have been allegations that the ruling party has taken advantage of state control over programming. Some journalists also allege that government advertising is used as a political tool. Internet access is not restricted, and new network capabilities introduced in 2010 brought the promise of increased access.

Freedom of religion is constitutionally protected and respected in practice, and academic freedom is generally honored. Access to higher education is limited but improving, as the University of the West Indies initiates degree programs with community colleges in Saint Vincent and throughout the Organization of Eastern Caribbean States.

Freedoms of assembly and association are constitutional protected, and nongovernmental organizations are free from government interference. Labor unions are active and permitted to strike.

The government generally respects judicial independence, though the Saint Vincent and the Grenadines Human Rights Association (SVGHRA) has charged that the executive branch at times exerts inordinate influence over the courts. The highest court is the Saint Lucia-based Eastern Caribbean Supreme Court, which includes a court of appeals and a high court. Under certain circumstances, litigants have a right of ultimate appeal to the Trinidad-based Caribbean Court of Justice. The SVGHRA has criticized long judicial delays and a large backlog of cases caused by personnel shortages in the local judiciary. At the end of 2011, there were 39 males awaiting trial for murder. Prison conditions remain poor. In October 2009, Saint Vincent opened the Belle Isle Correctional Facility to alleviate pressure on long-overcrowded correctional facilities. Murder convictions carry a mandatory death sentence, though executions have not taken place in over 15 years.

Women hold approximately 18 percent of seats in the elected House of Assembly and the appointed Senate. Violence against women, particularly domestic violence, is a major problem. The Domestic Violence Summary Proceedings Act, which provides for protective orders, offers some tools that benefit victims. Homosexuality remains a criminal offense, and Saint Vincent rejected a 2011 call by the UN Human Rights Council to repeal laws criminalizing same-sex relations.

Samoa

Political Rights: 2
Civil Liberties: 2
Status: Free

Population: 191,000
Capital: Apia

Ten-Year Ratings Timeline For Year Under Review (Political Rights, Civil Liberties, Status)

2002	2003	2004	2005	2006	2007	2008	2009	2010	2011
2,2F	2,2F	2,2F	2,2F	2,2F	2,2F	2,2F	2,2F	2,2F	2,2F

Overview: **The Human Rights Protection Party (HRPP) captured the most seats in the March 2011 legislative elections. The HRPP's Tuila'epa Aiono Sailele Milielegaoi was elected to a third term as prime minister. In January, the government ended its monopoly on telephone and internet services with the privatization of the state-owned telecommunications provider, SamoaTel.**

Germany controlled what is now Samoa between 1899 and World War I. New Zealand administered the islands under a UN mandate after World War II. The country gained independence in 1962.

The centrist Human Rights Protection Party (HRPP) has dominated politics since independence. Tuila'epa Aiono Sailele Malielegaoi of the HRPP secured a second term as prime minister in the 2006 legislative elections, in which the HRPP won 35 seats, the Samoa Democratic United Party captured 10 seats, and independents took the remainder. Former prime minister Tuiatua Tupua Tamasese Efi was elected head of state by the legislature in June 2007.

In the March 4, 2011, parliamentary elections, the HRPP took 36 seats, while the Tautua Somoa Party (TSP) captured the remaining 13 seats. The elections were generally regarded as fair and open, though the electoral court found four lawmakers from both the HRPP and TSP—including the head of the TSP—guilty of bribing voters, and stripped them of their seats. Twelve candidates from the HRPP and three from the TSP competed for the vacant seats in special by-elections in July. The HRPP captured all four seats, boosting its majority to 40 seats in the parliament. Tuila'epa was subsequently elected to a third term as prime minister.

Samoa depends heavily on annual remittances of $350 million from some 100,000 Samoans living abroad. The country has also been forging closer ties with China to benefit from financial aid, development loans, and the sale of fishing licenses, though the rapid expansion of Chinese presence in Samoan businesses has led local business leaders to warn of rising social tensions. To raise further revenue for the country, the government legalized casino gambling in 2010, though no casinos had opened by the end of the 2011. Samoans will be barred from the casinos to appease religious opponents who worry that gambling will have a corrupting influence on society. In December 2011, Samoa was admitted to the World Trade Organization (WTO); it has until June 2012 to ratify the agreement.

The role and powers of village chiefs continued to stir controversy in 2011. Matai, or chiefs of extended families, control local government and churches through the village fono, or legislature, which is open only to them. The Supreme Court ruled in 2000 that the village fono could not infringe on freedom of religion, speech, assembly, or association. However, entire families have been forced to leave their villages for allegedly insulting a matai, embracing a different religion, or voting for political candidates not endorsed by the matai. In June 2011, a matai who ran in the March general elections was banished by his village, which had backed another candidate.

Political Rights and Civil Liberties:

Samoa is an electoral democracy. Executive authority is vested in the head of state, who is elected for five-year terms by the Legislative Assembly. The head of state appoints the prime minister, who leads the government and names his own cabinet. All laws passed by the 49-member, unicameral Legislative Assembly must receive approval from the head of state to take effect. Approval of the matai is essential for most candidates for elected office. Two legislative seats are reserved for at-large voters, mostly citizens of mixed or non-Samoan heritage who have no ties to the 47 village-based constituencies. All lawmakers serve five-year terms. The main political parties are the HRPP and the TSP.

Official corruption and abuses are a source of increasing public discontent. In January 2011, a lawmaker was charged with 15 counts of theft and fraud related to the unlawful transfer of ownership of freehold land. In June, two former finance ministry employees were found guilty of stealing $400,000 and were sentenced to three years in jail. Samoa was ranked 69 out of 183 countries surveyed in Transparency International's 2011 Corruption Perceptions Index.

Freedoms of speech and the press are generally respected. The government operates one of three television stations, and there are several English-language and Samoan newspapers. A lawmaker who lost his seat in the 2011 elections sued TV3, a privately owned station, for defamation in its broadcasts prior to the elections. In December, TV3 was found guilty, and the station's manager and a reporter were fined $60,000. In January 2011, the government ended its monopoly on telephone and internet services by privatizing the national telecommunications provider SamoaTel.

The government respects freedom of religion in practice, and relations among religious groups are generally amicable. There were no reports of restrictions on academic freedom in 2011.

Freedoms of assembly and association are respected, and human rights groups operate freely. Approximately 60 percent of adults work in subsistence agriculture, and about 20 percent of wage earners belong to trade unions. Workers, including civil servants, can strike and bargain collectively.

The judiciary is independent and upholds the right to a fair trial. The Supreme Court is the highest court, with full jurisdiction over civil, criminal, and constitutional matters. The head of state, on the recommendation of the prime minister, appoints the chief justice. In January 2011, Mata Keli Tuatagaloa became the first woman named as district court judge. Prisons generally meet minimum international standards.

Samoa has no military, and the small police force has little impact in the villages, where the fono settles most disputes. The councils vary considerably in their decision-making styles and in the number of matai involved. Light offenses are usually punished with fines; serious offenses result in banishment from the village.

Domestic violence against women and children is common. Spousal rape is not illegal, and social pressure and fear of reprisal inhibit reporting of domestic abuse. In November 2011, Leatinu'u Salote Lesa became the first woman to head a political party in Samoa when she was elected to lead the TSP. In October 2011, the government rejected a call by the United Nations to decriminalize homosexuality, which it argues is contrary to Samoan culture and values.

San Marino

Political Rights: 1
Civil Liberties: 1
Status: Free

Population: 32,000
Capital: San Marino

Ten-Year Ratings Timeline For Year Under Review (Political Rights, Civil Liberties, Status)

2002	2003	2004	2005	2006	2007	2008	2009	2010	2011
1,1F	1,1F	1,1F	1,1F	1,1F	1,1F	1,1F	1,1F	1,1F	1,1F

Overview: **In 2011, the government canceled a referendum on joining the European Union (EU) in spite of popular support for becoming an EU member state. In a move to improve economic transparency, a law mandating greater cooperation with foreign governments that request financial information was adopted in July. In September, the government voted to establish a commission to fight organized crime.**

Founded in the year 301, according to tradition, San Marino is considered the world's oldest existing republic and is one of the world's smallest states. The papacy recognized San Marino's independence in 1631, as did the Congress of Vienna in 1815. In 1862, Italy and San Marino signed a treaty of friendship and economic cooperation. Despite its dependence on Italy, from which it currently receives budget subsidies, San Marino maintains its own political institutions. Tourism and banking dominate the country's economy.

In June 2008, the left-wing governing coalition—consisting of the Party of Socialists and Democrats (PSD), the Popular Alliance of Democrats (AP), the United Left (SU), and the new Democrats of the Center party (DdC)—collapsed when the AP withdrew its delegates. The move forced the Great and General Council, San Marino's legislature, to call early elections for November. In that poll, the center-right Pact for San Marino coalition—composed of the San Marino Christian Democratic Party (PDCS), the AP, the Freedom List, and the Sammarinese Union of Moderates—won 54 percent of the vote and 35 of the 60 seats in the legislature, with 22 seats going to the PDCS.

In July 2011, San Marino furthered its efforts to shed its image as a financially corrupt country, when the government voted in favor of a law that would require the republic to comply with foreign governments' requests for financial and banking information. The law would allow San Marino to offer information unilaterally, in compliance with Organization for Economic Cooperation and Development standards.

In March, the government canceled a referendum on joining the European Union (EU), despite popular support for accession. In June, the government chose to push for stronger adherence to EU standards without becoming a full-fledged EU member or giving the people the opportunity to vote in a referendum.

Political Rights and Civil Liberties: San Marino is an electoral democracy. The 60 members of the Great and General Council, the unicameral legislature, are elected every five years by proportional representation. Executive power rests with the 10-member Congress of State (cabinet), which is headed by two captains regent. As the joint heads of state, the captains regent are elected every six months by the Great and General Council from among its own members. Although there is no official prime minister, the secretary of state for foreign and political affairs is regarded as the head of government; Antonella Mularoni was elected to the post in December 2008. Under changes made to the electoral law in 2008, the winning coalition must capture a majority of 50 percent plus 1 and at least 30 of the 60 parliamentary seats.

The PDCS, the PSD, and the AP are the three dominant political groups in the country. There are several smaller groups, however, and majority governments are usually formed by a coalition of parties.

There are few problems with government corruption in the country, though financial corruption has led the government to continue exploring laws to provide greater financial transparency. In August 2010, San Marino became the 48th state to join the Council of Europe's Group of States against Corruption (GRECO). In June 2011, GRECO sent a team to evaluate San Marino and released a report on its findings in December in which it made a number of recommendations on how San Marino could develop more effective anticorruption programs. In September, the government voted to establish an antimafia commission to combat organized crime; its first official meeting was held in November.

Freedoms of speech and of the press are guaranteed. There are several daily private newspapers, a state-run broadcast system for radio and television called RTV, and a private FM station, Radio Titiano. The Sammarinese have access to all Italian print media and certain Italian broadcast stations. Access to the internet is unrestricted.

Religious discrimination is prohibited by law. Roman Catholicism is the dominant, but not the state, religion. Academic freedom is respected.

Freedom of assembly is respected, and civic organizations are active. Workers are free to strike, organize trade unions, and bargain collectively, unless they work in military occupations. Approximately half of the country's workforce is unionized.

The judiciary is independent. Lower court judges are required to be noncitizens—generally Italians—to assure impartiality. The final court of review is the Council of Twelve, a group of judges chosen for six-year terms from among the members of the Great and General Council. Civilian authorities maintain effective control over the police and security forces, and the country's prison system generally meets international standards.

The European Commission against Racism and Intolerance has raised some concerns in the past about the status of foreigners in the country. San Marino has no formal asylum policy, and a foreigner must live in the country for 30 years to be eligible for citizenship. The European Convention on Nationality recommends that such residence requirements not exceed 10 years.

Women are given legal protections from violence and spousal abuse, and gender equality exists in the workplace and elsewhere. There are, however, slight differences in the way men and women can transmit citizenship to their children. Abortion is permitted only to save the life of the mother, though abortion laws in neighboring Italy are more liberal, and some women living in San Marino seek abortions there. Under a 2008 electoral law, no more than two-thirds of candidates from each party can be of the same gender. Nine women were elected to the Great and General Council in 2008, and two to the 10-member Congress of State.

São Tomé and Príncipe

Political Rights: 2
Civil Liberties: 2
Status: Free

Population: 180,000
Capital: São Tomé

Ten-Year Ratings Timeline For Year Under Review (Political Rights, Civil Liberties, Status)

2002	2003	2004	2005	2006	2007	2008	2009	2010	2011
1,2F	2,2F	2,2F	2,2F	2,2F	2,2F	2,2F	2,2F	2,2F	2,2F

Overview: **Former president Manuel Pinto da Costa won the August 2011 presidential election, defeating the ruling party's candidate, Evaristo Carvalho, in a runoff vote. Meanwhile, the first**

international auction of oil explorations rights for the São Tomé Exclusive Economic Zone was held in May 2011.

São Tomé and Principe gained independence from Portugal in 1975. President Manuel Pinto da Costa's Movement for the Liberation of São Tomé and Principe—later the Movement for the Liberation of São Tomé and Principe/Social Democratic Party (MLSTP-PSD)—was the only legal political party until a 1990 referendum established multiparty democracy. Former prime minister Miguel dos Anjos Trovoada returned from exile and won the first democratic presidential election in 1991. He was reelected for a final term in 1996.

Fradique de Menezes, backed by Trovoada's Independent Democratic Action (ADI) party, won the 2001 presidential election. In 2003, a group of military officers briefly ousted Menezes, but he was returned to power one week later.

The Force for Change Democratic Movement-Liberal Party (MDFM-PL), in coalition with the Democratic Convergence Party (PCD), captured more seats than any other party in the 2006 parliamentary elections. While peaceful protesters had prevented thousands from voting in several parts of the country, a rerun for affected districts was subsequently held without incident. Negotiations on the formation of a new coalition government led to the appointment of a new prime minister, MDFM leader Tomé Soares da Vera Cruz. In the July presidential election, Menezes was chosen for a second term.

Following growing criticism over price increases and the handling of a police mutiny in 2007, the government collapsed twice in 2008. A new ruling coalition was formed in June with Joaquim Rafael Branco, leader of the MLSTP-PSD, as prime minister. The ADI refused to join, but the government gained a majority of seats in the National Assembly.

In the August 2010 parliamentary elections, the ADI captured 26 seats, followed by the MLSTP-PSD with 21 seats and the PCD with 7; the MDFM-PL captured only one seat. The Supreme Court validated the results, and ADI leader Patrice Trovoada was appointed prime minister.

After two unsuccessful electoral bids in 1996 and 2001, former president Pinto da Costa won the August 2011 presidential election. He defeated the ruling party's candidate, Evaristo Carvalho, in a runoff election with 52.9 percent of the vote. Foreign observers deemed the highly contested elections credible and fair. Pinto da Costa has sought to quell fears about human rights violations during his previous 15-year authoritarian rule by vowing to respect the rights of São Toméans during his presidential term.

Large oil and natural gas deposits are thought to lie off the nation's coast. The first international auction of oil explorations rights for the São Tomé Exclusive Economic Zone was held in May 2011; companies from the United States, Nigeria, and the British Virgin Islands were among those awarded rights. A 2001 agreement with Nigeria created the Joint Development Zone (JDZ), which provides São Tomé and Principe with 40 percent of oil and gas revenues. Corruption allegations have surrounded the process by which exploration blocks in the JDZ are awarded, and bonus funds intended for São Tomé's oil account were allegedly transferred to a Nigerian bank in 2008.

São Tomé and Principe's economy has seen steady growth since 2010, thanks to the expansion of trade and construction. However, according to the International Monetary Fund (IMF), despite the substantial debt relief São Tomé and Principe has received, the country remains at high risk of falling back into debt distress because of its limited export and production base.

Political Rights and Civil Liberties: São Tomé and Principe is an electoral democracy. The 2010 parliamentary elections were free and fair, as were the presidential elections in 2011. The president is elected for up to two five-year terms. Members of the unicameral, 55-seat National Assembly are elected by popular vote to four-year terms.

Development aid and potential oil wealth have fueled corruption among the ruling elite. In November 2010, the president was implicated in a scandal involving the sale of oil, after the cabinet secretary declared that records of revenues from these sales could not be located in the Treasury. The state prosecutor began an investigation into the matter in December 2010 but announced in February 2011 that it would not be able to pursue the matter further due to immunity. The National Assembly removed the national audit office's oversight of the sale of public property and goods in 2009. The office initiated trials against five former government officials charged with the misappropriation of social welfare money in late 2009, though Menezes pardoned 10 former officials imprisoned for embezzling food aid funds in January 2010. São Tomé and Principe was ranked 100 out of 183 countries surveyed in Transparency International's 2011 Corruption Perceptions Index.

Freedom of expression is guaranteed and respected. While the state controls a local press agency and the only radio and television stations, no law forbids independent broadcasting. Opposition parties receive free airtime, and newsletters and pamphlets criticizing the government circulate freely. Residents also have access to foreign broadcasters. Internet access is not restricted, though a lack of infrastructure limits penetration.

Freedom of religion is respected within this predominantly Roman Catholic country. The government does not restrict academic freedom.

Freedoms of assembly and association are respected. Citizens have the constitutional right to demonstrate with two days' advance notice to the government. Workers' rights to organize, strike, and bargain collectively are guaranteed and respected. In October 2011, the Union of State Workers threatened to paralyze the government if it did not respond to its demands, including a 400 percent wage increase; the 5,200 public workers are the largest workforce in São Tomé and Príncipe. Although the government included a 21 percent wage increase in the 2012 budget, the union organized a general strike on November 28 and threated to hold an antigovernment protest the following day. The latter was cancelled after the government and the union returned to the negotiating table.

The judiciary is independent, though occasionally subject to manipulation. The Supreme Court has ruled in the past against both the government and the president. The court system is understaffed and inadequately funded. Prison conditions are harsh.

The constitution provides equal rights for men and women, but women encounter discrimination in all sectors of society. Domestic violence is common and rarely prosecuted.

Saudi Arabia

Political Rights: 7
Civil Liberties: 7*
Status: Not Free

Population: 27,897,000
Capital: Riyadh

Ratings Change: Saudi Arabia's civil liberties rating declined from 6 to 7 due to new restrictions on the media and public speech as well as the severe treatment of religious minorities, including crackdowns on Shiite Muslim protests.

Ten-Year Ratings Timeline For Year Under Review (Political Rights, Civil Liberties, Status)

2002	2003	2004	2005	2006	2007	2008	2009	2010	2011
7,7NF	7,7NF	7,7NF	7,6NF	7,6NF	7,6NF	7,6NF	7,6NF	7,6NF	7,7NF

Overview: **In an effort to prevent popular uprisings similar to those that took place elsewhere in the Middle East in 2011, Saudi authorities announced over $130 billion in new social spending. Nevertheless, small protests occurred during the year, including in predominantly Shiite villages in the country's Eastern Province. Saudi women launched a highly visible campaign in May, calling for greater freedoms, including the right to drive, and King Abdullah announced that women would be allowed to vote in municipal elections in 2015 and hold seats in the country's Consultative Council, the Majlis al-Shura. Meanwhile, the King issued a royal decree in April amending the country's press law to criminalize criticism of religious scholars.**

Since its unification in 1932 by King Abdul Aziz Ibn Saud, Saudi Arabia has been governed by the Saud family in accordance with a conservative school of Sunni Islam. In the early 1990s, Saudi Arabia embarked on a limited program of political reform, introducing an appointed Consultative Council, or Majlis al-Shura. However, this did not lead to any substantial shift in political power. In 1995, King Fahd bin Abdul Aziz al-Saud suffered a stroke, and his half brother, Crown Prince Abdullah, took control of most decision making in 1997.

Following a series of terrorist attacks in 2003 and 2004, Saudi authorities intensified their counterterrorism efforts, killing dozens of suspects and detaining thousands of others over subsequent years. Officials also attempted to stem financial support for terrorist groups through new checks on money laundering and oversight of charitable organizations.

The formal transfer of power from King Fahd, who died in 2005, to King Abdullah led to increased expectations of political reform. However, Abdullah enacted few significant changes. The 2005 municipal council elections gave Saudi men a limited opportunity to select some of their leaders at the local level, but women were completely excluded. The eligible electorate consisted of less than 20 percent of the population: male citizens who were at least 21 years old, not serving in the military, and resident in their district for at least 12 months. Half of the council seats were open for election, and the other half were appointed by the monarchy. Candidates supported by conservative Muslim scholars triumphed in the large cities of Riyadh and Jeddah, and minority Shiite Muslim voters participated in large numbers. The government ultimately determined that the councils would serve only in an advisory capacity.

In 2006, Abdullah issued the bylaws for the Allegiance Commission, a new body to be composed of the sons (or grandsons, if sons are deceased, incapacitated, or unwilling) of the founding king. The commission, to be chaired by the oldest surviving son, would make decisions on appointing successors to the throne, using secret ballots and a quorum of two-thirds of the members. The commission was also granted the authority to deem a king or crown prince medically unfit to rule. With the death of Crown Prince Sultan bin Abdul Aziz in October 2011, the commission helped select former minister of the interior Nayef bin Abdul Aziz as heir apparent. A cabinet reshuffle in 2009 resulted in the appointment of the first-ever female cabinet member, Noura al-Fayez. The king also fired two controversial religious figures, one of whom headed the religious police force. The move was interpreted as a sign that the monarchy felt less beholden to hard-line religious leaders and was seeking to promote more moderate clerics. This trend continued in 2010, with King Abdullah decreeing in August that the issuing of religious edicts (fatwas) would be restricted to the Official Council of Senior Clergy. The decree was intended to outlaw the declaration of controversial fatwas and rein in radicalism.

In March 2011, over 1,000 members of Saudi Arabia's National Guard (SANG) were sent into Bahrain as part of the Gulf Cooperation Council's Peninsula Shield Force that helped to crack down on tens of thousands of Bahraini prodemocracy demonstrators.

Saudi Arabia did not experience the kind of popular protests that either toppled or threatened regimes elsewhere in the Middle East and North Africa in 2011. Saudi activists used social media to call for a "Day of Rage" to be held on March 11; however, authorities dispatched over 10,000 police and security personnel across the country as preemptive measures, and large protests failed to materialize. Nevertheless, smaller demonstrations occurred during the year, including in predominantly Shiite villages in the country's Eastern Province.

In an effort to prevent social unrest, King Abdullah committed over $130 billion to address some of the social and economic complaints of the country's citizens. Improvements included plans to construct affordable housing, provide unemployment benefits, and increase the salaries of government employees.

In September, the government held elections for half of the municipal council seats. While women were once again excluded from participating in these elections, and turnout was low, King Abdullah announced that women would be eligible to run and vote in the next round of municipal elections, scheduled for 2015, and would be allowed to hold seats in the country's Consultative Council, the Majlis al-Shura.

Saudi Arabia's growing youth population—which suffers from an unemployment rate estimated as high as 43 percent for those between the ages of 20 and 24—has placed additional pressure on the authorities to create new jobs. In response, the government has deployed its immense oil wealth to strengthen the nonpetroleum sector and sought to encourage private investment, though the results of these efforts remain unclear.

Political Rights and Civil Liberties: Saudi Arabia is not an electoral democracy. The 1992 Basic Law declares that the Koran and the Sunna (the guidance set by the deeds and sayings of the prophet Muhammad) are the country's constitution. The cabinet, which is appointed by the king, passes legislation that becomes law once ratified by royal decree. The king also appoints a 150-member Majlis al-Shura (Consultative Council) every four years, though it serves only in an advisory capacity. Limited elections for advisory councils at the municipal level were introduced in 2005, and the second round of elections was held in September 2011. In addition to the advisory councils, the monarchy has a tradition of consulting with select members of Saudi society, but the process is not equally open to all citizens. Political parties are forbidden, and organized political opposition exists only outside the country, with many London-based activists.

Corruption remains a significant problem. After widespread floods killed over 120 people in November 2009, King Abdullah in May 2010 ordered the prosecution of over 40 officials in the city of Jeddah on charges of corruption and mismanagement related to improper construction and engineering practices. A second round of floods in January 2011 killed over 10 people and displaced several thousands, sparking outrage and even small protests that alleged ongoing corruption. In March 2011, King Abdullah issued a royal decree establishing an anticorruption commission to monitor and observe government departments, though administrative obstacles hindered the commission's success in 2011.

The government tightly controls domestic media content and dominates regional print and satellite-television coverage, with members of the royal family owning major stakes in news outlets in multiple countries. Government officials have banned journalists and editors who publish articles deemed offensive to the religious establishment or the ruling authorities. In April 2011, the king issued a royal decree amending the country's press law, placing further restrictions on freedom of expression. The amendments criminalize any criticism of the country's Grand Mufti, the Council of Senior Religious Scholars, or government officials. Violations could result in fines and forced closure.

In March 2011, Khaled al-Johani, a teacher, was arrested after criticizing the government and calling for greater rights and democracy during an interview recorded in public in Riyadh, and broadcast by the television station BBC Arabic. He was imprisoned shortly afterwards and remained in jail at year's end. Also in March, authorities withdrew the press credentials of Ulf Laessing, a Reuters correspondent based in Riyadh, for attempting to cover the recent public protests. Saudi filmmaker Feras Bugnah was arrested in October and detained without charge for over two weeks after he posted a film documenting widespread poverty in Riyadh.

The regime has taken steps to limit the influence of new media, blocking access to over 400,000 websites that are considered immoral or politically sensitive. In January 2011, the kingdom issued a law requiring all blogs and websites, or anyone posting news or commentary online, to have a license from the Ministry of Information or face fines and/or the closure of the website.

Islam is the official religion, and all Saudis are required by law to be Muslims. The government prohibits the public practice of any religion other than Islam and restricts the religious practices of the Shiite and Sufi Muslim minority sects. Although the government recognizes the right of non-Muslims to worship in private, it does not always respect this right in practice. In 2009, authorities instituted a ban on the building of Shiite mosques, marking a significant reversal of policies that had offered Shiites some religious freedom in recent years.

Academic freedom is restricted, and informers monitor classrooms for compliance with curriculum rules, such as a ban on teaching secular philosophy and religions other than Islam. Despite changes to textbooks in recent years, intolerance in the classroom remains an important problem, as some teachers continue to espouse discriminatory and hateful views of non-Muslims and Muslim minority sects.

Freedoms of association and assembly are not upheld. The government frequently detains political activists who stage demonstrations or engage in other civic advocacy. While there were no large-scale protests in 2011, a number of smaller protests took place throughout the year. In spite of routine arrests, family members of political prisoners protested regularly outside the Ministry of the Interior (MOI) building in Riyadh, demanding information and the release of their loved ones. In July, over 20 people were arrested, including women and children, for protesting in front of the MOI, though they were later released. Protests also took place in predominantly Shiite villages in the country's Eastern Province throughout the year. Hundreds and sometimes thousands of Shiite demonstrators took to the streets demanding the release of political prisoners, political reform, and in support of the uprising in Bahrain. Authorities increased their security presence in Shiite villages in order to prevent larger protests. At least 14 people, including security personnel, were injured in clashes between police and protesters in al-Awamiyya village in October. Saudi security forces imposed a heavy security cordon in Shiite villages in the Eastern Province in the fall and early winter 2011, targeting activists and preventing media from reporting on events in the region.

A 2005 labor law extended various protections and benefits to previously unregulated categories of workers. The legislation also banned child labor, set provisions for resolving labor disputes, and established a 75 percent quota for Saudi citizens in each company's workforce. However, the more than six million foreign workers in the country have virtually no legal protections. Many are lured to the kingdom under false pretenses and forced to endure dangerous working and living conditions. Female migrants employed in Saudi homes as domestic workers report regular physical, sexual, and emotional abuse.

In 2007, Abdullah established a new Supreme Court and an Appeals Court, whose members are appointed by the king. The new higher courts replaced the old judiciary council, which was widely considered reactionary and inconsistent. A Special Higher Commission of judicial experts was formed in 2008 to write laws that would serve as the foundation for verdicts in the court system, which is grounded in Sharia (Islamic law). While Saudi courts have historically relied on the Hanbali school of Islamic jurisprudence, the commission incorporates all four Sunni Muslim legal schools in drafting the new laws. In 2009, the kingdom began a judicial training program and initiated the construction of new courts.

The penal code bans torture, but allegations of torture by police and prison officials are common, and access to prisoners by independent human rights and legal organizations is strictly limited. In July 2011, Saudi Arabia issued a draft of a sweeping new antiterrorism law, which Amnesty International criticized as an attempt to silence calls for reform; the draft law includes significant prison sentences for criticizing the government or questioning the integrity of the king or crown prince.

Substantial prejudice against ethnic, religious, and national minorities prevails. Shiites represent 10 to 15 percent of the population and are underrepresented in major government positions; no Shiite has ever served as a government minister. Shiites have also faced physical assaults.

Freedom of movement is restricted in some cases. The government punishes activists and critics by limiting their ability to travel outside the country. Reform advocates are routinely stripped of their passports.

Saudis have the right to own property and establish private businesses. While a great deal of business activity is connected to members of the government, the ruling family, or other elite families, officials have given assurances that industrial and commercial zones currently being built will be free from royal family interference.

Women are not treated as equal members of society, and many laws discriminate against them. They were not permitted to vote in the 2005 or 2011 municipal elections, they may not legally drive cars, and their use of public facilities is restricted in some cases when men are present. By law and custom, Saudi women cannot travel within or outside of the country without a male relative. Unlike Saudi men, Saudi women cannot pass their citizenship to their children or foreign-born husbands. According to interpretations of Sharia in Saudi Arabia, daughters generally receive half the inheritance awarded to their brothers, and the testimony of one man is equal to that of two women. Moreover, Saudi women seeking access to the courts must be represented by a male. The religious police enforce a strict policy of gender segregation and often harass women, using physical punishment to ensure that they meet conservative standards of dress in public. In May 2011, Saudi women launched a highly visible campaign demanding the expansion of their rights, including the right to drive. A 32-year-old Saudi woman, Manal al-Sharif, was arrested on May 21 after posting a video of herself driving on YouTube; she was released 10 days later.

Education and economic rights for Saudi women have improved somewhat in recent years. More than half of the country's university students are now female, though they do not have equal access to classes and facilities. Women gained the right to hold commercial licenses in 2004, and Saudi state television began using women as newscasters in 2005. That same year, two women became the first females elected to Jeddah's chamber of commerce. In 2008, the Saudi Human Rights Commission established a women's branch to investigate cases of human rights violations against women and children; it has not consistently carried out any serious investigations or brought cases against violators. A 2009 law imposes fines of up to $266,000 for those found guilty of human trafficking.

Senegal

Political Rights: 3
Civil Liberties: 3
Status: Partly Free

Population: 12,767,000
Capital: Dakar

Ten-Year Ratings Timeline For Year Under Review (Political Rights, Civil Liberties, Status)

2002	2003	2004	2005	2006	2007	2008	2009	2010	2011
2,3F	2,3F	2,3F	2,3F	2,3F	2,3F	3,3PF	3,3PF	3,3PF	3,3PF

Overview: **Tensions rose in 2011 in the run-up to the February 2012 presidential election, in which President Abdoulaye Wade planned to run for a constitutionally questionable third term. Protests and riots broke out in Dakar in June as the parliament debated constitutional changes, sponsored by Wade, that would have reduced the threshold needed to win in the first round of a presidential election and created the post of vice president. The bills were withdrawn in response to the protests. Sporadic demonstrations and opposition campaigns against Wade's candidacy continued through the end of 2011.**

Since independence from France in 1960, Senegal has avoided military or harsh authoritarian rule and has never suffered a successful coup d'état. President Leopold Senghor exercised de facto one-party rule through the Socialist Party (PS) for nearly two decades after independence. Most political restrictions were lifted after 1981, when Abdou Diouf of the PS succeeded Senghor. Diouf went on to win large victories in elections in 1988 and 1993.

Four decades of PS rule ended when Senegalese Democratic Party (PDS) leader Abdoulaye Wade defeated Diouf in the 2000 presidential runoff vote, which was deemed free and fair by international observers. A new constitution was approved in 2001, reducing presidential terms from seven to five years, setting the maximum number of terms at two, and abolishing the Senate. A coalition led by the PDS won a majority of seats in the 2001 legislative elections.

After taking office in 2000, Wade worked to increase the power of the presidency and demonstrated a willingness to persecute those threatening his authority. Idrissa Seck was dismissed as prime minister in 2004 based on accusations of embezzlement and threatening national security, though charges against him were later dropped. In 2006, Wade led a successful drive to amend the constitution to postpone legislative elections by a year and reestablish the Senate, where most of the members would be appointed by the president.

Wade secured a second term in the 2007 presidential election, which saw 70.5 percent turnout and fervent opposition accusations of vote rigging. Wade claimed 56 percent of the vote, compared with 15 percent for Seck, the runner-up. The opposition coalition, including the PS and 11 other parties, boycotted legislative polls later that year, leading to an overwhelming victory for the PDS, whose Sopi (Change) coalition secured 131 of 150 seats; turnout was just 35 percent. The National Assembly in 2008 approved Wade's proposal to restore the seven-year presidential term beginning in 2012.

In September 2009, Wade announced his intention to run for a third term in 2012, prompting critics to allege that he was trying to circumvent the constitution, which set a two-term limit. Supporters contended that Wade's current term was his first under the 2001 constitution, which introduced term limits, making his run for a possible a third term legal. In October 2010, Wade appointed his son, Karim, as energy minister, in addition to his existing role as minister of international cooperation, national planning, air transport, and infrastructure. The move prompted fears that the president was positioning his son to succeed him.

Protests and riots broke out in Dakar and other towns on June 23, 2011, as the PDS-dominated parliament considered constitutional amendments, introduced by Wade, that would lower the threshold for victory in the first round of a presidential election from 50 percent to 25 percent and create the position of vice president. Those changes would have virtually assured Wade victory in the first round against the fractured opposition, and, the protesters alleged, allowed the octogenarian incumbent to appoint his son as vice president and then pass the presidency on to him. The protests—unusual for Senegal—escalated during the day and prompted the PDS to withdraw the bill. More than 100 people were injured as police used rubber bullets, tear gas, and water cannons to subdue stone-throwing demonstrators, who were also angered by the declining standard of public services and the rising cost of living. Four days later, protesters ransacked the offices of the state electricity company, Senelec, in response to chronic, prolonged power cuts. In early October, a spokesman confirmed that Wade would be the PDS's presidential candidate in 2012.

The separatist conflict in the Casamance region remained unresolved at the end of 2011. The peace process had wavered since the 2007 death of the head of the separatist Movement of the Democratic Forces of Casamance, Augustin Diamacoune Senghor. Although there were no major clashes in 2011, about 83 people were reported killed in connection with the conflict during the year. Progress has been made in recent years in clearing the region of land mines, which have caused nearly 800 deaths and 60,000 displacements since 1988.

Political Rights and Civil Liberties: Senegal is an electoral democracy. The National Observatory of Elections has credibly overseen legislative and presidential polls since its creation in 1997. The president is elected by popular vote for up to two terms, and the length of the term was extended from five to seven years by a constitutional amendment in 2008. However, there were widespread fears in 2011 that the Constitutional Council would rule in early 2012 in favor of President Abdoulaye Wade's bid to run for a third term in the February 2012 election, a move that many legal scholars believed to be unconstitutional. The president appoints the prime minister. In April 2009, Wade appointed his former spokesman, Souleymane Ndéné Ndiaye, to the post.

Constitutional amendments that took effect in 2007 converted the National Assembly into a 150-seat lower house and created an upper house, the 100-member Senate. Members of the National Assembly are popularly elected every five years, though the most recent vote was postponed from 2006 to 2007 as part of the amendments. The Senate consists of 65 members appointed by the president and 35 members elected by public officials.

There are more than 75 legally registered political parties in Senegal. Major parties include the ruling PDS and the opposition PS. The PDS currently controls most national political offices, but the opposition performed well in the 2009 municipal elections. The June 23 Movement (M23)—comprising about 60 opposition parties and nongovernmental organizations (NGOs) and formed out of the June 23, 2011, protests—was created in an effort to prevent Wade from running in the 2012 presidential election. The June 23 protests were sparked in part by a new, younger group of activists led by rap musicians known as the Y'en A Marre (Enough Is Enough) movement. Both groups have drawn comparisons to the Arab Spring movements that swept across North Africa and the Middle East beginning in early 2011.

Corruption remains a serious problem. Wade sparked considerable controversy in August 2010 when he asserted his right to royalties on a $27 million monument constructed in Dakar in celebration of Senegal's 50th year of independence; the monument itself is viewed by many as an abuse of public funds, especially as public services and living standards continue to erode. In response to chronic power outages and public criticism, Wade called for an audit of the state-run electricity company in October 2010. Blackouts remained problematic throughout 2011. Senegal was ranked 112 out of 183 countries surveyed in Transparency International's 2011 Corruption Perceptions Index.

Freedom of expression is generally respected, and members of the independent media are often highly critical of the government despite the risk of criminal defamation charges; however, self-censorship is said to be rising. There are a variety of public, private, and community radio stations and many independent print outlets. The government operates a television station, and there are several private television stations, which are subject to government censorship. In February 2011, Transparency International and its Senegalese chapter, Forum Civil, expressed concern over the ongoing "prosecution for criminal defamation and harassment" of Abdou Latif Coulibaly, an investigative journalist and critic of Wade, for his reporting on government corruption. In November 2010, Coulibaly had been found guilty of defamation against a special adviser to Wade and given a two-month suspended sentence. In April 2011, he again was convicted of defamation in a separate case related to his stories about alleged fraudulent government dealings, and given a three-month suspended sentence. In October 2011, opposition activist Malick Noël Seck—who was aligned with the PS—was sentenced to two years in prison for issuing a death threat, assault, and contempt of court, after sending a letter to the Constitutional Council in which he criticized the body for its silence on the controversy over Wade's candidacy. Access to the internet is not restricted.

Religious freedom is respected, and the government provides free airline tickets to Senegalese Muslims and Christians undertaking pilgrimages overseas. Senegal is a predominantly Muslim country, with 94 percent of the population practicing Islam. The country's Sufi Muslim brotherhoods are very influential; Wade has close ties with the most powerful brotherhood, the Mouride. Academic freedom is legally guaranteed and respected in practice.

Freedoms of association and assembly are guaranteed. The number of street protests and demonstrations has been on the rise in recent years, and the government has taken action to repress some of them. There were sporadic demonstrations throughout 2011 in Dakar and other towns against Wade's bid for a third term; citizens also protested against lengthy power cuts and an increase in basic living expenses. In the June 23 protest, two rights activists, Alioune Tine and Oumar Diallo, were assaulted, and identified their attackers as young PDS supporters. In July and September, the government attempted to cancel protests against Wade's 2012 candidacy, but the demonstrations went ahead as planned.

Human rights groups and other NGOs had previously operated freely in Senegal, but the rising political tensions in 2011 resulted in some efforts by the government to curb their work. Wade's office in October said it would bar Senegalese rights group the African Encounter for the Defense of Human Rights, headed by Tine, from acting as a monitor in the February 2012 presidential election because it had become a leading member of M23. Although workers' rights to organize, bargain collectively, and strike are legally protected for all except security employees, the labor code requires the approval of the Interior Ministry for the initial formation of a trade union.

The judiciary is independent by law, but poor pay and lack of tenure expose judges to external influences and prevent the courts from providing a proper check on the other branches of government. Uncharged detainees are incarcerated without legal counsel far beyond the lengthy periods already permitted by law. Prisons are overcrowded, often leading to hygiene and health issues for inmates.

Women's constitutional rights are often disregarded, especially in rural areas, and women enjoy fewer opportunities than men for education and formal employment. In May 2010, the National Assembly passed legislation requiring parity between men and women on candidate lists for public office. Women hold 34 seats in the 150-seat National Assembly, and 40 of 100 seats in the Senate. Many elements of Islamic and local customary law, particularly regarding inheritance and marital relations, discriminate against women. Rape and domestic abuse are widespread problems.

Child trafficking is a problem in Senegal. In particular, boys are often drawn in by Koranic teachers' promises to provide religious education, only to be physically abused and forced to beg in the streets. According to the U.S. State Department's 2011 Trafficking in Persons Report, approximately 50,000 child beggars lived under these circumstances. In September 2010, seven Koranic teachers were arrested and convicted of using children to beg, marking the first application of a 2005 law banning organized child begging. A conference held in Dakar in January 2011 sought to address the problem by educating the population about the issue via Islamic texts and religious leaders.

Serbia

Political Rights: 2
Civil Liberties: 2
Status: Free

Population: 7,257,000
Capital: Belgrade

Note: The ratings through 2002 are for the Federal Republic of Yugoslavia, of which Serbia was a part, and those from 2003 through 2005 are for the State Union of Serbia and Montenegro. Kosovo is examined in a separate report.

Ten-Year Ratings Timeline For Year Under Review (Political Rights, Civil Liberties, Status)

2002	2003	2004	2005	2006	2007	2008	2009	2010	2011
3,2PF	3,2F	3,2F	3,2F	3,2F	3,2F	3,2F	2,2F	2,2F	2,2F

Overview: **Serbia in 2011 arrested the last fugitive war crimes suspects from the conflicts of the 1990s, allowing the country to progress on its path to European Union candidacy. However, the deadlock between Belgrade and Pristina over Kosovo's sovereignty remained unresolved. Separately, in October, the government barred a gay pride parade on the grounds that related violence by extremist groups would jeopardize national security.**

Serbia was recognized as an independent state in 1878 after several centuries under Ottoman rule. It formed the core of the Kingdom of Serbs, Croats, and Slovenes proclaimed in 1918. After World War II, Serbia became a constituent republic of the Socialist Federal Republic of Yugoslavia, under the rule of Josip Broz Tito. Within the boundaries of the Serbian republic as drawn at that time were two autonomous provinces: the largely Albanian-populated Kosovo in the south, and Vojvodina, with a significant Hungarian minority, in the north.

Following the disintegration of socialist Yugoslavia in 1991, the republics of Serbia and Montenegro in 1992 formed the Federal Republic of Yugoslavia (FRY). Slobodan Miloševic and his Socialist Party of Serbia (SPS, the former League of Communists of Serbia) ruled Serbia throughout the 1990s by controlling the country's security forces, financial institutions, and state-owned media. An avowed Serb nationalist, Miloševic oversaw extensive Serbian involvement in the 1991–95 wars that accompanied the old federation's breakup, supporting local Serb forces both in Bosnia and Herzegovina and in Croatia.

In 1998–99, an ethnic Albanian insurgency in Kosovo provoked increasingly violent reprisals by state forces against the guerrillas and the civilian population. In March 1999, NATO launched a 78-day bombing campaign to force the withdrawal of FRY and Serbian forces. A NATO-led force then occupied Kosovo, and the United Nations oversaw institution-building efforts there.

Miloševic was forced from office in October 2000, after his attempt to steal the September Yugoslav presidential election from opposition candidate Vojislav Koštunica of the Democratic Party of Serbia (DSS) triggered massive protests. An anti-Miloševic coalition took power following Serbian parliamentary elections in

December, and Zoran Đindic of the Democratic Party (DS) became Serbia's prime minister. The FRY was replaced with a looser State Union of Serbia and Montenegro in 2003, and each republic was granted the option of holding an independence referendum after three years.

Đindic was assassinated by organized crime groups allied with Miloševic-era security structures in March 2003, and after parliamentary elections in December, Koštunica became Serbia's prime minister at the head of a fragile coalition government. The new DS leader, Boris Tadic, won the Serbian presidency in a June 2004 election.

Montenegro held a successful referendum on independence in May 2006, formally declaring independence the following month. This necessitated new Serbian elections, and in January 2007 the main anti-Miloševic parties—including the DS, the DSS, and the liberal G17 Plus—collectively outpolled the ultranationalist Serbian Radical Party (SRS) and the SPS. In May, Koštunica formed another coalition government. Tadic won a second term as president in early February 2008, taking 51 percent of the vote.

Later that month, Kosovo unilaterally declared its independence from Serbia. Debate over the proper response increased tensions in the Koštunica government, which ultimately resigned in March, prompting new elections. The May balloting resulted in an undisputed victory for the DS and its smaller allies, which favored economic reform and European Union (EU) integration. The DS-led bloc won 102 of 250 seats and formed a coalition government with an SPS-led bloc (20 seats), the Hungarian Coalition (4 seats), and the Bosniak List for European Sandžak (2 seats). The SRS took 78 seats, followed by the DSS with 30; the smaller Liberal Democratic Party took 13 seats, and the Coalition of Albanians of the Preševo Valley won the remaining seat.

The new government, led by Mirko Cvetkovic, was the first since 2000 to include the SPS, which had sought to reinvent itself as a mainstream center-left party. The outcome also marked the first time since 2000 that a single party, the DS, controlled the presidency, the premiership, and a working majority in the parliament. In another sign of political normalization, hard-liners in the SRS were further isolated when the moderate wing of the party broke off to form the Serbian Progressive Party (SNS) in September.

In 2009, the parliament passed legislation to improve conditions for nongovernmental organizations (NGOs) and a statute that defined and expanded Vojvodina's autonomy. The country also received praise for its cooperation with the International Criminal Tribunal for the former Yugoslavia (ICTY), and secured visa-free travel to EU countries for Serbian citizens. By year's end, Serbia had formally submitted its application for EU membership, and the government's regional reconciliation efforts continued in 2010. However, the country suffered a major diplomatic defeat in July of that year, when the International Court of Justice (ICJ) ruled that Kosovo's declaration of independence did not violate international law.

In May 2011, Serbian authorities arrested and extradited former Bosnian Serb military commander Ratko Mladic, a longtime fugitive who was wanted by the ICTY for alleged war crimes. Croatian Serb wartime leader Goran Hadžic, the last of 161 suspected war criminals indicted by the ICTY to remain at large, was arrested and extradited from Serbia in July. The two arrests marked a major step forward for Serbia's bid for EU candidacy.

While EU-brokered negotiations yielded progress on trade and travel issues between Serbia and Kosovo during 2011, Belgrade maintained its opposition to Kosovo's sovereignty. In August, German chancellor Angela Merkel warned that Serbia must abolish its parallel governing structures in the Serb-populated northern portion of Kosovo before it could join the EU. The country's formal status as an EU candidate had yet to be confirmed at year's end. Meanwhile, the SRS asked Serbian prosecutors to initiate criminal proceedings against Tadic and Cvetkovic for negotiating terms with the Kosovo authorities that "endangered Serbia's territorial integrity," though no charges were brought by year's end.

Political Rights and Civil Liberties: Serbia is an electoral democracy. The president, elected to a five-year term, plays a largely ceremonial role. The National Assembly is a unicameral, 250-seat legislature, with deputies elected to four-year terms according to party lists. The prime minister is elected by the assembly. Both the presidential and parliamentary elections in 2008 were deemed largely free and fair by international monitoring groups.

In addition to the main political parties, numerous smaller parties compete for influence. These include factions representing ethnic minorities, two of which belong to the current coalition government. In April 2011, the Constitutional Court clarified and extended its 2010 decision to prohibit a practice whereby politicians elected on a party ticket were obliged to deposit a letter of resignation with the party before taking office. This had allowed party leaders to eliminate and replace elected officials who proved disloyal. The court declared the system unconstitutional and invalidated any postelection reallocation of parliamentary seats.

Corruption remains a serious concern. A new Anti-Corruption Agency that began operating in January 2010 is tasked with conflict-of-interest monitoring, oversight of political party funding, and other preventive activities. A new law adopted in June 2011 requires political parties to report all financial contributions they receive, and stipulates that these contributions must be made through official bank transfers. Despite several high-profile arrests in 2011, a systematic legislative effort and the political will to tackle large-scale corruption in public tenders are still seen to be lacking. Serbia was ranked 86 out of 183 countries surveyed in Transparency International's 2011 Corruption Perceptions Index.

The press is generally free, although most media outlets are thought to be aligned with specific political parties. In May 2011, public broadcaster RTS formally apologized for its role in supporting authoritarian governments during the 1990s, but advocacy groups noted that RTS remains subject to strong government influence. A 2011 study by the Anti-Corruption Agency found that private media are influenced by state advertising purchases, and that many of Serbia's leading media outlets are owned by offshore companies with limited transparency. Libel is a criminal offense punishable by fines, but not imprisonment. The 2010 Law on Electronic Communications allows police and security services to view personal electronic communications, which press freedom groups have criticized as a threat to the confidentiality of journalists' sources. Journalists continue to encounter threats and physical violence, and perpetrators rarely face significant penalties. In October 2011, the car of Tihomir Trišic, editor of the weekly *Akter*, was set on fire. Police were still investigating the incident at year's end. There were no reports of the government restricting access to the internet during the year.

The constitution guarantees freedom of religion, which is generally respected in practice. However, increases in ethnic tension often take the form of religious intolerance. Critics charge that the 2006 Law on Churches and Religious Communities privileges seven "traditional" religious communities by giving them tax-exempt status and forcing other groups to go through cumbersome registration procedures. Application of many aspects of the law is considered to be arbitrary. Relations between factions within the Islamic community in the Sandžak region, and between one of the factions and the Serbian government, have been deteriorating in recent years. There were no reports of government restrictions on academic freedom in 2011.

Citizens enjoy freedoms of assembly and association, though a 2009 law banned meetings of fascist organizations and the use of neo-Nazi symbols. A 2010 gay pride parade in Belgrade was attacked by several thousand counterdemonstrators, but police successfully protected the marchers. Extremist groups threatened violence ahead of the 2011 parade, and police said they were underequipped for any clashes, with some reportedly considering a boycott. The government consequently banned the event, calling it a threat to national security. Foreign and domestic NGOs are generally free to operate without government interference, and the 2009 Law on Associations clarified their legal status. The laws and constitution allow workers to form or join unions, engage in collective bargaining, and strike, but the International Confederation of Trade Unions (ITUC) has reported that organizing efforts and strikes are substantially restricted in practice.

Serbia's judicial structure underwent major changes in 2010, including the merger of 138 municipal courts into 34 basic courts. The system suffers from a large backlog of cases, including some 7,000 at the Constitutional Court alone. Prisons are generally considered to meet international standards, but overcrowding remains a serious problem and a contributing factor behind inmate riots and protests.

Ethnic minorities are underrepresented in government. The country's main minority groups are the Bosniaks (Muslim Slavs), concentrated in the Sandžak region; an ethnic Albanian population in the Preševo Valley; and the Hungarian community in Vojvodina. There is concern about the spread of extreme forms of Islam in the Sandžak. In June 2010, elections to the Council of Bosniaks in Sandžak gave 17 of 35 seats to a group led by the populist mufti Muamer Zukorlic. Two elected members from the Bosnian Renaissance party subsequently defected, joining Zukorlic's group. One day before the vote, the government made an amendment to the council's election rules, requiring the ruling party or coalition to win at least a two-thirds majority of seats before a new council could be legally constituted. Under Zukorli 's leadership, the council has since operated in defiance of Belgrade. Discrimination against the Romany community is common. Amnesty International reported multiple forced evictions—conducted without warning and "under appalling circumstances"—of Romany families from public and privately owned buildings in 2011.

Women make up about 22 percent of the parliament, and five women currently serve as cabinet ministers. Just three of Serbia's 150 municipalities have female mayors. According to electoral regulations, women must account for at least 30 percent of a party's candidate list. Although women are legally entitled to equal pay for equal work, traditional attitudes often limit their roles in the economy. A 2009 law on gender equality provides a wide range of protections in employment, health, education, and politics. Domestic violence remains a serious problem, and is reportedly on the rise. Some towns in southern Serbia have become transit points for the trafficking of women from the former Soviet Union to Western Europe for the purpose of forced prostitution.

Seychelles

Political Rights: 3
Civil Liberties: 3
Status: Partly Free

Population: 88,100
Capital: Victoria

Ten-Year Ratings Timeline For Year Under Review (Political Rights, Civil Liberties, Status)

2002	2003	2004	2005	2006	2007	2008	2009	2010	2011
3,3PF	3,3PF	3,3PF	3,3PF	3,3PF	3,3PF	3,3PF	3,3PF	3,3PF	3,3PF

Overview: **President James Michel won a May 2011 presidential election, defeating opposition leader Wavel Ramkalawan. In parliamentary balloting in September, Michel's People's Party captured all but one of the seats in the National Assembly, after Ramkalawan's Seychelles National Party boycotted the vote in protest of the government's failure to implement electoral reforms.**

The Seychelles gained independence from Britain in 1976 as a multiparty democracy and remained a member of the Commonwealth. In 1977, Prime Minister France-Albert René seized power from President James Mancham. René then made his Seychelles People's Progressive Front (SPPF) the sole legal party. In 1992, however, the SPPF passed a constitutional amendment legalizing opposition parties, and many exiled leaders returned. René won multiparty elections in 1993.

The Seychelles National Party (SNP), led by Wavel Ramkalawan, emerged as the strongest opposition group in 1998 elections. René won a narrow victory in the 2001 presidential election, leading to opposition complaints of fraud. René called for early legislative elections in 2002, and although the SPPF won, the SNP made significant gains.

René stepped down in 2004 and was replaced by Vice President James Michel. An Indian Ocean tsunami struck later that year, causing about $30 million in damage to public infrastructure; the vital tourism and fishing industries also suffered. Michel defeated Ramkalawan in the July 2006 presidential election, and the SPPF retained its majority in May 2007 legislative elections.

Michel, running for the People's Party (Parti Lepep, or PP)—the new name for the SPPF—won a new term in the May 2011 presidential election. He defeated Ramkalawan, 55 percent to 41 percent. Ramkalawan accused the PP of bribing voters; however, observers from the Commonwealth called the election "credible." The SNP boycotted parliamentary elections held in late September and early October, citing alleged misconduct by the PP in the presidential vote and Michel's failure to implement promised electoral reforms. That allowed the PP to claim all

25 directly elected seats and 8 of the 9 proportional seats available; the Popular Democratic Movement, formed by a dissident SNP member who disagreed with its decision to boycott the elections, took the remaining proportional seat. Observers from the Southern African Development Community said the voting was "credible and transparent."

In 2011 the Seychelles continued to take action to combat Indian Ocean piracy. In February, a Seychellois court sentenced 10 Somalis to 20 years in prison for piracy. In September, the Seychelles hosted an antipiracy conference that was attended by representatives of the European Union, NATO, regional governments, and the maritime industry.

Political Rights and Civil Liberties: The Seychelles is an electoral democracy. The 2011 presidential and parliamentary elections were generally viewed as having met basic international norms, despite the opposition boycott of the latter. However, the ruling PP's control over state resources and most media gives it a significant advantage. The president and the unicameral National Assembly are elected by universal adult suffrage for five-year terms. The head of government is the president, who appoints the cabinet. Of the National Assembly's 34 members, 25 are directly elected, and 9 are allocated on a proportional basis to parties gaining at least 10 percent of the vote.

The PP remains the dominant party, and the opposition SNP has claimed that its sympathizers are harassed by police and victimized by job-related security investigations in the public sector.

Concerns over government corruption have focused on the lack of transparency in the privatization and allocation of government-owned land. Seychelles was ranked 50 out of 183 countries surveyed in Transparency International's 2011 Corruption Perceptions Index.

The government controls much of the nation's media sector, operating radio and television stations. The daily newspaper, the *Seychelles Nation*, is government owned, and the PP publishes a weekly newspaper, the *People*. The opposition weekly, *Regar*, has been sued for libel by government officials under broad constitutional restrictions on free expression. The board of directors of the officially multipartisan Seychelles Broadcasting Corporation (SBC) includes several non-PP members, though coverage is biased in favor of the ruling party. Despite the passage of a new Broadcasting Act in March 2011 that was intended to make the SBC more independent, the outlet continues to be dominated by the government. High licensing fees have discouraged the development of private broadcast media. Internet access is not limited, though there have been reports that the state monitors e-mail, chat rooms, and blogs.

Religious freedom is constitutionally protected and respected in practice. Churches in this predominantly Roman Catholic country have been strong voices for human rights and democratization, and they generally function without government interference. Academic freedom is generally respected, though PP loyalists are reportedly favored in high-level academic appointments.

The constitution endorses freedoms of assembly and association. Private human rights groups and other nongovernmental organizations operate in the country. While public demonstrations are generally tolerated, the government has occasionally impeded opposition gatherings. Workers have the right to strike. The PP-aligned Seychelles Federation of Workers' Unions remains the main active trade union.

Judges generally decide cases fairly but face interference in those involving major economic or political interests. The majority of the members of the Seychellois judiciary are foreign nationals from other Commonwealth countries, and the impartiality of the non-Seychellois magistrates can be compromised by the fact that they are subject to contract renewal. Chief Justice Frederick Egonda-Ntende of Uganda has committed to reducing the number of pending court cases and accelerating judgment of new cases. Security forces have at times been accused of using excessive force, including torture and arbitrary detention.

The country's political and economic life is primarily dominated by people of European and South Asian origin. Islanders of Creole extraction face de facto discrimination, and prejudice against foreign workers has been reported. The government does not restrict domestic travel but may deny passports for unspecified reasons of "national interest."

The Seychelles boasts one of the world's highest percentages of women in parliament, reaching 45 percent in 2011. Inheritance laws do not discriminate against women. In general, however, women enjoy fewer educational opportunities. While nearly all adult females are classified as "economically active," most are engaged in subsistence agriculture. Rape and domestic violence remain widespread. The government adopted a National Strategy on Domestic Violence in 2008, but it has had little success.

Sierra Leone

Political Rights: 3
Civil Liberties: 3
Status: Partly Free

Population: 5,364,000
Capital: Freetown

Ten-Year Ratings Timeline For Year Under Review (Political Rights, Civil Liberties, Status)

2002	2003	2004	2005	2006	2007	2008	2009	2010	2010
4,4PF	4,3PF	4,3PF	4,3PF	4,3PF	3,3PF	3,3PF	3,3PF	3,3PF	3,3PF

Overview: **Despite efforts by ruling and opposition parties to dissuade violence and encourage tolerance, tensions mounted in the lead-up to the 2012 elections. In July, the main opposition party elected former junta leader Julius Maada Bio as their candidate to face incumbent Ernest Koroma in the 2012 presidential race. During the year, the government passed a series of laws to increase protections and incentives for investors, businesses, and entrepreneurs to engage in agricultural and industrial development.**

Founded by Britain in 1787 as a haven for liberated slaves, Sierra Leone achieved independence in 1961. Siaka Stevens, who became prime minister in 1967 and then president in 1971, transformed Sierra Leone into a one-party state under his

All People's Congress (APC) party. In 1985, Stevens retired and handed power to his designated successor, General Joseph Momoh. The Revolutionary United Front (RUF) launched a guerrilla insurgency from Liberia in 1991, sparking a civil war that would last for more than a decade. Military officer Valentine Strasser ousted Momoh the following year, but failed to deliver on the promise of elections. Brigadier-General Julius Maada Bio deposed Strasser in 1996, and elections were held despite military and rebel intimidation. Voters chose former UN diplomat Ahmad Tejan Kabbah of the Sierra Leone People's Party (SLPP) as president.

In 1997, Major Johnny Paul Koroma toppled the Kabbah government and invited the RUF to join his ruling junta. Nigerian-led troops under the aegis of the Economic Community of West African States Monitoring Group (ECOMOG) restored Kabbah to power in 1998, and the 1999 Lomé peace agreement led to the deployment of UN peacekeepers. By 2002, the 17,000-strong UN peacekeeping force had started disarmament in rebel-held areas and the war was declared over.

Kabbah won a new term in the 2002 presidential elections, defeating the APC's Ernest Koroma (no relation to Johnny Paul Koroma). The SLPP took 83 of 112 available seats in parliamentary elections that month. However, the SLPP government failed to adequately address the country's entrenched poverty, dilapidated infrastructure, and endemic corruption, and in 2007, Ernest Koroma won a presidential runoff election with 55 percent of the vote, leaving SLPP candidate Solomon Berewa with 45 percent. In the legislative polls, the APC led with 59 seats, followed by the SLPP with 43, and the People's Movement for Democratic Change (PMDC) with 10.

Chieftaincy elections and parliamentary and local council by-elections held between 2009 and 2011 were marred by political violence initiated by APC and SLPP supporters. Following serious clashes in the lead-up to a local by-election in the Pujehun district in March 2009, a UN-facilitated joint communiqué was issued by the APC and SLPP calling for an end to all acts of political violence. A Commission of Inquiry was launched in 2009 to investigate incidences of rape and sexual violence that allegedly occurred during the March attacks, and an independent review was conducted in 2010 to investigate the causes of the political violence. However, by the end of 2011, the government had yet to release the results of the review, and had failed to implement numerous communiqué recommendations, including calls for the establishment of an independent police complaints commission.

By-elections confirmed a regional polarization, whereby the ruling APC enjoys support in the north and west, while the opposition SLPP dominates the south and east. In December 2010, President Koroma reshuffled his cabinet in an attempt to diversify geographical representation and include more SLPP partisans.

Political violence continued in 2011. In May, clashes were reported during a parliamentary by-election in Kailahun district. The opposition SLPP held its national convention in July amidst intra-party dissension and elected retired brigadier general Julius Maada Bio, who deposed Strasser in 1996, as their 2012 presidential candidate. A political fracas occurred in the district of Kono in September, when the convoy of the Minister of Internal Affairs was attacked, causing his security and police to discharge their weapons. That same month, SLPP presidential candidate Bio was attacked with stones in the city of Bo, and APC party buildings were torched in response.

The government was quick to launch investigations into the September incidents, which resulted in the identification for prosecution of more than 50 people from both political parties. The police also placed a moratorium on political rallies in September. The ban was lifted in December, however, following the signing of an agreement among the country's main political parties to promote cooperation with the police and increase security during political processions. The SLPP and the National Democratic Alliance (NDA) did not sign the agreement, arguing that the government does not have the right to ban political party rallies. Koroma requested International Criminal Court prosecutors to monitor the Sierra Leonean electoral environment in the lead-up to the 2012 elections.

Renewed calls were made in 2011 for a formal inquest into the military junta's 1992 executions of the former police inspector-general and 27 others. The APC government first announced plans to launch an inquest in May 2010, but went silent on the matter following criticism from civil society and the international community that such a move would inflame political intolerance and target current opposition SLPP members who served with the junta. Family members of the victims, however, argue that the Truth and Reconciliation Commission did not thoroughly investigate the extra-judicial killings.

Political Rights and Civil Liberties: Sierra Leone is an electoral democracy. International observers determined that the 2007 presidential and parliamentary elections were free and fair, and that power was transferred peacefully to the opposition. Of the unicameral Parliament's 124 members, 112 are chosen by popular vote and 12 are reserved for indirectly elected paramount chiefs. Parliamentary and presidential elections are held every five years, and presidents may seek a second term.

The APC and SLPP are the main political parties. Other parties include the PMDC, the NDA, and United Democratic Movement (UDM). Both the All Political Parties Women's Association and the All Political Parties Youth Association, which became operational in 2011, play key roles in promoting peaceful electoral campaigning, dialogue, and participation.

Much of the administration's efforts in 2011 were focused on cementing the electoral framework in preparation for the 2012 elections. The government finalized key management capacity support agreements to ensure that the National Elections Commission (NEC) will be able to credibly undertake electoral administration and voter registration. In March, a critical consultative workshop was held regarding electoral law reform, and resulting recommendations called for the need to address the legal deficiencies that occurred during the 2007 elections, including the authority of the NEC to nullify votes, rules for the election of the president, and forfeiture of parliamentary seats. Measures were also taken to reform the Political Parties Registration Commission to ensure sanctions are in place for any breaches of the code of conduct by political parties. The country's first biometric voting registration system was also established. President Ernest Koroma has also pledged to promote a 30 percent quota for women to be represented in elective positions, and a draft gender equality bill to that effect was introduced in Parliament in September 2011; however, it had not passed by year's end.

While corruption remains a serious problem, Koroma has actively encouraged and supported the work of the Anti-Corruption Commission. Several key cases were concluded in 2011, including the acquittal of the director-general of the National Revenue Authority and the conviction of numerous public officials. In August, senior civil servants signed performance contracts, and the new Civil Service Code of Conduct was put into effect. In September, a public sector pay reform program was also launched. Sierra Leone was ranked 134 out of 183 countries surveyed in Transparency International's 2011 Corruption Perceptions Index.

Freedoms of speech and the press are constitutionally guaranteed, but these rights are occasionally restricted. In June 2010, the Sierra Leone Broadcasting Corporation (SLBC) was officially launched as the independent national broadcaster. The APC and SLPP relinquished control of their radio stations in 2010, allowing for incorporation into the SLBC, and in 2011, the High Court upheld decisions made by the Independent Media Commission (IMC) to deny a license to the APC-run Freetown City Council and to close down the SLPP radio station. In June 2011, a journalist with the *Exclusive*, a private daily newspaper, was murdered by protestors participating in a violent dispute over land outside of Freetown. The police arrested three suspects, including a police officer; the investigation was ongoing at year's end. The IMC is working with the SLBC to determine coverage policies and regulatory mechanisms for the 2012 elections. Numerous independent newspapers circulate freely, and there are dozens of public and private radio and television outlets. The government does not restrict internet access, though the medium is not widely used. A proposed Freedom of Information bill remained pending in Parliament at year's end.

Freedom of religion is protected by the constitution and respected in practice. Academic freedom is similarly upheld.

Freedoms of assembly and association are constitutionally guaranteed and generally observed in practice. However, police used force, including tear gas and live ammunition, to break up the September 2011 demonstrations in Bo. The government also implemented a ban on all political demonstrations and meetings from September to December in the wake of the protests. Workers have the right to join independent trade unions, but serious violations of core labor standards occur regularly. Nongovernmental organizations (NGOs) and civic groups operate freely, though a 2008 law requires NGOs to submit annual activity reports and renew their registration every two years.

The judiciary has demonstrated a degree of independence, and a number of trials have been free and fair. However, corruption, poor salaries, police unprofessionalism, prison overcrowding, and a lack of resources threaten to impede judicial effectiveness.

Drug trafficking and other crimes pose a threat to the rule of law and the stability of the wider Mano River region. The Sierra Leone Transnational Organized Crime Unit continued to register success in 2011 in carrying out substantial drug interceptions.

The Special Court for Sierra Leone (SCSL), a hybrid international and domestic war crimes tribunal, has been working since 2004 to convict those responsible for large-scale human rights abuses during the civil war. The trial that began in 2007 of former Liberian president Charles Taylor, accused of fostering the RUF insurgency, concluded in March 2011. However, judgment regarding the 11 counts of war crimes, crimes against humanity, and other gross violations of international law had not been delivered by year's end. Efforts continued in 2011 to transfer the SCSL to a Residual Special Court for Sierra Leone in the Hague as a follow-up mechanism to the SCSL.

The Human Rights Commission of Sierra Leone continued its work in 2011, despite funding and logistical shortcomings. In June, the Commission held its first public hearing for 235 former soldiers who had been forcibly retired, ostensibly due to chronic illness and/or mental imbalances. The Commission found that the retirees had been subject to discrimination, inhumane treatment, and violation of their privacy. The government did not appeal the decision, and has been supportive of the Commission's independence.

Continued progress was made in 2011 in rendering Sierra Leone more attractive for business. Infrastructure investments were made in thermal and hydro-power plants, and major roads were upgraded. In July, Parliament passed the 2011 Finance Act, the revised Petroleum Exploration and Production Act, and the Intellectual Property Rights Law, while the National Electricity Act regulating electricity and water usage was adopted in November. This bundle of legislation has created increased incentives for investors, businesses, and entrepreneurs to engage in agricultural and industrial development, particularly in the manufacturing sector. It also safeguards against piracy, makes it easier to pay taxes, and to register businesses. Major investments were made in the iron ore and oil industry in 2011, and production will begin in 2012; GDP is consequently expected to increase by 51 percent in 2012.

Laws passed in 2007 prohibit domestic violence, grant women the right to inherit property, and outlaw forced marriage. Despite these laws and constitutionally guaranteed equality, gender discrimination remains widespread and female genital mutilation and child marriages are common.

Singapore

Political Rights: 4*
Civil Liberties: 4
Status: Partly Free

Population: 5,167,000
Capital: Singapore

Ratings Change: Singapore's political rights rating improved from 5 to 4 due to parliamentary and presidential elections that featured more active campaigning and increased support for opposition parties.

Ten-Year Ratings Timeline For Year Under Review (Political Rights, Civil Liberties, Status)

2002	2003	2004	2005	2006	2007	2008	2009	2009	2010
5,4PF	5,4PF	5,4PF	5,4PF	5,4PF	5,4PF	5,4PF	5,4PF	5,4PF	4,4PF

Overview: **After a campaign period that featured a more open media environment and greater freedom of assembly than in previous years, opposition parties made unprecedented gains in May 2011 parliamentary elections, though the ruling People's Action Party (PAP)**

remained comfortably in control of the legislature. In another indication of the opposition's increased ability to compete, a PAP-backed candidate won the presidency by an extremely narrow margin in August.

The British colony of Singapore obtained home rule in 1959, entered the Malaysian Federation in 1963, and gained full independence in 1965. During his three decades as prime minister, Lee Kuan Yew and his People's Action Party (PAP) transformed the port city into a regional financial center and exporter of high-technology goods but restricted individual freedoms and stunted political development.

Lee transferred the premiership to Goh Chok Tong in 1990 but stayed on as "senior minister," and the PAP retained its dominance. Lee's son, Lee Hsien Loong, became prime minister in 2004, and the elder Lee assumed the title of "minister mentor." In 2005, President Sellapan Ramanathan, also known as S. R. Nathan, began a second term as the largely ceremonial head of state.

The 2006 parliamentary elections resembled past elections in serving more as a referendum on the prime minister's popularity than as an actual contest for power, with both the electoral framework and the restrictive media environment favoring the ruling party. The PAP retained 82 of 84 elected seats, though the opposition offered candidates for a greater number of seats and secured a larger percentage of the vote than in previous years.

Lee Hsien Loong continued to pursue economic growth while using the legal system and other tools to keep media criticism and the opposition in check. The government maintained that racial sensitivities and the threat of Islamist terrorism justified draconian restrictions on freedoms of speech and assembly, but such rules were repeatedly used to silence criticism of the authorities. The *Far Eastern Economic Review*, owned by the U.S.-based News Corporation, was forced to pay some US$300,000 in 2009 to settle a defamation case brought by the Lees. Similarly, in March 2010, the *International Herald Tribune* apologized and paid US$122,400 in fines for an article on dynastic politics in Asia that the Lees considered defamatory.

The May 2011 parliamentary elections featured a more vigorous and coordinated campaign effort by the opposition, which fielded candidates for 82 of the 87 directly elected seats, the highest number since independence. The opposition Workers' Party took an unprecedented six directly elected seats, plus two under a system that guarantees the opposition at least nine seats in Parliament. Another party, the Singapore People's Party (SPP), was awarded the remaining seat allocated to the opposition. That left the PAP with 81 seats, though it had secured only 60 percent of the overall vote. Shortly thereafter, Lee Kuan Yew resigned from his "minister mentor" position, ending over half a century in government.

The first contested presidential election since 1993 was held in August, with all candidates running as independents in keeping with the constitution. Former deputy prime minister Tony Tan, the PAP-backed candidate, won with 35.2 percent of the vote, narrowly defeating three opponents. His closest challenger, former PAP lawmaker Tan Cheng Bock, took 34.9 percent, and the opposition-backed Tan Jee Say placed third with 25.1 percent. Businessman Tan Kin Lian, a former PAP district official, secured the remainder. The results confirmed the growing strength of the opposition, and the increased willingness of the electorate to vote against the ruling party.

Political Rights and Civil Liberties: Singapore is not an electoral democracy. The country is governed through a parliamentary system, and elections are free from irregularities and vote rigging, but the ruling PAP dominates the political process. The prime minister retains control over the Elections Department, and the country lacks a structurally independent election authority. Opposition campaigns have typically been hamstrung by a ban on political films and television programs, the threat of libel suits, strict regulations on political associations, and the PAP's influence on the media and the courts.

The largely ceremonial president is elected by popular vote for six-year terms, and a special committee is empowered to vet candidates. The prime minister and cabinet are appointed by the president. Singapore has had only three prime ministers since independence. Of the unicameral legislature's 87 elected members, who serve five-year terms, 12 are elected from single-member constituencies, while 75 are elected in Group Representation Constituencies (GRCs), a mechanism intended to foster minority representation. Historically, the top polling party in each GRC won all of its four to six seats, so the system effectively bolstered the majority of the dominant party. However, the 2011 election demonstrated that this system could be challenged. Notably, the opposition Workers' Party captured a five-seat GRC in the May 2011 elections. As of 2011, up to nine members can be appointed from among leading opposition parties to ensure a minimum of opposition representation, up from three in previous years, though only three of these seats needed to be awarded in the latest elections. Up to nine additional, nonpartisan members can be appointed by the president.

Singapore has traditionally been lauded for its lack of corruption, and was ranked 5 out of 183 countries surveyed in Transparency International's 2011 Corruption Perceptions Index. However, issues of transparency remain a concern.

Singapore's media remain tightly constrained. All domestic newspapers, radio stations, and television channels are owned by companies linked to the government. Although editorials and news coverage generally support state policies, newspapers occasionally publish critical pieces. Mainstream media offered more balanced coverage of the opposition ahead of the 2011 elections. Self-censorship is common among journalists. The Sedition Act, in effect since the colonial period, outlaws seditious speech, the distribution of seditious materials, and acts with "seditious tendency." Popular videos, music, and books that reference sex, violence, or drugs are also subject to censorship. Foreign broadcasters and periodicals can be restricted for engaging in domestic politics, and all foreign publications must appoint legal representatives and provide significant financial deposits.

Recent high-profile cases illustrate the reach of Singapore's defamation and censorship laws, and the government's broader efforts to restrict speech. In November 2010, British author Alan Shadrake was convicted of defamation for a book in which he questioned the judicial system's impartiality in meting out capital punishment. He was sentenced to six weeks in prison, fined approximately US$16,000, and charged for legal fees of more than US$38,000. His appeal was rejected by Singapore's highest court in May 2011, and he was deported in July.

The internet is widely accessible, but the authorities monitor online material and block some content through directives to licensed service providers. Singaporeans' increased use of Facebook and Twitter, among other social-networking websites, has sparked interest in social activism and opposition parties, contributing to opposition electoral gains in 2011. Enforcement of internet restrictions was eased in the run-up to the voting, allowing broader online discussion of political issues.

The constitution guarantees freedom of religion as long as its practice does not violate any other regulations, and most groups worship freely. However, religious actions perceived as threats to racial or religious harmony are not tolerated, and unconventional groups, like the Jehovah's Witnesses and the Unification Church are banned. All religious groups are required to register with the government under the 1966 Societies Act. Adherents of the Falun Gong spiritual movement have been arrested and prosecuted on vandalism charges in recent years for displaying posters in a public park that detail the persecution of their fellow practitioners in China.

All public universities and political research institutions have direct government links that bear at least some influence. Academics engage in political debate, but their publications rarely deviate from the government line on matters related to Singapore.

The Societies Act restricts freedom of association by requiring most organizations of more than 10 people to register with the government, and only registered parties and associations may engage in organized political activity. Political speeches are tightly regulated, and public assemblies must be approved by police. A 2009 law eliminated a previous threshold requiring permits for public assemblies of five or more people, meaning political events involving just one person could require official approval. Permits are not needed for indoor gatherings, as long as the topic of discussion does not relate to race or religion. In the 2011 campaign period, opposition parties held rallies without significant interference.

Unions are granted fairly broad rights under the Trade Unions Act, though restrictions include a ban on government employees joining unions. A 2004 amendment to the law prohibits union members from voting on collective agreements negotiated by union representatives and employers. Strikes are legal for all except utility workers, but they must be approved by a majority of a union's members, as opposed to the internationally accepted standard of at least 50 percent of the members who vote. In practice, many restrictions are not applied. Nearly all unions are affiliated with the National Trade Union Congress, which is openly allied with the PAP. Singapore's 180,000 household workers are excluded from the Employment Act and regularly exploited. A 2006 standard contract for foreign household workers addresses food deprivation and entitles replaced workers to seek other employment in Singapore, but it fails to provide other basic protections, such as rest days.

The government's overwhelming success in court cases raises questions about judicial independence, particularly because lawsuits against opposition politicians and parties often drive them into bankruptcy. It is unclear whether the government pressures judges or simply appoints those who share its conservative philosophy. The judiciary is efficient, and defendants in criminal cases enjoy most due process rights.

The government generally respects citizens' right to privacy, but the Internal

Security Act (ISA) and Criminal Law Act (CLA) allow warrantless searches and arrests to preserve national security, order, and the public interest. The ISA, previously aimed at communist threats, is now used against suspected Islamist terrorists. Suspects can be detained without charge or trial for an unlimited number of two-year periods. A 1989 constitutional amendment prohibits judicial review of the substantive grounds for detention under the ISA and of the constitutionality of the law itself. The CLA is mainly used to detain organized crime suspects; it allows preventive detention for an extendable one-year period. The Misuse of Drugs Act empowers authorities to commit suspected drug users, without trial, to rehabilitation centers for up to three years. The penal code mandates caning, in addition to imprisonment, for about 30 offenses, though the punishment is applied inconsistently.

There is no legal racial discrimination. Despite government efforts, ethnic Malays have not on average reached the schooling and income levels of ethnic Chinese or ethnic Indians, and they reportedly face discrimination in both private and public sector employment.

Citizens enjoy freedom of movement, though the government occasionally enforces its policy of ethnic balance in public housing, in which most Singaporeans live, and opposition politicians have been denied the right to travel.

Women enjoy the same legal rights as men on most issues, and many are well-educated professionals. Few women hold top positions in government and the private sector. Twenty women won seats in the 2011 parliamentary elections, though Lim Hwee Hua, who became the first female cabinet minister in 2010, lost her seat. Despite the presence of an open gay community, acts of "gross indecency" between men are punishable by up to two years in prison.

↑ Slovakia

Political Rights: 1
Civil Liberties: 1
Status: Free

Population: 5,440,000
Capital: Bratislava

Trend Arrow: Slovakia received an upward trend arrow due to an amendment to the Press Act that helps protect media from political influence and intimidation, as well as improvements in the independence of the judiciary.

Ten-Year Ratings Timeline For Year Under Review (Political Rights, Civil Liberties, Status)

2002	2003	2004	2005	2006	2007	2008	2009	2010	2011
1,2F	1,2F	1,1F	1,1F	1,1F	1,1F	1,1F	1,1F	1,1F	1,1F

Overview: **A lack of consensus over Slovakia's contribution to a eurozone bailout fund led to the collapse of Prime Minister Iveta Radicová's government and the scheduling of early elections for March 2012. Radicová, together with Justice Minister Lucia Žitnanská, had worked to reduce corruption, especially in procurement procedures and**

the judiciary. In September, the parliament passed an amendment to the 2008 Press Act, partially undoing the controversial law's infringements on editorial freedom by limiting politicians' "right of reply."

Czechoslovakia was created in 1918 amid the collapse of the Austro-Hungarian Empire, and Soviet forces helped establish a communist government after World War II. A series of peaceful anticommunist demonstrations in 1989 brought about the collapse of the communist regime, and open elections were held the following year. In 1992, negotiations began on increased Slovak autonomy within the Czech and Slovak Federative Republic. This process led to a peaceful dissolution of the federation and the establishment of an independent Slovak Republic in 1993.

From 1993 to 1998, Vladimír Meciar—who served twice as prime minister during this period—and his Movement for a Democratic Slovakia (HZDS) dominated politics, flouted the rule of law, and intimidated independent media. In the 1998 parliamentary elections, voters rejected Meciar's rule and empowered a broad right-left coalition. The new parliament selected Mikuláš Dzurinda as prime minister and worked to enhance judicial independence, combat corruption, undertake economic reforms, and actively seek membership in the European Union (EU) and NATO.

The HZDS led the 2002 parliamentary elections, but Dzurinda's Slovak Democratic and Christian Union (SDKU) formed a center-right government with three other parties, allowing the country to complete reforms associated with EU and NATO membership. Slovakia formally joined both organizations in 2004.

Meciar lost the 2004 presidential election to a former HZDS ally, Ivan Gašparovic. The governing coalition fractured in February 2006 amid unpopular economic reforms, prompting early parliamentary elections in June. The leftist, populist Smer (Direction–Social Democracy) led the voting and formed an unusual coalition with the HZDS—now allied with the People's Party (LS)—and the far-right Slovak National Party (SNS).

Supported by Smer and the SNS, President Gašparovic won a second term in a two-round election held in March and April 2009, narrowly defeating Iveta Radicová of the SDKU (now allied with the Democratic Party, or DS).

Smer won the largest share of votes in parliamentary elections held in June 2010, taking 62 of the 150 seats. The SDKU-DS placed a distant second with 28 seats, followed by the center-right Freedom and Solidarity (SaS) with 22, the Christian Democratic Movement (KDH) with 15, the new ethnic Hungarian party Most-Híd with 14, and the SNS with 9. For the first time since 1991, Meciar's party did not win any seats, having failed to reach the 5 percent vote threshold for representation. Despite Smer's plurality, the SDKU-DS was able to form a center-right majority in July with the SaS, the KDH, and Most-Híd, and Radicová became the country's first female prime minister.

Slovakia attracted international attention in October 2011, when it became the only EU member state to reject the expanded European Financial Stability Facility (EFSF)—a proposed bailout fund necessitated by an ongoing eurozone public-debt crisis. Radicová combined the parliamentary vote for the bailout with a vote of confidence in her government so as to persuade the SaS to support the measure. The strategy failed, and the government collapsed. Smer then successfully organized support for the EFSF expansion in a second vote, in return for early elections. The bailout package was ultimately approved, and elections, originally planned for 2014, were scheduled for March 2012. Radicová and her cabinet would serve in a caretaker capacity until the elections.

Political Rights and Civil Liberties: Slovakia is an electoral democracy. Voters elect the president for up to two five-year terms and members of the 150-seat, unicameral National Council for four-year terms. The prime minister is appointed by the president but must have majority support in the parliament to govern.

Slovakia's political party system is fragmented. The current ruling coalition of SDKU-DS, KDH, Most-Híd and the opposition party Smer was brought together to pass the EFSF, and left SaS in political isolation.

In 2010 the government passed the State Citizenship Act, which featured a ban on dual citizenship in response to Hungary's decision to allow ethnic Hungarians living abroad to apply for Hungarian citizenship. Ethnic Hungarians make up roughly 10 percent of Slovakia's population. In February 2011, the parliament amended the Citizenship Act, allowing for some citizens to hold dual citizenship if they are long-term residents of another country or their parents were born in another state.

Corruption remains a problem in Slovakia. Throughout 2011, Prime Minister Iveta Radicová pushed an anticorruption agenda, beginning with a new law in January that requires mandatory online disclosure of contracts involving public authorities and state-owned companies. Several high-profile corruption scandals were unveiled during 2011, including charges against Radicová's former adviser, Martin Novotný, over his alleged involvement in the granting of a state subsidy to build the Osrblie sports facility. Novotný was released from pretrial detention in October, but the case was ongoing at year's end. A larger scandal emerged in late December, when the "Gorilla file," purportedly a leaked intelligence document, raised allegations of secret privatization deals involving millions of euros in bribes paid to Slovak politicians by associates of the country's largest private equity firm, Penta, during former prime minister Mikuláš Dzurinda's second term. An anticorruption law passed in 2010 allows state police and prosecutors to investigate the origin of anyone's assets if they amount to more than $630,000; assets of undetermined origin can be confiscated by the courts. Slovakia was ranked 66 out of 183 countries surveyed in Transparency International's 2011 Corruption Perceptions Index.

Slovakia's media are largely free but have been vulnerable to political interference. In recent years, journalists have faced an increasing number of verbal attacks and libel suits by public officials. In March 2010, Slovakia's largest financial group, J&T, purchased *Pravda*, the country's second-largest daily; the firm had acquired a popular television station in 2007, raising concerns about ownership concentration. A September 2011 amendment to the controversial Press Act removed a requirement that media publish responses or corrections from public officials if they are criticized for their performance in office.

The government respects religious freedom. Registered religious organizations are eligible for tax exemptions and government subsidies. The Roman Catholic Church is the largest denomination and consequently receives the largest share of subsidies. A 2007 law requires religious groups to have at least 20,000 members to register, effectively excluding the small Muslim community and other groups. Academic freedom is respected in Slovakia.

Authorities uphold freedoms of assembly and association. In May 2010, Slovakia's first gay rights rally was attacked by neo-Nazi counterdemonstrators, and the police were widely criticized for failing to provide adequate security. In June 2011, a gay pride march in Bratislava was conducted without incident due to a stronger police presence. Nongovernmental organizations (NGOs) generally operate without government interference. Private funding is encouraged by a program allowing companies to donate up to 2 percent of their corporate income taxes to support NGOs. Labor unions are active in Slovakia, and organized workers freely exercise their right to strike. In October, a metalworkers' union blocked six border crossings to protest raising the retirement age, tax increases, and payroll reform.

The constitution provides for an independent judiciary, and an independent Judicial Council oversees the assignment and transfer of judges. However, the court system has long suffered from corruption, intimidation of judges, and a significant backlog of cases. The parliament and the Justice Ministry took strides to crack down on the lack of transparency and oversight in 2011. In February, the parliament overturned a presidential veto on judicial reform legislation designed to ensure greater transparency in the vetting of judges and public access to court proceedings, including through the publication of court decisions on the internet. In May, a revision of the Act on Judges and Judicial Assistants allowed Justice Minister Lucia Žitnanská to remove 14 judges for failing to process cases in a timely manner—a common grievance among the public. Štefan Harabin, the Supreme Court president and a political opponent of Žitnanská, accused her of "political cleansing." Žitnanská lodged several additional disciplinary complaints during the year, and Harabin attempted to delay them. In June the Constitutional Court ruled in favor of a November 2010 complaint by Žitnanská, finding that Harabin had obstructed the Justice Ministry's attempts to conduct an audit of the Supreme Court and ordering a 70 percent reduction in Harabin's pay for one year. In December, Žitnanská proposed that the Constitutional Court merge the multiple, ongoing complaints against Harabin into one hearing, and called for his removal as head of the Supreme Court. Žitnanská also pushed for transparency in the prosecutor's office in 2011, submitting legislation—passed by the parliament in June—that requires prosecutors to publish their decisions on the internet, limits their service to a single term, and reforms the selection process for new prosecutors.

Roma, who comprise roughly 10 percent of Slovakia's population, continue to experience widespread discrimination and inequality. Discriminatory practices include forced evictions and segregation of Romany children in special education programs. In 2010, the government formally committed to ending the segregation of Roma in schools. However, a draft strategy that the Ministry of Education released in June 2011 was criticized for failing to adequately address the problem. Amnesty International expressed concerns that the document used language that blamed Roma for being "disinterested" in quality education. However, a Prešov district court set a promising precedent in December, when it ruled against a school in eastern Slovakia for intentionally segregating Romany children into separate classrooms without justification.

Although women enjoy the same legal rights as men, they continue to be underrepresented in senior-level business positions and in the government. Although Radicová became Slovakia's first female prime minister in 2010, only 23 women hold seats in the 150-seat parliament. Domestic violence is punishable by imprisonment but remains widespread. Romany women have been sterilized by doctors without their consent. In November 2011, the European Court of Human Rights delivered a landmark ruling against Slovakia for its forced sterilization of a Romany woman, clarifying that the practice violated the prohibition on inhuman and degrading treatment and respect for private and family life. Human trafficking from and through Slovakia, mainly for the purpose of sexual exploitation, remains a problem.

Slovenia

Political Rights: 1
Civil Liberties: 1
Status: Free

Population: 2,052,000
Capital: Ljubljana

Ten-Year Ratings Timeline For Year Under Review (Political Rights, Civil Liberties, Status)

2002	2003	2004	2005	2006	2007	2008	2009	2010	2011
1,1F	1,1F	1,1F	1,1F	1,1F	1,1F	1,1F	1,1F	1,1F	1,1F

Overview: **In September 2011, Prime Minister Borut Pahor's government collapsed after a no confidence vote, leading to early elections in December. Ljubljana mayor Zoran Jankovic's center-left Positive Slovenia won in an upset but failed to form a government. A pension reform package was rejected in a June referendum. October saw protests outside the Ljubljana Stock Exchange amid Slovenia's ongoing economic troubles.**

The territory of modern Slovenia, long ruled by the Austro-Hungarian Empire, became part of the Kingdom of Serbs, Croats, and Slovenes (renamed the Kingdom of Yugoslavia in 1929) after World War I, and a constituent republic of the Socialist Federal Republic of Yugoslavia following World War II. After decades of relative prosperity in Josip Broz Tito's Yugoslavia, various elements in Slovene civil society began to break with the communist system in the 1980s. In 1990, the Democratic United Opposition defeated the ruling League of Communists in democratic elections, although former Communist leader Milan Kucan was elected president. The country declared independence in June 1991 and secured its status after a 10-day conflict.

After 1990, center-left governments generally led Slovenia, and Janez Drnovšek's Liberal Democracy of Slovenia (LDS) was dominant. Drnovšek served as prime minister almost continuously from 1992 to 2002, when he was elected president. In the 2004 parliamentary elections, Janez Janša's center-right Slovenian Democratic Party (SDS) finally unseated the LDS-led government, and Janša became prime minister.

Slovenia is considered one of postcommunist Europe's success stories. In

2004, Slovenia joined the European Union (EU) and NATO. It was the first former communist bloc state to adopt the euro, in 2006, and to hold the EU's rotating presidency, in 2008.

In the 2007 presidential election, Danilo Türk, a law professor and former diplomat, ran as an independent, backed by the Social Democrats (SD) and several other parties. He defeated the government's candidate, Alojz Peterle, in the November runoff.

In the September 2008 parliamentary elections, the SD captured 29 seats, followed by the SDS with 28. SD leader Borut Pahor became prime minister and formed a coalition government with three small parties.

Partly due to the effects of the global economic crisis, the Pahor government weakened in 2010, and the SDS had a strong showing in the October municipal elections. Ghanian-born doctor Peter Bossman was elected mayor of Piran, making him the first black mayor of an Eastern European city.

At the urging of the International Monetary Fund and other economic watchdogs, the government proposed reforms in December 2010 to reduce public debt by increasing the retirement age to 65, implementing pension reform, and cutting social benefits. However, voters rejected the measures in a June 2011 referendum. Pahor's government fell after two coalition partners, critical of his handling of the economy, departed his ruling coalition that summer, leading to a parliamentary no-confidence vote in September. After parliament failed to elect a new premier, President Türk called early elections for December 4. Though Janša's SDS led in preelection polling, Ljubljana mayor Zoran Jankovic's center-left Positive Slovenia won with 28 seats, followed by the SDS followed with 26 seats, and the SD with 10. However, Jankovic failed to secure a parliamentary majority to form a government or become prime minister by year's end.

After two decades, a border dispute with Croatia remains a key foreign policy issue in Slovenia. The dispute concerns the delineation of the countries' maritime border in the Bay of Piran, and parts of their common territorial border. In 2009, Pahor and his Croatian counterpart, Jadranka Kosor, agreed that Slovenia would lift its veto of Croatia's EU accession and allow an international arbitration panel to settle the dispute, pending ratification by both states' Parliaments. Slovenia's Parliament ratified the agreement in April 2010, but the opposition requested a referendum. Voters narrowly approved the agreement in June, and it entered into force in November 2010. The agreement was submitted to the UN in May 2011.

Political Rights and Civil Liberties: Slovenia is an electoral democracy. The country has a bicameral Parliament. Members of the 90-seat National Assembly, which chooses the prime minister, are elected to four-year terms. Members of the 40-seat National Council, a largely advisory body representing professional groups and local interests, are elected to five-year terms. The president is directly elected for up to two five-year terms. One seat each is reserved in the National Assembly for Slovenia's Hungarian and Italian minorities, and Roma are automatically given seats on 20 municipal councils.

Corruption, while less extensive than in some other Central European countries, remains a problem in Slovenia, usually taking the form of conflicts of interest and contracting links between government officials and private businesses. Only 5,000 of the country's 80,000 public servants are subject to financial disclosure laws. In August 2011, Interior Minister Katarina Kresal resigned over corruption allegations in a ministry deal to rent office space to the National Investigative Agency in 2010. Slovenia was ranked 35 out of 183 countries surveyed in Transparency International's 2011 Corruption Perceptions Index.

Freedoms of speech and of the press are constitutionally guaranteed. However, newspapers that criticize the government have faced difficulty securing advertising revenue, and journalists reportedly avoid coverage that could complicate relations with advertisers. The privatization of print media that began in the 1990s remains incomplete, with state-owned companies and other interests maintaining stakes in several newspapers. In 2011, there were reports of political pressure and harrasment against journalists, including anonymous death threats against Blaž Zgaga and Matej Šurc, who have reported extensively on the arms trade in Slovenia during the conflicts of the 1990s. Internet access is unrestricted.

The constitution guarantees freedom of religion and contains provisions that prohibit incitement to religious intolerance or discrimination. Approximately 58 percent of Slovenians identify themselves as Roman Catholics. In June 2010, the Constitutional Court annulled certain provisions of the 2007 Religious Freedoms Law, including requirments for legal registration of religious communities and the payment of social security contributions to priests working in prisons and hospitals. Though societal discrimination against the small Muslim community has been problematic in the past and 2011 saw isolated reports of faith-based discrimination, interfaith relations were generally civil during the year. After a 40-year struggle to build a mosque in Ljubljana, a design was selected in November 2011, with construction to begin once the Muslim community finalizes funding. There were no reports of government restrictions on academic freedom during the year.

The government respects freedoms of assembly and association. Numerous nongovernmental organizations operate freely, and the government generally supports the role they play in policymaking. Workers have the right to establish and join trade unions, strike, and bargain collectively, though police and military do not share these rights. The Association of Free Trade Unions of Slovenia (ZSSS) has some 300,000 members and controls the four trade union seats in the National Council. The ZSSS demonstrated its political strength by successfully pushing for the June 2011 referendum on pension reform, stymying pension reform legislation. In October 2011, over 100 people gathered for days outside the Ljubljana Stock Exchange to protest corporate greed.

The constitution provides for an independent judiciary, and the government respects judicial freedom. Although the judiciary has an extensive backlog of cases, the government has taken steps in recent years with the Lukanda Project, an intitiative begun in 2005 to reduce the backlog. As of June 2010, 266,221 cases were still backlogged. Prison conditions meet international standards, though overcrowding has been reported.

Incitement to racial hatred is a criminal offense. However, tensions remain between police and various minorities, including Italians, Muslim residents and guest workers, and citizens of the former Yugoslavia. Some 18,000 non-Slovene citizens of the former federation who remained in Slovenia after independence had been removed from official records after they failed to apply for citizenship or permanent residency during a brief window of opportunity in 1992. However, in 2009, Pahor's government began enforcing a 2003 Constitutional Court ruling intended to provide retroactive permanent residency status to the estimated 4,000 to 6,000 people among "the erased." In March 2010, Parliament adopted legislation to reinstate the legal status of those "erased" in 1992. In February 2011, Parliament passed a declaration recognizing the right of groups belonging to the former Yugoslavia to organize based on ethnicity and to use their native language to bolster multiculturalism in Slovenia. Roma are on the margins of society. In March 2011, Amnesty International admonished the government to protect the rights of Roma after publishing a report revealing that many Roma lack access to adequate housing and clean water.

Women hold the same legal rights as men but remain underrepresented in political life. Following the December 2011 elections, there are 28 women in the 90-seat National Assembly and 1 in the 40-seat National Council. More than 65 percent of Slovenia's women are in the workforce, the largest proportion of any of the 10 countries that joined the EU in 2004. Domestic violence remains a concern. Prostitution has been decriminalized in Slovenia. Slovenia is a transit point and destination for women and girls trafficked for the purpose of prostitution.

Solomon Islands

Political Rights: 4
Civil Liberties: 3
Status: Partly Free

Population: 545,000
Capital: Honiara

Ten-Year Ratings Timeline For Year Under Review (Political Rights, Civil Liberties, Status)

2002	2003	2004	2005	2006	2007	2008	2009	2010	2011
3,3PF	3,3PF	3,3PF	3,3PF	4,3PF	4,3PF	4,3PF	4,3PF	4,3PF	4,3PF

Overview: **Danny Philip resigned as prime minister in November 2011 over corruption charges and was replaced by former minister of finance Gordon Darcy Lilo. Jimmy Lusibaea, a former militant leader and elected lawmaker, was stripped of his seat in Parliament following his conviction on charges, including attempted murder in 2000.**

The Solomon Islands gained independence from Britain in 1978. Tensions between the two largest ethnic groups—the Gwale and the Malaitans—over jobs and land rights turned into open warfare in 1998. Scores were injured or killed before peace was gradually restored through the 2000 Townsville Peace Agreement, brokered by Australia and New Zealand. A UN mission initially maintained order, while the Australian-led Regional Assistance Mission to the Solomon Islands (RAMSI) has kept the peace since 2003.

In 2007, Derek Sikua was elected prime minister and made political stability and national reconciliation priorities of his government. A Truth and Reconciliation Commission, modeled after South Africa's, was launched in 2009 to investigate crimes and address impunity connected to the 1998–2003 violence. In 2010, the commission began its first hearings, during which witnesses told stories of threats, torture, and death. More hearings were held in 2011 to collect information for a final report expected to be released in 2012.

In the August 2010 general elections, independents won 19 seats, the Solomon Islands Democratic Party (SIDP) captured 13 seats, the Reform Democratic Party (RDP) and the Ownership, Unity, and Responsibility Party each took 3 seats, and smaller parties captured the remainder. Approximately 100 international observers and police officers monitored the elections and maintained order. As is common in the Solomon Islands, new parties formed before the elections and disbanded afterward; legislators aligned themselves with these parties, but the groupings were fluid. RDP leader Danny Philip was chosen as the new prime minister, narrowly defeating SIDP leader Steve Abana. Philip, who served in Parliament from 1994 to 2001, reaffirmed the country's ties with Taiwan and pledged to work with RAMSI, fight corruption, and promote gender equality and development.

Philip resigned on November 10, 2011, in response to corruption allegations. On November 15, Parliament chose Philip's former finance minister, Gordon Darcy Lilo, as the new prime minister. His selection resulted in rioting throughout the capital. Malaitans, in particular, opposed Lilo's selection because he had previously proposed termination of government allocations to Malaita. Within two days, Lilo faced a no-confidence vote, which was withdrawn due to lack of support.

In November 2010, Jimmy Lusibaea—the former leader of a militant group during the country's civil war—was convicted on charges including assault and attempted murder in 2000 and sentenced to almost three years in prison. Lusibaea challenged his conviction in January 2011, claiming that his crimes had occurred during a period covered under an amnesty for atrocities committed during the war. In October, his sentence was drastically reduced, though a High Court stripped him of his seat in Parliament.

In December 2011, the cabinet endorsed a phased withdrawal of RAMSI, which has shifted its emphasis from direct policing to a capacity-building mission for the Solomon Island police force.

Political Rights and Civil Liberties:

The Solomon Islands are not an electoral democracy. A governor general, appointed on the advice of the National Parliament for a five-year term, represents the British monarch as head of state. Members of the 50-seat, unicameral National Parliament are elected for four-year terms. A parliamentary majority elects the prime minister, and the governor-general appoints the cabinet on the advice of the prime minister. New parties often form before elections and are disbanded afterward, as lawmakers switch allegiance after taking office. Political activity is driven more by personalities and clan identities than party affiliation.

Corruption is rampant at all levels of government. In February 2011, Minister of Mines and Energy Mark Kemakeza was charged with corruption and abuse of office and stripped of his post in April. The court had not ruled on the charges against him by year's end. In July, 14 senior officials were fired for misusing government funds. In November, a government audit discovered widespread document falsification and forgery in the finance ministry, and the opposition party alleged misuse of nearly $900,000 of $1.3 million in discretionary funds controlled by the prime minister, leading to his resignation. Solomon Islands ranked 120 out of 183 countries in Transparency International's 2011 Corruption Perceptions Index.

Freedoms of expression and of the press are generally respected, but politicians and elites sometimes use legal and extralegal means to intimidate journalists. The print media include a privately owned daily, a weekly, and two monthly publications. The government operates the only radio station. There is no local television station, but foreign broadcasts can be received via satellite. Internet use is growing, but access is limited by lack of infrastructure and high costs.

Freedom of religion is generally respected, as is academic freedom.

The constitution guarantees freedom of assembly, and the government generally recognizes this right in practice. Organizers of demonstrations must obtain permits, which are typically granted. Civil society groups operate without interference. Workers are free to organize, and strikes are permitted. In August 2011, a nationwide strike by public sector union workers ended after just one day when it accepted the government's offer of a 4 percent increase in the cost of living allowance.

Threats against judges and prosecutors have weakened the independence and rigor of the judicial system. Judges and prosecutors have also been implicated in scandals relating to corruption and abuse of power. A lack of resources limits the government's ability to provide legal counsel and timely trials. The ombudsman's office has far-reaching powers to investigate complaints of official abuse and unfair treatment, but generally lacks the funds to do so. Poor training, abuse of power, and factional and ethnic rivalries are common in the police force.

Discrimination limits the economic and political roles of women; none were elected in the 2010 elections, and there are no female judges on the High Court. Rape and other forms of abuse against women and girls are widespread. While rape is illegal, no law prohibits domestic violence. In October 2011, the government rejected a call by the United Nations to decriminalize homosexuality, saying that it is against traditional values.

Somalia

Political Rights: 7
Civil Liberties: 7
Status: Not Free

Population: 9,900,000
Capital: Mogadishu

Note: The numerical ratings and status listed above do not reflect conditions in Somaliland, which is examined in a separate report.

Ten-Year Ratings Timeline For Year Under Review (Political Rights, Civil Liberties, Status)

2002	2003	2004	2005	2006	2007	2008	2009	2010	2011
6,7NF	6,7NF	6,7NF	6,7NF	7,7NF	7,7NF	7,7NF	7,7NF	7,7NF	7,7NF

Overview: **In 2011, a crippling drought in the Horn of Africa converged with continuing insecurity, the lack of an effec-**

tive central government, and gaps in international aid to put 4 million people in need of emergency assistance in Somalia and created famine conditions in the parts of the south controlled by the main insurgent group, the Shabaab. In June, the international community reluctantly agreed to extend the mandate of the weak Transitional Federal Government for another year. After African Union peacekeepers ousted the Shabaab from Mogadishu in August, the group responded by launching its most deadly bomb attack on the capital to date in October.

Somalia gained independence in 1960 as an amalgam of former British and Italian colonies populated largely by ethnic Somalis. A 1969 coup by General Siad Barre led to two decades of instability, civil strife, and the manipulation of clan loyalties for political purposes. After Barre's regime was finally toppled in 1991, the country descended into warfare between clan-based militias, and an effective national government was never restored.

Famine and fighting killed approximately 300,000 people in 1991 and 1992, prompting a UN humanitarian mission led by U.S. forces. The intervention soon deteriorated into urban guerrilla warfare with Somali militias. Over 100 UN peacekeepers, including 18 U.S. soldiers, were killed. The international community withdrew, largely turning its back on Somalia's civil strife for the next decade.

Attempts to revitalize the political process began in 2000 with a peace conference in Djibouti, where many of Somalia's factional leaders agreed to participate in a three-year transitional government. While this initiative quickly unraveled, a fresh effort in 2004 resulted in the establishment of a 275-seat Transitional Federal Assembly (TFA), in which the leading clans took an equal number of seats, and a new Transitional Federal Government (TFG). That year, TFA members elected the Ethiopian-backed warlord Abdullahi Yusuf Ahmed to serve a five-year term as president. Divisions soon emerged within the TFG between his supporters and an alliance of Islamists and clan leaders. The Islamic Courts Union (ICU), a broad coalition of Islamists, eventually emerged as the dominant force within Mogadishu, and the group gained control of most of southern Somalia during 2006. The TFG retreated to the town of Baidoa, north of Mogadishu. Meanwhile, hard-liners within the ICU, backed by Eritrea, grew increasingly hostile toward neighboring Ethiopia. With tacit U.S. support, Ethiopia invaded Somalia to oust the ICU in December 2006, forcing the Islamists to the extreme south of the country.

The departure of the ICU prompted an insurgency against the Ethiopian-backed TFG by groups including the Shabaab, a radical ICU faction. All sides in the conflict committed severe human rights abuses, and as many as 400,000 people were displaced from Mogadishu during 2007.

Hopes for a political breakthrough were raised when a group of moderate exiled ICU leaders joined forces with non-Islamist opposition members to form the Alliance for the Reliberation of Somalia (ARS). UN-sponsored negotiations between the TFG and a faction of the ARS led to a 2008 power-sharing arrangement that doubled the size of the TFA. The Shabaab did not participate in negotiations and vowed to fight on. Ethiopian forces withdrew from Somalia in early 2009, and the expanded TFA was sworn in, electing the chairman of the ARS, Sheikh Sharif Sheikh Ahmed, as its new president.

Islamist insurgents kept up their attacks, led by the Shabaab, which declared a formal alliance with al-Qaeda at the start of 2010. Mogadishu was the epicenter of the fighting; at least 2,000 civilians were killed there in 2010, including 5 government officials and 6 members of parliament who were caught up in an attack on a hotel.

Despite ongoing assaults, the Shabaab was unable to oust the TFG from Mogadishu, which relied upon a contingent of African Union (AU) troops to shift the momentum in its favor. The troops, which numbered almost 10,000 by 2011, forced the Shabaab into what it described as a "tactical withdrawal" from Mogadishu in August. In response, the group launched an October suicide bombing that killed more than 70 people near a government building. Nevertheless, the Shabaab was under increasing strain, deeply unpopular with the public, militarily weak, and undermined by internal splits. It came under further pressure in October, when in response to a series of kidnappings across its border, Kenyan troops invaded southern Somalia. Ethiopian forces entered Somali territory from the west, squeezing the area under direct control of the Shabaab. Military operations were ongoing at year's end.

Meanwhile, rampant corruption and infighting among the TFG's leaders paralyzed government business and destroyed much of the TFG's credibility. Prime Minister Omar Abdirashid Ali Sharmarke resigned in September 2010, and his replacement, Mohamed Abdullahi Mohamed, became caught up in a dispute between President Sharif and the speaker of parliament over whether to extend the mandates of the Transitional Federal Institutions, which were due to expire in August 2011. Under a deal negotiated by Uganda in June, Mohamed was fired, and the president, the Speaker, and his deputies had their terms extended until August 2012, when elections would be held. A new prime minister, Abdiweli Mohamed Ali, was appointed.

The crisis in Somalia was further exacerbated in 2011 by the Horn of Africa's worst drought in six decades, which combined with the absence of security and a functioning government to create a humanitarian emergency. According to the United Nations, four million people were affected in Somalia, including three million in the parts of the south controlled by the Shabaab. By September, famine conditions had been declared in six regions of south-central Somalia, and the United Nations was warning that the lives of 750,000 people were in the balance. The Shabaab impeded efforts to assist the victims, banning 16 international organizations from operating in areas under its control in November. Although the international relief effort began to have an impact by the end of the year, an estimated 250,000 Somalis remained at imminent risk of starvation. Nearly one million people had abandoned their homes to seek assistance, many of them fleeing across the border to the Dadaab refugee camp in Kenya. The population of Dadaab, originally designed to hold 90,000, tipped 440,000 by the end of the year.

In the semiautonomous region of Puntland in northeastern Somalia, the security situation deteriorated in 2011, as the authorities struggled to contain pro-Shabaab militias. In August, at least 16 people were killed in Galkaiyo in clashes between the two sides, including a senior police officer. A spate of assassinations of public officials added to the sense of insecurity. Meanwhile, pirates continued to use Puntland as a launch pad for attacks. The International Maritime Bureau recorded

237 piracy incidents off the coast of Somalia in 2011, including 28 successful hijackings. Twenty-five people had been killed in the process. By the end of the year, approximately 270 crew members were being held hostage.

Political Rights and Civil Liberties: Somalia is not an electoral democracy. The state has ceased to exist in most respects, and there is no governing authority with the ability to protect political rights and civil liberties. The TFG is recognized internationally but is deeply unpopular domestically, and its actual territorial control is minimal. The TFA was expanded from 275 to 550 seats in 2009 following an agreement between the TFG and a wing of the opposition ARS. The TFA elects the president, choosing the moderate Islamist Sheikh Sharif Sheikh Ahmed in 2009. The TFG was given a five-year mandate when it was established in 2004. A new constitution and national elections were to follow, but the TFA voted in 2009 to extend the TFG's mandate until 2011. The mandates of both the TFA and the TFG were extended for another year in 2011. No effective political parties exist, and the political process is driven largely by clan loyalty.

The Transitional Federal Charter (TFC), the organizing document for Somalia that was approved in 2004, calls for a new constitution to be drawn up and approved in a national referendum. A draft version of a permanent constitution was completed in July 2010 but failed to win widespread support and had not been passed by the end of 2011.

Since 1991, the northwestern region of Somaliland has functioned with relative stability as a self-declared independent state, though it has not received international recognition. The region of Puntland has declared a temporary secession until Somalia is stabilized, although calls for full independence have been on the rise. Elections for Puntland's 66-member legislature were held in 2008. The new parliament elected Abdirahman Muhammad Mahmud "Farole" for a four-year term as president in January 2009. The result was seen as a fair reflection of the will of the legislature, and power was transferred peacefully from the defeated incumbent. The Puntland authority broke off cooperation with the TFG in January 2011 in frustration at the under-representation of its interests in Mogadishu. The two sides were reconciled at a conference in August, but relations remain tense.

Corruption in Somalia is rampant, especially among TFG officials and parliamentarians. An internal audit from the prime minister's office released in May 2011 estimated that more than $72 million in donor assistance was stolen between 2009 and 2010, and a further $250 million in revenues could not be accounted for. TFG-affiliated militias in Mogadishu have diverted emergency food aid meant for victims of Somalia's famine. The UN Monitoring Group on Somalia and Eritrea reported in June that arms and weapons supplied to the TFG found their way into Mogadishu's main market, and from there into the hands of the Shabaab. It said it was possible that TFG commanders were selling up to one-half of their ammunition. Corruption is also pervasive in Puntland, where the authorities have been complicit in piracy.

The TFC calls for freedoms of speech and the press, but these rights do not exist in practice. A press law passed in 2008 allowed for significant government control over the media. Somalia is one of the most dangerous countries in the world for journalists. According to the Committee to Protect Journalists, 22 media workers have been killed since 2007 in Somalia and Somaliland. In September 2011, a Malaysian journalist reporting on the famine was shot and killed, and a colleague injured, when the convoy they were travelling in came under fire from AU troops. Four soldiers were suspended following an investigation. In December, Abdisalan Sheikh Hassan of Horn Cable TV was shot in the head by a gunman in military uniform while driving through central Mogadishu; he had reportedly received several death threats. Radio is the primary news medium in Somalia. Somalis living abroad maintain a rich internet presence, and internet and mobile-telephone services are widely available in large cities. Nevertheless, poverty, illiteracy, and displacement limit access to these resources.

Journalists also faced a difficult and dangerous media environment in Puntland. A female journalist with Radio Galkaiyo was shot and wounded as she left her office in September 2011. In November, the authorities closed down two independent broadcasters, Universal TV and Somali Channel TV, accusing them of undermining security. An online journalist received a pardon in July 2011 following his conviction for endangering state security for an article which said that two murdered men had been members of the president's security detail.

Nearly all Somalis are Sunni Muslims, but there is a very small Christian community. Both Somalia's TFC and Puntland's charter recognize Islam as the official religion. The TFC provides for religious freedom, though this right is not respected in practice. The Shabaab has imposed crude versions of Islamic law in areas under its control, banning music, films, certain clothing, and in one area prohibiting men and women from walking together or talking in public. Anyone accused of apostasy risks execution. The Christian nongovernmental organization (NGO) Compass Direct recorded at least three cases in 2011 where Muslims were murdered for renouncing their faith. The Shabaab has also denied religious freedom to moderate Muslims and caused deep offense among many Somalis by destroying the graves of Sufi saints.

The education system is severely degraded due to the breakdown of the state. The Shabaab interferes with schools in areas under its control, demanding that all classes be taught in Arabic and ordering the removal from schools of UN-distributed textbooks it considers to be "un-Islamic." The October 2011 suicide bombing in Mogadishu targeted a group of students who had gathered to find out whether they had been awarded scholarships to study abroad.

Freedom of assembly is not respected amid the ongoing violence. The conflict forced many NGOs and UN agencies operating in Somalia to either reduce or suspend their activities. According to the UN Office for the Coordination of Humanitarian Affairs, 53 aid workers have been killed since 2008. In December 2011, three employees working on World Food Programme projects were shot dead in the town of Mataban. A week later, two staff with the medical charity Médicins Sans Frontières were killed in Mogadishu. Efforts have been made to resume emergency relief operations in the wake of the famine, but the Shabaab has blocked or impeded international aid agencies from getting supplies to the victims, particularly those living in rural areas. Somalia's insecurity has had spillover effects on relief efforts in neighboring countries. In October, two Spanish aid workers were kidnapped at gunpoint from Kenya's Dadaab camp, forcing NGOs to scale back their operations; it is believed that the hostages were taken to Somalia.

Existing labor laws are not adequately enforced. With the exception of a journalists' association, unions in the country are not active.

There is no judicial system functioning effectively at the national level. The TFA passed a law to implement Sharia (Islamic law) in 2009, but the government has been unable to implement the legislation. In reality, authorities administer a mix of Sharia and traditional Somali forms of justice and reconciliation. The harshest codes are enforced in areas under the control of the Shabaab, where people convicted of theft or other minor crimes are flogged or have their limbs amputated, usually in public. In January 2011, a man was executed by firing squad in Mogadishu after the Shabaab accused him of being a CIA spy. Three more alleged spies, including a boy of 16, met the same fate in August. The TFG has also carried out summary executions of suspected Shabaab loyalists. Independent monitors have been denied access to the detention facility run by the TFG's National Security Agency in Mogadishu, where interrogations of Shabaab suspects take place.

The rights of Somali citizens are routinely abused by the various warring factions. The TFG, the AU, and insurgent groups have fired shells indiscriminately into neighborhoods in Mogadishu. Children make up a large proportion of the civilian casualties. The United Nations said in May that half the injured patients it treated in Mogadishu were under the age of five. According to Amnesty International, both the TFG and the Shabaab have unlawfully recruited child soldiers, some as young as eight. By restricting the movement of the population in the drought-hit areas it controls, the Shabaab has exposed hundreds of thousands of people to risk of starvation.

Most Somalis share the same ethnicity and religion, but clan divisions have long fueled violence in the country. The larger, more powerful clans continue to dominate political life and are able to use their strength to harass weaker clans.

Women in Somalia face considerable discrimination. Although outlawed, female genital mutilation is still practiced in some form on nearly all Somali girls. Sexual violence is rampant due to lawlessness and impunity for perpetrators, and rape victims are often stigmatized. While the TFC stipulates that women should make up at least 12 percent of parliamentarians, the current TFP fails to meet this quota; there are just 37 women among the 550 members of parliament.

South Africa

Political Rights: 2
Civil Liberties: 2
Status: Free

Population: 50,460,000
Capital: Tshwane/Pretoria

Ten-Year Ratings Timeline For Year Under Review (Political Rights, Civil Liberties, Status)

2002	2003	2004	2005	2006	2007	2008	2009	2010	2011
1,2F	1,2F	1,2F	1,2F	2,2F	2,2F	2,2F	2,2F	2,2F	2,2F

Overview: **The passage by the lower house of the controversial Protection of Information Bill in November 2011 un-**

derscored recent threats against media rights and freedom of information in South Africa. Laws and practices dealing with asylum seekers and illegal immigrants—including the renewed deportation of Zimbabwean immigrants—were toughened in 2011. A series of strikes by public sector and other workers, along with a continued rise in protests over the scope and pace of service delivery, increased fiscal pressures on the ruling African National Congress. The year also saw a number of corruption scandals and legal actions involving high-ranking government officials.

In 1910, the Union of South Africa was created as a self-governing dominion of the British Empire. The Afrikaner-dominated National Party (NP) came to power in 1948 on a platform of institutionalized racial separation, or "apartheid," that was designed to maintain white minority rule. Facing growing British and regional pressure to end apartheid, South Africa declared formal independence in 1961 and withdrew from the Commonwealth. The NP went on to govern South Africa under the apartheid system for 33 years. Mounting domestic and international pressure prompted President F. W. de Klerk to legalize the antiapartheid African National Congress (ANC) and release ANC leader Nelson Mandela from prison in 1990. Between then and the first multiracial elections in 1994, almost all apartheid-related legislation was abolished, and an interim constitution was negotiated and enacted.

The ANC won the 1994 elections in a landslide, and Mandela was elected president. As required by the interim constitution, a national unity government was formed, including the ANC, the NP, and the Zulu-nationalist Inkatha Freedom Party (IFP). A Constitutional Assembly produced a permanent constitution, which was signed into law in 1996. The ANC claimed almost two-thirds of the vote in 1999 elections, and Thabo Mbeki, Mandela's successor as head of the ANC, won the presidency. In 2004 the ANC won an even greater victory, taking nearly 70 percent of the national vote and majorities in seven of nine provincial legislatures. Mbeki easily secured a second five-year term.

In late 2007, former deputy president Jacob Zuma defeated Mbeki in a heated battle for the ANC presidency, and Zuma's allies were elected to a majority of ANC executive positions; Mbeki had sacked Zuma in 2005, after he was implicated in the corruption trial of his financial adviser, Schabir Shaik. Relations between the ANC and Mbeki's government were strained throughout 2008, and in September—after a High Court judge set aside the remaining corruption charges against Zuma due to prosecutorial misconduct—the ANC's national executive committee forced Mbeki to resign as state president. The party nominated its deputy president, Kgalema Motlanthe, to serve as interim state president, and he was quickly confirmed by the National Assembly, the lower house of Parliament. After Mbeki's ouster, recently resigned defense minister Mosiuoa "Terror" Lekota quit the ANC and formed the opposition Congress of the People (COPE) party; he was joined by a series of ANC leaders, nearly all of them Mbeki allies.

Despite new competition from COPE, the ANC won another sweeping victory in the April 2009 elections, taking 65.9 percent of the national vote, 264 seats in the 400-seat National Assembly, and clear majorities in eight of nine provinces. The Democratic Alliance (DA) retained its status as the largest opposition party, winning 67 National Assembly seats and outright control of Western Cape Province. COPE won 30 seats, and the IFP took 18. Zuma was easily elected state president by the National Assembly the following month, winning 277 of the 400 votes.

May 2011 municipal elections—marked by relatively high voter turnout—saw the ANC win 62 percent of the vote and the DA win just under 24 percent, including outright control of Cape Town and 11 of 24 municipalities in the Western Cape. The ANC won the vast majority of municipalities in every other province. The IFP won just over 3.5 percent of the vote, and COPE took just over 2 percent.

In November 2011, the National Assembly passed the Protection of Information Bill, 229 votes to 107, despite vociferous protests from the private media sector, most opposition parties, and a raft of civil society organizations. The bill allows state agencies to classify a wide range of information on extremely vague bases—including "all matters relating to the advancement of the public good" and "the survival and security of the state"—as in the "national interest" and thus subject to significant restrictions on publication and disclosure. It mandates prison terms of 3 to 25 years for violations, and does not allow a "public interest" defense. The bill's debate and passage were met with frequent demonstrations in Cape Town, Durban, and Johannesburg. It still required approval by the National Council of Provinces (NCOP), the upper house, at year's end.

Some 5.5 million South Africans, about 11 percent of the population, are infected with HIV. A 2008 Harvard University study claimed that 330,000 people had died between 2000 and 2005 as a result of the Mbeki government's skepticism about the link between HIV and AIDS and resistance to supporting the use of antiretroviral drugs (ARVs). State-funded access to ARVs has since expanded greatly, and prices of the drugs have halved. In June 2011, 1.4 million South Africans were taking ARVs, 400,000 of whom had gained access in the previous 12 months. The government also appeared to have met its goal of testing 15 million people a year, while mother-to-child transmission fell to 3.5 percent in 2011.

Political Rights and Civil Liberties: South Africa is an electoral democracy. Elections for the 400-seat National Assembly are determined by party-list proportional representation, and the 90 members of the NCOP are selected by the provincial legislatures. The National Assembly elects the president to serve concurrently with its five-year term.

The ANC, which is part of a tripartite governing alliance with the Congress of South African Trade Unions (COSATU) and the South African Communist Party, dominates the political landscape. Factionalism within the ANC and COSATU, as well as tensions between the alliance partners, increased significantly in 2011, tied generally to the upcoming ANC elective conference in December 2012. In November, ANC Youth League President Julius Malema was suspended by the ANC for "sowing divisions and bringing the party into disrepute." The DA is the leading opposition party, followed by COPE and the IFP.

Several agencies are tasked with combating corruption, but enforcement is inadequate. Public servants regularly fail to declare their business interests as required by law, and the ANC has been criticized for charging fees to business leaders for access to top government officials. In several instances, the tender process for contracts associated with the 2010 World Cup was alleged to have been corrupt or nontransparent. In October 2011, Public Works Minister Gwen Mahlangu-Nkabinde and Cooperative Governance and Traditional Affairs Minister Sicelo Shiceka were replaced, and police chief Bheki Cele was suspended; all three had been implicated in corruption. Political motivations have tinged a number of government-sponsored corruption investigations. Following a Constitutional Court challenge calling for an independent inquiry into a 1990s "arms deal" scandal, the government in September reopened an official inquiry into the affair. Between 2005 and 2009, current president Jacob Zuma had been charged with corruption three times in connection with the scandal, but was cleared of those charges on procedural grounds. In October, the government released the long-awaited Donen report, detailing findings of corruption by top ANC and government officials—including potential Zuma rivals Tokyo Sexwale, the minister of human settlements, and Deputy President Kgalema Motlanthe—related to the UN oil-for-food program in Iraq in the 1990s. South Africa was ranked 64 out of 183 countries surveyed in Transparency International's 2011 Corruption Perceptions Index.

Freedoms of expression and the press are protected in the constitution and generally respected in practice. A number of private newspapers and magazines are sharply critical of powerful figures and institutions. Most South Africans receive the news via radio outlets, a majority of which are controlled by the South African Broadcasting Corporation (SABC). The SABC also dominates the television market, but two commercial stations are expanding their reach. Internet access is unrestricted and growing rapidly, though many South Africans cannot afford the service fee.

The government is highly sensitive to media criticism and has increasingly encroached on the editorial independence of the SABC. Government critics have been barred or restricted from SABC airwaves, while a number of documentaries and special programs produced by the broadcaster have been canceled due to political considerations. The makeup and financing of the SABC board have become increasingly politicized in recent years. The government has recently enacted and proposed a series of potentially restrictive laws. In November 2011, the Constitutional Court accepted a multiparty legal challenge to the 2009 Film and Publications Amendment Act, which requires any publisher not recognized by the press ombudsman—or any person who wishes to distribute, broadcast, or exhibit a film or game—to submit potentially pornographic or violence-inciting materials to a government board for approval. The law also allows for the banning of such materials, which are broadly defined. In June, the government announced a R1 million ($148,000), cabinet-approved advertising budget to be spent at newspapers that "assist the government in getting its message across"; the government's media advertising operations were also consolidated within the Ministry of Communication. In November, a *Mail & Guardian* report on alleged corrupt dealings by Zuma's spokesman Mac Maharaj was censored by legal order, with the newspaper and two reporters charged with illegally accessing documents.

In September, Malema was convicted of hate speech by a Johannesburg High Court for leading crowds in singing a song containing the lyrics "shoot the boer," which the court alleged promoted the killing of white farmers.

Freedom of religion and academic freedom are constitutionally guaranteed and actively protected by the government.

Freedoms of association and peaceful assembly are secured by the constitution. South Africa hosts a vibrant civil society. Nongovernmental organizations (NGOs) can register and operate freely, and lawmakers regularly accept input from NGOs on pending legislation. A recent trend of protests over the pace and extent of public-service delivery—including housing, electricity, and water—continued in 2011. In April, a man in Ficksburg in Free State was killed after police beat him during a violent service delivery protest; two officers were later charged with murder, and four with assault. In August, thousands of protesters opposed to an ANC disciplinary hearing for Malema clashed with police.

South Africans are free to form, join, and participate in independent trade unions. COSATU, the nation's largest trade union federation, claims about two million members. Strike activity is very common. In July 2011, a series of large strikes by workers in the metals, engineering, chemical, and energy sectors resulted in widespread petrol shortages for at least half the month. The National Union of Metalworkers SA workers won a 10 percent wage increase, while counterparts in the chemical, paper, and pulp industries won wage increases between 8.5 and 10 percent. Zuma and the ANC remain under heavy pressure by COSATU to raise workers' salaries, deliver better social services, and improve economic performance to help reduce the country's high levels of unemployment.

Judicial independence is guaranteed by the constitution, and the courts—particularly the Constitutional Court and the Supreme Court—operate with substantial autonomy. Nevertheless, judicial and prosecutorial independence has come under pressure in recent years amid the Zuma corruption cases, prompting several instances of both judicial and political misconduct. Zuma's September 2011 appointment of Judge Mogoeng Mogoeng as chief justice of the Constitutional Court was contentious. An ordained minister who has expressed controversial opinions on homosexuality and rape, Mogoeng's nomination was opposed by numerous legal advocacy groups, as well as by COSATU. Judicial staff and resource shortages undermine defendants' procedural rights, including the rights to a timely trial and state-funded legal counsel. While pretrial detainees wait an average of three months before trial, some wait up to two years. The lower courts have proven more susceptible to corruption than the higher panels, and there have been reports of violent intimidation of judges and magistrates.

In advance of the 2010 World Cup, the government set up a number of "dedicated courts" to deal with tournament-related cases. The courts were widely lauded for their efficiency, and the justice minister announced that some elements of the temporary system would remain intact, though details were pending at year's end. The government also hired and trained an additional 40,000 police officers, who remained on the job after the World Cup to bolster the undermanned police force.

Despite constitutional prohibitions and government countermeasures, there have been many reports of police torture and excessive force during arrest, interrogation, and detention. According to the Independent Complaints Directorate, there were 257 deaths in police custody between April 2010 and March 2011, 64 of which were linked to injuries sustained while in custody. The Judicial Inspectorate of Prisons investigates prisoners' assault allegations but has limited resources and capacity. Prisons often fail to meet international standards and feature overcrowding, inadequate health care, and abuse of inmates by staff or other prisoners; both HIV/AIDS and tuberculosis are problems. Recent inquiries have found that corruption, maladministration, and sexual violence are rife in the penal system. In August 2011, the country's first prison unit for mothers and their babies was opened near Cape Town. South Africa has one of the highest violent crime rates in the world. However, in 2011, rates of murder, attempted murder, and carjacking declined significantly, though rape and sexual assault rates increased. The Zuma administration has given the police more latitude to use force against criminals. Mostly due to police incapacity, vigilante activity is a problem.

The constitution prohibits discrimination based on a range of categories, including race, sexual orientation, and culture. State bodies such as the South African Human Rights Commission and the Office of the Public Prosecutor are empowered to investigate and prosecute cases of discrimination. Affirmative-action legislation has benefited previously disadvantaged groups (defined as "Africans," "Coloureds," "Asians," and as of 2008, "Chinese") in public and private employment as well as in education. Racial imbalances in the workforce persist, and a majority of the country's business assets remain white owned. The government's Black Economic Empowerment program aims to increase the black stake in the economy, mostly by establishing race-based ownership thresholds for government tenders and licenses.

Increased illegal immigration, particularly from Zimbabwe and Mozambique, has been met by a rise in xenophobic violence by police and vigilantes, and sporadic attacks have continued. In May 2011, residents in two Port Elizabeth townships attacked scores of Somali-owned shops, causing about 200 Somali immigrants to flee the area. In July, the African Peer Review Mechanism gave South Africa the lowest possible rating for its handling of xenophobia in the country.

The number of foreign nationals in South Africa is contested, with estimates ranging from two to seven million, including between one and three million Zimbabweans. In general, South Africa receives the largest number of asylum applications in the world; according to the Office of the UN High Commissioner for Refugees, over 400,000 were present in the country by year's end 2011, mostly from Zimbabwe. In March 2011, Parliament passed the Immigration Amendment Bill, which reduces the period asylum seekers have to make a formal application at refuge reception centers after entering the country from 14 days to 5 days, along with other restrictions. In October, the government resumed deportations of Zimbabwean migrants, halted in 2009. According to the International Organization of Migration, only 275,000 of an estimated 1.5 million Zimbabweans had applied to have their status regularized through the government's Zimbabwe Documentation Process, which ended in July 2011. Only half of the applicants received permits to remain in South Africa.

Separately, the nomadic Khoikhoi and Khomani San peoples, indigenous to South Africa, suffer from social and legal discrimination.

South Africa has one of the world's most liberal legal environments for homosexuals. The 2006 Civil Unions Act legalized same-sex marriage, and a 2002 Constitutional Court ruling held that homosexual couples should be allowed to adopt children. Nevertheless, societal bias remains strong. Homosexuals are routinely subject to physical attacks, including an increase in instances of so-called "corrective rape," whereby lesbians are raped by men seeking to change their sexual orientation. The state generally protects citizens from arbitrary deprivation of their property. However, some 80 percent of farmland is owned by white South Africans, who make up 14 percent of the population. As a result, thousands of black and colored farmworkers suffer from insecure tenure rights; illegal squatting on white-owned farms is a serious problem, as are attacks on white owners. The government has vowed to transfer 30 percent of land to black owners by 2014; however, only about 6 percent of land had been transferred by the end of 2011, and about 90 percent of the redistributed farms had failed or were failing, according to the Ministry for Land Reform and Rural Development.

Equal rights for women are guaranteed by the constitution and promoted by the Commission on Gender Equality. While the constitution allows the option and practice of customary law, it does not allow such law to supersede women's rights as South African citizens. Nevertheless, women suffer de facto discrimination with regard to marriage (including forced marriage), divorce, inheritance, and property rights, particularly in rural areas. Despite a robust legal framework, domestic violence and rape, both criminal offenses, are extremely grave problems. South Africa has one of the world's highest rates of sexual abuse, which increased further in 2011. More than 56,000 women reported having been raped from March 2010 to March 2011, with many more cases likely unreported. Women are also subject to sexual harassment and wage discrimination in the workplace, and are not well represented in top management positions. Women are better represented in government, holding 45 percent of the seats in the National Assembly and leading five of nine provincial governments. The main opposition DA party is led by Helen Zille, the premier of Western Cape Province.

South Korea

Political Rights: 1
Civil Liberties: 2
Status: Free

Population: 48,989,000
Capital: Seoul

Ten-Year Ratings Timeline For Year Under Review (Political Rights, Civil Liberties, Status)

2002	2003	2004	2005	2006	2007	2008	2009	2010	2011
2,2F	2,2F	1,2F	1,2F	1,2F	1,2F	1,2F	1,2F	1,2F	1,2F

Overview: **After escalating provocations on the Korean peninsula in 2010, inter-Korean relations remained at a stalemate for the first half of 2011. While bilateral talks resumed in February, attempts at dialogue were largely unsuccessful. Criticism of President Lee's hardline stance against North Korea and on other key domestic issues weakened his influence and that of the ruling Grand National Party. The opposition Democratic Party made key gains in both the April and October by-elections, including winning the mayoral seat of Seoul.**

The Republic of Korea (ROK) was established on the southern portion of the Korean Peninsula in 1948, three years after the Allied victory in World War II ended Japan's 35-year occupation. U.S. and Soviet forces had divided the peninsula between them, initially to accept the surrender of the Japanese army. The subsequent Korean

War (1950–53) pitted the U.S.- and UN-backed ROK, or South Korea, against the Soviet- and Chinese-backed Democratic People's Republic of Korea, or North Korea, and left some three million Koreans dead or wounded. In the decades following the 1953 armistice, South Korea's mainly military rulers crushed dissent and maintained tight control over society in response to the continuing threat from the North. During this period, South Korea implemented an export-led industrialization drive that transformed the poor, agrarian country into one of the world's leading economies.

South Korea began its democratic transition in 1987, when military strongman Chun Doo-hwan acceded to widespread protests, allowing his successor to be chosen in a direct presidential election. In the December balloting, Chun's ally and fellow general Roh Tae-woo defeated the country's two best-known dissidents, Kim Young-sam and Kim Dae-jung.

After joining the ruling party in 1990, Kim Young-sam defeated Kim Dae-jung in the 1992 presidential election, becoming South Korea's first civilian president since 1961. He sacked hard-line military officers, curbed domestic security services, and successfully prosecuted former presidents Chun and Roh for corruption and treason. However, the government's inability to mitigate a regional financial crisis led South Koreans to elect Kim Dae-jung as president in 1997.

Kim Dae-jung's efforts to reach out to North Korea culminated in a historic Inter-Korean summit in 2000 with North Korean leader Kim Jong-il. Roh Moo-hyun, a human rights lawyer and former cabinet minister who won the 2002 presidential election on the ruling liberal party's ticket, took office in February 2003 facing an economic slowdown, an opposition-led parliament, and North Korea's revival of its nuclear weapons program. Former Seoul mayor Lee Myung-bak of the conservative Grand National Party (GNP) won the 2007 presidential election. The GNP also won the majority of seats in the 2008 parliamentary elections, while the opposition Democratic Party (DP) and four smaller parties and independents accounted for the remainder.

Lee's foreign policy has focused on strengthening relations with the United States while taking a hard-line stance against North Korea. However, the president and his party have been heavily criticized for their alleged "authoritarian style" of governance, business-friendly reform agenda, and other deviations from previous presidential policies. Nevertheless, with aggressive fiscal intervention and heavy spending, the Lee administration was able to stabilize the financial sector, save the job market from massive layoffs, and steer the economy toward recovery after being hit by the 2008 global financial crisis.

Relations with North Korea grew tense in April 2009, after Pyongyang announced its withdrawal from the multilateral Six-Party Talks on its nuclear weapons program and proceeded to test a long-range missile. It then conducted its second nuclear weapons test in May. The UN Security Council responded by tightening sanctions on the North.

North Korea denied involvement in the March 2010 sinking of the South Korean naval vessel Cheonan, which killed 46 crew members. An international group of experts—which did not include members from North Korea, China, or Russia—concluded that the ship had been struck by a North Korean torpedo. South Korea vowed retaliation and demanded that Pyongyang apologize and prosecute the officers responsible. Pyongyang proclaimed that it would not engage in dialogue with the South until after Lee left office.

In June 2010, South Korea brought its case against North Korea to the UN Security Council, and in July the council issued a presidential statement to condemn the attack, without explicitly naming North Korea as the attacker. However, in response to joint U.S.-South Korean live-fire naval exercises in November, North Korea launched a surprise attack on South Korea's Yeonpyeong Island on November 23. The South mounted a counterattack, with the entire exchange lasting an hour and causing a number of South Korean casualties, including the first civilian deaths since the Korean War.

North Korea also revealed to the international community in November 2010 that it had built a modern uranium enrichment facility, heightening fears that it would produce weapons grade uranium. This revelation sparked public debate in the South whether it should reintroduce U.S. tactical nuclear weapons or pursue a nuclear weapons program of its own.

Inter-Korean talks resumed again in February 2011, though there was little progress. Lee's hard-line stance against the North, insisting on preconditions to meaningful engagement, continued to attract domestic and international criticism.

The DP made important gains in the April 2011 by-elections, in which three parliamentary seats, one provincial governor and several local councilor seats were contested. In August, Seoul Mayor Oh Se-hoon of the GNP resigned from office after losing a referendum to reduce free school lunches in the city's school system—a referendum that was at the center of an emerging debate on public welfare. DP candidate Park Won-soon defeated the GNP's Na Kyung-won for Seoul's mayoral seat in October.

On October 12, 2011, the U.S. Congress ratified the Korea-United States Free Trade Agreement (KORUS FTA), which was first signed by the two countries in June 2007, and renegotiated in December 2010. While ratification of the agreement was met with heated debate in the Korean National Assembly, it was approved on November 22, and KORUS FTA is expected to go into force in early 2012.

In November, South Korea, Japan, and the United States held trilateral strategy coordination talks and reaffirmed their commitment to cooperate in their dealings with North Korea. Inter-Korean relations are expected to improve, as South Korea made plans to resume humanitarian aid to the North through third-party organizations at year's end.

Political Rights and Civil Liberties: South Korea is an electoral democracy. The 1988 constitution vests executive power in a directly elected president, who is limited to a single five-year term. Of the unicameral National Assembly's 299 members, 245 are elected in single-member districts, and 54 are chosen through proportional representation, all for four-year terms.

Political pluralism is robust, with multiple parties competing for power. The two largest parties have been the conservative GNP and the liberal DP, which merged with the Citizens Unity Party in December 2011 to become the Democratic United Party.

Despite the overall health of the political system, bribery, influence peddling, and extortion have not been eradicated from politics, business, and everyday life. South Korea was ranked 43 out of 183 countries surveyed in Transparency International's 2011 Corruption Perceptions Index.

The news media are free and competitive. Newspapers are privately owned and report fairly aggressively on government policies and alleged official and corporate wrongdoing. Although media censorship is illegal, official censorship has increased under the administration of Lee Myung-bak, particularly of online content. The government has also attempted to influence the news of media outlets and interfered with the management of major broadcast media. The National Security Law stipulates that South Koreans may not listen to North Korean radio, though no effective measures are in place to block access to North Korean broadcasts.

The constitution provides for freedom of religion. However, Buddhist groups have accused the Lee government of religious bias. On January 10, 2011, some 230 monks and lay staff from the Jogye Order staged a three-hour peaceful protest at Chonggye Plaza in Seoul, intensifying criticism of the ruling GNP for budget cuts affecting social welfare and Buddhist activities. Academic freedom is unrestricted, with the exception of limits on statements of support for the North Korean regime or communism, in accordance with the National Security Law. This law is applied selectively and only rarely.

The government generally respects citizens' right to privacy. An Anti-Wiretap Law sets the conditions under which the government can monitor telephone calls, mail, and e-mail. Nevertheless, political and business elites often carry two mobile phones and change their numbers frequently to evade what they perceive as intrusive government eavesdropping. In June 2011, a Korean Broadcasting System reporter was investigated on allegations of illegal wiretapping of the DP chief's office. However, the police investigation ended in November for lack of evidence. Travel both within South Korea and abroad is unrestricted. The only exception is travel to North Korea, for which government approval is required.

South Korea respects freedom of assembly. The law requires that police be informed in advance of all demonstrations and that assemblies not undermine public order. Local nongovernmental organizations (NGOs) have alleged that while protesters are convicted under this law, police have not been equally penalized for mistreating demonstrators. Antimilitary and environmental activists staged ongoing protests since construction began of a ROK naval base at Gangjeong (on Jeju Island) in January 2011. Protests intensified in August and September, and police detained 35 protestors for illegally obstructing a government project. Thousands of students also participated in protests in Seoul throughout the year to demand that the government fulfill its promise to reduce college tuition fees. In September, police used water cannons to disperse student protesters for what authorities considered to be illegal demonstrations; 49 protesters were taken into custody. Water cannons were also used by the authorities in response to mass protests that took place in Seoul in November over the Korea-United States Free Trade Agreement.

Human rights groups, social welfare organizations, and other NGOs are active and for the most part operate freely. The country's independent labor unions advocate workers' interests, organizing high-profile strikes and demonstrations that sometimes lead to arrests. However, labor unions in general have been diminishing in strength and popularity, especially amid the economic downturn. In December 2010, Hanjin Heavy Industries and Construction cut 400 jobs from its Busan shipyard. Kim Jin-suk, a member of the Korean Confederation of Trade Unions, waged a solitary protest in a crane bed 35 meters in the air that lasted 309 days. After an 11-month deadlock, Hanjin reached an agreement with labor activists to reinstate

94 of the laid-off workers within one year. Kim was arrested at the end of her protest for trespassing and disturbing business.

South Korea's judiciary is generally considered to be independent. There is no trial by jury; judges render verdicts in all cases. Police occasionally engage in verbal and physical abuse of detainees. While South Korea's prisons lack certain amenities, such as hot water in the winter, there have been few reports of beatings or intimidation by guards.

The country's few ethnic minorities face legal and societal discrimination. Residents who are not ethnic Koreans face extreme difficulties obtaining citizenship, which is based on parentage rather than place of birth. Lack of citizenship bars them from the civil service and limits job opportunities at some major corporations. In April 2011, the National Assembly approved revisions to the Korean Nationality Law, allowing dual citizenship to be granted to certain populations, including foreigners married to Koreans and Koreans who gained foreign nationality through marriage or adoption. Excluded from eligibility were Chinese residents, causing some controversy.

Although women in South Korea enjoy legal equality, they face discrimination in practice, with men enjoying more social privileges and better employment opportunities. However, a 2005 Supreme Court ruling granted married women equal rights with respect to inheritance. Women continue to be underrepresented in government following the 2008 elections, comprising just 14 percent of National Assembly seats. South Korea is one of the few countries outside the Muslim world where adultery is a criminal offense.

South Sudan

Political Rights: 6
Civil Liberties: 5
Status: Not Free

Population: 8,260,000
Capital: Juba

Ten-Year Ratings Timeline For Year Under Review (Political Rights, Civil Liberties, Status)

2002	2003	2004	2005	2006	2007	2007	2009	2010	2010
--	--	--	--	--	--	--	--	--	6,5NF

Overview: **The people of South Sudan voted overwhelmingly in favor of independence from Sudan in a referendum held in January 2011. Independence was formally declared on July 9, amid celebrations in the capital, Juba. However, tensions continued with the North, particularly in the contested region of Abyei, where a separate referendum was canceled. The new nation also struggled to contain internal violence, prevent abuses by its security forces, and tackle corruption.**

The Republic of South Sudan achieved independence on July 9, 2011, completing its formal separation from Sudan. The event marked the end of an independence struggle that had begun on the eve of Sudan's own independence from Britain and

Egypt in 1956. The South's revolt led to Africa's longest civil war, from 1955 to 1972 and 1983 to 2005, with a decade-long interlude during which the South enjoyed substantial autonomy. The second bout of fighting claimed the lives of up to 2 million people. The war was motivated by Southern alienation from the Northern government in Khartoum and attempts by successive regimes in the North to impose an Arab and Islamic identity on the South. South Sudan's more than 60 cultural and linguistic groups are predominantly African and practice Christianity or indigenous religions.

Resistance to the Northern government was led by the Sudan Peoples' Liberation Army (SPLA) and its political arm, the Sudan Peoples' Liberation Movement (SPLM). The group's leader, John Garang, declared his intention to fight not for the separation of the South but for a new Sudan, governed under more inclusive, secular principles. The Southern struggle was undermined by divisions over strategy and splits fomented by Khartoum, which often played out along ethnic lines. Shortly after the signing of the Comprehensive Peace Agreement (CPA) that ended the war in 2005, Garang died in a helicopter crash. His successor, Salva Kiir, pursued a more overtly separatist agenda for the South.

The CPA formalized a system of power sharing between the SPLM and the ruling political faction in Khartoum, the National Congress Party (NCP). The two parties held seats in a national unity government, and the South, ruled by the SPLM-dominated Government of Southern Sudan (GOSS) in Juba, was granted a large degree of autonomy. While the aim of the CPA was to "make unity attractive," neither side was committed to the system it established. The GOSS focused on a provision that allowed the South to hold a referendum on self-determination after six years.

As the referendum date approached, the SPLM accused the NCP of holding up the preparations, and anxiety mounted that Khartoum would refuse to recognize a Southern vote in favor of independence. However, the plebiscite was held on time, on January 9, 2011. Voting took place over the course of a week and was largely peaceful. A total of 3.9 million Southern Sudanese had registered to vote, including 116,000 people living in the North. Voter turnout was 99 percent in the South and 58 percent in the North. On February 7, election officials confirmed that almost 99 percent of the votes cast were in favor of independence. The U.S.-based Carter Center, which monitored the referendum, declared the exercise to have been "orderly, pleasant, and productive." Sudan's president, Omar al-Bashir, pledged to recognize the result.

In Abyei, a contested area on the North-South border, residents were due to vote in a separate referendum on which country they would join. However, the plans were derailed by arguments between the NCP and SPLM over issues including the voting eligibility of the Misseriya, a nomadic Arab group—perceived as friendly to the NCP regime—that migrates to Abyei for part of the year. Clashes between Misseriya and the local police broke out in January, killing at least 30 people. In May, an attack by Southern forces on a northern military unit prompted a full-scale occupation of Abyei by the North, causing approximately 100,000 people to flee. Under a deal negotiated in June, both sides agreed to withdraw their forces to make way for UN peacekeepers, which had begun to be deployed by year's end.

The failure to determine Abyei's status contributed to tense relations between North and South. Although independence day passed peacefully in July, with al-

Bashir attending the handover ceremony in Juba, the terms of Southern separation remained unresolved. Negotiations stalled over issues including border demarcation, management of the oil sector, and the status of Southerners living in the North.

Insecurity within the South was a serious problem both before and after independence. The SPLA faced a series of armed rebellions in Unity, Upper Nile, and Jonglei States. According to the United Nations, nearly 2,400 people were killed in 330 separate incidents during the first six months of the year. In February, rebels led by George Athor killed up to 200 people in Jonglei, most of them civilians. In August, at least 600 people were killed, also in Jonglei, during cattle raiding between rival groups. More than 75 people were killed in October, when rebels attacked the SPLA in Unity State. Athor was killed in December in an SPLA operation in the southwest of the country.

The Southern government also struggled to meet the overwhelming challenge of building a new state in the face of citizens' expectations of rapid improvements to their daily lives. South Sudan is desperately poor, lacks basic infrastructure, and is highly dependent on revenue from oil that is exported mainly through Northern pipelines.

Political Rights and Civil Liberties: South Sudan is not an electoral democracy. Its first national elections are due to be held in 2015. During the interim period, the country will be governed according to the results of the 2010 presidential and legislative elections, when South Sudanese voted for state representatives, the GOSS, and the unity government in Khartoum. In the run-up to that voting, the ruling SPLM used intimidation and, in some cases, violence to ensure victory. Non-SPLM candidates were detained and prevented from campaigning, and voters were threatened.

The transitional constitution, passed in July 2011, gives broad powers to the executive. The president cannot be impeached and has the authority to fire state governors and dissolve the parliament and state assemblies. Some opposition politicians boycotted the constitutional consultation process, claiming it was insufficiently inclusive and dominated by SPLM loyalists. A permanent constitution is due to be passed by 2015.

A new Southern parliament was convened in August 2011. The SPLM holds 90 percent of the 332 seats in the lower house, the National Legislative Assembly (NLA). In addition to members of the old Southern legislature, the chamber includes 96 former members of the National Assembly in Khartoum and 66 additional members appointed by political parties. The upper chamber, the Council of States, consists of 20 former members of Sudan's Council of States, plus 30 members appointed by President Salva Kiir. The SPLM was given all but 5 posts in a 29-member cabinet, also appointed in August. South Sudan has a decentralized system, with significant powers devolved to the 10 state assemblies. Nine of the 10 state governors are members of the SPLM.

Five opposition parties are represented in the NLA, but they lack both the resources to operate effectively and the necessary experience to formulate policy and set party platforms. The SPLM is intolerant of opposition. In July 2011, two leading members of the largest opposition party, SPLM–Democratic Change, said they were arrested and tortured by SPLM security agents.

Accusations persist that members of the country's largest ethnic group, the

Dinka, dominate the leadership of the SPLM to the detriment of other groups, such as the Nuer. South Sudan's new cabinet lineup reflected an attempt to address these concerns, with portfolios spread more equitably among the main regions and ethnic groups.

Corruption is a serious problem and a major source of public frustration. Government appointments are typically handed out to SPLM loyalists or potential spoilers with little regard to merit, and corrupt officials take advantage of inadequate budget monitoring to divert public funds. In September 2011, the head of the newly formed UN Mission in South Sudan (UNMISS) called on the international community to help trace and repatriate funds she said had been deposited abroad by corrupt GOSS officials. Kiir responded with a five-point plan to tackle the problem. The interim constitution gives authority to the country's Anti-Corruption Commission to launch prosecutions.

South Sudan has seen an explosion of private media in recent years, with 37 FM radio stations, more than half a dozen newspapers, and several online news sites in operation. The sole national television channel is owned by the government. There is also one private satellite television channel, Ebony TV. Journalists currently operate in a legal vacuum. The government has yet to pass a media bill establishing the right of journalists to operate freely. Many officials, particularly from the SPLA, view journalists' activities with suspicion. In February 2011, security officials assaulted an employee of the *Citizen* newspaper and raided its offices following the publication of an article exposing police corruption. Copies of the *Juba Post* were seized in March, after the paper carried an interview with the rebel leader George Athor. In November, the editor and a journalist with Destiny newspaper were detained following the publication of an editorial that was critical of the president. Both were held without charge for two weeks before being released. According to the Union of Journalists of Southern Sudan, media workers face harassment, assault, and arrest in the course of their work, and avoid covering sensitive subjects such as human rights abuses and official corruption.

Religious freedom is guaranteed by the interim constitution and generally respected in practice. The constitution also guarantees the right to free education, although access to schools is a problem outside the state capitals. There are no restrictions on academic freedom.

Freedoms of association and assembly are enshrined in the interim charter, and the authorities typically uphold them in practice. South Sudan is highly dependent on the assistance of foreign nongovernmental organizations (NGOs), which operate freely in the country. Domestic civil society organizations, including unions, remain at an early stage of development. A Workers' Trade Union Federation was formed in late 2010, and the GOSS pledged to support its work.

The interim constitution provides for an independent judiciary, headed by a Supreme Court. The president's Supreme Court appointments must be confirmed by a two-thirds majority in the NLA. The embryonic court system is under huge strain. In September 2011, the chief justice said the courts had the capacity to handle 100,000 cases a year, but faced four times that number. He called for greater use of traditional dispute-resolution systems to ease the burden.

The South Sudan Police Service (SSPS) is ill-equipped, unprofessional, and overwhelmed by the country's security challenges. In February 2011, UN inspectors uncovered evidence of brutality and rape at the main police training academy. At least two recruits died of their injuries. There were frequent reports during the year of arbitrary arrest, torture, and long periods of pretrial detention in substandard facilities. Children and the mentally ill were routinely detained with adult prisoners. In July, two police officers were arrested after a female suspect claimed she was tortured and sexually assaulted at Juba's main police station. In August, the director of public security and criminal investigation was arrested for alleged involvement in torture, the disappearance of a suspect, and the use of illegal detention centers. Also that month, the country's most senior UN human rights official required five days of hospital treatment after he was beaten by SSPS officers.

The army is often called upon to perform policing functions, and the SPLA committed serious abuses while carrying out such duties, according to Human Rights Watch and Amnesty International. These included extrajudicial killings, the destruction of homes, and looting. Hundreds of civilians were killed during fighting between the SPLA and rebel groups operating in the South during 2011.

Since 2005, more than two million refugees and internally displaced people have moved back to the South. The GOSS encouraged their return but has largely failed to provide them with even the most basic assistance.

Land use and ownership are frequent causes of conflict in South Sudan, and the return of refugees has exacerbated the problem. Unclear or nonexistent laws have been exploited by SPLM officials and overseas investors to uproot people from their land.

The interim constitution guarantees the rights of women to equal pay and property ownership. In reality, women are routinely exposed to discriminatory practices and domestic abuse. More than 80 percent of women are illiterate. Women hold a quarter of the posts in the cabinet, fulfilling a gender quota laid out in the constitution. The SPLA continues to use child soldiers, despite a pledge to end the practice by the end of 2010.

Spain

Political Rights: 1
Civil Liberties: 1
Status: Free

Population: 46,178,000
Capital: Madrid

Ten-Year Ratings Timeline For Year Under Review (Political Rights, Civil Liberties, Status)

2002	2003	2004	2005	2006	2007	2007	2009	2010	2010
1,1F	1,1F	1,1F	1,1F	1,1F	1,1F	1,1F	1,1F	1,1F	1,1F

Overview: **The conservative Popular Party won a resounding victory in national elections held in November 2011, after the introduction of unpopular austerity measures undermined the government of the ruling Spanish Socialist Workers' Party. Spain's borrowing rate rose rapidly in November, and concerns persisted that the country would not be able to meet its deficit-cutting targets.**

Peninsular Spain's current borders were largely established by the 16th century, and after a period of great colonial expansion and wealth, the country declined in relation to its European rivals. The Spanish Civil War of 1936–39 ended in victory for General Francisco Franco's right-wing Nationalists, who executed, jailed, and exiled the leftist Republicans. During Franco's long rule, many countries cut off diplomatic ties, and his regime was ostracized by the United Nations from 1946 to 1955. The militant Basque separatist group Euskadi Ta Askatasuna (ETA), or Basque Fatherland and Freedom, was formed in 1959, with the aim of creating an independent Basque homeland, and went on to carry out a campaign of terrorist bombings and other illegal activities. After a transitional period following Franco's death in 1975, Spain emerged as a parliamentary democracy, joining the European Economic Community, the precursor to the European Union (EU), in 1986.

In the 2004 parliamentary elections, the Spanish Socialist Workers' Party (PSOE) defeated the conservative Popular Party (PP), which had been in power for 11 years. However, lacking an outright majority, the PSOE relied on regionalist parties to support its legislation. The elections came only days after multiple terrorist bombings of commuter trains in Madrid that killed almost 200 people. The PP government initially blamed ETA, sparking anger from voters after it was discovered that the attacks had been carried out by Islamic fundamentalists in response to the government's support of the U.S.-led war in Iraq. After becoming prime minister, the PSOE's José Luis Rodríguez Zapatero pulled Spain's troops out of Iraq. In 2007, a Spanish court handed down long prison sentences to 21 of the 28 defendants charged in connection with the bombings; 7 were acquitted. In 2008, another key suspect in the bombings was sentenced to 20 years in prison.

ETA announced a ceasefire in 2006, but peace talks with the government broke down in January 2007, after the group claimed responsibility for a December 2006 bombing in a parking garage at Madrid's Barajas Airport. The Supreme Court banned hundreds of candidates with alleged links to ETA from participating in 2007 local elections in the Basque region. In March 2009, the Basque Nationalist Party lost its absolute majority in the Basque parliament elections for the first time in 30 years. The coalition of the PSOE and the PP pledged to focus on security and the economy in the Basque region, and not press for regional autonomy. In October 2011, ETA declared a "definitive cessation of armed activities," which was just shy of a full surrender and disarmament. The announcement came after a campaign by the police over the previous few years—including the arrests of the group's top operatives and foot soldiers and the seizure of weapons and bomb-making materials—had weakened the group considerably.

In May 2011, the PSOE suffered several losses in local elections. In July, Zapatero called for early general elections in November. Zapatero had been suffering from low approval ratings that were attributed to the country's economic difficulties, which included a 20 percent unemployment rate and 45 percent youth unemployment rate. Additionally, the debt crisis in Europe had led to the implementation of unpopular austerity measures, such as increasing the retirement age from 65 to 67. The conservative PP trounced the PSOE in the November elections. The PP won 186 out of 350 seats in the lower house, while the PSOE took only 111 seats, its worst showing in 30 years. PP leader Mariano Rajoy replaced Zapatero as prime minister. In May, the "Indignant" movement began as protesters, led by unemployed youth, occupied a central square in Madrid. By October, the movement had inspired similar international movements, such as Occupy Wall Street, that also focused on the disproportionate political power of the wealthy.

In November, Spain's debt crisis worsened as interest rates on the country's debt rose drastically. In December, the new government announced a package of 8.9 billion (US$11.2 billion) in spending cuts and 6.2 billion in tax increases to address the country's economic woes. The measures were imposed after the new government discovered that the deficit was 8 percent of gross domestic product (GDP), rather than the 6 percent calculated by the previous government; Spain had pledged to the EU that it would cut its deficit to 4.4 percent in 2012.

Political Rights and Civil Liberties: Spain is an electoral democracy. The Congress of Deputies, the lower house of the bicameral Parliament, has 350 members elected in multimember constituencies, except for the North African enclaves of Ceuta and Melilla, which are each assigned one single-member constituency. The Senate has 264 members, with 208 elected directly and 56 chosen by regional legislatures. Members of both the Senate and Congress serve four-year terms. Following legislative elections, the prime minister is selected by the monarch and is usually the leader of the majority party or coalition. The candidate must also be elected by Parliament. The country's 50 provinces are divided into 17 autonomous regions with varying degrees of power.

People generally have the right to organize in political parties and other competitive groups of their choice. The Basque separatist Batasuna party, which had previously garnered between 5 and 10 percent of the regional vote, was permanently banned in 2003 for its alleged ties to the armed group ETA. In September 2011, Arnaldo Otegi, the former leader of Batasuna, was sentenced to 10 years in jail for trying to revive the party.

In September 2010, the largest corruption trial in the country's history began in the summer resort town of Marbella. The 95 defendants—including two former mayors and 15 town counselors—were accused of participating in a widespread system of graft, with local businesspeople bribing town officials for favorable decisions, primarily in city planning. Spain was ranked 31 out of 183 countries surveyed in Transparency International's 2011 Corruption Perceptions Index.

Spain has a free and lively press, with more than 100 newspapers covering a wide range of perspectives and actively investigating high-level corruption. Daily newspaper ownership, however, is concentrated within large media groups like Prisa and Zeta. Journalists who oppose the political views of ETA have in the past been targeted by the group. Newspapers objected to a proposed government regulation announced in July 2010 that would prohibit advertising prostitution in the classified section. The explicit advertisements bring in over 40 million euros (approximately US$57 million) annually for the newspaper industry, which is struggling economically. The law was passed in December 2011.

Freedom of religion is guaranteed through constitutional and legal protections. Roman Catholicism is the dominant religion and enjoys privileges that other religions do not, such as financing through the tax system. Jews, Muslims, and Protestants have official status through bilateral agreements with the state, while other groups (including Jehovah's Witnesses and Mormons) have no such agreements. The government does not restrict academic freedom.

The constitution provides for freedom of assembly, and the government respects this right in practice. Domestic and international nongovernmental organizations operate without government restrictions. With the exception of members of the military, workers are free to strike and organize and join unions of their choice. About 15 percent of the workforce is unionized. Antiausterity protests took place across the country throughout 2011.

The constitution provides for an independent judiciary. However, there have been recent concerns over the functioning of the judicial system, including the impact of media pressure on sensitive issues such as immigration and Basque terrorism. Spain's universal jurisdiction law allows for the trial of suspects for crimes committed abroad if they are not facing prosecution in their home country. However, in June 2009, Spain's lower house voted in favor of limiting the universal jurisdiction law to cases involving either victims with Spanish citizenship or some other link to Spain, as well as cases where the alleged perpetrators are in Spain. In August 2011, a Spanish judge indicted nine Salvadoran soldiers under the country's universal jurisdiction law for the murder of six priests in El Salvador in 1989 during that country's civil war.

Police abuse of prisoners, especially immigrants, has been reported. Those suspected of certain terrorism-related crimes can be held by police for up to five days with access only to a public lawyer. Prison conditions generally meet international standards.

Women enjoy legal protections against rape, domestic abuse, and sexual harassment in the workplace. However, violence against women, particularly within the home, remains a serious problem. Women currently hold 36 percent of the seats in the lower house. In February 2010, the Senate approved a measure liberalizing abortion laws to allow for the termination of a pregnancy on demand during the first 14 weeks. Legislation enacted in 2005 legalized same-sex marriages and allowed gay couples to adopt children. Trafficking in men, women, and children for the purpose of sexual exploitation and forced labor remains a problem.

Sri Lanka

Political Rights: 5
Civil Liberties: 4
Status: Partly Free

Population: 20,700,000
Capital: Colombo

Ten-Year Ratings Timeline For Year Under Review (Political Rights, Civil Liberties, Status)

2002	2003	2004	2005	2006	2007	2008	2009	2010	2011
3,4PF	3,3PF	3,3PF	3,3PF	4,4PF	4,4PF	4,4PF	5,4PF	5,4PF	5,4PF

Overview: **President Mahinda Rajapaksa maintained a firm grip on power in 2011, with his coalition winning landslide victories in local elections. The government continued to reject credible allegations of war crimes committed in the final phase of its military campaign against the Tamil Tiger rebel group in 2009, and the United Nations called**

for an independent international mechanism to investigate these issues. The situation for human rights defenders and journalists remained grim during the year, with numerous attacks and cases of intimidation occurring amid a climate of nationalist rhetoric and impunity. Although the majority of civilians displaced by the war had returned to their home districts, many resettled away from their original homes and faced multiple threats to their physical and economic security. Meanwhile, the Tamil minority's long-standing grievances went largely unaddressed by the government.

After Sri Lanka gained independence from Britain in 1948, political power alternated between the conservative United National Party (UNP) and the leftist Sri Lanka Freedom Party (SLFP). While the country made impressive gains in literacy, basic health care, and other social needs, its economic development was later stunted and its social fabric tested by a long-running civil war between the government and ethnic Tamil rebels. The conflict was triggered by anti-Tamil riots in 1983 that claimed hundreds of lives, but it came in the context of broader Tamil claims of discrimination in education and employment by the Sinhalese majority. By 1986, the Liberation Tigers of Tamil Eelam (LTTE, or Tamil Tigers), which called for an independent Tamil homeland in the northeast, had eliminated most rival Tamil guerrilla groups and was in control of much of the northern Jaffna Peninsula. At the same time, the government was also fighting an insurgency in the south by the leftist People's Liberation Front (JVP). The JVP insurgency, and the brutal methods used by the army to quell it in 1989, killed an estimated 60,000 people.

Following a 2002 ceasefire accord (CFA), the government and LTTE agreed to explore a political settlement based on a federal system. However, the peace process was weakened by the Tigers' pullout from negotiations in 2003, as well as infighting between the main political parties about how to approach the LTTE.

After parliamentary elections held in 2004, President Chandrika Kumaratunga's United People's Freedom Alliance (UPFA) coalition, led by the SLFP and bolstered by the support of the JVP, formed a minority government. The addition of the JVP to the ruling coalition and the presence of Sinhalese nationalist forces in Parliament further hampered the peace process, as did the emergence of a breakaway faction of the Tigers, the Tamil People's Liberation Tigers (TMVP). The splinter group was led by Colonel Karuna Amman (the nom de guerre of Vinayagamoorthi Muralitharan), who accused the LTTE leadership of discrimination against eastern Tamils. By 2006, the Karuna faction had become loosely allied with the government. Prime Minister Mahinda Rajapaksa of the SLFP narrowly won the 2005 presidential election, largely due to an LTTE boycott enforced by voter intimidation in the areas under its influence. Rajapaksa cultivated a more authoritarian style of rule, relegating Parliament to a secondary role, and appointed his brothers to key positions.

Fighting with the LTTE escalated in 2007, and the government formally annulled the CFA in January 2008. A sustained government offensive, accompanied by a deepening humanitarian crisis, culminated in a final battle in May 2009, in which the Tigers' leadership was annihilated. At least 100,000 people had been killed in the 26-year conflict, including as many as 40,000 in May 2009 alone, according to the United Nations. Approximately 300,000 civilians were displaced during the final phase of the war, and many of those were interned in government-run camps, where they faced severe food shortages and outbreaks of disease. The government initially limited aid groups' access to the camps and did not allow inmates to leave, with the primary aim of screening all residents for any rebels hiding among them. At the end of 2009, more than 100,000 internally displaced persons (IDPs) remained in the camps, while thousands more had left but were unable to return to their homes due to war damage and mines.

The SLFP strengthened its political position ahead of the 2010 parliamentary balloting by winning a number of local and provincial elections—seen as a public endorsement of the government's military successes—and drawing several senior TMVP defectors, including Karuna himself, into its ranks. Rajapaksa called a presidential election for January 2010, almost two years early, and went on to win nearly 58 percent of the vote. His main opponent, former head of the armed forces Sarath Fonseka, received around 40 percent. Voting was divided along ethnic lines, with most Tamils and Muslims supporting Fonseka and most Sinhalese supporting the president. Fonseka alleged irregularities and requested that the vote be annulled. In February, he was arrested on charges of plotting a coup, though most analysts viewed the charges as politically motivated. In September, a court martial found him guilty of engaging in politics while still an active service member and of not adhering to procurement rules. After Rajapaksa endorsed the verdict, the former general began a 30-month prison sentence. In addition to harassment of political opponents, the government continued to crack down on dissent from other quarters, applying pressure to prominent journalists, human rights advocates, and international critics.

In parliamentary elections held in April 2010, the ruling UPFA secured 144 of 225 seats, but fell short of a two-thirds majority. The opposition UNP won 60 seats, while the Democratic National Alliance (DNA) coalition, led by the JVP, won seven (including one for Fonseka), and the Tamil National Alliance (TNA) took 14. Turnout was considerably lower than in the previous elections, at just over 50 percent. The president's brother, Chamal Rajapaksa, was elected as speaker of Parliament. The government was further strengthened by the defection of several lawmakers from opposition parties in August.

Parliament passed the government-backed 18th Amendment to the constitution in September 2010. The package of revisions extended political control over state institutions by abolishing the constitutional council mandated by the 17th Amendment and replacing it with a government-dominated parliamentary council tasked with selecting key members of the judiciary and nominally independent commissions. The new amendment also reduced the powers of the electoral and police commissions and removed the two-term limit on presidents. The opposition boycotted the parliamentary vote on the changes, which were criticized by a range of civil society and watchdog groups.

In July 2011, the ruling coalition swept local council elections in most of the country. But in a sign of continued ethnic polarization, the TNA, long allied with the Tigers, won most council contests in the north and east despite alleged intimidation and attempted electoral manipulation by the army.

The issue of whether war crimes were committed in the final phases of the civil conflict remained a source of contention in 2011. In April, an expert panel formed by the UN secretary general released a report assigning blame to both sides for a range of atrocities, and recommending the establishment of an international mechanism to ensure justice. The panel also recommended that the government immediately commence investigations into the alleged breaches of international law committed by both sides and urged the government to issue a formal acknowledgment of its involvement in the killings of civilians during the last stages of the civil war. A documentary broadcast in June by Britain's Channel 4 television station showed a range of apparent violations, including the shelling of civilians, attacks on hospital facilities, and summary executions by army units. Although the government maintained that a full international investigative mechanism or tribunal was unnecessary, the dossier of the UN expert panel was forwarded to the UN Human Rights Council in September. Largely as a result of disagreement over this issue, Sri Lanka's relations with the United Nations and major world democracies soured further during the year, and the government increasingly turned to nondemocratic powers such as China, Iran, and Russia for foreign investment and diplomatic support.

Meanwhile, the Lessons Learnt and Reconciliation Commission (LLRC), a government-backed investigative body whose primary mandate was to assess the reasons behind the collapse of the 2002 ceasefire, held a number of hearings to gather testimony from witnesses, but analysts warned that the panel's composition left serious doubts as to its independence. The final report, publicly released in December 2011, called on the government to gradually remove security forces from civilian affairs and activity, establish a more distanced relationship between the police and institutions managing armed forces, and commence investigations into the myriad abductions, disappearances, and harassment of journalists.

Political Rights and Civil Liberties:

Sri Lanka is not an electoral democracy. The 1978 constitution vested strong executive powers in the president, who is directly elected for six-year terms and can dissolve Parliament. The prime minister heads the leading party in Parliament but has limited powers. The 225-member unicameral legislature is elected for six-year terms through a mixed proportional-representation system.

In the January 2010 presidential election, monitoring groups alleged inappropriate use of state resources—particularly transport, infrastructure, police services, and media—to benefit the incumbent, in violation of orders issued by election officials. More than 1,000 incidents of violence, including at least four deaths, were reported in the preelection period. In the northern and eastern provinces, inadequate provisions for transport and registration of IDPs contributed to a low turnout. Election officials' orders were similarly disregarded prior to the April 2010 parliamentary elections, which also featured extensive misuse of state resources. The independent Center for Monitoring Election Violence (CMEV) noted that the elections were considerably less beleaguered by violence than the presidential vote, with 84 major and 202 minor incidents reported. Nevertheless, irregularities led to the nullification or suspension of results in several districts. Local council elections held in 2011, though mostly peaceful, were marred by some violence and killings, and civil society groups accused the government and party cadres of engaging in intimidation prior to the voting, particularly in the northern and eastern provinces. They also cited continuing problems with voter documentation, misuse of state resources by the ruling party, and other violations of election laws.

Some observers charge that President Mahinda Rajapaksa's centralized, authoritarian style of rule has led to a lack of transparent, inclusive policy formulation. The Centre for Policy Alternatives (CPA) and others have noted the concentration of power in the hands of the Rajapaksa family. The president himself holds multiple ministerial portfolios, and his brothers serve in other key posts: Gotabaya serves as defense secretary, Basil is minister for economic development, and Chamal is speaker of Parliament. A growing number of other relatives, including the president's son Namal, also hold important political or diplomatic positions. The president and his family consequently control approximately 70 percent of the national budget. During 2011, the president took steps to enhance Namal's profile in international and domestic forums, fueling speculation that he was being groomed as a potential successor.

The 18th Amendment to the constitution in 2010 effectively reversed efforts to depoliticize certain institutions under the 17th Amendment, giving a government-dominated parliamentary council powers to advise the president regarding appointments to independent commissions that oversee the police, the judiciary, human rights, and civil servants.

Official corruption is a continuing concern. The current legal and administrative framework is inadequate for promoting integrity and punishing corrupt behavior, and weak enforcement of existing safeguards has been a problem. For example, legislators routinely ignore wealth-declaration requirements stipulated in the 1994 Bribery Amendment Act. In June 2011, the Commission to Investigate Allegations of Bribery or Corruption (CIABOC) was reinstated after more than a year of inaction, with a new chairman and two commissioners appointed by the president. The commissioners immediately started work on clearing a backlog of more than 3,000 pending cases, as well as proposing amendments to existing laws; by year's end fiv prosecutions had been secured in different cases. Corruption cases can only be initiated by members of the public, who have been reluctant to do so because of a lack of whistle-blower protections; although in 2011 the government proposed amending the law to allow officials to initiate investigations, this had not taken place by year's end. Sri Lanka was ranked 86 out of 183 countries surveyed in Transparency International's 2011 Corruption Perceptions Index.

Although freedom of expression is guaranteed in the constitution, a number of laws and regulations restrict this right, including the Official Secrets Act, the Prevention of Terrorism Act (PTA), additional antiterrorism regulations issued in 2006, and laws on defamation and contempt of court. State-run media outlets have fallen under government influence, while official rhetoric toward critical journalists and outlets has grown more hostile, often equating any form of criticism with treason.

Journalists throughout Sri Lanka, particularly those who cover human rights or military issues, encounter considerable levels of intimidation, which has led over the past several years to increased self-censorship. A number of journalists received death threats in 2011, while others were assaulted. Staff at the independent *Uthayan* newspaper, based in Jaffna, faced threats and attacks in response to critical coverage of the government and paramilitary groups operating in the north, including a brutal attack on editor Gnanasundaram Kuhanathan in July. Past attacks on journalists and media outlets, such as the murder of Lasantha Wickrematunga in 2009, have not been adequately investigated, leading to a climate of complete impunity. In July 2011, Wickrematunga's brother, who heads the *Sunday Leader* newspaper, received a threatening telephone call from President Rajapaksa in response to an article. The paper's editor, Frederica Jansz, also received threats in October.

The government has stepped up efforts to censor the internet, temporarily blocking access to independent news sites such as Lanka eNews and Groundviews, as well as the website of Transparency International. In January 2011, the offices of *Lanka eNews* were destroyed in an arson attack by unknown assailants. Its staff have faced a range of threats and harassment over the past two years, including arrests and the unexplained 2010 disappearance of journalist and cartoonist Prageeth Eknaligoda, who remained missing at the end of 2011.

Religious freedom is respected, and members of all faiths are generally allowed to worship freely. However, the constitution gives special status to Buddhism, and there is some discrimination and occasional violence against religious minorities. Tensions between the Buddhist majority and the Christian minority—particularly evangelical Christian groups, who are accused of forced conversions—sporadically flare into attacks on churches and individuals by Buddhist extremists. In September 2011, a Muslim shrine was destroyed by Buddhist monks in the town of Anuradhapura, prompting condemnations by Muslim leaders but only a lukewarm response from government officials. Work permits for foreign clergy, formerly valid for five years, are now being issued for only one year with the possibility of extension. Conditions for Muslims in the north and east improved with the demise of the LTTE, but relations between Muslims and the predominantly Hindu Tamils remain somewhat tense. In recent years, the minority Ahmadiyya Muslim sect has faced increased threats and attacks from Sunni Muslims who accuse Ahmadis of being apostates.

Academic freedom is generally respected. However, some commentators have warned of increasing politicization on university campuses, lack of tolerance for antigovernment views, and a rise in self-censorship by professors and students. In May 2011, the authorities introduced mandatory "leadership training" for all university undergraduates, conducted by the army at military camps, despite protests from student unions and a Supreme Court order recommending that the plan be suspended. Concerns have been raised that the curriculum promotes Sinhalese nationalist viewpoints and discourages respect for ethnic diversity and political dissent.

Emergency regulations that empowered the president to restrict rallies and gatherings lapsed in August 2011, and permission for demonstrations is usually granted. However, police occasionally use excessive force to disperse protesters, as was the case when trade unions staged a massive protest against pension reform in May 2011. In June, a journalist and two others were arrested and interrogated by police after they attempted to display posters advertising a public discussion forum and were accused of conspiring against the government. The army has placed some restrictions on assembly, particularly for planned memorial events in the north and east concerning the end of the war, according to the International Crisis Group.

Nongovernmental organizations (NGOs) face some official harassment and curbs on their activities. In April 2010, the president gave the Defense Ministry control over the registration of NGOs, both local and foreign. Human rights and peace-seeking NGOs—particularly those willing to document abuses of human rights or accountability, such as the CPA, National Peace Council, or the local branch of Transparency International—faced surveillance, smear campaigns, threats, and criminal investigations into their funding and activities in 2011. Many of these

NGOs had difficulty acquiring work permits in the northern and eastern areas of the country. However, the UN and other humanitarian organizations were generally given adequate access to conflict zones. The body of human rights defender Pattani Razeek, who disappeared in February 2010, was found in July 2011. In August, activist Perumal Sivakumara died after being assaulted by police.

Most of Sri Lanka's 1,500 trade unions are independent and legally allowed to engage in collective bargaining, but this right is poorly upheld in practice. Except for civil servants, most workers can hold strikes, though the 1989 Essential Services Act allows the president to declare a strike in any industry illegal. While more than 70 percent of the mainly Tamil workers on tea plantations are unionized, employers routinely violate their rights. Harassment of labor activists and official intolerance of union activities, particularly in export processing zones, are regularly reported. The government has increased penalties for employing minors, and complaints involving child labor have risen significantly. Nevertheless, thousands of children continue to be employed as household servants, and many face abuse.

Successive governments have respected judicial independence, and judges can generally make decisions without overt political intimidation. However, concerns about politicization of the judiciary have grown in recent years. A 2009 International Crisis Group report highlighted a number of problems, including the executive's power to make high-level judicial appointments; the chief justice's control over the Judicial Service Commission, which makes lower-level appointments; and the lack of a mechanism to sanction biased or corrupt judges. Judicial independence was further eroded by the 18th amendment, which granted a parliamentary council advisory powers and the president greater responsibility to make judicial appointments. Corruption remains fairly common in the lower courts, and those willing to pay bribes have better access to the legal system.

The last years of the war featured a sharp rise in human rights abuses by security forces, including arbitrary arrest, extrajudicial execution, forced disappearance, custodial rape, and prolonged detention without trial, all of which predominantly affected Tamils. Torture occurred in the context of the insurgency but also takes place during routine interrogations. Abusive practices have been facilitated by the emergency regulations, the PTA, and the 2006 antiterrorism regulations. Under the PTA, suspects can be detained for up to 18 months without trial. These laws have been used to detain a variety of perceived enemies of the government, including political opponents, critical journalists, members of civil society, and Tamil civilians suspected of supporting the LTTE. The government allowed the emergency regulations to lapse in August 2011, but shortly thereafter authorized the expansion of law enforcement powers under the PTA. An estimated 6,000 people were in detention under the emergency regulations at the time of their expiration, according to Human Rights Watch, and remained in detention without charge at year's end. Separately, of the roughly 11,000 Tiger cadres who surrendered in the war's final stages, some 3,000 remained in military-run "rehabilitation" programs in 2011.

Most past human rights abuses are not aggressively prosecuted, and victims and witnesses are inadequately protected. The National Human Rights Commission (NHRC) is empowered to investigate abuses, but it has traditionally suffered from insufficient authority and resources. The independence of the NHRC and other commissions was weakened by the adoption of the 18th Amendment in 2010.

Tamils maintain that they face systematic discrimination in areas including government employment, university education, and access to justice. Legislation that replaced English with Sinhala as the official language in 1956 continues to disadvantage Tamils and other non–Sinhala speakers. Tensions between the three major ethnic groups (Sinhalese, Tamils, and Muslims) occasionally lead to violence, and the government generally does not take adequate measures to prevent or contain it. However, no major incidents were reported in 2011.

Since the end of the war, the government has ostensibly concentrated on rehabilitating former LTTE-controlled territory in the north and east (about 10–15 percent of the country) through economic development programs, but Tamil hopes for greater political autonomy remained unfulfilled. LTTE rule has been replaced by that of the army, which controls most aspects of daily life, including local government in some districts.

Human rights groups have claimed that insufficient registration policies in the postwar IDP camps contributed to widespread disappearances and removals without accountability, and the status of hundreds of Tamils who disappeared during the war's final phase remains unclear. While most IDPs had returned to their home districts by the end of 2011, in many cases they were unable to occupy their former property due to land mines, destruction of their homes, or appropriation of their land by the military or government. According to the Internal Displacement Monitoring Centre, as of December 31, 2011, 95,534 people remained displaced, the vast majority of whom were residing with host families. In September, authorities announced the closure of Menik Farm, the largest internment camp, and the relocation of its 7,400 remaining inmates to a newly created transit camp in Kompavil. According to the State Department Human Rights Report, it remained uncertain as to whether these IDPs that resettled in Kompavil would be allowed to go back to their home areas when demining was finished or whether they would be forced to permanently settle in Kompavil. Other former residents of the conflict area live as refugees in India. Muslims forcibly ejected from the north by the LTTE in the early 1990s noted during the course of LLRC hearings in 2010 that many were unable to return to their homes, as their land was still being occupied by Tamils. In general, there are few official attempts to help this group of returnees.

Observers have expressed concern that government appropriation of land in the north and east as part of economic development projects or "high security zones" has impinged on freedom of movement and the ability of local people to return to their property, and that the land will be allotted to southerners or on politically motivated grounds. The military has expanded its economic activities in the north and east, running shops and growing agricultural produce for sale in the south, while local businesspeople are pushed out of the market. Throughout the country, the military's role in a variety of economic activities—from tourism to agriculture and infrastructure projects—has expanded significantly, providing jobs and revenue for a force that has tripled in size under the current president.

Women are underrepresented in politics and the civil service. Female employees in the private sector face some sexual harassment and discrimination in salary and promotion opportunities. Rape and domestic violence remain serious problems, with hundreds of complaints reported annually; existing laws are weakly enforced. Violence against women increased along with the general fighting in the civil conflict, and has also affected female prisoners and interned IDPs. The entrenchment of the army in the north and east has increased the risk of harassment and sexual abuse for female civilians (many of whom are widows) in those areas. Although women have equal rights under civil and criminal law, matters related to the family—including marriage, divorce, child custody, and inheritance—are adjudicated under the customary law of each ethnic or religious group, and the application of these laws sometimes results in discrimination against women. The government remains committed to ensuring that children have access to free education and health care, and it has also taken steps to prosecute those suspected of sex crimes against children.

Sudan

Political Rights: 7
Civil Liberties: 7
Status: Not Free

Population: 44,600,000 [Note: This figure includes South Sudan.]
Capital: Khartoum

Trend Arrow: Sudan received a downward trend arrow due to a surge in arrests of opposition political activists and leaders, the banning of a leading political party, the violent response to public demonstrations in Khartoum and other cities, and a crackdown on the activities of journalists.

Note: The numerical ratings and status listed above do not reflect conditions in South Sudan, which became an independent country in 2011 and is examined in a separate report.

Ten-Year Ratings Timeline For Year Under Review (Political Rights, Civil Liberties, Status)

2002	2003	2004	2005	2006	2007	2008	2009	2010	2011
7,7NF	7,7NF	7,7NF	7,7NF	7,7NF	7,7NF	7,7NF	7,7NF	7,7NF	7,7NF

Overview: **Sudan experienced political, economic, and social upheaval in 2011, including the loss of one-third of its territory when South Sudan became independent in July. Faced with the threat of political spillover from popular uprisings in other Arab countries and an economic crisis triggered by the secession of the oil-rich South, the embattled regime launched a harsh crackdown on any sign of dissent. New conflicts erupted in the border states of Southern Kordofan and Blue Nile, prompting a heavy-handed response by government forces, which were accused of committing war crimes. Meanwhile, the conflict in Darfur continued despite the signing of a peace agreement with one of the rebel groups.**

Sudan has been embroiled in nearly continuous civil wars since gaining independence from Britain and Egypt in 1956. Between 1956 and 1972, the Anyanya movement, representing mainly black Africans in southern Sudan, battled Arab Muslim–dominated government forces. In 1969, General Jafar Numeiri took power in a coup. The South gained extensive autonomy under a 1972 accord, but Numeiri reneged on the deal in 1983 and imposed Sharia (Islamic law), igniting a civil war with the main rebel group, the Sudan People's Liberation Army (SPLA). The fighting lasted until 2004, causing the deaths of an estimated two million people. Numeiri was ousted in a popular uprising in 1985, and a civilian government elected in 1986 was overthrown three years later by General Omar al-Bashir. Over the next decade, al-Bashir governed with the support of senior Muslim clerics including Hassan al-Turabi, who served as leader of the ruling National Islamic Front (NIF).

Al-Bashir fired al-Turabi in 1999 and oversaw flawed presidential and parliamentary elections a year later, which the National Congress Party (NCP) (formerly the NIF) won overwhelmingly. The government ended the civil war with the South in January 2005 by signing the Comprehensive Peace Agreement (CPA) with the SPLA and its political arm, the Sudan People's Liberation Movement (SPLM). The pact established a power-sharing government in Khartoum between the SPLM and the NCP, granted autonomy to a Government of Southern Sudan (GoSS) led by the SPLM, and allowed for a referendum on Southern independence to be held after a six-year transitional period.

While the CPA was being negotiated, a separate conflict erupted in Darfur. Rebels from Muslim but non-Arab ethnic groups attacked military positions in 2003, citing discrimination and marginalization by the government. In 2004, government-supported Arab militias known as janjaweed began torching villages, massacring the inhabitants, and raping women and girls. The military also bombed settlements from the air. More than two million civilians were displaced. The scale of the violence led to accusations of genocide by international human rights groups and the United States.

The government reached a peace agreement with one of Darfur's multiple rebel groups in 2006, but the others refused to sign the pact, and fighting continued despite the presence of international peacekeepers. In March 2009, the International Criminal Court (ICC) issued an arrest warrant for al-Bashir on charges of war crimes and crimes against humanity in Darfur. A charge of genocide was added in 2010.

National elections mandated by the CPA were held in 2010. The process was undermined by intimidation, vote rigging, and restrictions on freedom of expression by the NCP in the North and the SPLM in the South. The SPLM and other parties ultimately boycotted the national presidential election, citing unfair campaign conditions. As a result, al-Bashir won convincingly, capturing 68 percent of the vote. The NCP won 323 of 450 seats in the National Assembly, the lower house of parliament, 91 percent of the state assembly seats in the North, and 32 seats in the 50-seat upper chamber, the Council of States, which is indirectly elected by the state legislatures. In the South, Salva Kiir of the SPLM was elected president of the GoSS with 93 percent of the vote.

After the elections, attention turned to the task of organizing the Southern referendum on independence, scheduled for January 2011. Preparations were far behind schedule, but international pressure and technical assistance helped get the process back on track, ensuring that 3.9 million Southerners registered to vote. The referendum was held on time and was largely peaceful. The result, announced in February, showed a vote of almost 99 percent in favor of independence. In the North, where 116,000 Southerners had registered to vote, nearly 58 percent voted for independence. Turnout in the North, at 59 percent, was also significantly lower than in the South. The U.S.-based Carter Center, which monitored the referendum, declared the exercise to have been "successful and broadly consistent with international standards." Al-Bashir pledged to recognize the result.

A separate referendum in the contested border enclave of Abyei did not go ahead as planned. Residents were set to decide whether to remain in the North or join the South, but the NCP and SPLM could not agree on who should be eligible to vote. Amid rising tensions, a convoy of Northern troops came under attack, allegedly by the SPLA, in May. The North responded with overwhelming force, launching a full-scale occupation of Abyei that caused more than 100,000 residents to flee. Under a deal negotiated in June, both sides agreed to withdraw their forces to make way for UN peacekeepers, which began deploying in September.

The state of Southern Kordofan, close to the border with the South, became the next flashpoint. State elections scheduled for 2010 had been delayed over suspicions of census fraud in favor of the NCP. The election was eventually held in May 2011, resulting in a narrow victory for the NCP candidate, incumbent governor, Ahmed Haroun, who had been indicted by the ICC in 2007 for crimes against humanity and war crimes. The Carter Center said the result was credible despite some irregularities, but the SPLM candidate rejected the outcome. Clashes erupted in June when Khartoum brought forward a deadline for Southern-aligned forces in the state to disarm. In the following weeks, aerial bombardments and indiscriminate shelling by Northern forces caused more than 150,000 people to flee their homes. A leaked UN report accused Northern troops of carrying out "targeted killings and summary executions" and called for an independent investigation, with perpetrators to be referred to the ICC. A framework agreement to end the Southern Kordofan conflict was publicly disowned by al-Bashir, and the fighting continued. In November, the United Nations accused Sudan of launching an air raid on a camp in South Sudan housing refugees from Southern Kordofan; at least 12 people were killed.

Violence spread to neighboring Blue Nile State in September, displacing more than 100,000 people. Khartoum accused the SPLM-North (SPLM-N), an offshoot of the liberation movement in the South, of leading a rebellion. Al-Bashir declared a state of emergency, replaced the SPLM-N governor with a military appointee, and banned the SPLM-N as a political party, shutting its offices and detaining scores of its members throughout the country. For its part, the SPLM-N pledged to work for regime change in Khartoum.

The border conflicts in Abyei, Southern Kordofan, and Blue Nile soured relations with the South, which formally became the independent Republic of South Sudan on July 9. Khartoum accused the SPLM of interfering in the conflicts, and negotiations stalled on a host of bilateral issues, including border demarcation, management of the oil industry, and defining citizenship in the two new countries.

With many of its regions in full-scale revolt and its northern neighbors, Egypt and Libya, in the midst of revolution, the NCP focused on regime survival, launching a crackdown on any signs of unrest in Khartoum. Sporadic protests against the government's economic austerity measures in January and February were met with force and mass arrests. Tensions within the ruling party became increasingly evident. In February, al-Bashir announced that he would not contest the next presidential election, due in 2015. Sudanese analysts noted the increased prominence of the military faction in the regime; some argued that it had launched a "soft coup" in the weeks leading up to Southern independence, taking over the essential functions of the state.

Meanwhile, the conflict in Darfur continued. There was a sharp rise in fighting at the turn of 2011 after the only rebel group to sign the 2006 peace deal returned to the battlefield. In July, the NCP signed a peace agreement with another of the rebel groups, the Liberation and Justice Movement. But the more influential factions refused to join the process and rejected Khartoum's moves to impose a settlement, which included the appointment of a Darfuri vice president to the government in Khartoum in September. Khalil Ibrahim, leader of the Justice and Equality Movement (JEM), a major rebel group, was killed by Sudanese forces in December.

Political Rights and Civil Liberties: Sudan is not an electoral democracy. Although the first multiparty elections in 24 years were held in 2010, they were plagued by irregularities and failed to meet international standards, according to monitors from the United States, the European Union, and Sudan itself.

The country is governed according to the 2005 interim constitution, but this document is being redrafted following the independence of South Sudan. Members of the opposition and civil society have so far been excluded from consultations over the constitution-writing process and claim that proposed revisions would lead to a more repressive system of governance. The president is currently elected to serve five-year terms. Members of the lower house of the bicameral legislature, the 450-seat National Assembly, were elected in 2010 using a mixed majoritarian and party-list system. State legislatures chose the 50 members of the upper house, the Council of States. All lawmakers are to serve six five-year terms. As a result of South Sudan's secession, the two chambers were reduced to 354 and 30 seats, respectively.

Ahead of the 2010 elections, the NCP manipulated the census used to compile the electoral roll, overstating the population in areas of core support and undercounting opposition strongholds. Although 72 political parties nominated candidates for the elections, many of them were not allowed to campaign freely and rarely received official permission to hold public events. The leading opposition parties boycotted the presidential election in the North, and several also withdrew from the legislative polls. The voting period was plagued by irregularities, with reports of inaccurate voter rolls, ballot stuffing, and cash handouts to NCP voters.

By contrast, during the referendum on Southern independence held in January 2011, there were few reports of intimidation of Southern voters in the North, and although turnout was lower than in the South, monitors said this may have been because large numbers of Southerners decided to move to the South before polling day.

The NCP's dominance of the political system in the North was reinforced by the independence of South Sudan, which signaled the end of the Government of National Unity and the withdrawal of the South's representatives from the parliament. The Khartoum government also launched a crackdown on other political parties. The SPLM-N was banned from operating in September following the outbreak of fighting in Blue Nile State, and the leader of the Popular Congress Party, former NCP chief Hassan al-Turabi, was arrested in January and held without charge before being released in May. Members of other opposition parties were also detained for criticizing the government and making reference to the Arab Spring protests.

Sudan is considered one of the world's most corrupt countries. Power and resources are concentrated in and around Khartoum, while outlying states are neglected and impoverished. Members of the NCP, particularly those from favored ethnic groups, tightly control the national economy and use the wealth they have amassed in banking and business to buy political support. The International Crisis Group estimates that the party's top leadership owns more than 164 companies, which get the pick of the government's contracts.

The 2005 interim constitution recognizes freedom of the press, but the media face significant obstacles in practice. The 2009 Press and Publication Act allows a government-appointed Press Council to prevent publication or broadcast of material it deems unsuitable, temporarily shut down newspapers, and impose heavy fines for violations of media regulations. These powers were widely used in 2011. In addition, the National Intelligence and Security Services (NISS) forced the closure of six, mainly Southern newspapers following the independence of South Sudan and curtailed the distribution of three others. The government justified the move by saying it could not allow foreign-owned papers to operate in Sudan.

Journalists risk prosecution for doing their jobs. Ten reporters were charged with defamation in May 2011 for reporting on the alleged gang rape of a female student by agents from the NISS. At least three of the reporters were found guilty, and two spent a month in prison rather than pay a fine. A presidential decree was issued in August to release all journalists held in custody. Soon afterward, the editor of the newspaper *Al-Sahafa*, who had been detained since November 2010, was set free. Seven members of the Darfur radio channel Radio Dabanga who had been behind bars since October 2010 were released without charge in December 2011. However, four journalists remained in custody at year's end, according to the Committee to Protect Journalists.

International media are available in Sudan, but they are becoming more difficult to access. The government suspended the license of the British Broadcasting Corporation's Arabic service in 2010 and refused to renew the license of Radio France Internationale's Arabic service.

Religious freedom, though guaranteed by the 2005 interim constitution, is not upheld in practice. Sudan's population is predominantly Sunni Muslim, but there is a Christian minority. President Omar al-Bashir has signaled that the new constitution will establish Sharia as the main source of law and Islam as the national religion. The government uses religious laws as a means to persecute political opponents. In July 2011, 150 people from Darfur were rounded up by police in Khartoum. Of those arrested, 129 were charged with apostasy, which carries a maximum sentence of death. They were released in September, after agreeing to follow the government's interpretation of Islam. The United States has designated Sudan a "country of particular concern" for its violations of religious freedom.

Respect for academic freedom is limited. The government administers public universities, monitors appointments, and sets the curriculum. Authorities do not directly control private universities, but self-censorship among instructors is common. Student associations are closely monitored for signs of antigovernment activities. In one incident, 36 students from Shendi University, north of Khartoum, were arrested in April 2011, after they organized a strike. Some were tortured in custody, and several were charged with rioting. Protests by students at Kassala University were violently broken up by the authorities in October, leaving at least five people injured and one dead.

Freedom of assembly is restricted. In January and February 2011, a series of demonstrations broke out in Khartoum and other cities against the government's economic austerity measures, some of them inspired by the revolutions in North Africa. The government responded harshly, beating protesters and arresting more than 100 people. At least one person was killed. Police used tear gas to break up a similar demonstration in Khartoum in September.

The operating environment for nongovernmental organizations (NGOs) is difficult. In Darfur, government-backed forces and the main rebel groups place restrictions on the movements of aid workers and peacekeepers. Eight members of the joint United Nations–African Union peacekeeping force in Darfur were killed in 2011 by unknown assailants, bringing to 33 the number of deaths since the mission was established in 2007. In August, four members of the UN Interim Security Force for Abyei died from injuries sustained in a landmine explosion. The UN accused the authorities of delaying permission for a medical evacuation to take place. Independent NGOs were denied access to Southern Kordofan and Blue Nile following the outbreak of fighting in those states.

Trade union rights are minimal, and there are no independent unions. The Sudan Workers' Trade Unions Federation has been co-opted by the government.

The judiciary is not independent. Lower courts provide some due process safeguards, but the higher courts are subject to political control, and special security and military courts do not apply accepted legal standards. Sudanese criminal law is based on Sharia and allows punishments such as flogging.

The National Security Act, which took effect in 2010, gives the NISS sweeping authority to seize property, conduct surveillance, search premises, and detain suspects for up to four and a half months without judicial review. The police and security forces routinely exceed these broad powers, carrying out arbitrary arrests and holding people at secret locations without access to lawyers or their relatives. Human rights groups accuse the NISS of systematically detaining and torturing opponents of the government, including Darfuri activists, journalists, and students. Protesters arrested following demonstrations in January and February 2011 told Human Rights Watch that they were tortured and that female detainees were raped or sexually humiliated. In July, state media reported that 66 political detainees had been released from NISS custody. The NISS said this figure represented all the detainees being held, but others are thought to remain in custody.

It is widely accepted that the government has directed and assisted the systematic killing of tens or even hundreds of thousands of people in Darfur since 2003, including through its support for militia groups that have terrorized civilians. Human rights groups have documented the widespread use of rape, the organized burning of villages, and the forced displacement of entire communities. The government also waged war against its own citizens in Abyei, Southern Kordofan, and Blue Nile in 2011, using indiscriminate force against civilians, including aerial bombardments. Ethnic groups considered unfriendly to the government were targeted for attack, notably the Nuba people, who largely sided with the SPLM during the civil war. Humanitarian access was denied to populations caught up in the fighting in Southern Kordofan and Blue Nile, causing severe food shortages and raising the prospect of famine. The government refused to renew the mandate of the UN Mission in Sudan (UNMIS) after it expired in July, adding to the difficulties of monitoring the situation along the North-South border.

The approximately one million Southerners who remained in the North following South Sudan's independence face serious discrimination. Under proposed changes to the Sudan Nationality Act, effective from 2012, Southerners will be stripped of their citizenship and reclassified as foreigners, irrespective of how long they have lived in the North.

The ongoing dispute over the new international boundary between Sudan and South Sudan has led to the border being sealed. This has curtailed freedom of movement and trade, and caused serious hardship to nomadic groups whose migratory routes have been severed.

Female politicians and activists play a role in public life in Sudan, and women are guaranteed a quarter of the seats in the National Assembly. In daily life, however, women face extensive discrimination. Islamic law denies women equitable rights in marriage, inheritance, and divorce. Police use provisions of Sudan's Criminal Act outlawing "indecent and immoral acts" to prohibit women from wearing clothing of which they disapprove. Female genital mutilation is widely practiced. Rape has been used as a weapon of war in Darfur and other conflict zones in Sudan.

The U.S. State Department considers Sudan to be a source, transit, and destination country for persons trafficked for forced labor and sexual exploitation. The Sudanese military and Darfur rebel groups continue to use child soldiers.

Suriname

Political Rights: 2
Civil Liberties: 2
Status: Free

Population: 529,400
Capital: Paramaribo

Ten-Year Ratings Timeline For Year Under Review (Political Rights, Civil Liberties, Status)

2002	2003	2004	2005	2006	2007	2008	2009	2010	2011
1,2F	1,2F	1,2F	2,2F	2,2F	2,2F	2,2F	2,2F	2,2F	2,2F

Overview: **Suriname's strained relations with the Netherlands and the United States improved somewhat in 2011, following the 2010 election of former dictator Desiré Bouterse as president. He had been convicted on drug-trafficking charges in the Netherlands, and has been accused of killing his political opponents in the 1980s.**

The Republic of Suriname achieved independence from the Netherlands in 1975, after more than three centuries of colonial rule. A 1980 military coup led by Desiré Bouterse established a regime that brutally suppressed civic and political opposition and initiated a decade of military intervention in politics. In 1987,

Bouterse permitted elections, which were handily won by the center-right New Front for Democracy and Development (NF), a coalition of mainly East Indian, Creole, and Javanese parties. The National Democratic Party (NDP), organized by the military, won just 3 out of 51 seats in the National Assembly.

The army ousted the elected government in 1990, and Bouterse again took power in a bloodless coup, but international pressure led to new elections in 1991. The NF again won a majority in the parliament, which chose the NF's candidate, Ronald Venetiaan, as president. Power passed to the NDP in the 1996 elections, with Bouterse ally Jules Wijdenbosch as president, then returned to the NF and Venetiaan after early elections in 2000.

In 2001, Fred Derby—the star witness in the trial of Bouterse and others for 15 political killings committed in December 1982—suffered a fatal heart attack that initially appeared to rob the prosecution of key testimony. However, the government vowed that testimony given by Derby during a preliminary hearing would be submitted at trial.

In 2004, the NF government's fiscal austerity program helped to stabilize prices and the economy, though the policy's negative side effects led to increased voter discontent. In the May 2005 elections, the NF managed to remain the single largest political force, but its failure to win a two-thirds majority in the National Assembly prevented it from electing a president. In August, a United People's Assembly consisting of 891 members—including national, regional, and local lawmakers—gave Venetiaan his third term as president, with 560 votes for the incumbent versus 315 for the NDP's Rabindre Parmessar.

In 2007, Suriname's courts ordered officials to proceed with the long-delayed prosecution of Bouterse and nine other suspects for the 1982 "December murders." Bouterse denied involvement in the killings, although in March 2007, he accepted political responsibility and offered a public apology. The trial, regarded as a landmark test for Suriname's judicial system, began in November 2008. It advanced during 2009, following frequent delays, and featured the testimony of six bystanders who had fled the country and settled in the Netherlands after witnessing the executions.

Bouterse's Mega Combination coalition—comprising the NDP and three smaller parties—won legislative elections held in May 2010, capturing 40 percent of the vote and 23 seats in the parliament. The NF placed second, with approximately 32 percent of the vote and 14 seats. In the July presidential election, Bouterse won with 70.6 percent of the parliamentary vote, defeating NF candidate Chandrikapersad Santokhi. As president, Bouterse had the power to grant amnesty to those involved in the 1982 murders, but the charges had not been dropped by the end of 2011. The ongoing trial was suspended again in October, when 19 defense witnesses failed to appear.

Only Bharrat Jagdeo, neighboring Guyana's president, attended Bouterse's August 2010 inauguration. International travel was also difficult for Bouterse, with an Interpol warrant out for his arrest and a drug-trafficking conviction in the Netherlands still outstanding. However, he remained protected from arrest in Suriname because the country lacked an extradition treaty with the Netherlands, and as head of state, he was immune from prosecution abroad.

Foreign relations, which had been damaged following Bouterse's election, underwent some improvements in 2011. In August, the Netherlands announced that it would cooperate with Suriname on trade and economic issues, as well as on containing illegal immigration. The United States announced its intentions to normalize relations with Suriname after the country repaid a portion of its U.S. debt; in October, the two governments signed a antinarcotics agreement. Suriname also hosted several international conferences during the year that helped raise its stature before the international community.

Political Rights and Civil Liberties: Suriname is an electoral democracy. The Organization of American States reported that the 2010 legislative and presidential elections met international standards. The 1987 constitution provides for a unicameral, 51-seat National Assembly, elected by proportional representation for five-year terms. The body elects the president to five-year terms with a two-thirds majority. If it is unable to do so, a United People's Assembly—consisting of lawmakers from the national, regional, and local levels—convenes to choose the president by a simple majority. A Council of State made up of the president and representatives of major societal groupings—including labor unions, business, the military, and the legislature—has veto power over legislation deemed to violate the constitution.

Political parties largely reflect the cleavages in Suriname's ethnically diverse society, although political-racial discord is much less acute than in neighboring Guyana. Suriname's major parties include the NDP, the National Party of Suriname (NPS), and the People's Alliance for Progress. The NF is a coalition of the NPS and several smaller parties.

Suriname has been plagued by corruption cases in recent years, and organized crime and drug networks continue to hamper governance. In December 2010, President Desiré Bouterse fired Martinus Sastroredjo, his minister of spatial planning, land, and forestry management, after Sastroredjo refused to resign over a controversy involving his wife and a land application.

The constitution provides for freedoms of expression and of the press, and the government generally respects these rights in practice. Some media outlets engage in occasional self-censorship due to fear of reprisal from members of the former military leadership or pressure from senior government officials and others who object to critical stories about the administration. However, the trial of Bouterse for the "December murders" has been freely covered by the local press. There are two privately owned daily newspapers, *De Ware Tijd* and *De West*. A number of small commercial radio stations compete with the government-owned radio and television broadcasting systems, resulting in a generally pluralistic range of viewpoints. Public access to government information is legally recognized, though it is very limited in practice. The government does not restrict access to the internet.

The authorities generally respect freedom of religion and do not infringe on academic freedom.

Freedoms of assembly and association are provided for by the constitution, and the government respects these rights in practice. Workers can join independent trade unions, though civil servants have no legal right to strike. Collective bargaining is legal and conducted fairly widely. The labor movement is active in politics.

The judiciary is susceptible to political influence and suffers from a significant shortage of judges and a large backlog of cases. The courts and prisons are seriously overburdened by the volume of people detained for narcotics trafficking. Police abuse detainees, particularly during arrests. Suriname is a signatory to the 2001 agreement establishing the Trinidad-based Caribbean Court of Justice (CCJ) as the final venue of appeal for member states of the Caribbean Community, but has yet to ratify the CCJ as its own final court of appeal. Suriname is a major transit point for cocaine en route to Europe, and poor law enforcement capabilities have resulted in a rising tide of drug money entering the country.

Discrimination against indigenous and tribal groups is widespread, and Surinamese law offers such groups no special protection or recognition. As a result, Amerindians, who live mostly outside urban areas, have only a marginal ability to participate in decisions affecting their lands, cultures, traditions, and natural resources. Tribal people known as Maroons are the descendants of escaped African slaves who formed autonomous communities in the interior during the 17th and 18th centuries. Their rights to lands and resources, cultural integrity, and the autonomous administration of their affairs are not recognized in Surinamese law. In September 2009, some 65 Guyanese migrants were forcefully deported from the western districts of Suriname during "Operation Koetai." The deportations, while aimed at cracking down on smuggling and other illegal border activity, fueled tensions between Guyana and Suriname. However, a November 2010 agreement to seek Chinese investment to build a bridge between the two countries indicated that the incident had not damaged relations.

Constitutional guarantees of gender equality are not adequately enforced. Human trafficking remains a problem, and the country lacks a comprehensive law specifically banning the practice. However, several organizations address violence against women and related issues. In July 2011, a member of parliament denounced homosexuality and called on the government to state its position, but it has not adopted an antigay policy to date.

Swaziland

Political Rights: 7
Civil Liberties: 5
Status: Not Free

Population: 1,203,300
Capital: Mbabane

Ten-Year Ratings Timeline For Year Under Review (Political Rights, Civil Liberties, Status)

2002	2003	2004	2005	2006	2007	2008	2009	2010	2011
6,5NF	7,5NF	7,5NF	7,5NF	7,5NF	7,5NF	7,5NF	7,5NF	7,5NF	7,5NF

Overview: **A combination of reduced customs duties, profligate spending by the royal family, and government corruption contributed to a stark financial crisis in 2011. Austere economic conditions and the monarchy's continued resistance to political reforms spurred a rash of antigovernment protests in March and April.**

Swaziland regained its independence from Britain in 1968, and an elected Parliament was added to the traditional monarchy. In 1973, King Sobhuza II repealed the 1968 constitution, ended the multiparty system in favor of a tinkhundla (local council) system, and declared himself an absolute monarch. After Sobhuza's death in 1982, a protracted power struggle ended with the coronation of King Mswati III in 1986.

A new constitution implemented in 2006 removed the king's ability to rule by decree, but reaffirmed his absolute authority over the cabinet, Parliament, and judiciary. It also maintained the tinkhundla system—in which local chiefs control elections for 55 of the 65 seats in the House of Assembly, the lower house of Parliament—and did not overturn the ban on political parties. The charter provided for limited freedoms of speech, assembly, and association, as well as limited rights for women, but the king could suspend those rights at his discretion.

Also in 2006, 16 members of the prodemocracy People's United Democratic Movement (PUDEMO) were arrested and charged in connection with bomb attacks in 2005, but all were later freed on bail. In 2008, there were over 10 bomb attacks on government targets, and while there were no casualties, one blast killed the bomber, a member of PUDEMO. The government banned PUDEMO and four other groups under the newly enacted Suppression of Terrorism Act (STA).

In 2010 the Swaziland Federation of Trade Unions (SFTU) and the Swaziland Democracy Campaign organized two days of protests in Manzini, calling for political, civil, and economic reforms. Security personnel detained some 50 activists.

The year 2011 saw more antigovernment protests, most of which were violently dispersed by security forces. In March, thousands of civil servants marched in Mbabane to protest a pay freeze and government corruption amid the country's worsening financial crisis, which had been brought on by a sharp drop in revenue from a regional customs union and lavish spending by the royal family. The crisis had led to massive cuts in public services, including pensions, education, and health care. In April, prodemocracy demonstrations were met with a massive security presence and dispersed with tear gas, arrests, and assaults. PUDEMO leader Mario Masuku was placed under house arrest. In August, South Africa agreed to extend a R2.4 billion (US$355 million) loan if Swaziland met fiscal reforms approved by the International Monetary Fund and "confidence-building measures" on democracy and human rights; by year's end, the kingdom had yet to accept the loan due to these conditions.

Swaziland has the world's highest rate of HIV infection. The financial crisis has led to shortages in antiretroviral drugs, as well as HIV testing.

Political Rights and Civil Liberties: Swaziland is not an electoral democracy. King Mswati III is an absolute monarch with ultimate authority over the cabinet, legislature, and judiciary. Of the House of Assembly's 65 members, 55 are elected by popular vote within the tinkhundla system, in which local chiefs vet all candidates; the king appoints the other 10 members. The king also appoints 20 members of the 30-seat Senate, with the remainder selected by the House of Assembly. Members of the bicameral Parliament, all of whom serve five-year terms, are not allowed to initiate legislation. Traditional chiefs govern designated localities and typically report directly to the king.

Political parties are illegal, but there are political associations, the two largest being the banned PUDEMO and the Ngwane National Liberatory Congress.

Corruption is a major problem, and government corruption was widely blamed for contributing to Swaziland's financial crisis. In October 2011, the minister of finance reported that the country loses $10.6 million to corruption every month, about double its annual social services budget. Swaziland was ranked 95 out of 183 countries surveyed in Transparency International's 2011 Corruption Perceptions Index.

Constitutional rights to free expression are severely restricted in practice and can be suspended by the king. Publishing criticism of the ruling family is banned. Self-censorship is widespread, as journalists are routinely threatened and attacked by the authorities. In March 2011, the government banned all state media from covering antigovernment demonstrations. In July, the *Times of Swaziland* received a court order to stop reporting on the case of a judge suspended for criticizing the king in a court ruling. In June, after a 14-year effort by local media organizations, the Swaziland Media Complaints Commission, a self-regulatory body, was registered with the government. South African media are available, and both the *Swazi Observer* and the independent *Times of Swaziland* occasionally criticize the government. Swaziland's only independent radio station broadcasts religious programming. The government does not restrict access to the internet, but few Swazis can afford access.

Freedom of religion is not explicitly protected under the constitution, but is respected in practice. Academic freedom is limited by prohibitions against criticizing the monarchy.

The government restricts freedoms of assembly and association, and permission to hold political gatherings is frequently denied. Demonstrators routinely face violence and arrests by police. The government has sweeping powers under the STA to declare any organization a "terrorist group," a practice that has been abused by authorities. Police harassment and surveillance of civil society organizations has increased in recent years, as have forced searches of homes and offices, torture in interrogations, and the use of roadblocks to prevent demonstrations.

Swaziland has active labor unions, with the largest, the SFTU, leading demands for democratization. However, government pressure and crackdowns on strikes have limited union operations. The government is the country's largest employer, and recent retrenchments in the public sector have spurred increased activism by government employees. Workers in all areas of the economy can join unions, and 80 percent of the private workforce is unionized.

The dual judicial system includes courts based on Roman-Dutch law and traditional courts using customary law. The judiciary is independent in most civil cases, though the king has ultimate judicial powers, and the royal family and government often refuse to respect rulings with which they disagree. However, the Swazi High Court has made a number of notable antigovernment rulings in recent years. In June 2011, Judge Thomas Masuku—head of the Judicial Services Commission—was suspended for allegedly insulting the king in a ruling.

There were numerous incidents of police torture, beatings, and suspicious deaths in custody in 2011, particularly of leaders and participants in antigovernment protests. Security forces generally operate with impunity. Prisons are overcrowded, and inmates are subject to rape, beatings, and torture.

The constitution grants women equal rights and legal status as adults, but these rights remain restricted in practice. While both the legal code and customary law provide some protection against gender-based violence, it is common and often tolerated with impunity.

Sweden

Political Rights: 1
Civil Liberties: 1
Status: Free

Population: 9,447,000
Capital: Stockholm

Ten-Year Ratings Timeline For Year Under Review (Political Rights, Civil Liberties, Status)

2002	2003	2004	2005	2006	2007	2008	2009	2010	2011
1,1F	1,1F	1,1F	1,1F	1,1F	1,1F	1,1F	1,1F	1,1F	1,1F

Overview: **Opposition party leader Håkan Juholt was under investigation for fraud in 2011 regarding improper reimbursements he received for housing costs beginning several years earlier. Also during the year, Prime Minister Frederik Reinfeldt's center-right coalition reached an agreement with the Green Party to rework existing immigration policies and improve immigrants' access to public services and education.**

After centuries of wars and monarchical unions with its neighbors, Sweden emerged as a liberal constitutional monarchy in the 19th century. Norway ended its union with the country in 1905, leaving Sweden with its current borders. Its tradition of neutrality, beginning with World War I, was altered somewhat by its admission to the European Union (EU) in 1995, and was further eroded by a more pragmatic approach to security in 2002. However, Sweden has continued to avoid military alliances, including NATO.

Voters rejected adoption of the euro currency in a 2003 referendum, despite support from government and business leaders. The rejection was attributed to skepticism about the EU and fears regarding the possible deterioration of welfare benefits and damage to the economy. Just days before the referendum, Foreign Minister Anna Lindh was killed in a knife attack in Stockholm. Her killer, a Swedish national of Serbian descent who had no clear political agenda, was sentenced to life in prison.

In the 2006 parliamentary elections, a four-party, center-right alliance headed by Fredrik Reinfeldt of the Moderate Party defeated the Social Democratic Party (SAP), which had been in power for 12 years.

Parliament passed the Signals Intelligence Act in 2008, giving Sweden's National Defense Radio Establishment the authority to monitor communications without a court order. Following widespread public protest, the law was changed to allow such wiretapping only in cases where external military threats were suspected. While the law went into effect in January 2009, continued protest led Parliament to pass an amended version in October. Among other changes, the weakened legislation specified that only the government and military can request surveillance, and that those who have been monitored must be notified.

In the September 2010 parliamentary elections, Reinfeldt won a second term as prime minister, though his coalition failed to win an outright majority and would instead rule as a minority government. The four parties in the coalition captured a total of 173 seats: the Moderate Party won 107; the Center Party, 23; the Liberal

Party, 24; and the Christian Democrats, 19. The opposition SAP took 112 seats, while the Green Party (MP) captured 25, and the Left Party (VP) won 19. The controversial right-wing Swedish Democrats (SD) entered Parliament for the first time with 20 seats, though the other seven parties represented in Parliament vowed not to rely on the SD for significant votes, which left it politically isolated.

In March 2011, the minority government reached an agreement with the MP on a framework for immigration reform that would increase immigrants' access to public services. Separately, in October, SAP leader Håkan Juholt became the subject of a fraud investigation over housing reimbursements he received beginning in 2007.

Political Rights and Civil Liberties: Sweden is an electoral democracy. The unicameral Parliament, the Riksdag, has 349 members elected every four years by proportional representation. A party must receive at least 4 percent of the vote nationwide or 12 percent in one of the 29 electoral districts to win representation. The prime minister is appointed by the speaker of the Riksdag and confirmed by the body as a whole. King Carl XVI Gustaf, crowned in 1973, is the ceremonial head of state.

Eight political parties are currently represented in the Riksdag. The largest single party is the opposition SAP, also known as the Workers' Party, which ruled for most of the last century with the aid of the VP and, in the later decades, the MP.

The country's principal religious, ethnic, and immigrant groups are represented in Parliament. Since 1993, the indigenous Sami community has elected its own parliament, which has significant powers over community education and culture and serves as an advisory body to the government. In April 2011, the Supreme Court issued a landmark ruling in the so-called Nordmaling case, granting Sami reindeer herders common-law rights to disputed lands; the case had been ongoing for 14 years.

Corruption rates are low in Sweden, which was ranked 4 out of 183 countries surveyed in Transparency International's 2011 Corruption Perceptions Index. SAP leader Håkan Juholt faced intense political pressure in 2011 over charges of housing allowance fraud. He had illegally received double the allotted reimbursement for his residence in Stockholm by failing to notify the authorities that he shared the apartment with his partner. Juholt paid back roughly $23,500 and apologized to Parliament, but denied that the improper claims had been intentional.

Freedom of speech is guaranteed by law, and the country has one of the most robust freedom of information statutes in the world. However, hate-speech laws prohibit threats or expressions of contempt based on race, color, national or ethnic origin, religious belief, or sexual orientation.

Sweden's media are independent. Most newspapers and periodicals are privately owned, and the government subsidizes daily newspapers regardless of their political affiliation. Public broadcasters air weekly radio and television programs in several immigrant languages. The ethnic press is entitled to the same subsidies as the Swedish-language press. Under the 2009 Intellectual Property Rights Enforcement Directive, internet service providers must reveal information about users who are found to be engaged in illegal file sharing. However, the first case was referred to the European Court of Justice to determine whether the law is in accordance with European law on privacy and data protection. In 2011, Sweden postponed implementing the EU Data Retention Directive for the fifth straight year, citing privacy concerns. The directive requires Swedish telecommunications carriers to store data, including call records and internet traffic, for three years.

Religious freedom is constitutionally guaranteed. Although the population is 87 percent Lutheran, all churches, as well as synagogues and mosques, receive some state financial support. The number of reported hate crimes against the Jewish community has slowly declined in recent years, but the figures for those targeting the Muslim community have remained steady. Academic freedom is ensured for all.

Freedoms of assembly and association are respected in law and in practice. Peaceful protests were mounted against the SD and racism in the period surrounding the 2010 elections. The rights to strike and organize in labor unions are guaranteed. Trade union federations, which represent about 80 percent of the workforce, are strong and well organized. The Swedish labor code was amended in 2010 after the European Court of Justice ruled that employees at the Swedish branches of foreign companies are subject to their home country's collective agreements, and not those of Swedish unions.

The judiciary is independent. Swedish courts are allowed to try suspects for genocide committed abroad. In 2011, Sweden sought the extradition of controversial WikiLeaks founder Julian Assange from the United Kingdom so that he could be questioned regarding rape and sexual assault allegations stemming from two incidents in Stockholm in 2010. At year's end, Assange was appealing his arrest warrant in the British courts.

In 2007, Sweden changed its immigration policy, disallowing family reunification for "quota refugees." Family members must now apply separately for visas. A new Equality Ombudsman position was created in 2008 to oversee efforts to prevent discrimination on the basis of gender, ethnicity, disability, and sexual orientation, and a permanent national hate crime police unit was established in 2009. In recent years the government has faced resistance from local communities in its efforts to establish temporary housing for asylum seekers.

Gay couples were legally allowed to adopt for the first time in 2003. The country granted lesbian couples the same rights to artificial insemination and in vitro fertilization as heterosexual couples in 2005.

Sweden is a global leader in gender equality. Approximately 45 percent of Riksdag members are women. Of the 24 government ministers, 11 are women. Although 80 percent of women work outside of the home, they still earn only 70 percent of men's wages in the public sector and 76 percent in the private sector. The country is a destination and transit point for women and children trafficked for the purpose of sexual exploitation. The 2004 Aliens Act helped to provide more assistance to trafficking victims, and a special ambassador has been appointed to aid in combating human trafficking.

Switzerland

Political Rights: 1
Civil Liberties: 1
Status: Free

Population: 7,868,000
Capital: Bern

Ten-Year Ratings Timeline For Year Under Review (Political Rights, Civil Liberties, Status)

2002	2003	2004	2005	2006	2007	2008	2009	2010	2011
1,1F	1,1F	1,1F	1,1F	1,1F	1,1F	1,1F	1,1F	1,1F	1,1F

Overview: The October 2011 elections for the Federal Assembly saw the right wing Swiss People's Party lose seats in the National Council for the first time since 1975 as centrist parties made gains. In response to UN concerns about the use of excessive force in asylum detention centers and in forced repatriation cases, the government instituted a number of measures in 2011, including a monitoring system and trained observers, to ensure proper treatment of deportees.

Switzerland, which has existed as a confederation of cantons since 1291, emerged with its current borders and a tradition of neutrality at the end of the Napoleonic wars in 1815. The country's four official ethnic communities are based on language: German, French, Italian, and Romansh (the smallest community).

Switzerland remained neutral during the wars of the 20th century, and it joined the United Nations only after a referendum in 2002. Membership in international institutions has long been a controversial issue in Switzerland. The Swiss have resisted joining the European Union (EU), and even rejected membership in the European Economic Area, a free-trade area that links non-EU members with the EU. However, Switzerland has joined international financial institutions and signed a range of free-trade agreements.

During the 2003 federal elections, the far-right Swiss People's Party (SVP), hostile to both EU membership and immigration, made blatantly xenophobic appeals. It led the vote, followed closely by the center-left Social Democratic Party (SPS).

The SVP successfully championed a 2006 referendum on tightening asylum and immigration laws. The new laws required asylum seekers to produce an identity document within 48 hours of arrival or risk repatriation, effectively limiting immigration to those coming from EU countries; prospective immigrants from outside the EU would have to possess skills lacking in the Swiss economy.

In the October 2007 federal elections, the SVP captured 29 percent of the vote, more than any party since 1919. The SVP campaign received international attention for its anti-immigrant appeals, and an SVP rally and counterdemonstration in Bern resulted in violence rarely seen in Switzerland.

In December 2007, the SVP temporarily placed itself in opposition to the government after the parliament refused to reappoint Christoph Blocher to the cabinet, choosing instead Eveline Widmer-Schlumpf, from the party's more moderate wing. The SVP subsequently expelled Widmer-Schlumpf, who then became part of the new center-right Conservative Democratic Party (BDP).

Following successful petitioning by the SVP, a referendum calling for a ban on the future construction of minarets on mosques was held in November 2009. Nearly 58 percent of the population and 22 out of 26 cantons voted in favor of the ban. However, the four mosques with existing minarets would not be affected. In November 2010, a referendum mandating the automatic deportation of foreigners convicted of certain crimes passed with 53 percent of the vote. Both referendums met with considerable domestic and international criticism.

The federal elections held on October 23, 2011, saw a modest strengthening of the political center in Switzerland. In National Council elections, the SVP, while still the most represented party, lost seats for the first time since 1975, retaining 54 seats—8 fewer than the 2007 election. The SPS gained seats reaching a total of 46. The Free Democratic Party (FDP) was reduced to 30 seats. The Christian Democratic People's Party (CVP) also lost seats, coming away with 28. The Green Party (GPS) and the Green Liberal Party (GLP) won 15 and 12 seats, respectively, and the BDP took 9 seats, with the remaining 6 seats going to other parties. In the Council of States elections, the CVP retained 13 seats, followed by the FDP and SPS with 11 each, the SVP with 5, the GLP with 2, the BDP with 1, and the remaining seats going to other parties. A by-election for all seven members of the Federal Council was held on December 14, with six of the seven members being reelected and Alain Berset filling the seat of the retiring Micheline Calmy-Rey. Widmer-Schlumpf was elected president of the Confederation and will preside over the Federal Council during 2012.

As a major banking center, Switzerland was hit hard by the global financial crisis in 2008, leading to renewed international criticism of the country's strict bank secrecy laws. In 2009, Switzerland agreed to adopt international transparency standards established by the Organization for Economic Cooperation and Development (OECD) by providing foreign governments with financial information in tax evasion cases and tax fraud investigations. Switzerland reached tax agreements with Germany, the United Kingdom, and the United States in 2010 and India in 2011, most of which involved untaxed money held in Swiss bank accounts.

Political Rights and Civil Liberties: Switzerland is an electoral democracy. The 1848 constitution, significantly revised in 1874 and 2000, provides for a Federal Assembly with two directly elected chambers: the 46-member Council of States (in which each canton has two members and each half-canton has one) and the 200-member National Council. All lawmakers serve four-year terms. The Federal Council (cabinet) is a seven-person executive council, with each member elected by the Federal Assembly. The presidency is largely ceremonial and rotates annually among the Federal Council's members.

The Swiss political system is characterized by decentralization and direct democracy. The cantons and half-cantons have significant control over economic and social policy, with the federal government's powers largely limited to foreign affairs and some economic matters. Referendums, which have been used extensively since the 1848 constitution, are mandatory for any amendments to the Federal Constitution, the joining of international organizations, or major changes to federal laws.

The government is free from pervasive corruption. As the world's largest offshore financial center, the country had long been criticized for failing to comply with recommended international norms on money laundering and terrorist financing. However, Switzerland has reached bilateral deals with several countries on financial information sharing and was removed from the OECD's "grey list" of tax havens in 2009. Switzerland was ranked 8 out of 183 countries surveyed in Transparency International's 2011 Corruption Perceptions Index.

Freedom of speech is guaranteed by the constitution. Switzerland has a free media environment, although the state-owned Swiss Broadcasting Corporation dominates the broadcast market. Consolidation of newspaper ownership in large media conglomerates has forced the closure of some small and local newspapers. The law penalizes public incitement to racial hatred or discrimination and denying crimes against humanity. In 2007, the Swiss Federal Court found Doqu Perinçek of the Turkish Workers' Party guilty of denying the Armenian genocide in a public speech in 2005. There is no government restriction on access to the internet.

Freedom of religion is guaranteed by the constitution, and most cantons support one or several churches. The country is split roughly between Roman Catholicism and Protestantism, though some 400,000 Muslims form the largest non-Christian minority, according to the 2000 census. A 2008 law requires that immigrant clerics receive integration training, including language instruction, before practicing. Most public schools provide religious education, depending on the predominant creed in each canton. Religion classes are mandatory in some schools, although waivers are regularly granted upon request. The government respects academic freedom.

Freedoms of assembly and association are provided by the constitution. The right to collective bargaining is respected, and approximately 25 percent of the workforce is unionized.

The judiciary is independent, and the rule of law prevails in civil and criminal matters. Most judicial decisions are made at the cantonal level, except for the federal Supreme Court, which reviews cantonal court decisions when they pertain to federal law. Prison and detention center conditions generally meet international standards, and the Swiss government permits visits by independent human rights observers. Some incidents of police discrimination and excessive use of force have been documented. In response to concerns put forward by the UN Committee against Torture in 2010, the government took steps in 2011 to address the treatment of asylum seekers, including the training of observers present during repatriation flights and instituting a monitoring system in cases of forced repatriation.

The rights of cultural, religious, and linguistic minorities are legally protected. However, increasing anxiety about the growing foreign-born population has led to a tightening of asylum laws. Further societal discriminations are mounting towards minorities, especially against those of African and Central European descent, as well as Roma.

Women were only granted universal suffrage at the federal level in 1971, and the half-canton of Appenzell-Innerrhoden denied women the right to vote until 1990. Fifty-eight women sit on the 200-member National Council and 9 in the Council of States. The constitution guarantees men and women equal pay for equal work, but pay differentials remain. Switzerland was ranked 10 out of 135 countries surveyed in the World Economic Forum's 2011 Gender Gap Report, which analyzes equality in the division of resources and opportunities between men and women. Abortion in the first 12 weeks of pregnancy was decriminalized following a 2002 referendum.

Syria

Political Rights: 7
Civil Liberties: 7*
Status: Not Free

Population: 22,518,000
Capital: Damascus

Ratings Change: Syria's civil liberties rating declined from 6 to 7 due to increased government efforts to divide the country along sectarian lines, the complete deterioration of the rule of law, and increased restrictions on freedom of movement.

Ten-Year Ratings Timeline For Year Under Review (Political Rights, Civil Liberties, Status)

2002	2003	2004	2005	2006	2007	2008	2009	2010	2011
7,7NF	7,7NF	7,7NF	7,6NF	7,6NF	7,6NF	7,6NF	7,6NF	7,6NF	7,7NF

Overview: **Responding to persistent popular protests that began in March, the government used the military and other security forces to pursue a violent campaign of repression in 2011, periodically besieging towns and killing several thousand people by year's end. The regime offered some nominal reforms, such as the repeal of the emergency law, but they had little practical effect as authorities continued to attack, detain, and abuse tens of thousands of Syrians, including journalists, political activists, and members of certain ethnic and religious groups.**

The modern state of Syria was established as a League of Nations mandate under French control after World War I and gained formal independence in 1946. Periods of military and elected civilian rule alternated until the Arab Socialist Baath Party seized power in a 1963 coup, transforming Syria into a one-party state governed under emergency law. During the 1960s, power shifted from the party's civilian ideologues to army officers, most of whom were Alawites (adherents of a heterodox Islamic sect who make up 12 percent of the population). This trend culminated in General Hafez al-Assad's rise to power in 1970.

The regime cultivated a base of support that spanned sectarian and ethnic divisions, but relied on Alawite domination of the security establishment and the forcible suppression of dissent. In 1982, government forces stormed the city of Hama to crush a rebellion by the opposition Muslim Brotherhood, killing as many as 20,000 insurgents and civilians.

Bashar al-Assad took power after his father's death in 2000, pledging to liberalize Syria's politics and economy. The first six months of his presidency featured the release of political prisoners, the return of exiled dissidents, and open discussion of the country's problems. But in February 2001, the regime began to reverse this so-called Damascus Spring. Leading reformists were arrested and sentenced to lengthy prison terms, while others faced constant surveillance and intimidation by the secret police.

Reinvigorated by the toppling of Iraq's Baathist regime in 2003, Syria's dissidents began cooperating and pushing for the release of political prisoners, the cancellation of the emergency law, and the legalization of opposition parties. Syria's

Kurdish minority erupted into eight days of rioting in March 2004, during which at least 30 people were killed and about 2,000 were arrested.

Despite hints that sweeping political reforms would be drafted at a major Baath Party conference in 2005, no substantial measures were taken. In October 2005, representatives of all three segments of the opposition—Islamists, Kurds, and secular liberals—signed the Damascus Declaration for Democratic National Change (DDDNC), which called for the country's leaders to step down and endorsed a broad set of liberal democratic principles.

In May 2006, a number of Syrian political and human rights activists signed the Beirut-Damascus Declaration, which called for a change in Syrian-Lebanese relations and the recognition of Lebanese sovereignty. Many who signed were detained or sentenced to prison in a renewed crackdown on personal freedoms.

Al-Assad won another presidential term in 2007, with 97.6 percent of the vote. In results that were similarly predetermined, the ruling Baath-dominated coalition won the majority of seats in that year's parliamentary and municipal polls. Meanwhile, supporters of the DDDNC formed governing bodies for their alliance and renewed their activities, prompting another government crackdown that extended into 2008.

In 2010, the state continued to suppress dissenting views and punish government opponents. Nevertheless, the United States and European countries took tentative steps to improve relations with Damascus during the year.

A massive antigovernment uprising in 2011 dashed any hopes of further progress in Syria's foreign relations. The protests were sparked by the detention and reported torture of several children for writing antigovernment graffiti in the southern city of Dara'a in March, and they soon spread to central cities like Hama and Homs as well as towns along the Syrian-Turkish border. The authorities' extensive use of live fire and military hardware against civilian demonstrators led small groups of soldiers to desert and organize antigovernment militias, raising fears of a civil war. The United Nations estimated in December that over 5,000 people had died in the uprising, with tens of thousands injured or detained.

Throughout the year, the government maintained that it was under attack from armed, foreign-backed terrorists, rather than a domestic, civilian protest movement. Still, it made a few largely symbolic concessions, repealing the country's long-standing emergency law and promising future constitutional changes. Attempts to establish a dialogue between the government and opposition collapsed amid the ongoing violence.

The regime's actions increasingly drew objections and punitive measures from the international community, including the United States, Europe, the Arab League, and Turkey, which had previously built close ties with the Assad administration. By year's end, Turkey was hosting thousands of Syrian refugees, as well as a civilian opposition Syrian National Council and representatives of the Free Syrian Army, which claimed to be coordinating antigovernment militias inside Syria. However, Russia and China blocked proposed actions against Syria by the UN Security Council. An Arab League monitoring mission to Syria in December did little to halt the unrest.

Political Rights and Civil Liberties: Syria is not an electoral democracy. Under the 1973 constitution, the president is nominated by the ruling Baath Party and approved by popular referendum for seven-year terms. In practice, these referendums are orchestrated by the regime, as are elections for the 250-seat, unicameral People's Council, whose members serve four-year terms and hold little independent legislative power. Almost all power rests in the executive branch.

The only legal political parties are the Baath Party and its several small coalition partners in the ruling National Progressive Front (NPF). Independent candidates, who are heavily vetted and closely allied with the regime, are permitted to contest about a third of the People's Council seats, meaning two-thirds are reserved for the NPF. The government promised in 2011 to initiate a process of constitutional reform with the aim of easing the Baath Party's political dominance, but constitutional changes made toward year's end took a vague approach to political parties and aimed instead at reinforcing President Bashar al-Assad's own power.

Corruption is widespread and rarely carries serious punishment, and bribery is often necessary to navigate the bureaucracy. Regime officials and their families benefit from a range of illicit economic activities. Syria was ranked 129 out of 183 countries surveyed in Transparency International's 2011 Corruption Perceptions Index.

Freedom of expression is heavily restricted. The penal code and a 2001 Publications Law criminalize the publication of material that harms national unity, tarnishes the state's image, or threatens the "goals of the revolution." Many journalists, writers, and intellectuals have been arrested under these laws. Apart from a few radio stations with non-news formats, all broadcast media are state owned. However, satellite dishes are common, giving most Syrians access to foreign broadcasts. More than a dozen privately owned newspapers and magazines have sprouted up in recent years, but during the 2011 turmoil, even the most established of them dealt only obliquely with domestic political issues. The 2001 press law permits the authorities to arbitrarily deny or revoke publishing licenses and compels private print outlets to submit all material to government censors. It also imposes punishment on reporters who do not reveal their sources in response to government requests.

During 2011, journalists frequently went missing or were jailed. In December, Reporters Without Borders estimated that at least 15 journalists remained in extended detention, including bloggers and online dissidents. Foreign journalists also faced detention and travel restrictions. In late March and early April, four Reuters journalists were detained for several days. A reporter for the Qatar-based satellite television station Al-Jazeera was released in May after being held for three weeks and deported to Iran. In September, a journalist from the pan-Arab newspaper *Al-Hayat* was arrested, and as of December, his fate remained unclear. The prominent blogger Razan Ghazzawi was also arrested in early December and released two weeks later.

Syrians access the internet only through state-run servers, which block more than 200 sites associated with the opposition, Kurdish politics, Islamic organizations, human rights, and certain foreign news services, particularly those in Lebanon. Social-networking and video-sharing websites are also blocked. E-mail correspondence is reportedly monitored by intelligence agencies, which often require internet café owners to monitor customers. The government has also been successful in fostering self-censorship through intimidation. In 2011, the risks of citizen journalism via the internet increased, with two citizen journalists killed in Homs in

November and December. The Syrian Electronic Army, a progovernment hacking group, also attacked a series of antigovernment websites with apparent backing from the Assad regime.

Although the constitution requires that the president be a Muslim, there is no state religion in Syria, and freedom of worship is generally respected. However, the government tightly monitors mosques and controls the appointment of Muslim religious leaders. All nonworship meetings of religious groups require permits, and religious fundraising is closely scrutinized. Mosques frequently became sites of violence in 2011, as government forces attempted to prevent gatherings of worshipers from turning into protests. The Alawite minority dominates the internal security forces and the officer corps of the military, while the military rank and file tends to be Sunni. Sunni soldiers face pressure and persecution from their Alawite superiors, and it is believed that hundreds of Sunni troops deserted or mutinied in 2011 in response to orders to fire on mostly Sunni protesters. Some activists interpreted the October assassination of the son of Ahmad Hassoun, Syria's leading Sunni cleric, as an attempt by the regime to incite sectarian violence. Other signs of sectarian polarization included apparent tit-for-tat killings between neighborhoods dominated by different religious groups in Syria's more restive cities.

Academic freedom is heavily restricted. Several private universities have been founded in recent years, and the extent of academic freedom within them varies. University professors have been dismissed or imprisoned for expressing dissent, and some were killed during the 2011 uprising. In one week in September, for example, four professors in Homs were assassinated.

Freedom of assembly is closely circumscribed. Public demonstrations are illegal without official permission, which is typically granted only to progovernment groups. The security services intensified their ban on public and private gatherings starting in 2006, forbidding any group of five or more people from discussing political and economic topics. Surveillance and extensive informant networks have enforced this rule and, until antigovernment sentiment erupted in 2011, ensured that a culture of self-censorship and fear prevailed. Illegal protests throughout the year were met with gunfire, arrests, and alleged torture.

Freedom of association is severely restricted. All nongovernmental organizations must register with the government, which generally denies registration to reformist or human rights groups. Leaders of unlicensed human rights groups have frequently been jailed for publicizing state abuses.

Professional syndicates are controlled by the Baath Party, and all labor unions must belong to the General Federation of Trade Unions, a nominally independent grouping that the government uses to control union activity. Strikes in nonagricultural sectors are legal, but they rarely occur.

While the lower courts in previous years operated with some independence and generally safeguarded ordinary defendants' rights, politically sensitive cases were usually tried by the Supreme State Security Court (SSSC), an exceptional tribunal appointed by the executive branch that denied the right to appeal, limited access to legal counsel, tried many cases behind closed doors, and routinely accepted confessions obtained through torture. State media reported in April 2011 that the SSSC had been abolished in response to the uprising, though this did not bring any tangible gains in the rights of the accused.

The security agencies, which operate independently of the judiciary, routinely extract confessions by torturing suspects and detaining their family members. The government lifted its emergency law in April 2011, but security agencies still had virtually unlimited authority to arrest suspects and hold them incommunicado for prolonged periods without charge. Political activists are often monitored and harassed by security services even after release from prison. As of mid-December 2011, an estimated 12,000 to 40,000 people had been detained for political reasons. Extrajudicial killings also increased significantly in 2011 in the course of the government's crackdown against popular protests.

The Kurdish minority faces severe restrictions on cultural and linguistic expression. The 2001 press law requires that owners and top editors of print publications be Arabs. Kurdish exile groups estimate that as many as 300,000 Syrian Kurds have traditionally been unable to obtain citizenship, passports, identity cards, or birth certificates, preventing them from owning land, obtaining government employment, and voting. Suspected Kurdish activists are routinely dismissed from schools and public sector jobs. While the government pledged in April 2011 to give citizenship to thousands of Kurds in eastern Syria, conditions for Kurds remained harsh. Opposition groups claimed that the regime was behind the killing of prominent Kurdish activist Mishaal al-Tammo in October, and government forces shot and killed several Kurds at al-Tammo's funeral.

Though Syria provides relatively generous educational and medical benefits to Iraqi refugees, they face obstacles to employment and owning property. Many young Iraqi women have been forced into Syria's sex trade. The Syrian government estimated that there were about one million Iraqi refugees in Syria as of January 2011. Iraqis maintained a low profile during the 2011 uprising, but the state's violent response, international economic sanctions, and a degree of Iraqi government support for the Syrian regime left refugees in a difficult position.

Opposition figures, human rights activists, and relatives of exiled dissidents are often prevented from traveling abroad. The government did allow a longtime human rights activist to leave the country in July 2011, though it blocked another who tried to travel to Germany for cancer treatment. Amnesty International reported in October that Syrian dissidents in many foreign countries had been subjected to intimidation by Syrian embassy officials, as well as threats or real harm to their relatives in Syria. The government's crackdown, security checkpoints, and military deployments during the year severely restricted internal travel, in some cases blockading restive towns for extended periods.

While Syria was one of the first Arab countries to grant female suffrage, women remain underrepresented in Syrian politics and government. They hold 12 percent of the seats in the legislature, though the government has appointed some women to senior positions, including one of the two vice presidential posts. The government provides women with equal access to education, but many discriminatory laws remain in force. A husband may request that the Interior Ministry block his wife from traveling abroad, and women, unlike men, are generally barred from taking their children out of the country without proof of the spouse's permission. Violence against women is common, particularly in rural areas. The government imposed two-year minimum prison sentences for killings classified as "honor crimes" in 2009, and in early 2011 changed the law to mandate sentences of five to seven years.

Women's rights groups estimate that there are about 200 such killings each year. Personal status law for Muslims is governed by Sharia (Islamic law) and is discriminatory in marriage, divorce, and inheritance matters. Church law governs personal status issues for Christians, in some cases barring divorce.

Taiwan

Political Rights: 1
Civil Liberties: 2
Status: Free

Population: 23,176,000
Capital: Taipei

Ten-Year Ratings Timeline For Year Under Review (Political Rights, Civil Liberties, Status)

2002	2003	2004	2005	2006	2007	2008	2009	2010	2011
2,2F	2,2F	2,1F	1,1F	2,1F	2,1F	2,1F	1,2F	1,2F	1,2F

Overview: **A series of convictions were handed down in high-profile corruption cases during 2011, with defendants including judges, a diplomat, and former president Chen Shui-bian. Chen's predecessor, Lee Teng-hui, was indicted on embezzlement and money-laundering charges. At year's end, the national media regulator was evaluating a China-friendly media conglomerate's bid to purchase the country's second-largest cable television company. Academics and civil society groups warned that the merger could undermine the diversity of Taiwan's media environment.**

Taiwan became home to the Chinese nationalist Kuomintang (KMT) government-in-exile in 1949 and is still formally known as the Republic of China (ROC). Although the island is independent in all but name, the People's Republic of China (PRC) considers it a renegade province and has threatened to take military action if de jure independence is declared.

Taiwan's transition to democracy began in 1987, when the KMT ended 38 years of martial law. In 1988, Lee Teng-hui became the first Taiwanese-born president, breaking the mainland émigrés' stranglehold on politics. The media were liberalized and opposition political parties legalized in 1989. Lee oversaw Taiwan's first full multiparty legislative elections in 1991–92 and won the first direct presidential election in 1996.

Chen Shui-bian's victory in the 2000 presidential race, as a candidate of the proindependence Democratic Progressive Party (DPP), ended 55 years of KMT rule. Chen narrowly won reelection in 2004, but the KMT-led opposition retained its majority in the legislature.

Thanks in part to a new seat allocation system adopted in 2005, the KMT secured an overwhelming majority in the January 2008 legislative elections, taking 81 of 113 seats. The DPP took 27, and the remainder went to independents and smaller parties. Taipei mayor Ma Ying-jeou of the KMT won that year's presidential election, which marked the island's second peaceful, democratic transfer of power. Both elections were deemed generally free and fair.

Chen was indicted on corruption charges in December 2008, and in November 2010, the Supreme Court finalized bribery convictions for him and his wife, sentencing them to 17 and a half years in prison. In October 2011, the High Court overturned a lower court's acquittal of Chen on separate bribery charges, handing down an additional 18-year sentence. Some observers viewed the prison terms as a positive demonstration that presidents are not above the law, but there were also concerns about possible political bias and procedural irregularities in the earlier stages of the cases.

The latter part of 2011 was dominated by campaigns for the upcoming presidential and parliamentary elections, both scheduled for January 2012. Ma was seeking reelection, and his main challengers were DPP candidate Tsai Ing-wen, Taiwan's first female presidential candidate, and James Soong of the People First Party (PFP). At year's end, the campaigns appeared to be proceeding fairly, though the opposition and some outside observers voiced concerns about potential interference from Beijing and fears of political instability between the January elections and the May presidential inauguration should the DPP win.

On the issue of relations with China, the Ma administration has pursued closer cross-strait ties while continuing to reject unification, independence, and the use of force. Since 2008, bilateral talks have led to agreements on matters including transportation, tourism, food safety, financial cooperation, and intellectual-property protection. In June 2010, both sides signed the Economic Cooperation Framework Agreement (ECFA), which was expected to bring about greater economic integration by reducing trade barriers. In 2011, the government launched a program allowing Chinese tourists to visit as individuals rather than strictly in tour groups, and local universities began accepting Chinese students. Though many Taiwanese supported improving economic ties with China, critics argued that the administration was conceding elements of Taiwan's sovereignty, and moving too quickly with minimal transparency. The country remained under threat from China's military strength, with over 1,000 missiles aimed at the island. In 2011 the United States agreed to upgrade its older U.S.-built F-16 fighter planes instead of selling newer models—a decision that came as a disappointment for many in Taiwan.

Political Rights and Civil Liberties:

Taiwan is an electoral democracy. The 1946 constitution created a unique government structure comprising five distinct branches (yuan). The president, who is directly elected for up to two four-year terms, wields executive power, appoints the prime minister, and can dissolve the legislature. The Executive Yuan, or cabinet, consists of ministers appointed by the president on the recommendation of the prime minister. The prime minister is responsible to the national legislature (Legislative Yuan), which consists of 113 members serving four-year terms. The three other branches of government are the judiciary (Judicial Yuan), a watchdog body (Control Yuan), and a branch responsible for civil-service examinations (Examination Yuan).

The two main parties, the proindependence DPP and the Chinese nationalist KMT, dominate the political landscape. In general, opposition parties are able to function freely, as evident from the vibrant campaign ahead of the January 2012 elections.

Though significantly less pervasive than in the past, corruption remains a problem. A number of high-profile indictments and convictions were handed down during 2011, and some were subject to accusations of selective prosecution or political bias. In June, three senior judges were sentenced to up to 20 years in prison for taking bribes from a former lawmaker in exchange for an acquittal. A former diplomat was sentenced in August to six months in prison for forging official expense claims, and in October several customs officials were indicted for accepting bribes.

The various corruption cases involving former president Chen Shui-bian, his family, and his associates continued to make their way through the courts in 2011. Although the Taiwan High Court's October reversal of a lower court's acquittal added an 18-year prison sentence to Chen's previous sentence of 17 and a half years on separate bribery convictions, several banking executives indicted in the case at hand were acquitted. Some observers expressed concerns that the reversal and inconsistent legal arguments between the first and second rulings damaged the image of the judiciary and gave the appearance of political bias.

Another former president, Lee Teng-hui, was indicted in June along with an aide on embezzlement and money-laundering charges. Lee was accused of siphoning US$7.79 million from a secret diplomatic fund in the 1990s to establish a research institute where he now serves as honorary chairman. Lee denied the charges, and the case was pending at year's end. Critics questioned the timing of the indictment, given Lee's close association with DPP presidential candidate Tsai Ing-wen.

As part of its efforts to combat corruption among mid- and low-level public officials, the government in July established the Agency Against Corruption, to be administered by the Ministry of Justice. It does not have the authority to prosecute ministerial-level officials. Taiwan was ranked 32 out of 183 countries surveyed in Transparency International's 2011 Corruption Perceptions Index.

Taiwanese media reflect a diversity of views and report aggressively on government policies and corruption allegations. The state has relatively little influence over the media, though partisan influence is strong. In response to public concerns over "embedded marketing," in which government entities pay for promotional items that are presented as news, the legislature amended the Budget Law in January 2011 to prohibit the use of public funds for such purposes; the law did not explicitly address "embedded marketing" paid for by PRC entities. Occasional cases of Chinese state-run news appearing in Taiwanese papers continued to surface during the year. In April, *China Post*, an English-language newspaper in Taiwan, was found to have inserted articles originally published by the PRC's state-run *China Daily* without citing their source. An amended Children and Youth Welfare and Rights Protection Act passed in November banned excessively detailed newspaper coverage of rape, suicide, or drug abuse, as well as the publication of photographs depicting violent or erotic subject matter.

Also during 2011, the National Communications Commission (NCC) was weighing a bid by Want Want China Broadband—part of a media conglomerate owned by a businessman with mainland commercial interests and a record of friendly relations with the Chinese government—to purchase China Network Systems (CNS), Taiwan's second-largest cable television provider. International media watchdogs and local academics urged the regulator to reject the bid, claiming that it could undermine the diversity of news content. A final decision was pending at year's end. Meanwhile, a KMT legislator sued a reporter for criminal defamation in October after he wrote an article charging that the legislator had pressured the NCC to expedite its decision. Pending a final ruling, the reporter faced a provisional seizure of US$82,600 by the court. Separately, in July the NCC approved a bid by Hong Kong–based Next Media to launch a television news channel in Taiwan, after its owner agreed to omit sexual and violent content; the licensing request had been denied multiple times since 2009.

In another case that raised concerns about increased Chinese influence over Taiwanese media, in April Taiwan's partly government-owned satellite company Chunghwa Telecom (CHT), which has joint ventures with Chinese state-run counterparts, announced the termination of its contract with New Tang Dynasty Television, a station operated by practitioners of the Falun Gong spiritual movement, which is persecuted in China. The station relied on CHT's satellite to broadcast uncensored news into the PRC. Following pressure from press freedom groups, Taiwanese officials, and foreign lawmakers, the company renewed the contract in August.

Taiwanese of all faiths can worship freely. Religious organizations that choose to register with the government receive tax-exempt status.

Educators in Taiwan can generally write and lecture without interference, though the 2009 Act Governing the Administrative Impartiality of Public Officials bars scholars at public academic facilities from engaging in certain political activities.

Freedom of assembly is generally respected, and several large-scale demonstrations and campaign rallies took place in 2011. However, under the Assembly and Parade Law, protesters can be prosecuted for failing to obtain a permit or obey police orders to disperse. A professor charged in 2008 for organizing peaceful protests surrounding a Chinese envoy's visit was acquitted in November 2011. A constitutional review of the law requested in 2010 was still pending at year's end.

All civic organizations must register with the government, though registration is freely granted. While nongovernmental organizations (NGOs) generally operate without harassment, in August 2011, a human rights association and several grassroots groups assisting farmers in land expropriation cases reported visits by police or Ministry of Justice investigators, who inquired about plans to attend demonstrations or otherwise engage in social activism.

Trade unions are independent, and most workers enjoy freedom of association. However, government employees, military personnel, and defense-industry workers are barred from joining unions or bargaining collectively. An amended version of the Trade Union Act that took effect in May 2011 allows teachers to join or form unions, though they are not allowed to stage strikes. The measure also stipulates that the authorities can no longer dissolve unions for activities that "disturb public order." Separately in May, the government launched an arbitration committee to handle disputes over improper labor practices.

According to official statistics, 425,660 foreign workers were working in Taiwan in 2011. About half are covered by the Labor Standards Law, but more than 196,000 foreign household workers lack institutional protection from abuses by employers. In February, the government briefly imposed punitive measures, such as tightening visa procedures, on migrant workers from the Philippines after the Philippine government triggered a diplomatic row by extraditing 14 Taiwanese nationals to mainland China to face charges of fraud.

Taiwan's judiciary is independent, and trials are generally fair. However, in recent years there have been concerns over the selection of judges for high-profile cases and the quality of the disciplinary system amid corruption scandals and controversial rulings in child abuse cases. In June 2011, the legislature passed a long-stalled Judges Law that would create a complaint and removal mechanism for incompetent judges. Although the law was generally seen as a step forward for judicial reform, civil society groups argued that the disciplinary and evaluation committees did not include enough members from outside the judiciary, while some judges warned that including any external evaluators could undermine judicial independence. The law was scheduled to take effect in 2012.

Police largely respect the ban on arbitrary detention, and attorneys are allowed to monitor interrogations to prevent abuses. However, a number of prominent cases have exposed flaws in the protection of defendants' rights. In September 2011, a military court posthumously acquitted air force private Chiang Kuo-ching of raping and murdering a five-year-old girl in 1996. He had been executed in 1997, after a confession was extracted by torture as part of a flawed investigation, and in January 2011, another man implicated by forensic evidence was arrested and charged with the murder. Chiang's family was awarded US$3.4 million in compensation The ruling was issued amid a growing public debate on whether to abolish the death penalty, after the government ended a five-year moratorium in 2010. In a separate case in July, the Supreme Court rejected the appeal of a death row inmate who had allegedly been tortured to extract a confession for crimes including the 1987 abduction and murder of a nine-year-old boy, and had endured 11 retrials over 23 years.

Corruption in the police force remains a problem in parts of Taiwan. In March 2011, a group of 30 current and retired officers in the northern city of Keelung were arrested for accepting millions of dollars in bribes related to illegal gambling parlors over 18 years. In December, nine officers were convicted and received sentences ranging from 2 to 13 and a half years.

The constitution provides for the equality of all citizens. Six seats in the legislature are reserved for indigenous people, giving them representation that exceeds their share of the population. Their self-governance is guaranteed under the Indigenous Peoples Basic Law, but issues surrounding ownership of ancestral lands and the use of natural resources remain unresolved. A draft Indigenous Autonomy Act introduced in the legislature in May 2011 would allow indigenous people to establish tribal offices and councils, but critics noted that the bill would not delineate autonomous tribal lands or remove the tribal entities from the authority of existing administrative districts.

Taiwanese law does not allow for the granting of asylum or refugee status, though the cabinet drafted a refugee law in early 2010 as part of an effort to honor two UN human rights treaties—the International Covenant on Civil and Political Rights and the International Covenant on Economic, Social, and Cultural Rights—that Taiwan had ratified in March 2009. The ratifications were rejected by the United Nations, which cited the PRC as the only recognized representative of China. The refugee bill remains pending in the legislature.

Amid warming relations with the PRC, the government launched a program in June 2011 that allows a quota of 500 Chinese tourists per day from select cities to travel to Taiwan without the supervision of organized tour groups.

After the 2008 elections, women held 30 percent of the legislature's seats. DPP chairwoman Tsai Ing-wen, who announced in March 2011 that she would be running for president in January 2012, is Taiwan's first female candidate for the position. Taiwanese women face job discrimination and lower pay than men on average. Rape and domestic violence remain problems. Local women's rights groups criticized an amendment to the Social Order and Maintenance Act that took effect in November. Under the amendment, local governments are allowed to set up designated districts in which prostitution is legal. The island continues to be a destination for human trafficking. Some women from China and Southeast Asian countries arrive through fraudulent marriages and deceptive employment offers for purposes of sex trafficking and forced labor.

Tajikistan

Political Rights: 6
Civil Liberties: 5
Status: Not Free

Population: 7,535,000
Capital: Dushanbe

Ten-Year Ratings Timeline For Year Under Review (Political Rights, Civil Liberties, Status)

2002	2002	2004	2005	2006	2007	2008	2009	2010	2011
6,5NF	6,5NF	6,5NF	6,5NF	6,5NF	6,5NF	6,5NF	6,5NF	6,5NF	6,5NF

Overview: **Citing the need to curb extremism, the government in 2011 pushed through legislation that prohibits minors' participation in regular religious activities unless they receive state-supervised religious education. Scores of mosques were closed for alleged registration problems during the year, and the government announced that sermons in registered mosques could only be given on a short list of preapproved topics. The authorities continued to pressure journalists and curb freedom of speech through detentions, prosecutions, and the threat of heavy fines.**

Former Communist Party leader Rakhmon Nabiyev was elected president of Tajikistan, after the country declared independence from the Soviet Union in 1991. Long-simmering tensions between regional elites, combined with various anti-Communist and Islamist movements, soon plunged the country into a five-year civil war. In September 1992, Communist hard-liners forced Nabiyev's resignation; he was replaced later that year by Emomali Rakhmonov, a leading Communist Party member.

Rakhmonov was elected president in 1994, after most opposition candidates either boycotted or were prevented from competing in the poll. Similarly, progovernment candidates won the 1995 parliamentary elections amid a boycott by the United Tajik Opposition (UTO), a coalition of secular and Islamist groups that had emerged as the main force fighting against Rakhmonov's government.

After a December 1996 ceasefire, Rakhmonov and UTO leader Said Abdullo Nuri signed a formal peace agreement in 1997, with a reintegration process to be overseen by a politically balanced National Reconciliation Commission. A September 1999 referendum that permitted the formation of religion-based political parties paved the way for the legal operation of the Islamist opposition, including the Islamic Renaissance Party (IRP). The referendum also extended the president's term from five to seven years. In November, Rakhmonov was reelected with a reported 97 percent of the vote in a poll that was criticized by international observers for widespread irregularities.

In February 2000 parliamentary elections, Rakhmonov's People's Democratic Party (PDP) received nearly 65 percent of the vote. Although the participation of six parties provided some political pluralism, a joint monitoring mission by the Organization for Security and Cooperation in Europe (OSCE) and the United Nations cited serious electoral problems. After the elections, the National Reconciliation Commission was formally disbanded. However, important provisions of the 1997 peace accord remained unimplemented, with demobilization of opposition factions incomplete and the government failing to meet a 30 percent quota for UTO members in senior government posts.

A 2003 constitutional referendum cleared a path for Rakhmonov to seek two additional terms and remain in office until 2020. The PDP easily won 2005 parliamentary elections amid reports of large-scale irregularities. Separately in 2005, Russian border guards who had long patrolled the frontier with Afghanistan completed their withdrawal. However, a Russian army division dating to the Soviet period remained in the country.

Rakhmonov won the November 2006 presidential election with more than 70 percent of the vote, although the OSCE noted a lack of real competition. The president broadened his influence to the cultural sphere in 2007, de-Russifying his surname to "Rahmon" in March and signing legislation in May to establish spending limits on birthday and wedding celebrations.

The country suffered extreme economic hardship in 2008 and 2009 due to severe weather, power outages, and falling remittances from Tajiks working abroad. The ruling PDP nevertheless won 55 of 63 lower-house seats in February 2010 parliamentary elections, which failed to meet basic democratic standards, according to OSCE monitors.

Also during 2010, the security situation experienced its worst deterioration since the 1992–97 civil war, with violence including a mass prison break, an attack on a police station in Khujand that featured the country's first suicide bombing, and a guerrilla ambush that killed 30 soldiers in the remote Rasht Valley. In 2011, the government dispatched special forces to Rasht in a bid to extend its control over one of the last areas left unofficially to former opposition commanders. The operations resulted in the deaths of several of these local strongmen, including Ali Bedaki, who was apparently killed after being captured in January.

In September, Russia successfully negotiated a 49-year lease extension on its base in Tajikistan, which houses the largest Russian military presence in Central Asia. Russia also sought joint control of the Tajik-Afghan border and use of the Ayni airbase near Dushanbe, in which India was also reportedly interested. Iran, meanwhile, continued to fund construction of the Sangtuda-2 hydropower plant.

Political Rights and Civil Liberties:

Tajikistan is not an electoral democracy. The 1994 constitution provides for a strong, directly elected president who enjoys broad authority to appoint and dismiss officials. A full-time, bicameral parliament was created in 1999, while amendments in 2003 allowed current president Emomali Rahmon to serve two additional seven-year terms beyond the 2006 election. In the Assembly of Representatives (lower chamber), 63 members are elected by popular vote to serve five-year terms. In the 33-seat National Assembly (upper chamber), 25 members are chosen by local assemblies, and 8 are appointed by the president, all for five-year terms. Elections are neither free nor fair.

Patronage networks and regional affiliations are central to political life, with officials from the president's native Kulyob region dominant in government. In 2009 Rahmon's daughter Ozoda was appointed deputy foreign minister, while by 2011, his son Rustam had attained the rank of major and been appointed to a newly created post in the Customs Agency in charge of fighting contraband, in addition to holding a significant number of other positions.

Corruption is reportedly pervasive. Members of the president's family allegedly maintain extensive business interests, and major irregularities at the National Bank and the country's largest industrial company, TALCO Aluminum, have been documented. Tajikistan was ranked 152 out of 183 countries surveyed in Transparency International's 2011 Corruption Perceptions Index.

Despite constitutional guarantees of freedom of speech and the press, independent journalists face harassment and intimidation, and the penal code criminalizes defamation. Crippling libel judgments are common, particularly against newspapers that are critical of the government. In October 2011, a court convicted *Nuri Zindagi* reporter Makhmadyusuf Ismoilov of slander and other charges but released him under an amnesty. He had been detained in late 2010 after publishing articles that accused local officials of corruption, and spent 11 months in detention. Also in October, British Broadcasting Corporation (BBC) correspondent Urunboy Usmonov was convicted of failing to report contacts with the banned Islamist group Hizb ut-Tahrir, having interviewed and covered the trials of some of its members. He, too, was released under an amnesty; he claimed to have been tortured after his arrest in June. The government controls most printing presses, newsprint supplies, and broadcasting facilities, leaving little room for independent news and analysis. Most television stations are state owned or only nominally independent, and the process of obtaining broadcast licenses is cumbersome. Internet penetration is low. The government blocks some critical websites, and online news outlets are subject to criminal libel laws.

The government has imposed a number of restrictions on religious freedom. Wearing of the hijab (headscarf) in schools and higher educational institutions has been banned since 2005. In 2007, the authorities shut down large numbers of unauthorized mosques and instituted more restrictive rules for licensing religious leaders, and a 2009 law banned the promotion of any religion except the traditional Hanafi form of Islam. The country's limited religious education institutions have failed to integrate most of the 1,500 students who were pressured to return from religious schools abroad in 2010, and some have faced prosecution. In January 2011, a new wave of mosque closures began, shuttering dozens of houses of worship, and the government announced plans to issue a list of some 60 approved topics on which imams could deliver Friday sermons. Unprecedented new legislation on "parental responsibility" that came into force in August banned minors from attending regular religious services in mosques unless they received officially sanctioned religious education. It was unclear how the government would enforce the law; many religious leaders criticized it or quietly refused to obey it.

The government limits freedoms of assembly and association. Local government approval is required to hold public demonstrations, and officials reportedly refuse to grant permission in virtually all cases. All nongovernmental organizations must register with the Ministry of Justice. Citizens have the legal right to form and join trade unions and to bargain collectively, but trade unions are largely subservient to the authorities and indifferent to workers' interests.

The judiciary lacks independence. Many judges are poorly trained and inexperienced, and bribery is reportedly widespread. Police frequently make arbitrary arrests and beat detainees to extract confessions. Overcrowding and disease contribute to often life-threatening conditions in prisons.

Tajikistan is a major conduit for the smuggling of narcotics from Afghanistan to Russia and Europe. A side effect has been an increase in drug addiction within Tajikistan, as well as a rise in the number of cases of HIV/AIDS.

Sexual harassment, discrimination, and violence against women, including spousal abuse, are reportedly common, but cases are rarely investigated. Reports indicate that women sometimes face societal pressure to wear headscarves, even though official policy discourages the practice. Despite some government efforts to address human trafficking, Tajikistan remains a source and transit country for persons trafficked for prostitution. Child labor, particularly on cotton farms, also remains a problem.

Tanzania

Political Rights: 3
Civil Liberties: 3
Status: Partly Free

Population: 46,219,000
Capital: Dar-es-Salaam

Ten-Year Ratings Timeline For Year Under Review (Political Rights, Civil Liberties, Status)

2002	2003	2004	2005	2006	2007	2008	2009	2010	2011
4,3PF	4,3PF	4,3PF	4,3PF	4,3PF	4,3PF	4,3PF	4,3PF	3,3PF	3,3PF

Overview: **After holding successful presidential and parliamentary elections in 2010, Tanzania in November 2011 passed legislation to begin the process of reforming the constitution. However, further advances in civil and political rights have stalled in the face of continued impunity for the security forces, widespread corruption, and government interference in the media.**

Three years after mainland Tanganyika gained independence from Britain in 1961, the Zanzibar archipelago merged with Tanganyika to become the United Republic of Tanzania. The ruling Chama Cha Mapinduzi (CCM) party, under longtime president Julius Nyerere, dominated the country's political life. Nyerere's collectivist economic philosophy—known in Swahili as ujaama—promoted a sense of community and nationality, but also resulted in significant economic dislocation and decline. During Nyerere's tenure, Tanzania played an important role as a "frontline state" in the international response to white-controlled regimes in southern Africa. Nyerere's successor, Ali Hassan Mwinyi, was president from 1985 to 1995 and oversaw a carefully controlled political liberalization process.

CCM victories in the 1995 and 2000 presidential and parliamentary elections on the mainland and on Zanzibar were tainted by fraud and irregularities. The CCM captured a majority of seats in the 2005 elections, and Foreign Minister Jakaya Kikwete, a CCM stalwart, was elected president. The postelection atmosphere was tense, as the opposition Civic United Front (CUF) once again accused the CCM of electoral fraud. Negotiations to legitimize the 2005 elections remained deadlocked, until a July 2010 referendum led to a constitutional change creating two vice-presidential positions to be divided between the CCM and CUF.

The campaign period for the October 2010 national polls was characterized by lively policy debate and active campaigning by a range of parties. Kikwete was reelected to a second five-year term as president with 61 percent of the vote, defeating five opposition candidates. While the CCM retained its majority in concurrent National Assembly elections, winning 186 seats, the opposition gained its largest representation in Tanzania's history. The CUF took 24 seats, and Chama Cha Demokrasia na Maendeleo (CHADEMA) won 23. While there were some protests alleging vote rigging and poor administration of the elections, the 2010 polls represented a considerable improvement over previous elections. In the separate Zanzibar polls, the CCM presidential candidate also won a narrow victory.

In November 2011, the National Assembly passed the Constitution Review Act, which calls for the creation of a commission to begin reforming the constitution. The opposition protested that the public had not been adequately consulted about the new law, and expressed concern that members of the commission are appointed by the president. Later that month, the police refused to grant Jukwaa la Katiba (Constitutional Forum), an umbrella group of civil society organizations, permission to hold a demonstration in Dar es Salaam against Kikwete signing the bill.

In January 2011, two people were killed by police at a CHADEMA-led antigovernment protest in Arusha. Thirteen CHADEMA officials were arrested for inciting violence; the case was pending at year's end. In early November, the police banned demonstrations by CHADEMA nationwide, on the grounds that the party's previous gatherings had become violent.

Political Rights and Civil Liberties: Tanzania is an electoral democracy. The October 2010 national elections were judged to be the most competitive and legitimate in Tanzania's history. Unlike past elections, the opposition accepted the 2010 results in Zanzibar, due in large part to a July referendum providing for the creation of a national unity government after the poll. Executive power rests with the president, who is elected by direct popular vote for a maximum of two five-year terms. Legislative power is held by a unicameral National Assembly, the Bunge, which currently has 357 members serving five-year terms. Of these, 239 are directly elected in single-seat constituencies; 102 are women chosen by the political parties according to their representation in the Bunge; 10 are appointed by the president; 1 is awarded to the attorney general;

and 5 are members of the Zanzibar legislature, whose 50 deputies are elected to five-year terms. Along with the legislature, Zanzibar has its own president and cabinet with largely autonomous jurisdiction over the archipelago's internal affairs.

Although opposition parties were legalized in 1992, the ruling CCM continues to dominate the country's political life. The constitution prohibits political coalitions, which has impeded efforts by other parties to seriously contest the CCM's dominance. Opposition politics have also tended to be highly fractious. To register in Tanzania, political parties must not be formed on religious, ethnic, or regional bases and cannot oppose the union of Zanzibar and the mainland.

Corruption remains a serious problem. A 2007 anticorruption bill gave the government greater power to target abuses in procurement and money laundering, but critics claim it is insufficient. Several high-profile scandals, particularly the controversial purchase of radar equipment from the United Kingdom involving alleged kickbacks to Tanzanian government officials and businessmen, were the focus of considerable press attention through 2010 and into 2011. Tanzania was ranked 100 out of 183 countries surveyed in Transparency International's 2011 Corruption Perceptions Index.

Although the constitution provides for freedom of speech, it does not specifically guarantee freedom of the press. Current laws allow authorities broad discretion to restrict media on the basis of national security or public interest. Print and electronic media are active, though hindered by a difficult government registration process and largely limited to major urban areas. The growth of broadcast media has been slowed by a lack of capital investment, both public and private. However, a number of independent television and private FM radio stations have gone on the air in recent years. Government-owned media outlets are largely biased toward the ruling party. Journalists were arbitrarily arrested, threatened, and assaulted in 2011, leading to self-censorship. In December, authorities charged the managing editor and a columnist with the daily *Tanzania Daima* with incitement over an article claiming that the government misused police to block demonstrators. The case was pending at year's end.

Press freedom rights in Zanzibar are constrained by its semiautonomous government. The Zanzibari government owns the only daily newspaper, but three of the four newspapers that publish periodically are privately owned. Many islanders receive mainland broadcasts and read the mainland press. The government largely controls radio and television content; mainland television broadcasts are delayed in Zanzibar to allow authorities to censor content. The Zanzibari government often reacts to media criticism by accusing the press of being a "threat to national unity." Internet access, while limited to urban areas, is growing. While previously unrestricted, authorities now monitor and reportedly engage in cyberattacks on websites that are critical of the government.

Freedom of religion is generally respected, and relations between the various faiths are largely peaceful. In recent years, however, religious tensions, especially between Muslims and Christians, have increased. The Zanzibari government appoints a mufti, a professional jurist who interprets Islamic law, to oversee Muslim organizations. Some Muslims have criticized this practice, arguing that it represents excessive government interference. Academic freedom is respected.

The constitution guarantees freedoms of assembly and association. However, these rights are not always respected. Organizers of political events are required to obtain permission from the police, and critical political demonstrations are actively discouraged. Many nongovernmental organizations (NGOs) are active, and some have influenced the public policy process. However, the 2002 NGO Act has been criticized for increasing government control over NGOs and restricting their operation. Essential public service workers are barred from striking, and other workers are restricted by complex notification and mediation requirements. Strikes are infrequent on both the mainland and in Zanzibar. There were reports in 2011 of employers using discriminatory hiring practices, actively discouraging unionization, and making threats of violence against union leaders.

Tanzania's judiciary is subject to political influence, underfunding, and corruption. The president exercises considerable influence over which cases are presented to the courts. Arrest and pretrial detention rules are often ignored. Prisons suffer from harsh conditions, including overcrowding and safety and health concerns, and police abuse is common. Narcotics trafficking is a growing problem, especially given the challenge of controlling Tanzania's borders. Security forces reportedly routinely abused, threatened, and mistreated civilians with limited accountability throughout 2011. By December, 25 people had been killed and over 40 injured by police and other security forces during the year.

The 2002 Prevention of Terrorism Act has been criticized by NGOs for its inconsistencies and anomalies. Acts of terrorism include attacks on a person's life, kidnapping, and serious damage to property. The law gives the police and immigration officials sweeping powers to arrest suspected illegal immigrants or anyone thought to have links with terrorists.

Tanzania has enjoyed relatively tranquil relations among its many ethnic groups. A large number of refugees from conflicts in Burundi, the Democratic Republic of Congo, and Somalia—311,150 as of September 2011—live in Tanzania. Tanzania won praise in 2010 for granting citizenship to 162,000 Burundian refugees, the largest-ever single naturalization of refugees.

Albinos are subject to violence and discrimination. There were at least five attempted murders of albinos to obtain their body parts in 2011, though there were no reported killings. The first albino murder convictions were obtained in September 2009, and the first albino was elected to parliament in 2010.

Women's rights are constitutionally guaranteed but not uniformly protected. Nevertheless, women are relatively well represented in parliament, with over 30 percent of seats. Traditional or Islamic customs that discriminate against women prevail in family law, especially in rural areas and in Zanzibar, and women enjoy fewer educational and economic opportunities than men. Domestic violence is reportedly common and rarely prosecuted. Human rights groups have sought laws to bar forced marriages, which are most common among Tanzania's coastal peoples. According to a 2011 UNICEF survey, almost 33 percent of girls and 13.4 percent of boys under the age of 18 had been victims of sexual violence. In 2011, over 1,000 deaths due to mob violence and allegations of witchcraft were reported.

Thailand

Political Rights: 4*
Civil Liberties: 4
Status: Partly Free

Population: 69,519,000
Capital: Bangkok

Ratings Change: Thailand's political rights rating improved from 5 to 4 due to relatively free and fair national elections in July, which resulted in a transfer of power to the opposition.

Ten-Year Ratings Timeline For Year Under Review (Political Rights, Civil Liberties, Status)

2002	2003	2004	2005	2006	2007	2008	2009	2010	2011
2,3F	2,3F	2,3F	3,3PF	7,4NF	6,4PF	5,4PF	5,4PF	5,4PF	4,4PF

Overview: **Thailand's political temperature cooled in 2011 following deadly street violence between security forces and antigovernment protesters the previous year. The opposition Puea Thai Party won relatively free and fair parliamentary elections in July 2011, and Yingluck Shinawatra, the younger sister of exiled former premier Thaksin Shinawatra, became prime minister. Despite the new government, prosecutors and security agencies continued to employ *lèse-majesté* laws to curb freedom of expression and political speech. Also during the year, rights abuses associated with the insurgency and counterinsurgency in southern Thailand persisted, and the government faced criticism over its response to massive flooding that killed hundreds of people in the fall.**

Known as Siam until 1939, Thailand was the only Southeast Asian country to avoid European colonial rule. A 1932 coup transformed the kingdom into a constitutional monarchy, but Thailand endured multiple military coups, constitutional overhauls, and popular uprisings over the next six decades. The army dominated the political scene during this period, with intermittent bouts of unstable civilian government. Under the leadership of General Prem Tinsulanonda in the 1980s, the country underwent a rapid economic expansion and a gradual transition toward democratic rule. The military seized power again in 1991, but Thailand's revered monarch, King Bhumipol Adulyadej, intervened to appoint a civilian prime minister in 1992. Fresh elections held in September of that year ushered in a 14-year period of elected civilian leadership.

Thaksin Shinawatra, a former deputy prime minister who built his fortune in telecommunications, unseated the ruling Democratic Party (DP) in the 2001 elections. He and his Thai Rak Thai (TRT, or Thais Love Thais) party mobilized voters in rural areas in part by criticizing the government for favoring urban, middle-class Thais. As prime minister, Thaksin won praise for pursuing populist economic policies designed to stimulate aggregate demand. However, critics accused him and his government of undercutting the 1997 reformist constitution. Human rights groups also condemned Thaksin for media suppression and a violent counternarcotics campaign that resulted in at least 2,500 killings in a three-month period in 2003.

In 2004 separatist violence surged in Thailand's four southernmost provinces, home to most of the country's four million Muslims. Thaksin mounted a hard-line response, and the government placed the provinces of Narathiwat, Yala, and Pattani under martial law that year. The government was accused of human rights abuses in its effort to put down the insurgency.

The TRT swept the February 2005 parliamentary elections, making Thaksin the first prime minister to serve out a full four-year term and be elected to two consecutive terms. However, anti-Thaksin sentiment rose markedly during the year, particularly in Bangkok and the south. Facing a wave of protests led by the People's Alliance for Democracy (PAD)—a right-wing grouping of royalists, business elites, and military leaders with support in the urban middle class—the prime minister called snap elections in early April 2006. All three opposition parties boycotted the vote, and a fresh round of elections was ultimately scheduled for October.

A military coup in September 2006 preempted the new vote and ousted Thaksin, who was abroad at the time. The coup leaders' Council for National Security (CNS) abrogated the constitution, dissolved the parliament, and replaced the Constitutional Court with its own tribunal. In May 2007, the tribunal found the TRT guilty of paying off smaller parties in the April 2006 elections and dissolved it, specifically prohibiting Thaksin and 111 other party leaders from participating in politics for the next five years. About 57 percent of referendum voters in August 2007 approved a new constitution that contained a number of antidemocratic provisions.

Former TRT members regrouped under the banner of the People's Power Party (PPP) and won the December 2007 parliamentary elections. Throughout 2008, yellow-shirted PAD supporters led protests accusing the new government of serving as a corrupt proxy for Thaksin and demanding its dissolution. Meanwhile, in October the Supreme Court sentenced Thaksin in absentia to two years in prison for abuse of office.

The PPP-led government—under intense pressure from the PAD, military commanders, and the judiciary—finally fell in December 2008, when the Constitutional Court disbanded the ruling party on the grounds that it had engaged in fraud during the December 2007 elections. DP leader Abhisit Vejjajiva subsequently formed a new coalition and won a lower-house vote to become prime minister. The red-shirted United Front for Democracy Against Dictatorship (UDD), which had opposed the 2006 coup, mounted large protests against the PPP's dissolution and the new government. Abhisit imposed emergency rule in Bangkok for nearly two weeks in April 2009, arresting red-shirt leaders and shutting down pro-UDD radio stations.

Reconciliation efforts later in 2009 made little progress, and UDD protests escalated again in the spring of 2010, with red shirts occupying the heart of Bangkok's commercial district in April. The government, which accused the UDD of intending to overthrow the monarchy, declared another state of emergency, and the army finally dispersed the entrenched protesters in May, at times using live fire. Between March and the end of May, a total of 92 people were killed in clashes between protesters and security forces.

Abhisit established two committees on national reform to advance reconciliation, and his government attempted to garner public support with populist economic policies. However, these efforts largely failed to win over opposition supporters, and in early 2011, Abhisit called new elections for July.

In the run-up to the elections, many elements of the Thai elite, including the military, clearly indicated to voters their preference for the DP, with the army chief appearing on national television to essentially advise voters not to vote for Puea Thai, the successor to the PPP, led by Thaksin's younger sister Yingluck Shinawatra. The military also allegedly worked behind the scenes to convince smaller parties to ally themselves with the DP following the vote. Within Puea Thai, some expressed worries that Yingluck would become a proxy for Thaksin, who called her his "clone." Political tensions were further heightened by concerns about the future of the monarchy, as the king's health was reportedly fading, and the crown prince was seen as more divisive figure.

Puea Thai ultimately won the parliamentary elections outright, taking 265 of 500 seats in the lower house. The DP placed second with 159 seats, and small parties divided the remainder. The army accepted the results, in part because Puea Thai leaders reportedly assured the military that they would not interfere in military promotions or seek trials for anyone involved in the 2010 political violence. Yingluck became prime minister and installed several Thaksin loyalists in top cabinet positions. They began advocating an amnesty for Thaksin, but no such action was taken, and he remained in exile throughout the year. However, some red shirts who had been arrested after the 2010 violence were released by the courts.

Yingluck suggested that she would consider reforming the country's lèse-majesté laws, which had been enforced more aggressively since 2006, and revising the constitution to bring it closer to the 1997 charter. However, she had apparently set aside both proposals by year's end, as she engages in a delicate balancing game with military and royalist foes who oppose the changes.

Flooding that destroyed many of the industrial estates in the outskirts of Bangkok during the year resulted in the deaths of more than 800 people and caused some $45 billion in damage. The disaster added to the rivalry between Yingluck and her opponents, as the army used its national resources to help with flood aid.

Political Rights and Civil Liberties: Thailand is an electoral democracy. The July 2011 elections were considered relatively free and fair, yielding a victory for the opposition and replacing a government that had come to power as a result of judicial action and lacked a popular mandate. Although the influential military weighed in against Puea Thai during the run-up to the vote, it was unable to alter the outcome. However, the Asian Network for Free Elections, a leading monitoring organization, reported that several political parties had representatives inside polling stations trying to influence voters' choices, and that vote buying had increased compared to previous parliamentary polls. The Thai Election Commission postponed certifying the election results after receiving complaints of fraud and irregularities in the election of one-quarter of candidates.

The current constitution was drafted under the supervision of a military-backed government and approved in an August 2007 referendum. It included an amnesty for the 2006 coup leaders, and in a clear response to the premiership of Thaksin Shinawatra, whose government the coup overthrew, the charter limited prime ministers to two four-year terms and set a lower threshold for launching no-confidence motions. The constitution also reduced the role of elected lawmakers. Whereas the old Senate was fully elected, the Senate created by the new charter consists of

77 elected members and 73 appointed by a committee of judges and members of independent government bodies. Senators, who serve six-year terms, cannot belong to political parties. For the 500-seat lower chamber, the House of Representatives, the new constitution altered the system of proportional representation to curtail the voting power of the northern and northeastern provinces, where support for Thaksin remains strong.

Corruption is widespread at all levels of Thai society. Both the DP and Puea Thai include numerous lawmakers who have been linked to corruption charges during their time in power. Thailand was ranked 80 out of 183 countries surveyed in Transparency International's 2011 Corruption Perceptions Index, a drop of nearly twenty points from a decade earlier.

The 2007 constitution restored freedom of expression guarantees that were eliminated by the 2006 coup, though the use of laws to silence critics is growing. The 2007 Computer Crimes Act assigns significant prison terms for the publication of false information deemed to endanger the public or national security. In 2011, Tanthawut Taweewarodomkul was sentenced to 13 years in prison for posting items on a site critical of the palace. In recent years, the government has blocked as many as 100,000 websites for allegedly insulting the monarchy, and this blocking continued under the new government in 2011. The authorities did ease restrictions on some red-shirt websites and community radio stations, but DP supporters argued that Prime Minister Yingluck Shinawatra's government had begun trying to shut down radio stations associated with their political camp.

The government and military control licensing and transmission for Thailand's six main television stations and all 525 radio frequencies. Community radio stations are generally unlicensed. Print publications are for the most part privately owned and have been subject to fewer restrictions than the broadcast media. However, most print publications take a clear position on either side of the country's political divide.

The past five years have featured a surge in use of the country's lèse-majesté laws to stifle freedom of expression. According to the National Human Rights Commission, more than 400 lèse-majesté cases went to trial in 2010 and 2011. The laws prohibit defamation of the monarchy, but the authorities have increasingly used them to target activists, scholars, students, journalists, foreign authors, and politicians who are critical of the government, exacerbating self-censorship. Some of the accused face decades in prison for multiple counts. Others, such as Reuters reporter Andrew Marshall, flee the country, as Marshall did in 2011 after writing an extensive series on the monarchy.

The constitution prohibits discrimination based on religious belief. There is no official state religion, but the constitution requires the monarch to be a Buddhist, and speech considered insulting to Buddhism is prohibited by law. The conflict in the south, which pits ethnic Malay Muslims against ethnic Thai Buddhists, continues to undermine citizens' ability to practice their religion. Buddhist monks report that they are unable to travel freely through southern communities to receive alms, while Muslim academics and imams face government scrutiny.

The 2007 constitution restored freedom of assembly guarantees, though the government may invoke the Internal Security Act (ISA) or declare a state of emergency to curtail major demonstrations, as it did for much of 2010. In 2011, the state of emergency was lifted for most of the country, though it remained in place in the restive south. Political parties and organizations campaigned and met openly and freely in the run-up to the July election and engaged in pro- or anti-government demonstrations after the election.

Thailand has a vibrant nongovernmental organization (NGO) community, with groups representing farmers, laborers, women, students, environmentalists, and human rights interests. In 2011, armed men shot and killed environmental activist Thongnak Sawekchinda, who had led a local campaign against pollution created by coal companies

Thai trade unions are independent, and more than 50 percent of state-enterprise workers belong to unions, but less than 2 percent of the total workforce is unionized. Antiunion discrimination in the private sector is common, and legal protections for union members are weak and poorly enforced. Exploitation and trafficking of migrant workers from Burma, Cambodia, and Laos are serious and ongoing problems, as are child and sweatshop labor. The UN Human Rights Council reported in 2011 that trafficking of forced labor into Thailand was growing in the agricultural, construction, and fishing industries.

The 2007 constitution restored judicial independence and reestablished an independent Constitutional Court. A separate military court adjudicates criminal and civil cases involving members of the military, as well as cases brought under martial law. Sharia (Islamic law) courts hear certain types of cases pertaining to Muslims. The Thai courts have played a decisive role in determining the outcome of political disputes, for example in the ouster of the PPP government in 2008, generating complaints of judicial activism and political bias.

A combination of martial law and emergency rule remains in effect in the four southernmost provinces. Military sweeps have involved the indiscriminate detention of thousands of suspected insurgents and sympathizers, and there are credible reports of torture and other human rights violations, including extrajudicial killings, by security forces. To date there have been no successful criminal prosecutions of security personnel for these transgressions. Separatist fighters and armed criminal groups regularly attack government workers, police, teachers, religious figures, and civilians. More than 5,000 people have been killed in the conflict in the past decade.

Thailand's hill tribes are not fully integrated into society and face restrictions on their freedom of movement. Many reportedly lack citizenship, which renders them ineligible to vote, own land, attend state schools, or receive protection under labor laws. Thailand has not ratified UN conventions on refugees, and the authorities have forcibly repatriated Burmese and Laotian refugees.

While women have the same legal rights as men, they remain subject to economic discrimination in practice, and vulnerable to domestic abuse, rape, and sex trafficking. Sex tourism remains a problem. Yingluck Shinawatra is the country's first female prime minister, but she has not made women's rights a priority of her administration.

Togo

Political Rights: 5
Civil Liberties: 4
Status: Partly Free

Population: 5,847,000
Capital: Lomé

Ten-Year Ratings Timeline For Year Under Review (Political Rights, Civil Liberties, Status)

2002	2003	2004	2005	2006	2007	2008	2009	2010	2011
6,5PF	6,5NF	6,5NF	6,5NF	6,5NF	5,5PF	5,5PF	5,4PF	5,4PF	5,4PF

Overview:

President Faure Gnassingbé's government coalition between his Rally of the Togolese People party and a faction of the opposition Union of Forces for Change party continued to hold in 2011. A 2010 ban on political demonstrations continued in 2011 as security forces cracked down on several protests throughout the year. However, the government made some reform efforts, including an audit of government ministries, and a truth and reconciliation commission began hearing testimonies during the year.

Originally part of a German colony that fell under the control of France after World War I, Togo gained its independence in 1960. Gnassingbé Eyadéma, a demobilized sergeant, overthrew the civilian government in a bloodless coup in 1967. Using mock elections and a loyal military, he then presided over close to 40 years of repressive rule.

In 1991, under pressure from European governments, Eyadéma agreed to set up a transitional government and prepare for free elections. However, security forces attacked opposition supporters, forcing thousands to flee abroad, and the transitional government was later dissolved. A series of elections were held during the 1990s, but military harassment and legal manipulation ensured that Eyadéma and his Rally of the Togolese People (RPT) party remained in power. Eyadéma secured a new five-year term in 2003. Gilchrist Olympio, the most prominent opposition politician from the Union of Forces for Change (UFC), was prevented from running through a manufactured technicality.

Eyadéma died in February 2005, and the military quickly installed his son, Faure Gnassingbé, as president. While protests and opposition activity were formally banned, demonstrations remained frequent, and the police response was brutal.

Under international pressure, Gnassingbé held an April 2005 election that confirmed him as president. The poll was marred by over a million phantom voters on the electoral rolls, widespread intimidation, and a complete communications blackout on election day. Subsequent clashes between opposition supporters and security forces killed almost 500 people, injured thousands, and forced 40,000 to flee the country.

In 2006, the promise of renewed economic aid from the European Union (EU)—which had cut off support in 1993—spurred the RPT and opposition parties to schedule legislative elections. In the October 2007 polls, the RPT won 50 of the 81 National Assembly seats, the UFC secured 27 seats, and the Action Committee for Renewal captured the remainder. Polls were deemed to have been transparent and relatively fair, although the lopsided electoral system enabled the RPT to win 62 percent of the seats with just 39 percent of the vote. By the end of 2008, the EU, World Bank, and International Monetary Fund (IMF) had restored economic aid.

The electoral code was reformed in 2009 in preparation for the 2010 elections, lifting the residency requirements that previously barred Olympio from running. Nonetheless, in February Olympio was disqualified again for having missed a mandatory physical, leading the UFC to back Jean-Pierre Fabre instead. The UFC's inability to unite the opposition behind Fabre, the president's refusal to allow a second round in the election, and the RPT's dominance over the state media resulted in Gnassingbé's reelection in March with more than 60 percent of the vote. While the elections were deemed relatively free and fair by observers, a number of irregularities were observed, including vote-buying by the RPT and partisanship within the electoral commission. However, the problems were not considered serious enough to have influenced the outcome of the vote. Fabre immediately contested the results and led a series of weekly protests in Lomé. The Ministry of Security responded by banning demonstrations in Lomé and dispersing Fabre's supporters with tear gas and water cannons.

The UFC splintered in May 2010, following disagreements over how to address the contested election results. Fabre, refusing to accept the results, boycotted parliament, while a faction led by Olympio agreed to enter into a coalition government with the RPT. UFC members were subsequently appointed to high-level cabinet and ministry positions. The RPT-UFC coalition agreement included a Monitoring Committee chaired by Olympio to help resolve interparty disputes and marked the first time the opposition had been included in the government since 1990.

The coalition government held throughout 2011, as Gnassingbé's administration took steps towards reform, including moving forward with the first census in a decade, conducting an audit of government ministries and public service agencies, and exploring the possibility of universal health care. These moves have attracted international donors, including the West African Development Fund, the World Bank and France, to help fund infrastructure improvements and other development projects.

Political Rights and Civil Liberties: Togo is not an electoral democracy. Despite international consensus that the 2007 legislative elections and the 2010 presidential elections were carried out in a relatively free and fair manner, the structure of the electoral system largely ensures that President Faure Gnassingbé will remain in power. The president is elected to five-year terms and appoints the prime minister. Members of the 81-seat, unicameral National Assembly are also elected to five-year terms, using a party-list system that favors the RPT.

Corruption continues to be a serious problem, with nepotism and bribery commonplace. In 2011, the government worked toward improving transparency with a large-scale audit of all ministries and public services to trim government spending. Togo was ranked 143 out of 183 countries surveyed in Transparency International's 2011 Corruption Perceptions Index.

Freedom of the press is guaranteed by law, though it is often disregarded in practice. Impunity for crimes against journalists and frequent defamation suits encourage self-censorship. A 2009 law gives the state broadcasting council, the High Authority of Broadcasting and Communications, the power to impose severe penalties—including the suspension of publications or broadcasts and the confiscation of press cards—if journalists are found to have made "serious errors." This law is frequently used, and in November 2010, the Posts and Telecommunications Regulation Agency (ART&P) suspended the operations of three independent radio stations for not having the right permits. The stations remained shut down throughout 2011, provoking public protests by media workers. In August, a demonstration by press freedom advocates criticizing the country's National Intelligence Agency for threatening and attacking journalists with impunity was dispersed by police using tear gas. Private print and broadcast outlets are limited in capacity and often heavily politicized. Access to the internet is generally unrestricted, but few people use the medium due to high costs.

Constitutionally protected religious freedom is generally respected. Islam and Christianity are recognized as official religions, but other religious groups must register as associations. While political discussion is prohibited on religious radio and television outlets, and government informers are known to watch the streets, ordinary citizens are now able to speak more openly than in previous years.

Government security forces are believed to maintain a presence on university campuses. In 2011, students at the University of Lomé protested government-enacted education reforms. For over eight weeks, students staged sit-ins, refusing to attend classes. In June, police attempts to disperse the student protesters resulted in violent clashes. By August, however, international pressure led the government to hold talks with leaders of the student union and agree to their core demands, including an increase in the number of exams and lectures available to help students transition to a new academic system and finish their studies more quickly, improved facilities in the library and lecture halls, and a new information and communication technology center.

Freedoms of assembly and association were challenged throughout 2011. The Ministry of Security's 2010 temporary ban on demonstrations was extended into 2011, and security forces blocked access to protest locations and used force to disperse a diverse array of demonstrations, including those supporting former presidential candidate Jean-Pierre Fabre, demonstrations advocating for press freedom, and student protests against education reforms and lack of adequate facilities. In March 2011, the Council of Ministers adopted a draft law allegedly aimed at improving the rights of freedom of assembly and demonstration. The new law, which was adopted by the National Assembly in May and heavily criticized by civil society, requires that demonstrations receive prior authorization and only be held during certain times of the day. Togo's constitution guarantees the right to form and join labor unions, and most workers have the right to strike. A number of strikes occurred in 2011, including by the student union, teachers' union, and doctors' union. The government eventually met with each of these striking groups. While the government agreed to the students' demands, the doctors eventually abandoned their strike when the government appointed a new health minister.

The judicial system, including the Constitutional Court, lacks resources and is heavily influenced by the presidency. The high-profile trial of leaders of the alleged 2009 coup attempt concluded in 2011 with the conviction of 33 defendants, including the president's half-brother, Kpatcha Gnassingbé. Kpatcha and others were sentenced to life imprisonment despite a lack of evidence against them and verified accounts of their torture while in detention. Overcrowding is a serious problem in Togolese prisons, and prisoners lack adequate food and access to medical care.

After widespread domestic and international demands for investigations into the political violence that scarred Togo between 1958 and 2005, the Truth, Justice and Reconciliation Commission (TJRC)—including a diverse array of civil society representatives—was finally launched in 2009, but did not begin hearing testimonies until 2011. The TJRC has no punitive power and can only recommend prosecutions and reparations, though none were made in 2011, as the commission focused on holding public hearings and gathering statements from over 20,000 people. Formal hearings for the 523 accepted cases began in August, and the TJRC is expected to release its recommendations by May 2012.

Discrimination is common among the country's 40 ethnic groups, and tensions have historically divided the country between north and south along political, ethnic, and religious lines. The army is traditionally composed of soldiers from the northern Kabyè group, and ethnic minorities are underrepresented in the civil service.

Togolese citizens are typically free to travel overseas and around the country, despite numerous roadblocks set up by vigilante groups or unemployed youths attempting to extort money. Citing security concerns, the government temporarily closed all international borders prior to the 2010 presidential election.

Despite constitutional guarantees of equality, women's opportunities for education and employment are limited. Customary law discriminates against women in divorce and inheritance, giving them the legal rights of minors. Spousal abuse is a widespread problem due to a family code making men the legal head of household, and spousal rape is not a crime. Child trafficking for the purpose of slavery remains a serious problem, and prosecutions under a 2005 child-trafficking law are rare.

Tonga

Political Rights: 3
Civil Liberties: 3
Status: Partly Free

Population: 104,000
Capital: Nuku'alofa

Ten-Year Ratings Timeline For Year Under Review (Political Rights, Civil Liberties, Status)

2002	2003	2004	2005	2006	2007	2008	2009	2010	2011
5,3PF	5,3PF	5,3PF	5,3PF	5,3PF	5,3PF	5,3PF	5,3PF	3,3PF	3,3PF

Overview: **Prime Minister Lord Tu'ivakano named his new cabinet in January 2011; the appointment of two cabinet members who did not hold any elected positions at the time stirred controversy, and a prominent party leader quit his cabinet position in protest. In December, House Speaker Lord Lasike, who was facing a charge of unlawful possession**

of ammunition, violated the conditions of his bail agreement and traveled to the United States; a warrant was issued for his arrest.

Tonga consists of 169 islands that King Siaosi I united under his rule in 1845. It became a constitutional monarchy in 1875 and a British protectorate in 1900, gaining independence in 1970 as a member of the Commonwealth. King Taufa'ahau Tupou IV ruled from 1945 to 2006. His son, Crown Prince Tupouto'a, assumed the title King Siaosi Tupou V in 2006 and was officially crowned in 2008.

Politics and the economy are dominated by the monarchy, hereditary nobles, and a few prominent commoners. Strife between the government and activists promoting democratic reforms resulted in street protests in 2006 that escalated into violent rioting and led to the declaration of a state of emergency. The king eventually entered into talks with the activists, and an agreement was reached in December 2009 providing for the creation of a new 26-member parliament with 17 popularly elected representatives.

Parliamentary elections were held under the new government structure in November 2010. Prodemocracy candidates of the Democratic Party of the Friendly Islands (DPFI) won 12 of the 17 commoners' seats. In December, parliament chose Lord Tu'ivakano over the DPFI's Samuela 'Akilisi Pohiva as the new prime minister.

In January 2011, Tu'ivakano's 12-member cabinet was announced, with 7 members selected by the king and 5 by Tu'ivakano. Two of Tu'ivakano's selections were not members of parliament, including former lawmaker Clive Edwards, who was named head of the public enterprise and revenue portfolio, and a female academic, 'Ana Maui Taufe'ulungaki, with no previous government experience, as head of the education, women's affairs, and culture department. Just one day into his term, Pohiva quit the cabinet to protest the cabinet appointments of these nonelected officials.

On February 3, the prime minister officially lifted a state of emergency that had been in effect since the 2006 protests.

In December, House Speaker Lord Lasike, who was to face a court hearing on one charge of unlawful possession of ammunition, breached his bail agreement and defied a court order by traveling to the United States, where he was married. A warrant for his arrest was issued on December 23, and he had not returned to Tonga by year's end.

The economy is heavily dependent on foreign aid and remittances from Tongans living abroad. The global economic downturn has reduced tourist arrivals, overseas remittances, and returns from government investments. In October, the government imposed steep increases for many compulsory government license and service fees in order to raise revenues. In November, China pledged $8 million in technology and economic assistance to Tonga.

Political Rights and Civil Liberties:

Tonga is an electoral democracy. The unicameral Legislative Assembly has 26 members, including 17 popularly elected representatives and 9 nobles elected by their peers; all members serve four-year terms. The king retains the power to appoint the chief justice, judges of the court of appeal, and the attorney general on the advice of the privy council. The privy council, whose members are appointed by the king, lost its power to pass legislation following changes to the government structure in 2010. Additionally, the Legislative Assembly—rather than the king—now selects the prime minister.

Prodemocracy candidates have typically aligned with the Human Rights and Democracy Movement, which is not a formal party. Several new parties were formed to compete in the 2010 general elections, including the DPFI, the Democratic Labor Party, the Sustainable Nation-Building Party, and the People's Democratic Party.

Corruption is widespread, with royals, nobles, and their top associates allegedly having used state assets for personal benefit, and transparency and accountability are lacking. In 2011, the government conducted its first audit of parliament since 1999. The report, which covered the second half of 2010, found evidence that fraud and mismanagement had resulted in financial losses for 8 of 13 state enterprises. In June 2011, Lord Tu'ilakepa, a noble and lawmaker, was charged with conspiracy to import illicit drugs. He was alleged to have accepted bribes from Colombian drug lords to use Tonga as conduit to bring tons of cocaine to Australia. He already faced multiple charges of illegal possession of a firearm, ammunition, and illicit drugs from 2010. His case was pending at year's end.

The constitution guarantees freedom of the press. Although commentaries critical of the government appear regularly in all newspapers, including those owned by the state or in which the state owns shares, the government has a history of suppressing media criticism. In 2011 cabinet member Clive Edwards filed a civil lawsuit against the newspaper *Kele'a*, claiming that an unfavorable article in the paper had cost him his seat in parliament. In May, the court found Kele'a, its publisher, and its editor guilty of defamation and fined them $8,100 for publishing a false election story. Internet access is not restricted, and the number of users has increased despite high costs and lack of infrastructure.

Freedom of religion is generally respected, but the government requires all religious references on broadcast media to conform to mainstream Christian beliefs. Academics reportedly practice self-censorship to avoid conflicts with the government.

Freedoms of assembly and association are upheld. The 1963 Trade Union Act gives workers the right to form unions and to strike, but regulations for union formation were never promulgated.

The judiciary is generally independent, though a shortage of judges has created serious case backlogs. Traditional village elders frequently adjudicate local disputes. Nobles have increasingly faced scrutiny in society and the courts. Prisons are basic, and are only lightly guarded, as violent crimes are rare. There have been no reports of prisoner abuse.

Women enjoy equal access to education and hold several senior government jobs, though no women were elected in the 2010 elections. Women cannot own land, and domestic violence is common.

Trinidad and Tobago

Political Rights: 2
Civil Liberties: 2
Status: Free

Population: 1,325,000
Capital: Port-of-Spain

Ten-Year Ratings Timeline For Year Under Review (Political Rights, Civil Liberties, Status)

2002	2003	2004	2005	2006	2007	2008	2009	2010	2011
3,3PF	3,3PF	3,3PF	3,2F	2,2F	2,2F	2,2F	2,2F	2,2F	2,2F

Overview: **In August 2011, Prime Minister Kamla Persad-Bissessar declared a state of emergency in response to a spike in violent crime. The measure, which led to nearly 4,000 arrests and significant drug seizures, also raised concerns about violations of fundamental rights in the country.**

Trinidad and Tobago, a member of the Commonwealth, achieved independence from Britain in 1962 and became a republic in 1976.

Patrick Manning of the People's National Movement (PNM) was reelected prime minister in the November 2007 elections; he had held the position since 2001, and was also prime minister from 1991 to 1995. The 2007 elections were considered free and fair. A Caribbean Community observer mission reported that voting was orderly and peaceful, representing a marked reduction in tension compared with previous elections.

In the face of a no-confidence vote, Manning dissolved Parliament in April 2010 and called elections for May. Kamla Persad-Bissessar's People's Partnership (PP) coalition—comprising the United National Congress (UNC), the Congress of the People, and the Tobago Organization of the People—won 29 of 41 seats, while Manning's PNM captured only 12. Persad-Bissessar's campaign was based on pledges to bring transparency and accountability to all areas of government. The PP's victory ended nearly 40 years of rule by the PNM.

Soon after becoming prime minister, Persad-Bissessar in July allowed the first local elections since 2003; they had been postponed four times by the Manning government. The PP dominated in the country's 14 city, borough, and regional corporations.

In August 2011, a state of emergency was imposed to address an increase in violent crime. Related provisions included an 11 p.m. curfew and police authority to conduct searches and seizures without warrants. In September, the state of emergency was extended by three months, with the government citing continued security concerns. By early October, almost 4,000 people had been arrested and about TT$750 million (US$117 million) in drugs had been seized. The state of emergency was criticized by the opposition and civic groups. The Trinidad & Tobago Transparency Institute demanded the names and locations of detainees, and the Law Association of Trinidad and Tobago called on the police to crack down on officers who used excessive force during the state of emergency.

Political Rights and Civil Liberties: Trinidad and Tobago is an electoral democracy. Tobago is a ward of Trinidad. The president is elected to a five-year term by a majority of the combined houses of Parliament, though executive authority rests with the prime minister. Parliament consists of the 41-member House of Representatives, elected to five-year terms, and the 31-member Senate, also serving five-year terms. The president appoints 16 senators on the advice of the prime minister, 6 on the advice of the opposition, and 9 at his or her own discretion.

Political parties are technically multiethnic, though the PNM is favored by Afro-Trinidadians, while the UNC is affiliated with Indo-Trinidadians. The PP coalition was multiethnic.

The country is believed to suffer from high levels of official corruption. Trinidad's Integrity Commission, established in 2000, has the power to investigate the financial and ethical performance of public functionaries. Following the resignations of several commission members in 2009 after their legal eligibility to serve came under scrutiny, a new Integrity Commission was appointed in 2010. Trinidad and Tobago was ranked 91 out of 183 countries surveyed in Transparency International's 2011 Corruption Perceptions Index.

Freedom of speech is constitutionally guaranteed. Press outlets are privately owned and vigorous in their pluralistic views. There are four daily newspapers and several weeklies, as well as both private and public broadcast media outlets. Access to the internet is not restricted.

Freedom of religion is guaranteed under the constitution, and the government honors this provision in practice. Foreign missionaries are free to operate, but the government allows only 35 representatives of each denomination. Academic freedom is generally observed.

Freedoms of association and assembly are respected. Civil society is relatively robust, with a range of interest groups engaged in the political process. Labor unions are well organized and politically active, though union membership has declined in recent years. Strikes are legal and occur frequently.

The judicial branch is independent, though subject to some political pressure and corruption. As a result of rising crime rates, the court system is severely backlogged, with thousands of criminal cases awaiting trial. The government permits human rights monitors to visit prisons, which are severely overcrowded.

The government has struggled in recent years to address the problem of violent crime. Many Trinidadians of East Indian descent, who are disproportionately the targets of abduction, blame the increase in violence and kidnapping on government corruption and police collusion. Most abuses by the authorities go unpunished. In October 2011, Amnesty International released a report criticizing the use of excessive force by police, and noted that such violence was seldom investigated.

Drug-related corruption extends to the business community, and a significant amount of money is believed to be laundered through front companies. The 2000 Proceeds of Crime Act imposes severe penalties for money laundering and requires that major financial transactions be strictly monitored. The government works closely with U.S. law enforcement agencies to track drug shipments in and out of the country. Corruption in the police force, which is often drug related, is endemic, and law enforcement inefficiency results in the dismissal of some criminal cases.

The population is multiethnic, consisting of Afro-Trinidadians, Indo-Trinidadians, and those of mixed race. The Indo-Trinidadian community continues to edge toward numerical, and thus political, advantage. Racial disparities persist, with Indo-Trinidadians making up a disproportionate percentage of the country's upper class.

Women participate in high-level politics, holding 12 seats in the House of Representatives and 8 seats in the Senate. Domestic violence remains a significant concern. The Amnesty International 2011 report on Trinidad and Tobago noted that while violence against women and girls has increased, the conviction rate for sexual offenses was only 3 percent in 2009. A draft National Policy on Gender and Development, first proposed in 2009, has still not been implemented.

Tunisia

Political Rights: 3*
Civil Liberties: 4*
Status: Partly Free

Population: 10,676,000
Capital: Tunis

Status Change: Tunisia's political rights rating improved from 7 to 3, its civil liberties rating improved from 5 to 4, and its status improved from Not Free to Partly Free due to the free and fair elections for the transitional Constituent Assembly held in October; increased freedoms of speech, press, assembly, and religious expression; and greater freedom for academics and nongovernmental organizations, all of which followed the ouster of longtime president Zine el-Abidine Ben Ali in January.

Ten-Year Ratings Timeline For Year Under Review (Political Rights, Civil Liberties, Status)

2002	2003	2004	2005	2006	2007	2008	2009	2010	2011
6,5NF	6,5NF	6,5NF	6,5NF	6,5NF	7,5NF	7,5NF	7,5NF	7,5NF	3,4PF

Overview: **Nationwide antigovernment demonstrations that broke out in late December 2010 escalated in January 2011, leading to the ouster of President Zine el-Abidine Ben Ali on January 14 and the formation of a transitional government. The government was reshuffled several times during the year in the face of continuing protests. Elections held in October for a Constituent Assembly were deemed to be free and fair, and the new body produced a governing coalition of Islamist and secular parties. Hamadi Jebali, an Islamist, was chosen to serve as prime minister, and secular politician Moncef Marzouki was selected as president.**

Tunisia, which had been a French protectorate since 1881, gained its independence in 1956. The country was then ruled for more than 30 years by President Habib Bourguiba, a secular nationalist who favored economic and social modernization along Western lines but severely limited political liberties. Bourguiba succeeded in advancing women's rights and economic development, and his government maintained strong relations with the West and fellow Arab states.

In 1987, Prime Minister Zine el-Abidine Ben Ali ousted Bourguiba and seized the presidency in a bloodless coup. Ben Ali's rise to power had little effect on state policy. He continued to push market-based economic development and women's rights, but he also repressed political opponents. Independent journalists, secular activists, and Islamists faced imprisonment, torture, and harassment. Many Islamists, particularly supporters of the banned movement Ennahda, were jailed following sham trials in the early 1990s.

Ben Ali's hold on government institutions remained strong over subsequent years, and he won a fifth five-year term in the October 2009 presidential election, taking nearly 90 percent of the vote amid tight media and candidacy restrictions.

The government's repressive measures continued through 2010 and included a harsh crackdown on critical journalists and bloggers. In June, the parliament passed a law that criminalized opposition activities deemed to be fomented by "agents of a foreign power." A state media campaign during the year advocated constitutional amendments that would allow Ben Ali to run for a sixth term in 2014.

The strict state controls enforced by the Ben Ali regime, combined with an economic environment marked by high unemployment and few opportunities for young adults, led to nationwide antigovernment protests in December 2010 and January 2011. The uprising was triggered by the self-immolation of a fruit vendor protesting police harassment. As a result of the protests, which led to at least 219 deaths as demonstrators clashed with police, Ben Ali was forced to flee to Saudi Arabia on January 14.

Prime Minister Mohammed Ghannouchi assumed the role of head of state after Ben Ali's departure, but he too was forced from office by the continuing protests. Ben Ali's party, the Democratic Constitutional Rally (RCD), was dissolved by court order in March, all members of the party were forced to resign from the transitional government, and a court decision in June found Ben Ali guilty of theft and sentenced him in absentia to 35 years in prison and a $65 million fine.

Originally scheduled for June, elections for a Constituent Assembly were held in October. The voting was observed by international monitoring groups, and they were widely touted as the first orderly, free, and fair elections in the country's history. There were isolated reports of irregularities, and one case of a campaign finance rules violation, but the transitional authorities made attempts to act quickly on those problems, in some instances invalidating seats that were gained unfairly. Turnout was 52 percent, according to the Tunisian High Authority of the Elections; this is substantially higher than previous Tunisian elections.

Ennahda, the formerly outlawed Islamist party, won a plurality of the vote and 89 of the 217 seats. Two left-leaning parties, the Congress for the Republic (CPR) and Ettakatol, joined Ennahda in a governing coalition after winning 29 and 20 seats, respectively. Other major parties included the Popular Petition for Freedom, Justice, and Development (PP), with 26 seats, and the secularist Progressive Democratic Party (PDP), with 16. Ennahda's Hamadi Jebali became prime minster, Ettakatol's Mustafa Ben Jaafar was chosen as speaker of the assembly, and the CPR's Moncef Marzouki was named to hold the largely ceremonial presidency. The Constituent Assembly was tasked with drafting a new constitution and holding new elections within a year, and would serve as a legislature in the interim.

Political Rights and Civil Liberties: Tunisia is an electoral democracy. The balloting of October 2011 represented a dramatic improvement in electoral freedoms and practices. Under the former regime of Zine el-Abidine Ben Ali, the cabinet, much of the legislature, and many regional officials had been appointed directly by the president. Elections were tightly controlled, and term limits were extended to allow Ben Ali to remain in power.

By contrast, in the 2011 elections, all 217 members of the Constituent Assembly were directly elected through party-list voting in 33 multimember constituencies, and voters were able to choose from political parties representing a wide range of ideologies and political philosophies, including Islamist and secularist groups. Many of the parties that competed were excluded from political participation under Ben Ali.

The removal of Ben Ali and his close relatives and associates, who had used their positions to create private monopolies in several sectors of the economy, represented an important first step in combating corruption and conflicts of interest. An anticorruption commission was established soon after the former president's ouster, the unelected transitional cabinet was far more subject to popular scrutiny than its predecessors, and the government elected in October also seemed inclined to operate with greater transparency. However, a strong legal framework and systematic practices aimed at curbing corruption had yet to take shape at year's end. Tunisia was ranked 73 out of 183 countries surveyed in Transparency International's 2011 Corruption Perceptions Index.

The Ben Ali regime had used an array of legal, penal, and economic measures to silence dissenting voices in the media, and the transitional government almost immediately proclaimed freedom of information and expression as a foundational principle for the country. Conditions improved significantly in practice, but many problems persisted, and it remained uncertain whether legal or institutional frameworks would be established to guarantee media freedoms. The transitional government appointed Slim Amamou, a dissident blogger who was imprisoned by the Ben Ali regime, as secretary of state for youth and sport in January 2011. However, after the government acted on the army's request to censor websites, Amamou resigned in May. While the state television and radio networks made an effort to include opposition voices during the year, the transitional government issued no new radio or television broadcasting permits, and there were reports of police and criminal attacks on journalists. For instance, during continuing protests in Tunis in May and July, police allegedly targeted journalists while attempting to disperse the crowds. Isolated criminal attacks reportedly struck radio stations in the southern town of Gafsa in August. In September, a blogger who had been critical of the transitional government was banned from leaving the country, detained, and questioned without access to a lawyer. Also during the year, however, police protected Nessma TV facilities after Islamist demonstrators threatened to attack the network in retaliation for what they deemed to be offensive programming.

Muslims form the dominant religious group in Tunisia, but the small populations of Jews and Christians have generally been free to practice their faiths. After Ben Ali's ouster, conservative and fundamentalist Muslims had more freedom to express their beliefs without state interference and to openly discuss the role that religion should play in the public sphere.

Authorities limited academic discussion of sensitive topics under the Ben Ali regime, and its removal created a more open environment for students and faculty, but substantial institutional changes were still pending in 2011.

The antigovernment demonstrations that swept the country in early 2011 started in the underdeveloped towns of the interior, after fruit vendor Mohamed Bouazizi burned himself to death to protest police harassment in December 2010. The self-immolation became a symbol for wider political frustration and economic dislocation. The unrest quickly spread to larger coastal cities, and while the police attempted to crack down, the military generally declined to intervene. After the Ben Ali administration collapsed, further demonstrations on various issues took place throughout 2011, as citizens exercised their new ability to engage in open political expression.

Nongovernmental organizations (NGOs) were legally prohibited from pursuing political objectives and activities under the Ben Ali regime. However, new NGOs have begun to form and operate, such as the Tunisian Human Rights League (LTDH). A number of conferences were held by NGOs across the country during 2011, and different groups held protests outside government offices to draw attention to women's rights, the role of religion in the state, and challenges facing nomadic Berber communities. No formal registration process has been instated for these organizations, and their existence is not protected by legal frameworks.

State-sanctioned trade unions supported government policies and electoral candidates during the Ben Ali era, but new unions were established in 2011, including the Union of Tunisian Labor (UTT) and the General Confederation of Tunisian Labor (UCGT). Their future role in politics and the economy remains the subject of debate, even within the left-leaning CPR.

Under Ben Ali, the judicial system was carefully managed by the executive branch, which controlled the appointment and assignment of judges. Trials of suspected Islamists, human rights activists, and journalists were typically condemned as grossly unfair and politically biased by domestic and international observers. Politicized imprisonment and other similar abuses declined significantly in 2011, and the judiciary experienced some changes, reflected partly in the trial of Ben Ali in absentia. However, the court system and law enforcement agencies have been criticized for lagging behind other institutions in their pace of reform, and there is a significant backlog of cases related to abuses by members of the former regime and security forces that have yet to be officially addressed.

After the fall of Ben Ali and the end of restrictions on leaving the country, tens of thousands of Tunisians fled to Europe. With a police force that is significantly more accountable to the people following the Bouazizi suicide, travel within the country has become more liberalized, though this right is not yet protected by legal frameworks.

Tunisia has long been praised for relatively progressive social policies, especially in the areas of family law and women's rights. The country ratified the Optional Protocol to the UN Convention on the Elimination of All Forms of Discrimination against Women (CEDAW) in late 2008, and women in Tunisia have enjoyed more social freedoms and legal rights than in most other countries in the region. The personal status code grants women equal rights in divorce, and children born to Tunisian mothers and foreign fathers are automatically granted citizenship. The country legalized medical abortion in 1973. There are currently 49 women in the Constituent Assembly, representing the largest proportion of female representatives in the Arab world, though only 7 are from a secular party. Human rights groups have called on all of Tunisia's transitional authorities to uphold women's rights and ensure that women and children are protected under the new constitution.

Turkey

Political Rights: 3
Civil Liberties: 3
Status: Partly Free

Population: 73,950,000
Capital: Ankara

Ten-Year Ratings Timeline For Year Under Review (Political Rights, Civil Liberties, Status)

2002	2003	2004	2005	2006	2007	2008	2009	2010	2011
3,4PF	3,4PF	3,3PF	3,3PF	3,3PF	3,3PF	3,3PF	3,3PF	3,3PF	3,3PF

Overview: **The ruling Justice and Development Party (AKP) won a strong majority in June 2011 parliamentary elections, securing another term for Prime Minister Recep Tayyip Erdogan. In July, Turkey's top military commanders resigned en masse following the arrest of dozens of officers suspected of conspiring to stage a coup, giving the civilian government an unprecedented opportunity to assert control over the historically dominant military.**

Turkey emerged as a republic following the breakup of the Ottoman Empire at the end of World War I. Its founder and the author of its guiding principles was Mustafa Kemal, dubbed Atatürk (Father of the Turks), who declared that Turkey would be a secular republic. He sought to radically modernize the country through measures such as the pursuit of European-style education, use of the Latin alphabet instead of Perso-Arabic script for writing Turkish, and the abolition of the Muslim caliphate.

Following Atatürk's death in 1938, Turkey remained neutral for most of World War II, joining the Allies only in February 1945. In 1952, the republic joined NATO to secure protection from the Soviet Union. However, Turkey's domestic politics remained unstable, and the military—which saw itself as a bulwark against both Islamism and Kurdish separatism—forced out civilian governments on four occasions between 1960 and 1997. In the most recent of these incidents, the military forced the resignation of a government led by the Welfare Party, an Islamist group that had won parliamentary elections in 1995.

The governments that followed failed to stabilize the economy, leading to growing discontent among voters. As a result, the Justice and Development Party (AKP) won a sweeping majority in the 2002 elections. The previously unknown party had roots in the Welfare Party, but it sought to distance itself from Islamism. Abdullah Gül initially served as prime minister because the AKP's leader, Recep Tayyip Erdogan, had been banned from politics while serving as Istabul's mayor in 1998, due to a conviction for crimes against secularism; he had read a poem that seemed to incite religious intolerance. Once in power, the AKP majority amended the constitution, allowing Erdogan to replace Gül in 2003.

Erdogan oversaw a series of reforms linked to Turkey's bid to join the European Union (EU). Accession talks officially began in 2005, but difficulties soon arose. Cyprus, an EU member since 2004, objected to Turkey's support for the Turkish Republic of Northern Cyprus, which is not recognized internationally. EU public opinion and some EU leaders expressed opposition to Turkish membership for a variety of other reasons. This caused the reform process to stall, and Turkish popular support for membership declined. The AKP government gradually shifted its foreign policy attention to the Middle East and Central Asia, where it sought to take on a leadership role.

In 2007, President Ahmet Necdet Sezer, a staunch secularist and a perceived check on the AKP-dominated parliament, was due to complete his nonrenewable term in office. Despite objections from the military and the secularist Republican People's Party (CHP), the AKP nominated Gül to replace him. In a posting on its website, the military tacitly threatened to intervene if Gül's nomination were approved, and secularists mounted street demonstrations opposing his candidacy. An opposition boycott invalidated the parliament's presidential vote in April, and Erdogan called early parliamentary elections for July.

The AKP won a landslide victory, increasing its share of the vote to nearly 47 percent, for 341 of 550 seats. The opposition CHP and the new Nationalist Action Party (MHP) also won seats, and a group of 20 candidates from the pro-Kurdish Democratic Society Party (DTP) gained seats for the first time by running as independents, since their party did not reach the legal threshold for formal representation. The MHP decided not to boycott the subsequent presidential vote, and Gül was elected president in August.

In 2008, tensions between the AKP and the secularist opposition erupted into an ongoing investigation centered on an alleged secretive nationalist group called Ergenekon. A total of 194 people were charged in three indictments in 2008 and 2009, including military officers, academics, journalists, and union leaders. A trial against 86 suspects began in October 2008, and a second trial against an additional 56 suspects began in July 2009. Turkish authorities linked Ergenekon to a number of terrorist attacks and conspiracies dating back to the 1990s. The alleged goal of the attacks was to raise the specter of Islamist violence so as to provoke a political intervention by the military. However, critics argued that the AKP was using unsubstantiated charges to suppress its political opponents. More arrests followed in 2010, as military officers were accused of plotting a coup in 2003. In December, approximately 200 active and retired military officers went on trial in that case, known as Sledgehammer.

Meanwhile, in September 2010, the government called a referendum on a new package of constitutional amendments aimed at bringing the charter in line with EU standards and curtailing the exceptional power of the military and judiciary. The reforms expanded the size of the Constitutional Court and the Supreme Board of Judges and Prosecutors, giving the parliament a greater say in their composition, and made all closures of political parties subject to parliamentary approval. The latter change would potentially make it more difficult to disband both Islamist and Kurdish parties. However, the Peace and Democracy Party (BDP), which succeeded the DTP after it was disbanded by the Constitutional Court in late 2009, boycotted the referendum because it did not address the prohibitive 10 percent vote threshold that had thwarted the election of Kurdish parties to date. The proposed amendments ultimately passed with 58 percent of the vote.

Parliamentary elections were held in June 2011, and the AKP won easily with nearly 50 percent of the vote and 326 of 550 seats. The CHP placed second with 135 seats, followed by the MHP with 53 and independents backed by the BDP with 36. Erdogan was confirmed for a new term as prime minister.

Fresh arrests of military officers in the Sledgehammer case in July prompted the resignation of Turkey's military chief of staff and the heads of the army, navy, and air force. The move was apparently designed to undermine the AKP's legitimacy, but in effect it gave the civilian authorities greater control, allowing Erdogan's government to appoint new commanders of its choosing. Arrests in the Ergenekon case also continued during the year, and trials in both cases were ongoing at year's end. Neither investigation had yet produced any convictions.

In October, President Gül announced the formation of a multiparty Constitution Reconciliation Commission tasked with negotiating the framework for a new draft charter. The subsequent process was conducted behind closed doors and was marred by tension between the BDP and AKP over ongoing detentions and trials of the pro-Kurdish party's members. Nonetheless, a working document was scheduled to be released in 2012, ostensibly giving time for civic groups and the public to provide input before any final approval.

Political Rights and Civil Liberties: Turkey is an electoral democracy. The 1982 constitution provides for a 550-seat unicameral parliament, the Grand National Assembly. Constitutional reforms approved in a 2007 referendum reduced members' terms from five to four years. The reforms also provided that the president would be elected by popular vote for a once-renewable, five-year term, replacing the existing system of election by the parliament for a single seven-year term. The new system will take effect in 2014, upon the expiration of the current president's term. The prime minister is head of government, while the president has powers including a legislative veto and the authority to appoint judges and prosecutors. The June 2011 elections were widely judged to have been free and fair, with an 83 percent voter turnout. They also featured the first legally permissible campaigns in Kurdish, the reduction of the minimum age for candidacy from 30 to 25, and upgraded ballot boxes.

A party must win at least 10 percent of the nationwide vote to secure representation in the parliament. Political parties are disbanded with relative frequency for having a program that is not in agreement with constitutional parameters, a condition that could be interpreted broadly and has generally been applied to Islamist and pro-Kurdish parties.

AKP-led reforms have increased civilian oversight of the military, but restrictions persist in areas such as civilian supervision of defense expenditures. A 2009 law restricting the use of military courts brought Turkey closer to EU norms, and 2010 constitutional amendments limited the jurisdiction of military courts to military personnel. These amendments also removed an article that had prevented the prosecution of the leaders of the 1980 military coup.

Turkey struggles with corruption in government and in daily life. The AKP government has adopted some anticorruption measures, but reports by international organizations continue to raise concerns, and graft allegations have been lodged against both AKP and CHP politicians. Prime Minister Recep Tayyip Erdogan has been accused of involvement in a number of scandals involving political and economic cronyism and nepotism. Turkey was ranked 61 out of 183 countries surveyed in Transparency International's 2011 Corruption Perceptions Index.

The right to free expression is guaranteed in the constitution, but legal impediments to press freedom remain. A 2006 antiterrorism law reintroduced jail sentences for journalists, and Article 301 of the penal code allows journalists and others to be imprisoned for discussing subjects such as the division of Cyprus and the 1915 mass killings of Armenians by Turks, which many consider to have been genocide. Defendants have been charged under the same article for crimes such as insulting the armed services and denigrating the Turkish nation; very few have been convicted, but the trials are time-consuming and expensive, encouraging self-censorship. In March 2011, two journalists were arrested for alleged connections to Ergenekon, though critics said they were being persecuted for their political reporting. One of the journalists, Ahmet Sık, had written a book alleging deep ties between Turkish security forces and the Islamic movement of Fethullah Gülen. The other, Nedim Sener, had written a book about police complicity in the 2007 murder of ethnic Armenian journalist Hrant Dink. Sık, Sener, and several other journalists were on trial in the case at year's end. Roughly 100 journalists were behind bars in Turkey at the end of 2011, with most in pretrial detention and charged under antiterrorism laws. About 40 were arrested in December during a series of raids targeting suspected members of the Union of Kurdish Communities (KCK), an alleged affiliate of the Kurdistan Workers' Party (PKK) militant group.

Nearly all media organizations are owned by giant holding companies with interests in other sectors and political parties, contributing to self-censorship. The internet is subject to the same censorship policies that apply to other media, and a 2007 law allows the state to block access to websites deemed to insult Atatürk or whose content includes criminal activities. An internet filtration system was introduced in November 2011, with optional settings designed to protect minors. The system was widely criticized for a lack of transparency and blockage of innocuous sites, such as those of underwear brands. Kurdish-language publications and television broadcasts are now permitted. However, Kurdish newspapers in particular often face closure or website blocking.

The constitution protects freedom of religion, but the state's official secularism has led to considerable restrictions on the Muslim majority and others. Observant men are dismissed from the military, and women are barred from wearing headscarves in public universities and government offices. However, in practice, universities and sometimes individual professors make their own decisions as to whether students can wear headscarves. Three non-Muslim groups—Jews, Orthodox Christians, and Armenian Christians—are officially recognized, and attitudes toward them are generally tolerant, although they are not integrated into the Turkish establishment. Other groups, including non-Sunni Muslims like the Alevis, lack legal status, and Christian minorities have sometimes faced hostility. In the 2011 elections, independent candidate Erol Dora became both the first Christian and the first Assyrian deputy elected to the parliament since the 1960 coup.

Academic freedom is limited by self-censorship and legal or political pressure regarding sensitive topics such as Kurdish rights, the Armenian massacres, and the legacy of Atatürk. Scholars linked to the Kurdish issue by academic interest, political solidarity, or humanitarian concern were subject to increased intimidation and in some cases detention during 2011. Most notable were the arrests of publisher Ragıp Zarakolu and political science professor Bürsa Ersanlı, who were detained in October along with 70 other BDP members for alleged associations with the KCK.

Freedoms of association and assembly are protected in the constitution. Prior restrictions on public demonstrations have been relaxed, but violent clashes with police still occur. While a 2004 law on associations has improved the freedom of civil society groups, legislation passed in 2005 allows the state to restrict groups that might oppose its interests. Members of local human rights groups have received death threats and sometimes face prosecution. Nevertheless, civil society is active on the Turkish political scene.

Laws to protect labor unions are in place, but union activity remains limited in practice. Under the 2010 constitutional amendments, workers are entitled to enroll in more than one trade union in a single sector, and state employees for the first time were granted the right to collective bargaining. Regulations for the recognition of legal strikes are onerous, and penalties for participating in illegal strikes are severe.

The constitution establishes an independent judiciary. In practice the government can influence judges through appointments, promotions, and financing, though much of the court system is still controlled by strict secularists who oppose the AKP government. A 2009 scandal revealed official wiretapping of judges, which reflected mutual distrust between the AKP executive branch and the judiciary. The court system in general is undermined by procedural delays, with some trials lasting so long as to become a financial burden for the defense.

The current government has enacted laws and introduced training to prevent torture, but reports of mistreatment remain common. In the first half of 2010, the Turkish Human Rights Presidency, which is part of the prime minister's office, received 3,461 complaints, mostly related to health and patient rights, the right to fair trial, and torture. Prison conditions can be harsh, with overcrowding and practices such as extended isolation in some facilities.

The state claims that all Turkish citizens are treated equally, but because recognized minorities are limited to the three defined by religion, other minorities, Kurds in particular, have faced legal restrictions on language, culture, and freedom of expression. The situation has improved with EU-related reforms. However, the AKP's 2009 initiative to improve Kurdish rights faltered in the face of political opposition and divisive events like the Constitutional Court's dissolution of the DTP. The government has since stepped up nationalist rhetoric and cracked down on alleged PKK collaborators. According to the BDP, by the end of 2011, roughly 4,000 people had been arrested in an anti-KCK campaign that began in 2009. About 1,000 BDP officials and members were detained in raids on party offices during 2011. The PKK, meanwhile, has continued to engage in violent attacks. In February 2011, the group ended a unilateral ceasefire it had declared ahead of the September 2010 referendum, and armed clashes during the year killed hundreds of soldiers, police, militants, and civilians.

Gay and transgender people in Turkey are subject to widespread discrimination, police harassment, and in some cases violence. Nongovernmental organizations focused on these communities often face the threat of closure by the authorities. Advocates for the disabled have noted the lack of implementation of a law designed to reduce discrimination. Amnesty International in 2009 criticized Turkey's asylum policy, which does not recognize non-Europeans as refugees.

Property rights are generally respected in Turkey, with the exception of the southeast, where tens of thousands of Kurds as well as thousands of Assyrians were driven from their homes during the 1990s. Increasing numbers have returned under a 2004 program, and some families have received financial compensation, but progress has been slow. Local paramilitary "village guards" have been criticized for obstructing the return of displaced families through intimidation and violence.

The amended constitution grants women full equality before the law, but the World Economic Forum ranked Turkey 122 out of 135 countries surveyed in its 2011 Global Gender Gap Index. Only about a third of working-age women participate in the labor force. Women hold just 78 seats in the 550-seat parliament, though that represents an increase from 48 after the 2007 elections. Domestic abuse is reportedly common, and so-called honor crimes continue to occur. Suicide among women has been linked to familial pressure, as stricter laws have made honor killings less permissible. Penal code revisions in 2004 included increased penalties for crimes against women and the elimination of sentence reductions in cases of honor killing and rape. In 2009 the government introduced a policy whereby police officers responding to calls for help regarding domestic abuse would be held legally responsible should any subsequent abuse occur.

Turkmenistan

Political Rights: 7
Civil Liberties: 7
Status: Not Free

Population: 5,105,000
Capital: Ashgabat

Ten-Year Ratings Timeline For Year Under Review (Political Rights, Civil Liberties, Status)

2002	2003	2004	2004	2006	2007	2008	2009	2010	2011
7,7NF	7,7NF	7,7NF	7,7NF	7,7NF	7,7NF	7,7NF	7,7NF	7,7NF	7,7NF

Overview: **All the candidates who registered in 2011 for Turkmenistan's February 2012 presidential election were members of the ruling party, and the tightly controlled process was widely expected to result in a new term for President Gurbanguly Berdymukhammedov. Also during the year, the authorities sought to silence independent reports of massive explosions at an arms depot in July, and they took greater repressive measures against human rights activists inside and outside the country.**

Turkmenistan gained formal independence from the Soviet Union in 1991. Saparmurat Niyazov, the former head of the Turkmenistan Communist Party, had been the sole candidate in elections to the newly created post of president in October 1990. He won reelection in 1992 with a reported 99.5 percent of the vote. A 1994 referendum extended his term until 2002. In the December 1994 elections to the Mejlis (National Assembly), only Niyazov's Democratic Party of Turkmenistan (DPT), the former Communist Party, was permitted to field candidates.

In the 1999 Mejlis elections, every candidate was selected by the government and virtually all were members of the DPT. The Organization for Security and Cooperation in Europe (OSCE), citing numerous procedural inadequacies, refused to send even a limited assessment mission. The Mejlis unanimously voted in late December to make Niyazov president for life.

In 2002, Niyazov survived an alleged assassination attempt in Ashgabat. The incident sparked a crackdown on the opposition and perceived critics of the regime, drawing condemnation from foreign governments and international organizations. Mejlis elections in 2004 followed the established pattern of executive control.

Niyazov's rule was marked by frequent government reshuffles, the gutting of formal institutions, the muzzling of media, and an elaborate personality cult. The *Ruhnama*, a rambling collection of quasi-historical and philosophical writings attributed to Niyazov, became the core of educational curriculums. The limited available information about the true state of affairs in Turkmenistan pointed to crises in health care, education, and agriculture.

Niyazov's death in December 2006 from an apparent heart attack was followed by the rapid and seemingly well-orchestrated ascent of Deputy Prime Minister Gurbanguly Berdymukhammedov to the position of acting president. The succession appeared to circumvent constitutional norms, as criminal charges were brought against Mejlis speaker Ovezgeldy Atayev, who would have become acting president according to the constitution. Berdymukhammedov subsequently cemented his formal status, easily besting five obscure ruling-party candidates in a February 2007 presidential election that was not monitored by any international observers.

Berdymukhammedov gradually removed high-ranking Niyazov loyalists and took steps to replace Niyazov as the subject of the state's cult of personality. In August 2008, the Halk Maslahaty (People's Council), the country's supreme representative body, voted without public debate to approve a new constitution, effectively dissolving itself and dispersing its powers to the Mejlis and the president. Elections for an expanded Mejlis were held in December 2008, but as with previous votes, all of the nearly 300 candidates were preapproved by the presidential administration.

In June 2011, the authorities announced that the next presidential election would be held in February 2012, and that the polls would include opposition parties and adhere to international norms. However, no steps were taken to fulfill those pledges, and all seven challengers facing the incumbent at the end of 2011 were minor figures associated with the ruling party.

Under Berdymukhammedov, Turkmenistan's foreign policy has become less isolationist, though it remains focused on natural gas exports. China became Turkmenistan's leading export market following the completion of a pipeline that is slated to reach full capacity in 2012.

Political Rights and Civil Liberties: Turkmenistan is not an electoral democracy. The late president Saparmurat Niyazov wielded almost absolute power until his death. None of the country's elections—including the February 2007 vote that gave Niyazov's successor, Gurbanguly Berdymukhammedov, a five-year term in office—have been free or fair. Berdymukhammedov has maintained all the means and patterns of repression established by Niyazov.

Under a new constitution approved in 2008, the Mejlis (National Assembly) became the sole legislative body and expanded from 50 to 125 seats, with members serving five-year terms. The new charter also gave citizens the right to form political parties, though only one party, the ruling DPT, is officially registered. Berdymukhammedov made several references to the possibility of forming new political parties in 2010 and 2011, but no actual changes had taken place by the end of 2011. Local elections held in July 2009 and December 2010 mimicked the country's previous stage-managed polls amid reports of low voter turnout.

Corruption is widespread, with public officials often forced to bribe their way into their positions. Allocation of state profits from gas exports remains opaque. According to a 2011 report by Crude Accountability, only 20 percent of revenues from the sale of hydrocarbons are transferred to the state budget. An August 2011 law expanded even further the president's near-total control over the hydrocarbon sector and the revenue it produces. Turkmenistan was ranked 177 out of 183 countries surveyed in Transparency International's 2011 Corruption Perceptions Index. The government's lack of transparency affects a variety of public services, including medical care. An April 2010 report by Doctors Without Borders found that Turkmen authorities were concealing, "a dangerous public health situation, in which government officials actively deny the prevalence of infectious disease, medical data is systemically manipulated, and international standards and protocols are rarely applied in practice."

Freedom of the press is severely restricted by the government, which controls all broadcast and print media. Internet access has expanded somewhat since Niyazov's death, though the sole service provider, run by the government, reportedly blocks undesirable websites. The authorities remained hostile to news reporting in 2011, and sought to suppress any independent sources of information. In July, explosions at a weapons warehouse in Abadan were portrayed as a minor accident in official news reports, whereas the Vienna-based Turkmenistan Initiative for Human Rights (TIHR), a group composed of exiles from Turkmenistan with extensive sources in the country, reported 1,382 deaths stemming from the explosions and provided eyewitness reports and mobile-telephone videos from the city to support its account of the disaster. The TIHR website became the target of denial-of-service attacks, and police scoured Abadan in search of the group's sources. In late 2010, TIHR director Farid Tukhbatullin had been the subject of death threats in Vienna after appearing on the London-based satellite television station K+, which could be viewed in Turkmenistan.

The government restricts freedom of religion, and independent groups face persecution. Practicing an unregistered religion remains illegal, with violators subject to fines. Islamic cleric Shiri Geldimuradov reportedly died in prison under unclear circumstances in 2010.

The government places significant restrictions on academic freedom. The *Ruh-*

nama is still used in the school system and remained part of university entrance exams in 2011. Since 2009, students bound for university study abroad have routinely been denied exit visas.

The constitution guarantees freedoms of peaceful assembly and association, but these rights are severely restricted in practice. Sporadic protests, usually focused on social issues, have taken place. A 2003 law on nongovernmental organizations (NGOs) deprived all such groups of their registration; the handful that were subsequently reregistered are tightly controlled. Turkmenistan is still home to a few dedicated activists, but there is virtually no organized civil society sector.

The government-controlled Colleagues Union is the only central trade union permitted. There are no legal guarantees protecting workers' rights to form unions and strike, though the constitution does not specifically prohibit such activities. Strikes in Turkmenistan are extremely rare.

The judicial system is subservient to the president, who appoints and removes judges without legislative review. The authorities frequently deny rights of due process, including public trials and access to defense attorneys.

Prisons suffer from overcrowding and inadequate nutrition and medical care, and international organizations are not permitted to visit. The government has released some two dozen political prisoners since Niyazov's death, but many others remain behind bars. Nothing is known about the condition of jailed former foreign ministers Boris Shikhmuradov and Batyr Berdyev. Rights activists Annakurban Amanklychev and Sapardurdy Khajiev, convicted on dubious espionage charges in 2006, remained in prison in 2011. The UN Working Group on Arbitrary Detention stated in 2010 that their continued detention violated international law. Unanswered questions still surround the 2006 death in custody of Radio Free Europe/Radio Liberty correspondent Ogulsapar Muradova. A June 2011 report by the UN Committee Against Torture expressed deep concern "over the numerous and consistent allegations about the widespread practice of torture and ill-treatment of detainees."

Employment and educational opportunities for ethnic minorities are limited by the government's promotion of Turkmen national identity.

Freedom of movement is restricted, with a reported blacklist preventing some individuals from leaving the country. A few activists who hold dual citizenship and continue to reside in Turkmenistan are able to travel abroad using their Russian passports, but even this window is closing, as activists, including Natalia Shabunts were denied new Turkmen passports in 2011 in a bid to make them choose either Russian or Turkmen citizenship.

A Soviet-style command economy and widespread corruption diminish equality of opportunity. The new constitution establishes the right to private property, but the deeply flawed judiciary provides little protection to businesses and individuals. Arbitrary evictions and confiscation of property are common practices.

Traditional social and religious norms, inadequate education, and poor economic conditions limit professional opportunities for women, and NGO reports suggest that domestic violence is common.

Tuvalu

Political Rights: 1
Civil Liberties: 1
Status: Free

Population: 11,200
Capital: Funafuti

Ten-Year Ratings Timeline For Year Under Review (Political Rights, Civil Liberties, Status)

2002	2003	2004	2005	2006	2007	2008	2009	2010	2011
1,1F	1,1F	1,1F	1,1F	1,1F	1,1F	1,1F	1,1F	1,1F	1,1F

Overview: **In January 2011, the government implemented a brief ban on public gatherings of three or more people following public protests against a lawmaker for his failure to meet with community leaders. In September, the government declared a two-week state of emergency to impose strict control on the use of fresh water to alleviate the effects of a severe rain shortage.**

The Gilbert and Ellice Islands, situated in the central South Pacific Ocean, became a British protectorate in 1892 and a British colony in 1916. Polynesian Ellice Islanders voted to separate themselves from the Micronesian Gilbertese in 1974. In 1978, the Ellice Islands became independent under the name of Tuvalu, while the Gilbert Islands become part of Kiribati.

Politics in Tuvalu have been marked by intense personal and political rivalries and the use of no-confidence votes to unseat incumbents. In the September 2010 elections, 26 candidates—all independents—competed for 15 seats in Parliament. The elections were considered free and fair, with no reported incidents of fraud or violence. In December 2010, Prime Minister Maatia Toafa was ousted in a no-confidence vote and was replaced by Home Affairs Minister Willy Telavi.

In January 2011, amid public protests over Finance Minister Lotoala Metia's refusal to meet with community leaders—a breach of traditional protocol—Telavi banned public meetings involving more than 10 people; the government said that rumors of threats to burn down lawmakers' residences had made the ban necessary. The emergency order was revoked after four weeks, with the provision that public meetings could be held only with permission from the police commissioner.

Global climate change and rising sea levels pose significant challenges for Tuvalu and other low-lying island states. Tuvalu's highest point is just five meters above sea level. Meanwhile, the weather pattern known as La Niña resulted in far less rainfall than usual in 2011, causing a severe freshwater shortage for Tuvalu. In September, the government declared a two-week state of emergency when about 50 percent of the population had only a two-day supply of freshwater; water usage was strictly monitored and rationed in some areas. New Zealand and the United States sent desalination equipment, which turns saltwater into freshwater, to help alleviate the shortage.

Political Rights and Civil Liberties: Tuvalu is an electoral democracy. Britain's Queen Elizabeth II is the head of state and is represented by a governor general, who must be a citizen of Tuvalu. The prime minister, chosen by Parliament, leads the government. The unicameral, 15-member Parliament is elected to four-year terms. A six-person council administers each of the country's nine atolls. Council members are chosen by universal suffrage for four-year terms.

There are no formal political parties, though there are no laws against their formation. Political allegiances revolve around geography, tribal loyalties, and personalities, with elected representatives frequently changing sides and building new alliances.

Tuvalu is one of the few places in the Pacific Islands where corruption is not a serious problem, though international donors have called for improvements in governance.

The constitution provides for freedoms of speech and the press, and the government generally respects these rights in practice. The semi-public Tuvalu Media Corporation (TMC) operates the country's sole radio and television stations, as well as the biweekly newspaper *Tuvalu Echoes* and the government newsletter *Sikuelo o Tuvalu*. Human rights groups have criticized the TMC for its limited coverage of politics and human rights issues, but there have been no allegations of censorship or imbalances in reporting. Many residents use satellite dishes to access foreign programming. Internet use is largely limited to the capital because of cost and connectivity challenges, but authorities do not restrict access.

Religious freedom is upheld in this overwhelmingly Christian country, where religion is a major part of life. Academic freedom is generally respected.

The constitution provides for freedoms of association and assembly, and the government upholds these rights in practice. However, on January 13, 2011, the government for the first time invoked the Public Order Act for two weeks to ban public gatherings of three or more people on the main island of Funafuti. The decision was made after hundreds of protestors demanded the immediate resignation of Finance Minister Lotoala Metia for refusing to meet with traditional elders. The government cited a rumored arson threat against Metia as the reason for the ban. Two weeks later, the ban was replaced by a regulation requiring organizers of protests to obtain prior permission from police; this requirement was lifted after two weeks. Nongovernmental organizations (NGOs) provide a variety of health, education, and other services. A 2007 law allowing the incorporation of NGOs strengthened legal protection for civil society groups. Workers have the right to strike, organize unions, and choose their own representatives for collective bargaining. Public sector employees, numbering fewer than 1,000, are members of professional associations that do not have union status. With two-thirds of the population engaged in subsistence farming and fishing, Tuvalu has only one registered trade union—the Tuvalu Overseas Seamen's Union—with about 600 members who work on foreign merchant vessels. Remittances from these and other Tuvaluans working overseas are a major source of income for the country.

The judiciary is independent and provides fair trials. Tuvalu has a two-tier judicial system. The higher courts include the Privy Council in London, the Court of Appeal, and the High Court. The lower courts consist of senior and resident magistrates, the island courts, and the land courts. The chief justice, who is also the chief justice of Tonga, visits Tuvalu twice a year to preside over the High Court. A civilian-controlled constabulary force maintains internal order. There are no reports of abuse in the prison system.

About 10 percent of Tuvalu's annual budget is derived from the Tuvalu Trust Fund, a well-run overseas investment fund set up by Britain, Australia, and South Korea in 1987 to provide development assistance.

Traditional customs and social norms condone discrimination against women and limit their role in society. Women enjoy equal access to education, but they remain underrepresented in positions of leadership in business and government. There are currently no women in Parliament. There have been few reports of violence against women. Rape is illegal, but spousal rape is not included in the definition. No law specifically addresses sexual harassment.

↓ Uganda

Political Rights: 5
Civil Liberties: 4
Status: Partly Free

Population: 34,543,000
Capital: Kampala

Trend Arrow: Uganda received a downward trend arrow due to the poor conduct of the February national elections, the government's violent response to protests over corruption and inflation, and a crackdown on journalists.

Ten-Year Ratings Timeline For Year Under Review (Political Rights, Civil Liberties, Status)

2002	2003	2004	2005	2006	2007	2008	2009	2010	2011
6,4PF	5,4PF	5,4PF	5,4PF	5,4PF	5,4PF	5,4PF	5,4PF	5,4PF	5,4PF

Overview: **In February 2011, after a quarter-century in power, President Yoweri Museveni won reelection in polls that were marred by administrative defects and massive government spending in favor of incumbents. In April, protests over corruption and deteriorating economic conditions were violently suppressed by the government, causing at least 10 deaths. Attempts to resume the demonstrations in October were also crushed by the authorities. The government showed a growing intolerance for dissent during the year, and critical journalists faced harassment.**

Following independence from Britain in 1962, Uganda experienced considerable political instability. President Milton Obote, an increasingly authoritarian leader, was overthrown by Major General Idi Amin in 1971. Amin's brutality made world headlines as hundreds of thousands of people were killed. His 1978 invasion of Tanzania led to his ouster by Tanzanian forces and Ugandan exiles. After Obote returned to power in 1980 through fraudulent elections, opponents, primarily from southern Ugandan ethnic groups, were savagely repressed.

Obote was overthrown again in a 1985 military coup, and in 1986 the rebel National Resistance Army, led by Yoweri Museveni, took power. Museveni introduced a "no party" system, under which only one supposedly nonpartisan political organization—the National Resistance Movement (NRM)—was allowed to operate unfettered. This system lasted for two decades.

Museveni and the NRM won presidential and legislative elections in 2001, though a ban on most formal party activities restricted the opposition, which decided to boycott the legislative polls.

In 2005, voters approved constitutional amendments that lifted the ban on political parties and abolished presidential term limits. A leading Museveni opponent, Kizza Besigye of the Forum for Democratic Change (FDC), returned from exile to contest the 2006 presidential election. However, he was arrested on charges including treason and rape, and was defeated at the polls by Museveni, who took 59 percent of the vote. The NRM won a large majority in concurrent parliamentary elections.

Growing tensions between the government and the Buganda region concerning land reform legislation erupted into violence in September 2009, when at least 40 people were killed in rioting in Kampala, and hundreds were arrested, after police stopped Ronald Muwenda Mutebi II, monarch of the Baganda ethnic group, from attending a rally. In March 2010, a suspicious fire destroyed much of the Kasubi Tombs, the burial ground of the Baganda monarchs and a UNESCO World Heritage Site. Security forces fired into crowds that gathered following the fire, killing three and injuring five others. A government commission of inquiry produced a report in 2011, but it had yet to be made public by the end of the year.

Separately, in July 2010, the Somalia-based Islamist militia group known as the Shabaab bombed two venues in Uganda where crowds had gathered to watch the final 2010 World Cup soccer match, killing some 76 people and injuring 70 others. The Shabaab opposes Uganda's contribution of peacekeeping troops to the African Union mission in Somalia.

Museveni won the February 2011 presidential election with 68 percent of vote. Besigye, whom the Constitutiona Court had cleared of treason, terrorism, murder, and firearms charges in October 2010, placed second with 26 percent. In the concurrent parliamentary elections, the ruling NRM took 263 of 375 elected seats, followed by the FDC with 34, and smaller parties or independents with the remainder. International observers noted that the elections had been peaceful but marred by widespread administrative failings that led to mass disenfranchisement. Turnout, at 59 percent, was about eight points lower than in 2006 elections. Museveni and his party exploited the advantages of incumbency; observers criticized the passage of a special $256 million supplementary budget shortly before the election, with much of the funds going to the president's office.

Although Besigye's calls for protests after the elections were not immediately successful, he went on to lead a "walk to work" campaign of marches against corruption and the rising cost of living, prompting police violence in April and May that killed at least 10 people. Hundreds of others were arrested, and Besigye's eyes were injured after police sprayed his face with a chemical agent.

The government maintained its intolerance for opposition for the rest of the year. In September, Vincent Nzaramba, the author of a book advocating peaceful protest to overthrow Museveni, was detained for several days and said he was physically abused in custody. Attempts to renew the April–May protests in October led to 40 arrests and treason charges—which can carry the death penalty—for three of the organizers. The charges were pending at year's end.

Separately in October, the United States dispatched 100 military advisers to Uganda to assist regional efforts to eliminate the Lord's Resistance Army (LRA), a cult-like rebel group established in 1988 and led by Joseph Kony that is accused of killing, raping, and abducting tens of thousands of people. Although the LRA continued to operate in neighboring countries, it has not staged attacks in Uganda itself since 2005.

Political Rights and Civil Liberties: Uganda is not an electoral democracy. The February 2011 elections were undermined by flawed administration, extensive media bias, and government spending on behalf of incumbents. The introduction of a multiparty system in 2005 has not yet delivered democracy, because the playing field remains tilted heavily in the ruling party's favor.

The single-chamber National Assembly and the powerful president, who faces no term limits, are elected for five-year terms. Of the legislature's 386 members, 238 are directly elected, and 137 are indirectly elected from special interest groups including women, the military, youth, the disabled, and trade unions. Eleven ex-officio seats are held by cabinet ministers, who are not elected members and do not have voting rights.

The National Assembly has asserted some independence, censuring high-level executive officials and exercising oversight to influence a number of government actions and policies. However, significant concerns remain over the ability of opposition parties to compete with the ruling NRM. The opposition is hindered by restrictive party registration requirements, voter and candidate eligibility rules, the use of government resources to support NRM candidates, a lack of access to media coverage, and paramilitary groups—such as the Kiboko Squad and the Black Mambas—that intimidate voters and government opponents. Army representatives in the National Assembly have openly campaigned for President Yoweri Museveni. Despite questions over the independence of the electoral commission, Museveni renewed the panel and its chairman for a second seven-year term in 2009.

Although Uganda has a variety of laws and institutions tasked with combating corruption, enforcement is weak in practice. In 2010, foreign donors announced a 10 percent cut in budget support for the next fiscal year, citing concerns over the country's failure to address high-level corruption. Uganda has recently discovered large oil reserves, which could create new opportunities for graft. In October 2011, three ministers resigned pending an investigation into multimillion-dollar bribes allegedly paid by the British firm Tullow Oil, and the parliament voted to suspend all new oil deals until a new law for the sector is passed, marking a setback for the executive branch. Uganda was ranked 143 out of 183 countries surveyed in Transparency International's 2011 Corruption Perceptions Index.

The constitution provides for freedom of speech, and the media sector has flourished in the last decade, with over 250 radio stations, 50 television stations, and about 50 print outlets now in operation. Independent journalists are often critical of the government, but in recent years, they have faced substantial, escalating government restrictions and intimidation, which encourage self-censorship. In November 2011, Amnesty International reported that up to 30 journalists faced criminal charges for their reporting, including two radio journalists—Patrick Otim, detained since 2009, and Augustine Okello, detained in July 2011—who are charged with treason, which carries the death penalty. During the February elections, the government exploited the state-run media to marginalize the opposition, and one editor at the state broadcasting corporation was fired for attempting to offer more even-handed coverage. Independent journalists reported being pressured to keep opposition candidates off the air. Journalists were also threatened and beaten by police during the April–May protests.

The authorities have begun to restrict internet usage. During the 2011 "walk to work" protests, the Ugandan Communications Commission ordered internet service providers to temporarily block the social media sites Facebook and Twitter to "prevent the sharing of information that incites the public," though the services generally remained accessible.

There is no state religion, and freedom of worship is constitutionally protected and respected in practice. Various Christian sects and the country's Muslim minority practice their creeds freely. Academic freedom is also generally respected.

Freedoms of association and assembly are officially recognized but often restricted in practice, as illustrated by the police violence and criminal charges against protesters during 2011. Nongovernmental organizations (NGOs) are willing to address politically sensitive issues. However, their existence and activities are vulnerable to legal restrictions, including the manipulation of onerous registration requirements under the 2006 NGO Registration Amendment Act. Kenyan human rights activist Al-Amin Kimathi, who had traveled to Uganda to provide legal aid to Kenyan suspects in the July 2010 terrorist bombings, was arrested in September of that year and charged with complicity in the attacks. Under international pressure, the government dropped the charges against him in September 2011.

Workers' rights to organize, bargain collectively, and strike are recognized by law, except for those providing essential government services, but legal protections often go unenforced. Many private firms refuse to recognize unions, and strikers are sometimes arrested.

Executive influence undermines judicial independence. Prolonged pretrial detention, inadequate resources, and poor judicial administration impede the fair exercise of justice. The country has also faced criticism over the military's repeated interference with court processes. Rape, vigilante justice, and torture and abuse of suspects and detainees by security forces remain problems. The Joint Anti-Terrorism Task Force has committed many of the worst rights abuses. The prison system is reportedly operating at nearly three times its intended capacity, with pretrial detainees constituting more than half of the prison population.

Although the constitution enshrines the principle of gender equality, discrimination against women remains pronounced, particularly in rural areas. Women hold nearly 35 percent of the National Assembly seats, and one-third of local council seats are reserved for women. The law gives women the right to inherit land, but discriminatory customs often trump legal provisions in practice. Cultural practices such as female genital mutilation persist. Sexual abuse of minors is a significant problem. Ritual sacrifice of abducted children has reportedly increased in recent years, with wealthier individuals paying for the killings to secure good fortune. The charity Jubilee Campaign claimed in 2011 that about 900 cases of child sacrifice had gone uninvestigated by police. Uganda continues to be a source and destination country for men, women, and children trafficked for the purposes of forced labor and prostitution.

Ugandan society and government remain exceptionally homophobic. In October 2010, a local paper published the names, photographs, and some addresses of gay Ugandans, including the activist David Kato, who was subsequently murdered in January 2011. His killer pleaded guilty and was sentenced to 30 years in prison in November. Since 2009, international controversy has surrounded an Anti-Homosexuality Bill that would make some sex acts capital crimes; it had yet to pass at the end of 2011.

Ukraine

Political Rights: 4*
Civil Liberties: 3
Status: Partly Free

Population: 45,700,000
Capital: Kyiv

Ratings Change: Ukraine's political rights rating declined from 3 to 4 due to the authorities' efforts to crush the opposition, including the politicized use of the courts, a crackdown on media, and the use of force to break up demonstrations.

Ten-Year Ratings Timeline For Year Under Review (Political Rights, Civil Liberties, Status)

2002	2003	2004	2005	2006	2007	2008	2009	2010	2011
4,4PF	4,4PF	4,3PF	3,2F	3,2F	3,2F	3,2F	3,2F	3,3PF	4,3PF

Overview: **During 2011, President Viktor Yanukovych's administration systematically sought to eliminate opposition to the ruling Party of the Regions. Former prime minister Yuliya Tymoshenko, Yanukovych's main political opponent, was convicted of abuse of power in October and jailed. In addition, the authorities increased restrictions on peaceful assembly, media outlets, opposition organizations, and private businesses. A number of political prisoners remained behind bars, and there were increased reports of police torture and the use of psychiatry for political repression. The government revised the electoral law to improve its chances in the 2012 parliamentary elections, while rampant corruption gave incumbents a strong incentive to retain power and avoid possible prosecution by their successors.**

In December 1991, Ukraine's voters approved independence from the Soviet Union in a referendum and elected Leonid Kravchuk as president. Leonid Kuchma defeated Kravchuk in the 1994 presidential poll, and won reelection in 1999 amid media manipulation, intimidation, and the abuse of state resources. Kuchma faced growing criticism for high-level corruption and the erosion of political rights and civil liberties. Evidence implicating him in the 2000 murder of independent journalist

Heorhiy Gongadze fueled mass demonstrations and calls for the president's ouster, but propresidential factions retained a majority in 2002 parliamentary elections.

In the significantly tainted first round of the October 2004 presidential election, reformist former prime minister Viktor Yushchenko led a field of 24 candidates, followed by Prime Minister Viktor Yanukovych, a representative of the eastern, Russian-speaking Donbas region who enjoyed backing from Russian president Vladimir Putin. In the November runoff, the official results showed Yanukovych to be the winner by less than three percentage points, but voting irregularities in Yanukovych's home region led the domestic opposition and international monitors to declare his apparent victory "not legitimate."

In what became known as the Orange Revolution because of Yushchenko's ubiquitous campaign color, millions of people massed peacefully in Kyiv and other cities to protest fraud in the second-round vote. The Supreme Court on December 4 struck down the results and ordered a rerun on December 26. In the middle of the crisis, the parliament ratified constitutional reforms that shifted crucial powers from the president to the parliament, effective January 1, 2006. Although technically adopted in an unconstitutional manner, the compromise changes effectively lowered the stakes of the upcoming rerun, making it more palatable to Yushchenko's opponents. However, they also created an unclear division of power, which later led to constant conflict between the president and prime minister.

The repeat of the second round was held in a new political and social atmosphere. The growing independence of the media, the parliament, the judiciary, and local governments allowed for a fair and properly monitored ballot. Yushchenko won easily, and his chief ally, former deputy prime minister Yuliya Tymoshenko, became prime minister. However, their alliance quickly broke down, leading to a multilateral stalemate that prevented implementation of comprehensive political and economic reform. The unproductive wrangling continued during a short-lived Yanukovych premiership (2006–2007) and another stint as prime minister for Tymoshenko (2007–2010) after parliamentary elections in September 2007, seriously eroding public support for the Orange Revolution.

In the 2010 presidential election, which met most international standards, Yanukovych defeated Tymoshenko in the second round of voting in February, 49 percent to 46 percent. He quickly reversed many of the changes adopted in the wake of the Orange Revolution, securing Constitutional Court rulings that enabled him to oust Tymoshenko as prime minister and replace her with a loyalist and annul the 2004 constitutional compromise that had reduced the power of the presidency. In October 2010, Ukraine held local elections that were widely viewed as less free and fair than elections held under Yushchenko.

In 2011, Yanukovych launched a systematic campaign to eliminate any viable opposition to the ruling Party of the Regions ahead of parliamentary elections set for 2012. Most importantly, prosecutors brought a series of varying charges against Tymoshenko, Yanukovych's strongest opponent, in a bid to secure a criminal conviction. In October, a Kyiv court finally convicted her of abusing her office as prime minister by signing an allegedly unfavorable gas deal with Russia without seeking cabinet approval. She was sentenced to seven years in prison, banned from public office for an additional three years, and levied a fine of about $190 million. Most observers did not consider her acceptance of Russia's demands in the gas deal a crime. The Security Service of Ukraine (SBU) leveled two more charges against her after the conviction, and on December 30, she was moved to the Kachanivska Penal Colony in Kharkiv, where her lawyer claims she is denied proper medical care.

Attempts to mount street protests against Tymoshenko's prosecution and other government actions were met with brutal crackdowns and arrests by police, whose ranks were increased during the year. Other political prisoners who were placed or remained behind bars in 2011 included 9 leaders of protests against the administration's tax policies, 14 or more nationalists involved in beheading a Joseph Stalin monument, and numerous former members of the Tymoshenko government. The highest-ranking Tymoshenko ally in custody, former interior minister Yuriy Lutsenko, was on trial at year's end for abuse of office and misappropriation of funds—charges that were widely seen as politically motivated.

Political Rights and Civil Liberties: Ukraine is an electoral democracy at the national level, with the opposition winning in the four most recent presidential and parliamentary elections. However, the October 2010 local elections showed serious flaws under newly elected president Viktor Yanukovych's leadership.

Citizens elect delegates to the Verkhovna Rada (Supreme Council), the 450-seat unicameral parliament, for four-year terms. The 2004 constitutional amendments, which were annulled in 2010, had extended this term to five years. Under the ruling Party of the Regions, the parliament has largely become a rubber-stamp body. According to a new electoral law adopted on December 8, Ukraine returned to a system in which half the members of parliament are elected by proportional representation and half in single-member districts; blocs of parties are not allowed to participate. The Party of the Regions supported the new law because it believes that it will improve its prospects in the 2012 parliamentary elections. Meanwhile, some members of the opposition favored the new legislation because they maintain that it contains new anti-fraud features and will help stimulate the consolidation of opposition parties.

The president is elected to a maximum of two five-year terms. With the return to the 1996 constitution in October 2010, the president now dominates the political system. He issues decrees; exercises power over the courts, the military, and law enforcement agencies; appoints the prime minister with the Rada's approval and removes the prime minister at will; appoints and fires all other ministers without the Rada's approval; and appoints regional governors without consulting the prime minister. The Rada can dismiss the entire cabinet, but not individual ministers.

Political parties are typically little more than vehicles for their leaders and financial backers, and they generally lack coherent ideologies or policy platforms. Yanukovych is systematically eliminating opposition to his party, either through repression (as with Yuliya Tymoshenko's Fatherland party) or cooptation (as with Deputy Prime Minister Serhiy Tyhypko's Strong Ukraine party).

Corruption, one of the country's most serious problems, continues to worsen. Business magnates are presumed to benefit financially from their close association with top politicians. Yanukovych himself has become de facto owner of a huge estate outside of Kyiv, raising suspicions of illicit wealth, while his two sons have amassed both power and personal fortunes. The apparent corruption of his administration, and the precedent set by its politicized pursuit of charges against Tymoshenko and former members of her government, have increased Yanukovych's incentives to remain in power indefinitely.

The constitution guarantees freedoms of speech and expression, and libel is not a criminal offense. Business magnates with varying political interests own and influence many outlets, while local governments often control the local media. Conditions for the media have worsened since Yanukovych's election, and the president threatened one reporter at a December press conference who asked about his family's growing wealth while many in the country face financial hardships. Some 69 percent of Ukrainians get their news from television, and the medium now features fewer alternative points of view, open discussions, and expert opinions. In April 2011, government pressure led the owner of the *Kyiv Post* to fire its editor, but the decision was reversed after the staff walked off the job and the international community expressed outrage. Three opposition channels in Kharkiv that were co-owned by Fatherland member Arsen Avakov were taken off the air in September. Journalists who investigate wrongdoing at the local level face physical intimidation, and local police and prosecutors do not energetically pursue such cases. Vasyl Klymentyev, a journalist who investigated local corruption in Kharkiv, disappeared in August 2010 and is presumed dead. In July 2011, unknown assailants barricaded the door and set fire to the apartment of the chief editor of the Donetsk regional website *News of Donbass*, Oleksiy Matsuka, but he was not home at the time; the site frequently criticizes corruption among the local elite. Former Interior Ministry official Oleksiy Pukach is currently on trial for the 2000 murder of independent journalist Heorhiy Gongadze. In March 2011, prosecutors formally charged former president Leonid Kuchma with taking actions that led to the killing, but the case was dismissed in December, after the main evidence was ruled inadmissible.

Internet access is not restricted and is generally affordable; lack of foreign-language skills is the main barrier. While the Access to Public Information Act passed in January 2011, it did little to improve the overall environment.

The constitution and the 1991 Law on Freedom of Conscience and Religion define religious rights in Ukraine, and these are generally well respected. However, among other problems, Yanukovych publicly associates himself with one of the country's competing branches of the Orthodox Church, and there have been some signs of anti-Semitism in political campaigns in recent years.

Academic freedom has come under pressure since Yanukovych took power. Education Minister Dmytro Tabachnyk has curtailed many programs designed to promote Ukrainian language and culture, and in 2010 he began a process aimed at bringing Ukrainian textbooks into line with those in Russia. Ministry budget cuts have focused heavily on schools with liberal reputations and universities in western Ukraine, while universities in the Donetsk region have gained more funding.

The constitution guarantees the right to peaceful assembly but requires organizers to give the authorities advance notice of any demonstrations. Yanukovych's government has made it more difficult to assemble, and in 2011 there was a significant increase in the number of court rulings prohibiting peaceful assembly. The administration is also collecting extensive information on all protest organizers, including details about their professional activities, in order to exert pressure on them.

Although the vibrancy of Ukraine's civil society has declined since the height of the Orange Revolution, social, political, cultural, and economic movements of different sizes and with various agendas remain active. Despite an increasing number of hooligan gangs that intimidate and destroy the property of anyone who supports the opposition, civic activism seems to be on the rise. Intellectuals, students, and Ukrainian speakers are mobilizing against Tabachnyk's policies; the women's organization Femen has drawn attention to corruption and social injustice; entrepreneurs are rallying against economic stagnation and the government's tax policies; veterans have protested cuts to their benefits; journalists have protested crackdowns on the media; a new leftist movement is emerging in Kyiv; and teachers have protested budget cuts. Nevertheless, the Ukrainian Helsinki Human Rights Union has expressed concern that civil society is not active enough in opposing the repressive actions by the government. Trade unions function, but strikes and worker protests are infrequent. Factory owners are still able to pressure their workers to vote according to the owners' preferences.

The judiciary is subject to intense political pressure, as the Tymoshenko case demonstrated in 2011. Under the previous administration, the judiciary was an important arbiter in political battles between the president and prime minister, and all political factions attempted to manipulate courts, judges, and legal procedures. The Constitutional Court had largely remained silent in the face of politicians' attempts to grab power. Under Yanukovych, however, the Constitutional Court has sided with the president, allowing him to form a parliamentary majority and overturn the 2004 constitutional amendments in 2010. Three Constitutional Court judges who were critical of Yanukovych resigned in September of that year, clearing the way for more supportive replacements ahead of the ruling on the 2004 amendments. Also during 2010, the parliament adopted a new law giving the Supreme Council of Justice the right to appoint and dismiss judges from their positions, in violation of the constitution. The council is now used as a tool of blackmail and pressure against judges, according to Valentyna Telychenko, the lawyer representing Gongadze's wife in the trial of his alleged killers. Supreme Court chairman Vasyl Onopenko, a longtime ally of Tymoshenko, survived a no-confidence vote in March 2011, but his term expired on September 29. He decided not to run for a second term after the Pechersk District Court dropped criminal charges against his son-in-law, though he publicly denies a connection. On December 23, Petro Pylypchuk was elected head of the Supreme Court; he is expected to be more supportive of Yanukovych.

Reports of police torture grew during 2011. The number of raids by tax police and the security service against opposition-aligned businesses also increased. Since 2010, Ukrainian authorities have misused psychiatry to intimidate civil society activists.

While the country's Romany population suffers from discrimination, the government has actively interceded to protect the rights of most ethnic and religious minorities, including the Crimean Tatar community. Tatars continue to suffer discrimination at the hands of local authorities and communities in Crimea in terms of land ownership, access to employment, and educational opportunities. Members of the gay and lesbian community also report discrimination.

Gender discrimination is prohibited under the constitution, but women's rights have not been a priority for government officials. The current cabinet does not include any women, making it the first of 14 Ukrainian governments to be exclusively male. Human rights groups have complained that employers openly discriminate on the basis of gender, physical appearance, and age. The trafficking of women abroad for the purpose of prostitution remains a major problem.

United Arab Emirates

Political Rights: 6
Civil Liberties: 6*
Status: Not Free

Population: 7,891,000
Capital: Abu Dhabi

Ratings Change: The United Arab Emirates' civil liberties rating declined from 5 to 6 due to the government's arrest of proreform political activists, its disbanding of the prominent professional advisory boards of certain nongovernmental organizations, and its decision to strip citizenship from notable Islamist leaders.

Ten-Year Ratings Timeline For Year Under Review (Political Rights, Civil Liberties, Status)

2002	2003	2004	2005	2006	2007	2008	2009	2010	2011
6,5NF	6,6NF	6,6NF	6,6NF	6,5NF	6,5NF	6,5NF	6,5NF	6,5NF	6,6NF

Overview: **The United Arab Emirates continued to crack down on advocates of political change throughout 2011. After more than 100 intellectuals and activists submitted a petition to the country's rulers calling for reforms, five prominent democracy activists were arrested and convicted of insulting the country's leadership, though they were pardoned by the president in November. Meanwhile, the government replaced the elected boards of two civil society organizations with appointed councils.**

Attacks on shipping off the coast of what is now the United Arab Emirates (UAE) led the British to mount military expeditions against the local tribal rulers in the early 19th century. A series of treaties followed, including a long-term maritime truce in 1853 and an 1892 pact giving Britain control over foreign policy. The seven sheikhdoms of the area subsequently became known as the Trucial States. In 1971, Britain announced that it was ending its treaty relationships in the region, and six of the seven Trucial States formed the UAE federation. Ras al-Khaimah, the seventh state, joined in 1972. The provisional constitution left significant power in the hands of each emirate.

After the 2001 terrorist attacks on the United States, the government strengthened antiterrorism legislation, including introducing reforms in the financial services and banking sectors to block the financing of terrorism.

In 2006, Sheikh Mohammed bin Rashid al-Maktoum succeeded his late brother as ruler of the emirate of Dubai and prime minister of the UAE. The first-ever elections for 20 of the 40-seat, largely advisory Federal National Council were held that year, with participation limited to a small electoral college appointed by the emirates' seven rulers. The UAE government appointed the remaining 20 members in February 2007.

In May 2009, UAE police detained Sheikh Issa bin Zayed al-Nahyan, brother of the current UAE president, after he was videotaped torturing an Afghani merchant in 2008. In 2010, all charges against al-Nahyan were dropped after a court ruled that he had been drugged and therefore had committed the crime unknowingly. The court awarded the Afghani victim approximately $2,700 in compensation.

While the UAE did not experience the kinds of demonstrations that characterized the Arab Spring elsewhere, in March and April 2011, activists began calling for greater political rights and a move toward a more democratic political system. Authorities responded by arresting the most outspoken proreform voices. In March, the UAE, along with Saudi Arabia, provided support for the military force that helped crush Bahrain's pro-democracy movement. In December, authorities cited security concerns in their decision to revoke the citizenship of six men, including the scholar Mohammed Abdel-Razzaq al-Siddiq. Those targeted were affiliated with the Islamic Reform and Social Guidance Association. While the UAE claimed they had links to extremists, critics charged that their punishment was more likely the result of their having been outspoken in calling for political reform; the six men had signed a petition earlier in the year in favor of legislative reform and free elections.

In contrast to many of its neighbors, the UAE has achieved some success in diversifying its economy to reduce dependency on the petroleum sector. The country has built a leading free-trade zone in Dubai and a major manufacturing center in Sharjah, and it has invested resources to expand its tourism industry.

Political Rights and Civil Liberties: The UAE is not an electoral democracy. All decisions about political leadership rest with the dynastic rulers of the seven emirates, who form the Federal Supreme Council, the highest executive and legislative body in the country. The seven leaders select a president and vice president, and the president appoints a prime minister and cabinet. The emirate of Abu Dhabi, the major oil producer in the UAE, has controlled the federation's presidency since its inception.

The UAE has a 40-member Federal National Council (FNC), half of which was elected for the first time in 2006 by a 6,689-member electoral college chosen by the seven rulers. The other half of the council is directly appointed by the government for two-year terms. The council serves only as an advisory body, reviewing proposed laws and questioning federal government ministers. In September 2011, the UAE held elections to the FNC after having expanded the electoral college to 129,000-members; however, only 36,000 voters participated.

There are no political parties in the country; the allocation of positions in the government is determined largely by tribal loyalties and economic power. Citizens have limited opportunities to express their interests through traditional consultative sessions.

The UAE is considered one of the least corrupt countries in the Middle East. It was ranked 28 out of 183 countries surveyed in Transparency International's 2011 Corruption Perceptions Index.

Although the UAE's constitution provides for some freedom of expression, the government has historically restricted this right in practice. The 1980 Printing and Publishing Law applies to all media and prohibits "defamatory material and negative material about presidents, friendly countries, [and] religious issues, and [prohibits] pornography." Consequently, journalists commonly practice self-censorship, and the leading media outlets frequently publish government statements without criticism or comment. However, Dubai has a "Media Free Zone," where print and broadcast media is produced for audiences outside of the UAE with relatively few restrictions. Throughout 2011, the government continued to consider a restrictive press law that would replace prison sentences with fines of up to $136,000 for articles deemed harmful to UAE's economy and up to $1.35 million for those considered "insulting" to the ruling family or government. The draft law would also force journalists to reveal their sources. The law had not been adopted by year's end. Government officials ban a variety of publications and internet websites. In April 2011, the government banned most small businesses and individuals from using secure and encrypted e-mail and internet settings on their mobile phones, allowing authorities to access most private correspondence.

The constitution provides for freedom of religion. Islam is the official religion, and the majority of citizens are Sunni Muslims. The minority Shiite Muslim sect and non-Muslims are free to worship without interference. The government controls content in nearly all Sunni mosques. Academic freedom is limited, with the Ministry of Education censoring textbooks and curriculums in both public and private schools.

The government places restrictions on freedoms of assembly and association. Public meetings require government permits. Nongovernmental organizations (NGOs) must register with the Ministry of Labor and Social Affairs, and registered NGOs reportedly receive subsidies from the government. After members of two prominent teachers' and lawyers' associations publicly pledged support for democratic reform in the UAE, authorities in April 2011 dissolved their elected boards of directors and replaced them with proregime sympathizers. In March 2011, over 130 intellectuals and activists signed a petition calling for political reforms, including the expansion of legislative powers for the FNC. Five of the country's most outspoken reform advocates—Nasser bin Gaith, Ahmed Mansoor, Fahad Salim Dalk, Hassan Ali Al-Khamis, and Ahmed Abdul Khaleq—were subsequently arrested and convicted of insulting the country's leaders, though they were pardoned by the president in November.

The UAE's mostly foreign workers do not have the right to organize, bargain collectively, or strike. Workers occasionally protest against unpaid wages and poor working and living conditions, to which the government reportedly responds with military force.

The judiciary is not independent, with court rulings subject to review by the political leadership. The legal system is divided into Sharia (Islamic law) courts, which address family and criminal matters, and secular courts, which cover civil law. Sharia courts sometimes impose flogging sentences for drug use, prostitution, and adultery. While the federal Interior Ministry oversees police forces in the country, each emirate's force enjoys considerable autonomy. Violence within the nonindigenous community has led to arbitrary arrests and detention. Prisons in the larger emirates are overcrowded.

Discrimination against noncitizens and foreign workers, who comprise more than 80 percent of the UAE's population, is common. Foreign workers are often subjected to harsh working conditions, physical abuse, and the withholding of passports. Stateless residents, known as bidoon, are unable to secure regular employment and face systemic discrimination. While the Interior Ministry has established methods for the bidoon to apply for citizenship, the government uses unclear criteria in approving or rejecting requests for citizenship.

The constitution does not address gender equality. Muslim women are forbidden to marry non-Muslims and are eligible for only half of their brother's inheritance. Women are underrepresented in government, though they have received appointments at various levels in recent years. In 2008 two new women were added to the cabinet, and Abu Dhabi swore in the country's first woman judge after the judicial law was amended to allow women to serve as prosecutors and judges. Despite a 2006 antitrafficking law and the opening of two shelters for female victims, the government has failed to adequately address human trafficking. In 2010, Anti-Slavery International posted images of alleged child jockeys used in the popular sport of camel racing, a practice that was officially banned in 2005.

United Kingdom

Political Rights: 1
Civil Liberties: 1
Status: Free

Population: 62,736,000
Capital: London

Ten-Year Ratings Timeline For Year Under Review (Political Rights, Civil Liberties, Status)

2002	2003	2004	2005	2006	2007	2008	2009	2010	2011
1,1F	1,1F	1,1F	1,1F	1,1F	1,1F	1,1F	1,1F	1,1F	1,1F

Overview: **In 2011 widespread telephone hacking by *News of the World* journalists was uncovered, leading the paper's owner, U.S.-based News Corporation, to close it in July. The ensuing investigations also revealed that police had failed to properly investigate earlier reports of hacking, and that officers had received money from *News of the World* reporters. Separately, voters rejected altering the electoral system in a national referendum held in May, and in July, London and other cities were rocked by youth riots, which the police struggled to contain.**

The English state emerged before the turn of the first millennium and was conquered by Norman French invaders in 1066. Wales, Scotland, and lastly Ireland were subdued or incorporated into the kingdom over the course of centuries, culminating in the creation of the United Kingdom of Great Britain and Ireland in 1801. The Glorious Revolution of 1688–89 began a gradual—but eventually total—assertion of the powers of Parliament vis-à-vis the monarchy, as Britain became one of the modern world's first democracies. A significant extension of voting rights was passed in 1832, and subsequent reforms led to universal adult suffrage.

Most of Ireland won independence after World War I, with Protestant-majority counties in the north remaining a restive part of what became, as of 1927, the United Kingdom of Great Britain and Northern Ireland. Significant powers were devolved to a Scottish Parliament, and fewer to a Welsh Assembly, in 1997. Peace negotiations tentatively restored home rule to Northern Ireland in 1998.

The Labour Party won the 1997 general elections, ending nearly two decades of Conservative Party rule. Prime Minister Tony Blair led Labour to another major victory in 2001, though he faced opposition within the party for his support of the U.S.-led war in Iraq beginning in 2003. A combination of slow progress in improving public services and the continuation of the Iraq war led to a far less decisive Labour victory in May 2005 elections.

On July 7, 2005, coordinated suicide bombings in London killed over 50 people and wounded hundreds more. The four culprits were British Muslims. The attacks set off a public debate about the integration of immigrants and racial and religious minorities into British society. They also led to wide-ranging government proposals to tighten antiterrorism laws, which in turn sparked concerns about civil liberties.

In previous decades, Britain's main source of internal violence had been the struggle between unionists and Irish nationalists in Northern Ireland. This largely ended with the 1998 peace agreement. However, the Northern Ireland Assembly established by the agreement was suspended in 2002 after Sinn Fein—the political party linked to the Irish Republican Army (IRA), an outlawed Irish nationalist militant group—was caught spying on rival politicians and security officials. Further peace talks and the formal disarmament of the IRA paved the way for fresh elections to the assembly in March 2007 and the formation of a power-sharing local government between Sinn Fein and the Democratic Unionist Party (DUP).

In June 2007, Blair resigned, and Chancellor of the Exchequer Gordon Brown took office as prime minister. Brown acted decisively to counter the international financial crisis in late 2008 and early 2009 by shoring up ailing banks with public money, and his approach was for a time hailed abroad as a model response. Nevertheless, in the June 2009 European Parliament elections, Labour was outperformed by both the Conservatives and the UK Independence Party (UKIP), which strongly opposes British membership in the European Union. Voters also handed the far-right, xenophobic British National Party (BNP) its first two seats.

Parliamentary elections were called for May 2010, and the opposition Conservatives led the field with 306 seats. Labour placed second with 258, the Liberal Democrats took 57, and smaller parties divided the remainder. Conservative leader David Cameron, lacking a majority, formed a rare coalition government with the Liberal Democrats.

The new government faced a daunting economic situation, including a ballooning budget deficit. In October, Prime Minister Cameron announced a severe program of tax increases and spending cuts, prompting large public protests. The austerity measures came into full swing in 2011, and economic growth barely remained in positive territory.

In March 2011, referendum voters in Wales endorsed a reform that increased the autonomy of the Welsh Assembly, giving it authority to make laws in 20 subject areas without consulting Parliament.

In a national referendum in May, proposed by the Liberal Democrats and carried out as part of the coalition agreement, voters considered a new "instant runoff" electoral system under which they would rank parliamentary candidates by preference, and a candidate would have to receive more than 50 percent of the first-choice votes to win outright. Some 40 percent of eligible voters turned out for the plebiscite, and two-thirds rejected the new method in favor of the existing first-past-the-post system. Elections were held the same day for the legislatures of Northern Ireland and Scotland. Sinn Fein and the DUP consolidated their control in Northern Ireland, and the ruling Scottish National Party (SNP) made major gains in Scotland.

In July, the weekly tabloid *News of the World* was closed by its owner—media mogul Rupert Murdoch's News Corporation—amid mounting allegations that its reporters had hacked into the telephone messages of hundreds of public figures and crime victims over the past several years. Related investigations, including those by other media outlets, exposed corrupt links between reporters and police, who had failed to adequately pursue previous reports of hacking or alert possible victims, and allegedly sold favors and information to *News of the World* journalists in some cases.

Shortly after the paper was closed, News Corporation withdrew its bid to acquire the British satellite broadcaster BSkyB, in which it already held a minority stake. The deal had raised concerns about the growth of News Corporation's perceived power within Britain's media and political establishments. Highlighting those concerns, Andy Coulson, Cameron's communications director until January, was arrested in July for his alleged role in the phone hacking while serving as a *News of the World* editor prior to 2007. Responding to public criticism, the prime minister launched a series of official inquiries into the hacking scandal. One probe found in November that other papers had engaged in hacking, and that the number of hacking requests by *News of the World* staff was larger than originally thought. The inquiries and parallel criminal cases were ongoing at year's end.

Separately, on August 4, the fatal police shooting of a 29-year-old suspect in London led to four nights of rioting in the capital and a number of other cities. The police appeared unprepared to deal with the outbreak, and failed to stop looting and other criminality in many instances. The riots sparked new discussions in Parliament over changes to policing in the country, as well as debates about economic inequality and the social integration of the children of immigrants.

Political Rights and Civil Liberties:

The United Kingdom is an electoral democracy. Each of the members of the House of Commons, the dominant lower chamber of the bicameral Parliament, is elected in a single-member district. Parliamentary elections must be held at least every five years. Executive power rests with the prime minister and cabinet, who must have the support of the Commons.

The House of Lords, Parliament's upper chamber, can delay legislation initiated in the Commons. If it defeats a measure passed by the Commons, the Commons must reconsider, but it can ultimately overrule the Lords. The Lords membership, currently about 800, consists mostly of "life peers" nominated by successive governments. There are also 92 hereditary peers (nobles) and some two dozen bishops and archbishops of the Church of England. The monarch, Queen Elizabeth II, plays a largely ceremonial role as head of state.

In addition to the Labour and Conservative parties and the left-leaning Liberal Democrats, other parties include the Welsh nationalist Plaid Cymru and the SNP. In Northern Ireland, the main Catholic and republican parties are Sinn Fein and the Social Democratic and Labour Party, while the leading Protestant and unionist parties are the Ulster Unionist Party and the DUP. Parties that have never won seats in Parliament, such as the UKIP and BNP, fare better in races for the European Parliament, which feature proportional representation voting.

Corruption is not pervasive in Britain, but high-profile scandals have damaged the reputation of the political class under both Labour and Conservative governments. In January 2011, a former Labour member of Parliament, David Chaytor, received an 18-month prison sentence for lying about mortgage payments on property he owned outright. In May, Lord Taylor of Warwick, a Conservative, was sentenced to 12 months in prison for lying about travel and property expenses. After a series of delays, a 2010 antibribery law, which has been called one of the most sweeping in the world, was implemented in July. Following accusations that London police officials had received bribes from *News of the World* reporters, the commissioner and assistant commissioner of the Metropolitan Police both resigned in July. Britain was ranked 16 out of 183 countries surveyed in Transparency International's 2011 Corruption Perceptions Index.

The law provides for press freedom, and the media are lively and competitive. Daily newspapers span the political spectrum, though the economic downturn and rising internet use have driven some smaller papers out of business. The state-owned British Broadcasting Corporation is editorially independent and faces significant private competition. England's libel laws are among the most claimant-friendly in the world, leading wealthy foreign litigants—known as libel tourists—to use them to silence critics; a suit is possible as long as the allegedly libelous material was accessed in Britain, and the burden of proof falls on the defendant. In some cases, this practice has led to self-censorship. A bill that would significantly overhaul the country's libel laws was unveiled in March 2011, but it was still under discussion at year's end. On rare occasions, the courts impose so-called superinjunctions, which forbid the media from reporting certain information or even the existence of the injunction itself. The government has faced criticism for rampant delays in fulfilling freedom of information requests, and in January 2011, it introduced plans for a Public Data Corporation to make public information more accessible. Internet access has not been restricted by the government, though the amount of information that internet firms must store on user activities, including visits to foreign websites, was increased in 2009.

Although the Church of England and the Church of Scotland have official status, freedom of religion is protected in law and practice. Nevertheless, minority groups, particularly Muslims, report discrimination, harassment, and occasional assaults. A 2006 law banned incitement to religious hatred, with a maximum penalty of seven years in prison. Academic freedom is respected by British authorities.

Freedoms of assembly and association are respected, though the authorities' use of "kettling," in which protesters are surrounded and tightly confined, has recently been criticized for discouraging peaceful demonstrations. Civic and nongovernmental organizations are allowed to operate freely. Workers have the right to organize trade unions, which have traditionally played a central role in the Labour Party.

A new Supreme Court began functioning in 2009, replacing an appellate body within the House of Lords. The police maintain high professional standards, and prisons generally adhere to international guidelines. However, the government came under criticism from UNICEF in October 2011 for potentially breaching the UN Convention on the Rights of the Child by jailing a large number of minors with no prior criminal records following the August riots.

Britain's antiterrorism laws are some of the strongest in the democratic world, and are frequently criticized by rights groups. In January 2011, the government proposed reforms that would reduce its existing powers to detain terrorism suspects for 28 days without charge and impose "control orders"—which include monitoring and restrictions on freedom of movement—on others, also without formal charges. However, critics said the changes were largely superficial, and the issue remained a matter of debate throughout the year.

The government has been accused of "outsourcing" torture—particularly during the years after 2001 terrorist attacks on the United States—by extraditing terrorism suspects to their home countries, where they could be abused in custody. In 2010, the Cameron government agreed to investigate these allegations, but human rights organizations in 2011 criticized the terms of the inquiry as "secretive, unfair, and deeply flawed," as the government said evidence would not be requested from foreign governments and victims would not have the opportunity to question British intelligence officials. In July, victims' lawyers and human rights groups announced that they would boycott the inquiry.

Violence in Northern Ireland has been rare in recent years, and the last provisions of a 2009 law delegating responsibility for policing and criminal justice to the government of Northern Ireland came into effect in 2010. However, a Catholic recruit for the Police Service of Northern Ireland (PSNI) was killed in a car bomb attack outside his home in April 2011; members of an IRA splinter group claimed responsibility. Other Catholics who have joined the PSNI have faced threats from republican militants. In June, fighting broke out in Belfast between police and extremists on both sides. The riots spread across the territory and lasted several nights.

Britain has large numbers of immigrants and locally born descendants of immigrants, who receive equal treatment under the law. In practice, their living standards are lower than the national average, and they complain of having come under increased suspicion amid the terrorist attacks and plots of recent years. In October 2011, Cameron called on the public to report suspected illegal immigrants to the authorities.

A 2010 equality act consolidated previous antidiscrimination laws and covers categories including age, disability, race, religion, sex, and sexual orientation. Since 2005, same-sex couples have been able to form civil partnerships with the same rights as married couples.

While women receive equal treatment under the law, they remain underrepresented in top positions in politics and business. Women won 143 seats in the House of Commons in the 2010 elections. Abortion is legal in Great Britain but heavily restricted in Northern Ireland, where it is allowed only to protect the life or the long-term health of the mother.

United States of America

Political Rights: 1
Civil Liberties: 1
Status: Free

Population: 311,695,000
Capital: Washington, D.C.

Note: The numerical ratings and status listed above do not reflect conditions in Puerto Rico, which is examined in a separate report.

Ten-Year Ratings Timeline For Year Under Review (Political Rights, Civil Liberties, Status)

2002	2003	2004	2005	2006	2007	2008	2009	2010	2011
1,1F	1,1F	1,1F	1,1F	1,1F	1,1F	1,1F	1,1F	1,1F	1,1F

Overview: **President Barack Obama encountered stiff resistance to his legislative agenda from congressional Republicans during 2011. The result was legislative gridlock, with little or no progress on a series of measures designed to reduce the federal budget deficit. Meanwhile, civil libertarians and others grew increasingly critical of the administration's use of remotely piloted aircraft overseas to kill suspected terrorists, including American citizens. In the fall, police sometimes employed aggressive tactics in response to a protest movement fueled by growing economic inequality.**

The United States declared independence in 1776, during a rebellion against British colonial rule. The current system of government began functioning in 1789, following ratification of the country's constitution. Because the founders of the United States distrusted concentrated government authority, they set up a system in which the federal government has three coequal branches—executive, legislative, and judicial—and left many powers with state governments and the citizenry.

For most of the country's history, power has alternated between the Democratic and Republican parties. In 2008, then senator Barack Obama, a Democrat, became the first black American to win a presidential election, taking 53 percent of the popular vote. Senator John McCain, the Republican nominee, took 46 percent. In concurrent legislative elections, the Democrats increased their majorities in both the House of Representatives and the Senate.

Obama entered the White House with an ambitious domestic agenda dictated in part by fears of economic collapse in the wake of the financial crisis of 2008. During his first 18 months in office, he pushed through measures to stimulate the economy, revive the automobile industry, and, after a lengthy and bitter struggle, overhaul the nation's health-care system. In response, Republicans accused the president of improperly expanding the involvement of the federal government in economic affairs, and of implementing policies that irresponsibly increased an already large budget deficit.

In the November 2010 congressional elections, Republicans recaptured control of the House of Representatives, taking 242 seats, and narrowed the Democratic majority in the Senate, securing a new total of 47 seats. This left the Democrats with 193 House seats and 51 seats in the Senate. There were also two independent senators who voted with the Democratic caucus. Many of the successful Republican candidates aligned themselves with the Tea Party movement, a loose grouping of citizen and lobbying organizations that demanded reductions in the federal budget, a much smaller role for government in domestic affairs, and tax cuts.

The Republican electoral gains acted as a check on Obama's domestic agenda. Indeed, the following year was notable for what most observers described as legislative gridlock. Several efforts to forge compromises aimed at reducing the budget deficit ended in failure, leading to a pattern of crises and grudging, temporary solutions. One rating agency downgraded the credit rating for U.S. bonds after a particularly damaging budget standoff in August.

The administration stepped up the use of remotely piloted drone aircraft to attack alleged terrorist leaders in countries including Pakistan and Yemen, reportedly killing U.S. citizens in at least two cases. The campaign drew criticism from U.S. civil liberties organizations, as did various other aspects of the government's counterterrorism efforts. While Obama had made a number of changes to the counterterrorism policies of his predecessor, George W. Bush, including an explicit ban on the use of torture by U.S. personnel, he declined to roll back other Bush-era practices, such as the collection of Americans' voice and internet communications by the National Security Agency. The administration also blocked information requests in several security-related court cases; made no effort to amend the USA PATRIOT Act, aspects of which have been criticized by civil libertarians; continued to rely on the use of indefinite detention of terrorism suspects; and, in the face of political and popular resistance, abandoned efforts to close down the military detention facility in Guantanamo Bay, Cuba. Obama also drew criticism from press freedom and other groups for the aggressive prosecution of leaks of classified information, which in some cases led to pressure on journalists to reveal the identity of confidential sources.

The United States has avoided the hard-edged debates over Muslim immigrants that have afflicted a number of European societies, but a series of controversies over the assimilation of Muslims have occurred since the 2001 terrorist attacks. During 2011, the media revealed the New York Police Department's monitoring of mosques, Muslim student organizations, and other institutions of the Muslim community throughout the Northeast. While relations between black and Hispanic Americans and local police departments have improved over the years, civil rights organizations criticized police in various cities in 2011 for "stop-and-frisk" tactics that disproportionately target young black and Hispanic men.

Also in 2011, growing wealth disparities and a perceived decline in equality of opportunity gave rise to the "Occupy" protest movement. The movement began in September as Occupy Wall Street, featuring a round-the-clock encampment in a small park in New York City's financial district. Similar encampments were then established in other cities. While the Occupy forces drew considerable publicity, they failed to exert serious influence on the political process. After a few months, municipalities began to remove the protesters from their sites. While police generally used nonviolent tactics to contain marches and clear public spaces, in several cities, most notably New York, law enforcement authorities at times resorted to rougher methods that led to clashes with the Occupy participants.

Political Rights and Civil Liberties: The United States is an electoral democracy with a bicameral federal legislature. The upper chamber, the Senate, consists of 100 members—two from each of the 50 states—serving six-year terms, with one-third coming up for election every two years. The lower chamber, the House of Representatives, consists of 435 members serving two-year terms. All national legislators are elected directly by voters in the districts or states they represent. The president and vice president are elected to four-year terms. Under a 1951 constitutional amendment, the president is limited to two terms in office.

Presidential elections are decided by an Electoral College, meaning it is possible for a candidate to win the presidency while losing the national popular vote. Electoral College votes are apportioned to each state based on the size of its congressional representation. In most cases, all of the electors in a particular state cast their ballots for the candidate who won the statewide popular vote, regardless of the margin. Two states, Maine and Nebraska, have chosen to divide their electoral votes between the candidates based on their popular-vote performance in each congressional district, and other states are now considering similar systems.

A great deal of government responsibility rests with the 50 states. Most criminal cases are dealt with at the state level, as are education, family matters, gun ownership policies, and many land-use decisions. States also have the power to raise revenues through taxation. In some states, citizens have a wide-ranging ability to influence legislation through referendums, which have been conducted on issues including tax rates, affirmative action, and immigrant rights. Such direct-democracy mechanisms, often initiated by signature campaigns, have been hailed by some as a reflection of the openness of the U.S. system. However, they have also been criticized on the grounds that recalling elected officials in the middle of their terms or making policy through referendums can lead to incoherent governance, undermine representative democracy, and weaken the party system.

The intensely competitive U.S. political environment is dominated by the two major parties, the right-leaning Republicans and the left-leaning Democrats. The country's "first-past-the-post" or majoritarian electoral system discourages the emergence of additional parties, as do a number of specific legal and other hurdles. However, on occasion, independent or third-party candidates have significantly influenced politics at the presidential and state levels, and a number of newer parties, such as the Green Party or parties aligned with organized labor, have modestly affected politics in certain municipalities in recent years. While the majoritarian system has discouraged the establishment of parties based on race, ethnicity, or religion, religious groups and minorities have been able to gain political influence through participation in the two main parties. A number of laws have been enacted to ensure the political rights of minorities. However, a major controversy has been triggered by new laws in a number of states that require voters to present certain types of identification documents at the polls. Sponsors of the laws claim that the intent is to combat voter fraud. But critics contend that voter fraud is a minor problem at most, and accuse Republicans of adopting the laws to suppress voting by demographic groups that tend to support Democratic candidates by heavy margins, particularly low-income blacks.

Election campaigns are long and expensive. Serious candidates frequently find themselves in a "permanent campaign," with a never-ending process of fund-raising. The two parties and the constituency and interest groups that support them have used various methods to circumvent legal restrictions on campaign spending, and the Supreme Court on several occasions has struck down such restrictions, finding that they violated free speech rights. Election spending for the 2008 contests easily surpassed that of previous years, reaching over $5 billion; the presidential race alone cost $2.4 billion.

American society has a tradition of intolerance toward corrupt acts by government officials, corporate executives, or labor leaders. In recent years, the most serious instances of political corruption have been uncovered among state-level officials. In the most notable case, former Illinois governor Rod Blagojevich was convicted in 2011 on multiple counts of corruption, including attempts to benefit financially from his appointment of a replacement for Barack Obama after he vacated his Senate seat to become president. The U.S. media are aggressive in reporting on cases of corporate and official corruption; newspapers often publish investigative articles that delve into questions of private or public malfeasance. However, there are concerns that financial difficulties in the newspaper industry have reduced the press's willingness to devote resources to investigative journalism. At the same time, the expanding influence of interest groups and lobbyists on the legislative and policymaking processes, combined with their crucial role in campaign fund-raising, has given rise to public perceptions of enhanced corruption in Washington.

The federal government has a high degree of transparency. A substantial number of auditing and investigative agencies function independently of political influence. Such bodies are often spurred to action by the investigative work of journalists. Federal agencies regularly place information relevant to their mandates on websites to broaden public access. In an action widely praised by scholars and civil libertarians, Obama in 2009 ordered that millions of government documents from the Cold War era be declassified, and ordered federal agencies to adopt a cooperative attitude toward public information requests. A Knight Foundation study released in March 2011 found that about half of federal government agencies had adhered to the new standard.

The United States has a free, diverse, and constitutionally protected press. A long-standing debate over the impact of ownership consolidation—either by sprawling media companies with outlets in many states and formats, or by corporate conglomerates with little or no previous interest in journalism—has evolved into doubts about the financial viability of newspapers. A number of newspapers have carried out major staff reductions over the past decade while instituting various format changes. Nevertheless, circulation and especially advertising revenue continue to erode. Meanwhile, news websites have begun to assume the role once played by newspapers and newsmagazines, and the traditional news divisions of broadcast television networks have increasingly given way to 24-hour cable news stations. News coverage has also grown more polarized, with particular outlets and their star commentators providing a consistently right- or left-leaning perspective.

Controversy has emerged in recent years over attempts by federal prosecutors and private attorneys to compel journalists to divulge the names of confidential sources or turn over notes and background material. While laws that protect the media from such pressures have been adopted in many states, a similar measure at the federal level has yet to win congressional approval.

The United States has a long tradition of religious freedom. Adherents of practically every major religious denomination, as well as many smaller groupings, can be found throughout the country, and rates of both religious belief and religious service attendance are high. The constitution protects religious freedom while barring any official endorsement of a religious faith, and there are no direct government subsidies to houses of worship. The debate over the role of religion in public life is ongoing, however, and religious groups often mobilize to influence political discussions on the diverse issues in which they take an interest, including gay marriage, abortion, civil rights, and immigration. There is also a long-running debate over the possible use of public money to enable students from impoverished backgrounds to attend private schools with religious affiliations.

The academic sphere enjoys a healthy level of intellectual freedom. There are regular discussions on university campuses over such issues as the global economy, Israel and the Palestinians, and the alleged politicization of curriculums on Middle Eastern affairs.

In general, officials respect the right to public assembly. Protest demonstrations in opposition to government policies are frequently held in Washington, New York, and other major cities. Over the past decade, local authorities have often placed restrictions on large protests directed at meetings of international institutions, political party conventions, or targets in the financial sector. These restrictions, which generally limit the time and route of marches, were instituted in the wake of violent episodes at antiglobalization rallies. The United States gives wide freedom to trade associations, nongovernmental organizations, and issue-oriented pressure groups to organize and argue their cases through the political process.

Federal law guarantees trade unions the right to organize workers and engage in collective bargaining with employers. The right to strike is also guaranteed. Over the years, however, the strength of organized labor has declined, so that less than 8 percent of the private sector workforce is currently represented by unions. The country's labor code and decisions by the National Labor Relations Board (NLRB) during Republican presidencies have been regarded as impediments to organizing efforts. Union organizing is also hampered by strong resistance from private employers. Under Obama, a prolabor majority on the NLRB has issued decisions deemed favorable to unions. In 2011, state-level measures to roll back the rights of public employee unions were adopted in Wisconsin, Ohio, and Indiana. Despite its institutional decline, organized labor continues to play a vigorous role in electoral politics.

Judicial independence is respected. Although the courts have occasionally been accused of intervening in areas that are best left to the political branches, most observers regard the judiciary as a linchpin of the American democratic system. In recent years, much attention has been paid to the ideological composition of the Supreme Court, which has issued a number of significant decisions by a one-vote margin and is currently seen as having a conservative majority. Concern has also been raised about a trend toward the politicization of judicial elections in some states.

While the United States has a strong rule-of-law tradition, the criminal justice system's treatment of minority groups has long been a problem. A disproportionately large percentage of defendants in criminal cases involving murder, rape, assault, and robbery are black or Hispanic. Minority groups also account for an outsized share of the prison population.

Indeed, civil liberties organizations and other groups have advanced a broad critique of the criminal justice system, arguing that there are too many Americans in prison, that prison sentences are often excessive, that too many prisoners are relegated to solitary confinement or other maximum-security arrangements, and that too many people are prosecuted for minor drug offenses. Over two million Americans are behind bars in federal and state prisons and local jails at any given time, producing the highest national incarceration rate in the world. The number of incarcerated Americans has continued to increase even as the national rate of violent crime has declined. There is also a large number of juveniles serving lengthy prison terms in adult penitentiaries. Concerns have been raised about prison conditions, especially the incidence of violence and rape.

The United States has the highest rate of legal executions in the democratic world. Reflecting growing doubts about the death penalty, a number of states have formally abandoned executions, while others have announced a moratorium pending studies on the practice's fairness. The number of executions has declined since a peak in the late 1990s. Of particular importance in the trend has been the exoneration of some death-row inmates based on new DNA testing. The Supreme Court has ruled out the death penalty in cases where the perpetrator is a juvenile or mentally handicapped.

The United States is one of the world's most racially and ethnically diverse societies. In recent years, residents and citizens of Latin American ancestry have replaced black Americans as the largest minority group, and the majority held by the non-Hispanic white population has declined. An array of policies and programs are designed to protect the rights of minorities, including laws to prevent workplace discrimination, affirmative-action plans for university admissions, quotas to guarantee representation in the internal affairs of some political parties, and policies to ensure that minorities are not treated unfairly in the distribution of government assistance. The black population, however, continues to lag in overall economic standing, educational attainment, and other social indicators. Affirmative action in employment and university admissions remains a contentious issue. The Supreme Court has given approval to the use of race or ethnicity as a factor in university admissions under certain narrow conditions. However, affirmative action has been banned, in whole or in part, through referendums in five states.

The United States has generally maintained liberal immigration policies in recent decades. Most observers believe that the country has struck a balance that both encourages assimilation and permits new legal immigrants to maintain their religious and cultural customs. Many Americans remain troubled by the large number of illegal immigrants in the country, and the federal government has responded by strengthening security at the border with Mexico and stepping up efforts to deport illegal immigrants, especially those found guilty of criminal offenses or apprehended while crossing the border. Some states have enacted laws to restrict various economic and civil rights of undocumented immigrants, though the federal courts have struck down key sections of these laws, partly because of their potential side effects on the rights of U.S. citizens.

Citizens of the United States enjoy a high level of personal autonomy. The right to own property is protected by law and is jealously guarded as part of the American way of life. Business entrepreneurship is encouraged as a matter of government policy.

The United States prides itself as a society that offers wide access to economic and social advancement and favors government policies that enhance equality of opportunity. Historically, the opportunities for economic advancement have played a key role in the successful assimilation of new immigrants. Recently, however, studies have shown a widening inequality in wealth and a narrowing of access to upward mobility. Among the world's prosperous, stable democracies, the United States is unique in having a large underclass of poor people who have at best a marginal role in economic life.

Women have made important strides toward equality over the past several decades. They now constitute a majority of the American workforce and are well represented in professions like law, medicine, and journalism. Although the average compensation for female workers is roughly 80 percent of that for male workers, women with recent university degrees have effectively attained parity with men. Nonetheless, many female-headed families continue to live in conditions of chronic poverty.

Federal antidiscrimination legislation does not include homosexuals as a protected class, though many states have enacted such protections. Since Massachusetts's highest court ruled in 2003 that the state constitution gave homosexual couples the same right to marry as heterosexual couples, many states have passed laws or constitutional amendments explicitly banning same-sex marriage. At the same time, an increasing number of states have granted gay couples varying degrees of family rights, and a handful have endorsed full marriage rights, the most recent being New York in 2011.

Uruguay

Political Rights: 1
Civil Liberties: 1
Status: Free

Population: 3,369,000
Capital: Montevideo

Ten-Year Ratings Timeline For Year Under Review (Political Rights, Civil Liberties, Status)

2002	2003	2004	2005	2006	2007	2008	2009	2010	2011
1,1F	1,1F	1,1F	1,1F	1,1F	1,1F	1,1F	1,1F	1,1F	1,1F

Overview: **Uruguay finally annulled the country's long-standing amnesty for members of the 1973-1985 dictatorship in November 2011. President José Mujica, who lost standing within his Frente Amplio coalition due in part to his indecisive handling of the issue, also struggled to push forward a proposal to increase taxes on large landholdings.**

After gaining independence first from Spain and then later Brazil, the Republic of Uruguay was established in 1828. The ensuing decades brought a series of revolts, civil conflicts, and incursions by neighboring states, followed by a period of relative stability in the first half of the 20th century. The rival Colorado and Blanco parties vied for political power in the 1950s and 1960s, but economic troubles and an insurgency by the leftist Tupamaros National Liberation Front led to a military takeover in 1973. For the next 22 years, the country remained under the control of a military regime whose reputation for incarcerating the largest proportion of political prisoners per capita in the world earned Uruguay the nickname "the torture chamber of Latin America."

The military era came to an end after the 1984 elections, in which Julio María Sanguinetti of the Colorado Party won the presidency. Sanguinetti, the military's favored candidate, promoted a 1986 amnesty law—also known as the "Expiry Law"—that granted members of the armed forces immunity for human rights violations committed during the years of dictatorship. The military extracted the concession as its price for allowing the democratic transition the year before.

The 1990s were marked by relative economic stability and prosperity. Dr. Jorge Batlle of the Colorado Party, who was elected president in 1999, immediately sought an honest accounting of the human rights situation under the former military regime, while showing equally firm determination to reduce spending and privatize state monopolies. In 2001, crises in the rural economy and an increase in violent crime, as well as growing labor unrest, set off alarms in what was still one of Latin America's safest countries.

In October 2004, Tabaré Vázquez of the Broad Front (FA) coalition was elected president in the first round of voting, dealing a crushing blow to the Colorado Party. Vázquez's coalition also captured a majority of seats in both houses of parliament in concurrent legislative elections. Vázquez began his term by implementing a floating exchange rate, fiscal discipline, and an inflation-targeted monetary policy in a growing economy. His administration also introduced a personal income tax in 2007. Aided by increased commodity prices, Vázquez tripled foreign investment, maintained steady inflation, reduced poverty, and cut unemployment in half.

In October 2009 parliamentary elections, the FA coalition won slim majorities in both houses, securing 16 of 30 seats in the Senate and 50 of 99 seats in the Chamber of Representatives. Aided by Vázquez's ongoing popularity, José Mujica of the FA coalition was elected president in November 2009. Mujica, a socialist senator who spent 14 years in prison for waging a guerilla movement against the military regime, focused his first year on national reconciliation and maintaining moderate policies. Mujica's diverse FA coalition complicated reform efforts during his first two years in office, as the president aimed to appease the multiple elements of his coalition, as well as the right-leaning opposition. Public disagreement between Mujica and Vice President Danilo Astori delayed the administration's controversial proposal to tax large land holdings. The bill was finally sent to Congress on August 22, but had not been debated by year's end.

Uruguay's efforts to bring to justice those responsible for human rights violations committed during its military regime have been inconsistent and at times contradictory. The 1986 amnesty law gives the executive rather than the judicial branch final say over what cases can be tried. A majority of Uruguayans have supported the amnesty and voted to maintain it in two separate referendums in 1989 and 2009. However, recent administrations and court rulings have undermined its reach, reinterpreting the law to allow for higher-level officers to be tried. Since the

FA coalition took office in 2005, an estimated 20 former military officers have been tried and convicted. Former military dictator Gregorio Álvarez was convicted in October 2009 of abducting political opponents and for 37 counts of murder during the period of military rule, and was sentenced to 25 years in prison. In February 2010, former president Juan María Bordaberry received a 30-year prison sentence for the 1976 kidnapping and murder of two parliamentary leaders; he died in July 2011 while under house arrest.

Notwithstanding these convictions, lawmakers continued to push to eliminate the amnesty bill, especially in light of the February 2011 Inter-American Court ruling that Uruguay should investigate alleged crimes from its dirty war. After failing to overturn the law in a close parliamentary vote in May 2011, both houses of parliament voted to nullify the law in October. Despite going against popular opinion, Mujica signed the bill into law on November 1. His overall indecisive handling of the amnesty issue, however, caused him to lose standing within the FA coalition.

Political Rights and Civil Liberties:

Uruguay is an electoral democracy. The 2009 elections were free and fair. The 1967 constitution established a bicameral General Assembly, consisting of the 99-member Chamber of Representatives and the 30-member Senate, with all members directly elected for five-year terms. The president is directly elected for a single five-year term.

The major political parties and groupings are the Colorado Party, the Independent Party, the Blanco Party, and the ruling FA coalition. The latter includes the Movement of Popular Participation, the New Space Party, the Socialist Party, and the Uruguayan Assembly, among other factions.

The Transparency Law criminalizes a broad range of potential abuses of power by officeholders, including the laundering of funds related to public corruption cases. Uruguay was ranked 25 out of 183 countries surveyed in Transparency International's 2011 Corruption Perceptions Index, making it one of the least corrupt countries in Latin America.

Constitutional guarantees regarding free expression are respected, and violations of press freedom are rare. The press is privately owned, and broadcasting includes both commercial and public outlets. There are numerous daily newspapers, many of which are associated with political parties. A June 2009 bill eliminated criminal penalties for the defamation of public officials. The government does not place restrictions on internet usage.

Freedom of religion is a cherished political tenet of democratic Uruguay and is broadly respected. The government does not restrict academic freedom.

Rights to freedom of assembly and association are provided for by law, and the government generally observes these in practice. Civic organizations have proliferated since the return of civilian rule. Numerous women's rights groups focus on problems such as violence against women and societal discrimination. Workers exercise their right to join unions, bargain collectively, and hold strikes. Unions are well-organized and politically powerful. The national umbrella trade union, the PIT-CNT, held a nationwide general strike in October 2010, demanding wage increases and protesting against proposed reforms to the bloated and inefficient public administration. The guiding principles for these reforms included ending the immobility of public servants, reforming the civil service, and establishing a new pay system. The decision to hold the first general strike under José Mujica's government was divisive within the union movement and reflected an increase in opposition from the radical left within the president's alliance. In 2011, workers in the transportation, metalwork, public health, and education sectors engaged in strikes to demand better working conditions and higher wages.

Uruguay's judiciary is relatively independent, but the court system remains severely backlogged. Pretrial detainees often spend more time in jail than they would if convicted of the offense in question and sentenced to the maximum prison term. Overcrowded prisons, poor conditions, and violence among inmates remained problems in 2011. Medical care for prisoners is substandard, and many rely on visitors for food.

The small Afro-Uruguayan minority, comprising an estimated 4 percent of the population, continues to face economic and social inequalities and is underrepresented in the government.

Women enjoy equal rights under the law but face traditional discriminatory attitudes and practices, including salaries averaging approximately two-thirds those of men. Violence against women remained a problem in 2011. Women held only 12 percent of the seats in the Chamber of Representatives and 13 percent of the Senate following 2009 elections. However, under a 2009 quota law, women must comprise one-third of a party's political candidate list beginning in 2014. Congress approved same-sex civil unions in 2007, making Uruguay the first South American country to approve these rights nationwide.

Uzbekistan

Political Rights: 7
Civil Liberties: 7
Status: Not Free

Population: 28,463,000
Capital: Tashkent

Ten-Year Ratings Timeline For Year Under Review (Political Rights, Civil Liberties, Status)

2002	2003	2004	2005	2006	2007	2008	2009	2010	2011
7,6NF	7,6NF	7,6NF	7,7NF	7,7NF	7,7NF	7,7NF	7,7NF	7,7NF	7,7NF

Overview: **As in previous years, Uzbekistan's government suppressed all political opposition and restricted independent business activity in 2011, and the few remaining civic activists and critical journalists in the country faced prosecution, hefty fines, and arbitrary detention. Nevertheless, the regime continued to improve relations with the United States and Europe as it provided logistical support for NATO operations in Afghanistan.**

Uzbekistan gained independence from the Soviet Union through a December 1991 referendum. In a parallel vote, Islam Karimov, the former Communist Party leader and chairman of the People's Democratic Party (PDP), the successor to the Communist Party, was elected president amid fraud claims by rival candidate Mohammed Solih of the Erk (Freedom) Party. Solih fled the country two years later, and his party was forced underground. Only progovernment parties were allowed to compete in elections to the first post-Soviet legislature in December 1994 and January 1995. A February 1995 referendum extended Karimov's first five-year term until 2000, allegedly with 99 percent voter support.

The government's repression of the political opposition and of Muslims not affiliated with state-sanctioned religious institutions intensified after a series of deadly bombings in Tashkent in February 1999. The authorities blamed the attacks on the Islamic Movement of Uzbekistan (IMU), an armed group seeking to overthrow the secular government and establish an Islamic state.

All of the five parties that competed in the December 1999 parliamentary elections, which were strongly criticized by international monitors, supported the president. In the January 2000 presidential poll, Karimov defeated his only opponent, allegedly winning 92 percent of the vote. The government refused to allow the participation of genuine opposition parties. A 2002 referendum extended presidential terms from five to seven years.

A series of suicide bomb attacks and related violent clashes in late March and early April 2004 killed some 50 people. Police appeared to be the main targets. The authorities blamed radical international Islamist groups—particularly the al-Qaeda-linked IMU and the banned Hizb ut-Tahrir (Party of Liberation). Suicide bombers killed several people outside the U.S. and Israeli embassies in July 2004 amid conflicting claims of responsibility. In December, elections for the lower house of a new bicameral parliament were held, with only the five legal, proresidential parties allowed to participate.

In May 2005, a popular uprising in the Ferghana Valley city of Andijon triggered a violent government crackdown. The incident began on May 10 and 11, when family members and supporters of 23 local businessmen charged with involvement in a banned Islamic group staged a peaceful demonstration in anticipation of the trial verdict. The situation turned violent on the night of May 12, when armed men stormed a prison, freed the 23 businessmen and other inmates, and captured the local government administration building. Thousands of local residents subsequently gathered in the city center, where people began to speak out on political and economic issues, often making antigovernment statements.

Security forces responded by opening fire on the crowd, which included many women and children. Although the authorities maintained that the protesters were the first to open fire, eyewitnesses reported that the security forces began shooting indiscriminately. Official figures put the death toll at 187, but unofficial sources estimated the dead at nearly 800, most of them unarmed civilians.

Karimov repeatedly rejected calls from the European Union (EU), the Organization for Security and Cooperation in Europe (OSCE), and the United States for an independent international inquiry into the violence. In July 2005, Uzbekistan gave the United States six months to leave its military base at Karshi-Khanabad, which it had used to support operations in Afghanistan since late 2001. Russia and China endorsed the official Uzbek account of the violence.

The Uzbek authorities pursued a wide-ranging crackdown after the Andijon incident, targeting nongovernmental organizations (NGOs) with foreign funding, potential political opposition figures, human rights defenders, and even former officials.

Karimov's seven-year term ended in January 2007, and the constitution barred him from running for reelection. Nevertheless, he won a new term in December 2007 with an official 88 percent of the vote. Parliamentary elections in December 2009 offered voters no meaningful choice, though the four legal political parties, all of which supported the government, indulged in mild criticism of one another. In June 2010, Uzbekistan briefly took in over 100,000 ethnic Uzbek refugees fleeing ethnic violence in neighboring Kyrgyzstan. However, the authorities quickly returned them to Kyrgyzstan amid some reports of coercion.

Uzbekistan has largely repaired relations with the EU and United States in recent years, in part by agreeing to the overland transportation of nonmilitary supplies to support NATO operations in Afghanistan. The rapprochement gained new momentum in 2011, as NATO increased transit traffic, the United States approved waivers for Uzbekistan on some human-rights related sanctions, and high-level visits between U.S., European, and Uzbek officials resumed.

Political Rights and Civil Liberties: Uzbekistan is not an electoral democracy. President Islam Karimov uses the dominant executive branch to suppress all political opposition, and his December 2007 reelection appeared to flout constitutional rules on term limits. Under electoral legislation adopted in 2008, the bicameral parliament's lower house now has 150 seats, with 135 members directly elected in single-member constituencies and 15 representing the newly formed Ecological Movement of Uzbekistan, which holds separate indirect elections. The 100-member upper house, or Senate, has 84 members elected by regional councils and 16 appointed by the president. All members of the parliament serve five-year terms.

Only four political parties, all progovernment, are currently registered, and no genuine opposition parties function legally. A 2007 law intended to expand the role of registered parties had no real effect on the moribund political arena. Unregistered opposition groups function primarily in exile. In October 2011, the exiled opposition group Birdamlik attempted to hold a national event to bring complaints against local officials in several cities. Local activists faced harassment from the authorities, and leaders of the campaign reported that neighborhood committee (mahalla) officials threatened residents who wanted to participate.

Corruption is pervasive. Uzbekistan was ranked 177 out of 183 countries surveyed in Transparency International's 2011 Corruption Perceptions Index.

Despite constitutional guarantees, freedoms of speech and the press are severely restricted. The state controls major media outlets and related facilities. Although official censorship was abolished in 2002, it has continued through semiofficial mechanisms that strongly encourage self-censorship. U.S.-funded Radio Free Europe/Radio Liberty was forced out of Uzbekistan in December 2005. By 2010, Agence France-Presse was the only major international news agency with an accredited reporter in Uzbekistan. State-controlled television has aired "documentaries" that smear perceived opponents of the government, including a program in 2007 on journalist Alisher Saipov, who was subsequently murdered in Kyrgyzstan. In

June and July 2011, two former journalists from Uzbekistan's Yoshlar television channel, Saodat Omonova and Malohat Eshonkulova, held a multiweek hunger strike after they were arrested and fined for protesting censorship.

The OpenNet Initiative has found that the government systematically blocks websites with content that is critical of the regime. For a period in August 2011, many mainstream news and information sites based outside the country, including approved domestic sites hosted on Russian domains, were suddenly blocked as well, without explanation. Also during the year, the government reportedly ordered mobile-telephone operators to monitor their networks for "suspicious" texting and internet activity, and national security officers began seizing laptops in airports to check travelers' browsing histories for visits to critical media websites.

The government permits the existence of mainstream religions, including approved Muslim, Jewish, and Christian denominations, but treats unregistered religious activities as a criminal offense. The state exercises strict control over Islamic worship, including the content of sermons. Suspected members of banned Muslim organizations and their relatives have been subjected to arrest, interrogation, and torture. In 2011, members of legally registered Christian organizations were frequently targeted in raids, with authorities seizing religious literature, and members were arrested for unauthorized private gatherings. In March, the last remaining bookstores legally permitted to sell approved religious literature in Tashkent were raided and closed.

The government reportedly limits academic freedom. Bribes are commonly required to gain entrance to exclusive universities and obtain good grades. Open and free private discussion is limited by the mahalla committees, traditional neighborhood organizations that the government has turned into an official system for public surveillance and control.

Despite constitutional provisions for freedom of assembly, the authorities severely restrict this right in practice, breaking up virtually all unsanctioned gatherings and detaining participants.

Freedom of association is tightly constrained, and unregistered NGOs face extreme difficulties and harassment. A local advocate in 2008 described membership in the government-controlled association for NGOs as "voluntary but compulsory." After the 2005 unrest in Andijon, the government shut down virtually all foreign-funded organizations in Uzbekistan; Human Rights Watch, the last international monitoring group with a presence in the country, was forced to close its office in March 2011. Independent rights activist Abdullo Tojiboy Ogli was arrested and fined about $2,100 in April 2011 for holding an "unsanctioned gathering" on labor and residency rights, and had received similar fines for the same offense on multiple occasions in the previous year. The Council of the Federation of Trade Unions is dependent on the state, and no genuinely independent union structures exist. Organized strikes are extremely rare.

The judiciary is subservient to the president, who appoints all judges and can remove them at any time. The creation in 2008 of a Lawyers' Chamber with compulsory membership increased state control over the legal profession. Law enforcement authorities routinely justify the arrest of suspected Islamic extremists or political opponents by planting contraband or filing dubious charges of financial wrongdoing. In May 2011, the president amnestied political prisoner and critical poet Yusuf

Juma, who had been sentenced to five years in prison in 2008, allegedly for injuring police during a demonstration. He left for the United States after his release.

Prisons suffer from severe overcrowding and shortages of food and medicine. As with detained suspects, prison inmates—particularly those sentenced for their religious beliefs—are often subjected to abuse or torture.

Although racial and ethnic discrimination is prohibited by law, the belief that senior positions in government and business are reserved for ethnic Uzbeks is widespread. Moreover, the government appears to be systematically closing schools for the Tajik-speaking minority.

Permission is required to move to a new city, and bribes are commonly paid to obtain the necessary registration documents. A committee was formed in 2011 to overhaul the residency permit system for Tashkent, resulting in reports of increasing denial of basic services to unregistered residents and their resettlement in less-developed provincial areas. Restrictions on foreign travel include the use of exit visas, which are often issued selectively. Despite such controls, millions of Uzbeks, primarily men of working age, seek employment abroad, particularly in Russia and Kazakhstan.

Widespread corruption and the government's tight control over the economy limit equality of opportunity. The country's agricultural sector has undergone few reforms since the Soviet period. A series of regulations and decrees have placed numerous restrictions on market traders. Small businesses are freer to develop than large enterprises, which are often enmeshed in high-level corruption schemes. However, a campaign to "modernize" several cities ahead of the 20th anniversary of the country's independence justified the seizure and destruction, without compensation, of hundreds of privately owned shops in Tashkent and the Samarqand region.

Women's educational and professional prospects are limited by cultural and religious norms and by ongoing economic difficulties. Victims of domestic violence are discouraged from pressing charges against perpetrators, who rarely face prosecution. The trafficking of women abroad for prostitution remains a serious problem. The parliament passed legislation in November 2009 that imposed tougher penalties for child labor, but the practice reportedly remained widespread during subsequent cotton harvests.

Vanuatu

Political Rights: 2
Civil Liberties: 2
Status: Free

Population: 250,000
Capital: Port Vila

Ten-Year Ratings Timeline For Year Under Review (Political Rights, Civil Liberties, Status)

2002	2003	2004	2005	2006	2007	2008	2009	2010	2011
1,2F	2,2F	2,2F	2,2F	2,2F	2,2F	2,2F	2,2F	2,2F	2,2F

Overview:

Intense factional rivalries continued to fragment politics in 2011, resulting in three different prime ministers dur-

ing the first six months of the year. Although in November the World Trade Organization approved Vanuatu's application to join the group, Vanuatu's parliament did not ratify the agreement by year's end due to significant opposition from churches and civil society groups.

Vanuatu was governed as an Anglo-French "condominium" from 1906 until independence in 1980. The Anglo-French legacy continues to split society along linguistic lines in all spheres of life, including politics, religion, and economics. Widespread corruption and persistent political fragmentation have caused governments to collapse or become dysfunctional. No-confidence votes have forced several changes of government in recent years, and parliamentary coalitions are frequently formed and dissolved.

In the 2008 parliamentary elections, the Vanua'aku Party (VP) won 11 seats, the National United Party (NUP) took 8, while the Union of Moderate Parties (UMP) and the Vanuatu Republican Party (VRP) each captured 7. Parliament chose Edward Natapei of the VP as prime minister.

Natapei was ousted by a no-confidence vote in December 2010, and replaced by Sato Kilman. On April 24, 2011, Kilman was ousted by a 26 to 25 no-confidence vote, and the Speaker of Parliament appointed Serge Vohor to replace him. Kilman asserted that a minimum of 27 votes is required for his removal, and a court of appeal reinstalled Kilman as prime minister on May 13. On June 16, however, the Supreme Court declared Kilman's election in 2010 null and void on the grounds that the Speaker of Parliament violated constitutional requirements to hold a secret parliamentary ballot. On the same day, the speaker named Natapei as interim prime minister. The court also ordered a new parliamentary ballot to elect a new prime minister, and Kilman was chosen to another term on June 26.

While the economy has improved somewhat in recent years, it has suffered setbacks amid global economic troubles. In July 2011, Vanuatu asked China for $32 million to meet its budget shortfall in return for pledging to support China in the United Nations and other international forums. Vanuatu threatened to switch formal recognition to Taiwan if China did not meet its demand. Shortly thereafter, the Chinese ambassador to Vanuatu said China would pay a portion of this sum under the condition that Vanuatu recognizes only China.

In November 2011, the World Trade Organization approved Vanuatu's application to join the group. The decision was controversial in Vanuatu due to concerns over the possible impact on the country's poor, and churches and civil society groups held rallies against the move. Parliament did not ratify the agreement by year's end.

Vanuatu suffered a shortage of fresh drinking water in 2011 amid a sever drop in rainfall due to the La Niña weather pattern. The United Nations University's Institute for Environment and Human Security ranks Vanuatu as the Pacific island most at risk of natural disasters.

Political Rights and Civil Liberties: Vanuatu is an electoral democracy. The constitution provides for parliamentary elections every four years. The prime minister, who appoints his own cabinet, is chosen by the 52-seat unicameral Parliament from among its members. Members of Parliament and the heads of the six provincial governments form an electoral college to select the largely ceremonial president for a five-year term. The National Council of Chiefs works in parallel with the Parliament, exercising authority mainly over language and cultural matters.

Many political parties are active, but politicians frequently switch affiliations. Politics is also driven by linguistic and tribal identity. The leading parties are the VP, the NUP, the UMP, and the VRP. The Vanuatu Progressive Development Party was launched in May 2011.

Corruption is a serious problem. Allegations of bribery of both voters and parliament members are common. Accusations surfaced in early 2011 that Henry Iauko and Carlot Korman, the current and former ministers of lands, respectively, along with other senior officials, were involved in illicit land deals; all land leases ceased in March pending investigation and review. The practice of politicians distributing passports to foreign nationals in exchange for personal gain has long been a concern of local critics and international aid donors. In April 2011, the government approved creation of a commission to audit all Vanuatu passports. Vanuatu was ranked 77 out of 183 countries surveyed in Transparency International's 2011 Corruption Perceptions Index.

The government generally respects freedoms of speech and the press, though elected officials have been accused of threatening journalists for critical reporting. The state-owned Television Blong Vanuatu broadcasts in English and French. Newspapers include the state-owned *Vanuatu Weekly* and several privately-owned daily and weekly papers. In March 2011, government official Henry Iauko assaulted the *Daily Post*'s publisher and threatened the newspaper's staff over articles reporting his legal troubles. Although Iauko was found guilty of assault, he was fined only $150 and kept his cabinet position. In August, journalists from the Vanuatu Broadcasting and Television Corporation alleged that Pastor Don Ken, the Minister of Ni-Vanutau Business, demanded suppression of a story on his drunken behavior and arrest in July. State monopoly of telecommunications services ended in 2008. The number of internet users is growing, but access is limited by cost and lack of infrastructure.

The government generally respects freedom of religion in this predominantly Christian country. There were no reports of restrictions on academic freedom in 2011.

The law provides for freedoms of association and assembly, and the government typically upholds these rights. Public demonstrations are permitted by law and generally allowed in practice. Civil society groups are active on a variety of issues. Five independent trade unions are organized under the umbrella Vanuatu Council of Trade Unions. Workers can bargain collectively and strike. One hundred Aviation Vanuatu workers went on strike in May 2011.

The judiciary is largely independent, but a lack of resources hinders the hiring and retention of qualified judges and prosecutors. Long pretrial detentions are common, and prisons fail to meet minimum international standards. Tribal chiefs often adjudicate local disputes, but their punishments are sometimes deemed excessive. Harsh treatment of prisoners and police brutality provoke frequent prison riots and breakouts. In March 2011, the justice minister released a report by the Commission of Inquiry that criticized the police's handling of 2007 riots involving Tanna and Ambryn islanders; the report called for a major revamp of the police force and a national summit on security and policing.

Discrimination against women is widespread. No laws prohibit spousal rape, domestic abuse, or sexual harassment, which women's groups claim are common and increasing. Most cases go unreported due to victims' fear of reprisal or family pressure, and the police and courts rarely intervene or impose strong penalties.

Venezuela

Political Rights: 5
Civil Liberties: 5
Status: Partly Free

Population: 29,278,000
Capital: Caracas

Ten-Year Ratings Timeline For Year Under Review (Political Rights, Civil Liberties, Status)

2002	2003	2004	2005	2006	2007	2008	2009	2010	2011
3,4PF	3,4PF	3,4PF	4,4PF	4,4PF	4,4PF	4,4PF	5,4PF	5,5PF	5,5PF

Overview: **President Hugo Chávez Frías sought treatment for an undisclosed form of cancer in 2011, fueling speculation about his future as the country's dominant political figure. Meanwhile, several contenders jockeyed to emerge as the opposition's unity candidate for the 2012 presidential campaign. Harassment of nongovernmental organizations and journalists persisted, and criminal violence continued to rise on the streets and in the prisons.**

The Republic of Venezuela was founded in 1830, nine years after independence from Spain. Long periods of instability and military dictatorship ended with the establishment of civilian rule in 1958 and approval of a democratic constitution in 1961. Until 1993, the center-left Democratic Action (AD) party and the Social Christian Party (COPEI) dominated politics under an arrangement known as the Punto Fijo pact. President Carlos Andrés Pérez (1989–93) of the AD, already weakened by the violent political fallout from his free-market reforms, was nearly overthrown by Lieutenant Colonel Hugo Chávez Frías and other nationalist military officers in two 1992 coup attempts, in which dozens of people were killed. Pérez was subsequently impeached as a result of corruption and his inability to stem the social consequences of economic decline, which had coincided with lower oil prices beginning in the 1980s. Rafael Caldera, a former president (1969–74) and founder of COPEI, was elected president in late 1993 as head of the 16-party Convergence coalition, which included both left- and right-wing groups.

Chávez won the 1998 presidential contest on a populist, anticorruption platform, and in 1999 voters approved a new constitution that strengthened the presidency and introduced a unicameral National Assembly. Although Chávez retained his post in elections held under the new charter in 2000, opposition parties won most governorships, about half of the mayoralties, and a significant share of the National Assembly seats.

In April 2002, following the deaths of 19 people in a massive antigovernment protest, dissident military officers attempted to oust Chávez, the vice president, and the National Assembly with backing from some of the country's leading business and labor groups. However, the coup was resisted by loyalist troops and protesters, and Chávez moved swiftly to regain control of the military, replacing dozens of senior officers.

The country was racked by continued protests, and in December 2002 opposition leaders called a general strike that lasted 62 days but ultimately weakened their political position as well as the economy. While fending off his opponents with legal maneuvers and intimidation tactics, Chávez launched bold social-service initiatives, including urban health and literacy projects, many of which were staffed by thousands of experts from Cuba. He also continued to increase his influence over the judiciary, the media, and other institutions of civil society. Chávez survived a 2004 presidential recall referendum triggered by an opposition signature campaign, taking 58 percent of the vote amid high turnout.

National Assembly elections in 2005 were boycotted by the opposition, which accused the National Electoral Council (CNE) of allowing violations of ballot secrecy. A mere 25 percent of eligible voters turned out, and all 167 deputies in the resulting National Assembly were government supporters, though a small number defected to the opposition in subsequent years.

In the 2006 presidential election, Chávez defeated Zulia state governor Manuel Rosales of the opposition A New Time party, 61 percent to 38 percent. The incumbent exploited state resources during the campaign and drew on enduring support among poorer Venezuelans who had benefited from his social programs.

Soon after the vote, Chávez pressed forward with his program of radical institutional changes. Nearly all progovernment parties merged into the Unified Socialist Party of Venezuela (PSUV), and the socialist "Bolivarian revolution" deepened economically with a series of nationalizations of private assets. At the end of January 2007, the National Assembly voted to allow the president to issue decrees on a broad array of topics for 18 months.

Referendum voters in December 2007 narrowly defeated a package of constitutional amendments, among them the removal of presidential term limits. The vote reflected robust opposition participation, public disappointment with rising inflation and crime rates, and a degree of disaffection among current and former Chávez supporters. However, a set of 26 new laws decreed by Chávez in July 2008 appeared designed to institute measures that were rejected in the referendum, including presidential authority to name new regional officials and the reorganization of the military hierarchy.

State and local elections in November 2008 were preceded by the disqualification of over 300 candidates, including some opposition leaders, by the nominally independent but government-friendly comptroller. PSUV and other Chávez-aligned candidates enjoyed massive resource advantages and state publicity, while opposition candidates focused on perceived failures in public services and benefited from coverage in the opposition press. The opposition captured the mayoralty of greater Caracas as well as 5 of 22 states, including the 3 richest and most populous. Government candidates won 17 states and some 80 percent of the mayoralties.

A government-backed referendum in February 2009 abolished term limits, with over 54 percent of participating voters endorsing Chávez's proposal. In March and April 2009, the legislature passed laws allowing the national government to strip states of key governing functions and cut budget allocations; in practice, opposition-governed states and particularly the Caracas mayor's office were most affected. A new electoral law enacted in August was generally perceived to favor government candidates.

In the run-up to National Assembly elections in September 2010, the PSUV benefitted from significant exposure on state-run media, pressure on public employees and neighborhood groups, and the provisions of the 2009 electoral law. The opposition, grouped together as the Unity Roundtable (MUD), took more than 47 percent of the vote, the PSUV captured 48 percent, and the opposition-leaning Fatherland for All (PPT) party obtained over 3 percent. Due to the revised electoral rules, however, PSUV candidates secured 98 of the 165 seats, MUD candidates took 65, and the PPT won the remaining 2.

With the PSUV facing the loss of its supermajority in the new legislature, Chávez urged the outgoing chamber to enact a raft of new legislation before dissolving. Over 20 laws were passed or modified in December, including highly controversial regulations related to the internet, funding for civil society groups, education, procedural issues within the National Assembly, territorial reorganization, and the distribution of resources to subnational governments and community groups. In addition, the legislature again voted to grant Chávez wide-ranging decree powers for 18 months.

In 2011, the opposition began its primary campaign for the 2012 presidential contest, setting a primary election date for February 2012. Miranda state governor Henrique Capriles maintained a lead in the polls throughout the year, with Zulia governor Pablo Pérez and well-known politician Leopoldo López running second and third, respectively. In September, the Inter-American Court of Human Rights ruled that López, who was on the comptroller's list of disqualified candidates, must be allowed to run due to the absence of any formal charges against him. However, Venezuela's Supreme Tribunal of Justice (TSJ) ruled in October that the Inter-American Court's binding decision could not be carried out because, in the court's interpretation, it conflicted with the Venezuelan constitution and violated Venezuelan sovereignty. While López remained in the race, it remained unclear whether he would be allowed to take office in the event of an electoral victory.

Also during the year, it was revealed that Chávez was being treated for an undisclosed form of cancer. After weeks of rumors surrounding an operation he underwent while visiting Cuba, allegedly to remove a pelvic abscess, Chávez acknowledged in late July that he was indeed being treated for cancer, though he refused to divulge specifics. The government insisted that Chávez's prognosis was excellent, and he made clear his intention to run for reelection in 2012. Critics bemoaned the lack of transparency, particularly given Chávez's personalized style of rule and the absence of a clear line of succession within the PSUV.

Unstable social and economic conditions continued to pose difficulties for the government. Though the economy grew at a rate of 4 percent, inflation remained at 27 percent, electrical blackouts struck parts of the country in early 2011, industrial production stagnated, and shortages of some food items continued. Legislation passed in November that allowed the government to set prices on consumer goods seemed to increase shortages. Meanwhile, according to local rights groups, violent crime reached unprecedented levels despite the introduction of a new military anticrime unit, the People's Guardians. In June and July, the forcible suppression of a riot in one part of the El Rodeo prison complex led to a month-long standoff in another part; the conflict ended without the massacre that prisoners' family members feared, though the episode cast new light on Venezuela's horrifically violent prisons.

Relations with the United States were stable but tense, and the United States remained without an ambassador in Caracas throughout the year. Venezuela's improved relations with Colombia since 2010 have indirectly aided its ties with Washington. Although Venezuela continued to reject cooperation with the U.S. Drug Enforcement Agency, it extradited an accused Colombian drug kingpin to the United States in December. The bilateral friction is also attributable to Chávez 's creation of ostensible leftist alternatives to U.S.-backed regional trade pacts; his weapons purchases from Russia; and his rhetorical support for and economic cooperation with Cuba, Iran, and other nondemocratic states. In December 2011, Venezuela hosted the first meeting of the Community of Latin American and Caribbean Nations, a new regional body that pointedly excludes the United States and Canada.

Political Rights and Civil Liberties: Venezuela is not an electoral democracy. While the act of voting is relatively free and the count is fair, the political playing field favors government-backed candidates, and the separation of powers is nearly nonexistent.

The opposition boycotted the 2005 National Assembly elections due to concerns that ballot secrecy would be compromised. After the failed 2004 presidential recall referendum, tens of thousands of people who had signed petitions in favor of the effort found that they could not get government jobs or contracts, or qualify for public assistance programs; they had apparently been placed on an alleged blacklist of President Hugo Chávez Frias's political opponents. The opposition decided to actively contest the 2006 presidential and 2010 National Assembly elections, and the voting was generally considered free and fair, but the CNE failed to limit use of state resources by Chávez and the ruling PSUV. They enjoyed a massive advantage in television exposure, and the promotion of social and infrastructure projects often blurred the line between their official roles and their electoral campaigns. Public employees were also subjected to heavy pressure to support the government.

The unicameral, 165-seat National Assembly is popularly elected for five-year terms. Chávez's control of the 2006–10 assembly allowed him to further curb the independence of institutions including the judiciary, the intelligence services, and the Citizen Power branch of government, which was created by the 1999 constitution to fight corruption and protect citizens' rights. The December 2010 grant of decree powers to Chávez was the third time he received such authority. He used this power to enact 23 laws in 2011, compared with 19 laws passed by the National Assembly. The president serves six-year terms, but due to the results of the 2009 referendum, he and other elected officials are no longer subject to term limits.

The merger of government-aligned parties into the PSUV is largely complete, though several groups retain nominal independence. Opposition leadership in some states and localities has been blunted by laws allowing the national government to strip important functions from subnational administrations. In 2009, opposition parties established the MUD, which selected unity candidates—in part via primaries—for the 2010 elections and maintained cohesion during the campaign.

The MUD is also coordinating the opposition's efforts leading up to the 2012 presidential campaign.

The government plays a major role in the economy and has done little to remove vague or excessive regulatory restrictions that increase opportunities for corruption. Several large development funds are controlled by the executive branch without independent oversight. Balance sheets for two of the largest funds, FONDEN and the Chinese Fund, were released in 2011, but a $29 billion discrepancy between the stated total expenditure and the sum of individual line items remained unexplained at year's end. Anticorruption efforts are a low government priority; Comptroller General Clodosbaldo Russián died in June, and no permanent replacement had been selected by year's end. Several Venezuelans were convicted in U.S. courts during the year for their roles in a Ponzi scheme that pilfered money from the pension fund of the national oil company, PDVSA. Venezuela was ranked 172 out of 183 countries surveyed in Transparency International's 2011 Corruption Perceptions Index.

Although the constitution provides for freedom of the press, the media climate is permeated by intimidation, sometimes including physical attacks, and strong antimedia rhetoric by the government is common. The 2004 Law on Social Responsibility of Radio and Television gives the government the authority to control radio and television content. Opposition-oriented outlets make up a large portion of the print media, but their share of the broadcast media has declined in recent years. The television station RCTV's terrestrial broadcast frequency and equipment was seized in 2007, based on what Chávez claimed were the station's ongoing efforts to destabilize the government. In July 2010, the National Telecommunications Commission (CONATEL) stripped 32 radio stations of their licenses for what it described as procedural and administrative problems. Also during the year, the president of Globovisión, the primary opposition-aligned television broadcaster, was charged with several violations, prompting him to take refuge in the United States. In October 2011 Globovisión was fined $2.1 million for its reporting on a prison riot. Coverage of election campaigns by state media has been overwhelmingly biased in favor of the government; private outlets have also exhibited bias, though to a somewhat lesser degree.

The government does not restrict internet access, but in 2007 the government nationalized the dominant telephone company, CANTV, giving the authorities a potential tool to hinder access. In addition, a law passed during the December 2010 lame-duck legislative session extended the 2004 broadcasting law's restrictions to the internet. In 2011 a number of prominent opposition activists and journalists found that their Twitter microblog accounts had been hacked and used to disseminate anti-opposition messages. In addition, the offices of the freedom of expression advocacy group Public Space were burglarized twice in November, with computers and other valuable items stolen.

Constitutional guarantees of religious freedom are generally respected, though government tensions with the Roman Catholic Church remain high. Government relations with the small Jewish community have also been strained, but have improved recently. Academic freedom has come under mounting pressure since Chávez took office, and a school curriculum developed by his government emphasizes socialist concepts. A new Organic Education Law enacted in 2009 included ambiguities that could lead to restrictions on private education and increased control by the government and communal councils. In universities, elections for student associations and administration positions have become more politicized, and rival groups of students have clashed repeatedly over both academic and political matters. In December 2011, a student election at the Central University of Venezuela in which progovernment students were defeated decisively was followed by violence that caused damage to the university's concert hall.

Freedom of peaceful assembly is guaranteed in the constitution. However, the right to protest has become a sensitive topic in recent years, and rights groups have criticized legal amendments that make it easier to charge protesters with serious crimes. According to the rights group Provea, the number of protests rose considerably in 2011, while police repression of demonstrations declined. Workers, particularly employees of state-owned enterprises, demonstrated most frequently, followed by citizens protesting poor public-services delivery and high crime rates. The state's harsh rhetorical and legal response has fallen most heavily on the labor sector.

Nongovernmental organizations (NGOs) are also frequent antagonists of the government, which has sought to undermine the legitimacy of human rights and other civil society organizations by questioning their ties to international groups. In December 2010, the lame-duck parliament passed the Law on Political Sovereignty and National Self-Determination, which threatens sanctions against any "political organization" that receives foreign funding or hosts foreign visitors who criticize the government. Dozens of civil society members have been physically attacked in recent years, and other forms of harassment are common, including bureaucratic hurdles to registration and intimidation of activists. During the El Rodeo prison riots in 2011, noted prison activist Humberto Prado was repeatedly harassed and accused of orchestrating the uprising.

Workers are legally entitled to form unions, bargain collectively, and strike, with some restrictions on public sector workers' ability to strike. Control of unions has increasingly shifted from traditional opposition-allied labor leaders to new workers' organizations. Antigovernment groups allege that Chávez intends to create government-controlled unions, while the president's supporters maintain that the old labor regime was effectively controlled by the AD, COPEI, and employers. The growing competition has contributed to a substantial increase in labor violence as well as confusion during industry-wide collective bargaining. According to Provea, labor violence caused the deaths of 36 workers between October 2010 and September 2011. Labor strife has also risen due to the addition of thousands of employees of nationalized companies to the state payroll, and the government's failure to implement new collective-bargaining agreements in a context of reduced state resources.

Politicization of the judicial branch has increased under Chávez, and high courts generally do not rule against the government. Conviction rates remain low, the public-defender system is underfunded, and nearly half of all judges and prosecutors lack tenure. The National Assembly has the authority to remove and appoint judges to the TSJ, which controls the rest of the judiciary. In December 2010 the outgoing legislature appointed nine new TSJ judges who are generally viewed as friendly to the government. Judge Maria Lourdes Afiuni remained in confinement throughout 2011, though in February, she was moved from jail to house arrest for medical reasons. She had been arrested on corruption charges in December 2009, just hours after ordering the release of a prominent banker who had been held without conviction for more than the maximum of two years.

Although exact figures remain disputed, Venezuela's murder rate is among the world's highest. One local NGO, the Venezuelan Violence Observatory, offered a "conservative" estimate of over 19,000 homicides in 2011, or over 65 per 100,000 citizens. The police and military have been prone to corruption, widespread arbitrary detention and torture of suspects, and extrajudicial killings. In 2009, the justice minister admitted that police were involved in up to 20 percent of crimes. Although hundreds of officers are investigated each year, few are convicted, partly due to a shortage of prosecutors. The government claims that units trained in human rights and deployed in 2010 and 2011 have cut crime rates substantially in some zones. Despite the April 2011 announcement of a new Ministry of Prisons, prison conditions in Venezuela remain among the worst in the Americas. The NGO Venezuelan Prison Observatory reported 487 violent deaths within prison walls between January and October 2011, up from the 2010 tally of 476.

The increasingly politicized military has stepped up its participation in social development and the delivery of public services. While a faction of the military is perceived as wary of the Bolivarian project, Chávez's institutional control is considered solid. Military salaries were raised by 50 percent in October 2011. Foreign officials assert that the military has adopted a permissive attitude toward drug trafficking and Colombian rebel activity inside Venezuela, though improved relations with Colombia led Venezuela to deport an alleged rebel leader in April. In recent years, the division of responsibility between the military and civilian militias has become less clear, and informal progovernment groups have been responsible for attacks on press outlets and, occasionally, individual journalists and opposition supporters.

Property rights are affected by the government's penchant for nationalization, and the fast pace of nationalization continued in 2011, though the firms affected were less prominent than those seized in past years. Accusations of mismanagement, corruption, and politicized hiring practices within nationalized businesses are common.

The formal and constitutional rights of indigenous people, who make up about 2 percent of the population, have improved under Chávez, though such rights are seldom enforced by local political authorities. The constitution reserves three seats in the National Assembly for indigenous people. Indigenous communities trying to defend their land rights are subject to abuses, particularly along the Colombian border. In October 2011, the government agreed to formally transfer nearly 35,000 acres of ranchland to members of the Yukpa indigenous group.

Women enjoy progressive rights enshrined in the 1999 constitution, as well as benefits offered under a major 2007 law. However, despite some improvements on implementation, domestic violence and rape remain common and are rarely punished in practice. The problem of trafficking in women remains inadequately addressed by the authorities. Women are poorly represented in government, with just 17 percent of the seats in the National Assembly, but hold a number of important offices in the executive branch.

Vietnam

Political Rights: 7
Civil Liberties: 5
Status: Not Free

Population: 87,850,000
Capital: Hanoi

Ten-Year Ratings Timeline For Year Under Review (Political Rights, Civil Liberties, Status)

2002	2003	2004	2005	2006	2007	2008	2009	20010	2011
7,6NF	7,6NF	7,6NF	7,5NF	7,5NF	7,5NF	7,5NF	7,5NF	7,5NF	7,5NF

Overview: **The government in 2011 pursued a crackdown on dissent that had been ongoing for several years. The 11th Communist Party Congress, held in January, confirmed promotions for officials linked to the military and security forces and generally heralded a continuation of existing policies. Elections for the country's one-party legislature were held in May. In July, the new chamber approved Nguyen Tan Dung for another term as prime minister and chose Truong Tan Sang as state president.**

Vietnam won full independence from France in 1954, but it was divided into a Western-backed state in the south and a Communist-ruled state in the north. Open warfare between the two sides erupted in the mid-1960s. A 1973 peace treaty officially ended the war, but fighting did not cease until 1975, when the north completed its conquest of the south. Vietnam was formally united in 1976.

War and unsound economic policies mired Vietnam in deep poverty, but economic reforms that began in 1986 drastically transformed the country over the next two decades. Tourism became a major source of revenue, as did the export of foodstuffs and manufactured products. However, the ruling Communist Party of Vietnam (CPV) rejected any parallel political reforms that would threaten the one-party system. Criticism of the government continued to be harshly suppressed, and official corruption remained widespread.

Vietnam secured entry into the World Trade Organization in 2007, and the government subsequently embarked on a serious and extended crackdown on peaceful dissent, displaying a sharply reduced tolerance for open criticism and prodemocracy activism. Dozens of dissidents were arrested, and many were sentenced to lengthy prison terms. This process continued unabated in 2011. Among other cases during the year, former CPV member and activist Vi Duc Hoi was sentenced to prison in January for posting prodemocracy articles on the internet, a prominent scholar was sentenced in April for criticizing the government, four activists received prison terms in August for protesting against land confiscations, and multiple bloggers and online activists were arrested.

At the 11th Communist Party Congress in January, party members generally approved a continuation of the current policies of gradual economic opening and rejection of political reform. The congress chose hard-liner Nguyen Phu Trung as CPV general secretary, and picked other officials with strong security and military ties for top positions, sidelining some more moderate figures.

Tightly controlled elections for the one-party National Assembly were held in May, with the CPV taking 454 seats, officially vetted nonparty members securing 42 seats, and self-nominated candidates garnering the remaining four. In July, the new legislature approved Nguyen Tan Dung, the prime minister since 2006, for another term, and elected Truong Tan Sang as the new state president.

In response to ongoing tensions with China over disputed territory in the South China Sea, Vietnam allowed months of anti-China protests in Hanoi and other cities in 2011. Meanwhile, the United States continued to upgrade its defense ties with Vietnam despite concerns about the country's poor human rights record.

Political Rights and Civil Liberties: Vietnam is not an electoral democracy. The CPV, the sole legal political party, controls politics and the government, and its Central Committee is the top decision-making body. The National Assembly, whose 500 members are elected to five-year terms, generally follows CPV dictates. The Vietnam Fatherland Front, essentially an arm of the CPV, vets all candidates. The president, elected by the National Assembly for a five-year term, appoints the prime minister, who is confirmed by the legislature.

Corruption and abuse of office are serious problems. Although senior CPV and government officials have acknowledged growing public discontent, they have mainly responded with a few high-profile prosecutions of corrupt officials and private individuals rather than comprehensive reforms. Government decisions are made with little transparency, and revelations of contracts with Chinese and other foreign companies for major mining or development projects have generated considerable controversy. The sons of several senior CPV leaders were appointed to top positions during the 11th Party Congress in 2011, suggesting that nepotism is becoming a serious problem in Vietnam.

The government tightly controls the media, silencing critics through the courts and other means of harassment. A 1999 law requires journalists to pay damages to groups or individuals found to have been harmed by press articles, even if the reports are accurate. A 2006 decree imposes fines on journalists for denying revolutionary achievements, spreading "harmful" information, or exhibiting "reactionary ideology." Foreign media representatives in theory cannot travel outside Hanoi without government approval, though they often do in practice. The CPV or state entities control all broadcast media. Although satellite television is officially restricted to senior officials, international hotels, and foreign businesses, many homes and businesses have satellite dishes. All print media outlets are owned by or are under the effective control of the CPV, government organs, or the army.

The government restricts internet use through legal and technical means, and this effort was stepped up significantly in 2010 and 2011, particularly in the period directly before and after the 11th Party Congress. A 2003 law bans the receipt and distribution of antigovernment e-mail messages, websites considered "reactionary" are blocked, and owners of domestic websites must submit their content for official approval. Internet cafés must register the personal information of and record the sites visited by users. Internet service providers face fines and closure for violating censorship rules. The government detained numerous bloggers and online writers during 2011, and cyberattacks disabled websites and blogs that were critical of the authorities or provided independent information about sensitive topics, including

Roman Catholicism, human rights, and the party congress. Nevertheless, online criticism of government scandals and corruption has increased in recent years, and official pressure on the medium eased somewhat after the May 2011 elections.

Religious freedom remains restricted. All religious groups and most individual clergy members must join a party-controlled supervisory body and obtain permission for most activities. The Roman Catholic Church can now select its own bishops and priests, but they must be approved by the government. In early 2011, the government allowed the Vatican to appoint its first official representative to Vietnam, which was seen as a breakthrough in relations between Hanoi and the Holy See. Many restrictions on charitable activities have been lifted, and clergy enjoy greater freedom to travel domestically and internationally.

However, harassment, arrests, and occasional attacks directed at religious minorities continue to occur. Activist organizations reported in 2011 that Vietnamese and Lao troops killed four Hmong Christians near the border in April, and that detentions of Christian leaders remained common, particularly in central Vietnam. In May, security forces reportedly dispersed a gathering of thousands of Hmong Christians in Dien Bien. Foreign observers were prevented from visiting the site of the unrest.

Academic freedom is limited. University professors must refrain from criticizing government policies and adhere to party views when teaching or writing on political topics. Although citizens enjoy more freedom in private discussions than in the past, the authorities continue to punish open criticism of the state, and this climate of repression increased in the period surrounding the party congress in 2011. In April, legal scholar Cu Huy Ha Vu was sentenced to seven years in prison for "propagandizing against the government."

Freedoms of association and assembly are restricted. Organizations must apply for official permission to obtain legal status and are closely regulated and monitored by the government. A small but active community of nongovernmental groups promotes environmental conservation, land rights, women's development, and public health. Human rights organizations and other private groups with rights-oriented agendas are banned.

The Vietnam General Conference of Labor (VGCL), closely tied to the CPV, is the only legal labor federation. All trade unions are required to join the VGCL. In recent years, the government has permitted hundreds of independent "labor associations" to represent workers at individual firms and in some service industries. Farmer and worker protests against local government abuses, including land confiscations and unfair or harsh working conditions, have become more common. The central leadership uses such demonstrations to pressure local governments and businesses to comply with tax laws, environmental regulations, and wage agreements. Enforcement of labor laws covering child labor, workplace safety, and other issues remains poor. Critics also allege that the government has intentionally kept minimum wages low to attract foreign investment, although wages have been rising as multinational companies migrate to Vietnam due to labor unrest in China.

Vietnam's judiciary is subservient to the CPV, which controls courts at all levels. Defendants have a constitutional right to counsel, but lawyers are scarce, and many are reluctant to take on human rights and other sensitive cases for fear of harassment and retribution—including arrest—by the state. Defense attorneys cannot call or question witnesses and are rarely permitted to request leniency for their clients. Police can hold individuals in administrative detention for up to two years on suspicion of threatening national security. The police are known to abuse suspects and prisoners, and prison conditions are poor. Many political prisoners remain behind bars, and political detainees are often held incommunicado. Human rights groups in 2011 expressed concern that jailed blogger Nguyen Van Hai appeared to have been seriously injured while in custody, and that Thaddeus Nguyen Van Ly, a veteran rights activist who had been released on medical grounds in 2010, was returned to prison in July.

Ethnic minorities, who often adhere to minority religions as well, face discrimination in mainstream society, and some local officials restrict their access to schooling and jobs. Minorities generally have little input on development projects that affect their livelihoods and communities. In March 2011, Human Rights Watch reported that the government had increased repression of Montagnard Christians over the past year, detaining asylum seekers, confiscating land, and closing down worship groups.

Land disputes have become more frequent as the government seizes property to lease to domestic and foreign investors. Affected residents and farmers rarely find the courts helpful, and their street protests often result in state harassment and arrests.

Women hold 122 seats in the National Assembly. Although economic opportunities have grown for women, they continue to face discrimination in wages and promotion. Many women are victims of domestic violence, and thousands each year are trafficked internally and externally and forced into prostitution. A number of cases of international adoption fraud have been exposed in recent years.

Yemen

Political Rights: 6
Civil Liberties: 6*
Status: Not Free

Population: 23,833,000
Capital: Sanaa

Ratings Change: Yemen's civil liberties rating declined from 5 to 6 due to the regime's violent response to public protests throughout the year and a deterioration of the rule of law amid the protracted effort to remove and replace President Ali Abdullah Saleh.

Ten-Year Ratings Timeline For Year Under Review (Political Rights, Civil Liberties, Status)

2002	2003	2004	2005	2006	2007	2008	2009	2010	2011
6,5NF	5,5PF	5,5PF	5,5PF	5,5PF	5,5PF	5,5PF	6,5NF	6,5NF	6,6NF

Overview: **Hundreds of thousands of Yemenis demonstrated throughout 2011 to demand democratic change and an end to the 33-year rule of President Ali Abdullah Saleh. Security and military forces loyal to Saleh used brutal violence in repeated attempts to crush the prodemocracy movement. Amid the political uncertainty, Yemeni and U.S.**

officials warned that Islamist militants, including an affiliate of al-Qaeda, were growing in strength. The United States began a series of airstrikes targeting alleged al-Qaeda operatives in May. After months of international pressure, Saleh finally signed a Saudi-brokered agreement in November that transferred his powers to Yemen's vice president, though he formally remained president at year's end. Clashes continued after the pact was announced. The humanitarian costs of Yemen's political conflict and related violence were high, with hundreds killed and thousands displaced.

For centuries after the advent of Islam, a series of dynastic imams controlled most of northern Yemen and parts of the south. The Ottoman Empire exercised some influence over Yemeni territory from the 16th to the early 20th century, and the British controlled the southern portion of the country, including the port of Aden, beginning in the 19th century.

After the reigning imam was ousted in a 1960s civil war and the British left the south in 1967, Yemen remained divided into two countries: the Yemen Arab Republic (North Yemen) and the People's Democratic Republic of Yemen (South Yemen). The two states ultimately unified in 1990, and northern forces put down a southern attempt to secede in 1994. In the face of widespread poverty and illiteracy, tribal influences that limited the central government's authority in certain parts of the country, a heavily armed citizenry, and the threat of Islamist terrorism, Yemen took limited steps to improve the status of political rights and civil liberties in the years after unification.

In 2006, Yemen held its second presidential election since unification. President Ali Abdullah Saleh was reelected with 77 percent of the vote, and the ruling General People's Congress (GPC) party won by a similar margin in concurrent provincial and local council elections. The 2006 presidential race was the first in which a serious opposition candidate challenged the incumbent. Saleh's main opponent, Faisal Ben Shamlan, was supported by a coalition of Islamist and other opposition parties and received 22 percent of the vote.

In May 2008, Yemen held its first-ever elections for 20 provincial governorships, which had previously been appointed. Opposition groups refused to participate, claiming electoral manipulation by the government. Progovernment candidates were elected in 17 of the 20 provinces that participated, and independents won in the remaining 3. One province did not hold elections due to protests by unemployed Yemenis.

Tensions between the government and opposition escalated in late 2008, and the opposition Joint Meeting Parties (JMP)—a coalition that included the Yemeni Socialist Party and Islah, an Islamist party—threatened to boycott parliamentary elections scheduled for April 2009. The two sides agreed in February 2009 to postpone the vote by two years pending the outcome of a national dialogue. Yemen's opposition grew increasingly frustrated in 2010, as Saleh ignored calls for electoral reform and appeared set on installing his son Ahmed as his successor.

Any possibility for elections in 2011 was upended after Yemenis launched a sustained protest campaign in January to call for Saleh's immediate ouster. The demonstrations started in the capital, Sanaa, and quickly spread to Aden, Hodeidah, and other parts of Yemen. In March, the parliament approved a set of emergency laws that gave the president sweeping powers to imprison critics and censor speech. The laws suspended constitutional protections, outlawed protests, and gave security forces the power to arrest and detain without judicial review. The most intense periods of protest were between February and June, and in September, as hundreds of thousands of Yemenis repeatedly took to the streets in opposition to the regime. The protests, led by young activists, were not coordinated by the JMP, although the latter eventually supported them.

In spite of high-profile defections from the government and military, the president retained some pillars of support. Pro-Saleh security services and military units used deadly violence in attempts to break up opposition protests, including sniper fire, shelling, and even airstrikes. Yemen's Ministry of Human Rights estimated that 2,000 people were killed as a result of the political crisis over the course of the year. Tribal groups, urban militias, and other anti-Saleh forces, including rogue army general Ali Mohsen al-Ahmar and his troops, also resorted to violence to oust Saleh and protect their own interests. The president was gravely wounded in an explosion at his presidential compound in June. He was evacuated to Saudi Arabia, where he was treated for severe burns.

Saleh returned to Yemen in September, but under sustained pressure from the United States, the United Nations, and the Gulf Cooperation Council, he signed a Saudi-brokered agreement in late November that transferred his powers to Yemen's vice president. A unity cabinet with both GPC and JMP ministers was formed in early December, and a single-candidate election designed to officially install Vice President Abed Rabbo Mansour al-Hadi as president was scheduled for February 2012. However, clashes between pro- and anti-Saleh forces continued through year's end, and Saleh formally remained president.

The lengthy political crisis of 2011 seriously exacerbated existing centrifugal forces within Yemen, including autonomous tribal groups, a southern secessionist movement that had grown increasingly militant in recent years, a seven-year-old rebel movement rooted in the Zaidi Shiite Muslim community of the northern province of Saada, and Sunni Islamist militant groups affiliated with al-Qaeda. All four of these elements asserted themselves more openly during 2011, in many cases clashing with government forces and seizing territory.

The Saleh government at times sought to highlight the al-Qaeda threat to bolster its international support. The United States, responding to the growing disorder, began a series of drone aircraft strikes against suspected al-Qaeda militants in May. The attacks killed a number of alleged terrorist operatives, including the U.S. citizens Anwar al-Awlaki and Samir Khan in September. It was unclear how many civilians were killed in the U.S. strikes.

Political Rights and Civil Liberties:

Yemen is not an electoral democracy. Past elections, while more competitive than in many Arab countries, have been marred by flaws, including vote-buying, the partisanship of public officials and the military, and exploitation of state control over key media platforms. Moreover, the original six-year mandate of the current parliament expired in 2009, and elections were postponed again amid the turmoil of 2011. The political system has long been dominated by the ruling GPC party, and there are few limits on the authority of the executive branch. President Ali Abdullah Saleh has been serving continuously since 1978, when he became president of North Yemen through a military coup. Under the political agreement signed in November 2011, Saleh's vice president is set to replace him through a single-candidate presidential election in February 2012.

The president is elected for seven-year terms, and appoints the 111 members of the largely advisory upper house of parliament, the Majlis al-Shura (Consultative Council). The 301 members of the lower house, the House of Representatives, are elected to serve six-year terms. Provincial councils and governors are also elected. In the last parliamentary elections in 2003, the GPC took 238 lower-house seats, and the two main opposition parties, the Islamist party Islah and the Yemeni Socialist Party, took 46 and 8 seats, respectively. There is also a handful of smaller factions and independent lawmakers. Yemen's relatively well-developed and experienced opposition parties have historically been able to wring some concessions from the government.

Corruption is an endemic problem. Despite some recent efforts by the government to fight graft, Yemen lacks most legal safeguards against conflicts of interest. Auditing and investigative bodies are not sufficiently independent of the executive authorities.

The state maintains a monopoly over the media that reach the most people—terrestrial television and radio. Article 103 of the Press and Publications Law bans direct personal criticism of the head of state and publication of material that "might spread a spirit of dissent and division among the people" or that "leads to the spread of ideas contrary to the principles of the Yemeni Revolution, [is] prejudicial to national unity or [distorts] the image of the Yemeni, Arab, or Islamic heritage." *Al-Ayyam*, Yemen's most popular newspaper until its forcible closure by the government in 2009, remained out of operation in 2011, and its editor was on trial at year's end. It and other publications had been targeted for their reporting on the southern secessionist movement. The political crisis of 2011 led to multiple raids or attacks by progovernment forces on various news outlets, including the bureaus of foreign satellite television broadcasters like Al-Jazeera. Copies of print media were frequently seized during distribution, and a number of journalists faced intimidation, arrest, and physical violence. In March, Yemen expelled at least four foreign journalists who were covering the protest movement. Yemeni sources, including the Yemeni Journalist Syndicate and the Center for the Rehabilitation and Protection of Freedom of the Press, estimated nearly 500 cases of government harassment against local journalists during the first half of 2011; journalists staged demonstrations in Sanaa in July to protest the harassment. Access to the internet is not widespread, and the authorities block websites they deem offensive.

The constitution states that Islam is the official religion and declares Sharia (Islamic law) to be the source of all legislation. Yemen has few non-Muslim religious minorities, and their rights are generally respected in practice. The government has imposed some restrictions on religious activity in the context of the rebellion in the northern province of Saada. Mosques' hours of operation have been limited in the area, and imams suspected of extremism have been removed. Strong politicization of campus life, including tensions between supporters of the ruling GPC and the opposition Islah party, infringes on academic freedom at universities.

Yemenis have historically enjoyed some freedom of assembly, with periodic restrictions and sometimes deadly interventions by the government. The 2011 protest movement posed a serious challenge to the government's tolerance for public dissent. In spite of brutal violence, protesters persisted in taking to the streets, and continuously occupied certain locations in the capital and other major cities. Over the past three years, southern Yemenis have mounted growing protests to challenge the government's alleged corruption and abuse of power, the marginalization of southerners in the political system, and the government's inability to address pressing social and economic concerns. The protest movement has increasingly called for secession by the south. The push for secession was partly subsumed in 2011, as many southerners joined the broader anti-Saleh movement. Tens of thousands regularly protested in Aden and elsewhere. As in previous years, authorities responded with mass arrests of organizers and attempts to break up demonstrations by force. State security forces justified their harsh response by linking the southern movement to Islamist militant groups that also operated in the south.

Yemenis have the right to form associations under Article 58 of the constitution. Several thousand nongovernmental organizations operate in the country, although their freedom to operate is restricted in practice. The law acknowledges workers' right to form and join trade unions, but some critics claim that the government and ruling party elements have stepped up efforts to control the affairs of these organizations. Virtually all unions belong to a single labor federation, and the government is empowered to veto collective-bargaining agreements.

The judiciary is nominally independent, but in practice it is susceptible to interference from the executive branch. Authorities have a poor record on enforcing judicial rulings, particularly those issued against prominent tribal or political leaders. Lacking an effective court system, citizens often resort to tribal forms of justice or direct appeals to executive authorities.

Arbitrary detention occurs, partly because law enforcement officers lack proper training and senior government officials lack the political will to eliminate the problem. Security forces affiliated with the Political Security Office (PSO) and the Ministry of the Interior torture and abuse detainees, and PSO prisons are not closely monitored. As part of the November agreement for him to step down from power, Ali Abdullah Saleh was granted immunity from prosecution for his role in the country's deadly crackdown in 2011.

Yemen is relatively homogeneous ethnically and racially. However, the Akhdam, a small minority group, live in poverty and face social discrimination.

Thousands of refugees seeking relief from war and poverty in the Horn of Africa are smuggled annually into Yemen, where they are routinely subjected to theft, abuse, and even murder.

Women continue to face pervasive discrimination in several aspects of life. A woman must obtain permission from her husband or father to receive a passport and travel abroad. Unlike men, women do not have the right to confer citizenship on a foreign-born spouse, and they can transfer Yemeni citizenship to their children only in special circumstances. Yemen's penal code allows lenient sentences for those convicted of "honor crimes"—assaults or killings of women by family members for alleged immoral behavior. In April 2008, the parliament voted down legislation that would have banned female genital mutilation. Women are vastly underrepresented in elected office; there is just one woman in the lower house of parliament. School enrollment and educational attainment rates for girls fall far behind those for boys. In a positive development, the protest leader Tawakul Karman, a journalist, rights activist, and member of the Islah political party, was a co-recipient of the 2011 Nobel Peace Prize for her role in the Arab Spring.

↑ Zambia

Political Rights: 3
Civil Liberties: 4
Status: Partly Free

Population: 13,475,000
Capital: Lusaka

Trend Arrow: Zambia received an upward trend arrow due to the conduct of the September presidential election and the peaceful transfer of power to opposition leader Michael Sata, ending two decades of rule by the Movement for Multiparty Democracy.

Ten-Year Ratings Timeline For Year Under Review (Political Rights, Civil Liberties, Status)

2002	2003	2004	2005	2006	2007	2008	2009	2010	2011
4,4PF	4,4PF	4,4PF	4,4PF	3,4PF	3,4PF	3,3PF	3,4PF	3,4PF	3,4PF

Overview: **The September 2011 presidential election led to a peaceful handover of power to the opposition Patriotic Front's Michael Sata, ending two decades of rule by the Movement for Multiparty Democracy. In his first months in office, Sata took steps to reinvigorate anticorruption efforts and loosen restrictions on journalists.**

Zambia gained independence from Britain in 1964. President Kenneth Kaunda and his United National Independence Party subsequently ruled Zambia as a de facto—and, from 1972, a de jure—one-party state. In the face of domestic and international pressure, Kaunda agreed to a new constitution and multiparty democracy in 1991. In free elections that October, former labor leader Frederick Chiluba and his Movement for Multiparty Democracy (MMD) captured both the presidency and the National Assembly by wide margins. However, in the 1996 elections, the MMD-led government manipulated candidacy laws, voter registration, and media coverage in favor of the incumbents. Most opposition parties boycotted the polls, and the MMD renewed its parliamentary dominance.

Dissent within the MMD, as well as protests by opposition parties and civil society, forced Chiluba to abandon an effort to change the constitution and seek a third term in 2001. Instead, the MMD nominated Levy Mwanawasa, who went on to win the 2001 elections. The MMD also captured a plurality of elected parliament seats amid charges of vote rigging and other serious irregularities. In September 2006, Mwanawasa won a second term with about 42 percent of the vote. In concurrent legislative elections, the MMD won 72 seats in the 150-seat parliament, and the opposition Patriotic Front (PF) took 44. The polls were deemed the freest and fairest in 15 years.

Mwanawasa suffered a stroke in June 2008 and died in August; he was succeeded by Vice President Rupiah Banda. A presidential by-election followed in October, with Banda winning around 39 percent of the vote, the PF's Michael Sata claiming 38 percent, and Hakainde Hichilema of the United Party for National Development (UPND) taking 20 percent. Sata claimed that the election was fraudulent and filed a legal challenge calling for a recount, but his request was rejected by the Supreme Court in March 2009.

Banda's presidency was characterized by contentious politics, increasing infringements on civil liberties, and weakened anticorruption efforts. A 2008 National Constitutional Conference—boycotted by elements of civil society and the opposition—completed a draft constitution that was distributed to the public for commentary in June 2010. While the draft was praised for expanding protections for economic, social, and cultural rights, it was criticized for failing to sufficiently curtail executive powers and expanding the size of the parliament. In March 2011, the Constitution Amendment Bill failed to achieve the required two-thirds majority in the legislature. Meanwhile, the government and MMD supporters took aggressive and violent actions against the political opposition and elements of civil society that they considered hostile to the president.

In the September 2011 presidential election, Sata defeated Banda, 43 percent to 36 percent. Banda accepted the result, marking the second time in Zambian history that an incumbent peacefully surrendered the presidency after losing an election. In concurrent parliamentary elections, the PF won a small majority, taking 61 seats, to 55 for the MMD and 29 for the UPND. Although the elections were characterized by fierce campaigning, the misuse of state resources by the MMD, and isolated rioting that claimed at least two lives, the polls were deemed free and credible by international observers. Shortly after his election, Sata pledged to appoint a committee to rewrite the constitution.

Sata is often described as a populist, and in his previous campaigns, he had harshly criticized the growing role of Chinese companies in Zambia's mining sector, even threatening to expel them if elected. However, he moderated his tone in 2011, focusing instead on improving conditions at Chinese-owned mines and ensuring that Chinese companies followed Zambian labor laws.

Political Rights and Civil Liberties:

Zambia is an electoral democracy. While the opposition had alleged fraud and harassment in recent elections, the ruling MMD relinquished control of both the presidency and the parliament in 2011, and local and international observers declared the year's voting to be generally free and credible. The president and the unicameral National Assembly are elected to serve concurrent five-year terms. The National Assembly includes 150 elected members, as well as 8 members appointed by the president.

Prior to the election of opposition PF leader Michael Sata as president in September 2011, opposition parties had been able to operate, but often faced intimidation and violence. Sata had been arrested and charged with various offenses, including sedition, since 2001. In March 2009, the PF joined forces with the UPND to challenge the MMD in the 2011 elections, and the leaders of both parties subsequently faced threats of violence and sexual assault by MMD cadres. In 2010, members of the opposition were harassed and detained by the police, while others were violently attacked by individuals associated with the MMD. In 2011, however, the preelection period was generally calm.

Corruption is believed to be widespread. The government of Sata's predecessor, Rupiah Banda, proved willing to protect political figures and weaken the legal regime against graft. Most visibly, Banda aided the political rehabilitation of former president Frederick Chiluba, who died in June 2011 after being acquitted of embezzlement by a Zambian court, even though a 2007 finding in a separate case by the High Court in London indicated that he had stolen $57 million during his presidency. In June 2010, the Global Fund to Fight AIDS, Malaria and Tuberculosis suspended $300 million in funding out of concern over corruption, and the Dutch and Swedish aid agencies, as well as the European Union, have also withheld some funds for the same reason. In October 2010, the National Assembly passed legislation to remove an "abuse of office" clause from the Anti-Corruption Act. However, Sata soon after taking office fired several high-ranking officials who had been implicated in corruption. He also dismissed Godfrey Kayukwa, the director general of the Anti-Corruption Commission (ACC), who had been accused by the local chapter of Transparency International (TI) of destroying the reputation of that institution. Zambia was ranked 91 out of 183 countries surveyed in TI's 2011 Corruption Perceptions Index.

Freedom of speech and the press is constitutionally guaranteed. The MMD government had often restricted these rights in practice; however, there were signs that Sata and the PF would provide for a more open media environment. The government controls two widely circulated newspapers, and owing to prepublication review, journalists commonly practice self-censorship. The state-owned, progovernment Zambia National Broadcasting Corporation (ZNBC) dominates the broadcast media, although several independent stations have the capacity to reach large portions of the population. The government has the authority to appoint the management boards of ZNBC and the Independent Broadcasting Authority, which regulates the industry and grants licenses to prospective broadcasters. The Banda government had delayed the passage of a freedom of information bill, but Sata's government promised to advance the measure.

While the independent media play a significant role in Zambia, journalists have faced aggression from law enforcement officials, threats of violence from MMD members, and persistent warnings from government authorities that they might enact legislation to regulate the media. Criminal libel and defamation suits have been brought against journalists by MMD leaders in response to stories on corruption. In July 2011, more than 100 MMD supporters violently attacked members of a crew from the independent Muvi TV station and seized their equipment.

Constitutionally protected religious freedom is respected in practice. However, the Catholic clergy, occasional critics of the MMD government, became the target of threats by MMD activists in 2010, and one priest known for political activism was briefly detained by police. Sata became the country's first Catholic president in 2011. The government does not restrict academic freedom.

Under the Public Order Act, police must receive a week's notice before all demonstrations. While the law does not require permits, the police have frequently broken up "illegal" protests because the organizers lacked permits. The police can choose where and when rallies are held, as well as who can address them. Although nongovernmental organizations (NGOs) have operated freely in the past, legislation passed in 2009 placed new constraints on their activities, such as requiring registration and reregistration every five years. The law also established a board to provide guidelines and regulate NGO activity in the country.

The law provides for the right to join unions, strike, and bargain collectively. Zambia's trade unions are among Africa's strongest. The Zambia Congress of Trade Unions operates democratically without state interference. About two-thirds of the country's 300,000 formal-sector employees are union members. However, there is significant labor exploitation in some sectors of the economy. Tensions between workers and management at Chinese-owned mines have been increasing. In November 2011, Human Rights Watch (HRW) released a report on labor abuses in Chinese-operated copper mines, detailing unsafe working conditions, resistance to unionization, and much lower pay than at other Zambian mines.

Judicial independence is guaranteed by law. However, several recent decisions, especially those concerning Chiluba, tainted the public image of the judiciary and raised concerns that the executive branch was exercising undue influence. Legislation passed in 2009 allowed the executive to increase the number of judges serving on the High and Supreme Courts. However, the courts continue to lack qualified personnel, in part because of poor working conditions, which contributes to significant trial delays. Pretrial detainees are sometimes held for years under harsh conditions, and many of the accused lack access to legal aid owing to limited resources. In rural areas, customary courts of variable quality and consistency—whose decisions often conflict with the constitution and national law—decide many civil matters.

Allegations of police corruption, brutality, and even torture are widespread, and security forces have generally operated with impunity. In 2010, HRW, the Prisons Care and Counseling Association, and the AIDS and Rights Alliance for Southern Africa released a report that decried forced labor, abuse of inmates by authorities, and deplorable health conditions in Zambia's prisons.

In January 2011, two people were reported killed, and several others wounded, in clashes between police and activists demanding secession for an area of western Zambia called Barotseland. Sata after his inauguration appointed a commission to look into the killings. Secession activists have been denied permission to hold public meetings, and some media outlets have been threatened for covering the issue.

Societal discrimination remains a serious obstacle to women's rights. Women won just 17 of the 150 elected seats in the National Assembly in the September 2011 polls; 2 were later appointed to the 20-member cabinet, and 5 to the 11-member Supreme Court. Women are denied full economic participation and usually require male consent to obtain credit. Discrimination against women is especially prevalent in customary courts, where they are considered subordinate with respect to property, inheritance, and marriage. Domestic violence and rape are major problems, and traditional norms inhibit many women from reporting assaults. In 2005, an amended penal code banned the traditional practice of "sexual cleansing," in which a widow is obliged to have sex with relatives of her deceased husband. In an alleged effort to intimidate members of civil society, then vice president George Kunda stated in 2009 that the government could prosecute known homosexuals in the country using 2005 legislation against homosexuality. People living with HIV/AIDS are routinely discriminated against in society and for employment.

Zimbabwe

Political Rights: 6
Civil Liberties: 6
Status: Not Free

Population: 12,084,000
Capital: Harare

Ten-Year Ratings Timeline For Year Under Review (Political Rights, Civil Liberties, Status)

2002	2002	2004	2005	2006	2007	2008	2009	2010	2011
6,6NF	6,6NF	7,6NF	7,6NF	7,6NF	7,6NF	7,6NF	6,6NF	6,6NF	6,6NF

Overview: **While the national unity government held together in 2011, political violence continued and little progress was made toward a new constitution. President Robert Mugabe and his Zimbabwe African National Union–Patriotic Front (ZANU-PF) party pushed for elections in early 2012, though no dates were set. An international entity that oversees the diamond trade approved diamond exports from the country despite the reported abuse of miners and graft by ZANU-PF power brokers. Also during the year, the authorities expanded their crackdown on the mainstream Anglican Church, which does not recognize a pro-Mugabe splinter faction.**

In 1965, a white-minority regime in what was then colonial Southern Rhodesia unilaterally declared independence from Britain. A guerrilla war led by black nationalist groups, as well as sanctions and diplomatic pressure from Britain and the United States, contributed to the end of white-minority rule in 1979 and the recognition of an independent Zimbabwe in 1980. Robert Mugabe and the Zimbabwe African National Union–Patriotic Front (ZANU-PF), first brought to power in relatively democratic elections, have since ruled the country.

Zimbabwe was relatively stable in its first years of independence, but from 1983 to 1987, the Shona-dominated government violently suppressed opposition among the Ndebele ethnic minority, and between 10,000 and 20,000 civilians were killed by government forces. Widespread political unrest in the 1990s, spurred by increasing authoritarianism and economic decline, led to the creation in 1999 of the opposition Movement for Democratic Change (MDC), an alliance of trade unions and other civil society groups, including many white farmers. However, President Mugabe and ZANU-PF claimed victory over the MDC in parliamentary elections in 2002 and 2005, as well as in a 2002 presidential poll. All three elections were seriously marred by political violence aimed at MDC supporters, fraudulent electoral processes, and the abuse of state resources and state-run media. Security forces crushed mass protests and strikes called by MDC leader Morgan Tsvangirai in 2003.

The 2005 parliamentary elections left the ruling party with a two-thirds majority and the ability to amend the constitution. It subsequently enacted amendments that nationalized all land, brought all schools under state control, and reintroduced an upper legislative house, the Senate. The MDC split over whether to participate in November 2005 elections for the chamber, allowing ZANU-PF to win an overwhelming majority amid voter turnout of less than 20 percent.

Also in 2005, the government implemented a slum-clearance effort known as

Operation Murambatsvina, which means "drive out the trash" in the Shona language. It resulted in the destruction of thousands of informal businesses and dwellings as well as thousands of arrests. According to the United Nations, approximately 700,000 people were made homeless, and another 2.4 million were directly or indirectly affected. Initially moved into transit camps near cities, many displaced residents were forced to return to the rural areas designated on their national identity cards. Analysts maintain that the operation, billed as part of a law-and-order campaign, actually targeted urban MDC strongholds.

Violence before the March 2008 elections, though serious, was less severe than expected. In the parliamentary polls, the Tsvangirai-led MDC won 99 seats in the lower house, followed by ZANU-PF with 97 seats, and a breakaway faction of the MDC, led by Arthur Mutambara, with 10. The results denied ZANU-PF a legislative majority for the first time in the country's 28-year history. In the Senate, ZANU-PF took half of the 60 elected seats, but it also controlled the chamber's 33 unelected seats. The MDC and its splinter faction won 24 and 6 Senate seats, respectively.

When the Zimbabwe Election Commission (ZEC) finally released the presidential results in May, it found that Tsvangirai had outpolled Mugabe, 47.9 percent to 43.2 percent, requiring a runoff between the two. The MDC accused the ZEC of fraud and claimed that Tsvangirai had won the election outright with 50.3 percent of the vote. As evidence, the party cited an extensive parallel vote count conducted by a network of civic groups.

Following the election, ZANU-PF militias and state security forces began a brutal campaign of violence aimed at punishing and intimidating MDC members and their suspected supporters in civil society and the press. Tsvangirai ultimately withdrew from the June runoff, allowing the unopposed Mugabe to win 85 percent of the vote amid low turnout and many spoiled ballots. Political violence continued after the election. According to international and domestic human rights organizations, some 200 MDC activists and supporters were killed over the course of 2008, about 5,000 were tortured, and more than 10,000 required medical treatment for injuries.

In September 2008, ZANU-PF and the MDC reached a power-sharing agreement brokered by the Southern African Development Community (SADC)—known as the Global Political Agreement, or GPA—that allowed Mugabe to remain president, created the post of prime minister for Tsvangirai, and distributed ministries to ZANU-PF (14, including defense, state security, and justice), Tsvangirai's MDC faction (13, including finance, health, and constitutional and parliamentary affairs), and Mutambara's faction (3). A constitutional amendment creating the post of prime minister was enacted in February 2009, and the new government was sworn in that month.

In practice, Mugabe retained control of the powerful executive branch, and in 2009 and 2010, he unilaterally appointed the central bank governor, the attorney general, and the police commissioner, as well as a number of senior judges and diplomats. Mugabe also refused to swear in some MDC ministers and all of its provincial governors, appointing ZANU-PF loyalists instead.

The GPA set a February 2011 deadline for the adoption of a new constitution, but attempts to hold public meetings on the charter in 2009 and 2010 were undermined by political violence that was overwhelmingly perpetrated by ZANU-PF supporters.

In July 2011, the MDC and ZANU-PF agreed on a road map toward elections, including reforms of the electoral laws within 45 days. However, no such reforms were made by year's end, nor were any agreements reached on the composition of the ZEC or security reforms. In October, the ZEC announced that it would need an additional US$220 million to hold a constitutional referendum and administer future elections. No date had been set for either by year's end, though Mugabe called for the elections to be held in early 2012. ZANU-PF was generally pushing to hold elections earlier than Tsvangirai and the MDC, apparently due to concerns about Mugabe's health and the likelihood of internal ZANU-PF rifts if balloting were to be held after his death. In December, ZANU-PF once again endorsed Mugabe as its presidential candidate.

The Kimberly Process, an international mechanism designed to prevent the use of diamonds to fund armed conflicts, decided in November to lift a suspension of Zimbabwean diamond exports from a number of mines in the Marange diamond fields. The ban had been imposed in 2009, following reports of military control of the mines and severe human rights abuses against both miners and locals. In August, the British Broadcasting Corporation (BBC) had reported that security forces ran a "torture camp" near the mines to punish those caught mining for themselves or demanding higher payment. Also that month, Human Rights Watch (HRW) found that mining companies were employing police and private security guards who used shootings, beatings, and attack dogs to deter unlicensed miners. The *Financial Times* reported in December that significant amounts of diamond revenues were not being reported or sent to the MDC-controlled Finance Ministry, but were directed instead to high-ranking ZANU-PF officials.

Political Rights and Civil Liberties: Zimbabwe is not an electoral democracy. President Robert Mugabe and the ZANU-PF party have dominated the political landscape since independence in 1980, overseeing 18 amendments to the constitution that have expanded presidential power and decreased executive accountability. Presidential and legislative elections in March 2008 were marred by a wide-ranging campaign of violence and intimidation, flawed voter registration and balloting, biased media coverage, and the use of state resources—including food aid—to bribe and threaten voters. The period leading up to the presidential runoff in June 2008 featured accelerated violence against the opposition, prompting a UN Security Council resolution declaring the impossibility of a fair poll. Mugabe ultimately ran unopposed, and the vote was declared illegitimate by observers from the African Union and the SADC. Although the September 2008 GPA called for a new constitution and the formation of an independent election commission, neither goal had been achieved by the end of 2011. In June, the South African Institute for Race Relations reported on a leaked Zimbabwean voter roll that contained some two million extra names, including children and people aged over 100.

Since the restoration of the Senate in 2005, Zimbabwe has had a bicameral legislature. A 2007 constitutional amendment removed appointed seats from the House of Assembly, increased the size of both chambers (to 210 elected seats in the House of Assembly and 60 elected seats in the Senate), and redrew constituency boundaries. In the Senate, at least 33 additional seats are still held by traditional chiefs, presidential appointees, and other unelected officials. The president and elected lawmakers serve five-year terms. A 2009 constitutional amendment stemming from the GPA created the post of prime minister (and two deputy prime ministers) while retaining the presidency, leaving the country with a split executive branch.

In 2011, MDC-affiliated ministers and officials continued to face obstruction and harassment from state entities controlled by ZANU-PF. Most notably, in March the Supreme Court nullified the 2009 election of the MDC's Lovemore Moyo as speaker of the lower house based on a claim by ZANU-PF that the vote had been "disorderly." Later in the month, Moyo was reelected Speaker. In June, MDC deputy media minister Jameson Timba was arrested for "insulting the president" in a South African newspaper; he was soon released from detention. The following month, a number of employees of the MDC-controlled Finance Ministry were briefly detained on charges of inappropriate travel.

State-sponsored political violence is a serious and chronic problem, and worsened in 2011. In general, MDC-affiliated politicians, activists, and supporters are subject to harassment, assault, and arbitrary detention by security forces and militias allied with ZANU-PF. Some attacks have also been perpetrated by affiliates of the MDC. In January, the Southern African Coalition reported a surge in ZANU-PF-inspired violence, particularly surrounding meetings of MDC supporters and MDC-controlled local authorities in Harare and the Budiriro and Mbare townships. In February, hundreds of MDC supporters who sought refuge in a church from an outbreak of MDC–ZANU-PF violence in Mbare were briefly detained by police. In June, the Zimbabwe Elections Support Network reported that ZANU-PF militants had begun setting up bases in disputed rural voting districts, many of which were used as so-called "torture camps" during the 2008 elections. Police raided the offices of the MDC in Harare in November, sealing the office of Prime Minister Morgan Tsvangirai and firing tear gas into the building.

Corruption is rampant throughout the country, including at the highest levels of government. The collapse in public-service delivery and the politicization of food and agricultural aid has made the problem ubiquitous at the local level. In May 2011, the World Bank reported that almost half of Zimbabwe's civil servants are either not qualified for their positions or not working at all. Also in 2011, reports by both the Finance Ministry and international observers alleged that the bulk of proceeds from the Marange diamond fields had bypassed the national treasury, fueling speculation of official enrichment and patronage. In March, Energy Minister Elton Mangoma of the MDC was arrested on charges of making irregular fuel purchases and violating tender procedures, though a court cleared him of the charges in June. An anticorruption commission envisioned in the GPA has yet to be formed. Zimbabwe was ranked 154 out of 183 countries surveyed in Transparency International's 2011 Corruption Perceptions Index.

Freedom of the press is restricted. The country's draconian legal framework includes the Access to Information and Protection of Privacy Act (AIPPA), the Official Secrets Act, the Public Order and Security Act (POSA), and the Criminal Law (Codification and Reform) Act. In general, these laws restrict who may work as a journalist, require journalists to register with the state, severely limit what they may publish, and mandate harsh penalties—including long prison sentences—for violators. As mandated by the GPA, in 2010 the newly formed and quasi-independent Zimbabwe Media Commission (ZMC) replaced the state-controlled Media and Information Commission (MIC). However, former MIC head Tafataona Mahoso was appointed chief executive of the new body. The ZMC granted a number of new licenses, including to two news agencies and the long-shuttered *Daily News*, the country's most widely read independent daily until it was closed for violating AIPPA in 2003. The paper returned to print in March 2011.

The government continues to dominate the broadcast sector via the state-controlled Zimbabwe Broadcasting Corporation (ZBC) and the NewZiana news agency. Access to international news via satellite television is prohibitively expensive for most Zimbabweans. In 2009, the government lifted a ban on foreign news organizations such as the BBC, but the MIC significantly raised the accreditation fees for these outlets. Accreditation and license fees for foreign outlets were raised again in January 2011. Government jamming of domestic and foreign-based shortwave radio has decreased in recent years, but is still a problem. The 2007 Interception of Communications Act empowers the state to monitor telephonic and electronic communication. Journalists are routinely subjected to verbal intimidation, physical attacks, arrest and detention, and financial pressure by the police and ZANU-PF supporters.

Restrictions on freedom of expression have extended to the art world. In 2011, the cast of a play about the 2008 election violence was arrested and detained for two days for "beating a drum in public" and undermining the authority of the president. While freedom of religion has generally been respected in Zimbabwe, church attendance has become increasingly politicized, and 2011 featured a stark increase in restrictions on and harassment of religious groups—particularly the mainstream Anglican Church—that are not aligned with ZANU-PF. Throughout the year, a pro-Mugabe Anglican splinter faction led by excommunicated bishop Nolbert Kunonga mounted a campaign to seize hundreds of church properties and other assets, including orphanages and Harare's main cathedral. In October, Archbishop of Canterbury Rowan Williams gave Mugabe a report on alleged abuses against Anglicans, including death threats against bishops; denial of access to churches, schools, clinics, and missions stations; the violent dispersal of congregations; evictions of priests; and one murder. In September, South Africa's *Mail & Guardian* reported on efforts by ZANU-PF to court the leaders of popular evangelical churches ahead of upcoming elections.

Academic freedom is limited. All schools are under state control, and education aid has often been based on parents' political loyalties. Security forces and ZANU-PF thugs harass dissident university students, who have been arrested or expelled for protesting against government policy. Teachers, especially in rural areas, are often targets of political violence. In 2008, thousands of teachers—many of whom served as polling officials—were beaten by ZANU-PF militias, and many rural schools were closed. According to the Progressive Teachers' Union of Zimbabwe, 7 teachers were killed, 60 were tortured, about 600 were hospitalized, and over 230 teachers' houses were burned down. In October 2011, Amnesty International reported that thousands of children evicted during Operation Murambatsvina in 2005 were still attending makeshift schools in their new settlements. The nongovernmental organization (NGO) Plan International reported in November that one-third of Zimbabwean girls were not attending primary school, and two-thirds were not attending secondary school due to poverty, abuse, and cultural practices. The small nongovernmental sector is active, but NGOs face legal restrictions and extralegal harassment. The 2004 Non-Governmental Organizations Act increased scrutiny of human rights groups and explicitly prohibited them from receiving foreign funds. Among other instances of harassment in 2011, Abel Chikomo, director of the Zimbabwe Human Rights NGO Forum, was arrested in April and charged with running an illegal organization; Chikomo was harassed repeatedly throughout the year. In September, Jenni Williams and Magodonga Mahlangu, leaders of Women of Zimbabwe Arise (WOZA), were arrested along with 10 other activists during a demonstration in Bulawayo. While others were released without charge, Williams and Mahlangu were held for 13 days on charges of kidnapping and theft. According to Amnesty International, WOZA leaders and members had also faced a targeted intimidation campaign by security forces in February, ahead of their annual Valentine's Day protest march in Bulawayo.

The 2002 POSA requires police permission for public meetings and demonstrations. Such meetings are often broken up, and participants are subject to arbitrary arrest as well as attacks by ZANU-PF militias. The POSA allows police to impose arbitrary curfews and forbids criticism of the president. In March 2011, police raided a meeting of civil society activists inspired by the popular uprising in Egypt. While 46 people were initially arrested and charged with treason, which can carry the death penalty, the cases against all but 6 were dropped, and the remaining charges were reduced to "inciting public violence" in July. The six defendants' trial had not begun by year's end.

The Labor Relations Act allows the government to veto collective-bargaining agreements that it deems harmful to the economy. Strikes are allowed except in "essential" industries. Because the Zimbabwe Congress of Trade Unions (ZCTU) has led resistance to Mugabe's rule, it has become a particular target for repression. In recent years, Gertrude Hambira, secretary general of the General Agriculture and Plantation Workers' Union (GAPWUZ), has also been subject to focused harassment by the authorities.

Pressure from the executive branch has substantially eroded judicial independence, though the situation has improved somewhat since the GPA. The accused are often denied access to counsel and a fair, timely trial, and the government has repeatedly refused to enforce court orders. It has also replaced senior judges or pressured them to resign by stating that it could not guarantee their security; judges have been subject to extensive physical harassment. Vacancies for scores of magistrate posts have caused a backlog of tens of thousands of cases.

Security forces abuse citizens with impunity, often ignoring basic rights regarding detention, searches, and seizures. The government has taken no clear action to halt the rising incidence of torture and mistreatment of suspects in custody. Security forces have also taken on major roles in crop collection and food distribution, and both the police and the military remain heavily politicized toward ZANU-PF despite the GPA. Meanwhile, ZANU-PF militias operate as de facto enforcers of government policy and have committed assault, torture, rape, extralegal evictions, and extralegal executions without fear of punishment. In March 2011, HRW accused the government of willfully failing to investigate and prosecute political violence perpetrated during the 2008 elections, and alleged that this failure was fueling further acts of violence. In September, in a rare exception to the prevailing impunity, a court sentenced ZANU-PF militia commander Gilbert Mavhenyengwa to 20 years in prison for the 2008 rape of the wife of an MDC supporter.

Lengthy pretrial detention remains a problem, and despite some improvements in recent years, and prison conditions remain harsh and sometimes life-threatening. Overcrowding and funding shortages have contributed to HIV and tuberculosis infections among inmates and poor sanitation facilities.

People living in the two Matabeleland provinces continue to suffer political and economic discrimination, and security forces often target these areas as MDC strongholds. Restrictive citizenship laws discriminate against Zimbabweans born in neighboring African countries.

The state has extensive control over travel and residence. The government has seized the passports of its domestic opponents, and foreign critics are routinely expelled or denied entry. High passport fees inhibit legal travel. At the same time, badly underfunded immigration and border authorities lack the capacity to effectively enforce travel restrictions.

Property rights are not respected. Operation Murambatsvina in 2005 entailed the eviction of hundreds of thousands of city dwellers and the destruction of thousands of residential and commercial structures, many of which had been approved by the government. Despite the advent of a government resettlement program (Operation Garikai), by 2011 the majority of victims still lacked adequate housing and had no means of redressing the destruction of their property. Most victims have moved into existing, overcrowded urban housing stock or remained in rural areas.

The 2007 Indigenization Law, which stipulates that 51 percent of shares in all companies operating in Zimbabwe must be owned by black Zimbabweans, came into effect in 2010. September 2011 was the deadline for foreign companies to submit plans on share sales to the government. Over 700 companies did not submit plans or had their plans rejected by the government; many complained of lack of clarity over the procedures and requirements. By year's end, details concerning the implementation and enforcement of the law remained murky. In February 2011, a ZANU-PF-sponsored rally against foreign ownership of companies spurred a series of violent attacks on foreign traders (mostly Chinese and Nigerian) in Harare; eight people were arrested.

Fewer than 400 white-owned farms remain out of the 4,500 that existed when land invasions started in 2000, and any avenues of legal recourse for expropriated farmers have been closed. In November 2011, a study by researchers at Sussex University found that only 35 percent of recipients of the redistributed land were pursuing farming full time, with the rest either farming part time or having abandoned the land altogether.

Women enjoy extensive legal protections, but societal discrimination and domestic violence persist. Women serve as ministers in national and local governments and hold 32 and 24 seats in the House of Assembly and Senate, respectively. The World Health Organization has reported that Zimbabwean women's "healthy life expectancy" of 34 years is the world's shortest. Sexual abuse is widespread, including the use of rape as a political weapon. Female members of the opposition often face particular brutality at the hands of security forces. The prevalence of customary laws in rural areas undermines women's civil rights and access to education.

Homosexuality is illegal, and police raided the offices of a gay rights NGO in 2010. In October 2011, Tsvangirai called for gay rights to be enshrined in the new constitution, but the suggestion was rejected by Justice Minister Patrick Chinamasa.

Abkhazia

Political Rights: 5 **Population:** 216,000
Civil Liberties: 5
Status: Partly Free

Ten-Year Ratings Timeline For Year Under Review (Political Rights, Civil Liberties, Status)

2002	2003	2004	2005	2006	2007	2008	2009	2010	2011
6,5NF	6,5NF	6,5NF	5,5PF	5,5PF	5,5PF	5,5PF	5,5PF	5,5PF	5,5PF

Overview: **Abkhazia held a snap presidential election in August following the unexpected death of President Sergei Bagapsh in May. Incumbent vice president Aleksandr Ankvab won with 55 percent of the vote in balloting that was widely lauded as generally free and fair, and took office in September. In contrast to previous elections, Russia did not endorse a candidate, though the Kremlin continued to exert economic and military pressure on the territory.**

Annexed by Russia in 1864, Abkhazia became an autonomous republic within Soviet Georgia in 1930. After the 1991 collapse of the Soviet Union, Abkhazia declared its independence from Georgia in 1992, leading to a year-long war that left thousands dead and displaced more than 200,000 residents, mainly ethnic Georgians. Abkhaz forces won de facto independence for the republic in 1993, and an internationally brokered ceasefire was signed in Moscow in 1994.

Incumbent Abkhaz president Vladislav Ardzinba ran unopposed for reelection in 1999, and a reported 98 percent of voters supported independence in a concurrent referendum. Deputies loyal to Ardzinba won all 35 seats in the 2002 parliamentary elections after the opposition withdrew to protest bias by the election commission and state-backed media.

Under pressure from a powerful opposition movement, Prime Minister Gennady Gagulia resigned in April 2003 and was succeeded by Defense Minister Raul Khadjimba, though Ardzinba refused to step down as president.

An opposition candidate, former prime minister Sergei Bagapsh, defeated Khadjimba in the December 2004 presidential election, but he was pressured into a January 2005 rerun with Khadjimba—who was backed by Ardzinba and Moscow—as his vice presidential running mate. The new ticket won the rerun with 91 percent of the vote. In July 2006, Georgian troops occupied the strategic Kodori Gorge, the only portion of Abkhazia still under Georgian control, after a Kodori-based Georgian paramilitary group refused orders from Tbilisi to disarm its fighters. The pro-Tbilisi government-in-exile for Abkhazia, composed of ethnic Georgians, was transferred to the gorge later that year.

Members of three pro-Bagapsh parties captured more than 20 seats in the 2007 parliamentary elections, and a number of opposition candidates also won seats, despite claims that Bagapsh interfered with the electoral process.

In April 2008, Moscow increased its deployment of peacekeepers in Abkhazia to more than 2,500, drawing sharp international criticism. After years of rising tension, war broke out in August between Georgian forces on one side and Russian, South Ossetian, and Abkhaz forces on the other. Although the brief conflict centered on South Ossetia, another Russian-backed Georgian territory that had won de facto independence in the early 1990s, Abkhaz troops succeeded in capturing the Kodori Gorge and additional territory on the Georgian-Abkhaz border.

In late August, following a French-brokered ceasefire, Russia formally recognized both Abkhazia and South Ossetia as independent states, though nearly all of the international community continued to view the territories as de jure parts of Georgia. A 2009 Russian-Abkhaz agreement authorized Moscow to build and upgrade military bases and reinforce the Abkhaz-Georgian border. Abkhazia later announced that it would transfer control of its airport to Russia, and the government licensed Russia's state-owned oil company Rosneft to explore for oil in the territory.

Bagapsh won reelection in December 2009, capturing more than 59 percent of the vote amid 73 percent turnout. Khadjimba placed a distant second with just 15 percent. Though all five candidates reportedly endorsed Russia's preeminent role in the territory, Abkhaz opposition journalists and politicians, led by Khadjimba, accused the government of ceding undue control to Moscow.

In February 2010, Bagapsh signed a second agreement with Russia, allowing it to build three new bases for naval, air, and ground forces. About 3,500 Russian soldiers and 1,500 border guards were stationed in the territory as of August 2011. In October, Russia's parliament passed an agreement to maintain the bases for 49 years, followed by automatic 15-year extensions.

In May 2011, Bagapsh died unexpectedly after lung surgery, leading to a snap presidential election in August between Vice President Aleksandr Ankvab, Prime Minister Sergei Shamba, and Khadjimba, running as an opposition candidate. Amid 70 percent turnout, Ankvab won with 55 percent of the vote, followed by Shamba with 21 percent and Khadjimba with 19.5 percent. The election was considered genuinely competitive, and Moscow did not publicly endorse a candidate, though all three promised to maintain strong ties with Russia.

The small Pacific states of Vanuatu and Tuvalu recognized Abkhazia's independence during 2011, joining Russia, Venezuela, Nicaragua, and Nauru. In October, the territory hosted the World Domino Championship, previously reserved for UN member states, as part of an ongoing bid to gain broader recognition.

Political Rights and Civil Liberties: Residents of Abkhazia can elect government officials, but the more than 200,000 Georgians who fled the region during the war in the early 1990s cannot vote in the elections held by the separatist government. Most of the ethnic Georgians who remain in Abkhazia are also unable to vote in local polls, as they lack Abkhaz passports, though 9,000 passports were issued to mostly ethnic Georgian residents of Gali for the 2011 presidential election, compared with 3,000 in 2009. None of the separatist government's elections have been recognized internationally.

The 1999 constitution established a presidential system, stating that only ethnic Abkhaz can be elected to the post. The president and vice president are elected for five-year terms. The parliament, or People's Assembly, consists of 35 members elected for five-year terms from single-seat constituencies.

Corruption in Abkhazia is believed to be extensive, and government officials are not required to provide declarations of income. In January 2011, Russia's Audit Chamber accused Abkhaz leaders of misappropriating $12 million allocated by Moscow for infrastructure development.

Local broadcast media are largely controlled by the government, which operates the Abkhaz State Television and Radio Company (AGTRK). In July 2010, opposition journalists and politicians proposed a package of reforms that would turn AGTRK into an independent public-service broadcaster, though it remained state run at the end of 2011. All the major Russian television stations also broadcast into the territory. Private broadcasters received increased government scrutiny ahead of the 2009 elections, and the opposition complained of inadequate access to broadcast media. By contrast, during the 2011 election campaign the three presidential candidates received equal airtime on state television and agreed to televised debates.

The print media are considered more influential, consisting of several weekly newspapers. The government publication *Respublika Abkhazii* competes with two main independent papers, *Chegemskaya Pravda* and *Novaya Gazeta*.

Internet access has increased since 2008, with an estimated 25 percent of the population online. Some legal restrictions apply to both traditional and online media, including criminal libel statutes.

Religious freedom in Abkhazia is affected by the political situation. The Abkhaz Orthodox Church declared its separation from the Georgian Orthodox Church in 2009, and a number of Georgian Orthodox clerics have been expelled for alleged spying or refusal to recognize separatist authorities. In 2011, the Abkhaz church was split into two factions when a group of clerics formed a new diocese, having objected to the leadership's more deferential stance toward the Russian Orthodox Church. Neither faction is internationally recognized as independent from the Georgian church. Though a 1995 decree bans Jehovah's Witnesses, they continue to practice openly in Abkhazia, as do other denominations. Abkhazia's Muslims, who make up about 30 percent of the population, are allowed to practice freely.

The Abkhaz constitution offers some protection to ethnic minorities seeking education in their native languages. Armenian-language schools generally operate without government interference, but many of Gali's Georgian-language schools have been converted to instruction in Russian, leaving the future status of the remaining Georgian-language schools uncertain. Some of Gali's ethnic Georgian students regularly travel to Georgian-controlled territory to attend classes. Ethnic Georgian residents who do not hold Abkhaz passports are restricted from studying at Sukhumi State University.

Although most nongovernmental organizations (NGOs) rely on funding from outside the territory, the NGO sector exerts a significant degree of influence on government policies. Freedom of assembly is somewhat limited, but the opposition and civil society groups mounted several protests in 2009 and 2010 to challenge the government's increasing dependence on Russia as well as a proposal to offer citizenship to some ethnic Georgian returnees.

Abkhazia's judicial code is based on Russia's, and the criminal justice system suffers from chronic problems, including limited defendant access to qualified legal counsel, violations of due process, and lengthy pretrial detentions. Local NGOs have petitioned for significant judicial reform.

Gali's ethnic Georgian residents reported an improvement of their human rights situation in 2011, though they continued to suffer from widespread poverty and their undefined legal status within Abkhazia. Ethnic Georgians are eligible for Abkhaz passports—entitling them to vote, own property, run a business, and obtain Russian citizenship and pensions—but on the condition that they give up their Georgian passports, which provide significant economic and legal benefits.

Travel and choice of residence are limited by the ongoing separatist dispute. Most ethnic Georgians who fled Abkhazia during the early 1990s live in Tbilisi and western Georgia. As many as 47,000 former Gali residents have returned to Abkhazia since 1994, with an additional 5,000 who commute between Abkhazia and Georgia, though the process of obtaining travel permits remains expensive and burdensome for Gali Georgians. Under a law preventing foreigners from buying Abkhaz property, ethnic Russians have been barred from acquiring residences in the territory, and some have reported that their homes have been confiscated.

Since the 2008 war, ethnic Abkhaz have had greater difficulty receiving visas to travel abroad, including to the United States and European Union countries. About 90 percent of Abkhazia's residents hold Russian passports, since Abkhaz travel documents are not internationally recognized. In April 2011, Russia implemented an agreement on visa-free travel between Abkhazia and Russia.

Equality of opportunity and normal business activities are limited by corruption, criminal organizations, and economic reliance on Russia, which pays for half the state budget and accounts for 99 percent of foreign investment.

A strong NGO sector has contributed to women's involvement in business and civil society. However, Abkhaz women complain of being underrepresented in government positions, holding only 4 of the 35 seats in Abkhazia's parliament.

Gaza Strip

Political Rights: 6
Civil Liberties: 6
Status: Not Free

Population: 1,710,000

Note: Whereas past editions of *Freedom in the World* featured one report for Israeli-occupied portions of the West Bank and Gaza Strip and another for Palestinian-administered portions, the latest two editions divide the territories based on geography, with one report for the West Bank and another for the Gaza Strip. As in previous years, Israel is examined in a separate report.

Ten-Year Ratings Timeline For Year Under Review (Political Rights, Civil Liberties, Status)

2002	2003	2004	2005	2006	2007	2008	2009	2010	2011
--	--	--	--	--	--	--	--	6,6NF	6,6NF

Overview: **In May 2011, Egypt opened the Rafah border crossing to certain categories of Gaza residents, easing the Israeli-led blockade of the territory and increasing Gazans' access to external**

trade. Exchanges of artillery fire between Gazan militants and Israeli forces continued sporadically during 2011. In October, the territory's ruling faction, Hamas, released a captive Israeli soldier in exchange for hundreds of Palestinians held by Israel. Despite a May political agreement between Hamas and the West Bank–based Fatah faction, no date for overdue Palestinian elections had been set by year's end.

The Gaza Strip was demarcated as part of a 1949 armistice agreement between Israel and Egypt following the 1948 Arab-Israeli war. Populated mostly by Palestinian Arab refugees of that war, the territory was occupied by Egypt until 1967. Israel conquered Gaza, along with the West Bank and other territories, in the 1967 Six-Day War, and ruled it thereafter through a military administration.

In 1968, Israel began establishing Jewish settlements in Gaza, a process regarded as illegal by most of the international community. Israel maintained that the settlements were legal since under international law Gaza was a disputed territory. In what became known as the first intifada (uprising), in 1987 Palestinians living in the West Bank and Gaza staged massive demonstrations, acts of civil disobedience, and attacks against Israeli settlers and Israel Defense Forces (IDF) troops in the territories, as well as attacks within Israel proper. Israel and Yasser Arafat's Palestine Liberation Organization (PLO) reached an agreement in 1993 that provided for a PLO renunciation of terrorism and recognition of Israel, Israeli troop withdrawals, and phased Palestinian autonomy in Gaza and the West Bank. In 1994, the newly formed Palestinian Authority (PA) took control of most of the Gaza Strip; the PA also came to control about 40 percent of the West Bank.

As negotiations on a final settlement and the creation of a Palestinian state headed toward collapse, a second intifada began in September 2000, and the Israeli government responded by staging military raids into PA territory.

After Arafat died in November 2004, the PA in January 2005 held its second-ever presidential election, which had been repeatedly postponed; the first voting for president and the Palestinian Legislative Council (PLC) had taken place in 1996. Mahmoud Abbas of Arafat's Fatah faction won the 2005 contest with 62 percent of the vote. In subsequent municipal voting in Gaza, the Islamist group Hamas won 77 out of 118 seats in 10 districts, to Fatah's 26 seats. Each group accused the other of fraud, and there was some election-related violence.

In 2005, Israel unilaterally "disengaged" from Gaza, withdrawing all settlers and military personnel. However, it retained control of the territory's airspace, its coastline, and most of its land border, including the passage of goods and people.

Hamas won the 2006 elections for the PLC, securing 74 of 132 seats, while Fatah took 45. Hamas was particularly dominant in Gazan districts. Fatah and Hamas formed a unity government headed by Prime Minister Ismail Haniya of Hamas. Israel, the United States, and the European Union (EU) refused to recognize the new government, citing Hamas's involvement in terrorism and its refusal to recognize Israel or past Israel-PA agreements. The United States and the EU, then the largest donors to the PA, cut off assistance to the government.

In June 2006, in response to the killing of eight Palestinian civilians by an artillery shell (the source of which was disputed), Hamas declared an end to a 2005 truce with Israel and accelerated the firing of Qassam rockets at Israel from Gaza. Hamas and other militant groups subsequently carried out a raid near Gaza, killing two IDF soldiers and capturing a third, Corporal Gilad Shalit. Israel responded by invading Gaza, where the IDF destroyed Qassam launchers and ammunition sites but failed to locate Shalit. The fighting killed dozens of civilians.

Armed clashes between Hamas and Fatah supporters in Gaza escalated in 2007, and in June Hamas militants took over Fatah-controlled institutions in the territory. Some 600 Palestinians were killed in the fighting, and thousands of Gazans fled—along with most Fatah militants—to the West Bank. Abbas accused Hamas of staging a coup in Gaza, dismissed the Hamas-led government, and appointed an emergency cabinet led by former finance minister Salam Fayad. This resulted in a bifurcated PA, with Hamas governing Gaza and Abbas, and Fayad governing the roughly 40 percent of the West Bank not directly administered by Israel. Hamas security forces and militants subsequently pursued a major crackdown on Fatah in Gaza, closing Fatah-affiliated civic organizations and media outlets, and allegedly torturing detainees.

Meanwhile, Israel declared the Gaza Strip a "hostile entity" in response to ongoing rocket attacks, and imposed an economic blockade on the territory, granting passage only to food and certain other humanitarian supplies. However, arms and goods were regularly smuggled through a developing tunnel network between Egypt and Gaza. The blockade was eased after Hamas and Israel declared a six-month truce in June 2008.

War erupted between Hamas and Israeli forces in December 2008, after the truce expired, and Hamas ramped up its rocket bombardment of Israeli towns near the Gaza border. The IDF launched near-daily air strikes and an almost three-week ground invasion of the Gaza Strip. Israel declared a unilateral ceasefire in late January 2009, and Hamas soon did the same. During the conflict, Israeli forces damaged or destroyed large portions of Gaza's military, government, and civilian infrastructure. According to the United Nations, some 50,000 homes, 800 industrial properties, 200 schools, and 39 mosques or churches were damaged or destroyed. For its part, Hamas launched over 700 rockets and mortar shells into Israeli civilian areas, often from civilian areas in Gaza. While the Palestinian Centre for Human Rights reported that 1,434 Palestinians were killed, including 960 noncombatants, the IDF reported that 1,166 Palestinians were killed, including 295 to 460 noncombatants. Thirteen Israelis were killed, including three noncombatants.

Israel tightened its blockade of Gaza during the war, allowing only humanitarian goods into the territory. Following the ceasefire, the restrictions were eased somewhat to allow the transfer of a limited number of authorized goods, as well as international aid workers and individuals with specified medical and humanitarian needs. Gaza's Rafah border crossing with Egypt opened on an ad hoc basis.

In 2010 and 2011, a series of private ships carrying food and other goods attempted to break Israel's coastal blockade of Gaza. In May 2010, Israeli soldiers intercepted a six-ship flotilla from Turkey and killed nine activists on one of the ships—the *Mavi Marmara*—in an ensuing confrontation. The Israeli government was widely condemned internationally for the incident, but claimed its soldiers were acting in self-defense. Israel later eased the blockade, allowing in virtually all consumer goods while continuing to ban weapons, fertilizer, gas tanks, drilling equipment, and water disinfectant, as well as all exports and almost all travel; prohibitions on construction materials were also slightly loosened. In May 2011, Egypt opened the Rafah border crossing to women, children, and men over 40; Gazan men between 18 and 40 required a permit to cross the border, which officially remained closed to overland trade.

A November 2010 report by 21 aid groups stated that there had been "little improvement" in economic conditions in Gaza since the easing of the blockade, citing in particular the continued restrictions on exports and construction materials. These findings were echoed in a 2011 report by the UN Relief and Works Agency (UNRWA), which criticized Israeli restrictions for impeding its projects to rebuild homes and schools. In August, the British Broadcasting Corporation (BBC) reported that the opening of the Rafah border crossing and the development of more sophisticated smuggling tunnels between Egypt and Gaza had begun to relieve shortages of construction and other goods, leading to a significant increase in construction by the Hamas authorities.

Fighting between Israel and Gazan militants broke out regularly during 2011. In most cases, rocket and mortar fire into Israel from Gaza prompted Israeli air strikes and artillery bombardments, killing both combatants and civilians, including children. According to the Israeli nongovernmental organization (NGO) B'Tselem, in 2011 the IDF killed a total of 105 Palestinians in the Gaza Strip, 37 of whom were noncombatants.

In October, Israel and Hamas negotiated a prisoner exchange, whereby Hamas freed IDF soldier Gilad Shalit and Israel would release 1,027 Palestinian prisoners. Of the latter, 447 were released immediately—mostly to Gaza, but some to the West Bank and foreign countries—and another 550 were freed in December.

Political Rights and Civil Liberties: Residents of Gaza were never granted citizenship by either Egypt or Israel, and are mostly citizens of the Palestinian Authority (PA). The current Hamas-controlled government in the territory claims to be the legitimate leadership of the PA. However, the authority—a quasi-sovereign entity created by the 1993 Oslo Accords—is effectively fractured, and the Hamas government implements PA law selectively.

The PA president is elected to four-year terms, and international observers judged the 2005 presidential election to be generally free and fair. However, PA president Mahmoud Abbas lost control over Gaza after the 2007 Fatah-Hamas schism, and Prime Minister Ismail Haniya continues to lead the Hamas government despite being formally dismissed by Abbas. Other Hamas ministers similarly remained in their posts in Gaza after almost all Fatah-affiliated ministers, government officials, and bureaucrats were expelled or fled to the West Bank. When Abbas's elected term expired in 2009, Hamas rejected the West Bank PA's legal justifications for his continued rule, arguing instead that the PA Basic Law empowered the head of the Palestinian Legislative Council (PLC)—Aziz Dweik of Hamas—to serve as acting president.

The unicameral, 132-seat PLC serves four-year terms. Voting in Gaza during the 2006 PLC elections was deemed largely fair by international observers, despite allegations that Hamas candidates campaigned in mosques in violation of electoral rules. However, the Hamas-Fatah rift, combined with Israel's detention of many (especially Hamas-affiliated) lawmakers, has prevented the PLC from meeting since 2007, and its term expired in 2010.

In May 2011, Hamas and Fatah agreed to form a national unity-government that would organize presidential and parliamentary elections and increase coordination between Hamas- and Fatah-aligned security forces. By year's end, however, the unity government had not yet been formed, and no date had been set for elections.

Humanitarian organizations and donor countries allege that Hamas authorities in Gaza exert almost total control over the distribution of funds and goods, and allocate resources according to political criteria with little or no transparency, creating ample opportunities for corruption. In March 2011, after authorities accused the Palestine Investment Bank in Gaza City of transferring money out of Gaza, gunmen allegedly supported by Hamas stormed the bank, taking $250 million.

The media are not free in Gaza. In 2008, Hamas replaced the PA Ministry of Information with a government Media Office and banned all journalists not accredited by it; authorities also closed down all media outlets that were not affiliated with Hamas. In 2011 officials continued to ban the import of three West Bank newspapers—*Al-Ayyam, Al-Quds*, and *Al-Hayat Al-Jadida*—that are generally associated with Fatah. In January, the UN news service IRIN reported a significant increase in Gaza-based blogs. The main telephone and data network in Gaza (and the West Bank) was temporarily disabled by computer hackers in November.

According to a 2011 report on conditions for journalists by the Palestinian Center for Development and Media Freedoms (MADA), physical attacks, arrests, detentions, and confiscation of equipment by Palestinian security forces increased by over 45 percent between 2009 and 2010, a trend that continued in 2011. According to MADA, in 2011 there were 53 such violations by Palestinian authorities in Gaza. In March, Hamas security forces routinely harassed journalists covering demonstrations in favor of Palestinian unity. In one incident, plainclothes policemen raided the Gaza bureau of Reuters, beating and threatening journalists and destroying equipment. In September, the BBC reported new restrictions on foreign journalists, including a requirement that they obtain five-day advance permission to work in the territory and sign forms noting that local Palestinian colleagues will be held responsible for coverage that is critical of Hamas.

Freedom of religion is restricted in Gaza. The PA Basic Law declares Islam to be the official religion of Palestine and states that "respect and sanctity of all other heavenly religions (Judaism and Christianity) shall be maintained." Under Hamas, the authorities—including quasi-official "morality police" and Hamas-affiliated volunteer dawa groups—increasingly enforce orthodox Sunni Islamic practices and conservative dress. In addition, security forces and militants routinely harass worshippers at non-Hamas-affiliated mosques. Christians continued to suffer routine harassment in 2011, though violent attacks decreased from a peak in 2009.

The Israeli blockade has restricted access to school supplies. While university students are ostensibly allowed to leave Gaza, they must be escorted by foreign diplomats or contractors. A March 2011 report by the Palestinian Centre for Human Rights noted that Gazans—who recently constituted 35 percent of the student body at West Bank universities—were now mostly absent from those institutions because of the blockade. Hamas has taken over the formal education system, aside from schools run by UNRWA. A teachers' strike in 2009 led to the replacement of many strikers with new, Hamas-allied teachers. In 2010, Islamist militants burned down UNRWA summer camps, accusing the organizers of teaching young girls "dancing and immorality." In March 2011, Hamas security officials began confiscating copies of "immoral" novels from (mostly university) bookstores, according to Human Rights Watch (HRW).

Since 2008, Hamas has significantly restricted freedoms of assembly and association, with security forces violently dispersing public gatherings of Fatah and other groups. In January 2011, police arrested six women who had gathered in Gaza City for a demonstration in solidarity with antigovernment protesters in Egypt. In late February and early March, police forcibly broke up several protests calling for unity between Hamas and Fatah, sealing off public squares and university campuses and beating demonstrators.

There is a broad range of Palestinian NGOs and civic groups, and Hamas itself operates a large network that provides social services to certain Palestinians. However, following the 2009 conflict between Hamas and Israel, Hamas restricted the activities of aid organizations that would not submit to its regulations or coordinate with its relief efforts, and many civic associations have been shut down for political reasons since the 2007 PA split. In July 2011, Hamas began enforcing its 2010 demand to audit the books of some 80 international NGOs in Gaza. Throughout the year, authorities harassed, detained, and summoned leaders of the Palestinian unity protests and signatories to the 2010 "Gaza Manifesto," which criticized both Israel and Hamas. Security officials also reportedly questioned Gazans who travelled to Western countries.

Independent labor unions in Gaza continue to function, and PA workers have staged strikes against Hamas-led management. However, the Fatah-aligned Palestinian General Federation of Trade Unions (PGFTU), the largest union body in the territories, has seen its operations greatly curtailed. Its main Gaza offices were taken over by Hamas militants in 2007, and the building was severely damaged in a December 2008 Israeli air raid.

Laws governing Palestinians in the Gaza Strip derive from Ottoman, British Mandate, Jordanian, Egyptian, PA, and Islamic law, as well as Israeli military orders. The judicial system is not independent, and Palestinian judges lack proper training and experience. In 2007, Abbas ordered judges to boycott judicial bodies in Gaza, and Hamas began appointing new prosecutors and judges in 2008. Hamas security forces and militants continued to carry out arbitrary arrests and detentions during 2011, and torture of detainees and criminal suspects is common. The Palestinian human rights ombudsman agency—the Independent Commission for Human Rights—has been banned from Hamas detention centers for the past three years, and from Gaza's central prison since December 2010. Nonetheless, the Independent Commission for Human Rights reported 102 torture complaints against security forces in Gaza in 2011.

Hamas-run military courts have sentenced 33 people to death since 2007 and carried out at least eight official executions, mostly for treason. In July 2011, two alleged collaborators with Israel—a father and a son convicted in 2004—were executed by firing squad.

Freedom of movement is severely restricted. Although Egypt opened the Rafah border crossing to women, children, and men over 40 in May 2011, with Gazan men between 18 and 40 requiring a permit to cross the border, the Israeli border remains sealed, with exceptions for medical cases, students, and aid workers. The regular clashes between Israeli forces and Gaza-based militants greatly restrict freedom of movement within the Gaza Strip, as does the presence of unexploded ordnance.

Freedom of residence has been limited by the violent conflicts in and around Gaza. Following the 2007 schism in the PA, thousands of Fatah-affiliated residents fled to the West Bank. Moreover, the conflict with Israel that ended in January 2009 was fought to a large extent in civilian neighborhoods, leading to the damage or destruction of some 50,000 homes.

The blockade has greatly reduced economic freedom and choice in the territory, though these conditions improved slightly in 2011. Much economic activity is conducted through a dense network of tunnels beneath Gaza's border with Egypt. The tunnels are also used to transport weapons and are routinely bombed by Israel.

Under Hamas, personal status law is derived almost entirely from Sharia (Islamic law), which puts women at a stark disadvantage in matters of marriage, divorce, inheritance, and domestic abuse. Rape, domestic abuse, and "honor killings," in which relatives murder women for perceived sexual or moral transgressions, are common, and these crimes often go unpunished. A December 2009 study by the Palestinian Woman's Information and Media Center found that 77 percent of women in Gaza had experienced violence of various sorts, 53 percent had experienced physical violence, and 15 percent had suffered sexual abuse. Women's dress and movements in public have been increasingly restricted under Hamas rule. The government has barred women from wearing trousers in public and declared that all women must wear hijab in public buildings, though these policies are enforced sporadically. In 2010, the government banned women from smoking water pipes and men from cutting women's hair. In July 2011, police began arresting male hairdressers who violated this ban.

Hong Kong

Political Rights: 5
Civil Liberties: 2
Status: Partly Free

Population: 7,100,000

Ten-Year Ratings Timeline For Year Under Review (Political Rights, Civil Liberties, Status)

2002	2003	2004	2005	2006	2007	2008	2009	2010	2011
5,3PF	5,3PF	5,2PF	5,2PF	5,2PF	5,2PF	5,2PF	5,2PF	5,2PF	5,2PF

Overview: **Hong Kong experienced a series of protests in 2011 due to growing public frustration over soaring property prices, a widening income gap, and limited democratic rights. As in the previous year, the authorities' response indicated a reduced respect for freedom of assembly. In August, during a visit by Chinese vice premier Li Keqiang, the government took unprecedented measures to limit reporters' ability to cover the visit. The well-financed pro-Beijing political camp swept district council elections held in November 2011, amid allegations of vote rigging and division within the prodemocracy camp over recent electoral reforms.**

Hong Kong Island was ceded in perpetuity to Britain in 1842; adjacent territories were subsequently added, and the last section was leased to Britain in 1898 for a period of 99 years. In the 1984 Sino-British Joint Declaration, London agreed to restore the entire colony to China in 1997. In return, Beijing—under its "one country, two systems" formula—pledged to maintain the enclave's legal, political, and economic autonomy for 50 years.

Under the 1984 agreement, a constitution for the Hong Kong Special Administrative Region, known as the Basic Law, took effect in 1997. The Basic Law stated that universal suffrage was the "ultimate aim" for Hong Kong, but it allowed direct elections for only 18 seats in the 60-member Legislative Council (Legco), and provided for the gradual expansion of elected seats to 30 by 2003. After China took control, it temporarily suspended the Legco and installed a provisional legislature that repealed or tightened several civil liberties laws during its 10-month tenure.

Tung Chee-hwa was chosen as Hong Kong's chief executive by a Beijing-organized election committee in 1997, and his popularity waned as Beijing became increasingly involved in Hong Kong's affairs, raising fears that civic freedoms would be compromised. Officials were forced to withdraw a restrictive antisubversion bill after it sparked mass protests in July 2003.

Pro-Beijing parties retained control of the Legco in 2004 elections, which were marred by intimidation that was thought to have been organized by Beijing. In 2005, with two years left to serve, the deeply unpopular Tung resigned. He was replaced by career civil servant Donald Tsang, and China's National People's Congress (NPC) decided that Tsang would serve out the remainder of Tung's term before facing election. Tsang won a new term as chief executive in 2007, garnering 82 percent of the votes in the mostly pro-Beijing election committee.

Pro-Beijing parties again won Legco elections in September 2008, taking 30 seats, though few of those members were elected by popular vote. The prodemocracy camp won 23 seats, including 19 by popular vote, enabling them to retain a veto on constitutional changes.

In November 2009, the government published a consultation document on draft electoral reforms that would ostensibly serve as a transitional arrangement until the adoption of universal suffrage. Following months of public debate and closed-door negotiations, the Legco approved a compromise version of the reforms in June 2010. The new system would enable a narrow majority of Legco members to be elected by popular vote for the first time, but many in the prodemocracy camp criticized the plan for largely preserving the semidemocratic status quo and providing no guarantees of future universal suffrage.

In 2011, a string of demonstrations indicated public frustration over soaring property prices, a growing income gap, and slowly evolving restrictions on democratic rights. Continuing a pattern from the previous year, police adopted a more confrontational approach in dealing with protesters and journalists, especially during the official visit of Chinese vice premier Li Keqiang in August. During the second half of the year, attention turned toward chief executive and Legco elections scheduled for 2012. In November, Leung Chun-ying, a member of a mainland government advisory body, and Henry Tang, a high-ranking Hong Kong civil servant with ties to both the Beijing-friendly business sector and the Chinese Communist Party, announced that they would run for chief executive in March. Local media reported that Tang was the Chinese Communist Party's preferred candidate. However, by year's end, Tang's popularity had fallen after several gaffes and scandals, causing observers to speculate that the central government might switch its backing to Leung.

Political Rights and Civil Liberties: Hong Kong's Basic Law calls for the election of a chief executive and a unicameral Legislative Council (Legco). The chief executive, who serves a five-year term, is elected by an 800-member committee: some 200,000 "functional constituency" voters—representatives of various elite business and social sectors, many with close ties to Beijing—elect 600 of the committee's members, and the remaining 200 consist of Legco members, Hong Kong delegates to the NPC, religious representatives, and 41 members of the Chinese People's Political Consultative Conference (CPPCC), a mainland advisory body.

The Legco consists of 30 directly elected members and 30 members chosen by the functional constituency voters. All serve four-year terms. The Basic Law restricts the Legco's lawmaking powers, prohibiting legislators from introducing bills that would affect Hong Kong's public spending, governmental operations, or political structure. In the territory's multiparty system, the five main parties are the prodemocracy Civic Party, Democratic Party, and League of Social Democrats; the pro-Beijing Democratic Alliance for the Betterment and Progress of Hong Kong; and the business-oriented Liberal Party.

The NPC ruled in 2007 that universal suffrage might be adopted in 2017 for the chief executive election and 2020 for the Legco. The issue's omission from the 2010 electoral reforms heightened fears that the transition would be pushed further into the future. Under the 2010 changes, the election committee for the chief executive will expand from 800 to 1,200 members in 2012, but will otherwise retain its existing composition. The Legco will expand from 60 to 70 seats. Five of the new members will be chosen through direct elections based on geographical constituencies. Members of Hong Kong's 18 district councils will nominate the other five candidates from among themselves, and nominees will then face a full popular vote.

The reforms increased the importance of the district council elections held in November 2011, prompting a record voter turnout rate of 41 percent. Candidates from the pro-Beijing camp won a large majority of contested seats, amid reports of increased funding from Beijing-friendly businessmen, allegations of vote rigging, and a growing split within the prodemocracy camp over the compromise behind the 2010 reform package. Separately, the government announced in September that it would reduce the district councils' appointed seats in phases, with full abolition intended by 2020, reportedly backtracking from an earlier promise to eliminate them sooner. In the November 2011 elections, the total number of appointed seats was reduced from 102 to 68, while elected seats increased from 405 to 412.

Hong Kong is generally regarded as having low rates of corruption, though business interests have considerable influence on the Legco. In December 2011, the territory's Independent Commission Against Corruption (ICAC) detained at least 22 individuals after prodemocracy legislators reported instances of voters registering under nonexistent addresses. By year's end, six people had been charged with vote rigging, and the others remained under investigation. Hong Kong was ranked 12 out of 183 polities surveyed in Transparency International's 2011 Corruption Perceptions Index.

Under Article 27 of the Basic Law, Hong Kong residents enjoy freedoms of speech, press, and publication. These rights are generally respected in practice, and political debate is vigorous. There are dozens of daily newspapers, and residents have access to international radio broadcasts and satellite television. Foreign media operate without interference. Nonetheless, Beijing's growing influence has led to self-censorship. This stems in part from the close relationship between Hong Kong media owners and central authorities; at least 10 such owners sit on the CPPCC. Of the respondents to a University of Hong Kong survey released in April 2011, a record high 54 percent said the media practice self-censorship. In September, two news executives at Asia Television (ATV) resigned after the station erroneously announced the death of former Chinese leader Jiang Zemin. The Broadcasting Authority fined the station HK$300,000 (US$38,600) in December and revealed that a senior executive had pressured staff to air the unverified news. In another set of incidents, Beijing-friendly media vigorously attacked two professors, rival media owner Jimmy Lai, the local head of the Roman Catholic Church, and a talk show host—all of whom had been critical of the central government, supported the prodemocracy camp, or granted interviews to independent Chinese news outlets.

Several cases emerged in 2011 of the Hong Kong authorities obstructing journalists' ability to cover certain events. In July, 19 journalists were pepper-sprayed by police during a demonstration marking the anniversary of the 1997 handover. Police also detained a citizen journalist and an intern photographer, the latter for "obstructing a public place"; the charges against her were dropped in September, after she filed a lawsuit for unlawful arrest and detention. In August, during the visit by Chinese vice premier Li Keqiang, authorities kept journalists far from Li, granted them permission to cover fewer than half of the events he attended, and reportedly barred several cameramen from filming. After the Legco moved to a new complex in July, reporters were required to remain in a designated press area, limiting their ability to report on proceedings and interview lawmakers.

The selection in September 2011 of a former government official as director of broadcasting at the state-owned Radio Television Hong Kong (RTHK)—the first time since the 1930s that a non–media professional was appointed to the post—heightened concerns over RTHK's editorial independence. In November, two longtime hosts of RTHK current affairs programs who were known for their criticism of the government were told that their contracts would not be renewed in 2012.

The Basic Law provides for freedom of religion, which is generally respected in practice. Religious groups are excluded from the Societies Ordinance, which requires nongovernmental organizations (NGOs) to register with the government. Adherents of the Falun Gong spiritual movement remain free to practice and hold occasional demonstrations, though government pressure on them to remove banners from public places reportedly increased in 2011.

University professors can write and lecture freely, and political debate on campuses is lively. However, students who protested Li Keqiang's visit to the University of Hong Kong in August 2011 were manhandled by the police, and one was briefly detained.

The Basic Law guarantees freedoms of assembly and association. Police permits for demonstrations are required but rarely denied, and protests on politically sensitive issues are held regularly. Nevertheless, in recent years, police have become more confrontational with protesters. When a group of 40 demonstrators gathered in front of the central government's liaison office in February 2011, responding to online calls for a Tunisian-style "Jasmine Revolution" in China, they were outnumbered by 100 police officers; the police attempted to confiscate banners, claiming they were "blocking the view" of officers. The annual protest march held on July 1 to mark the territory's handover drew the largest crowd since 2004, with estimates ranging from 50,000 to 200,000. In the early hours of the following morning, police briefly detained over 200 participants for "illegal assembly" and "obstructing public places." The director of a local human rights group was also detained while filming the police clearing the crowd. In August, during Li Keqiang's visit, police blocked a group of 100 protesters from approaching the new government headquarters, where Li was attending a ceremony, and attempted to confiscate a mock coffin that commemorated victims of the 1989 Tiananmen Square massacre.

Hong Kong hosts a vibrant and largely unfettered NGO sector, and trade unions are independent. However, there is limited legal protection for basic labor rights. Collective-bargaining rights are not recognized, protections against antiunion discrimination are weak, and there are few regulations on working hours. The territory's first minimum-wage law took effect in May 2011.

The judiciary is independent, and the trial process is generally fair. The NPC reserves the right to make final interpretations of the Basic Law, effectively limiting the power of Hong Kong's Court of Final Appeals. In June 2011, the court departed from legal decisions made under British rule by adopting Beijing's more stringent guarantee of sovereign immunity, in a lawsuit involving a U.S. investment fund and the Congolese government. The court then asked the NPC to confirm its interpretation of the Basic Law, marking the first such referral by the Hong Kong judiciary. The NPC Standing Committee approved the decision in August.

Police are forbidden by law to employ torture and other forms of abuse. They generally respect this ban in practice, and complaints of abuse are investigated. Arbitrary arrest and detention are illegal; suspects must be charged within 48 hours of their arrest. Prison conditions generally meet international standards.

Citizens are treated equally under the law, though Hong Kong's 200,000 foreign household workers remain vulnerable to abuse, and South Asians routinely complain of discrimination in employment. Since foreign workers face deportation if dismissed, many are reluctant to bring complaints against employers. A Race Discrimination Ordinance that took effect in 2009 created an independent Equal Opportunities Commission to enforce its protections, but it has been criticized for excluding discrimination through government actions and against immigrants. In September 2011, the High Court struck down a law banning foreign household workers from applying for permanent residency after it was challenged as discriminatory by a Filipina maid who had lived in the territory for more than 25 years. Other types of foreign workers were allowed to apply for permanent residency after seven years.

The government does not control travel, choice of residence, or employment within Hong Kong, but documents are required to travel to the mainland, and employers must apply to bring in workers from China; direct applications from workers are not accepted. Hong Kong maintains its own immigration system, but periodic denials of entry to democracy activists, Falun Gong practitioners, and others have raised suspicions that the government is enforcing a Beijing-imposed political blacklist, particularly at sensitive times. In January 2011, the authorities denied visas to prominent exiled democracy activists Wang Dan and Wu'er Kaixi, who had planned to attend the funeral of a Hong Kong democrat, without explanation. In a rebuke to such practices, the High Court ruled in March that the Immigration Department was incorrect in its 2010 decision to refuse visas to technical staff of Shen Yun Performing Arts, a U.S.-based dance company whose performances include portrayals of China's persecution of Falun Gong.

Women are protected by law from discrimination and abuse, and they are entitled to equal access to schooling and to property in divorce settlements. However, they continue to face discrimination in employment opportunities, salary, inheritance, and welfare. Only 11 out of the 60 Legco members are women, and all 21 judges on the Court of Final Appeals are men. Despite robust efforts by the government, Hong Kong remains a point of transit and destination for persons trafficked for sexual exploitation or forced labor.

Indian Kashmir

Political Rights: 4
Civil Liberties: 4*
Status: Partly Free

Population: 12,549,000

Ratings Change: Indian Kashmir's civil liberties rating improved from 5 to 4 due to an unprecedented increase in online media, a significant decline in state violence, and greater space for open public discussion.

Ten-Year Ratings Timeline For Year Under Review (Political Rights, Civil Liberties, Status)

2002	2003	2004	2005	2006	2007	2008	2009	2010	2011
5,5PF	5,5PF	5,5PF	5,5PF	5,5PF	5,4PF	5,4PF	4,4PF	4,5PF	4,4PF

Overview: **After a surge in violence between security forces and demonstrators in 2010, Indian-controlled Kashmir experienced markedly more stable and peaceful conditions in 2011. Local council elections in the spring drew a turnout of 80 percent, as voters defied the instructions of separatist groups to boycott the state-organized polls.**

When British India was partitioned into India and Pakistan in 1947, the Hindu maharajah of Jammu and Kashmir tried to maintain his principality's independence, but he eventually ceded it to India in return for autonomy and future self-determination. Within months, India and Pakistan went to war over the territory. As part of a UN-brokered ceasefire in 1949 that established the present boundaries, Pakistan gained control of roughly one-third of Jammu and Kashmir, leaving India with the remainder. The territory received substantial autonomy under Article 370 of India's constitution and a 1952 accord, but India annulled such guarantees in 1957 and formally annexed the portion of Jammu and Kashmir under its control. Since then, it has largely been governed as other Indian states, with an elected legislature and a chief minister. Under the 1972 Simla accord, New Delhi and Islamabad agreed to respect the Line of Control (LOC) dividing the region and to resolve Kashmir's status through negotiations.

The pro-India National Conference (NC) party won state elections in 1987 that were marred by fraud, violence, and arrests of members of a new, Muslim-based opposition coalition, leading to widespread unrest. An armed insurgency against Indian rule gathered momentum after 1989, waged by the Jammu and Kashmir Liberation Front (JKLF) and other proindependence groups that consisted largely of Kashmiris, as well as Pakistani-backed Islamist groups seeking to bring Kashmir under Islamabad's control.

New Delhi placed Jammu and Kashmir under federal rule in 1990 and attempted to quell the uprising. The Armed Forces Special Powers Act (AFSPA) was extended to the territory, allowing the army to make arrests and conduct searches without a warrant, and to use deadly force with virtual impunity. The JKLF abandoned its armed struggle in 1994, and Pakistani-backed extremist groups, which included fighters from elsewhere in the Muslim world, thereafter dominated the insurgency.

Although opposition parties joined together to form the All Parties Hurriyat Conference (APHC) in 1993, they boycotted the 1996 state elections, and the NC was able to form a government. The APHC also declined to participate in the 2002 elections, but the NC nevertheless lost more than half of its assembly seats, allowing the Congress Party and the People's Democratic Party (PDP) to form a coalition government.

Despite several setbacks, relations between the Indian government and moderate Kashmiri separatist groups generally improved after the 2002 elections. In 2004, talks were held for the first time between Kashmiri separatists and the highest levels of the Indian government. Moderate APHC leaders reiterated their renunciation of violence in 2005 and called for Kashmiris to become more deeply involved in the negotiating process. However, the talks were hampered by an emerging split within the APHC between those who favored a continuation of the insurgency and those who favored a political and diplomatic solution.

The coalition government collapsed in June 2008, when the PDP withdrew its support amid a high-profile dispute over land set aside for a Hindu pilgrimage site. State elections were held in November and December. Turnout was higher than expected, exceeding 60 percent on most polling dates, as voters largely ignored separatist groups' calls for a boycott. While early voting dates were generally peaceful, some violence pervaded later polling—particularly in early December—when antielection protesters clashed with security forces. The elections were considered mostly free and fair, however, with significantly reduced levels of voter intimidation, harassment, and violence compared with previous elections. The NC won a plurality of 28 seats, followed by the PDP with 21 seats and Congress with 17. The NC allied itself with Congress to form a governing coalition.

The security situation improved during 2009, with the number of militancy-related fatalities decreasing for the seventh consecutive year. In October, New Delhi announced plans to withdraw 15,000 troops from the Jammu region, granting local police more responsibility over the area. Nevertheless, there were several incidents of violence, including bombings in public places and other attacks directed at security forces, politicians, and minority groups.

In 2010, prompted by the police killing of a 17-year-old boy in June, opposition groups organized a protest movement called Quit Kashmir. They demanded that the Indian government recognize the Kashmir dispute as an international conflict, demilitarize the region, release all political prisoners, and revoke the AFSPA. For about three months, police and soldiers engaged in regular clashes with youthful, stone-throwing protesters, leaving more than 100 civilians dead. Tensions began to ease in September, when the central government announced plans to reduce the security presence in the territory, release jailed protesters, compensate the families of slain civilians, and reopen schools and universities. However, police arrested protest organizer Masrat Alam in October, and curfews and unrest continued sporadically for the rest of the year.

Calm was largely restored in 2011, and the year featured the lowest level of violence since 1989. The new stability had economic benefits, as hundreds of thousands of tourists visited the territory. From April to June, local council elections were held across Kashmir for the first time in a decade. Separatist groups urged citizens to boycott the polls, but turnout was reported at about 80 percent. In August, Chief Minister Omar Abdullah issued an amnesty for roughly 1,200 protesters accused of throwing stones at security forces during 2010.

Political Rights and Civil Liberties: Jammu and Kashmir, like India's other states, is governed by an elected bicameral legislature and a chief minister entrusted with executive power. An appointed governor serves as symbolic head of state. Members of the 87-seat lower house, or state assembly, are directly elected, while the 46-seat upper house has a combination of members elected by the state assembly and nominated by the governor.

India has never held a referendum allowing Kashmiri self-determination as called for in a 1948 UN resolution. The state's residents can change the local administration through elections, which are supposed to be held at least once every five years. The Election Commission of India (ECI) monitors the polls, but historically they have been marred by violence, coercion, and ballot tampering. Militants have enforced boycotts called for by separatist political parties, threatened election officials and candidates, and killed political activists and civilians during balloting. The 2002 campaign period was especially violent, but the 2008 legislative elections were considered generally free and fair, being largely peaceful despite some violence.

Corruption remains widespread, though the government has taken some steps to combat it. The legislature enacted the Jammu and Kashmir State Vigilance Commission (SVC) Bill in February 2011, establishing an anticorruption commission with the power to investigate alleged offenses under the state's 2006 Prevention of Corruption Act.

India's 1971 Newspapers (Incitement to Offences) Act, which is in effect only in Jammu and Kashmir, gives district magistrates the authority to censor publications in certain circumstances, though it is rarely invoked. The protest-related violence in 2010 led some newspapers to suspend circulation, and curfews inhibited journalists from covering important stories. However, conditions improved in 2011. Foreign journalists are generally able to travel freely, meet with separatist leaders, and file reports on a range of issues, including government abuses. As in the rest of India, print media are thriving in Kashmir, and online media have proliferated, providing new platforms for public discussion.

Journalists remain subject to pressure from militants and the authorities. In August 2011, two photojournalists were reportedly detained and beaten at a police station after attempting to cover a confrontation between protesters and security forces. Both were released, but required hospital treatment for their injuries. A newspaper reporter who inquired about the incident was allegedly threatened by police commanders. One of the two photographers was reportedly beaten by police again in November, along with three colleagues who were also covering protests.

Freedom of worship and academic freedom are generally respected by the authorities. Since 2003, the state government has permitted separatist groups to organize a procession marking the prophet Muhammad's birthday. However, militants at times attack Hindu and Sikh temples.

Freedoms of assembly and association are often restricted. Although local and national civil rights groups are permitted to operate, they sometimes encounter harassment by security forces. The separatist APHC is allowed to function, but its leaders are frequently subjected to short-term preventive detention, and its requests for permits for public gatherings are often denied. Although police repeatedly clashed with protesters during 2011, there was far less violence and repression than in the previous year. Protection of labor union rights in Kashmir is generally poor and has resulted in prolonged strikes by both public and informal sector workers.

The courts in Kashmir, already backlogged by thousands of pending cases, were further hampered in 2011 by intermittent lawyers' strikes triggered in part by the July 2010 arrest of Kashmir High Court Bar Association president Mian Abdul Qayoom under the Public Safety Act (PSA). Qayoom, who was accused of speaking out against Indian rule and fomenting protests, was released from detention in April 2011. Separately, in November 2011, members of the Jammu and Kashmir High Court Bar Association went on strike for 27 days to demand the revocation of a cabinet decision transferring the power to register land and property from judicial officers to the revenue department. In December, the High Court intervened in the matter with a stay order on the transfer of powers, and directed the lawyers to resume work. Also in December, lawyers held a one-day strike calling for the revocation of harsh security laws in the region, such as the AFSPA.

The government and security forces frequently disregard court orders. Broadly written legislation such as the AFSPA and the Disturbed Areas Act allow security forces to search homes and arrest suspects without a warrant, shoot suspects on sight, and destroy buildings believed to house militants or arms. Under the AFSPA, prosecutions of security personnel cannot proceed without the approval of the central government, which is rarely granted. Hundreds of people are detained each year under the PSA, which permits police to hold suspects without charge for up to two years. Critics have argued that the law facilitates forced disappearances.

Indian security personnel based in Kashmir carry out arbitrary arrests and detentions, torture, forced disappearances, and custodial killings of suspected militants and their alleged civilian sympathizers. Meanwhile, militant groups based in Pakistan continue to kill pro-India politicians, public employees, suspected informers, members of rival factions, soldiers, and civilians. The militants also engage in kidnapping, extortion, and other forms of intimidation. However, violence associated with the struggle between security forces and militant groups continued a multiyear decline in 2011. According to the South Asia Terrorism Portal (SATP), a total of 183 civilians, security personnel, and militants were killed during the year, down from 375 in 2010.

Violence targeting Pandits, or Kashmiri Hindus, is part of a pattern dating to 1990 that has forced several hundred thousand Hindus to flee the region; many continue to reside in refugee camps near Jammu. Other religious and ethnic minorities such as Sikhs and Gujjars have also been targeted.

As in other parts of India, women face some societal discrimination as well as domestic violence and other forms of abuse. Female civilians continue to be subjected to harassment, intimidation, and violent attacks, including rape and murder, at the hands of both the security forces and militant groups.

Nagorno-Karabakh

Political Rights: 6
Civil Liberties: 5
Status: Not Free

Population: 141,400

Ten-Year Ratings Timeline For Year Under Review (Political Rights, Civil Liberties, Status)

2002	2003	2004	2005	2006	2007	2008	2009	2010	2011
6,5NF	5,5PF	5,5PF	5,5PF	5,5PF	5,5PF	5,5PF	5,5PF	6,5PF	6,5NF

Overview: **In June 2011, Russian-brokered negotiations on Nagorno-Karabakh between the presidents of Armenia and Azerbaijan ended in deadlock after the latter refused the terms of a proposed agreement, raising the possibility of renewed violence. Nagorno-Karabakh's sole airport, closed in 1991, was set to reopen in May, but the event was delayed indefinitely following threats from Baku. In September, a drone aircraft was shot down by Karabakh forces near the de facto border with Azerbaijan.**

Nagorno-Karabakh, populated largely by ethnic Armenians, was established as an autonomous region inside Soviet Azerbaijan in 1923. In February 1988, the regional legislature adopted a resolution calling for union with Armenia. The announcement led to warfare over the next several years between Armenian, Azerbaijani, and local Nagorno-Karabakh forces.

In 1992, Nagorno-Karabakh's new legislature adopted a declaration of independence, which was not recognized by the international community. By the time a Russian-brokered ceasefire was signed in May 1994, Karabakh Armenians, assisted by Armenia, had captured essentially the entire territory and seven adjacent Azerbaijani districts. Virtually all ethnic Azeris had fled or been forced out of the region. The fighting resulted in thousands of deaths and created an estimated one million refugees and internally displaced persons (IDPs).

In December 1994, the head of Nagorno-Karabakh's state defense committee, Robert Kocharian, was selected as president by the territory's National Assembly. He won a popular vote for the presidency in 1996, but became prime minister of Armenia in March 1997. Foreign Minister Arkady Ghukassian was elected to replace him that September, and Kocharian went on to become Armenia's president in 1998.

Ghukassian easily secured a second term as president in 2002, and his ruling Democratic Party of Artsakh (AZhK) led the 2005 parliamentary elections, though the opposition accused the authorities of misusing state resources to influence the outcome. In 2006, a reported 98 percent of voters supported a referendum affirming Nagorno-Karabakh's independence. The referendum was not recognized by the international community.

Nagorno-Karabakh security chief Bako Saakian reportedly took more than 85 percent of the vote in the 2007 presidential election. His main opponent, Deputy Foreign Minister Masis Mailian, received 12 percent. The government subsequently absorbed or co-opted most of the political opposition.

Hope for progress on a peace agreement was shaken in 2008 by a series of external political developments. In March the UN General Assembly passed a resolution identifying Nagorno-Karabakh as part of Azerbaijan and calling on Armenia to withdraw its troops. The measure was supported by 39 member states and rejected by 7, including Russia, France, and the United States, the three co-chairs of the Minsk Group, a body established by the Organization for Security and Cooperation in Europe (OSCE) in the 1990s to facilitate negotiations on Nagorno-Karabakh's status. Also during the year, Kosovo declared independence from Serbia, and Russia recognized the independence of the breakaway Georgian regions of Abkhazia and South Ossetia, raising awkward questions about Nagorno-Karabakh. In addition, postelection violence in Armenia was followed by skirmishes along the ceasefire line that killed 16 soldiers on both sides, marking one of the worst violations of the ceasefire in years.

In October 2009, the governments of Turkey and Armenia signed an agreement to establish diplomatic relations and reopen their shared border, which Turkey had sealed in 1993 to show solidarity with Azerbaijan over Nagorno-Karabakh. However, ratification plans foundered on the lingering dispute over the territory.

Nagorno-Karabakh held parliamentary elections in May 2010. In contrast to the more competitive legislative polls of previous years, no genuine opposition candidates participated, and the balloting was swept by the three parties of the ruling coalition. Azat Hayrenik (Free Fatherland), the party of Prime Minister Ara Harutiunian, won 14 of the 33 seats, followed by AZhK with 10 and the Armenian Revolutionary Federation–Dashnaktsutiun party with 6. The remaining seats were captured by Hayrenik loyalists with no formal party affiliation.

The presidents of Armenia and Azerbaijan met with Russian president Dmitry Medvedev in June 2011 for highly anticipated talks on a peace agreement, but the summit ended in disappointment when Baku refused to sign the proposed draft. With negotiations stalled and both sides engaged in a rapid military buildup, international observers expressed concerns about the threat of open warfare.

Stepanakert's airport, closed in 1991 during the war, was set to reopen in May, but the decision was delayed indefinitely amid threats from Baku to shoot down any aircraft entering the territory. Azerbaijan later softened its statements after sharp international criticism. In September, Karabakh forces shot down a drone aircraft that they said had crossed the de facto border from Azerbaijan, which Baku denied.

Also in September, Nagorno-Karabakh held local elections, with a reported turnout of 59 percent. Government-backed candidate Suren Grigorian was elected as Stepanakert's mayor with 62.5 percent, replacing outgoing mayor Vazgen Mikaelian, who did not run for reelection.

Political Rights and Civil Liberties: Nagorno-Karabakh has enjoyed de facto independence from Azerbaijan since 1994 and retains close political, economic, and military ties with Armenia. Parliamentary and presidential votes held in 2005 and 2007 were criticized by the opposition for alleged fraud and other irregularities, and were seen as less free and fair than previous polls. In the 2010 parliamentary elections, there were no opposition candidates, administrative resources were used to support progovernment candidates, and the election commission was entirely composed of progovernment officials. All Karabakh elections are considered invalid by the international community, which does not recognize the territory's independence.

The president, who is directly elected for up to two five-year terms, appoints the prime minister. Of the unicameral National Assembly's 33 members, 17 are elected by party list and 16 from single-mandate districts, all for five-year terms. The main political parties in Nagorno-Karabakh are Azat Hayrenik, the AZhK, and the Armenian Revolutionary Federation–Dashnaktsutiun, all of which currently support the government. Given the territory's uncertain status, dissent, including political opposition, is generally regarded as a sign of disloyalty and a security risk. As a consequence, opposition groups have either disappeared or been brought into the government.

Nagorno-Karabakh continues to suffer from significant corruption, particularly in the construction industry, as well as favoritism in filling civil service positions.

The territory officially remains under martial law, which imposes restrictions on civil liberties, including media censorship and the banning of public demonstrations. However, the authorities maintain that these provisions have not been enforced since 1995, a year after the ceasefire was signed.

The government controls many of Nagorno-Karabakh's media outlets, and most journalists practice self-censorship, particularly on subjects related to the peace process. The territory's public television station, which has no local competition, broadcasts only three hours a day. Internet access is limited. The popular independent newspaper *Demo* and *Karabakh-Open.com*, the territory's only independent news website, were both closed by their publishers in 2008.

Most Karabakh residents belong to the Armenian Apostolic Church, and the religious freedom of other groups is limited. A 2009 law banned religious activity by unregistered groups and proselytism by minority faiths, and made it more difficult for minority religious groups to register. Although at least three minority groups were subsequently registered, a Protestant group and the Jehovah's Witnesses were reportedly denied registration. Unregistered groups have been fined for their religious activities, and Baptists and Jehovah's Witnesses have been jailed for refusing to serve in the Karabakh army.

Freedoms of assembly and association are limited, but trade unions are allowed to organize. The handful of nongovernmental organizations (NGOs) that are active in the territory are virtually all progovernment, and they suffer from lack of funding and competition from government-organized groups.

The judiciary is not independent in practice. The courts are influenced by the executive branch as well as powerful political, economic, and criminal groups.

In August 2011, to mark the 20th anniversary of the creation of the Nagorno-Karabakh Republic, the parliament approved a general amnesty law that allowed the release of up to 20 percent of the prison population, mainly inmates convicted of minor crimes, and the commutation of sentences of other prisoners on the condition that they took part in the 1991–94 war or had family members killed in the conflict.

The amnesty also stipulated the closure of at least 60 percent of pending criminal cases and the release of suspects from pretrial detention.

In June, a Karabakh soldier was tried in Armenian criminal court for the murder of four soldiers in his unit and was found guilty, receiving life imprisonment. The Karabakh army suffered from a series of noncombat deaths in 2011, including two shooting sprees that left 10 soldiers dead, and a number of Karabakh soldiers faced criminal charges.

The majority of Azeris who fled the territory during the separatist conflict continue to live in poor conditions in IDP camps in Azerbaijan. Land-mine explosions in the conflict zone cause deaths and injuries each year. According to the International Committee of the Red Cross, at least 50,000 antipersonnel mines were laid during the war. In many cases, records of minefield locations were lost or never created.

The continued control of major economic activity by powerful elites limits opportunities for most residents, though the government has instituted a number of economic rehabilitation projects in recent years.

Men and women have equal legal status, though women are underrepresented in government and the private sector. Women are not conscripted. The government administers a "birth-encouragement program," with the goal of repopulating the territory. Couples receive roughly $780 when they marry and additional money for the birth of each child.

Northern Cyprus

Political Rights: 2
Civil Liberties: 2
Status: Free

Population: 329,500

Note: See also the country report for Cyprus.

Ten-Year Ratings Timeline For Year Under Review (Political Rights, Civil Liberties, Status)

2002	2003	2004	2005	2006	2007	2008	2009	2010	2011
2,2F	2,2F	2,2F	2,2F	2,2F	2,2F	2,2F	2,2F	2,2F	2,2F

Overview: **In October 2011, the latest round of UN-sponsored unification talks between the Turkish Cypriot president and his Greek Cypriot counterpart failed to reach a tangible settlement. Also during the year, Northern Cyprus was the focal point of a dispute between Turkey and Cyprus regarding drilling for natural resources in waters surrounding the island.**

Cyprus gained independence from Britain in 1960, after a five-year guerrilla campaign by partisans demanding union with Greece. In July 1974, Greek Cypriot National Guard members, backed by the military junta that ruled Greece, staged an unsuccessful coup aimed at accomplishing the union. Five days later, Turkey invaded from the north, seized control of 37 percent of the island, and expelled 200,000 Greek Cypriots from the portion it occupied. Since then, a buffer zone, called the Green Line has divided Cyprus, including the capital city of Nicosia. UN resolutions stipulate that Cyprus is a single country of which the northern third is illegally occupied. In 1983, Turkish-controlled Cyprus declared its independence as the Turkish Republic of Northern Cyprus (TRNC), an entity recognized only by Turkey.

Reunification talks accelerated after a more receptive Turkish government was elected in 2002, and under added pressure for an agreement from the European Union (EU), the United States, and the United Nations. A prounification TRNC government led by Prime Minister Mehmet Ali Talat was elected in late 2003.

In April 2004, a reunification plan proposed by then UN secretary general Kofi Annan was put to a vote in simultaneous, separate referendums on both sides of the island. Amid accusations that the proposal favored the Turkish side, 76 percent of Greek Cypriots voted against it, while 65 percent of Turkish Cypriots voted in favor. With the island still divided, only Greek Cyprus joined the EU as planned in May 2004.

Talat's Republican Turkish Party (CTP) retained power at the head of a coalition government after winning February 2005 legislative elections, with the antiunification National Unity Party (UBP) placing second. Rauf Denktas, who had held the presidency since the TRNC declared independence, did not seek a new term in the April 2005 presidential election. Instead, Talat emerged as the victor in a field of seven candidates, defeating UBP leader Dervis Eroglu, 56 percent to 23 percent.

The UBP won legislative elections in April 2009, capturing 26 of 50 seats. Polls indicated that voters turned against the CTP, which secured just 15 seats, due to its failure to achieve reunification and because of an economic downturn that began in 2008. The Democratic Party, headed by Serdar Denktas, son of the former president, won five seats, while the Free Party and the Communal Democracy Party each captured two. Eroglu became prime minister, having previously held the post from 1985 to 1994 and 1996 to 2004.

In April 2010, Eroglu defeated Talat in a presidential election, capturing more than 50 percent of the vote. Eroglu's election was seen as a mandate for maintaining the status quo. Nevertheless, in October the two sides opened a seventh border crossing near the northwestern town of Limnitis, increasing the permeability of the Green Line.

Pressure on the TRNC government to implement fiscal austerity measures continued in 2011, and protesters demonstrated against benefit cuts in October. Also that month, the latest round of UN-backed reunification negotiations between the island's two governments concluded without a breakthrough. In November, Turkey and the TRNC signed an energy agreement giving the Turkish Petroleum Corporation permission to explore for natural gas in Turkish Cypriot territory, despite Greek Cypriot complaints that it would not be recognized as legal by the international community.

Political Rights and Civil Liberties: Elections in the TRNC are generally free and fair. The president and the 50-seat Assembly are elected to five-year terms. The prime minister is the head of the government. The main parties are the ruling UBP, which has opposed unification, and the opposition CTP, which has supported it.

The TRNC's roughly 1,000 Greek and Maronite Christian residents are disenfranchised, but many vote in elections in the southern Republic of Cyprus. Minorities are not represented, and women are underrepresented, in the TRNC Assembly.

The government has made efforts to combat corruption in recent years, but graft and lack of transparency remain problems. After the 2009 elections, Democratic Party leader Serdar Denktas asserted that all TRNC political parties had bought votes, and admitted to distributing 10,000 euros (US$13,300) himself.

Freedom of the press is generally respected, though some problems persist. The criminal code allows authorities to jail journalists for what they write, and the government has been hostile to independent outlets. Some journalists report threats in connection with their work and difficulty accessing public information. The government does not restrict access to the internet.

A 1975 agreement with Greek Cypriot authorities provides for freedom of worship, which is generally respected. The TRNC is an officially secular state. In 2011, the opening of a school with ties to the movement inspired by the teachings of Turkish Islamic theologian Fethullah Gülen was met with resentment by secularists and teachers' unions. The government does not restrict academic freedom. In 2004, Turkish Cypriot schools began teaching a less partisan account of Cypriot history, in accordance with Council of Europe recommendations.

The rights of freedom of assembly and association are typically upheld, though police were criticized for disrupting union protests during 2011, making several arrests and allegedly using excessive force. Civic groups and nongovernmental organizations generally operate without restrictions. Workers may form independent unions, bargain collectively, and strike, though union members have been subject to harassment.

The judiciary is independent, and trials generally meet international standards of fairness. Turkish Cypriot police, under the control of the Turkish military, sometimes fail to respect due process rights, and there have been allegations of abuse of detainees. Lawyers' associations and journalists have actively worked to expose and remedy irregularities in the justice system.

Census results released in 2007 showed that about half of the TRNC's population consisted of indigenous Turkish Cypriots. The rest included people of mainland Turkish origin and many foreign workers, as well as Greek Cypriots and Maronites. The latter three groups face discrimination, difficulties at Green Line checkpoints, and alleged surveillance by the Turkish Cypriot authorities. A census planned for November 2011 was indefinitely postponed amid widespread concerns that the native Turkish Cypriot population is rapidly diminishing.

There are no direct flights between the TRNC and the rest of the world due to Greek Cypriot resistance and international regulations that restrict the operation of the north's ports and airports. However, trade between the two sides of the island has continued to increase since restrictions were loosened in 2004. In addition, all EU citizens, including Greek Cypriots, can now travel to the north by presenting identity cards and no longer require passports or visas. Most governments do not recognize TRNC travel documents, so thousands of Turkish Cypriots have obtained Republic of Cyprus passports since the option became available in 2004. However, in 2008, Turkey began forbidding Turkish Cypriots from leaving the country through Turkey without TRNC passports.

A property commission formed by the TRNC in 2006 has resolved hundreds of restitution claims by Greek Cypriots who owned property in the north before the island's division, though critics have claimed that the compensation amounts were inadequate. The European Court of Human Rights (ECHR) recognized the commission in 2010 as an "accessible and effective" mechanism, and claims must now pass through the commission and a local appeals process before they can be appealed to the ECHR.

According to Articles 171 and 173 of the criminal code, male homosexuality is punishable with jail time. Reports show an increase in the number of arrests based on the law in recent years, and homosexuals face societal discrimination. Three men were arrested in October 2011 on charges of conspiring to engage in a homosexual act. President Dervis Eroglu subsequently announced plans to repeal the laws in question, and on October 25 the Communal Democracy Party submitted a proposal to repeal Chapter 154 of the criminal code, which criminalizes homosexual acts. However, the three men had not been released from prison as of the end of 2011.

Legal provisions for equal pay for women are not always enforced, especially in blue-collar jobs. A 2007 survey found that three-quarters of women were victims of violence at least once in their lives, with most attacks occurring at home. There are no laws specifically concerning domestic violence or sexual harassment, and incidents typically go unreported. According to the Turkish Cypriot Human Rights Foundation, the TRNC is a destination for trafficking in women, particularly from Eastern Europe and Russia, and little effort has been made to address this problem.

Pakistani Kashmir

Political Rights: 6
Civil Liberties: 5
Status: Not Free

Population: 9,584,600

Ten-Year Ratings Timeline For Year Under Review (Political Rights, Civil Liberties, Status)

2002	2003	2004	2005	2006	2007	2008	2009	2010	2011
7,5NF	7,5NF	7,5NF	7,5NF	7,5NF	7,5NF	7,5NF	6,5NF	6,5NF	6,5NF

Overview: **In Gilgit-Baltistan, nationalist groups' demands for greater autonomy remained unfulfilled in 2011, and there was an increase in demonstrations as well as harassment and targeted killings of Shiites and political activists during the year. Meanwhile, June elections in Azad Kashmir produced a new government led by the Azad Kashmir People's Party. As ongoing talks between India and Pakistan yielded little substantive progress on the Kashmir dispute, China expanded its military presence and involvement in development projects in the region.**

When British India was partitioned into India and Pakistan in 1947, the Hindu maharajah of Jammu and Kashmir tried to maintain his principality's independence, but he eventually ceded it to India in return for autonomy and future self-determination. Within months, India and Pakistan went to war over the territory. Following a UN-brokered ceasefire in 1949, Pakistan refused to withdraw troops from the roughly one-third of Jammu and Kashmir that it had occupied, but unlike India, it never formally annexed its portion. The Karachi Agreement of April 1949 divided Pakistani-administered Kashmir into two distinct entities—Azad (Free) Kashmir and the Northern Areas. Pakistan retained direct administrative control over the Northern Areas, while Azad Kashmir was given a degree of nominal self-government.

A legislative assembly for Azad Kashmir was set up in 1970, and the 1974 interim constitution established a parliamentary system headed by a president and a prime minister. However, the political process was disrupted for long periods by military rule in Pakistan as a whole. Even when elections were held, Islamabad's influence over the voting and governance in general remained strong, and few observers considered the region's elections to be free or fair. The opposition Muslim Conference (MC) party won the 2001 elections, defeating the Azad Kashmir People's Party (AKPP), but within weeks, Pakistani leader General Pervez Musharraf installed his own choice of president. In 2006 the MC again won a majority of the 41 directly elected seats in the legislature, and MC candidate Raja Zulqarnain Khan emerged as president. MC leader Sardar Attique Ahmed Khan became prime minister after receiving Musharraf's nomination, though he was eventually deposed in a 2009 no-confidence vote. Political instability and factional struggles led to a succession of several prime ministers in 2009 and 2010, with some alleging that the federal authorities had a hand in the turmoil.

In June 2011 legislative elections, the AKPP won 20 of 41 seats, followed by the Pakistan Muslim League–Nawaz (PML-N) with 9 seats and the MC with 5. AKPP leader Chaudhry Abdul Majid became prime minister in July, and Sardar Muhammad Yaqoob Khan was installed as president in August.

Meanwhile, in the Northern Areas, the lack of political representation fueled demands for both formal inclusion within Pakistan and self-determination. In 1999, the Pakistani Supreme Court directed the administration to act within six months to give the Northern Areas an elected government with an independent judiciary, and to extend fundamental rights to the region's residents. The Pakistani government then announced a package that provided for an appellate court as well as an expanded and renamed Northern Areas Legislative Council (NALC). Elections to the NALC were held in 2004, but the body had few real fiscal or legislative powers. The court of appeals was established in 2005.

Nationalist and proindependence groups in the Northern Areas continued to agitate for increased political rights, and in August 2009 Islamabad issued the Gilgit-Baltistan Empowerment and Self-Governance Order (GBESGO), which renamed the region and replaced the Northern Areas Legal Framework Order (LFO) of 1994. It provided for a somewhat more powerful legislative body, the Gilgit-Baltistan Legislative Assembly (GBLA), with the authority to choose a chief minister and introduce legislation on 61 subjects. While the government argued that the GBESGO established full internal autonomy, nationalist groups noted that a governor appointed by the Pakistani president would still be the ultimate authority and could not be overruled by the new assembly. Moreover, many subjects were excluded from the assembly's purview.

In November 2009 elections for the GBLA, the Pakistan People's Party (PPP), the ruling party at the federal level, won 12 of 24 directly elected seats; 10 of the remainder were divided among four other parties and four independents, and voting for 2 seats was postponed. Syed Mehdi Shah, head of the PPP's Gilgit-Baltistan chapter, became chief minister. Following the death of Governor Shama Khalid from cancer in September 2010, Pir Karam Ali Shah, a member of the GBLA, was appointed as governor in January 2011. In a by-election held in April, Nawaz Khan Naji, leader of the Balawaristan National Front (BNF), became the first member of the GBLA from a separatist party, defeating PPP and PML-N candidates by a large margin.

Despite periodic talks between India and Pakistan, little progress has been made toward a comprehensive resolution of the Kashmir dispute. Negotiations continued during 2011 without any significant breakthroughs. In recent years, there has been an expanding Chinese military and economic presence in Gilgit-Baltistan, including troops involved in large-scale development and construction projects in the region. Some locals have expressed concerns that the increasingly close relationship between Pakistan and China could pose a risk to peace and stability in the area.

Political Rights and Civil Liberties: The political rights of the residents of Pakistani-administered Kashmir remain severely limited, despite a number of improvements tied to the end of military rule and the election of a civilian government at the federal level in 2008, and elections for the new GBLA in 2009. Neither Gilgit-Baltistan nor Azad Kashmir has representation in Pakistan's Parliament.

Gilgit-Baltistan, previously known as the Northern Areas, is still directly administered by the Pakistani government, meaning its status falls short of compliance with a 1999 Supreme Court ruling on the issue. Because the region is not included in the Pakistani constitution and has no constitution of its own, its people have no fundamental guarantee of civil rights, democratic representation, or separation of powers.

Under the August 2009 GBESGO, Gilgit-Baltistan's political structure includes the 33-member GBLA and a chief minister, as well as a 15-member Gilgit-Baltistan Council (GBC) headed by the Pakistani prime minister and vice-chaired by the federally appointed governor. The GBC consists of six members of the GBLA and nine Pakistani Parliament members appointed by the governor. The GBLA in turn is composed of 24 directly elected members, six seats reserved for women, and three seats reserved for technocrats; the reserved seats are filled through a vote by the elected members. Ultimate authority rests in the hands of the governor, who has significant powers over judicial appointments and whose decisions cannot be overruled by the GBLA. Many fiscal powers remain with the GBC rather than the elected assembly. A majority of high-level positions in the local administration are reserved under the GBESGO for Pakistani bureaucrats.

No proindependence candidates won seats in the 2009 GBLA elections. Local nationalist leaders accused the authorities of preventing their parties from holding public gatherings, and a number of nationalist leaders and candidates were arrested during the campaign period. Although two people were killed and some 40 injured in violence between supporters of rival candidates, the elections themselves were largely peaceful. Independent observer missions characterized the elections as competitive, despite flaws including an inaccurate voter list, allegations of rigging and interference, and misuse of state resources to benefit the ruling PPP.

Azad Kashmir has an interim constitution, an elected unicameral assembly, a prime minister, and a president who is elected by the assembly. Both the president and the legislature serve five-year terms. Of the 49 assembly seats, 41 are filled through direct elections: 29 with constituencies based in Azad Kashmir and 12 representing Kashmiri "refugees" throughout Pakistan. Another eight are reserved seats: five for women and one each for representatives of overseas Kashmiris, technocrats, and religious leaders. However, Pakistan exercises considerable control over the structures of government and electoral politics. Islamabad's approval is required to pass legislation, and the federal minister for Kashmir affairs handles daily administration and controls the budget. The Kashmir Council—chaired by the president of Pakistan and composed of federal officials, Kashmiri assembly members, and the Azad Kashmir president and prime minister—also holds a number of key executive, legislative, and judicial powers, such as the authority to appoint superior judges and the chief election commissioner. The Pakistani military retains a guiding role on issues of politics and governance.

Those who do not support Azad Kashmir's accession to Pakistan are barred from the political process, government employment, and educational institutions. They are also subject to surveillance, harassment, and sometimes imprisonment by Pakistani security services. The 2011 legislative elections in Azad Kashmir were marred by allegations of rigging and vote-buying, as well as some violence and harassment, with at least three election-related killings reported. Following the elections, the PML-N accused the ruling PPP of fraud and misappropriation of development funds to buy votes.

Azad Kashmir receives a large amount of financial aid from Islamabad, but successive administrations have been tainted by corruption and incompetence. Aid agencies have also been accused of misusing funds. A lack of official accountability has been identified as a key factor in the poor socioeconomic condition of both Azad Kashmir and Gilgit-Baltistan. However, the region has benefited from improvements in accountability at the federal level and the transfer of some budgetary powers to the GBLA in 2009.

The Pakistani government uses the constitution and other laws to curb freedom of speech on a variety of subjects, including the status of Kashmir and sectarian violence. Media owners cannot publish in Azad Kashmir without permission from the Kashmir Council and the Ministry of Kashmir Affairs. Several dailies and weeklies operate in Gilgit-Baltistan, mostly under the auspices of the K-2 publishing house, and provide some scrutiny of official affairs. However, authorities have banned a number of local newspapers and detained or otherwise harassed journalists in recent years. In August 2011, security agents raided the offices of the K-2 newspaper, damaging equipment, harassing staff, and arresting two journalists. Also during the year, two prominent Gilgit-Baltistan journalists were jailed for contempt of court after collaborating on an article that alleged nepotism in judicial appointments. Local journalists have sometimes faced harassment and attacks from nonstate actors. In the aftermath of a devastating 2005 earthquake in the region, local press freedom organizations set up private radio stations that focus on news and humanitarian information, contributing to greater media diversity. Internet access is not usually restricted but remains confined to urban centers. Both phone and internet services in Gilgit-Baltistan are under the control of the Pakistani military, which has unfettered powers of surveillance.

Pakistan is an Islamic republic, and there are numerous official restrictions on religious freedom. Religious minorities also face unofficial discrimination, and are occasionally subject to violent attack. Since 2009 there has been an upsurge in sectarian violence between Shiite Muslims, who form a majority in Gilgit-Baltistan, and Sunni Muslims who have migrated to the region with the tacit support of federal authorities. A rise in sectarian killings, mostly targeting Shiites, was reported in Gilgit city late in 2011. Many such incidents have allegedly been instigated or encouraged by Pakistani security services.

Academic freedom and opportunities are limited. Local groups continue to call for the right to learn Shiite and Sufi teachings, as well as local languages and scripts, in government-run schools. Such practices are discouraged by the Pakistani authorities. Many areas do not have schools for girls, and in September 2010, the only university in Gilgit-Baltistan was closed due to lack of funds. The university resumed its operations in 2011 after its financial problems were resolved.

Freedoms of association and assembly are restricted. The constitution of Azad Kashmir forbids individuals and groups from engaging in activities that are prejudicial to the region's accession to Pakistan. In July 2011, Manzoor Parwana, chairman of the proindependence Gilgit-Baltistan United Movement (GBUM), was arrested and charged with sedition for a recent speech, and was barred from leaving the country. Police in recent years have regularly suppressed antigovernment demonstrations and protests concerning economic hardship and displacement, sometimes violently. In August 2011, police fired on a protest rally demanding compensation for displacement due to flooding in the Hunza Valley, killing two people. Following the incident, several dozen other protesters and political activists were detained under sedition and antiterrorism provisions; a number alleged that they were tortured in custody.

Nongovernmental organizations (NGOs) that work on humanitarian issues are generally able to operate freely, while those focused on political or human rights issues face more scrutiny and occasional harassment. The situation for labor rights is similar to that in Pakistan, but with even fewer protections for workers. Unions and professional associations have routinely been banned by the authorities.

The chairman of the GBC appoints Gilgit-Baltistan's chief judge and other judges on the advice of the governor. All judicial appointments in Gilgit-Baltistan are based on three-year contracts subject to discretionary renewal by the bureaucracy, leaving the judiciary largely subservient to the executive. In addition, the judiciary is not empowered to hear cases concerning fundamental rights or cases against the executive. Meanwhile, as the 1999 Supreme Court ruling has not yet been fully implemented, cases concerning Gilgit-Baltistan are considered outside the jurisdiction of the Supreme Court of Pakistan.

Azad Kashmir has its own system of local magistrates and high courts, whose heads are appointed by the president of Azad Kashmir in consultation with the Kashmir Council and the prime minister of Pakistan. Appeals are adjudicated by the Supreme Court of Pakistan. There are also Islamic judges who handle criminal cases concerning Islamic law. Disputes over the politicization of judicial appointments remain a concern, according to a detailed 2010 report by the Human Rights Commission of Pakistan. In February 2011, the Azad Jammu and Kashmir Bar Council called for the establishment of a judicial commission to handle appointments to the Azad Kashmir superior judiciary, noting that favoritism and delays in appointments hindered the courts' ability to function effectively and independently.

The High Court had been virtually nonfunctional for the prior 14 months due to unfilled vacancies.

Pakistan's Inter-Services Intelligence Directorate reportedly engages in extensive surveillance—particularly of proindependence groups and the press—as well as arbitrary arrests and detentions. In some instances, those detained by the security forces are tortured, and several cases of death in custody have been reported. Impunity for such abuses remains the norm. Under the colonial-era Frontier Crimes Regulations, residents are required to report to local police stations once a month. A large number of Pakistani military personnel are stationed in Gilgit-Baltistan, particularly at times of potential unrest, such as the 2009 elections.

Islamist militant groups operate from bases in Pakistani-administered Kashmir. Groups that once focused on attacks in Indian-administered Kashmir are reportedly expanding their local influence and activities, including the establishment of religious schools. They have also increased cooperation with militants based in Pakistan's tribal areas. Tension between pro-Pakistan Islamist groups and proindependence Kashmiri groups—as well as some local residents—has reportedly grown in recent years, contributing to the rise in attacks against local Shiites.

Since the 1970s, the Pakistani government has encouraged the settlement of Pakistanis in Gilgit-Baltistan in an effort to shift the demographic and ethnic balance in the region. Under the GBESGO, many of these settlers were given formal citizenship rights in Gilgit-Baltistan.

Several hundred families displaced by shelling between Indian and Pakistani forces prior to a 2003 ceasefire remain unable to return to their homes and have largely been excluded from assistance schemes launched after the 2005 earthquake. The Azad Kashmir government manages camps for refugees from Indian-administered Kashmir, the bulk of whom arrived after the situation on the Indian side worsened in 1989. Many more of the refugees (roughly 1.5 million) live elsewhere in Azad Kashmir and Pakistan. A bus service linking the capitals of Indian and Pakistani Kashmir was launched in 2005, allowing some civilians to reunite with family members. A second intra-Kashmir bus route was launched in 2006, and limited trade across the Line of Control resumed in 2008 for the first time in over 60 years.

The status of women in Pakistani-administered Kashmir is similar to that of women in Pakistan. While honor killings and rape reportedly occur less frequently than in Pakistan, domestic violence, forced marriage, and other forms of abuse are issues of concern. Women are also at risk of molestation and attack by Pakistani troops, and such attacks often go unpunished. Women are not granted equal rights under the law, and their educational opportunities and choice of marriage partners remain circumscribed. As in some parts of Pakistan, suspected Islamists occasionally mount attacks against NGOs that employ women and on their female employees.

Puerto Rico

Political Rights: 1
Civil Liberties: 2*
Status: Free

Population: 3,700,000

Ratings Change: Puerto Rico's civil liberties rating declined from 1 to 2 due to reports of serious police misconduct and brutality.

Ten-Year Ratings Timeline For Year Under Review (Political Rights, Civil Liberties, Status)

2002	2003	2004	2005	2006	2007	2008	2009	2010	2011
1,2F	1,2F	1,2F	1,1F	1,1F	1,1F	1,1F	1,1F	1,1F	1,2F

Overview: **In September 2011, a U.S. Justice Department report accused the Puerto Rican police force of systematic patterns of civil rights violations, as well as attacks on civilians and journalists. In November, Governor Luis Fortuño announced that a referendum would be held in 2012 for voters to decide whether Puerto Rico would remain a commonwealth, pursue U.S. statehood, or opt for independence.**

Having been captured by U.S. forces during the Spanish-American War in 1898, Puerto Rico acquired the status of a commonwealth of the United States following approval by plebiscite in 1952. As a commonwealth, Puerto Rico exercises approximately the same control over its internal affairs as do the 50 states. Although they are U.S. citizens, residents of Puerto Rico cannot vote in presidential elections and are represented in the U.S. Congress by a delegate to the House of Representatives with limited voting rights.

Power has alternated between the pro-commonwealth Popular Democratic Party (PPD) and the pro-statehood New Progressive Party (PNP) for several decades. Aníbal Acevedo-Vilá of the PPD won the 2004 gubernatorial election, defeating his PNP opponent by a razor-thin margin. He was indicted on corruption charges by a U.S. grand jury in March 2008, but refused to withdraw his candidacy ahead of the November 2008 elections. The result was a major shift in Puerto Rican politics. PNP gubernatorial candidate Luis Fortuño, who had served as the island's representative in the U.S. Congress, firmly defeated the incumbent, while the PNP secured overwhelming majorities in both chambers of the legislature.

Fortuño moved to raise taxes and cut 30,000 workers from the public payroll in order to combat a fiscal crisis that was exacerbated by the global economic downturn; the initiatives triggered a series of protests from trade unions in 2009. Layoffs continued in 2010, with an additional 17,000 public jobs cut, leading to further protests. From April to June 2010, students mounted a strike at the University of Puerto Rico, closing down 10 of the system's 11 campuses to protest tuition increases and cuts in public spending for higher education. Some violence broke out at the largest campus after police intervened in an effort to halt the protests.

In September 2011, the U.S. Justice Department published a report accusing the Puerto Rico Police Department of "profound" and "longstanding" patterns of civil rights violations and other illegal practices that have left it in a state of "institutional dysfunction." The report accused the police of attacking nonviolent protesters and journalists in a manner that compromised their constitutionally protected rights to freedom of speech and assembly, as well as using unnecessary or gratuitous force, especially in low-income and Dominican communities. The report also stated that unwarranted searches and seizures were common.

Political Rights and Civil Liberties: The commonwealth constitution, modeled after that of the United States, provides for a governor elected for four-year terms and a bicameral legislature, currently consisting of a 27-member Senate and a 51-member House of Representatives, elected for four-year terms. As U.S. citizens, Puerto Ricans are guaranteed all civil liberties granted in the United States.

Puerto Rico is represented in the U.S. Congress by a single delegate, who is allowed to vote on floor amendments to legislation, but not on the final passage of bills.

The major political parties are the pro-commonwealth PPD, the pro-statehood PNP, and the Puerto Rican Independence Party (PIP). For years, Puerto Ricans have been nearly equally divided between those who support the continuation of commonwealth status and those who favor full U.S. statehood. A third option, independence, has little popular support; the PIP candidate for governor received just 2 percent of the popular vote in 2008.

In December 2011, Governor Luis Fortuño approved a referendum on Puerto Rico's status to be held in November 2012. The referendum will consist of two questions, both asked on the same day. The first will ask voters if they want Puerto Rico to maintain its current status as a commonwealth, and the second will ask if voters would prefer Puerto Rico to pursue statehood, independence, or sovereign free association. Critics argued that, due to the wording of the questions, asking them both at the same time was an attempt from Puerto Rican leaders to manipulate voters into choosing for statehood.

Corruption is an endemic problem in Puerto Rican politics. A number of leading political figures have been indicted in recent years on various corruption charges. Puerto Rico was ranked 39 out of 183 countries and territories surveyed in Transparency International's 2011 Corruption Perceptions Index.

Puerto Rico's tradition of varied and vigorous news media has been under strain due to a decline in newspapers stemming from the economic crisis and other factors.

Freedom of religion is guaranteed in this predominantly Roman Catholic territory. A substantial number of Evangelical churches have been established on the island in recent years. Academic freedom is guaranteed.

Freedom of assembly is protected by law, and Puerto Ricans frequently mount protests against local or federal government policies. There is a robust civil society, with numerous nongovernmental organizations representing the interests of different constituencies. The government respects trade union rights, and unions are generally free to organize and strike.

The legal system is based on U.S. law, and the island's Supreme Court heads an independent judiciary. However, concerns about politicization at the Supreme Court emerged in November 2010, when the four justices appointed by Fortuño approved a resolution asking the legislature to expand the court from seven to nine members, ostensibly to deal with a heavy caseload. The three-justice minority dissented, arguing that the expansion had been unnecessary and approved without sufficient debate. The legislature quickly passed the measure, and Fortuño was appointed the two new justices in 2011, giving his picks an overwhelming majority on the court, potentially for many years to come.

Crime is a growing problem. By late December 2011, there had been 1,130 homicides in Puerto Rico—147 more than in the previous year—with a large proportion being drug-related. The center of the narcotics trade has shifted from San Juan to smaller communities, leaving housing projects in some towns under virtual siege by drug gangs.

In recent years, there has been an upsurge in attempts by illegal migrants from various Caribbean countries to reach Puerto Rico; many are brought to the island by smugglers. There is evidence that Puerto Rico law enforcement officers have routinely discriminated against Dominicans living in the island.

Although women enjoy equal rights under the law, the September 2011 Justice Department report cited evidence that police officers failed to investigate incidents of sexual assault and domestic violence, including spousal abuse by fellow officers.

Somaliland

Political Rights: 4
Civil Liberties: 5
Status: Partly Free

Population: 3,500,000

Ten-Year Ratings Timeline For Year Under Review (Political Rights, Civil Liberties, Status)

2002	2003	2004	2005	2006	2007	2008	2009	2010	2011
--	--	--	--	4,4PF	4,4PF	5,4PF	5,5PF	4,5PF	4,5PF

Overview: **Somaliland celebrated the twentieth anniversary of its declaration of independence from Somalia in May 2011, though international recognition of its claims for statehood remained elusive. Relations with neighboring Puntland deteriorated following heavy fighting in a contested border area.**

The modern state of Somalia was formed in 1960, when the newly independent protectorates of British Somaliland and Italian Somaliland agreed to unite. In 1969, General Siad Barre seized power, ushering in a violent era of clan rivalries and political repression. Barre was deposed in 1991. The current Somaliland, largely conforming to the borders of the former British Somaliland in the northwestern corner of the country, took advantage of the resulting political chaos and declared independence later that year.

In a series of conferences, Somaliland's leaders formed a government system combining democratic elements, including a parliament, with traditional political structures, such as an upper house consisting of clan elders. Somaliland's first two presidents were appointed by clan elders. In 2003, Dahir Riyale Kahin became

Somaliland's first elected president, and direct elections for members of the lower house of parliament were held for the first time in 2005, with no reports of widespread intimidation or fraud. The president's United People's Democratic Party (UDUB) captured the most seats, followed closely by the Peace, Unity, and Development Party (Kulmiye) and the Justice and Development Party (UCID).

In 2006, Riyale violated the constitution by postponing elections for the upper house and extending its term by four years. The presidential election was repeatedly delayed, until June 2010, eight months after Riyale's extended term officially expired. The leader of Kulmiye, Ahmed Mohamed Silanyo, captured almost 50 percent of the vote, comfortably ahead of Riyale, who received 33 percent. Monitors from Europe and the United States identified some irregularities, but declared the vote to have been free and fair. While the presidential elections were a success, long overdue legislative elections were postponed once again in September 2010, and had yet to be held by the end of 2011.

Somaliland's democratic progress and steady economic development added impetus to its campaign for international recognition. Hopes were raised when South Sudan was granted independence in July 2011, which was seen by many in Somaliland as an important precedent. But formal recognition remained elusive, and international partners continued to express their preference for a united Somalia.

Somaliland has had difficult relations with the rest of Somalia, particularly the autonomous region of Puntland. The two neighbors have rival claims to the Sool, Sanaag, and Cayn regions, currently under the control of Somaliland. In February 2011, clashes between Somaliland's military and a pro-Puntland militia led to the deaths of at least 30 people and the displacement of over 3,000. Approximately 150 soldiers from Somaliland's army defected in protest of the operation, which they said was directed at members of their sub-clan. The Puntland president accused Somaliland of massacring civilians and harboring terrorists from the Shabaab, a radical Islamist militant group that controlled parts of southern and central Somalia. In August, a court in Puntland sentenced four Somaliland officials from Sool to 10 years for political sabotage.

The most devastating drought to hit the Horn of Africa in six decades caused serious hardship in Somaliland, though the authorities responded fairly well to the crisis, assisted by international aid organizations.

Political Rights and Civil Liberties: According to Somaliland's constitution, the president is directly elected for a maximum of two five-year terms and appoints the cabinet. The presidential election of 2010, originally scheduled for 2008, resulted in the smooth transfer of power from the UDUB party to the main opposition party Kulmiye. Members of Somaliland's 82-seat lower house of parliament, the House of Representatives, are directly elected for five-year terms, while members of the 82-seat upper house (Guurti) are indirectly elected by local communities for six-year terms. Both houses extended their terms in September 2010, arguing that Somaliland could not organize another election so soon after the presidential poll. The Guurti voted to increase its term by another three years in addition to the four it had already been granted. The House of Representatives, whose term was supposed to expire in December 2010, gave itself an extension of two years and eight months.

A constitutional restriction that allowed for a maximum of three political parties was relaxed in 2011 following a vote in parliament. The new multiparty law was criticized for excluding anyone under the age of 36 from forming a new party. In August, Somaliland's interior minister resigned, reportedly to launch a new opposition movement. In October, a new party, Waddani, was formed by breakaway members of the UCID party. Although parties defined by region or clan are technically prohibited, party and clan affiliations tend to coincide.

Corruption in Somaliland was a serious problem under the government of President Dahir Riyale Kahin, but there are signs of improvement under his successor. President Ahmed Mohamed Silanyo has set up an anticorruption commission, and efforts have been made to crack down on the misuse of public funds. In August 2011, two public officials were given prison sentences of five years each for misappropriating money.

While freedoms of expression and the press are guaranteed by Somaliland's constitution, these rights are limited in practice. It is not acceptable for citizens to express views in support of union with Somalia. Journalists faced increased interference and harassment in 2011 despite the new government's pledge to uphold press freedom. The editor of the daily newspaper *Waheen* was jailed for three years in January after being found guilty of defaming two senior officials he accused of nepotism; he was pardoned a month later. In September, a *Waheen* reporter was arrested and detained without charge for one week after publishing a story about a political dispute involving a regional governor. The security forces prevented journalists from attending public events, attacking a reporter who tried to cover the swearing-in of the new interior minister in September. In October, a television reporter was beaten by police in Hargeisa, who took exception to some photographs he had taken. Defamation charges were filed against the Somaliland Journalist Association, after it condemned the decision to temporarily suspend the registration of new private media outlets, and its chairman was arrested and briefly detained in December. The government owns the only radio station in Somaliland, Radio Hargeisa, and prohibits the establishment of private stations. There are seven private daily newspapers in Somaliland in addition to the state-owned *Mandeeq*, although they have limited circulations. The government does not restrict access to the internet.

Nearly all Somaliland residents are Sunni Muslims, and Islam is the state religion. Proselytizing by members of other faiths is prohibited. Academic freedom in Somaliland is less restricted than in neighboring Somalia. The territory has at least 10 universities and colleges of higher learning, although none are adequately resourced.

Freedoms of assembly and association are constitutionally guaranteed. International and local nongovernmental organizations (NGOs) operate without serious interference. However, concerns were raised about a new NGO Act, signed into law in May 2011. International NGOs complained that a provision compelling them to partner with local organizations would limit their effectiveness given the lack of technical expertise on the ground. They also expressed unease that the new law could open the way for increased government interference in the delivery of humanitarian aid. The constitution does not specifically mention the right to strike, though it does permit collective bargaining. The right to belong to a union is generally respected, though there was one arrest of a union leader in 2011.

Somaliland's constitution allows for three legal systems, based on Sharia (Islamic law), civil law, and customary law. The Riyale government bypassed the courts and used secret security committees to try many defendants without due process. Upon taking office, Silanyo pledged to uphold the rule of law, strengthen the independence of the judiciary, and release all prisoners who had not been charged with a crime, apart from those accused of terrorism or theft. The president followed through on that promise in May 2011, when 751 prisoners were pardoned to mark Somaliland's twentieth anniversary. Somaliland arrests approximately 200 children each month, who are often detained with adults and tried in the adult criminal justice system, in violation of a 2007 juvenile justice law.

The judiciary is underfunded and lacks independence, while the Supreme Court is largely ineffective. Somaliland has approximately 100 judges, most of whom do not have formal legal training. Silanyo fired the chairman of the high court and eight high court judges in June 2011, accusing them of nepotism and corruption. Somaliland's police and security forces, while more professional than those in Somalia, have at times used excessive force. For example, in October, police fired on civilians protesting their forceful eviction from a site in Hargeisa, killing one and injuring three.

Societal fault lines are largely clan based. Larger, wealthier clans have more political clout than the less prominent groups, and clan elders often intervene to settle conflicts. There has been increased discrimination against foreigners. In September 2011, the government threatened to expel all unregistered foreigners within a month. In Sool, where outsiders have been blamed for fomenting disorder, the authorities in October rounded up and deported 100 internally displaced people who had fled famine-affected areas of southern Somalia.

While society in Somaliland is patriarchal, women have made modest advances in public life. Silanyo appointed two women to his 20-member cabinet. There are two women in the House of Representatives, one woman in the Guurti, and a woman was elected chairperson of the Somaliland Human Rights Commission. Female genital mutilation, while illegal, is practiced on the vast majority of women.

South Ossetia

Political Rights: 7
Civil Liberties: 6
Status: Not Free

Population: 70,000

Ten-Year Ratings Timeline For Year Under Review (Political Rights, Civil Liberties, Status)

2002	2003	2004	2005	2006	2007	2008	2009	2010	2011
--	--	--	--	--	--	7,6NF	7,6NF	7,6NF	7,6NF

Overview: **As South Ossetia's November 2011 presidential election approached, officials loyal to outgoing president Eduard Kokoity jailed and threatened opposition figures and changed legislation to prevent the registration of certain candidates. Leading opposition candidate Alla Dzhioyeva appeared to come out ahead in a November 27 runoff against Moscow-backed candidate Anatoly Bibilov, but the Supreme Court annulled the vote over significant electoral violations and called for a repeat election in**

March 2012, touching off a series of protests. The parliament rejected the terms of a Russian-brokered compromise, and the dispute remained unresolved at year's end. The political standoff took place in a general atmosphere of intimidation and occasional violence, with both Russian officials and the South Ossetian leadership suggesting the annexation of the territory by Russia.

South Ossetia first declared its independence from Georgia in 1920, igniting a war that left thousands dead. Both Georgia and South Ossetia were incorporated into the Soviet Union in 1922, with South Ossetia designated an autonomous oblast (region) within Georgia.

As Georgian nationalism grew toward the end of the Soviet era, a South Ossetian independence movement called unsuccessfully for the oblast to be upgraded to a republic in 1989. South Ossetia declared full independence from Georgia in 1990, prompting Tbilisi to abolish its autonomous status. Fierce fighting broke out in January 1991, resulting in a thousand deaths and civilian displacement on both sides; some 40,000 to 100,000 Ossetians fled to North Ossetia in Soviet Russia. In March 1991, a reported 99 percent of South Ossetian referendum voters endorsed independence, and 90 percent voted in favor of seeking to join Russia in a January 1992 referendum, after the final dissolution of the Soviet Union. Both plebiscites were rejected by Tbilisi.

In June 1992, a ceasefire agreement established a Russian-led peacekeeping force, and the Organization for Security and Cooperation in Europe was put in charge of monitoring the ceasefire and facilitating negotiations on a permanent resolution of the conflict.

Torez Kulumbegov led separatist South Ossetia from 1992 to 1993. He was succeeded by Lyudvig Chibirov, who went on to win the newly created post of president in 1996. After a period of relatively cordial relations with Tbilisi, the 2001 election of hard-liner Eduard Kokoity as president of South Ossetia renewed tensions. His Unity Party took the majority of seats in 2004 parliamentary elections; though four seats were reserved for the territory's ethnic Georgian population, only five Georgian villages were able to vote. All of the separatist regime's elections went unrecognized by Georgia and the international community.

In May 2004, recently elected Georgian president Mikheil Saakashvili ordered a campaign to dismantle the multimillion-dollar smuggling operation controlled by Kokoity's regime, triggering skirmishes and causing Ossetians to rally around Kokoity. The two sides agreed to a ceasefire in August, but the separatist government in Tskhinvali rejected Saakashvili's proposal for expanded South Ossetian autonomy in September.

South Ossetia held a joint referendum and presidential election in November 2006, with 99.8 percent of voters on Ossetian-controlled territory reaffirming the bid for independence, according to Tskhinvali. Kokoity, who faced no genuine opposition, was reelected with a reported 98.1 percent of the vote. On the same day, Tbilisi organized a similarly lopsided election and referendum in South Ossetia's Georgian-controlled areas, but the resulting pro-Georgian government was never able to draw significant support away from separatist institutions.

Following weeks of skirmishes along the border, Tbilisi launched an attack on Tskhinvali on August 7, 2008. Russia immediately retaliated by sending troops into South Ossetia, pushing back Georgian forces. Russia also invaded Georgia via Abkhazia, another breakaway Georgian territory in the northwest. Both sides had signed a French-brokered ceasefire by August 16, and Russia eventually withdrew its troops to the confines of South Ossetia and Abkhazia. However, separatist forces retained some territory that was previously controlled by Tbilisi. Moscow, defying international criticism, formally recognized South Ossetia and Abkhazia as independent states on August 26 and subsequently concluded bilateral security agreements with the separatist governments, augmenting its long-term military presence.

In May 2009, South Ossetia held parliamentary elections that resulted in a legislature dominated by Kokoity supporters. The victory came amid accusations that Kokoity had shut out and threatened opposition parties. Public discontent with Kokoity increased further during the postwar reconstruction process, which remained painfully slow throughout 2009 and 2010 despite an influx of Russian aid. Many Ossetians accused Kokoity of embezzlement, and in December 2009, Russian officials released a report finding that only a fraction of the money had been used for its intended purposes. Tskhinvali residents mounted several protests over the reconstruction issue in 2010.

In June 2011, the parliament rejected efforts by Kokoity supporters to lift term limits and allow him to participate in a presidential election set for November. Eleven candidates ultimately ran in the first round of voting on November 13, including several Kokoity loyalists; six other candidates were forced or pressured to withdraw. Opposition candidate Alla Dzhioyeva, a former education minister, and Moscow-backed candidate Anatoly Bibilov, South Ossetia's emergency situations minister, each won about 25 percent of the vote and advanced to the November 27 runoff.

Preliminary results on November 28 gave Dzhioyeva nearly 57 percent, but the Supreme Court annulled the balloting after finding significant electoral violations, ordering a new vote in March 2012. The ruling triggered protests by opposition supporters. Under a Russian-brokered deal reached in early December, Dzhioyeva agreed to accept the court's ruling so long as Kokoity stepped down immediately and the parliament fired the prosecutor general and the Supreme Court chairman. Kokoity duly handed power to prime minister Vadim Brovtsev, but the parliament rejected the other conditions, leading to a standoff that remained unresolved at year's end.

Russia significantly expanded its control over the territory during 2011, and talk of annexation gained momentum in August, when Putin himself raised the possibility of a merger. The issue was politically divisive in South Ossetia, with Dzhioyeva and the opposition firmly against joining Russia, and Bibilov and many Tskhinvali officials already pushing to start the unification process.

Political Rights and Civil Liberties: Under the separatist constitution, the president and the 33-seat parliament are elected for five-year terms. South Ossetian elections are not monitored by independent observers or recognized by the international community. Most ethnic Georgians have either declined or been unable to participate in such elections.

During the May 2009 parliamentary elections, opposition parties reported significant violations, including alleged coercion of voters in favor of President Eduard Kokoity's supporters. Opposition representation was also reduced as a result of 2008 election laws, which set a 7 percent vote threshold for parties to enter the parliament and required all lawmakers to be elected by proportional representation. The 2011 presidential election campaign period featured violence and other abuses by Kokoity's government. The leading opposition candidates were prevented from registering after a 10-year residency requirement was added to the constitution in April. Other opposition candidates were beaten or jailed, and one senior member of a recently disqualified candidate's party was murdered in North Ossetia in October.

Russia exerts a dominant influence on South Ossetian politics, and its degree of control increased substantially after the 2008 war. Russians reputedly endorsed by Moscow held key cabinet positions in 2011, including the premiership. Also during the year, the South Ossetian parliament signed a 49-year agreement allowing Russia to build and operate a new military base in Tskhinvali; there were already over 4,000 Russian troops stationed in the territory.

Corruption is believed to be extensive. In 2010, Kokoity's administration faced pressure from Russia and the public to curb the alleged embezzlement of funds earmarked for postwar reconstruction, which became a major pledge of the 2011 presidential candidates. Before the war, the territory reportedly hosted large-scale smuggling and black-market activities.

South Ossetia's local electronic and print media are almost entirely controlled by separatist authorities, and private broadcasts are prohibited. Foreign media, including broadcasts from Russia and Georgia, are accessible. Independent or opposition-oriented journalists in the territory face various forms of intimidation. In March 2011, in what was seen as a politically motivated case, the son of opposition journalist Fatima Margiyeva was convicted of manslaughter for his friend's death by drug overdose and was sentenced to 15 months in jail. Margiyeva had received a two-year suspended prison sentence for weapons possession in 2010.

Freedom of religion has sometimes been adversely affected by the political and military situation. While the majority of the population is Orthodox Christian, there is a sizeable Muslim community, many members of which migrated from the North Caucasus. The educational system reflects government views, and many South Ossetians receive higher education in Russia.

While antigovernment protests were extremely rare before the 2008 war, opposition groups mounted demonstrations following the flawed 2009 elections, and Tskhinvali residents have protested repeatedly in response to the slow postwar construction of new homes and alleged government corruption. In 2011, one human rights activist was beaten and another threatened after leading such demonstrations. Opposition supporters held persistent peaceful protests after the presidential runoff was annulled in late November, though Kokoity at one point said they were unauthorized gatherings and security officials warned of possible violence. Civil society groups operate under the close scrutiny of the authorities, and activists are subject to intimidation.

South Ossetia's justice system has been manipulated to punish perceived opponents of the separatist leadership, while government allies allegedly violate the law with relative impunity. Russian prosecutors have attempted to curb malfeasance by local officials, but the Russian court system itself remains deeply flawed.

Indiscriminate attacks by both sides in the 2008 war killed and displaced civilians, and Ossetian forces seized or razed property in previously Georgian-controlled villages. Authorities in South Ossetia have barred ethnic Georgians from returning to the territory unless they renounce their Georgian citizenship and accept Russian passports. The de facto border with Georgia was tightened in 2011, with several Georgians subjected to detention by Ossetian and Russian border guards. Russian authorities have prevented ethnic Ossetians from entering Georgia, but travel to Russia is unimpeded.

Tibet

Political Rights: 7
Civil Liberties: 7
Status: Not Free

Population: 3,000,000 [Note: This figure from China's 2010 census covers only the Tibet Autonomous Region. Areas of eastern Tibet that were incorporated into neighboring Chinese provinces are also assessed in the report below.]

Ten-Year Ratings Timeline For Year Under Review (Political Rights, Civil Liberties, Status)

2002	2003	2004	2005	2006	2007	2008	2009	2010	2011
7,7NF	7,7NF	7,7NF	7,7NF	7,7NF	7,7NF	7,7NF	7,7NF	7,7NF	7,7NF

Overview: **The security clampdown established after an uprising in 2008 was generally maintained during 2011. Between March and the end of the year, 12 Tibetans set themselves on fire to protest Chinese Communist Party (CCP) rule, mostly in the Tibetan regions of Sichuan Province. The authorities responded with mass detentions, "patriotic education" campaigns, and communications blackouts, continuing a trend in recent years of growing repression in Tibetan areas outside the Tibetan Autonomous Region (TAR) where government policies had previously been less severe. Also in 2011, the top CCP official in the TAR was replaced, though the change appeared unlikely to significantly reduce state repression in the region.**

The Tibetan plateau, or a substantial portion of it, was ruled by a Dalai Lama or his government from the mid-17th century onward. Chinese Communist forces entered Tibet in 1950 and defeated the Tibetan army. The region was formally incorporated into the People's Republic of China the following year. In 1959, Chinese troops suppressed a major uprising in Lhasa, reportedly killing tens of thousands of people. Tibet's spiritual and political leader—the 14th Dalai Lama, Tenzin Gyatso—was forced to flee to India with some 80,000 supporters.

During the next six years, China closed 97 percent of the region's Buddhist monasteries and defrocked about 100,000 monks and nuns. Most Tibetan territory was reorganized as the Tibet Autonomous Region (TAR) in 1965, but some eastern portions of the Tibetan plateau were included in separate Chinese provinces. During the Chinese Cultural Revolution (1966–76), nearly all of Tibet's estimated 6,200 monasteries were destroyed.

Under reforms introduced in 1980, limited religious practice was allowed again. Between 1987 and 1989, some 200 mostly peaceful demonstrations were mounted in

Lhasa and surrounding areas. After the antigovernment protests escalated in March 1989, martial law was imposed until May 1990.

In the 1990s, Beijing reinvigorated its efforts to control religious affairs and undermine the exiled Dalai Lama's authority. Six-year-old Gendun Choekyi Nyima was detained by the authorities in 1995, and his selection by the Dalai Lama as the 11th Panchen Lama was rejected. He subsequently disappeared from public view, and Beijing orchestrated the selection of another six-year-old boy as the Panchen Lama. Since one of the roles of the Panchen Lama is to identify the reincarnated Dalai Lama, the move was widely seen as a bid to control the eventual selection of the 15th Dalai Lama.

China hosted envoys of the Dalai Lama in 2002, marking the first formal contact since 1993. The Tibetan government in exile sought genuine autonomy for Tibet, particularly to ensure the survival of its Buddhist culture, but the Chinese side said repeatedly that it would only discuss the return of the Dalai Lama and not broader conditions in Tibet. Meanwhile, other Tibetan exile groups increasingly demanded independence.

Under Zhang Qingli, who was appointed as secretary of the Chinese Communist Party (CCP) in the TAR in 2005, the authorities amplified their repressive policies. In March 2008, after security agents suppressed a march by monks to mark the anniversary of the 1959 uprising, a riot erupted. Some Tibetans attacked ethnic Chinese residents and burned Chinese- or Hui-owned businesses and government offices. Over 150 other protests, most of them reportedly peaceful, soon broke out in Tibetan-populated areas of the TAR and other provinces. The government responded with a massive deployment of armed forces, who opened fire on protesters on at least four occasions, according to Human Rights Watch. The authorities reported that 19 people were killed in Lhasa, primarily in fires, and admitted to the death of 3 Tibetan protesters in the city. Overseas Tibetan groups claimed that between 100 and 218 Tibetans were killed as security forces suppressed the demonstrations.

Although the region was accessible to tourists and journalists under special conditions for parts of the next three years, the high level of repression established in 2008 was generally maintained. Security measures were especially tight surrounding politically sensitive dates. In 2011, these included the March anniversary of the 1959 and 2008 uprisings, and the 60th anniversary of Chinese rule in July. On both occasions, the authorities imposed a month-long ban on travel to the area by foreign tourists.

In the Tibetan areas of Sichuan Province, repression intensified beginning in March 2011, after a young monk set himself on fire to protest CCP rule. By year's end, 10 more Tibetans in Sichuan and 1 in the TAR had self-immolated, and at least 6 of them died from their injuries. The crackdown after the first self-immolations spurred clashes between security forces and Tibetan residents, and according to some observers, was a motivating factor for the subsequent acts of protest.

The intermittent talks between the government and representatives of the Dalai Lama ceased again in 2011, as the atmosphere for dialogue deteriorated. At a July rally in Lhasa to mark the 60th anniversary of Chinese rule in the region, Chinese vice president Xi Jinping, expected to become China's top leader in 2012, touted the CCP's deeply unpopular policies in Tibet and praised the work of security units that have played a leading role in violent crackdowns. Both state-run media and "patriotic education" campaigns continued to vilify the Dalai Lama, and Beijing continued its aggressive policy of pressuring foreign leaders to refrain from meeting with him and endorse the official Chinese position on Tibet.

The government's extensive economic development programs in Tibet have disproportionately benefited ethnic Chinese and increased Chinese migration to the region, stoking Tibetan fears of cultural assimilation.

Political Rights and Civil Liberties: The Chinese government rules Tibet through administration of the TAR and 12 Tibetan autonomous prefectures or counties in the nearby provinces of Sichuan, Qinghai, Gansu, and Yunnan. Under the Chinese constitution, autonomous areas have the right to formulate their own regulations and implement national legislation in accordance with local conditions. In practice, decision-making power is concentrated in the hands of senior, ethnic Chinese CCP officials. In August 2011, Zhang Qingli was replaced as TAR party secretary by Chen Quanguo, a CCP veteran with no previous experience dealing with ethnic minorities. Some observers speculated that Chen might not pursue repressive measures with as much zeal as Zhang, but such a shift appeared unlikely without a policy change in Beijing. The few ethnic Tibetans who occupy senior positions serve mostly as figureheads and echo official doctrine on Tibet. Padma Thrinley (known as Pema Choling in the Chinese press), a Tibetan, has served as chairman of the TAR government since January 2010.

Since 1960, the Dalai Lama has overseen the partial democratization of the government in exile in Dharamsala, India. Current institutions include an elected parliament serving five-year terms, a Supreme Justice Commission that adjudicates civil disputes, and—since 2001—a directly elected prime minister, also serving five-year terms. The unelected Dalai Lama, who served as head of state, renounced his political role in March 2011, and the parliament made the necessary changes to the exile government's charter in May. Separately, Lobsang Sangay was elected prime minister in April, replacing a two-term incumbent.

Corruption is believed to be extensive in Tibet, as in the rest of China. Nevertheless, little information was available during the year on the scale of the problem or official measures to combat it.

Chinese authorities control the flow of information in Tibet, tightly restricting all media. International broadcasts are jammed. The internet has provided educated residents with more access to information, but the online restrictions and surveillance in place across China are enforced even more stringently in the TAR. Security forces periodically confiscate communications devices and raid internet cafés, and routinely monitor calls in and out of the region. Tibetans who transmit information abroad often suffer repercussions including long prison sentences, while some internet users have been arrested solely for accessing banned information. Near the sites of self-immolations in 2011, the authorities at times cut off the internet entirely. Several Tibetan websites and a social-networking site were shut down within days of the first self-immolation. Also during 2011, security forces continued a recent campaign of arrests aimed at cultural figures whose work—often circulated by hand within Tibet and shared with the outside world—emphasizes Tibetan identity. According to overseas Tibetan groups, more than 60 writers, intellectuals, and musicians have been arrested since 2008, with some sentenced to lengthy prison terms, including a number of convictions in 2011.

Authorities continued to restrict foreign journalists' access to the TAR in 2011. Like other foreigners, they were denied entry around politically sensitive dates in March and July. During other periods, they were required to travel in groups and obtain official permission to visit the TAR. Foreign journalists periodically report being expelled from Tibetan areas of Sichuan and other provinces, though no permission is technically required for travel there. Residents who assist foreign journalists are reportedly harassed.

The authorities regularly suppress religious activities, particularly those seen as forms of dissent or advocacy of Tibetan independence. Possession of Dalai Lama–related materials can lead to official harassment and punishment, though many Tibetans secretly possess such items. CCP members, government employees, and their family members are not allowed to practice Buddhism, at least within the TAR. The Religious Affairs Bureaus (RABs) control who can study in monasteries and convents. Officials allow only men and women over age 18 to become monks and nuns, and they are required to sign a declaration rejecting Tibetan independence, expressing loyalty to the Chinese government, and denouncing the Dalai Lama. Regulations announced in 2007 require government approval for the religious recognition and education of reincarnated Buddhist clergy. The government manages the daily operations of monasteries through Democratic Management Committees (DMCs) and the RABs. Only monks and nuns deemed loyal to the CCP may lead DMCs, and laypeople have also been appointed to these committees. New regulations in effect as of August 2011 in approximately half of the Tibetan areas outside the TAR will further increase government control over the personnel decisions and daily affairs of monasteries in those regions.

Ideological education campaigns that had been conducted sporadically since 1996 began to escalate under Zhang Qingli in 2005 and intensified after 2008. They have occasionally been extended beyond monasteries to Tibet's general population, forcing students, civil servants, farmers, and merchants to recognize the CCP claim that China "liberated" Tibet and to denounce the Dalai Lama. Monks and nuns who refuse face expulsion from their religious institutions, while others risk loss of employment or arrest.

University professors cannot lecture on certain topics, and many must attend political indoctrination sessions. The government restricts course materials to prevent the circulation of unofficial versions of Tibetan history.

Freedoms of assembly and association are severely restricted in practice. Independent trade unions and human rights groups are illegal, and even nonviolent protests are often harshly punished. Nongovernmental organizations (NGOs) focused on development and public health operate under highly restrictive agreements. Despite the risks, Tibetans continue to seek avenues for expressing dissatisfaction with government policies. In 2011, a new form of protest took gained prominence as 12 Tibetans, mostly monks and nuns, set themselves on fire and shouted slogans calling for freedom in Tibet and the return of the Dalai Lama. In March and April, police detained numerous people tangentially linked to the first self-immolator, Phuntsog, a monk from Kirti monastery in Sichuan's Aba (Ngaba) prefecture. A tighter lockdown was imposed on the monastery in April, sparking protests by local residents who tried to stop police from taking monks away for "patriotic education." After a standoff of several days, security forces suppressed the protests and detained 300 monks; two lay Tibetans reportedly died in the clashes. At least 100 of the detained monks were later released, but were required to return to their homes in Qinghai rather than continue their monastic studies. In September, six people linked to Phuntsog were sentenced: three monks accused of aiding and sheltering him received 10 to 13 years in prison, while three others received two to three years in "reeducation through labor" camps.

In addition to the self-immolations and related protests in Aba, clerics and lay Tibetans in Ganzi (Kardze), also in Sichuan, staged a series of small protests throughout the month of June. On an almost daily basis, a pair or small group would go to a public space, distribute leaflets, and call for the return of the Dalai Lama. By the end of the month, between 40 and 60 people had reportedly been arrested. Seventeen were apparently released in August, while the whereabouts of the others were unknown at year's end. Meanwhile, rural Tibetans in the TAR continued to stage periodic protests against Chinese mining operations on the plateau.

The judicial system in Tibet remains abysmal, and torture is reportedly widespread. Several cases of detainees dying in custody or shortly after release were reported in 2011. Defendants lack access to meaningful legal representation. Trials are closed if state security is invoked, and sometimes even when no political crime is listed. Chinese lawyers who offer to defend Tibetan suspects have been harassed or disbarred. Security forces routinely engage in arbitrary detention, and the families of detainees are often left with little information as to their whereabouts or well-being. A partial list of political prisoners published by the U.S. Congressional-Executive Commission on China included over 500 Tibetans as of September 2011.

Heightened restrictions on freedom of movement—including troop deployments, roadblocks, and passport restrictions—were employed sporadically during 2011, particularly surrounding politically sensitive anniversaries and in areas of Sichuan where self-immolations took place. Increased security efforts kept the number of Tibetans who successfully crossed the border into Nepal at around 700 during the year, compared with some 800 in 2010 and over 2,000 in 2007.

As members of an officially recognized minority group, Tibetans receive preferential treatment in university admission examinations, but this is often not enough to secure entrance. The dominant role of the Chinese language in education and employment limits opportunities for many Tibetans. Private sector employers favor ethnic Chinese for many jobs, especially in urban areas. Tibetans reportedly find it more difficult than Chinese residents to obtain permits and loans to open businesses.

Since 2003, the authorities have intensified efforts to resettle rural Tibetans—either by force or with inducements—in permanent-housing areas with little economic infrastructure. According to state-run media reports, by July 2011, a total of 1.4 million farmers and herders had been resettled within the TAR. Many have reportedly tried to return to their previous lands, risking conflict with officials if they are discovered. China's restrictive family-planning policies are more leniently enforced for Tibetans and other ethnic minorities than for ethnic Chinese. Officials limit urban Tibetans to having two children and encourage—but do not usually require—rural Tibetans to stop at three children. As a result, the TAR is one of the few areas of China where the prevailing preference for male children along with the restrictive regulations has not led to a skewed sex ratio in the population.

Transnistria

Political Rights: 6
Civil Liberties: 6
Status: Not Free

Population: 523,000

Ten-Year Ratings Timeline For Year Under Review (Political Rights, Civil Liberties, Status)

2002	2003	2004	2005	2006	2007	2008	2009	2010	2011
6,6NF	6,6NF	6,6NF	6,6NF	6,6NF	6,6NF	6,6NF	6,6NF	6,6NF	6,6NF

Overview:

Former parliament speaker Yevgeny Shevchuk defeated longtime incumbent Igor Smirnov and a Russian-backed candidate, current parliament speaker Anatoly Kaminsky, in the December presidential election. Shevchuk pledged to reduce barriers to trade and travel with Moldova while promoting Transnistria's independence and close ties to Russia. All of the parties to the multilateral talks on Transnistria's status had agreed in September to resume active negotiations after a five-year lull, and an official meeting of the group was held on December 1, with further talks set for February 2012. Also during the year, Transnistrian authorities, under international pressure, pardoned a journalist and a former tax inspector who had both been imprisoned as Moldovan spies.

The Pridnestrovskaya Moldavskaya Respublika (PMR), bounded by the Dniester River to the west and the Ukrainian border to the east, is a breakaway region in eastern Moldova with a large population of ethnic Russians and ethnic Ukrainians. In the rest of Moldova, where the dominant language is essentially identical to Romanian, the separatist region is commonly known as Transnistria. It was attached to the territory that became Moldova when the borders were redrawn under Soviet leader Joseph Stalin in 1940. As the Soviet Union began to collapse in 1990, pro-Russian separatists in Transnistria, fearing that Moldova would unite with neighboring Romania, declared independence from Moldova and established the PMR under an authoritarian presidential system.

With weapons and other assistance from the Russian army, the PMR fought a military conflict with Moldova that ended with a 1992 ceasefire. A new Moldovan constitution in 1994 gave the territory substantial autonomy, but the conflict remained unresolved, and the separatist regime continues to maintain a de facto independence that is not recognized internationally. The Organization for Security and Cooperation in Europe, Russia, and Ukraine have attempted to mediate a final settlement between Moldova and the PMR. In 2005, the United States and the European Union (EU) were invited to join the negotiations as observers, creating the so-called 5+2 format.

The formal multilateral talks collapsed in early 2006 and remained dormant for the next several years. In the absence of active 5+2 negotiations, Moldovan president Vladimir Voronin pursued bilateral talks with Russia and took a number of steps to bring Moldova's foreign policy into line with the Kremlin's. However, an alliance of pro-European parties swept Voronin and his Communist Party from power in Moldova's July 2009 elections, and international pressure for renewed talks on Transnistria's status subsequently increased.

The pro-Russian Obnovleniye (Renewal) party maintained its majority in Transnistria's December 2010 legislative elections, winning 25 of 43 seats. Party leader Anatoly Kaminsky was reelected as Speaker.

As the December 2011 presidential election approached, Russia's ruling party endorsed Kaminsky's candidacy. In October, the Russian presidential chief of staff openly urged longtime PMR president Igor Smirnov not to seek a fifth term, arguing that the territory needed new leadership. Analysts said the Kremlin was seeking a more pliable figure to engage in renewed 5+2 talks.

Smirnov was eliminated in the election's first round on December 11, taking 24 percent of the vote in a field of six. Former parliament Speaker Yevgeny Shevchuk led with 39 percent, followed by Kaminsky with 26 percent. Smirnov claimed numerous electoral violations, but his complaints were rejected by the election commission. He later said he would accept the results in the interest of unity and stability. Shevchuk went on to win the December 25 runoff against Kaminsky, securing 74 percent of the vote.

Shevchuk had stepped down as Speaker in 2009 after a disagreement with Smirnov over constitutional reform. He was expelled from Obnovleniye in July 2011, and formed the Vozrozhdeniye (Revival) movement to back his presidential bid. He ran on pledges to tackle corruption and improve the economy, and after the election, he laid out plans for reducing barriers to travel and trade, including with Moldova. Shevchuk also said he would work toward international recognition of the PMR, maintain strong ties with Russia, and also pursue good relations with Moldova and neighboring Ukraine.

The parties to the 5+2 talks agreed in September 2011 to resume formal negotiations, and a first official meeting was held on November 30 and December 1. The next gathering was set for February 2012.

Political Rights and Civil Liberties: Residents of Transnistria cannot choose their leaders democratically, and they are unable to participate freely in Moldovan elections. While the PMR maintains its own legislative, executive, and judicial branches of government, no country recognizes its independence. Both the president and the 43-seat, unicameral Supreme Council are elected to five-year terms. In June 2011, the legislature approved constitutional amendments that created a relatively weak post of prime minister and set a two-term limit on the presidency. The latter provision was not retroactive, leaving four-term incumbent Igor Smirnov free to run again. While the December presidential election was not recognized internationally, it featured increased competition and a somewhat broader choice for voters compared with previous polls.

The majority party in the legislature is Obnovleniye, which has pressed the government for business-oriented reforms but—like other parties operating in the territory—is generally viewed as part of the PMR establishment. It is associated with Transnistria's monopolistic business conglomerate, Sheriff Enterprises, and maintains a close relationship with the ruling party in Russia.

Native Moldovan speakers are not represented in government. PMR authorities detained the mayor and a councilman in a contested border village for several days in March 2011, reportedly because they had displayed a Moldovan flag. As in previous years, the authorities did not allow voting in Moldovan elections to take place in PMR-controlled territory in 2011, but the large number of PMR residents with Russian citizenship were free to vote in Russia's tightly controlled parliamentary elections in December.

Corruption and organized crime are serious problems in Transnistria. The authorities are entrenched in the territory's economic activities, which rely in large part on smuggling schemes designed to evade Moldovan and Ukrainian import taxes. The EU assists Ukraine and Moldova in efforts to maintain customs controls along their mutual border. Russia also has a major stake in the Transnistrian economy and supports the PMR through loans, direct subsidies, and low-cost natural gas. Upon resigning as parliament Speaker in 2009, Yevgeny Shevchuk reportedly accused the government of corruption, nepotism, and economic mismanagement. Russia suspended social subsidies, such as funding for pensions, for several months in 2010 and 2011 because of transparency concerns. In 2011, Russian prosecutors sought to question Smirnov's son, Oleg Smirnov, about his alleged embezzlement of over $5 million in Russian aid.

The media environment is restrictive. Nearly all media are state owned or controlled and refrain from criticizing the authorities. The few independent print outlets have small circulations. Critical reporting draws harassment by the government, which also uses tactics such as bureaucratic obstruction and the withholding of information to inhibit independent media. Independent journalist Ernest Vardanean, who had worked for outlets including a Moldovan newspaper and Radio Free Europe/Radio Liberty, was arrested in April 2010. In an apparently coerced video recording televised in May, he confessed to spying for Moldovan authorities. He was sentenced in December to 15 years in prison, but was pardoned under international pressure in May 2011 in exchange for an admission of guilt. Sheriff Enterprises, which dominates the private broadcasting and cable television sectors, is the territory's only internet service provider. The government is not known to restrict internet access.

Religious freedom is limited. Orthodox Christianity is the dominant faith, and authorities have denied registration to several smaller religious groups, at times in defiance of court decisions. Other court rulings in favor of minority faiths have been overturned in recent years. Unregistered groups, including Jehovah's Witnesses and Pentecostals, have difficulty renting space for prayer meetings and face harassment by police and Orthodox opponents. There are no legal exemptions from military service for conscientious objectors, leading to criminal punishment of Jehovah's Witnesses and others.

Although a small minority of students study Moldovan using the Latin script, this practice is restricted; the Moldovan language and Latin alphabet are associated with support for unity with Moldova, while Russian and the Cyrillic alphabet are associated with separatist goals. Parents who send their children to schools using Latin script, and the schools themselves, have faced routine harassment from the security services.

The authorities severely restrict freedom of assembly and rarely issue required permits for public protests. Freedom of association is similarly circumscribed. All nongovernmental activities must be coordinated with local authorities, and groups that do not comply face harassment, including visits from security officials. The region's trade unions are holdovers from the Soviet era, and the United Council of Labor Collectives works closely with the government.

The judiciary is subservient to the executive and generally implements the will of the authorities. Defendants do not receive fair trials, and the legal framework falls short of international standards. Politically motivated arrests and detentions are common. Both Vardanean and tax official Ilie Cazac, another espionage suspect arrested in March 2010, were reportedly denied access to lawyers of their choice, and access to their trials was restricted. Cazac purportedly confessed in June 2010, but both his and Vardanean's confessions were widely seen as coerced. Cazac was sentenced to 14 years in prison in February 2011, and reportedly refused to admit guilt to win a pardon. He was pardoned nonetheless in late October. Human rights groups have received accounts of torture in custody, and prison conditions are considered harsh and unsanitary. Suspicious deaths of military conscripts occur periodically amid reports of routine mistreatment.

Authorities discriminate against ethnic Moldovans, who make up over 30 percent of the population. Ethnic Russians and ethnic Ukrainians together account for some 60 percent. A significant minority of the region's residents hold Russian passports. Travelers are frequently detained and questioned by the PMR authorities.

Women are underrepresented in most positions of authority, and domestic violence against women is a problem. Transnistria is a significant source and transit point for trafficking in women for the purpose of prostitution. Homosexuality is illegal in Transnistria.

West Bank

Political Rights: 6
Civil Liberties: 5
Status: Not Free

Population: 2,623,000

Note: Whereas past editions of Freedom in the World featured one report for Israeli-occupied portions of the West Bank and Gaza Strip and another for Palestinian-administered portions, the latest two editions divide the territories based on geography, with one report for the West Bank and another for the Gaza Strip. As in previous years, Israel is examined in a separate report.

Ten-Year Ratings Timeline For Year Under Review (Political Rights, Civil Liberties, Status)

2002	2003	2004	2005	2006	2007	2008	2009	20010	2011
--	--	--	--	--	--	--	--	6,5NF	6,5NF

Overview: **In 2011, state-building efforts by the Palestinian Authority (PA) further strengthened the rule of law in Palestinian-ruled areas of the West Bank. At the same time, the PA government continued to operate without an electoral mandate or a functioning legislature. By year's end, a May national-unity agreement between the PA and Gaza-based Hamas failed to produce a new caretaker government or a date for elections. Israeli construction of West Bank settlements continued in 2011, mostly in areas near Jerusalem, and the year featured an uptick in attacks by Jewish settlers. While large demonstrations occurred throughout the year, both Israeli and Palestinian security forces used legal and coercive means to prevent or disperse them.**

The West Bank was demarcated as part of the 1949 armistice agreement between Israel and Jordan following the 1948 Arab-Israeli war. It consists of the land between the armistice line in the west and the Jordan River in the east. The territory was subsequently occupied and annexed by Jordan. During the 1967 Six-Day War, Israel conquered the West Bank along with the Gaza Strip and other territories, and later annexed East Jerusalem, leaving the rest of the West Bank and Gaza under a military administration.

After 1967, Israel began establishing Jewish settlements in the West Bank, a process that—along with the annexation of East Jerusalem—was regarded as illegal by most of the international community. Israel maintained that the settlements were legal since under international law the West Bank was a disputed territory. In what became known as the first intifada (uprising), in 1987 Palestinians living in the West Bank and Gaza staged massive demonstrations, acts of civil disobedience, and attacks against Israeli settlers and Israel Defense Forces (IDF) troops in the territories, as well as attacks within Israel proper. Israel and Yasser Arafat's Palestine Liberation Organization (PLO) reached an agreement in 1993 that provided for a PLO renunciation of terrorism and recognition of Israel, Israeli troop withdrawals, and phased Palestinian autonomy in the West Bank and Gaza.

In subsequent years, the new Palestinian Authority (PA) took control of 40 percent of West Bank territory, including 98 percent of the Palestinian population outside of East Jerusalem. As stalled negotiations on a final settlement and the creation of a Palestinian state headed toward collapse, a second intifada began in September 2000, and the IDF reentered most PA-administered areas.

After Arafat died in November 2004, the PA in January 2005 held its second-ever presidential election, which had been repeatedly postponed; the first voting for president and the Palestinian Legislative Council (PLC) had taken place in 1996. Mahmoud Abbas of Arafat's Fatah faction won the 2005 contest with 62 percent of the vote. In municipal voting in the West Bank, Fatah won most municipalities, but the Islamist faction Hamas posted impressive gains. Each group accused the other of fraud, and there was some election-related violence.

Hamas won the January 2006 elections for the PLC with 74 of 132 seats, while Fatah took 45. Fatah and Hamas then formed a unity government headed by Prime Minister Ismail Haniya of Hamas. Israel, the United States, and the European Union (EU) refused to recognize the new government, citing Hamas's involvement in terrorism and its refusal to recognize Israel or past Israel-PA agreements. The United States and the EU, then the largest donors to the PA, cut off assistance to the government.

Armed clashes between Hamas and Fatah supporters escalated in 2007, and in June, Hamas militants seized Fatah-controlled facilities in Gaza. Thousands of Gazans, particularly those loyal to Fatah, fled to the West Bank. Abbas subsequently dismissed the Hamas-led government, declared a state of emergency, and appointed an emergency cabinet led by former finance minister Salam Fayad. This resulted in a bifurcated PA, with Hamas governing Gaza and Abbas and Fayad governing the roughly 40 percent of the West Bank not directly administered by Israel. Fatah later cracked down on Hamas in the West Bank, arresting its officials and supporters, shutting down its civic organizations and media outlets, and allegedly torturing some detainees.

In the years after the split, the Fatah-controlled PA in the West Bank benefited from renewed U.S. and EU aid as well as tax revenues released by Israeli authorities.

So-called confidence-building measures between Israel and the PA in the West Bank included the release of hundreds of Palestinian prisoners held in Israel, the wider deployment of Palestinian security forces, and the removal of a number of Israeli checkpoints.

Nevertheless, the IDF reportedly still controlled about 60 percent of the West Bank, and construction continued on a security barrier that ran roughly along the West Bank side of the 1949 armistice line and often jutted farther into the territory to place densely populated Jewish settlements on the Israeli side, often expropriating private Palestinian land and greatly reducing freedom of movement nearby. The barrier, which by the end of 2011 was about 75 percent complete and had reduced attacks inside Israel by about 90 percent, was declared illegal by the International Court of Justice in 2004.

After a temporary freeze on settlement construction during most of 2010, in 2011 Israel expanded Jewish settlements in the territory. According to the Israeli nongovernmental organization (NGO) Peace Now, between October 2010 and July 2011, there were 2,598 new housing starts in the settlements. The government also approved plans for thousands more, particularly in and around East Jerusalem. While Israel dismantled a number of settler "outposts" on private Palestinian land during the year, Peace Now reported that scores remained, and that the Israeli authorities demolished unlicensed Palestinian buildings at a far greater rate than Jewish buildings in the IDF-controlled area of the West Bank.

In April 2011, a UN report argued that recent improvements in governance, rule of law, social services, and infrastructure in the West Bank would allow the PA to effectively govern an independent state. The following month, Hamas and Fatah agreed to form a national-unity government and end the schism in the PA, but no such government was formed during the year. In September, the PA applied to the UN Security Council for recognition of a Palestinian state—including East Jerusalem, the West Bank, and the Gaza Strip—with full UN membership. In November, Palestine won membership in UNESCO. To protest the agreement with Hamas and the PA's moves at the United Nations, Israel withheld or threatened to withhold hundreds of millions of dollars in tax revenues from the PA.

Political Rights and Civil Liberties: In 1988, Jordan rescinded citizenship for West Bank Palestinians, and Israel never granted them citizenship. Most Palestinian residents are citizens of the Palestinian Authority (PA), a quasi-sovereign entity created by the 1993 Oslo Accords. Jewish settlers in the West Bank are Israeli citizens.

The PA president is elected to four-year terms. The prime minister is nominated by the president but requires the support of the unicameral, 132-seat Palestinian Legislative Council (PLC), which also serves four-year terms. Voting in the West Bank during the 2005 presidential and 2006 PLC elections was deemed largely free and fair by international observers. However, after the bifurcation of the PA in 2007, elected officials on both sides were prevented from performing their duties. President Mahmoud Abbas appointed a new cabinet in the West Bank that lacked the PLC's approval. In 2008, PA security forces aligned with Abbas arrested hundreds of Hamas members and supporters. The rift, combined with Israel's detention of many Palestinian lawmakers, prevented the PLC from functioning, and its term expired in 2010.

Abbas's elected term as president expired in 2009, and the PLO indefinitely extended his term in December of that year. Moreover, Abbas issued a law permitting the Fatah-affiliated minister of local government to dissolve municipal councils, leading to the replacement of nearly all Hamas-affiliated municipal officials with Fatah loyalists. The May 2011 agreement between Hamas and Fatah envisioned a unity government that would organize presidential and parliamentary elections, but no date for such polls had been set by year's end.

After Israel annexed East Jerusalem in 1967, Arab residents were issued Israeli identity cards and given the option of obtaining Israeli citizenship. However, many have rejected this option because they do not recognize Israeli sovereignty in East Jerusalem. They can vote in municipal elections as well as PA elections, but are subject to restrictions imposed by the Israeli municipality of Jerusalem. In the 2006 PLC elections, Israel barred Hamas from campaigning in the city. By law, Israel strips Arabs of their Jerusalem residency if they remain outside the city for more than three months. East Jerusalem's Arab population does not receive a share of municipal services proportionate to its size.

Corruption remains a major problem in the West Bank, though Abbas has overseen some improvements. Prime Minister Salam Fayad has been credited with significantly reducing corruption at the higher levels of the PA. In January 2011, Abbas initiated a corruption investigation against a Fatah rival, Mohammed Dahlan, after removing him from the Fatah Central Committee amid rumors of a coup plot.

The media are not free in the West Bank. Under a 1995 PA press law, journalists may be fined and jailed, and newspapers closed, for publishing "secret information" on PA security forces or news that might harm national unity or incite violence. Several small media outlets are routinely pressured to provide favorable coverage of the PA and Fatah. Journalists who criticize the PA or Fatah face arbitrary arrests, threats, and physical abuse. Since 2007, both the PA and Israeli forces have shut down most Hamas-affiliated radio and television stations in the West Bank. In January 2011, Abbas ordered the closure of a television station affiliated with Dahlan. According to a 2011 report on conditions for journalists by the Palestinian Center for Development and Media Freedoms (MADA), physical attacks, arrests, detentions, and confiscation of equipment by Palestinian security forces increased by over 45 percent between 2009 and 2010, a trend that continued in 2011. According to MADA, in 2011 there were 100 violation of press freedom by Israeli forces (97 in West Bank, 3 in Gaza) and 106 violations by Palestinian authorities (53 in West Bank, 53 in Gaza). International press freedom groups regularly criticize Israel for blocking journalists' access to conflict zones, harming and sometimes killing reporters during battles, and harassing Palestinian journalists. Israel insists that reporters risk getting caught in crossfire but are not targeted deliberately. Both Palestinian and Israeli security forces were accused of assaulting and arbitrarily detaining several journalists in 2011.

The PA generally respects freedom of religion, though no law specifically protects religious expression and there are criminal blasphemy laws against defaming Islam. The Basic Law declares Islam to be the official religion of Palestine and states that "respect and sanctity of all other heavenly religions (Judaism and Christianity) shall be maintained." Synagogues are occasionally attacked by Palestinian militants. Some Palestinian Christians have experienced intimidation and harassment by radical Islamist groups and PA officials.

Israel generally recognizes freedom of religion in the West Bank, though recent years have featured a spike in mosque vandalism and other attacks by radical Israeli settlers. Citing the potential for violent clashes, Israel occasionally restricts Muslim men under age 50 from praying at the Temple Mount/Haram al-Sharif compound in Jerusalem.

The PA has authority over all levels of Palestinian education. Israeli military closures, curfews, and the West Bank security barrier restrict access to academic institutions, particularly those located between Israel and the barrier. Schools have sometimes been damaged during military actions, and student travel between the West Bank and the Gaza Strip has been limited. Israel accuses the PA of teaching anti-Semitism and advocating the destruction of Israel in public schools. Israeli academic institutions in the West Bank are increasingly subject to international and domestic boycotts. Primary and secondary education in West Bank settlements is administered by Israel, though religious schools have significant discretion over curriculum. According to the Association for Civil Rights in Israel (ACRI), East Jerusalem's schools are badly underfunded compared with schools in West Jerusalem.

The PA requires permits for demonstrations, and those against PA policies are generally disallowed and forcibly dispersed. Hamas has been effectively banned from holding demonstrations in the West Bank. There were a number of large demonstrations in support of antigovernment protests in Egypt in February 2011, and in March thousands of Palestinians demonstrated for national unity between Fatah and Hamas. According to Human Rights Watch (HRW), Palestinian security officials "harassed, interrogated, arbitrarily detained and assaulted peaceful demonstrators" on a number of occasions during this period.

The IDF sometimes respects freedom of assembly, though permission is required and demonstrations are routinely broken up with force. Israel's Military Order 101 requires an IDF permit for all "political" demonstrations of more than 10 people. In 2011, Israeli forces continued to restrict and disperse frequent and sometimes violent demonstrations in opposition to the security barrier, especially those near the towns of Bil'in and Nil'in. The IDF declared many of these protest areas to be closed military zones every Friday, and regularly used rubber-coated bullets, stun grenades, and tear gas to break up demonstrations. The IDF has reported hundreds of injuries to its personnel.

A broad range of Palestinian NGOs and civic groups operate in the West Bank, and their activities are generally unrestricted. Since 2007, however, many Hamas-affiliated civic associations have been shut down for political reasons. Workers may establish and join unions without government authorization. Palestinian workers seeking to strike must submit to arbitration by the PA Labor Ministry. There are no laws in the PA-ruled areas to protect the rights of striking workers. Palestinian workers in Jerusalem are subject to Israeli labor law.

The PA judicial system is only somewhat independent in practice, and Palestinian judges lack proper training and experience. Laws in effect in the West Bank derive from Ottoman, British Mandate, Jordanian, Israeli, and PA legislation, as well as Israeli military orders. The High Judicial Council handles most legal proceedings. Israel's Supreme Court hears petitions from non-Israeli residents of the West Bank regarding home demolitions, land confiscations, road closures, and IDF tactics. Decisions in favor of Palestinian petitioners, while rare, have increased in recent years. Though most applications have been rejected, the Israeli Supreme Court has repeatedly ordered changes to the route of the West Bank security barrier after hearing petitions from NGOs and Palestinians. By the end of 2011, the Ministry of Defense had altered or pledged to alter the route in response to four of six such rulings. The IDF dismantled a section of the barrier near Bil'in in June, four years after the relevant ruling.

The PA also has a military court system, which lacks almost all due process rights, including the right to appeal sentences, and can impose the death penalty. These courts handle cases on a range of security offenses, collaborating with Israel, and drug trafficking. There are reportedly hundreds of administrative detainees in Palestinian jails. According to the Palestinian Human Rights Monitoring Group, alleged collaborators are routinely tortured. These practices are not prohibited under Palestinian law. According to an April 2011 HRW report, Palestinian rights groups reported more than 200 torture complaints against PA security agencies in 2010, up from 164 in 2009, but only one case has led to the prosecution of security officers, all five of whom were acquitted. The Independent Commission for Human Rights in Palestine reported 112 torture complaints in the West Bank in 2011.

Palestinians accused of security offenses by Israel are tried in Israeli military courts, which grant some due process protections but limit rights to counsel, bail, and appeal. Administrative detention without charge or trial is widely used. According to the human rights group B'Tselem, by the end of 2011 there were 4,772 Palestinians in Israeli jails: 3,753 serving sentences, 131 detainees, 609 being detained until the conclusion of legal proceedings, 278 administrative detainees, and one detained under the Illegal Combatants Law. A temporary order in effect since 2006 permits the detention of suspects accused of security offenses for 96 hours without judicial oversight, compared with 24 hours for other detainees. Most convictions in Israeli military courts are based on confessions, sometimes obtained through coercion. Israel outlawed the use of torture to extract security information in 2000, but milder forms of coercion are permissible when the prisoner is believed to have vital information about impending terrorist attacks. Human rights groups criticize Israel for continuing to engage in what they consider torture. Interrogation methods include binding detainees to a chair in painful positions, slapping, kicking, and threatening violence against detainees and their relatives.

According to the Israeli Prison Service, as of October 2011, there were 164 Palestinian minors (ages 12–17) in Israeli jails, including 35 aged 12–15. Most were serving two-month sentences—handed down by a Special Court for Minors created in 2009—for throwing stones or other projectiles at Israeli troops in the West Bank; acquittals on such charges are very rare. East Jerusalem Palestinian minors are tried in Israeli civil juvenile courts. In July 2011, a B'Tselem report criticized the IDF for unfairly arresting and judging minors; the IDF denied the allegations.

While violence in the West Bank has dropped precipitously since the 2007 PA schism, there were a number of clashes in 2011. The IDF staged numerous raids, mostly aimed at Hamas militants and officials. Israeli soldiers and civilians were frequently and at times fatally attacked by Palestinian militants, while settler militants targeted people and property in several Palestinian villages, mosques, and farms. Clashes between Israeli soldiers and radical settlers grew more common in 2011. In December, settler militants rioted through an IDF base in the West Bank. According to B'Tselem, violent acts by Jewish settlers against Palestinian civilians increased significantly in 2011.

Israeli soldiers accused of harassing or assaulting Palestinian civilians are subject to Israeli military law. A September 2010 report by B'Tselem accused the IDF of failing to adequately investigate and prosecute cases of civilian deaths in the West Bank, citing only 23 criminal investigations out of the 148 recommended by the group between 2006 and 2009. Several soldiers were prosecuted in 2010 and 2011 for a range of offenses, although most received relatively light sentences.

The easing of checkpoints and roadblocks and the wider deployment of PA security forces continued to improved economic conditions in the West Bank, particularly in Nablus, Ramallah, and Jenin. However, the IDF maintained a monthly average of 92 permanently and partially staffed checkpoints, 519 staffed obstacles, and an additional 414 "flying" or random checkpoints in the West Bank, according to the UN Office for the Coordination of Humanitarian Affairs (OCHA). These impose extensive delays on local travel, stunt internal and external trade, and restrict Palestinian access to jobs, hospitals, and schools. Israel's security barrier has also cut off many Palestinians from their farms and other parts of the West Bank. While most roads are open to both Israelis and Palestinians, about 10 are open only to drivers with Israeli documents, ostensibly for security reasons.

All West Bank residents must have identification cards to obtain entry permits to Israel, including East Jerusalem. In 2010, the IDF broadened the definition of "infiltrator" in the West Bank to include Palestinians who are not in the PA population registry and do not have a permit to live in the territory, exposing them to deportation within 72 hours, imprisonment, and other penalties. Human rights groups alleged that the change could subject thousands of Palestinians with Gaza residency permits to sudden deportation; Israel claimed that the change affected only a small number of people and was intended to speed up military hearings for potential deportees. By the end of 2010, five people had been deported under the new rule.

According to Peace Now and B'Tselem, Israel denies construction permits and demolishes unauthorized housing at a far higher rate for Palestinian residents than for Israeli settlers in the Israeli-controlled portion of the West Bank, known as Area C. OCHA reported that in the first six months of 2011 Israeli authorities demolished 342 Palestinian-owned structures in Area C, including 125 residential structures. Israel disputed these figures, claiming that authorities have only demolished illegal structures, and that Jewish and Palestinian residents in Area C are subject to the same restrictions.

In 2010 B'Tselem found that while built-up settlements occupy 1 percent of the West Bank's land, 21 percent of that is private, Palestinian land. A property dispute in the East Jerusalem neighborhood of Sheikh Jarrah—where a number of Palestinian families have been evicted in favor of Jewish residents—continued to draw protests by both Palestinians and Israelis. In January 2011, Israeli authorities started the controversial demolition of the Shepherds Hotel in East Jerusalem to make way for 20 homes for Jewish families; the ownership of the property is in dispute. According to the United Nations, 35 percent of the land in East Jerusalem has been designated as state land by Israel. A 2010 UNRWA report stated that Palestinians can legally build in an area comprising about 13 percent of East Jerusalem, and that over 28 percent of Arab homes are built illegally.

While Palestinian women are underrepresented in most professions and encounter discrimination in employment, they have full access to universities and to many professions. Palestinian laws and societal norms, derived in part from Sharia (Islamic law), put women at a disadvantage in matters of marriage, divorce, and inheritance. For Christians, such personal status issues are governed by ecclesiastical courts. Rape, domestic abuse, and "honor killings," in which women are murdered by relatives for perceived sexual or moral transgressions, are not uncommon. These murders often go unpunished.

Western Sahara

Political Rights: 7
Civil Liberties: 7*
Status: Not Free

Population: 507,000

Ratings Change: Western Sahara's civil liberties rating declined from 6 to 7 due to the inability of civil society groups to form and operate, as well as serious restrictions on property rights and business activity.

Ten-Year Ratings Timeline For Year Under Review (Political Rights, Civil Liberties, Status)

2002	2003	2004	2005	2006	2007	2008	2009	2010	2011
7,6NF	7,6NF	7,6NF	7,6NF	7,6NF	7,6NF	7,6NF	7,6NF	7,6NF	7,7NF

Overview: **Morocco and the proindependence Polisario Front failed to make progress in mediated talks on Western Sahara's status in 2011. Informal negotiations failed once again, with no future round scheduled. Meanwhile, Sahrawis continued to be denied basic political, civil, and economic rights.**

Western Sahara was ruled by Spain for nearly a century until Spanish troops withdrew in 1976, following a bloody guerrilla conflict with the proindependence Popular Front for the Liberation of Saguia el-Hamra and Rio de Oro (Polisario Front). Mauritania and Morocco both claimed the resource-rich region, agreeing to a partition in which Morocco received the northern two-thirds. However, the Polisario Front proclaimed an independent Sahrawi Arab Democratic Republic (SADR) and continued its guerrilla campaign. Mauritania renounced its claim in 1979, and Morocco filled the vacuum by annexing the entire territory.

Moroccan and Polisario forces engaged in a low-intensity armed conflict until the United Nations brokered a ceasefire in 1991. The agreement called for residents of Western Sahara to vote in a referendum on independence the following year, to be supervised by the newly established UN Mission for the Referendum in Western Sahara (MINURSO). However, the vote never took place, with the two sides failing to agree on voter eligibility.

Morocco tried to bolster its annexation by offering financial incentives for Moroccans to move to Western Sahara and for Sahrawis to move to Morocco. Morocco also used more coercive measures, engaging in forced resettlements of Sahrawis and long-term detention and "disappearances" of proindependence activists. Neighboring Algeria will not accept Moroccan control of the territory and hosts refugee camps in Tindouf, Algeria, which are home to an estimated 90,000 Sahrawis as well as the SADR government in exile.

In 2004, the Polisario Front accepted a UN Security Council plan that called for up to five years of autonomy followed by a referendum on the territory's status. However, Morocco rejected the plan, fearing it could lead to independence, and in 2007 offered its own autonomy plan.

Because the Polisario Front remains committed to an eventual referendum with independence as an option, while Morocco continues to push for autonomy, the two sides have failed to make meaningful progress in a series of negotiations that started in 2007 and continued in 2011. A November 2010 meeting was overshadowed by a confrontation in the Gadaym Izik protest camp outside Western Sahara's main city, Laayoune, in which Moroccan forces violently dispersed residents who had mobilized within the camp. Around a dozen people were killed and scores were injured in the fighting, although the precise numbers are difficult to verify. The talks were reconvened on July 19–21, 2011, and brokered by the UN special envoy, Christopher Ross. These talks, which also included Algeria and Mauritania, failed as well.

Political Rights and Civil Liberties:

As the occupying force in Western Sahara, Morocco controls local elections and works to ensure that independence-minded leaders are excluded from both the local political process and the Moroccan Parliament.

Reports of corruption are widespread. Although the territory possesses extensive natural resources, including phosphate, iron ore deposits, hydrocarbon reserves, and fisheries, the local population remains largely impoverished.

The Moroccan constitution provides for freedom of the press, but this is severely limited in Western Sahara, and there is little independent Sahrawi media activity. Moroccan law bars the media and individuals from challenging Morocco's sovereignty over Western Sahara, leading to self-censorship. The authorities expel or detain Sahrawi, Moroccan, and foreign reporters who attempt to conduct first-hand reporting on the issue. The internet and independent satellite broadcasts are largely unavailable due to economic constraints.

Nearly all Sahrawis are Sunni Muslims, as are most Moroccans, and Moroccan authorities generally do not interfere with their freedom of worship. There are no major universities or institutions of higher learning in Western Sahara.

Sahrawis are not permitted to form independent political or nongovernmental organizations, and their freedom of assembly is severely restricted. As in previous years, activists supporting independence and their suspected foreign sympathizers were subject to harassment. In April 2010, activists faced harassment at the Laayoune airport upon their return from the Polisario-controlled refugee camps in Tindouf. Sahrawis are technically subject to Moroccan labor laws, but there is little organized labor activity in the territory.

International human rights groups have criticized Morocco's record in Western Sahara for decades. In the aftermath of the November 2010 clashes outside Laayoune, Amnesty International renewed its call for independent monitoring of human rights violations. Three Sahrawi activists who had been arrested in Morocco in October 2009—Brahim Dahane, Ali Salem Tamek, and Ahmed Naciri—were released from prisons in Salé and Casablanca in April 2011.

In October 2011, Moroccan police prohibited two Spanish members of the European Parliament, Willy Meyer and Jose Pérez Ventura, from disembarking from an airplane at the Laayoune airport; they were seeking to observe the human rights situation in Western Sahara. Spain lodged a formal protest about the treatment of the men, who reportedly sustained injuries in an altercation on the airplane stairway.

The Polisario Front has also been accused of disregarding human rights. In September 2010, the Polisario Front arrested a Sahrawi dissenter, Mostapha Selma Sidi Mouloud, as he returned to the Tindouf camps after publicly endorsing Morocco's autonomy plan in Western Sahara. A former police chief, Sidi Mouloud, was held by the Polisario for more than two months before being released in December 2010 to the UN High Commissioner for Refugees; he now lives in exile in Mauritania and has kept a low profile.

Morocco and the Polisario Front both restrict free movement in potential conflict areas. Morocco has been accused of using force and financial incentives to alter the composition of Western Sahara's population.

The SADR government routinely signs contracts with firms for the exploration of oil and gas, although these cannot be implemented given the territory's status, and no credible free market exists within the territory.

Sahrawi women face much of the same cultural and legal discrimination as Moroccan women. The significant reform in 2004 of the Moroccan Mudawwana—a law governing issues including marriage, divorce, inheritance, and child custody—does not appear to have been applied to Western Sahara. Conditions are generally worse for women living in rural areas, where poverty and illiteracy rates are higher.

Freedom in the World 2012 Methodology

INTRODUCTION

The *Freedom in the World* survey provides an annual evaluation of the state of global freedom as experienced by individuals. The survey measures freedom—the opportunity to act spontaneously in a variety of fields outside the control of the government and other centers of potential domination—according to two broad categories: political rights and civil liberties. Political rights enable people to participate freely in the political process, including the right to vote freely for distinct alternatives in legitimate elections, compete for public office, join political parties and organizations, and elect representatives who have a decisive impact on public policies and are accountable to the electorate. Civil liberties allow for the freedoms of expression and belief, associational and organizational rights, rule of law, and personal autonomy without interference from the state.

The survey does not rate governments or government performance per se, but rather the real-world rights and freedoms enjoyed by individuals. Thus, while Freedom House considers the presence of legal rights, it places a greater emphasis on whether these rights are implemented in practice. Furthermore, freedoms can be affected by government officials, as well as by nonstate actors, including insurgents and other armed groups.

Freedom House does not maintain a culture-bound view of freedom. The methodology of the survey is grounded in basic standards of political rights and civil liberties, derived in large measure from relevant portions of the Universal Declaration of Human Rights. These standards apply to all countries and territories, irrespective of geographical location, ethnic or religious composition, or level of economic development. The survey operates from the assumption that freedom for all peoples is best achieved in liberal democratic societies.

The survey includes both analytical reports and numerical ratings for 195 countries and 14 select territories.[1] Each country and territory report includes an overview section, which provides historical background and a brief description of the year's major developments, as well as a section summarizing the current state of political rights and civil liberties. In addition, each country and territory is assigned a numeri-

1. These territories are selected based on their political significance and size. Freedom House divides territories into two categories: related territories and disputed territories. Related territories consist mostly of colonies, protectorates, and island dependencies of sovereign states that are in some relation of dependency to that state, and whose relationship is not currently in serious legal or political dispute. Disputed territories are areas within internationally recognized sovereign states whose status is in serious political or violent dispute, and whose conditions differ substantially from those of the relevant sovereign states. They are often outside of central government control and characterized by intense, longtime, and widespread insurgency or independence movements that enjoy popular support. Generally, the dispute faced by a territory is between independence for the territory or domination by an established state.

cal rating—on a scale of 1 to 7—for political rights and an analogous rating for civil liberties; a rating of 1 indicates the highest degree of freedom and 7 the lowest level of freedom. These ratings, which are calculated based on the methodological process described below, determine whether a country is classified as Free, Partly Free, or Not Free by the survey.

The survey findings are reached after a multilayered process of analysis and evaluation by a team of regional experts and scholars. Although there is an element of subjectivity inherent in the survey findings, the ratings process emphasizes intellectual rigor and balanced and unbiased judgments.

HISTORY OF THE SURVEY

Freedom House's first year-end reviews of freedom began in the 1950s as the *Balance Sheet of Freedom*. This modest report provided assessments of political trends and their implications for individual freedom. In 1972, Freedom House launched a new, more comprehensive annual study called *The Comparative Study of Freedom*. Raymond Gastil, a Harvard-trained specialist in regional studies from the University of Washington in Seattle, developed the survey's methodology, which assigned political rights and civil liberties ratings to 151 countries and 45 territories and—based on these ratings—categorized them as Free, Partly Free, or Not Free. The findings appeared each year in Freedom House's *Freedom at Issue* bimonthly journal (later titled *Freedom Review*). The survey first appeared in book form in 1978 under the title *Freedom in the World* and included short, explanatory narratives for each country and territory rated in the study, as well as a series of essays by leading scholars on related issues. *Freedom in the World* continued to be produced by Gastil until 1989, when a larger team of in-house survey analysts was established. In the mid-1990s, the expansion of *Freedom in the World*'s country and territory narratives demanded the hiring of outside analysts—a group of regional experts from the academic, media, and human rights communities. The survey has continued to grow in size and scope; the 2012 edition is the most exhaustive in its history.

RESEARCH AND RATINGS REVIEW PROCESS

This year's survey covers developments from January 1, 2011, through December 31, 2011, in 195 countries and 14 territories. The research and ratings process involved 59 analysts and 20 senior-level academic advisers—the largest number to date. The analysts used a broad range of sources of information—including foreign and domestic news reports, academic analyses, nongovernmental organizations, think tanks, individual professional contacts, and visits to the region—in preparing the country and territory reports and ratings.

The country and territory ratings were proposed by the analyst responsible for each related report. The ratings were reviewed individually and on a comparative basis in a series of six regional meetings—Asia-Pacific, Central and Eastern Europe and the Former Soviet Union, Latin America and the Caribbean, Middle East and North Africa, sub-Saharan Africa, and Western Europe—involving the analysts, academic advisers with expertise in each region, and Freedom House staff. The ratings were compared to the previous year's findings, and any major proposed numerical shifts or category changes were subjected to more intensive scrutiny. These reviews were followed by cross-regional assessments in which efforts were made to ensure comparability and consistency in the findings. Many of the key country reports were also reviewed by the academic advisors.

CHANGES TO THE 2012 EDITION OF FREEDOM IN THE WORLD

The survey's methodology is reviewed periodically by an advisory committee of political scientists with expertise in methodological issues. Over the years, the committee has made a number of modest methodological changes to adapt to evolving ideas about political rights and civil liberties. At the same time, the time series data are not revised retroactively, and any changes to the methodology are introduced incrementally in order to ensure the comparability of the ratings from year to year.

This year, South Sudan was added to the list of countries surveyed in *Freedom in the World* following its independence from Sudan in July 2011.

RATINGS PROCESS

(*NOTE: see the complete checklist questions and keys to political rights and civil liberties ratings and status at the end of the methodology essay.*)

Scores–The ratings process is based on a checklist of 10 political rights questions and 15 civil liberties questions. The political rights questions are grouped into three subcategories: Electoral Process (3 questions), Political Pluralism and Participation (4), and Functioning of Government (3). The civil liberties questions are grouped into four subcategories: Freedom of Expression and Belief (4 questions), Associational and Organizational Rights (3), Rule of Law (4), and Personal Autonomy and Individual Rights (4). Scores are awarded to each of these questions on a scale of 0 to 4, where a score of 0 represents the smallest degree and 4 the greatest degree of rights or liberties present. The political rights section also contains two additional discretionary questions: question A (For traditional monarchies that have no parties or electoral process, does the system provide for genuine, meaningful consultation with the people, encourage public discussion of policy choices, and allow the right to petition the ruler?) and question B (Is the government or occupying power deliberately changing the ethnic composition of a country or territory so as to destroy a culture or tip the political balance in favor of another group?). For additional discretionary question A, a score of 1 to 4 may be added, as applicable, while for discretionary question B, a score of 1 to 4 may be subtracted (the worse the situation, the more that may be subtracted). The highest score that can be awarded to the political rights checklist is 40 (or a total score of 4 for each of the 10 questions). The highest score that can be awarded to the civil liberties checklist is 60 (or a total score of 4 for each of the 15 questions).

The scores from the previous survey edition are used as a benchmark for the current year under review. In general, a score is changed only if there has been a real world development during the year that warrants a change (e.g., a crackdown on the media, the country's first free and fair elections) and is reflected accordingly in the narrative.

In answering both the political rights and civil liberties questions, Freedom House does not equate constitutional or other legal guarantees of rights with the on-the-ground fulfillment of these rights. While both laws and actual practices are factored into the ratings decisions, greater emphasis is placed on the latter.

For states and territories with small populations, the absence of pluralism in the political system or civil society is not necessarily viewed as a negative situation unless the government or other centers of domination are deliberately blocking its operation. For example, a small country without diverse political parties or media outlets or significant trade unions is not penalized if these limitations are determined to be a function of size and not overt restrictions.

Political Rights and Civil Liberties Ratings–The total score awarded to the political rights and civil liberties checklist determines the political rights and civil liberties rating. Each rating of 1 through 7, with 1 representing the highest and 7 the lowest level of freedom, corresponds to a range of total scores (see tables 1 and 2).

Status of Free, Partly Free, Not Free–Each pair of political rights and civil liberties ratings is averaged to determine an overall status of "Free," "Partly Free," or "Not Free." Those whose ratings average 1.0 to 2.5 are considered Free, 3.0 to 5.0 Partly Free, and 5.5 to 7.0 Not Free (see table 3). The designations of Free, Partly Free, and Not Free each cover a broad third of the available scores. Therefore, countries and territories within any one category, especially those at either end of the category, can have quite different human rights situations. In order to see the distinctions within each category, a country or territory's political rights and civil liberties ratings should be examined. For example, countries at the lowest end of the Free category (2 in political rights and 3 in civil liberties, or 3 in political rights and 2 in civil liberties) differ from those at the upper end of the Free group (1 for both political rights and civil liberties). Also, a designation of Free does not mean that a country enjoys perfect freedom or lacks serious problems, only that it enjoys comparably more freedom than Partly Free or Not Free (or some other Free) countries.

Indications of Ratings and/or Status Changes–Each country or territory's political rights rating, civil liberties rating, and status is included in a statistics section that precedes each country or territory report. A change in a political rights or civil liberties rating since the previous survey edition is indicated with a symbol next to the rating that has changed. A brief ratings change explanation is included in the statistics section.

Trend Arrows–Positive or negative developments in a country or territory may also be reflected in the use of upward or downward trend arrows. A trend arrow is based on a particular development (such as an improvement in a country's state of religious freedom), which must be linked to a score change in the corresponding checklist question (in this case, an increase in the score for checklist question D2, which covers religious freedom). However, not all score increases or decreases warrant trend arrows. Whether a positive or negative development is significant enough to warrant a trend arrow is determined through consultations among the report writer, the regional academic advisers, and Freedom House staff. Also, trend arrows are assigned only in cases where score increases or decreases are not sufficient to warrant a ratings change; thus, a country cannot receive both a ratings change and a trend arrow during the same year. A trend arrow is indicated with an arrow next to the name of the country or territory that appears before the statistics section at the top of each country or territory report. A brief trend arrow explanation is included in the statistics section.

GENERAL CHARACTERISTICS OF EACH POLITICAL RIGHTS AND CIVIL LIBERTIES RATING

POLITICAL RIGHTS

Rating of 1–Countries and territories with a rating of 1 enjoy a wide range of political rights, including free and fair elections. Candidates who are elected actually rule, political parties are competitive, the opposition plays an important role and enjoys real power, and minority groups have reasonable self-government or can participate in the government through informal consensus.

Rating of 2–Countries and territories with a rating of 2 have slightly weaker political rights than those with a rating of 1 because of such factors as some political corruption, limits on the functioning of political parties and opposition groups, and foreign or military influence on politics.

Ratings of 3, 4, 5–Countries and territories with a rating of 3, 4, or 5 include those that moderately protect almost all political rights to those that more strongly protect some political rights while less strongly protecting others. The same factors that undermine freedom in countries with a rating of 2 may also weaken political rights in those with a rating of 3, 4, or 5, but to an increasingly greater extent at each successive rating.

Rating of 6–Countries and territories with a rating of 6 have very restricted political rights. They are ruled by one-party or military dictatorships, religious hierarchies, or autocrats. They may allow a few political rights, such as some representation or autonomy for minority groups, and a few are traditional monarchies that tolerate political discussion and accept public petitions.

Rating of 7–Countries and territories with a rating of 7 have few or no political rights because of severe government oppression, sometimes in combination with civil war. They may also lack an authoritative and functioning central government and suffer from extreme violence or warlord rule that dominates political power.

CIVIL LIBERTIES

Rating of 1–Countries and territories with a rating of 1 enjoy a wide range of civil liberties, including freedom of expression, assembly, association, education, and religion. They have an established and generally fair system of the rule of law (including an independent judiciary), allow free economic activity, and tend to strive for equality of opportunity for everyone, including women and minority groups.

Rating of 2–Countries and territories with a rating of 2 have slightly weaker civil liberties than those with a rating of 1 because of such factors as some limits on media independence, restrictions on trade union activities, and discrimination against minority groups and women.

Ratings of 3, 4, 5–Countries and territories with a rating of 3, 4, or 5 include those that moderately protect almost all civil liberties to those that more strongly protect some civil liberties while less strongly protecting others. The same factors that undermine freedom in countries with a rating of 2 may also weaken civil liberties in those with a rating of 3, 4, or 5, but to an increasingly greater extent at each successive rating.

Rating of 6–Countries and territories with a rating of 6 have very restricted civil liberties. They strongly limit the rights of expression and association and frequently hold political prisoners. They may allow a few civil liberties, such as some religious and social freedoms, some highly restricted private business activity, and some open and free private discussion.

Rating of 7–Countries and territories with a rating of 7 have few or no civil liberties. They allow virtually no freedom of expression or association, do not protect the rights of detainees and prisoners, and often control or dominate most economic activity.

Countries and territories generally have ratings in political rights and civil liberties that are within two ratings numbers of each other. For example, without a well-developed civil society, it is difficult, if not impossible, to have an atmosphere supportive of political rights. Consequently, there is no country in the survey with a rating of 6 or 7 for civil liberties and, at the same time, a rating of 1 or 2 for political rights.

ELECTORAL DEMOCRACY DESIGNATION

In addition to providing numerical ratings, the survey assigns the designation "electoral democracy" to countries that have met certain minimum standards. In determining whether a country is an electoral democracy, Freedom House examines several key factors concerning the last major national election or elections.

To qualify as an electoral democracy, a state must have satisfied the following criteria:

1. A competitive, multiparty political system;
2. Universal adult suffrage for all citizens (with exceptions for restrictions that states may legitimately place on citizens as sanctions for criminal offenses);
3. Regularly contested elections conducted in conditions of ballot secrecy, reasonable ballot security, and in the absence of massive voter fraud, and that yield results that are representative of the public will;
4. Significant public access of major political parties to the electorate through the media and through generally open political campaigning.

The numerical benchmark for a country to be listed as an electoral democracy is a subtotal score of 7 or better (out of a possible total score of 12) for the political rights checklist subcategory A (the three questions on Electoral Process) *and* an overall political rights score of 20 or better (out of a possible total score of 40). In the case of presidential/parliamentary systems, both elections must have been free and fair on the basis of the above criteria; in parliamentary systems, the last nationwide elections for the national legislature must have been free and fair. The presence of certain irregularities during the electoral process does not automatically disqualify a country from being designated an electoral democracy. A country cannot be an electoral democracy if significant authority for national decisions resides in the hands of an unelected power, whether a monarch or a foreign international authority. A country is removed from the ranks of electoral democracies if its last national election failed to meet the criteria listed above, or if changes in law significantly eroded the public's possibility for electoral choice.

Freedom House's term "electoral democracy" differs from "liberal democracy" in that the latter also implies the presence of a substantial array of civil liberties. In the survey, all Free countries qualify as both electoral and liberal democracies. By contrast, some Partly Free countries qualify as electoral, but not liberal, democracies.

FREEDOM IN THE WORLD 2012
CHECKLIST QUESTIONS AND GUIDELINES

Each numbered checklist question is assigned a score of 0-4 (except for discretionary question A, for which a score of 1-4 may be added, and discretionary question B, for which a score of 1-4 may be subtracted), according to the survey methodology. The bulleted sub-questions are intended to provide guidance to the writers regarding what issues are meant to be considered in scoring each checklist question; the authors do not necessarily have to consider every sub-question when scoring their countries.

POLITICAL RIGHTS CHECKLIST
A. ELECTORAL PROCESS

1. Is the head of government or other chief national authority elected through free and fair elections?

- Did established and reputable national and/or international election monitoring organizations judge the most recent elections for head of government to be free and fair? (Note: Heads of government chosen through various electoral frameworks, including direct elections for president, indirect elections for prime minister by parliament, and the electoral college system for electing presidents, are covered under this and the following sub-questions. In cases of indirect elections for the head of government, the elections for the legislature that chose the head of government, as well as the selection process of the head of government himself, should be taken into consideration.)
- Have there been undue, politically motivated delays in holding the most recent election for head of government?
- Is the registration of voters and candidates conducted in an accurate, timely, transparent, and nondiscriminatory manner?
- Can candidates make speeches, hold public meetings, and enjoy media access throughout the campaign free of intimidation?

• Does voting take place by secret ballot or by equivalent free voting procedure?

• Are voters able to vote for the candidate or party of their choice without undue pressure or intimidation?

• Is the vote count transparent, and is it reported honestly with the official results made public? Can election monitors from independent groups and representing parties/candidates watch the counting of votes to ensure their honesty?

• Is each person's vote given equivalent weight to those of other voters in order to ensure equal representation?

• Has a democratically elected head of government who was chosen in the most recent election subsequently been overthrown in a violent coup? (Note: Although a peaceful, "velvet coup" may ultimately lead to a positive outcome—particularly if it replaces a head of government who was not freely and fairly elected—the new leader has not been freely and fairly elected and cannot be treated as such.)

• In cases where elections for regional, provincial, or state governors and/or other subnational officials differ significantly in conduct from national elections, does the conduct of the subnational elections reflect an opening toward improved political rights in the country, or, alternatively, a worsening of political rights?

2. Are the national legislative representatives elected through free and fair elections?

• Did established and reputable domestic and/or international election monitoring organizations judge the most recent national legislative elections to be free and fair?

• Have there been undue, politically motivated delays in holding the most recent national legislative election?

• Is the registration of voters and candidates conducted in an accurate, timely, transparent, and nondiscriminatory manner?

• Can candidates make speeches, hold public meetings, and enjoy media access throughout the campaign free of intimidation?

• Does voting take place by secret ballot or by equivalent free voting procedure?

• Are voters able to vote for the candidate or party of their choice without undue pressure or intimidation?

• Is the vote count transparent, and is it reported honestly with the official results made public? Can election monitors from independent groups and representing parties/candidates watch the counting of votes to ensure their honesty?

• Is each person's vote given equivalent weight to those of other voters in order to ensure equal representation?

• Have the representatives of a democratically elected national legislature who were chosen in the most recent election subsequently been overthrown in a violent coup? (Note: Although a peaceful, "velvet coup" may ultimately lead to a positive outcome—particularly if it replaces a national legislature whose representatives were not freely and fairly elected—members of the new legislature have not been freely and fairly elected and cannot be treated as such.)

• In cases where elections for subnational councils/parliaments differ significantly in conduct from national elections, does the conduct of the subnational elections reflect an opening toward improved political rights in the country, or, alternatively, a worsening of political rights?

3. Are the electoral laws and framework fair?

• Is there a clear, detailed, and fair legislative framework for conducting elections? (Note: Changes to electoral laws should not be made immediately preceding an election if the ability of voters, candidates, or parties to fulfill their roles in the election is infringed.)

• Are election commissions or other election authorities independent and free from government or other pressure and interference?

• Is the composition of election commissions fair and balanced?

• Do election commissions or other election authorities conduct their work in an effective and competent manner?

• Do adult citizens enjoy universal and equal suffrage? (Note: Suffrage can be suspended or withdrawn for reasons of legal incapacity, such as mental incapacity or conviction of a serious criminal offense.)

• Is the drawing of election districts conducted in a fair and nonpartisan manner, as opposed to gerrymandering for personal or partisan advantage?

• Has the selection of a system for choosing legislative representatives (such as proportional versus majoritarian) been manipulated to advance certain political interests or to influence the electoral results?

B. POLITICAL PLURALISM AND PARTICIPATION

1. Do the people have the right to organize in different political parties or other competitive political groupings of their choice, and is the system open to the rise and fall of these competing parties or groupings?

• Do political parties encounter undue legal or practical obstacles in their efforts to be formed and to operate, including onerous registration requirements, excessively large membership requirements, etc.?

• Do parties face discriminatory or onerous restrictions in holding meetings, rallies, or other peaceful activities?

• Are party members or leaders intimidated, harassed, arrested, imprisoned, or subjected to violent attacks as a result of their peaceful political activities?

2. Is there a significant opposition vote and a realistic possibility for the opposition to increase its support or gain power through elections?

• Are various legal/administrative restrictions selectively applied to opposition parties to prevent them from increasing their support base or successfully competing in elections?

• Are there legitimate opposition forces in positions of authority, such as in the national legislature or in subnational governments?

• Are opposition party members or leaders intimidated, harassed, arrested, imprisoned, or subjected to violent attacks as a result of their peaceful political activities?

3. Are the people's political choices free from domination by the military, foreign powers, totalitarian parties, religious hierarchies, economic oligarchies, or any other powerful group?

• Do such groups offer bribes to voters and/or political figures in order to influence their political choices?

• Do such groups intimidate, harass, or attack voters and/or political figures in order to influence their political choices?

• Does the military control or enjoy a preponderant influence over government policy and activities, including in countries that nominally are under civilian control?

• Do foreign governments control or enjoy a preponderant influence over government policy and activities by means including the presence of foreign military troops, the use of significant economic threats or sanctions, etc.?

4. Do cultural, ethnic, religious, or other minority groups have full political rights and electoral opportunities?

• Do political parties of various ideological persuasions address issues of specific concern to minority groups?

• Does the government inhibit the participation of minority groups in national or subnational political life through laws and/or practical obstacles?

• Are political parties based on ethnicity, culture, or religion that espouse peaceful, democratic values legally permitted and de facto allowed to operate?

C. FUNCTIONING OF GOVERNMENT

1. Do the freely elected head of government and national legislative representatives determine the policies of the government?

• Are the candidates who were elected freely and fairly duly installed in office?

• Do other appointed or non-freely elected state actors interfere with or prevent freely elected representatives from adopting and implementing legislation and making meaningful policy decisions?

• Do nonstate actors, including criminal gangs, the military, and foreign governments, interfere with or prevent elected representatives from adopting and implementing legislation and making meaningful policy decisions?

2. Is the government free from pervasive corruption?

• Has the government implemented effective anticorruption laws or programs to prevent, detect, and punish corruption among public officials, including conflict of interest?

• Is the government free from excessive bureaucratic regulations, registration requirements, or other controls that increase opportunities for corruption?

• Are there independent and effective auditing and investigative bodies that function without impediment or political pressure or influence?

• Are allegations of corruption by government officials thoroughly investigated and prosecuted without prejudice, particularly against political opponents?

• Are allegations of corruption given wide and extensive airing in the media?

• Do whistle-blowers, anticorruption activists, investigators, and journalists enjoy legal protections that make them feel secure about reporting cases of bribery and corruption?

• What was the latest Transparency International Corruption Perceptions Index score for this country?

3. Is the government accountable to the electorate between elections, and does it operate with openness and transparency?

• Are civil society groups, interest groups, journalists, and other citizens able to comment on and influence pending policies of legislation?

• Do citizens have the legal right and practical ability to obtain information about government operations and the means to petition government agencies for it?

• Is the budget-making process subject to meaningful legislative review and public scrutiny?

• Does the government publish detailed accounting expenditures in a timely fashion?

• Does the state ensure transparency and effective competition in the awarding of government contracts?

• Are the asset declarations of government officials open to public and media scrutiny and verification?

ADDITIONAL DISCRETIONARY POLITICAL RIGHTS QUESTIONS:

A. For traditional monarchies that have no parties or electoral process, does the system provide for genuine, meaningful consultation with the people, encourage public discussion of policy choices, and allow the right to petition the ruler?

• Is there a non-elected legislature that advises the monarch on policy issues?

• Are there formal mechanisms for individuals or civic groups to speak with or petition the monarch?

• Does the monarch take petitions from the public under serious consideration?

B. Is the government or occupying power deliberately changing the ethnic composition of a country or territory so as to destroy a culture or tip the political balance in favor of another group?

• Is the government providing economic or other incentives to certain people in order to change the ethnic composition of a region or regions?

• Is the government forcibly moving people in or out of certain areas in order to change the ethnic composition of those regions?

• Is the government arresting, imprisoning, or killing members of certain ethnic groups in order change the ethnic composition of a region or regions?

CIVIL LIBERTIES CHECKLIST

D. FREEDOM OF EXPRESSION AND BELIEF

1. Are there free and independent media and other forms of cultural expression? (Note: In cases where the media are state controlled but offer pluralistic points of view, the survey gives the system credit.)

• Does the government directly or indirectly censor print, broadcast, and/or internet-based media?

• Is self-censorship among journalists common, especially when reporting on politically sensitive issues, including corruption or the activities of senior officials?

• Does the government use libel and security laws to punish those who scrutinize government officials and policies through either onerous fines or imprisonment?

• Is it a crime to insult the honor and dignity of the president and/or other government officials? How broad is the range of such prohibitions, and how vigorously are they enforced?

• If media outlets are dependent on the government for their financial survival, does the government withhold funding in order to propagandize, primarily provide official points of view, and/or limit access by opposition parties and civic critics?

• Does the government attempt to influence media content and access through means including politically motivated awarding of broadcast frequencies and newspaper registrations, unfair control and influence over printing facilities and distribution networks, selective distribution of advertising, onerous registration requirements, prohibitive tariffs, and bribery?

• Are journalists threatened, arrested, imprisoned, beaten, or killed by government or nongovernmental actors for their legitimate journalistic activities, and if such cases occur, are they investigated and prosecuted fairly and expeditiously?

• Are works of literature, art, music, or other forms of cultural expression censored or banned for political purposes?

2. Are religious institutions and communities free to practice their faith and express themselves in public and private?

• Are registration requirements employed to impede the free functioning of religious institutions?

• Are members of religious groups, including minority faiths and movements, harassed, fined, arrested, or beaten by the authorities for engaging in their religious practices?

• Does the government appoint or otherwise influence the appointment of religious leaders?

• Does the government control the production and distribution of religious books and other materials and the content of sermons?

• Is the construction of religious buildings banned or restricted?

• Does the government place undue restrictions on religious education? Does the government require religious education?

3. Is there academic freedom, and is the educational system free of extensive political indoctrination?

• Are teachers and professors free to pursue academic activities of a political and quasi-political nature without fear of physical violence or intimidation by state or nonstate actors?

• Does the government pressure, strongly influence, or control the content of school curriculums for political purposes?

• Are student associations that address issues of a political nature allowed to function freely?

• Does the government, including through school administration or other officials, pressure students and/or teachers to support certain political figures or agendas, including pressuring them to attend political rallies or vote for certain candidates? Conversely, does the government, including through school administration or other officials, discourage or forbid students and/or teachers from supporting certain candidates and parties?

4. Is there open and free private discussion?

• Are people able to engage in private discussions, particularly of a political nature (in places including restaurants, public transportation, and their homes) without fear of harassment or arrest by the authorities?

• Does the government employ people or groups to engage in public surveillance and to report alleged antigovernment conversations to the authorities?

E. ASSOCIATIONAL AND ORGANIZATIONAL RIGHTS

1. Is there freedom of assembly, demonstration, and open public discussion?

• Are peaceful protests, particularly those of a political nature, banned or severely restricted?

• Are the legal requirements to obtain permission to hold peaceful demonstrations particularly cumbersome and time consuming?

• Are participants of peaceful demonstrations intimidated, arrested, or assaulted?

• Are peaceful protestors detained by police in order to prevent them from engaging in such actions?

2. Is there freedom for nongovernmental organizations? (Note: This includes civic organizations, interest groups, foundations, etc.)

• Are registration and other legal requirements for nongovernmental organizations particularly onerous and intended to prevent them from functioning freely?

• Are laws related to the financing of nongovernmental organizations unduly complicated and cumbersome?

• Are donors and funders of nongovernmental organizations free of government pressure?

• Are members of nongovernmental organizations intimidated, arrested, imprisoned, or assaulted because of their work?

3. Are there free trade unions and peasant organizations or equivalents, and is there effective collective bargaining? Are there free professional and other private organizations?

• Are trade unions allowed to be established and to operate free from government interference?

• Are workers pressured by the government or employers to join or not to join certain trade unions, and do they face harassment, violence, or dismissal from their jobs if they do?

• Are workers permitted to engage in strikes, and do members of unions face reprisals for engaging in peaceful strikes? (Note: This question may not apply to workers in essential government services or public safety jobs.)

• Are unions able to bargain collectively with employers and able to negotiate collective bargaining agreements that are honored in practice?

• For states with very small populations or primarily agriculturally based economies that do not necessarily support the formation of trade unions, does the government allow for the establishment of peasant organizations or their equivalents? Is there legislation expressively forbidding the formation of trade unions?

• Are professional organizations, including business associations, allowed to operate freely and without government interference?

F. RULE OF LAW

1. Is there an independent judiciary?

• Is the judiciary subject to interference from the executive branch of government or from other political, economic, or religious influences?

• Are judges appointed and dismissed in a fair and unbiased manner?

• Do judges rule fairly and impartially, or do they commonly render verdicts that favor the government or particular interests, whether in return for bribes or other reasons?

• Do executive, legislative, and other governmental authorities comply with judicial decisions, and are these decisions effectively enforced?

• Do powerful private concerns comply with judicial decisions, and are decisions that run counter to the interests of powerful actors effectively enforced?

2. Does the rule of law prevail in civil and criminal matters? Are police under direct civilian control?

• Are defendants' rights, including the presumption of innocence until proven guilty, protected?

• Are detainees provided access to independent, competent legal counsel?

• Are defendants given a fair, public, and timely hearing by a competent, independent, and impartial tribunal?

• Are prosecutors independent of political control and influence?

• Are prosecutors independent of powerful private interests, whether legal or illegal?

• Is there effective and democratic civilian state control of law enforcement officials through the judicial, legislative, and executive branches?

• Are law enforcement officials free from the influence of nonstate actors, including organized crime, powerful commercial interests, or other groups?

3. Is there protection from political terror, unjustified imprisonment, exile, or torture, whether by groups that support or oppose the system? Is there freedom from war and insurgencies?

• Do law enforcement officials make arbitrary arrests and detentions without warrants or fabricate or plant evidence on suspects?

• Do law enforcement officials beat detainees during arrest and interrogation or use excessive force or torture to extract confessions?

• Are conditions in pretrial facilities and prisons humane and respectful of the human dignity of inmates?

• Do citizens have the means of effective petition and redress when their rights are violated by state authorities?

• Is violent crime either against specific groups or within the general population widespread?

• Is the population subjected to physical harm, forced removal, or other acts of violence or terror due to civil conflict or war?

4. Do laws, policies, and practices guarantee equal treatment of various segments of the population?

• Are members of various distinct groups—including ethnic and religious minorities, homosexuals, and the disabled—able to exercise effectively their human rights with full equality before the law?

• Is violence against such groups widespread, and if so, are perpetrators brought to justice?

• Do members of such groups face legal and/or de facto discrimination in areas including employment, education, and housing because of their identification with a particular group?

• Do women enjoy full equality in law and in practice as compared to men?

• Do noncitizens—including migrant workers and noncitizen immigrants—enjoy basic internationally recognized human rights, including the right not to be subjected to torture or other forms of ill-treatment, the right to due process of law, and the rights of freedom of association, expression, and religion?

• Do the country's laws provide for the granting of asylum or refugee status in accordance with the 1951 UN Convention Relating to the Status of Refugees, its 1967 Protocol, and other regional treaties regarding refugees? Has the government established a system for providing protection to refugees, including against refoulement (the return of persons to a country where there is reason to believe they fear persecution)?

G. PERSONAL AUTONOMY AND INDIVIDUAL RIGHTS

1. Do citizens enjoy freedom of travel or choice of residence, employment, or institution of higher education?

• Are there restrictions on foreign travel, including the use of an exit visa system, which may be issued selectively?

• Is permission required from the authorities or nonstate actors to move within the country?

• Do state or nonstate actors determine or otherwise influence a person's type and place of employment?

• Are bribes or other inducements needed to obtain the necessary documents to travel, change one's place of residence or employment, enter institutions of higher education, or advance in school?

2. Do citizens have the right to own property and establish private businesses? Is private business activity unduly influenced by government officials, the security forces, political parties/organizations, or organized crime?

• Are people legally allowed to purchase and sell land and other property, and can they do so in practice without undue interference from the government or nonstate actors?

• Does the government provide adequate and timely compensation to people whose property is expropriated under eminent domain laws?

• Are people legally allowed to establish and operate private businesses with a reasonable minimum of registration, licensing, and other requirements?

• Are bribes or other inducements needed to obtain the necessary legal documents to operate private businesses?

• Do private/nonstate actors, including criminal groups, seriously impede private business activities through such measures as extortion?

3. Are there personal social freedoms, including gender equality, choice of marriage partners, and size of family?

• Is violence against women, including wife-beating and rape, widespread, and are perpetrators brought to justice?

• Is the trafficking of women and/or children abroad for prostitution widespread, and is the government taking adequate efforts to address the problem?

• Do women face de jure and de facto discrimination in economic and social matters, including property and inheritance rights, divorce proceedings, and child custody matters?

• Does the government directly or indirectly control choice of marriage partners through means such as requiring large payments to marry certain individuals (e.g., foreign citizens) or by not enforcing laws against child marriage or dowry payments?

• Does the government determine the number of children that a couple may have?

• Does the government engage in state-sponsored religious/cultural/ethnic indoctrination and related restrictions on personal freedoms?

• Do private institutions, including religious groups, unduly infringe on the rights of individuals, including choice of marriage partner, dress, etc.?

4. Is there equality of opportunity and the absence of economic exploitation?

• Does the government exert tight control over the economy, including through state ownership and the setting of prices and production quotas?

• Do the economic benefits from large state industries, including the energy sector, benefit the general population or only a privileged few?

• Do private interests exert undue influence on the economy through monopolistic practices, cartels, or illegal blacklists, boycotts, or discrimination?

• Is entrance to institutions of higher education or the ability to obtain employment limited by widespread nepotism and the payment of bribes?

• Are certain groups, including ethnic or religious minorities, less able to enjoy certain economic benefits than others? For example, are certain groups restricted from holding particular jobs, whether in the public or the private sector, because of de jure or de facto discrimination?

• Do state or private employers exploit their workers through activities including unfairly withholding wages and permitting or forcing employees to work under unacceptably dangerous conditions, as well as through adult slave labor and child labor?

KEY TO SCORES, PR AND CL RATINGS, AND STATUS

Table 1		Table 2	
Political Rights (PR)		**Civil Liberties (CL)**	
Total Scores	**PR Rating**	**Total Scores**	**CL Rating**
36–40	1	53–60	1
30–35	2	44–52	2
24–29	3	35–43	3
18–23	4	26–34	4
12–17	5	17–25	5
6–11	6	8–16	6
0–5*	7	0–7	7

Table 3

Combined Average of the PR and CL Ratings	Country Status
1.0–2.5	Free
3.0–5.0	Partly Free
5.5–7.0	Not Free

* It is possible for a country's total political rights score to be less than zero (between -1 and -4) if it receives mostly or all zeros for each of the 10 political rights questions *and* it receives a sufficiently negative score for political rights discretionary question B. In such a case, a country would still receive a final political rights rating of 7.

Tables and Ratings

Table of Independent Countries

Country	PR	CL	Freedom Rating
⬇ Afghanistan	6	6	Not Free
⬇ Albania*	3	3	Partly Free
Algeria	6	5	Not Free
Andorra*	1	1	Free
Angola	6	5	Not Free
Antigua and Barbuda*	3	2	Free
Argentina*	2	2	Free
Armenia	6	4	Partly Free
Australia*	1	1	Free
Austria*	1	1	Free
⬇ Azerbaijan	6	5	Not Free
Bahamas*	1	1	Free
Bahrain	6	6▼	Not Free
⬇ Bangladesh*	3	4	Partly Free
Barbados*	1	1	Free
Belarus	7	6	Not Free
Belgium*	1	1	Free
Belize*	1	2	Free
Benin*	2	2	Free
Bhutan	4	5	Partly Free
Bolivia*	3	3	Partly Free
Bosnia and Herzegovina*	4	3	Partly Free
Botswana*	3	2	Free
Brazil*	2	2	Free
Brunei	6	5	Not Free
Bulgaria*	2	2	Free
Burkina Faso	5	3	Partly Free
Burma	7	6▲	Not Free
Burundi	5	5	Partly Free
Cambodia	6	5	Not Free
Cameroon	6	6	Not Free
Canada*	1	1	Free
Cape Verde*	1	1	Free
Central African Republic	5	5	Partly Free
Chad	7	6	Not Free
Chile*	1	1	Free
⬇ China	7	6	Not Free
Colombia*	3	4	Partly Free
Comoros*	3	4	Partly Free
Congo (Brazzaville)	6	5	Not Free
Congo (Kinshasa)	6	6	Not Free
Costa Rica*	1	1	Free
Côte d'Ivoire	6▲	6	Not Free
Croatia*	1	2	Free
Cuba	7	6	Not Free
Cyprus*	1	1	Free
Czech Republic*	1	1	Free
Denmark*	1	1	Free
⬇ Djibouti	6	5	Not Free
Dominica*	1	1	Free
Dominican Republic*	2	2	Free
East Timor*	3	4	Partly Free
⬇ Ecuador*	3	3	Partly Free
⬆ Egypt	6	5	Not Free
El Salvador*	2	3	Free
Equatorial Guinea	7	7	Not Free
Eritrea	7	7	Not Free
Estonia*	1	1	Free
⬇ Ethiopia	6	6	Not Free
Fiji	6	4	Partly Free
Finland*	1	1	Free
France*	1	1	Free
Gabon	6	5	Not Free
The Gambia	6▼	5	Not Free▼
Georgia	4	3	Partly Free
Germany*	1	1	Free
Ghana*	1	2	Free
Greece*	2▼	2	Free
Grenada*	1	2	Free
Guatemala*	3▲	4	Partly Free
Guinea	5	5	Partly Free
Guinea-Bissau	4	4	Partly Free
Guyana*	2	3	Free
Haiti	4	5	Partly Free
Honduras	4	4	Partly Free
Hungary*	1	2▼	Free
Iceland*	1	1	Free
India*	2	3	Free
Indonesia*	2	3	Free
⬇ Iran	6	6	Not Free
Iraq	5	6	Not Free
Ireland*	1	1	Free
⬇ Israel*	1	2	Free
Italy*	1	1▲	Free
Jamaica*	2	3	Free
Japan*	1	2	Free
Jordan	6	5	Not Free
⬇ Kazakhstan	6	5	Not Free
Kenya	4	3	Partly Free
Kiribati*	1	1	Free
Kosovo	5	4	Partly Free
Kuwait	4	5	Partly Free
Kyrgyzstan	5	5	Partly Free
Laos	7	6	Not Free
Latvia*	2	2	Free
Lebanon	5	4▼	Partly Free
Lesotho*	3	3	Partly Free
Liberia*	3	4	Partly Free

Country	PR	CL	Freedom Rating
Libya	7	6▲	Not Free
Liechtenstein*	1	1	Free
Lithuania*	1	1	Free
Luxembourg*	1	1	Free
Macedonia*	3	3	Partly Free
Madagascar	6	4	Partly Free
⬇ Malawi*	3	4	Partly Free
Malaysia	4	4	Partly Free
Maldives*	3	4	Partly Free
Mali*	2	3	Free
Malta*	1	1	Free
Marshall Islands*	1	1	Free
Mauritania	6	5	Not Free
Mauritius*	1	2	Free
Mexico*	3	3	Partly Free
Micronesia*	1	1	Free
Moldova*	3	3	Partly Free
Monaco*	2	1	Free
Mongolia*	2	2	Free
Montenegro*	3	2	Free
Morocco	5	4	Partly Free
Mozambique	4	3	Partly Free
Namibia*	2	2	Free
Nauru*	1	1	Free
Nepal	4	4	Partly Free
Netherlands*	1	1	Free
New Zealand*	1	1	Free
Nicaragua	5▼	4	Partly Free
Niger*	3▲	4	Partly Free
Nigeria	4	4	Partly Free
North Korea	7	7	Not Free
Norway*	1	1	Free
Oman	6	5	Not Free
⬇ Pakistan	4	5	Partly Free
Palau*	1	1	Free
Panama*	1	2	Free
Papua New Guinea*	4	3	Partly Free
Paraguay*	3	3	Partly Free
Peru*	2	3	Free
Philippines*	3	3	Partly Free
Poland*	1	1	Free
Portugal*	1	1	Free
Qatar	6	5	Not Free
Romania*	2	2	Free
Russia	6	5	Not Free
Rwanda	6	5	Not Free
St. Kitts and Nevis*	1	1	Free
St. Lucia*	1	1	Free
St. Vincent and the Grenadines*	1	1	Free
Samoa*	2	2	Free
San Marino*	1	1	Free
São Tomé and Príncipe*	2	2	Free
Saudi Arabia	7	7▼	Not Free
Senegal*	3	3	Partly Free
Serbia*	2	2	Free
Seychelles*	3	3	Partly Free
Sierra Leone*	3	3	Partly Free
Singapore	4▲	4	Partly Free
⬆ Slovakia*	1	1	Free
Slovenia*	1	1	Free
Solomon Islands	4	3	Partly Free
Somalia	7	7	Not Free
South Africa*	2	2	Free
South Korea*	1	2	Free
South Sudan	6	5	Not Free
Spain*	1	1	Free
⬇ Sri Lanka	5	4	Partly Free
Sudan	7	7	Not Free
Suriname*	2	2	Free
Swaziland	7	5	Not Free
Sweden*	1	1	Free
Switzerland*	1	1	Free
Syria	7	7▼	Not Free
Taiwan*	1	2	Free
Tajikistan	6	5	Not Free
Tanzania*	3	3	Partly Free
Thailand*	4▲	4	Partly Free
Togo	5	4	Partly Free
Tonga*	3	3	Partly Free
Trinidad and Tobago*	2	2	Free
Tunisia*	3▲	4▲	Partly Free▲
Turkey*	3	3	Partly Free
Turkmenistan	7	7	Not Free
⬇ Tuvalu*	1	1	Free
Uganda	5	4	Partly Free
Ukraine*	4▼	3	Partly Free
United Arab Emirates	6	6▼	Not Free
United Kingdom*	1	1	Free
United States*	1	1	Free
Uruguay*	1	1	Free
Uzbekistan	7	7	Not Free
Vanuatu*	2	2	Free
Venezuela	5	5	Partly Free
Vietnam	7	5	Not Free
⬆ Yemen	6	6▼	Not Free
Zambia*	3	4	Partly Free
Zimbabwe	6	6	Not Free

PR and CL stand for Political Rights and Civil Liberties, respectively; 1 represents the most free and 7 the least free rating.

▼▲ up or down indicates an improvement or decline in ratings or status since the last survey.

⬆⬇ up or down indicates a trend of positive or negative changes that took place but were not sufficient to result in a change in political rights or civil liberties ratings.

* indicates a country's status as an electoral democracy.

Note: The ratings reflect global events from January 1, 2011, through December 31, 2011.

Table of Related Territories

Territory	PR	CL	Freedom Rating
Hong Kong	5	2	Partly Free
Puerto Rico	1	2▼	Free

Table of Disputed Territories

Country	PR	CL	Freedom Rating
Abkhazia	5	5	Partly Free
Gaza Strip	6	6	Not Free
Indian Kashmir	4	4▲	Partly Free
Nagorno-Karabakh	6	5	Not Free
Northern Cyprus	2	2	Free
Pakistani Kashmir	6	5	Not Free
Somaliland	4	5	Partly Free
South Ossetia	7	6	Not Free
Tibet	7	7	Not Free
Transnistria	6	6	Not Free
West Bank	6	5	Not Free
Western Sahara	7	7▼	Not Free

Combined Average Ratings: Independent Countries

FREE

1.0

Andorra
Australia
Austria
Bahamas
Barbados
Belgium
Canada
Cape Verde
Chile
Costa Rica
Cyprus
Czech Republic
Denmark
Dominica
Estonia
Finland
France
Germany
Iceland
Ireland
Italy
Kiribati
Liechtenstein
Lithuania
Luxembourg
Malta
Marshall Islands
Micronesia
Nauru
Netherlands
New Zealand
Norway
Palau
Poland
Portugal
Saint Kitts and Nevis
Saint Lucia
Saint Vincent and the Grenadines
San Marino
Slovakia
Slovenia
Spain
Sweden
Switzerland
Tuvalu
United Kingdom
United States
Uruguay

1.5

Belize
Croatia
Ghana
Grenada
Hungary
Israel
Japan
Mauritius
Monaco
Panama
South Korea
Taiwan

2.0

Argentina
Benin
Brazil
Bulgaria
Dominican Republic
Greece
Latvia
Mongolia
Namibia
Romania
Samoa
São Tomé and Principe
Serbia
South Africa
Suriname
Trinidad and Tobago
Vanuatu

2.5

Antigua and Barbuda
Botswana
El Salvador
Guyana
India
Indonesia
Jamaica
Mali
Montenegro
Peru

PARTLY FREE

3.0

Albania
Bolivia
Ecuador
Lesotho
Macedonia
Mexico
Moldova
Paraguay
Philippines
Senegal
Seychelles
Sierra Leone
Tanzania
Tonga
Turkey

3.5

Bangladesh
Bosnia-Herzegovina
Colombia
Comoros
East Timor
Georgia
Guatemala
Kenya
Liberia
Malawi
Maldives
Mozambique
Niger
Papua New Guinea
Solomon Islands
Tunisia
Ukraine
Zambia

4.0

Burkina Faso
Guinea-Bissau
Honduras
Malaysia
Nepal
Nigeria
Singapore
Thailand

4.5

Bhutan
Haiti
Kosovo
Kuwait
Lebanon
Morocco
Nicaragua
Pakistan
Sri Lanka
Togo
Uganda

5.0

Armenia
Burundi
Central African Republic
Fiji
Guinea
Kyrgyzstan
Madagascar
Venezuela

NOT FREE

5.5

Algeria
Angola
Azerbaijan
Brunei
Cambodia
Congo (Brazzaville)
Djibouti
Egypt
Gabon
The Gambia
Iraq
Jordan
Kazakhstan
Mauritania
Oman
Qatar
Russia
Rwanda
South Sudan
Tajikistan

6.0

Afghanistan
Bahrain
Cameroon
Congo (Kinshasa)
Côte d'Ivoire
Ethiopia
Iran
Swaziland
United Arab Emirates
Vietnam
Yemen
Zimbabwe

6.5

Belarus
Burma
Chad
China
Cuba
Laos
Libya

7.0

Equatorial Guinea
Eritrea
North Korea
Saudi Arabia
Somalia
Sudan
Syria
Turkmenistan
Uzbekistan

Combined Average Ratings: Related Territories

FREE

1.5

Puerto Rico

PARTLY FREE

3.5

Hong Kong

Combined Average Ratings: Disputed Territories

FREE

2.0

Northern Cyprus

PARTLY FREE

4.0

Indian Kashmir

4.5

Somaliland

5.0

Abkhazia

NOT FREE

5.5

Nagorno-Karabakh
Pakistani Kashmir
West Bank

6.0

Gaza Strip
Transnistria

6.5

South Ossetia

7.0

Tibet
Western Sahara

Electoral Democracies (117)

Albania
Andorra
Antigua and Barbuda
Argentina
Australia
Austria
Bahamas
Bangladesh
Barbados
Belgium
Belize
Benin
Bolivia
Bosnia-Herzegovina
Botswana
Brazil
Bulgaria
Canada
Cape Verde
Chile
Colombia
Comoros
Costa Rica
Croatia
Cyprus
Czech Republic
Denmark
Dominica
Dominican Republic
East Timor
Ecuador
El Salvador
Estonia
Finland
France
Germany
Ghana
Greece
Grenada
Guatemala
Guyana
Hungary
Iceland
India
Indonesia
Ireland
Israel
Italy
Jamaica
Japan
Kiribati
Latvia
Lesotho
Liberia
Liechtenstein
Lithuania
Luxembourg
Macedonia
Malawi
Maldives
Mali
Malta
Marshall Islands
Mauritius
Mexico
Micronesia
Moldova
Monaco
Mongolia
Montenegro
Namibia
Nauru
Netherlands
New Zealand
Niger
Norway
Palau
Panama
Papua New Guinea
Paraguay
Peru
Philippines
Poland
Portugal
Romania
St. Kitts and Nevis
St. Lucia
St. Vincent and the Grenadines

Samoa
San Marino
São Tomé and Principe
Senegal
Serbia
Seychelles
Sierra Leone
Slovakia
Slovenia
South Africa
South Korea
Spain
Suriname
Sweden
Switzerland
Taiwan
Tanzania
Thailand
Tonga
Trinidad and Tobago
Tunisia
Turkey
Tuvalu
Ukraine
United Kingdom
United States
Uruguay
Vanuatu
Zambia

The Survey Team

CONTRIBUTING AUTHORS

MICHAEL E. ALLISON is an associate professor of political science at the University of Scranton in Pennsylvania. He received his master's degree and PhD in political science from Florida State University. His teaching and research interests include the comparative study of civil war and civil war resolution, particularly as it relates to the transition of former armed opposition groups to political parties in Latin America. His work has appeared in *Latin American Politics and Society, Conflict Management and Peace Science*, and *Studies in Comparative International Development*. He also blogs at *Central American Politics*. He served as a Central America analyst for *Freedom in the World*.

ROOP BHATTI is a juris doctor candidate at the Washington University in St. Louis School of Law. Previously, she worked as a legal intern at the Human Rights Law Network in New Delhi, India. She also interned at the Chicago Council on Global Affairs, and was a foreign language interpreter for several South Asian languages in the Circuit Court of Cook County. She holds a bachelor's degree with honors in both international studies and South Asian languages and civilization from the University of Chicago. She served as a South Asia analyst for *Freedom in the World*.

JACLYN BURGER is a peace-building consultant based in South Africa. She previously served with the United Nations Stabilization Mission in Haiti and the United Nations Mission in Liberia. She has also worked on bilateral security-sector reform and training programs in Liberia and the Democratic Republic of the Congo. Her research interests include security-sector reform, transitional justice, national reconciliation, and governance issues in sub-Saharan Africa. She holds a master's degree in international peace and conflict resolution with a specialization in postconflict peace building from American University. She served as a West Africa analyst for *Freedom in the World*.

S. ADAM CARDAIS is a contributing editor at *Transitions Online*, a Prague-based internet magazine covering politics, economics, and society in postcommunist Europe and the former Soviet Union. He holds an MA in European studies, with a focus on postconflict peace building in the former Yugoslavia, from New York University. He served as a Balkans analyst for *Freedom in the World*.

FOTINI CHRISTIA is an associate professor of political science at the Massachusetts Institute of Technology. Her book, *Alliance Formation in Civil War*, is forthcoming in 2012 from Cambridge University Press. She has done extensive ethnographic, survey, and experimental research in the field, addressing the effects of institutions of cooperation in postconflict, multiethnic societies. Her current collaborative research project is a randomized impact evaluation of a $1 billion community-driven development program in Afghanistan, which examines the effects of development aid on local governance and economic well-being. She served as a South Asia analyst for *Freedom in the World.*

CATHERINE CONAGHAN is a professor of political studies at Queen's University, Canada, where she focuses on the Andean region. She is the author of several books on topics dealing with democracy in Latin America, including *Fujimori's Peru: Deception in the Public Sphere.* Her publications include articles in the *Journal of Latin American Studies, Latin American Research Review,* and *Studies in Comparative International Development.* She has conducted extensive fieldwork in Ecuador, Bolivia, and Peru. She received a PhD from Yale University. She served as an Andean region analyst for *Freedom in the World.*

SARAH COOK is a senior research analyst at Freedom House. She serves as assistant editor for *Freedom on the Net,* an index that tracks internet freedom around the world, and is an editor of the *China Media Bulletin,* a weekly news digest of media freedom developments related to China. She coedited the English version of Chinese attorney Gao Zhisheng's memoir, *A China More Just,* and was a delegate to the UN Human Rights Commission for an organization working on religious freedom in China. She holds a master's degree in politics and an LLM in public international law from the School of Oriental and African Studies in London, where she was a Marshall Scholar. She served as an East Asia analyst for *Freedom in the World.*

BRITTA H. CRANDALL teaches at Davidson College in North Carolina. She completed her PhD at the Johns Hopkins University School of Advanced International Studies and is the author of *Hemispheric Giants: The Misunderstood History of U.S.-Brazilian Relations.* Prior to her doctoral studies, she was associate director for Latin American sovereign risk analysis at Bank One and worked as a Latin American program examiner for the Office of Management and Budget. She served as a South America analyst for *Freedom in the World.*

JAKE DIZARD is a PhD candidate in political science at the University of Texas at Austin. He was previously the managing editor of *Countries at the Crossroads,* Freedom House's annual survey of democratic governance. His area of focus is Latin America, with a specific emphasis on the Andean region and Mexico. He is a 2005 graduate of the Johns Hopkins University School of Advanced International Studies. He served as a Latin America analyst for *Freedom in the World.*

RICHARD DOWNIE is deputy director and a fellow of the Africa program at the Center for Strategic and International Studies. Previously, he was a journalist for the British Broadcasting Corporation (BBC). He received a master's degree in international public policy at the Johns Hopkins University School of Advanced International Studies. He served as a Horn of Africa analyst for *Freedom in the World.*

JENNIFER DUNHAM is a research analyst for *Freedom in the World* and *Freedom of the Press at Freedom House.* Previously, she was the managing editor and Africa writer for *Facts On File World News Digest.* She holds a master's degree in international relations from New York University's Center for Global Affairs, where she wrote her thesis on transitional justice in Rwanda and Sierra Leone. She served as a sub-Saharan Africa analyst for *Freedom in the World.*

MICHAEL DZUBIAN is a student at Harvard Law School. From 2009 to 2012, he worked as a research assistant in the Middle East Program at the Center for Strategic and International Studies. He served as a Middle East analyst for *Freedom in the World.*

DAVID FOWKES is an adjunct professor at American University and Johns Hopkins University's School of Advanced International Studies. He holds a PhD from the latter, attained with the support of a Fulbright scholarship. He served as a Southern and East Africa analyst for *Freedom in the World.*

AMY FREEDMAN is a professor and the department chair of political science and international studies at Long Island University, C. W. Post Campus. She received her master's degree and PhD in political science from New York University. Her research touches on various questions relating to democratization. She has a forthcoming book on the internationalization of domestic conflicts and is a coeditor of the journal *Asian Security.* She served as a Southeast Asia analyst for *Freedom in the World.*

CAROL JEAN GALLO is a PhD student in the Politics and International Studies Department at the University of Cambridge, and holds a master's degree in African studies from Yale University. Her research is concerned with local knowledge and the ways in which international institutions and local people may understand concepts related to peace building. Previously, she worked as a consultant in the UN Department of Peacekeeping Operations in New York. She served as a sub-Saharan Africa analyst for *Freedom in the World.*

NATASHA GEBER is a New York–based independent researcher. She previously contributed to Freedom House's *Nations in Transit* publication. She holds a BA in political science and Slavic studies from McGill University, where she has also worked as a researcher in the Political Science Department. She served as a Central and Eastern Europe analyst for *Freedom in the World.*

THOMAS W. GOLD is currently the director of strategic initiatives and external affairs at the Research Alliance for New York City Schools at New York University. He is a former assistant professor of comparative politics at Sacred Heart University and the author of *The Lega Nord and Contemporary Politics in Italy.* He earned his PhD in political science from the New School for Social Research and received a Fulbright Fellowship to conduct research in Italy. He served as a Western Europe analyst for *Freedom in the World.*

EVA HOIER GREENE is a former research assistant at Freedom House. She completed her bachelor's degree in international development in Denmark. Prior to her work at Freedom House, she covered nuclear disarmament, among other issues, at the Permanent Mission of Denmark to the United Nations. She served as a Western Europe analyst for *Freedom in the World.*

ARMAN GRIGORYAN is an assistant professor of international relations at Lehigh University. His research interests revolve around interstate and intrastate conflicts, interventions, and post-Soviet politics. His articles have appeared in *International Studies Quarterly*, *International Security*, and *Ethnopolitics*. He served as a Caucasus analyst for *Freedom in the World.*

SYLVANA HABDANK-KOŁACZKOWSKA is the project director of *Nations in Transit*, Freedom House's annual survey of democratic governance from Central Europe to Eurasia. She also writes reports on Central Europe for the *Freedom of the Press* survey. Previously, she was the managing editor of the *Journal of Cold War Studies*, a peer-reviewed quarterly. She holds an MA from Harvard University in regional studies of Eastern Europe and Eurasia, and a BA in political science from the University of California, Berkeley. She served as a Central Europe and Balkans analyst for *Freedom in the World.*

HOLGER HENKE is assistant provost at York College (CUNY) and a political scientist with a variety of research interests in international relations. He has authored and edited six books, including *Constructing Vernacular Culture in the Trans-Caribbean*, and has published numerous articles in journals such as *Cultural Critique and Latin American Perspectives*. He is the editor of *Wadabagei: A Journal of the Caribbean and its Diasporas*. He received a PhD in government from the University of the West Indies (Mona) and a master's degree in political science from the Geschwister-Scholl-Institute of Political Science at the Ludwig Maximilians University of Munich. He served as a Caribbean analyst for *Freedom in the World.*

ANNE HENOCHOWICZ is the translation coordinator for the bilingual website *China Digital Times*. She has contributed to *Foreign Policy* and the blog *China Beat*. She received master's degrees from the University of Cambridge and Ohio State University, where she studied Mongolian folk music in contemporary China. She served as an East Asia analyst for *Freedom in the World.*

DANIEL HOLODNIK is the Middle East program coordinator and research associate at the Center for Strategic and International Studies. He holds a master's degree in Islamic studies from Duke University and a bachelor's degree in religion from Cornell University. He served as a Middle East analyst for *Freedom in the World.*

MAÏTÉ HOSTETTER is a program coordinator for the West Africa Department at the International Foundation for Electoral Systems, where she focuses on human rights, civic and voter education, and electoral management. Previously, she worked at Freedom House in the West and Central Africa Department. She holds a master's degree in the social sciences from the University of Chicago, with a concentration on human rights, and a bachelor's degree in international studies and anthropology from the University of California, San Diego. She served as a West Africa analyst for *Freedom in the World.*

RACHEL JACOBS is a PhD candidate in political science at the University of Wisconsin, Madison. Her research focuses on regime consolidation in Southeast

Asia. Previously, she was a research analyst for *Countries at the Crossroads*, Freedom House's annual survey of democratic governance. She holds a master's degree in international relations from the University of Chicago and a bachelor's degree in government and Asian studies from Cornell University. She served as a Southeast Asia analyst for *Freedom in the World*.

TOBY CRAIG JONES is an associate professor of history and the director of the Center for Middle Eastern Studies at Rutgers University, New Brunswick. From 2012 to 2014, he will serve as co-director of the Rutgers Center for Historical Analysis. He is also a nonresident scholar in the Middle East Program at the Carnegie Endowment for International Peace. He is the author of *Desert Kingdom: How Oil and Water Forged Modern Saudi Arabia* and is currently writing a new book entitled *America's Oil Wars*. He is an editor of *Middle East Report* and has published widely, including in the *International Journal of Middle East Studies*, the *Atlantic*, the *New York Times*, and *Foreign Affairs*. From 2004 to 2006 he was the Persian Gulf analyst at the International Crisis Group. He served as a Middle East analyst for *Freedom in the World*.

KARIN DEUTSCH KARLEKAR is the project director of *Freedom of the Press*, Freedom House's annual survey of global press freedom. A specialist on media freedom trends and measurement indicators, she also developed the methodology for and edited the pilot edition of *Freedom on the Net*, Freedom House's assessment of internet and digital media freedom. She has written South Asia reports for several Freedom House publications, and has been on research and advocacy missions to Afghanistan, Nigeria, Pakistan, Sri Lanka, South Africa, Uganda, Zambia, and Zimbabwe. She previously worked as a consultant for Human Rights Watch and as an editor at the *Economist Intelligence Unit*. She holds a PhD in Indian history from Cambridge University. She served as a South Asia analyst for *Freedom in the World*.

SANJA KELLY is the project director of *Freedom on the Net,* Freedom House's assessment of internet and digital media freedom. An expert on internet freedom, democratic governance, and women's rights, she has also directed the research and production of Freedom House publications including *Women's Rights in the Middle East and North Africa* and *Countries at the Crossroads*. She is the author of numerous reports and articles on these topics, and has been on research assignments in the former Yugoslavia, the Caucasus, South and Southeast Asia, Africa, and the Middle East. She served as a Balkans analyst for *Freedom in the World*.

JOSHUA KURLANTZICK is a fellow for Southeast Asia at the Council on Foreign Relations. Previously, he was a scholar at the Carnegie Endowment for International Peace, where he focused on Southeast Asian politics and economics and China's relations with Southeast Asia. He is a longtime journalist, whose articles have appeared in *Time*, the *New Republic*, the *Atlantic Monthly*, *Foreign Affairs*, and the *New Yorker*, among others. He is the author of the upcoming book *Democracy in Decline*. He served as a Southeast Asia analyst for *Freedom in the World*.

MIRIAM LANSKOY is the director for Russia and Eurasia at the National Endowment for Democracy. She has testified before Congress, been interviewed on NPR, and appeared on PBS's *Newshour*, in addition to publishing articles in periodicals including the Journal of *Democracy*, *SAIS Review*, and *Fletcher Forum*. In 2010, she published her first book, *The Chechen Struggle: Independence Won and Lost*, with former foreign minister of Chechnya Ilyas Akhmadov. She holds a PhD in international affairs from Boston University. She served as a Central Asia analyst for *Freedom in the World*.

ASTRID LARSON is the language center coordinator for the French Institute Alliance Française. She has served as an analyst for Western Europe, sub-Saharan Africa, and the South Pacific for Freedom House's *Freedom of the Press* survey. She received her MA in international media and culture from the New School University. She served as a Western Europe analyst for *Freedom in the World*.

PETER LICURSI is an editor at *Bidoun*, a magazine that deals with art, culture, and politics in the Middle East. He studied history at Columbia University and Turkish at Yeditepe University in Istanbul. He served as a Western Europe analyst for *Freedom in the World*.

TIMOTHY LONGMAN is an associate professor of political science and director of the African Studies Center at Boston University. He has researched and published extensively on state-society relations, human rights, religion, and politics in Burundi, Rwanda, and the Democratic Republic of Congo, and authored the book *Christianity and Genocide in Rwanda*. Prior to coming to Boston University, he taught for 13 years at Vassar College. He has served as a consultant for Human Rights Watch, the International Center for Transitional Justice, and USAID in Burundi, Rwanda, and Congo. He served as an East Africa analyst for *Freedom in the World*.

ELEANOR MARCHANT is a PhD candidate at the Annenberg School for Communications at the University of Pennsylvania, specializing in political communications and new technology in Africa. She is also a research associate at the Center for Global Communication Studies, where she advises on African and transnational media research projects. Previously, she worked at the Programme in Comparative Media Law and Policy at the University of Oxford, the Media Development Loan Fund, and the Media Institute in Nairobi. She also served as assistant editor for Freedom House's *Freedom of the Press* survey. She holds a master's degree in international relations from New York University. She served as a West Africa analyst for *Freedom in the World*.

KATHERIN MACHALEK is a research analyst for *Nations in Transit*, Freedom House's annual survey of democratic governance from Central Europe to Eurasia. A specialist on Eastern Europe, the Caucasus, and Central Asia, she has authored several articles on political developments and corruption. Previously, she worked for the Geneva-based Human Rights Information and Documentation Systems (HURIDOCS), helping civil society organizations in Eurasia improve their use of information and communication technologies and digital advocacy. She holds a master's degree in political science from the University of North Carolina, Chapel Hill. She served as a Central Europe analyst for *Freedom in the World.*

SUSANA MOREIRA is a PhD candidate at the Johns Hopkins University School of Advanced International Studies, where her research focuses on Chinese national oil companies' investment strategies in Latin America and sub-Saharan Africa. She is also involved in several other research projects, including the African Crisis Management in Comparative Perspective project sponsored by Africom. She served as a sub-Saharan Africa analyst for *Freedom in the World.*

BRET NELSON is a senior research assistant for *Freedom in the World* and *Freedom of the Press* at Freedom House. He holds a master's degree in political science from Fordham University and is completing a master's degree in Middle East studies at the Graduate Center, CUNY. He served as a Caribbean analyst for *Freedom in the World.*

ALYSSON A. OAKLEY is a senior adviser at the International Republican Institute. She has lived in Indonesia (with frequent postings to East Timor) for over ten years, five of which were spent working on political development with a focus on political parties and local legislatures. She holds a master's degree in international economics and Southeast Asian studies from Johns Hopkins University's School of Advanced International Studies. She served as a Southeast Asia analyst for *Freedom in the World.*

ROBERT ORTTUNG is assistant director of the Institute for European, Russian, and Eurasian Studies at George Washington University's Elliott School of International Affairs, president of the Resource Security Institute, and a visiting scholar at the Center for Security Studies at the Swiss Federal Institute of Technology (ETH) in Zurich. He is managing editor of *Demokratizatsiya: The Journal of Post-Soviet Democratization* and a coeditor of the *Russian Analytical Digest* and the *Caucasus Analytical Digest.* He received his PhD in political science from the University of California, Los Angeles. He served as a Central and Eastern Europe analyst for *Freedom in the World.*

FRANCOIS PIERRE-LOUIS is an associate professor of political science at Queens College, CUNY, and a senior adviser to the chancellor of the City University of New York for the Haiti-CUNY Program. His research interests include immigration and Haitian and Caribbean politics. He served in the private cabinets of President Jean Bertrand Aristide of Haiti in 1991 and Prime Minister Jacques Edouard Alexis in 2007–2008. He is the author of *Haitians in New York City: Transnationalism and Hometown Associations.* His articles have appeared in *Wadabagei: A Journal of the Caribbean and its Diasporas*, the *Journal of Haitian Studies*, and the *Journal of Black Studies.* He served as a Caribbean analyst for *Freedom in the World.*

ARCH PUDDINGTON is vice president for research at Freedom House and coeditor of *Freedom in the World.* He has written widely on American foreign policy, race relations, organized labor, and the history of the Cold War. He is the author of

Broadcasting Freedom: The Cold War Triumph of Radio Free Europe and Radio Liberty and *Lane Kirkland: Champion of American Labor*. He served as a North America analyst for *Freedom in the World*.

SARAH REPUCCI is an independent consultant based in New York City. She has previously worked as a senior research coordinator at Transparency International and a senior researcher at Freedom House. She holds a master's degree in European studies from New York University. She served as a Western Europe analyst for *Freedom in the World*.

MARK Y. ROSENBERG is the Southern Africa analyst for Eurasia Group. He received a PhD in political science from the University of California, Berkeley, where his research focused on single-party dominance and the political economy of heterogeneous societies, mostly in sub-Saharan Africa. He previously worked as a researcher at Freedom House and assistant editor of *Freedom in the World*. He served as a Southern Africa and Middle East analyst for *Freedom in the World*.

TYLER ROYLANCE is a staff editor at Freedom House and is involved in a number of its publications. Previously, he worked as a senior editor for *Facts On File World News Digest*. He holds a master's degree in history from New York University. He served as a Central and Eastern Europe analyst for *Freedom in the World*.

CLEMENT V. SALOMON holds a master's degree in politics from New York University, where he focused on European security and defense policy. He served as a Western Europe analyst for *Freedom in the World*.

YVONNE SHEN is an editor for the *China Media Bulletin*, Freedom House's weekly digest of media freedom developments related to China. Prior to joining Freedom House, she was a research fellow at the Taiwan Foundation for Democracy in Taipei. She holds a master's degree from New York University's Wagner School of Public Service. She served as an East Asia analyst for *Freedom in the World*.

SILVANA TOSKA is a PhD candidate in political science at Cornell University, focusing on the causes and spread of revolutions. She received a master's degree in African studies from Oxford University, where she wrote on the effects of foreign aid on ethnic conflict, and a master's degree in Arab studies from Georgetown University. She served as a sub-Saharan Africa analyst for *Freedom in the World*.

JENNY TOWN is a research associate at the U.S.-Korea Institute at Johns Hopkins University's School of Advanced International Studies. Previously, she worked for the Human Rights in North Korea Project at Freedom House. She holds a master's degree from Columbia University's School of International and Public Affairs, with a concentration in human rights. She served as an East Asia analyst for *Freedom in the World*.

NOAH TUCKER holds a master's degree from Harvard University's Davis Center for Russian and Eurasian Studies, and has worked both in the nonprofit sector and as a researcher on Central Asian religion, human rights, security, and conflict. He served as a U.S. embassy policy specialist for Kyrgyzstan in 2011 and returned to Central Asia for fieldwork most recently in the summer of 2012. He served as a Central Asia analyst for *Freedom in the World.*

VANESSA TUCKER is the director for analysis at Freedom House. Previously, she was the project director of *Countries at the Crossroads*, Freedom House's annual survey of democratic governance. Prior to joining Freedom House, she worked at the Harvard Kennedy School's Women and Public Policy Program, at the Kennedy School's Program on Intrastate Conflict, and with the Carter Center's Democracy Program. She holds a master's degree in international relations from Yale University. She served as a Middle East analyst for *Freedom in the World.*

ALI VAEZ is the director of the Iran Project at the Federation of American Scientists. Trained as a scientist, he has more than a decade of experience in journalism, including as a foreign correspondent for Radio Free Europe/Radio Liberty in Switzerland. He has written widely on Iranian affairs and is a regular contributor to media outlets such as the BBC, CNN, NPR, and Reuters. His work has appeared in the *International Herald Tribune*, *Foreign Policy*, the *Huffington Post*, and the *Atlantic*, among others. He received a PhD from the University of Geneva and a master's degree in international public policy from Johns Hopkins University's School of Advanced International Studies. He served as a Middle East analyst for *Freedom in the World.*

DARIA VAISMAN is a New York–based writer and producer. Her first book, a narrative nonfiction account of U.S. foreign policy in the former Soviet Union, will be published in 2013. She is also making a documentary on diplomatic recognition and sovereignty, which is currently in production. She holds a master's degree from Columbia University's School of International and Public Affairs. She served as a Caucasus analyst for *Freedom in the World.*

CHRISTINE WADE is an associate professor of political science and international studies at Washington College, where she is also the curator of the Louis L. Goldstein Program in Public Affairs. She has authored and coauthored numerous publications on Central American politics, and holds a PhD in political science from Boston University. She served as a Central America analyst for Freedom in the World.

CHRISTOPHER WALKER was vice president for strategy and analysis at Freedom House through mid-2012. He served as coeditor of *Countries at the Crossroads* and Nations in Transit and has written extensively on issues of democratic development. He holds a master's degree from Columbia University's School of International and Public Affairs. He served as a Caucasus analyst for *Freedom in the World.*

GREG WHITE is a professor of government and the faculty director of the Global Studies Center at Smith College. He is the author of *Climate Change and Migration: Borders and Security in a Warming World* and a recipient of a Mellon Foundation New Directions Fellowship, as well as Fulbright-IIE and Fulbright-Hays scholarships to Tunisia and Morocco, respectively. He received his PhD from the University of Wisconsin, Madison. He served as a North Africa analyst for *Freedom in the World.*

AIMEL RIOS WONG is as assistant program officer at the National Endowment for Democracy, where he assists in the evaluation of project proposals and monitors the work of grantees in Cuba, Paraguay, Peru, and Venezuela. He received a master's degree in international affairs, with a concentration in Latin America and the Caribbean, from American University. He served as a Caribbean analyst for *Freedom in the World.*

ANNY WONG is a political scientist with the RAND Corporation. Her research covers science and technology policy, international development, army manpower, and U.S. relations with states in the Asia-Pacific region. She holds a PhD in political science from the University of Hawaii at Manoa. She served as a Pacific Islands analyst for *Freedom in the World.*

ELIZA B. YOUNG is the Watchlist analyst for the International Rescue Committee's Emergency Preparedness and Response Unit in New York City. She previously worked as a research analyst at Freedom House. She holds a master's degree in international relations from King's College, London. She served as a Central and Western Europe analyst for *Freedom in the World.*

ACADEMIC ADVISERS

JON B. ALTERMAN is the Brzezinski Chair in Global Security and director of the Middle East Program at the Center for Strategic and International Studies.

GORDON BARDOS is a Balkan politics and security expert based in New York City.

JAVIER CORRALES is a professor of political science at Amherst College in Amherst, Massachusetts.

ROBERT LANE GREENE writes for the *Economist* and is an adjunct assistant professor of global affairs at New York University.

STEVEN HEYDEMANN is the senior adviser for Middle East initiatives at the U.S. Institute of Peace, and previously served as director of the Center for Democracy and Civil Society at Georgetown University.

DAVID HOLIDAY is the senior regional advocacy officer for the Latin America Program of the Open Society Foundations.

THOMAS R. LANSNER is an adjunct associate professor of international affairs at Columbia University's School of International and Public Affairs.

CARL LEVAN is an assistant professor at American University's School of International Service in Washington, DC.

PETER LEWIS is an associate professor and director of the African Studies Program at Johns Hopkins University's School of Advanced International Studies.

ELLEN LUST is an associate professor of political science at Yale University.

RAJAN MENON is the Anne and Bernard Spitzer Professor of Political Science, Department of Political Science, City College of New York/City University of New York.

JOHN S. MICGIEL is an adjunct professor of international affairs and executive director of the East Central European Center at Columbia University.

ALEXANDER J. MOTYL is a professor of political science at Rutgers University, Newark.

ANDREW J. NATHAN is the Class of 1919 Professor of Political Science at Columbia University.

PHILIP OLDENBURG is an adjunct associate professor in Columbia University's Department of Political Science and a research scholar at the university's South Asia Institute.

MARTIN SCHAIN is a professor of politics at New York University.

PETER SINNOTT is an independent scholar who has been working on Central Asia issues for more than 25 years.

SCOTT TAYLOR is an associate professor in the School of Foreign Service and director of the African Studies Program at Georgetown University.

BRIDGET WELSH is an associate professor of political science at Singapore Management University.

COLETTA A. YOUNGERS is an independent consultant specializing in human rights and democracy issues in Latin America and a senior fellow at the Washington Office on Latin America (WOLA).

PRODUCTION TEAM

IDA WALKER, Proofreader

MARK WOLKENFELD, Production Coordinator

Selected Sources for *Freedom in the World* 2012

PUBLICATIONS/BROADCASTS/BLOGS

ABC Color [Paraguay], www.abc.com.py
Africa Confidential, www.africa-confidential.com
Africa Daily, www.africadaily.com
Africa Energy Intelligence, www.africa intelligence.com
AFRICAHOME dotcom, www.africahome.com
Africa News, http://www.africanews.com
AfricaOnline.com, www.africaonline.com
African Elections Database, http://african elections.tripod.com
Afrol News, www.afrol.com
Aftenposten [Norway], www.aftenposten.no
Agence France-Presse (AFP), www.afp.com
Al-Arab al-Yawm [Jordan]: alarabalyawm.net
Al-Arabiya, www.alarabiya.net
Al-Ahram, http://www.ahram.org.eg/
Al-Ahram Weekly [Egypt], www.weekly.ahram.org.eg
Al-Akhbar [Beirut], www.al-akhbar.com
Al-Dustour [Egypt], http://www.addustour.com/
Al-Hayat, http://www.alhayat.com/
Al-Jazeera, http://english.aljazeera.net
allAfrica.com, www.allafrica.com
Al-Masry al-Youm [Egypt], http://www.almasryal youm.com/
Al-Ray Al-'am [Kuwait], www.alraialaam.com
Al-Raya [Qatar], www.raya.com
Al-Sharq al-Awsat, http://www.asharqalawsat.com/english/
Al-Quds al-Arabi, www.alquds.co.uk
Al-Thawra [Yemen], www.althawra.gov.ye
Al-Watan [Qatar], www.al-watan.com
American Broadcasting Corporation News (ABC), www.abcnews.go.com
American RadioWorks, www.americanpublic media.publicradio.org
The Analyst [Liberia], www.analystliberia.com
Andorra Times, www.andorratimes.com
An-Nahar [Lebanon], http://www.annahar.com/ http://web.naharnet.com/default.asp
Annual Review of Population Law (Harvard Law School), annualreview.law.harvard.edu
Arab Advisors Group, http://www.arabadvisors.com/
Arabianbusiness.com, www.arabianbusiness.com
Arabic Network for Human Rights Information (ANHRI), www.anhri.net
Arab Media, http://arab-media.blogspot.com/
Arab News [Saudi Arabia], www.arabnews.com
Arab Reform Bulletin, http://www.carnegieen dowment.org/
Asharq Alawsat, www.asharqalawsat.com
Asia Sentinel, http://www.asiasentinel.com/
Asia Times, www.atimes.com
As-Safir [Lebanon], www.assafir.com
Associated Press (AP), www.ap.org
The Atlantic Monthly, www.theatlantic.com
Austrian Times, www.austriantimes.at
Australia Broadcasting Corporation News Online, www.abc.net.au/news
The Australian, www.theaustralian.news.com.au
Awareness Times [Sierra Leone], www.news.sl
Bahrain Post, www.bahrainpost.com
Bahrain Tribune, www.bahraintribune.com
Balkan Insight, www.balkaninsight.com
The Baltic Times, www.baltictimes.com
Bangkok Post, www.bangkokpost.co.th
The Boston Globe, www.boston.com
British Broadcasting Corporation (BBC), www.bbc.co.uk
BruDirect.com [Brunei], www.brudirect.com/
The Budapest Sun, www.budapestsun.com
Budapest Times, http://www.budapesttimes.hu/
Business Day [South Africa], www.bday.co.za
Cabinda.net, www.cabinda.net
Cable News Network (CNN), www.cnn.com
Cameroon Tribune, www.cameroon-tribune.cm
The Caribbean & Central America Report (Intelligence Research Ltd.)
CBS News, www.cbsnews.com
The Central Asia-Caucasus Analyst (Johns Hopkins University), www.cacianalyst.org
Central News Agency [Taiwan], http://focus taiwan.tw/
The China Post, www.chinapost.com.tw
Chosun Ilbo [South Korea], http://english.chosun.com/
The Christian Science Monitor, www.csmonitor.com
CIA World Factbook, www.cia.gov/cia/publications/factbook
Civil Georgia, www.civil.ge
Congo Siasa, http://congosiasa.blogspot.co.uk/
The Contemporary Pacific, http://pidp.eastwest center.org/pireport/tcp.htm
The Copenhagen Post [Denmark], www.cphpost.dk
Corriere della Sera [Italy], www.corriere.it
Czech News Agency, http://www.ceskenoviny.cz/news/
Daily Excelsior [India-Kashmir], www.daily excelsior.com
Daily Star [Bangladesh], www.dailystar.net

Daily Star [Lebanon], www.dailystar.com.lb
The Daily Times, www.dailytimes.bppmw.com/
Danas [Serbia], http://www.danas.rs/danasrs/naslovna.1.html
Dani [Bosnia-Herzegovina], www.bhdani.com
Dawn [Pakistan], www.dawn.com
Der Spiegel [Germany], www.spiegel.de
Der Standard [Austria], www.derstandard.at
Die Zeit [Germany], www.zeit.de
Deutsche Presse-Agentur [Germany], www.dpa.de
Deutsche Welle [Germany], www.dwelle.de
The East Africa Standard [Kenya], www.eastandard.net
East European Constitutional Review (New York University), www.law.nyu.edu/eedr
East Timor Law Journal [East Timor], http://www.eastimorlawjournal.org/
The Economist, www.economist.com
The Economist Intelligence Unit reports, http://www.eiu.com/
EFE News Service [Spain], www.efenews.com
Election Watch, www.electionwatch.org
Election World, www.electionworld.org
El Mercurio [Chile], www.elmercurio.cl
El Nuevo Herald [United States], www.miami.com/mld/elnuevo
El Pais [Uruguay], www.elpais.com.uy
El Tiempo [Colombia], www.eltiempo.com
El Universal [Venezuela], www.eluniversal.com.ve
Epoch Times, http://www.theepochtimes.com/
Eurasia Review, http://www.eurasiareview.com/
Expreso [Peru], www.expreso.co.pe
Far Eastern Economic Review, www.feer.com
Federal Bureau of Investigation Hate Crime Statistics, www.fbi.gov ucr/2003/03semimaps.pdf
Federated States of Micronesia Congress press releases http://www.fsmcongress.fm/
Federated States of Micronesia Information Services http://www.fsmpio.fm/
Fijilive, www.fijilive.com
FijiSUN, www.sun.com.fj
Fiji Times Online, www.fijitimes.com
Fiji Village, www.FijiVillage.com
The Financial Times, www.ft.com
Finnish News Agency, http://virtual.finland.fi/stt
Folha de Sao Paulo, www.folha.com.br
Foreign Affairs, www.foreignaffairs.org
Foreign Policy, www.foreignpolicy.com
France 24, www.france24.com
Frankfurter Allgemeine Zeitung [Germany], www.faz.net
The Friday Times [Pakistan], www.thefridaytimes.com
The Frontier Post [Pakistan], www.frontierpost.com
FrontPageAfrica [Liberia], www.frontpageafrica.com
Gazeta.ru [Russia], gazeta.ru
Global Insight, http://www.globalinsight.com/
Global News Wire, www.lexis-nexis.com
Globus [Croatia], www.globus.com.hr
The Guardian [Nigeria], www.ngrguardiannews.com
The Guardian [United Kingdom], www.guardian.co.uk
Gulf Daily News [Bahrain], www.gulf-daily-news.com
Gulf News Online [United Arab Emirates], www.gulf-news.com
Gulf Times [Qatar], www.gulf-times.com
Haaretz [Israel], www.haaretz.com
Hankyoreh Shinmun [South Korea], http://english.hani.co.kr/kisa/
Harper's Magazine, www.harpers.org
Haveeru Daily [Maldives], www.haveeru.com.mv
The Hindustan Times [India], www.hindustantimes.com
Iceland Review, www.icelandreview.com
The Independent [United Kingdom], www.independent.co.uk
Index on Censorship, www.indexoncensorship.org
India Today, www.india-today.com
The Indian Express, www.indian-express.com
Info Matin [Mali], www.info-matin.com
Insight Magazine, www.insightmag.com
Insight Namibia Magazine, www.insight.com.na
Integrated Regional Information Networks (IRIN), www.irinnews.org
Inter Press Service, www.ips.org
Interfax News Agency, www.interfax-news.com
International Herald Tribune, www.iht.com
IRIN news, http://www.irinnews.org/
Irish Independent, www.unison.ie/irish_independent
Irish Times, www.ireland.com
Islands Business Magazine, www.islandsbusiness.com
Izvestia, www.izvestia.ru
The Jakarta Globe, http://www.thejakartaglobe.com/home/
The Jakarta Post, http://www.thejakartapost.com/
Jamaica Gleaner, http://www.jamaica-gleaner.com/
Jawa Pos [Indonesia], http://www.jawapos.co.id/utama/
Jeune Afrique [France], http://www.jeuneafrique.com/
Johnson's Russia List, www.cdi.org/russia/johnson/
Joongang Ilbo [South Korea], http://joongangdaily.joins.com/?cloc=home|top|jdaily
The Jordan Times, www.jordantimes.com
Journal of Democracy, www.journalofdemocracy.org
Jyllands-Posten [Denmark], www.jp.dk
The Kaselehlie Press [Micronesia], http://www.bild-art.de/kpress/
Kashmir Times [India-Kashmir], www.kashmirtimes.com
Kathmandu Post [Nepal], www.nepalnews.com.np/ktmpost.htm

Kedaulatan Rakyat [Indonesia], http://www.kedaulatan-rakyat.com/
Khaleej Times [United Arab Emirates], www.khaleejtimes.com
The Kiribati Independent, http://www.thekiribatiindependent.co.nz/
Kommersant [Russia], www.kommersant.ru
Kompas [Indonesia], http://www.kompas.com/
Korea Herald [South Korea], http://www.koreaherald.com/index.jsp
The Korea Times [South Korea], http://times.hankooki.com
Kuensel [Bhutan], www.kuenselonline.com
Kurier [Austria], www.kurier.at
Kuwait Post, www.kuwaitpost.com
L'Informazione di San Marino, http://www.libertas.sm/News_informazione/news_frameset.htm
La Jornada [Mexico], www.jornada.uam.nx
La Nacion [Argentina], www.lanacion.com.ar
La Repubblica [Italy], www.repubblica.it
La Semaine Africaine [Congo-Brazzaville], http://www.lasemaineafricaine.com/
La Tercera [Chile], www.tercera.cl
Lanka Monthly Digest [Sri Lanka], www.lanka.net/LMD
Latin American Regional Reports, www.latinnews.com
Latin American Weekly Reports, www.latinnews.com
Le Faso [Burkina Faso], www.lefaso.net
Le Figaro [France], www.lefigaro.fr
Le Messager [Cameroon], www.lemessager.net
Le Monde [France], www.lemonde.fr
Le Quotidien [Senegal], http://www.lequotidien.sn/
Le Temps [Switzerland], www.letemps.ch
Le Togolais [Togo], http://www.letogolais.com/
Lexis-Nexis, www.lexis-nexis.com
Liberia Media Center, http://www.lmcliberia.com/
The Local [Sweden], www.thelocal.se
L'Orient-Le Jour [Lebanon], www.lorientlejour.com
The Los Angeles Times, www.latimes.com
Mail & Guardian [South Africa], www.mg.co.za
Malaysiakini [Malaysia], http://www.malaysiakini.com/
The Manila Times, www.manilatimes.net/
Marianas Business Journal, http://www.mbjguam.net/
Marianas Variety [Micronesia], www.mvariety.com
Marlborough Express [New Zealand], http://www.stuff.co.nz/marlborough-express
Marshall Islands government press releases, http://www.rmigovernment.org/index.jsp
Matangi Tonga Magazine, www.matangitonga.to
The Messenger [Georgia], www.messenger.com.ge
The Miami Herald, www.miami.com/mld/miamiherald
Middle East Desk, www.middleeastdesk.org
Middle East Online, www.middle-east-online.com
Middle East Report, www.merip.org
Minivan News [Maldives], www.minivannews.com
Mirianas Variety [Micronesia], www.mvariety.com
Misr Digital, http://misrdigital.blogspirit.com/
Moldova Azi, www.azi.md
Mopheme News [Lesotho], www.lesoff.co.za/news
Mother Jones, www.motherjones.com
The Moscow Times, www.themoscowtimes.com
Nacional [Croatia], www.nacional.hr
The Namibian, www.namibian.com.na/
The Nation, www.thenation.org
The Nation [Thailand], www.nationmultimedia.com
The Nation Online [Malawi], www.nationmalawi.com
The National [Papua New Guinea], www.thenational.com.pg
The National [UAE], www.thenational.ae
National Business Review [New Zealand], http://www.nbr.co.nz
National Public Radio (NPR), www.npr.org
National Review, www.nationalreview.com
Neue Zurcher Zeitung [Switzerland], www.nzz.ch
The New Dawn [Liberia], http://www.thenewdawnliberia.com/
The New Democrat Online [Liberia], www.newdemocratnews.com
New Mandala, http://asiapacific.anu.edu.au/newmandala/
The New York Times, www.nytimes.com
The New Yorker, www.newyorker.com
The New Zealand Herald, www.nzherald.co.nz
New Zealand government press releases, http://www.beehive.govt.nz/
News Agency of the Slovak Republic, http://www.tasr.sk/30.axd?lang=1033
Nezavisimaya Gazeta [Russia], www.ng.ru
NIN [Serbia], http://www.nin.co.rs/
Nine O'Clock [Romania], www.nineoclock.ro
NiuFM News [New Zealand], http://www.niufm.com/
Noticias [Argentina], www.noticias.uolsinectis.com.ar
Notimex [Mexico], www.notimex.com
Novi Reporter [Bosnia-Herzegovina], http://www.novireporter.com
Nyasa Times [Malawi], www.nyasatimes.com
The Observer [Liberia], www.liberianobserver.com
O Estado de Sao Paulo, www.estado.com.br
O Globo [Brazil], www.oglobo.globo.com
OFFnews [Argentina], www.offnews.info
Oman Arabic Daily, www.omandaily.com
Oman Daily Observer, www.omanobserver.com
Oslobodjenje [Bosnia-Herzegovina], www.oslobodjenje.com.ba
Outlook [India], www.outlookindia.com
Pacific Business News, http://pacific.bizjournals.com/pacific/

Pacific Daily News, www.guampdn.com/
Pacific Islands Report, http://pidp.eastwest center.org/pireport
Pacific Magazine, http://www.pacificmagazine.net
Pacific Scoop [New Zealand], http://pacific.scoop.co.nz
Pagina/12 [Argentina], www.pagina12.com.ar
PANAPRESS, www.panapress.com
Papua New Guinea Post-Courier, www.post courier.com.pg
The Perspective Newspaper [Liberia], www.perspective.org
The Philippine Daily Inquirer, http://www.inquirer.net/
Phnom Penh Post, www.phnompenhpost.com
The Pioneer [India], www.dailypioneer.com
Planet Tonga, http://www.planet-tonga.com
Political Handbook of the World, http://phw.binghamton.edu
Politics.hu [Hungary], http://www.politics.hu/
Politika [Serbia], http://www.politika.rs/
Port Vila Presse [Vanuatu], www.news.vu/en/
The Post [Zambia], www.zamnet.zm/zamnet/post/post.html
The Prague Post, www.praguepost.com
Radio and Television Hong Kong, www.rthk.org.hk
Radio Australia, www.abc.net.au/ra
Radio France Internationale, www.rfi.fr
Radio Free Europe-Radio Liberty, www.rferl.org
Radio Lesotho, www.lesotho.gov.ls/radio/radiolesotho
Radio Okapi [Congo-Kinshasa], www.radioOkapi.net
Radio New Zealand, www.rnzi.com
Republika [Indonesia], http://www.republika.co.id/
Reuters, www.reuters.com
Ritzau [Denmark], www.ritzau.dk
Royal African Society's African Arguments, http://africanarguments.org/
Sahel Blog, http://sahelblog.wordpress.com/
Saipan Tribune, http://www.saipantribune.com
The Samoa News, www.samoanews.com
Samoa Observer, http://www.samoaobserver.ws/
San Marino Notizie, http://www.sanmarino notizie.com/
Savali Press [Samoa], www.savalipress.com
Semana [Colombia], www.semana.com
The Sierra Leone News, www.thesierraleone news.com
Slobodna Bosna [Bosnia-Herzegovina], www.slobodna-bosna.ba
The Slovak Spectator, www.slovakspectator.sk
Slovak News Agency, http://www.sita.sk/eng/services/online/en/content.php
SME [Slovakia], http://www.sme.sk/
Sofia Echo, www.sofiaecho.com
Solomon Islands Broadcasting Corporation, www.sibconline.com.sb
Solomon Star, www.solomonstarnews.com
The Somaliland Times, www.somalilandtimes.net
South Asia Tribune [Pakistan], www.satribune.com
South China Morning Post [Hong Kong], www.scmp.com
Star Radio News [Liberia], www.starradio.org.lr
The Statesman [India], www.thestatesman.net
Straits Times [Singapore], www.straitstimes.asia1.com.sg
Sub-Saharan Informer, http://www.ssinformer.com/
Suddeutsche Zeitung [Germany], www.sueddeutsche.de
Tageblatt [Luxembourg], www.tageblatt.lu
Tahiti Presse, www.tahitipresse.pf
Taipei Times, www.taipeitimes.com
Tamilnet.com, www.tamilnet.com
Tax-News.com, www.tax-news.com
Téla Nón Diário de São Tomé e Príncipe, http://www.telanon.info/
The Telegraph [United Kingdom], www.telegraph.co.uk
Tempo [Indonesia], http://www.tempointeraktif.com/
Texas in Africa, http://texasinafrica.blogspot.co.uk/
This Day [Nigeria], www.thisdayonline.com
The Tico Times [Costa Rica], www.ticotimes.net
Time, www.time.com
The Times of Central Asia, www.times.kg
The Times of India, www.timesofindia.net
Times of Zambia, www.times.co.zm/
TomPaine.com, www.TomPaine.com
Tonga USA Today, www.tongausatoday.com
Tongan Broadcasting Commission, http://tonga-broadcasting.com/
Transcaucasus: A Chronology, http://www.anca.org/resource_center/transcaucasus.php
Trinidad Express, http://www.trinidadexpress.com/
Tuvalu News, http://www.tuvalu-news.tv/
University World News, http://www.university worldnews.com/
U.S. News and World Report, www.usnews.com
U.S. State Department Country Reports on Human Rights Practices, www.state.gov/g/drl/rls/hrrpt
U.S. State Department Country Reports on Human Trafficking Reports, www.state.gov/g/tip
U.S. State Department International Religious Freedom Reports, www.state.gov/g/drl/irf
The Vanguard [Nigeria], www.vanguardngr.com
Vanuatu Daily Post, www.vanuatudaily.com
Venpres [Venezuela], www.venpres.gov.ve
Voice of America, www.voa.gov
The Wall Street Journal, www.wsj.com
The Washington Post, www.washingtonpost.com
The Washington Times, www.washingtontimes.com
The Weekly Standard, www.weeklystandard.com